PRACTICAL
REAL ESTATE
LAW | Sixth Edition

DELMAR CENGAGE Learning

Options.

Over 300 products in every area of the law: textbooks, online courses, CD-ROMs, reference books, companion websites, and more – helping you succeed in the classroom and on the job.

Support.

We offer unparalleled, practical support: robust instructor and student supplements to ensure the best learning experience, custom publishing to meet your unique needs, and other benefits such as Delmar Cengage Learning's Student Achievement Award. And our sales representatives are always ready to provide you with dependable service.

Feedback.

As always, we want to hear from you! Your feedback is our best resource for improving the quality of our products. Contact your sales representative or write us at the address below if you have any comments about our materials or if you have a product proposal.

Accounting and Financials for the Law Office • Administrative Law • Alternative Dispute Resolution • Bankruptcy Business Organizations/Corporations • Careers and Employment • Civil Litigation and Procedure • CLA Exam Preparation • Computer Applications in the Law Office • Constitutional Law • Contract Law • Court Reporting Criminal Law and Procedure • Document Preparation • Elder Law • Employment Law • Environmental Law • Ethics Evidence Law • Family Law • Health Care Law • Immigration Law • Intellectual Property • Internships Interviewing and Investigation • Introduction to Law • Introduction to Paralegalism • Juvenile Law • Law Office Management • Law Office Procedures • Legal Nurse Consulting • Legal Research, Writing, and Analysis • Legal Terminology • Legal Transcription • Media and Entertainment Law • Medical Malpractice Law Product Liability • Real Estate Law • Reference Materials • Social Security • Sports Law • Torts and Personal Injury Law • Wills, Trusts, and Estate Administration • Workers' Compensation Law

---

DELMAR CENGAGE Learning
5 Maxwell Drive
Clifton Park, New York 12065-2919

For additional information, find us online at:
www.delmar.cengage.com

PRACTICAL
REAL ESTATE
LAW | Sixth Edition

Daniel F. Hinkel

DELMAR
CENGAGE Learning™

Australia • Brazil • Japan • Korea • Mexico • Singapore • Spain • United Kingdom • United States

Title: Practical Real Estate Law, Sixth Edition

Author: Daniel F. Hinkel

Vice President, Career and Professional Editorial: Dave Garza

Director of Learning Solutions: Sandy Clark

Senior Acquisitions Editor: Shelley Esposito

Managing Editor: Larry Main

Senior Product Manager: Melissa Riveglia

Editorial Assistant: Danielle Klahr

Vice President, Career and Professional Marketing: Jennifer Baker

Marketing Director: Deborah Yarnell

Marketing Manager: Erin Brennan

Marketing Coordinator: Jonathan Sheehan

Production Director: Wendy Troeger

Production Manager: Mark Bernard

Senior Content Project Manager: Betty Dickson

Senior Art Director: Joy Kocsis

Senior Technology Product Manager: Joe Pliss

Library of Congress Control Number: 2010924582
ISBN-13: 978-1-4390-5720-9
ISBN-10: 1-4390-5720-6

Delmar
5 Maxwell Drive
Clifton Park, NY 12065-2919
USA

Cengage Learning is a leading provider of customized learning solutions with office locations around the globe, including Singapore, the United Kingdom, Australia, Mexico, Brazil, and Japan. Locate your local office at: **international.cengage.com/region**

Cengage Learning products are represented in Canada by Nelson Education, Ltd.

To learn more about Delmar, visit **www.cengage.com/delmar.**
Purchase any of our products at your local college store or at our preferred online store **www.ichapters.com.**

NOTICE TO THE READER

Publisher does not warrant or guarantee any of the products described herein or perform any independent analysis in connection with any of the product information contained herein. Publisher does not assume, and expressly disclaims, any obligation to obtain and include information other than that provided to it by the manufacturer. The reader is expressly warned to consider and adopt all safety precautions that might be indicated by the activities described herein and to avoid all potential hazards. By following the instructions contained herein, the reader willingly assumes all risks in connection with such instructions. The reader is notified that this text is an educational tool, not a practice book. Since the law is in constant change, no rule or statement of law in this book should be relied upon for any service to any client. The reader should always refer to standard legal sources for the current rule or law. If legal advice or other expert assistance is required, the services of the appropriate professional should be sought. The publisher makes no representations or warranties of any kind, including but not limited to, the warranties of fitness for particular purpose or merchantability, nor are any such representations implied with respect to the material set forth herein, and the publisher takes no responsibility with respect to such material. The publisher shall not be liable for any special, consequential, or exemplary damages resulting, in whole or part, from the readers' use of, or reliance upon, this material.

Printed in the United States of America
1 2 3 4 5 6 7 14 13 12 11 10

TO JOHN HENRY

contents

CHAPTER 16

REAL ESTATE CLOSING FORMS AND EXAMPLES 583

preface

As a former instructor for the National Center for Paralegal Training, I had the pleasure of teaching a real estate course to paralegal students for over two decades. This textbook, a greatly expanded version of that course material, is directed toward the training and practice of paralegals in the area of modern real estate transactions.

A paralegal cannot effectively assist a transactional real estate attorney unless he or she is fully aware of all the substantive legal issues involved and has a good command of the various legal forms in use. The treatment of the subject assumes that the reader has no knowledge of real property law. The text introduces the reader to the basics of real property law and then proceeds step by step through all the areas of a modern real estate practice.

The text is written for national use and tries to present the general concepts of real property law that are applied in most of the 50 states. Although the text is not state specific, it can be supplemented easily with state materials if the instructor so desires.

The book is designed to be used in two ways. It can be used as a classroom teaching source for the training of paralegals. It also can be used as a reference work by paralegals employed in a real estate legal practice. The book includes an explanation of legal principles, practical suggestions, and numerous forms. Using this text, the student or practicing paralegal possesses in a single source a collection of useful material.

It is time for a new edition of this book. Our country is suffering a severe real estate recession, and many new laws have been passed to assist homeowners facing foreclosure. The book discusses these new laws.

TEXTBOOK ORGANIZATION

Based on comments and suggestions from various teachers, students, and reviewers of the previous editions of this book, the text has been revised. Chapter 1 introduces students to the concept of property ownership and discusses the various types of ownership that can exist. Chapter 2 introduces the student to the situation in which real property is owned by more than one person and discusses all the forms of concurrent ownership. Chapter 3 is a discussion of the methods of describing real property and contains sample surveys and legal descriptions. Chapters 4 and 5 discuss government regulation of and various private encumbrances to the ownership of real property, with a special emphasis on easements. Chapter 6 begins a discussion on contracts, and Chapter 7 is devoted to contract forms and the explanation of standard provisions found in real estate contracts. Chapter 8 is a discussion of deeds, complete with many examples and sample forms. Chapters 9, 10, and 11 discuss real estate finance. Chapter 9 discusses the business aspect of real estate lending and is designed to acquaint the student with the economic and practical needs of lender and borrower clients. Chapter 10 is a discussion of the substantive law of notes, mortgages, and foreclosures. Chapter 11 explains the various note and mortgage forms, as well as other documents used by lenders to document and secure residential and commercial loans. Chapters 12 and 13 are devoted to title examinations and title insurance.

Chapters 14, 15, and 16 are devoted to the real estate closing. Chapter 14 is a full discussion of the substantive issues of real estate closings. Chapter 15 is a discussion of the government regulations that affect a residential real estate closing. Chapter 16 is devoted to forms and examples of closing documents, including a sample of a residential real estate closing transaction. Chapter 17 contains a discussion of condominiums, cooperatives, and time-shares. Chapter 18 is a discussion of leases, complete with residential and commercial lease forms.

CHANGES TO THE SIXTH EDITION

Forms

All forms have been updated where needed, and new forms have been added to the text.

Expanded Coverage

New examples and exhibits have been added to explain some of the more difficult legal concepts.

New material under the heading of Web News has been added to each chapter. This feature provides the student with Internet links to additional information.

New material discussing the recent real estate recession and the efforts being made by the federal and state governments to assist homeowners facing foreclosure and to support the market value of homes has been added to Chapters 9 and 10.

New title insurance forms have been added to Chapter 13.

New material has been added to Chapter 14 that explains the roles of the various participants in a real estate closing.

New material discussing the use and etiquette of e-mail correspondence has been added to Chapter 14.

The new RESPA, HOEPA, and Truth-in-Lending rules are discussed in Chapter 15.

New instructions on how to complete the new HUD-1 form have been added in Chapter 16.

STUDENT LEARNING FEATURES

- **Chapter objectives** open each chapter to focus students' attention on the key concepts they will learn.
- **Checklists** are found in most chapters and include task-specific steps that students can apply to many aspects of a paralegal's workday. For example, Chapter 7 contains a checklist for preparation and review of a commercial real estate contract, and Chapter 16 includes a checklist for a residential closing.
- **Terminology** is emphasized throughout each chapter. Key terms appear in boldface and are defined in context where they first appear. They are also listed at the end of each chapter for quick reference. Finally, a comprehensive glossary ends the text.
- The **Ethics** feature in each chapter takes the student into a hypothetical scenario that presents an ethical problem. The feature emphasizes the importance of professional responsibility in a law practice.

- A **chapter-ending summary** provides an excellent review of the chapter's main points.
- **Review questions, case problems**, and **practical assignments** at the end of each chapter provide students with more exercises and opportunities to consider how they would handle specific tasks. For example, a practical assignment in Chapter 5 asks students to draft an easement, and one in Chapter 10 asks students to draft a note and a deed to secure debt based on a hypothetical scenario.

SUPPLEMENTS AVAILABLE FOR THE SIXTH EDITION

Student StudyWARE™ CD-ROM

The new accompanying CD-ROM provides additional material to help students master the important concepts in the course. The CD-ROM includes additional quizzes, case studies, and key terms flash cards.

Instructor's Manual

The Instructor's Manual has been revised to incorporate changes in the text and to provide comprehensive teaching support. The Instructor's Manual contains the following:

- Introduction and Chapter Outline for each chapter
- Teaching Ideas
- Answers to Review Questions and Case Problems
- Testbank and Answer Key

Instructor Resources

INSTRUCTOR RESOURCES

Spend less time planning and more time teaching. With Delmar Cengage Learning's Instructor Resources to Accompany Practical Real Estate Law, preparing for class and evaluating students has never been easier!

This invaluable instructor CD-ROM allows you anywhere, anytime access to all of your resources:

- The **Instructor's Manual** contains various resources and answers for each chapter of the book.
- The **Computerized Testbank** in ExamView makes generating tests and quizzes a snap. With many questions and different styles to choose from, you can create customized assessments for your students with the click of a button. Add your own unique questions and print rationales for easy class preparation.
- Customizable **PowerPoint® Presentations** focus on key points for each chapter. (PowerPoint® is a registered trademark of the Microsoft Corporation.)

All of these instructor materials are also posted on our Web site in the Online Resources section.

WebTutor™

The WebTutor™ supplement allows you, as the instructor, to take learning beyond the classroom. This online courseware is designed to complement the text and benefit students and instructors alike by helping to better manage your time, prepare for exams, organize your notes, and more. WebTutor™ allows you to extend your reach beyond the classroom.

Online Companion™

The Online Companion™ can be found at *www.paralegal.delmar.cengage.com* in the Online Companion™ section of the Web site. The Online Companion™ contains:

- State Supplements
- Chapter Summaries
- Additional Forms
- Internet Resources
- Additional Court Decisions

Web Page

Come visit our Web site at *www.paralegal.delmar.cengage.com* where you will find valuable information such as hot links and sample materials to download, as well as other Delmar Cengage Learning products.

Supplements At-A-Glance

SUPPLEMENT	WHAT IT IS	WHAT'S IN IT
Student CD-ROM	Software program (CD-ROM in the back of the book). StudyWARE™ is like the student's own interactive private tutor, reinforcing the material in the text in an exciting and fun environment!	StudyWARE™ software with additional quizzes, case studies with multiple choice follow-up questions, and flash cards.
Online Instructor's Manual	Resources for the Instructor posted online at *www.paralegal.delmar.cengage.com* in the Online Resources section	• Instructor Manual with introductions and chapter outlines, teaching ideas, answers to review questions and case problems, and testbank and answer key • PowerPoint® Presentations
Instructor Resources CD-ROM INSTRUCTOR RESOURCES	Resources for the Instructor available on CD-ROM	• Instructor Manual with introductions and chapter outlines, teaching ideas, answers to review questions and case problems, and testbank and answer key • Computerized Test Bank in ExamView with many questions and styles to choose from to create customized assessments for your students • PowerPoint® Presentations
WebTUTOR™ WebTUTOR™	WebTUTOR™ supplemental courseware is the best way to use the Internet to turn everyone in your class into a front-row student. It complements Cengage Learning paralegal textbooks by providing interactive reinforcement that helps students grasp complex concepts. WebTUTOR™ allows you to know quickly what concepts your students are or are not grasping.	• Automatic and immediate feedback from quizzes and exams • Online exercises that reinforce what they have learned • Flash cards that include audio support • Greater interaction and involvement through online discussion forums

SUPPLEMENT	WHAT IT IS	WHAT'S IN IT
Online Companion ™	Additional resources for the student posted online at *www.paralegal.delmar.cengage.com* in the Online Companion™ section.	• State supplements • Chapter summaries • Additional forms • Internet resources • Additional court decisions
Real Estate Law Online Course	Robust Online Course available on both Blackboard and WebCT. (Availability upon request for eCollege, Angel, Desire2Learn, and more.) The course can be used along with this textbook or any book for the Introductory course. See a demo at *http://cengagesites.com/academic/?site=4074.*	Includes 16 lessons with an Introduction; Objectives; Lecture Outline; Video Activities; Journal Activities; Group Activities; Internet Activities; Discussion Questions; Ethics Question; Glossary Terms; Web Links; Study Notes; and Quizzing for the student. Instructor materials include PowerPoints and Testbanks.

This text covers all the important issues that a real estate paralegal will encounter in a modern real estate practice. I offer it to you with the sincere hope that you will find it useful.

acknowledgments

Acknowledgments are due John Henry Hinkel, who dedicated many hours to the typing of the manuscript, and to the following individuals for their fine efforts in reviewing the fifth edition in preparation for this sixth edition.

Daniel F. Hinkel

Gaila Anderson
City College
Fort Lauderdale, FL

Sally Bisson
College of Saint Mary
Omaha, NE

John DeLeo
Central Pennsylvania
College
Summerdale, PA

Dora Dye
City College of
San Francisco
San Francisco, CA

Annie Laurie I. Meyers
Northampton Community
College
Bethlehem, PA

Edwards O'Boyle
Gwinnett College
Lilburn, GA

> Please note that the Internet resources are of a time-sensitive nature and URL addresses may often change or be deleted.

chapter | 1

Introduction to the Law of Real Property

Objectives

After reading this chapter, you should be able to:

- Distinguish between real and personal property
- Understand the legal concept of property ownership
- Identify the modern estates of ownership for real property
- Understand and be able to explain the legal concept of adverse possession
- Identify various ways of becoming an owner of real property

Outline

> "For 'tis the only thing in the world that lasts.
> 'Tis the only thing worth working for, fighting for, dying for."
>
> Margaret Mitchell, *Gone with the Wind*

The sentiments of Scarlett O'Hara's father about Tara are shared by millions of homeowners throughout the world. Home ownership ranks high on most people's wish list, and a home is considered the most valuable asset in many households. The real estate industry with all its many facets, such as development, construction, sales, leasing, and finance, generates vast concentrations of wealth and creates millions of jobs. Real estate is a valuable commodity, and almost every aspect of its use, sale, and development is regulated by law. These laws are steeped in history and tempered with logic and practicality. Representation of real estate clients is a major area of practice for many law firms, and the opportunities for the trained real estate paralegal are numerous. Preparation for this work begins with an introduction to the basic principles of real property law.

REAL PROPERTY LAW

Laws That Govern Real Property Transactions

The law of the United States comprises two separate systems of law: federal law and state law. Federal law applies uniformly throughout the country, whereas state law, because of differences in local history and conditions, varies from state to state. The law of real property in general is governed by state law and, therefore, is somewhat different in each of the various states. The law of the state in which the real property is located usually governs. For example, if a New York couple owns a beach house on Cape Cod, the laws of the Commonwealth of Massachusetts control the couple's ownership rights to the property and the form and content of the various legal documents and procedures involved in the sale, leasing, financing, inheritance, and so on of the property.

There are, however, basic legal principles that govern real estate transactions, and the approach of this text is to describe these principles and to mention the more important instances in which the states do not agree.

Real Property versus Personal Property

The law recognizes two classifications of property: real and personal. John E. Cribbet, former dean of the University of Illinois College of Law, in his treatise *Principles of the Law of Real Property,* points out that "the terminology makes no semantic sense because a car is just as 'real' as a farm and the family mansion is more 'personal' to the owner than shares of stock. The explanation lies not in the history of property, but in the history of procedure. In early common law a real action, so called because it led to the return of the thing itself, was used when land was wrongfully detained by another; a personal action, which gave only a money claim against the wrongdoer, was proper when things other than land were involved. Thus the thing took the name of the action, and we have, to this day, real property and personal property." Real property relates to land and those things that are more or less permanently attached to the land, such as homes, office buildings, and trees.

Personal property is sometimes referred to as "chattels" or "goods." Personal property has its own set of legal rules and regulations, which govern the ownership of the property, the ability to sell the property, and the ability to pledge the property to secure a debt. Personal property may include living objects, such as animals, and inanimate objects, such as a television.

Tangible Personal Property

The property can be either tangible or intangible. Tangible personal property is property that has a physical substance—something you can hold, taste, see, or hear. Tangible personal property includes such things as automobiles, televisions, and clothes.

Intangible Personal Property

Intangible personal property is property that represents a set of rights that have no physical existence but that do represent control or ownership of something of value. A certificate of stock is an example of intangible personal property. Although the stock certificate itself is tangible, the stock certificate represents a fractional ownership in a company, and it is the intangible fractional ownership in the company that gives the stock certificate value. Other examples of intangible property are bonds, patents, copyrights, and intellectual property rights, such as software.

Fixtures

It usually is easy to tell if an item is personal property or real property, but in some situations, the determination may be difficult. Take, for example, a stove and a refrigerator that are located in the kitchen of a house. Are these items real property or personal property? The answer to this question is governed by the law of fixtures.

A **fixture** is an article of personal property, such as an air-conditioning unit or a dishwasher, that has been installed in or attached to land or a building and, on attachment, is regarded by the law as part of the real property. The term *trade fixtures* is used to describe shelving, counters, and other ornamental items installed on property by a tenant to assist the tenant in the conduct of its business. Most states permit a tenant to remove trade fixtures during the term of the lease and at the expiration of the lease. The removal may be conditioned upon the tenant repairing any damage to the property that results from the removal of the trade fixtures.

A number of judicial tests exist to determine if an article is a fixture. The tests are based upon the extent of the fixture's annexation to the real property and the adaptation of the fixture to the use of the real property. The more permanent the attachment or annexation, the more likely the court will determine that the item is a fixture. If it is clear that the item has been specifically constructed and adapted to enhance the use of a particular building, such as a hot tub spa on the deck of a house, then the item is more likely to be a fixture. In addition, courts pay strict attention to the intention of the parties. If it is clear from the circumstances surrounding the attachment of the item to the building that the parties intended for it to be a fixture and part of the real property, this will be given weight by the court. In addition, if the parties have indicated in writing an intention that an item shall be a fixture or shall not be a fixture, a court will enforce this written intention.

Often the question of whether an object is a fixture or not is really a question of "who gets the property," and the answer varies according to the context in which the question is asked. The question is raised in disputes between landlords and tenants, mortgagors and mortgagees, sellers and buyers, and lenders and creditors. For example, in a seller and purchaser dispute, the law generally favors the purchaser and holds that any personal property attached to the home or building are considered fixtures and will transfer with the real property unless the seller either has removed the fixtures before the sale or reserves ownership in the contract or deed. The requirements of justice and fairness in a particular case may determine the outcome of whether an object is a fixture or not, which makes it difficult to create any consistent body of law on the subject.

The classification of an item as a fixture is important because if the item is a fixture, it is part of the real property and will be transferred with the real property unless there clearly is an intent for it not to be transferred. This means that if a person buys a building, he or she also obtains all the fixtures within the building. Classification also is important in a loan transaction because if a person pledges real property as security for a debt, not only will the real property be pledged, but also any items deemed to be fixtures located on the real property.

Failure to identify an item as a fixture may send a person to jail, as shown by the case of *Ex Parte Brown.*

Physical Elements of Real Property

As previously discussed, real property is land and those things such as houses or buildings attached to the land. The definition of real property, however, includes more than land and things that are attached to the land. Real property includes everything beneath the surface

fixture

Item of personal property that becomes real property because of its attachment to the land or a building.

CASE

WRIGHT, Presiding Judge.

Ruby and Louis Brown were divorced by decree of the Lauderdale County Circuit Court in November 1983. As part of this decree, the husband was awarded the family home, "including all fixtures and realty appurtenant thereto." The wife was awarded all furniture in the home with the exception of the master bedroom suite, the dining room furniture, kitchen appliances, and one-half of all silver, silverware, and other kitchenware, which was awarded to the husband. The wife was to remove all of the furniture and personal property awarded to her prior to relinquishing possession of the home. In February 1984, the husband filed a petition with the circuit court asking that the wife be found to be in contempt for violating the property settlement provisions of the divorce decree. In May 1985, the court issued an order which specifically stated:

"The evidence shows that under the decree of divorce the Plaintiff [husband] was awarded certain items of personal property which the Defendant [wife] removed from the Plaintiff's home. A microwave of the value of $400.00 and a refrigerator of the value of $500.00. Further, the Plaintiff was awarded the family home and there was attached thereto a bookcase and china cabinets of the value of $2,000.00 which the Defendant removed from the home. Therefore, the Plaintiff was deprived of real and personal property of the value of $2,900.00 and the Defendant's action in removing these items is [a] violation of the decree and a contempt of the Court."

For her contempt, the court ordered the wife to serve ten days in the county jail, allowing, however, that she could purge herself of the contempt by making a payment of $2,900 to the Clerk of the Circuit Court of Lauderdale County. Thereafter, the wife filed this petition for certiorari asking that we review this finding of contempt.

We are perplexed by the wife's first argument for reversal. She admits that she acted in contempt of the court's order when she removed the microwave and refrigerator from the home, but argues that the bookcase and china cabinets were not fixtures appurtenant to the home and thus could be removed by her as furniture. She does not argue that the ten-day jail sentence was excessive, *see Williams v. Stumpe,* 439 So.2d 1297 (Ala. Civ. App.1983), nor that she is unable to pay the $2,900 necessary to purge herself of this contempt, *see Zeigler v. Butler,* 410 So.2d 93 (Ala. Civ. App.1982). Instead, the real issue she wishes this court to address is whether the $2,900 is an accurate assessment of the damage caused the husband by her contempt.

[1] It is settled that a trial court can assess damages in favor of an aggrieved party in civil contempt proceedings. *Lightsey v. Kensington Mortgage & Finance Corp.,* 294 Ala. 281, 315 So.2d 431 (1975); *Smith v. Smith,* 365 So.2d 8 (Ala. Civ. App.1978). It is also settled that "a party who has been found in contempt and who has been assessed compensatory damages should seek review of the finding of contempt by means of extraordinary writ (certiorari or habeas corpus), and should seek review of the question of the assessed amount of compensatory damages by appeal." *Smith, supra.* The wife has not appealed the $2,900 award. However, out of deference to the parties, we note that even if the wife had not admitted her contempt, there is ample evidence in the record to support the trial judge's determination that the bookcase and china cabinets were fixtures appurtenant to the house.

"A 'fixture' is an article that was once a chattel, but which, by being physically annexed or affixed to realty, has become accessory to it and 'part and parcel of it.'" *Milford v. Tennessee River Pulp and Paper Company,* 355 So.2d 687 (Ala. 1978). Whether an article is a fixture is a determination that must be made on the particular circumstances of each case. *Id.* The supreme court has articulated the criteria to be used in making this determination as follows:

"(1) Actual annexation to the realty or to something appurtenant thereto; (2) Appropriateness to the use or purposes of that part of the realty with which it is connected; (3) The intention of the party making the annexation of making permanent attachment to the freehold. This intention of the party making the annexation is inferred; (a) From the nature of the articles annexed; (b) The relation of the party making the annexation; (c) The structure and mode of annexation; (d) The purposes and uses for which the annexation has been made."

Id. (quoting *Langston v. State,* 96 Ala. 44, 11 So. 334 (1891)).

In her own testimony, the wife revealed that the articles had all been custom-built for the express purpose of being used with the family house, not just to be used in any house. All of the articles were anchored to the walls, and the china cabinets were each set into a permanent base. Under our limited scope of review, we cannot say that this testimony does not support a finding that the articles were intended to be fixtures, "part and parcel" of the house.

We are of the opinion that the trial court has not committed error in finding that the wife acted in contempt of the divorce decree. Further, her sentence of ten days in jail, with the opportunity to purge her contempt by paying to the clerk $2,900, is not unconstitutional. The decision of the trial court is affirmed.

AFFIRMED.

BRADLEY and HOLMES, JJ., concur.

of the earth and in the airspace above. Ancient laws decreed that an owner of the earth's surface rights of ownership extended from the surface downward to the center of the earth and upward indefinitely to the stars.

Airspace

The ability of humans to fly has reduced ownership from the surface to the stars, and there is now public domain airspace occurring at certain elevations above the surface of the earth. An owner of real property still owns the private airspace above the surface of the land. This private airspace is of a sufficient elevation to permit the construction of the tallest buildings and other structures found throughout the world.

This airspace can be quite valuable, especially as in a crowded city such as New York, where the airspace can be used for building purposes. For example, a charitable organization in New York City owned a four-story building that was located in the midst of multistory skyscrapers. The organization sold the airspace above its building to a developer for several million dollars. The developer used the building as a foundation and constructed a skyscraper within the airspace. Airspace also can be valuable in less populous areas to preserve a scenic view of a mountain or a shoreline. The advent of solar energy has increased the value of airspace, and most states provide for solar easements that create the right to purchase adjoining airspace to permit the sun to shine on solar heating or cooling units of a building.

Mineral Rights

Since the ownership of the surface of real property includes ownership extending from the surface to the center of the earth, an owner of real property usually owns all the minerals beneath the surface of the land. Some minerals, such as oil, gas, and coal, are more valuable than the land's surface. The law generally permits the ownership of real property to be divided horizontally; that is, ownership of the surface may be divided and be separate from ownership of the minerals beneath the surface. It is not uncommon for the owner of the surface to sell or lease the minerals separately from the surface to a company with the technology to extract the minerals, retaining a royalty or percentage of the profits on the sale of the minerals. Conversely, the surface of the land can be sold, and the owner can retain the rights to the minerals beneath the surface.

It is easy to see that tension can be created between the owner of the surface of land and a separate owner of the minerals beneath the surface. The mineral rights owner in its exploration efforts may disturb the surface of the land and make it unusable by the surface owner. Extensive mining underneath the surface for coal or other minerals can result in a collapse of improvements upon the surface, resulting in injury to both property and person. It is not uncommon for the sale of mineral rights to contain limitations upon the mineral rights owner's ability to disturb the surface in its exploration of minerals. States that have large mineral resources have enacted laws that not only define the rights of a mineral owner, but also resolve the conflicts between surface owners and mineral rights owners.

Trees, plants, and other things that grow in the soil may be considered real property. Trees, perennial bushes, grasses, and so on that do not require annual cultivation are considered real property. Annual crops produced by labor, such as wheat, corn, and soybeans, are considered personal property.

Water Rights

An owner of real property has certain ownership rights to use water that is located on or beneath the surface of the land. The users of water are diverse, such as governments, farmers, manufacturers, and consumers. Water pollution and changes in weather patterns that are responsible for below-average rainfall have combined to drastically reduce the amount of usable water available in many sections of the nation and have heightened competition among the users of water. Many states, in an effort to resolve this conflict, have enacted laws regulating the transfer, ownership, and use of water rights.

The source of water governs, to a great extent, a landowner's rights to own and use the water. The categories of water sources are (a) groundwater, such as an underground stream or spring; (b) surface water, which accumulates on the surface of the land from rain; and (c) water that accumulates in a river, stream, or natural lake.

Groundwater is water beneath the surface of the land. It is created by underground streams or by rain that soaks through the soil. A landowner's right to use an underground stream is governed by the same rules that govern rivers and streams on the surface of the land, which are hereinafter discussed. Groundwater that has been created by rain soaking through the soil is deemed to belong to the owner of the land on which the groundwater is found. The landowner has the right to use the groundwater in any way he or she chooses as long as the landowner does not use or divert the water in such a way as to intentionally harm an adjoining property owner.

A landowner can use *surface water* in any way he or she chooses as long as the use does not harm an adjoining property owner. The diversion of surface water by a landowner onto a neighbor's land may be a problem, especially when the terrain is hilly. For example, a property owner owns land that is at or near the bottom of a hill. Because of the natural flow of surface water, the property floods during rainy periods. The property owner decides to build a dam on the property to keep the surface water from flooding the land. The dam protects the property from flooding by diverting the water uphill onto a neighbor's property, causing the neighbor's property to flood. The flooding of the neighbor's property is unnatural because the flooding is caused by the artificial dam. The owner of the dam in this situation is liable to the neighbor for damages caused by the flooding because the dam altered the natural flow of the water. A property owner does not have the right to alter the natural flow of surface water.

Water located within a river, stream, or natural lake is owned by the state or federal government and not by the individual property owners whose properties adjoin the river, stream, or natural lake. Although an adjoining property owner to a river, stream, or natural lake does not have ownership rights of the water, in most states, the owner has a right to the beneficial use of the water. The right to the beneficial use of the water is governed by one of two areas of water law, known as **riparian rights** and **appropriation.** Riparian rights, derived from the Latin word *ripa,* for "river," are based on an ancient doctrine that all owners of riparian lands must share equally in the use of the water for domestic purposes. Riparian lands are those that border a stream, river, or natural lake. Under the riparian rights doctrine, an owner of riparian land has the right to use the water equally with other owners of riparian lands. This equal ownership means that a riparian owner does not have a right to interfere with the natural flow of the water in the river, stream, or lake. For example, an owner of riparian land could not create a dam across the river so that the water would cease to flow to other owners of riparian land. In addition, the riparian owner would not be able to channel the water from the river into a reservoir located on his or her property. Both the dam and the reservoir would alter the natural flow of the water and violate other owners' riparian rights to beneficial use of the water.

Appropriation, sometimes referred to as *prior appropriation,* is found in western states where water is scarce. This doctrine was developed in the nineteenth century to regulate the conflicts of water usage between settlers of the western states, predominantly miners,

riparian rights

Rights of the owners of lands adjoining streams, rivers, and lakes relating to the water and its use.

appropriation

In regard to water law, doctrine stating that water belongs to the person who first makes beneficial use of it.

farmers, and ranchers. Under the appropriation or prior appropriation water rights doctrine, the right to use the water is given to the landowner who uses the water first. The date of appropriation determines the user's priority to use water, with the earliest user having the superior right. If the water is insufficient to meet all needs, those earlier in time or first in time obtain all the allotted water and those who appropriate later receive only some or none of the water. The first in time, or first-right appropriation, concept contrasts sharply with the riparian tradition of prorating the entitlement to water among all users during times of scarcity.

In order to obtain rights to water, a landowner must prove that he has appropriated the water. Generally, this requires an intentional act by the landowner to use the water for a beneficial use. The intentional act is usually the construction of a channel or reservoir to move the water from its natural source and the storage or usage of the water on the landowner's property. The landowner must use the diverted water for a beneficial use. What is a "beneficial use" is usually determined by state law. Generally, domestic use such as drinking water, agricultural use such as irrigation, and water used in manufacturing are considered beneficial uses.

All states that follow the appropriation theory of water rights usage have established administrative agencies to issue water permits in connection with water usage. The chief purpose of the administrative procedures is to provide an orderly method for appropriating water and regulating established water rights. Water rights under the appropriation theory are transferable from one property owner to another. It is possible to transfer water rights without a transfer of land and to transfer land without a transfer of water rights. Each state has its own regulatory system and requirements for the transfer of water rights.

Ownership of Real Property

The legal profession, including paralegals, spends time and clients' money worrying about the ownership of real property. The basic principle that only the owner of real property can sell or pledge it as security for a debt means that on any typical sale or loan transaction, title examinations and other efforts are made by legal counsel for the purchaser or lender to determine the extent of the seller's or borrower's ownership of the real property.

The chief legal rights accorded an owner of real property are possession, use, and power of disposition. An owner of real property has the right to possess the property. **Possession** is occupation of the land evidenced by visible acts such as an enclosure, cultivation, the construction of improvements, or the occupancy of existing improvements. Possession gives the property owner the right to exclude others from the land. Occupancy of land by someone without the permission of the owner is a *trespass*. The owner may evict the trespasser from the land and/or sue the trespasser for money damages or even have the trespasser arrested.

A landowner has the right to use the land for profit or pleasure. Absolute freedom to use land has never existed, and the modern owner is faced with several limitations on the use of land arising from public demands of health, safety, and public welfare as well as the rights of neighbors to the safety and enjoyment of their property. The law, however, does favor the free use of land, and doubts will be resolved in favor of the owner.

An owner of property has the right to dispose of that ownership. The power of disposition may take place by inheritance or will at the owner's death, or it may take place during the owner's lifetime by contract, deed, or lease. The law favors the free right to transfer

possession

Occupation of land evidenced by visible acts such as enclosure, cultivation, the construction of improvements, or the occupancy of existing improvements.

ownership, and any restraint on this right will not be upheld unless the restraint supports some important public purpose or private right.

Private property rights are subject to the right of sovereignty exercised by federal, state, and local governments. Therefore, private ownership is subject to the powers to tax; to regulate the use of private property in the interest of public safety, health, and the general welfare; and to take private property for public use. A government's power to regulate, tax, and take private property for public use is discussed in Chapter 4.

METHODS OF ACQUIRING OWNERSHIP TO REAL PROPERTY

The main methods of acquiring ownership to real property are inheritance, devise, gift, sale, and adverse possession.

Inheritance and Devise

inheritance

Ability to acquire ownership to real property because of one's kinship to a deceased property owner who dies without a will.

devise

Transfer of real property by means of a last will and testament.

The first two methods, **inheritance** and **devise,** are ownership transfers that take place on the death of the previous owner. Inheritance, or descent, as it is also known, is the passage of title and ownership of real property from one who dies intestate (without a will) to people whom the law designates because of blood or marriage as the owner's heirs. Each state has its own inheritance statute, and the statutes vary slightly from state to state. The law of the state where the property is located decides who is to inherit.

An example of a typical inheritance statute is shown in Exhibit 1–1. The closest group of heirs to the deceased property owner will inherit all the property. For example, in Exhibit 1–1, if the deceased property owner is survived by a spouse and children, the spouse and children will inherit all the property. If the deceased property owner is not survived by a spouse or children, the deceased property owner's surviving parents and/or siblings, if any, will inherit the property.

The acquisition of ownership by devise is the passage of title of real property from one who dies *with* a will. A **will** is a legal document prepared during the property owner's lifetime that indicates where and how the owner's property is to be disposed of at the owner's death. The **conveyance** of real property in a will is referred to as a devise. The will must comply with the state law governing wills. Again, the state law where the real property is located will control.

will

Legal document by which a person disposes of his property. A will takes effect on the death of the maker of the will.

conveyance

The transfer of title of some or all of the ownership rights to real property from one person to another. A conveyance is usually by instrument such as a deed, lease, or mortgage.

Gift

Ownership to real property can be obtained by a gift. Once the gift is complete, and with real property this would be on the proper execution and delivery of a **deed** to the property, the gift is irrevocable. The promise to make a gift, however, usually is revocable. An exception to the revocation of gifts rule is in the event that the recipient of the gift has detrimentally relied on the belief that the gift would be made. The injured party may recover costs for the detrimental reliance. For example, you purchase insurance for a home based on someone's promise to give you that home. If the gift is not made, you would be able to recover the cost of the insurance.

deed

Written document that transfers ownership of real property from one person to another.

Contract and Sale

Property ownership can be obtained by buying the property. This is the transaction that involves most real estate paralegals and attorneys. A complete discussion of contracts and the sale of property is found in Chapters 6 and 7.

EXHIBIT 1–1

Example of a State
Inheritance Statute

RULES OF INHERITANCE WHEN DECEDENT DIES WITHOUT A WILL

(a) For purposes of this Code section:

(1) Children of the decedent who are born after the decedent's death are considered children in being at the decedent's death, provided they were conceived prior to the decedent's death, were born within ten months of the decedent's death, and survived 120 hours or more after birth; and

(2) The half-blood, whether on the maternal or paternal side, are considered equally with the whole-blood, so that the children of any common parent are treated as brothers and sisters to each other.

(b) When a decedent dies without a will, the following rules shall determine such decedent's heirs:

(1) Upon the death of an individual who is survived by a spouse but not by any child or other descendant, the spouse is the sole heir. If the decedent is also survived by any child or other descendant, the spouse shall share equally with the children, with the descendants of any deceased child taking that child's share, *per stirpes*; provided, however, that the spouse's portion shall not be less than a one-third share;

(2) If the decedent is not survived by a spouse, the heirs shall be those relatives, as provided in this Code section, who are in the nearest degree to the decedent in which there is any survivor;

(3) Children of the decedent are in the first degree, and those who survive the decedent shall share the estate equally, with the descendants of any deceased child taking, *per stirpes*, the share that child would have taken if in life;

(4) Parents of the decedent are in the second degree, and those who survive the decedent shall share the estate equally;

(5) Siblings of the decedent are in the third degree, and those who survive the decedent shall share the estate equally, with the descendants of any deceased sibling taking, *per stirpes*, the share that sibling would have taken if in life; provided, however, that if no sibling survives the decedent, the nieces and nephews who survive the decedent shall take the estate in equal shares, with the descendants of any deceased niece or nephew taking, *per stirpes*, the share that niece or nephew would have taken if in life;

(6) Grandparents of the decedent are in the fourth degree, and those who survive the decedent shall share the estate equally;

(7) Uncles and aunts of the decedent are in the fifth degree, and those who survive the decedent shall share the estate equally, with the children of any deceased uncle or aunt taking, *per stirpes*, the share that uncle or aunt would have taken if in life; provided, however, that if no uncle or aunt of the decedent survives the decedent, the first cousins who survive the decedent shall share the estate equally; and

(8) The more remote degrees of kinship shall be determined by counting the number of steps in the chain from the relative to the closest common ancestor of the relative and decedent and the number of steps in the chain from the common ancestor to the decedent. The sum of the steps in the two chains shall be the degree of kinship, and the surviving relatives with the lowest sum shall be in the nearest degree and shall share the estate equally. (Code 1981, § 53-2-1, enacted by Ga. L. 1996, p. 504, §10.)

Delmar/Cengage Learning

Adverse Possession

Possession of real property is given substantial legal protection. Even a party in unlawful possession of the real property has the right to exclude anyone else from possession except for the true owner. Possession, in and of itself, also engenders, through time, the inference that the possession began lawfully. The longer the continued possession, the stronger this inference. If possession is maintained long enough, it is possible that the person in

adverse possession

Method of acquiring ownership to real property by possession for a statutory time period.

possession becomes the owner through a process known as **adverse possession.** Adverse possession operates as a statute of limitations, in the sense that it precludes all others from contesting the title of the possessor.

The rules on adverse possession vary from state to state. Typically, the possessor must possess the property for a period ranging from 7 to 20 years. The possession also must be adverse, which means without the consent or permission of the true owner. In some states, it is necessary that an adverse possessor have knowledge that he is in adverse possession of the property. An example of how this works follows.

Assume that property owners Andy and Barbara are neighbors and that Andy has built a fence on what Andy believes to be the property line, but in fact, the fence encroaches 1 foot onto Barbara's property. Andy is unaware of this encroachment and maintains the fence for 20 years. In a state that requires Andy to have knowledge that he is an adverse possessor, Andy, even though he has satisfied the statute of limitations for adverse possession, would not become the owner of this additional 1 foot of Barbara's property.

In addition to the possession being adverse, it must be public, continuous, peaceful, exclusive, and uninterrupted.

tacking

The addition of possession periods by different adverse possessors.

Tacking of possession is permitted if there is some contractual or blood relationship between the two adverse possessors. Tacking is the adding of possession periods by different adverse possessors. For example, adverse possessor Andy enters into possession of the property, keeps it for 7 years, and then sells it to adverse possessor Barbara. Adverse possessor Barbara, in a state that requires 20 years of adverse possession, could tack or add onto adverse possessor Andy's period of possession because of the contractual relationship between the two. Then Barbara would have to stay in possession only 13 years to obtain ownership.

The meaning of possession for purposes of adverse possession varies from state to state. *Possession,* in a strict sense, means occupancy and use of the property. Acts of possession include residing in improvements located on the property; enclosing property by fences, walls, or other artificial barriers; or constructing permanent buildings, such as a home, on the land followed by occupancy. In addition, planting, cultivating, and harvesting crops and produce from the land are considered acts of possession. Some states, however, require that the adverse possessor pay taxes on the real property during the period of possession.

color of title

A form of adverse possession where the original possession of the property by a prescriber is based upon a written instrument such as a deed or court decree.

Adverse possession may also take place when there is **color of title.** Color of title is shown by a written instrument such as a deed, court decree, or judgment. States permit the color of title to be unrecorded but do require that it contain a sufficient description of the property to identify the property being possessed.

Generally, color of title is shown by a deed that for some reason is void and therefore did not legally transfer title to the grantee. In addition, the grantee of the deed must not have had knowledge that the deed was void. Color of title adverse possession requires a stated period of possession (usually 7 years) to transform into ownership. For example, if a person acquires property by a deed from a partnership signed by a partner who did not have authority to sell the property, the partner's lack of authority would cause the deed not to transfer title. The grantee of the deed, however, is unaware of the partner's lack of authority. He or she enters into possession under the deed. The possession would be adverse to the partnership but could evolve into ownership after 7 years.

Even though ownership to real property can be obtained through adverse possession, except for adverse possession under color of title, there is no written documentation or proof of this ownership. If the adverse possessor attempts to sell the real property, chances are he or she will have a difficult time establishing title. One means of establishing ownership through adverse possession is by bringing what is known as a "quiet title" action to perfect title to the real property. In a quiet title action, the adverse possessor sues the entire world and challenges anyone to step forward and object to the adverse possessor's claim of ownership. In the suit, the adverse possessor would then bring proof through affidavits or witnesses as to the adverse possessor's necessary period of possession and the nature of that possession. If the court finds that the adverse possessor is now the owner, it will issue a judgment adjudicating the adverse possessor's ownership. This judgment could then be used to establish ownership for purposes of future sales.

Generally, a person cannot obtain adverse possession against property that benefits the public, no matter how long his possession. Therefore, title by adverse possession cannot be obtained in any property owned by a city, county, state, or other public government entity, such as a public park or school.

HISTORY OF AMERICAN REAL PROPERTY LAW

The early settlers who came to America from Europe brought with them the laws of their native land, including the laws concerning land ownership. Except for Louisiana, Texas, and portions of the Southwest, where the civil laws of France and Spain have substantial influence, most modern real property law is the product of English feudal law, which developed into what is known as the common law.

Feudalism grew out of the chaos of the Dark Ages. Because of the collapse of all central law and order, people banded together for security and stability, with usually the strongest member of the group taking command. The stronger members became known as lords, and the weaker members became known as tenants or vassals of the lord. For the lord to keep the allegiance of the vassals, it became necessary to compensate them for their services. Because almost all the wealth of the lords at that time was in the form of land, the land was parceled out to the vassals for services. Tenures or rights to possession were created. The early tenures were of four main types: (1) *knight tenure,* land given in return for pledged armed services; (2) *serjeanty tenure,* land given in return for performance of ceremonial services for the lord (later this evolved into ordinary domestic services such as cook and butler); (3) *frankalmoign tenure,* land given for religious purposes to priests and other religious bodies; and (4) *socage tenure,* land given to farmers. These early field tenures evolved into the concept of estates (derived from the Latin word *status*), which became the primary basis of classification of interests in land. The word *estate* is still used today to express the degree, quantity, nature, duration, or extent of an owner's interest in real property.

The word "fee" is used to describe many modern-day estates evolved from the ancient English doctrine of tenure, which was based upon the notion of a lord giving up his land to a tenant in return for *homage* (rent) and service. The holding of the tenure by the tenant was called his *fief* or *fee.* So long as homage was paid by the tenant, the lord was bound to respect the tenant's rights for his lifetime. Over a period of several decades, the lords began to believe that the tenant's heirs had a right to take up the tenant's property upon the tenant's death and to continue to pay homage to the lord and keep the land. This created the ability to transfer the fee to heirs of the tenant at the tenant's death, and the concept of inheritance began to be associated with fee ownership.

The ability to transfer a fee during the tenant's life took longer to establish. The ability of the tenant to transfer the property during his lifetime was first viewed as a means of the tenant to deprive his heirs of their future ownership of the property, or to otherwise disinherit the heirs, and was at first considered against public policy.

The power to sell property during the tenant's lifetime was first recognized with purchased land, rather than inherited land. The idea was that one must not take advantage of the right of inheritance and then deprive one's own heirs of the same advantage. However, as the law continued to evolve in England, the right of transfer became well established and applied to both purchased and inherited land.

Modern-Day Estates in Real Property

There are six types of modern-day estates in real property: (1) fee simple or fee simple absolute, (2) fee simple determinable, (3) fee simple on condition subsequent, (4) life estate, (5) estate for years, and (6) estate at will.

Fee Simple or Fee Simple Absolute

Fee simple or **fee simple absolute** is the highest and best kind of estate an owner can have. It is one in which the owner is entitled to the entire estate, with unconditional powers of disposition during the owner's lifetime and the power to transfer the property to heirs and legal representatives on the owner's death.

Fee simple or fee simple absolute is maximum legal ownership and has a potentially infinite duration and unrestricted inheritability. In most states, no special language is needed to create a fee simple absolute. The presumption is that a fee simple estate is created at every conveyance unless a lesser estate is mentioned and limited in the conveyance. Most homes and commercial properties are owned in fee simple.

Fee Simple Determinable

A **fee simple determinable** is an ownership in real property that is limited to expire automatically on the happening or nonhappening of an event that is stated in the deed of conveyance or the will creating the estate. For example, Aaron conveys to Bill "to have and to hold to Bill so long as the land is used for residential purposes. When the land is no longer used for residential purposes, it shall revert to Aaron." The use of the words *so long as* to preface the condition under ancient English common law created a fee simple determinable, and in modern times, most states recognize that the use of these words preceding the statement of a condition in a deed or will creates a fee simple determinable. The estate granted is a fee, and like the fee simple absolute, it can be inherited and may last forever so long as the condition is not broken. Yet it is a determinable fee because there is a condition. The estate will automatically expire on the nonoccurrence or occurrence of the event, for example, the use of the land for nonresidential purposes. The estate conveyed to Bill will automatically end if and when the land is used for nonresidential purposes, and Aaron will again own the estate in fee simple absolute. During the existence of Bill's ownership of the fee simple determinable, Aaron retains a future interest in the land called a *possibility* or *right of reverter.* Aaron's possibility of reverter can be passed on to Aaron's heirs at Aaron's death. Aaron's possibility of reverter also may be transferred to a third party at the time of the conveyance to Bill. For example, Aaron conveys to Bill to "have and to hold so long as the land is used for residential purposes and then to Carol. If the land is not used for residential purposes, it will go to Carol, Aaron's possibility of reverter having been transferred to Carol."

Fee Simple on Condition Subsequent

A **fee simple on condition subsequent** exists when a fee simple is subject to a power in the grantor (person who conveyed the fee) to recover the conveyed estate on the happening of a specified event. "Aaron transfers to Bill on the express condition that the land shall not be used for nonresidential purposes, and if it is, Aaron shall have the right to reenter and possess the land." The use of the words *on the express condition that* under English common law created a fee simple on condition subsequent, and in modern times, most states recognize that the use of these words preceding the statement of a condition in a deed or will creates a fee simple on condition subsequent. Bill has a fee simple on condition subsequent, and

---

fee simple or **fee simple absolute**

Estate of real property with infinite duration and no restrictions on use.

fee simple determinable

Estate of real property with potential infinite duration. The ownership of a fee simple determinable is subject to a condition, the breach of which can result in termination of the estate. A fee simple determinable automatically expires on the nonoccurrence or occurrence of a condition.

fee simple on condition subsequent

Estate of real property with potential infinite duration. The ownership of a fee simple on condition subsequent is subject to a condition, the breach of which can result in termination of the estate. A fee simple on condition subsequent continues in existence until an action is brought to recover the property.

Aaron has the right of entry or power of termination. On the happening of the stated event, the granted estate will continue in existence until Aaron effectively exercises the option to terminate by making entry or bringing an action to recover the property. A breach of the condition does not cause an automatic termination of the fee simple on condition subsequent estate. The basic difference, therefore, between the fee simple determinable and the fee simple on condition subsequent is that the former automatically expires on violation of the specified condition contained in the instrument creating the estate, whereas the latter continues until it is terminated by the exercise of the grantor's power to terminate. Aaron's right to reenter can be transferred to a third party in the same manner as the possibility of reverter in a fee simple determinable.

Creation of a fee simple determinable or fee simple on condition subsequent gives a property owner the means of controlling the use of the property after the transfer or after the property owner's death. This element of control may be important to the property owner for a number of reasons. For example, a farmer owns a farm that has been in the family for generations. The farmer has three children. Two of the children have left the farm and live in the city. The third child has expressed an interest in staying on the farm and taking it over on the farmer's retirement or death. The farmer may be able to satisfy his objectives by transferring the family farm to the child who desires to continue farming in fee simple on condition subsequent or fee simple determinable, on the condition that the land always be used as a farm.

A conditional fee is also used in transfers of property to a charity. A property owner often is willing to transfer valuable land to a charity, provided it is used for specific charitable purposes. For example, a property owner is willing to convey land to her college, provided the land be used to expand the college's law school. The property owner could accomplish this by transferring a conditional fee to the college on the condition that the land be used for the expansion of the law school. The property owner may want to give the possibility of reverter or right of reentry to the property owner's family.

Fee simple determinable or fee simple on condition subsequent ownership, owing to the threat that ownership will terminate in the event the condition is breached, makes a property difficult to sell. In addition, most lending institutions who lend money on the security of real property will not make a loan or receive conditional fee title as security for a loan. These reasons have made the fee simple determinable and fee simple on condition subsequent somewhat uncommon forms of ownership.

Life Estate

A **life estate** has its duration measured by the life or lives of one or more persons. An estate for life may be for either the life of the owner or the life of some other person or people ("measuring life"). Life estates may be created by deed, will, or an express agreement of the parties. For example, an elderly woman owns a duplex home. Her daughter, to provide her mother with money, wants to buy the duplex. The daughter is willing to give to the mother a life estate in the side of the duplex that the mother has been living in for the past several years. Therefore, the mother will continue living in her portion of the duplex during her lifetime, and on her death, the daughter would have full fee simple title to all the duplex.

At the time of the creation of a life estate, there also is retained or created a reversion or remainder interest. For example, Aaron transfers to Bill a life estate for the life of Bill. As part of this transfer, a reversion right to Aaron is implicitly created. This means that on Bill's death, the property will revert back to Aaron. Aaron's reversion right is not contingent on Aaron's surviving Bill, and Aaron's reversion right can be transferred by Aaron during Aaron's lifetime, or it may be inherited by Aaron's heirs at his death or transferred by Aaron's will. This reversion right also can be transferred by Aaron to a third party, and

life estate

Estate of real property the duration of which is measured by the life or lives of one or more persons.

EXHIBIT 1–2

Difference between a Reversion
and a Remainder

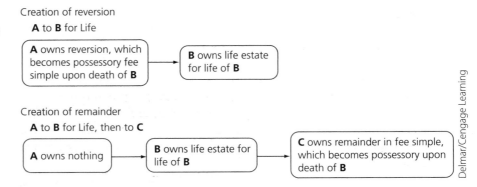

Creation of reversion

A to **B** for Life

> **A** owns reversion, which becomes possessory fee simple upon death of **B** → **B** owns life estate for life of **B**

Creation of remainder

A to **B** for Life, then to **C**

> **A** owns nothing → **B** owns life estate for life of **B** → **C** owns remainder in fee simple, which becomes possessory upon death of **B**

Delmar/Cengage Learning

this transfer could take place at the time of the transfer of the life estate to Bill. For example, Aaron transfers to Bill a life estate for the life of Bill, then to Carol. This means that on Bill's death, the property will go to Carol. Carol has what is known as a vested remainder in fee simple. Carol's right to own the property in fee simple on Bill's death is not dependent on Carol's surviving Bill. If Carol dies before Bill, Carol's vested remainder in fee simple will pass to Carol's heirs or the devisees under her will. Carol's heirs or the devisees under the will receive the property on Bill's death. The difference between a reversion and a remainder is illustrated in the life estate timeline diagrams in Exhibit 1–2.

The owner of a life estate is entitled to the full use and enjoyment of the real property so long as the owner exercises ordinary care and prudence for the preservation and protection of the real property and commits no acts intending to cause permanent injury to the person entitled to own the real property after the termination of the life estate. If the life estate owner of the real property does not take care of the real property, the owner will be deemed to commit **waste,** and the life estate will terminate, even though the measuring life is still alive. Failure to make needed repairs or improvements, the cutting of timber for sale, or the mining of minerals have all been held to be acts of waste. Because forfeiture of ownership is the penalty for waste, most courts are reluctant to find waste, and the decisions vary from state to state as to what acts of a life estate owner constitute waste.

As a general rule, the life estate owner is entitled to all income generated from the real property and is entitled to possession of the real property during the ownership of the life estate. Life estates are transferable, although the life estate owner can transfer only what he or she has, which is a life estate for the measuring life. A life estate owner usually has the obligation to pay taxes on the real property, keep the real property adequately insured, and pay debts secured by the real property. Because death terminates the life estate and death is so uncertain an event, a life estate ownership is difficult to sell or pledge as security for a loan.

waste

Action or nonaction that causes a loss of value to real property.

Future Interests

The fee simple determinable, fee simple on condition subsequent, and life estate all have the effect of creating different ownerships in the same property. This division of the property into different ownerships is known as the *creation of a future interest.* The example set forth under the discussion of fee simple determinable, where Aaron conveys to Bill "to have and to hold for as long as the land is used for residential purposes" and then to Carol, creates a future interest in Carol. It is possible that Carol at some future time will own the property in fee if it is not used for residential purposes. There is no certainty that Carol will ever own the property in the future in fee since there is no certainty that the condition will be broken.

Future interests are present ownership interests in the property, but the right to possession and use of the property is deferred until some future event occurs, such as the death of the life owner or the breach of a condition in a conditional fee.

Future interests generally are *reverters, reversions,* or *remainders.* The term *revert* describes the coming back of the land when one owner dies or when a condition is breached (in the case of a conditional fee).

By contrast with the word *revert,* the word *remain* is used to express the fact of land staying away from the grantor and remaining with some other person.

Future interests may be better understood if you view a property as this book. The present ownerships, that is, life estates, fee simple determinable, or fee simple on condition subsequent, and the future interests, that is, the reversions, possibilities of reverter, or remainders, are not chapters of the book. Rather, they identify persons who at one point in time may own the whole book.

For example, a property is transferred from A to B for life. Think of this book being given from A to B to own until B's death. Upon B's death, the book will be returned to A, and A will have the whole book again.

Consider also a transfer where the real property is transferred from A to B for life and then to C. Think of this book being given from A to B to own during B's lifetime. On the death of B, the book will be given to C, who at that time will have full ownership rights to the book and will have no obligation to deliver the book to A. Upon C's death, the ownership of the book will be transferred to the heirs of C.

Put simply, present ownerships and future interests own the entire book at different times.

Estate for Years

An **estate for years** is limited in its duration to a fixed period. For example, "Aaron to Bill for 20 years" would create an estate for years in Bill. The estate for years would continue until the period of ownership terminates. Next to the fee simple estate, the estate for years is the most common form of ownership. An estate for years may be a lease, but not all leases are estate for years. For a lease to be an estate for years, it must be clear that ownership to the real property is conveyed and not mere rights to possession.

A complete discussion on leases is contained in Chapter 18.

> **estate for years**
>
> Estate of real property the duration of which is for a definite period.

Estate at Will

An **estate at will** is an estate with no fixed term that is created by the express or implied agreements of the parties. An estate at will can automatically be terminated; however, under modern law, there may be some notice requirement (30- or 60-day notice) before termination. An estate at will may be created by implication. For example, Aaron transfers to Bill an estate for years for 20 years. At the expiration of the 20 years, Bill remains in possession of the real property and continues to pay rental to Aaron, which Aaron accepts. Once the estate for years has expired (i.e., the 20 years), Bill is not in possession as an owner of an estate for years, so the law usually will imply that Bill now has an estate at will, that is, Bill is in possession with the consent of Aaron. Aaron can terminate Bill's possession and ownership rights immediately or on any statutory notice if required in the state where the real property is located.

> **estate at will**
>
> Estate of real property the duration of which is for an indefinite period. An estate at will can be terminated at the will of the parties.

ROLE OF PARALEGAL IN REAL ESTATE LEGAL PRACTICE

The opportunities for a real estate paralegal are plentiful and diversified. Private law firms—large and small, urban and rural—employ real estate paralegals to assist with real estate transactions. Many corporations and government agencies also employ paralegals. For example, development and construction firms and major retailers, such as Walmart, Home Depot, and Gap, work on real estate matters as a major part of their business activities. Furthermore, banks and life insurance companies lend money for real estate projects and may have in-house legal departments that supervise their real estate lending activities. In addition, gas, telephone, and electric utility companies have corporate legal departments that deal with real estate matters. In the public sector, government agencies responsible for the regulation and development of real estate, including public housing authorities and public transportation authorities, also employ paralegals.

The skills used by paralegals in a real estate practice include preparation of legal documents, examination and review of real property titles, preparation of land descriptions, preparation and review of leases, and the fact-finding investigative work required to represent purchasers, sellers, and lenders in connection with real estate transactions. The role of a paralegal in each of these skill areas will be examined in more detail throughout various chapters of this book.

Research Materials for Real Property Law

The law of real property is generally governed by the state law of the state in which the real property is located. State law is generally divided into two classifications: statutes and judicial decisions. Statutes are laws passed by the state's elected legislature. These statutes are usually assembled into a code. Most codes are available in law libraries at law firms, law schools, and courthouses and may also be available at public libraries.

Decisions rendered by a state court such as a court of appeals or supreme court are published and bound together in the form of a reporter for each state. Reporters are generally found in the same law libraries as statutes.

Decisions of trial courts are generally not recorded or published. These decisions are usually not considered precedent for future decisions but can be helpful in understanding a particular trial court's interpretation of the law. Trial court decisions are unofficial and can only be obtained by going to the courthouse and reviewing files regarding the case in which the decision was issued.

Most state bar associations or local publishers publish practice books on areas of real property law. Because most states require attorneys to continue education in order to maintain a license to practice law, these continuing education programs often publish very valuable materials concerning both the law and practical aspects of real estate transactions. Many of these continuing education program books can be purchased through the sponsors of the programs, and many law firms purchase and keep continuing education books within their libraries.

Treatises—short comprehensive summaries of specific areas of law—are also published by many local state law publishers. These treatises may be written by a law professor or an attorney practicing in the topic area on which the treatise is focused. Most law libraries have copies of the major treatises published within the state.

Access to state statutes, judicial decisions, treatises, and other source information on real property law can also be obtained through online services. Programs such as Westlaw provide, for a fee, access to a wide range of legal source materials via the computer.

The Internet also contains a large amount of both free and subscriber-based information concerning real property law. The Real Property, Probate, and Trust Law Section of the American Bar Association maintains free information on the following Web site at *http://www.abanet.org*. A Web site known as Dirt provides worthwhile information for a fee at *http://cctr.umkc.edu*.

Real property sections of state bar associations also maintain Web pages that may provide valuable information concerning different areas of real property law within the state. The Legal Information Institute at Cornell University maintains a Web site that provides valuable information concerning all areas of the law, including real property law. It can be accessed at *http://www.law.cornell.edu*.

Search engines such as Google and Yahoo have links to Web pages that provide valuable information concerning a variety of real property subjects. To find these links, go to the search page and type in the keywords for the subject matter. For example, if you are interested in tenants in common, type in the words *tenants in common,* and the engine will provide a number of Web page links for the subject. Google can be found at *http://www .google.com,* and Yahoo can be accessed at the main Web page of *http://www.yahoo.com* or the less-cluttered search page at *http://search.yahoo.com.*

Blogs are also helpful in researching real property subjects. A blog is a log or journal of an individual's or institution's postings on the Internet. Blogs are generally presented in a journal style with a new entry each day. It is important in reviewing or reading a blog to remember that the information posted may be an individual's opinion with no peer review or guarantee of accuracy of content. Legal blogs are also called *blawgs.* Blawgs can be found on Law.com's Legal Blog Watch at *http://legalblogwatch.typepad.com* and Blawg at *http://www.blawg.org.*

🏛 ETHICS: Introduction

Ethics—service to others performed in a moral and honest manner—is the cornerstone of a professional practice. It is essential that the system for establishing and dispensing justice be developed and maintained in such a way that the public shall have absolute confidence in the integrity and impartiality of its administration. Such a system cannot exist unless the conduct and motives of the members of the legal profession merit the approval of all just and honest citizens. Not only is the future of this country and its justice system dependent on the ethical conduct of those who are licensed to administer justice, but also the future of the legal profession depends on its members acting in an ethical manner. Lawyers are asked daily to deal with the most intimate and serious problems that affect clients. Only a profession made up of members with the highest ethical considerations can continue to deliver the service and confidence demanded by the public.

Attorneys are governed by two sets of ethical rules: the American Bar Association's Model Rules of Professional Conduct and Model Code of Professional Responsibility and the ethical codes and rules of professional responsibility promulgated by state bar associations. A violation of these rules can result in disciplinary action being brought against the errant attorney, including such drastic penalties as the loss of a license to practice law.

It is not clear that paralegals are bound and covered by the various ethical codes and rules of professional conduct applicable to attorneys. Because paralegals are not licensed, there is no removal of license sanction that could be imposed against a paralegal for violation of ethical codes or rules of professional conduct. *Attorneys, however, who are responsible for and supervise the activities of the paralegal can be sanctioned and disciplined for the actions of the paralegal under the attorney's control and supervision.*

Several states have adopted guidelines to assist an attorney in the utilization of paralegals. These state guidelines generally try to provide answers in several areas of ethics where nonlawyers performing legal services deal indirectly with clients and the public. Most of these state guidelines cover such areas as unauthorized practice of law, disclosure of status as a paralegal, confidentiality, conflicts of interest, and those matters that can be supervised and delegated by an attorney to a paralegal. These areas of ethical concern will be revisited in ethics discussions throughout the book.

The two major paralegal professional associations, the NALA, The National Association of Paralegals and the National Federation of Paralegal Associations (NFPA) have adopted codes of ethics as guidelines for professional ethical conduct of their members. Copies of these ethical codes can be obtained on each association's Web site:

NALA, The National Association of Paralegals *www.nala.org*

National Federation of Paralegal Associations, Inc. *www.paralegals.org*

SUMMARY

The ability to possess property, use it, and dispose of it either by sale or at death by inheritance or will all depends upon the rules of ownership. These rules of ownership can be complex. Ownership can be divided horizontally to permit separate ownership of the airspace, the surface, and the minerals beneath the surface of land. Ownership of real property can also be held in different estates, such as fee simple, fee simple determinable, fee simple on condition subsequent, life estate, estate for years, and estate at will. Each of these estates provides the owner with different rights and limitations.

In any sale, lease, or loan transaction, it is important to determine who owns the real property in question and what estate is held by the owner. It is important in each transaction that the estate owned be sufficient to satisfy all the parties' expectations for the transaction. A fee simple absolute estate usually will be satisfactory under all circumstances. Other estates may not be satisfactory, and a paralegal must be conscious of the limitations that each of the lesser estates imposes on the ownership and use of the real property.

KEY TERMS

adverse possession	estate for years	inheritance
appropriation	fee simple or fee simple	life estate
color of title	absolute	possession
conveyance	fee simple determinable	riparian rights
deed	fee simple on condition	tacking
devise	subsequent	waste
estate at will	fixture	will

REVIEW QUESTIONS

1. What is real property, and how does it differ from personal property?

2. What is the difference between riparian rights and appropriation?

3. What test does the court use to determine if an item is a fixture?

4. What are the chief legal rights accorded to an owner of real property?

5. How does a fee simple determinable differ from a fee simple on condition subsequent?

6. What is the concept of waste, and how is it applicable to a life estate?

7. Name the various ways a person can become an owner of real property.

8. What is the difference between inheritance and receiving property by devise?

9. What are the elements of adverse possession?

10. Why would anyone want to create a life estate?

CASE PROBLEMS

1. Oscar is the owner in fee simple of Black Acre, on which is located a weather-beaten old house. Adam has asked Oscar if he, Adam, might move into the house on Black Acre. Oscar grants the request, and Adam moves in. Shortly thereafter, Oscar sells Black Acre to Barbara. The statute of limitations in the state where Black Acre is located is 10 years for adverse possession. Adam knew nothing about Oscar's sale to Barbara and occupies the house for 12 years after such sale. Adam, during the whole period of occupancy, thinks he is occupying the property with Oscar's permission. Barbara discovers Adam's occupancy of the house and demands that Adam leave the house. Adam refuses to leave. Barbara sues Adam for trespass, and Adam defends that he is an adverse possessor and is now the owner of Black Acre. Who wins?

2. Aaron transfers to Bob a life estate in a house with the remainder to Carol. Carol dies before Bob. On Bob's death, will the property go to Aaron or to Carol's heirs?

3. Aaron transfers a life estate to Bob for the life of Carol with the remainder to David. What interest does Carol have in the property? If Bob dies before Carol, who owns the property until Carol's death?

4. Aaron transfers property to Bill for the life of Carol, then to David. Bill sells his life estate to Susan. Carol dies before Bill. Until Bill's death, who owns the property?

5. Adam has entered into a contract to sell his home to Barbara. The home features a hot tub on its rear deck, a beautiful chandelier in the dining room, and a built-in home entertainment center in the den. These special features, among others, persuaded Barbara to enter into a contract to buy the home from Adam. The contract is not carefully written and does not expressly require Adam to sell these three items to Barbara. The contract only mentions that Adam will sell the home and all fixtures to Barbara. At the time the ownership of the home is to be transferred to Barbara, Adam takes the position that the spa, chandelier, and home entertainment center are not part of the sale. Can Barbara require Adam to sell these items to her pursuant to the contract? What are the main issues involved in such a determination?

PRACTICAL ASSIGNMENTS

1. Obtain a copy of your state's statutes of inheritance or descent and compare them with the inheritance statute shown as Exhibit 1–1.

2. What is required in your state for a person to obtain ownership to real property by adverse possession?

3. Research your state's law concerning waste by an owner of a life estate, and list three examples of things ruled to be waste by the courts of your state.

4. An elderly parent informs her daughter that if the daughter leaves her commercial real estate paralegal career in London, returns home, and takes care of the parent, that the parent will give to the daughter a valuable parcel of commercial real property. This communication is in the form of a letter signed by the parent. The daughter, upon receipt of the letter, quits her paralegal career in London and moves home to take care of the parent. The daughter moves in with the parent and takes care of all her daily needs for one year. At the end of the year, the daughter asks the parent about preparing a deed and transferring the commercial property as promised in the letter to the daughter. The parent refuses and states that she never intended to give the commercial property to the daughter; it was merely a trick to get the daughter to leave London and return home. Research your state's law to see if the daughter could, if she so chose, bring a successful civil action against the parent to honor the promise of the gift. Would the daughter be able to recover the commercial property and obtain damages, or would there be no recovery? Please prepare a brief memorandum stating what case authority you were able to find to support or defeat the daughter's case.

Student StudyWare™ CD-ROM

Interactive Student CD in the book includes additional quizzing, case studies, and key terms flashcards.

Online Companion™

For additional resources, please go to *www.paralegal.delmar.cengage.com*

chapter | 2

Concurrent Ownership

Objectives

After reading this chapter, you should be able to:

- Distinguish and explain the four types of concurrent ownership
- Identify the rights, duties, and liabilities of common owners
- Understand the difference between individual and community property
- Draft a cotenancy agreement

Outline

Real property may be owned by a single owner or by a group of owners. When a single owner owns real property, this is known as *ownership in severalty*. A single owner has all the attributes of ownership, that is, the sole exclusive right to possess and use the property, the right to transfer the property, and the responsibility for all expenses and other charges in connection with the property.

Real property often is owned by more than one person. The combinations are endless: married couples own homes together, family members inherit real property together, and partners join together in commercial investment. Ownership of real property by more than one person provokes some interesting questions. Can one owner sell his or her interest without the consent of the other owners? Will the debts of an owner attach to the real property as a whole, thereby affecting the interests of the other owners? How are the expenses and income of the real property divided among the owners? What happens if an owner does not pay his or her share of the expenses? Can the owners terminate the group ownership and divide the real property among themselves? Attorneys and paralegals face these and other questions daily when dealing with real property that is owned by more than one person.

To decide what rights group owners and third parties who deal with these owners have in the real property, it is necessary to determine how the concurrent ownership is held.

TYPES OF CONCURRENT OWNERSHIP

Four types of concurrent ownership exist: (1) joint tenancy with the right of survivorship, (2) tenancy in common, (3) tenancy by the entirety, and (4) community property. The law of the state in which the real property is located will determine how the concurrent ownership is held. For example, owners who reside in South Carolina but own property in California are bound by California concurrent ownership law.

The old common law term of *tenant* or *tenancy*, which is synonymous with the modern use of the word *owner* or *ownership*, is still used to describe some of the types of concurrent ownership.

Joint Tenancy with Right of Survivorship

A **joint tenancy with the right of survivorship** is recognized in most states. It can be created by a deed or a will. It usually occurs when real property is transferred to two or more persons with express language that they are to take the real property as "joint tenants with the right of survivorship," or similar language. Thus, when a joint tenancy is desired, most instruments use the following language: "to A and B as joint tenants with right of survivorship, not as tenants in common."

Under a joint tenancy with right of survivorship, each owner owns an equal and undivided interest in the whole of the real property. Each owner has the right to use and possess the entire real property; this right to use or possession is held in common with the other owners.

The existence of a single ownership as a unit rather than as separate interests in the individual units is the essence of joint tenancy with the right of survivorship. This emphasis on the estate as a unit led to the common law requirements that four items—interest, title, time, and possession—be present for the creation of a joint tenancy with the right of survivorship. In other words, each owner's interest must constitute an identical interest (e.g., fee simple or life estate), must accrue by the same conveyance (deed or will), must commence at the same time, and must be held in the same undivided possession. If any of these four items, also called *unities,* is lacking in a conveyance, the estate is not a joint tenancy with right of survivorship but is instead a tenancy in common.

For example, the four unities would be satisfied if Joseph and Susan each received an undivided one-half interest in fee simple from their father by one deed. On the other hand, if the father chose to convey by one deed a one-half undivided fee simple interest in the property to Joseph and in a second deed a one-half undivided fee interest in the property to Susan, Joseph and Susan would not be joint tenants but would be tenants in common. The four unities do not exist because Joseph and Susan did not receive their interest in the same deed.

The outstanding feature of the joint tenancy with right of survivorship is the right of survivorship. The right of survivorship provides that if one of the joint owners dies, title to the real property is transferred to the surviving joint owners. This process will continue until the sole survivor of the joint owners owns all the real property. For example, Aaron, Bob, and Carl are joint tenants with right of survivorship. Aaron dies and wills his property to Donna. Donna will actually receive nothing. Bob and Carl will be joint owners with the right of survivorship, each owning one-half interest in the real property. Later, Bob dies and wills all the property to Ellen. Again, Ellen will receive nothing. At this point, Carl will be the sole owner of the property. This survivorship feature is illustrated in Exhibit 2–1.

joint tenancy with right of survivorship

Ownership of real property by two or more persons. Joint tenants with the right of survivorship own equal interest in the real property, and on the death of any owner, the deceased owner's interest in the real property will pass to the surviving owner.

EXHIBIT 2–1

Right of Survivorship

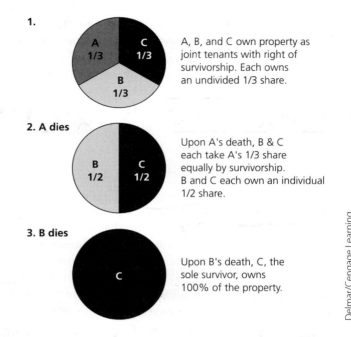

1.

A, B, and C own property as joint tenants with right of survivorship. Each owns an undivided 1/3 share.

2. A dies

Upon A's death, B & C each take A's 1/3 share equally by survivorship. B and C each own an individual 1/2 share.

3. B dies

Upon B's death, C, the sole survivor, owns 100% of the property.

Delmar/Cengage Learning

A severance of the joint tenancy means that the survivorship feature no longer takes effect. A joint tenancy with right of survivorship can easily be severed in most states. The sale of a joint tenant's interest in the real property will create a severance of the joint tenancy. In many states, a contract to sell or even the granting of a mortgage on the real property will sever the joint tenancy. An example of how this severance might work is as follows: Aaron, Bob, and Carl are joint tenants with the right of survivorship. Aaron, during the lifetime of Aaron, Bob, and Carl, conveys an undivided one-third interest to Donna. This conveyance will sever the joint tenancy as to the interest being conveyed to Donna, and Donna will be a tenant in common with Bob and Carl, who are still joint tenants with the right of survivorship. When Donna dies, Donna's interest will pass by will or by inheritance to Donna's heirs. When Bob dies, Bob's interest will pass to Carl. At such time, Donna (if living) and Carl would become tenants in common. Donna would own one-third, and Carl would own two-thirds.

Under a joint tenancy with right of survivorship, each owner owns an equal and undivided interest in the whole of the real property. Each owner has the right to use and possess the entire real property; this right to use or possession is held in common with the other owners.

For example, Aaron and Bob own a 20-acre farm as joint tenants with the right of survivorship. Aaron and Bob would each own an undivided 50 percent interest in the farm. Assume that a third party, Carl, wants to buy 5 acres of the farm. Neither Aaron nor Bob could sell the 5 acres to Carl because each of them individually owns only an undivided 50 percent of the 5 acres. Carl, therefore, would have to purchase the 5 acres from both Aaron and Bob.

Tenancy in Common

tenancy in common

Co-ownership of real property by two or more persons. Each owner's interest in the property is capable of inheritance.

Tenancy in common is a form of co-ownership in which two or more persons are each entitled to possession of the same real property. A tenancy in common may be created voluntarily by grant, lease, devise, or bequest or involuntarily by descent to heirs. Title does not have to arise at the same time or by the same instrument. Unlike a joint tenancy with right of survivorship, there is no right to survivorship in a tenancy in common. Each common owner's interest in the real property will pass by will or by inheritance on the common owner's death. In addition, under a tenancy in common, the owners may hold unequal shares, if so provided in the conveyance. For example, Aaron's deed conveys real property to Bob (an undivided one-quarter interest) and to Carl (an undivided three-quarters interest). Most states prefer a tenancy in common over a joint tenancy with right of survivorship. This means that if real property is conveyed to two or more persons and the deed or will does not indicate how the ownership is to be held, the ownership will be deemed a tenancy in common.

Rights, Duties, and Liabilities of Common Owners

Each common owner, whether it be a joint tenancy with right of survivorship or a tenancy in common, has a right to enter on the common real property and take possession of the whole property, subject only to the equal rights of the other common owners to do the same thing. Subject to the rights of the other common owners, a common owner of real property may use and enjoy the property as though he were the sole owner. A common owner may occupy and use every portion of the real property at all times and in all circumstances. The right to use and possess, however, is not exclusive, and each of the common owners has the same right. A common owner has been held to have a right to extract minerals, drill for oil, or cut timber from the common land. Any income produced from these activities that exceeds the common owner's proportionate share is to be distributed to the other common owners. A common owner is held to a standard of reasonable care and must take care of the real property as a prudent person would take care of his or her own property.

A common owner is entitled to his or her fractional proportionate share of rent or income produced from the real property. For example, a common owner with a 15 percent interest in the real property would be entitled to 15 percent of the income or rent from the real property. A common owner who has received money from a third party for the use of the common real property is a trustee of the amount collected for purposes of distribution to the other common owners for all sums over and above the common owner's share.

Rights of contribution

In a similar manner to rents and income, a common owner is responsible for expenses, such as taxes and repairs, in proportion to his or her respective interest in the real property. A common owner who pays more than his or her share of the common expenses is entitled to have the other common owners refund to him or her their proportionate shares of the amount paid. This right to reimbursement is known as the right of **contribution.** It is clear in most states (Alabama, Arkansas, California, Colorado, Delaware, Georgia, Idaho, Illinois, Indiana, Iowa, Kentucky, Maryland, Massachusetts, Michigan, Minnesota, Mississippi, Missouri, Nebraska, Nevada, New Hampshire, New Jersey, New York, North Carolina, Ohio, Oregon, Tennessee, Texas, Virginia, Washington, West Virginia, and Wisconsin) that payment of taxes or repairs made to preserve the property entitles a common owner to a right of contribution against the other common owners for their share of the taxes or repairs. It is not clear whether a co-owner is entitled to a contribution for the cost of an improvement if he or she has improved the real property without the consent of the other common owners. Some states (Illinois, Indiana, Kentucky, Michigan, Missouri, Texas, Virginia, and West Virginia) permit a common owner who improves real property in good faith to recover by contribution from the other common owners their share of the lesser of (a) the cost of the improvement or (b) the increase in value to the common property by the improvement. For example, a common owner builds a garage onto a home that is held in equal shares by three common owners. The cost of the garage is $15,000, but the garage increases the value of the property only by $9,000. Therefore, the improving common owner can recover only $3,000 from each of the other common owners because the increase in value is less than the cost of the improvement.

contribution

Right of a co-owner of real property to receive reimbursement from other co-owners for their share of expenses that are common to the real property.

Repairs usually are defined as expenditures for the purposes of keeping property in ordinary and efficient operating condition. Repairs do not add to the value of the property or appreciably prolong the property's life. Improvements, on the other hand, are defined as replacements, alterations, or additions to the property that prolong the life of the property, increase its value, or make it adaptable to a different use.

A common owner may enforce his or her right of contribution against other common owners by way of a lien on the other common owners' interests in the real property. This lien, if not voluntarily paid, can be enforced by a sale of the real property.

As to each common owner's undivided interest in the real property, he or she has a free right without the consent of the other common owners to sell, lease, or mortgage his or her undivided real property interest. A common owner, however, cannot convey a greater interest than he or she owns. A deed executed by a common owner will be treated as conveying only his or her undivided interest in the real property, even though the deed may, on its face, purport to convey the entire real property. A single common owner does not have the power to rent the common property, grant an easement across the property, sell the property, or mortgage the property without the consent of the other common owners. Common owners usually are not considered agents for one another, and one common owner cannot bind the other common owners to an agreement regarding the common property. The debts of a single common owner will bind his or her interest in the property but will not affect the common property. For example, a property is owned in common by Aaron, Bob, and Carol in equal shares. Aaron has substantial debts and judgments attached against him. Aaron's judgments will attach only to his undivided one-third interest in the property and will in no manner affect or attach to Bob's and Carol's interest in the common property. Common owners are, however, 100 percent responsible for injuries to a third person by reason of a dangerous condition on the common property.

Partition

The common owners may divide the common property into separate ownerships. This process is called **partition.** The partition may be by voluntary agreement of the common owners or by court action. The parties can voluntarily agree to a partition by executing an agreement allocating separate tracts to each owner or by exchanging deeds executed by all the common owners. A division by agreement or deed should be accompanied by a survey or plat showing the new agreed-on boundaries. No new consideration is necessary to support a written division.

If the common owners cannot agree on a voluntary division, the law in most states provides a judicial procedure for partitioning real property between common owners or selling it and dividing the proceeds. A suit to partition commonly owned real property can be brought by an owner of an undivided interest in the real property. Some states, however, do not permit a court-ordered partition for owners of a joint tenancy with survivorship. The defendants to the partition are each of the other people who own an interest in the real property. Holders of mortgages or other debt on the real property usually are joined in the partition. Notice of the partition normally is given personally to each owner.

The court usually divides the real property into parcels with a market value equivalent to each owner's undivided interest in the real property. For example, as tenants in common, Aaron owns 25 percent, Bob 25 percent, and Carol 50 percent. The court, on partition, will divide the property into parcels, of which Aaron's parcel will be equivalent to 25 percent of the value of all parcels, Bob's parcel will be equivalent to 25 percent of the value of all parcels, and Carol's parcel will be equivalent to 50 percent of the value of all parcels. The court usually has the authority to hire surveyors to describe the parcels and appraisers to establish

partition

Method by which co-owners of real property can divide the common property into separate ownerships. Partition may be by voluntary agreement of the co-owners or by court action.

values of each parcel. If the common owners do not want the real property divided or the real property is not capable of division, such as a single-family home, then the court will order the real property sold and the proceeds divided according to each owner's undivided interest in the real property.

Tenancy by the Entirety

A **tenancy by the entirety** is an estate held by husband and wife as a unit. Tenancy by the entirety is based on an old English common law view that a husband and wife are one person for the purpose of owning property. The married couple was treated as a single person, and the couple, both husband and wife, owned the property as a single unit. In this situation, neither the husband nor wife, so long as they were married, had an individual interest in the real property that could be sold, leased, or mortgaged. For example, the individual debt of a husband would not attach to the real property owned by the husband and wife as tenants by the entirety. Neither spouse could dispose of any interest in the tenancy by the entirety, and both spouses had to join in any sale, lease, or mortgage of the real property.

Several states recognize tenancy by the entirety (Arkansas, Delaware, Illinois, Indiana, Kentucky, Maryland, Massachusetts, New Hampshire, New Jersey, New York, North Carolina, Oregon, Pennsylvania, Tennessee, Vermont, Virginia, and Wisconsin). In a state that recognizes tenancy by the entirety, generally a conveyance to husband and wife automatically creates a tenancy by the entirety, unless the deed or will provides otherwise. A divorce will convert a tenancy by the entirety to a tenancy in common, with each party owning one-half interest in the real property.

A tenancy by the entirety contains a right of survivorship. On the death of one spouse, the surviving spouse owns the real property as a whole. Owners by the entirety have no individual interest that they can convey so as to break the unities of title and defeat survivorship. Thus, neither spouse can in any manner affect the right of survivorship with the other during their joint lives. For example, a husband and wife own a piece of property as tenancy by the entirety. The husband dies and wills all his property to his daughter by a first marriage. The daughter will not take an interest in the tenancy by the entirety property because the wife will, by the survival feature, own the entire interest in the real property.

tenancy by the entirety

Ownership of real property by a husband and wife. The husband and wife are treated as a single owner, and neither the husband nor the wife can transfer the property without the other's consent.

Community Property

Tenancy by the entirety, joint tenancy with the right of survivorship, and tenancy in common are all English common law concepts. The rules of **community property**, however, are borrowed from the civil laws of Spain and France and currently are found in the states that were founded by the Spanish or French (Arizona, California, Idaho, Louisiana, Nevada, New Mexico, Texas, Washington, and Wisconsin). The system is entirely statutory and varies from state to state. A few general propositions will give some notion of the differences between the common law and the community property forms of ownership.

The community property system creates a form of common ownership of property by the husband and wife similar to that of a partnership. During marriage, all property individually or jointly acquired by the husband or wife, other than by gift, bequest, devise, or descent, is held by them as a community property. The property may consist of the earnings of both spouses, borrowings, land or buildings purchased by them, or the rents and profits received from these land and buildings.

community property

Rule of law in states following the civil law of Spain and France, which provides that real property acquired during marriage is owned equally by the husband and wife.

States that follow community property law have a concept of separate property and community property. Property that is not part of the community property is termed separate property. It consists of all property owned by either spouse before marriage or acquired by one spouse during marriage by gift, inheritance, bequest, or devise. Income from separate property also is separate property in most states. Property acquired during marriage with funds derived from separate property usually will retain the separate property classification. If both community and separate funds are used, the property will be apportioned between the two spouses according to their respective contributions from each classification. For example, a husband and wife purchase a building during marriage. The husband contributes 50 percent of the purchase price from the sale of separate property. The other 50 percent is contributed through the joint earnings of husband and wife. The property will be deemed to be 50 percent separate property belonging to the husband and 50 percent community property, with the husband and wife each owning one-half interest. In other words, the husband will have a 75 percent interest in the new real property, and the wife will have a 25 percent interest.

Property that is deemed to be community property is owned equally by both husband and wife, and neither can convey the whole without the other's consent. On divorce, unless the parties agree otherwise, the property typically is divided equally and is held to be owned by the husband and wife as tenants in common, or the real property is partitioned, if partition is possible.

Most community property states provide a husband and wife certain presumptions of law to aid in the determination of ownership of marital property. Any property acquired by the married couple during the marriage and still owned by them at the end of the marriage is presumed to be community property. If separate and community property is so commingled that it is not possible to identify the separate property, then the commingled property is presumed to be community property. In order to rebut the presumption of community property in these circumstances, a husband or wife may need to keep written records of how the disputed property was acquired.

One main difference between community property and the English forms of concurrent ownership (tenancy by the entirety, joint tenancy with right of survivorship, and tenancy in common) is that community property is created by operation of law and not by operation of conveyance. A conveyance in a community property state could be to an individual person. If the person is married and the property is community property, however, an unnamed spouse will be deemed to be a one-half owner of the property. For example, Harold and Maude are married. Phillip conveys community property to Harold. The deed from Phillip is to Harold only, because the property is community property. Maude will own one-half interest in the property, even though Maude is not mentioned in the deed.

Community Property and Prenuptial Agreements

Although not a romantic idea, some husbands and wives in both community property states and non–community property states may enter into agreements before marriage concerning the ownership of real property by the married couple or by the individual spouses. In community property states, the spouses may enter into an agreement that will set forth in detail what property is deemed to be separate property owned by the individual spouses and what property is deemed to be community property. This type of agreement resolves disputes of property ownership at the time of divorce or on sale of the property. A sample community separate property agreement is included at the end of this chapter (see Exhibit 2–2).

Some married couples in non–community property states may enter into **prenuptial agreements** regarding the division and ownership of property in the event of separation or divorce. A prenuptial agreement is also referred to as an **antenuptial agreement.** It is

prenuptial (or antenuptial) agreement

Agreement entered into by a married couple that, among other things, outlines an agreement between the couple regarding the division and ownership of property in the event of separation or divorce.

common under these agreements for one spouse to renounce, waive, or give up claims to property owned by the other spouse.

Dower and Curtesy

A **dower** is an interest in real property of the husband that the law in some states gives to the widow to provide the widow with a means of support after the husband's death. A dower interest is either a life estate or a fee simple interest and some undivided fraction (usually one-third or one-quarter) of the real property that the husband owned during the marriage. The requirements for a dower interest are (a) a valid marriage, (b) the husband owned the real property during the marriage, and (c) the husband dies before the wife.

Although the dower right does not become a present interest until the husband dies, it is created at the time of the marriage. It is necessary in a state that recognizes dower that all conveyances of property owned by the husband be consented to by the wife to release the dower interest in the conveyed property.

Many states provide to a husband a right similar to dower in the wife's property. This right is called **curtesy.** The requirements for a curtesy interest are (a) a valid marriage, (b) the wife owned real property during the marriage, and (c) the wife dies before the husband.

Dower and curtesy rights have been substantially altered or abolished in many states. It is necessary in dealing with dower or curtesy to check a particular state's law before proceeding.

Elective Share

Many states in which dower exists give to the widow at her husband's death the right to elect between her dower and some fee simple ownership share of property owned by her husband. Depending on the state, this fee simple ownership is either one-fourth or one-third interest in the property owned by the husband. The widow's share in some states (e.g., Alaska, Colorado, Connecticut, Georgia, Mississippi, New York, North Dakota, Oklahoma, Oregon, South Dakota, and Wyoming) may be limited to property that the husband owned at his death, which would mean that the widow would have no claim on property conveyed by the husband during his lifetime without her signature.

In other states (e.g., Florida, Indiana, Iowa, Kansas, Maine, Maryland, Minnesota, Missouri, Nebraska, Pennsylvania, and Utah), the widow receives an ownership share in lieu of dower in all property owned during the lifetime of the husband. In these states, the wife's signature is necessary on any deed, mortgage, or contract of sale given by the husband.

Most states also provide for the husband a similar **elective share** in property owned by the wife.

Practice Note: Any time a transaction, such as a lease, sale, or loan, involves all the common real property, it will be necessary for each and every common owner of the property to sign all the legal documents involved. If the transaction involves property in a community property state or in a state that recognizes dower, curtesy, or elective share, it is necessary for both the owner of the property and the owner's spouse to sign all deeds, leases, sales, mortgages, contracts, or other legal documents involving the property. The safest approach is to treat all real property owned by a married person in a community property state as community property and to require both the husband and the wife to execute all the legal documents. A table summarizing the various types of co-ownerships and the rights of each individual co-owner under each co-ownership is set forth as Exhibit 2–3 at the end of this chapter.

A table summarizing the types of co-ownership recognized in each of the states is set forth as Exhibit 2–4 at the end of this chapter.

---

dower

Widow's interest in real property of her husband that provides a means of support after the husband's death.

curtesy

Interest in real property of the wife that the law in some states gives to the surviving husband at the time of the wife's death.

elective share

Right given to a widow in many states to elect, at her husband's death, to receive either dower or some ownership (fee simple) share of her husband's real property.

AGREEMENTS OF COTENANCY

Real property often is co-owned for investment or commercial purposes. A group of individual investors may become co-owners of raw land for speculation or investment or may join together to build or buy commercial property such as shopping centers, office buildings, or apartments. An interpretation of the tax laws now permits a tenant in common's ownership interest in one property to be exchanged or transferred for an interest in another property as a tax-free exchange. This new tax treatment of ownership in property by tenants in common has created a new market where many commercial properties are now being purchased and held by individual investors as tenants in common. When real property is co-owned for investment, the general rules of co-ownership discussed earlier in this chapter may not be totally appropriate for the investors' needs and purposes. Most states will permit the general rules to be altered and changed by contract among the co-owners. These agreements or contracts are called cotenancy or co-ownership agreements. The following checklist with examples and references to the discussions in this chapter may be used as a guide to the preparation of cotenancy agreements.

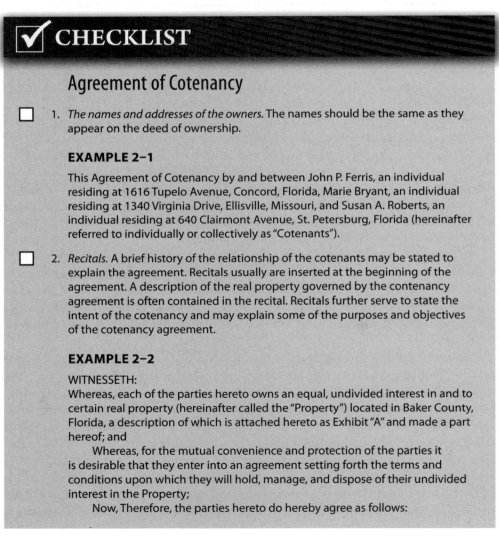

✓ CHECKLIST

Agreement of Cotenancy

☐ 1. *The names and addresses of the owners.* The names should be the same as they appear on the deed of ownership.

EXAMPLE 2–1

This Agreement of Cotenancy by and between John P. Ferris, an individual residing at 1616 Tupelo Avenue, Concord, Florida, Marie Bryant, an individual residing at 1340 Virginia Drive, Ellisville, Missouri, and Susan A. Roberts, an individual residing at 640 Clairmont Avenue, St. Petersburg, Florida (hereinafter referred to individually or collectively as "Cotenants").

☐ 2. *Recitals.* A brief history of the relationship of the cotenants may be stated to explain the agreement. Recitals usually are inserted at the beginning of the agreement. A description of the real property governed by the contenancy agreement is often contained in the recital. Recitals further serve to state the intent of the cotenancy and may explain some of the purposes and objectives of the cotenancy agreement.

EXAMPLE 2–2

WITNESSETH:
Whereas, each of the parties hereto owns an equal, undivided interest in and to certain real property (hereinafter called the "Property") located in Baker County, Florida, a description of which is attached hereto as Exhibit "A" and made a part hereof; and

Whereas, for the mutual convenience and protection of the parties it is desirable that they enter into an agreement setting forth the terms and conditions upon which they will hold, manage, and dispose of their undivided interest in the Property;

Now, Therefore, the parties hereto do hereby agree as follows:

(continued)

3. *Term of the agreement.* A cotenancy agreement may be formed for a definite term and may be subject to termination by mutual agreement.

EXAMPLE 2–3

This Agreement shall be effective and shall continue in full force and effect until July 5, 2013, or until terminated by agreement of all the Cotenants hereto, whichever is sooner.

4. *Not a partnership.* Co-ownership of real property does not in and of itself make the owners partners for one another. Partners in a partnership are responsible for each of the partners' activities in connection with the partnership and may be fully responsible for all partnership liabilities and debts. Most co-owners of real property do not want to assume or create partnership liability on the part of each of the owners. Therefore, it is not unusual for a cotenancy agreement to clearly state that the intent of the agreement is not to create a partnership.

EXAMPLE 2–4

The Cotenants do not intend by this agreement to create a partnership or a joint venture, but merely to set forth the terms upon which each cotenant shall hold, manage, and dispose of his or her undivided interest in the Property. No cotenant hereto is authorized to act as agent for any other cotenant hereto, to act on behalf of any other cotenant hereto, to do any act which will be binding on any other cotenant hereto, or to incur any expenditures with respect to the Property, except as specifically set forth herein.

5. *Managing cotenant.* Co-ownership of real property usually requires that all the owners consent to any activity that affects the real property as a whole. This unanimous consent may not be practical in all circumstances, and it is not unusual for cotenancy agreements to appoint a managing owner who has the authority to act within limited parameters without the consent of the other owners. The consent of the other owners has been indirectly given by the appointment of the managing owner in the cotenancy agreement.

EXAMPLE 2–5

Marie Bryant hereby agrees to accept and discharge her responsibility as property manager. At any time hereafter, Cotenants owning an interest in the Property totaling 50 percent or more of all interest in the Property shall have the right and authority to revoke such designation and designate a new property manager.

The property manager is authorized to pay ad valorem taxes on the Property and to pay principal and interest on indebtedness encumbering the Property; she is authorized to incur only such other expenditures as may be approved from time to time by all the Cotenants.

The property manager shall keep just and true books of account with respect to the Property. The books shall be maintained at the offices of the property manager, or such other place as the Cotenants shall agree, and each Cotenant shall at all reasonable times have access to such books. The books shall be kept on the basis of a calendar year using the cash method of accounting and shall be closed and balanced at the end of each year. An accounting of all items, receipts, income, profits, costs, expenses, and losses arising out of or resulting from the ownership of the Property shall be made by the property manager annually as of December 31 of each year, and also upon the death of any Cotenant hereto, and also upon termination of this agreement. A copy of each statement shall be delivered by the property manager to each tenant hereto.

(continued)

6. *Banking arrangements.* Bank accounts and other banking arrangements usually are stated in the agreement, including the people who are authorized to sign checks and to conduct banking transactions on behalf of the owners.

EXAMPLE 2–6

There shall be deposited in a checking account with First National Bank of Baker, Florida, all amounts deposited with the property manager by the Cotenants hereto as hereinafter provided. All rentals and income from the Property and amounts deposited with the property manager by the Cotenants hereto shall be received, held, and disbursed by the property manager as a trust fund to be applied only for the purposes herein specified. Withdrawals of such trust funds shall be made in said account only for the purpose of making payments herein authorized and only by the property manager.

7. *Owners' cash contributions and remedies for failure to make contributions.* Most cotenancies of property for investment require cash contributions from time to time from the various owners. A cotenancy agreement usually will outline the procedures and requirements for cash contributions by the various owners as well as the penalties for an owner's refusal or failure to make a required cash contribution.

EXAMPLE 2–7

(a) As monies are required from time to time to make payments as authorized herein, the property manager shall cause the monies to be withdrawn from said bank account and used to make such payments. In the event the trust fund shall be insufficient to make such payment, the Cotenants hereto shall, within thirty (30) days after written notice given by the property manager, deposit with the property manager in proportion to their respective interest in the Property, the funds required to make the payments.

(b) If any Cotenant should fail to so deposit his or her share of such funds with the property manager within the time required, then any one or more of the other Cotenants hereto may advance such funds, and the amounts so advanced shall be a loan from the Cotenant or Cotenants advancing such funds to the Cotenant so defaulting in his or her obligation hereunder. Such loan shall bear interest at the rate of 10 percent per annum from the day so advanced until paid. If such loan, together with interest thereon, has not been paid within thirty (30) days from the date of such advancement, then the Cotenant or Cotenants so advancing said funds shall have the option to purchase from the defaulting Cotenant the interest of the defaulting Cotenant in the Property as follows:

(i) the purchase price of such interest in the Property shall be an amount equal to one-half (1/2) of the total of all amounts actually paid by such defaulting Cotenant for his or her interest in the Property, consisting of the initial payment made by such Cotenant at the time this agreement is executed, plus all amounts actually deposited with the property manager under provisions of subparagraph (a) of this paragraph prior to the time such option is exercised; and

(ii) such purchase price shall be paid by canceling the indebtedness of the defaulting Cotenant under subparagraph (b), with the balance, if any, payable in cash at closing. If such indebtedness exceeds the purchase price, the balance of such indebtedness shall be paid by the defaulting Cotenant at closing; and

(iii) said option to purchase may be exercised by giving notice in writing at any time within sixty (60) days after the date of said advancement, said notice stating that said option is hereby exercised, specifying the place, in the City of Baker, State of Florida, and a time when such purchase shall be closed. Said notice shall be signed by the Cotenant or Cotenants sending the same, shall be sent by United States registered or certified mail, postage

(continued)

prepaid, addressed to the last known address of such defaulting Cotenant. The date of such notice shall be the date that same is deposited in the mail. The closing of said purchase and sale shall be within thirty (30) days after the date of such notice at the time and place specified in the notice.

(c) Each Cotenant hereto hereby constitutes and appoints each other Cotenant hereto as his or her agent and attorney-in-fact for the purposes of executing and delivering any and all documents necessary to convey his or her interest in the Property pursuant to the provisions of this paragraph, and any conveyance so made shall fully divest the Cotenant whose interest is so conveyed of all right, title, or equity in or to the Property, and his or her interest therein. The power of attorney herein granted, being coupled with an interest, is irrevocable and shall not be revoked by the death or dissolution of any Cotenant. Each Cotenant hereto hereby releases the Cotenant who conveys any interest in the Property provided in this paragraph from any and all claims or liabilities for so conveying such interest.

(d) Time is of the essence with respect to this paragraph.

8. *Allocation of income and profits.* The cotenancy agreement will allocate the income and profits among the various owners.

EXAMPLE 2–8

All receipts and income arising out of or resulting from the ownership, leasing, and sale of the Property shall belong to the Cotenants hereto in proportion to his or her respective interest in the property.

9. *Sale of the property as a whole.* Because all owners must consent to the sale of the co-owned property as a whole, most cotenancy agreements establish a procedure for obtaining such consent.

EXAMPLE 2–9

The Cotenants hereto agree that they shall hold the Property for investment. The Property shall not be developed, or any improvements constructed thereon, except with the unanimous consent of the Cotenants. If Cotenants owning interests in the Property totaling 50 percent or more of all interests in the Property shall notify the property manager in writing that they have received a written offer to purchase part or all of the Property and that they desire to accept the same, and shall enclose a copy of such offer to the property manager with such notice, then all Cotenants shall be obligated to sell the Property (or the portion thereof covered by such offer) to the purchaser making such offer and for the price and on the terms and conditions set forth in the offer. Each Cotenant hereby specifically covenants that he or she will execute and deliver to the purchaser making such offer a general warranty deed conveying the interest of the Cotenant in the Property to the purchaser. Notwithstanding the foregoing, no Cotenant hereto shall be obligated to sell his or her interest in the Property pursuant to the provisions of this paragraph, unless such notice to the property manager was signed by at least two Cotenants.

10. *Sale of an owner's undivided interest in the property.* A co-owner, as previously discussed, has a right to transfer his or her undivided interest in the property without the consent of the other owners. An unrestricted right to transfer an undivided interest in the common property often is an undesirable feature of co-ownership. Most people join together as co-owners because of a special relationship they have with one another. An owner usually trusts the other owners to do what is best for the entire group. The possibility of having one of these owners sell his or her undivided interest to a stranger is not welcomed. To protect against such an occurrence, most cotenancy agreements provide a procedure to prevent or at least make difficult the sale of an undivided interest in the property to a stranger.

(continued)

EXAMPLE 2–10

No Cotenant shall have the right to assign, transfer, sell, or in any way dispose of any part of his or her interest in the Property except as herein provided:

(a) Any Cotenant may, at any time or from time to time, transfer all or any part of his or her interest in the Property to any other Cotenant.

(b) If any Cotenant should desire to sell or assign his or her interest in the Property, or any portion thereof, to any person other than another Cotenant, he or she shall first offer to sell such interest to the other Cotenants at a price not to exceed the price at which such Cotenant proposes to sell his or her interest to any prospective purchaser other than a Cotenant, and on the same terms and conditions offered or proposed to be offered to such prospective purchaser. The offeree shall have a period of thirty (30) days from the time such offer is received within which to accept the same. Each of the offeree Cotenants shall be entitled to purchase the interest in the Property so offered to them in the same proportion as his or her interest at the time of such offer bears to the total interest of the several offeree Cotenants; in the event any such offeree declines to purchase the interest which he or she is entitled to purchase, the remaining offerees shall have a period of ten (10) days after the expiration of the thirty (30)-day period specified above within which to accept the offer with respect to the interest so declined, but in no event will time for accepting the offer be extended beyond said ten (10)-day extension.

(c) In the event one or more of the offerees elects to buy the interest so offered for sale during the time specified above, such offeree shall, prior to the expiration of said time, pay to the offeror in cash 10 percent of the down payment required to be made under the terms of the proposed sale, said 10 percent to be earnest money that will be applied against the sales price at the closing or will be forfeited in the event the purchasing party fails to consummate the purchase hereinafter provided. The purchasing party shall thereafter have sixty (60) days from the date of making said 10 percent payment in which to close the purchase.

(d) If any Cotenant should desire to mortgage or pledge his or her interest in the Property, or otherwise to encumber such interest by using the same as security for borrowed funds, then he or she shall give the other Cotenants at least thirty (30) days time in which to provide, upon the same terms and conditions, the funds proposed to be obtained by so encumbering such interest.

(e) Any offer required to be made by this agreement shall be in writing, signed by the offerer, shall be sent by registered or certified mail to each Cotenant. Any acceptance to an offer made hereunder shall be in writing, signed by the offeree, shall be sent by registered or certified mail to the offerer.

(f) If any interest in the Property held by a Cotenant is offered for sale to the other Cotenants or is offered to be encumbered, as provided in the foregoing paragraph, and within the time provided the acceptances received from the offerees combined do not cover the entire amount of such offer, then none of such acceptances shall be valid and the offerer shall have a period of sixty (60) days after the expiration of the time within which an offer hereunder could have been accepted, within which to complete the sale or encumbrance, as the case may be, to any person not a party hereto, on the terms and conditions set forth in such offer. If such sale or encumbrance shall not be completed within said sixty (60)-day period, a new offer must be made to the parties hereto as required by the above paragraphs.

11. *Remedies for an owner's failure to perform.* A cotenancy agreement usually provides rights and remedies to enforce the performance of an owner's obligations under the agreement.

EXAMPLE 2–11

The Cotenants intend that their obligations under this agreement shall be enforceable by specific performance. The remedies of the Cotenants under this agreement are cumulative and shall not exclude any other remedies to which any

(continued)

Cotenant may be lawfully entitled. The failure of any Cotenant to insist upon strict performance of a covenant hereunder or of any obligation hereunder shall not be a waiver of such Cotenant's right to demand strict compliance therewith in the future.

☐ 12. *Partition.* The general law in most states gives a co-owner the right to have the common property divided or partitioned. Partition of common property owned for investment, however, can work a hardship on the other owners. For example, it is difficult to partition in kind a high-rise office building. Therefore, permitting a co-owner the right to partition would result in the office building being sold and the proceeds partitioned. The sale could have adverse tax consequences for all the co-owners as well as being a sale of a valuable asset against their wishes. The general law in most states permits the right of partition to be waived by co-owners, and most cotenancy agreements do limit or prohibit the right of partition.

EXAMPLE 2–12

The Cotenants hereby agree that no individual Cotenant, or any successor in interest to a Cotenant, shall have the right while this agreement remains in effect to have the Property partitioned, or to file a complaint or institute any procedure in law or in equity to have the Property partitioned, and each Cotenant, on behalf of himself or herself, his or her successors, representatives, heirs, and assigns hereby waives any such right.

☐ 13. *Successors and assigns.* Most cotenancy agreements are not personal to the original owners, but instead affect the co-ownership relationship of the property until termination. Therefore, all terms and provisions should be binding on the original owners and their successors and assigns.

EXAMPLE 2–13

This agreement, each and every provision hereof, shall be binding upon and shall inure to the benefit of the Cotenants, their successors, representatives, heirs, and assigns, and each Cotenant agrees on behalf of himself or herself, his or her successors, representatives, heirs, and assigns to execute any instruments that may be necessary or proper to carry out and execute the purposes and intentions of this agreement, and hereby authorizes and directs his or her successors, representatives, heirs, and assigns to execute any and all such instruments. Each and every successor in interest to any Cotenant, whether such successor acquired an interest in the Property by way of gift, devise, purchase, foreclosure, or by any other method, shall hold such interest subject to all the terms and provisions in this agreement.

☐ 14. *Counterparts.* It is not unusual for co-owners to reside in different parts of the country. It is cumbersome for the single agreement to have all the signatures appear on the same document. Most cotenancy agreements provide that the agreement can be executed in counterparts. Counterpart execution means that different copies of the same document are executed by the different parties. The original signatures of all the owners appear on different copies of the agreement, but all the copies are read as a single document and are enforceable.

EXAMPLE 2–14

This agreement can be executed in several counterparts, each which shall be considered an original, and shall be enforced according to the laws of the State of Florida.

☐ 15. *Signature and witnessing.* Cotenancy agreements are executed by all the owners. It also is common practice to have the signatures witnessed and notarized. The parties may even desire to record the agreement in the public records of the county where the property is located.

(continued)

EXAMPLE 2–15

In witness whereof, the Cotenants have hereinto set their hands and seals, and set opposite their signature is the undivided interest in the Property owned by each, as of and effective this _____ day of _____.

Signed, sealed, and
delivered in the
presence of:

_____ (SEAL)
John P. Ferris, 33⅓ percent

_____
Witness

_____
Notary

Signed, sealed, and
delivered in the
presence of:

_____ (SEAL)
Marie Bryant, 33⅓ percent

_____
Witness

_____
Notary

Signed, sealed, and
delivered in the
presence of:

_____ (SEAL)
Susan A. Roberts, 33⅓ percent

_____
Witness

_____
Notary

CONCURRENT OWNERSHIP AND THE ROLE OF THE PARALEGAL

A paralegal will experience concurrent ownership when dealing with the sale, lease, or mortgage of real property. The paralegal might be asked to draft a deed that creates a form of concurrent ownership in the grantee of the deed. The paralegal will need to research state law to determine if special language is needed to create the form of concurrent ownership desired by the new owners of the property. This person may also be involved in reviewing the status of title to determine what form of concurrent ownership is held by the present owners. This determination will be helpful when preparing deeds, leases, contracts, mortgages, or other legal documents involving the ownership of the property. Any time a transaction such as a lease, sale, or loan involves all the common owners of the property, it will be necessary for each and every common owner of the property to sign all the legal documents in connection with the transaction. If the transaction involves property in a community property state or a state that recognizes dower and curtesy, it is necessary for both the owner of the property and the owner's spouse to sign all legal documents involving the property. The safest approach is to treat all real property owned by a married person in a community property state as community property and to require both the husband and wife to execute all the legal documents. A table summarizing the various types of concurrent ownership and the rights of each individual co-owner under each ownership is set forth as Exhibit 2–3 at the end of this chapter.

ETHICS: Unauthorized Practice of Law

You are a paralegal with a law firm that represents a bank. Your main responsibility is to assist the attorneys of the firm in the closing of real estate loans. Through these activities, you have become good friends with a number of loan officers at the bank. These loan officers often call you directly with questions or comments on the various files in your workload. One afternoon, one of these loan officers calls to inform you that she and her husband are buying a home. They intend to buy the home as joint tenants with the right of survivorship because they heard on a radio talk show that this form of ownership does away with the necessity of having a will and avoids all probate proceedings. She asks that you advise her as to whether she and her husband need a will. You believe that you know the answer to her question and can advise her of the proper way to proceed. Do you give the advice, or do you refer her to one of the attorneys in the firm? What is the ethical consideration of your choice?

The practice of law is defined in many states to include conveyancing, preparing legal documents, rendering opinions as to the validity or invalidity of titles to real or personal property, and giving legal advice. Most ethical codes of conduct prohibit a lawyer from aiding a nonlawyer in the unauthorized practice of law. Because paralegals are not licensed to practice law, the use of a paralegal in the preceding areas could result in a breach of ethics on the part of the attorney. A paralegal, on the other hand, is actively involved in many aspects of the preceding actions, which constitute the practice of law. This apparent conflict is resolved in most states by permitting the paralegal to be involved in these activities, provided the lawyer maintains a direct relationship with the client involved, supervises and directs the work delegated to the paralegal, and assumes complete and ultimate responsibility for the work product produced by the paralegal. Supervision of the paralegal's work by the attorney must be direct and constant to avoid any charges of aiding the unauthorized practice of law. Therefore, although it may be improper in many states for a paralegal to actually close a real estate transaction without the assistance or supervision of an attorney, it is not improper for the paralegal to prepare the closing documents and to arrange for other aspects of the closing, provided the paralegal's work is closely supervised by the attorney.

The paralegal in this example should refer the loan officer to an attorney at the firm for an answer to the question regarding the will. The answer involves the giving of legal advice, which, if given by the paralegal, would constitute an unauthorized practice of law.

[handwritten margin note: never give advice if you do this makes your attorney liable he can be fully responsible you get fired]

OTHER LEGAL ENTITIES

Persons who wish to group together and invest in commercial income-producing properties may form entities other than cotenancy arrangements through which to own the commercial properties. The property is owned by the legal entity, not the individual shareholders, members, or partners who make up the beneficial interest in the entity. Generally, these entities can be classified into four groups: corporations, general partnerships, limited partnerships, and limited liability companies.

Corporation

A **corporation** is a legal entity that can issue shares representing fractional ownership interests. The owners of these shares (*shareholders*) own the corporation. A corporation may have one or more shareholders, but the corporate legal entity is separate from the shareholders. This means that the shareholders do not have liability for corporate debts or corporate actions. This limitation of liability is an attractive feature of a corporation because it permits passive investment in a business. If the business fails, the investor or shareholder

corporation

A legal entity wherein the owners do not have personal liability for the debts or actions of the entity.

will lose only the price paid for their shares. Corporations are used to purchase, sell, and operate commercial properties.

Corporations are formed by the preparation and filing of articles of incorporation with the secretary of state of the state of incorporation. The articles of incorporation describe the business purpose of the corporation, the number of shares the corporation is authorized to issue, and other information. Corporations are generally governed by a board of directors. The board of directors may authorize other officers to execute contracts on behalf of the corporation and perform other acts that are binding on the corporation.

General Partnership

general partnership

An association of two or more persons to carry on a business for profit as co-owners.

A **general partnership** is generally defined as an association of two or more persons to carry on a business for profit as co-owners. The owners of a partnership are known as *partners*. The partners in a general partnership are responsible for the debts and obligations of the partnership. The partnership does not offer, as a corporation does, limited liability to the owners. Although general partnerships lack the advantage of limited liability, they offer the advantage of permitting partners to deduct losses from the partnership on their individual tax returns. This advantage has encouraged general partnerships to own and operate commercial real property.

Most states have adopted the Uniform Partnership Act, which provides that a general partnership is a legal entity for the purpose of owning real property. This means that the general partnership owns the property, not the individual partners. Generally, all partners in a general partnership must consent to a transfer of title to the real property unless the partnership agreement provides otherwise. General partnerships are informal legal entities. Usually it is not necessary for any formal document to be filed with the secretary of state or other government agency to create a general partnership. Although it is probably not wise to do so, a general partnership could be formed even without a written partnership agreement.

Limited Partnership

limited partnership

A legal entity made up of two classes of ownership: general partners and limited partners. The general partners have full liability for the debts and obligations of the limited partnership, and the limited partners have liability limited to the extent of their investment in the partnership.

A **limited partnership** is made up of two classes: general partners and limited partners. General partners, similar to members of a general partnership, have full liability for the debts and obligations of the limited partnership. The limited partners, however, like shareholders in a corporation, have limited liability. A limited partner's liability is limited to his or her investment in the partnership. A limited partnership is taxed like a general partnership in that losses are passed through to the partners and can be deducted on their individual tax returns. A combination of this attractive tax feature and the limited liability of the limited partners makes a limited partnership an attractive vehicle for the ownership of commercial property.

Limited partnerships are generally governed by the general partners, and the general partners have full authority to act on behalf of the partnership, including the authority to transfer ownership of the property owned by the limited partnership.

Most states have adopted the Uniform Limited Partnership Act, which requires a formal written limited partnership agreement and the filing of certain documents with the secretary of state of the state in which the limited partnership is formed.

Limited Liability Company

limited liability company

An entity which offers the tax advantages of a partnership and the limited liability of a corporation.

A **limited liability company** is a relatively new type of entity that offers the tax advantages of a partnership and the limited liability of a corporation. A limited liability company is owned by members who are not responsible for the debts or obligations of the limited liability company. Limited liability companies may acquire real property; the title vests in the limited liability company rather than in the members individually.

Limited liability companies are managed by the members. Every member of a limited liability company is an agent of the company for the purpose of its business affairs. A contract executed by any member is binding on the limited liability company. A limited liability company may be managed by a manager or managers who have similar authority to sign contracts and deeds on behalf of the limited liability company.

Limited liability companies are formal companies. Articles of organization must be filed with the secretary of state of the state in which the limited liability company is formed.

SUMMARY

Real property may be owned by a group of individuals. Ownership of real property by more than one owner creates several legal issues concerning the use, possession, and responsibility of the property among the common owners as well as several legal issues regarding the sale, mortgage, or lease of the real property to a person outside the ownership group. Four basic types of concurrent ownership are recognized in the United States: joint tenancy with right of survivorship, tenancy in common, tenancy by the entirety, and community property. Generally, tenancy by the entirety and community property involve co-ownership of property by a husband and wife. Ownership of real property as tenants in common or by joint tenancy with right of survivorship may involve a husband and wife but may also involve unmarried and even nonrelated parties. Often the tenancy in common ownership is used by commercial investors to own investment property such as an apartment complex or a shopping center. Joint tenancy with right of survivorship and tenancy by the entirety have rights of survivorship, which provide that upon the death of one of the common owners, his or her interest in the property will pass automatically to the surviving owner. Common owners may enter into agreements with each other to better define the rights and relationships among the owners. These agreements are often referred to as cotenancy agreements.

HELPFUL WEBSITES

Community Property
An excellent article on the ins and outs of community property law can be found at *http://www.legalzoom.com.*

Concurrent Ownerships
Excellent articles and summaries explaining the different types of concurrent ownerships can be found at *http://www.ndsu.nodak.edu.*

KEY TERMS

community property	elective share	limited partnership
contribution	general partnership	partition
corporation	joint tenancy with right	prenuptial (or antenuptial) agreement
curtesy	of survivorship	tenancy by the entirety
dower	limited liability company	tenancy in common

REVIEW QUESTIONS

1. What are the four unities required for a joint tenancy with right of survivorship?
2. What is the right of contribution, and why is it important to a co-owner of real property?
3. How is a tenancy in common different from a joint tenancy with right of survivorship?
4. What is the difference between a tenancy by the entirety and community property?
5. Explain the process of partition as it relates to the co-ownership of real property.
6. What property is considered to be separately owned property in a community property state?

7. What is an agreement of cotenancy, and when would it be used?

8. What is dower?

9. Explain the difference between the right of survivorship in a joint tenancy with right of survivorship and a tenancy by the entirety.

10. What are the advantages of a prenuptial agreement and a community/separate property agreement?

11. What is the difference between a general partnership and a limited partnership?

12. What are the advantages of owning an investment of real property in a limited liability company?

CASE PROBLEMS

1. Aaron conveys by deed a parcel of real property to John, Jane, and Susan as joint tenants with right of survivorship. John, during the lifetime of all the joint owners, transfers his interest in the property to Carol. After John's transfer to Carol, Jane dies and wills her interest in the property to Barbara. After Jane's death, Susan dies and wills her interest in the property to Stewart. Who are the owners of the property, and in what proportion?

2. You are reviewing a deed. The deed indicates that the ownership of property has been transferred from Ajax Realty Company to David Farris, Mary Farris, and John Farris. What form of co-ownership do David, Mary, and John own in the real property?

3. You are a paralegal working with a law firm that is representing a purchaser of a parcel of real property. The purchaser desires to purchase 100 percent of the property and has entered into a contract with Samuel Seller. The title examination of the property reveals that Samuel Seller owns the property together with Susan Seller and Sarah Seller. What additional precautions or safeguards must you take to protect the purchaser in this transaction?

4. You are a paralegal in a law firm that represents a creditor who has made a loan to Robert Black. You discover that Robert Black owns a parcel of real property together with his wife, Margo Black. Will the creditor be able to sell Robert Black's interest in the real property for purposes of satisfying the debt? What factors are important in answering this question?

5. You are a paralegal in a law firm that represents a number of investors who are purchasing a shopping center. The investors intend to own the shopping center as tenants in common and have asked the firm to prepare an agreement of cotenancy. You have been asked to prepare the first draft of the agreement. What information are you going to need from the client to prepare it?

6. A law firm where you work has been approached by a group of investors who wish to purchase an office building. They have requested the firm to advise them as to what type of legal entity should be formed to own the building. Research the advantages and disadvantages of owning an office building in the form of a corporation, a general partnership, a limited partnership, and a limited liability company. Considering the advantages and disadvantages of each of these entities as an owner of real property, what would your advice be to the investors as to which entity would be the best form in which to own the property?

PRACTICAL ASSIGNMENTS

Team up with two other classmates. Pretend these classmates are interested in forming a cotenancy agreement. By reviewing carefully the checklist for agreement of cotenancy in this chapter, prepare a list of questions that you would need to ask these individuals prior to preparing the cotenancy agreement. After the questions have been prepared, interview the two classmates to obtain answers to the questions. Then prepare, based on the cotenancy agreement form used in the checklist in this chapter, a cotenancy agreement covering the issues and concerns of your classmates that were obtained from the interview. The final product of this assignment should be the list of interview questions and answers, as well as the first draft of the agreement of cotenancy.

ADDENDUM

Exhibit 2–2 Community Property Agreement
Exhibit 2–3 Co-ownership Chart
Exhibit 2–4 State Co-ownership Chart

Student StudyWare™ CD-ROM
Interactive Student CD in the book includes additional quizzing, case studies, and key terms flashcards.

Online Companion™
For additional resources, please go to *www.paralegal.delmar.cengage.com*

This community property agreement made _____ , 20_____ , between Henry Husband, of _____ [address], City of _____ , County of _____ , State of _____ , and Wendy Wife, of _____ [address], City of _____ , County of _____ , State of _____.

This agreement is made in consideration of the contemplated marriage of the parties.

Section One
Intent of Parties

(a) *Setting Forth Property Rights.* The parties have the intent and desire to define and set forth the respective rights of each in the property of the other after their marriage.

(b) *Separate Property.* The parties intend and desire that all property owned respectively by each of them at the time of their marriage, and all property that may be acquired by each of them from any source during their marriage, shall be respectively their separate property, except as otherwise provided in this agreement.

Section Two
Property of Parties

The parties to this agreement own property as follows:

(a) *Henry Husband's Personal Property.* Henry Husband owns personal property described as follows:

Description	Location	Value
_____	_____	$ _____
_____	_____	$ _____
_____	_____	$ _____

(b) *Henry Husband's Real Property.* Henry Husband owns the real property described as follows: Legal

Description	Location	Value
_____	_____	$ _____
_____	_____	$ _____
_____	_____	$ _____

(a) *Wendy Wife's Personal Property.* Wendy Wife owns personal property described as follows:

Description	Location	Value
_____	_____	$ _____
_____	_____	$ _____
_____	_____	$ _____

(b) *Wendy Wife's Real Property.* Wendy Wife owns the real property described as follows: Legal

Description	Location	Value
_____	_____	$ _____
_____	_____	$ _____
_____	_____	$ _____

EXHIBIT 2–2

Community Property Agreement

Delmar/Cengage Learning

(continued)

EXHIBIT 2–2

Community Property
Agreement

(*continued*)

Section Three
Status of Separate
and Community Property

All real and personal property owned by either of the parties at the time of their marriage, and all real and personal property that either may acquire from any source whatsoever during their marriage, shall be their respective separate property, except as otherwise provided, [or if property is to be community property]. All real and personal property, wherever located, now owned or possessed by either of the parties, and all real and personal property that either of them may hereafter acquire from whatever source, _____ [if appropriate, add: with the exception of damages recovered for personal injury] shall be their community property.

Section Four
Management of Community Property

If, at any time during the marriage of the parties, any community property that is subject to the sole management, control, and disposition of either of the parties is mixed or combined with community property that is subject to the sole management, control, and disposition of the other party, the combined property shall be subject to the sole management, control, and disposition of Wendy Wife.

Section Five
Liability for Debts

The debts contracted by each party prior to their marriage are to be paid by the party who shall have contracted the debts, and the property of the other party shall not in any respect be liable for their payments.

Section Six
Execution of Instruments

Each party shall cooperate fully in executing, acknowledging, and delivering any instruments required to accomplish the intent of and to effectuate this agreement.

Section Seven
Effective Date

This agreement shall take effect on the date the marriage contemplated by the parties has been solemnized under the laws of the State of _____.

In witness whereof, the parties have executed and sealed this agreement at the day and year first above written.

_____(SEAL)

Henry Husband

_____(SEAL)

Wendy Wife

EXHIBIT 2–3

Co-ownership Chart

FORM OF CO-OWNERSHIP	JOINT TENANCY WITH SURVIVORSHIP	TENANCY IN COMMON	TENANCY BY ENTIRETY	COMMUNITY PROPERTY
Creation	By conveyance • Deed • Will	By conveyance • Deed • Will • Inheritance	By conveyance • Deed • Will	Operation of law
Identity of owner	Two or more persons identified in conveyance	Two or more persons identified in conveyance	Husband and wife identified in conveyance	Husband and wife by operation of law
Quantity of interest in property	Equal shares	Shares as set forth in conveyance may not be equal	Husband and wife as a unit own property; as individuals own nothing	Equal shares
Nature of interest	Undivided	Undivided	Undivided	Undivided
Responsibility for expenses of ownership (taxes, mortgages, and insurance)	Responsibility according to percentage of ownership	Responsibility according to percentage of ownership	Equal responsibility	Equal responsibility
Right of survivorship	Yes	No	Yes	No
Right of partition	Yes in some states; no in some states	Yes	No, except in event of divorce	No, except in event of divorce
Right to sell co-owner interest in common property	Yes	Yes	No	No
Debts of individual co-owner attach to co-owner's interest in property	Yes	Yes	No	Yes
Debts of individual co-owner attach to common property as a whole	No	No	No	No

EXHIBIT 2–4

State Co-ownership Chart

STATES	TENANCY IN COMMON	JOINT TENANCY WITH SURVIVORSHIP	TENANCY BY ENTIRETY	COMMUNITY PROPERTY
Alabama	√	√		
Alaska	√	√	√	
Arizona	√	√		√
Arkansas	√	√	√	
California	√	√		√
Colorado	√	√		
Connecticut	√	√		
Delaware	√	√	√	
District of Columbia	√	√	√	
Florida	√	√	√	
Georgia	√	√		
Hawaii	√	√	√	
Idaho	√	√		√
Illinois	√	√	√	
Indiana	√	√	√	
Iowa	√	√		
Kansas	√	√		
Kentucky	√	√	√	
Louisiana	√	√		√
Maine	√	√		
Maryland	√	√	√	
Massachusetts	√	√	√	
Michigan	√	√	√	
Minnesota	√	√		
Mississippi	√	√	√	
Missouri	√	√	√	
Montana	√	√		
Nebraska	√	√		
Nevada	√	√		√
New Hampshire	√	√		
New Jersey	√	√	√	
New Mexico	√	√		√
New York	√	√	√	
North Carolina	√	√	√	
North Dakota	√	√	√	
Ohio	√	√		
Oklahoma	√	√	√	
Oregon	√	√	√	
Pennsylvania	√	√	√	
Rhode Island	√	√	√	
South Carolina	√	√		
South Dakota	√	√		
Tennessee	√	√	√	
Texas	√	√		√
Utah	√	√		
Vermont	√	√	√	
Virginia	√	√	√	
Washington	√	√		√
West Virginia	√	√		
Wisconsin	√	√		√
Wyoming	√	√	√	

chapter | 3

Surveys and Land Descriptions

Objectives

After reading this chapter, you should be able to:
- Read and understand three types of legal descriptions: government rectangular survey description, platted description, and metes and bounds description
- Review surveys
- Review a land survey for the accuracy of a legal description
- Prepare a legal description from a land survey

Outline

In a scene from the classic film *Cocoanuts,* Groucho Marx explains real estate to Chico Marx. Groucho asks Chico if he knows what a lot is. Chico replies, "Yeah, too much." Groucho then says, "I don't mean a whole lot, just a little lot with nothing on it." Chico responds, with all of Chico's logic, "Anytime you gotta too much, you gotta whole lot. A whole lot is too much, too much is a whole lot; same thing."

Regardless of whether you have a whole lot or a small lot with nothing on it, the lot has to be described. Real estate often is described casually, such as the "big white house on the corner of Wilton and Lullwater" or "the Harris farm at the end of the road." The competent practice of real estate law, however, demands that parcels of land be referred to more precisely. Every deed, mortgage, lease, easement, or other document that deals with land must state the exact size and location of the land according to an established system of land description. The purpose of the description is to fix the boundaries of the land and to distinguish the land in question from other land. A description that is too vague will render void any document in which it is incorporated. Therefore, a specific or correct description is called a **legal description**, because it makes the document legal and enforceable. In many states, legal descriptions are prepared by registered land surveyors, and the real estate paralegal only needs to proofread the description for mistakes. In other states, the preparation of a legal description is the task of an attorney or a paralegal working under the supervision of an attorney. The land surveyor prepares a survey or drawing of the property showing the various boundaries, and it is the duty of the paralegal to prepare a written legal description locating and identifying the property's boundaries as shown on the survey.

legal description

Description of real property by a government survey, metes and bounds, or lot numbers of a recorded plat, which description is complete enough that a particular parcel of land can be located and identified.

THE SURVEY

The word **survey** is derived from an old French word meaning "to look over." It refers to the evaluation of real property evidence to locate the physical limits of a particular parcel of land. The real property evidence considered by the surveyor typically consists of physical field evidence, written record evidence, and field measurements. The surveyor, having made an evaluation of the evidence, forms an opinion as to where the lines would be located.

The surveyor then prepares a map, or plat of survey, to communicate his or her opinion to others. The map or plat is colloquially known as the survey.

A survey may be a boundary survey, which locates the boundaries of the land in question and provides a description of the land. A surveyor may, however, be asked to prepare an **as-built survey**. An as-built survey locates all physical improvements on the land in relation to the boundary lines. On an as-built survey, the surveyor usually locates all fences, walls, driveways, pavements, building structures, and natural features such as streams and ponds. This information is necessary to determine both the presence of features that may limit the value or use of the land and the conformity with local ordinances regarding minimum building setbacks and other requirements. An example of an as-built survey is shown in Exhibit 3–1.

Note that the as-built survey in Exhibit 3–1 reveals some interesting features of this property. For example, a 36-inch concrete pipe runs underneath the corner of the house. In addition, a sanitary sewer line runs underneath the house. Both the concrete pipe and the sewer line could cause substantial problems for the owner. These features may make it difficult for the owner to obtain a loan on the property or to sell the property. The utility companies that own rights to the concrete pipe and sanitary sewer line also could damage the house if they had to repair the pipe and line.

For purposes of land descriptions, a survey should provide the paralegal with the following information: (a) the state, county, land district, and section in which the property surveyed is located; (b) an indication of which direction on the survey is north; (c) a point of beginning for a land description; (d) courses and distances for each property line; (e) the name of the surveyor; (f) a scale for distances not shown on the survey; and (g) in most cases a legend of abbreviations or symbols used.

survey

Visual presentation of the physical boundaries of real property. The survey is used to describe real property.

as-built survey

Survey that locates all physical improvements on the land in relation to the boundary lines of the land.

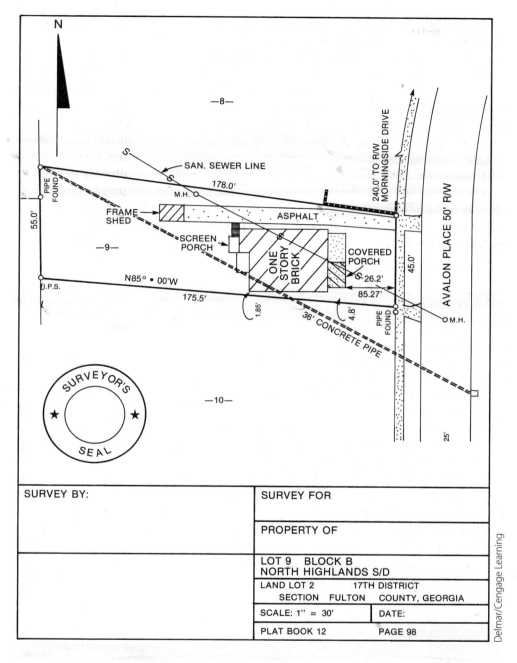

Delmar/Cengage Learning

EXHIBIT 3–1
As-Built Survey

PREPARATION OF SURVEYS AND SURVEY STANDARDS

Surveys are generally prepared by professionals known as land surveyors. Land surveyors are generally licensed by the state and must pass certain examinations for competency. Educational requirements generally are a college degree with a major in engineering or mathematics.

Most surveyors prepare surveys based on standards developed jointly by **title insurance** companies and surveyors. These standards are generally referred to as the

title insurance

Contract to indemnify the insured against loss through defects in the title to real property.

ALTA/ACSM standards. The ALTA/ACSM standards were last revised in 2005. A copy of the 2005 ALTA/ACSM standards are contained at the end of this chapter as Exhibit 3–18. For more information explaining the 2005 ALTA/ASCM Standards, you can visit the American Land Title Association's Web site at *http://www.alta.org/standards/standards.cfm*. The ALTA/ACSM requirements contain basic requirements with additional items that can be requested by the client. The more additional items that are required, the more expensive a survey will be, but the survey will also contain amore accurate picture, drawing, or representation of the property. Generally, a client or attorney, when ordering a survey, should provide the surveyor with (a) an accurate legal description of the property; (b) a current **title insurance commitment**; (c) copies of all recorded **easements**, servitudes, and covenants affecting the property; (d) copies of any appurtenant easements; and (e) names and deed data for all adjacent owners.

title insurance commitment

A commitment or a contract by a title insurance company to issue a title insurance policy.

easement

Right granted to a nonowner of real property to use the real property for a specific purpose. For example, a right to an electric utility company to locate an electric line on real property is an easement.

LAND DESCRIPTIONS

Three types of land description are in use in the United States: (1) government rectangular survey description, (2) platted description, and (3) metes and bounds description.

Government Rectangular Survey Description

When the United States was first being established, a standard system of describing land was needed to make areas of land easy to locate and available for sale by federal land offices. Thomas Jefferson headed a committee that in 1785 devised a method of dividing land into a series of rectangles. The rectangular survey system is used in describing land in Alabama, Alaska, Arizona, Arkansas, California, Colorado, Florida, Idaho, Illinois, Indiana, Iowa, Kansas, Louisiana, Michigan, Minnesota, Mississippi, Missouri, Montana, Nebraska, Nevada, New Mexico, North Dakota, Ohio, Oklahoma, Oregon, South Dakota, Utah, Washington, Wisconsin, and Wyoming (see Exhibit 3–2).

The rectangular survey system is based on sets of two intersecting hypothetical lines: **principal meridians** and **base lines.** Principal meridians are vertical lines that run north and south. Base lines are horizontal lines that run east and west. Using the principal meridians and base lines, a state can be divided into land areas that are easily identified. Within these identifiable areas of land, any particular section or parcel of land can be located.

principal meridians

Imaginary north and south lines used in a government survey system. Meridians intersect the base lines to form a starting point for the measurement of land under that system.

base line

Imaginary east-west survey line used in the government survey system to establish township lines.

Principal Meridians

A principal meridian is a surveyor's line that runs due north and south through a particular area or state. Principal meridians are identifiable in terms of their distance in degrees, minutes, and seconds west of the Greenwich meridian. The United States contains 35 principal meridians, and each is assigned a name or number for identification purposes. For example, the principal meridians running north and south in the state of Louisiana are called the Louisiana meridian and the St. Helena meridian.

Base Lines

A base line is a surveyor's line that runs due east and west and is identified as being a certain number of degrees north of the equator. Only one base line will cross each principal meridian; therefore, a parcel of land can be described as being a certain distance east or west of a given principal meridian and a certain distance north or south of a given base line.

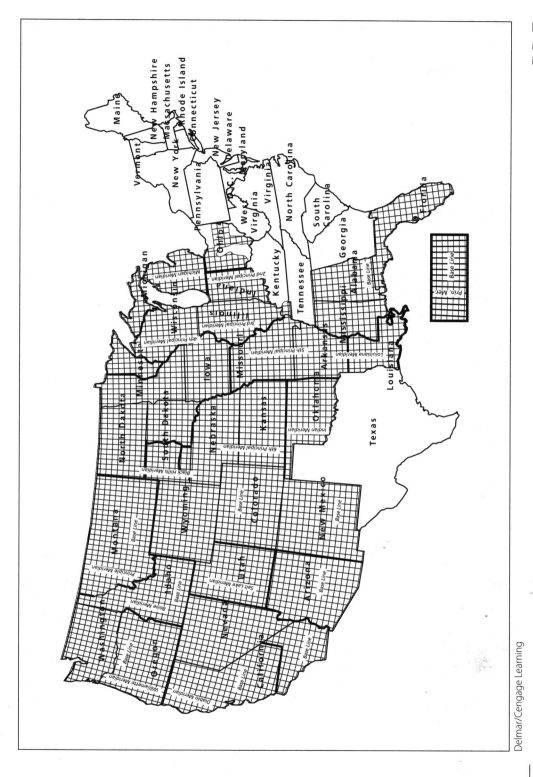

EXHIBIT 3–2

Methods of Land Description
in the United States

Township or Range Lines

Using only principal meridians and base lines, the areas of land are still large, and surveying a particular parcel within the areas would be difficult. To simplify the task of identifying a smaller parcel, township and range lines have been established. **Township lines** run east and west at 6-mile intervals parallel with base lines and form strips of land or tiers

---

township lines

Lines in a government rectangular survey system that run east and west at 6-mile intervals parallel with base lines and that form strips of land or tiers called townships.

range lines

Division of a state in a government survey system being a 6-mile-wide row of townships running north and south.

township

In a government survey, it is a square tract of land 6 miles on each side, containing 36 square miles.

called townships. Land on either side of the principal meridians is also divided into 6-mile strips by north and south lines called **range lines.** Squares of land formed by the intersecting township lines and range lines make up a grid, with each square within the grid having about 6 miles on each side. These squares, called **townships,** make up the basic units of the rectangular survey system. In theory, each township is 6 miles square and contains 36 square miles; in reality, a slight overage or shortage may exist because of difficulties encountered during surveying.

Correction Lines and Guide Meridians

Because the earth is round, all range lines gradually approach one another to the point where they eventually meet at the North Pole. Thus, an accurate survey of a township would show its north boundary line to be about 50 feet shorter than its south boundary line. In the case of the fourth township north of the base line, the difference is four times as great, or about 200 feet. The rectangular survey system uses *correction* lines to compensate for these resulting shortages. Each fourth township line (24 miles) north and south of a base line is designated as a correction line. At each correction line, the east and west range lines are remeasured to the full distance of 6 miles apart. Each correction line serves as a new base line for townships that lie between it and the next correction line. *Guide meridians* are lines running due north and south at 24-mile intervals (every fourth range line) on either side of the principal meridian. They begin at the base line and extend to the first correction line in either direction. Guide meridians are not parallel to the principal meridians or to one another. Combined with the correction lines, these guide meridians divide land territories into areas about 24 miles apart.

Township Squares

A *township square* is identified by using (a) the location of the township's strip in which the township is located; (b) the designation of the range strip; and (c) the name or number of the closest principal meridian. The first tier of squares immediately adjacent to and parallel with the base line is assigned Township 1, the second tier is assigned Township 2, and so on; therefore, each township in the first tier north of the base line is called Township 1 North of the base line; each in the second row is Township 2 North of the base line and so on. Likewise, each township square in the first tier south of the base line is called Township 1 South; each township in the second tier is Township 2 South and so on. Similarly, range numbers are assigned to each tier of township squares running parallel to a principal meridian, beginning with a row immediately adjacent to the principal meridian. Township squares in the first row east of the principal meridian are numbered Range 1 East of a particular principal meridian. Those in the second row east would be identified as Range 2 East and so on. Similarly, townships located within range lines on the west side of the principal meridian would be identified as Range 1 West, Range 2 West, Range 3 West, and so on.

For example, in Exhibit 3–3, the township marked x is described as Township 5 North, Range 2 East of the Louisiana meridian. It is Township 5 North because the township is located within the fifth strip north of the base line. It is Range 2 East because the township is located within the second strip of land running north and south east of the Louisiana meridian. Finally, references are made to the Louisiana meridian because it is the closest principal meridian. The description can be abbreviated as T5 North, R2 East, Louisiana meridian.

section

Division or parcel of land on a government survey comprising 1 square mile, or 640 acres.

Sections

The 36-mile township square is further subdivided into 36 **sections,** each section being 1 mile square and containing about 640 acres. The sections are numbered consecutively from 1 to 36, beginning in the northeast corner or upper right-hand corner of the township

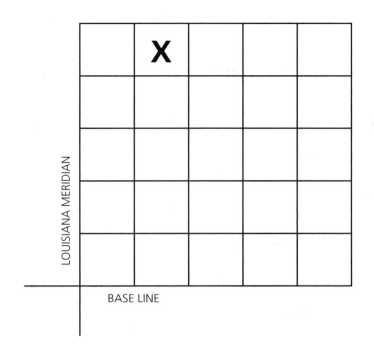

EXHIBIT 3–3

Principal Meridian and
Base Line

EXHIBIT 3–4

Sections in a Township

and proceeding west and east alternately through the township, ending in the southeast corner with the number 36 (Exhibit 3–4).

Sections are subdivided into quarter sections, and quarter sections can be further divided into halves or quarters. These halves of the quarter sections and quarter-quarter sections can be divided into smaller tracts. Exhibit 3–5 shows a section that has been subdivided. Note that in Exhibit 3–5, the SE 1/4 of the NE 1/4 of the section would be an area of land equal to 40 acres. The S 1/2 of the SW 1/4 of the NE 1/4 would be an area of land equal to 20 acres.

EXHIBIT 3–5

One Section of Land

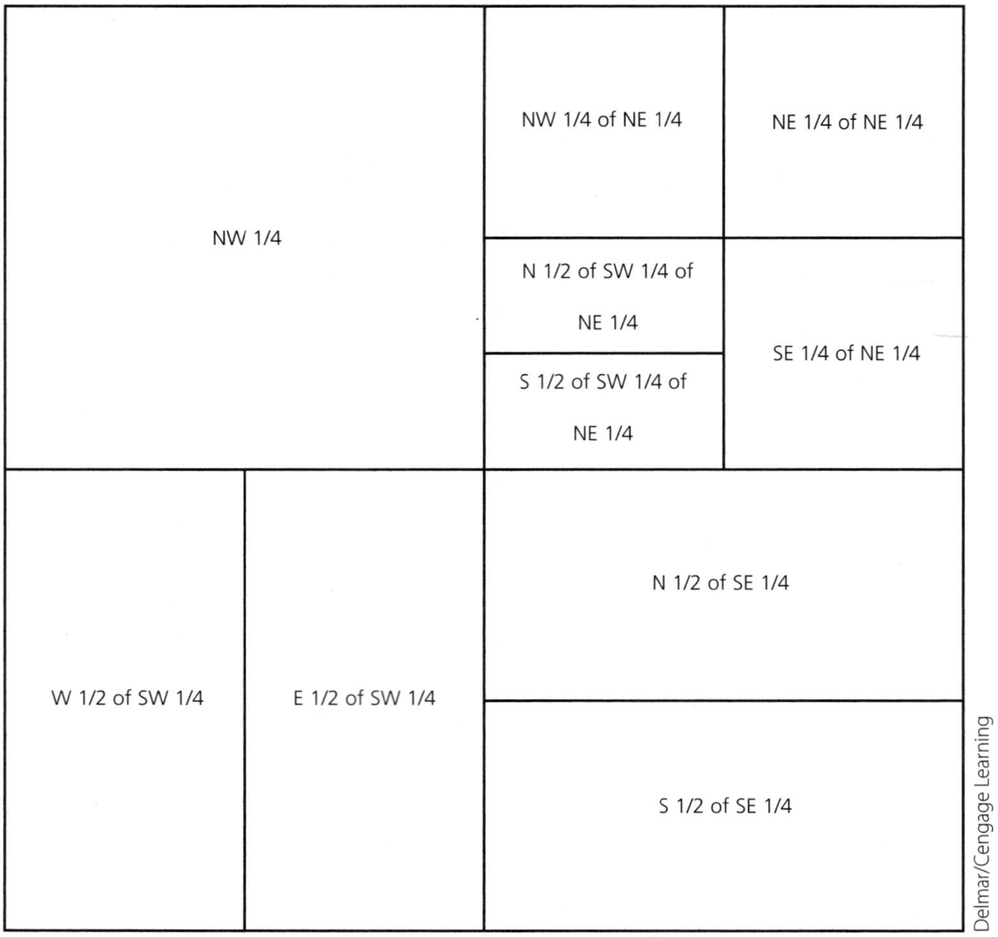

Exhibits 3–5 and 3–6 are helpful in visualizing land descriptions and understanding the rectangular survey system.

Practice Note in Reading Government Rectangular Survey Descriptions

A government rectangular survey description is read backward. That is, you read from the end of the description to the beginning to determine the location and size of the property. For example, consider the following description:

> The North 1/2 of the Northeast 1/4 of the Southeast 1/4 of Section 5, Township 3 North, Range 2 East of the Louisiana Principal Meridian.

To locate this tract of land from the preceding description, you read the description starting with the end. First search for the Louisiana principal meridian on the map of the United States. Then on a regional map, find the township in which the property is located by counting two range strips east to the Louisiana meridian and three townships north of its corresponding base line. After locating section 5 of the township on the map, divide the section into quarters, the southeast quarter into quarters, and then the northeast 1/4 of the southeast 1/4 into halves. The north half of the northeast 1/4 of the southeast 1/4 is the property in question. The property contains 20 acres. The description can be abbreviated as N 1/2, NE 1/4, SE 1/4 of Section 5, T 3N, R 2E, of the Louisiana principal meridian.

A SECTION OF LAND	ACRES	LINEAR CHAINS (1 Chain= 66 feet)	LINEAR RODS (1 Rod = 16 1/2 feet)	LINEAR FEET	SQUARE MILE
ONE FULL SECTION	640	80	320	5,280	1
QUARTER SECTION	160	40	160	2,640	1/2
QUARTER QUARTER SECTION	40	20	80	1,320	1/4
QUARTER QUARTER QUARTER SECTION	10	10	40	660	1/8
QUARTER QUARTER QUARTER QUARTER SECTION	21/2	5	20	330	1/16
QUARTER QUARTER QUARTER QUARTER QUARTER SECTION	5/8	21/2	10	165	1/32

EXHIBIT 3–6

A Section

Delmar/Cengage Learning

Platted Description

The platted, or short form, description describes a piece of land by reference to a recorded survey or plat. The first requirement for a platted legal description is that a land surveyor prepares a **plat** showing the dimensions and boundaries of the land. The plat is then recorded in the county records where the land is located. Platted descriptions commonly are used in single-family home subdivisions, condominiums, and industrial parks. The local custom in some areas also may dictate that almost all property be platted.

A paralegal preparing a platted legal description need only make reference to the plat, indicating the book and page numbers where the plat has been recorded. Example 3–1 is an example of a platted legal description.

plat

Survey of real property that often is recorded.

Example 3–1

ALL THAT TRACT or parcel of land lying and being in Land Lot 106 of the 18th district of DeKalb County, Georgia, and being Lot 3, Block A, Unit 1 of Farris Subdivision as shown on Plat of Subdivision recorded at Plat Book 10, Page 84, DeKalb County, Georgia Records.

Practice Note on Platted Description

The platted legal description refers to a certain lot being shown on a certain plat recorded in a certain plat book and page within the county. For the legal description to be correct, the land being described must in fact appear as designated in the brief reference. It is a good idea to obtain a copy of the recorded plat to make certain that the property is adequately and correctly described.

The requirements for a platted description are as follows:

- Land lot
- District
- County
- State
- Subdivision name and lot, block, and unit numbers
- Recorded reference to plat book and page numbers

Metes and Bounds Description

A metes and bounds description sets forth and completely describes the boundary lines of the land. Example 3–2 is an example of a metes and bounds description. The survey from which it was taken is shown in Exhibit 3–7.

Example 3–2

ALL THAT TRACT OR PARCEL OF LAND lying and being in Land Lot 99 of the 17th District of Fulton County, Georgia, and being more particularly described as follows:

TO FIND THE TRUE POINT OF BEGINNING, commence at a point formed by the intersection of the northerly side of Buckhead Avenue (a 60-foot right-of-way) and the easterly side of Peachtree Road; thence run east along the aforementioned right-of-way line of Buckhead Avenue a distance of 293.8 feet to an iron pin found and the TRUE POINT OF BEGINNING; thence running north 00 degrees 52 minutes 00 seconds west a distance of 82.13 feet to a nail found; thence north 21 degrees 48 minutes 38 seconds east a distance of 14.84 feet to a nail found on the southeasterly right-of-way line of Bolling Way; thence along the right-of-way line of Bolling Way north 37 degrees 19 minutes 27 seconds east a distance of 98.20 feet to a nail found; thence south 86 degrees 24 minutes 30 seconds east a distance of 13.5 feet to a nail found; thence south 00 degrees 52 minutes 00 seconds east a distance of 167.80 feet to an iron pin found on the northerly right-of-way line of Buckhead Avenue; thence south 86 degrees 02 minutes 22 seconds west along the northerly right-of-way line of Buckhead Avenue a distance of 80.0 feet to the TRUE POINT OF BEGINNING.

---

course

In a metes and bounds legal description, it is the direction of a property boundary line.

distance

In a metes and bounds legal description, it is the length of a property boundary line, usually measured in feet and hundredths of a foot; example: 82.13 feet.

Each boundary line, or "call," is described by a course and a distance. The **course** is the direction in which the boundary line travels, and the **distance** is the length of the boundary line. For example, the first call in Exhibit 3–7 measuring the eastern boundary of the property as it leaves Buckhead Avenue is north 00°52'00" west 82.13 feet. The course of the call is northwest, and the distance of the call is 82.13 feet.

A metes and bounds description usually begins with an introduction that locates the land in a general part of the state. For example, the state of Georgia is subdivided into

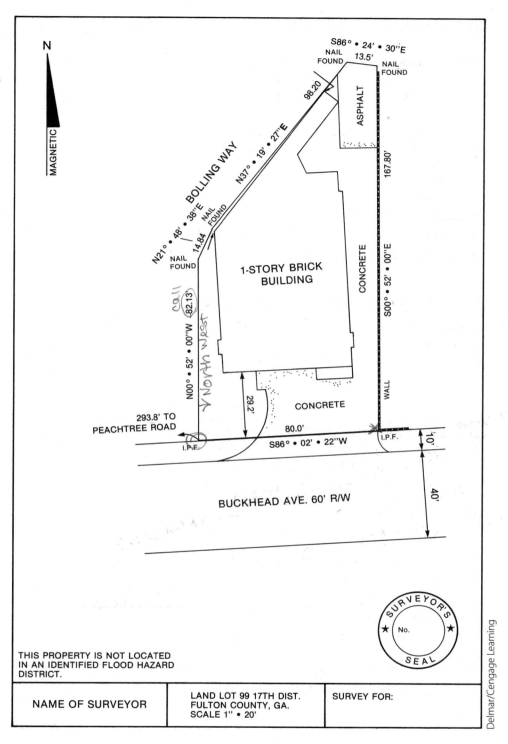

Delmar/Cengage Learning

EXHIBIT 3–7
Metes and Bounds Survey

counties, a county is further subdivided into land districts, and some districts are divided into sections. Within districts and sections are land lots that range from 40 to 490 acres. The boundaries of the counties, districts, sections, and land lots are all made definite by government survey. An example of an introduction to a metes and bounds description in Georgia is as follows in Example 3–3.

Example 3–3

All that tract or parcel of land lying and being in Land Lot 99 of the 17th District of Fulton County, Georgia, and being more particularly described as follows:

Each metes and bounds description must begin somewhere, and that somewhere is called the *point of beginning,* or *beginning point.* The beginning point must be precise or the entire description will be incorrect; it must be a definitely ascertainable point and a point that can be located on the ground. Therefore, a beginning point must be either (a) at a known point (a monument, man-made or natural), such as a land lot corner, street corner, street intersection, intersection of the street with a railroad, or intersection of a street with a stream; or (b) a certain course and distance from a monument. The beginning point for the survey in Exhibit 3–7 and the preceding legal description is the intersection of two streets, Buckhead Avenue and Peachtree Road. The beginning point is described as follows in Example 3–4.

Example 3–4

TO FIND THE TRUE POINT OF BEGINNING, commence at a point formed by the intersection of the northerly side of Buckhead Avenue (60-foot right-of-way) and the easterly side of Peachtree Road; thence run East along the aforementioned right-of-way line of Buckhead Avenue a distance of 293.8 feet to an iron pin found and the TRUE POINT OF BEGINNING.

Review the other sample metes and bounds legal descriptions at the end of this chapter and see how each of the beginning points was obtained. It is incorrect to say as a beginning point, "Begin at an iron pin (found on a certain street)" or "Begin at a point (on a certain street)" because there are an infinite number of iron pins or points along that street.

Once the beginning point has been fixed, the metes and bounds description proceeds along a series of calls, each **call** being a course and distance describing a boundary line of the land. Each of these calls is located on the survey by the land surveyor. A review of the legal description and the survey in Exhibit 3–7 as well as the sample legal descriptions and surveys at the end of this chapter show how the course and distances have been described. The course (the direction) of a boundary line usually is done by course bearings. These bearings are based on true north or true south compass readings, and each course is based on a north-south direction. The compass directions are based on a 360-degree radius, for which there are four 90-degree quadrants: northwest, northeast, southeast, and southwest (Exhibit 3–8). Each quadrant has 90 degrees; each degree has 60 minutes; and each minute has 60 seconds. For example, a line that is north 10°50′26″ west is a line that is 10°50′26″ west of due north and is a line that would be found in the northwest quadrant of the compass.

The distance of a call usually is measured in feet or hundredths of feet. A call that is 56.8 feet is 56 and 80/100ths of a foot in length. In some parts of the country, especially in rural areas, the distances may be measured in rods and chains. A rod is 16.5 feet. A chain is 100 links, with each link being 0.66 feet, so the entire chain is 66 feet. It is rare for a distance to be given in yards.

Curved Property Lines

Not all property can be measured in straight lines, and many times a metes and bounds description involves a curved land boundary. Whenever a legal description involves a curve,

call

Course and distance describing a boundary line of land in a metes and bounds land description.

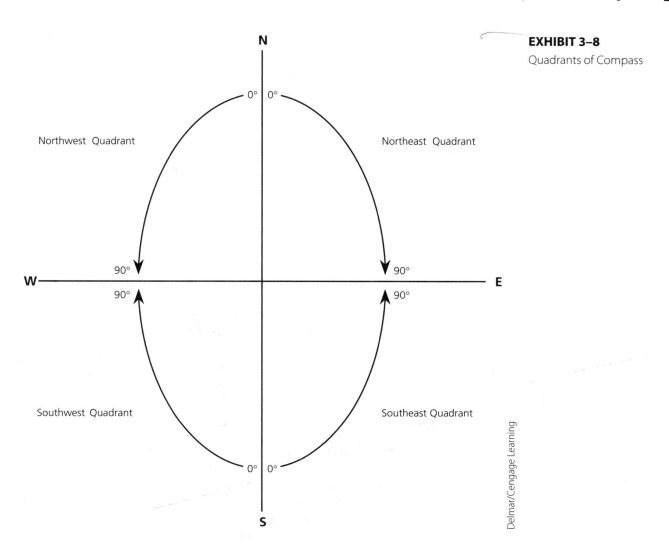

Delmar/Cengage Learning

EXHIBIT 3–8
Quadrants of Compass

the land surveyor should give the following information concerning each curve: (a) the arc distance of the curve; (b) the radius distance of the curve; (c) the chord course (**chord** being a straight line drawn from the beginning point of the arc to the ending point of the arc); and (d) the distance of the chord (Exhibit 3–9).

A paralegal who has been given the arc distance, the radius distance of the curve, and the chord course and distance can prepare a land description involving a curved boundary. An example of a curved land description taken from Exhibit 3–9 is given in Example 3–5.

chord

Straight line drawn from the beginning point of an arc to the ending point of an arc.

Example 3–5

THENCE, along the arc of a curve an arc distance of 583.49 feet to a point (said curve having a radius of 583.44 feet and being subtended by a chord bearing north 39°16′12″ east, a chord distance of 559.48 feet).

Measurement of Courses by Angles

Sometimes surveyors use angles to measure the exact direction of a property line instead of or in addition to bearings.

EXHIBIT 3–9

Elements of Curved Property
Description

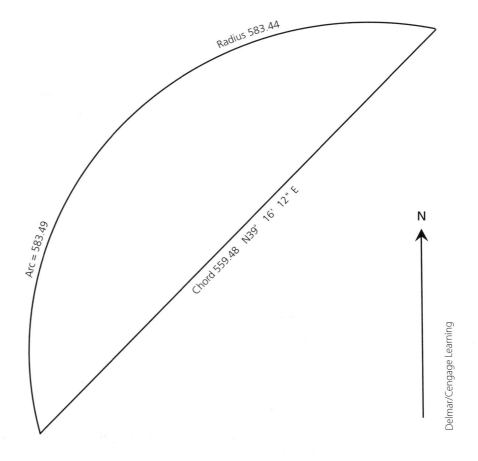

A circle has 360 degrees (each degree has 60 minutes and each minute has 60 seconds), and this is the basis for angles used in legal descriptions. The only thing an angle has in common with the bearings is the use of the terms *degrees, minutes,* and *seconds;* a line running northeasterly at an interior angle of 60°14′30″ is not the same thing as a line running north 60°14′30″ east.

An angle runs from the last described course and is either interior (inside the property boundary) or exterior (outside the property boundary).

When reviewing a survey in which angles are used to describe courses, think of a property corner as an intersection of two lines. At the point of intersection, draw a circle, using that point as a center of the circle. The arc of the circle within the property boundary is the interior angle, and the arc outside the property boundary is the exterior angle.

At one corner of the example shown in Exhibit 3–10, there is an interior angle of 85 degrees and an exterior angle of 275 degrees; at another corner, there is an interior angle of 270 degrees and an exterior angle of 90 degrees. The calls would be any one of the following: thence north at an interior angle of 85 degrees (exterior angle of 275 degrees from the last described course); thence east at an interior angle of 85 degrees (exterior angle of 275 degrees from the last described course); thence south at an interior angle of 270 degrees (exterior angle 90 degrees) from the last described course; thence east at an interior angle of 270 degrees (exterior angle 90 degrees) from the last described course.

When angles are used, the interior-exterior angles are always the same, even though the property lines are described from different directions. Most surveyors locate only one interior-exterior angle at a corner, not necessarily both; but a circle always has 360 degrees, and the omitted angle can easily be computed if necessary.

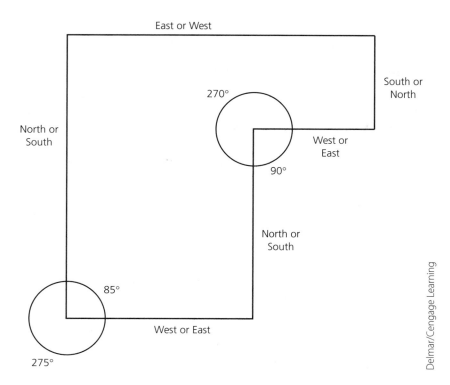

Delmar/Cengage Learning

EXHIBIT 3–10

Measurement of Courses
by Angles

Closure

A metes and bounds description must close. This means that the legal description starts at the beginning point, follows each boundary line by course and distance, and ends back at the beginning point. If the land description does not close, it is defective.

Practice Notes on Metes and Bounds Description

The basic requirements for a metes and bounds legal description are (a) identification of land lot, district, section, county, and state in which the property is located; (b) definite beginning point; (c) compass direction and distances from one point to the next; and (d) return to the beginning point.

A metes and bounds legal description usually cannot be prepared without a survey. Most surveyors locate the beginning point on the survey and also give a course and distance for each property boundary line. The main problem in the metes and bounds description is carelessness: mistakes in reading the survey and omission of a boundary line description. It is a good practice to proofread a metes and bounds description with another person. The other person should read the legal description, and the person responsible for the legal description should proof what is being read on the survey. Then roles should be swapped: the other person should read the survey, and the person responsible for the description should proof the description.

PRACTICE TIPS FOR REVIEWING A SURVEY

One of the duties of a real estate paralegal is to assist the attorney in the review of a survey. A survey review is generally conducted in connection with a transaction involving a sale or a loan secured by real property. Generally, the client for whom the survey is being reviewed will either be a purchaser of the real property being surveyed or a lender who is making a loan secured by the real property.

A paralegal, when reviewing a survey, should have a survey, a title commitment or title report, a survey checklist, and several colored marking pens. Most law firms have developed their own survey review checklist; however, one is included at the end of this chapter (Exhibit 3–19). Generally, when reviewing a survey, it is acceptable to write or mark on the survey. A paralegal should order several copies so that clean copies of the survey can be given to the client.

The paralegal should review the survey carefully to determine if the surveyor has provided the basic information on the survey. Basic survey information includes a north arrow indicating which direction is north and a legend describing any symbols the surveyor used to mark different items on the survey. In addition, a survey should be dated and contain the surveyor's seal and, in many states, should be personally signed by the surveyor.

One of the key objectives when reviewing a survey is to determine if the survey description of the property matches the description contained in either the deed from the current owner or the title insurance commitment. Most surveys will contain a printed legal description of the property and the description contained on the boundary lines of the property. The paralegal should locate the boundary on the survey and highlight the boundary to identify it. If the description for the property is a metes and bounds, the paralegal should trace each course and distance around the boundary from the point of beginning following each boundary until returning to the point of beginning. If there is insufficient information on the survey to permit the paralegal to trace the legal description, then the survey may be defective. If the legal description is a platted description referring to platted lots, the paralegal should locate the plat information and recording on the survey and match it with the legal description in the deed or title commitment. It is important that the survey legal description match the legal description used in the title insurance commitment and the legal documents used for the transaction. If there are differences between the legal descriptions in the survey and the title insurance commitment, an investigation needs to be done to determine why the differences exist, and then any discrepancies need to be resolved. The paralegal should confer with the attorney if he or she finds a difference between the survey description and the title insurance commitment description.

Another objective in a survey review is to locate on the survey each easement or other encumbrance shown in the title insurance commitment. The survey should show the recording number of each easement and the location of the easement on the survey. If the easements mentioned in the title commitment cannot be located on the survey, an inquiry needs to be made as to why these easements were not found. Occasionally, a surveyor will indicate by notes on the survey that certain easements cannot be located. These easements may be blanket easements covering the entire property, or the descriptions on the easements were so vague that the surveyor could not determine where they were located.

The location of any improvements on the property and a review of the survey to determine if there are encroachments either onto the property or from the property is an important objective when reviewing a survey. It is important to locate all buildings and other improvements and to trace around the property boundary to see that the improvements do not encroach onto an adjoining neighbor's property or over or upon easements located on the survey. It is also important to determine if improvements on adjacent properties do not encroach upon the property being surveyed. Any encroachments located by the paralegal should be brought to the attention of the attorney to determine if the encroachments constitute a serious problem.

Most property is serviced by utilities, so the survey should locate evidence of these utilities. The survey should be reviewed carefully to ensure that utility services such as electricity, water, storm sewer, sanitary sewer, telephone lines, and gas are shown and that the property is connected to such utilities.

In addition to utilities, a means of vehicular access to the property is important. A survey should show all adjacent streets, roads, and highways and indicate whether the accesses are public or private. The survey should be reviewed carefully to determine whether the property has access to a public street. The driveways and curb cuts drawn on the survey should be studied to determine how vehicles drive onto and leave the property from the public street.

Other issues to review on a survey include setback lines, which may be required by private restrictions or **zoning** regulations. The setback line requirements generally provide that improvements must be located a certain distance from the street or from the boundary of the property. If the improvements violate the setback lines, this could result in noncompliance of zoning or a violation of a restrictive covenant. Any encroachments or violations of setback lines should be brought to the attention of the attorney to determine if they are serious encroachments.

Surveyors should indicate whether the property is located in a flood hazard area. If this is the case, flood insurance may be required. The paralegal should carefully review the survey and notes to determine if any of the property is located in a flood hazard zone.

zoning

Legitimate police power of governments to regulate the use of real property.

ETHICS: Competency

You are a paralegal with a small general practice firm that represents clients in a number of areas, including real estate. You are working with an attorney on a complicated real property transaction. The land description for the property is complicated. The attorney you work with remarks to you that she is not very good at drafting land descriptions. She mentions that because you received formal paralegal training, you should be skilled in this area, and she requests that you do the land description. She does not know that you also have difficulty preparing land descriptions. You know that if you prepare the description, even though your supervising attorney will review it, it is questionable whether the attorney will be knowledgeable enough to catch any mistakes. Should you draft the land description and hope for the best?

The American Bar Association's Code of Professional Responsibility provides that a lawyer should represent a client competently. An attorney should strive to become and remain proficient in his or her practice and should accept employment only in matters in which he or she is or intends to become competent to handle. Although a paralegal is not directly regulated by the American Bar Association's Code of Professional Responsibility, an ethical and professional paralegal should act with competence and proper care in assisting attorneys in the representation of clients. When a paralegal undertakes the duty of assisting an attorney in the representation of a client, the paralegal should use proper care to safeguard the client's interest. If the paralegal is working in an area beyond his or her competence but in which he or she is expected to become competent, it is the paralegal's duty to diligently undertake the work and to study whatever is necessary to perform the work competently. Paralegals should take pride in their professional endeavors. Their obligation to act competently requires a higher motivation to be a professional.

In this factual situation, the paralegal should either decline to prepare the description and explain to the attorney his or her difficulty in preparing descriptions of this type or seek help from other members of the firm to see if someone else in the firm is competent in this area of practice. The paralegal may also obtain help from title insurance companies, surveyors, or other professionals who may be willing to assist the paralegal in gaining an understanding of the skills and tasks required to prepare the land description.

SUMMARY

A survey is an important part of any real estate transaction. A surveyor describes the boundaries of the property and either provides a legal description or a means for preparing a legal description of the real property. In addition, the land survey will also locate all improvements on the property and show any encroachment of improvements onto adjacent properties or encroachments of improvements from adjacent properties onto the surveyed property. The surveyor will also locate easements, utilities, means of access, and other important features of the property being surveyed.

Surveys are generally prepared by professional licensed surveyors according to standards developed by the survey profession and the title insurance industry.

Real estate paralegals come in daily contact with surveys and will use these surveys to either prepare or proof legal descriptions and to determine if the property, as represented on the survey, satisfies all the expectations and requirements of the client. A full knowledge of land descriptions and survey requirements is important to enable the paralegal to fully assist an attorney in a real estate transaction.

HELPFUL WEBSITES

American Congress on Surveying and Mapping
http://www.acsm.net
This site provides good technical information on the science of surveying and mapmaking. The site provides links to obtain copies of the ALTA/ACSM Standards. The site also provides access to copies of each state's minimum technical standards for land surveyors.

National Society of Professional Surveyors
http://www.nspsmo.org
This site provides interesting information regarding the surveying profession and business. The site contains a copy of the Surveyor's Creed and Canon of Ethics.

KEY TERMS

as-built survey	easement	survey
base line	legal description	title insurance
call	plat	title insurance commitment
chord	principal meridians	township
course	range lines	township lines
distance	section	zoning

REVIEW QUESTIONS

1. What information should a survey provide for the purpose of a land description?
2. Identify and describe the three types of land description.
3. What type of description commonly is used in a residential subdivision?
4. What is a base line, and what is its relation to a meridian line in a government rectangular survey?
5. How many acres are found in the north 1/2 of the northwest 1/4 of the southeast 1/4 of a section?
6. How many acres are found in the southeast 1/4 of the southwest 1/4 of the southeast 1/4 of a section?
7. What are the basic requirements for a platted description?
8. What information should a land surveyor give to prepare a legal description involving a curved land boundary?
9. What is required to have a correct point of beginning on a metes and bounds legal description?
10. In a metes and bounds legal description, each property boundary is described by a course and distance. What is a course, and what is a distance?

PRACTICAL ASSIGNMENTS

1. Prepare a metes and bounds legal description from the survey in Exhibit 3–14 at the end of this chapter.

2. Prepare a metes and bounds legal description from the survey in Exhibit 3–15 at the end of this chapter.

3. Prepare a metes and bounds legal description from the survey in Exhibit 3–16 at the end of this chapter.

4. The legal description for Exhibit 3–17 at the end of this chapter is incorrect. Please find the errors and prepare a correct legal description.

5. Obtain a copy of a commercial as-built real estate survey either from your instructor or from another source. Review the survey in conjunction with the ALTA/ACSM Land Title Survey Minimum Standard Detail Requirements 2005, shown as Exhibit 3–18. From this review, please list all the ALTA/ACSM Minimum Standard Detail Requirements that appear on the survey.

ADDENDUM

Exhibit 3–11 Platted Description Survey
Exhibit 3–12 Metes and Bounds Description (Including Curve with Description)
Exhibit 3–13 Metes and Bounds with Use of Interior Angles
Exhibit 3–14 Metes and Bounds Survey—E. Ponce de Leon Property

Exhibit 3–15 Metes and Bounds Survey—Mohawk Trail Property
Exhibit 3–16 Metes and Bounds Survey—West Pine Valley Road Property
Exhibit 3–17 Metes and Bounds Survey with Legal Description—Willow Creek Property
Exhibit 3–18 ALTA/ACSM 2005 Survey Standards
Exhibit 3–19 Survey Review Checklist

ACKNOWLEDGMENT

All publications of the American Land Title Association®, including ALTA® Policy Forms, Endorsements, and Related Documents, are copyrighted and are reprinted herein by specific permission from:
American Land Title Association® (ALTA®)
1828 L Street, N.W., Suite 705
Washington, DC 20036
Phone: 202-296-3671
E-mail: service@alta.org
Web: *http://www.alta.org*

Student StudyWare™ CD-ROM

Interactive Student CD in the book includes additional quizzing, case studies, and key terms flashcards.

Online Companion™

For additional resources, please go to *www.paralegal.delmar.cengage.com*

EXHIBIT 3–11

Platted Description Survey

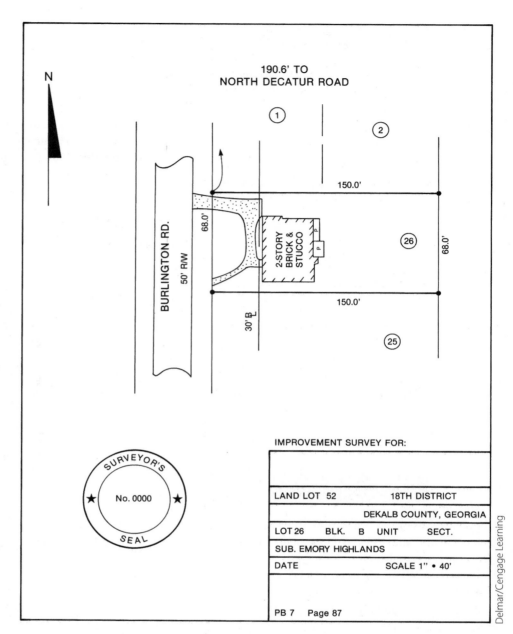

IMPROVEMENT SURVEY FOR:

LAND LOT 52	18TH DISTRICT
	DEKALB COUNTY, GEORGIA
LOT 26 BLK. B UNIT SECT.	
SUB. EMORY HIGHLANDS	
DATE	SCALE 1" • 40'

PB 7   Page 87

Delmar/Cengage Learning

ALL THAT TRACT or parcel of land lying and being in Land Lot 52 of the 18th District of DeKalb County, Georgia, being Lot 26, Block B, Emory Highlands, according to plat recorded in Plat Book 7 at page 87, in the office of the Clerk of the Superior Court of DeKalb County, Georgia.

EXHIBIT 3–12

Metes and Bounds Survey and Description (Including Curve with Description)

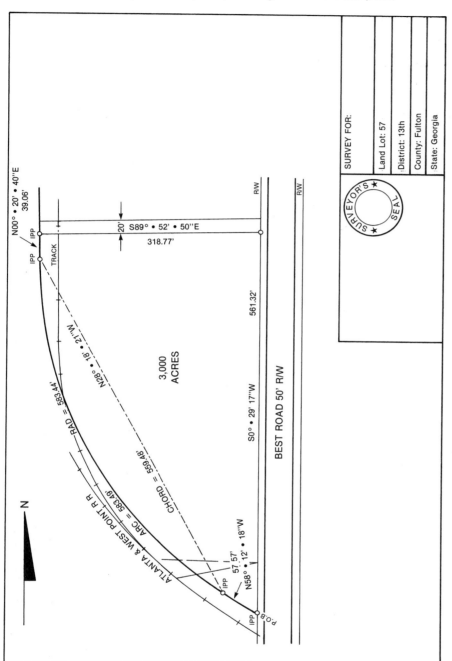

ALL THAT TRACT or parcel of land lying and being in Land Lot 37 of the 13th District of Fulton County, Georgia, and being more particularly described as follows:

BEGIN at an iron pin at the intersection of the western right-of-way at Best Road (50-foot right-of-way) and the northeastern right-of-way of the Atlanta & West Point Railroad; thence, run north 58 degrees 12 minutes 18 seconds west 57.57 feet to an iron pin placed; thence, run in a northwesterly direction along the arc of a curve an arc distance of 583.49 feet to an iron pin (said curve having a radius of 583.44 feet and being subtended by a chord bearing north 28 degrees 18 minutes 21 seconds west, a chord distance of 559.48 feet); thence, north 00 degrees 20 minutes 40 seconds east 39.06 feet to an iron pin; thence, south 89 degrees 52 minutes 50 seconds east 318.77 feet to an iron pin located on the western right-of-way of Best Road; thence, run along the western right-of-way of Best Road south 00 degrees 29 minutes 17 seconds west 561.32 feet to the POINT OF BEGINNING.

Delmar/Cengage Learning

EXHIBIT 3–13

Metes and Bounds Survey with
Use of Interior Angles

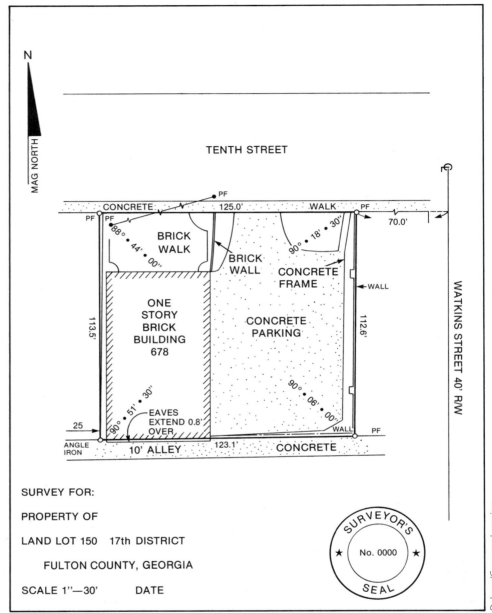

ALL THAT TRACT or parcel of land lying and being in Land Lot 150 of the 17th District of Fulton County, Georgia, and being more particularly described as follows:

BEGINNING at an iron pin found on the south side of 10th Street 70 feet west of the center line of Watkins Street (having a 40-foot right-of-way) as measured along the south side of 10th Street; thence south and forming an interior angle of 90 degrees 18 minutes 30 seconds from 10th Street 112.6 feet to a 3-inch steel fence post on the north side of an alley; thence, west along the north side of said alley and forming an interior angle of 90 degrees 06 minutes from the preceding call 123.1 feet to a 3-inch steel fence post; thence north and forming an interior angle of 90 degrees 51 minutes 30 seconds from the preceding call 113.5 feet to a 3-inch steel fence post on the south side of 10th Street; thence east along the south side of 10th Street and forming an interior angle of 88 degrees 44 minutes from the preceding call 125 feet to the point of BEGINNING; said property being known as 678 10th Street, N.W., according to the present system of numbering houses in the City of Atlanta, and being formerly known as Lots 4, 5, 6, 7 and 8, Block G of the Joe E. Brown Co. as per plat recorded in Plat Book 7, pages 86 and 87, Fulton County, Georgia Records; and being the same property shown on a plat of survey dated April 30, 1987.

TOGETHER WITH all of Grantor's right, title and interest, if any, in and to the ten (10) foot alley located along the rear line of the above-described property.

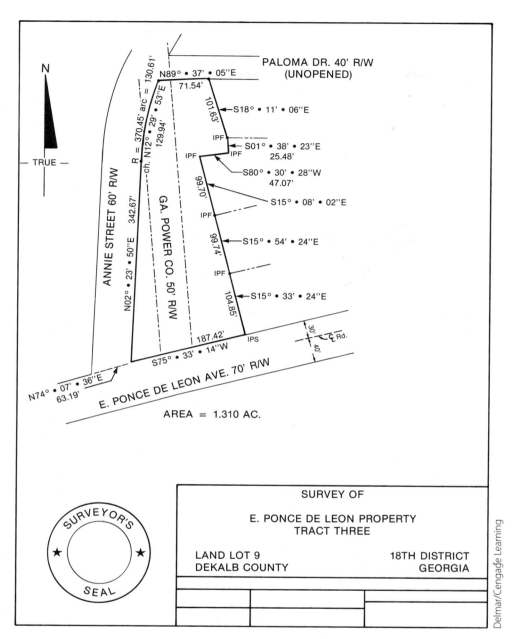

EXHIBIT 3–14

Metes and Bounds Survey—
E. Ponce de Leon Property

EXHIBIT 3–15

Metes and Bounds Survey—
Mohawk Trail Property

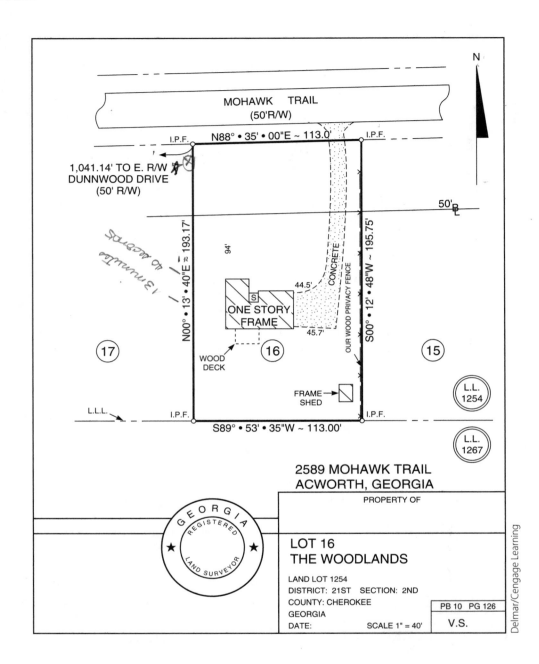

2589 MOHAWK TRAIL
ACWORTH, GEORGIA

PROPERTY OF

LOT 16
THE WOODLANDS

LAND LOT 1254
DISTRICT: 21ST   SECTION: 2ND
COUNTY: CHEROKEE
GEORGIA
DATE: SCALE 1" = 40'

PB 10   PG 126

V.S.

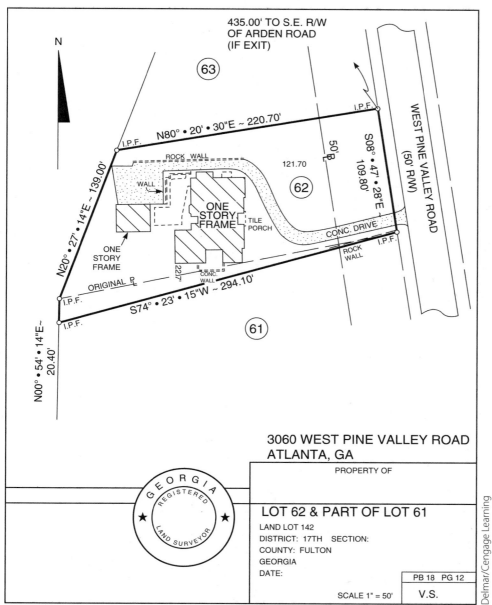

EXHIBIT 3–16

Metes and Bounds Survey—
West Pine Valley Road Property

EXHIBIT 3–17

Metes and Bounds Survey with Legal Description—Willow Creek Property

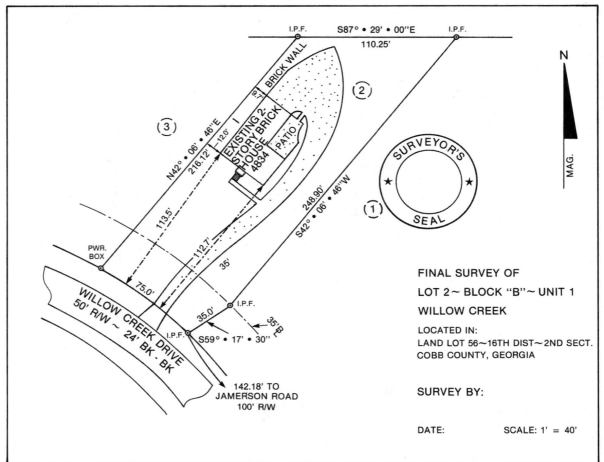

ALL THAT TRACT or parcel of land lying and being in Land 56 of the 16th District, 2nd Section, Cobb County, Georgia, and being more particularly described as follows:

BEGIN at an iron pin found on the northeastern right-of-way of Willow Creek Drive (50-foot right-of-way), said iron pin being located 142.18 feet northwest of the intersection of the northeastern right-of-way of Willow Creek Drive with the northern right-of-way of Jamerson Road (100-foot right-of-way); run thence in a northwesterly direction along the northeasterly right-of-way of Willow Creek Drive 75.0 feet to a power box; run thence North 42°06'46" East 261.12 feet to an iron pin found; thence run South 87°29'00" West 110.25 feet to an iron pin found; thence run South 24°06'46" West 248.90 feet to an iron pin found; run thence South 59°17'03" West 35.0 feet to an iron pin found being the POINT OF BEGINNING.

2005 MINIMUM STANDARD DETAIL REQUIREMENTS
FOR ALTA/ACSM LAND TITLE SURVEYS
as adopted by
American Land Title Association
and
National Society of Professional Surveyors
(*a member organization of the American Congress on Surveying and Mapping*)

It is recognized that members of the American Land Title Association (ALTA) have specific needs, peculiar to title insurance matters, which require particular information for acceptance by title insurance companies when said companies are asked to insure title to land without exception as to the many matters which might be discoverable from survey and inspection and not be evidenced by the public records. In the general interest of the public, the surveying profession, title insurers and abstracters, ALTA and the National Society of Professional Surveyors, Inc. (NSPS) jointly promulgate and set forth such details and criteria for standards. It is recognized and understood that local and state standards or standards of care, which surveyors in those respective jurisdictions are bound by, may augment, or even require variations to the standards outlined herein. Where conflicts between the standards outlined herein and any jurisdictional statutes or regulations occur, the more restrictive requirement shall apply. It is also recognized that title insurance companies are entitled to rely on the survey furnished to them to be of an appropriate professional quality, both as to completeness and as to accuracy. It is equally recognized that for the performance of a survey, the surveyor will be provided with appropriate data which can be relied upon in the preparation of the survey.

For a survey of real property and the plat or map of the survey to be acceptable to a title insurance company for purposes of insuring title to said real property free and clear of survey matters (except those matters disclosed by the survey and indicated on the plat or map), certain specific and pertinent information shall be presented for the distinct and clear understanding between the client (insured), the title insurance company (insurer), and the surveyor (the person professionally responsible for the survey). These requirements are:

1. The client shall request the survey or arrange for the survey to be requested and shall provide a written authorization to proceed with the survey from the person responsible for paying for the survey. Unless specifically authorized in writing by the insurer, the insurer shall not be responsible for any costs associated with the preparation of the survey. The request shall specify that an **"ALTA/ACSM LAND TITLE SURVEY"** is required and shall designate which of the optional items listed in Table A are to be incorporated. The request shall set forth the record description of the property to be surveyed or, in the case of an original survey, the record description of the parent parcel that contains the property to be surveyed. Complete copies of the record description of the property (or, in the case of an original survey, the parent parcel), any record easements benefiting the property; the record easements or servitudes and covenants burdening the property ("Record Documents"); documents of record referred to in the Record Documents; and any other documents containing desired appropriate information affecting the property being surveyed and to which the survey shall make reference shall be provided to the surveyor for notation on the plat or map of survey.

2. The plat or map of such survey shall bear the name, address, telephone number, and signature of the professional land surveyor who performed the survey, his or her official seal and registration number, the date the survey was completed, the dates of all of the surveyor's revisions and the caption "ALTA/ACSM Land Title Survey" with the certification set forth in paragraph 8.

3. An **"ALTA/ACSM LAND TITLE SURVEY"** shall be in accordance with the then-current "Accuracy Standards for Land Title Surveys" ("Accuracy Standards") as adopted, from time to time by the National Society of Professional Surveyors and the American Land Title Association and incorporated herein by reference.

(continued)

EXHIBIT 3–18

ALTA/ACSM 2005 Survey Standards

ALTA forms have been used by permission of the American Land Title Association.

EXHIBIT 3–18

ALTA/ACSM 2005 Survey
Standards

(*continued*)

4. On the plat or map of an **"ALTA/ACSM LAND TITLE SURVEY,"** the survey boundary shall be drawn to a convenient scale, with that scale clearly indicated. A graphic scale, shown in feet or meters or both, shall be included. A north arrow shall be shown and when practicable, the plat or map of survey shall be oriented so that north is at the top of the drawing. Symbols or abbreviations used shall be identified on the face of the plat or map by use of a legend or other means. If necessary for clarity, supplementary or exaggerated diagrams shall be presented accurately on the plat or map. The plat or map shall be a minimum size of 8½ by 11 inches.

5. The survey shall be performed on the ground and the plat or map of an **"ALTA/ACSM LAND TITLE SURVEY"** shall contain, in addition to the required items already specified above, the following applicable information:

(a) All data necessary to indicate the mathematical dimensions and relationships of the boundary represented, with angles given directly or by bearings, and with the length and radius of each curve, together with elements necessary to mathematically define each curve. The point of beginning of the surveyor's description shall be shown as well as the remote point of beginning if different. A bearing base shall refer to some well-fixed line, so that the bearings may be easily re-established. The North arrow shall be referenced to its bearing base and should that bearing base differ from record title, that difference shall be noted.

(b) When record bearings or angles or distances differ from measured bearings, angles or distances, both the record and measured bearings, angles, and distances shall be clearly indicated. If the record description fails to form a mathematically closed figure, the surveyor shall so indicate.

(c) Measured and recorded distances from corners of parcels surveyed to the nearest right-of-way lines of streets in urban or suburban areas, together with recovered lot corners and evidence of lot corners, shall be noted. For streets and highways abutting the property surveyed, the name, the width and location of pavement relative to the nearest boundary line of the surveyed tract, and the width of existing rights of way, where available from the controlling jurisdiction, shall be shown. Observable evidence of access (or lack thereof) to such abutting streets or highways shall be indicated. Observable evidence of private roads shall be so indicated. Streets abutting the premises, which have been described in Record Documents, but not physically opened, shall be shown and so noted.

(d) The identifying titles of all recorded plats, filed maps, right of way maps, or similar documents which the survey represents, wholly or in part, shall be shown with their appropriate recording data, filing dates and map numbers, and the lot, block, and section numbers or letters of the surveyed premises. For non-platted adjoining land, names, and recording data identifying adjoining owners as they appear of record shall be shown. For platted adjoining land, the recording data of the subdivision plat shall be shown. The survey shall indicate platted setback or building restriction lines which have been recorded in subdivision plats or which appear in Record Documents which have been delivered to the surveyor. Contiguity, gores, and overlaps along the exterior boundaries of the surveyed premises, where ascertainable from field evidence or Record Documents, or interior to those exterior boundaries, shall be clearly indicated or noted. Where only a part of a recorded lot or parcel is included in the survey, the balance of the lot or parcel shall be indicated.

(e) All evidence of monuments shall be shown and noted to indicate which were found and which were placed. All evidence of monuments found beyond the surveyed premises on which establishment of the corners of the surveyed premises are dependent, and their application related to the survey shall be indicated.

(f) The character of any and all evidence of possession shall be stated and the location of such evidence carefully given in relation to both the measured boundary lines and those established by the record. An absence of notation on the survey shall be presumptive of no observable evidence of possession.

(*continued*)

(g) The location of all buildings upon the plot or parcel shall be shown and their locations defined by measurements perpendicular to the nearest perimeter boundaries. The precision of these measurements shall be commensurate with the Relative Positional Accuracy of the survey as specified in the current Accuracy Standards for ALTA/ACSM Land Title Surveys. If there are no buildings erected on the property being surveyed, the plat or map shall bear the statement, "No buildings." Proper street numbers shall be shown where available.

(h) All easements evidenced by Record Documents which have been delivered to the surveyor shall be shown, both those burdening and those benefiting the property surveyed, indicating recording information. If such an easement cannot be located, a note to this effect shall be included. Observable evidence of easements and/or servitudes of all kinds, such as those created by roads; rights-of-way; water courses; drains; telephone, telegraph, or electric lines; water, sewer, oil, or gas pipelines on or across the surveyed property and on adjoining properties if they appear to affect the surveyed property, shall be located and noted. If the surveyor has knowledge of any such easements and/or servitudes, not observable at the time the present survey is made, such lack of observable evidence shall be noted. Surface indications, if any, of underground easements and/or servitudes shall also be shown.

(i) The character and location of all walls, buildings, fences, and other visible improvements within five feet of each side of the boundary lines shall be noted. Without expressing a legal opinion, physical evidence of all encroaching structural appurtenances and projections, such as fire escapes, bay windows, windows and doors that open out, flue pipes, stoops, eaves, cornices, areaways, steps, trim, etc., by or on adjoining property or on abutting streets, on any easement or over setback lines shown by Record Documents shall be indicated with the extent of such encroachment or projection. If the client wishes to have additional information with regard to appurtenances such as whether or not such appurtenances are independent, division, or party walls and are plumb, the client will assume the responsibility of obtaining such permissions as are necessary for the surveyor to enter upon the properties to make such determinations.

(j) Driveways, alleys, and other ways of access on or crossing the property must be shown. Where there is evidence of use by other than the occupants of the property, the surveyor must so indicate on the plat or map. Where driveways or alleys on adjoining properties encroach, in whole or in part, on the property being surveyed, the surveyor must so indicate on the plat or map with appropriate measurements.

(k) As accurately as the evidence permits, the location of cemeteries and burial grounds (i) disclosed in the Record Documents provided by client or (ii) observed in the process of performing the field work for the survey, shall be shown.

(l) Ponds, lakes, springs, or rivers bordering on or running through the premises being surveyed shall be shown.

6. As a minimum requirement, the surveyor shall furnish two sets of prints of the plat or map of survey to the title insurance company or the client. If the plat or map of survey consists of more than one sheet, the sheets shall be numbered, the total number of sheets indicated and match lines be shown on each sheet. The prints shall be on durable and dimensionally stable material of a quality standard acceptable to the title insurance company. The record title description of the surveyed tract, or the description provided by the client, and any new description prepared by the surveyor must appear on the face of the plat or map or otherwise accompany the survey. When, in the opinion of the surveyor, the results of the survey differ significantly from the record, or if a fundamental decision related to the boundary resolution is not clearly reflected on the plat or map, the surveyor may explain this information with notes on the face of the plat or map or in accompanying attachments. If the relative positional accuracy of the survey exceeds that allowable, the surveyor shall explain the site conditions that resulted in that outcome with a note on the face of the map or plat.

EXHIBIT 3–18
ALTA/ACSM 2005 Survey Standards
(*continued*)

(*continued*)

EXHIBIT 3–18

ALTA/ACSM 2005 Survey
Standards
(*continued*)

7. Water boundaries necessarily are subject to change due to erosion or accretion by tidal action or the flow of rivers and streams. A realignment of water bodies may also occur due to many reasons such as deliberate cutting and filling of bordering lands or by avulsion. Recorded surveys of natural water boundaries are not relied upon by title insurers for location of title.

When a property to be surveyed for title insurance purposes contains a natural water boundary, the surveyor shall measure the location of the boundary according to appropriate surveying methods and note on the plat or map the date of the measurement and the caveat that the boundary is subject to change due to natural causes and that it may or may not represent the actual location of the limit of title. When the surveyor is aware of changes in such boundaries, the extent of those changes shall be identified.

8. When the surveyor has met all of the minimum standard detail requirements for an ALTA/ACSM Land Title Survey, the following certification shall be made on the plat:

To (name of client), (name of lender, if known), (name of title insurance company, if known), (name of others as instructed by client):

This is to certify that this map or plat and the survey on which it is based were made in accordance with the "Minimum Standard Detail Requirements for ALTA/ACSM Land Title Surveys," jointly established and adopted by ALTA and NSPS in 2005, and includes items _____ of Table A thereof. Pursuant to the Accuracy Standards as adopted by ALTA and NSPS and in effect on the date of this certification, undersigned further certifies that in my professional opinion, as a land surveyor registered in the State of _____, the Relative Positional Accuracy of this survey does not exceed that which is specified therein.

Date: _____ (signed) _____ (seal) _____
                                                                            Registration No.

NOTE: If, as otherwise allowed in the Accuracy Standards, the Relative Positional Accuracy exceeds that which is specified therein, the following certification shall be made on the plat:

To (name of client), (name of lender, if known), (name of title insurance company, if known), (name of others as instructed by client):

This is to certify that this map or plat and the survey on which it is based were made in accordance with the "Minimum Standard Detail Requirements for ALTA/ACSM Land Title Surveys," jointly established and adopted by ALTA and NSPS in 2005, and includes items _____ of Table A thereof. Pursuant to the Accuracy Standards as adopted by ALTA and NSPS and in effect on the date of this certification, undersigned further certifies that in my professional opinion, as a land surveyor registered in the State of _____, the maximum Relative Positional Accuracy is _____ feet.

Date: _____ (signed) _____ (seal) _____
                                                                            Registration No.

The 2005 Minimum Standard Detail Requirements for ALTA/ACSM Land Title Surveys are effective January 1, 2006. As of that date, all previous versions of the Minimum Standard Detail Requirements for ALTA/ACSM Land Title Surveys are superseded by these 2005 standards.

Adopted by the American Land Title Association on October 5, 2005.
Adopted by the Board of Directors, National Society of Professional Surveyors on October 24, 2005. American Land Title Association, 1828 L St., N. W., Suite 705, Washington, D. C. 20036.
National Society of Professional Surveyors, Inc., 6 Montgomery Village Avenue, Suite 403, Gaithersburg, MD 20879

(*continued*)

TABLE A
OPTIONAL SURVEY RESPONSIBILITIES AND SPECIFICATIONS

NOTE: The items of Table A must be negotiated between the surveyor and client. It may be necessary for the surveyor to qualify or expand upon the description of these items, e.g., in reference to item 6, there may be a need for an interpretation of a restriction. The surveyor cannot make a certification on the basis of an interpretation or opinion of another party. Items 16, 17, and 18 are only for use on projects for the U.S. Department of Housing and Urban Development (HUD).

If checked, the following optional items are to be included in the ALTA/ACSM LAND TITLE SURVEY, except as otherwise negotiated:

1. _____ Monuments placed (or a reference monument or witness to the corner) at all major corners of the boundary of the property, unless already marked or referenced by an existing monument or witness to the corner.
2. _____ Vicinity map showing the property surveyed in reference to nearby highway(s) or major street intersection(s).
3. _____ Flood zone designation (with proper annotation based on federal Flood Insurance Rate Maps or the state or local equivalent, by scaled map location and graphic plotting only.)
4. _____ Gross land area (and other areas if specified by the client).
5. _____ Contours and the datum of the elevations.
6. _____ List setback, height, and floor space area restrictions disclosed by applicable zoning or building codes (beyond those required under paragraph 5d of these standards). If none, so state. The source of such information must be disclosed. See "Note" on the bottom of previous page.
7. _____ (a) Exterior dimensions of all buildings at ground level
   (b) Square footage of:
   _____ (1) exterior footprint of all buildings at ground level;
   _____ (2) gross floor area of all buildings; or
   _____ (3) other areas to be defined by the client.
   _____ (c) Measured height of all buildings above grade at a defined location. If no defined location is provided, the point of measurement shall be shown.
8. _____ Substantial, visible improvements (in addition to buildings) such as billboards, signs, parking structures, swimming pools, etc.
9. _____ Parking areas and, if striped, the striping and the type (e.g. handicapped, motorcycle, regular, etc.) and number of parking spaces.
10. _____ Indication of access to a public way on land such as curb cuts and driveways, and to and from waters adjoining the surveyed tract, such as boat slips, launches, piers, and docks.
11. _____ Location of utilities (representative examples of which are shown below) existing on or serving the surveyed property as determined by:
   _____ (a) Observed evidence
   _____ (b) Observed evidence together with evidence from plans obtained from utility companies or provided by client, and markings by utility companies and other appropriate sources (with reference as to the source of information)
   • railroad tracks and sidings;
   • manholes, catch basins, valve vaults, or other surface indications of subterranean uses;
   • wires and cables (including their function, if readily identifiable) crossing the surveyed premises, all poles on or within ten feet of the surveyed premises, and the dimensions of all crossmembers or overhangs affecting the surveyed premises; and
   • utility company installations on the surveyed premises.

EXHIBIT 3–18
ALTA/ACSM 2005 Survey Standards
(*continued*)

(*continued*)

EXHIBIT 3–18

ALTA/ACSM 2005 Survey
Standards

(*continued*)

12. _____ Governmental Agency survey-related requirements as specified by the client.
13. _____ Names of adjoining owners of platted lands.
14. _____ The distance to the nearest intersecting street as designated by the client.
15. _____ Rectified orthophotography, photogrammetric mapping, laser scanning, and other similar products, tools, or technologies may be utilized as the basis for the location of certain features (excluding boundaries) where ground measurements are not otherwise necessary to locate those features to an appropriate and acceptable accuracy relative to a nearby boundary. The surveyor shall (a) discuss the ramifications of such methodologies (e.g. the potential accuracy and completeness of the data gathered thereby) with the title company, lender, and client prior to the performance of the survey and, (b) place a note on the face of the survey explaining the source, date, relative accuracy, and other relevant qualifications of any such data.
16. _____ Observable evidence of earth moving work, building construction, or building additions within recent months.
17. _____ Any changes in street right of way lines either completed or proposed, and available from the controlling jurisdiction. Observable evidence of recent street or sidewalk construction or repairs.
18. _____ Observable evidence of site use as a solid waste dump, sump, or sanitary landfill.
19. _____

ACCURACY STANDARDS FOR ALTA/ACSM LAND TITLE SURVEYS

Introduction

These Accuracy Standards address Relative Positional Accuracies for measurements that control land boundaries on ALTA/ACSM Land Title Surveys.

In order to meet these standards, the surveyor must assure and certify that the Relative Positional Accuracies resulting from the measurements made on the survey do not exceed that which is allowable.

If the size or configuration of the property to be surveyed, or the relief, vegetation or improvements on the property will result in survey measurements for which the allowable Relative Positional Accuracies will be exceeded, the surveyor must alternatively certify as to the Relative Positional Accuracy that was otherwise achieved on the survey.

Definition

"Relative Positional Accuracy" means the value expressed in feet or meters that represents the uncertainty due to random errors in measurements in the location of any point on a survey relative to any other point on the same survey at the 95 percent confidence level.

Background

The lines and corners on any property survey have uncertainty in location which is the result of (1) availability and condition of reference monuments, (2) occupation or possession lines as they may differ from record lines, (3) clarity or ambiguity of the record descriptions or plats of the surveyed tracts and its adjoiners, and (4) Relative Positional Accuracy.

The first three sources of uncertainty must be weighed as evidence in the determination of where, in the professional surveyor's opinion, the boundary lines and corners should be placed. Relative Positional Accuracy is related to how accurately the surveyor is able to monument or report those positions.

Of these four sources of uncertainty, only Relative Positional Accuracy is controllable, although due to the inherent error in any measurement, it cannot be eliminated. The first three can be estimated based on evidence; Relative Positional Accuracy can be estimated using statistical means.

(*continued*)

The surveyor shall, to the extent necessary to achieve the standard contained herein, (1) compensate or correct for systematic errors, including those associated with instrument calibration, (2) select the appropriate equipment and methods, and use trained personnel, and (3) use appropriate error propagation and other measurement design theory to select the proper instruments, field procedures, geometric layouts, and computational procedures to control random errors.

If radial survey methods, GPS or other acceptable technologies or procedures are used to locate or establish points on the survey, the surveyor shall apply appropriate procedures in order to assure that the allowable Relative Positional Accuracy of such points is not exceeded.

Computation of Relative Positional Accuracy

Relative Positional Accuracy may be tested by:

(1) comparing the relative location of points in a survey as measured by an independent survey of higher accuracy or

(2) the results of a minimally constrained, correctly weighted least square adjustment of the survey.

Allowable Relative Positional Accuracy for
Measurements Controlling Land
Boundaries on ALTA/ACSM Land Title
Surveys

0.07 feet (or 20 mm) + 50 ppm

EXHIBIT 3–18

ALTA/ACSM 2005 Survey Standards

(*continued*)

Delmar/Cengage Learning

EXHIBIT 3–19

Survey Review Checklist

SURVEY REVIEW CHECKLIST

Date: _____

File name: _____

Reviewed by: _____

Survey date: _____ Last Revision _____

Surveyor: _____ Phone _____

Prepared for: _____

Type of Survey: _____

Title Report Reference: _____

SURVEY REQUIREMENTS

1. _____ Scale

2. _____ Basis of bearings

3. _____ North arrow

4. _____ Legend

5. _____ Signed, sealed, and dated

6. _____ Property description and location:

    A. _____ Legal Description (on survey; match title commitment): _____

    _____ Description closes: _____

    B. _____ Boundaries: _____

        _____ point of commencement/point of beginning shown (and description returns to POB)

        _____ corners set

        _____ iron pins placed at deflection points

        _____ curves (length and arc or radius, tangent)

        _____ monuments found

        _____ azimuth base line shown

        _____ platted property: lots, blocks, section, and recording numbers of plat

        _____ platted property; metes and bounds match plat

    C. _____ Adjoining properties (noted with any overlaps or gaps shown): _____

    D. _____ Multiple parcels contiguous: _____

7. _____ Easements and other physical encumbrances shown on title (locate all with corresponding number of title commitment; include appurtenant easements): _____

_____

8. _____ Improvements:

    A. _____ Building and structures (height, area, perimeter dimensions; frame, roof and exterior finish): _____

(continued)

B. _____ Other improvements or physical objects (fences—determine ownership and issues, rockeries, landscaping, planter boxes, out-buildings): _____

9. _____ Encroachments (improvements over easements/boundaries; subject property onto adjoiner, adjoiner onto subject property): _____

10. _____ Access:

A. _____ Roads (adjoining streets, highways, alleys—public vs. private, rights-of-way; labeled, distance to property and restrictions shown): _____

B. _____ Ingress and egress (curb cuts and driveways): _____

11. _____ Utilities (locate electricity, sewer—storm and sanitary, telephone, water, gas; all connected to public utility lines either through public street or easement over private adjoiner): _____

12. _____ Storm drainage ponds and systems (if any; easement for runoff): _____

13. _____ Parking (number and size of spaces): _____

14. _____ Building setback lines: _____

15. _____ Street address (of each building): _____

16. _____ Area of land and area of buildings: _____

17. _____ Water (locate including flow direction all creeks, rivers, ponds, bays, lakes adjacent to or on property, or within flood plain or flood-prone area): _____

18. _____ Cemeteries (if any): _____

19. _____ Vicinity sketch (show closest thoroughfare intersection): _____

20. _____ Field notes on survey: _____

21. _____ Flood Hazard Area Certification (map number, zone): _____

22. _____ Certification (compare with requirement; client named): _____

23. _____ Other: _____

EXHIBIT 3–19

Survey Review Checklist

(*continued*)

chapter | 4

Public Regulation and Private Encumbrances

Objectives

After reading this chapter, you should be able to:

- Understand public restrictions on the use of real property, such as zoning, building codes, eminent domain, and subdivision restrictions
- Identify the various private encumbrances

encumbrance

A claim, charge, or liability on property, such as a lien or mortgage that lowers its value.

Outline

I deally, a person who owns real property wants the use of the property to be unrestricted and the title to be debt-free. In real life, it is unusual for real property, especially urban real property, to be totally free of restrictions or debts. Most ownership to real property is burdened with encumbrances. An **encumbrance** is defined by *Oran's Dictionary of the Law* as a claim, charge, or liability on property, such as a lien or mortgage that lowers its value. The courts have defined *encumbrances* to encompass more than just liens and mortgages. The term may be used to describe any matter that may cause a property to be reduced in value or its use restricted. Encumbrances usually include such things as zoning restrictions, restrictive covenants, money judgments against the owner, taxes, mortgages, and easements. Although some encumbrances, such as zoning restrictions, may have a positive effect on the ownership of the property, an encumbrance usually is viewed as an unwanted item. Private encumbrances are discovered by title examinations, which are discussed later in this book, and it often is the paralegal's responsibility to review encumbrances that pose problems for the client. The paralegal normally works with an attorney to advise the client as to the acceptability of an encumbrance. This chapter is an overview of the types of public and private encumbrances that can affect real property. Many of the encumbrances are discussed in more detail in later chapters.

PUBLIC REGULATION

Federal, state, and local governments are vested with power to restrict or take private property for the purpose of promoting the health and welfare of the general public. This power to protect and promote the public welfare gives to governmental authorities the power to impose on private real property such things as zoning regulations, building codes, subdivision regulations, environmental protection laws, the power of eminent domain, and taxation.

Zoning

The power to regulate land use is within the legitimate power of a government, and it is not unusual for city and county governments to issue **zoning** regulations that restrict private land use. The main objective of zoning is to improve living and working conditions in congested areas by preventing the liberties of one property owner from interfering with the rights of another. For example, you can imagine how irate you would be as a property owner if you purchased a beautiful home in a quiet residential neighborhood and then discovered that your neighbor has sold his or her property to a company that intends to build a 24-hour diner on the property.

Zoning is considered constitutional as long as the zoning regulation bears some reasonable relation to the public welfare. If a zoning regulation is unreasonable, it may amount to the "taking" of the real property, and the owner may be entitled to compensation or to having the zoning regulation voided.

Zoning consists of (a) dividing the city or county into districts; (b) prescribing within each district the types of structures and architectural designs for buildings to be located there; and (c) prescribing the uses for the buildings within each district. Many counties and cities now post their zoning ordinances and maps on the Internet.

For example, a city council may divide the city into four districts. One district may be reserved for single-family residential use; another district may be reserved for multifamily use, such as apartments, condominiums, and town houses; a third district may be retail commercial, in which there can be stores and offices; and the fourth district may be industrial, in which there could be manufacturing plants. Examples of a residential zoning ordinance and a commercial zoning ordinance are included at the end of this chapter (Exhibits 4–1 and 4–2).

Zoning is a political process; it usually is considered a legislative function of a governmental authority. Zoning requires procedural due process. This means that notice must be given and a hearing held before a zoning regulation can be passed. The notice usually is by means of a sign on the property or a notice in the newspaper. It is not required that landowners be given personal notice of an intention to change the zoning on their property. All zoning hearings are public. Landowners, with or without legal counsel, have an opportunity to speak at these hearings. The governmental authorities must present evidence to support the zoning classifications. A property owner does have a right to appeal a zoning decision or classification to a court of law. The court, however, in reviewing the zoning decision, will not overturn the governmental authorities' decision unless it finds that there is a clear case of abuse by the government.

Real property that has been used for a particular purpose but is later changed by the zoning regulations is deemed to be a preexisting or nonconforming use. These uses are

zoning

Legitimate police power of government to regulate the use of real property.

allowed to continue, provided they are not expanded. Some zoning statutes provide a phaseout of nonconforming uses over a period of years. For example, you are the owner of a small neighborhood grocery in a residential neighborhood. The city decides to zone the entire neighborhood residential, making your retail grocery store a nonconforming use. You may continue to operate the grocery store as you have in the past under the nonconforming use protection. You would not, however, be able to change the grocery store into a restaurant or other use, nor would you be able to expand the grocery store. *Shackford & Gooch v. The Town of Kennebunk*, 486 A.2d 102, illustrates the problems a property owner has in expanding or altering a nonconforming use.

Zoning is enforced through injunction by the public authorities. For example, a property owner decides to operate a business from her home. The property is zoned single-family residential, and the operation of the business is in violation of the zoning ordinance. The government could obtain an injunction that would order the property owner to stop operating the business. If the property owner continues to operate the business, she could be held in contempt of court and face both fines and imprisonment. The issuance of building permits is another way to enforce a zoning ordinance. A building permit will be refused unless the proposed improvement and its intended use comply with zoning.

Building Codes and Subdivision Regulations

Building code regulations also are a legitimate use of a city's or county's police power to protect the health and welfare of its citizens. For example, most cities have codes that regulate the electrical wiring and plumbing of homes and buildings. **Building codes** regulate methods and materials to be used in construction of improvements. Most cities and counties do not permit a building to be constructed and occupied without a permit and a final inspection by the building department.

building codes

Public laws that regulate methods and materials to be used in the construction of improvements.

Most city and county governments can create and enforce subdivision laws. State and federal governments can create and enforce environmental protection laws. Subdivision laws require that streets and sewers be approved in advance by the government. The streets and sewers are not accepted for public maintenance by the government without a satisfactory inspection. Many counties and cities now post their business code and subdivision regulations on the Internet.

Environmental Protection Laws/CERCLA

Fifty years ago, "environmental law" was not a commonly used term in either legal literature or the common popular vernacular. During the 1960s, various conservation societies such as the Sierra Club, through their spirited crusades, prompted a deeper study of the ecology of nature and created a public awareness that we only enjoy the natural resources of earth as trustees for future generations and that we must protect them against pollution and exploitation. The result has been the creation of a wide body of both federal and state law designed to protect the quality of our earth, water, and air.

Water is one of the earth's most precious commodities. Without water, no life would exist. The quality of water is regulated by federal environmental laws such as the Clean Water Act, 33 U.S.C. §§ 1251–1387. The Clean Water Act empowers the federal government with enforcement powers to ensure the quality of water, as well as imposing fines on people who would contaminate or pollute our water sources.

Another concern regarding water is the preservation of marshlands or wetlands. Research has shown the importance of these areas as breeding and feeding grounds for migratory birds and as natural oxygen producers. It is believed that the entire ecological chain that leads from the microscopic life forms to our own life form is dependent upon the preservation of adequate marshlands or wetlands. Both federal and state laws protect the use and development of wetlands. This protection is generally in the form of denying a developer a permit or ability to develop property identified as wetlands; fines or injunctions are imposed on those developers who do disturb wetland properties. Generally, the identification of wetlands is determined by the United States Army Corps of Engineers. It is not uncommon for a developer who is attempting a project that may include wetlands to have a surveyor or other trained person carefully study Army Corps of Engineers maps to determine if any wetland properties are located within the project boundaries.

CASE

Shackford & Gooch, Inc. et al. v. The Town of Kennebunk et al.
486 A.2d 102 (Me. 1984)

GLASSMAN, Justice.

Shackford & Gooch, Inc. *et al.,* opponents to the issuance of a building permit to B. & B. Coastal Enterprises, Inc., appeal from a judgment of the Superior Court, York County, ordering the Kennebunk Zoning Board of Appeals to issue a permit to B. & B. Coastal Enterprises to build and use a deck on the roof of its restaurant. B. & B. Coastal Enterprises cross-appeals, challenging that portion of the judgment holding that the Zoning Board of Appeals was not estopped from enforcing its ordinance. We grant the appeal and deny the cross-appeal.

I.

B. & B. Coastal Enterprises, Inc. operates Bartley's Dockside Restaurant (Dockside) in a building that is nonconforming because its setbacks do not meet the requirements of the Kennebunk Zoning Ordinance. In March 1982, Dockside applied to the Kennebunk building inspector for a permit to build stairs on the outside of the restaurant. The inspector granted the permit, at the same time giving Dockside verbal authorization to build a deck on the flat roof of the restaurant, assuring Dockside that a building permit for the deck was not necessary. When Dockside began construction of the deck, Shackford & Gooch, Inc., owner of an abutting fish market, petitioned the building inspector to stop the work on the grounds that a building permit was necessary, and that the deck violated local zoning ordinances.

The controversy eventually came before the Kennebunk Zoning Board of Appeals (Board), which decided in June 1982 that, based on an estoppel theory, Dockside could retain and use the roof deck, subject to a restricted number of seats. On review of this decision, the Superior Court ruled that the Board's finding of estoppel was incorrect as a matter of law. The court vacated the decision of the Board and remanded the case for the Board to determine initially whether the deck met the requirements of the Kennebunk Zoning Ordinance and, if not, whether Dockside was entitled to a variance.

After a hearing in September 1983, the Board found that Dockside's deck constituted an expansion of a nonconforming structure and did not comply with the setback requirements of the ordinance. The Board denied Dockside's request for the necessary variances. On review of the Board's decision, the Superior Court held as a matter of law that the deck as a vertical addition to the building did not extend the nonconforming horizontal setbacks of Dockside. The court further held the deck created no increase in Dockside's seating capacity that would necessitate a parking variance. Declining to reconsider the Superior Court's earlier ruling on estoppel, the court ordered the Board to issue a permit to Dockside to build and use its deck in accordance with the seating restriction established in the June 1982 hearing.

When the Superior Court acts as an appellate court reviewing an action of an administrative board, we directly examine the record developed before the board. *See Driscoll v. Gheewalla,* 441 A.2d 1023, 1026 (Me. 1982); *see also Nancy W. Bayley, Inc. v. Maine Employment Security Commission,* 472 A.2d 1374, 1377 (Me. 1984). On review of an action taken by a zoning board of appeals, we may not make factual findings independent of those of the board, nor may we substitute our judgment for that of the board. *Mack v. Municipal Officers of the Town of Cape Elizabeth,* 463 A.2d 717, 719–20 (Me. 1983); *Driscoll,* 441 A.2d at 1026. Our role is to determine whether the board abused its discretion, committed an error of law, or made findings not supported by substantial evidence in the record. *Mack,* 463 A.2d at 719; *Driscoll,* 441 A.2d at 1026.

The Board found in its remand hearing that Dockside's roof deck was not in compliance with the side yard, rear yard, or shoreland zoning setback requirements of the Kennebunk ordinance. The Board thus considered the deck to be an expansion of a nonconforming structure requiring a variance. The ordinance provides:

> No lawfully non-conforming use of buildings or land shall be changed, extended, or enlarged in any manner for any purpose not permitted under this Ordinance, except as may be permitted as a variance, not as an exception.

Kennebunk, Me., Zoning Ordinance § 1.4(B) (1963). The section on variance appeals provides:

> The Board may allow a relaxation, in a moderate degree, of the lot area, lot width, yard depth, or percentage of lot covered requirements of this Ordinance. Such a relaxation may be granted only when the Board determines that, by reason of physical conditions [sic] peculiar to the land or building under appeal (conditions virtually unique to that property and not

(continued)

arising or applying as to other land and building(s) adjoining or nearby within the same zoning district), unusual difficulty or particular hardship would be caused by literal application and rigorous enforcement of the terms of the Kennebunk Zoning Ordinance. The Board may also permit modest expansion of any lawfully non-conforming building or use of land, but only on land occupied by such use at the time the use became lawfully non-conforming and not onto any additional lot adjoining.

Id. at § 7.6(C)(2).

[4–6] We agree with the Board that the addition of a roof deck, or indeed, any significant alteration of a nonconforming structure is an extension or expansion. *See* 1 R. Anderson, *American Law of Zoning* 2d § 6.43 at 455 (2d ed. 1976). Dockside argues that because the roof deck does not encroach any further into the nonconforming setbacks than do the lawfully nonconforming walls of the restaurant, it does not constitute an expansion of the nonconformity. To permit such an addition to a nonconforming structure without a variance, however, would offend the policy of zoning, which is to "gradually or eventually eliminate nonconforming uses as speedily as justice will permit." *See Keith v. Saco River Corridor Commission,* 464 A.2d 150, 154 (Me. 1983). When an ordinance prohibits enlargement of a nonconforming building, a landowner cannot as a matter of right alter the structure, even if the alteration does not increase the nonconformity.

Judgment vacated;

Remanded for entry of judgment as follows: appeal denied; decision of Zoning Board of Appeals affirmed.

All concurring.

Comprehensive Environmental Response, Compensation and Liability Act (CERCLA)

Also known as Superfund, this federal legislation created a trust fund designed to finance the activities of the Environmental Protection Agency and gave the Environmental Protection Agency the authority to recover cleanup costs for contaminated properties from the responsible parties for the contamination.

Air, like water, goes with the land but is not confined to it, and the landowner has a transient right to use the air as it flows over his boundaries. A landowner has a right to receive air in a reasonably clean and pure state from his neighbors and must let it pass over his property without adding pollution or debris. Air quality standards are established by the federal government under the Clean Air Act, 42 U.S.C. §§ 7401–7671. Many states have similar statutes that regulate the quality of air. Clean air acts are generally enforced through injunctions or fines. Excessive noise may also be regarded as a form of air pollution and is subject to similar controls by both federal and state legislation.

The problems of closed or abandoned disposal sites of hazardous waste are handled by the Environmental Protection Agency (EPA) under the **Comprehensive Environmental Response, Compensation and Liability Act (CERCLA)** passed in 1980, 42 U.S.C. § 9601 et seq. CERCLA, also known as Superfund, for the trust fund designed by the Act to finance the activities of the EPA under the Act, puts vigor and teeth into environmental law enforcement. CERCLA gave the EPA the authority to take notice of release of hazardous substances and to recover the cleanup costs from the responsible parties. In addition, CERCLA provides private parties with the ability both to sue responsible parties for hazardous waste cleanup and to claim government help if the government has ordered them to perform a cleanup and the responsible party has failed to do so.

Under CERCLA are four classes of parties potentially liable for the cleanup of hazardous substances: first, the present owners and operators of facilities that generate or create hazardous substances; second, owners and operators who in the past have created hazardous waste or disposed of hazardous waste; third, those who arrange for the treatment and transport of disposable hazardous waste; and finally, those parties who accept hazardous waste for treatment, transport, or disposal.

CERCLA makes each responsible party fully liable for the cost of cleaning up hazardous waste sites. The EPA has a variety of strong enforcement weapons to accomplish the cleanup responsibilities. The EPA may seek a court injunction ordering the responsible party to clean up the hazardous waste. In addition, the EPA can clean up the hazardous waste and assess the costs against the responsible party, including placing a lien on the property to secure payment of the cost. A responsible party who fails to comply with any order from the EPA to clean up hazardous waste may be subject to treble damages and penalties.

The EPA expects that there are thousands of contaminated sites throughout the United States. The average cost of cleaning up a Superfund (contaminated) site is now estimated to be in excess of $25 million.

It is easy to see why contaminated property could become an expensive liability for its owner. In many cases, the cost of cleaning up the property would exceed the value of the property. CERCLA has an "innocent purchaser" defense to protect an innocent purchaser or lender who makes a loan on contaminated property. This innocent purchaser defense provides an exception to the strict joint and several liability for cleanup costs under the Superfund law. It provides that anyone who purchases or makes a loan on contaminated property who at the time of the acquisition or making of the loan was not aware that the property was contaminated will not be liable for the cost of cleanup of the contamination.

To avail itself of the innocent party defense, a person must (1) have no actual knowledge of the contamination at the time of the purchase or making of the loan and (2) have undertaken at the time of acquisition or making of the loan all appropriate inquiry into the previous ownership and uses of the property consistent with good commercial or customary practice. Generally, a buyer or lender, at the time of acquisition or making of the loan, must have the property correctly investigated for the likelihood of subsurface contamination. This inquiry is generally done by hiring an environmental engineer to prepare a review of the property for possible contamination. This review is generally referred to as a **Phase I** environmental examination. Most Phase I environmental examinations are performed in accordance with the American Society of Testing and Materials (ASTM) standards for environmental assessments. The use of the ASTM standards is voluntary, but most environmental engineers adhere to them.

The ASTM standards generally require the environmental engineer to review a survey or site plan of the site to be examined and determine its exact boundaries. As a part of this review, the environmental engineer must determine the up gradient direction for the possible flow of contamination. Because contamination generally flows in a gravity direction, an up gradient of property would be property with a higher elevation to that of the property being examined. The environmental engineer also during the Phase I review will look at regulatory data concerning the property and the surrounding area of the property. The regulatory data usually include any state or county lists of hazardous waste generators and an examination of the public records to determine if environmental liens have been filed. The review also requires a search of the United States EPA database for a list of hazardous waste generators, transporters, and storage and treatment facilities. The environmental engineer will also look to see if there are any underground storage tanks, either on the property or within a reasonable vicinity of the property that might leak and contaminate the property. The environmental engineer will inspect the property, looking for any evidence of toxic materials, including their storage, handling, and disposal. Many times this review will involve looking at vegetation on the property to see if it is discolored or dying, which might indicate some subsurface contamination. If requested, the environmental engineer may, during the site inspection, also review the property for other contaminants such as asbestos, lead-based paint, and polychlorinate biphenyls (PCBs), which can be contained in hydraulic oils and found in electrical transformers. Another source of potential subsurface contamination is the cleaning fluids and solvents used for dry-cleaning plants. These solvents are highly toxic and quite capable of contaminating the underground water supply.

After all the historical data and government databases have been reviewed, including the site review, the engineer will then write a Phase I environmental assessment indicating the likelihood of contamination on the property. The Phase I environmental assessment, depending on the type of project being assessed, can cost several thousand dollars. The Phase I report may indicate that there is some concern regarding contamination of the property, which may require additional testing. The additional testing is generally referred to as the **Phase II** environmental assessment. The Phase II environmental assessment involves

Phase I

An examination of real property to determine if it contains environmental contamination.

Phase II

A more intensive environmental examination of property, usually including the testing of soil and water for evidence of contamination.

the environmental engineer obtaining soil and water samples from the property. These soil and water samples are then analyzed in a laboratory to determine if they contain elements of contamination in excess of the limits considered normal by federal and state government standards. Phase II environmental assessments are generally more intensive than Phase I and can be quite expensive.

Since an examination is necessary for a purchaser or lender to avail themselves of the innocent party defense under CERCLA, Phase I environmental examinations have become almost an absolute requirement in connection with the purchase or making of a loan on a commercial property. Many purchasers and lenders, in addition to the Phase I environmental assessment, will also require the seller or borrower to provide them with an environmental indemnity.

Real estate owners and lenders now have access to various insurance products to offset the financial consequences of different environmental risks. An *environmental site protection insurance policy* will protect the insured against third-party liability, bodily injury, and property damage caused by environmental conditions.

A *remediation cost cap policy* eliminates financial uncertainty from environmental remediation projects by establishing an upper limit for the costs the insured must pay for remediation activities. The insurance company pays for any remediation costs that exceed the estimated cap.

A *secured creditor insurance policy* insures real estate mortgage lenders against loss caused by environmental contamination. This policy generally pays the lender the lesser of (a) the cost of cleaning up the property on which the lender has a mortgage or (b) the loan balance, if the borrower defaults and environmental contamination is found on the property. The secured creditor insurance policy may also protect the mortgage lender against third-party claims asserted against the lender as a result of environmental contamination on the mortgaged property.

Underground Storage Tanks

Underground storage tanks containing gasoline, petroleum products, or other fluids are generally not regulated directly by CERCLA. Underground storage tanks containing petroleum are generally regulated by state law. These state laws usually impose liability for the owner of an underground storage tank for leaks that cause contamination to soil or water sources. Many states require an owner of property to remove, or to fill with sand, tanks not in use. Many states have trust funds that provide money for the purpose of remediating or cleaning up sites that have been contaminated by leaking underground storage tanks. The money to fund the trust fund is collected from owners of underground storage tanks through taxes or other assessments. Most owners of gasoline stations are required to pay a tax to the state for each gallon of gasoline sold, which is deposited into a fund for remediation of all leaking underground storage tanks within the state. By participating in the fund, the owner, in the event his or her tanks leak, will be eligible to receive monies from the fund for the purpose of remediation.

Radon and Lead-Based Paint

Other areas of environmental concern often found in residential transactions are radon and lead-based paint. Radon, which is a product of decaying uranium, is a tasteless, colorless, odorless gas that is typically found in areas with deposits of granite, phosphate, shale, and uranium ore. It is believed that exposure to high levels of radon gas may pose a threat to health, including a cause of cancer. It is prudent in states where radon may be prevalent for purchasers to have investigations or assessments of the property to determine if radon does exist. In addition, many states have required sellers of homes known to have radon to make full disclosure to a purchaser concerning the radon levels in the home. Radon can be mitigated through proper ventilation of the areas where radon is located.

Lead-based paint is also an environmental concern in many residences. Lead poisoning generally does not result in death but can result in brain damage and other serious health side effects. The highest risk is for children growing up in homes with lead-based paint, who may, as a result of exposure to the paint, not develop properly and suffer brain damage or other health problems as adults. Lead-based paint was commonly used in homes built prior to 1978. The federal government banned the sale of this type of paint in 1977. Federal government regulations require the owners of housing built before 1978 to notify buyers and tenants that the property was built before 1978 and may contain lead-based paint. The notice must also disclose the hazards of such paint and the symptoms and treatment of its poisoning. In addition, the notice must prescribe precautions that can be taken to avoid lead-based paint poisoning. The owners must give this notice to a prospective buyer or tenant before they purchase or rent the property. All contracts of sale, leases, or management agreements for such pre-1978 housing must include provisions insuring that buyers and tenants received the required notices. In addition to these federal regulations, some states have similar regulations concerning the disclosure and sale of residential properties containing lead-based paint. Inspections can be made by qualified inspectors to determine if a property contains lead-based paint.

Power of Eminent Domain

Federal, state, and local governments have a right, known as **eminent domain**, to take private property for public use. Thus, private ownership of all real property is held subject to a perpetual repurchase option in favor of the United States; the various states; the county, city, and other government agencies; and, in some cases, even privately owned public utilities. Because the taking of private property for public use can have a harsh and disastrous effect on the private owner, constitutional safeguards have been set up to protect the owner against arbitrary or unreasonable use of eminent domain power. The government cannot exercise its power of eminent domain without first establishing that the private property is needed for a public use and paying the private owner adequate compensation for the property.

A property owner is provided with a number of procedural safeguards in the event of an exercise of the power of eminent domain. The property owner is entitled to due notice and a hearing before the time the private property can be taken. The property owner, at the hearing, has an opportunity to be represented by counsel and to prove that the taking is not necessary for public use or that the compensation being offered is unreasonable. The government has a wide range of public uses that support the exercise of the power of eminent domain, such as the taking of private property for the purpose of constructing public streets, sewer facilities, airports, government buildings, slum clearance or redevelopment projects, forest reserves, and even recreational areas such as parks and wildlife preserves. Because of the wide range of public uses that support the exercise of the power of eminent domain, the main issue in most condemnation proceedings is that of compensation. A property owner is entitled to the fair market value of the property being taken.

A recent United States Supreme Court decision, *Kelo v. City of New London*, 545 U.S. 469, 125 S. Ct. 2655 (2005), has heightened public awareness of the government's power of eminent domain. The Supreme Court in *Kelo* upheld the use of a government's eminent domain power for economic development purposes. The city's development plan was considered to be a public use even though the plan provided for taking land from one private landowner and giving it to another private landowner for development. The plan's stated

eminent domain

Power of government to take private property for public use.

"public use" was to create new jobs in the community and generate higher tax revenues for the government.

The *Kelo* decision has struck a chord with private property advocates and has generated a flurry of public debate as well as proposals within various state legislatures to enact new laws that would mitigate the effect of *Kelo* and reduce the government's power of eminent domain. It will be interesting to observe over the next several years whether a proper balance is struck between the power of a government to take private property for public use and an owner's right to have private property protected from the arbitrary and unreasonable use of eminent domain power.

Taxation

ad valorem taxes

Taxes assessed against an owner of real property in an amount based upon the value of the property.

Governmental bodies have the right to tax real property that is located within their jurisdictional boundaries. It is not unusual to find real property taxed at both the city and the county levels. Sometimes real property taxes are called **ad valorem taxes.** This definition comes from the fact that the taxes are measured on the value of the real property being taxed.

These valuations are determined through an assessment method of valuation. The law requires that a government authority acting through its representatives examine and appraise all property for taxation on a fair and equitable basis. Most assessed values are based on a full fair market value of the property. Generally, tax assessors have available a database that provides them with sales information for properties within the community. The assessor then can take the value of a property being sold and determine if the taxable property is comparable to such property and therefore assign a similar value to each tax parcel. The tax assessor may separate the value of land and building. The land is valued on the basis of a standard lot, that is, a lot or unit of size usually marketed in the vicinity. The value of improvements generally depends upon the use of the improvements. If the improvements are income-producing, the assessor may assign a value based upon the rent the building is capable of producing. If the improvements consist of a home, the assessor may assign a value based upon replacement cost of the home, subtracting a value for the age and current condition of the home.

Generally, a property owner has the right to challenge any assessment of property for purposes of taxation. The challenge must be filed generally within a certain period of time, usually 30 to 60 days from the date a notice is given by the tax authority to the owner concerning the assessed valuation of the owner's property. Most states require that in order to protest an assessed tax valuation, the property owner must have an independent appraisal of the property value to contest or controvert the government's evaluation.

The city or county tax authorities have the power not only to value the real property for purposes of taxation, but also to establish a millage rate for purposes of computing the tax. For example, if you have real property that had a tax assessment value of $200,000 and a millage rate of .01125, you would multiply the millage rate by the assessed value, and the tax would be $2,250.00.

Most governmental bodies have a tax year, which may be the calendar year or some other period of time. The taxes become a lien or debt charged against the real property on the first day of the tax year. For example, if the tax year is the calendar year, then on January 1, the taxes for that year would become a lien, even though the taxes may not be due and payable until sometime later in the year. Tax liens have a superpriority over a mortgage or other property interest in connection with the real property and must be paid before all other debts, liens, or claims. Tax liens can be enforced by foreclosure and sale of the real property by the public authority.

Governmental authorities also have the right to levy special assessments against real property owners for the costs of such things as grading, curbing, paving, and establishing sewer and water lines or sidewalks, which benefit a person's real property. Special assessments are enforceable by foreclosure and public sale of the real property.

Federal and State Income Tax Liens

Federal and state governments have the right to file a lien against the property of any delinquent taxpayer. A **lien** is a money debt attached to real property. A federal tax lien is evidenced by a certificate or notice of tax lien which once filed in the county where the property is located becomes a lien on all property owned by the taxpayer at the time of filing, as well as all future property acquired by the taxpayer until the tax lien has been paid in full. A federal tax lien generally has a 10-year lifetime, although there is a procedure to renew the tax lien for a longer time period. State governments generally have the same rights as the federal government to place a lien against the property of any delinquent taxpayer. The procedures for creating state tax liens vary from state to state, as well as the lifetime of the tax lien. An examination of any state's laws regarding tax liens needs to be done to determine the effect of a state tax lien upon property.

Federal and state income tax liens are title problems and can be discovered during a title examination.

lien
Money debt attached to real property. The holder of the lien can sell the real property to pay the debt.

PRIVATE ENCUMBRANCES

Private encumbrances are voluntarily created by private parties who deal with the real property and consist of judgment liens, mechanic's and materialmen's liens, mortgages and trust deeds, easements, and restrictive covenants.

Judgment Liens

A lien is created when the property owner has been sued for a sum of money and a court has entered a **judgment** against the property owner. For example, a property owner is involved in an automobile accident. The property owner is sued for negligence and has assessed against him by a court of law a $50,000 judgment.

Judgment liens do not become liens on real property until they have been recorded in a special book, called the Judgment Book or General Execution Docket, in the county where the real property is located.

A judgment lien remains a lien on real property until it has been paid or expires by passage of time. Most states have laws that limit the duration of a judgment lien. These laws provide that a judgment lien, if not paid, will expire within 7 to 14 years after becoming a lien on real property.

Judgments attach at the time of recordation to all property then owned by the judgment debtor or to any property thereafter acquired by the judgment debtor. Judgments are potential title problems and can be discovered during a title examination. The method for dealing with judgments in a title examination is discussed in Chapter 12.

judgment
Money debt resulting from a lawsuit. Judgments are liens on real property owned by the judgment debtor.

Mechanic's and Materialmen's Liens

A **mechanic's** or **materialmen's lien** is imposed by law on real property to secure payment for work performed or materials furnished for the construction, repair, or alteration of improvements on the real property. Each state has its own laws for the creation of these

mechanic's or **materialmen's lien**
Lien imposed by law on real property to secure payment for work performed or materials furnished for the construction, repair, or alteration of improvements on the real property.

liens. Claimants under most mechanic's or materialmen's lien statutes include contractors, laborers, subcontractors, material suppliers, lessors of equipment and machinery, architects, professional engineers, and land surveyors.

Most privately owned real property is subject to mechanic's or materialmen's liens. The lien attaches to all real property, including improvements, and all real property contiguous to the improved real property. Public real property is not subject to mechanic's or materialmen's liens.

Special Mechanic's and Materialmen's Lien Situations

Sometimes special situations exist that prompt the creation of mechanic's and materialmen's liens.

Landlord and Tenant. Work performed for a tenant of real property only attaches to the tenant's interest in the real property unless the landlord of the real property consents to the work and agrees to pay for the work.

Contract Seller and Purchaser. Work performed for a purchaser of real property before the contract closes only attaches to the purchaser's interest unless the seller has consented to the work.

Husband and Wife. One spouse is ordinarily not an agent for the other spouse. Work performed at the request of one spouse is not a lien on the other spouse's real property interest unless the other spouse has consented or agreed to pay for the work.

Joint Tenants. A lien binds only the interest in the real property of the joint tenant who ordered the work. A joint tenant is not an agent for the other tenants, and unless the other tenants have consented or agreed to pay for the work, their interest in the real property is not liened.

Other Mechanic's and Materialmen's Lien Considerations

The amount of the lien depends upon two theories of law. The theories are referred to as the New York theory, since it was first established under New York law, or the Pennsylvania theory, which was first established under Pennsylvania law. Under the New York theory, the amount of the mechanic's or materialmen's lien is limited to the contract price between the owner and the general contractor. Payment of the contract price by the owner is a defense to a mechanic's or materialmen's lien claim by a subcontractor or material supplier. Under the Pennsylvania theory, the original contract between the owner and the general contractor does not limit the amount of lien claims that can be filed by subcontractors and material suppliers. Payment of the contract price, under the Pennsylvania theory, is not a defense to subcontractor or material supplier lien claims.

For example, an owner of real property enters into a contract with a general contractor to build a home. The contract price for the construction is $100,000. A general contractor hires a number of subcontractors to build the home. The owner pays to the general contractor $80,000 of the $100,000 contract price. After having paid the $80,000, the owner discovers that a number of lien claims are filed against the home by subcontractors and material suppliers. The subcontractors' and material suppliers' lien claims total $50,000. Under the New York theory, the owner would be responsible to the subcontractors and material suppliers only for $20,000 (the difference between the $100,000 contract price and the $80,000 previously paid to the general contractor). Under the Pennsylvania theory, the owner would be responsible to the subcontractors and material suppliers for the full amount of their claims, or $50,000.

The right to a mechanic's or materialmen's lien usually exists once the work is performed or the material is furnished. The lien right must be perfected by filing a notice or claim of lien in the public records where the real property is located. Most states require that this notice or claim of lien be recorded within a reasonable period of time after completion of the work (60 to 120 days). A claim or notice of lien requires the following information: (a) the amount of the claim, (b) the name of the lien claimant, (c) the name of the owner, (d) a description of real property to be liened, and (e) the notarized signature of the lien claimant.

The priority of a lien claim dates from the time the first work is performed or the material is furnished. It does not attach from the date the claim of lien is filed, except for architects, engineers, and land surveyors.

For example, a material supplier provides materials for the construction of a home on March 1. The material supplier is not paid and finally files a claim of lien on May 1 for the unpaid materials. The material supplier's lien claim dates from March 1, the date the materials were furnished. This also means that the material supplier is ahead in terms of priority and will be paid ahead of any other lien claims that date after March 1.

A mechanic's or materialmen's lien is enforced through a foreclosure suit or sale of the real property. States also impose time limits for filing the foreclosure suit. The most common time limit is one year from the date the claim is due.

A mechanic's or materialmen's lien can be waived and terminated by a written waiver or release of lien. Most states require that lien waivers or releases of lien be signed by the lien claimant and be witnessed or notarized.

Mortgages and Trust Deeds

Real property can be pledged as security to pay debts of the owner. Mortgages and trust deeds are fully discussed in Chapter 10.

Easements

An **easement** is the right to use real property for a special purpose, such as a roadway, and can be given by the owner to a nonowner.

easement

Right granted to a nonowner of real property to use the real property for a specific purpose. For example, the right given to an electric utility company.

Restrictive Covenants

It is possible for real property owners to restrict the use of their real property. These restrictive covenants may be in the form of restrictions or covenants found in deeds of conveyance to the real property or in restrictions that are recorded against the real property. It is not unusual for real property that has been subdivided, such as single-family home subdivisions, industrial parks, and condominiums, to have restrictions regarding the use of the property by future real property owners. Private restrictive covenants often perform the same function as public zoning regulations, but in many instances they may be more restrictive than public zoning regulations. The private restrictions attempt to regulate the development of the real property in such a manner as to enhance the value of each individual owner's lot or share of the real property. For example, restrictive covenants found in residential subdivisions usually restrict the size of the homes that can be built on the lots, subject the homes to architectural review committees, regulate the height of the homes, and require that certain portions of the property be left vacant for purposes of creating front, rear, and side yards. All these restrictions are designed to create a nice residential environment that will enhance the value of each owner's home.

Restrictive covenants are enforced by injunction or suit for damages. Enforcement may be brought by any person who bought real property with notice of the restrictions and in reliance on the restrictions. Therefore, any homeowner in a single-family subdivision can enforce the restrictive covenants against other homeowners.

ETHICS: Abandonment of Work

A paralegal works with a firm that represents real estate developers. She is working with an attorney representing a client who is purchasing vacant land for the purpose of developing the property into a warehouse club. The property is under contract with the closing only three weeks away. The paralegal has been asked by the attorney to inquire into the zoning classification for the property and to obtain a copy of the zoning ordinance that affects the property. The assignment is given the afternoon before the paralegal is scheduled to leave for a one-week vacation. On return from vacation, the paralegal forgets about the request to obtain a zoning ordinance. On the day before the scheduled closing, the attorney is going over the closing checklist and requests at that time a copy of the zoning ordinance. The paralegal mentions that she forgot to obtain the zoning ordinance, and the attorney becomes quite upset and irritated. Is the supervisory attorney overreacting?

Professional ethics require that legal work be performed competently and to a timely completion. A paralegal should not willfully abandon or willfully disregard any legal matter entrusted to him or her. When a paralegal is given an assignment by an attorney, he or she should carry out the assignment to the end and not neglect or fail to perform the work at hand in a timely manner. The client's interest in having the transaction performed promptly is paramount. In this particular transaction, the zoning classification for the property is important and could affect the client's plans for the development of the property. Failure to obtain the zoning ordinance as requested is unprofessional and justifiable grounds for the attorney's irritation.

SUMMARY

Most real property is regulated in some way for the general welfare of the public. These regulations include zoning laws, building codes, subdivision regulations, and environmental protection laws. All property is subject to a government's power to take the property for public use, and almost all property is subject to some form of governmental taxation. All these government regulations must be taken into account by any owner of real property or any prospective purchaser of real property. These public regulations not only have an impact upon the value of the real property, but also may restrict an owner's intended use of the property.

In addition to public regulation of property, most property is affected by private encumbrances. These encumbrances

include liens, mortgages, easements, and restrictive covenants. The encumbrances are generally considered to be an unwanted item in connection with real property and can impact the value and intended use of the property. Encumbrances such as liens or mortgages constitute debts against the real property that must be paid by the owner to save the real property from being foreclosed or sold by the holder of the debt. Restrictive covenants may reduce or restrict the use an owner may make of real property. An easement, although an encumbrance that may restrict an owner's use of property, may also be of benefit to real property. A full discussion of easements follows in Chapter 5.

HELPFUL WEBSITES

Zoning
The National Association of Realtors® Web site contains a field guide to zoning laws and ordinances. The site contains updated information on zoning basics, zoning boards, and legal issues; zoning reform issues; and the costs and benefits of zoning at *http:// www.realtor.org.*

Mechanic's and Materialmen's Liens
A very resourceful Web site for mechanic's and materialmen's liens is the National Lien Law site. The site contains information and forms for each state. The site also contains a very informative general information FAQ about lien law at *http://www.nationallienlaw.com.*

Environmental Law
A considerable amount of information concerning environmental law and environmental concerns can be found on the Internet. Most of this information can be accessed through the Environmental Protection Agency's home page at *http:// www.epa.gov.* The Environmental Protection Agency's legacy databases can also be accessed through *http://www.epa.gov/ enviro.* Web sites of most major international environmental organizations, such as Greenpeace, the Sierra Club, and the National Resources Defense Council, can be located using a search engine such as *http://www.google.com.*

KEY TERMS

ad valorem taxes
building codes
Comprehensive Environmental
   Response, Compensation and
   Liability Act (CERCLA)

easement
eminent domain
encumbrance
judgment
lien

mechanic's or materialmen's lien
Phase I
Phase II
zoning

REVIEW QUESTIONS

1. List and briefly discuss various types of government regulation of private property.

2. What general methods does a government authority use to enforce its zoning regulations?

3. What is a real property owner's general responsibility for hazardous waste located on the real property?

4. What are the main legal issues involved in an eminent domain proceeding?

5. What is a judgment lien, and why should a real property owner be concerned about it?

6. Who is entitled to claim a mechanic's or materialmen's lien?

7. Briefly explain the New York theory and the Pennsylvania theory of lien claims and how each of these theories impact on the claims of a subcontractor or material supplier.

8. What is the general rule for the priority of a mechanic's or materialmen's lien claim, and why is this priority important?

9. What is required for a formal notice or claim of lien?

10. How are private restrictive covenants enforced?

PRACTICAL ASSIGNMENTS

1. Research your state's mechanic's or materialmen's lien law. Prepare a memorandum outlining the following:
   (a) List of claimants entitled to file a mechanic's or materialmen's lien claim
   (b) Requirements for a claim of lien
   (c) Requirements for foreclosing a mechanic's or materialmen's lien

2. Search the Internet to see what information your county or city provides in regard to zoning ordinances, building codes, and real estate taxes. Make a detailed list of what information is available from these governmental sources on the Internet.

3. Research the procedures available in your state to challenge a county ad valorem tax assessment. Write a brief memorandum outlining all procedures a homeowner must follow in order to challenge a tax valuation assessment on his or her home. Obtain from the appropriate governmental tax assessment office or from the Internet all forms that must be filed by a homeowner to challenge a property tax valuation assessment.

4. Research your state's laws to see if there have been any new laws passed in reaction to *Kelo v. City of New London*. Review the new law(s) and discuss how they place limitations on a government's use of eminent domain.

ADDENDUM

Exhibit 4–1 R-4 Single-Family Residential District Regulations

Exhibit 4–2 C-1 Community Business District Regulations

Student StudyWare™ CD-ROM

Interactive Student CD in the book includes additional quizzing, case studies, and key terms flashcards.

Online Companion™

For additional resources, please go to
www.paralegal.delmar.cengage.com

EXHIBIT 4–1

R-4 Single-Family Residential
District Regulations

Section 16-06.001 Scope of provisions.
Section 16-06.002 Statement of intent.
Section 16-06.003 Permitted principal uses and structures.
Section 16-06.004 Permitted accessory uses and structures.
Section 16-06.005 Special permits.
Section 16-06.006 Transitional uses, structures, requirements.
Section 16-06.007 Minimum lot requirements.
Section 16-06.008 Minimum yard requirements.
Section 16-06.009 Maximum height.
Section 16-06.010 Minimum off-street parking requirements.
Section 16-06.011 Limitations on signs.

Section 16-06.001 Scope of provisions.

The regulations set forth in this chapter or set forth elsewhere in this part when referred to in this chapter are the regulations in the R-4 Single-Family Residential District. (Ord. No. 1981-95A, Sec. 1, 12/19/80)

Section 16-06.002 Statement of intent.

The intent of this chapter in establishing the R-4 Single-Family Residential District is as follows:

(1) To provide for the protection of existing single-family communities and the development of new communities on lots of medium size at a density of not more than one (1) dwelling unit per 9,000 square feet.

(2) To provide for the development of recreational, educational and religious facilities as basic elements of a balanced community. (Ord. No. 1981-95A, Sec. 1, 12/19/80)

Section 16-06.003 Permitted principal uses and structures.

A building or premises shall be used only for the following principal purposes, and in no case shall there be more than one (1) main building and one (1) main use on a lot:

(1) Churches, synagogues, temples and other religious worship facilities, having a minimum lot area of five (5) acres and located on at least a four-lane collector street.

(2) Public schools through the secondary level operated by the City Board of Education, having no dwelling or lodging facilities except for caretakers.

(3) Single-family detached dwellings.

(4) Structures and uses required for operation of the Rapid Rail Transit System, but not including uses involving storage, train yards, warehousing, switching, or maintenance shops as the primary purpose. (Ord. No. 1981-95A, Sec. 1, 12/19/80)

Section 16-06.004 Permitted accessory uses and structures.

Uses and structures which are customarily incidental and subordinate to permitted principal uses and structures are permitted. These include but are not limited to the following, subject to limitations and requirements set forth herein or elsewhere in this part:

(1) Greenhouses, garden sheds, private garages and similar structures.

(2) Barns for keeping of horses, provided that no such barns shall be within 50 feet of any lot line.

(3) Guest houses, servant quarters, or lodging facilities for caretakers or watchmen.

(4) Swimming pools, tennis courts and similar facilities.

(5) Home occupation, subject to limitations set forth in section 16-29.001(17).

(6) Structures necessary for active construction projects.

(7) Devices for the generation of energy, such as solar panels, wind generators and similar devices.

Except in the case of home occupation, no accessory use shall be of a commercial nature.

No accessory building shall be constructed until construction of the principal building has actually begun, and no accessory building shall be used or occupied until the principal building is completed and in use. (Ord. No. 1981-95A, Sec. 1, 12/19/80)

Delmar/Cengage Learning

(continued)

Section 16-06.005 Special permits.

The following uses are permissible only by special permits of the kinds indicated, subject to limitations and requirements set forth herein or elsewhere in this part:

(1) *Special use permits:*

(a) Cemeteries, mausoleums and columbariums. (Ord. No. 1981-96, Sec. 5, 12/15/81)

(b) Child care nurseries, day care centers, pre-kindergartens, kindergartens, play and other special schools or day care facilities for young children.

(c) Churches, synagogues, temples and other religious worship facilities, where lot area is less than five (5) acres but more than one (1) acre.

(d) Civic, service, garden, neighborhood or private clubs.

(e) Colleges and universities, other than trade schools, business colleges and similar uses.

(f) Extraction or removal of sand, gravel, topsoil, clay, dirt, or other natural resources.

(g) Group homes.

(h) Landfills.

(i) Line-of-sight relay devices for telephonic, radio or television communication, including broadcasting equipment, but not including broadcasting studios.

(j) Nursing homes, convalescent homes, and similar care facilities.

(k) Parks, playgrounds, stadiums, baseball or football fields, golf courses, sports arenas, recreational centers, community centers, community service facilities, and the like, when not owned or operated by a governmental agency.

(l) Private schools.

(m) Rehabilitation centers.

(2) *Special administrative permits:* None.

(3) *Special exceptions:*

(a) Churches, synagogues, temples and other religious worship facilities, where lot area is one (1) acre or less.

(b) Structures and uses required for operation of a public utility, except uses involving storage, train yards, warehousing switching, or maintenance shops as the primary purpose. (Ord. No. 1981-95A, Sec. 1, 12/19/80)

Section 16-06.006 Transitional uses, structures, requirements.

None. (Ord. No. 1981-95A, Sec. 1, 12/19/80)

Section 16-06.007 Minimum lot requirements.

The following minimum lot requirements shall apply to all uses approved by special permits as well as permitted uses:

(1) *Churches, temples, synagogues, and similar religious facilities, except when authorized by a special permit:* Every lot shall have an area of not less than five (5) acres and a frontage of not less than 200 feet.

(2) *Single-family detached dwellings and all other uses:* Every lot shall have an area of not less than 9,000 square feet and a frontage of not less than 70 feet.

(3) If a lot has less area of width than herein required and was a lot of record on the effective date of this part, that lot shall be used only for a single-family dwelling. (Ord. No. 1981-95A, Sec. 1, 12/19/80; Ord. No. 1981-96, Sec. 8, 12/15/81)

Section 16-06.008 Minimum yard requirements.

The following minimum yard requirements shall apply to all uses approved by special permits as well as permitted uses:

(1) *Front yard:* There shall be a front yard having a depth of not less than 35 feet.

(2) *Side yard:* There shall be two (2) side yards, one (1) on each side of the main building, each having a width of not less than seven (7) feet. (Ord. No. 1983-32, Sec. 1, 5/4/83)

(3) *Rear yard:* There shall be a rear yard having a depth of not less than seven (7) feet.

EXHIBIT 4–1

R-4 Single-Family Residential District Regulations

(*continued*)

(*continued*)

EXHIBIT 4–1

R-4 Single-Family Residential
District Regulations

(*continued*)

(4) *Accessory structures:* Accessory structures other than fences, when permitted, shall be placed to the side or rear of the main structure within the buildable area of the lot so as not to project beyond the front of the main structure. For fences, see section 16-28.008(5). (Ord. No. 1981-95A, Sec. 1, 12/19/80)

Amendment Note: Ord. No. 1983-32, section 1, adopted 5/2/83, approved 5/4/83, amended subsection (2) to require 7-foot minimum side yards rather than combined yards of 15 feet, with no yard to be less than 7 feet wide.

Section 16-06.009 Maximum height.

The following height limitations shall apply to all uses approved by special permits as well as permitted uses: No building shall exceed 35 feet in height. See section 16-28.022 for excluded portions of structures. (Ord. No. 1981-95A, Sec. 1, 12/19/80)

Section 16-06.010 Minimum off-street parking requirements.

The following parking requirements shall apply to all uses approved by special permits as well as permitted uses (see section 16-28.014):

(1) *Single-family detached dwellings:* One (1) space per dwelling.

(2) *Schools, colleges, churches, recreational or community centers and other places of assembly:* One (1) space for each four (4) fixed seats (with 18 inches of bench length counted as one (1) seat, or one (1) space for each 35 square feet of enclosed floor area for the accommodation of movable seats in the largest assembly room, whichever is greater, plus the following:

(a) *Public or private elementary or middle school:* Two (2) spaces for each classroom.

(b) *High school:* Four (4) spaces for each classroom.

(c) *Colleges and universities:* Eight (8) spaces for each classroom.

(3) *Nursing homes, convalescent homes, and similar care facilities:* One (1) space per four (4) beds.

(4) *Child care centers, day care centers, pre-kindergartens, kindergartens, play and other special schools or day care centers for young children:* One (1) space per 600 square feet of floor area. In addition to providing off-street parking, such establishments shall provide safe and convenient facilities for loading and unloading children, as approved by the director, bureau of traffic and transportation.

(5) *Other uses:* One (1) space for each 300 square feet of floor area. (Ord. No. 1981-95A, Sec. 1, 12/19/80)

Section 16-06.011 Limitations on signs.

The following sign regulations shall apply to all uses approved by special permits as well as permitted uses (see section 16-28.017):

(1) No freestanding sign shall be higher than 10 feet above ground level.

(2) No sign shall have or consist of any rotating, revolving or otherwise moving part.

(3) No sign shall be internally illuminated, nor shall any sign be animated or changing.

(4) No general advertising signs shall be permitted.

(5) Signs shall be mounted flat to the wall of the building or not nearer than 30 feet to the street property line.

(6) For a residential use, one (1) permanent sign shall be permitted. Such sign shall not exceed two (2) square feet in sign area.

(7) For other approved uses, one (1) permanent sign per street frontage shall be permitted. Such signs shall not exceed 20 square feet in sign area.

(8) One (1) permanent sign per street frontage listing the name of a subdivision shall be permitted. Such sign shall not exceed 35 square feet in sign area. (Ord. No. 1981-95A, Sec. 1, 12/19/80)

EXHIBIT 4–2

C-1 Community Business
District Regulations

Section 16-11.001 Scope of provisions.
Section 16-11.002 Statement of intent.
Section 16-11.003 Permitted principal uses and structures.
Section 16-11.004 Permitted accessory uses and structures.
Section 16-11.005 Special permits.
Section 16-11.006 Transitional uses, structures, requirements.
Section 16-11.007 Development controls.
Section 16-11.008 Minimum yard requirements.
Section 16-11.009 Maximum height limitations.
Section 16-11.010 Minimum off-street parking requirements.
Section 16-11.011 Limitations on signs.

Section 16-11.001 Scope of provisions.

The regulations set forth in this chapter, or set forth elsewhere in this part when referred to in this chapter, are the regulations in the C-1 Community Business District. (Ord. No. 1981-95A, Sec. 1, 12/19/80)

Section 16-11.002 Statement of intent.

The intent of this chapter in establishing C-1 Community Business District is as follows:

(1) To provide for medium-intensity retail and service activities in areas already committed to development of this character, or consistent with areas so specified on the comprehensive development plan.

(2) To encourage residential use either as single or mixed use development. (Ord. No. 1981-95A, Sec. 1, 12/19/80)

Section 16-11.003 Permitted principal uses and structures.

A building or premises shall be used only for the following principal purposes:

(1) Banks, savings and loan associations, and similar financial institutions.

(2) Broadcasting towers, line-of-sight relay devices for telephonic, radio or television communication.

(3) Business or commercial schools.

(4) Child care centers, kindergartens and special schools.

(5) Churches, synagogues, temples and other religious worship facilities, on lots of one (1) acre or more.

(6) Clubs and lodges.

(7) Commercial greenhouses.

(8) Commercial recreation establishments, including bowling alleys, theaters, convention halls, places of assembly, and similar uses, with primary activities conducted within fully enclosed buildings. Pool halls, billiard parlors and amusement arcades are allowed only by special use permits. (Ord. No. 1981-96, Sec. 18, 12/15/81; Ord. No. 1982-11, Sec. 1, 4/13/82)

(9) Dormitories, fraternities and sororities.

(10) Eating and drinking establishments.

(11) General advertising signs, subject to limitations herein on number and area.

(12) Group homes, rehabilitation centers.

(13) Hospitals.

(14) Hotels and motels, rooming houses, boardinghouses.

(15) Institutions of higher learning , including colleges and universities.

(16) Laundry and dry cleaning, collection stations or plants, limited to no more than 5,000 square feet floor area, laundry and dry cleaning establishments where equipment is operated by customers.

(17) Multifamily dwellings, two-family dwellings and single-family dwellings. (Ord. No. 1981-96, Sec. 19, 12/15/81)

Delmar/Cengage Learning

(continued)

EXHIBIT 4–2

C-1 Community Business
District Regulations
(*continued*)

(18) Museums, galleries, auditoriums, libraries and similar cultural facilities.

(19) Nursing homes and convalescent centers.

(20) Offices, clinics (including veterinary if animals are kept within soundproof buildings), laboratories, studios, and similar uses, but not blood donor stations except at hospitals. (Ord. No. 1983-12, Sec. 1, 3/11/83)

(21) Parking structures and lots. (Ord. No. 1981-96, Sec. 20, 12/15/81)

(22) Professional or personal service establishments, but not hiring halls.

(23) Repair establishments for home appliances, bicycles, lawn mowers, shoes, clocks and similar articles.

(24) Retail establishments, including catering establishments, delicatessens and bakeries without wholesale operations.

(25) Sales and leasing agencies for new passenger automobiles, bicycles, mopeds, and commercial vehicles not exceeding one (1) ton in rated capacity, selling, servicing and repairing new vehicles and dealing in the disposal, servicing or repairing of used vehicles in connection therewith and all located on the same site.

(26) Security storage centers not exceeding 7500 square feet of floor area and having all pickup and delivery of items by passenger automobile or van.

(27) Service stations and car washes.

(28) Structures and uses required for operation of the Rapid Rail Transit System or a public utility but not including uses involving storage, train yards, warehousing, switching or maintenance shop as the primary purpose.

(29) Tailoring, custom dressmaking, millinery and similar establishments limited to not more than 5000 square feet in area.

(30) Adult businesses as defined in section 16-29.001(3). See also section 16-28.016. (Ord. No. 1981-96, Sec. 21,12/15/81)

Except for off-street parking, automobile sales lots, and necessary activities at commercial greenhouses and service stations, or as authorized by special permit, all commercial sales and service activities shall be conducted within completely enclosed buildings, and there shall be no unenclosed displays of merchandise. No wholesaling or jobbing shall be conducted from within the district. No use or manner of operation shall be permitted which is obnoxious or offensive by reason of odor, smoke, noise, glare, fumes, gas, vibration, unusual danger of fire or explosion, emission of particulate matter, or interference with radio or television reception, or for other reasons is incompatible with the character of the district and its relation to adjoining residential districts. (Ord. No. 1981-95A, Sec. 1, 12/19/80)

Amendment Note: Section 1 of Ord. No. 1983-12, adopted 3/10/83, approved 3/11/83, amended subsection (20) to allow veterinary clinics.

Section 16-11.004 Permitted accessory uses and structures.

Uses and structures which are customarily incidental and subordinate to permitted principal uses and structures, to include devices for generation of energy such as solar panels, wind generators and similar devices, except as otherwise herein provided, no merchandise shall be stored other than that to be sold at retail on the premises; and no storage for such merchandise shall occupy more than 25 percent of the total floor areas on the premises. No off-premises storage of such merchandise shall be permitted in the district as either a principal or accessory use. (Ord. No. 1981-95A, Sec. 1, 12/19/80)

Section 16-11.005 Special permits.

The following uses are permissible only by special permit of the kind indicated, subject to limitations and requirements set forth herein or elsewhere in this part:

(1) *Special use permits:*

(a) Helicopter landing facilities or pickup or delivery stations.

(b) Mortuaries, funeral homes.

(*continued*)

EXHIBIT 4–2

C-1 Community Business
District Regulations
(*continued*)

(c) Outdoor amusement enterprises, exhibits, entertainments, meetings, displays or sales areas, or outdoor areas for religious ceremonies of 90 days' or more duration.

(d) Poolrooms, billiard parlors, amusement arcades. (Ord. No. 1981-95A, Sec. 1, 12/19/80; Ord. No. 1981-96, Sec. 22, 12/15/81)

(2) *Special administrative permits:*

(a) Outdoor amusement enterprises, exhibits, entertainments, meetings, displays or sales areas, or outdoor areas for religious ceremonies of less than 90 days' duration.

(b) Zero-lot-line development (see section 16-28.001(6)).

(3) *Special exceptions:*

(a) Churches, synagogues, temples and other religious worship facilities, where lot area is less than one (1) acre.

(b) Off-street parking within 500 feet of primary use. (Ord. No. 1981-95A, Sec. 1, 12/19/80)

Section 16-11.006 Transitional uses, structures, requirements.

(1) *Transitional Uses:* Where a lot in this district abuts a lot in any R-1 through R-G district at the side along the same street frontage, and without an intervening street, the first lot within this district, or the first 100 feet of such lot if it is wider than 100 feet, shall not be used for any drive-in facility, service station, mortuary or funeral home, sales lot for automobiles, or general advertising signs.

(2) *Transitional Height Planes:* Where this district adjoins a district in R-1 through R-G classification without an intervening street, height within the district shall be limited as follows: No portion of any structure shall protrude through a height-limiting plane beginning thirty-five (35) feet above the buildable area boundary nearest to the common district boundary and extending inward over this district at an angle of forty-five (45) degrees.

(3) *Transitional Yards:*

(a) *Side yard:* Adjacent to an R District without an intervening street, 20 feet is required which shall not be used for the purpose of parking, paving, loading, servicing or storage activity and shall be planted and/or maintained in a natural state. (Ord. No. 1981-96, Sec. 26, 12/15/81)

(b) *Rear Yard:* There shall be a rear yard of 20 feet when adjacent to an R District that shall not be used for parking, or paving or for purpose of parking, loading or servicing.

(c) *Screening:* Where a lot in this district abuts a lot in an "R" District on the side or rear lot lines without an intervening street, opaque fencing or screening not less than six (6) feet in height shall be provided and maintained in a sightly condition. See Section 16-28.008(9). (Ord. No. 1981-95A, Sec 1, 12/19/80, as amended by Ord. No. 1982-54, Sec. 3, 7/26/82)

Amendment Note: Ord. No. 1982-54, Sec. 3, adopted 7/19/82, approved 7/26/82, deleted former subsection 16-11.006(3*c) and enacted a new subsection 16-11.006(3*c) in lieu thereof.

Section 16-11.007 Development controls.

(1) *Bulk Limitations:* For nonresidential uses and lodging uses, floor area shall not exceed an amount equal to 2.0 times net lot area. Multifamily dwellings shall be permitted up to the maximum ratios established for sector 3 shown on table I, section 16-08.007.

(2) *Minimum Lot Width, Area, All Uses:* No fixed minimum lot widths or areas are established for these districts, except as follows:

(a) *Churches, synagogues, temples, and similar religious facilities:* Minimum net lot, one (1) acre except by special exception.

(b) *Single-family and two-family dwellings:* Minimum lot width of 50 feet; minimum net lot area of 5000 square feet.

(c) *Multifamily dwellings:* See section 11.007(1), "Bulk Limitations." (Ord. No. 1981-95A, Sec. 1, 12/19/80)

Section 16-11.008 Minimum yard requirements.

(a) *Front Yard:* 40 feet.

(b) *Side:* None, except if a building is not constructed to the lot line it shall be set back at least five (5) feet from the lot line and except as required in section 16-11.006.

(continued)

EXHIBIT 4–2

C-1 Community Business
District Regulations
(*continued*)

(c) *Rear:* None, except as required in section 16-11.006. (Ord. No. 1981-95A, Sec. 1, 12/19/80)

(d) *Side Street Side:* On corner lots there shall be a setback along the side street of not less than half the required depth of the front yard. (Ord. No. 1981-96, Sec. 23, 12/15/81)

Section 16-11.009 Maximum height limitations.

None, except as required in section 16-11.006. (Ord. No. 1981-95A, Sec. 1, 12/19/80)

Section 16-11.010 Minimum off-street parking requirements.

The following parking requirements shall apply to all uses approved by special permit as well as permitted uses (see section 16-28.104 and also section 16-28.015 for loading requirements):

(1) *Schools, colleges, churches, recreational or community centers, and other places of assembly:* One (1) space for each four (4) fixed seats with 18 inches of bench length counted as one (1) seat, or one (1) space for each 35 square feet of enclosed floor area for the accommodation of movable seats in the largest assembly room, whichever is greater, plus the following:

(a) *Public or private elementary or middle school:* Two (2) spaces for each classroom.

(b) *High school:* Four (4) spaces for each classroom.

(c) *Colleges and universities:* Eight (8) spaces for each classroom.

(2) *Nursing homes, convalescent homes, and similar care facilities:* One (1) space per four (4) beds.

(3) *Child care centers, day care centers, pre-kindergartens, kindergartens, play and other special schools, or day care centers for young children:* One (1) space per 600 square feet of floor area. In addition to providing off-street parking, such establishments shall provide safe and convenient facilities for loading and unloading children, as approved by the director, bureau of traffic and transportation.

(4) *Dwellings and lodgings:* See section 16-08.007, table I, for applicable ratios according to the appropriate floor area ratio.

(5) *Banks, savings and loan institutions, and the like:* One (1) space for each 200 square feet of floor area.

(6) *Business colleges, trade schools, conservatories, dancing schools, and the like:* One (1) space for each 200 square feet of floor area.

(7) *Drive-in establishments:* See section 16-28.021.

(8) *Fraternities, sororities, dormitories:* One (1) space for two (2) beds plus one (1) space for each 200 square feet of floor area designated or occupied other than for sleeping purposes.

(9) *Clubs, lodges:* One (1) space for each 200 square feet of floor area.

(10) *Retail establishments, including catering, delicatessens and bakeries, but not other uses as provided below:* One (1) space for each 200 square feet of floor area.

(11) *Eating and drinking establishments:* One (1) space for each 100 square feet of floor area.

(12) *Laundry and dry cleaning plants, collection stations, self-operated facilities:* One (1) space for each 200 square feet of floor area.

(13) *Tailoring, custom dressmaking, millinery, and similar establishments:* One (1) space for each 400 square feet of floor area.

(14) *Repair establishments for home appliances, bicycles, lawn mowers, shoes, clocks and watches, and the like:* One (1) space for each 200 square feet of floor area.

(15) *Bowling alleys, poolrooms, billiard parlors, and the like:* One (1) space for each 100 square feet of floor area.

(16) *Theaters:* One (1) space for each 100 square feet of floor area. (Ord. No. 1981-96, Sec. 24, 12/15/81)

(17) *Accessory uses:* All accessory uses cited in section 16-11.004 shall provide one (1) additional space per 300 square feet of floor area devoted to such space.

(18) *Other uses:* One (1) space for each 300 square feet of floor area. (Ord. No. 1981-95A, Sec. 1, 2/19/80)

(*continued*)

Section 16-11.011 Limitations on signs.

The following sign regulations shall apply to all uses approved by special permits as well as permitted uses (see section 16-28.017):

(1) Only three (3) business signs shall be permitted for each business establishment. Two (2) additional business signs shall be permitted for each additional street frontage.

(2) No animated or flashing signs shall be permitted.

(3) No sign, other than wall signs, shall extend over or project over the street property line.

(4) Only one (1) business sign, not exceeding 60 square feet in sign area, may encroach into the required front yard setback.

(5) A freestanding business sign shall not exceed 45 feet in height above ground level; provided, however, when the ground level is lower than the level of the adjoining street pavement, then a freestanding business sign may be raised so as to be not more than 25 feet above the level of the pavement.

(6) General advertising signs shall be permitted subject to the following restrictions:

(a) General advertising signs are prohibited within 100 feet of any residential district; provided, however, if the lot upon which the general advertising sign is to be located contains a depth of less than 200 feet, the general advertising sign shall be permitted within the buildable area of the lot at its furtherest possible distance from the residential district.

(b) All general advertising signs shall be restricted to the buildable area of the lot.

(c) A general advertising sign shall not be located within 200 feet of another general advertising sign on the same side of the street as measured point to point along the abutting right-of-way; provided, however, such a sign may be located within 200 feet of another sign when the signs are separated by buildings or other obstructions so that only one (1) sign facing located within the 200-foot zone is visible from the fronting street at any one (1) time. On streets which are a part of the interstate highway, limited-access freeway or expressway system within the city, no general advertising sign shall be located within 1000 feet of another general advertising sign on the same side of the highway as measured point to point along the abutting right-of-way; provided, however, such a sign may be located within 1000 feet of another sign when the signs are separated by buildings or other obstructions so that only one (1) sign facing located within 1000-foot zone is visible from the fronting highway at any one (1) time.

EXHIBIT 4–2

C-1 Community Business District Regulations

(*continued*)

chapter | 5

Easements and Licenses

Objectives

After reading this chapter, you should be able to:

- Understand the uses of an easement
- Identify the various kinds of easements and their methods of creation and termination
- Explain the purpose of a license and distinguish it from an easement

Outline

A s discussed in Chapter 4, real property can be encumbered by any number of things. An encumbrance is viewed by the property owner as an unwanted item. An easement, although an encumbrance, may be a benefit to real property. For example, Aaron and Carol own neighboring lots of lakefront property. They are both constructing vacation cottages on their respective lots. They discover during the construction process that it would be in their best interest to construct a driveway that would be located one-half on Aaron's property and one-half on Carol's property. Through the use of an easement, a joint driveway can be created for the benefit of Aaron and Carol. Aaron will give Carol an easement for the use of that portion of the driveway located on Aaron's property, and Carol will grant to Aaron an easement for the use of that portion of the driveway located on Carol's property. Aaron and Carol also could agree to share the costs of maintaining the driveway. Although the joint driveway easement restricts the use of both Aaron's and Carol's property, the restriction of use is minimal compared with the benefit that each owner receives through the use of the driveway.

Easements are common encumbrances. The paralegal will encounter easements on almost all urban real property transactions and on many rural transactions. It is not uncommon for paralegals to review easements and advise clients as to the restrictions and benefits of the easement. Paralegals who are involved with the development of real property also prepare easements. This chapter discusses the general law regarding easements and provides some practical suggestions for the preparation of easements, including examples of easement forms.

EASEMENTS

An **easement** is a right to use the real property of another owner for a specific purpose. It is considered an encumbrance on the real property on which the easement is located. Some common examples of easements are utility easements and access easements. *Utility easements* are rights given to utility companies, such as the gas, electric, and telephone companies, which permit them to install transmission lines over real property. *Access easements* give a party the right to travel over or across real property to a public street. Samples of both an access easement and a utility easement appear at the end of this chapter (Exhibits 5–4 and 5–5).

Easements are divided into two categories: **appurtenant easements** and **easements in gross.** An appurtenant easement is an easement created for the benefit of a particular tract of land. An example is shown in Exhibit 5–1.

An easement is created over Parcel A to provide access for Parcel B to the public street. Parcel B is known as the **dominant tenement,** the parcel of land benefited by the easement, and Parcel A is known as the **servient tenement,** the land on which the easement is located. This easement would be an encumbrance on Parcel A and a benefit to Parcel B.

Appurtenant easements are regarded as being so closely connected to the dominant tenement that on the sale of the dominant tenement, the easement passes automatically, even if the deed does not mention the easement. In other words, a sale of Parcel B, even with a deed that does not mention the easement over Parcel A, conveys Parcel B and the easement over Parcel A to the new owner.

An easement in gross does not benefit a particular parcel of land. Utility easements are easements in gross. For example, an electric power company acquires an easement to locate a high-tension electric power line across several owners' properties. The easement benefits the power company but does not benefit a particular parcel of real property owned by the power company. The power company easement is an easement in gross.

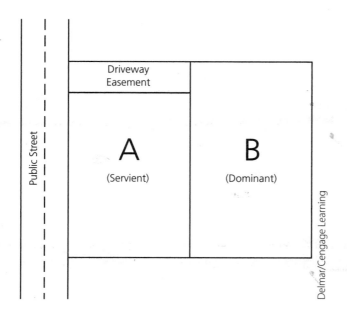

easement

Right granted to a nonowner of real property to use the real property for a specific purpose. For example, a right given to an electric utility company to locate an electric line on real property is an easement.

appurtenant easement

Easement created to benefit a particular parcel of real property. The easement transfers automatically with a transfer of the ownership of the real property benefited by the easement.

easement in gross

Easement granting the owner of the easement the right to use real property for a particular purpose. The easement does not benefit a parcel of real property owned by the owner of the easement.

dominant tenement

Parcel of land benefited by an appurtenant easement.

servient tenement

Parcel of land on which an appurtenant easement is located.

EXHIBIT 5–1

Appurtenant Easement

Public Street

Driveway Easement

A

(Servient)

B

(Dominant)

Delmar/Cengage Learning

Creation of Easements

An easement may be created by (a) express grant, (b) implication, (c) prescription, or (d) necessity.

Express Grant

An easement can be created by an express grant. The grant may be by a separate document or by a reservation of easement contained in a deed. The grant of an easement by a separate easement agreement is prepared with the same formality of requirements as a deed. The easement is in writing and describes the use of the easement and the real property on or over which the easement is located. It also is signed by the grantor (person giving the easement), witnessed, notarized, and delivered to the grantee (the recipient) of the easement. The easement forms at the end of this chapter are examples of easements created by express grant.

The grantor of the easement must be the owner of the real property on which the easement is located. The grantor cannot convey an easement for any longer term than the grantor's ownership of the real property. For example, a grantor who owns a life estate in a parcel of real property can grant an easement only for the period of the life estate and no longer. A title examination of the grantor's real property is conducted to determine what rights the grantor of the easement has to the real property.

Encumbrances on the real property, such as a mortgage or a deed of trust, can create problems for the holder of the easement. A mortgage or a trust deed on the easement property that is recorded before the express grant of the easement has priority over the easement, and if the mortgage or the deed of trust goes into default and is foreclosed, the foreclosure terminates the easement. If an easement is granted over real property that is encumbered by a mortgage or a trust deed, the grantee of the easement may obtain the consent of the mortgagee or subordination of the mortgage or trust deed to the easement. This consent or subordination will protect the grantee of the easement in the event of a foreclosure of the mortgage or trust deed.

The grantee of an appurtenant easement is the owner of the real property being benefited by the easement. The grantee of an easement in gross is the party to whom the special use is being granted, such as a utility company. Easements in gross in some states are not assignable unless the express grant of easement provides so.

The following is a discussion of other issues that should be considered in the preparation of a formal grant of easement.

Preparation of a Formal Grant of Easement

1. *Consideration.* The rules in various states differ as to whether something of value, known as *consideration,* must be given in exchange for a valid express grant of easement. Nominal consideration ("$1 and other good and valuable consideration") usually is sufficient in jurisdictions that require consideration. Therefore, it is a good idea, when preparing an express grant of easement, to include a recital of consideration. In addition, the grantor of an easement often will not grant the easement unless paid a sum of money. If money is being paid for the easement, the sum of money should be mentioned in the easement agreement.

2. *Location.* The location of the easement should be described with specificity. A survey of the easement area should be prepared, and a legal description should be taken from the survey. An easement that covers real property without a specific location is known as a **blanket easement.** Blanket easements commonly are found in utility company right-of-way easements.

blanket easement

Easement that covers real property without a specific location of the easement.

express grant

implication

prescription

necessity

3. *Use.* All intended uses of an easement should be carefully described in the agreement. In cases when the use description is vague, ambiguous, or uncertain, all doubts are decided in favor of the grantor of the easement. For example, an easement for pedestrian traffic does not permit vehicular traffic. The owner of an access easement does not have the right to install pipes for water, gas, oil, or any other liquid unless the right is given in the easement, and an easement for electric service may not convey the right to install telecommunication lines.

4. *Term.* An easement may be made for any term or duration. Easements may be created for a term of months or years, for the life of the owner of the servient tenement or dominant tenement, or for perpetuity. When no limitation on the term is mentioned in the grant of easement, the easement is interpreted to be perpetual and last forever.

5. *Exclusive or nonexclusive.* An easement may be for the exclusive use of the owner of the easement, or it may be nonexclusive, wherein a number of people may use the easement, including the grantor of the easement. An easement that is silent as to exclusivity is interpreted to create a nonexclusive easement.

6. *Liability for easement area.* Access and utility easements create the possibility that someone may get hurt in the exercise of the use of the easement. For example, automobile accidents may take place on an access easement. Gas lines located within utility easements may rupture. Any dangerous conditions that exist on the easement area are the responsibility of the grantor. The grantor of the easement, however, usually relinquishes control and dominion over the easement area to the grantee of the easement. If that is the case, it is not unusual for the grantor of the easement to require the grantee of the easement to indemnify and hold the grantor harmless against any harm to person or property that may result directly or indirectly from the use of the easement. The grantor of an easement often requires, in addition to the indemnity, proof that the grantee of the easement has liability insurance to cover such claims. The grantor of the easement may ask to be made a named insured on the grantee's liability insurance.

7. *Repair and maintenance.* Many easements require the easement area to be repaired and maintained during the term of the easement. Absent an express obligation to repair and maintain, the law is unclear as to whether the grantor or the grantee is responsible for repair and maintenance. Most easement agreements allocate the responsibilities for repair and maintenance. If the easement areas are exclusively used by the grantee of the easement, then the obligation to repair and maintain usually is shifted entirely to the grantee. In the event of an easement in which the use is shared between the grantor and the grantee, such as a joint driveway easement, then the repair and maintenance responsibilities may be equally divided between the parties.

Most easement agreements also provide that in the event a party responsible for repair and maintenance does not honor its obligations, the other party may perform the repair and maintenance responsibilities and assess the cost of doing so against the defaulting responsible party. For example, consider a driveway easement in which Aaron and Carol have each agreed to pay one-half the cost of maintenance and repair to the driveway. Aaron refuses to pay his share. Most easement agreements provide that Carol can pay Aaron's share and then assess the cost of doing so against Aaron. This assessment may be secured by a lien on Aaron's real property over which the easement travels. Easements also may provide that in the event Aaron does not pay his share of the repair and maintenance obligations, such failure will result in a termination of the easement.

The following checklist incorporates the previously discussed issues that are considered in the preparation or review of an easement.

✓ CHECKLIST

Preparation of an Easement

☐ I. Parties
  A. Grantor—fee owner of easement area
    1. Conduct title examination to verify ownership
  B. Grantee
    1. Appurtenant easement—fee owner of property benefited by easement
    2. Easement in gross—the person benefited from the use of the easement

☐ II. Description of Easement Area
  A. Blanket description of grantor's property with no specific location of actual area to be used
  B. Specific location of easement area
    1. Boundary survey of easement area
  C. Description of property to be benefited by easement (This is necessary for appurtenant easements, such as right-of-way or driveway easements.)

☐ III. Purpose of Easement
  A. General types of use
    1. Utility location (water, sewer, gas, electric)
    2. Access to and from public streets
    3. Parking
    4. Encroachment permission
  B. Describe totally the intended use of the easement (Easements are enforced as written.)

☐ IV. Purchase Price or Consideration
  A. Mutual benefit, as in case of joint driveways
  B. Nominal consideration ($1)
  C. Negotiated purchase price

☐ V. Term
  A. Perpetual
  B. Fixed terms (e.g., 5 years)
  C. Until the happening of some event, such as the dedication of a street or sanitary sewer line to public use

☐ VI. Exclusive or Nonexclusive Use

☐ VII. Maintenance Obligations
  A. Joint maintenance where easement provides mutual benefit (joint driveway)
    1. Method of collection and enforcement of joint obligations to maintain
      a. Forfeiture of easement
      b. Suit and lien
  B. Grantee of easement maintains
  C. Grantor of easement maintains, but grantee of easement reimburses grantor for expenses of maintenance

☐ VIII. Liability
  A. Cross-indemnities where easements provide mutual benefit (joint driveway)
  B. Grantee of easement indemnifies grantor of easement
  C. Requirement of liability insurance
    1. Both grantor and grantee of easement shown as named insureds

(continued)

Implied Easement

An easement may be created by implication. An **implied easement** can only be made in connection with a conveyance of the real property being served by the easement. Implied easements are based on a theory that when real property is conveyed, the conveyance contains whatever is necessary for the beneficial use and enjoyment of the real property or retains whatever is necessary for the beneficial use and enjoyment of real property retained by the grantor. In creating an implied easement, the law is attempting to arrive at the intent of the parties to the conveyance as shown by all the facts and circumstances under which the conveyance was made.

For example, Aaron received ownership to real property that is described as being bounded by a private street or right-of-way. Aaron receives an implied easement of access over the street. This easement is created provided that the seller of the real property owns the private street or road. In addition, a conveyance of real property by use of a platted description in which the plat describes certain rights-of-way and other easement rights benefiting the conveyed real property shall grant to the new owner an implied easement to these rights or other uses.

Another situation in which an implied easement is created is when the owner of two tracts of land sells one of the tracts without mention of an easement in the deed, and the result of the transaction is to cause the parcel sold to become landlocked. The courts in such a situation imply that there is an easement created over the remaining tract of land to benefit the land sold.

In the example shown in Exhibit 5–2, a single owner owns Tracts A and B and sells Tract B to a new owner without reference to any access or roadway easement over Tract A to the public street. Without the reservation or grant of an easement over Tract A to the public street, the owner of Tract B appears to have purchased a landlocked parcel of property without access to the public street. Generally, the law in this situation will imply that the owner of Tract A had intended to grant the owner of Tract B an easement over Tract A to gain access to the public street. An implied easement for access will be deemed given to the owner of Tract B over Tract A to gain access to the public street.

Implied easements, once created, are perpetual. They are also appurtenant easements and are transferred with the dominant tenement. As shown in Exhibit 5–2, the

implied easement

Easement created by the conduct of the parties to the easement, not by written agreement.

EXHIBIT 5–2

Implied Easement

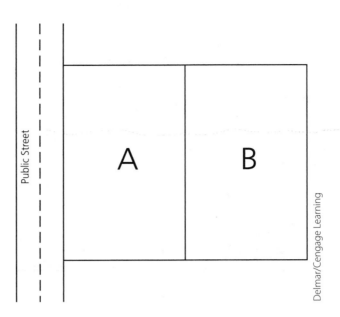

sale of Tract B, after the implied easement has been created, will transfer the implied easement over Tract A.

The reverse situation, however, does not always create a reserved right of an implied easement. Using Exhibit 5–2, if a person owns both Tracts A and B and sells Tract A without reference to a reservation of easement for the benefit of Tract B, the law is not uniform in granting the owner of Tract B a reserved implied easement over Tract A to reach the public street. The law in some states will grant the easement, whereas others will deny the easement. The denial of the easement will result in the owner of Tract B having a landlocked parcel of land without access.

Because implied easements are unwritten, they often have to be proven or perfected in order to be valid. A means of establishing ownership to an implied easement is the same as establishing ownership through adverse possession. This requires the owner of the implied easement to bring a lawsuit known as a "quiet title action" to prove ownership rights in the easement.

The court in *Russakoff v. Scruggs,* 241 Va. 135, 400 S.E.2d 529, applied both of the previously discussed elements of an implied easement in holding that certain property owners held an implied easement for access to and use of a lake.

Prescriptive Easement

prescriptive easement

Easement created when a person uses real property for a period of time without the owner's permission.

An easement may be acquired by prescription. **Prescriptive easements** are created when a person uses property without the permission of the owner for a period of time. A prescriptive easement is similar to the concept of adverse possession discussed in Chapter 1. A person who acquires a prescriptive easement, however, does not exercise such dominion and control over the real property in question as to become an owner of the real property through adverse possession. Instead, the owner of a prescriptive easement has used the real property only for a particular purpose and, therefore, acquires rights to continue to use the real property for that purpose. A prescriptive easement can be obtained over any private real property but cannot be acquired in real property belonging to the United States or any other governmental authority. A prescriptive easement requires that the prescriptive use take place for a period of time. This period varies from state to state, but periods of 10 to 20 years are common.

An important element of a prescriptive easement is that the use made of the easement must be adverse and hostile to the owner of the real property over which the use is being made. *Adverse use* means use without the owner's permission or consent. An owner's permission to the use before the time the prescriptive easement ripens (i.e., before the expiration of the term of years required to obtain a prescriptive easement) causes the prescriptive easement to terminate. Therefore, an owner can prevent prescriptive rights from being made to his or her real property by granting consent to the use. This consent can be given on conditions favorable to the owner of the real property. For example, a landowner notices that his neighbor is using a corner of his property as a right-of-way to a public street. The landowner grants the neighbor an express easement to use the corner of his property for a right-of-way. The express easement provides that the landowner can terminate the easement on 30 days notice. The express grant of permission to the neighbor prevents the neighbor from obtaining perpetual prescriptive rights, and the landowner still maintains, with the 30-day cancellation option, total control over his property.

In addition to the prescriptive use being adverse, the holder of the prescriptive easement must use and enjoy the easement on a continuous and uninterrupted basis. If at any time before the expiration of the term required to create a prescriptive easement the prescriptive use is interrupted by the owner of the land or is voluntarily abandoned by the party claiming the easement, the prescriptive easement is not created. The erection of gates and barriers as well as suits for trespass have all been held to be sufficient interruption by the landowner to defeat a claim of prescriptive use.

abandon by the party claiming the easement

Prescriptive use also must be open, visible, and notorious. The use must be apparent enough to give the owner of the land knowledge or full opportunity to assert his or her rights to interrupt the prescriptive use.

In the example of prescriptive use shown in Exhibit 5–3, B does not have access to the public highway but starts driving across A's property. B drives across A's property for the necessary prescriptive period but without A's consent and without being interrupted by A. B will acquire the right to continue driving across A's property.

Prescriptive easements, once created, are perpetual. They also are appurtenant easements and are transferred with the dominant tenement. In the example shown in Exhibit 5–3, the sale of Tract B will transfer the prescriptive easement over Tract A.

Because prescriptive easements are unwritten, they often have to be proven or perfected in order to be valid. A means of establishing ownership to a prescriptive easement is the same as establishing ownership through adverse possession. This requires the owner of the prescriptive easement to bring a quiet title action to prove ownership rights in the easement.

EXHIBIT 5–3

Prescriptive Use

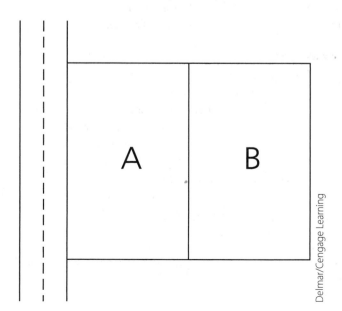

Delmar/Cengage Learning

 **CASE**

Russakoff v. Scruggs
241 Va. 135, 400 S.E.2d 529 (Va. 1991)

LACY, Justice.

The issue we must decide on this appeal is whether lot owners established an easement for access to and use of a lake.

In the 1960s, Richmond Real Estate Developers, Inc., which was owned by E. Carlton Wilton and his two brothers as sole stockholders, began constructing Canterbury East subdivision, located in the Tuckahoe District of Henrico County. The subdivision included a man-made lake with a waterline at the contour line of about the 136' elevation, as shown on the Canterbury East subdivision plat filed with the county. Richard L. and Diane Y. Russakoff, Edward E. Haddock, and Edwin M. Lohmann (collectively Russakoff) each own a lot in Canterbury East subdivision. Their rear lot lines abut the 140' contour, thus leaving a strip of land approximately 20 feet wide, between the lots and the lake. This strip was reserved for flood plains, sewer lines, and water lines.

Richmond Real Estate Developers ceased paying taxes on the lake property, and it escheated to the Commonwealth. A tax sale was held on September 16, 1983, where Kerry I. and Doris J. Scruggs (collectively Scruggs) were the highest bidders. On May 25, 1984, the Commonwealth conveyed the lake property to Scruggs pursuant to the tax sale. Scruggs then posted "no trespassing" signs, erected a fence around the lake, and sent all homeowners surrounding the lake a letter offering them use of the lake by renting or purchasing shares. Further, Scruggs testified that, since the lake was in "bad need of repair and hadn't had anything done to it for years," as of the date of trial he had spent $8,231.53 on improvements, which included approximately $3,000 in taxes and insurance.

By bill of complaint filed February 10, 1988, Russakoff alleged that the right to use the lake had been acquired under a number of legal theories, including adverse possession. The trial court sustained Scruggs' demurrer on the adverse possession claim, but overruled the demurrer as to the other theories. In an amended bill of complaint, Russakoff alleged a right to use the lake by virtue of prescriptive easement, oral agreement, license, easement by implication, and easement by necessity. After an *ore tenus* hearing, the trial court ruled that Russakoff was not entitled to any easement or other rights to use Canterbury Lake. The court dismissed the action, and Russakoff appeals.

In the amended bill of complaint, Russakoff advanced various theories in support of the right of access to and use of Canterbury Lake. The trial judge did not relate his factual findings to any theory Russakoff identified, but characterized the claims as ones based on easements, and stated in an opinion letter and final order that Russakoff was "not entitled to any easement rights" in Canterbury Lake or "to the use of" the lake. Therefore, we must review the record to determine whether Russakoff failed to establish an easement under any of the

three easement theories he pled, which were an easement created by prescription, by implication, or by necessity.*

[1, 2] We begin by reviewing the applicable legal principles. Easements are not ownership interests in the servient tract but "the privilege to use the land of another in a particular manner and for a particular purpose." *Brown v. Haley,* 233 Va. 210, 216, 355 S.E.2d 563, 567–68 (1987). Easements are appurtenant to, and run with, the dominant tract if they benefit the owner in his use and enjoyment of that tract. *See Scott v. Moore,* 98 Va. 668, 675, 37 S.E. 342, 344 (1900).

[3] There are a number of ways an easement can be created. "Easements may be created by express grant or reservation, by implication, by estoppel or by prescription." *Bunn v. Offutt,* 216 Va. 681, 684, 222 S.E.2d 522, 525 (1976). In the case of easements over streets and roads, we have recognized the creation of an easement by reference in the deed to a plat showing the road, even if the street or road had not been created or was not being used at the time of conveyance. *Walters v. Smith,* 186 Va. 159, 169–70, 41 S.E.2d 617, 622 (1947). Within the category of easements created by implication, we have recognized easements created by necessity, *see, e.g., Middleton v. Johnston,* 221 Va. 797, 802, 273 S.E.2d 800, 803 (1981), and by preexisting use (also referred to as quasieasements), *see, e.g., Brown,* 233 Va. at 218, 355 S.E.2d at 569. *See also* 1 R. Minor, *The Law of Real Property* § 99 (F. Ribble 2d ed. 1928).

[4, 5] Russakoff claims, *inter alia,* an easement arising by implication. Such an easement is based on the legal principle that when one conveys land, he is presumed to transfer all that is necessary to the use and enjoyment of the land conveyed. *Brown,* 233 Va. at 218, 355 S.E.2d at 569. While one cannot have an easement on land he owns, if, before severance, one part of the land was used for the benefit of another part, a "quasi-easement" exists over the "quasiservient" portion of the land. That easement is conveyed by implication when the dominant tract is severed; the grantee of the dominant tract obtains an easement over the servient tract, based on the previous use. *See generally Sanderlin v. Baxter,* 76 Va. 299 (1882); R. Minor, *supra,* § 99.

[6] While the extent of the easement right is determined by the circumstances surrounding the conveyance which divides the single ownership, the existence of the easement is established on a showing that (1) the dominant and servient tracts originated from a common grantor, (2) the use was in existence at the time of the severance, and (3) the use

---

*Scruggs argued to the trial court, and on appeal, that Russakoff sought an "implied easement (or easement by estoppel as it is sometimes called)." However, while any easement which is unwritten may be characterized as "implied," Russakoff neither pled nor sought a declaration that an easement was created by estoppel.

(continued)

is apparent, continuous, and reasonably necessary for the enjoyment of the dominant tract. *Brown,* 233 Va. at 219, 355 S.E.2d at 569; *Fones v. Fagan,* 214 Va. 87, 90–91, 196 S.E.2d 916, 919 (1973).

It is clear from the record before us that Russakoff's lots (dominant tracts), and the lake property (servient tract), were originally part of a single tract, thereby satisfying the first prong of the test. Next, the record is equally clear that, at the time Russakoff's predecessors in title took possession of the dominant tracts, the servient tract was a lake. Wilton testified as to the lake's existence, and the lake was reflected on the plat in the deeds conveying the dominant tracts to Russakoff's predecessors. The use of the servient tract as a lake, preexisting the severance, was established.

[7] Turning to the question of apparent and continuous use, the trial court identified Russakoff's use of a pump for lawn watering as the only use of the lake. This use, the trial court held, was not sufficient to establish an easement. Russakoff asserts that this holding is erroneous and that the record supports a finding that the use of the lake and strip of land to gain access to the lake was sufficient to establish an easement. We agree.

The record reflects that Russakoff and previous owners of the lots used the lake openly and continuously, through the construction of docks, piers, and sprinkler systems, and by using the lake for boating and ice skating. Mr. Lohmann, who purchased his lot in 1977, testified that he had a boat which his children used for fishing, frogging and "that type of thing," and when the lake was frozen in the winter they skated on the ice. Haddock testified that the lake was a "big consideration" in his purchase of his property in 1968. He "bought a boat along with the house so we could use it in the lake." The boat originally belonged to Mr. Sharp, Haddock's predecessor in title. Haddock testified that he used the lake for wading, built a pier (although it had disintegrated prior to Scruggs' purchase of the lake), and bought a canoe and used it on the lake. He also testified that his family as well as neighbors skated on the lake in the winter.

Dr. Stearns, Russakoff's predecessor in title, testified that he had used the lake since 1966. He constructed a pier, a lawn irrigation system, and a retaining wall. Additionally, he observed as many as 800 people ice skating on the lake in the winter. He had used the lake for almost 20 years before Scruggs demanded that he pay $250 a year for access to and use of the lake.

Diane Russakoff testified that, in viewing the property prior to purchasing it from Stearns, she saw boats in Stearns' yard, as well as in the neighbors' yards. Mrs. Russakoff also observed that the grass was cut all the way to the water. Dr. Stearns informed her that he had made uninterrupted use of the lake since he had purchased the property. Additionally, Dr. Stearns showed the Russakoffs the sprinkler system from the lake to the lawn. Although the system was disconnected at the time of the purchase from Stearns, the Russakoffs reconnected the system and used it.

Our review of this record shows that the trial judge's finding that the only use of the lake was Russakoff's lawn sprinkler system, which he found to be insufficient to support an easement, is clearly erroneous. Rather, the record supports a contrary conclusion that use of the lake was continuous and apparent.

[8] The third prong of the test also requires that the easement be reasonably necessary to the use and enjoyment of the dominant tract. This determination requires a showing of need which, by definition, may be less than that required for establishing an easement by necessity, but must be something more than simple convenience. We have recognized that whether this element is established "generally will depend upon the circumstances of the particular case." *Jones v. Beavers,* 221 Va. 214, 221, 269 S.E.2d 775, 779 (1980).

[9] Here, we hold that a purchaser of a lot would have a legitimate expectation of the right to access and use the lake where a visual inspection and reference to the plat incorporated in the deed of conveyance showed the existence of a lake within 20 feet of one's lot line, and where investigation would disclose that the 20-foot strip between the lake and the lot line was retained solely for certain utility and flood plain uses. The Canterbury East developers contemplated enjoyment of the lake, as a lake, by purchasers of the lots surrounding the lake. Under these circumstances, the easement at issue was reasonably necessary to the use and enjoyment of the lakeside lots.

[10] An easement created by implication, which, as here, is appurtenant to the land, may be vitiated if, when the servient estate is purchased by another, the purchaser of the servient tract does not have notice of the easement or the use is not apparent. Under those circumstances, the purchaser takes the land free from such easement or use. *Ricks v. Scott,* 117 Va. 370, 384, 84 S.E. 676, 681 (1915). As discussed above, the evidence in this case supports a finding of a use which was apparent, continuous, and reasonably necessary to the enjoyment of the dominant tract. The record also clearly shows Scruggs' knowledge of the use. In addition to sending a letter indicating the lot owners could *no longer* use the lake without payment of a fee, Scruggs agreed that "numerous property owners were using the lake and had pumps in the water for getting water up on their lot[s]." Furthermore, Scruggs testified that shortly after purchasing the lake, he traversed the lake in a canoe and disconnected at least two of the existing sprinkler systems which used the lake water for lawn watering purposes, and Scruggs' actions show that the use of the lake by surrounding property owners was apparent, and that he was aware of the use.

At the time Scruggs purchased the lake, its use was apparent, continuous, and reasonably necessary to the enjoyment of property surrounding the lake. Therefore, we conclude that an easement by implication was established in favor of Russakoff for access to and use of Canterbury Lake.

In view of this holding, it is unnecessary to review Russakoff's claims to an easement created by prescription or by necessity.

easement by necessity

Easement for access to a public street that is necessary for the use and enjoyment of the property benefited by the easement.

Easement by Necessity

Many states provide a landowner who does not have access to a public road or street the right to apply for the grant of a private way or an easement over adjacent lands to gain access. This is an **easement by necessity.** It grants to a landowner a quasi-private right to condemn an adjoining owner's land for purposes of acquiring an access easement to a public street or road. An easement by necessity generally requires that fair compensation be paid to the landowner of the condemned easement. Easements by necessity are created by statutory procedures or, in some states, by common law theory. These statutes limit the width of the right-of-way as well as provide a method to determine fair compensation. Because there are strict requirements concerning easements by necessity in some states, it is important to check a particular state's requirements before proceeding.

Termination of Easements

An easement, once granted, continues to exist until terminated by the operation of some rule of law or by the terms of the express grant. An easement may be terminated by (a) expiration of express term, (b) abandonment, (c) merger, (d) foreclosure of prior servient liens, or (e) express release or termination.

As mentioned, an easement by express grant can be made for any duration, or it can be terminated on the happening of a certain event. For example, a private road easement may be terminated on the dedication of the road to public use.

An easement may be terminated by abandonment. Abandonment is a matter of the intention of the grantee of the easement as evidenced by the acts of the grantee and surrounding circumstances. Abandonment is nonuse with the intent to never use again. Evidence of abandonment may be the permanent removal of physical installations, such as rails or bridges, which permit the use of the easement or actions that permit others to maintain obstructions to prevent the exercise of the easement. For example, a railroad has an easement for a spur/side track. After a number of years, the railroad stops using the spur/side track and even removes the rails and ties. A strong argument could be made that the railroad has abandoned the easement and that the easement has terminated. Although easements usually·cannot be lost by nonuse alone, nonuse is evidence of an intent to abandon.

An easement may be lost by the merger of the dominant and the servient tenement. For example, Aaron grants to Bob the right to cross over Aaron's property to the public road. The right-of-way over Aaron's property is an appurtenant easement to Bob's property. Later, Bob acquires the fee simple title to Aaron's property over which the easement travels. Bob now owns both the fee title and the easement over the former property of Aaron. This ownership of the dominant and servient tenements causes a merger, and the easement is terminated because Bob no longer needs the easement to travel over Bob's own property.

An easement also may be lost by the foreclosure of a mortgage or a deed of trust that was on the servient property before the time the easement was created. Easements in some states are terminated by a tax foreclosure sale of the servient estate.

An easement can be terminated by an express written release or termination given by the easement owner to the owner of the servient estate. Written releases of easements should be drafted with the same formality as the easement and be recorded in the public records of the county in which the easement is located.

license

A revocable privilege or permission to do an act or series of acts on land possessed by another.

LICENSES

A **license** is a revocable privilege or permission to do an act or a series of acts on land possessed by another. For example, an owner of a farm that has a lake located on it gives a neighbor permission to fish in the lake. The permission to fish in the lake includes permission to walk across the farm fields to reach the lake. It is understood that the permission to fish in the lake can be terminated at any time by the farmer and that the neighbor acquires no rights in the farmer's land. A license is distinguished from an easement in that an easement is a property interest and a license is mere permission to perform a certain act. Since an easement is a property interest, once granted, it generally cannot be terminated or revoked by the grantor. A license being a consensual privilege or permission to do a certain thing, it generally can be terminated or revoked by the grantor of the license.

A license can be created orally or in writing, or it can be implied from the conduct of the parties. An oral license without any consideration being paid for the license is revocable at the will of the person granting the license. On the other hand, a license in writing for which compensation and consideration have been paid usually is irrevocable. An implied license may come about from custom or from acts constituting an invitation, such as signs and advertisements. For example, the owner of a retail store extends a license to the customers of the store to enter on the land where the store is located, shop, buy merchandise, and so on. An implied license is revocable at any time, and once revoked, if the licensee does not leave the property, the licensee becomes a trespasser.

The terms of a license are strictly interpreted, and a licensee cannot extend or vary the terms. Third persons who interfere with the licensing or unlawful exercise of the license may be liable to the licensee in damages.

PRACTICE TIPS FOR THE PARALEGAL

A paralegal may be involved in the preparation or review of easements. The preparation of an easement requires the same skills as the preparation of any other legal document. The easement must be prepared to satisfy the requirements of the client and other parties to the agreement. The language used to create the use, location, and limitations of the easement should be concise and with clear meaning. Vague or indefinite language will only invite dispute as to the intent and meaning of the easement and may result in future problems or even litigation by the parties to the easement. The checklist for the preparation of an easement contained in this chapter is helpful as a drafting tool to ensure that all the issues concerning an easement have been resolved and contained in the final easement agreement.

A paralegal who assists in representing a purchaser or lender in connection with a real property transaction may be asked to review easements that have been reported in a title examination of the property. When an easement is reviewed on behalf of a purchaser or lender, the general objective is to determine if the easement will interfere with the use or value of the property.

It is important when reviewing an easement to determine the exact location of the easement on the property. Often a survey may be required to determine that location. Once the exact location has been determined, the easement must then be discussed with the client to decide if the location will interfere with existing use of the property or any future plans the client may have for the property.

An easement should also be reviewed to determine what rights of use the easement holder has to the easement property and what obligations the parties have concerning maintenance of the easement area and liability for accidents which may occur therein. Liability insurance may be required to cover certain events happening in the easement area.

An easement should also be carefully reviewed to determine its duration. Most easements are perpetual unless there is a stated time period for termination set forth in the easement agreement. Generally stated, property should not be purchased unless all easements affecting the property have been carefully reviewed.

⛉ ETHICS: False Witness

Your supervising attorney has just had a difficult closing. The closing lasted a day and has occupied a couple of conference rooms. It is near the end of the day, and the attorney brings you a stack of documents. The attorney asks you to witness a number of signatures on the documents. You indicate that you have not seen these people sign. The attorney apologizes but states that the people have already gone home and that the signatures must be witnessed. To avoid a confrontation, you witness the documents. Was this the proper thing to do?

It is unethical for an attorney or paralegal to give false witness or commit perjury on behalf of a client. Few attorneys or paralegals intentionally lie or misrepresent the facts involving a real estate transaction. These same honest attorneys and paralegals, however, may routinely witness or notarize the unseen signature of parties to various legal documents.

Most legal documents, such as deed and mortgages, require a witness for the document to be recorded or be valid. They also require that the witness actually see the person sign the document. Witnessing a document in which the witness has not seen the party sign the document is a misrepresentation of fact and a breach of legal ethics. The notarization of a signature without having seen the party sign is an even more serious matter. When notarizing a signature, a notary is swearing under the notarial oath that she or he has seen the person sign the document. A notarization of the signature is, therefore, a witness under oath, and if the notary has not seen the person sign the document, the notary is committing perjury.

It is advisable that a paralegal in the beginning of an employment situation confer with his or her supervising attorney concerning what procedures will be followed in the witness or notarization of legal documents. The paralegal should strongly stress that he or she will not witness or notarize documents unless he or she has seen the signing of the documents.

SUMMARY

Knowledge of the law of easements and licenses is essential for any paralegal involved in a real estate practice. The use of easements and licenses is commonplace. Easements may be essential for the use and enjoyment of a parcel of real property. Easements for the benefit of electric, gas, and telecommunications utility companies are routinely found in both urban and rural properties. Easements may be created in a number of ways, such as express creation, implication, prescription, and, in some situations, by necessity. The use of an easement may be limited to an express period of time, or it may be perpetual. Easements may generally be terminated by an expiration of express term, abandonment, merger, or foreclosure of a prior lien or may be by express release or termination. A license grants the holder permission to do something upon the grantee's land. A license is different from an easement in that a license is not a property interest and may be terminated with notice.

HELPFUL WEBSITES

Easement Checklist

The American Bar Association has an excellent article on "15 Things to Remember in Drafting Real Property Easements" at *http://www.abanet.org.*

Conservation Easements

Interesting information on conservation easements can be found on The Ohio State University Web site at *http://ohioline.osu.edu.*

Historic Preservation Easements

A good article on Historic Preservation Easements can be found on the National Park Service Web site at *http://www.nps.gov/history/HPS/TPS/tax/easement.htm.*

KEY TERMS

appurtenant easement
blanket easement
dominant tenement
easement

easement by necessity
easement in gross
implied easement
license

prescriptive easement
servient tenement

REVIEW QUESTIONS

1. Explain the difference between an appurtenant easement and an easement in gross, and give an example of each.

2. What are the four ways in which an easement can be created?

3. The owner of Parcel A gives to the owner of Parcel B an easement to use a driveway located on Parcel A. Which parcel is the dominant tenement, and which parcel is the servient tenement?

4. What is a license, and how does it differ from an easement?

5. What is an easement by necessity, and how does it differ from a prescriptive easement?

6. Is there any written proof of a prescriptive or implied easement?

7. What is a blanket easement?

8. What are the requirements for an abandonment of an easement?

9. Explain how an easement can be lost by merger of the dominant and servient tenements.

10. Are prescriptive and implied easements appurtenant or easements in gross?

CASE PROBLEMS

1. You are a paralegal in a law firm representing a property owner. The property owner is negotiating to purchase a driveway easement from a neighbor. You have been asked to prepare the easement agreement. What information do you need to prepare the easement?

2. You are a paralegal in a law firm that represents a real estate developer. The developer has obtained a necessary driveway easement to her property. After the easement was obtained, it was discovered that the property over which the driveway is located had been earlier pledged as security for a debt to the First Bank and Trust. It also has been discovered that the First Bank and Trust debt is in default and that the First Bank and Trust is having a public auction of the property to pay the debt. Should the real estate developer be concerned? If so, what steps can be taken to protect the developer?

3. Aaron owns two lots of real property, Lot 1 and Lot 2. Lot 1 is located next to a public right-of-way, but Lot 2 is landlocked from the public lot right-of-way by Lot 1. Aaron conveys Lot 2 to Bob with a deed, making no reference to any right-of-ways or any other kinds of easement benefiting Lot 2. Bob then sells Lot 2 to Carol. Carol claims against Aaron that she has a right-of-way easement over Lot 1 for the purposes of providing access from the public street to Lot 2. Does Carol have a valid claim?

4. David has a driveway easement over Carol's property. By the terms of the easement, the driveway easement expired six months ago. David continues to use the driveway easement. Can Carol sue David for trespass?

PRACTICAL ASSIGNMENTS

1. Research the law of your state regarding the requirements for an easement by necessity, and write a short memorandum outlining the findings of your research.

2. Sea View Development Corporation is the owner of a certain parcel of property that fronts or joins onto the right-of-way of U.S. Highway 98. The property is more particularly described as follows: "A portion of Tract 7, Chase Heights No. 3 as recorded on Plat Book 14, Page 32, current Public Records, Walton County, Florida." Walton Construction Company owns a tract of land directly behind the property owned by Sea View Development Company. The property is described as follows: "Tract 6, Chase Heights No. 3 as recorded on Plat Book 14, Page 32, Public Records, Walton County, Florida." It is important to the development of the Walton Construction Company property that it obtain an easement for access about 20 feet in width over and across the property owned by Sea View Development Corporation. The location of the easement will be drawn by a specific survey and can be described on an exhibit to the easement agreement. Walton Construction Company intends to pay Sea View Development Corporation $1,000 for the easement. The easement will be perpetual and for the purpose of pedestrian and vehicular access from U.S. Highway 98 to the property owned by Walton Construction Company. The easement will be nonexclusive in that owners and tenants of Tracts 6 and 7 may use the easement. Walton Construction Company intends to be fully responsible for the repair and maintenance of any road constructed on the easement area.

   You are a paralegal in the firm representing Walton Construction Company. You have been asked to prepare a first draft of an easement for the purposes set forth above. Prepare the first draft. You may want to use the easement set forth as Exhibit 5–4 as an example. Note that this assignment requires only an ingress and egress easement, so you will need to delete any references to the sanitary sewer easement set forth in Exhibit 5–4.

3. Go to the real property record room of your local courthouse. Search the records, find, and make a copy of each of the following: (a) an easement to your local electric utility company, (b) an ingress and egress easement, (c) an easement to permit the drainage of water over an adjoining property owner's land, (d) an easement for your local telephone company, and (e) a sanitary sewer easement. Compare the easements you found in your local record room with those easements set forth as Exhibits 5–4 and 5–5 of this chapter. Briefly discuss how they are similar and how they are different.

ADDENDUM

Exhibit 5–4 Sanitary Sewer Easement and Ingress and Egress Easement

Exhibit 5–5 Electric Power Company Right-of-Way Easement

Student StudyWare™ CD-ROM

Interactive Student CD in the book includes additional quizzing, case studies, and key terms flashcards.

Online Companion™

For additional resources, please go to *www.paralegal.delmar.cengage.com*

THIS SANITARY SEWER EASEMENT AND INGRESS AND EGRESS EASEMENT is made this <u>21st</u> day of April, 20___, by and between

(herein with his heirs and assigns called "Grantor") and
(herein with their heirs and assigns called "Grantee").

WITNESSETH:

WHEREAS, Grantee has requested that Grantor convey to Grantee a nonexclusive twenty (20) foot permanent easement over real property described on Exhibit "A" (the "Sewer Easement Property") for the purpose of installing and maintaining a sanitary sewer line; and

WHEREAS, Grantor is willing to grant such a sewer easement upon all of the terms and conditions set forth in this Sanitary Sewer Easement and Ingress and Egress Easement; and

WHEREAS, Grantor desires to grant an ingress and egress easement over the property described on Exhibit "B" attached hereto; and

WHEREAS, Grantee desires to grant an ingress and egress easement over the property described on Exhibit "C" attached hereto; and

WHEREAS, Grantor and Grantee desire to grant such mutual ingress and egress easement on the terms and conditions set forth in this Sanitary Sewer Easement and Ingress and Egress Easement; and

WHEREAS, Grantor and Grantee desire to set forth herein and effectuate hereby their agreements in this regard;

NOW, THEREFORE, for and in consideration of the premises and other valuable consideration, the receipt and sufficiency of which is hereby acknowledged by each of the undersigned, Grantor and Grantee hereby agree as follows:

1. Upon all terms and conditions set forth in this Agreement, Grantor hereby grants and conveys to Grantee a twenty (20) foot permanent nonexclusive easement ("Sewer Easement") over, through and across the Sewer Easement Property, the Sewer Easement being designated "San. Sew. Esmt. 'A'" on that plat of survey for   and Acme Title Insurance Company prepared by Richard A. Scott, Georgia Registered Land Surveyor Number 1075 dated March 2, 20___, last revised April 15, 20___, for the purpose of installing, using, repairing, maintaining and replacing an underground sanitary sewer line. Grantor hereby retains the right to landscape the surface of the Sewer Easement and otherwise use said Sewer Easement in any manner whatsoever so long as such use shall not interfere with the use and maintenance of the easement granted herein. Without limitation to the foregoing, Grantor shall have the right to use the Sewer Easement to the fullest extent possible, including, without limitation: (a) paving the surface of the Sewer Easement for use as pedestrian and vehicular access ways, vehicle parking and sidewalks, (b) landscaping and installing irrigation systems on the Sewer Easement, (c) placing permanent structural supports in the Sewer Easement for walkways and construction of improvements in air space over the Sewer Easement, (d) installing, maintaining, repairing and replacing storm sanitary sewer lines and other utility lines and conduits in the Sewer Easement, (e) grading and adding fill to the surface of the Sewer Easement, (f) placing street lighting, fencing and signage in the Sewer Easement, (g) conveying to County, State or other governmental bodies for roads and streets and (h) placing a retention pond on the surface of the Sewer Easement.

2. After each entry by Grantee on the Sewer Easement for the purpose of repair, maintenance or replacement of said sanitary sewer line, Grantee shall, at the expense of Grantee, return the surface of the Sewer Easement within a reasonable time to the condition in which such surface existed immediately prior to such installation or entry with proper compaction of the soil and proper ground cover to prevent erosion. All installations, repair, maintenance or replacements shall be conducted so as to minimize the interruption and interference of the Grantor's use of the Sewer Easement.

3. Grantor, his heirs and assigns, shall have the right to install one or more tap-ons to the sanitary sewer line constructed within the Sewer Easement, without payment of any fee or charge to Grantee, at any time chosen by Grantor, subject only to the following conditions:

(a) Each tap-on must comply with all applicable governmental regulations;

(b) The installation of the connection must be performed in a manner which does not substantially disrupt sanitary sewer service being provided by the sanitary sewer line within the Sewer Easement; and

(c) Grantor shall pay any and all costs related to such tap-ons. Grantor hereby indemnifies Grantee and agrees to hold Grantee harmless from and against any and all mechanic's and materialmen's liens and

Delmar/Cengage Learning

EXHIBIT 5–4

Sanitary Sewer Easement and Ingress and Egress Easement

(continued)

any other loss, damage or liability which Grantee may incur as a result of the exercise by Grantor of its rights under this Paragraph 3.

4. Grantee hereby indemnifies Grantor and agrees to hold Grantor harmless from and against any and all mechanic's and materialmen's liens which may arise out of or in any way relate to the maintenance and repair of the sewer line by Grantee.

5. Grantee agrees not to dedicate the easement granted hereby to DeKalb County, Georgia, without the prior written approval by Grantor.

6. Grantor hereby reserves the right at any time and from time to time to relocate all or any portion of the sanitary sewer line contained in the Sewer Easement and to relocate at any time and from time to time the location of the Sewer Easement as Grantor may deem expedient and necessary or prudent with respect to the development of the property of the Grantor. Grantee hereby acknowledges and recognizes that Grantor reserves the right to develop the property of the Grantor in any manner that Grantor may deem prudent or expedient and, accordingly, Grantor reserves the right to relocate the Sewer Easement in any manner whatsoever so as to accommodate any development of the property of the Grantor. The Grantee shall not be responsible for any costs and expenses associated with relocation of the sanitary sewer line. Upon such relocation, Grantor shall deliver to Grantee an easement in recordable form for such relocated sewer line after which the sewer easement herein conveyed shall terminate. Any relocation shall be subject to the prior written approval of any first mortgagee having its deed to secure debt recorded in DeKalb County deed records.

7. This Sanitary Sewer Easement and Ingress and Egress Easement shall bind and inure to the benefit of the parties hereto and their respective heirs, executors, personal representatives, mortgagees, successors and assigns.

8. Grantor grants and conveys unto Grantee a perpetual nonexclusive easement for automobile and pedestrian ingress and egress over, upon and across the land described on Exhibit "B" hereto. Grantee grants and conveys unto Grantor a perpetual nonexclusive easement for automobile and pedestrian ingress and egress over, upon and across the land described on Exhibit "C" hereto. Included in the foregoing easements granted to Grantor is an easement for the construction and maintenance of a driveway. Grantor shall maintain the driveways so located thereon. The easements granted by this Paragraph 8 may be terminated by Grantor upon Grantor filing upon the deed records on the Courts of DeKalb County, a cancellation of this Easement. Upon such cancellation being filed the easements granted by this Paragraph 8 shall terminate. Any cancellation shall be subject to the prior written consent of any first mortgagee having a recorded deed to secure debt conveying the property described on Exhibit "A" hereto.

This Sanitary Sewer Easement and Ingress and Egress Easement shall be interpreted and construed in accordance with the laws of the State of Georgia.

IN WITNESS WHEREOF, Grantor and Grantee have executed and sealed this Sanitary Sewer Easement and Ingress and Egress Easement the day and year first above written.

EXHIBIT "A"

ALL THAT TRACT or parcel of land lying and being in Land Lots 298 and 309 of the 18th District of DeKalb County, Georgia, and being a portion of Lots 18 and 19, Block "3" of the subdivision of Camp Gordon as shown on plat recorded in Plat Book 14, Page 51, DeKalb County, Georgia, records, and being more particularly described as follows:

Starting at a point on the center line of New Peachtree Road and the intersection of the center line of West Hospital Avenue and running thence northeast along the center line of New Peachtree Road, 440.35 feet to a point and the true point of beginning; running thence northeast along the center line of New Peachtree Road 445.0 feet to a point; thence southeast at an interior angle of 89 degrees 29 minutes 30 seconds from the center line of New Peachtree Road a distance of 563.9 feet to an iron pin; thence southwest at an interior angle of 90 degrees 30 minutes 30 seconds from the preceding course a distance of 416.00 feet to a point; thence northwest at an interior angle of 90 degrees from the last mentioned course a distance of 187.9 feet to a point; thence southwest at an interior angle of 270 degrees from the last mentioned course a distance of 24.0 feet to a point; thence northwest at an interior angle of 90 degrees from the last mentioned course a distance of 376.00 feet to the center line of New Peachtree Road and the point of beginning.

(continued)

Excepted from the above described property is that portion lying within the right-of-way of New Peachtree Road and Brogdon Court.

EXHIBIT 5–4

Sanitary Sewer Easement and Ingress and Egress Easement (*continued*)

EXHIBIT "B"

ALL THAT TRACT or parcel of land lying and being in Land Lots 298 and 309 of the 18th District of DeKalb County, Georgia, and being a portion of Lots 18 and 19, Block "3" of the sub-division of Camp Gordon as shown on plat recorded in Plat Book 14, Page 51, DeKalb County, Georgia, records, and being more particularly described as follows:

Starting at a point on the center line of New Peachtree Road and the intersection of the center line of West Hospital Avenue and running thence northeast along the center line of New Peachtree Road, 440.35 feet to a point and the true point of beginning; running thence northeast along the center line of New Peachtree Road 6.0 feet to a point; thence southeast at an interior angle of 90 degrees from the center line of New Peachtree Road a distance of 376.0 feet to a point; thence southwest at an interior angle of 90 degrees from the preceding course a distance of 6.0 feet to a point; thence northwest at an interior angle of 90 degrees from the last mentioned course a distance of 376.0 feet to the center line of New Peachtree Road and the point of beginning.

Excepted from the above described property is that portion lying within the right-of-way of New Peachtree Road.

EXHIBIT "C"

ALL THAT TRACT or parcel of land lying and being in Land Lots 298 and 309 of the 18th District of DeKalb County, Georgia, and being a portion of Lots 18 and 19, Block "3" of the sub-division of Camp Gordon as shown on plat recorded in Plat Book 14, Page 51, DeKalb County, Georgia, records, and being more particularly described as follows:

Starting at a point on the center line of New Peachtree Road and the intersection of the center line of West Hospital Avenue and running thence northeast along the center line of New Peachtree Road, 440.35 feet to a point and the true point of beginning; thence southeast at an interior angle of 90 degrees from the center line of New Peachtree Road a distance of 376.0 feet to a point; thence southwest at an interior angle of 90 degrees from the preceding course a distance of 24.0 feet to a point; thence northwest at an interior angle of 90 degrees from the last mentioned course a distance of 376.0 feet to a point on the center line of New Peachtree Road; running thence northeast along the center line of New Peachtree Road 24.0 feet to the point of beginning.

Excepted from the above described property is that portion lying within the right-of-way of New Peachtree Road.

EXHIBIT 5–5

Electric Power Company Right-of-Way Easement

STATE OF_____, _____ COUNTY.

    In consideration of the sum of _____, ($_____) Dollars in hand paid by The American Power Company, hereinafter called the Company, the receipt and sufficiency whereof is hereby acknowledged, the undersigned, _____, whose post office address is _____, _____, does hereby grant and convey to said Company, its successors and assigns, the right, privilege and easement to go in, upon and along the tract of land owned by the undersigned to Land Lot _____, of the _____ District of _____ County, known as No. _____ in or near the City or Town of _____, _____ , together with the right to construct, operate, and maintain upon said land its lines for transmitting electric current, erected on one line of poles, with wire and other necessary apparatus, fixtures, and appliances; with the right to permit the attachment of the wires and appliances of any other company or person to said poles; together with the right at all times to enter upon said premises for the purpose of inspecting the lines, making repairs, removals, alterations, or extensions thereon, thereto, or therefrom; also the right to cut away or trim and keep clear of said lines all trees, limbs of trees, and other obstructions that may interfere or be likely to interfere with the proper operation of said lines; also the right of ingress and egress over said lines to and from said lines.

    The undersigned does not convey any land, but merely grants the hereinabove described rights, privileges, and easements.

    Said Company shall not be liable for, or bound by, any statement or agreement or understanding not herein expressed.

    IN WITNESS WHEREOF, the said _____, has hereinto set _____ hand_____ and seal_____, this _____ day of _____, 20_____.

                               _____ (SEAL)

                               By: _____ (SEAL)

                               Title: _____ (SEAL)

Grantors

Signed, sealed and delivered in the presence of:

_____

Witness

_____

Notary Public

My Commission Expires:

_____

This document to be signed in the presence of two (2) witnesses, one of whom should be a notary public.

chapter | 6

Contracts

Objectives

After reading this chapter, you should be able to:

- Explain the requirements of a valid real estate contract
- Identify the remedies for default of a real estate contract
- Understand the role of a real estate agent in the procurement of a real estate contract
- Distinguish the three types of real estate agency listing agreements
- Explain the federal tax consequences of a sale of real property

Outline

O ne of the main areas of a paralegal's involvement in real estate is assistance in representing a purchaser or seller in the sale and purchase of real property. When ownership to real property is acquired through purchase and sale, the transaction requires the negotiation and preparation of a contract before the actual transfer of ownership to the real property. The contract sets forth the terms for the purchase and sale. A paralegal who participates in a real estate contract transaction should be aware of the general legal rules governing the validity of a contract as well as the remedies available for an injured party in the event of a default under a contract. This chapter reviews the law regarding the validity of a real estate contract and the remedies for breach of a real estate contract. In addition, it briefly discusses the role of a real estate agent in procuring a real estate contract.

REQUIREMENTS OF A VALID CONTRACT

contract

Agreement between two or more persons consisting of a promise or mutual promises that the law will enforce or the performance of which the law recognizes as a duty.

A **contract** is an agreement between two or more persons consisting of a promise or mutual promises that the law will enforce or the performance of which the law will in some way recognize as a duty. For a valid real estate contract to exist and the promises therein to be enforceable, a number of legal requirements exist. These requirements are (a) legal capacity of the parties, (b) mutual agreement, (c) consideration, (d) lawful purpose, and (e) written agreement. All the requirements must be present or the contract is invalid and the promises unenforceable.

Legal Capacity to Contract

The legal capacity means that the parties entering into the contract are responsible in such a way that the law will make them bound by their promises. In this section, we examine how this concept relates to minors or infants, mental incompetents, corporations, partnerships, limited liability companies, personal representatives, trustees, and agents.

Minors or Infants

The law protects a minor or infant from his or her contractual promises. A minor is deemed to be a person under a certain age (18 years in most states). A minor's contract is voidable at the election of the minor. The minor can void or fail to perform the contract if the minor so desires, but if the minor performs, the other party is bound. For example, an adult enters into a contract to purchase a car from a sixteen-year-old. If the sixteen-year-old decides not to sell the car, the adult has no legal recourse. On the other hand, if the adult decides not to buy the car, the sixteen-year-old can legally enforce the contract and require the adult to buy the car or pay damages.

An exception to the voidability rule of contracts entered into by minors is a contract for necessities of the minor. A minor who is independent and living apart from his or her parents may be responsible for contracts entered into for necessities of life such as food, medical care, or even shelter. Generally, the purchase of real property is not considered as necessary, and most real estate contracts entered into by a minor are voidable at the election of the minor.

Mental Incompetents

Mental incompetents do not understand the essence of the contract. They are protected from their promises in most states. They do not understand that they own property, the value of the property, or the value of what the purchaser is offering. A mental incompetent may be a person who does not understand that by signing the contract, he or she is obligated to perform some task, such as sell or purchase property. The test for mental incompetence has a high standard. Mere lack of knowledge or failure to read a contract does not make a person a mental incompetent. Likewise, illiteracy is not mental incompetence.

Persons adjudicated incompetent cannot enter into contracts after the adjudication, and any contracts entered into by them will be void. The adjudication of incompetency is a formal court proceeding, and a final adjudication will be part of the public court record. This adjudication, however, is generally not recorded in the real property records and therefore can only be determined by a search of the court records.

A person who is, in fact, incompetent at the time of entering into a contract but has not been formally adjudicated incompetent has a defense to the contract. The contract will be void if the person can prove incompetency at the time of the contract's signature.

Corporations

A contract entered into by a corporation presents special legal capacity problems. A corporation is created by state statute and only has the power granted to it by state corporate law or its corporate charter. Most business corporations have the authority to buy and sell real property, and therefore, capacity is not a problem. Many nonprofit corporations, on the other hand, have limited powers. A nonprofit corporation's corporate charter should be examined to determine if the corporation has the legal authority to buy and sell real property.

Even though the corporation probably has the authority to enter into a contract, human representatives of the corporation negotiate and sign the contract. Do these representatives truly represent the corporation, and do they have the authority to make the contract binding on the corporation? These questions of authority and capacity should be carefully examined by the paralegal. A corporate officer's authority is set forth in a resolution passed by the board of directors of the corporation. These board resolutions or corporate resolutions are obtained at the time the contract is signed. An example of a corporate resolution authorizing a contract and empowering representatives of the corporation to sign the contract is shown in Exhibit 6–1.

Partnerships

General partnerships and limited partnerships also create special authorization problems. A general partnership formed under the Uniform Partnership Act has the power to enter into contracts for the sale and purchase of real property. Unless the partnership agreement designates a managing partner, all partners must consent to any contracts entered into by the partnership. A review of the partnership agreement is necessary to determine what authority the partners have if less than all the partners are negotiating and signing the contract.

Limited partnerships formed under the Uniform Limited Partnership Act authorize the general partners to act on behalf of the partnership and to buy and sell partnership real property. The consent or agreement of the limited partners is not required. The powers of the general partners, however, can be limited by the partnership agreement, and a review

---

EXHIBIT 6–1

Certification of Resolution

I, Ardene J. Thompson, the duly elected Assistant Secretary for First Arizona Savings, FSB (the "Bank") do hereby certify that all the Members of the Executive Committee of the Bank adopted the following action by written consent in lieu of a meeting, pursuant to Article IV, Section 6 of the Bylaws of the Bank, which resolution has not been amended or revoked as of the date hereof.

"BE IT RESOLVED, that the Executive Committee hereby approves the sale of that certain property known as Pace's Ferry Place, more particularly described in the attached Exhibit "A" (the "Property"), to Village Properties, an Arizona general partnership, for the sum of $2,200,000.00 pursuant to the terms of the Purchase Agreement dated June 6, 20____ ; and

BE IT FURTHER RESOLVED, that James J. Connor, Administrative Vice President, or Ruth K. McGuire, Executive Vice President, are each hereby authorized to execute on behalf of the Bank any and all documents as may be necessary and proper to contract for and to close on the sale of the "Property."

IN WITNESS WHEREOF, I, Ardene J. Thompson, have duly set my hand and seal of the Bank.

September 9, 20____

_____
Assistant Secretary
[SEAL]

Delmar/Cengage Learning

of the agreement is necessary to determine what authority the general partners have to sign contracts binding on the limited partnership. In addition, general partners do not have the authority, without limited partners' consent, to sell all the assets of the limited partnership. A real property limited partnership may have only one asset, such as an apartment project or a shopping center. A careful examination of the affairs of the limited partnership as well as the agreement is necessary in these situations.

Limited Liability Companies

A limited liability company consists of members of the company who either collectively act on behalf of the company or appoint managers or managing members to act on behalf of the company. Generally, any contract entered into by a limited liability company will need the consent or agreement of all members, evidenced either by their signatures on the contract or by giving authority to a manager or group of members to sign the contract. A careful examination of the limited liability company articles of organization and operating agreement is necessary to determine which members have authority to sign contracts on behalf of the company.

Personal Representatives

An executor or executrix of an estate has limited power to enter into contracts to buy and sell real property on behalf of the estate. An executor or executrix only has the power given by state law and under the will. An executor or executrix cannot act in violation of the will without a court order. Therefore, when reviewing contracts entered into with estates of deceased people, it is necessary to review not only state law regarding the executor's or executrix's powers, but also the actual will that appoints the executor or executrix.

An administrator of an intestate estate (one in which the deceased died without a will) has limited power to buy and sell property. In many states, an administrator cannot enter into a contract to sell estate property without a court order or without consent from all the heirs who would be entitled to inherit the property.

Trustees

Trustees of a trust have problems similar to those of executors or executrixes and administrators. A trustee only has the authority given by state law and by the actual trust instrument. A contract entered into with a trust requires that the trust document be carefully reviewed to see if the trustee has the authority to bind the trust to the contract.

Trustees also have a fiduciary responsibility to the beneficiaries of the trust. This means that the trustee cannot deal with trust property in such a way as to be detrimental to the beneficiaries. For example, a trustee could not enter into a contract to sell trust property to herself, her relatives, or any other entity in which the trustee has a financial interest. This would be self-dealing and a breach of fiduciary duty. In addition, a trustee cannot enter into a contract to sell trust property if the trustee intends to use the proceeds for purposes other than to benefit the beneficiaries. In any situation where a trustee would potentially be breaching his or her fiduciary duty, the trustee does not have the authority to act unless all the beneficiaries consent to the action. Beneficiaries who are under legal age cannot give their consent without the appointment of a guardian.

Agents

agent

A person who has the power and authority to act on behalf of another person. An authorized agent's actions will bind the person on whose behalf the agent is acting.

principal

A person who appoints an agent to act on his or her behalf.

An **agent** is a person who has the power and authority to act on behalf of another person. A person who appoints an agent to act on his or her behalf is known as a **principal.** An authorized agent's actions will bind the principal. For example, if an agent is authorized to sign a contract, then it will be the principal, not the agent, who is responsible for the performance of the contract.

A person occasionally appoints an agent or an attorney-in-fact to sign real estate contracts on his or her behalf. This is done by the use of a written agency agreement known as a **power of attorney.** A person who appoints an agent is the principal under the power of attorney, and the agent is known as an attorney-in-fact. Although the agent is known as an attorney-in-fact, the agent need not be a licensed lawyer. Any person competent to enter into a binding contract can be an attorney-in-fact under a power of attorney. An attorney-in-fact only has the power granted to it by the express written agency appointment. A power of attorney is generally prepared in recordable form and is recorded along with any deed or other recorded document signed by the attorney-in-fact. An example of a broad general power of attorney is set out in Exhibit 6–2.

In reviewing contracts signed by an attorney-in-fact, it is necessary to review the power of attorney carefully to make sure the attorney-in-fact is acting within the scope of authority. Powers of attorney cannot be expanded on, nor can any powers be implied. The language must be carefully drawn to provide the attorney with the power to act. For example, a power of attorney that gives the attorney the authority to sell property does not give the attorney the authority to purchase property. When dealing with real property contracts, it is necessary that the agency appointment or power of attorney be written and have the same formality as the contract. For example, if the contract is under seal (usually designated by the word *seal* at the end of the signature lines), the power of attorney must likewise have the same formality and be under seal.

A power of attorney can be revoked at any time by the person appointing the agent. In addition, powers of attorney are automatically revoked by the death of the principal or by the appointment of a new agent for the same purpose. Generally, a power of attorney, unless it is a so-called durable power of attorney, is also revoked by the insanity or incompetence of the principal. Durable powers of attorney have been created to provide that the appointment of the agent will continue despite the later incompetence or insanity of the principal. It is essential to establish, as best one can, that the power of attorney has not been revoked at the time the agent signs the contract. Due to the uncertainties involved when a contract or other legal document is signed by a power of attorney, many institutions and other parties are reluctant to enter into agreements with a party using a power of attorney.

Mutual Agreement

A valid contract requires that an agreement and bargain be struck between the parties to the contract. The parties must agree on the same thing, on the same terms, and at the same time. This situation is referred to as "meeting of the minds." This mutual consent may be manifested by an offer on the part of one party and an acceptance of the offer on the part of the other party.

An **offer** is a promise to do something. A person who makes an offer is often called an **offeror,** and a person to whom an offer has been made is often called an **offeree.** In the case of a real estate contract, an offer can be an offer to purchase made by a buyer or an offer to sell made by a seller. An offer generally must be sufficiently clear to determine what is being offered and must be communicated to the other party. An offer does not result in a contract until the offer has been accepted by the person to whom the offer has been made. The acceptance of the offer must be in response to the offer and, in the case of a real estate contract, must be an acceptance of the exact same terms as the offer. The acceptance must also be communicated by the offeree to the offeror. Generally, an offer can be withdrawn by the offeror at any time prior to receipt of a notice of an acceptance of the offer from the offeree. In addition, an acceptance made by an offeree of the offer that is on different terms is a **counteroffer,** which has the effect of terminating or rescinding the original offer and

power of attorney
Written document authorizing another person to act as one's agent.

offer
A contractual promise to do something.

offeror
A person who makes an offer to contract.

offeree
A person to whom an offer to contract has been made.

counteroffer
A response to an offer by the offeree stating terms of acceptance different from the offer. Counteroffer terminates the original offer and becomes an offer of its own to be accepted or rejected.

EXHIBIT 6–2

Power of Attorney

KNOW ALL MEN BY THESE PRESENTS:

That I, ANDREW J. NELSON, resident of Clay County, Illinois, being desirous of arranging for the transaction of my business through an attorney-in-fact, have appointed, named and consti- tuted, and by these presents do name, constitute and appoint SUSAN T. BRAXTON, a resident of Clay County, Illinois, as my true and lawful attorney-in-fact, and do authorize said attorney- in-fact, for me in my name, place and stead: to execute, and deliver, any and all sale documen- tation necessary in order to close a sale of my property known as the Clay County Office Park and being more particularly described on Exhibit "A" attached hereto and made a part hereof to BURTON INVESTMENTS COMPANY, INC. pursuant to a real estate contract by and between Andrew J. Nelson and Burton Investments Company, Inc. dated December 6, 20____, said sale documents to include but not be limited to, affidavits, general warranty deeds, assignment of warranties, assignment of leases and rents, and general warranty bill of sale.

I hereby further give and grant unto my said attorney-in-fact full power and authority to execute and deliver any and all other instruments and documents and to do and perform any and all other acts necessary and proper to be done in the exercise of any of the foregoing pow- ers as largely, fully, and amply as I might or could do if I were personally present, with full power of substitution and revocation, and I hereby ratify and confirm all that my said attorney-in-fact shall lawfully do or cause to be done by virtue hereof.

It is my intent, and it is expressly understood, that the powers herein granted to my said attorney-in-fact shall not be terminated in the event that I become physically or mentally incompetent to manage my affairs. Said attorney-in-fact shall be authorized to exercise all powers herein granted notwithstanding said incompetency. Said attorney-in-fact shall not be required to seek the appointment of a guardian of my person or property, but may instead exercise all of the powers herein granted.

And I hereby declare that any act or thing lawfully done hereunder by my said attorney-in- fact shall be binding on myself, and my heirs, legal and personal representatives, and assigns, whether the same shall have been done before or after my death or other revocation of this instrument, unless and until notice thereof shall have been received by my said attorney-in- fact. Unless any person has notice of the revocation of this power of attorney, any person rely- ing on these presents shall presume that such power continues to be in full force and effect.

Any banks, bankers, trust companies, savings and loan associations, fiduciaries, deposito- ries, or other institutions, persons, firms, or corporations may act in reliance hereon and shall be fully protected.

My attorney-in-fact herein named shall not be liable for any loss resulting from any action taken by said attorney-in-fact if done in good faith and in the absence of fraud.

Notwithstanding anything contained herein to the contrary, this power may be revoked, and notice of such revocation shall be deemed received by all the world, by written instrument recorded in the Office of the Clerk of the Superior Court of Clay County, Illinois.

IN WITNESS WHEREOF the undersigned hereunto set his hand and seal, this _____ day of _____, _____ .

Signed, sealed and delivered in the
presence of:

_____
Witness

_____ (SEAL)
ANDREW J. NELSON

_____
Notary Public
My Commission Expires:

_____
[NOTARY SEAL]

becoming an offer on its own, which then must be accepted or rejected. For example, Aaron offers to sell a house to Bill for $200,000. Bill responds with an offer to buy the house for $185,000. At this stage of negotiations, Aaron has offered to sell for $200,000, and Bill has offered to buy for $185,000. Bill's offer to buy for $185,000 is a counteroffer to Aaron's offer to sell for $200,000. Bill's counteroffer revokes Aaron's original offer. The only offer that now can be accepted or rejected is Bill's offer to buy for $185,000. Until such time as Aaron and Bill agree on the same price, there is no mutual agreement and no contract.

Consideration

A contract must state the **consideration** flowing from one party to the other or from each to both. Consideration may be money, something of value, or, in many states, just a recital of the agreement of the parties to buy and sell.

consideration

Something of value given to make the promises in a contract enforceable.

Lawful Purpose

A contract must be for a lawful purpose to be enforceable. Generally, all real estate contracts are for a lawful purpose and thus satisfy this test. Contracts to commit crimes or that are against public policy are unenforceable. For example, assume that the owner of a home believes that she would be able to get a better price for the home if she raffled it off in a lottery. The owner sells tickets or chances to win the home, hoping to sell enough tickets to recover more than the sale price for the home. If this type of lottery takes place in a state that makes gambling or lotteries either a crime or against public policy, the agreement would be unenforceable. The winner of the lottery, even though having paid money for the winning ticket, would be unable to require the owner of the home to transfer the home to him or her for the price of the lottery ticket.

Written Agreements

Not every contract must be in writing to be enforceable; however, early in the development of contract law, it was observed that oral agreements were subject to much abuse. Consequently, in 1677, the statute of frauds was enacted in England. Its purpose was to prevent any fraudulent practices as were commonly upheld by perjury in the law courts. The statute of frauds, which has been adopted in almost every state, basically provides that certain contracts are not enforceable unless there exists some written memorandum or agreement that is signed by the party to be charged with the obligation. The statute of frauds requires various categories of contracts to be in writing. These categories are (a) a contract to answer for the debt of another person (guaranty or surety contract); (b) an agreement made on consideration of marriage; (c) any agreement that is not to be performed within one year from the date thereof; and (d) any contract for the sale or transfer of land or any interest in land.

Unless a state's statute of frauds requires a contract to be in writing to be enforceable, an oral contract will be enforceable. Therefore, any contract not listed within a state's statute of frauds as requiring a writing will be enforceable without a writing. The main problem with an oral contract is the ability to prove what the terms of the contract were. Therefore, even in areas where a written contract is not required to be enforceable, people are well advised to reduce the contract to writing so that later if there is a dispute, the terms of the contract can be proven.

Although real estate contracts are generally required to be in writing, there is an exception to this rule. This exception is known as the *doctrine of part performance.* Most states will provide that an oral contract to buy or sell property is enforceable if one of the parties to the contract has partially performed in reliance upon the contract. For example, there is an oral contract between a seller and purchaser to sell a home for $200,000. The purchaser, in reliance upon the contract, tenders payment to the seller of the $200,000. Under these circumstances, the purchaser could require the seller to sell the home for $200,000. One problem with the doctrine of part performance is the ability to prove the performance was made in relation to an oral contract. The purchaser in this example would have to prove by some means that he or she had a contract with the seller to purchase the home in question for $200,000. If the seller denies that such a contract existed, the purchaser will have a difficult burden of proof in establishing its oral contract for the sale of the property and the application of the doctrine of part performance to make such oral contract enforceable. The issue would probably be determined by a jury and would depend on the credibility of the seller's and purchaser's testimony in regard to the alleged contract.

A written real estate contract should contain at least the following essential details: (a) names of the parties (seller and buyer); (b) stated agreement to buy and sell; (c) description of the real property to be bought and sold; (d) purchase price; (e) terms of payment; (f) amount and disposition of the earnest money paid by the purchaser; (g) date of closing (when the transfer of ownership is to take place); (h) statement that "time is of the essence"; (i) if the parties so desire, a list of conditions before the sale; and (j) signature of the parties. Chapter 7 contains a thorough discussion of contract provisions and sample forms of contracts.

REMEDIES FOR BREACH OF A REAL ESTATE CONTRACT

In the event one of the parties to a contract for the purchase and sale of real estate breaches the contract and fails to perform the obligations under the contract, the injured party is entitled to one of the following remedies: (a) specific performance, (b) money damages, (c) rescission, or (d) liquidated damages.

Specific Performance

specific performance

Remedy for breach of real estate contract that requires a defaulting party to perform the promises made in the contract.

The remedy of **specific performance** follows a theory that real property is unique; therefore, when a party defaults under a contract, that party should be required to perform the obligations under the contract. Under the remedy of specific performance, the party in default is ordered by the court to perform. For example, if a seller defaults on a contract, the court orders the seller to sell the real property to the purchaser pursuant to the terms of the contract. This is an ideal remedy for the purchaser because he or she receives what was originally bargained for—the real property at the agreed-to purchase price. Specific performance also can be awarded to a seller against a defaulting purchaser. In this case, the court orders the purchaser to pay the contract price to the seller and receive title to the real property.

One limitation on the use of specific performance is the ability of the defaulting party to perform. For example, a person who does not own a parcel of real property contracts to sell the real property to a purchaser. The seller, then, because of lack of title, fails to perform. The court cannot order specific performance because performance is impossible; therefore, the injured party is left with money damages or rescission.

Specific performance is limited to situations where the contract for the sale of the property is clear and definite as to its terms and is free from fraud or mistake. Specific performance has been denied where the property description in the contract was so vague and uncertain that it would be difficult to tell what property was intended to be bought or sold. Specific performance has been denied where there is a question of fairness in the adequacy of consideration and the enforcement of the contract would not be equitable. For example, if a purchaser and seller entered into a contract whereby property worth $1,000,000 was to be sold, through some mistake of the seller's, for a value of $100,000, the inadequacy of the price may justify a court's decision to deny specific performance.

Money Damages

The theory for money damages is that the injured party is to be placed in the same situation he or she would be in if the contract had been performed, insofar as money can do it. The amount of money damage is the difference between the contract price and the market value of the real property at the time and place of default. For example, a seller can only recover damages for the purchaser's default if the fair market value of the real property is less than the contract price at the time of default. It is only in this circumstance that the seller has lost money as a result of the sale not closing. On the other hand, a purchaser can only recover from a seller for money damages if the fair market value of the real property is more than the purchase price at the time of the default. It is only under this circumstance that the purchaser has lost money as a result of the sale not going through. The determination of fair market value usually is done by expert witnesses such as appraisers.

Assume, for example, that a parcel of property has a fair market value of $200,000. A contract is entered into between a seller and purchaser to sell the property for $180,000. The seller refuses to sell the property to the purchaser and breaches the contract. The purchaser can therefore recover the difference between the fair market value of the property and the purchase price of the property from the seller. This difference would be $200,000 fair market value less $180,000 purchase price, or $20,000 that could be recovered. The seller, under the same set of factual circumstances, could not recover from the purchaser if the purchaser defaulted on the contract. The reason for this is that the purchaser has a contract to buy the property for less than its fair market value. A default by the purchaser under the rule of damages has not damaged the seller. In fact, the seller has received a benefit by the purchaser not buying the property at a price which is $20,000 less than its fair market value. In this situation, the seller would not be able to recover any damages from the purchaser. If the purchaser had agreed to pay $220,000 for the home and then defaulted, then the seller would have suffered damage. The damage would be the difference between fair market value of $200,000 and the purchase price of $220,000. The seller would be entitled to receive $20,000 from the defaulting purchaser.

Rescission

Rescission operates under a different theory than money damages or specific performance. Here, instead of trying to put the injured party in the position he or she would have been in had the contract been performed, the law attempts to place the injured party in the position he or she would have been in had the contract not been entered into. That is, restore the "status" to the time before entering into the contract. The remedy of rescission provides that the contract is to be terminated and the injured party reimbursed for expenses incurred in preparation for the performance of the contract. For example, the seller breaches the obligation to sell property to a purchaser. The purchaser, in preparation of performance of the contract, has hired an attorney to do a title examination and prepare the contract and a surveyor to survey the property. The purchaser has bills totaling $2,000. If the purchaser is awarded rescission, the contract is terminated, and the seller is ordered to pay the purchaser $2,000 as reimbursement for expenses.

The remedy of rescission is also used when a seller or purchaser has committed fraud in connection with a real estate sale. For example, a seller of a home represented verbally to the purchasers that the basement did not leak. Following the purchase of the home, the purchasers found that there were severe flooding problems in the basement. The purchasers may sue the seller for damages caused by the flooding, or decide they do not want the home and sue to rescind the contract. If the rescission is successful, the purchasers would return the home to the seller and would receive from the seller the purchase price paid for the home.

rescission

Remedy for default of a real estate contract wherein the contract is terminated and the defaulting party must reimburse the injured party for expenses incurred in connection with the contract.

Rescission can be waived. Rescission may be waived when the purchaser's conduct amounts to a recognition of the transaction or the purchaser acts in a manner inconsistent with a repudiation of a contract. Once rescission is waived, it cannot be revived. Improvements made to the property by a purchaser may constitute a waiver of the right of rescission.

Failure to timely rescind can also result in a waiver of the right of rescission. A purchaser generally must rescind the contract in a timely fashion as soon as the facts supporting the rescission are discovered.

It is easy to see why money damages, specific performance, and rescission are inconsistent remedies. It is impossible to require a party to perform and collect money damages at the same time. A party cannot rescind or terminate the contract and also have the court order the performance under the contract. Because these remedies are inconsistent, the injured party is entitled to only one of the remedies. However, at the time of suit, to enforce the contract, the party need not "elect" a certain remedy but instead may ask the court to award in the alternative all three forms of relief. The courts then will decide, after all the evidence is presented, which remedy will be awarded. For example, if the seller does not own the real property or the real property has serious title defects that cannot be corrected, then performance is not granted. Instead, the purchaser is left with the remedy of either money damages or rescission. In the same example, if it turns out that the fair market value of the real property and the contract price are the same, then the purchaser cannot recover money damages but is left with rescission as the only remedy.

Liquidated Damages

liquidated damages

Amount of money agreed on by the parties to a contract to be the damages in the event of a default of the contract.

Sometimes the parties do not want to rely on money damages, specific performance, or rescission as a remedy for breach of contract and instead agree within the contract that a certain sum of money is to be paid in the event of default. This agreed-upon sum, called **liquidated damages,** is enforceable, provided it does not result in a penalty. The amount agreed on must be reasonable—close to what actual money damages would be in the event of default. When liquidated damages are included within a contract, they typically are the exclusive remedy. The parties can only collect liquidated damages, unless for some reason the provision is not enforceable. It is not unusual for contracts to provide that the purchaser will forfeit earnest money as liquidated damages in the event of the purchaser's default.

A sample contract liquidated damages provision is shown in Example 6–1.

Example 6–1

In the event the transaction contemplated hereby is not closed because of Purchaser's default, the Earnest Money Deposit shall be paid to Seller as full liquidated damages for such failure to close, the parties acknowledging the difficulty of ascertaining Seller's damages in such circumstances, whereupon neither party hereto shall have any further rights, claims, or liabilities under this Agreement except for the provisions that are made to survive the termination or cancellation of this Agreement. Said liquidated damages shall be Seller's sole and exclusive remedy, and Seller shall expressly not have the right to seek specific performance.

These contract provisions must be drafted carefully or the forfeiture may result in an unenforceable liquidated damage provision. This problem is illustrated in the case *Southeastern Land Fund, Inc. v. Real Estate World, Inc.,* 227 S.E.2d 340.

 **CASE**   Southeastern Land Fund, Inc. v. Real Estate World, Inc.
237 Ga. 227, 227 S.E.2d 340 (Ga. 1976)

INGRAM, Justice.

Certiorari was granted in this case[1] for this court to consider whether a provision in a real estate sales contract, providing for the payment of earnest money, should be considered as a provision for liquidated damages. The Court of Appeals concluded this provision was a penalty and could not be enforced.

The litigation began when the seller filed suit against the buyer who defaulted under the contract. The buyer had paid $5,000 in cash as earnest money when the contract was signed. Thereafter, a promissory note for $45,000, representing additional earnest money, was executed and delivered by the buyer to the seller pursuant to the contract. The buyer defaulted at closing and the seller sued the buyer to collect the $45,000 note. The seller obtained a summary judgment in the trial court and the buyer's motion for summary judgment and counterclaim for return of the $5,000 earnest money were denied.

On appeal to the Court of Appeals, that court reversed in a 6–3 decision and held the earnest money provision of the contract amounted to a penalty. The Court of Appeals also ruled that the buyer's motion for summary judgment should have been granted by the trial court.

The contract provides: "In the event purchaser defaults hereunder after having paid the additional earnest money [$45,000] . . . seller shall be entitled to retain all original earnest money [$5,000] paid hereunder as partial liquidated damages occasioned by such default, to collect the proceeds of the indebtedness owed by purchaser as additional earnest money as further partial liquidated damages occasioned by such default, and to pursue any and all remedies available to him at law or equity including, but not limited to, an action for specific performance of this contract."

[1, 2] If, as the Court of Appeals found, this provision in the contract was a penalty, or is unenforceable as a liquidated damages provision, then the buyer can prevail in asserting a defense to the enforcement of the $45,000 note. If, on the other hand, this is a proper provision for liquidated damages, then the seller can prevail in enforcing the note. Of course, whether a provision represents liquidated damages or a penalty does not depend upon the label the parties place on the payment but rather depends on the effect it was intended to have and whether it was reasonable. See *Lytle v. Scottish American Mortgage Co.,* 122 Ga. 458, 50 S.E. 402 (1905). Where the parties do not undertake to estimate damages in advance of the breach and instead provide for both a forfeiture [penalty] plus actual damages, the amount, even though called

liquidated damages, is instead an unenforceable penalty. See *Foote & Davis Co. v. Malony,* 115 Ga. 985, 42 S.E. 413 (1902).

[3] The seller argues that a seller who is not in default may *always* retain the earnest money paid by the buyer and sue for actual damages above the amount of earnest money received under the contract. We do not agree with this argument and the seller cites no authority that support it. While it is true that the earnest money feature of a real estate contract distinguishes it to some extent from a wholly executory contract, the same basic contract rules are used to determine available remedies for the breach of a real estate sales contract as for the breach of other contracts. This general contract law of remedies for a breach, as well as the intent of the parties in providing specific remedies in the contract, must be used in analyzing and deciding each particular case.

[4] Depending on the language used in the contract and the discernible intent of the parties, the existence of an earnest money provision in a real estate sales contract can have one of three effects in the case of a breach by the buyer. First, the money could be considered as partial payment of any actual damages which can be proven as the result of the buyer's breach.[2] Second, the money could be applied as part payment of the purchase price in the enforcement of the contract in a suit for specific performance by the seller. Third, the money could be liquidated damages for breach of the contract by the buyer. A provision for earnest money cannot, however, under Georgia law, be used for all three results as we shall see.

[5–7] Of course, if the real estate sales contract is silent on the remedy to be provided, the non breaching seller is entitled to his proven actual damages. The ordinary measure of damages is the difference between the contract price and the market value of the property at the time of the buyer's breach. *Shives v. Young,* 81 Ga. App. 30, 57 S.E.2d 874 (1950). If the nonbreaching seller sues for actual damages, the earnest money then becomes a fund out of which those damages are partially paid if the proven damages exceed the amount of the earnest money.[3]

[8] Even if the real estate contract is silent as to the remedy of specific performance, it is still available as a remedy unless it is specifically excluded as a remedy. In the cases in

---

[1]The decision of the Court of Appeals is reported in 137 Ga. App. 771, 224 S.E.2d 747 (1976).

[2]We do not decide in this case whether a breaching buyer may sue in the first instance for recovery of earnest money if the seller suffers no actual damages.

[3]Apparently, in many instances where real estate sales contracts provide that earnest money will be retained by the seller to be applied toward the seller's damages, as a result of the buyer's default, no suit is brought by the seller to prove his actual damages and likewise the buyer does not contest whether the seller has actually suffered damages or the extent of them. In these circumstances, the earnest money is really treated by the parties as liquidated damages, after a breach by the buyer, even though the parties did not agree to liquidate the damages in their contract.

(continued)

which rescission has been used as a remedy the parties are put as nearly as is possible back to the status quo ante. See *Lightfoot v. Brower*, 133 Ga. 766, 66 S.E. 1094 (1909); *Walter Tally, Inc. v. Council*, 109 Ga.App.100, 135 S.E.2d 515 (1964); *Woodruff v. Camp*, 101 Ga. App. 124, 112 S.E. 2d 831 (1960). Cf. *Higgins v. Kenney*, 159 Ga. 736 S.E. 827 (1924).

[9] Of course, Georgia law also recognizes that the parties may agree in their contract to a sum to liquidate their damages. Code Ann. §§ 20-1402 provides: "Damages are given as compensation for the injury sustained. If the parties agree in their contract what the damages for a breach shall be, they are said to be liquidated, and unless the agreement violates some principle of law, *the parties are bound thereby*." (Emphasis supplied.) See also Code Ann. §§ 20-1403.

[10] In deciding whether a contract provision is enforceable as liquidated damages, the court makes a tripartite inquiry to determine if the following factors are present:

"First, the injury caused by the breach must be difficult or impossible of accurate estimation; second, the parties must intend to provide for damages rather than for a penalty; and third, the sum stipulated must be reasonable pre-estimate of the probable loss." Calamari & Perillo, *The Law of Contracts*, 367 (1970). See *Tuten v. Morgan*, 160 Ga. 90, 92, 127 S.E. 143 (1924), and *Bernhardt v. Federal Terra Cotta Co.*, 24 Ga. App. 635, 101 S.E. 588 (1919). See also *Martin v. Lott*, 144 Ga. 660, 87 S.E. 902 (1915).

[11] Another feature implicit in the concept of liquidated damages in addition to the above actors is that both parties are bound by their agreement. See Code Ann. §§ 20-1402. See e.g., *Jarro Building Industries Corp. v. Schwartz*, 54 Misc. 2d 13, 281 N.Y.S.2d 420 (1967). A nonbreaching party who has agreed to accept liquidated damages cannot elect after a breach to take actual damages should they prove greater than the sum specified. The breaching party cannot complain that the actual damages are less than those specified as liquidated damages. The liquidated damages become the "maximum as well as the minimum sum that can be collected." *Mayor etc. of Brunswick v. Aetna Indemnity Co.*, 4 Ga. App. 722, 727,62 S.E. 475, 477 (1908).

The problem that this particular contract provision raises is whether the seller has tried to retain a right to elect to sue for actual damages rather than liquidated damages and in so doing has rendered the purported liquidated damages provision unenforceable. This particular paragraph in the contract provides for "partial" liquidated damages. This can be read that the parties intended for the two "partial" liquidated damages

provisions to comprise the whole. However, it is also susceptible to the construction that these two partial liquidated damages were not intended to be the sole damages remedy for this particular breach of contract.

[12] The contract provision that included the retention of the right to elect specific performance as an alternative remedy to damages poses no problem in our analysis as it does not render a valid liquidated damages provision unenforceable. See, e.g., *Wells v. First National Exhibitor's Circuit, Inc.*, 149 Ga. 200, 99 S.E. 615 (1919). "The law is now well settled that a liquidated damages provision will not in and of itself be construed as barring the remedy of specific performance." *Rubenstein v. Rubenstein*, 23 N.Y.2d 293, 296, N.Y.S.2d 354, 244 N.E.2d 49 (1968). To bar specific performance there should be explicit language in the liquidated damages provision that it is to be the sole remedy. See also Restatement, Contracts §§ 378. Thus the retention of the right to elect specific performance in this contract does not render the purported liquidated damages provision invalid. The answer must be found elsewhere in the construction of these contract provisions.

[13, 14] We think a correct resolution of this issue must be found in the doctrine that "in cases of doubt the courts favor the construction which holds the stipulated sum to be a penalty, and limits the recovery to the amount of damages actually shown, rather than a liquidation of the damages." *Mayor & Council of Brunswick v. Aetna Indemnity Co.*, supra, 4 Ga. App. p. 728, 62 S.E. p. 478. If the parties intended for the $5,000 and the $45,000 to represent the "maximum as well as the minimum sum that can be collected," from the buyer's breach, the contract should have made it clear that this was the effect intended by these provisions. It is the lingering ambiguity inherent in these provisions of the contract that persuades us to affirm the result reached by the Court of Appeals in construing the contract.

In summary, we hold that these contract provisions are not enforceable under Georgia law as proper liquidated damages provisions in this real estate sales contract. It follows that the trial court erred in granting summary judgment in favor of the seller and we affirm the Court of Appeals reversal of that portion of the trial court's order. However, the existence of the actual damages, if any, to be proven by the nonbreaching seller precludes the grant of the buyer's motion for summary judgment. Therefore, that portion of the Court of Appeals opinion directing the grant of the buyer's motion for summary judgment must be reversed.

JUDGMENT AFFIRMED IN PART; REVERSED IN PART.

REAL ESTATE BROKER

Although real estate may be sold without the services of a real estate broker, many sale transactions are arranged by a real estate broker, who earns a commission in matching a buyer and seller.

A real estate broker is subject to license by various state agencies. The aims of licensing are to protect the public from unscrupulous practices and to establish professional standards of conduct. Most licensing criteria require that the real estate broker demonstrate a certain degree of competence in the area of real property law and maintain continuing education credits. Generally, a real estate license authority may deny a license to a person applying to be a broker if the person does not have a good reputation for honesty, trustworthiness, and integrity; has been convicted of certain enumerated crimes; or has been sanctioned by any regulatory agency for violating a law regulating the sale of real estate. A broker who does not have a license or whose license has been suspended is not entitled to receive a real estate commission.

The National Association of Realtors™ is a trade association for real estate agents. Interesting information can be found on its Web page, including a code of ethics, membership information, and current events of interest to real estate agents and brokers. The Web page can be visited at *http://www.realtor.org*.

Agency Relationship

The relationship between a real estate broker and his or her client is known as an *agency relationship*. An agency relationship is one based on trust and confidence of the parties and is a fiduciary relationship. The client who can either be a seller or buyer of real property is known as the principal in the relationship, and the real estate broker is the agent. The broker is also a fiduciary. A **fiduciary** is a person who holds a special relationship of confidence and trust to a principal and owes to the principal a duty to exercise all of the affairs of the principal in good faith and with loyalty. An agent or fiduciary also has the obligation to do what is best for the principal and not to self-deal or seek any benefit from a transaction that would be a detriment to the principal. For example, an agent who is hired by a principal to seek out and identify commercial properties that the principal would be interested in buying cannot, while in the employment of the principal, find such commercial property and then, as an agent, invest in such properties on his or her own behalf. This type of self-dealing would be a breach of the fiduciary obligation that the agent owes to the principal.

Generally, an agent owes certain other duties or responsibilities to a principal. In several states these duties comprise (1) a duty to follow the instructions of the principal, (2) a duty to exercise reasonable care and skill and performance of the agent's duties, (3) a duty to fully disclose all matters the agent becomes aware of relating to the agency relationship, and (4) a duty to account for any money belonging to the principal that comes into the agent's possession.

An agency relationship is a bilateral relationship, and a principal owes certain duties and obligations to the agent. Generally, these duties are (1) a duty to compensate the agent for his or her work, (2) a duty to reimburse the agent for any expenditures the agent has reasonably incurred in connection with the performance of the agency, and (3) a duty to indemnify the agent against any third-party claims that may be made against the agent due to his or her performance under the agency agreement.

An agent may also have the power and authority to bind the principal to agreements entered into or actions taken by the agent on behalf of a principal. The authority of an agent to bind a principal may be divided into both express authority and implied authority. **Express authority** is authority that has been clearly given by the principal to the agent. This authority generally is given in written form, such as a listing agreement or property management agreement. For example, it is not unusual for owners of apartments to hire a property manager to manage the leasing and maintenance of the apartment units. Generally, the owner will enter into a property management agreement with the agent outlining the terms under which the agent may lease apartments to prospective tenants. The actual leasing and in many cases the execution of the leases will be done by

fiduciary

Person who holds a special relationship of confidence and trust to a principal and owes to the principal a duty to exercise all of the affairs of the principal in good faith and with loyalty.

express authority

Authority that has been clearly given by the principal to the agent.

the agent. Although the agent signs the leases, the principal is responsible to the tenant for the lease terms.

Implied authority, on the other hand, is not authority expressly given to an agent by the principal. Instead, implied authority is implied by law to be those things necessary and proper for the agent to carry out the duties of the agency. For example, an agent or property manager hired by a property owner to lease apartments may also have the implied authority to advertise the rental of such apartments in newspapers and to contract for office supplies and other materials necessary to enable them to lease the apartments. The principal as the party responsible for all acts of the agent, including acts done by implied authority, would be responsible to pay the cost of the advertising as well as honor the contract for the office supplies and other materials.

Traditionally, real estate brokers represented owners of properties who were interested in selling their property. These brokers would find a purchaser to buy the property and would collect a commission from the seller. The broker, although he or she spent most of his or her time with prospective purchasers of the property, was really an agent for the seller, and it was the seller to whom the agent had a fiduciary obligation.

Recently, there has been a growth of real estate brokers who specialize in representing purchasers. These brokers will work with persons who are interested in purchasing property. Their services may involve identifying potential of properties to purchase as well as negotiating the terms of the purchase. A purchaser's agent may be paid a commission from the owner of the property once the sale is completed or may receive a commission from the purchaser.

Many states also recognize dual agents. A *dual agent* is a broker who simultaneously has a client relationship with both the seller and purchaser in the same real estate transaction. Although a dual agency may be legal, it is easy to see how it is difficult for a dual agent to perform fiduciary obligations to two principals who do not have a mutual interest in the transaction. A dual agent trying to get the best price for a property on behalf of the seller and, at the same time, get a fair price for the purchaser may find his or her duties of loyalty and good faith strained. Generally, a broker may only act as a dual agent after a full disclosure of the relationship and with the written consent of both buyer and seller.

Services Provided by a Real Estate Broker

A real estate broker can provide a number of useful services that can assist an owner in the sale of real property. A broker may specialize in a special type of property such as high priced homes or commercial shopping centers or property located in certain geographic areas of the community. This specialization enables a broker to assist an owner in determining a correct price for the property, as well as to identify potential purchasers who might be interested in the property.

Pricing property for sale is a very important aspect of the transaction and one where a broker can provide a valuable service. Ideally, the owner wants the best price that he or she can receive from the sale of the property; however, one must be realistic concerning this price. Property which is placed on the market at too high a price may not sell for a long period of time or until the price is reduced. Both a delay in sale and a reduction in price are unpleasant for the owner. On the other hand, if a property is priced too low, even though a sale might quickly take place, the owner may likewise be unhappy because of money that was lost in pricing the property. A real estate broker generally has access to figures concerning what similar properties have sold for in the community. Using a database that shows comparison pricing, as well as both new listings and sales, enables a broker to provide an owner with pricing information to accomplish the owner's objectives of both a quick sale and a fair price.

---

implied authority

Implied authority is implied by law to be those things necessary and proper for the agent to carry out the duties of the agency.

A real estate broker can also help an owner prepare a property for sale. A homeowner who has lived in a home for several years cannot see it with the same eyes as a harried house-hunter. A skilled real estate broker can quickly take in the scene and suggest ways to improve the property's appearance for sale. For example, new paint will brighten up the house or walls and make it more attractive. Removing clutter from the home will make it appear more spacious. A broker can also compile a sale booklet for prospective purchasers containing information about taxes, utility rates, nearby schools, parks, and available transportation.

A broker can assist an owner in advertising a property for sale and hold "open house" tours of the property. Generally, during these "open house" tours, the owner of the home is not present. A broker will generally prefer to work without the owner so that the broker can present the home for sale in an objective and professional manner.

A real estate broker's main service to an owner is to find a purchaser. A good broker who is constantly working with a group of potential purchasers will become familiar with their needs or wants with respect to property. For example, a residential broker may work with a young couple who is looking for their first home. The broker may have shown the couple a number of houses that did not meet their tastes, requirements, or budget. Over a period of time spent with the couple, the broker will learn what types of properties they are interested in, what they do not like, and what they can afford. Once a property comes on the market that seems to satisfy all of the couple's requirements, the broker can quickly identify the property and hopefully assist in the consummation of the sale.

Although real estate brokers are not attorneys, they do many things that resemble the practice of law. It is not unusual for many states to permit real estate brokers to prepare contracts for the sale of real property. A broker may also act as an escrow agent for the purpose of holding earnest money deposits or other payments in connection with the contract. Real estate brokers are experienced in closing sales for real estate and often assist both sellers and purchasers in preparing for the closing. It is not unusual for a real estate broker to arrange for the preparation of title examinations, surveys, insurance, inspection reports, and other matters that must be attended to in order for the sale to take place.

LISTING AGREEMENTS

Owners hire brokers to sell real property with a **listing (agency) agreement.** A form of listing agreement is shown as Exhibit 6–3. The main types of listing agreements are open, exclusive, and exclusive right to sell. Brokers' listing agreements usually provide that the real property is to be sold during a period of time (a listing period). These agreements also state that if the real property is introduced to a number of people during the listing period and sold to one of the people after the listing period, the agent is entitled to a commission. A seller should require that the agent submit to the seller a list of people to whom the real property has been shown before the expiration of the listing agreement. The agent also should agree that if the real property is sold to one of these people within some reasonable period of time (e.g., six months) after the listing expiration, a commission will be due and payable.

listing agreement

Agreement entered into between an owner and a real estate broker retaining the real estate broker to assist the owner in selling real property.

Open Listing

Under an open listing, an owner of property hires an agent or a broker to sell the real property, but the owner still reserves the right to hire other agents or brokers and to sell the real property on his or her own efforts. The first agent or broker to bring a purchaser who is

EXHIBIT 6–3

Exclusive Seller Listing Agreement

Reprinted with permission of Georgia Association of Realtors, Inc.

EXCLUSIVE SELLER LISTING AGREEMENT
(ALSO REFERRED TO AS EXCLUSIVE SELLER BROKERAGE AGREEMENT)

2005 Printing

**State law prohibits Broker from representing Seller as a client without first entering into a written agreement
with Seller under O.C.G.A. § 10-6A-1 et. seq.**

For and in consideration of the mutual promises contained herein and other good and valuable consideration, _____
_____ as seller (hereinafter referred to as "Seller"), and _____ _____
_____ as broker and its affiliated licensees (hereinafter collectively referred to as "Broker") do hereby enter into this Agreement, this
_____ day of _____, 20 _____.

1. **Exclusive Listing Agreement.** Seller hereby grants to Broker the exclusive right and privilege as the agent of the Seller to show and offer for sale
    the following described property as the real estate broker for Seller: All that tract of land lying and being in Land Lot _____ of the _____
    District, _____ Section of _____ County, Georgia, and being known as Address _____, _____ City,
    Georgia Zip Code _____, according to the present system of numbering in and around this area, being more particularly described as
    Lot _____, Block _____, Unit _____, Phase/Section _____ of _____
    ____ Subdivision, as recorded in Plat Book _____, Page _____, _____ County, Georgia records together with all fixtures,
    landscaping, improvements, and appurtenances, all being hereinafter collectively referred to as the "Property." The full legal description of the
    Property is the same as is recorded with the Clerk of the Superior Court of the county in which the Property is located and is made a part of this
    Agreement by reference. The term of this Agreement shall begin on the _____ day of _____, 20 _____ and shall continue
    through the _____ day of _____, 20 _____ (hereinafter referred to as "Listing Period").

2. **Independent Contractor Relationship.** This Agreement shall create an independent contractor relationship between Broker and Seller. Broker
    shall at no time be considered an employee of Seller. Seller acknowledges that the real estate licensees affiliated with Broker are independent
    contractors of Broker, and are not Broker's employees.

3. **Broker's Duties to Seller.** Broker's sole duties to Seller shall be to:
    A. Use Broker's best efforts to procure a buyer ready, willing, and able to purchase Property at a sales price of at least $ _____ (which
        amount includes the commission) or any other price acceptable to Seller;
    B. Assist to the extent requested by Seller, in negotiating the terms of and filling out a pre-printed real estate purchase and sale
        agreement; and
    C. Comply with all applicable laws in performing its duties hereunder including the Brokerage Relationships in Real Estate Transaction Act,
        O.C.G.A. § 10-6A-1 et. seq.

4. **Seller's Duties.** Seller represents that Seller:
    A. presently has title to Property or has full authority to enter into this Agreement;
    B. will cooperate with Broker to sell Property to prospective buyers and will refer all inquiries concerning the sale of Property to the Broker
        during the terms of this agreement;
    C. will make Property available for showing at reasonable times as requested by Broker; and
    D. will provide Broker with accurate information regarding Property (including information concerning all adverse material facts pertaining to
        the physical condition of Property); and
    E. must fully comply with all state and federal laws.

5. **Marketing.**
    A. **Advertisements:** Broker may advertise Property for sale in all media and may photograph and/or videotape and use the photographs and/
        or videotapes in connection with Broker's marketing efforts. Seller agrees not to place any advertisements on the property or to advertise
        the property for sale in any media except with the prior written consent of Broker. Broker is also hereby authorized to place Broker's "For
        Sale" sign on Property. Broker is authorized to procure buyers to purchase Property in cooperation with other real estate brokers and their
        affiliated licensees. Broker may distribute listing and sales information (including the sales price) to them and other members of the mul-
        tiple listing service(s), and said cooperating brokers and their licensees may with permission of Broker (which permission may be granted
        or denied in the sole discretion of Broker) republish such information on their Internet web sites. Broker and other real estate brokers and
        their affiliated licensees may show Property without first notifying Seller.

(continued)

EXHIBIT 6–3

Exclusive Seller Listing Agreement *(continued)*

B. **Lockboxes:** A lockbox may be used in connection with the marketing of Property. There have been isolated instances of reported burglaries of homes on which lockboxes have been placed and for which the lockbox has been alleged to have been used to access the home. In order to minimize the risk of misuse of the lockbox, Broker recommends against the use of lockboxes on door handles that can be unscrewed from the outside or on other parts of the home from which the lockbox can be easily removed. Since others will have access to Property, Seller agrees to either remove all valuables or put them in a secure place.

C. **Multiple Listing Service(s):** Seller acknowledges that Broker is a member of the following multiple listing service(s): _____ _____ ("Service(s)"). Broker agrees to file this listing with said Service(s) within forty-eight hours after Seller signs the same (excepting weekends, federal holidays and postal holidays). Seller acknowledges that the Service(s) is/are not a party to this Agreement and is/are not responsible for errors or omissions on the part of Seller or Broker. Seller agrees to indemnify Service(s) from and against any and all claims, liabilities, damages or losses arising out of or related to the listing and sale of Property.

6. **Commission.**

A. Seller agrees to pay Broker at closing a commission (hereinafter "Commission") of _____ percent (%) of the sales price of Property or $ _____ in the event that during the term of this Agreement:

 1. Broker procures a buyer ready, willing, and able to purchase Property at the price described above; or

 2. Seller enters into a contract for the sale or exchange of Property with any buyer, whether through the efforts of Broker or any other person, including Seller.

B. Broker shall share this Commission with a cooperating broker, if any, who procures the buyer of Property by paying such cooperating broker _____ percent (%) of the sales price of Property OR $ _____. Cooperating brokers are expressly intended to be third-party beneficiaries under this Agreement.

C. In the event that Seller sells or contracts to sell Property to any buyer introduced to Property by Broker within _____ days after the expiration of the Listing Period, then Seller shall pay the commission referenced above to Broker at the closing of the sale or exchange of Property. Notwithstanding the above, in the event that Property is sold to the prospective buyer by or through another licensed broker with whom Seller has signed an exclusive right to sell listing agreement, then no commission shall be owed to Broker by virtue of this Agreement. The commission obligations set forth herein shall survive the termination of this Agreement.

7. **Limits on Broker's Authority and Responsibility.** Seller acknowledges and agrees that Broker:

A. may show other properties to prospective buyers who are interested in Property;

B. shall not be responsible to advise Seller on any matter including but not limited to the following: any matter which could have been revealed through a survey, title search or inspection of Property; the condition of Property, any portion thereof, or any item therein; building products and construction techniques; the necessity or cost of any repairs to Property; mold; hazardous or toxic materials or substances; termites and other wood destroying organisms; the tax or legal consequences of this transaction; the availability and cost of utilities or community amenities; the appraised or future value of Property; any condition(s) existing off Property which may affect Property; the terms, conditions and availability of financing; and the uses and zoning of Property whether permitted or proposed. Seller acknowledges that Brokers are not experts with respect to the above matters and that, if any of these matters or any other matters are of concern to them, they should seek independent expert advice relative thereto. Seller acknowledges that Broker shall not be responsible to monitor or supervise any portion of any construction or repairs to Property and that such tasks clearly fall outside the scope of real estate brokerage services;

C. shall owe no duties to Seller nor have any authority to act on behalf of Seller other than what is set forth in this Agreement;

D. may make all disclosures required by law;

E. may disclose all information about Property to others; and

F. shall, under no circumstances, have any liability greater than the amount of the real estate commission paid hereunder to Broker (excluding any commission amount paid to a cooperating real estate broker, if any).

G. shall be held harmless from any and all claims, causes of action, or damages arising out of or relating to:

 1. inaccurate and/or incomplete information provided by Broker to a prospective buyer;

 2. earnest money handled by anyone other than Broker; or

 3. any injury to persons on Property and/or loss of or damage to Property or anything contained therein.

8. **Extension.** If during the term of this Agreement, Seller and a prospective buyer enter into a real estate sales contract which is not consummated for any reason whatsoever, then the original expiration date of this Agreement shall be extended for the number of days that the Property was under contract.

9. **Seller's Property Disclosure Statement and Official Georgia Wood Infestation Report.** Within _____ days of the date of this Agreement, Seller agrees to provide Broker with a current, fully executed Seller's Property Disclosure Statement. Additionally, within _____ days of the date of this Agreement, Seller agrees to provide Broker with an Official Georgia Wood Infestation Report dated not more than 180 days prior to the date of this Agreement. Broker is hereby authorized to distribute the same to prospective buyers interested in Property.

(continued)

EXHIBIT 6–3

Exclusive Seller Listing Agreement *(continued)*

10. <u>Required State Law Disclosures.</u>
   A. Broker agrees to keep confidential all information that Seller asks to be kept confidential by express request or instruction unless the Seller permits such disclosure by subsequent word or conduct or such disclosure is required by law.
   B. Broker may not knowingly give customers false information.
   C. In the event of a conflict between Broker's duty not to give customers false information and the duty to keep the confidences of Seller, the duty not to give customers false information shall prevail.
   D. Unless specified below, Broker has no other known agency relationships with other parties which would conflict with any interests of Seller (except that Broker may represent other buyers, sellers, landlords, and tenants in buying, selling or leasing property).

11. <u>Disclosure of Potentially Fraudulent Activities.</u>
   A. To help prevent fraud in real estate transactions, Seller does hereby give Broker permission to report any suspicious, unusual and/or potentially illegal or fraudulent activity (including but not limited to mortgage fraud) to:
      1. Governmental officials, agencies and/or authorities and/or
      2. Any mortgage lender, mortgage insurer, mortgage investor and/or title insurance company which could potentially be harmed if the activity was in fact fraudulent or illegal.
   B. Seller acknowledges that Broker does not have special expertise with respect to detecting fraud in real estate transactions. Therefore, Seller acknowledges that:
      1. Activities which are fraudulent or illegal may be undetected by Broker and
      2. Activities which are lawful and/or routine may be reported by Broker as being suspicious, unusual or potentially illegal or fraudulent.

12. <u>Broker's Policy on Agency.</u> Unless Broker indicates below that Broker is not offering a specific agency relationship, the types of agency relationships offered by Broker are: seller agency, buyer agency, designated agency, dual agency, landlord agency, and tenant agency.

   The agency relationship(s), if any, **NOT** offered by Broker is/are the following: _____ .

13. <u>Dual Agency Disclosure.</u> *[Applicable only if Broker's agency policy is to practice dual agency]* If Seller and a prospective buyer are both being represented by the same Broker, Seller is aware that Broker is acting as a dual agent in this transaction and consents to the same. Seller has been advised that:
   A. In serving as a dual agent, Broker is representing two clients whose interests are or at times could be different or even adverse;
   B. Broker will disclose all adverse, material facts relevant to the transaction and actually known to the dual agent to all parties in the transaction except for information made confidential by request or instructions from either client which is not otherwise required to be disclosed by law;
   C. Seller does not have to consent to dual agency and, the consent of the Seller to dual agency has been given voluntarily and the Seller has read and understands the brokerage engagement agreement.
   D. Notwithstanding any provision to the contrary contained herein, Seller hereby directs Broker, while acting as a dual agent, to keep confidential and not reveal to the other party any information which could materially and adversely affect their negotiating position.
   E. Broker or Broker's affiliated licensees will timely disclose to each client the nature of any material relationship with other clients other than that incidental to the transaction. A material relationship shall mean any actually known personal, familiar, or business relationship between Broker and a client which would impair the ability of Broker to exercise fair and independent judgment relative to another client. The other party whom Broker may represent in the event of dual agency may or may not be identified at the time Seller enters into this Agreement. If any party is identified after the Agreement and has a material relationship with Broker, then Broker shall timely provide to Seller a disclosure of the nature of such relationship.

14. <u>Designated Agency Disclosure.</u> *[Applicable only if Broker's agency policy is to practice designated agency]* Seller does hereby consent to Broker acting in a designated agency capacity in transactions in which Broker is representing Seller and a prospective buyer. With designated agency, the Broker assigns one or more of its affiliated licensees exclusively to represent the Seller and one or more of its other affiliated licensees exclusively to represent the prospective buyer.

15. <u>Notices.</u> Except as otherwise provided herein, all notices required or permitted hereunder shall be in writing, signed by the party giving the notice and delivered either:
   A. in person;
   B. by an overnight delivery service, prepaid;
   C. by facsimile transmission (FAX) to Broker and Seller at their respective FAX telephone numbers, if any, identified on the signature page of this Agreement (provided that an original of the notice shall be promptly sent thereafter if so requested by the party receiving the same); or
   D. by the United States Postal Service, postage prepaid, registered or certified return receipt requested.

   The parties agree that a faxed signature of a party constitutes an original signature binding upon that party. Notices shall be deemed to be given as of the date and time they are actually received, except for Fax notices which shall be deemed to have been given and received as of the date and time they are transmitted provided that the sending FAX produces a written confirmation showing the correct date and time of

(continued)

EXHIBIT 6–3

Exclusive Seller Listing Agreement *(continued)*

the transmission and the telephone number referenced herein to which the notice should have been sent. All notice requirements referenced herein shall be strictly construed. Any notice sent by FAX shall be sent to such other FAX number as the receiving party may from time to time specify by notice to the party sending the FAX.

16. <u>Early Termination.</u> Broker or Seller shall have the right to terminate this Agreement at any time by giving the other party written notice; how-ever, such a termination shall not limit Broker's right to collect any commission earned or owing as of the date of termination or to which Broker is entitled to collect herein after the termination of this Agreement. It being expressly agreed that such rights shall survive the termination of this Agreement.

17. <u>Governing Law.</u> This Agreement may be signed in multiple counterparts and shall be governed by and interpreted pursuant to the laws of the State of Georgia.

18. <u>Entire Agreement.</u> This Agreement constitutes the sole and entire agreement between the parties. No representation, promise or induce-ment not included in this Agreement shall be binding upon any party hereto. This Agreement and the terms and conditions herein may not be amended, modified or waived except by the written agreement of Seller. The failure of the parties to adhere strictly to the terms and conditions of this Agreement shall not constitute a waiver of the right of the parties later to insist on such strict adherence.

SPECIAL STIPULATIONS: The following Special Stipulations, if conflicting with any exhibit, addendum, or preceding paragraph, shall control:

BY SIGNING THIS AGREEMENT, SELLER ACKNOWLEDGES THAT: (1) SELLER HAS READ ALL PROVISIONS AND DISCLOSURES MADE HEREIN; (2) SELLER UNDERSTANDS ALL SUCH PROVISIONS AND DISCLOSURES AND HAS ENTERED INTO THIS AGREEMENT VOLUNTARILY; AND (3) SELLER IS NOT SUBJECT TO A CURRENT LISTING AGREEMENT WITH ANY OTHER BROKER.

RECEIPT OF A COPY OF THIS AGREEMENT IS HEREBY ACKNOWLEDGED BY SELLER.
The above Agreement is hereby accepted, _____ o'clock _____ .m., on the _____ day of _____, 20 _____.

_____ _____
Broker Seller's Signature

_____ _____ _____
MLS Office Code Brokerage Firm License Number Print or Type Name

Broker's Phone# _____ & FAX# _____

             _____
             Seller's Signature

By: _____
   Broker or Broker's Affiliated Licensee Print or Type Name

_____ Phone# _____ FAX# _____
Print or Type Name

_____ Address: _____
Agent's Georgia Real Estate License Number

ready, willing, and able to purchase the real property at the price demanded by the seller earns the commission. Because open listings can result in a free-for-all, with a number of brokers and agents competing for the commission, most brokers or agents shy away from open listings. They would prefer to use energy and time on listings that increase their chances for a commission.

Exclusive Listing

Under an exclusive listing, an owner hires only one broker or agent to assist in the sale of the real property. The owner still reserves the right to sell the real property, and if the owner's efforts result in a sale, no commission is earned.

Exclusive Right-to-Sell Listing

Under an exclusive right-to-sell listing, an owner hires only one broker or agent to assist in selling the real property, and the owner agrees that if the real property is sold, even through the owner's efforts, a commission is earned. Brokers and agents prefer this type of listing, which assures a commission if the real property is sold during the listing period.

Many brokers and agents participate in a multiple-listing service. A multiple-listing service is a cooperative of brokers who pool all their listings and make them available to all members of the service. By doing this, a seller's real property is made available to all brokers in the community, and the chances for a quick sale are greatly enhanced.

A broker or an agent earns a real estate commission if the broker or agent produces a person who is ready, willing, and able to purchase the real property at the price and on the terms required by the seller in the listing agreement. The broker or agent must be the procuring cause of the sale. This means that the broker or agent must find a purchaser within the time agreed in the listing, and the purchaser's offer must meet the terms of the listing unless modifications are agreed to by the real property owner. The term "able to buy" means that the purchaser has the financial ability as well as the legal and mental capacity to enter into an enforceable contract to purchase the real property. The broker or agent earns the commission once a purchaser who meets the terms of the seller's offer to sell the property is presented to the seller. The commission is earned even if the seller refuses the purchaser's offer, or if the seller and purchaser go to contract but the contract does not close.

Although the commission is earned at the time the purchaser and seller contract, it typically is not paid until the contract closes and the purchase money is received by the seller. The real estate commission typically is a percentage of the sales price and is paid by the seller. The real estate contract usually outlines the commission rights of a broker or agent, and the broker or agent is made a party to the contract for the purpose of enforcing the commission rights.

Some states provide for a broker to have a lien on the property being sold in the event the broker's commission is not paid. Generally, real estate broker lien laws apply only to the sale of commercial property and not to the sale of condominiums and homes. Usually a broker, in order to perfect a lien for a commission, must file a written notice of lien upon the property providing information concerning the amount of the unpaid commission and other factual information regarding the claim of lien. Once the lien is recorded, it becomes a monetary charge against the property and cannot be removed until either payment of the commission or a settlement with the broker. The broker has the right to require the liened property to be sold to pay the commission.

Real Estate Brokers and the Internet

Real estate brokers have embraced the Internet for purposes of advertising properties for sale. Using digital photography, a broker is able to provide to a prospective purchaser with a virtual tour of any home listed with the broker for sale. A prospective purchaser, using the Internet, can review both the exterior and the interior of a number of homes in a very short period of time. Homes that appear attractive on the Internet can then be viewed in person at a later time.

Recently there has been a growth of low-cost Internet realtors who operate entire brokerage companies on the Internet. These Internet brokers may acquire listings for placement on the Internet or may contract with other, more traditional brokers for listings with an agreement that, if the home sells through the Internet broker, the traditional broker will receive a share of the commission. While most buyers use online listings essentially for background information, using the Internet to facilitate the sale of a property is a growth industry, and as both buyers and sellers become more familiar with its use, it may become a major method of selling real property.

TAXATION AND THE SALE OF REAL PROPERTY

Federal Income Tax

The sale of real property may result in the owner having a gain for purposes of taxation and owing an income tax to both the federal and state governments based upon the proceeds received from the sale. Although real estate paralegals are generally not involved in calculating an owner's taxable gain on the sale of the property or in preparing the owner's tax return, knowledge regarding the tax consequences of a sale is important. Generally, the tax consequences of the sale of real property depend to a large part on the use of the property, whether it was used as a home for the owner or as commercial income-producing property.

Federal Income Tax on the Sale of a Home

The sale of a home can create federal and state income tax consequences. The Internal Revenue Code generally defines a home as a house, houseboat, mobile home, cooperative apartment, or condominium. It is necessary for the owner to have resided in the home at the time of the sale for at least two of the past five years prior to the date of the sale. If an owner has more than one home, such as a vacation home, the owner can only treat one home under the home sale taxation rules. Generally, it would be the home where the owner lives most of the time.

The formula for computing a taxable gain on the sale of a home is the selling price, less selling expenses, less adjusted basis of the home. The amount left over would be the owner's taxable gain.

The selling price is defined as the total amount the owner receives from the sale of the home. It includes all money, notes, mortgages, and other debts assumed by the buyer as part of the sale. To arrive at the amount that would be a taxable gain from the sale of a home, an owner may subtract selling expenses from the selling price. The selling expenses would include commissions for real estate brokers, any advertising fees, legal fees, and loan charges paid by the owner, such as loan placement fees or points.

In addition to subtracting selling expenses from the selling price, the owner may also subtract the adjusted basis of the home from the selling price.

An owner's basis for a home is his or her purchase price for the home. The purchase price includes not only the actual contract price paid for the home, but also any settlement fees or closing costs. For example, if the purchaser had to pay an attorney, surveyor, and title insurance company in order to buy the home, the cost of all of those items could be added to the purchase price to determine the basis for the property. This basis may also be adjusted by other factors. For example, the basis may be increased by the cost of any additions or improvements made to the home that have a useful life of more than one year. In addition, any amounts net of insurance proceeds an owner may have spent after a casualty to restore damaged property may be added to the basis.

The amount left over after subtracting selling expenses and adjusted basis from the selling price is the owner's taxable gain from the sale. If the amount left over is a loss, the loss may not be deducted on an owner's income tax return for the sale of a home. If the amount is a gain, the amount may be taxed at capital gain rates. Under current tax laws, a property owner may exclude up to $250,000 of gain from the sale of a home, or $500,000 if the owner files a joint return with his or her spouse. Exhibit 6–4 shows how gain would be computed on the sale of a home.

Federal Income Tax on the Sale of Commercial Property

The sale of commercial property also has income tax consequences. The method of arriving at the taxable gain is similar to that of the sale of a home. That is, it is selling price, less selling expenses, less adjusted basis. The amount left over, if a positive amount, is a taxable gain. Unlike the sale of a home, an owner of commercial property may subtract from his or her income any losses received from the sale of a commercial property.

The main difference between the taxable consequences from the sale of a home and that of commercial property is the requirement that an owner of commercial property deduct depreciation from the basis in order to arrive at an adjusted basis of the property. Depreciation is a tax method that permits a property owner to recover the cost of income-producing property through yearly deductions. By depreciating property, the property owner may deduct some of his or her costs from the acquisition of the property on the tax return for each year of ownership. Depreciation is only permitted on property that is used for rental or income-producing purposes. Only the value of improvements can

EXHIBIT 6–4

Example: Computation of Taxable Gain for Sale of a Home

Example: Computation of Taxable Gain for the Sale of a Home	
Contract Sales Price	$200,000.00
Less Brokerage Commission (6%)	$ 12,000.00
Less Closing Costs Attributed to Seller	$ 2,000.00
Net Selling Price	$186,000.00
Less Owner's Adjusted Basis	$135,000.00 (calculated below)
Taxable Gain	$ 51,000.00
Calculation of Owner's Basis:	
Owner's Purchase Price	$125,000.00
Plus Legal Fees, Title Insurance, and Survey Costs in Connection with the Purchase	$ 5,000.00
Plus Capital Improvements: New Roof with a Life of 10 years	$ 5,000.00
Adjusted Basis	$135,000.00

be depreciated, not the land itself. There are a number of depreciation systems available to a property owner. Depreciation is generally permitted over a period of time, such as 20 years. For example, an owner of an apartment project is depreciating the property over a period of 20 years with a straight-line depreciation method. The owner would be permitted to depreciate 5 percent of the cost of the improvements for each year of ownership. If the improvements were purchased for $1,000,000, the apartment owner could subtract 5 percent (1/20th) of the cost of these improvements, or $50,000, from the owner's income on his or her income tax return each year. The depreciation deduction of $50,000, however, does reduce the owner's basis in the property by $50,000. For example, if the apartment owner has owned the apartments for five years, the adjusted basis of the property would be $1,000,000 less $250,000 accrued depreciation, or $750,000. It would be this adjusted basis that would be subtracted from a selling price for the apartments in order to arrive at a taxable gain. It is easy to see that in many cases, although the property owner is getting a tax deduction for each year of ownership, a portion of these taxes are recaptured at the time of sale through an increase in the taxable gain due to the adjustment in basis by the accrued depreciation.

🏛 ETHICS: Commingling of Client Funds

A paralegal is employed by a law firm. One of the firm's clients is purchasing a home. The attorney, with the paralegal's help, has been requested to prepare the contract. The contract requires a down payment of $5,000 to be made at the time the contract is signed. The client signs the contract and gives to the paralegal a check with the paralegal shown as the payee for the down payment. The intent is that the check would be endorsed by the paralegal into the firm's escrow account and that a check would be issued to the seller as an earnest money down payment. The paralegal receives the check on Friday, noticing that it is made out to him. The paralegal endorses the check and places it into his personal checking account, fully intending on Monday to write a check from the account to the firm's escrow account. Are the acceptance of the check made out to the paralegal as payee and the depositing of the check into his personal account breaches of ethics?

One of the main ethical requirements for the practice of law is to separate client funds from personal funds. An attorney who commingles client funds with personal funds can face suspension or even loss of license to practice law. A paralegal, likewise, should never, under any circumstances, commingle funds received by a client with his or her own funds. A paralegal must always account for all monies or properties entrusted into his or her possession, and such money or property should be kept separate and apart from his or her own personal account. Acceptance of a check made payable to the paralegal in this case is a breach of ethics. In addition, the deposit of the check into the paralegal's own personal account, even though it may have been an innocent mistake on the paralegal's part, is also a breach of ethics.

SUMMARY

A contract is an important legal document in the transfer of ownership to real property. It is the "legal glue" that binds seller and purchaser together. Real estate contracts, in order to be enforceable, require that both the buyer and seller have legal capacity to contract, that there are both an offer and a mutual acceptance of that offer for the purchase and sale of the property, that consideration is given, that the contract is for a lawful purpose, and that the terms of the contract are written. All these requirements are necessary for the contract to be enforceable by either seller or purchaser. If any one of the elements is missing, the contract will be unenforceable.

If either a purchaser or seller defaults on the obligations under a contract, then the injured party may recover certain relief from the defaulting party. This relief may be in the form of specific performance that requires the defaulting party to perform the contract as agreed to, or it may be in the form of money damages or recovery of expenses. In addition, many real estate contracts contain liquidated damage provisions that specify that a certain sum of money will be paid in the event either the seller or the buyer defaults.

Although all real estate contracts have buyers and sellers as parties, many are often procured by real estate agents or brokers, and these brokers become a party to the contract. Real estate brokers may represent both purchasers and sellers in connection with a contract and generally perform services pursuant to a listing or agency agreement. These agreements may be either exclusive or nonexclusive.

Although most real estate contracts contain basic information regarding the purchase price, the description of the real property, and the date for the transfer of title, they also address numerous other issues of importance to the purchaser and seller. A full discussion of real estate contracts, including sample contract clauses and complete sample contracts, follows in Chapter 7.

HELPFUL WEBSITES

The National Association of Realtors® Web sites contain interesting information for the prospective homebuyer or seller. The sites contain information about the value of real estate brokers and how to work with a broker to buy or sell a home. The sites also contain some excellent calculators on such topics as home affordability, rent versus buy, how much mortgage a person can afford, and home value projections. See *http://www.realtor.org* and *http://www.realtor.com*.

KEY TERMS

agent	implied authority	power of attorney
consideration	liquidated damages	principal
contract	listing agreement	rescission
counteroffer	offer	specific performance
express authority	offeree	
fiduciary	offeror	

REVIEW QUESTIONS

1. What are the requirements of a valid real estate contract?
2. What is the statute of frauds, and what effect does it have on the validity of contracts?
3. Explain the difference between an exclusive listing and an exclusive right-to-sell listing.
4. Explain the three remedies available for the breach of a real estate contract.
5. Under what circumstances would a liquidated damage provision be unenforceable?
6. Why must contracts entered into with partnerships, executors, and trustees be carefully examined?
7. When is a real estate broker entitled to a commission?
8. Under what circumstances can a power of attorney be revoked?
9. Why is the contract of a mental incompetent unenforceable?
10. If a seller defaults on a contract, what is the most desirable remedy for the purchaser?

CASE PROBLEMS

1. Seller and purchaser enter into a contract for the sale and purchase of real property for a price of $175,000. The property has a value of $190,000. The purchaser fails to perform. What is the amount of money damages to be awarded to the seller? What is the amount of money damages owed to the purchaser if the seller fails to perform?

2. Susan Seller has contracted to sell her home to Bob Buyer. The sale is for $150,000 cash with no conditions except that title be marketable and the sale must close on July 20 at Susan's attorney's office. On July 18, Bob calls Susan and informs her that he had planned to buy the property by a "loan assumption" (i.e., he had assumed that his rich uncle would lend him the money). The rich uncle, however, has refused, and Bob does not have the cash to go ahead with the deal. Bob further mentions that he owns some other real estate worth about $500,000 and perhaps he could sell or get a loan against this real estate and have enough cash to go ahead

with the deal sometime in the future. Bob asks Susan if she will extend the closing for a month, until August 20. Susan says no and further informs Bob that she is ready, willing, and able to perform on July 20. On July 20, no closing takes place. On July 21, Susan sues Bob for breach of contract. Please answer the following questions with full discussion: (a) Has Bob breached the contract? (b) Does Susan have the right to sue Bob on July 21? (c) If Susan can sue Bob on July 21, what remedies are available to Susan for Bob's breach of contract?

3. You are a paralegal with a law firm. One of the firm's clients, a corporation, has entered into a contract to purchase property from Dwight Sneed. The client, after entering into the contract, has discovered that Dwight Sneed is 16 years old. The client is worried that Dwight Sneed's promises under the contract are unenforceable, and to avoid problems, the client wants to get out of the contract. Is the contract enforceable by Dwight Sneed against the corporate client?

4. You are assisting in the negotiation and preparation of a contract for the purchase and sale of real property. The seller of the property is a partnership composed of two partners. The partners are XYZ Realty Company, also a Texas corporation, and ABC Realty Company, also a Texas corporation. You have been asked to obtain proper documentation to demonstrate that the seller has the authority to enter into the contract and will be bound by the terms of the contract. What documentation will you need?

5. Alice Skinflint has retained Honest Broker to assist her in selling her vacation home. Skinflint and Broker enter into a listing agreement wherein the property is to be offered for sale for $300,000 cash. The listing is to expire on May 1. On April 25, Honest Broker receives an offer to purchase Skinflint's vacation home from I. M. Rich. The offer is for $300,000 cash, and Mr. Rich is a multimillionaire. Honest Broker calls Alice Skinflint and tells her that he has a purchaser for her vacation home and that he would like to meet with her before May 1 to have a contract signed. Alice Skinflint informs Honest Broker that she is going out of town for a vacation and will not be back until May 5 and that she cannot enter into a contract before the expiration of the listing on May 1. Alice Skinflint returns from her vacation on May 6, calls I. M. Rich, and signs a contract with I. M. Rich to sell the vacation home for $300,000. Honest Broker requests that Skinflint pay him a 6 percent commission on the sale. Skinflint refuses, saying that the property had not been sold before the expiration of the listing on May 1. What are the chances of Honest Broker recovering the commission from Skinflint?

6. Sam Seller offers to sell his home to Pat Purchaser for the sum of $160,000. Pat Purchaser responds that she will only purchase the home for $150,000. Sam Seller rejects Pat Purchaser's offer to purchase for $150,000. Pat Purchaser then offers $160,000 for Sam Seller's home. Is there a contract between Sam Seller and Pat Purchaser for the sale and purchase of the home at $160,000?

PRACTICAL ASSIGNMENTS

1. Research your state's statute of frauds law and prepare a brief memorandum summarizing what contracts are required to be in writing in your state.

2. Research your state's law concerning liquidated damages. What is required in your state for a liquidated damage provision in a real estate contract to be enforceable? Prepare a short memorandum regarding the conclusions of your research.

3. Research your state's law regarding powers of attorney and their use in the transfer of ownership to real property. Prepare a brief memorandum outlining the requirements for a power of attorney authorizing a person to sign a deed and discuss whether your state law requires the power of attorney to be recorded with the deed. Obtain from your instructor or an attorney a power of attorney form used in your state and compare it to the one shown as Exhibit 6–2. How is it similar, and how is it different?

4. Can a real estate broker act as a dual agent in your state? Please research the law carefully and prepare a short memorandum outlining what is required, in the form of disclosure or otherwise, for a real estate broker to represent both the seller and purchaser. This information is probably codified as part of the real estate brokerage statutes. Make a copy of the appropriate statute and add it as an appendix to your memorandum.

Student StudyWare™ CD-ROM

Interactive Student CD in the book includes additional quizzing, case studies, and key terms flashcards.

Online Companion™

For additional resources, please go to *www.paralegal.delmar.cengage.com*

chapter | 7

Preparation and Review of a Real Estate Contract

Objectives

After reading this chapter, you should be able to:

- Review a real estate contract for the sale and purchase of a home and understand its contents
- Prepare a real estate contract for the sale and purchase of a home
- Review a real estate contract for the sale and purchase of commercial real property and understand its contents
- Prepare a real estate contract for the sale and purchase of commercial real property

Outline

Paralegals prepare real estate contracts for an attorney's final review or assist the attorney in a review of contracts prepared by other counsel or by real estate brokers. During the process of preparing or reviewing a contract, one should remember that the contract is the primary controlling document in a real estate sale transaction. It follows the negotiations of the parties and, it is hoped, captures their agreements in writing. It dictates the rights and responsibilities of the parties, and in most instances, its effect goes well beyond the consummation of the transaction it contemplates. Because of its vital importance to the transaction, a paralegal must pay close attention to the contents of the real estate contract.

SYDNEY'S REAL ESTATE CONTRACT

It is Friday afternoon. The attorney you work for, Susan Barrister, has just received a call from Sydney Brownstreet, one of the firm's real estate developer clients. Susan has asked that you sit in on a telephone conversation with Sydney because she wants you to assist her in preparing whatever legal documents Sydney requires. When you enter her office, you hear Sydney's voice on the telephone speakerphone. "Listen, Susan, I need your help over the weekend. I've got a chance to buy a nice piece of property out on Delk Road that will be ideal for this new shopping center concept of mine. I need you to prepare a contract so that I will have it on Monday to present to the owner. The owner's name is Delk Road Development, Inc., and I want to offer $750,000 for the property. I can fax over to you a copy of the legal description. I also would like to close the deal by April 1. Is there anything else you need to know, Susan?"

Susan looks at you with a slight roll of her eyes toward the ceiling and then asks Sydney the following questions.

"Sydney, do you intend to buy the property in your name or in the name of your corporation, Brownstreet Shopping Centers, Inc.? Or are you going to form a new limited liability company to take title? Is the property vacant? Are there any easements that are necessary for your development of the property?

"How do you intend to pay for the property? Are you going to pay all cash at closing, or are the sellers going to take back a note? Do you need to line up financing for the purchase, and if so, should this be a condition to closing?

"Is there any debt existing on the property? If so, do you want to try to assume that debt?

"Are you satisfied with insurable title for the property? Do you want us to do a title examination? Do you want the seller to pay for it?

"Do you want to take possession of the property at closing? Before closing? Are taxes and all other expenses to be prorated as to the date of closing? Do you have any conditions that you want satisfied before closing? Are you satisfied with the zoning? Do you think that you can get a curb cut onto Delk Road? Do you need to do any soil tests to see if the soil will support your shopping center concept? Have you had the property examined for hazardous wastes? Are there sanitary sewer and other utilities to the property?

"Do you want a survey? Do you want the seller to pay for the survey? How much earnest money are you going to put down? Do you want to make it part of the purchase price? Are you willing to forfeit the earnest money if you do not go ahead and buy the property? Do you want the seller to hold the earnest money? Is there a real estate broker involved? Do you want the broker to hold the earnest money? Do you want to be able to assign the contract to some partnership that you are going to form in the future?"

As the conversation continues, it is easy to see that the preparation of a real estate contract requires the answers to more questions than just the identity of the seller and the purchaser, a description of the real property to be bought and sold, a purchase price, and a time for performance.

ELEMENTS IN A REAL ESTATE CONTRACT

The Parties

Obviously, the contract will have a seller and a purchaser. Other parties may join in the execution of the contract, such as a real estate broker for the purpose of enforcing commission rights or an escrow agent to acknowledge receipt of funds. All parties signing the contract should be clearly and distinctly identified by name and capacity (i.e., seller, buyer, and agent). In addition, it is helpful to put the parties' addresses, telephone and facsimile numbers, and e-mail addresses on the contract. In the event that a party to a contract, such as a corporation, partnership or limited liability company, is not a natural person, the authority of the representative who signs on its behalf should be revealed in the contract. For example, in a corporate contract, the corporation should be made a party to the contract, but the officer signing on behalf of the corporation should be identified, as well as the office he or she holds with the corporation.

A seller should be identified in the contract exactly the way the seller holds title to the real property. Purchasers should be identified the way in which they desire to take title. The name of each person signing the contract should be typed underneath the signature line (Examples 7–1 and 7–20).

Example 7–1

THIS AGREEMENT OF PURCHASE AND SALE (the "Agreement") is made and entered into as of the Effective Date, as hereinafter defined, by and between JOANNE SELLER, ALICE SELLER LONGWORTH, AND WARREN SELLER (hereinafter collectively "Seller"); and PURCHASER, INC., a Colorado corporation (hereinafter "Purchaser") and AMERICAN REALTY COMPANY, a Colorado corporation (hereinafter "Broker").

Consideration

A contract must state the consideration flowing from one party to the other or from each to both (Example 7–2). Consideration may be money or something of value. In many states, a recital of the agreement of the parties to buy and sell is sufficient.

Example 7–2

That for and in consideration of the mutual promises and covenants herein contained and the mutual advantages accruing to Seller and Purchaser hereunder and the sum of $10.00 and other good and valuable consideration paid by Purchaser to Seller, receipt of which is hereby acknowledged by Seller, it is mutually covenanted and agreed by the parties hereto as follows:

The Agreement

At a minimum, a contract should contain statements whereby the seller agrees to sell and the buyer agrees to buy the property. Typically, the contract also contains other agreements between the parties, but without an agreement to buy and sell, a sales contract is not valid.

The Property

A contract should adequately describe the real property being bought and sold. A true and correct description of the real property prepared from a survey is preferable, but the minimum requirement in most states is that the real property be clearly and distinctively identified (Example 7–3). Does the description of the property point to a particular parcel of identifiable property? If so, the description is adequate. If anything other than unimproved real property is the subject matter of a contract, it should so indicate. Any personal property to be included with the purchase should be accurately described. Although fixtures are included as part of the realty by operation of law, if there is any question as to whether an item is a fixture, the contract should cover the questioned item with certainty. It is better practice to clearly list all items included in the sale than to rely on items being included as fixtures by the operation of law. Likewise, if some items are to be excluded from the contract, they should be expressly excluded rather than relying on the operation of law to exclude them. If personal property items are to be excluded from the sale, the contract should discuss the method and time of removal and the means for repair to the real property if such repairs are required as a result of the removal of the excluded.

Example 7–3

Property. Seller hereby agrees to sell and convey to Purchaser and Purchaser hereby agrees to purchase from Seller, subject to the terms and conditions hereinafter set forth, the property located in Land Lot 99, 17th District, Colorado Springs, Elk County, Colorado, described on Exhibit A attached hereto and made a part hereof containing approximately 2.544 acres (the "Land") as shown on that certain survey of the Land prepared by D. W. Transit, Colorado Registered Land Surveyor No. 1845, for JoAnne Seller et al., dated July 25, 20__, last revised December 17, 20__ (the "Existing Survey"), together with the following:

(a) *Improvements.* All improvements on the Land owned by Seller, including, without limitation, a two-story retail shopping center containing approximately 54,520 net rentable square feet more commonly known as the "Mountain Square," together with drives, sidewalks, drainage, sewerage and utility facilities, and surface parking areas (collectively the "Improvements");

(b) *Tangible Personal Property.* All fixtures, equipment, machinery, building supplies, tools, furniture, and other personal property, if any, and all replacements thereof, located on or about the Land and Improvements and used exclusively in the operation and maintenance thereof (the "Tangible Personal Property"), but expressly excluding any and all property owned by tenants occupying the Improvements;

(c) *Intangible Property.* Any and all of the Seller's rights and interests in and to all intangible property pertaining to the Land, the Improvements or the Tangible Property or the use thereof, including without limitation, any trade names used in connection therewith, the landlord's interest in all leases regarding the Property to the extent assignable, and all other licenses, franchises, permits, tenant security deposits (unless Purchaser receives a credit for same), contract rights, agreements, transferable business licenses, tenant lists, correspondence with tenants and suppliers, booklets, manuals, advertising materials, transferable utility contracts, and transferable telephone exchange numbers (the "Intangible Property");

(d) *Easements.* Any and all of Seller's rights in and to all easements, if any, benefiting the Land or the Improvements; and

(e) *Rights and Appurtenances.* All rights and appurtenances pertaining to the foregoing, including any right, title, and interest of Seller in and to adjacent streets, alleys, or rights-of-way. All of the property described in Subsections (a), (b), (c), (d), and (e) of this Section together with the Land, are hereinafter sometimes collectively referred to as the "Property."

The Price

A contract should state the purchase price of the real property or provide for an exact method by which the purchase price can be computed (Example 7–4). The easiest approach is to always have a fixed price for the real property, but that may not always be appropriate for the transaction. In dealing with commercial real property or undeveloped acreage, the price often is expressed in terms of dollars per acre, square foot, or feet of road frontage. If such is the case, the contract needs to speak to the following questions: (a) What method will be used to determine the area or frontage (a survey)? (b) Does either party have the right to question the accuracy of such a method? (c) Are all areas within the boundary of the survey to be used in the computation, or are certain areas (e.g., flood plains, easements, and public or private right-of-ways) excludable? (d) Is the seller warranting a minimum area or amount of frontage that is acceptable to the purchaser?

Example 7–4

(a) *Purchase Price.* The Purchase Price (the "Purchase Price") to be paid for the Property shall be Seven Million Three Hundred Thousand and No/100 Dollars ($7,300,000.00) to be paid in the following manner:

(i) Purchaser shall take subject to a first mortgage loan on the Property held by Wearever Life Assurance Company in the original Principal amount of Five Million Five Hundred Thousand Dollars ($5,500,000.00), which mortgage loan currently bears interest at the rate of ten percent per annum (10%) and is due and payable in full on January 1, 20__. Seller agrees to pay one-half of any and all transfer, assumption, or other fees assessed by the holder of the mortgage loan in connection with the transfer of the Property subject to the mortgage loan; and

(ii) Purchaser shall deliver to Seller a purchase money note ("Note") in the amount of Six Hundred Fifty-Four Thousand Dollars ($654,000.00). Said Note shall bear interest at ten percent per annum (10%) and shall be payable interest-only quarterly with a final payment of all unpaid principal and accrued and unpaid interest being due and payable two years from the Closing Date (hereinafter defined). The Note shall provide that it can be prepaid in whole or in part at any time without premium or penalty. The Note shall provide that the holder of the Note shall give the Maker of the Note at least twenty (20) days written notice of default prior to any acceleration of the Note for default or exercise of any other remedies that the holder may have to collect the indebtedness evidenced by the Note; provided, however, the Note shall be cross-defaulted with the Wearever Life Assurance Company loan ("Wearever Loan") and defaults under the Wearever Loan are to be governed by the notice and cure periods provided for in the Wearever Loan. The Note shall be secured by a second priority Deed of Trust ("Deed") on the Property. The Deed shall provide that insurance and condemnation proceeds shall be used for restoration of the Property; shall provide for twenty (20) days written notice of default prior to any exercise of remedies thereunder; shall not provide for any tax or insurance escrows; shall not have any restrictions on the transfer of the Property or upon any further financing or encumbrancing of the Property. The Note and Deed shall be nonrecourse to Purchaser and shall contain no personal guaranty whatsoever. The Note shall be in the form of the Note attached hereto as Exhibit ____ and the Deed shall be in the form of the Deed of Trust attached hereto as Exhibit __.

(iii) The balance of the Purchase Price in the approximate amount of One Million One Hundred Forty-Six Thousand Dollars ($1,146,000.00) shall be payable in cash or by bank check drawn on the Federal Reserve Bank of Denver or by wire transfer or good funds on the Closing Date (hereinafter defined). Upon request by Purchaser prior to closing, Seller shall designate the account of Seller into which the net proceeds of the sale are to be deposited.

The Method of Payment

Closely related to the price is the way in which the price will be paid and received. A contract should provide for an exact method of payment and the medium of payment (e.g., cash, certified funds, notes, or personal checks). The most common methods of payment are (a) cash; (b) the seller accepting a note, usually secured by the real property; (c) the purchaser assuming preexisting encumbrances or debts against the real property or taking title subject thereto; and (d) the seller accepting other property, either real or personal, in exchange for the real property that is the subject matter of the contract. Many transactions involve a combination of these methods (Example 7–4).

Cash

The simplest situation is one in which the purchaser is paying all cash for the real property. Although drafting and reviewing an all-cash contract requires less attention to the method of payment, there are some points that require thought. Do the parties in fact mean cash, or do they mean cash or its equivalent? It is unusual for purchasers to bring $100 bills to a closing. Cash equivalents often are the method of payment. Cash equivalents can be certified funds, a cashier's or treasurer's check, or a bank wire transfer. A **certified check** is a personal check in which the bank certifies that the funds are in the account and that the check will be honored upon presentment for payment. A **cashier's check,** or treasurer's check, is a check issued by a bank. A **bank wire transfer** is when one bank electronically transfers funds from its account to another bank account.

Seller Financing ✕ #7

The seller financing method of payment requires a great deal of skill and thought on the part of the paralegal in drafting or reviewing the contract. It involves a continuation of rights and obligations between the parties subsequent to the closing of the purchase and sale. The contract should carefully detail each aspect of the financing instruments that will be executed at closing and, if possible, attach copies of these instruments as exhibits to the contract. At a minimum, a contract should touch on the following aspects of seller financing: (a) the security for the note (usually this is the real property being sold); (b) the priority of the lien created (is it a first mortgage lien or a junior lien?); (c) when installment payments are due under the note; (d) late penalties for payments not timely made; (e) prepayment penalties or privileges; (f) will the obligation be due on the subsequent sale by the purchaser of the property? (g) interest rates payable; (h) if the transaction so dictates, release provisions if the purchaser should desire to have a portion of the real property released from the lien before payment of the full loan; (i) maintenance of insurance on the real property for benefit of the seller; (j) personal liability to purchaser under the note and security instrument; and (k) the amount of the note and the exact method by which the amount of the note will be determined at closing.

Preexisting Obligations

The term *loan assumption* often is used to cover both the situation in which the purchaser is in fact assuming liability under some preexisting debt and the situation in which a purchaser is taking title to the property subject to a preexisting debt. The difference is one of liability for the purchaser. A purchaser who "assumes" a preexisting debt is personally obligated to pay the debt. A purchaser who takes "subject to" a preexisting debt is not personally responsible for payment. The maximum risk to a purchaser who takes "subject to" a preexisting obligation is the loss of the real property through foreclosure in the event the obligation is not paid. A thorough discussion of the differences between "assumption" and

certified check

Personal check in which the bank certifies that the funds are in the account and that the check will be honored on presentment for payment. Also called a *treasurer's check*.

cashier's check

Check issued by a bank, the payment of which is guaranteed by the full faith and credit of the bank.

bank wire transfer

Electronic transfer of money from one bank account to another bank account.

"subject to" appears in Chapter 10. A contract should clearly identify the preexisting obligation by giving the name of the holder thereof, the amounts and due dates of payments, the interest rates, the account or loan number (if any), and the loan balances as of a given date. In addition, information concerning the assumability of the loan should be included in the contract. Certain representations concerning the preexisting obligation should be required from the seller, such as representations that the loan is not in default, that the seller will comply with all the terms and conditions of the financing documents in the normal course before closing, and of the existence or lack of any condition that the holder of such loan may impose on the purchaser.

Exchanges

An exchange of one parcel of real property for another parcel of real property is done for tax purposes to postpone the occurrence of a taxable event (e.g., the recognition of gain on the sale of appreciated real property). Contracts that contemplate a tax-free exchange should be carefully drafted and reviewed from both a tax and a real property law perspective. Paralegals seldom are involved in the drafting or negotiation of tax-free exchange contracts.

Quality of Title

A contract should contain a description of the quality of title the seller is obligated to convey and the purchaser is obligated to accept at the time of closing (Example 7–5). The terms usually used in contracts are "marketable title" and "insurable title." A purchaser can agree to accept some lesser quality of title. In drafting or reviewing a contract, the inclusion of catchwords such as *marketable title* and *insurable title* without a clear definition can create problems. Marketable title usually means title that a prudent purchaser with full knowledge of all the facts would accept. Insurable title means title that is insurable by a title insurance company as being marketable. Real property may be "marketable" for a particular purpose even though numerous liens and encumbrances exist against the title, and title to any property is insurable, provided the owner is willing to pay a sufficient premium or accept insurance that excepts to any and every defect in title. A complete discussion of title insurance is set forth in Chapter 13.

Example 7–5

(a) Seller shall sell, convey, and assign to Purchaser at Closing good and marketable fee simple title to the Property subject only to the Permitted Title Exceptions as defined and set forth on Exhibit B attached hereto.

(b) Within thirty (30) days after the effective date of this contract, Purchaser shall cause title to the Property to be examined and shall furnish Seller with a written statement of any and all title matters, other than the Permitted Title Exceptions to which Purchaser objects. Purchaser shall also have the right to examine, or cause to be examined, title to the Property at any time or times after such initial title examination and prior to Closing and to furnish Seller with a written statement or statements of any and all additional matters, other than the Permitted Title Exceptions that affect the title to the Property or the use thereof and that arise, or first appear on record from and after the date of the initial title examination hereunder and to which Purchaser objects. Seller shall cooperate with Purchaser after receipt of any such written statement to correct, cure, or remove all matters described in such statement, and covenants to exercise diligent and good faith efforts to do so. Notwithstanding the above or the terms of this Section, in the event that any such matter results from any affirmative action taken by Seller subsequent to the date hereof, Seller covenants to expend such money and to take such other actions as may be necessary to correct, cure, or remove same. The Closing Date shall be postponed automatically for thirty (30) days, if necessary, to permit Seller to cure. If Seller shall fail to correct, cure, or remove all such matters within the time allowed by this Section, then Purchaser, at its option exercised by written notice, may:

(i) decline to purchase the Property; or

(ii) waive such matter and proceed to close the purchase and sale of the Property without a reduction in the Purchase Price and allow Seller to convey title to the Property in accordance with the terms hereof; or

(iii) in the event the matter results from affirmative action of Seller subsequent to the effective date of this contract, require Seller by action of specific performance or otherwise to exercise diligent and good faith efforts to correct, cure, or remove such matters and convey the Property in accordance with the terms of this Agreement, in which case the Closing Date shall be postponed until such correction, cure, or removal by Seller has been completed (provided, however, that at any time during such period Purchaser may exercise its options as set forth in Section (b)(i) or Section (b)(ii) above).

Should Purchaser accept, by written waiver, its interest in the Property subject to matters in addition to the Permitted Title Exceptions, such acceptable matters shall be added to the list now set forth in Exhibit B and shall thereafter be deemed to be Permitted Title Exceptions except that, in the event any of such matters result from any affirmative action taken by Seller subsequent to the date hereof, such acceptance shall be without prejudice to Purchaser's thereafter seeking monetary damages from Seller for any such matter. If Purchaser shall decline to accept the Seller's interest in the Property subject to such matters, pursuant to Section (b) above, then Escrowee shall refund to Purchaser the Deposit and the parties hereto shall have no further rights, obligations, duties, or liabilities hereunder whatsoever, except for those rights, obligations, duties, and liabilities that, by the express terms hereof, survive any termination hereof and except for Purchaser's right to seek monetary damages from Seller for any matter which Seller shall have failed so to correct and which shall have resulted from any affirmative action taken by Seller after the date hereof.

(c) Purchaser may, at its expense, elect to obtain a standard ALTA Form 1990 owner's policy of title insurance pursuant to which fee simple title to the Property shall be insured. Seller covenants to Purchaser that title to the Property shall at Closing not only be good and marketable, but, in the event Purchaser elects so to purchase such an owner's policy of title insurance, shall be insurable by an ALTA title insurer or other title insurance company reasonably acceptable to Purchaser at its regular rates, without exceptions or reservations to coverage of any type or kind, other than the Permitted Title Exceptions.

The contract should clearly set forth exceptions to title that the purchaser is willing to accept. All permitted exceptions should be specifically stated in the contract. Most purchasers are unwilling to accept title "subject to utility easements and other restrictions of record." Such a broad statement could include many title exceptions that are unacceptable or that would be detrimental to the real property. Be especially careful of standard permitted title exceptions, which often appear in preprinted forms. These preprinted form exceptions include (a) utility easements of record serving the real property, (b) zoning ordinances that affect the property, (c) subdivision restrictions of record, and (d) leases. The real property may be so heavily burdened by utility easements as to prevent any improvements from being constructed on it. Zoning ordinances may preclude a purchaser from using the real property in the way he or she desires. Subdivision restrictions may place financial burdens on the purchaser or may require approval of owners' associations before the consummation of the transaction. Finally, agreeing to accept title subject to leases without first reviewing the leases can create serious problems.

A contract should require the purchaser to notify the seller of any unacceptable title exceptions disclosed as a result of an examination of the public records and afford the seller the opportunity to cure these defects. A contract should provide either a reasonable time to search title and reasonable time to cure defects or a stated period of time for the purchaser to examine title and a stated period of time required for curative action by the seller. The contract should contain provisions dealing with the failure of the parties to meet their obligations with reference to the title.

A contract should provide that the seller shall not alter or encumber the title to the property after the date of the contract without the written consent of the purchaser.

Possession of the Property

A definite date and time for the purchaser to take possession of the property should be included in every contract. Ideally, the time of possession should follow immediately after the closing. In many situations, however, sellers may have legitimate business or personal reasons for remaining in possession for a few days after closing. For example, in a home sale, it is not unusual for the seller to remain in possession for a few days after the sale to remove his or her personal effects from the property. If possession is delayed until after closing, the contract should address the issues of maintenance, insurance, loss through fire or other casualty, and rent for the period of the seller's possession after closing.

Closing or Settlement

closing

Date set forth in a real estate contract on which the parties agree to perform all the promises of the contract. The date on which ownership of the real property is transferred from seller to purchaser and the purchaser pays the seller the purchase price for the real property.

The **closing** of a contract is the date on which the parties agree to perform all their promises under the contract. In some states, this date is referred to as *settlement*. It is the time when the purchaser is required to pay the purchase price and the seller is required to transfer title and ownership to the purchaser. The date, time, and, if possible, the place for the closing should be established in the contract (Example 7–6). If the closing date is omitted from the contract, the courts will impose on the parties a reasonable time and place to close the transaction.

Example 7–6

Closing Date. Unless this Agreement is terminated by Purchaser pursuant to the terms of this Agreement, the Closing shall take place at the offices of Purchaser's attorneys, or such location as is mutually agreeable to Purchaser and Seller, beginning at 10:00 A.M. on a business day (in Colorado Springs, Colorado) selected by Purchaser on or before November 11, 20__. The date of Closing shall hereinafter be referred to as the "Closing Date." Purchaser shall give Seller notice of the Closing Date at least five (5) business days prior thereto; provided, however, if Purchaser gives Seller no such notice of the Closing Date, then the Closing Date shall be November 11, 20__.

Closing or Settlement Documents

A contract should list the documents that the parties will be expected to sign at closing (Example 7–7). Because, in most cases, a comprehensive list is not available before the closing itself, the parties should be obligated to execute such other documents as are reasonably necessary to carry out the purpose and intent of the contract. Closing documents usually include affidavits of title, settlement statements, deeds of conveyance, and bills of sale, and assignments of warranty; notes, security instruments, and assignments of leases also may be included. Ideally, all closing forms are identified in and attached as exhibits to the contract; however, time and cost requirements and the fact that most of these documents have taken on a relatively standard format have made that somewhat unnecessary. The contract should, however, identify the type of deed that will be executed at closing to convey title to the real property. The deed usually is a general warranty deed, wherein the seller warrants to the purchaser that the title to the real property is free from liens and claims by any parties other than those listed therein and the seller covenants to defend the title represented against any claims. If a contract is silent regarding the form of deed, a general warranty deed will be required. A lesser type of deed, however, can be contracted for. Deeds are discussed fully in Chapter 8.

Example 7–7

Seller's Obligations. At Closing, Seller shall:

(a) Execute, acknowledge, and deliver to Purchaser a general warranty deed in recordable form, the form of which is attached hereto as Exhibit _____, conveying the Property to Purchaser subject only to (i) taxes for the years subsequent to the year of Closing; (ii) the zoning classification as of the Effective Date; and (iii) the Permitted Exceptions;

(b) Execute and deliver to Purchaser the following additional conveyance documents: (A) an Affidavit reciting Seller's non-foreign status within the meaning of Section 1445(f)(3) of the Internal Revenue Code of 1986; (B) an Assignment and Assumption of Leases assigning to Purchaser Seller's interest in the Leases, a form of which is attached hereto as Exhibit _____; and (C) an Assignment of Contracts, Other Rights, and Intangible Property assigning to Purchaser the Intangible Property, the form of which is attached hereto as Exhibit _____; and (D) a Lender Estoppel Letter from the holder of the Mortgage Loan, a proposed form of which is attached hereto as Exhibit _____; (E) Subordination, Attornment, and Non-Disturbance Agreements satisfactory to Lender, signed by tenants leasing at least eighty-five percent (85%) of the net rentable square footage of the Property, a proposed form of which is attached hereto as Exhibit _____;

(c) Execute and deliver to Purchaser a Closing Statement setting forth the adjustments and prorations to the Purchase Price as well as the costs pursuant to this Agreement as elsewhere specifically provided herein (the "Closing Statement");

(d) Deliver to Purchaser a certified and updated rent roll reflecting all the tenants under Leases to the Property as of the Closing Date and indicating thereon any delinquencies with respect to rent due;

(e) Deliver to Purchaser all permits, certificates of occupancy, and licenses issued by Governmental Authorities or utility companies in connection with the occupancy and use of such of the Improvements as are in the possession of Seller;

(f) Deliver to Purchaser a form letter to all tenants under Leases stating that Purchaser has acquired the Property from Seller, that future rents should be paid as specified by Purchaser, and that Purchaser will be responsible for all tenants' security deposits, if any;

(g) A certificate of Seller stating (A) that Seller has no knowledge of any pending or threatened condemnation proceedings or any taking by any Governmental Authority that in any way affects the Property, (B) that there are no Leases (other than Leases approved by Purchaser), no Service Contracts (whether written or oral), no employees, no insurance policy endorsements or claims, no other notices from any Governmental Authority regarding any violations of any Requirements of Law affecting the Property except as heretofore provided to Purchaser as required elsewhere in this Agreement;

(h) The plans and specifications for such of the Improvements, including all amendments thereto, as are in the possession of Seller;

(i) The originals of all Leases, including all amendments thereto;

(j) All information and materials required for full compliance under the Foreign Investors in Real Property Tax Act;

(k) All keys to the Improvements in Seller's possession and a list of all other persons who, to the best of Seller's knowledge, are in possession of keys to the Improvements, other than keys to tenant space in the possession of tenants;

(l) Such other documents, instruments, and agreements as Purchaser may reasonably require to effect and complete the transactions contemplated herein and to obtain an owner's title insurance policy insuring the interest of Purchaser, as owner, in the amount of $7,300,000.00, free and clear of all exceptions except the Permitted Exceptions, for a premium calculated at standard rates, including, without limitation, a Seller's Affidavit of Title in the form attached hereto as Exhibit _____ and a Bill of Sale in the form attached hereto as Exhibit _____; and

Purchaser's Obligations at Closing. On the Closing Date, subject to the terms, conditions, and provisions hereof, Purchaser shall:

(a) Execute and deliver to Seller an assumption agreement whereby Purchaser assumes all liabilities and agrees to perform all obligations of Seller under all the Leases, the form of which is contained in Exhibit _____, and the Service Contracts and all employee contracts assumed by Purchaser pursuant hereto, the form of which is contained in Exhibit _____. Said assumption agreements shall contain an indemnification by Purchaser of Seller and an agreement to hold Seller harmless from and against any and all claims, debts, liabilities, and the like affecting or relating to the Property, or any part thereof, and the Leases after the Closing Date. Likewise, said assumption agreements shall contain an agreement to hold Purchaser harmless from and against any and all claims, debts, liabilities, and the like affecting or relating to the Property, or any part thereof, and the Leases prior to and including the Closing Date.

(b) Execute and deliver to Seller a copy of the Closing Statement.

Proration, Closing Costs, and Financial Adjustments

Any item that will be prorated between the parties at the time of sale should be listed in the contract, along with the date of such proration (Example 7–8). These items usually include insurance premiums; property taxes for the current year; rents; interest on any loans against the real property that the purchaser is assuming; special assessments, such as sanitation fees, which are liens against the real property; utility charges; and mandatory owners' association fees. The contract should provide for the handling of any items that will be credits to either party and debits to the other, such as fees for utility deposits. Furthermore, a contract should designate which party will pay the costs involved in closing the transaction. These costs include document recording, taxes on transfer, title examination charges, legal fees for each party, survey, title insurance, intangibles tax, recording fees, assumption fees, and loan costs. Closing costs usually are negotiable, and the allocation of these costs will be whatever the parties agree to.

Example 7–8

Closing Costs. In connection with Closing, Seller shall pay the Colorado real estate transfer tax and all costs relating to the satisfaction, cure, and removal of all title defects (except the Permitted Exceptions) undertaken by Seller as herein required and the payment of one-half (1/2) of all transfer, assumption, or other fees due the holder of the Mortgage Loan to obtain the consent to the transfer of the Property to the Purchaser and the consent to the Note and Deed of Trust. Purchaser shall pay the costs of the premiums payable or costs incurred in connection with the issuance of the owner's title insurance commitment and the owner's title insurance policy in favor of Purchaser and all costs of recording the general warranty deed. The Purchaser shall be solely responsible for the new survey costs. Each party shall pay its own attorney's fees.

Prorations. The following items shall be apportioned and prorated (based on a 30-day month, unless otherwise indicated) between the Seller and the Purchaser as of the Closing Date so that credits and charges for all days prior to the Closing Date shall be allocated to the Seller and credits and charges for the Closing Date and for all days thereafter shall be allocated to the Purchaser: .

(a) *Taxes.* At the Closing, all ad valorem property taxes, water and sewer charges, and assessments of any kind on the Property for the year of the Closing shall be prorated between Purchaser and Seller as of 12:01 a.m. on the Closing Date. Such proration shall be based upon the latest ad valorem property tax, water, sewer charge, and assessment bills available. If, upon receipt of the actual ad valorem property tax, water, sewer, and assessment bills for the Property, such proration is incorrect, then either Purchaser or Seller shall be entitled, upon demand, to receive such amounts from the other as may be necessary to correct such malapportionment. This obligation so to correct such malapportionment shall survive the Closing and not be merged into any documents delivered pursuant to the Closing.

(b) *Rents.* Purchaser shall receive a credit for all amounts due under the Leases in effect at Closing, hereinafter referred to as the "Rents," collected by Seller prior to Closing and allocable in whole or in part to any period following the Closing Date. Seller shall deliver to Purchaser any Rents received after Closing. Purchaser shall deliver to Seller any Rents received after Closing that relate to periods prior to and through the Closing Date; provided, however, that any such Rents collected by Purchaser after the Closing shall be applied first toward Rents due which shall have accrued after the Closing Date and then toward Rents that accrued prior to the Closing Date. Purchaser shall use its best efforts (short of incurring legal fees and expenses or taking other action that would not be in its best interest as owner of the Property) to collect all such delinquent Rents.

In the event that Purchaser is unable to collect delinquent Rents due Seller within thirty (30) days after the Closing Date, then Seller may pursue collection of such delinquent Rents from the respective Tenants in accordance with its rights under Colorado law; provided, however, Seller shall have no right to collect Rents in any manner that would result in an interference with the Tenant's rights of possession under its lease or in any way interfere with the landlord/tenant relationship between Purchaser and the Tenant. (For example, Seller shall have no rights to dispossess Tenant in an effort to collect delinquent Rents.)

(c) *Other Expense Prorations.* All other reasonable expenses normal to the operation and maintenance of the Property that require payments either in advance or in arrears for periods that begin prior to the Closing Date and end thereafter. Without limiting the generality of the foregoing, such expenses shall include water; electric; telephone and all other utility and fuel charges; fuel on hand (at cost plus sales tax); any deposits with utility companies; employee wages, salaries, benefits and pension, health and welfare insurance, Social Security, and such other contributions; and charges under employee contracts and/or Service Contracts.

(d) *Security Deposits.* Purchaser shall receive a credit for the security deposits paid under the Leases in existence and in effect on the Closing Date.

(e) *Leasing Commissions.* Seller warrants and represents that there are no leasing commissions due and owing or to become due and owing under any of the Leases or any renewals and extensions thereof, as of the Closing Date. Seller agrees to hold harmless from and to indemnify and defend Purchaser from and against any and all such leasing commissions and all other fees, charges, and compensation whatsoever due any person or entity in connection with the procuring of any Lease together with all extensions and renewals thereof or otherwise relating to any Lease. This provision shall survive the Closing and the consummation of the transactions contemplated herein.

Condition of the Property and Risk of Loss

Most contracts provide that the real property will be in substantially the same condition at the time of closing as at the time of contract, natural wear and tear excepted. It is suggested this warranty be extended to the time of possession, if possession should occur after closing. In addition, contracts usually provide that heating, plumbing, and electrical systems will be in normal working order at the time of closing and further provide that the purchaser has the right and obligation to make inspection of these systems before closing. Many contracts provide the purchaser with a right of inspection or "walk-through" before closing and require the seller to repair any items found in need of repair as a result of that inspection. Sellers often put language in the contract limiting their responsibility to make repairs to the expenditure of a fixed sum of money; if the repairs exceed the fixed sum, the purchaser does not have to purchase the real property.

A contract also should indicate which party bears the risk of loss by fire or other casualty to the real property during the contract period (Example 7–9). In many states, the purchaser bears the risk of loss unless the contract provides otherwise. Most purchasers are unaware of this rule, and many do not buy insurance until the day before closing. The contract should allocate the risk of loss during the contract period to the seller. The contract should indicate whether options are available to the purchaser if the real property should be partially damaged or totally destroyed before closing. These options might include consummating the transaction and receiving the proceeds of any insurance settlement resulting from the loss or requiring the seller to restore the real property with insurance proceeds or termination of the contract.

Example 7–9

Risk of Loss. Risk of loss or damage to the Property or any part thereof by condemnation, eminent domain, or similar proceedings, or by deed in lieu or under threat thereof (collectively, a "Taking"), or by fire, flood, or other casualty from the effective date of the contract until delivery of the limited warranty deed will be on Seller and after the delivery of the limited warranty deed will be on Purchaser. In the event of any such loss or damage to all or to a material part of the Property or any part of the Improvements prior to the delivery of the general warranty deed, this Agreement may, at the option of Purchaser to be exercised by written notice to Seller, be declared null and void and Purchaser shall be returned the Deposit and both parties hereto shall be released from any further rights and duties hereunder, or this Agreement shall remain in full force and effect and Seller shall transfer to Purchaser on the Closing Date all insurance proceeds or condemnation awards received by Seller because of such casualty or Taking and all of Seller's right, title, and interest in and to any recovery or claims under any insurance policies or condemnation awards relating to the Property.

Upon the happening of one of the events in the preceding paragraph, subsequent to the Inspection Deadline and prior to delivery of the general warranty deed, if the cost of repair or replacement or, in the event of a Taking, if the reduction in the value of the project is TWENTY-FIVE THOUSAND DOLLARS ($25,000.00) or less, Purchaser shall close and take the Property as diminished by such events and Seller shall transfer to Purchaser on the Closing Date all insurance proceeds or condemnation awards received by Seller because of such casualty or Taking and all of Seller's right, title, and interest in and to any recovery or claim under any insurance policies or condemnation awards relating to the Property together with a credit to Purchaser for the amount of any deductibles contained in any insurance policy.

Earnest Money

earnest money

Money paid by the purchaser at the time the real estate contract is signed. The money may be used as a down payment on the purchase price or may be retained by the seller for damages in the event the purchaser defaults on the contract.

Earnest money is money paid by the purchaser at the time the contract is signed. It is not easy to describe what role in the contract the earnest money plays. Earnest money is not consideration for the contract unless the contract specifically provides so. Earnest money is not a partial payment of the purchase price unless so designated and delivered to the seller. Earnest money is not a prepaid penalty unless so provided in the contract. At best, earnest money seems to be a token deposit made to evidence the purchaser's intent to be bound by the terms of the contract (i.e., a showing of good faith). The contract should provide for the disposition of the earnest money in every possible situation (e.g., consummation of the transaction, default by seller, default by purchaser, failure of a contingency, exercise of an election to void the contract granted to either party, mutual termination of the contract) and for what purpose the earnest money deposit is to be used (Example 7–10). In addition, if real estate brokers are involved, a contract should take into account what claims, if any, the brokers may have on the earnest money deposit in all such events. Earnest money often is placed in a trust or an escrow interest-bearing account. Contracts should provide what quality of account it is to be invested in, for example, FDIC (Federal Deposit Insurance Corporation)-insured deposits. In addition, the contract should make it clear who is to get the interest. The party who is entitled to the interest should provide the holder of the escrow deposit with their federal tax identification number.

Example 7–10

Earnest Money Deposits. Purchaser shall deliver its earnest money deposit to Colorado Title Company (the "Escrowee") upon Purchaser's execution of this Agreement in the form of a cashier's check (drawn on a Colorado financial institution) in the sum of SEVENTY-FIVE THOUSAND DOLLARS ($75,000.00) (the "Earnest Money"), made payable to Escrowee in trust said Earnest Money together with any interest earned thereon shall hereinafter be referred to as(the "Deposit "). The Deposit shall be held and disbursed by Escrowee as provided in this Agreement.

The Escrowee is directed to hold the Deposit as escrowed funds in an FDIC-insured, interest-bearing account at The Second National Bank in Colorado Springs, Colorado. Purchaser represents that its U.S. federal tax identification number is 86-11314. Purchaser's tax identification number shall be credited with any interest earned on the Earnest Money prior to its being disbursed by Escrowee. Purchaser shall complete and execute a Payer's Request for Taxpayer Identification Number (Form W-9). Seller and Purchaser hereby agree to hold Escrowee harmless from any loss of escrowed funds, including the Deposit, for any reason whatsoever except for Escrowee's fraud or gross negligence or for loss of interest caused by any delay in the deposit or early withdrawal of the Deposit from the interest-bearing account. This Agreement shall serve as escrow instructions and an executed copy of this Agreement shall be deposited by Purchaser with Escrowee. At Closing, the Deposit shall be delivered to Seller and applied against the Purchase Price. In the event of a termination of this Agreement or a default under this Agreement, the Deposit shall be delivered or disbursed by the Escrowee as provided in this Agreement. If any dispute or difference arises between the Purchaser and Seller or if any conflicting demands are made upon the Escrowee, the Escrowee shall not be required to determine the same or to take any action thereon. Rather, the Escrowee may await settlement of the controversy or deposit the Deposit into the Registry of the Superior Court of Elk County, Colorado, in an interpleader action or otherwise for the purpose of having the respective rights of the parties adjudicated. Upon making such deposit or upon institution of such interpleader action or other actions, the Escrowee shall be fully relieved and discharged from all further obligations hereunder with respect to the sums so deposited.

Should any party terminate this Agreement, as permitted herein, or declare the other party in default of its obligations hereunder, and demand payment of the Deposit to it, then Escrowee shall pay to it the Deposit, provided that declaring party provides evidence of the other party's receiving its demand notice, and within seven (7) business days following the other party's receipt of same, the nondeclaring party has not delivered written objection to Escrowee's disbursing the Deposit. If any dispute arises that is not resolved within thirty (30) days after such written objection, Escrowee shall deposit the Deposit into the Registry of the Superior Court of Elk County, Colorado, whereupon Escrowee's obligations and liabilities hereunder shall cease and terminate.

Brokers

If a real estate broker is involved, the contract should provide for the rights of the broker to a commission and the obligations incumbent on the broker under the contract (Example 7–11). It is not unusual for contracts to provide that the commission will be payable only on the closing of the transaction and in accordance with the terms of the contract. In addition, if the seller should not receive full proceeds at closing, the payment of the commission might be tied to the subsequent receipt of such proceeds. This usually is done by requiring the broker to accept a note from the seller as part payment of the commission.

The note requires a payment in the same ratio and at the same time that the seller receives payment from the purchaser and conditions the seller's obligations to pay on purchaser's receipt of buyer's payments. For example, if the sales price is being paid in four equal annual installments, the contract may provide that the real estate commission will be paid by the seller to the broker in four equal annual installment payments at the same time the seller receives payment from the purchaser.

Example 7–11

Brokerage Commissions. Each party further represents to the other that except for American Realty Company ("Broker"), no broker has been involved in this transaction. Seller shall be solely responsible for paying any commission due to the Broker in connection with this transaction. Seller shall pay in cash or good funds at Closing brokerage commissions of one percent (1%) to Broker. No commission shall be due and owing Broker should the sale and purchase of the Property fail to close for any reason whatsoever, including, without limitation, the breach of this Agreement by Seller or Purchaser. Under no circumstances whatsoever shall Broker be entitled to retain any portion of the Deposit. In the event any other claims for brokerage commissions or fees are ever made against the Seller or the Purchaser in connection with this transaction, all such claims shall be handled and paid by the party whose actions or alleged commitments form the basis of such claim. Seller further agrees to indemnify and hold harmless the Purchaser from and against any and all such claims or demands with respect to any brokerage fees or agent's commissions or other compensation asserted by any person, firm, or corporation in connection with this Agreement or the transactions contemplated hereby arising from actions or alleged commitments of the Seller. Purchaser further agrees to indemnify and hold harmless the Seller from and against any and all such claims or demands with respect to any brokerage fees or agent's commission or other compensation asserted by any person, firm, or corporation in connection with this Agreement or the transaction contemplated hereby arising from actions or alleged commitments of the Purchaser. This provision shall survive Closing and the conveyance of the Property by Seller to Purchaser.

Many preprinted contract forms used by realty or broker associations provide that the commission will be payable to the broker in full at closing. They also provide that a default of either purchaser or seller will enable the broker to enforce commission rights against the defaulting party, usually by application of the earnest money. In addition, the contract may include statements to the effect that neither party has relied on warranties or representations made by the broker, but rather only those made by the other parties; that the broker is acting for the accommodation of the parties in holding earnest money and is therefore indemnified by each against any claims in connection therewith; and that the broker is the procuring cause of the contract. A broker should be made a party of the contract to enforce commission rights.

If no broker is involved in the transaction, a contract should so indicate and have the parties mutually indemnify each other against the possible claims of brokers resulting from the actions of each.

Merger

The law in many states provides that all the promises, conditions, and covenants contained in a contract are merged into the deed of conveyance at the time of closing and do not survive the closing of the sale. This rule can be circumvented by providing in the contract that all provisions shall survive closing or by having the parties sign at closing an agreement for the survival of warranties, representations, and obligations of the parties contained in the contract (Example 7–12).

Example 7–12

Survival. The provisions of this Agreement shall survive Closing and the execution and delivery of the deed and instruments conveying the Property.

Assignment of Contract

The general rule is that contracts are freely assignable by the purchaser and seller unless assignment is prohibited in the contract. Most sellers do not agree to the unlimited assignability of the contract by the purchaser. This is particularly true when a unique relationship exists between the parties that is, at least in part, the reason the seller has entered into the contract (e.g., when the seller is extending credit for a portion of the price and is relying on the financial strength of the purchaser or when the seller is giving preferential price or terms to a friend or relative). It is, therefore, not uncommon for a contract to contain a provision requiring the seller's written consent before the assignment of the purchaser's interest. The giving of consent to assignment can be conditioned on, among other things, the proposed assignees' agreeing to assume all obligations binding on the assignor under the contract and being bound by all terms of the contract as if an original party. In addition, a seller may require the original purchaser to agree to remain liable for damages if the assignee should default under the contract. If, at the time of contracting, there exists a possibility that the purchaser may desire to close the sale in some name other than that in which the contract is executed, for example, a general or limited partnership or a corporation or limited liability company not yet in existence, the contract also should provide for the seller's consent (Example 7–13).

Example 7–13

Assignability. Purchaser shall not have the right to assign this Agreement to any person(s), partnership, or corporation, including a partnership or corporation to be formed hereafter, without the consent of Seller. In the event of such assignment, the assignee shall assume the obligations of Purchaser under this Agreement, and Purchaser shall have no further obligation or liability under this Agreement. Seller may assign its rights but shall remain bound under the terms of this Agreement and the representations, warranties, and covenants contained herein.

Time Is of the Essence

The general rule is that time limits set forth in a contract are not strictly enforceable unless **time is of the essence.** If time is not of the essence, then a date for performance is not an exact critical date. The courts will permit performance to take place within a reasonable period of time after the date specified in the contract. For example, if the closing date is August 15 and time is not of the essence, the courts will permit the parties to close within a reasonable period of time after August 15. Most sellers and purchasers do not want to operate within the nebulous realm of reasonable time and so desire that dates set forth in a contract be critical and strictly enforceable. Therefore, every contract should contain a provision that time is of the essence for the contract and for each and every obligation of the purchaser and seller (Example 7–14). The phrase most often used is simply "time is of the essence."

time is of the essence

Provision contained in a contract that requires strict performance of the contract by the date or dates provided therein.

strictly enforceable

Example 7–14

Time. Time is of the essence of this Agreement and of each of its provisions.

Warranties of the Parties

Any warranty, statements, or representations made by either the seller or the purchaser that were relied on by the other in deciding to enter the contract for purchase and sale of the property should be affirmatively set out in the contract (Example 7–15). Warranties commonly required of a seller include the following: (a) that the seller holds title to the real property of equal quality to that which the seller is required to convey; (b) that the seller will perform all duties and obligations of the contract; (c) that the seller has the right and full authority to enter into the contract; (d) that no other party is expressing any claim to any portion of the real property and the seller will take no action before closing that would diminish the quality of title; (e) that the seller will make no change in the zoning of the real property; (f) that the seller is aware of no pending governmental action that will affect the real property or burden it with additional assessments; (g) that utilities are available to the real property; (h) that the real property is accessible by way of public roads; and (i) that the real property contains a minimum number of acres or square feet or has a minimum amount of frontage on a public street.

Warranties commonly asked for from a purchaser are (a) that the purchaser has the right and authority to enter into the agreement; (b) that the purchaser has financial resources to meet the financial obligations required under the contract; (c) that the purchaser will perform his or her duties in accordance with the agreement; (d) that no parties have initiated or threatened any action that might affect the purchaser's ability to perform; and (e) that the purchaser will take no action that would diminish the quality of the seller's title before closing.

It is a good idea to have the parties reaffirm the warranties and representations at closing by separate instrument. The contract should provide that the parties will sign such a separate instrument at closing. Contracts also usually provide for the rights and obligations of the parties in the event that any warranty proves untrue. Specifically, the contract will provide that in the event a warranty proves untrue, a party can either terminate the contract or treat such failure as a default under the contract and exercise all its remedies for default.

Example 7–15

(a) *Seller's Covenants and Representations.*

(i) Seller has obtained all consents, approvals, or authorizations necessary to execute this Agreement and to consummate the transaction contemplated hereby, and all documents referred to herein will be validly executed and delivered and binding upon Seller.

(ii) Seller has no knowledge of any material defect in the Improvements or any part thereof and has no knowledge of and has received no notice from any Governmental Authority (as defined below) of any violation of any Requirement of Law (as defined below) relating to the Property or any part thereof;

(iii) Seller has no knowledge of and has received no notice from any insurance company or board of fire underwriters or similar agency that there exists any condition or circumstances on the Property or any part thereof, which must be corrected in order to maintain the effectiveness, or as a condition precedent to the issuance of, any insurance policy affecting the Property or any part thereof or which is in violation of, any applicable fire code or similar rule, regulation, or order for such board of fire underwriters or similar agency;

(iv) Seller has no knowledge of and has received no notice of any litigation, claim, or suit that is pending or threatened that could adversely affect the Property or any part thereof or title thereto (exclusive of any litigation, claim, or suit brought against a tenant of the Property after the effective date of the contract wherein Seller is not named a defendant or a third-party defendant and wherein no counterclaims are alleged against Seller, provided, however, that Seller will give Purchaser prompt notice of all such litigation, claims, and suits);

(v) Neither Seller nor, to the best of Seller's knowledge, any previous owner of the Property or any part thereof has used, generated, stored, or disposed of any Hazardous Materials (as defined below) in or on the Property or any part thereof; or has used or disposed of any Hazardous Materials in connection with the use, operation, construction, or repair of the Property or any part thereof. Seller shall hold Purchaser harmless and shall indemnify and defend Purchaser from and against any and all losses, damages, claims, and liabilities whatsoever in any way relating to or arising out of any breach of the foregoing representation. This provision shall survive Closing and the consummation of the transactions contemplated hereby:

(vi) Seller owns good and unencumbered title to the Tangible Personal Property and Intangible Personal Property, and Seller has done nothing to encumber same during Seller's ownership thereof other than those certain Loan Documents listed on Exhibit ___ attached hereto;

(vii) Seller has not operated the Property within the past five (5) years under any other name or trade name of which it has not notified Purchaser;

(viii) Seller shall not cause or permit to exist (A) any mortgage, deed to secure debt, security deed, security agreement, assignment, or other similar instrument or agreement or any lien or encumbrance whatsoever (other than the Permitted Exceptions or those listed on Exhibit ___) to attach to or affect title to the Property or any part thereof from and after the Effective Date except for the Leases approved by Purchaser; or (B) any matters not shown on the new survey;

(ix) Seller represents, to the best of its knowledge, that the mechanical, electrical, plumbing, heating, ventilation, and air conditioning systems (HVAC), roofing, drainage, sanitary sewerage, and utility equipment facilities and systems servicing the Property and the improvements thereon are in operational order and shall be so maintained through and including the Closing Date. Seller represents that it is aware of no defects in any of said systems;

(x) Seller covenants that it shall not enter into any leases pertaining to the Property after the Effective Date without prior written approval of Purchaser. Purchaser shall approve leases containing reasonable business terms, including base rentals of at least $16.00 per square foot and $1.75 of common area maintenance (CAM) changes. Seller covenants and represents that it shall incur no brokerage commissions pertaining to leases entered into prior to the Closing Date on any leases negotiated in any respect by Seller prior to the Closing Date;

(xi) Seller represents that it has no notice of and is not aware of any violation of the Property and improvements of any applicable zoning laws, ordinances, or regulations including, without limitation, all parking requirements and building setback requirements (except as shown on the existing survey, which Purchaser has the right to consider during the inspection period);

(xii) Seller shall continue to operate, manage, and maintain the Property in good condition and in a good businesslike manner, such operation and maintenance to include the undertaking of any reasonably necessary capital improvements or repairs, through and including the Closing Date. Such continuous operation and maintenance shall also be a condition precedent to Closing; and

(b) *Purchaser's Covenants and Representations*. Purchaser hereby represents and warrants to Seller that Purchaser has obtained all consents, approvals, or authorizations necessary to execute this Agreement and to consummate the transaction contemplated hereby, and all documents referred to herein will be validly executed and delivered and binding upon Purchaser.

Contingencies

A **condition precedent** in a contract is a situation that must be resolved in accordance with the terms of the contract before one or both of the parties are required to perform their contractual obligations. These elements are also called *conditional clauses* of the contract, or *contingencies*. A contract can be made conditional on virtually anything. Some of the more common contingencies include financing, rezoning, sale of other property,

condition precedent

Condition in a contract that must be satisfied in accordance with the terms of the contract before one or both of the parties are required to perform their contractual obligations.

inspection of property for physical defects, purchase of adjacent property, engineering reports, issuance of building or use permits, and review of documents affecting title to the property. In drafting conditional clauses, exact standards by which the parties can determine when and if the condition has been met must be provided. In addition, the contract should require the parties to use due diligence and good faith in attempting to meet the contingency. For example, a common contingency found in contracts is the financing contingency. This contingency means that the purchaser does not have an obligation to purchase the property unless the purchaser can obtain an acceptable loan for a large portion of the purchase price. Financing contingencies usually require that the contingency set forth the amount of the loan, the interest rate, and the repayment term of the loan that the purchaser is seeking to obtain. A financing contingency also requires the purchaser to make an application for a loan and to diligently try to obtain the loan. A failure to meet a condition precedent would make a contract unenforceable. Most contracts provide for repercussions in the event a contingency fails with regard not only to the contract as a whole, but also to any earnest money as well. The contract also should indicate for whose benefit the condition applies and provide if either party has a right to waive the conditions.

Definitions

Although most terms and phrases used in a contract take on their ordinary meanings, many contracts include a definitions section that carefully and clearly defines key words and phrases. This is particularly important when the parties are not from the same geographical area and the possibility exists for misunderstanding as to the exact meaning of certain terms.

Default

A contract should provide the exact rights and obligations of the parties in the event that one party fails to perform in accordance with the terms of the contract. The contract also should list the events that constitute a default. The remedies for breach of contract are discussed in Chapter 6.

Notice

Because most contracts provide that parties need to notify each other of different events, such as title objections, date for closing, and results of inspection reports, there should be a paragraph that outlines when and how notices are to be given (Example 7–16). Most notice provisions deal with personal delivery and certified mail, although under modern practice, contracts provide for notice to be sent by overnight express carriers, fax, and even e-mail. If one of the parties is a partnership, corporation, or limited liability company the contract should specify an individual to receive notice.

Example 7–16

Notification. Any notice or demand under which the terms of this Agreement or under any statute must or may be given or made by the parties hereto shall be made in writing and shall be deemed to have been delivered when hand delivered; as of the date sent by an overnight courier; or as of the date of postmark affixed by the U.S. Postal Service, by mailing the same by certified mail return receipt requested addressed to the respective parties at the following addresses:

To Purchaser: Purchaser, Inc.
535 East Paces Ferry Road
Denver, Colorado
Attn: George Purchaser

To Seller: c/o JoAnne Seller
2970 Crabtree Road, N.W.
Suite 500
Colorado Springs, Colorado

Such addresses may be changed by the giving of written notice as provided in this paragraph; provided, however, that any mailed notice of changed address shall not be effective until the fifth (5th) day after the date of postmark by the U.S. Postal Service.

Entire Agreement

The **parol evidence rule** that is applicable in most states provides that a written agreement is the best and only evidence of the agreement between the parties and that the parties are not permitted to bring in oral testimony regarding other agreements concerning the transaction. The law in many states, however, requires that the contract contain a clause that indicates that it is the entire agreement and that no other written or oral agreements affecting the transaction exist (Example 7–17). Typically, the clause states that "the contract contains the entire agreement of the parties thereto concerning the subject matter thereof and that representations, inducements, promises, or agreements oral or otherwise not expressly set forth therein shall be of any force or effect."

In addition, the contract should provide that it cannot be amended or modified unless in writing and executed by all parties to it.

parol evidence rule

Rule of evidence that provides that a written agreement is the best and only evidence of the agreement between the parties and that the parties are not permitted to bring in oral testimony regarding other agreements concerning the transaction.

Example 7–17

Entire Agreement. No agreements, representations, or warranties unless expressly incorporated or set forth in this Agreement shall be binding upon any of the parties.

Applicable Law

The general rule in most states is that a contract for the sale and purchase of real property will be governed by the law of the state in which the real property is located. Despite this general rule, most contracts do specify the law of the state that will govern the construction and enforcement of the contract (Example 7–18).

Example 7–18

This Agreement shall be construed and interpreted under the Laws of the State of Colorado.

Additional Provisions

It is not unusual, when using a preprinted form, to find additional provisions added to the contract by way of addendum or exhibit. It is important that there be a provision in the contract that provides that if conflict between the preprinted portion of the contract and the special stipulations contained in the addendum or exhibit should arise, the special stipulations will control.

Offer and Acceptance

Because most contracts are not signed at the same time by both seller and purchaser but are prepared by the seller or the purchaser and presented to the other party for consideration, it is important that the contract contain a clause that addresses the issue of when and how the offer is to be accepted and converted into a contract. This usually is done by a provision that indicates that the contract represents an offer that must be accepted by the signature of the other party to the contract on or before a certain date (Example 7–19).

Example 7–19

This instrument shall be regarded as an offer by the Purchaser or Seller who first signs to the other and is open for acceptance by the other until ___ o'clock ___ .m., on this ___ day of ___, 20 ___ by which time written acceptance of such offer must have been actually received.

    The above offer is hereby accepted, _____ o'clock _____.m. on this _____ day of _____ 20 _____.

In addition, it is preferable to make the date of the contract a certain date, especially if other dates, such as the date for doing a title examination or inspection of the property, are calculated from the date of the contract. For example, the purchaser must examine title and present objections to the seller not later than thirty days from the date of the contract.

Execution

execution

Signature of a party to a legal document. The act of signing a legal document.

The seller, purchaser, and other parties to a contract should **execute** the contract properly and in accordance with their authority (Example 7–20). It is not necessary for real estate contracts to be witnessed and notarized, and real estate contracts usually are not recorded. From the seller's perspective, recording of the contract is not advisable because if the contract is not closed, the record of the contract might represent a cloud on the property title, thus creating future problems for the seller.

Example 7–20

IN WITNESS WHEREOF, the parties hereto have set their hands and seals as of the Effective Date.

PURCHASER:
PURCHASER, INC., a Colorado corporation

_____

By: (SEAL)
    George W. Purchaser,
    President
Date Executed: _____

SELLER:

_____ (SEAL)
JoAnne Seller

_____ (SEAL)
Alice Seller Longworth

_____ (SEAL)
Warren Seller

Date Executed: _____

The undersigned as Escrowee hereby acknowledges receipt of a copy of this Agreement and of the initial Earnest Money deposit by check $___ drawn on ___, subject to collection, and agrees to hold said funds pursuant to the terms of this Agreement.

COLORADO TITLE COMPANY

Dated: _____   By: _____

Charles B. Jares, as
Executive Vice President

The preceding list is by no means exhaustive of all possible areas of concern in preparing or reviewing a real estate sales contract. The outline does touch on the major issues that a paralegal can expect a real estate contract to address. A paralegal should remember that each contract is unique and should reflect the agreement between the parties to that particular transaction. Drafting and reviewing a comprehensive sales contract requires time and careful attention to detail but should ultimately reduce the possibility of later misunderstanding between the parties.

An example of a contract for the purchase and sale of a home is shown in Exhibit 7–1 at the end of this chapter. An example of a contract for the purchase and sale of a large tract of vacant land is shown in Exhibit 7–2 at the end of this chapter.

Caveat Emptor and the Seller Disclosure Form

✱ buyer beware

Usually, real estate transactions have been governed by the common law doctrine of *caveat emptor,* which means "let the buyer beware." The doctrine of **caveat emptor** provides that a seller, absent some express warranty, is not liable to a buyer for any conditions regarding the title to the land existing at the time of transfer or any physical conditions concerning the improvements located on the land. *Caveat emptor* requires that buyers bear the burden of examining and finding any defects in both the title and condition of improvements on real estate they purchase. A buyer who fails to obtain any express warranties from a seller buys the property "as is" and "at risk."

Most states have modified the rule of caveat emptor, at least as it applies to residential property, by requiring that a seller of residential real estate complete a disclosure form to inform the buyer about the condition of the property. A sample of a seller disclosure form is shown as Exhibit 7–3 at the end of this chapter. The form requires the seller to make a good faith disclosure of all information available to the seller at the time the disclosure statement is given. Most states require that the seller disclosure statement be delivered to the buyer either prior to the seller accepting a written offer from the buyer or the buyer accepting a written offer from the seller in the sale of residential real estate. Disclosure statements require that a seller disclose all known conditions materially affecting the property and any information pertaining to basements, foundations, wells, pumps, roofs, septic tanks, sewer systems, heating systems, plumbing, electrical systems, asbestos, and structural damage, among others. Cases that have interpreted the effect of a seller disclosure statement generally hold that a seller who intentionally misrepresents the property in the seller disclosure statement may be liable in damages to the buyer. A seller who was unaware of structural damage is not usually liable for misrepresentation if the statement was given in good faith and without knowledge of the problem.

caveat emptor

A doctrine which provides that a seller, absent some express warranty, is not liable to a buyer or any conditions regarding the title or improvements to the land existing at the time of transfer.

SPECIAL COMMERCIAL CONTRACT ISSUES

The purchase and sale of a commercial investment property, such as a shopping center, office building, or apartment project, presents some special concerns for the purchaser and seller. The purpose of the following discussion is to itemize and briefly describe some of the provisions and issues that need to be addressed in the commercial real estate sale contract.

Description of the Property

The sale of a commercial real property includes more than just the real estate. Most apartment projects and office buildings contain a number of personal property items that are used in the maintenance and repair of the real property. These personal property items, such as snow removal equipment, irrigation systems, landscaping, and washing and dryer services, all need to be described and included within the description of the property being bought and sold. In addition, many times a parcel of commercial real property is being operated under a certain trade name, such as Brook Tree Apartments or Corporate Campus Office Center. The purchaser should obtain the rights to these trade names, and a provision for this assignment and transfer should be contained in the contract (see Example 7–3).

Representations, Warranties, and Covenants

In addition to the normal representations, warranties, and covenants made by a seller in a real estate contract, a number of additional representations, warranties, and covenants are normally part of a commercial contract (see Example 7–15).

Warranties Regarding Leases

Most commercial properties are income-producing, which means that the real property has been leased to tenants. There usually is a warranty on the part of the seller that all the leases, agreements, rent rolls, and income and expense statements that had been previously delivered to the purchaser are true and correct. The seller also usually agrees not to enter into any new leases during the contract period before closing without the purchaser's consent, or in the alternative, the contract will provide certain rental guidelines, such as how much rent and how long the lease must be for the seller to follow.

Service Contracts

Many commercial properties involve contracts for such services as janitorial, landscaping, and pest control. The seller should warrant that the copies of the service contracts that have been provided to the purchaser are true and correct copies. The seller also should warrant that it will not enter into any new service contracts before closing or, in the alternative, will not enter into any service contracts that are not terminable within thirty days notice.

No Litigation Affecting Seller or Property

The owners of commercial properties are more likely to have litigation filed against them than the owners of homes. It is not unusual in large commercial projects for there to be litigation between the owner and one or more of the tenants. There also may be litigation against the seller in regard to accidents, such as a slip and fall in a supermarket. Most commercial contracts require the seller to warrant that there is no litigation either pending or threatened against the seller or the real property. If there is litigation, a full disclosure of the litigation should be made in the contract. If litigation is threatened or pending, the purchaser usually wants indemnities from the seller regarding the outcome of the litigation.

Purchaser's Inspection or "Free Look"

Most purchasers of commercial properties require that they be given a period of time after the contract has been signed to inspect the real property. If during this inspection the property is found to be unacceptable, the purchaser can terminate the contract and receive a return of his earnest money. This inspection period is called a "free look" because the purchaser has a period of time to decide whether to buy the real property and can terminate during this period of time without any liability. Most inspections by purchasers of commercial properties go beyond just an inspection of the physical condition of the real property. During the inspection period, the purchaser requires the seller to furnish copies of all leases, service contracts, tenant correspondence files, tax notices, insurance premiums, operating and expense reports, and any other documentation that in any way has an effect on the operation or ownership of the real property.

Most contracts provide that the inspection period will not begin to run until the items have been furnished by the seller to the purchaser. The contract usually provides that because this information regarding the real property is private and of a sensitive nature that the purchaser agrees to keep such information confidential and will not disseminate the information to anyone without the seller's permission. Practically speaking, permission to provide the financial information concerning the property to a lender usually is required because most purchasers require institutional lender financing to purchase the commercial real property.

Closing Documents

The sale of a commercial real property requires several special closing documents in addition to the normal closing documents. Most purchasers require that the seller provide at closing a certified current rent roll and expense report. Purchasers also require that all leases be assigned, together with credits for all security deposits and prepaid rents (see Example 7–7). Purchasers also may require that each tenant sign an **estoppel letter** (Example 7–21). The average tenant estoppel letter has the tenant certify as to the accuracy of certain things regarding a lease, such as the date of the lease, date of amendments or modifications, term of the lease, renewal options, monthly rents, and security deposits. The estoppel letter also requires the tenant to swear that there are no defaults under the lease either by tenant or landlord and that the tenant has no claims, counterclaims, defenses, or setoffs against the landlord arising from the lease. A copy of the lease with all amendments is attached to the letter, and the tenant certifies that it is a true and correct copy of the lease. If the lease is guaranteed, the guarantor joins in the tenant estoppel letter.

estoppel letter
Sworn statement of fact.

Example 7–21

Date: , 20____
Office Park Investments, Inc.
P.O. Box 510
Andersonville, Indiana

          Re: *Farris Center Office Park*

Gentlemen:
     It is our understanding that Office Park Investments, Inc. (hereinafter called "Purchaser") intends to purchase the above-captioned premises, and as a condition precedent, such Purchaser requires that this certification be made by the undersigned (hereinafter called "Tenant").

(continued)

As an inducement to Purchaser to purchase the premises, and knowing that Purchaser will rely upon the information and agreements contained herein in making said purchase, Tenant hereby acknowledges, certifies, warrants, and covenants that:

1. Tenant presently leases approximately _____ square feet of space located on the above-referenced premises, pursuant to the terms and provisions of that certain Lease Agreement dated _____ 20_____, by and between _____, as Landlord, and Tenant, as Lessee, a copy of said Lease being attached hereto and made a part hereof as Exhibit A (the "Lease").

2. Said Lease is in full force and effect and Tenant is primarily liable as Lessee thereunder, and the documents attached hereto as Exhibit A constitute a full, complete, and accurate copy of said Lease, and said Lease has not been modified, supplemented, or amended in any way, and there are no other promises, obligations, understandings, agreements, or commitments between Landlord and Tenant with respect to said premises other than as expressly set forth in said Lease.

3. All contingencies and conditions precedent to the commencement, effectiveness, validity, and enforceability of said Lease have been satisfied, and Tenant hereby ratifies said Lease. All duties of an inducement nature and all work required under said Lease to be performed by Landlord have been satisfactorily completed in accordance with the provisions of said Lease, and Tenant claims no offsets, rebates, concessions, abatements, recoupments, or defenses against or with respect to rent, additional rent, or other sums payable under the terms of said Lease, and there are no breaches or defaults under the terms of said Lease, and no event has occurred that, with the passage of time or the giving of notice, or both, shall constitute a default by Landlord or Tenant under the terms of said Lease.

4. The base monthly rental currently payable by Tenant under the terms of said Lease is _____ ($_____) Dollars per month, and no other rent has been prepaid to Landlord or any other party, and there has been no security deposit paid to or currently held by Landlord with respect to said Lease.

5. The Lease Term pursuant to said Lease commenced on _____ 20_____, and shall expire on _____, 20_____.

6. Tenant has no interest, rights, or claims with respect to said premises other than the interest, rights, or claims arising out of or with respect to said lease.

7. Tenant is a corporation and is in good standing with the State of Indiana, and has full authority to execute the within document.

8. The undersigned officers of Tenant have full authority to execute and deliver this certificate as agents for and on behalf of Tenant.

9. Tenant is currently in actual, full, and complete physical occupancy and possession of said premises, and Tenant has accepted said premises as suitable for all uses and purposes contemplated or intended under said Lease.

10. Upon acquisition of said premises by Purchaser, Tenant shall attorn to Purchaser or any successor assign of Purchaser's and recognize such party as Tenant's Lessor and Landlord pursuant to said Lease.

Very truly yours,

_____

By: _____
President

Lender's Estoppel

Many commercial real properties are sold subject to existing debt. The purchaser assumes or takes subject to the prior mortgage. Most commercial purchasers require that the prior mortgage holder sign an estoppel certificate and that the certificate be provided to the purchaser at closing (Example 7–22). A lender's estoppel usually requires the lender to attach a copy of the note and mortgage to the certificate and to certify that the attachments are true and correct copies and that there are no amendments or modifications to the note and mortgage. The estoppel also requires a certification as to the outstanding balance of the loan and a certification as to the balance of any escrows that may be held for taxes or insurance. The lender also certifies that the loan is not in default and that the sale of the real property to the purchaser will not constitute a default. The lender acknowledges the purchaser's address for purposes of sending notices under the note and mortgage. An example of a lender estoppel letter is set forth as Example 7–22.

Example 7–22

STATE OF _____
COUNTY OF _____

ESTOPPEL CERTIFICATE

The undersigned hereby certifies as of the date of execution hereof as follows:

(a) That the undersigned (the "Holder") is the holder of a certain Promissory Note dated May 11, 1998, from ACME DEVELOPMENT, INC., a California corporation, in the original principal amount of $3,560,000.00 (the "Note");

(b) That the Note is secured by a Deed of Trust from ACME DEVELOPMENT, INC. to Holder (the "Lender") dated May 11, 1998, and recorded in Deed Book 7244, Page 301, Oil County, California, records (the "Security Deed"), which encumbers certain property located in Oil County, California (the "Property"), more particularly described on Exhibit A attached hereto and made a part hereof;

(c) That true and correct copies of the Note and Security Deed are attached hereto as Exhibits B and C;

(d) That the Note and Security Deed are in full force and effect and there have been no events of default in connection therewith;

(e) That all payments of interest and principal under the Note and Security Deed are current; that as of this date the outstanding principal balance due on the Note is $____, that the last payment received on the Note was on the ____ day of ____, 20____; and that the next payment on the Note is due on ____;

(f) Holder understands that HAMMOND CENTER, INC. is purchasing the property subject to the Security Deed; the purchase of the property is hereby consented to and approved and shall not constitute an event of default in connection with the Note or Security Deed;

(g) That there is no failure of compliance, breach, default, or event of default that has occurred in the Note or Security Deed as of this date;

(h) Holder agrees to provide to HAMMOND CENTER, INC., Suite 120, 450 Glenlake Parkway, San Diego, California, notice of any default under the Note or Security Deed and permit HAMMOND CENTER, INC. fifteen (15) days to cure any default under the Note or Security Deed, prior to Holder's acceleration of the Note. The undersigned acknowledges that Hammond Center, Inc. is relying on this Certificate in connection with its purchase of the property.

WITNESS my hand and seal this ____ day of _____, 20_____.

THE SECOND NATIONAL BANK

By _____ (SEAL)

Signed, sealed, and delivered   [CORPORATE SEAL]
in the presence of:

_____
Witness

Sworn to before me
this _____ day of
_____, 20____.

_____
Notary Public
My Commission Expires:

_____

Rent Prorations

The proration between purchaser and seller of rent received from tenants occupying commercial real property is always contained in a commercial contract (Examples 7–23 through 7–25). Rent proration questions can be dealt with in a number of ways. The following issues, however, should be at least considered and addressed in any commercial rent proration provision: (a) Are rents to be prorated on the basis of rent paid or rent payable; that is, is the seller to receive credit at closing for rents that are delinquent or due but unpaid? (b) If the seller does not receive credit at closing for delinquent or due but unpaid rents, is the seller to be permitted to proceed against tenants of the project after closing to collect such rents allocable to periods before the closing date? The purchaser may object to permitting the seller to do this because it can unreasonably interfere with the purchaser's tenants at that time. (c) If the seller is not permitted to proceed against the tenants after closing to collect delinquent or due but unpaid rents, is the purchaser to have any obligation to the seller to make an effort with respect to this collection? In what order are funds received from tenants owing delinquent or due but unpaid rents to be applied?

Example 7–23

All paid rents under the existing leases and the new leases shall be prorated as of the closing date. In the event that, at the time of closing, there are any past due or delinquent rents owing by any tenants of the project, Buyer shall have the exclusive right to collect such past due or delinquent rents and shall remit to Seller its pro rata share thereof, to the extent, and only to the extent, that the aggregate rents received by Buyer from each such tenant owing past due or delinquent rents exceeds the sum of (i) the aggregate rents and other sums payable by such tenant for periods from and after the closing date, (ii) any amount expended by Buyer to collect such past due or delinquent rents. Buyer shall have no obligation to collect or enforce collection of any such past due or delinquent rents from or against a tenant.

Example 7–24

Current rent paid under the existing leases and the new leases for the month in which the closing date occurs shall be prorated as of the closing date. The proration of such current rent paid shall be affected so that Seller shall be credited with all such rent accruing prior to but not including the closing date, and Buyer shall be credited with all such rent accruing thereafter. Buyer shall receive a credit in the amount of any prepaid rents paid to Seller as of the closing date. No proration shall be made for rents delinquent or due but unpaid as of the closing date; provided, however, that Seller shall deliver to Buyer on the closing date a schedule identifying the tenants who owe delinquent rents, and Buyer shall make reasonable efforts to collect for Seller such delinquent rents, and shall remit to Seller any rents for periods prior to the closing date actually paid to Buyer. All monies collected by Buyer from tenants owing delinquent rents shall be applied first to delinquent rents owed to Seller for the month during which the closing date occurs and the one preceding month, then to rent owed to Buyer for the period from and after the closing date to the date of collection and then to any other delinquent rents owed to Seller.

Example 7–25

Rents under the existing leases and the new leases (and that of brokerage commissions) shall be prorated as of the closing date. Seller shall pay to Buyer that portion of the rent paid by the tenants under the existing leases and new leases applicable to periods subsequent to the closing date. No proration shall be made for rent delinquent or due but unpaid as of the closing date. All monies collected by Buyer from tenants owing delinquent or due but unpaid rents as of the closing date shall be applied first to current rents owing to Buyer by such tenants for periods from and after the closing date. From and after the closing date, Buyer shall use its best efforts to collect any delinquent or due but unpaid rents owing to Seller for periods prior to the closing date, and shall promptly remit to Seller any amounts collected by Buyer from tenants owing delinquent or due but unpaid rents, in excess of current rents owing to Buyer. Buyer shall have no obligation to incur any expense or to institute any litigation against any tenant, to collect any such delinquent or due but unpaid rent, but Seller shall have the right to exercise such rights and remedies as may be provided for or allowed by law or in equity to collect such rents other than the right to evict or dispossess such tenant.

Lease Commissions

It is quite common in commercial real estate transactions for the leases to involve commissions to brokers who obtained the leases for the seller. These brokerage commissions usually are a percentage of each month's rent for the remaining term of the lease and, in some cases, extensions or renewals of the lease. Brokerage commissions can be prorated between purchaser and seller in a number of ways. The purchaser can assume and pay all lease commissions earned and due in connection with the leases after the date of closing, whereas the seller is responsible to pay all lease commissions before the date of closing. The purchaser may want the seller to "cash out," or pay off, the lease commissions in full before the time of closing. Most brokers are quite willing to discount future lease commissions to a current value and receive a lump sum cash payment at the time of closing. If the lease commissions are to be cashed out by the seller at closing, it is prudent for the contract to provide that the seller will provide proof that such commissions have been paid. This proof can be in the form of a release from all the brokers of any claim for commissions under the leases that are assigned in connection with the sale of the property.

Security Deposits

Most tenants of commercial properties deliver to the landlord at the time the lease is signed a security deposit securing the tenant's performance under the lease. On expiration of the lease, the security deposits are refundable to the tenant. Therefore, in most commercial contracts, the purchaser requires that it receive a credit for all security deposits that may be owed after the closing to the tenants (Example 7–26).

Example 7–26

Buyer shall receive a credit against the purchase price in the amount of all security deposits paid by tenants, and interest accrued thereon contingently payable to the tenant for his or her account there maintained, and Seller shall retain such funds free and clear of any and all claims on the part of the tenants. Buyer shall be responsible for maintaining a security deposit in the aggregate amounts so credited to Buyer in accordance with the provisions of the existing leases and the new leases relevant thereto.

Many states require that security deposits for tenants of apartment projects be placed in a special escrow account to ensure their return on expiration of the lease. The provision shown in Example 7–27 may be found in an apartment project contract to handle the special escrow arrangement.

> ## Example 7–27
>
> Seller shall deliver to Buyer a certified or cashier's check drawn upon or by a national bank having offices in the city where the property is located, payable to Buyer, in an amount equal to the total of all tenants security deposits held by Seller "as landlord" under the existing leases and the new leases, together with a schedule setting forth the name of each tenant for whose account a deposit is being held, the apartment unit with respect to which deposit is being held, and the amount of such deposit. Buyer shall promptly deposit the proceeds of such check into an escrow account, shall hold such deposits in trust for the benefit of the tenants of the project, and shall comply in all respects with the provisions of state law respecting security deposits. Buyer shall and hereby indemnify and hold Seller harmless from, against, and in respect of any and all liabilities, damages, losses, costs, expenses (including attorney's fees and expenses), causes of action, suits, judgments, claims, demands, and liens of any nature whatsoever arising in connection with such security deposit from and after the closing date.

Seller's Covenants Regarding Operation of Property

A critical issue regarding the operation of commercial property during the pendency of the contract is that of limitations on the seller's ability to enter into new leases with respect to the property and the requirement of the seller to maintain the status quo regarding insurance policies. The provision shown in Example 7–28 addresses these concerns.

> ## Example 7–28
>
> Between the date hereof and the closing date, Seller shall operate the project in an orderly course of business; shall maintain and repair the project so that, on the closing date, the project will be in the same condition as it now exists, natural wear and tear and loss by insured casualty alone excepted; shall comply with all obligations of the lessor or landlord under the existing leases and the new leases; shall continue to carry and maintain and enforce all existing policies of casualty and public liability insurance with respect to the property; shall not make or enter into any lease or other agreement for the use, occupancy, or possession of all or any part of the land or improvements except for leases that (1) are for a term including option renewal in terms that are no longer than three years; (2) provide for a rental rate not less than the rental rate being charged for some rent spaces in the project as of the date of Seller's execution of this agreement; and (3) are on a standard form of lease used by Seller and approved by purchaser with respect to the project.

Hazardous Materials

The presence of hazardous waste materials on real property can create serious problems for the property owner. Federal and state law imposes on the owner of real property liability for all damage caused by hazardous waste as well as the cost of hazardous waste cleanup. An owner of real property may be responsible regardless of whether the owner created the hazardous waste material. Most purchasers will not purchase real property without having a hazardous waste inspection done by a professional inspection firm. These hazardous waste inspections are typically a Phase I, which is a general inspection of land records and a site visit to the property, or a Phase II, which involves the laboratory testing of soil and water conditions at the property. In addition, most purchasers require that the contract contain certain representations, warranties, and indemnifications from the seller regarding hazardous waste materials. The provision shown as Example 7–29 addresses these concerns.

Example 7–29

Hazardous Waste Indemnity. Purchaser's obligation to purchase the Property pursuant to this Contract is contingent upon there being no petroleum hydrocarbons or contaminants contained in the soil, surface, or subterranean water that are in violation of local, state, or federal statutes and regulations and that there be no other existence of any hazardous substances or waste located upon the Property. For purposes of this Agreement, the term "hazardous substances or wastes" shall mean petroleum, including crude oil or any fraction thereof, flammable explosives, radioactive materials, asbestos, any material containing polychlorinated biphenyls, and any of the substances defined as "hazardous substances" or "toxic substances" in the Comprehensive Environmental Response, Compensation and Liability Act of 1980, as amended, 42 U.S.C. Section 9601 et seq., the Hazardous Materials Transportation Act, 49 U.S.C. Section 1802 et seq., the Resource Conservation and Recovery Act, 42 U.S.C. Section 6901 et seq., and in the Toxic Substance Control Act of 1976, as amended, 15 U.S.C. Section 2601 et seq., or any other federal, state, local or other governmental legislation, statute, law, code, rule, regulation, or ordinance identified by its terms as pertaining to the disposal, storage, generation, or presence of hazardous substances or waste (the "Environmental Laws"). Purchaser shall at Seller's expense have the Property inspected for purposes of discovering if hazardous substances or wastes exist. Seller's share of the cost of the inspection shall not exceed $_____ (1) _____; if the inspection cost exceeds $_____ (2) _____, Seller shall pay $_____ (3) _____ and Purchaser shall pay the excess cost above $_____ (4) _____. If, upon inspection, hazardous wastes or substances are found to exist, Purchaser shall have the option of terminating this contract and receiving a refund of the earnest money down payment. In the alternative, Seller shall have the right at its own expense to remove all hazardous substances or wastes from the Property and to conclude the sale with Purchaser, or Seller may terminate this Contract without penalty.

Seller warrants, represents and agrees that (a) neither Seller nor any person has violated any of the applicable Environmental Laws as defined in the paragraph above relating to or affecting the Property; (b) the Property is presently in compliance with all Environmental Laws, and there are no facts or circumstances presently existing upon or under the Property or relating to the representations and warranties which violate any of the applicable Environmental Laws, and there is not now pending nor threatened any action, suit, investigation, or proceeding against Seller or the Property (or against any other party related to the Property); (c) Seller or tenant has obtained all licenses, permits or other governmental regulatory approvals necessary to comply with Environmental Laws and Seller is in full compliance with the terms and provisions of all such licenses, permits, or other governmental regulatory approvals; and (d) Seller has received no notice that any municipality or any governmental or quasi-governmental authorities are investigating or have determined that there are any violations of zoning, health, building, fire, pollution, environmental, or other statutes, ordinances, or regulations affecting the Property.

Indemnification

Most purchasers of commercial properties require indemnification from the seller with respect to liabilities pertaining to the property arising before the closing date. Most sellers likewise require an indemnification from the purchaser for such liabilities arising subsequent to the closing date. When drafting indemnification language, particular attention should be paid to the description of the liabilities covered and as to whether each party's indemnification is to be limited to the period of that party's actual ownership of the property or to extend to all periods before the closing date (with respect to the seller's indemnification) and all periods subsequent to the closing date (with respect to the buyer's indemnification). An indemnity provision is shown in Example 7–30.

> ### Example 7–30
>
> The Seller and Buyer shall and do each hereby indemnify, defend, and hold each other harmless from, against, and in respect to any and all liabilities, damages, losses, expenses (including counsel fees and expenses and disbursements of counsel), amounts of judgment, assessments, fines or penalties, and amounts paid in compromise or settlement, suffered, incurred, or sustained by the indemnified party on account, by reason, as a result of or in connection with any matter pertaining to the ownership, use, occupancy, management, maintenance, or operation of the property arising during the period of ownership of the property by the indemnifying party.

Seller's Disclaimer of Warranty

Although the purchaser tries to obtain as many warranties as possible from a seller, the seller often will only make warranties set forth in the contract and disclaim any and all other warranties. The provision shown in Example 7–31 is designed to allow the seller to achieve that result.

> ### Example 7–31
>
> Except for the warranties of title to be included in Seller's instruments of conveyance to the project, Seller does not, by the execution and delivery of this agreement, and Seller shall not, by the execution and delivery of any document or instrument executed and delivered in connection with the closing, make any warranty, expressed or implied, of any kind or nature whatsoever, with respect to the project and all such warranties are hereby disclaimed. Without limiting the generality of the foregoing, Seller makes, and shall make, no expressed or implied warranty of suitability or fitness of any of the property for any purpose, or as to the merchantability of title, value, quality, quantity, condition, or salability of any of the property, or that the use or sale of any of the property will not violate the copyright, trademark, or patent rights of any person. Sale of the property by Seller to Buyer hereunder shall be "as is" and "where is."

Real property usually is sold without any warranty concerning its physical condition unless the warranties are expressed in the contract or required by state law. The law in many states does require that certain warranties regarding the fitness and suitability of the improvement on the real property be given by the seller of a new residential home.

An example of a contract for the purchase and sale of a retail shopping center is shown as Exhibit 7–4 at the end of this chapter. A checklist for the preparation of a real estate contract is found on the following pages.

OPTIONS

option

A contract by which an owner of property, usually called the optionor, agrees with another person, usually called the optionee, that the optionee shall have the right to buy the owner's real property at a fixed price within a certain time on agreed terms and conditions.

Buyers and sellers of real property occasionally use an option initially instead of entering into a contract for the purchase and sale of the property. An **option** is a contract by which an owner of property, usually called the optionor, agrees with another person, usually called the optionee, that the optionee shall have the right to buy the owner's real property at a fixed price within a certain time on agreed terms and conditions. The effect of an option is to bind an owner of real property to an agreement to sell the property to the optionee in the event the optionee elects to purchase the property at the fixed price and on the terms set forth in the option. The decision to enter into the contract to purchase the property is entirely at the discretion of the optionee. An option usually is based on valuable consideration and is an irrevocable offer to sell by the owner of the real property. Option agreements must be in writing and be supported by something of value, usually money paid as an option price. An option form is shown as Exhibit 7–5 at the end of this chapter.

CONTRACTS AND COMPUTERS

The preparation of contracts has been affected by the use of computers and the Internet. Most law firms and corporations have abandoned preprinted, fill-in-the-blank contracts in favor of computer-generated contracts. Standard contract provisions are stored on a computer hard drive and controlled using word processing software such as WordPerfect or Microsoft Word. This word processing technology creates flexibility in the drafting and redrafting of contracts. As contract terms are negotiated, the changes to the contract from the previous draft can be shown in some highlighted or underlined form on the current draft. Drafts can also be time- or date-stamped on each page so that parties do not become confused by multiple drafts of the agreement.

✓ CHECKLIST

Preparation or Review of Commercial Real Estate Contract

The issues to be covered by a real estate contract are so numerous that without a checklist, it is easy to leave some issues out of the contract. A checklist for the preparation of a commercial contract follows.

☐ I. Parties to the Contract
- ☐ A. Seller should be the current owner of the property.
- ☐ B. Purchaser should sign the contract in exactly the same form as he or she wants to obtain title. If the purchaser intends to have an entity such as a limited partnership or partnership to be formed to take title to the property, the contract should provide for the transfer and assignment of the contract to the new entity.
- ☐ C. Brokers and agents usually are made a party to the contract to enforce commission rights.

☐ II. Description of Property to Be Purchased
- ☐ A. Adequate description of real property and associated personal property
- ☐ B. Include easements appurtenant to the property
  - 1. Cross-easement agreements (shopping center)
  - 2. Off-site utility easements
  - 3. Access easements

☐ III. Purchase Price and Earnest Money
- ☐ A. Earnest money
  - 1. Specify amount and who holds the earnest money
  - 2. Additional earnest money payments for extensions of time to close
  - 3. What happens to any interest on earnest money
  - 4. Application of earnest money to the purchase price
  - 5. Application of earnest money in the event of default under contract

(continued)

☐ B. Purchase price
    1. Calculation of purchase price
        a. Predetermined fixed amount
        b. Amount to be determined based on amount of acreage or square footage of property
            i. Establish method for determining acreage or square footage
            ii. Method of payment
                (a) All cash
                (b) Cash in excess of existing debt
                    (i) Consider due on sale clause
                    (ii) Which party bears expenses of transfer due holder of existing loan
                (c) Seller financing
                    (i) All terms of seller financing, including amount, interest rate, and terms, should be identified.
                    (ii) Terms of the note and mortgage should be negotiated and copies attached as exhibits.
                (d) New loan to be obtained by the purchaser

☐ IV. Title Examination
    ☐ A. Which party conducts examination
    ☐ B. Quality of title to be delivered by seller
        1. Marketable
        2. Insurable
        3. Free and clear of all matters of record
    ☐ C. Obligation of seller to correct title objections
        1. Defects curable by payment of money
        2. Other defects
            a. Defects existing before execution of contract
            b. Defects created after execution of contract

☐ V. Closing
    ☐ A. Which party establishes closing date
    ☐ B. Minimum or maximum periods to close
    ☐ C. Right to extend closing date
        1. Purchaser's right to extend closing by payment of money
        2. Seller's right to extend closing by reason of acts of purchaser
    ☐ D. Who bears closing cost
    ☐ E. Prorations
        1. Rent
            a. Fixed rent
            b. Overage or percentage rent
            c. Rent in arrears
        2. Interest on the existing debt
        3. Utilities and taxes
            a. Prorations when utilities and taxes are paid by landlord
            b. Prorations when utilities and taxes are paid by tenant
        4. Credits to purchaser for prepaid rents and security deposits
    ☐ F. Possession of property
        1. Normally delivered at closing
        2. When possession is delivered to purchaser before closing
            a. For limited purposes of installing fixtures
            b. For purpose of conducting business
                i. Specify what amounts are to be paid by purchaser for early occupancy
                ii. Specify risk of loss

(continued)

        3. When possession is delivered to purchaser after closing
          a. For limited purpose of permitting seller to remove personal property from the premises
          b. Specify what amounts are to be paid by seller for continued possession
          c. Specify risks or losses due to possession by seller

☐   G. Documents to be delivered at closing
        1. Warranty deed
          a. General or limited
          b. Legal description to be based on new survey
        2. Assignment of leases
        3. Bill of sale to personal property
        4. Owner's affidavit
        5. General assignment of warranties
        6. Certified rent roll
        7. Termite bond
        8. Foreign person affidavit
        9. Escrow agreements for tenant work and tenant allowances
        10. Covenant not to compete
        11. Prior lender and tenant estoppel letters
        12. As-built survey
        13. Notice to tenants
        14. Copies of leases
        15. Evidence of payment of brokerage commission
          a. Brokerage commission arising out of purchase and sale
          b. Cash out of the leasing commissions

☐ VI. Covenants and Warranties of the Parties
    ☐   A. Purpose of warranties is to ensure accuracy of information on property
    ☐   B. Typical issues covered by warranties
        1. Seller's title to property
        2. Seller's authority to sign and carry out contract
        3. Removal of encumbrances
        4. Compliance of property with laws and ordinances
        5. No condemnation suit pending
        6. Right to possession
        7. True and correct copies of leases and agreements delivered to purchaser
        8. Accuracy of rent roll and expense statements
        9. Absence of mechanic's and materialmen's liens
        10. No litigation against seller or property
        11. Condition of property
        12. No encroachments
        13. No prior use from manufacture or storage of toxic or hazardous waste
    ☐   C. Limitations on warranties
        1. Best of knowledge
        2. Materiality
        3. Limited period of survival after closing

☐ VII. Conditions to Closing
    ☐   A. Purpose of conditions to closing
        1. Limitation on purchaser's obligation to close until seller completes certain items
        2. Substitute for complete warranties of seller
    ☐   B. Which parties have right to waive conditions

(continued)

☐ C. Typical conditions
1. Satisfactory inspection of property
2. Satisfactory inspection of records involving the property
3. Ability to obtain new loan
4. Approval of board of directors of purchaser
5. Receipt of estoppel certificates from lenders and tenants
6. Truth and accuracy of seller's warranties on closing date

☐ VIII. Inspection by Purchaser
☐ A. Right to inspect physical condition of the property
1. Time in which to exercise inspection
2. Right to terminate after inspection
☐ B. Right to inspect seller's books and records related to property
1. Place of inspection
2. Right to copy records
3. Permitted use of materials inspected
☐ C. Right to inspect property for possible environmental contamination
1. Phase I examination
2. Phase II examination
☐ D. Enforceability of free-look cancellation clauses

☐ IX. Casualty and Condemnation
☐ A. Purchaser's options on casualty or condemnation
1. Materiality limitation on purchaser's right to terminate
2. Time limits on exercise of option to terminate by purchaser
☐ B. Seller's obligations on casualty or condemnation
1. Timely notice to purchaser of event of casualty or condemnation
2. Is seller obligated to restore premises
☐ C. Should seller be required to carry insurance

☐ X. Remedies on Default
☐ A. Default by seller or purchaser
1. Suit for damages or specific performance
2. Liquidated damages

☐ XI. Brokerage
☐ A. Obtain warranties from each party as to brokers involved
☐ B. Specify which party pays brokerage commissions
☐ C. Cross-indemnity for brokerage claims

☐ XII. Confidentiality
☐ A. No recording the contract
☐ B. All information delivered to purchaser shall be kept confidential or delivered to other people only with seller's consent.

☐ XIII. Miscellaneous Provisions
☐ A. Right to sign a contract
☐ B. Provisions for date and manner of delivering notices
☐ C. Time is of essence
☐ D. Survival of contract provisions
☐ E. Contract represents entire agreement between parties
☐ F. Severability of contract provisions
☐ G. Method of offer and acceptance
☐ H. Provide for approval and counterpart form

With the recent technology explosion, more and more people are communicating through the use of computers. Most legal documents such as contracts, leases, and mortgage documents are being sent electronically from one computer to another over the Internet. Using the Internet, paralegals can now e-mail word processing files, spreadsheets, and even computer programs to and from clients, lawyers, and other paralegals. For the paralegal, all of this means that large amounts of information can be located, reviewed, and retrieved on the computer screen, filed away, or printed. Most law firms, corporations, and other organizations connected to the Internet have obtained their own unique domain names.

Not only can drafts and correspondence be sent electronically from one computer to another, but also the legal recognition of **electronic signatures** now permits valid and enforceable documents to be sent electronically. Most states have passed laws that authorize electronic signatures on real estate documents such as contracts, options, leases, deeds, easements, and mortgages. An electronic signature is generally defined to mean a signature created, transmitted, received, and restored by electronic means and includes, but is not limited to, a secure electronic signature. A *secure electronic signature* is defined as an electronic or digital method executed or adopted by a party with the intent to be bound or to authenticate a record which is unique to the person using it that is capable of verification, is under the sole control of the person using it, and is linked to data in such a manner that if the data is changed, the electronic signature is invalid. For example, if a person signs a mortgage with a secure electronic signature and the mortgage is electronically changed after the secure signature has been affixed, the signature would be invalid, and the mortgage is likewise invalid.

> **electronic signature**
>
> A person's signature created electronically by a computer.

Most states also recognize electronic signatures by notaries. Even if the notary notarizes a document electronically, the notary must physically witness the person's signature being notarized.

Many states protect consumers in residential real estate transactions and provide that a consumer cannot be required to use electronic documents and signatures without the consumer's consent.

🏛 ETHICS: Illegal or Fraudulent Activity

A paralegal is employed with a law firm. A client of the firm is a real estate developer who builds and sells single-family homes. The developer is generally honest but is having trouble selling one of its homes. The developer finally has a purchaser who is willing to buy the home, but the purchaser does not have any money. The developer wants to prepare a contract that will show that the purchaser is making a down payment of 20 percent of the purchase price, which should enable the purchaser to go to a lending institution and get a loan for the other 80 percent. The developer, however, will not actually receive the 20 percent down payment. The developer instead will take a note from the purchaser for the 20 percent, which will be paid out over a period of time. This means that the purchaser actually will not have any money invested in the property at the time of the sale. This activity on the part of the developer and purchaser constitutes a fraud on the lending institution that will be making a loan to the purchaser.

The developer has explained all of this to an attorney who works at the firm. The attorney has decided that he will go ahead and prepare a contract that will show that a down payment of 20 percent has been made and received by the developer. The attorney has asked a paralegal at the firm to assist in the preparation of the contract. Does the preparation of the contract, which shows that a down payment of 20 percent has been made when in fact it has not, constitute a breach of ethics on the part of the attorney as well as the paralegal?

An attorney or a paralegal should never assist a client in conduct that is illegal or fraudulent. Assisting a client to commit fraud can result in a loss of license to practice law on the part of the attorney and could subject both the attorney and the paralegal to civil and criminal penalties. The participation by the attorney and paralegal in the preparation of the contract to assist the developer in perpetrating a fraud on the lending institution is a serious breach of ethics.

The Internet has also changed many of the ways in which notices are to be given pursuant to a real estate contract. Although first-class mail and a more established technological method, facsimile (fax) transmission, may still be required in a real estate contract, it is not uncommon for buyers and sellers to now agree that notices can be sent via e-mail. Many contracts provide for e-mail addresses in the notice section of the contract.

One risk in allowing notices to be sent by e-mail is that it is often difficult to determine if an e-mail message has in fact been received. This problem in acknowledging receipt may be satisfied by providing that notice can be sent electronically but must be followed up by a written notice sent by another means, such as mail or fax.

Another area of concern when sending e-mail or fax messages in regard to a contract is the privacy issue. Electronically sent notices are not as private as notices sent by other means. E-mails between attorneys and their clients may not be privileged communications. Many bar associations have been counseling attorneys to obtain consents from their clients before sending e-mail messages to the clients. The consent basically is an acknowledgment by the client that the e-mail may not be a privileged communication, but that the client desires e-mail communication even though the privilege may not exist.

SUMMARY

A purchaser and seller of real property each have a number of issues and concerns that must be addressed and agreed to in the contract for purchase and sale. A paralegal who participates in the preparation and review of a real estate contract must not only be aware of the general issues and concerns of purchasers and sellers of real property, but also must ask the client about any special issues or concerns. The contract is the agreement that outlines responsibilities and duties of the respective seller and purchaser and is the blueprint that will be followed at the time of the closing of the sale and purchase. Careful thought and attention to detail must be given to the preparation and review of real estate contracts.

The real estate contract is the mutual promise of both purchaser and seller regarding the future transfer of ownership to real property. The contract does not transfer ownership but merely promises to do so at some future date and time. At the time that ownership is to be transferred, the transfer is accomplished by a separate legal document known as a deed. Deeds are the subject of Chapter 8.

HELPFUL WEBSITES

Legal Guide to Buying and Selling a Home
An excellent legal guide to buying and selling a home can be found at the American Bar Association Web site at *http://www.abalawinfo.org*.

Home Buying Purchase Contract Contingencies
General information about the legal and practical aspects of buying a home can be found on the About.com Web site.

The site contains a list with explanation of the common home buying purchase contract contingencies at *http://homebuying.about.com*.

KEY TERMS

bank wire transfer	condition precedent	option
cashier's check	earnest money	parol evidence rule
caveat emptor	electronic signature	time is of the essence
certified check	estoppel letter	
closing	execution	

REVIEW QUESTIONS

1. Why is careful attention to detail required in the preparation of a real estate contract?
2. Briefly describe the various methods of payment for real property.
3. What does the "time is of the essence" phrase mean in a real estate contract?
4. What is a "free look," and in what circumstances would you expect to find a free-look provision in a real estate contract?
5. Explain the difference between marketable title and insurable title.
6. What items usually are prorated in a real estate contract?
7. If, under a real estate contract, the seller is to provide financing to the purchaser, what issues should be discussed concerning seller financing?
8. At what time do most real estate contracts provide that the purchaser will take possession of the property?
9. What is a closing, and why is its date important in a real estate contract?
10. What is earnest money, and what is its role in a real estate contract?
11. What is the doctrine of *caveat emptor,* and how does it apply to a real estate purchase and sale contract?
12. Why would a real estate broker want to be a party to a real estate contract?
13. What warranties commonly are required of a seller in a real estate contract?
14. What warranties commonly are required of a purchaser in a real estate contract?
15. What is a tenant estoppel letter, and when would one be required in a real estate contract?

CASE PROBLEMS

1. The following is a list of contract provisions. Do these provisions favor the seller or the purchaser?
   a. Seller is to convey insurable title to the real property at closing.
   b. Seller is to convey title to the real property subject to utility easements and other restrictions of record.
   c. Seller shall not alter or encumber the title to the real property after the date of the contract without the prior written consent of purchaser.
   d. The real estate contract is freely assignable.
   e. The contract is silent as to risk of loss between date of contract and date of closing.
2. Harold and Maude entered into negotiations with Sam to purchase Sam's home. The home was not new, and Harold and Maude had some concerns that the roof might leak. Sam verbally assured them that the roof did not leak. The written contract entered into between Sam and Harold and Maude, however, did not contain any written warranties concerning the roof. The contract also contained a provision that stated that no agreements, representations, or warranties, unless expressly incorporated or set forth in the contract, would be binding on any of the parties. After Harold and Maude purchased the home, they discovered that the roof leaked every time it rained. Harold and Maude have come to the law firm where you are a paralegal and have asked for advice concerning their rights to sue Sam for his misrepresentation concerning the condition of the roof. You have been asked to research the issue and to report to your supervising attorney your conclusions concerning Harold and Maude's rights against Sam for the roof leak. What would be your conclusion?

PRACTICAL ASSIGNMENTS

1. Review the contract for purchase and sale of a retail shopping center shown as Exhibit 7–4, and answer the following questions. Answer the questions in detail, making reference to the contract paragraph number you used as authority for your answer.

   a. How much is the brokerage commission in connection with this sale, and who is responsible for paying it?

   b. Who is the holder of the real estate note and deed to secure debt that is going to be assumed by the purchaser in connection with this transaction?

   c. What is the name of the property being sold?

   d. What percentage of the tenant estoppels must the seller obtain?

   e. Under what terms is the purchaser willing to consent to new leases on the property from the date of contract to the date of closing?

   f. How many net rentable square feet are contained in the property being bought and sold?

   g. Where is the closing to take place?

   h. What amount of gross rental income from the property is guaranteed by the seller for the first year after closing date?

   i. On what basis does the seller agree to pay the purchaser any income shortfall from the actual income generated from the property and the seller's guarantee of income?

   j. Is Saturday considered a business day under the agreement?

   k. What is the amount of the earnest money deposit?

   l. When is the effective date as that term is defined under the contract?

   m. What type of deed will be delivered to the purchaser at the time of the sale?

   n. When will possession of the property be delivered to the purchaser pursuant to the agreement?

   o. What is the seller's remedy for the purchaser's default?

   p. Can the purchaser assign its rights under the contract to a partnership of which the purchaser is not a general partner?

   q. If there is damage to the property before closing in the amount of $15,000, does this give the purchaser the right to terminate the agreement and not purchase the property?

   r. Is the earnest money to be held in an interest-bearing or a non-interest-bearing account?

   s. If the purchaser desires title insurance, who will pay for the title insurance?

   t. What is the earliest date that the tenant estoppels required by seller can be dated?

   u. Does the purchaser have a free look under this agreement, and when is the last date for fully exercising its free look?

   v. If the holder of the existing mortgage loan charges an assumption fee, who will pay the assumption fee?

   w. What is to happen to leasing brokerage agreements in connection with the property before closing?

   x. Who has the risk of loss and damage to the property before closing?

   y. How are security deposits paid under the leases to be prorated at time of closing?

2. Obtain a copy of a contract for sale of residential real estate from a local realtor or other source. Compare it carefully with the contract shown as Exhibit 7–1. Discuss in writing the similarities and differences between the two contracts.

3. Research your state's law to determine what seller disclosure forms are required. Are the seller disclosure forms required only for residential transactions or commercial transactions, or both? Is the giving of a seller disclosure form voluntary or mandatory?

4. Research your state's law to determine if it recognizes electronic signatures on real estate documents. Make a copy of your state's statute and review it to see if there are limitations on the use of electronic signature.

ADDENDUM

Exhibit 7–1 Contract for Purchase and Sale of a Home
Exhibit 7–2 Contract for Purchase and Sale of a Large Tract of Vacant Land
Exhibit 7–3 Seller's Property Disclosure Statement
Exhibit 7–4 Contract for Purchase and Sale of a Retail Shopping Center

Exhibit 7–5 Option to Purchase
The exhibits referred to in the contracts are not included in the materials presented.

ACKNOWLEDGMENT

Portions of this chapter have been excerpted from *The Sales Contract: Real Practice and Procedures Program Materials* by Donald Lee Mize "Pages 2.1–2.45; Institute of Continuing Legal Education in Georgia, 1985, Athens, Georgia." Used by permission of the Publisher.

Student StudyWare™ CD-ROM

Interactive Student CD in the book includes additional quizzing, case studies, and key terms flashcards.

Online Companion™

For additional resources, please go to *www.paralegal.delmar.cengage.com*

EXHIBIT 7–1

Contract for Purchase and Sale of a Home

Reprinted with permission of Georgia Association of Realtors, Inc.

PURCHASE AND SALE AGREEMENT

Offer Date: _____, 20_____

2005 Printing

1. <u>Purchase and Sale</u>. The undersigned buyer ("Buyer") agrees to buy and the undersigned seller ("Seller") agrees to sell all that tract or parcel of land, with such improvements as are located thereon, described as follows: All that tract of land lying and being in Land Lot _____ of the _____ District, _____ Section of _____ County, Georgia, and being known as Address _____, City _____, Georgia, Zip Code _____, according to the present system of numbering in and around this area, being more particularly described as Lot _____, Block _____, Unit _____, Phase/Section _____ of _____ Subdivision, as recorded in Plat Book _____, Page _____, _____ County, Georgia records, together with all fixtures, landscaping, improvements, and appurtenances; all being hereinafter collectively referred to as the "Property." The full legal description of Property is the same as is recorded with the Clerk of the Superior Court of the county in which Property is located and is made a part of this Agreement by reference.

2. <u>Purchase Price and Method of Payment</u>. Buyer warrants that Buyer will have sufficient cash at closing, which when combined with the loan(s), if any, referenced herein, will allow Buyer to complete the purchase of Property. Buyer does not need to sell or lease other real property in order to complete the purchase of Property. The purchase price of Property to be paid by Buyer at closing is: _____ U.S. Dollars, $_____

   subject to the following: *[Select sections A, B, C and/or D below. The sections not marked are not a part of this Agreement.]*

❏**A. All Cash at Closing:** Buyer shall pay the purchase price to Seller in cash, or its equivalent. Buyer's obligation to close shall not be subject to any financial contingency. Buyer shall pay all closing costs.

❏**B. Loan to be Assumed:** See Exhibit "_____."

❏**C. New Loan to be Obtained:**

   1.**Type of Loan:** This Agreement is conditioned upon Buyer's ability to obtain a loan to be repaid in consecutive monthly payments with the terms described below, (hereinafter "the Primary Loan") secured by a first priority security deed on Property:
     a. Loan Amount: _____ percent (%) of the purchase price of Property
     b. Term: _____ years
     c. Interest rate at par of _____ percent (%) per annum
     d. Loan Type: ❏ Conventional ❏ FHA (see exhibit) ❏ VA (see exhibit) ❏ Other (see exhibit)
     e. Rate Type: ❏ Fixed Rate Mortgage ❏ Adjustable Rate Mortgage ❏ Interest Only Mortgage
   "Ability to obtain" as used herein shall mean that Buyer, as of the closing date, is qualified to obtain the loan based upon the lender's customary and standard underwriting criteria. If the basis of the loan denial is either or both of the following, Buyer shall still be deemed to have the ability to obtain the Primary Loan: (1) Buyer lacks sufficient funds to close; or (2) Buyer is required to lease or sell other real property as a condition of obtaining the Primary Loan.
   2.**Seller's Contributions at Closing:** Seller shall, at the time of closing, contribute a sum not to exceed $_____ to be used by Buyer to pay for:
     a. preparation of the warranty deed and owner's affidavit by the closing attorney;
     b. at Buyer's discretion any of the following (if allowed by the lender): closing costs, prepaid items, escrow establishment charges, loan discount points, survey costs, and insurance premiums (including flood insurance, if applicable) relating to Property and/or loan.
   Buyer shall pay all other costs, fees, and amounts for the above referenced items and to fulfill lender requirements to otherwise close this transaction.
   3.**Closing Attorney:** This transaction shall be closed by the law firm of _____
   _____. If Buyer is given the right to select a law firm from a mortgage lender's approved list of closing attorneys, Buyer agrees to select said law firm. If the law firm named above is not on the mortgage lender's approved list, and cannot be added in time to close this transaction, Buyer may select another law firm from lender's approved list to close this transaction.
   4.**Loan Obligations:** Buyer shall: (a) make application for the Primary Loan within _____ days from the Binding Agreement Date; (b) immediately give notice to Seller of having applied for such loan (or any subsequent loan), and provide the name and telephone number of the lender and the name and telephone number of the loan originator; and (c) pursue qualification for and approval of such loan diligently and in good faith. Buyer hereby authorizes Buyer's lender to release information to Seller and Seller's Broker verifying the amount and terms of any loan for which Buyer has applied. Should Buyer not timely apply for the Primary Loan, Seller may terminate this Agreement if Buyer does not cure the default within five days after receiving written notice thereof by providing Seller with written evidence of having applied for such loan. Notwithstanding the above, Buyer may fulfill the obligation to apply for the Primary Loan by applying for any other available loan with terms for which Buyer may more easily qualify. Buyer shall be obligated to close this transaction if Buyer has the ability to obtain the Primary Loan or any other loan for which Buyer has applied and been approved. Prior to closing, Buyer shall not intentionally make any material changes in Buyer's financial condition which would adversely affect Buyer's ability to obtain the Primary Loan or any other loan referenced herein. In the event any application of Buyer for a loan on Property is denied, Buyer shall immediately give notice of the same to Seller and promptly thereafter provide Seller with a letter from the lender denying the loan detailing all of the reasons for the denial.

❏ **D. Second Loan to be Obtained:** see Exhibit "_____."

Copyright© 2005 by Georgia Association of REALTORS®, Inc.   F20, Purchase and Sale Agreement, Page 1 of 7 01/01/05

(continued)

EXHIBIT 7–1

Contract for Purchase and Sale of a Home (*continued*)

---

3. <u>Earnest Money.</u>
   A. **Receipt:** Buyer has paid to _____ ("Holder") earnest money of $_____ check, **OR** $_____ cash, which has been received by Holder. The earnest money shall be deposited in Holder's escrow/trust account (with Holder retaining the interest if the account is interest bearing) within five banking days from the Binding Agreement Date. If Buyer writes a check for earnest money and the same is deposited into Holder's escrow/trust account, Holder shall not be required to return the earnest money until the check has cleared the account on which the check was written. In the event any earnest money check is dishonored, for any reason, by the bank upon which it is drawn, Holder shall promptly give notice to Buyer and Seller. Buyer shall have three banking days after notice to deliver good funds to Holder. In the event Buyer does not timely deliver good funds, Seller shall have the right to terminate this Agreement upon written notice to Buyer.
   B. **Entitlement to Earnest Money:** Subject to the Disbursement of Earnest Money paragraph below:
      1. Buyer shall be entitled to the earnest money upon: a) failure of the parties to enter into a binding agreement; b) failure of any contingency or condition to which this Agreement is subject; c) termination of this Agreement due to the default of Seller; d) the termination of this Agreement in accordance with a specific right to terminate set forth in the Agreement; or e) upon the closing of Property; and
      2. Seller shall be entitled to the earnest money if this Agreement is terminated due to the default of Buyer. In such event, Holder may pay the earnest money to Seller by check, which if accepted and deposited by Seller, shall constitute liquidated damages in full settlement of all claims of Seller. It is agreed to by the parties that such liquidated damages are not a penalty and are a good faith estimate of Seller's actual damages, which damages are difficult to ascertain.
   C. **Disbursement of Earnest Money:** Holder shall disburse the earnest money upon: a) the closing of Property; b) a subsequent written agreement of Buyer and Seller; c) an order of a court or arbitrator having jurisdiction over any dispute involving the earnest money; or d) the failure of the parties to enter into a binding agreement (where there is no dispute over the formation or enforceability of the Agreement). In addition, Holder may disburse the earnest money upon a reasonable interpretation of the Agreement, provided that Holder first gives all parties 15 days notice stating to whom and why the disbursement will be made. Any party may object to the proposed disbursement by giving written notice of the same to Holder within the 15 day notice period. Objections not timely made in writing shall be deemed waived. If Holder receives an objection and, after considering it, decides to disburse the earnest money as originally proposed, Holder may do so and send notice to the parties of Holder's action. If Holder decides to modify its proposed disbursement, Holder shall first send a new 15 day notice to the parties stating the rationale for the modification and to whom the disbursement will now be made.
   D. **Interpleader:** If there is a dispute over the earnest money which the parties cannot resolve after a reasonable period of time, and where Holder has a bona fide question as to who is entitled to the earnest money, Broker may interplead the earnest money into a court of competent jurisdiction. Holder shall be reimbursed for and may deduct from any funds interpleaded, its costs and expenses, including reasonable attorney's fees actually incurred. The prevailing defendant in the interpleader lawsuit shall be entitled to collect its attorney's fees and court costs and the amount deducted by Holder from the non-prevailing defendant.
   E. **Hold Harmless:** All parties hereby agree to indemnify and hold Holder harmless from and against all claims, causes of action, suits and damages arising out of or related to the performance by Holder of its duties hereunder. All parties further covenant and agree not to sue Holder for damages relating to any decision of Holder to disburse earnest money made in accordance with the requirements of this Agreement.

4. <u>Closing and Possession.</u>
   A. **Property Condition:** Seller warrants that at the time of closing or upon the granting of possession if at a time other than at closing, Property will be in substantially the same condition (including conditions disclosed in the Seller's Property Disclosure Statement) as on the Binding Agreement Date, except for normal wear and tear, and changes made to the condition of Property pursuant to the written agreement of Buyer and Seller. Seller shall deliver Property clean and free of debris at time of possession. If Property is destroyed or substantially damaged prior to closing, Seller shall promptly give notice to Buyer of the same and provide Buyer with whatever information Seller has regarding the availability of insurance and the disposition of any insurance claim. Buyer or Seller may terminate this Agreement not later than fourteen days from receipt of the above notice. If Buyer or Seller do not terminate this Agreement, Seller shall cause Property to be restored to substantially the same condition as on the Binding Agreement Date. The date of closing shall be extended until the earlier of:
      1. one year from the original date of closing, or
      2. seven days from the date that Property has been restored to substantially the same condition as on the Binding Agreement Date and a new certificate of occupancy (if required) is issued.
   B. **Taxes:** Real estate taxes on said Property for the calendar year in which the sale is closed shall be prorated as of the date of closing. Seller shall pay State of Georgia property transfer tax.
   C. **Timing of Closing:** This transaction shall be closed on the _____ day of _____, 20_____ or on such other date as may be agreed to in writing by the parties. In the event the loan described herein is unable to be closed on or before said date or Seller fails to satisfy valid title objections, then Buyer or Seller may, by unilateral notice to the other party (which notice must be received on or before the closing date) extend the closing date and the date for surrender of occupancy up to seven days.
   D. **Possession:** Buyer agrees to allow Seller to retain possession of Property through: *[Select sections 1, 2, or 3 below. The sections not marked are not a part of this Agreement.]*
      ❏ 1. the closing; or ❏ 2. _____ hours after the closing; or ❏ 3. _____ days after the closing at _____o'clock _____.m.
   E. **Warranties Transfer:** Seller agrees to transfer to Buyer, at closing, subject to Buyer's acceptance thereof, (and at Buyer's expense, if there is any cost associated with said transfer) Seller's interest in any existing manufacturer's warranties, service contracts, termite bond or treatment guarantee and/or other similar warranties which, by their terms, may be transferable to Buyer.
   F. **Prorations:** Seller and Buyer agree to prorate all utility bills between themselves, as of the date of closing (or the day of possession of Property by Buyer, whichever is the later) which are issued after closing and include service for any period of time Property was owned/occupied by Seller or any other person prior to Buyer.

Copyright© 2005 by Georgia Association of REALTORS®, Inc.   F20, Purchase and Sale Agreement, Page 2 of 7   01/01/05

(continued)

EXHIBIT 7-1

Contract for Purchase and Sale of a Home (*continued*)

G. Closing Certifications: Buyer and Seller shall execute and deliver such certifications, affidavits, and statements as are required at closing to meet the requirements of the lender and of federal and state law.

5. **Seller's Property Disclosure.** Seller's Property Disclosure Statement is attached hereto and incorporated herein. Seller warrants that to the best of Seller's knowledge and belief, the information contained therein is accurate and complete as of the Binding Agreement Date.

6. **Title.**
   A. **Warranty:** Seller warrants that, at the time of closing, Seller will convey good and marketable title to said Property by general warranty deed subject only to: (1) zoning; (2) general utility, sewer, and drainage easements of record as of the Binding Agreement Date and upon which the improvements do not encroach; (3) subdivision and/or condominium declarations, covenants, restrictions, and easements of record on the Binding Agreement Date; and (4) leases and other encumbrances specified in this Agreement. Buyer agrees to assume Seller's responsibilities in any leases specified in this Agreement.
   B. **Examination:** Buyer may, prior to closing, examine title and furnish Seller with a written statement of objections affecting the marketability of said title. If Seller fails to satisfy valid title objections prior to closing or any extension thereof, then Buyer may terminate the Agreement upon written notice to Seller. Good and marketable title as used herein shall mean title which a title insurance company licensed to do business in Georgia will insure at its regular rates, subject only to standard exceptions.
   C. **Survey:** Any survey of Property attached hereto by agreement of the parties prior to the Binding Agreement Date shall be a part of this Agreement. Buyer shall have the right to terminate this Agreement upon written notice to Seller if a new survey performed by a surveyor licensed in Georgia is obtained which is materially different from any attached survey with respect to Property. The term "materially different" shall not apply to any improvements constructed by Seller in their agreed-upon locations subsequent to Binding Date Agreement. Matters revealed in said survey shall not relieve the warranty of title obligations of Seller referenced above.

7. **Termite Letter.**
   A. **Report:** An official Georgia Wood Infestation Report (the "Report") prepared by a licensed pest control operator, covering each dwelling (including attachments thereto) and garage on Property and dated within 180 days of the Binding Agreement Date is ❑, **OR,** is NOT ❑ attached to this Agreement as an exhibit. If the Report is not attached, Seller shall provide such Report to Buyer within seven days from the Binding Agreement Date. Buyer shall have the right to terminate this Agreement within ten days from the Binding Agreement Date if either of the following events occur:
      1. The Report is not timely provided to Buyer; or
      2. The Report provided after the Binding Agreement Date indicates present infestation of, or damage to, Property from termites or other wood destroying organisms.
   B. **Rights:** If Buyer does not timely give Seller notice of Buyer's decision to terminate this Agreement, Buyer's right to terminate the Agreement pursuant to this paragraph shall be waived. Notwithstanding the above, Buyer shall continue to have whatever other rights to terminate this Agreement, if any, that exist elsewhere in this Agreement. Unless otherwise noted on the Seller's Property Disclosure Statement, to the best of Seller's knowledge, the information contained in any attached or later provided Report is accurate and complete, and no other termite inspections have been performed or reports issued, the findings of which are inconsistent with the Report attached hereto.
   C. **Closing:** Prior to closing, Seller shall treat active infestation of termites and other wood destroying organisms, if any. At closing, Seller shall provide Buyer with a Report prepared by a licensed pest control operator dated within 30 days of the closing, stating that each dwelling and garage has been found to be free from active infestation of termites and other wood destroying organisms.

8. **Inspection.**
   A. **Right to Inspect:** Buyer and/or Buyer's representatives shall have the right to enter Property at Buyer's expense and at reasonable times (including immediately prior to closing) to thoroughly inspect, examine, test and survey Property. This shall include the right to inspect and test for lead-based paint and lead-based paint hazards for not less than ten days from the Binding Agreement Date. Seller shall cause all utility services and any pool, spa, and similar items to be operational so that Buyer may complete all inspections under this Agreement. Buyer agrees to hold Seller and all Brokers harmless from all claims, injuries, and damages arising out of or related to the exercise of these rights.
   B. **Rights of Buyer in Addition to Inspection:** [*Select Section 1, 2 or 3 below. The sections not marked are not a part of this Agreement.*]

   ❑ 1. **Property Sold with Right to Request Repairs.**
      a. Buyer shall have the right to request that Seller repair and/or replace Defects, if any, in Property identified by Buyer's Inspector(s) in a written report(s). Within _____ days from Binding Agreement Date, Buyer shall provide Seller with: (1) a signed written amendment to this Agreement requesting Defects to be repaired and/or replaced, and (2) a copy of all reports of Inspectors describing those Defects. If Buyer does not timely present the written amendment and inspection report(s), Buyer shall be deemed to have accepted Property "as is."
      b. If Buyer timely submits the written amendment and accompanying inspection reports, Buyer and Seller shall have _____ days from the Binding Agreement Date (hereinafter "Defect Resolution Period") to attempt to negotiate the Defects to be repaired and/or replaced, sign an amendment to the Agreement regarding the same and have it delivered to Buyer and Seller. If the requirements of the preceding sentence have not occurred before the end of the Defect Resolution Period, then within one day thereafter: (1) Buyer or Seller may accept in writing the other party's last written offer or counteroffer regarding the repair and/or replacement of Defects (regardless of whether the same has expired, or has previously been rejected, it being the express intent of the parties to override any common law to the contrary); or (2) Buyer may accept Property in "as-is" condition. A final agreement regarding the Defects to be repaired and/or replaced shall be formed by the first party to give such notice of acceptance to the other party. All parties shall then promptly execute an amendment to the Agreement reflecting the accepted offer or counteroffer. If neither party timely accepts the other party's last offer or counteroffer or Buyer does not buy Property "as-is", this Agreement shall terminate.

F20, Purchase and Sale Agreement, Page 3 of 7 01/01/05

(continued)

EXHIBIT 7–1

Contract for Purchase and Sale of a Home (*continued*)

c. Notwithstanding any other provision to the contrary, in the event the Inspector, in a written report provided to Seller, recommends any additional test, study, inspection or evaluation of any product, item or condition in Property, then the time period to inspect Property and the Defect Resolution Period may be extended once by Buyer, upon notice to Seller, delivered prior to the expiration of the original period to inspect Property, for up to seven additional days. The date of closing shall also be extended for the same number of days but only if the original closing date would, as a result of the above time periods being extended, fall within the new Defect Resolution Period.

d. All agreed upon repairs and replacements shall be completed in a good and workmanlike manner prior to closing. Nothing herein shall require Seller to replace a product or item (or portion thereof) in Property if it can be repaired such that at closing it is reasonably fit for the purpose(s) for which it was intended.

e. Definitions:

(1) Inspector – The term "Inspector" shall mean a person or company with specific, professional expertise in property inspections or in an item, building product or condition contained therein for which the Inspector is inspecting, examining, testing and/or surveying.

(2) Defects – The term "Defects" shall mean any condition, building product or item in Property, or portion thereof identified by an Inspector in a written report, which: (a) is in a condition which represents a significant health risk or an imminent risk of injury or damage to persons or property; (b) constitutes a violation of current laws, governmental codes or regulations except if it is "grandfathered" because it was initially installed or constructed prior to or in accordance with all applicable laws, codes or regulations; or (c) is not at the present time in good working order and repair, excepting normal wear and tear. All parties acknowledge that certain building products are or have been the subject of class action lawsuits and are generally considered by Inspectors to be defective ("Defective Product"). Notwithstanding the above, all parties agree that if the existence of a particular Defective Product has been disclosed by Seller to Buyer in the Seller's Property Disclosure Statement prior to Buyer contracting to purchase Property, then that Defective Product, or any portion thereof, as the case may be, shall not be considered to be a Defect if at the time of the inspection it is functioning in accordance with manufacturer's specifications and is reasonably fit for the purposes for which it was intended. However, if a particular building product is identified by the Inspector in a written report as generally being a Defective Product and the particular building product is not disclosed in the Seller's Property Disclosure Statement as set forth above, all parties agree that such a Defective Product shall be considered a Defect which Buyer can request Seller to repair and/or replace.

OR

☐ 2. **Property Sold with Right to Terminate.**

a. In consideration of Ten Dollars and other good and valuable consideration, the receipt and sufficiency of which is hereby acknowledged, Seller does hereby grant Buyer a _____ day right ("Termination Right") from Binding Agreement Date during which Buyer may do any or all of the following: (1) conduct at Buyer's sole expense whatever due diligence, inspections, examinations, surveys and testing, if any, Buyer deems appropriate; (2) seek to amend this Agreement to address any concerns with Property; (3) terminate this Agreement without penalty.

b. If Buyer decides to exercise Buyer's right to terminate this Agreement, Buyer must give notice of the same to Seller prior to the expiration of the Termination Right. If Buyer fails to give such notice timely, the Termination Right shall automatically expire and shall no longer be a part of this Agreement and Buyer shall be deemed to have accepted Property "as-is". The expiration of the Termination Right shall not, however, remove or terminate any other contingencies to which this Agreement may be subject or limit any other rights which Buyer may have under this Agreement. All parties agree that the Binding Agreement Date shall not be affected by Buyer's Termination Right.

c. Buyer warrants that Buyer is not currently under contract (including option contracts) to purchase other real property and agrees not to enter into any other such contracts during the time period that Buyer has a Termination Right. All parties agree that this Agreement shall constitute an option agreement until such time as the Termination Right has expired, lapses or has otherwise been terminated.

OR

☐ 3. **Property Sold "As Is."** All parties agree that Property is being sold "as is," with all faults including but not limited to lead-based paint and lead-based paint hazards and damage from termites and other wood destroying organisms. Seller shall have no obligation to make repairs to Property.

9. **Disclaimer.** Buyer and Seller acknowledge that they have not relied upon any advice, representations or statements of Brokers and waive and shall not assert any claims against Brokers involving the same. Buyer and Seller agree that Brokers shall not be responsible to advise Buyer and Seller on any matter including but not limited to the following: any matter which could have been revealed through a survey, title search or inspection of Property; the condition of Property, any portion thereof, or any item therein; building products and construction techniques; the necessity or cost of any repairs to Property; mold; hazardous or toxic materials or substances; termites and other wood destroying organisms; the tax or legal consequences of this transaction; the availability and cost of utilities or community amenities; the appraised or future value of Property; any condition(s) existing off Property which may affect Property; the terms, conditions and availability of financing; and the uses and zoning of Property whether permitted or proposed. Buyer and Seller acknowledge that Brokers are not experts with respect to the above matters and that, if any of these matters or any other matters are of concern to them, they should seek independent expert advice relative thereto. Buyer and Seller acknowledge that Brokers shall not be responsible to monitor or supervise any portion of any construction or repairs to Property and that such tasks clearly fall outside the scope of real estate brokerage services. Buyer further acknowledges that in every neighborhood there are conditions which different buyers may find objectionable. Buyer shall therefore be responsible to become fully acquainted with neighborhood and other off site conditions which could affect Property.

F20, Purchase and Sale Agreement, Page 4 of 7   01/01/05

EXHIBIT 7–1

Contract for Purchase and Sale of a Home (*continued*)

10. <u>Agency and Brokerage.</u>
   A. **Agency Disclosure:** In this Agreement, the term ΑBrokerΘ shall mean a licensed Georgia real estate broker or brokerage firm and, where the context would indicate, the broker's affiliated licensees. No Broker in this transaction shall owe any duty to Buyer or Seller greater than what is set forth in their brokerage engagements and the Brokerage Relationships in Real Estate Transactions Act, O.C.G.A. § 10-6A-1 et. seq.;
      1. **No Agency Relationship.** Buyer and Seller acknowledge that, if they are not represented by a Broker, they are each solely responsible for protecting their own interests, and that Broker's role is limited to performing ministerial acts for that party.
      2. **Listing Broker.** Broker working with the Seller is identified on the signature page as the "Listing Broker";

         and said Broker is ❑, **OR,** is NOT ❑ representing Seller;
      3. **Selling Broker.** Broker working with Buyer is identified on the signature page as "Selling Broker";

         and said Broker is ❑, **OR,** is NOT ❑ representing Buyer; and
      4. **Dual Agency or Designated Agency.** If Buyer and Seller are both being represented by the same Broker,

         a relationship of either designated agency ❑, **OR,** dual agency ❑ shall exist.
         a. **Dual Agency Disclosure.** [*Applicable only if dual agency has been selected above*]
            Buyer and Seller are aware that Broker is acting as a dual agent in this transaction and consent to the same. Buyer and Seller have been advised that:
            (1) In serving as a dual agent, Broker is representing two clients whose interests are or at times could be different or even adverse;
            (2) Broker will disclose all adverse, material facts relevant to the transaction and actually known to the dual agent to all parties in the transaction except for information made confidential by request or instructions from each client which is not otherwise required to be disclosed by law;
            (3) Buyer and Seller do not have to consent to dual agency and, the consent of Buyer and Seller to dual agency has been given voluntarily and the parties have read and understand their brokerage engagement agreements.
            (4) Notwithstanding any provision to the contrary contained herein, Buyer and Seller each hereby direct Broker, while acting as a dual agent, to keep confidential and not reveal to the other party any information which could materially and adversely affect their negotiating position.
         b. **Designated Agency Assignment.** [*Applicable only if the designated agency has been selected above*]
            Broker has assigned _____ to work exclusively with Buyer as Buyer's designated agent and _____ to work exclusively with Seller as Seller's designated agent. Each designated agent shall exclusively represent the party to whom each has been assigned as a client and shall not represent in this transaction the client assigned to the other designated agent.
   B. **Brokerage:** Broker(s) identified herein have performed valuable brokerage services and are to be paid a commission pursuant to a separate agreement or agreements. Unless otherwise provided for herein, Listing Broker will be paid a commission by Seller, and the Selling Broker will receive a portion of the Listing Broker's commission pursuant to a cooperative brokerage agreement. The closing attorney is directed to pay the commission of the Broker(s) at closing out of the proceeds of the sale. If the sale proceeds are insufficient to pay the full commission, the party owing the commission will pay any shortfall at closing. If more than one Broker is involved in the transaction, the closing attorney is directed to pay each Broker its respective portion of said commission. In the event the sale is not closed because of Buyer's and/or Seller's failure or refusal to perform any of their obligations herein, the non-performing party shall immediately pay the Broker(s) the full commission the Broker(s) would have received had the sale closed, and the Selling Broker and Listing Broker may jointly or independently pursue the non-performing party for their portion of the commission.
   C. **Disclosure of Commission, Rebate, or Direct Profit:** Broker hereby discloses that Broker may receive a commission, rebate or direct profit for procuring a mortgage loan, insurance or other services on behalf of Buyer or Seller.
   D. **Material Relationship Disclosure:** Broker and/or affiliated licensees have no material relationship with either Buyer or Seller except as follows: _____

11. <u>Other Provisions.</u>
   A. **Binding Effect, Entire Agreement, Modification, Assignment:** This Agreement constitutes the sole and entire agreement between the parties and shall be binding upon the parties and their successors, heirs and permitted assigns. No representation, promise or inducement not included in this Agreement shall be binding upon any party hereto. This Agreement may not be amended, modified or waived except by the written agreement of Buyer and Seller. This Agreement may not be assigned by Buyer except with the written agreement of Seller. Any assignee shall fulfill all the terms and conditions of this Agreement.
   B. **Survival of Agreement:** All conditions and stipulations in this Agreement, which the parties agree shall be performed or fulfilled after the closing, shall survive closing until such time as said conditions or stipulations are performed or fulfilled.
   C. **Governing Law:** This Agreement may be signed in multiple counterparts and shall be interpreted in accordance with the laws of the State of Georgia.
   D. **Time of Essence:** Time is of the essence of this Agreement.
   E. **Terminology:** As the context may require in this Agreement: (1) the singular shall mean the plural and vice versa; and (2) all pronouns shall mean and include the person, entity, firm, or corporation to which they relate.
   F. **Responsibility to Cooperate:** All parties agree to take all actions and do all things reasonably necessary to fulfill in good faith and in a timely manner the terms and conditions of this Agreement.

F20, Purchase and Sale Agreement, Page 5 of 7 01/01/05

(continued)

EXHIBIT 7-1
Contract for Purchase and Sale of a Home (*continued*)

G. Notices:
1. **All Notices Must Be In Writing.** All notices, including, but not limited to, offers, counteroffers, acceptances, amendments, notices to terminate and demands, required or permitted hereunder shall be in writing, signed by the party giving the notice and delivered either: (a) in person; (b) by an overnight delivery service, prepaid; (c) by facsimile transmission (FAX); or (d) by the United States Postal Service, postage prepaid, registered or certified return receipt requested.
2. **When Notice to Broker Is Notice to Client.** Except in transactions where Broker is practicing designated agency, notice to Broker shall for all purposes be deemed to be notice to the party being represented by Broker as a client. In transactions where Broker is practicing designated agency, notice to the designated agent shall be deemed to be notice to the party being represented by the designated agent. Notice to Broker shall not be deemed to be notice to any party who is only a customer of Broker.
3. **Faxed Notices.** All FAX notices to Listing Broker or Selling Broker shall be sent to their respective FAX numbers identified on the signature page of this Agreement. FAX notices to the designated agent for Buyer shall be sent to the FAX number of Selling Broker. FAX notices to the designated agent for Seller shall be sent to the FAX number of Listing Broker. All FAX notices to an unrepresented Buyer or unrepresented Seller shall be sent to the following facsimile numbers:

   Unrepresented Buyer: _____ ; Unrepresented Seller: _____ .

   Notice sent by FAX shall be deemed to be given and received as of the date and time it is transmitted provided that the sending FAX produces a written confirmation showing the correct date and the time of the transmission and the telephone number referenced herein to which the notice should have been sent. Any notice sent by FAX shall be sent to such other FAX number as the receiving party may from time to time specify by notice to the party sending the FAX. Any party sending notice by FAX shall send an original copy of the notice if so requested by the other party. A faxed signature of a party shall constitute an original signature binding upon that party.
4. **Miscellaneous.** Except as may be provided herein, notices shall be deemed to be given as of the date and time they are received. The notice requirements referenced herein shall be strictly construed.

H. Binding Agreement Date: The Binding Agreement Date shall be the date when the party making the last Offer receives notice that the Offer has been accepted. This party (or the Broker representing this party) shall fill in the Binding Agreement Date below and promptly give notice of this date to the other party.

12. <u>**Exhibits and Addenda**</u>. All exhibits and/or addenda attached hereto, listed below, or referenced herein are made a part of this Agreement. If any such exhibit or addendum conflicts with any proceeding paragraph, said exhibit or addendum shall control:

SPECIAL STIPULATIONS: The following Special Stipulations, if conflicting with any exhibit, addendum, or preceding paragraph, shall control:

(continued)

EXHIBIT 7–1

Contract for Purchase and Sale of a Home (*continued*)

☐ Mark box if additional Special Stipulations are attached.

Time Limit: The terms of this Agreement shall constitute an offer ("Offer") which shall be open for acceptance until _____ o'clock _____.m. on the _____ day of _____, 20_____.

Acceptance: This Offer is hereby accepted, without change, at _____ o'clock _____.m. on the _____ day of _____, 20_____.

_____
Selling Broker

Buyer's Signature
_____

_____   _____
MLS Office Code   Brokerage Firm License Number

Print or Type Name
_____

Broker's Phone#_____ & FAX#_____

By: _____
    Broker or Broker's Affiliated Licensee

Buyer's Signature
_____

Print or Type Name
_____

_____
Print or Type Name

_____
Selling Agent's Georgia Real Estate License Number

Multiple Listing Number _____

_____
Listing Broker

Seller's Signature
_____

_____   _____
MLS Office Code   Brokerage Firm License Number

Print or Type Name
_____

Broker's Phone#_____ & FAX#_____

By: _____
    Broker or Broker's Affiliated Licensee

Seller's Signature
_____

Print or Type Name
_____

_____
Print or Type Name

_____
Listing Agent's Georgia Real Estate License Number

Binding Agreement Date: The Binding Agreement Date shall be the date when the party making the last Offer receives notice that the Offer has been accepted. This party (or the Broker representing this party) shall fill in the Binding Agreement Date and promptly give notice of this date to the other party. The Binding Agreement Date in this transaction is the _____ day of _____, 20_____.

F20, Purchase and Sale Agreement, Page 7 of 7 01/01/05

EXHIBIT 7–2

Contract for Purchase and Sale of a Large Tract of Vacant Land

STATE OF
COUNTY OF BAKER

CONTRACT FOR PURCHASE AND SALE

THIS IS A CONTRACT for the purchase and sale of certain real estate by and between <u>JOHN J. JOHNS</u>, a resident of <u>Baker</u> County (hereinafter called "Seller"), <u>THOMAS T. TOMS</u>, a resident of <u>Charlie</u> County (hereinafter called "Purchaser"), and **Community & Home Properties** (hereinafter called "Broker").

In consideration of the mutual covenants herein contained, and other good and valuable consideration, the receipt and sufficiency of which is hereby acknowledged, the parties hereby agree as follows:

1. Agreement to Buy and Sell

Seller hereby agrees to sell and Purchaser hereby agrees to buy all that tract or parcel of land described on Exhibit A attached hereto and made a part hereof lying and being in Land Lot <u>172</u> of the <u>14th</u> District of <u>Baker</u> County, and being the same property conveyed to Seller by warranty deed dated <u>January 4, 2000</u> and recorded in Deed Book <u>140</u>, Page <u>28</u>, <u>Baker</u> County Records, which deed is incorporated herein by reference. The property which is the subject of this Contract (hereinafter called "the Property") includes the land, all crops, plants, trees and shrubbery thereon, all buildings thereon and all fixtures therein.

2. Survey

Prior to date of closing as hereinafter provided in Paragraph 7, Purchaser shall at Purchaser's expense cause an accurate survey to be made of the Property by a reputable surveyor registered under the laws of the State of   . The plat of such survey ("the plat") shall show the boundaries of the Property and the acreage therein computed to the nearest one-hundredth of an acre. Purchaser shall promptly furnish Seller with a copy of the plat and the plat shall conclusively determine as between Purchaser and Seller the acreage in the Property. Seller's conveyance to Purchaser shall be in accordance with said survey.*

3. Purchase Price

The purchase price for the Property shall be $5,000.00 per acre, and the total purchase price for the Property shall be determined by multiplying by said purchase price per acre the number of acres determined by the plat. Provided, however, that any portion of the Property lying within the rights-of-way of any road, street or easement, or below the high water mark of any streams and creeks, and all other areas to which Seller cannot convey title as provided herein, shall be excluded for purposes of determining the purchase price.

4. Payment

The purchase price of the Property shall be paid as follows:

(a) At the time of closing, Purchaser shall pay to Seller in cash or by Purchaser's [certified or cashier's] check an amount of money equal to twenty-nine percent (<u>29%</u>) of the purchase price, less a credit for all earnest money paid hereunder.

(b) The balance of the purchase price shall be paid by Purchaser's Promissory Note [in the form attached hereto as Exhibit B], which Note shall provide <u>ten</u> equal annual installments of principal, the first of which shall be due and payable on the fifth anniversary of closing hereunder and subsequent installments shall be due on each anniversary thereafter until paid in full.

(c) The Note shall bear interest on the unpaid balance of principal at the rate of <u>eight</u> percent (<u>8%</u>) per annum, which interest shall be payable on each anniversary of the closing hereunder.

(d) The Note shall provide that, after the last day of the calendar year in which closing hereunder takes place, the principal sum of said Note may be prepaid in whole or in part without penalty

---

*If Purchaser or Seller have the right to review the plat of survey, see alternative provisions.

Delmar/Cengage Learning

(continued)

EXHIBIT 7–2

Contract for Purchase and Sale of a Large Tract of Vacant Land (*continued*)

and without further interest on the amounts prepaid from the date of such prepayment. All partial prepayments shall be credited to installments of principal in the inverse order of maturity.

(e) The Note shall be secured by a Purchase Money Deed to Secure Debt conveying the Property to Seller as security. The form of said Deed to Secure Debt is attached hereto as Exhibit C and made a part hereof.

(f) The Note and Deed to Secure Debt shall provide that Seller shall not exercise any of Seller's remedies for Purchaser's default thereunder (including without limitation the right of acceleration of the balance of Purchaser's indebtedness thereunder) until the <u>tenth</u> day after written notice of said default (which written notice shall specify the nature of all such defaults and set out the method of cure of such defaults by Purchaser) is provided by Seller to Purchaser. If Purchaser has not cured all such defaults within <u>ten</u> days after receipt of such notice, Seller shall then be empowered to exercise all of Seller's remedies under the Note and Deed to Secure Debt.

(g) The Deed to Secure Debt shall provide for the release of the property described therein as set forth in Exhibit C attached hereto.

5. <u>Warranties of Seller</u>

Seller hereby warrants and represents that:

(a) Seller owns unencumbered fee simple title to the property, free and clear of all restrictions, liens and encumbrances except as set forth on Exhibit A hereto and herein called "the Permitted Title Exceptions," that no assessments have been made against said property which are unpaid (except ad valorem taxes for the current year) whether or not they have become liens, that the Property is not subject to any other leases nor to the claims of any tenants in possession, and that so long as this Contract remains in force, Seller will not lease or convey any portion of the Property or any rights therein, nor enter into any agreements or amendments to agreements granting to any person or entity any rights with respect to the Property or any part thereof.

(b) The Property contains not less than <u>20</u> acres.

(c) The Property has not previously been used as a landfill or as a dump for garbage or refuse, and that no portion of the Property is subject to flood plain restrictions.

(d) Access to the streets and roads adjoining the Property is not limited or restricted except by applicable zoning laws.

(e) All utilities, including but not limited to water, gas, sewer and electricity, are located within or at the boundary lines of the Property.

(f) The Property is now zoned <u>AG–1</u> under the present zoning laws of Baker County.

6. <u>Title Objections</u>

Purchaser shall have <u>30</u> calendar days from the date of this Agreement in which to examine Seller's title. If Purchaser finds any legal defects to title other than the Permitted Title Exceptions, Seller shall be furnished with a written statement thereof and shall have <u>30</u> calendar days in which to correct such defects, and Seller shall take all steps, including payment of money, necessary to correct said legal defects. If Seller shall fail to correct such legal defects within <u>30</u> days, then Purchaser shall have the choice of (a) accepting the Property with such legal defects after deduction from the purchase price otherwise payable hereunder the cost of correction of such legal defects which can be corrected by the payment of money; (b) postponing closing hereunder for not more than <u>ninety</u> calendar days until said defects are corrected or (c) declining to accept the Property with such legal defects, such choice to be exercised by written notice to Seller mailed within <u>10</u> calendar days following the end of the period provided above for the correction by Seller of such legal defects. Should Purchaser elect to postpone closing under (b) above and should, at the end of said ninety-calendar–day postponement period, said legal defects remain uncorrected, Purchaser shall have the further choice of options (a) and (c) set forth above in this paragraph, such choice to be exercised by written notice to Seller mailed within ten calendar days following the end of such postponement period. If Purchaser shall decline to so accept the Property subject to such legal defects, then this Contract shall, at Purchaser's option, be null and void and Purchaser's earnest money deposit shall be promptly refunded to Purchaser. Also, an amount of money equal to Purchaser's expenses in obtaining the title examination and the survey shall be paid by Seller to Purchaser.

7. Closing

(a) Unless extended as provided herein, Purchaser and Seller shall consummate and close the sale contemplated by this Agreement on or before the 120th calendar day following the date of this Agreement or the "final zoning" or defined in Paragraph 13 hereof, whichever is later, at such time, date and location as is designated by Purchaser in a written notice to Seller and Broker.

(b) At the closing each party shall execute and deliver all documents necessary to effect and complete the closing. The general warranty deed to be executed by Seller shall be on the form [attached hereto as Exhibit D] then generally used by Security Mortgage Company and shall convey to Buyer unencumbered fee simple title, free and clear of all liens, restrictions and encumbrances except the Permitted Title Exceptions [and insurable as such by Title Company at standard rates on American Land Title Association Owner's Policy Standard Form B–1987]. All blanks in all of the closing documents shall be filled in at the closing, and all documents shall otherwise be conformed to meet the requirements of the parties as expressed in this Contract.

(c) Seller shall pay the tax imposed on the warranty deed and shall pay the cost of recording and the Intangibles tax on the Deed to Secure Debt from Purchaser. Purchaser shall pay the cost of recording the warranty deed, the cost of examining and insuring title to the Property, and all other closing costs incurred by Purchaser.

(d) As of the date of closing, Purchaser and Seller shall prorate ad valorem taxes on the Property for the year in which the closing occurs, premiums, for hazard insurance on the Property, utility bills, soil bank payments and rents prepaid to Seller under any leases which are assigned to Purchaser. Seller shall assign and transfer to Buyer at the closing any leases or tenant contracts specified in the Permitted Title Exceptions and Purchaser shall assume Seller's obligations under such leases or contracts.

(e) At closing Seller shall execute a written statement of the warranties and representations contained herein.

8. Inspection

Commencing upon the date of this Agreement Purchaser shall have the right to go on the Property personally or through agents, employees and contractors for the purposes of making boundary line and topographical surveys of same, soil tests and such other tests, analyses and investigations of the Property as Purchaser deems desirable. Purchaser shall pay all costs incurred in making such surveys, tests, analyses and investigations.

9. Condition and Possession of the Property

At closing Seller shall deliver to Purchaser possession of the Property in the same condition as on the date of this Contract. If all or any material portion of the Property shall be condemned, damaged or destroyed prior to the closing, Purchaser may elect to (i) terminate this Contract, or (ii) reduce the purchase price in the amount of the condemnation award or the decrease in value caused by the damage or destruction to the property, or (iii) receive such insurance proceeds or condemnation award as may be paid or payable with respect to such damage or destruction. Purchaser's election under this paragraph shall be exercised by written notice to Seller within 10 days after receipt of written notice from Seller of such taking, damage or destruction or of written notice of the amount of the insurance or condemnation award payable with respect to such taking, damage or destruction, whichever is later. If Purchaser elects to terminate this Contract under this paragraph, all earnest money paid hereunder shall be immediately refunded to Purchaser.

10. Default

If the sale contemplated by this Contract is not consummated through default of Seller, Purchaser's earnest money deposit shall be promptly refunded to Purchaser. If said sale is not consummated

EXHIBIT 7–2

Contract for Purchase and Sale of a Large Tract of Vacant Land

(*continued*)

(continued)

because of Purchaser's default, then Seller shall be entitled to retain Purchaser's earnest money deposit as full liquidated damages for such default of Purchaser. Nothing contained in this paragraph shall eliminate or limit Purchaser's right to sue for, and obtain, damages caused by Seller's default or specific performance of Seller's obligations hereunder. If Seller fails to consummate this sale for any reason other than Seller's inability to furnish to Purchaser marketable and insurable title to the Property as provided herein, Seller shall pay to Broker the real estate commission as provided in paragraph 11.

11. Commission

Seller shall at closing pay to Broker a real estate commission in the amount of ten percent of the purchase price. Purchaser and Seller hereby acknowledge that Broker has rendered a valuable service by negotiating this Contract, and Broker is therefore made a party to this Contract for the enforcement of Broker's rights to such commission. Purchaser shall have no obligations to pay any commissions.

12. Assignment

Purchaser shall have the right to assign this Contract in whole or in part only with the consent of Seller, which consent shall not be unreasonably withheld, and the terms and provisions hereof shall be binding upon and shall inure to the benefit of the parties hereto, their successors, representatives, heirs and assigns. Upon the occurrence of an assignment of this entire Contract, Purchaser shall be relieved of Purchaser's obligations hereunder.

13. Zoning

(a) Commencing on the date hereof, Seller and Purchaser shall use their best efforts to obtain rezoning for all of the Property to the zoning classification of A-1 under the applicable Zoning Ordinances of Baker County, so as to permit the development of the Property for apartment use in accordance with plans prepared by Purchaser at Purchaser's expense and submitted for use in connection with said rezoning. Purchaser [Seller] shall on or before the 60th calendar day following the date hereof properly execute and file at [Seller's] Purchaser's expense an Application for Rezoning of the Property with the proper officials of said County, attached to which shall be the plans prepared by the Purchaser. [Seller] Purchaser shall diligently and vigorously pursue said Application until a final decision has been made thereon by the governing body of said County and thereafter until all appeals and suits filed in connection with said rezoning have been finally disposed of. Seller and Purchaser shall cooperate in obtaining such rezoning and shall in no event either oppose or interfere with such rezoning.

(b) Said rezoning shall become "final zoning," as the term "final zoning" is used herein, on the date that such rezoning has been granted by the appropriate officials of said County pursuant to said Application of Purchaser [Seller], and any and all appeal periods as provided by law have expired without an appeal or suit having been filed, or, if filed, with such suit or appeal dismissed or resolved finally and conclusively in favor of such rezoning, and, at the expiration of such appeal periods, or at the conclusion of any such appeal or suit, the rezoning of the Property shall not have been further changed or withdrawn by the appropriate officials of said County.

(c) If said Application for Rezoning is not filed by Purchaser [Seller] within said 60-day period, then and in that event [Purchaser] Seller shall have the right to terminate this Contract by giving [Seller] Purchaser written notice of termination. Upon such termination, Purchaser's earnest money shall be promptly refunded in full to Purchaser.

(d) If Purchaser [Seller] complies with all of Purchaser's [Seller's] obligations as to rezoning set forth in this paragraph and if nevertheless said rezoning has been denied, or has neither been denied nor has become "final zoning" on or before 180 calendar days following the date hereof, then Purchaser shall have the right by written notice to Seller or Broker (i) to terminate this Contract and receive a prompt refund of Purchaser's earnest money or (ii) to postpone closing hereunder for not more than ninety calendar days thereafter until said "final zoning" is obtained or (iii) to terminate this Contract at the end of such postponement period if said "final zoning" remains unobtained and receive a prompt refund of Purchaser's earnest money or (iv) to waive the provisions of this paragraph and accept the Property without the "final zoning" described hereinabove.

(*continued*)

14. <u>Conditions to Closing</u>

Unless waived by Purchaser, obligations of Purchaser under this Contract are expressly made subject to the following conditions:

(a) The truth and accuracy as of the date of this Contract and as of the date of closing of each and every warranty or representation herein made by Seller.

(b) The final rezoning of the Property as provided in Paragraph 13 hereof within the time specified, as such time may be extended.

(c) Purchaser's obtaining at or prior to the closing an easement for pedestrian and vehicular ingress and egress to and from the property across the adjoining property owned by Sam Smith, such easement to be in the form attached hereto as Exhibit E. Purchaser agrees to use Purchaser's best efforts to obtain such easement, to pay the cost of same (not to exceed $2,000.00), and to accept such easement if it is available.

15. <u>Notice</u>

Any notice required or permitted to be given hereunder shall be sufficient if in writing and sent by U.S. Certified Mail, postage prepaid, to the party being given such notice at the following addresses:

Seller: _____

_____

_____

Purchaser: _____

_____

_____

Broker: _____

_____

_____

Any party may change said address by giving the other parties hereto notice of such change of address. Notice given as hereinabove provided shall be deemed received by the party to whom it is addressed on the third calendar day following the date on which said notice is deposited in the mail.

16. <u>Survival of Contract</u>

All the terms and conditions of this Contract not performed at or prior to closing shall survive the closing hereunder and shall not be merged into the closing documents.

This instrument shall be regarded as an offer by the Purchaser or Seller who first signs to the other and open for acceptance by the other until <u>5:00</u> o'clock <u>P.M.</u> on the <u>13th</u> day of <u>November, 20_____</u>, by which time written acceptance of such offer must have been actually received by Broker, who shall promptly notify the other party in writing of such acceptance. The date of this Contract shall be the date of such acceptance.

Signed, sealed and delivered as to Purchaser this <u>11th</u> day of November,

_____

Witness

_____   _____ (SEAL)

Notary Public   Thomas T. Toms, Purchaser

Signed, sealed and delivered as to Seller

this <u>12th</u> day of November, 20__

(*continued*)

EXHIBIT 7–2

Contract for Purchase and Sale of a Large Tract of Vacant Land (*continued*)

_____

Witness

_____   _____ (SEAL)

Notary Public   John J. Johns, Seller
Signed, sealed and delivered as to Seller   COMMUNITY & HOME
this 12th day of November, 20_____   PROPERTIES
Witness

_____   By _____ (SEAL)

Notary Public

Alternate Survey Provision

Prior to date of closing as hereinafter provided, Purchaser shall at Purchaser's expense cause an accurate survey to be made of the Property by a reputable surveyor registered under the laws of the State of _____. The plat of such survey shall show the boundaries of the Property and the acreage contained therein, computed to the nearest one-tenth of an acre. Within five calendar days after Purchaser's receipt of a plat of said survey, Purchaser shall mail a copy of said Plat to Seller in the manner hereinafter provided for giving notice, and, within ten calendar days after receipt of said copy, Seller shall notify Purchaser in writing if such plat is not acceptable to Seller. If Seller does not, within said ten-day period, so notify Purchaser that such plat is not acceptable, said survey shall conclusively determine as between Purchaser and Seller the final acreage to be conveyed hereunder, and Seller's conveyance to Purchaser shall be in accordance with said survey.

If Seller does, within said ten-day period, so notify Purchaser that such plat is not acceptable, Seller shall, simultaneously with the giving of such notification, cause at Seller's expense an accurate second survey of said Property to be made by a reputable surveyor registered under the laws of the State of _____. The plat of such second survey shall show the boundaries of the Property and the acreage contained therein, computed to the nearest one-tenth of an acre. Within five calendar days after Seller's receipt of a plat of said second survey, Seller shall mail a copy thereof to Purchaser in the manner hereinafter provided for giving notice, and, within ten calendar days after receipt of such copy, Purchaser shall notify Seller in writing if such plat is not acceptable to Purchaser. If Purchaser does not, within said ten-day period, so notify Seller that such plat is not acceptable, said second survey shall conclusively determine as between Purchaser and Seller the final acreage to be conveyed hereunder, and Seller's conveyance to Purchaser shall be in accordance with said second survey.

If Purchaser does, within said ten-day period, so notify Seller that such plat is not acceptable, and if, within fourteen calendar days after receipt by Purchaser of such survey of Seller, Seller and Purchaser are unable to agree upon a survey, then both Seller and Purchaser shall cause their respective surveyors to name a third surveyor who shall be a reputable surveyor registered under the laws of the State of _____. If said two surveyors have not named such third surveyor within seven calendar days following the last day of said fourteen-day period, then said third surveyor shall be a reputable surveyor, registered under the laws of the State of _____ and named by the Superior Court Judge senior in point of service serving the county in which the Property (or the majority of said Property, if it lies in more than one county) lies.

Said third surveyor shall be promptly employed by Purchaser and Seller to make an accurate third survey of said Property, the cost of which third survey shall be borne equally by Purchaser and Seller. Said third surveyor shall furnish copies of the plat of said third survey to Purchaser and Seller upon completion of same; said plat shall show the boundaries of the Property and the acreage contained therein, computed to the nearest one-tenth of an acre. Said third survey shall conclusively determine as between Purchaser and Seller the final acreage to be conveyed hereunder, and Seller's conveyance to Purchaser shall be in accordance with said third survey.

The survey which, in accordance with provisions of this Paragraph 2, does in fact conclusively determine the final acreage to be conveyed hereunder shall be hereinafter referred to in this Agreement as "the Survey."

EXHIBIT 7-3

Seller's Property Disclosure Statement

Reprinted with permission of Georgia Association of Realtors, Inc.

SELLER'S PROPERTY DISCLOSURE STATEMENT
EXHIBIT "_____"

2005 Printing

For property located at _____, _____ Georgia, _____
together with all improvements thereon ("Property")

NOTICE TO BUYER AND SELLER: This disclosure statement is designed to assist Seller in disclosing to prospective buyers all known material adverse facts relating to the physical condition of Property that may not be readily observable, disclosing historical information and past problems with Property, and identifying those fixtures/items that are included with the sale of Property. All questions are to be answered with respect to the above referenced Property.

IF THE ANSWERS TO ANY OF THE QUESTIONS LISTED BELOW ARE "YES," PLEASE EXPLAIN IN DETAIL IN THE "ADDITIONAL EXPLANATIONS" SECTION.

		Yes	No	Don't Know
1.	**OCCUPANCY:**			
(a)	Is Property vacant?	___	___	___
	If yes, how long has it been since Seller occupied Property? _____			
(b)	Are there any leases, written or verbal, on Property or any part thereof?	___	___	___
2.	**SOIL, TREES, SHRUBS AND BOUNDARIES:**			
(a)	Are there any landfills (other than foundation backfill), graves, mine shafts, trash dumps or wells (in use or abandoned)on Property?	___	___	___
(b)	Is there any sliding, settling (other than normal settling), earth movement, sinkholes, upheaval, or earth stability/expansive soil problems?	___	___	___
(c)	Are there any diseased or dead trees on Property?	___	___	___
(d)	Are there any encroachments, leases, unrecorded easements, or boundary line disputes?	___	___	___
3.	**ROOF, GUTTERS AND DOWNSPOUTS:**			
(a)	Approximate age of roof: _____ years.			
(b)	Has the roof, or any part thereof, been repaired during your ownership?	___	___	___
(c)	Are there any roof leaks or other problems with the roof, roof flashing, gutters or downspouts?	___	___	___
4.	**TERMITES, DRY-ROT, PESTS, AND WOOD-DESTROYING ORGANISMS:**			
(a)	Is there any past or present damage to Property caused by infiltrating pests, termites, dry-rot, or other wood-destroying organisms?	___	___	___
(b)	Is your Property currently under a transferable bond, warranty or other coverage for termites or other wood destroying organisms by a licensed pest control company?	___	___	___
	If yes, check type of coverage: ❑ re-treatment and repair; or ❑ re-treatment only			
(c)	Is there a cost to transfer the bond, warranty or other coverage?	___	___	___
	If yes, what is the cost? $_____			
(d)	Is there a cost to maintain the bond, warranty or other coverage? If yes, what is the annual cost? $ _____	___	___	___
(e)	Have any termite/pest control reports or treatments for Property been done in the last five years?	___	___	___
(f)	Does any dwelling or garage on Property have any untreated wood or exterior siding/cladding, such as rigid board insulation, foam plastic, synthetic stucco, hard coat stucco, wood or masonry siding (excluding brick), below grade or within six inches of finished grade?	___	___	___
5.	**STRUCTURAL ITEMS, ADDITIONS AND ALTERATIONS:**			
(a)	What year was the main residential dwelling constructed? _____			
(b)	Has there been any movement, shifting, settling (other than normal settling), cracking, deterioration, or other structural problems with any dwelling or garage on Property?	___	___	___
(c)	Has there been any additional structural bracing, underpinning, or other structural reinforcement added to any dwelling or garage on Property?	___	___	___
(d)	Are there any problems with driveways, walkways, patios, or retaining walls on Property?	___	___	___
(e)	Have there been any additions, structural changes, or any other major alterations to the original improvements on the Property?	___	___	___
(f)	Has there been any work done on the Property where required permits and/or approvals (public or private) were not obtained?	___	___	___
(g)	Has any work been done to Property that was not in compliance with building codes or zoning regulations?	___	___	___
(h)	Does any part of the exterior siding or cladding of any dwelling or garage on Property consist of synthetic stucco?	___	___	___

Copyright© 2005 by Georgia Association of REALTORS®, Inc   F50, Seller's Property Disclosure Statement Exhibit, Page 1 of 5 01/01/05

(continued)

EXHIBIT 7–3

Seller's Property Disclosure Statement (*continued*)

		Yes	No	Don't Know

6. DRAINAGE, FLOODING AND MOISTURE:
(a) Has there been any water leakage, water accumulation, or dampness within the basement, crawl space or other parts of the main dwelling at or below grade?
(b) Have any repairs been made to control any water or dampness problems in the basement, crawl space, or other parts of the main dwelling at or below grade?
(c) Is the Property or any improvements thereon located in a flood zone?
(d) Does water regularly stand on Property for more than one day after it has rained?
(e) Has there been any past flooding on Property?
(f) Are there any problems with siding or exterior cladding, swelling, chipping, delaminating or retaining moisture?
(g) Does mold appear on interior heated and cooled portions of any dwelling on Property other than on the walls, floors or ceilings of showers, sinks, and bathtubs?

7. PLUMBING RELATED ITEMS:
(a) What is your drinking water source: ❑ Public ❑ Private ❑ Well on Property
(b) If your drinking water is from a well, has it been tested within the past twelve months?
(c) Do you have a water softener, filter or purifier? If yes, ❑ Leased ❑ Owned
(d) What is the type of sewage system: ❑ Public ❑ Private ❑ Septic Tank
(e) Is the main dwelling served by sewage pump or lift system?
(f) Do you know if any septic tank or cesspool on Property has ever been professionally serviced? If yes, please give the date of last service: _____, _____
(g) Do you know of any past or present leaks, backups, or other similar problems relating to any of the plumbing, water and/or sewage-related items?
(h) Is there any polybutylene plumbing, other than primary service line, on Property?

8. OTHER SYSTEMS AND COMPONENTS:
(a) What type of heating system(s) serve the main dwelling? ❑ gas ❑ electric ❑ other
(b) What is the approximate age of heating system(s): _____years
(c) What type of air conditioning system(s) serve the main dwelling? ❑ gas ❑ electric ❑ other
(d) What is the approximate age of air conditioning system(s) _____ years
(e) Is any portion of the main dwelling not served by a central or zoned heating and/or air conditioning system?
(f) How is water heated in the main dwelling? ❑ Electric ❑ Gas ❑ Solar
(g) What is the approximate age of water heater: _____years
(h) Does the main dwelling have aluminum wiring other than the primary service line?
(i) Is there any system or appliance which is leased or for which the buyer must pay a transfer fee to continue to use? If yes, what is the transfer fee? $_____ If yes, what is the current use fee to be paid by the buyer? $_____
(j) Are any fireplaces not working or in need of repair?
(k) When was each fireplace, wood stove or chimney/flue last cleaned? Date: _____

9. TOXIC SUBSTANCES:
(a) Are there any underground tanks, toxic or hazardous substances on Property (structure or soil) such as asbestos, urea-formaldehyde, methane gas, radioactive material, radon, mold, benzene or other environmental contaminates?
(b) Has Property ever been tested for radon, lead, mold or any other potentially toxic substances?

10. COVENANTS, FEES AND ASSESSMENTS:
(a) Is Property part of a condominium, community association or subject to covenants, conditions and restrictions (CC & Rs)?
(b) Is there a mandatory community association fee or assessment? If yes, what is the amount? $_____ per _____. Is there an initiation fee? If yes, what amount? $_____.
(c) Are there any recreational facilities in the community for which the obligation to pay and the right to use are optional? If yes, please describe the nature of the facilities and the optional fee or charge. _____ _____
(d) In purchasing Property, will any initiation, transfer, or other similar fee be owed to the Association? If yes, what is the amount? $_____.
(e) Are there any special assessments approved by but yet not owing or due to a community Association that are not yet owed or due?

F50, Seller's Property Disclosure Statement Exhibit, Page 2 of 5 01/01/05

(continued)

EXHIBIT 7–3

Seller's Property Disclosure Statement (*continued*)

		Yes	No	Don't Know

11. OTHER MATTERS:

(a) Have there been any inspections of Property in the past year?
If yes, by whom and of what type? _____

(b) Does Property contain any building products which are or have been the subject of class action lawsuits, litigation or legal claims alleging that the product is defective?
If yes, please identify the product or products and the general location of each on Property:
_____

(c) Is there or has there been in the past any litigation involving Property or any improvement therein alleging negligent or improper construction defects, termites, and/or title problems?

(d) Has there been any award or payment of money in lieu of repairs for such a defective building product?

(e) Has any release been signed that would limit a future owner from making any claims in connection with Property?

(f) Has there been any fire, flood or wind damage which required repairs to Property in excess of $500.00?

(g) Approximately how many insurance claims have been filed on Property since you owned it? _____

(h) Are any fixtures or appliances included in the sale in need of repair?

(i) Have any repairs been made to the electrical, plumbing, or heating and air condition systems, or any part thereof?

(j) Was any dwelling on Property or portion thereof (excluding mobile, modular and manufactured dwelling) moved to the site from another location?

12. FIXTURES/ITEMS: (Check (T) only those fixtures/items below that are included in the sale of Property. Unless otherwise indicated, if there is more than one item (such as a second refrigerator or two chandeliers or three smoke detectors), all such fixtures/items checked are included in the sale of Property. Those fixtures/items listed below that are not checked shall not be included in the sale of Property.

❑ Air Conditioning Window Unit
❑ Air Purifier
❑ Alarm System (Burglar)
  ❑ Leased ❑ Owned
❑ Alarm System (Smoke/Fire)
  ❑ Leased ❑ Owned
❑ Arbor
❑ Attic Fan (Whole House Fan)
❑ Attic Ventilator Fan
❑ Awning
❑ Basketball Post & Goal
  ❑ Built-In ❑ Free Standing
❑ Birdhouses
❑ Boat Dock
❑ Carbon Monoxide Detector
❑ Ceiling Fan
❑ Chandelier
❑ Closet Shelving System
  ❑ Built-In ❑ Free Standing
❑ Dehumidifier
  ❑ Built-In ❑ Free Standing
❑ Dishwasher
  ❑ Built-In ❑ Free Standing
❑ Dog House
❑ Door & Window Hardware
❑ Dryer
  ❑ Gas ❑ Electric
❑ Fence (Invisible)
❑ Fence Pet Collar
❑ Fireplace
  ❑ Gas Logs
  ❑ Screen/Door
  ❑ Wood Burning Insert
❑ Flag Pole

❑ Garage Door Opener
  ❑ Remote Control
❑ Garbage Disposal
❑ Gas Grille
  ❑ Built-In ❑ Free Standing
❑ Gazebo
❑ Hot Tub
❑ Humidifier
❑ Ice Maker
  ❑ Built-In ❑ Free Standing
❑ Intercom
❑ Jetted Tub
❑ Landscaping Lights
❑ Light Fixtures
  (Except Chandeliers)
❑ Mailbox
❑ Microwave Oven
  ❑ Built-In ❑ Free Standing
❑ Mirror (Attached)
❑ Outbuilding
❑ Outdoor Bench
❑ Playhouse
❑ Porch swing
❑ Propane Gas Tanks
  ❑ Above ground ❑ Buried
  ❑ Leased ❑ Owned
❑ Radio (Built-In)
❑ Refrigerator
❑ Satellite Dish/Receiver
❑ Sauna
❑ Septic Pump
❑ Shelving Unit & System
  ❑ Built-In ❑ Free Standing
❑ Shower Head/Sprayer
❑ Smoke Detector
  ❑ Battery Operated ❑ Hard Wired

❑ Speakers (Built-In)
❑ Sprinkler System
❑ Statuary
❑ Stepping Stones
❑ Storage Building
❑ Stove
  ❑ Gas ❑ Electric
  ❑ Built-In ❑ Free Standing
❑ Sump Pump
❑ Surface Unit Cook Top
  ❑ Gas ❑ Electric
❑ Swimming Pool
  ❑ Above Ground
❑ Swimming Pool Equipment
  (List below)
❑ Swing Set
❑ Switch Plate Covers
❑ Telephone Jacks/Wires
❑ Television Antenna
❑ Television Cable/Jacks
❑ Thermostat (Programmable)
❑ Trash Compactor
  ❑ Built-In ❑ Free Standing
❑ Tree House
❑ Trellis
❑ Vacuum System (Built-In)
  ❑ Vacuum Attachments
❑ Vent Hood
❑ Washing Machine
❑ Water Purification System
❑ Water Softener System
❑ Weather Vane
❑ Well Pump
❑ Window Screens
❑ Window Treatments
❑ Wine Cooler

F50, Seller's Property Disclosure Statement Exhibit, Page 3 of 5 01/01/05

(continued)

EXHIBIT 7-3

Seller's Property Disclosure Statement (*continued*)

Other fixtures/items included in the sale of Property:
_____
_____

Other fixtures/items not included in the sale of Property:
_____
_____

The common law of fixtures shall apply to fixtures not addressed herein. Those fixtures/items that are not included in the sale of Property shall remain Property of Seller and shall be removed prior to closing or the transfer of possession of Property to Buyer, whichever is later. Seller shall lose the right to remove any such fixtures/items not timely removed. In removing all fixtures/items, Seller shall use reasonable care to prevent damage and, if necessary, to restore Property to its original condition.

13. **LEAD-BASED PAINT:** Was any part of the residential dwelling on Property constructed prior to 1978?

❑ **Yes** ❑ **Don't Know** ❑ **No** (If no, proceed to paragraph 14.)

If you have answered "Yes" above, Seller does hereby provide the following warning and shall disclose the following information regarding lead-based paint and lead-based paint hazards.

PURCHASE AND SALE TRANSACTION LEAD WARNING STATEMENT.

Every purchaser of any interest in residential property on which a residential dwelling was built prior to 1978 is notified that such property may present exposure to lead from lead-based paint that may place young children at risk of developing lead poisoning. Lead poisoning in young children may produce permanent neurological damage, including learning disabilities, reduced intelligence quotient, behavioral problems, and impaired memory. Lead poisoning also poses a particular risk to pregnant women. The seller of any interest in residential real property is required to provide the buyer with any information on lead-based paint hazards from risk assessments or inspections in the seller's possession and notify the buyer of any known lead-based paint hazards. A risk assessment or inspection for possible lead-based paint hazards is recommended prior to purchase.

Seller's Disclosure. *[Seller to mark and initial sections A and B below]*

☐   A. Presence of lead-based paint and/or lead paint hazard (check one below):
Seller Initials

     ❑ Known lead-based paint and/or lead-based paint hazards are present in the housing (explain below):
_____
_____

     ❑ Seller has no knowledge of lead-based paint and Seller Initials based paint hazards in the housing.

☐   B. Records and Reports available to the Seller (check one below):
Seller Initials

     ❑ Seller has provided the Buyer with all the available records and reports pertaining to lead-based paint and/or lead-based paint hazards in the housing (list document below):
_____
_____

     ❑ Seller has no reports or records pertaining to lead-based paint and/or lead-based paint hazards in the housing.

Buyer's Acknowledgment. *[Buyer to mark and initial sections C, D, and E below]*

☐   C. Buyer has received copies of all information listed above regarding lead-based paint and/or lead-based paint hazards
Buyer Initials

☐   D. Buyer has read and understands the above lead warning statement and has received the pamphlet "Protect Your Family From Lead in Your Home."
Buyer Initials

☐   E. Buyer has (check one below):
Buyer Initials

     ❑ Received a 10-day opportunity (or mutually agreed upon period) to conduct a risk assessment inspection for the presence of lead-based paint and/or lead-based paint hazards; or

     ❑ Waived the opportunity to conduct a risk assessment inspection for the presence of lead-based paint and/or lead-based paint hazards.

Broker Acknowledgment. *[Broker to initial section F below]*

☐   F. Broker has informed the Seller of the Seller's obligations under 42 U.S.C. § 4852(d) and is aware of his/her responsibility to ensure compliance.
Broker Initials

_____ Broker's (or Broker's Affiliated Licensee's) signature

The lead-based paint disclosures must occur prior to Seller's acceptance of Buyer's written offer to purchase; if the potential Buyer makes the offer to purchase before the requisite disclosures are provided to Buyer, Seller can not accept the offer until: 1) the disclosure is made; and 2) the potential Buyer has had an opportunity to review the information and consider whether to amend the offer.

(continued)

EXHIBIT 7–3

Seller's Property Disclosure Statement (*continued*)

14. **AGRICULTURAL DISCLOSURE:** Is Property within, partially within, or adjacent to any property zoned or identified on an approved county land use plan as agricultural or forestry use? ❑ **Yes** ❑ **Don't Know** ❑ **No**

It is the policy of this state and this community to conserve, protect, and encourage the development and improvement of farm and forest land for the production of food, fiber, and other products, and also for its natural and environmental value. This notice is to inform prospective property owners or other persons or entities leasing or acquiring an interest in real property that property in which they are about to acquire an interest lies within, partially within, or adjacent to an area zoned, used, or identified for farm and forest activities and that farm and forest activities occur in the area. Such farm and forest activities may include intensive operations that cause discomfort and inconveniences that involve, but are not limited to, noises, odors, fumes, dust, smoke, insects, operations of machinery during any 24 hour period, storage and disposal of manure, and the application by spraying or otherwise of chemical fertilizers, soil amendments, herbicides, and pesticides. One or more of these inconveniences may occur as the result of farm or forest activities which are in conformance with existing laws and regulations and accepted customs and standards.

15. **ADDITIONAL EXPLANATIONS OR DISCLOSURES:**

❑ **Mark box if additional pages are attached.**

16. **SELLER'S REPRESENTATION:**
To the best of Seller's knowledge and belief, the information contained in this Seller's Property Disclosure Statement is accurate and complete as of the date signed by Seller. It should not be a substitute for Buyer inspecting Property or obtaining any warranties with regard to Property that Buyer may wish to obtain. Seller hereby authorizes Broker to provide this Seller's Property Disclosure Statement to prospective buyers of Property and to real estate brokers and their affiliated licensees. **Seller agrees to promptly update this Seller's Property Disclosure Statement and to provide any Buyer and Broker with a revised copy of the same if there are any material changes in the answers to the questions contained herein.**

Is each individual named below a U. S. Citizen or resident alien?   ❑ Yes ❑ No
Has each individual named below been a Georgia resident for the past two years?   ❑ Yes ❑ No
Has Property been Seller's primary residence for at least two of the last five years? ❑ Yes ❑ No

Seller: _____   Date:_____, 20_____

Seller: _____   Date:_____, 20_____

17. **RECEIPT AND ACKNOWLEDGMENT BY BUYER:**
I acknowledge receipt of this Seller's Property Disclosure Statement. I understand that, except as stated in the Purchase and Sale Agreement, Property is being sold in its present condition, without warranties or guarantees of any kind by Seller or Brokers. No representations concerning the condition of Property are being relied upon by Buyer except as disclosed herein or stated in the Purchase and Sale Agreement.

Buyer: _____   Date:_____, 20_____

Buyer: _____   Date:_____, 20_____

F50, Seller's Property Disclosure Statement Exhibit, Page 5 of 5 01/01/05

EXHIBIT 7–4

Contract for Purchase and Sale
of a Retail Shopping Center

AGREEMENT OF PURCHASE AND SALE

THIS AGREEMENT OF PURCHASE AND SALE (the "Agreement" is made and entered into as of the Effective Date, as hereafter defined, by and between _____

_____

_____ (hereinafter collectively "Seller"); and _____

_____, a corporation (hereinafter "Purchaser").

WITNESSETH:

That for and in consideration of the mutual promises and covenants herein contained and the mutual advantages accruing to Seller and Purchaser hereunder and the sum of $10.00 and other good and valuable consideration paid by Purchaser to Seller, receipt of which is hereby acknowledged by Seller, it is mutually covenanted and agreed by the parties hereto as follows:

1. Property.

Seller hereby agrees to sell and convey to Purchaser and Purchaser hereby agrees to purchase from Seller, subject to the terms and conditions hereinafter set forth, the property located in Land Lot _____, _____ District, My Town, Great County, State described on Exhibit A attached hereto and made a part hereof containing approximately 2.544 acres (the "Land") as shown on that certain survey of the Land prepared by _____, Registered Land Surveyor No. 1845, for _____, dated July 25, 20____, last revised December 17, 20____ (the "Existing Survey"), together with the following:

(a) *Improvements.* All improvements on the Land owned by Seller, including, without limitation, a two-story retail shopping center containing approximately 54,520 net rentable square feet, more commonly known as the "Village Square," together with drives, sidewalks, drainage, sewerage and utility facilities and surface parking areas (collectively the "Improvements");

(b) *Tangible Personal Property.* All fixtures, equipment, machinery, building supplies, tools, furniture and other personal property, if any, and all replacements thereof, located on or about the Land and Improvements and used exclusively in the operation and maintenance thereof (the "Tangible Personal Property"), but expressly excluding any and all property owned by tenants occupying the Improvements;

(c) *Intangible Property.* Any and all of the Seller's rights and interests in and to all intangible property pertaining to the Land, the Improvements or the Tangible Property or the use thereof, including without limitation any trade names used in connection therewith, the Landlord's interest in all leases regarding the Property to the extent assignable, and all other licenses, franchises, permits, tenant security deposits (unless Purchaser receives a credit for same), contract rights, agreements, transferable business licenses, tenant lists, correspondence with tenants and suppliers, booklets, manuals, advertising materials, transferable utility contracts, and transferable telephone exchange numbers (the "Intangible Property");

(d) *Easements.* Any and all of Seller's rights in and to all easements, if any, benefiting the Land or the Improvements; and

(e) *Rights and Appurtenances.* All rights and appurtenances pertaining to the foregoing, including any right, title and interest of Seller in and to adjacent streets, alleys or right-of-way. All of the property described in Subsections (a), (b), (c), (d), and (e) of this Section 1 together with the Land are hereinafter sometimes collectively referred to as the "Property."

2. Purchase Price and Earnest Money Deposits.

(a) *Purchase Price.* The Purchase Price (the "Purchase Price") to be paid for the Property shall be Seven Million Three Hundred Thousand and No/100 Dollars ($7,300,000.00) to be paid in the following manner:

(i) Purchaser shall take subject to a first mortgage loan on the Property held by Wearever Life Assurance Company in the original principal amount of Five Million Five Hundred Thousand Dollars ($5,500,000.00), which mortgage loan currently bears interest at the rate of ten percent per annum (10%) and is due and payable in full on January 1, 20____. Seller agrees to pay one-half of any and all

(continued)

EXHIBIT 7–4

Contract for Purchase and Sale of a Retail Shopping Center

(*continued*)

transfer, assumption, or other fees assessed by the holder of the mortgage loan in connection with the transfer of the Property subject to the mortgage loan; and

(ii) Purchaser shall deliver to Seller a purchase money note ("Note") in the amount of Six Hundred Fifty-Four Thousand Dollars ($654,000.00). Said Note shall bear interest at ten percent per annum (10%) and shall be payable interest only quarterly with a final payment of all unpaid principal and accrued and unpaid interest being due and payable two years from the Closing Date (hereinafter defined). The Note shall provide that it can be prepaid in whole or in part at any time without premium or penalty. The Note shall provide that the holder of the Note shall give the Maker of the Note at least twenty (20) days written notice of default prior to any acceleration of the Note for default or exercise of any other remedies which the holder may have to collect the indebtedness evidenced by the Note; provided, however, the Note shall be cross-defaulted with the Wearever Life Assurance Company loan ("WLA Loan") and defaults under the WLA Loan are to be governed by the notice and cure periods provided for in the WLA Loan. The Note shall be secured by a second priority Deed to Secure Debt ("Deed") on the Property. The Deed shall provide that insurance and condemnation proceeds shall be used for restoration of the property; shall provide for twenty (20) days' written notice of default prior to any exercise of remedies thereunder; shall not provide for any tax or insurance escrows; and shall not have any restrictions on the transfer of the Property or upon any further financing or encumbrancing of the Property. The Note and Deed shall be nonrecourse to Purchaser and shall contain no personal guaranty whatsoever. The Note shall be in the form of the Note attached hereto as Exhibit L and the Deed shall be in the form of the Deed to Secure Debt attached hereto as Exhibit L–1.

(iii) The balance of the Purchase Price in the approximate amount of One Million One Hundred Forty-Six Thousand Dollars ($1,146,000.00) shall be payable in cash or by bank check drawn on a Federal Reserve Bank or by wire transfer or good funds on the Closing Date (hereinafter defined). Upon request by Purchaser prior to closing, Seller shall designate the account of Seller into which the net proceeds of the sale are to be deposited.

(b) *Earnest Money Deposits.* Purchaser shall deliver its earnest money deposit to Ajax Realty, Inc. (the "Escrowee") upon Purchaser's execution of this Agreement in the form of a cashier's check (drawn on a State financial institution) in the sum of SEVENTY FIVE THOUSAND DOLLARS ($75,000.00) (the "Earnest Money"), made payable to Escrowee in trust. (said Earnest Money together with any interest earned thereon shall hereinafter be referred to as the "Deposit.") The Deposit shall be held and disbursed by the escrowee as provided in this Agreement.

The Escrowee is directed to hold the Deposit as escrowed funds in an FDIC-insured, interest-bearing account, at The Bank in My Town, State. Purchaser represents that his U.S. federal tax identification number is _____. Purchaser's tax identification number shall be credited with any interest earned on the Earnest Money prior to its being disbursed by Escrowee. Purchaser shall complete and execute a Payer's Request for Taxpayer Identification Number (Form W–9). Seller and Purchaser hereby agree to hold Escrowee harmless from any loss of escrowed funds, including the Deposit, for any reason whatsoever except for the Escrowee's fraud or gross negligence or for loss of interest caused by any delay in the deposit or early withdrawal of the Deposit, from the interest-bearing account. This Agreement shall serve as escrow instructions and an executed copy of this Agreement shall be deposited by Purchaser with the Escrowee. At Closing, the Deposit shall be delivered to Seller and applied against the Purchase Price. In the event of a termination of this Agreement or a default under this Agreement, the Deposit shall be delivered or disbursed by the Escrowee as provided in this Agreement. If any dispute or difference arises between the Purchaser and Seller or if any conflicting demands be made upon the Escrowee, the Escrowee shall not be required to determine the same or to take any action thereon. Rather, the Escrowee may await settlement of the controversy or deposit the Deposit into the Registry of the Superior Court of Great County, State, in an interpleader action or otherwise for the purpose of having the respective rights of the parties adjudicated. Upon making such deposit or upon institution of such interpleader action or other actions, the Escrowee shall be fully relieved and discharged from all further obligations hereunder with respect to the sums so deposited.

(c) Should any party terminate this Agreement, as permitted herein, or declare the other party in default of its obligations hereunder, and demand payment of the Deposit to it, then the Escrowee shall pay to it the Deposit, provided that the declaring party provides evidence of the other party's receiving

EXHIBIT 7–4

Contract for Purchase and Sale
of a Retail Shopping Center
(*continued*)

its demand notice, and within seven (7) business days following the other party's receipt of same, the nondeclaring party has not delivered written objection to the Escrowee's disbursing the Deposit. If any dispute arises that is not resolved within thirty (30) days after such written objection, the Escrowee shall deposit the Deposit into the Registry of the Superior Court of Great County, State, whereupon Escrowee's obligations and liabilities hereunder shall cease and terminate.

3. Inspection Period.

Purchaser shall have until 11:59 P.M. of August 26, 20____; (the "Final Inspection Date") within which to make an inspection of: the Property, all of Seller's operating financial records of the Property for the period of Seller's ownership of the Property (including the current year) pertaining to the Property, and all items required to be delivered by Seller pursuant to this Agreement. All such records and items shall be made available to Purchaser at the office of the Seller in My Town, State. Purchaser shall have the right to enter upon the Property and make a complete inspection of the Property. Purchaser shall upon reasonable notice to Seller have the right to talk with all tenants, lenders' representatives (if any), and all service personnel involved with or connected with the Property. If for any reason the results of Purchaser's inspection are not deemed by Purchaser to be satisfactory for any reason whatsoever, in its sole discretion, then Purchaser may elect to terminate this Agreement by written notice of such election to Seller no later than the Final Inspection Date, in which event neither Purchaser nor Seller shall have any further rights or obligations hereunder, and Escrowee shall return to Purchaser the Deposit together with accrued interest and thereafter this Agreement shall be deemed terminated and of no further force or effect. If Purchaser fails to make such election to terminate this Agreement as aforesaid by the Final Inspection Date, then Purchaser shall be deemed to have waived its right to terminate this Agreement pursuant to this Section.

4. Title of the Property.

(a) Seller shall sell, convey and assign to Purchaser at Closing good and marketable fee simple title to the Property subject only to the Permitted Title Exceptions as defined and set forth on Exhibit B attached hereto.

(b) Within thirty (30) days following the Effective Date, Purchaser shall cause title to the Property to be examined and shall furnish Seller with a written statement of any and all title matters, other than the Permitted Title Exceptions to which Purchaser objects. Purchaser shall also have the right to examine, or cause to be examined, title to the Property at any time or times after such initial title examination and prior to Closing and to furnish Seller with a written statement or statements of any and all additional matters, other than the Permitted Title Exceptions which affect the title to the Property or the use thereof and which arise, or first appear of record from and after the date of the initial title examination hereunder and to which Purchaser objects. Seller shall cooperate with Purchaser after receipt of any such written statement to correct, cure, or remove all matters described in such statement, and covenants to exercise diligent and good faith efforts to do so. Notwithstanding the above or the terms of this Section 4(b), in the event that any such matter results from any affirmative action taken by Seller subsequent to the date hereof, Seller covenants to expend such money and to take such other actions as may be necessary to correct, cure, or remove same. The Closing Date shall be postponed automatically for thirty (30) days, if necessary, to permit Seller to cure. If Seller shall fail to correct, cure, or remove all such matters within the time allowed by this Section 4(b), then Purchaser, at its option exercised by written notice may:

(i) decline to purchase the Property; or

(ii) waive such matter and proceed to close the purchase and sale of the Property without a reduction in the Purchase Price and allow Seller to convey title to the Property in accordance with the terms hereof; or

(iii) in the event the matter results from affirmative action of Seller subsequent to the Effective Date, require Seller by action of specific performance or otherwise to exercise diligent and good faith efforts to correct, cure, or remove such matters and convey the Property in accordance with the terms of this Agreement in which case the Closing Date shall be postponed until such correction, cure, or

(*continued*)

removal by Seller has been completed (provided, however, that at any time during such period Purchaser may exercise its options as set forth in Section 4(b)(i) or Section 4(b)(ii) previous page). Should Purchaser accept, by written waiver, its interest in the Property subject to matters in addition to the Permitted Title Exceptions, such acceptable matters shall be added to the list now set forth in Exhibit B and shall thereafter be deemed to be Permitted Title Exceptions except that, in the event any of such matters results from any affirmative action taken by Seller subsequent to the date hereof, such acceptance shall be without prejudice to Purchaser's thereafter seeking monetary damages from Seller for any such matter. If Purchaser shall decline to accept the Seller's interest in the Property subject to such matters, pursuant to Section 4(b) above, then Escrowee shall refund to Purchaser the Deposit and the parties hereto shall have no further rights, obligations, duties, or liabilities hereunder whatsoever, except for those rights, obligations, duties, and liabilities which, by the express terms hereof, survive any termination hereof and except for Purchaser's right to seek monetary damages from Seller for any matter which Seller shall have failed so to correct and which shall have resulted from any affirmative action taken by Seller after the date hereof.

(c) Purchaser may, at its expense, elect to obtain a standard ALTA Form 1987–B owner's policy of title insurance pursuant to which fee simple title to the Property shall be insured. Seller covenants to Purchaser that title to the Property shall at Closing not only be good and marketable, but, in the event Purchaser elects so to purchase such an owner's policy of title insurance, shall be insurable by Ticor Title Insurance Company of California or by Chicago Title Insurance Company or other title insurance company reasonably acceptable to Purchaser at its regular rates, without exceptions or reservations to coverage of any type or kind, other than the Permitted Title Exceptions.

5. Survey.

(a) Purchaser shall have within thirty (30) days from the Effective Date the option to obtain a current accurate as-built survey of the Premises (the "New Survey") and such New Survey discloses any matter which is not set forth on the Existing Survey to which Purchaser objects (any such matter being herein referred to as "New Survey Objections"), then Purchaser shall give Seller notice of such New Survey Objections. Purchaser shall be entitled to make its best efforts to cure said New Survey Objections and Seller covenants that it shall cooperate with Purchaser to the extent necessary to effectuate said cures.

(b) If Seller shall have failed to correct, cure or remove all such New Survey Objections prior to time set for closing, then Purchaser, at its option, exercised by written notice, may:

(i) decline to purchase the Property; or

(ii) waive such matter and proceed to close the purchase and sale of the Property without a reduction in the Purchase Price and allow Seller to convey title to the Property in accordance with the terms hereof; or

(iii) if such New Survey Objection should arise by affirmative action of Seller after the Execution Date, require Seller by action of specific performance or otherwise to exercise diligent and good faith efforts to correct, cure or remove such New Survey Objections and convey the Property in accordance with the terms of this Agreement, in which case the Closing Date shall be postponed until such correction, cure or removal by Seller has been completed (provided, however, that at any time during such period Purchaser may exercise its options as set forth in Section 5(b)(i) or Section 5(b)(ii) above).

Should Purchaser accept, by written waiver, its interest in the Property subject to New Survey Objections, such acceptable matters shall be added to the list now set forth in Exhibit B and shall thereafter be deemed to be Permitted Title Exceptions except that, in the event any of such matters results from any affirmative action taken by Seller subsequent to the date hereof, such acceptance shall be without prejudice to Purchaser's thereafter seeking monetary damages from Seller for any such matter. If Purchaser shall decline to accept the Seller's interest in the Property subject to such matters, pursuant to Section 5(b)(i) above, then the Escrowee shall refund to Purchaser the Deposit and the parties hereto shall have no further rights, obligations, duties or liabilities hereunder whatsoever, except for those rights, obligations, duties and liabilities which, by the express terms hereof, survive any termination hereof, and except for Purchaser's right to seek monetary damages from Seller for any matter that Seller shall have failed so to correct and that shall have resulted from any affirmative action taken by Seller after the date hereof.

EXHIBIT 7–4

Contract for Purchase and Sale of a Retail Shopping Center (*continued*)

(continued)

EXHIBIT 7–4

Contract for Purchase and Sale
of a Retail Shopping Center
(*continued*)

6. Seller's Deliveries.

(a) Seller shall deliver to Purchaser or Purchaser's designee the following items, in possession of Seller or any entity related to Seller, as soon as reasonably possible after the Effective Date, but in any event within five (5) days after the Effective Date, unless another time period is otherwise indicated below:

(i) True, correct and complete copies of all leases of space on the Property together with any amendments thereto and all brokerage commission agreements relating thereto and together with all lease abstracts, tenant correspondence files, and other relevant information; all necessary information and documentation necessary to establish the base index, such as the consumer price index, for the base year of such lease and for any escalation clause in any lease; and copies of all written correspondence to or received from any lessee regarding such additional rental charges or rental escalation provisions. (All leases of space on the Property, together with any amendments thereto and such brokerage commission agreements and other documents described hereinabove, are hereinafter collectively referred to as the "Leases," and each lease of space on the Property, together with any amendments thereto and such brokerage commission agreements, is hereinafter individually referred to as a "Lease");

(ii) A true, correct and complete rent roll concerning all Leases as of the Effective Date or a more current date, indicating thereon any delinquencies with respect to rent due and owing and indicating all brokerage commissions and similar fees owing and relating to the Leases;

(iii) True, correct and complete copies of all contracts other than Leases, if any, pertaining to the Property (the "Service Contracts") in existence as of the Effective Date or a more current date, including but not limited to all management contracts, maintenance contracts, contracts or agreements relating to any unfinished improvements to the Property, service leases, and contracts for parking on a monthly or yearly basis, together with a list of those contracts that cannot be unilaterally terminated by Purchaser as of the Closing Date without further payment;

(iv) A true, correct and complete inventory of all the Tangible Personal Property as of the Effective Date or a more current date;

(v) [INTENTIONALLY DELETED]

(vi) True, correct and complete copies of the latest personal property and real estate tax bills for the Property and all tax bills, notices, assessments and communications relating to the Property, or any part thereof, promptly upon receipt of same by Seller;

(vii) True, correct, and complete copies of the most recent title insurance policy relating to the Land, if any, in the possession of Seller; together with true, correct, and complete copies of all exceptions listed on Schedule B thereof that are not inchoate liens or survey exceptions;

(viii) True, correct, and complete copies of all matters listed on Exhibit B attached hereto that are not inchoate liens or survey exceptions (to the extent that such copies are not furnished to Purchaser pursuant to Section 6(a)(vii) above);

(ix) True, correct, and complete copies of all inspection reports and tests and studies relating to the Property, including, without limitation, engineering studies, environmental assessments or reports, and maintenance schedules;

(x) A true, correct, and complete copy of any offering circular, private placement memorandum, registration statement, or other similar information or materials relating to the Property, which is in the possession of the Seller;

(xi) True, correct, and complete copies of all existing insurance policies relating to the Property (or, if the Property is insured pursuant to a master policy, true, correct, and complete copies of all certificates issued pursuant to such master policies that evidence the insurance coverages relating to the Property), and true, correct, and complete copies of all records and communications concerning all claims, losses, and demands made under any insurance policy relating to the Property since Seller acquired the Property and otherwise in possession of Seller, together with a listing of the names, addresses, and account representatives of all insurance companies that have issued policies relating to the Property since Seller acquired the Property and otherwise in the possession of Seller;

(xii) A memorandum, which Seller shall prepare if presently not in Seller's possession, describing all oral contracts and agreements pertaining to the Property, if any, which memorandum shall include, without limitation, the names, address and telephone numbers of all persons or entities that are parties

(continued)

to such contracts or agreements, together with a detailed description of the terms, conditions, and provisions of such contracts and agreements;

(xiii) True, complete, and correct copies of all documents, including, but not limited to, plans, specifications, contracts, budgets, schedules, and certificates pertaining to the current construction, renovation, paving, and all other improvements to the Property;

(xiv) On or before November 1, 20____, tenant estoppel letters subsequentially in the form attached hereto as Exhibit C (the "Tenant Estoppels Letter"), each dated no earlier than October 1, 20____, duly executed by all tenants of the Property or in such form as required by Lender. Seller shall use its best efforts to obtain the Tenant Estoppels from all tenants. If Seller is unable to obtain Tenant Estoppels from tenants occupying at least eighty-five percent (85%) of the net rented square footage of the Improvements under leases existing as of October 1, 20____, as required above, then Purchaser may either (A) accept those Tenant Estoppels obtained by Seller and close the subject transaction otherwise in accordance with the terms of the Agreement; or (B) decline to purchase the Property. If Purchaser elects to close the subject transaction pursuant to its option set forth in Section 6(a)(xiv)(A) above, then with respect to all those Leases for which a tenant estoppel letter is not obtained and delivered to Purchaser at or before Closing, Seller shall deliver to Purchaser at Closing a certificate setting forth the status of each such Lease and providing the information set forth in the Tenant Estoppel letters;

(xv) True, correct, and complete copies of all Permits (as defined below), certificates of occupancy, and licenses issued by any Governmental Authority (as defined below) or utility company in connection with the occupancy and use of such Improvements as are in the possession of Seller;

(xvi) True, correct, and complete copies, if any, of all notes and other unrecorded documents, agreements, and instruments relating to indebtedness secured by the Property or any part thereof; and

(b) In the event any event or circumstance shall occur that renders any documents, materials, or other information provided by Seller to Purchaser pursuant to Section 6(a) no longer true, correct, and complete, Seller shall immediately deliver to Purchaser all documentation, material, and information necessary to supplement the same so as to render such documents, material, and information true, correct, and complete. Purchaser shall have seven (7) business days in which to review such supplemental material and, in the event that such supplemental materials differ materially and adversely, in Purchaser's sole opinion, from the information and materials previously furnished or made available to Purchaser, and are not deemed by Purchaser to be satisfactory, then Purchaser may elect to terminate this Agreement by delivering written notice of such election to Seller no later than seven (7) business days after the receipt by Purchaser of such necessary material, to permit the running of such period of seven (7) business days. If, however, any such documents, materials, or other information provided by Seller to Purchaser pursuant to Section 6(a) are untrue, incorrect, or incomplete as of the date provided pursuant to Section 6(a), Seller shall be deemed to have breached this Agreement, and Purchaser shall be entitled to all remedies provided in Section 20 of this Agreement.

7. Legal Description.

In the event that the legal description of the Land as set forth in the New Survey differs from the legal description of the Land as set forth in the Existing Survey, Seller shall convey at Closing to Purchaser by quitclaim deed all Seller's right, title, and interest in and to the Land as described in the New Survey, together with all Property relating thereto or existing therein; provided, however, that nothing in the preceding sentence shall limit Purchaser's right to deem any such material differences a New Survey Objection, thereby entitling Purchaser to the rights and remedies set forth in Section 5 above. In any event, Seller must convey by a legal description for which Purchaser may obtain standard title insurance through Chicago Title Insurance Company, Ticor Title Insurance Company of California or Lawyers Title Insurance Company, at standard rates.

8. Purchaser's Access to the Property and Seller's Records.

At any time prior to Closing (unless this Agreement is terminated as herein provided), the Purchaser, its agents, employees, and contractors, shall have the right to enter upon the Property after reasonable notice to Seller for purposes of surveying, inspecting, and testing the Property; provided,

EXHIBIT 7–4

Contract for Purchase and Sale
of a Retail Shopping Center
(*continued*)

however, that in the event this Agreement fails to close for any reason, Purchaser shall (on or before the scheduled Closing Date) restore the Property to its original condition, and further provided that Purchaser shall use its best efforts not to disrupt the ordinary course of business of Seller or any of the tenants under Leases. Purchaser agrees to indemnify and hold Seller harmless against any property damage or personal injury or claim of lien against the Property resulting from the activities permitted by this Section (including, without limitation, reasonable attorney's fees and expenses paid or incurred by the Seller during litigation and appeals thereof, if any). All inspections, tests, investigations, and other activities carried on by Purchaser pertaining to the Property shall be at Purchaser's sole cost and expense. In addition to and not in limitation of Purchaser's rights elsewhere set forth herein, Purchaser shall have the right upon three (3) business days' prior written notice to Seller to inspect all property, books, leases, and records of Seller pertaining directly to the operation of the Property, for the period of Seller's ownership of the Property, provided that the cost of copying such items shall be borne by Purchaser and such items shall be made available to Purchaser by Seller at the Office of Seller in My Town, State, or such other location in My Town, State, where said items are normally stored.

9. Covenants and Representations.

(a) *Seller's Covenants and Representations.*

(i) Seller has obtained all consents, approvals or authorizations necessary to execute this Agreement and to consummate the transaction contemplated hereby, and all documents referred to herein will be validly executed and delivered and binding upon Seller;

(ii) Seller has no knowledge of any material defect in the Improvements or any part thereof and has no knowledge of and has received no notice from any Governmental Authority (as defined below) of any violation of any Requirement of Law (as defined below) relating to the Property or any part thereof;

(iii) Seller has no knowledge of and has received no notice from any insurance company or board of fire underwriters or similar agency that there exists any condition or circumstances on the Property, or any part thereof, which must be corrected in order to maintain the effectiveness, or as a condition precedent to the issuance of, any insurance policy affecting the Property or any part thereof or which is in violation of any applicable fire code or similar rule, regulation, or order for such board of fire underwriters or similar agency;

(iv) Seller has no knowledge of and has received no notice of any litigation, claim or suit that is pending or threatened and that could adversely affect the Property or any part thereof or title thereto (exclusive of any litigation, claim, or suit brought against a tenant of the Property after the Effective Date wherein Seller is not named as a defendant or a third-party defendant and wherein no counterclaims are alleged against Seller, provided, however, that Seller will give Purchaser prompt notice of all such litigation, claims and suits);

(v) Neither Seller, nor, to the best of Seller's knowledge, any previous owner of the Property or any part thereof has used, generated, stored, or disposed of any Hazardous Materials (as defined below) in or on the Property or any part thereof; or has used or disposed of any Hazardous Materials in connection with the use, operation, construction or repair of the Property or any part thereof. Seller shall hold Purchaser harmless and shall indemnify and defend Purchaser from and against any and all losses, damages, claims and liabilities whatsoever in any way relating to or arising out of any breach of the foregoing representation. This provision shall survive Closing and the consummation of the transactions contemplated hereby;

(vi) Seller owns good and unencumbered title to the Tangible Personal Property and Intangible Personal Property, and Seller has done nothing to encumber same during Seller's ownership thereof other than those certain Loan Documents listed on Exhibit K attached hereto;

(vii) Seller has not operated the Property within the past five (5) years under any other name or trade name of which it has not notified Purchaser;

(viii) All documents, materials, and information delivered to Purchaser pursuant to Section 6(a), as supplemented by such documents, materials and information delivered to Purchaser pursuant to Section 6(b), are true, correct, and complete;

(ix) Seller shall not cause or permit to exist (A) any mortgage, deed to secure debt, security deed, security agreement, assignment, or other similar instrument or agreement or any lien or encumbrance

(continued)

EXHIBIT 7–4

Contract for Purchase and Sale
of a Retail Shopping Center
(*continued*)

whatsoever (other than the Permitted Exceptions or those listed on Exhibit K) to attach to or affect title to the Property or any part thereof from and after the Effective Date except for the Leases approved by Purchaser; or (B) any matters not shown on the New Survey;

(x) Seller represents, to the best of its knowledge, that the mechanical, electrical, plumbing, HVAC, roofing, drainage, sanitary sewerage, and utility equipment facilities and systems servicing the Property and the improvements thereon are in operational order and shall be so maintained through and including the Closing Date. Seller represents that it is aware of no defects in any of said systems;

(xi) Seller covenants that it shall not enter into any leases pertaining to the Property after the Effective Date without prior written approval of Purchaser. Purchaser shall approve leases containing reasonable business terms, including base rentals of at least $16.00 per square foot and $1.75 of common area maintenance charges (CAMs). Seller covenants and represents that it shall incur no brokerage commissions pertaining to leases entered into prior to the Closing Date on any leases negotiated in any respect by Seller prior to the Closing Date;

(xii) Seller represents that it has no notice of and is not aware of any violation on the Property or improvements of any applicable zoning laws, ordinances or regulations including, without limitation, all parking requirements and building setback requirements (except as shown on the Existing Survey, which Purchaser has the right to consider during the Inspection Period);

(xiii) [INTENTIONALLY DELETED]

(xiv) Seller shall continue to operate, manage, and maintain the Property in good condition and in a good businesslike manner, such operation and maintenance to include the undertaking of any reasonably necessary capital improvements or repairs, through and including the Closing Date. Such continuous operation and maintenance shall also be a condition precedent to Closing; and

(b) *Purchaser's Covenants and Representations*. Purchaser hereby represents and warrants to Seller that Purchaser has obtained all consents, approvals, or authorizations necessary to execute this Agreement and to consummate the transaction contemplated hereby, and all documents referred to herein will be validly executed and delivered and binding upon Purchaser.

10. Additional Conditions Precedent.

(a) This Agreement is contingent upon Purchaser being able to Purchase the Property subject to the current mortgage loan in the original principal amount of FIVE MILLION FIVE HUNDRED THOUSAND AND NO/100 DOLLARS ($5,500,000.00) held by Wearever Life Assurance Company (the "Mortgage Loan") being evidenced by (a) certain Real Estate Note, dated December 17, 20____, from Seller to Wearever Life Assurance Company, (b) Deed to Secure Debt and Security Agreement by and between the same parties dated December 17, 20____, recorded at Deed Book 11234, Page 137, Great County, State Records, and (c) an Assignment of Leases and Rents by and between the same parties dated December 17, 20____, recorded at Deed Book 11234, Page 162, Great County, State Records (hereinafter referred to as the "Mortgage Loan Documents"). One-half (½) of all costs, assumption fees, and transfer fees paid to the holder of the Mortgage Loan to obtain permission to transfer the Property to Purchaser shall be paid by Seller and the other one-half (½) by Purchaser. The tax and insurance provisions contained in the Mortgage Loan Documents are to be waived upon the same terms and conditions under which they are presently being waived for Seller. The terms of the Mortgage Loan, including but not limited to the rate of interest, the amount of the monthly installments, and the Maturity Date, are to remain unchanged. Seller shall provide Purchaser with an Estoppel Agreement from the holder of the Mortgage Loan in substantially the same form as that attached hereto as Exhibit "I". Purchaser agrees to provide the holder of the Mortgage Loan with any financial information necessary to enable the holder of the Mortgage Loan to approve the transfer of the Property from Seller to Purchaser. This Agreement shall remain contingent upon the ability of Purchaser to obtain the Property subject to the Mortgage Loan and the consent by the holder of the Mortgage Loan to the Note and Deed.

If the Seller has not obtained the permission from the holder of the Mortgage Loan to transfer the Property to Purchaser subject to the Mortgage Loan and upon the terms set forth therein and the consent to the Note and Deed on or before September 26, 20____, then Purchaser may by written notice to Seller notify Seller of its election to terminate this Agreement, whereupon this Agreement shall terminate and the Deposit together with accrued interest thereon shall be returned to Purchaser, and thereafter the parties hereto shall have no further rights, duties, obligations, or liabilities hereunder.

(b) Seller shall continuously operate and maintain the Property in good condition and continue businesslike management through and including the Closing Date.

11. Closing Date.

Unless this Agreement is terminated by Purchaser pursuant to the terms of this Agreement, the Closing shall take place at the offices of Purchaser's attorneys, Winkom, Blinkholm and Nodd, 1400 Crabtree Place Tower, My Town, State, or such location as is mutually agreeable to Purchaser and Seller, beginning at 10:00 A.M. on a business day (in My Town, State) selected by Purchaser on or before November 11, 20____. The date of Closing shall hereinafter be referred to as the "Closing Date." Purchaser shall give Seller notice of the Closing Date at least five (5) business days prior thereto; provided, however, if Purchaser gives Seller no such notice of the Closing Date, then the Closing Date shall be November 11, 20____.

12. Seller's Obligations.

At Closing, Seller shall:

(a) Execute, acknowledge and deliver to Purchaser a limited warranty deed in recordable form, the form of which is attached hereto as Exhibit D, conveying the Property to Purchaser subject only to: (i) taxes for the years subsequent to the year of Closing; (ii) the zoning classification as of the Effective Date; and (iii) the Permitted Exceptions;

(b) Execute and deliver to Purchaser the following additional conveyance documents: (A) an Affidavit reciting Seller's non-foreign status within the meaning of Section 1445(f)(3) of the Internal Revenue Code of 1986; (B) an Assignment and Assumption of Leases assigning to Purchaser Seller's interest in the Leases, a form of which is attached hereto as Exhibit E; and (C) an Assignment of Contracts, Other Rights and Intangible Property assigning to Purchaser the Intangible Property, the form of which is attached hereto as Exhibit F; and (D) a Lender Estoppel Letter from the holder of the Mortgage Loan, a proposed form of which is attached hereto as Exhibit I; (E) Subordination, Attornment, and Non-Disturbance Agreements satisfactory to Lender signed by tenants leasing at least eighty-five percent (85%) of the net rentable square footage of the Property, a proposed form of which is attached hereto as Exhibit J; and (F) a certificate that Seller knows of no defects in the system referred to in Sections 9(a) (x) and (xi) of this Agreement as of the Closing Date;

(c) Execute and deliver to Purchaser a Closing Statement setting forth the adjustments and prorations to closing as well as the costs pursuant to this Agreement as elsewhere specifically provided herein (the "Closing Statement");

(d) Deliver to Purchaser a certified and updated rent roll reflecting all the tenants under Leases to the Property as of the Closing Date and indicating thereon any delinquencies with respect to rent due;

(e) Deliver to Purchaser all Permits, certificates of occupancy, and licenses issued by any Governmental Authorities or utility companies in connection with the occupancy and use of the Improvements as are in the possession of Seller;

(f) Deliver to Purchaser a form letter to all tenants under Leases stating that Purchaser has acquired the Property from Seller, that future rents should be paid as specified by Purchaser, and that Purchaser will be responsible for all tenants' security deposits, if any;

(g) A certificate of Seller stating (A) that Seller has no knowledge of any pending or threatened condemnation proceedings or any taking by any Governmental Authority which in any way affects the Property; and (B) that there are no Leases (other than Leases approved by Purchaser), no Service Contracts (whether written or oral), no employees, no insurance policy endorsements or claims, and no other notices from any Governmental Authority regarding any violations of any Requirements of Law affecting the Property except as heretofore provided to Purchaser as required under Section 6 above and elsewhere in this Agreement;

(h) The plans and specifications for the Improvements, including all amendments thereto, as are in the possession of Seller;

(i) The originals of all Leases, including all amendments thereto;

(continued)

EXHIBIT 7–4

Contract for Purchase and Sale
of a Retail Shopping Center
(*continued*)

(j) All information and materials required for full compliance under the Foreign Investors in Real Property Tax Act;

(k) All keys to the Improvements in Seller's possession and a list of all other persons which, to the best of Seller's knowledge, are in possession of keys to the Improvements, other than keys to tenant space in the possession of tenants;

(l) Such other documents, instruments, and agreements as Purchaser may reasonably require to effect and complete the transactions contemplated herein and to obtain an owner's title insurance policy insuring the interest of Purchaser, as owner, in the amount of $7,300,000.00, free and clear of all exceptions except the Permitted Exceptions, for a premium calculated at standard rates, including, without limitation, a Seller's Affidavit of Title in the form attached hereto as Exhibit G and a Bill of Sale in the form attached hereto as Exhibit H; and

(m) Seller's estoppel certificates to the extent required by Section 6(a)(xiv) above.

13. Purchaser's Obligations at Closing.

On the Closing Date, subject to the terms, conditions, and provisions hereof, Purchaser shall:

(a) Execute and deliver to Seller an assumption agreement whereby Purchaser assumes all liabilities and agrees to perform all obligations of Seller under all the Leases, the form of which is contained in Exhibit E, and the Service Contracts and all employee contracts assumed by Purchaser pursuant hereto, the form of which is contained in Exhibit F. Said assumption agreements shall contain an indemnification by Purchaser of Seller and an agreement to hold Seller harmless from and against any and all claims, debts, liabilities, and the like affecting or relating to the Property, or any part thereof, and the Leases after the Closing Date. Likewise, said assumption agreements shall contain an agreement to hold Purchaser harmless from and against any and all claims, debts, liabilities, and the like affecting or relating to the Property, or any part thereof, and the Leases prior to and including the Closing Date.

(b) Execute and deliver to Seller a copy of the Closing Statement.

(c) Deliver to Seller pursuant to the terms of Section 2 herein the Note and Deed and, pursuant to Section 2 herein, the sums required to be paid hereinunder, and Purchaser shall execute such other documents, instruments, affidavits, and agreements as may be required to close the transaction contemplated herein.

14. Closing Costs.

In connection with Closing, Seller shall pay the State real estate transfer tax and all costs relating to the satisfaction, cure and removal of all title defects (except the Permitted Exceptions) undertaken by Seller as herein required and the payment of one-half (½) all transfer, assumption or other fees due the holder of the Mortgage Loan to obtain the consent to the transfer of the Property to the Purchaser and the consent to the Note and Deed. Purchaser shall pay the costs of the premiums payable or costs incurred in connection with the issuance of the owner's title insurance commitment and the owner's title insurance policy in favor of Purchaser and all costs of recording the limited warranty deed. The Purchaser shall be solely responsible for the New Survey costs. Each party shall pay its own attorney's fees.

15. Prorations.

The following items shall be apportioned and prorated (based on a 30-day month, unless otherwise indicated) between the Seller and the Purchaser as of the Closing Date so that credits and charges for all days prior to the Closing Date shall be allocated to the Seller and credits and charges for the Closing Date and for all days thereafter shall be allocated to the Purchaser:

(a) *Taxes*. At the Closing, all ad valorem property taxes, water and sewer charges, and assessments of any kind on the Property for the year of the Closing shall be prorated between Purchaser and Seller as of 12:01 A.M. on the Closing Date. Such proration shall be based upon the latest ad valorem property tax, water, sewer charge, and assessment bills available. If, upon receipt of the actual ad valorem property tax, water, sewer and assessment bills for the Property, such proration is incorrect, then either Purchaser or Seller shall be entitled, upon demand, to receive such amounts from the other as may be necessary

EXHIBIT 7–4

Contract for Purchase and Sale
of a Retail Shopping Center
(*continued*)

to correct such malapportionment. This obligation to correct such malapportionment shall survive the Closing and not be merged into any documents delivered pursuant to the Closing.

(b) *Rents*. Purchaser shall receive a credit for all amounts due under the Leases in effect at Closing, hereinafter referred to as the "Rents," collected by Seller prior to Closing and allocable in whole or in part to any period following the Closing Date. Seller shall deliver to Purchaser any Rents received after Closing. Purchaser shall deliver to Seller any Rent received after Closing that relates to periods prior to and through the Closing Date; provided, however, that any such Rents collected by Purchaser after the Closing shall be applied first toward Rents due that shall have accrued after the Closing Date, and then toward Rents that accrued prior to the Closing Date. Purchaser shall use its best efforts (short of incurring legal fees and expenses or taking other action which would not be in its best interest as owner of the Property) to collect all such delinquent Rents.

In the event that Purchaser is unable to collect delinquent Rents due Seller within thirty (30) days after the Closing Date, then Seller may pursue collection of such delinquent Rents from the respective Tenants in accordance with its rights under State law; provided, however, Seller shall have no right to collect Rents in any manner which would result in an interference with the Tenant's rights of possession under its lease or in any way interfere with the landlord/tenant relationship between Purchaser and the Tenant (for example, Seller shall have no rights to dispossess Tenant in an effort to collect delinquent Rents).

(c) *Other Expense Prorations*. All other reasonable expenses normal to the operation and maintenance of the Property that require payments either in advance or in arrears for periods which begin prior to the Closing Date and end thereafter. Without limiting the generality of the foregoing, such expenses shall include water, electric; telephone and all other utility and fuel charges; fuel on hand (at cost plus sales tax); any deposits with utility companies; employee wages, salaries, benefits and pension, health and welfare insurance, social security, and such other contributions; and charges under employee contracts and/or Service Contracts.

(d) *Security Deposits*. Purchaser shall receive a credit for the security deposits paid under the Leases in existence and in effect on the Closing Date.

(e) *Leasing Commissions*. Seller warrants and represents that there are no leasing commissions due and owing or to become due and owing under any of the Leases or any renewals and extensions thereof, as of the Closing Date. Seller agrees to hold harmless from and to indemnify and defend Purchaser from and against any and all such leasing commissions and all other fees, charges, and compensation whatsoever due any person or entity in connection with the procuring of any Lease, together with all extensions and renewals thereof, or otherwise relating to any Lease. This provision shall survive the Closing and the consummation of the transactions contemplated herein.

16. Employees and Service Contracts.

Seller represents and warrants that there are no employees or employment contracts relating to the Property which cannot be terminated on or prior to Closing because of contractual terms or applicable law. From and after the Effective Date, Seller will not enter into or extend or renew any contracts relating to the Property which cannot by their express terms terminate with thirty (30) days' notice, without the prior written approval of Purchaser. With respect to all other employees and contracts relating to the Property, Purchaser shall not be obligated to continue the employment of all such employees and to continue all such contracts and to assume all obligations therefor as of the Closing Date, unless Purchaser notifies Seller of its intention to continue the employment of employees under any or all of such employee agreements and/or contracts prior to Closing, in which event Seller shall be responsible for terminating the employment of such personnel and such contracts capable of being terminated and designated for termination by Purchaser's notice. With respect to any leasing brokerage agreements in connection with the Property, Seller shall terminate and obtain release of same prior to or on the Closing Date.

17. Brokerage Commissions.

Each party further represents to the other that except for_____
_____ (collectively "Brokers"), no broker has been involved in this transaction. Seller shall be solely responsible for paying

EXHIBIT 7–4

Contract for Purchase and Sale of a Retail Shopping Center

(*continued*)

any commission due to the Brokers in connection with this transaction. Seller shall pay in cash or good funds at Closing brokerage commissions of one percent (1%) to _____ ____ _____ and one percent (1%) of the Purchase Price to _____. No commission shall be due and owing Brokers should the sale and purchase of the Property fail to close for any reason whatsoever, including, without limitation, the breach of this Agreement by Seller or Purchaser. Under no circumstances whatsoever shall Brokers be entitled to retain any portion of the Deposit. In the event any other claims for brokerage commissions or fees are ever made against the Seller or the Purchaser in connection with this transaction, all such claims shall be handled and paid by the party whose actions or alleged commitments form the basis of such claim. Seller further agrees to indemnify and hold harmless the Purchaser from and against any and all such claims or demands with respect to any brokerage fees or agent's commissions or other compensation asserted by any person, firm, or corporation in connection with this Agreement or the transactions contemplated hereby arising from actions or alleged commitments of the Seller. Purchaser further agrees to indemnify and hold harmless the Seller from and against any and all such claims or demands with respect to any brokerage fees or agent's commissions or other compensation asserted by any person, firm, or corporation in connection with this Agreement or the transaction contemplated hereby arising from actions or alleged commitments of the Purchaser. This provision shall survive Closing and the conveyance of the Property by Seller to Purchaser.

18. Risk of Loss.

Risk of loss or damage to the Property or any part thereof by condemnation, eminent domain, or similar proceedings, or by deed in lieu or under threat thereof (collectively, a "Taking"), or by fire, flood or other casualty from the Effective Date until delivery of the limited warranty deed will be on Seller and after the delivery of the limited warranty deed will be on Purchaser. In the event of any such loss or damage to all or to a material part of the Property or any part of the Improvements prior to the delivery of the limited warranty deed, this Agreement may, at the option of Purchaser to be exercised by written notice to Seller, be declared null and void and Purchaser shall be returned the Deposit and both parties hereto shall be released from any further rights and duties hereunder, or this Agreement shall remain in full force and effect and Seller shall transfer to Purchaser on the Closing Date all insurance proceeds or condemnation awards received by Seller because of such casualty or Taking and all of Seller's rights, title and interest in and to any recovery or claims under any insurance policies or condemnation awards relating to the Property.

Upon the happening of one of the events in the preceding paragraph, subsequent to the Inspection Deadline and prior to delivery of the limited warranty deed, if the cost of repair or replacement or, in the event of a Taking, if the reduction in the value of the project is TWENTY–FIVE THOUSAND DOLLARS ($25,000.00) or less, Purchaser shall close and take the Property as diminished by such events and Seller shall transfer to Purchaser on the Closing Date all insurance proceeds or condemnation awards received by Seller because of such casualty or Taking and all of Seller's right, title, and interest in and to any recovery or claim under any insurance policies or condemnation awards relating to the Property, together with a credit to Purchaser for the amount of any deductibles contained in any insurance policy.

19. Purchaser's Default.

In the event the transaction contemplated hereby is not closed because of Purchaser's default, the Deposit shall be paid to Seller as full liquidated damages for such failure to close, the parties acknowledging the difficulty of ascertaining Seller's damages in such circumstances, whereupon neither party hereto shall have any further rights, claims, or liabilities under this Agreement except for the provisions which are made to survive the termination or cancellation of this Agreement. Said liquidated damages shall be Seller's sole and exclusive remedy, and Seller shall expressly not have the right to seek specific performance.

20. Seller's Default.

If the Seller fails to perform any of the covenants of this Agreement, or if Seller otherwise defaults hereunder, the Purchaser shall have the right, in addition to all rights and remedies herein provided, to

EXHIBIT 7–4

Contract for Purchase and Sale
of a Retail Shopping Center
(*continued*)

pursue any right or remedy it may have against Seller at law or in equity for such breach and/or default, including, without limitation, the right of specific performance of all provisions of this Agreement. Purchaser's monetary damages in the event of such breach and/or default by Seller shall be limited to $100,000.00. The parties hereto acknowledge the difficulty of ascertaining Purchaser's monetary damages in such event.

21. Assignability.

Purchaser shall have the right to assign this Agreement to any person(s), partnership or corporation, including a partnership or corporation to be formed hereafter, with notice to but without the consent of Seller, and the transaction contemplated by this Agreement shall be consummated in the name of such assignee. In the event of such assignment, the assignee shall assume the obligations of Purchaser under this Agreement, and Purchaser shall have no further obligation or liability under this Agreement. Seller shall have the right to assign its interest in this Agreement, only with the written consent of Purchaser, except insofar as such assignment is made to effectuate a tax-free exchange. In the latter instance, Seller may assign its rights but shall remain bound under the terms of this Agreement and the representations, warranties, and covenants contained herein.

Seller is entering into this contract with the intention of disposing of the Property through a like-kind exchange of properties, pursuant to Section 1031 of the Internal Revenue Code of 1954, as amended. Purchaser agrees that, upon request of Seller, Purchaser will convey or cause to be conveyed to Seller at closing other like-kind property acceptable to Seller in lieu of paying cash to Seller, or will pay the purchase price for the property to a third party, who will convey like-kind property to Seller. At the election of Seller, Seller may convey the Property to a third party prior to closing as part of a like-kind exchange of properties with such third party, provided that such third party agrees to be bound by all of the terms and provisions of this contract, and provided further that no such conveyance to any third party shall relieve Seller of any of its obligations hereunder. Anything contained herein to the contrary notwithstanding, Purchaser shall not be obligated to incur any additional liability or expense in connection with any exchange of properties by Seller. Furthermore, Seller shall indemnify Purchaser for any liability or expense incurred in any respect in connection with its cooperation with Seller in effectuating a tax-free exchange. Subject to the foregoing, this Agreement shall inure to the benefit of and shall be binding upon Seller and Purchaser and their respective successors and assigns.

22. Entire Agreement.

No agreements, representations, or warranties unless expressly incorporated or set forth in this Agreement shall be binding upon any of the parties.

23. Notification.

Any notice or demand under which the terms of this Agreement or under any statute must or may be given or made by the parties hereto shall be made in writing and shall be deemed to have been delivered when hand delivered; as of the date sent by an overnight courier; or as of the date of postmark affixed by the U.S. Postal Service, by mailing the same by certified mail return receipt requested addressed to the respective parties at the following addresses:

To Purchaser:

With Copies to:

To Seller:

With Copy to:

(continued)

Such addresses may be changed by the giving of written notice as provided in this paragraph; provided, however that any mailed notice of changed address shall be not be effective until the fifth (5th) day after the date of postmark by the U.S. Postal Service.

24. Time.

Time is of the essence of this Agreement and of each of its provisions.

25. Survival and Last Execution Date.

The provisions of this Agreement shall survive Closing and the execution and delivery of the deed and instruments conveying the Property. If this Agreement is not executed by all parties hereto on or before 5:00 P.M. on August 17, 20____, this Agreement shall be null and void.

26. Headings.

Descriptive headings are for convenience only and shall not control or affect the meaning or construction of any provision of this Agreement.

27. Binding Effect.

This Agreement shall be binding upon and shall inure to the benefit of the parties hereto and their successors and assigns subject to the provisions of Section 21 above.

28. Severability.

In case any one or more of the provisions contained in this Agreement shall for any reason be held to be invalid, illegal, or unenforceable in any respect, such invalidity, illegality, or unenforceability shall not affect any other provision hereof, and this Agreement shall be construed as if such invalid, illegal, or unenforceable provision had never been contained herein.

29. Effective Date of this Agreement.

The Effective Date of this Agreement shall be the last date upon which either the Purchaser or Seller shall have executed this Agreement, as demonstrated by the date(s) below their respective signatures on the signature page to this Agreement.

30. Business Day.

If the Closing is to occur on a holiday or other non-business day, or if any period of time set forth in this Agreement expires on a holiday or other non-business day, then the Closing or the expiration date of such period shall be the next business day. For purposes of this Agreement, the term "business day" shall mean any day which is not a Saturday, Sunday or other day on which banks in My Town, State, are not open for business during regular business hours.

31. Certain Definitions.

As used herein, the following terms are defined as follows:

(a) *Governmental Authority* means any nation or government, any state, municipal or other political subdivision thereof, and any entity exercising executive, legislative, judicial, regulatory, or administrative functions of or pertaining to government.

(b) *Hazardous Materials* means all hazardous wastes, polychlorinated biphenyls (commonly known as "PCBs"), toxic substances, and similar substances, including, without limitation, substances defined as "hazardous substances" or "toxic substances" in the Comprehensive Environmental Response and Liability Act of 1980, as amended, 42 U.S.C. § 9601 et seq., or the Hazardous Materials Transportation Act, and Recovery Act, as amended, 42 U.S.C. § 6901 et seq.

(c) *Permits* means all consents, certificates, authorizations, licenses, approvals, and permits required for the removal, alteration, or demolition of any structure or improvement, or any part thereof, on the Property or for construction, completion, use, occupancy, and operation of the Improvements in accordance

EXHIBIT 7–4

Contract for Purchase and Sale of a Retail Shopping Center (*continued*)

(*continued*)

EXHIBIT 7–4

Contract for Purchase and Sale
of a Retail Shopping Center
(*continued*)

with all Requirements of Law affecting the Property, including, without limiting the generality of the fore-going, demolition permits; building permits; drainage permits; curb cut, access and traffic permits and approvals; sewerage, waste and drainage permits; and environmental approvals and permits.

(d) *Requirements of Law* means any person or entity, the certificate of incorporation and by-laws or partnership agreement or limited partnership agreement or other organizational or governing documents of such person or entity, and any law, treaty, rule or regulation, or determination, judgment, or order of an arbitrator or a court or other Governmental Authority, in each case applicable to or binding upon such person or entity or any of its property or to which such person or entity or any of its property is subject; and, as to the Real Property, any applicable environmental, zoning, building, or land use laws; any requirements, standards, or regulations of the fire marshal and similar agencies; any ordinances, rules or regulations of any governmental authority or agency; and any applicable covenants and restrictions.

32. Possession.

Seller shall deliver actual possession of the Property to Purchaser at Closing.

33. Seller's Guaranty of Income.

At closing, Seller will execute and deliver to Purchaser a Guaranty ("Guaranty") that guarantees the gross rental income from the Property as hereinafter set forth. For a period commencing with the Closing Date and ending one year from the Closing Date, Seller shall guarantee that the gross rental income from the Property shall not be less than Eight Hundred Fifty Thousand and No/100 Dollars ($850,000.00). Seller agrees to pay to Purchaser a sum equal to the difference of Eight Hundred Fifty Thousand Dollars ($850,000.00) and the actual gross rental income received from the Property during the one-year period. Seller agrees to pay Purchaser the income shortfall on a quarterly basis. For example, during the first calendar quarter following the Closing Date if gross rental income from the Property does not equal $212,500.00, Seller shall pay to Purchaser on the last day of the quarter the difference between $212,500.00 and the gross rental income actually received during that period of time. The Seller's obligation to pay Purchaser for rental income shortfall pursuant to this paragraph shall not exceed $100,000.00 during the year succeeding the Closing Date. Purchaser shall provide Seller with a written itemized statement of all rentals received certified to be true and correct by Purchaser. Seller shall further agree that in the event that Seller does not pay Purchaser any rental deficit on a quarterly basis, Purchaser shall have the right to set off said amount due from Seller against the payments under the Note.

Commencing one year from the Closing Date and ending on the same day which is two years from the Closing Date, Seller guarantees that the gross rental income from the Property shall be Eight Hundred Seventy Five Thousand and No/100 Dollars ($875,000.00). Seller agrees to pay to Purchaser a sum equal to the difference between Eight Hundred Seventy Five Thousand Dollars ($875,000.00) and the actual gross rental income received from the Property during that period. Seller agrees to pay Purchaser the income shortfall on a quarterly basis. For example, during the first calendar quarter of the second year following the Closing Date if gross rental income from the Property does not equal $218,750.00, Seller shall pay to Purchaser on the last day of said quarter the difference between $218,750.00 and the gross rental income actually received during that period of time. The Seller's obligation to pay Purchaser for rental income shortfall pursuant to this paragraph shall not exceed $100,000.00 during the second year from Closing Date. Purchaser shall provide Seller with a written itemized statement of all rentals received certified to be true and correct by Purchaser. Seller shall further agree that in the event that Seller does not pay Purchaser any rental deficit on a quarterly basis, Purchaser shall have the right to set off said amount due from Seller against the payments under the Note.

Seller's obligation to pay Purchaser for the rental income shortfall shall be adjusted annually and, in the event the rental income shortfall is less than the sum of the quarterly payments Purchaser has received from Seller, then Purchaser shall refund the difference between the annual rental income shortfall and the amount of rental guaranty payments received from Seller. The annual adjustment shall take place within thirty days from a date that is one year from the Closing Date, and a second annual adjustment shall take place within thirty days from a date that is two years from the Closing Date.

(continued)

During the rental guaranty period as set forth herein, Purchaser shall make every effort to lease existing vacant spaces, including but not limited to, paying full commissions to outside brokers, marketing the Property in a quality manner, and maintaining the Property in a neat and professional manner. If Purchaser relocates any of the existing tenants in Village Square to another property owned by or affiliated with Purchaser, then the tenant's rental income, based on the rental being paid by the tenant prior to relocation, which would have been received by Purchaser had tenant not been relocated shall be credited against the annual gross rental income guaranteed by Seller (i.e. against the $850,000.00 during year one or the $875,000.00 during year two).

Any new space that is leased on the Property during the two-year guaranty period will be created toward the income guaranty (i.e. toward the $850,000.00 during year one or the $875,000.00 during year two). Also, the credit will be the greater of $15.00 per square foot of annual gross rental or the actual gross rental amount received under the lease. Credit for new leases against Seller's income guaranty will commence the earlier of when rental payments begin or six months following occupancy by the tenant.

If Purchaser elects to terminate or not to renew any of the existing leases whereby the tenant wants to stay at the Property and is willing to pay the lesser of the tenant's present rent or fair market rent, then Seller shall receive a credit against the guaranteed income amounts of the amount of the lost rental (i.e. against the $850,000.00 during year one or the $875,000.00 during year two).

34. Additional Provisions.

(a) In the event that Lender requires a form of Tenant Estoppel letter different from the form attached hereto as Exhibit C or in the event that Lender requires a form of Subordination, Attornment, and Non-Disturbance Agreement difference from the form attached hereto as Exhibit J, then Purchaser shall deliver such different form(s) to Seller on or before October 1, 20_____.

(b) In the event that the sale and purchase of the Property does not close for any reason other than Seller's default, Purchaser will provide Seller with copies of all surveys, reports, tests, and other materials relating to the Property obtained by Purchaser pursuant to the terms of this Agreement.

35. Miscellaneous.

(a) This Agreement shall be construed and interpreted under the Laws of the State.

(b) No failure of Purchaser or Seller to exercise any power given either party hereunder or to insist upon strict compliance by either party of its obligations hereunder, and no custom or practice of the parties at variance with the terms hereof shall constitute a waiver of either party's right to demand exact compliance with the terms hereof. Any condition, contingency or right of termination or recision granted by this Agreement to either Purchaser or Seller may be waived in writing by the party for whose benefit such condition or right was granted.

(c) This Agreement may be signed in number of counterparts. Each counterpart shall be an original but all such counterparts shall constitute one agreement. It shall be fully executed when each party whose signature is required has signed at least one counterpart, even though no one counterpart contains the signatures of all the parties.

IN WITNESS WHEREOF, the parties hereto have set their hands and seals as of the Effective Date.

PURCHASER:
Date Executed: _____

SELLER:
Date Executed: _____

The undersigned as Escrowee hereby acknowledges receipt of a copy of this Agreement and of the initial Earnest Money deposit by check $_____ drawn on _____, subject to collection, and agrees to hold said funds pursuant to the terms of this Agreement. The undersigned as Broker hereby agrees to the terms of Section 17 of this Agreement.

Dated: _____

EXHIBIT 7–4

Contract for Purchase and Sale of a Retail Shopping Center (*continued*)

EXHIBIT 7–5

Option to Purchase

STATE OF _____)
)   SS:
COUNTY OF _____)

OPTION TO PURCHASE

IN CONSIDERATION OF ONE HUNDRED AND NO/100 DOLLARS ($100.00) (herein called "Option Consideration") in hand paid, the receipt and sufficiency of which are hereby acknowledged, the undersigned FARRIS DEVELOPMENT CORPORATION, a _____ corporation (hereinafter referred to as "Optionor") hereby grants, conveys and extends to JAMES B. MILLER and ALICE C. MILLER (hereinafter collectively called "Optionee"), the exclusive right and option to purchase upon the terms and conditions set forth herein all that tract or parcel of land lying and being in Land Lots 31 and 32 of the 13th District, _____ County, _____(state)_____, and being known as the Birch Hill Apartments, a 284 unit apartment complex, and being more particularly described on Exhibit A attached hereto and made a part hereof, together with all improvements situated thereon and appurtenances thereto (hereinafter called "Property").

1. Option Term. This Option shall begin on September 1, 20____ and terminate at 11:30 P.M. on December 15, 20____.

2. Exercise of Option. This Option may be exercised by Optionee any time prior to the expiration of the Option, by the execution and delivery to Optionor of that certain Real Estate Contract attached hereto as Exhibit B and made a part hereof. Upon the exercise of the Real Estate Contract by Optionee and submission to Optionor, Optionor shall sign the Agreement and it shall become a binding Agreement between the parties hereto. The executed Real Estate Contract is to be sent to Optionor at the following address:

      604 Clairemont Avenue
      _____(city)_____, _____(state)_____ 30060

3. Purchase Price. The Purchase Price for the sale of the Property shall be ONE MILLION FIVE HUNDRED THOUSAND AND NO/100 DOLLARS ($1,500,000.00) and shall be paid pursuant to the terms set forth in the Real Estate Contract attached hereto as Exhibit B and made a part hereof.

4. No Assignment. This Option is personal to the Optionee and is not assignable.

5. Miscellaneous. This agreement constitutes the entire agreement between the parties hereto and it is understood and agreed that all undertakings and agreements heretofore had between the parties have merged herein. No representation, promise, or inducement not included herein shall be binding upon any party hereto.

IN WITNESS WHEREOF, the parties have hereunto set their hands and seals this _____ day of _____, 20____.

OPTIONOR:
FARRIS DEVELOPMENT CORPORATION
By: _____
David H. Farris, President
OPTIONEE:
_____ (SEAL)
JAMES B. MILLER
_____ (SEAL)
ALICE C. MILLER

Delmar/Cengage Learning

chapter | 8

Deeds

Objectives

After reading this chapter, you should be able to:
- Identify the types of deeds used in modern real estate practice
- Explain the basic requirements of a valid deed
- Prepare a deed

Outline

HISTORICAL DEVELOPMENT OF DEEDS

conveyance

The transfer of title or some or all of the ownership rights to real property from one person to another. A conveyance is usually by an instrument such as a deed, lease, mortgage, or other encumbrance.

After the Norman Conquest in 1066, English land titles were transferred by the actual physical delivery of land. Naturally, it was difficult to hand over a tract of land in the same way one handed over a horse, but the law encouraged the **conveyance** of land to be in the same manner as delivery of personal property. This required the actual delivery of vacant possession to the land. Typically, the seller and the purchaser would gather on the land in the presence of witnesses, and the seller would place or "seise" the purchaser with possession of the land.

As time passed, it became evident to landowners that documentary evidence was valuable to establish the terms of the land transfer. A document would be useful to identify the land, the names of the parties to the conveyance, the interest transferred (e.g., fee simple or life estate), and any warranties of title. The document could be signed and sealed by the grantor and a list of witnesses attached. Thus, it became the practice to prepare a deed or charter after the transfer of land. The early deeds were not necessary to transfer the ownership but were used as a chronicle or memorandum proving that the transfer had taken place.

The deed or charter became evidence of real property ownership, and the safety of the original document was a continuous source of worry to medieval landowners because both theft and forgery of deeds or charters were common. In one fifteenth-century case, a deed was kept in a chest too heavy to be brought into court. No doubt the chest was used to discourage theft of the deed. Other efforts were used to increase the safety of deeds. One effort was to pay royal clerks to record or transcribe a copy of the deed in the rolls where the office copies of royal communications were preserved. Another method was to execute duplicate deeds on the same piece of parchment, cutting the two copies apart with a ragged cut. Before the tear would be made, the word "chirographum" would be written across the line of the tear. If forgery were alleged, then it would be seen if the two documents fitted together. Such deeds or charters were called indentures, from the indented line of the cut.

The evolution of conveyancing continued, and the fine became the preferred method of conveyance. The fine was a written tri-party indenture. Two of the parts would be sent to the parties to the fine, the grantor and the grantee, and the third part was reserved among the court records. The fine method continued to evolve until the present-day system of conveyancing, in which written **deeds,** recorded in the public land records of the county or parish in which the land is located, are used to convey title of land from one person to another. Deeds are important legal documents in a real estate transaction because they are the only written instrument that can transfer real property ownership during an owner's lifetime.

deed

Written document that transfers ownership of real property from one person to another.

In most law firms, paralegals prepare deeds. For this reason, this chapter discusses the general law involving deeds and offers practical suggestions for the preparation of deeds and samples of deed forms.

TYPES OF DEEDS

Three types of deeds commonly are used in the United States: (1) general warranty deed, (2) limited (special) warranty deed, and (3) quitclaim deed. Quitclaim deeds signed by an executor, administrator, or trustee are also in common use.

General Warranty Deed

Caveat emptor ("let the buyer beware") applies to the law of real property transfers. In the absence of some express covenant for title, the full risk of title failure falls on the purchaser of real property. Therefore, the prudent purchaser will ask for and obtain certain covenants of title. These covenants usually are found in a deed known as a **general warranty deed.** The form of a general warranty deed varies from state to state. Some states require the warranties to be expressly set forth in the deed; in other states, the warranties may be included merely with the use of such words as "grant," "bargain and sell," or "warrant."

A general warranty deed contains six **covenants or warranties**: (1) covenant of seisin, (2) covenant of right to convey, (3) covenant against encumbrances, (4) covenant of further assurance, (5) covenant of quiet enjoyment, and (6) covenant of warranty. The covenants are made by the **grantor,** the person who is transferring ownership of the land, to the **grantee,** the person who is receiving ownership of the land.

Covenant of Seisin

Seisin has its roots in the feudal law of England. There is a great deal of argument among legal scholars as to the exact meaning of seisin. Practically speaking, seisin means the right to possession of property. The grantor (the seller) under a general warranty deed will warrant that the grantor has possession of the land being transferred or has a right to the possession of the land. The covenant of seisin also warrants that the grantor has ownership of or title to the land.

seller

Covenant of Right to Convey

The covenant of the right to convey is a promise made on behalf of the grantor of the deed that the grantor owns the land and has the right to transfer ownership of the land. An interest in the land held by a person other than the grantor would cause a breach of this covenant.

Covenant against Encumbrances

The covenant against encumbrances is a promise or warranty by the grantor that the land is unencumbered; that is, the land is free and clear from mortgages, liens, taxes, leases, easements, or any other restrictions that might restrict the use of the land or be a debt on the land.

Covenant of Further Assurance

The covenant of further assurance is a promise by a grantor that in the future, the grantor will make any conveyance necessary to vest in the grantee of the deed the title intended to be conveyed. For example, if the grantor intends to convey fee simple absolute title by the deed but later discovers that he has only a conditional fee, through the covenant of further assurance he agrees to satisfy or remove the conditions so that the title to the land conveyed is fee simple absolute.

NO Claims

Covenants of Quiet Enjoyment and Warranty *buyer*

The covenants of quiet enjoyment and warranty usually are the same and involve a warranty that the grantee of the deed will be able to use the land without fear of eviction and without fear of any third-party assertions of adverse claims.

They are in all warranty deed contracts

Present versus Future Covenants

The covenants of seisin, right to convey, and against encumbrances are called *present covenants* because if they are breached, it is at the time the deed is delivered. The immediate grantee (original purchaser or recipient of the land) is the only person who can sue for breach of a present covenant. Present covenants are not transferable when the land is subsequently sold.

buyer

The covenants of further assurance, quiet enjoyment, and warranty are called *future covenants* because they may be breached at some time in the future. Future covenants are transferable and run with the land. Any owner of the land has standing to sue for breach of a future covenant contained in a general warranty deed.

The following example illustrates the distinction between present and future covenants. Aaron transfers land by general warranty deed to Bob. Bob transfers the same land by general warranty deed to Carol. Carol later transfers the same land again by general warranty deed to David. Each deed is a general warranty deed with all six of the covenants. After the transfers have been made, David, the current owner of the land, discovers that there is a mortgage on the land that had been created by Aaron at the time Aaron owned the property. The mortgage, at the time of its discovery, is a breach of the covenant against encumbrances. Because the covenant against encumbrances is a present covenant, David can only recover losses as a result of the mortgage from Carol for the breach. If the holder of the mortgage attempts to foreclose and to evict David from possession of the land, the foreclosure and attempted eviction will become a breach of the covenant of quiet enjoyment (a future covenant). David, on breach of the future covenant, will have the right to recover from Carol, Bob, and Aaron because the covenant of quiet enjoyment is a future covenant that runs with the land and is transferable. A claim under a future covenant can be asserted by any owner of the land against any person who has given a general warranty deed in the chain of title. Exhibit 8–1 illustrates the difference between present and future covenants.

EXHIBIT 8–1

Present versus Future Covenants

Present Covenants	*Future Covenants*
Can only be enforced by the immediate grantee of a deed	Can be enforced by any owner of the property against the grantor of the deed
• covenant of seisin	• covenant of further assurance
• covenant of right to convey	• covenant of quiet enjoyment
• covenants against encumbrances	• covenant of warranty

Delmar/Cengage Learning

 **CASE**

Lunsford v. King
132 Ga. App. 749, 209 S.E.2d 27 (1974)

STOLZ, Judge.

Plaintiff Lunsford, vendee of a certain tract of land in Fulton County, Georgia, described in a contract of sale by metes and bounds, brought an action against Fulton County, Mrs. King (his vendor), and the vendor's predecessors in title, seeking to enjoin the county from taking or interfering with, without condemnation, the plaintiff's use of a strip of said tract which one of the defendant predecessors in title had dedicated to the defendant county for road-widening purposes, but which had been included in all of the legal descriptions in all of the subsequent warranty deeds, including the plaintiff's. The complaint prayed alternatively, if it be judicially determined that the county could legally proceed under its right-of-way deed, for damages from the remaining defendants, his predecessors in title, jointly and severally, for breach of warranty in the amount of $2,475. The plaintiff appeals from the grant of the summary judgment in favor of the defendant vendor and defendant King-Williams Land Co., Inc., now King Williams Realty & Mortgage, Inc. (the vendor's immediate predecessor in title). The plaintiff's appeal from the trial court's judgment denying the injunctive relief against Fulton County had been dismissed previously for lack of a certificate

for immediate review. *Lunsford v. Fulton County,* 227 Ga. 547, 181 S.E.2d 865. *Held*

"Where, as here, a certain tract of land is described in a contract of sale by definite boundaries, and it later appears that the vendor has no title to a portion of the tract contained within the described boundaries, this is a defect in the vendor's title as contemplated by Code § 29-202 rather than a deficiency in quantity as contemplated by Code § 29–201." *Lawton v. Byck,* 217 Ga. 676(2), 124 S.E.2d 369. The plaintiff's right to recovery of damages under Code § 29-202 is not defeated by his constructive knowledge of the prior recorded deed to the county. "A general warranty of title in a deed against the claims of all persons covers defects in the title though known to the purchaser at the time of taking the deed." Code § 29-304.

Accordingly, the plaintiff is entitled to prove his case before a jury, including the amount of the unliquidated damages for the "reduction of the price according to the relative value of the land so lost." Code § 29–202. Therefore, the trial judge erred in granting the summary judgment in favor of the defendant vendor, Mrs. King, and defendant King-Williams Land Co., Inc., now King Williams Realty & Mortgage, Inc.

JUDGMENT REVERSED.

A breach of a covenant in a warranty deed may be sued on by the grantee of the deed, even though the grantee was aware of, or should have been aware of, the defect at the time the grantee received the deed. This principle of law is illustrated in *Lunsford v. King,* 209 S.E.2d 27.

Limited (Special) Warranty Deed

A **limited** or **special warranty deed** is a warranty deed in which the grantor covenants only against the lawful claims of people claiming by, through, or under the grantor. For example, a grantor of a limited warranty deed would be liable only if the ownership of the land by the grantee of the deed is disturbed by some claim arising from some act of the grantor. For example, if the grantor has placed an easement on the property and warrants in the limited warranty deed an express covenant against encumbrances, then the grantor of the limited warranty deed would be responsible and could be sued for the easement. If the easement already existed on the land at the time the grantor of the limited warranty deed received title to the land and the easement was created by some person prior in title to the grantor, the grantor, by giving a limited warranty deed, would not be responsible for the easement. Remember that in this same example, if the grantor had given a general warranty deed, which is an absolute warranty against encumbrances, the grantor would have been responsible for the easement, regardless of whether the grantor was the cause or creation of the easement or the easement was created by a predecessor in title.

limited or **special warranty deed**

Deed wherein the grantor covenants and warrants only against the lawful claims of people claiming by, through, or under the grantor.

Grant Deed

A **grant deed** is a type of limited warranty deed commonly used in California. By California statute, unless otherwise restricted by the express terms contained in the deed, there are two implied covenants in a grant deed. The first covenant is that previous to the time of the execution of the grant deed, the grantor has not conveyed the same estate, or any right, title or interest therein, to any person other than the grantee. The second covenant is that the estate being transferred in the grant deed at the time of the execution of the grant deed is free from encumbrances done, made, or suffered by the grantor, or any person taking under him. The grant deed and the quitclaim deed, hereinafter discussed, are the only two forms of deeds commonly used in California. A form of California grant deed is shown as Exhibit 8–11.

grant deed

A type of limited warranty deed commonly used in California.

Quitclaim Deed

A **quitclaim deed** transfers only the interest the grantor has in the land and not the land itself. If the grantor of a quitclaim deed has complete ownership at the time of the execution of the deed, a quitclaim deed will pass complete ownership to the grantee. A quitclaim deed contains no covenants or warranties of title. If a grantor of a quitclaim deed conveys land that is encumbered or land not owned by the grantor, the grantee usually, absent some evidence of fraud, is without claim against the grantor. Quitclaim deeds often are found in other forms of deeds, such as foreclosure deeds (deeds received from foreclosures of property by mortgage or tax foreclosures), executor's deeds (deeds executed by the executor of an estate), administrator's deeds (deeds executed by an administrator of an intestate estate), and trustee's deeds (deeds executed by the trustee of a trust). A quitclaim deed is referred to in some states as a release deed or bargain and sale deed. Independent investigation of the title to the land is essential in a transaction that involves a quitclaim deed.

quitclaim deed

Deed that contains no warranties of title. A quitclaim deed transfers only the interest that the grantor has in the land without warranty.

Generally speaking, purchasers of land will want the best kind of deed: the general warranty deed. The type of deed typically is negotiated within the contract for sale of the land, and every effort is made to obtain the best deed.

Executor's and Administrator's Deeds

Most states provide that when a person dies owning real property that the decedent's title to the property is transferred at death to either the decedent's estate or to an executor or administrator handling the estate. If a person dies testate (with a will), an executor will be appointed to conserve and administer the decedent's testate estate. The executor generally is a person identified in the will as executor. If a person dies intestate (without a will), the court will appoint an administrator to conserve and administer the decedent's intestate estate. A transfer of title to real property from the estate will be by either executor's deed or administrator's deed. An administrator's deed generally must be based upon a valid order of the probate court authorizing the sale of the property. In the case of an executor, the will may authorize the executor to sell the property of the estate. If the will is clear on this authorization, the executor may not need a court order to sell the property or sign the executor's deed. If the authority is unclear, or as common practice, the executor may seek authorization by the probate court to sell the property and execute the appropriate deed.

Executor's and administrator's deeds are quitclaim deeds without any warranty of title. A form of executor's deed is shown as Exhibit 8–14. A form of administrator's deed is shown as Exhibit 8–15.

Trustee Deeds

Title to real property may be placed into a trust. A trust is an arrangement in which title to property is placed in the name of a person, the trustee, for the beneficial enjoyment of another person, the beneficiary. The trust agreement is generally a tri-party agreement with a grantor who is the creator of the trust, a trustee who holds legal title to the property in trust, and one or more beneficiaries. For example, a parent may transfer commercial real property in trust to a bank for the benefit of the parents' minor children. Pursuant to the trust, the children would be entitled to income from the commercial property during their minority, and then when the children reach the age of majority, the property would be sold and all proceeds distributed to them. In this example, the parent would be the grantor of the trust, the bank would be the trustee, and the children would be the beneficiaries. The trustee of a trust holds legal title to the property, and it is the trustee who signs any deeds transferring ownership of the trust property. The transfer may be authorized by the trust, or the trustee may obtain a court order authorizing the transfer to the property. Trustee deeds are generally quitclaim deeds without warranty. A form of trustee deed is shown as Exhibit 8–16.

BASIC REQUIREMENTS OF A VALID DEED

The basic requirements of a valid deed are (a) written instrument, (b) competent grantor, (c) identity of the grantee, (d) words of conveyance, (e) adequate description of land, (f) consideration, (g) signature of grantor, (h) witnesses, and (i) delivery of the completed deed to the grantee.

Written Instrument

A deed must be in writing, but no generally prescribed form is essential to the validity of a deed. Even a letter in most states could constitute a valid deed, provided all the requirements are met.

Some states—for example, New York—prescribe by statute the form of a deed and the specific language that must be used for the deed to be valid. The law of the state in which the real property to be transferred is located will control as to the form required for the deed. Paralegals should review the appropriate law before a deed is prepared.

Competent Grantor

The deed must be signed by a party who is competent. Deeds executed by minors (people under the age of eighteen years) are voidable, and deeds executed by mentally incompetent people usually are void. Partnership deeds should be executed by all the partners, and corporate deeds should have proper corporate authority from the board of directors. The grantor also must be the owner or have an ownership interest in the land conveyed by the deed.

Identity of the Grantee

A deed must identify with certainty the grantee. A deed to a nonexistent grantee is thought to be void. Every effort should be made to correctly identify the name of the grantee for both individual and corporate deeds. For corporations, the correct name is obtained from the corporate records division of the secretary of state's office in the state of incorporation.

Legal I.D.

Words of Conveyance

A deed must contain words of conveyance that indicate the grantor's intent to make a present conveyance of the land by the instrument. No special words are needed, but words such as *grant, convey, assign, set over, transfer,* and *give* have all been held to express the intent to pass title and are sufficient to make an instrument a deed.

Description of the Property

The deed must describe the land being conveyed with specificity. A platted description, government rectangular survey description, or metes and bounds description based on a registered land surveyor's survey should be used. A deed conveys only the land described in the deed. The deed will convey all improvements, buildings, air rights, mineral rights, fixtures, and other appurtenances that belong to the owner of the land unless excluded by express reference.

Consideration

A deed must have **consideration** to be valid. Consideration is defined as something of value given for the deed. This value is the purchase price of the land being conveyed, although gift deeds for love and affection are recognized in all states. A recital of consideration is sufficient. A typical recital of consideration may be "for Ten Dollars and other good and valuable consideration."

consideration

Something of value given to make the promises of a contract enforceable. Consideration also is something of value given by the grantee for a deed.

Signature of Grantor

The grantor is the only person required to sign the deed. Deeds are not signed by the grantee. Some states, however, require that the grantee sign if the grantee is assuming the payment of a mortgage on the land or is purchasing a condominium and intends to be bound by the covenants and restrictions of the condominium. Although a few states dictate where the deed must be signed, deeds typically are signed in the lower right-hand corner. States that recognize dower or curtesy require a signature of the grantor's spouse in order for the dower or curtesy interest to be released from the conveyed property.

Witnesses of Deeds

The requirement for the witnessing, attestation, or acknowledgment of the grantor's signature to a deed varies from state to state. Some states require that deeds be witnessed only to permit the deed to be recorded. In these states, a deed is valid between the parties without recordation and therefore valid without witnessing. Other states require that the grantor's signature must be witnessed for the deed to be valid. Therefore, within these states, all deeds must be witnessed. Each state has its own witnessing requirements in terms of number and who may be a witness to a deed. A witness may be a notary public or other disinterested person. An interested witness, such as the grantee, cannot witness the grantor's signature to a deed. The usual number of required witnesses is two. Some states do not require that the grantor's signature be witnessed. States that do not require witnesses usually require that the signature be authenticated by a notary public.

Delivery to Grantee

The deed does not transfer title to land until the deed is delivered to the grantee or someone on the grantee's behalf. A deed is delivered when the grantor places the deed in the possession of the grantee with the intention that the deed passes present title of the land to the grantee and the grantee accepts this delivery. There are many presumptions regarding the delivery or nondelivery of a deed. Possession of the deed by the grantee is a presumption of delivery. Possession of the deed by the grantor is presumption of nondelivery. Recordation of a deed in the public records is presumption of delivery. All these presumptions are rebuttable if facts can be shown to the contrary.

PREPARATION OF A VALID DEED

Real property law is local law, and the law of deeds is no exception. The law of the state in which the land to be conveyed by the deed is located controls the form as well as the formal requirements of the deed. It is important to check local and state law before preparing a deed.

The preparation of a valid deed is a simple process. It is advisable to use the forms that are available from state bar associations, title companies, or law firms. Several examples of deed forms are included at the end of this chapter.

Most deed forms have the following formal parts: caption, premises or preamble, granting clause, description, **habendum,** warranty clause, and testimonium. The location of each of the formal parts of the deed is keyed by number on the sample deed form shown in Exhibit 8–2.

Caption

The **caption** or heading of a deed is designed to show the place of execution of the deed. The caption indicates the county and state in which the deed was signed by the grantor. The caption does *not* refer to the county and state in which the land is located.

Premises or Preamble

The premises or **preamble** to a deed is the section that sets forth the parties to the deed and the date of the deed. A deed is valid without a date, but most deeds are dated. The date should be the date of execution by the grantor. The parties to the deed are the grantor and grantee. Every effort should be made to use the correct name for both the grantor and the grantee. Titles such as Mr., Mrs., and Ms., are seldom used.

Granting Clause

The granting clause contains the language indicating that the instrument is a deed and that the land is being granted or conveyed. Few states require any particular words, and therefore, any words indicating a present intent to transfer the land are sufficient. The granting clause in many deeds also contains a recital of consideration.

---

habendum

Clause found in a deed that indicates what estate in real property is being transferred by the deed.

caption

Portion of the deed that indicates the county and state in which the deed was signed by the grantor.

preamble

Portion of the deed that sets forth the parties to the deed and the date of the deed.

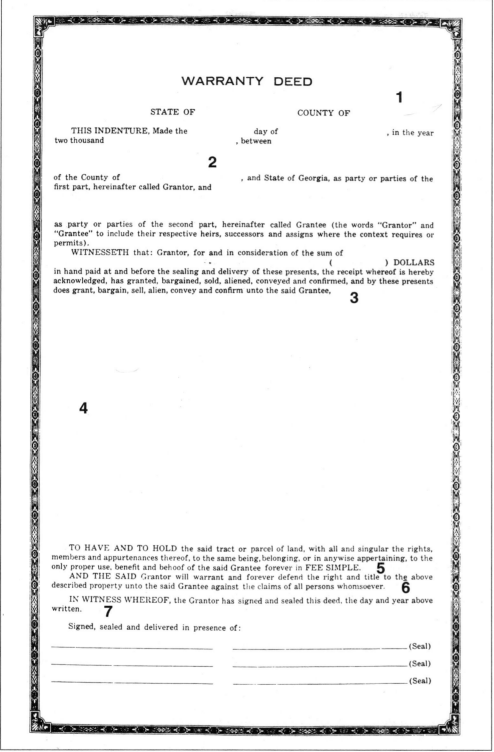

Delmar/Cengage Learning

EXHIBIT 8–2

Formal Parts of a Deed
(1) caption, (2) premises or preamble, (3) granting clause, (4) description, (5) habendum clause, (6) warranty clause, and (7) testimonium

Description

The main portion of any deed is the description of the land to be conveyed. It is important to use the best description available, which usually is a description prepared by a registered land surveyor or a description prepared from a registered land survey.

Habendum

The habendum clause indicates what estate is being transferred, such as life estate or fee simple.

Warranty Clause

The warranty clause usually contains words of warranty or, in the case of quitclaim deeds, a lack thereof.

Testimonium

testimonium

Portion of the deed where the grantor signs and the signature is witnessed or notarized.

The **testimonium** is the execution portion of the deed. Most deeds are signed under hand and seal and are witnessed. A recital of this action is found in the testimonium.

COMPLETING SECTIONS OF A DEED

The following are examples for completing the sections of a deed.

Preamble

The grantor and grantee designations, which appear in the preamble of a deed, may be completed as follows:

Grantor Designations

If the grantor is an individual, the preamble may read as follows:

> Joseph R. Snead, an individual

If the grantors are husband and wife, the preamble may read as follows:

> Joseph R. Snead and Mary T. Snead, husband and wife

If the grantor is an unmarried individual in a community property state, the preamble may read as follows:

> Joseph R. Snead, an unmarried individual

If the grantor is a corporation, the preamble may read as follows:

> The Farris Corporation, an Ohio corporation

If the grantor is a general partnership, the preamble may read as follows:

> Farris Associates, a North Carolina general partnership

If the grantor is a limited partnership, the preamble may read as follows:

> Farris Associates, Ltd., a North Carolina limited partnership

If the grantor is a limited liability company, the preamble may read as follows:

> Farris Investment Company, LLC, a Delaware limited liability company

If the grantor is the trustee of a trust, the preamble may read as follows:

> David H. Farris, Trustee of Trust created by Joseph R. Snead for the benefit of Mary T. Snead, pursuant to Trust Agreement dated July 26, 2001

If the grantor is the executor of an estate, the preamble may read as follows:

> David H. Farris, Executor under the Last Will and Testament of Joseph R. Snead, deceased of Richland County, Illinois

If the grantor is the administrator of the estate of a person who has died without a will, the preamble may read as follows:

> David H. Farris, Administrator of the intestate estate of Joseph R. Snead, deceased of Richland County, Illinois

Grantee Designations

If the grantee of a deed is an individual, married couple, corporation, partnership, limited liability company trustee, executor, or administrator, the same language as that shown previously may be used to describe the grantee.

If the grantees of a deed are husband and wife and the property conveyed by the deed is located in a state that recognizes the tenancy by entirety form of ownership, the preamble for the grantee may read as follows:

> Joseph R. Snead and Mary T. Snead, husband and wife and as tenants by the entirety

If the grantees of a deed want to hold title as joint tenants with the right of survivorship, the grantee preamble may read as follows:

> Joseph R. Snead and Mary T. Snead, as joint tenants with the right of survivorship

If the grantees of a deed want to hold title as tenants in common, the grantee preamble may read as follows:

> Joseph R. Snead and Mary T. Snead, as tenants in common

If the grantees of a deed are tenants in common and want to own unequal shares of the property, the grantee preamble may read as follows:

> Joseph R. Snead (an undivided 75 percent) and Mary T. Snead (an undivided 25 percent), as tenants in common

If the grantee of a deed is a corporation, the grantee preamble may read as follows:

> The Farris Corporation, an Ohio corporation

If the grantee of a deed is a general partnership, the grantee preamble may read as follows:

> Farris Associates, a North Carolina general partnership

If the grantee of a deed is a limited partnership, the grantee preamble may read as follows:

> Farris Associates, Ltd., a North Carolina limited partnership

If the grantee of a deed is a limited liability company, the grantee preamble may read as follows:

> Farris Investment Company, LLC, a Delaware limited liability company

Granting Clause

An example of a recital of nominal consideration in the granting clause is as follows:

> Ten and No/100 Dollars ($10.00) and other good and valuable consideration

A deed of gift contains a recital of consideration such as the following:

> For love and affection

Description

The legal description of the land conveyed by the deed should be described with full certainty on the face of the deed. If the description is too long to fit on the first page of the deed, it must be attached as an exhibit to the deed. A deed that uses an exhibit description should refer to the exhibit on the face of the deed. This reference can be as follows:

> All that tract or parcel of land lying and being in Land Lot 75 of the 5th District of Hall County, Georgia, and being more particularly described on Exhibit "A" attached hereto and by reference incorporated herein.

A general warranty deed warrants that the land is unencumbered. Often the land is encumbered, and exceptions to the warranty must be created. These exceptions often are stated in the description portion of the deed. The exceptions may be shown as follows:

> This conveyance is subject to the following title exceptions:

> (a) Taxes for the current year and subsequent years.

> (b) Easement from The Farris Corporation to Alabama Power Company; dated August 12, 1996, and recorded August 18, 1996, at Deed Book 35, Page 749, Montgomery County, Alabama.

> Title exceptions to a general warranty deed also may be shown on an exhibit to the deed.

> This conveyance is subject to the title exceptions shown on Exhibit "A" attached hereto and by reference incorporated herein.

It is the custom in some states to refer to title exceptions in general terms, such as:

> This conveyance is subject to all easements, restrictions, and encumbrances of record.

If the land conveyed in a deed is encumbered by a mortgage and the purchaser-grantee is willing to accept the land with the mortgage but not willing to assume personal responsibility for payment of the mortgage, the mortgage is described in the deed as follows:

> This conveyance is subject to a mortgage from The Farris Corporation to First Bank and Trust, dated April 12, 2009, recorded April 22, 2009, at Mortgage Book 632, Page 58, Carl County, North Dakota, securing the original principal indebtedness of $76,500.00.

If the purchaser-grantee is willing to assume personal responsibility for payment of the mortgage, the following language may be used in the deed:

> This conveyance is subject to a Mortgage from The Farris Corporation to First Bank and Trust, dated April 12, 2009, recorded April 12, 2009, at Mortgage Book 632, Page 58, Carl County, North Dakota, securing the original principal indebtedness of $76,500.00, and the Grantee by the acceptance of this deed assumes and agrees to pay the outstanding indebtedness according to its terms and assumes and agrees to be bound by all other terms and covenants contained in the Mortgage.

Testimonium

If the grantor is an individual, the deed may be prepared for signature as follows:

_____ (SEAL)
DAVID F. FARRIS

Deeds executed by partnerships are executed by all the partners.

D & F REALTY COMPANY, a
Georgia general partnership

By: _____ (SEAL)
DAVID A. FARRIS
General Partner

By: _____ (SEAL)
FRANCIS F. FARRIS
General Partner

A deed executed by a limited partnership is signed by all the general partners.

D & F Realty Company, Ltd., a New Jersey
limited partnership by all the general
partners:

By: _____ (SEAL)
DAVID F. FARRIS
General Partner

By: _____ (SEAL)
FRANCIS F. FARRIS
General Partner

Corporate deeds are executed by duly authorized officers on behalf of the corporation.

D & F REALTY COMPANY, INC.,
a Georgia corporation

By: _____ (SEAL)
DAVID F. FARRIS
President

Attest: _____ (SEAL)
FRANCIS F. FARRIS
Secretary

A deed executed by a limited liability company is signed by the authorized members of the limited liability company.

D & F REALTY LLC, a Georgia limited
liability company

By: _____ (SEAL)
David F. Farris, authorized member

By: _____ (SEAL)
Francis F. Farris, authorized member

[CORPORATE SEAL]

It is a good idea with corporate deeds to identify the names and titles of the officers who are signing the deeds and to affix the corporate seal to the deed.

A deed from a trust is executed by the trustee. The execution usually identifies the trustee and the trust instrument under which the trustee operates.

By: _____ (SEAL)
DAVID F. FARRIS, Trustee under agreement with JANE FARRIS dated June 1,
2009, for the benefit of MARY S. FARRIS

Deeds executed by estates are done by the executor in the case of a testate estate and by the administrator in the case of an intestate estate. Again, the execution usually identifies the estate under which the deed is being signed.

(Testate estate)

_____ (SEAL)

DAVID F. FARRIS, Executor under the Will of SUSAN F. FARRIS, Deceased, duly probated and recorded

(Intestate estate)

_____ (SEAL)

DAVID F. FARRIS, Administrator of the Estate of SUSAN F. FARRIS, who died intestate under Letters of Administration issued August 15, 2008

Deeds executed by an attorney in fact pursuant to a power of attorney usually identify the principal, attorney in fact, and power of attorney by date and recording information, if the power of attorney is recorded.

_____

DAVID F. FARRIS, by his duly appointed attorney in fact, SUSAN F. FARRIS pursuant to power of attorney dated September 25, 2009

PRACTICAL EXERCISES IN DEED PREPARATION

Experience teaches competence in the preparation of deeds. It is helpful for a paralegal who is first starting to prepare deeds to review deeds that have been used in other transactions.

In the deed shown in Exhibit 8–3, Alice Miller and David Miller are transferring ownership of their home to Susan Dickson and William Dickson. The home is encumbered by (a) an easement from Acme Land and Development Co. to Georgia Power and Light, dated June 8, 1996, recorded June 12, 1996, at Book 418, Page 292, Morris County, Georgia; and (b) unpaid real estate taxes for the current year. The land is described as follows:

ALL THAT TRACT or parcel of land lying and being in Land Lot 341 of the 8th Land District of Morris County, Georgia, and being more particularly described as Lot 6, Block C of The Oaks Subdivision, as per plat recorded at Plat Book 6, Page 23, Morris County, Georgia Plat Records, which Plat is incorporated herein and made a part of this description by reference.

Exhibit 8–4 is an example of a deed to transfer ownership of land from the Knox Land Development Company, an Illinois corporation, to Carole S. Jackson. The land is encumbered by (a) unpaid real estate taxes for the current year and (b) a mortgage from Knox Land Development Company to First National Bank of Salem, dated October 14, 1996, recorded October 14, 1996, at Mortgage Book 21, Page 466, Knox County, Illinois. The mortgage secures an original principal indebtedness of $84,000. Carole Jackson is willing to assume the mortgage.

The land is described as property lying and being in the northeast quarter of Section 27, Township 24 South, Range 35 East, Knox County, Illinois. The description is too long to be included on the first page of the deed.

EXHIBIT 8–3

Miller-Dickson Deed

WARRANTY DEED

STATE OF   COUNTY OF

THIS INDENTURE, Made the   day of   , in the year
two thousand   , between

Alice Miller and David Miller

of the County of   , and State of Georgia, as party or parties of the
first part, hereinafter called Grantor, and

Susan Dickson and William Dickson

as party or parties of the second part, hereinafter called Grantee (the words "Grantor" and
"Grantee" to include their respective heirs, successors and assigns where the context requires or
permits).

WITNESSETH that: Grantor, for and in consideration of the sum of Ten Dollars
and other good and valuable consideration   ($10.00   ) DOLLARS
in hand paid at and before the sealing and delivery of these presents, the receipt whereof is hereby
acknowledged, has granted, bargained, sold, aliened, conveyed and confirmed, and by these presents
does grant, bargain, sell, alien, convey and confirm unto the said Grantee,

ALL THAT TRACT or parcel of land lying and being in Land Lot
341 of the 8th Land District of Morris County, Georgia being more
particularly described as Lot 6, Block C of The Oaks Subdivision
as per plat recorded at Plat Book 6, Page 23, Morris County, Georgia
Plat Records, which Plat is incorporated herein and made a part of
this description by reference.

THIS CONVEYANCE IS SUBJECT TO THE FOLLOWING TITLE EXCEPTIONS:

(a)   Real estate taxes for the current year and subsequent years,
(b)   An easement from ACME Land & Development Co., to Georgia
      Power and Light, dated June 8, 1996, recorded June 12, 1996
      at Deed Book 418, Page 292 Morris County, Georgia Records.

TO HAVE AND TO HOLD the said tract or parcel of land, with all and singular the rights,
members and appurtenances thereof, to the same being, belonging, or in anywise appertaining, to the
only proper use, benefit and behoof of the said Grantee forever in FEE SIMPLE.

AND THE SAID Grantor will warrant and forever defend the right and title to the above
described property unto the said Grantee against the claims of all persons whomsoever.

IN WITNESS WHEREOF, the Grantor has signed and sealed this deed, the day and year above
written.

Signed, sealed and delivered in presence of:

_____ _____   _____ (Seal)
Witness   Alice Miller
_____ _____   _____ (Seal)
Notary Public   David Miller
                                            _____ (Seal)
My Commission Expires:

    [NOTARIAL SEAL]

Delmar/Cengage Learning

Using the deed shown in Exhibit 8–5 in the Addendum section of this chapter as a
guide or a deed form from your state, practice preparing deeds for the following hypothetical transfer situations.

EXHIBIT 8–4

Knox-Jackson Deed

Associated – Champaign Office ● Chicago Title Insurance Company
201 North Neil – Champaign, Illinois 61820 – Phone 356-0501

DOCUMENT NO. _____

For Recorder's Certificate Only

WARRANTY DEED

THE GRANTOR__, _____

Knox Land Development Company, an Illinois corporation

of the _____ of _____, in the County

of __Knox__, and State of __Illinois__,

for and in consideration of Ten Dollars ($10.00) and other good and

valuable consideration in hand paid, **CONVEY__** AND **WARRANT__** to

the **GRANTEE__,** _____

Carole S. Jackson

of the _____ of _____, County of __Knox__, and State

of __Illinois__, the following described real estate:

ALL THAT TRACT or parcel of land lying and being in the Northwest quarter
of Section 27, Township 24 South, Range 35 East, Knox County, Illinois and
being more particularly described on Exhibit "A" attached hereto and by
reference incorporated herein.

THIS CONVEYANCE IS SUBJECT TO THE FOLLOWING TITLE EXCEPTIONS:

(a) Mortgage from Knox Land Development Company to First National Bank
of Salem, dated October 14, 1996, recorded October 14, 1996 at
Mortgage Book 21, Page 466, Knox County, Illinois, securing the
original principal indebtedness of $84,000.00. The Grantee by
the acceptance of this deed assumes and agrees to pay the
outstanding indebtedness according to its terms and assumes and
agrees to be bound by all other terms and covenants contained in
the Mortgage.

Subject to: (1) Real estate taxes for the year 19___ and subsequent years;
(2) Covenants, conditions, restrictions and easements apparent or of record
(3) All applicable zoning laws and ordinances;

Dated this _____ day of _____, 20___.

_____

_____

Knox Land Development Company, an
Illinois corporation

By: _____ (SEAL)

Attest: _____, Its President
Its Secretary

STATE OF ILLINOIS }
                   } SS
CHAMPAIGN COUNTY }

(SEAL)

I, the undersigned, a Notary Public in and for said County and State
aforesaid, **DO HEREBY CERTIFY,** that _____ [CORPORATE SEAL]

personally known to me to be the same person__ whose name__ _____
subscribed to the foregoing instrument, appeared before me this day in
person and acknowledged that __h___ signed, sealed and delivered the said
instrument as _____ free and voluntary act, for the uses and purposes
therein set forth, including the waiver of the right of homestead.

Given under my hand and Notarial Seal, this _____
day of _____, A.D. 20____.

Notary Public

Deed Prepared By: _____	Send Tax Bill To:
	__ _____
	_____
Exempt under provisions of Paragraph _____	Section 4, Real Estate Transfer Tax Act.
Date _____	Signature _____
	Buyer, Seller or Representative

Practice Assignment 1

Hodges Development Co., Inc., a South Carolina corporation, is purchasing land from Mills Brothers Associates, a South Carolina general partnership, with Edward S. Mills and Thomas C. Mills as the general partners. The land is encumbered by (a) unpaid real estate taxes for the current year; (b) an easement from Harrison Maddox to South Carolina Power & Light, dated January 14, 1990, recorded January 26, 1990, at Book 253, Page 4, Spring County, South Carolina Records; and (c) restrictive covenants created by Declaration of Restrictive Covenants from Mills Brothers Associates, dated March 23, 1991, recorded at Book 261, Page 419, Spring County, South Carolina Records. The land is described as follows:

> ALL THAT TRACT or parcel of land lying and being in Land Lots 14, 15, and 16 of the 4th Land District of Spring County, South Carolina, and being more particularly described as Lots 21, 22, 23, and 24, Block C, Lots 15, 16, 19, and 22, Block D, and Lots 3, 4, 5, 8, 10, and 14, Block E, of The Mills Plantation Subdivision as per plat recorded at Plat Book 10, Page 103, Spring County, South Carolina Plat Records, which plat is incorporated herein and made a part of this description by reference.

Practice Assignment 2

Charles D. Hoover and Martha L. Hoover are transferring ownership of their home to James C. Brooks and Doris L. Brooks. James and Doris want to take the property as joint tenants with the right of survivorship. The home is encumbered by (a) unpaid real estate taxes for the current year and (b) a mortgage from Charles D. Hoover and Martha L. Hoover to First Federal Savings and Loan Association securing the original principal indebtedness of $116,412, dated August 15, 2008, recorded August 16, 2008, at Mortgage Book 212, Page 82, Todd County, Wisconsin. The purchasers are willing to assume the mortgage. The land is described as follows:

> ALL THAT TRACT or parcel of land lying and being in the Southeast Quarter of Township 14 North, Section 3, Range 15 West, Todd County, Wisconsin, and being more particularly described as Lot 14, Block A, of The Blue Springs Subdivision as per Plat recorded at Plat Book 3, Page 47, Todd County, Wisconsin Plat Records, which Plat is incorporated herein and made a part of this description by reference.

CORRECTION OF DEEDS

Although every attempt should be made to avoid mistakes, they do happen, and many times deeds must be corrected. The customary method of correcting an error in a deed is for the grantor to execute and deliver to the grantee a corrective deed. A corrective deed is valid without any additional consideration. Acceptance by the grantee is admission of the error found in the original deed.

Reformation and Cancellation of Deed

If a mutual mistake of fact is involved in the preparation, execution, and delivery of a deed, equity will reform the deed to its correct status. If there is some unilateral mistake of fact (only one party is mistaken) or fraud involved in the execution and delivery of a deed, the deed can be rescinded by the party who is mistaken or on whom the fraud was perpetrated.

Destruction of a deed does not return legal title to the grantor, nor does the return of a deed by the grantee to the grantor deliver title to the grantor. If it is desired for some reason that the grantee return the land to the grantor, the proper method is for the grantee to prepare, sign, and deliver a new deed to the grantor.

Practice Assignment 3

The deed shown in Exhibit 8–6 was prepared for the described transaction that follows and contains mistakes. Please review the deed, list all the mistakes, and prepare a corrective deed.

EXHIBIT 8–6

Deed Containing Mistakes

WARRANTY DEED

STATE OF GEORGIA   COUNTY OF FULTON

THIS INDENTURE, Made the 11th day of December , in the year two thousand , between

PINETREE DEVELOPMENT COMPANY, INC.

of the County of Fulton , and State of Georgia, as party or parties of the first part, hereinafter called Grantor, and

JACOB WILSON and ALICE WILSON

as party or parties of the second part, hereinafter called Grantee (the words "Grantor" and "Grantee" to include their respective heirs, successors and assigns where the context requires or permits).

WITNESSETH that: Grantor, for and in consideration of the sum of TEN AND NO/100 and other good and valuable consideration ($10.00) DOLLARS in hand paid at and before the sealing and delivery of these presents, the receipt whereof is hereby acknowledged, has granted, bargained, sold, aliened, conveyed and confirmed, and by these presents does grant, bargain, sell, alien, convey and confirm unto the said Grantee, all that tract or parcel of land lying and being in Land Lot 48 of the 14th District of Fulton County, Georgia, and being more particularly described as follows:

COMMENCING on the north side of Ponce de Leon Avenue, 653.5 feet east from the northeast corner of Ponce de Leon Avenue and Bedford Place (formerly Fort Street), running thence east along the north side of Ponce de Leon Avenue, 90 feet; running thence north 356 feet; running thence west 89.5 feet; running thence south 381.9 feet to the POINT OF BEGINNING on Ponce de Leon Avenue, and being improved property known as 368 Ponce de Leon Avenue, N.E., in the City of Atlanta, Georgia.

TO HAVE AND TO HOLD the said tract or parcel of land, with all and singular the rights, members and appurtenances thereof, to the same being, belonging, or in anywise appertaining, to the only proper use, benefit and behoof of the said Grantee forever in FEE SIMPLE.

AND THE SAID Grantor will warrant and forever defend the right and title to the above described property unto the said Grantee against the claims of all persons whomsoever.

IN WITNESS WHEREOF, the Grantor has signed and sealed this deed. the day and year above written.

PINETREE DEVELOPMENT CO., INC.

Signed, sealed and delivered in presence of:

_____
Unofficial Witness

By: _____ (Seal)
     Carol Tree, President

_____ (Seal)

_____
Notary Public

Attest: _____ (Seal)
     Susan Pine, Secretary

(Corporate Seal)

Pine Tree Development Company, Inc. is transferring title to Jacob Willson and Alice Willson. The property is unencumbered and described as follows:

ALL THAT TRACT or parcel of land lying and being in Land Lot 48 of the 14th District of Fulton County, Georgia and being more particularly described as follows:

COMMENCING on the north side of Ponce de Leon Avenue 653.5 feet east from the northeast corner of Ponce de Leon Avenue and Bedford Place (formerly Fort Street), running east along the north side of Ponce de Leon Avenue, 90 feet; run thence north 365 feet; running thence west 89.5 feet; run thence south 381.9 feet to the POINT OF BEGINNING on Ponce de Leon Avenue and being improved property known as 638 Ponce de Leon Avenue, N.E., in the City of Atlanta, Georgia.

PRACTICAL TIPS FOR THE PARALEGAL

One of the duties of a paralegal is to prepare deeds. The preparation of a deed requires careful attention to the following key parts of the deed: the grantor, the grantee, and the description of the property.

Grantor

The grantor must be the owner of the property being transferred. This ownership may need to be verified through a title report or other means. It is important to correctly spell or identify the grantor's name. It is possible that a grantor's current name may not have been the same name used to receive title to the property. If this is the case, the deed should be prepared in the grantor's present name but should also indicate the former name as "formerly known as" or "also known as." For example, Carol Brown received property in her name of Carol Brown. Carol later married and took the name of Carol Stone. In preparing a deed to the property, the grantor would be identified as "Carol Stone, formerly known as Carol Brown." Deeds for corporations, partnerships, and other entities require the same attention to detail. It is important to determine the correct name of the corporation, partnership, or entity transferring the property. It may be necessary to obtain copies of the organizational documents or evidence from the state's secretary of state as to the proper name.

Grantee

The grantee, or person receiving the property, should be properly identified as well. It is important that all names be properly spelled and all persons who intend to be owners be identified as grantees in the deed. If the grantees are receiving the property in some form of common ownership such as joint tenancy with right of survivorship or tenancy by the entirety, then it may be necessary for the deed to contain special language to create such form of ownership. It is possible in the case of a tenancy in common that the co-owners may hold disproportionate shares of ownership. If this is the case, the deed should identify in the grantee provision the form of ownership and the measure of ownership owned by each grantee. For example, a deed to Carol Brown, William Brown, and Joe Brown as tenants in common, where each have a different share of ownership, could be identified as "Carol Brown (an undivided 25 percent ownership), William Brown (an undivided 25 percent ownership), and Joe Brown (an undivided 50 percent ownership)." It is also important when deeds are given to an organization or entity such as a corporation or partnership that the entity exist at the time the deed is given and that the name be correctly identified.

Legal Description

A deed will only transfer the property that is described in it. It is important when drafting a legal description that it be the correct description of the property to be transferred. This description should come from a survey or other source such as a previous deed.

Witnessing a Deed

A paralegal will often be asked to witness the signature on a deed. If he or she is acting as a witness and not as a notary, it is important that the paralegal actually see the person sign the deed. If the paralegal is acting as a notary on a deed, not only must he or she actually see the person sign, but most notary statutes also require the notary to properly identify the person signing the deed. Identification may be by production of a driver's license or other means of photo identification. Notarizing a deed that the paralegal did not actually see signed is a violation of the notary oath and in many states may be perjury.

A checklist to help in the preparation of a deed is shown as follows. Deed forms vary from state to state, and a paralegal should be familiar with the forms used in the state in which he or she works. Several deed forms from various states are also included at the end of this chapter.

✓ CHECKLIST

Preparing a Deed

☐ I. Research before Preparation
- ☐ A. Review the contract or other agreement covering the transfer of ownership to the property.
- ☐ B. Review the title examination to make sure of the correct name of the title owner to the property.
- ☐ C. Confirm the correct spellings of all names of the grantor and grantee.
- ☐ D. Carefully review the title examination and determine what title exceptions should be identified in the deed.
- ☐ E. Confirm if prospective purchasers have any special requirements for taking title, such as joint tenancy with the right of survivorship and tenancy in common in a tenancy by entirety state or unequal shares.
- ☐ F. Review survey legal description with description in grantor's current deed to make sure no difference exists between the two descriptions.

☐ II. Preparing the Deed
- ☐ A. Draft the caption and preamble.
  1. Indicate the county and state in which the deed is signed.
  2. Date the deed with the date of execution and delivery.
  3. Indicate the correct name of the grantor, who should be the record titleholder of the property.
  4. Indicate the correct name of the grantee or grantees, indicating any special forms of ownership, such as joint tenancy, right of survivorship, and unequal shares.
- ☐ B. Draft the consideration. In most instances, use a nominal recital of consideration.
- ☐ C. Draft the legal description.
  1. Use the correct legal description verified by survey and title examination.

(continued)

2. If the legal description is too long to be included on the face of the deed, use an exhibit and identify the exhibit on the face of the deed.
3. List all title exceptions that are being transferred with the property.

☐ D. Draft signature blanks.

1. The grantor is the only person who signs the deed.
2. Correctly identify the grantor's name and confirm that it is the same as that shown in the preamble of the deed.
3. Type all names underneath the signature lines.
4. The deed must be signed and sealed.
5. Make certain the deed contains the proper number of witnesses and the notary designation is correct.

ETHICS: Falsification of Documents

A paralegal is helping an attorney represent a client in the transfer of ownership to real property. The transfer is taking place on October 2. During the closing of the transfer of ownership, the seller, a corporation, informs the attorney and paralegal that its tax year ended on September 30 and that it had intended for this transfer of ownership to take place during its past tax year. The seller requests that the deed be backdated to September 30 so that the sale and transfer of ownership would appear to take place during the past tax year. Should the attorney and paralegal backdate the deed?

The American Bar Association's Code of Professional Responsibility prohibits an attorney from falsifying a document for any reason. Likewise, a paralegal should not, under any circumstances, falsify a document for a client. Changing the date of a deed to reflect a different time for transfer of ownership, especially one that may affect the taxable consequences of the transfer, would be a violation of ethics. The attorney and paralegal in this situation should inform the client that they cannot falsify the document.

SUMMARY

Ownership to real property is transferred by deed. The deed may be a warranty deed containing the covenants or warranties of seisin, right to convey, covenant against encumbrances, covenant of further assurance, and covenants of quiet enjoyment and warranty. The deed may also be a quitclaim deed that does not contain any warranties or covenants of title. All deeds in order to be valid must be in writing and must identify properly the grantor, grantee, and the description of the property to be transferred. Deeds are generally signed only by the grantor, and most states require some form of witnessing of the grantor's signature. A deed does not transfer title until it is delivered to the grantee or someone on the grantee's behalf.

Every transaction that involves the sale and purchase of real property requires a deed. Most sales of real property also require that the purchaser borrow a portion of the purchase price. A number of financial institutions engage in the lending of funds for the purchase of real property. These financing sources are discussed in Chapter 9.

HELPFUL WEBSITE

Property Law
Good articles on property law can be found on PropertyProf Blog. The blog is updated weekly and is located at *http://www.lawprofessors.typepad.com.*

KEY TERMS

caption	general warranty deed	limited or special warranty deed
consideration	grant deed	preamble
conveyance	grantee	quitclaim deed
covenant or warranty	grantor	testimonium
deed	habendum	

REVIEW QUESTIONS

1. What six covenants or warranties are included in a general warranty deed?

2. What is the difference between a general warranty deed and a limited warranty deed?

3. What are the basic requirements of a valid deed?

4. List and briefly describe the formal parts of a deed.

5. What is the difference between a present covenant and a future covenant contained in a general warranty deed?

6. What is a quitclaim deed, and what are some of its uses?

7. Which state's law will control the legal requirements for a deed?

8. When can a deed be rescinded?

9. Briefly list three presumptions regarding the delivery of a deed.

10. What is the importance of having a grantor's signature witnessed?

CASE PROBLEMS

1. Samuel Adams is selling his Boston townhouse to Harrison Stone. Who is required to sign the deed in connection with the transfer of ownership?

2. Aaron owns a farm. Aaron has given First Bank and Trust a mortgage on the farm. Aaron transfers ownership of the farm to Bob and gives Bob a general warranty deed. The general warranty deed to Bob warrants that there are no encumbrances on the farm and does not mention the mortgage to First Bank and Trust. Bob owns the farm only a short time and sells the farm by limited warranty deed to Carol. Carol decides that farm life is not for her and sells the farm by general warranty deed to David. The general warranty deed does not mention the mortgage to First Bank and Trust. One week after David purchased the farm, First Bank and Trust notifies David of the mortgage. Is there a breach of any deed warranty or covenant and, if so, which covenant? At this stage,

can David sue Carol? Can David sue Bob? Can David sue Aaron?

First Bank and Trust, after notifying David of its mortgage, commences foreclosure proceedings to sell David's farm to pay the debt. At this stage, what deed covenant has been violated, if any? At this stage, can David sue Carol for breach of covenant? Bob? Aaron?

3. You are a paralegal involved in a closing of a purchase of real property. The real property is owned by Ruth White. Purchasers of the property are Albert Green and Linda Green. You have prepared the deed for Ruth White's signature, and you are in a state that requires two witnesses to Ruth White's signature. Can Timothy White, Ruth White's husband, witness her signature on the deed? Can Linda Green witness Ruth White's signature on the deed? Can you witness Ruth White's signature on the deed?

PRACTICAL ASSIGNMENTS

1. Research your state's law to determine what form of witnessing or notarization to a signature on a deed is required.
2. Martha Jones writes her daughter, Betsy Jones, the following letter:

Dear Betsy Jones:

Thank you for your last letter and the attention you have given me for years. You are truly a comfort to your mother in her old age, and I would like to show my appreciation. As you are aware, I have moved from my home at 1357 Morningside Drive in Smalltown into an apartment that is smaller and easier to take care of. My home on Morningside is now vacant, and I wish for you to have it. You can consider the home as your property.

> Best wishes.

> Please write soon.

> Love,

> Martha Jones

This letter was signed by Martha Jones and sent by regular mail to Betsy Jones, who received the letter and in reliance thereon immediately moved from her home more than 100 miles away to the home in Smalltown.

Please research your state's law and write a memorandum discussing whether the letter from Martha Jones to Betsy Jones is a valid deed and would transfer title to the home. Review carefully the requirements for a valid deed in your state and match them up with the facts set forth in this assignment. Write your conclusion citing proper statutory or case authority.

ADDENDUM

Exhibit 8–5 Sample Warranty Deed
Exhibit 8–7 General Warranty Deed—North Carolina
Exhibit 8–8 General Warranty Deed—Texas
Exhibit 8–9 Warranty Deed Joint Tenancy—Illinois
Exhibit 8–10 Limited Warranty Deed—Georgia
Exhibit 8–11 Grant Deed—California

Exhibit 8–12 Quitclaim Deed—Georgia
Exhibit 8–13 Quitclaim Deed—California
Exhibit 8–14 Executor's Deed—New York
Exhibit 8–15 Administrator's Deed—Georgia
Exhibit 8–16 Trustee Deed—Georgia

Student StudyWare™ CD-ROM

Interactive Student CD in the book includes additional quizzing, case studies, and key terms flashcards.

Online Companion™

For additional resources, please go to *www.paralegal.delmar.cengage.com*

EXHIBIT 8–5

Warranty Deed

WARRANTY DEED

STATE OF   COUNTY OF

THIS INDENTURE, Made the   day of   , in the year
two thousand   , between

of the County of   , and State of Georgia, as party or parties of the
first part, hereinafter called Grantor, and

as party or parties of the second part, hereinafter called Grantee (the words "Grantor" and
"Grantee" to include their respective heirs, successors and assigns where the context requires or
permits).

WITNESSETH that: Grantor, for and in consideration of the sum of
                                                        (   ) DOLLARS
in hand paid at and before the sealing and delivery of these presents, the receipt whereof is hereby
acknowledged, has granted, bargained, sold, aliened, conveyed and confirmed, and by these presents
does grant, bargain, sell, alien, convey and confirm unto the said Grantee,

TO HAVE AND TO HOLD the said tract or parcel of land, with all and singular the rights,
members and appurtenances thereof, to the same being, belonging, or in anywise appertaining, to the
only proper use, benefit and behoof of the said Grantee forever in FEE SIMPLE.

AND THE SAID Grantor will warrant and forever defend the right and title to the above
described property unto the said Grantee against the claims of all persons whomsoever.

IN WITNESS WHEREOF, the Grantor has signed and sealed this deed, the day and year above
written.

Signed, sealed and delivered in presence of:

_____   _____ (Seal)

_____   _____ (Seal)

_____   _____ (Seal)

EXHIBIT 8–7

General Warranty Deed—
North Carolina

Excise Tax   Recording Time, Book and Page

Tax Lot No. .... Parcel Identifier No. ....

Verified by .... County on the .... day of .... , 20............

by ....

Mail after recording to ....
....

This instrument was prepared by ....
Brief description for the Index

NORTH CAROLINA GENERAL WARRANTY DEED

THIS DEED made this .... day of .... , 20........ , by and between

GRANTOR   GRANTEE

Enter in appropriate block for each party: name, address, and, if appropriate, character of entity, e.q. corporation or partnership.

The designation Grantor and Grantee as used herein shall include said parties, their heirs, successors, and assigns, and shall include singular, plural, masculine, feminine or neuter as required by context.

WITNESSETH, that the Grantor, for a valuable consideration paid by the Grantee, the receipt of which is hereby acknowledged, has and by these presents does grant, bargain, sell and convey unto the Grantee in fee simple, all that certain lot or parcel of land situated in the City of .... , ... Township,

.... County, North Carolina and more particularly described as follows:

Delmar/Cengage Learning

(continued)

EXHIBIT 8–7

General Warranty Deed—
North Carolina (*continued*)

The property hereinabove described was acquired by Grantor by instrument recorded in ....

....

A map showing the above described property is recorded in Plat Book .... page.......................

TO HAVE AND TO HOLD the aforesaid lot or parcel of land and all privileges and appurtenances thereto belonging to the Grantee in fee simple.

And the Grantor covenants with the Grantee, that Grantor is seized of the premises in fee simple, has the right to convey the same in fee simple, that title is marketable and free and clear of all encumbrances, and that Grantor will warrant and defend the title against the lawful claims of all persons whomsoever except for the exceptions hereinafter stated. Title to the property hereinabove described is subject to the following exceptions:

IN WITNESS WHEREOF, the Grantor has hereunto set his hand and seal, or if corporate, has caused this instrument to be signed in its corporate name by its duly authorized officers and its seal to be hereunto affixed by authority of its Board of Directors, the day and year first above written.

(Corporate Name)

By: --

------------------------------------President

ATTEST:

-------------------------------Secretary (Corporate Seal)

USE BLACK INK ONLY

--(SEAL)

--(SEAL)

--(SEAL)

--(SEAL)

SEAL-STAMP

NORTH CAROLINA, -----------------------------------County.

I, a Notary Public of the County and State aforesaid, certify that ---

--- Grantor,

personally appeared before me this day and acknowledged the execution of the foregoing instrument. Witness my

hand and official stamp or seal, this ---------- day of ---, 20------.

My commission expires: --- Notary Public

SEAL-STAMP

NORTH CAROLINA, -----------------------------------County.

I, a Notary Public of the County and State aforesaid, certify that ---,

personally came before me this day and acknowledged that ---- he is ---------------------------- Secretary of

-- a North Carolina corporation, and that by authority duly

given and as the act of the corporation, the foregoing instrument was signed in its name by its ----------------

President, sealed with its corporate seal and attested by ----------- as its ---------------------------- Secretary.

Witness my hand and official stamp or seal, this -------day of -------------------------,20----------

My commission expires: --- Notary Public

The foregoing Certificate(s) of --

----

is/are certified to be correct. This instrument and this certificate are duly registered at the date and time and in the Book and Page shown on the first page hereof.

---REGISTER OF DEEDS FOR--COUNTY

By ---Deputy/Assistant - Register of Deeds

TEXAS STANDARD FORM

The State of Texas,
County of

{ **Know All Men by These Presents:**

That

of the County of   State of   for and in consideration

of the sum of

DOLLARS

to   in hand paid by

as follows:

have Granted, Sold and Conveyed, and by these presents do Grant, Sell and Convey unto the said

of the County of   State of   all that certain

TO HAVE AND TO HOLD the above described premises, together with all and singular the

rights and appurtenances thereto in anywise belonging unto the said

heirs and assigns forever and   do hereby bind

heirs, executors and administrators, to Warrant and Forever Defend, all and singular the said premises

unto the said

heirs and assigns, against every person whomsoever lawfully claiming, or to claim the same, or any

part thereof.

WITNESS   hand   at

this   day of

Witnesses at Request of Grantor: 20

....

....

EXHIBIT 8–8

General Warranty Deed—Texas

Delmar/Cengage Learning

(continued)

EXHIBIT 8–8

General Warranty Deed—Texas
(*continued*)

Mailing address of grantee:

Name:
Address:
_____

(Acknowledgment)

STATE OF TEXAS   }
COUNTY OF

    This instrument was acknowledged before me on the   day of   , 20   ,
by

My commission expires:
_____
_____
                     Notary Public, State of Texas
                     Notary's printed name:

(Acknowledgment)

STATE OF TEXAS   }
COUNTY OF

    This instrument was acknowledged before me on the   day of   , 20   ,
by

My commission expires:
_____
_____
                     Notary Public, State of Texas
                     Notary's printed name:

(Acknowledgment)

STATE OF TEXAS   }
COUNTY OF

    This instrument was acknowledged before me on the   day of   , 20   ,
by

My commission expires:
_____
_____
                     Notary Public, State of Texas
                     Notary's printed name:

128

Warranty Deed

FROM

TO

FILED FOR RECORD

This _____ day of _____ A.D. 20 _____

at _____ o'clock _____ M.

_____ County Clerk.

By _____ Deputy

RECORDED _____ A.D. 20 _____

In _____ County Records

In Book _____ on Page _____

_____ County Clerk.

By _____ Deputy

Recording Fee $ _____

This instrument should be filed immediately with the County Clerk for record.

WHEN RECORDED RETURN TO

The Odee Company, Dallas, TX 75238

Associated — Champaign Office ● Chicago Title Insurance Company
201 North Neil — Champaign, Illinois 61820 — Phone 356-0501

WARRANTY DEED — Joint Tenancy

DOCUMENT NO._____

For Recorder's Certificate Only ____

THE **GRANTOR**__, _____

_____

_____

of the _____ of _____, in the County

of _____, and State of _____,

for and in consideration of Ten Dollars ($10.00) and other good and

valuable consideration in hand paid, **CONVEY**__ and **WARRANT**__ to

the **GRANTEES**, _____

_____,

of the _____ . of _____, County of _____, and State

of _____, not in **TENANCY IN COMMON**, but in **JOINT TENANCY**, the following described

real estate, to-wit:

Subject to: (1) Real estate taxes for the year 20____ and subsequent years;
(2) Covenants, conditions, restrictions and easements apparent or of record;
(3) All applicable zoning laws and ordinances;

hereby releasing and waiving all rights under and by virtue of the Homestead Exemption Laws of the State of Illinois.

To Have and to Hold, the above granted premises unto the said Grantees forever, not in **TENANCY IN COMMON**, but in **JOINT TENANCY**.

Dated this _____ day of _____, 20____.

_____   _____

_____   _____

STATE OF ILLINOIS }
                   } SS
CHAMPAIGN COUNTY   }

I, the undersigned, a Notary Public in and for said County and State aforesaid, **DO HEREBY CERTIFY**, that

personally known to me to be the same person__ whose name__ _____
subscribed to the foregoing instrument, appeared before me this day in person and acknowledged that __h____ signed, sealed and delivered the said instrument as _____ free and voluntary act, for the uses and purposes therein set forth, including the waiver of the right of homestead.

(SEAL)

Given under my hand and Notarial Seal, this _____
day of _____, A.D. 20____.

_____ Notary Public

Deed Prepared By: _____	Send Tax Bill To:
	_____
	_____

Exempt under provisions of Paragraph _____, Section 4, Real Estate Transfer Tax Act.

Date _____   Signature _____
                                      Buyer, Seller or Representative

EXHIBIT 8–9

Warranty Deed Joint Tenancy—Illinois

EXHIBIT 8–10

Limited Warranty Deed—
Georgia

STATE OF GEORGIA

COUNTY OF

LIMITED WARRANTY DEED

THIS INDENTURE made this _____ day of _____ 20___ , by and between

party or parties of the first part, hereinafter referred to as "Grantor", and

party or parties of the second part, hereinafter referred to as "Grantee", the words "Grantor" and "Grantee" to include the neuter, masculine and feminine genders, the singular and the plural;

WITNESSETH :

FOR AND IN CONSIDERATION of the sum of Ten Dollars ($10.00) in hand paid and other good and valuable consideration delivered to Grantor by Grantee at and before the execution, sealing and delivery hereof, the receipt and sufficiency of which is hereby acknowledged, the Grantor has and hereby does grant, bargain, sell and convey unto Grantee, and the heirs, legal representatives, successors and assigns of Grantee

TO HAVE AND TO HOLD said tract or parcel of land, together with any and all of the rights, members and appurtenances thereof to the same being, belonging or in anywise appertaining to the only proper use, benefit and behoof of the Grantee and the heirs, legal representatives, successors and assigns of Grantee, forever, in fee simple.

GRANTOR SHALL WARRANT and forever defend the right and title to said tract or parcel of land unto the Grantee and the heirs, legal representatives, successors and assigns of Grantee, against the claims of all persons whomsoever claiming by, through or under Grantor.

IN WITNESS WHEREOF, the Grantor has signed and sealed this deed the day and year first above written.

Signed, sealed and delivered in the presence of:

_____   _____ (SEAL)
(Unofficial Witness)

_____   _____ (SEAL)
(Notary Public)

3

EXHIBIT 8–11
Grant Deed—California

RECORDING REQUESTED BY AND
WHEN RECORDED MAIL TO:

_____

(Space Above for Recorder's Use)

MAIL TAX STATEMENTS TO:

DOCUMENTARY TRANSFER TAX $_____

____ Computed on the consideration or value of property conveyed; OR

____ Computed on the consideration or value less liens or encumbrances remaining at time of sale.

_____
Signature of Declarant or Agent determining tax – Firm Name

GRANT DEED

FOR VALUABLE CONSIDERATION, receipt of which is hereby acknowledged, _____, a _____ ("**Grantor**"), hereby grants to _____, a _____ ("**Grantee**"), the real property (the "**Property**") in the City of _____, County of _____, State of California, described as:

Grantor has caused this Grant Deed to be duly executed on _____, 2006.

GRANTOR:

_____

a _____

By: _____

Name: _____

Title: _____

(ALL SIGNATURES MUST BE ACKNOWLEDGED)

Delmar/Cengage Learning

(continued)

EXHIBIT 8–11

Grant Deed—California (*continued*)

STATE OF CALIFORNIA

COUNTY OF _____

On _____ , before me, _____ , Notary Public,

(Print Name of Notary Public)

personally appeared _____

☐ personally known to me
   -or-

☐ proved to me on the basis of satisfactory evidence to be the person(s) whose name(s) is/are
   subscribed to the within instrument and acknowledged to me that he/she/they executed the same
   in his/her/their authorized capacity(ies), and that by his/her/their signature(s) on the instrument the
   person(s), or the entity upon behalf of which the person(s) acted, executed the instrument.

WITNESS my hand and official seal.

_____

Signature Of Notary

OPTIONAL

Though the data below is not required by law, it may prove valuable to persons relying on the document and could prevent
fraudulent reattachment of this form.

CAPACITY CLAIMED BY SIGNER	DESCRIPTION OF ATTACHED DOCUMENT

☐ Individual
☐ Corporate Officer

_____   _____
Title(s)   Title Or Type Of Document

☐ Partner(s)   ☐ Limited
                 ☐ General
☐ Attorney-In-Fact
☐ Trustee(s)   _____
☐ Guardian/Conservator   Number Of Pages
☐ Other: _____

Signer is representing:
Name Of Person(s) Or Entity(ies)

_____
Date Of Documents

_____

_____   _____
                                     Signer(s) Other Than Named Above

QUITCLAIM DEED

STATE OF

COUNTY OF

THIS INDENTURE, made the   day of   in the year
two thousand   , between

of the County of   , and State of   , as party
or parties of the first part, hereinafter called Grantor, and

of the County of   , and State of   , as party
or parties of the second part, hereinafter called Grantee (the words "Grantor" and "Grantee" to include their respective
heirs, successors and assigns where the context requires or permits).

WITNESSETH that: Grantor, for and in consideration of the sum of one dollar ($1.00) and other valuable
considerations in hand paid at and before the sealing and delivery of these presents, the receipt whereof is hereby
acknowledged, by these presents does hereby remise, convey and forever QUITCLAIM unto the said grantee

TO HAVE AND TO HOLD the said described premises to grantee, so that neither grantor nor any person or
persons claiming under grantor shall at any time, by any means or ways, have, claim or demand any right or title
to said premises or appurtenances, or any rights thereof.

IN WITNESS WHEREOF, Grantor has signed and sealed this deed, the day and year first above written.

Signed, sealed and delivered in the presence of:

_____(Seal)

_____   _____(Seal)
(Unofficial witness)

_____   _____(Seal)
(Notary Public)

EXHIBIT 8–13

Quitclaim Deed—California

AND WHEN RECORDED MAIL TO

NAME

ADDRESS

CITY &
STATE

Title Order No. _____ Escrow No. _____

MAIL TAX STATEMENTS TO

NAME

STREET
ADDRESS

CITY &
STATE

——————— SPACE ABOVE THIS LINE FOR RECORDER'S USE ———————

Quitclaim Deed

THE UNDERSIGNED GRANTOR(s) DECLARE(s)
DOCUMENTARY TRANSFER TAX is $ _____
☐ _____ unincorporated area ☐ City of _____
Parcel No. _____
☐ computed on full value of property conveyed, or
☐ computed on full value less value of liens or encumbrances remaining at time of sale, and

FOR A VALUABLE CONSIDERATION, receipt of which is hereby acknowledged,

hereby REMISE, RELEASE AND FOREVER QUITCLAIM to

the following described real property in the
county of _____ , state of California:

Dated _____

STATE OF CALIFORNIA
COUNTY OF _____ } SS.

On this _____ day of _____ , in the year
_____ , before me, the undersigned, a Notary Public in
and for said County and State, personally appeared _____
_____ ,
personally known to me (or proved to me on the basis of satisfactory
evidence) to be the person _____ whose name
_____ subscribed to the within instrument and
acknowledged that _____ executed the
same.

Signature _____

Name (Typed or Printed)
Notary Public in and for said County and State

(This area for official notarial seal)

MAIL TAX STATEMENT AS DIRECTED ABOVE 1-103 REV. 6/83 PRINTCO

EXHIBIT 8–14

Executor's Deed—New York

Standard N.Y.B.T.U. Form 8005—10M   Executor's Deed—Individual or Corporation (single sheet)

CONSULT YOUR LAWYER BEFORE SIGNING THIS INSTRUMENT — THIS INSTRUMENT SHOULD BE USED BY LAWYERS ONLY

THIS INDENTURE, made the   day of   , two thousand and

BETWEEN

as executor   of   the last will and testament of
                                                                                                                  , late of
                                                                                                                  , deceased,

party of the first part, and

party of the second part,

WITNESSETH, that the party of the first part, by virtue of the power and authority given in and by said last will and testament, and in consideration of

dollars,
paid by the party of the second part, does hereby grant and release unto the party of the second part, the heirs or successors and assigns of the party of the second part forever,

ALL that certain plot, piece or parcel of land, with the buildings and improvements thereon erected, situate, lying and being in the

TOGETHER with all right, title and interest, if any, of the party of the first part in and to any streets and roads abutting the above described premises to the center lines thereof; TOGETHER with the appurtenances, and also all the estate which the said decedent had at the time of decedent's death in said premises, and also the estate therein, which the party of the first part has or has power to convey or dispose of, whether individually, or by virtue of said will or otherwise; TO HAVE AND TO HOLD the premises herein granted unto the party of the second part, the heirs or successors and assigns of the party of the second part forever.

AND the party of the first part covenants that the party of the first part has not done or suffered anything whereby the said premises have been incumbered in any way whatever, except as aforesaid.
AND the party of the first part, in compliance with Section 13 of the Lien Law, covenants that the party of the first part will receive the consideration for this conveyance and will hold the right to receive such consideration as a trust fund to be applied first for the purpose of paying the cost of the improvement and will apply the same first to the payment of the cost of the improvement before using any part of the total of the same for any other purpose.
The word "party" shall be construed as if it read "parties" whenever the sense of this indenture so requires.

IN WITNESS WHEREOF, the party of the first part has duly executed this deed the day and year first above written.

IN PRESENCE OF:

(continued)

EXHIBIT 8–14

Executor's Deed—New York
(*continued*)

STATE OF NEW YORK, COUNTY OF   SS:

On the   day of   20   , before me
personally came

to me known to be the individual   described in and who
executed the foregoing instrument, and acknowledged that
executed the same.

STATE OF NEW YORK, COUNTY OF   SS:

On the   day of   20   , before me
personally came

to me known to be the individual   described in and who
executed the foregoing instrument, and acknowledged that
executed the same.

STATE OF NEW YORK, COUNTY OF   SS:

On the   day of   20   , before me
personally came
to me known, who, being by me duly sworn, did depose and
say that   he resides at No.   ;

that   he is the
of
                    , the corporation described
in and which executed the foregoing instrument; that   he
knows the seal of said corporation; that the seal affixed
to said instrument is such corporate seal; that it was so
affixed by order of the board of directors of said corporation, and that   he signed h   name thereto by like order.

STATE OF NEW YORK, COUNTY OF   SS:

On the   day of   20   , before me
personally came
the subscribing witness to the foregoing instrument, with
whom I am personally acquainted, who, being by me duly
sworn, did depose and say that   he resides at No.   ;

that   he knows
                    to be the individual
described in and who executed the foregoing instrument;
that   he, said subscribing witness, was present and saw
          execute the same; and that   he, said witness,
at the same time subscribed h   name as witness thereto.

Executor's Deed

TITLE NO. _____

TO

STANDARD FORM OF NEW YORK BOARD OF TITLE UNDERWRITERS
Distributed by
**CHICAGO TITLE
INSURANCE COMPANY**

SECTION

BLOCK

LOT

COUNTY OR TOWN

Recorded at Request of
CHICAGO TITLE INSURANCE COMPANY

Return by Mail to

Zip Code

RESERVE THIS SPACE FOR USE OF RECORDING OFFICE

Form 10-11

Lawyers Title Insurance Corporation

ATLANTA BRANCH OFFICE

GEORGIA STATE OFFICE
TITLE BUILDING
ATLANTA 3, GEORGIA

ADMINISTRATOR'S DEED

STATE OF GEORGIA, COUNTY OF

THIS INDENTURE, Made the   day of   , in the year
two thousand   , between

of the County of
of the estate of   , and State of Georgia, as administrat
called Grantor, and   deceased, hereinafter

hereinafter called Grantee (the words "Grantor" and "Grantee" to include their respective heirs, successors and assigns where the context requires or permits).

WITNESSETH that: Grantor, for and in consideration of the purchase price hereinafter set forth in hand paid at and before the sealing and delivery of these presents, the receipt whereof is hereby acknowledged, has granted, bargained, sold, aliened, conveyed and confirmed, and by these presents does grant, bargain, sell, alien, convey and confirm unto the said Grantee,

Said property is sold and conveyed by virtue of an order of the Court of Ordinary of
county entered after due notice of the application
thereof by publication as required by law; grantor having on the first Tuesday of the month and year above set forth, within the legal hours of sale, at the place of public sales in said county, put up and exposed said property to sale at public outcry to the highest bidder, after said sale had been duly advertised by publication as required by law, and after all requirements of law had been fully complied with; and said property having been bid off by the grantee at the price or sum of
dollars, grantee being
the highest and best bidder.

TO HAVE AND TO HOLD the said tract or parcel of land, with all and singular the rights, members and appurtenances thereof, to the same being, belonging, or in anywise appertaining, to the only proper use, benefit and behoof of the said Grantee forever in FEE SIMPLE.

IN WITNESS WHEREOF, the Grantor has signed and sealed this deed, the day and year above written.

Signed, sealed and delivered
in the presence of the undersigned:

....
(Unofficial Witness)

....
(Notary Public)

....(Seal)
As administrat   aforesaid

Delmar/Cengage Learning

EXHIBIT 8–15
Administrator's Deed—
Georgia

EXHIBIT 8–16

Trustee Deed—Georgia

TRUSTEE DEED

STATE OF

COUNTY OF

THIS INDENTURE, made the   day of   in the year two thousand   , between

David F. Farris, Trustee Under Trust Agreement with Jane Farris dated June 1, 2002

of the County of   , and State of   , as party or parties of the first part, hereinafter called Grantor, and

of the County of   , and State of   , as party or the parties of the second part, hereinafter called Grantee (the words "Grantor") and "Grantee" to include their respective heirs, successors and assigns where the context requires or permits).

WITNESSETH that: Grantor, for and in consideration of the sum of one dollar ($1.00) and other valuable considerations in hand paid at and before the sealing and delivery of these presents, the receipt whereof is hereby acknowledged, by these presents does hereby remise, convey and forever QUITCLAIM unto the said grantee

TO HAVE AND TO HOLD the said described premises to grantee, so that neither grantor nor any person or persons claiming under grantor shall at any time, by any means or ways, have, claim or demand any right or title to said premises or appurtenances, or any rights thereof.

IN WITNESS WHEREOF, Grantor has signed and sealed this deed, the day and year first above written.

Signed, sealed and delivered in the presence of:

_____   (Seal)

_____
(Unofficial Witness)   David F. Farris, Trustee Under Trust
                                              Agreement with Jane Farris dated June 1,
                                              2002

_____
(Notary Public)

chapter | 9

Financing Sources in Real Estate Transactions

Objectives

After reading this chapter, you should be able to:

- Identify the various sources of mortgage loans
- Understand the difference between a conventional and an insured loan
- Explain the role of the Federal Housing Administration (FHA) and Veterans Administration (VA) in real estate financing
- Explain the purposes of Fannie Mae and Freddie Mac
- Understand the difference between a permanent loan and a construction loan and their relation to each other
- Identify and understand the various forms of mortgage loan payment plans

mortgage loan
Loan secured by real property.

Outline

It is unusual for real property to be purchased on an all-cash basis. The buyer in a real estate transaction usually borrows a major portion of the purchase price by pledging the real property involved as security for a loan. This is known as a **mortgage loan.** The mortgage is given by the debtor (the property owner) to the lender. Mortgage loans on both residential and commercial properties usually are made by institutional lenders, such as savings banks, commercial banks, life insurance companies, credit unions, pension funds, mortgage banking companies, mortgage brokers, and issuers of mortgage-backed bonds.

The closing of mortgage loans constitutes a major part of the practice of a real estate attorney or paralegal. In this chapter, the business aspects of real estate finance are discussed.

SOURCES OF MORTGAGE LOANS

Most mortgage loans are granted by lending institutions, such as savings banks, commercial banks, life insurance companies, credit unions, pension funds, mortgage banking companies, and issuers of mortgage-backed bonds.

Savings Banks

Savings banks or "thrifts" are federally chartered institutions that generally invest in long-term home loans. Most savings banks evolved from federal savings and loan associations. The savings and loan associations were formed originally as organizations designed to lend only to their members and only to finance the purchase of their members' homes. In the latter part of the twentieth century, the savings and loan industry moved away from safe home loans into riskier higher yielding commercial loans. During the late 1980s and early 1990s, these commercial loans went into default, causing the savings and loan industry to collapse and to be bailed out by the federal government. The institutions that survived were converted into federal savings banks.

Commercial Banks

Commercial banks usually are considered a main source of short-term (loans of less than three years maturity) real estate financing. The short-term nature of bank lending is due to bank assets being tied up in demand deposits (checking accounts) rather than in long-term savings accounts. Commercial banks primarily make loans for construction of improvements and short-term bridge loans for the acquisition of property. A **bridge loan** for the acquisition of property with a maturity of one or two years enables the borrower to have the necessary financing to purchase real property. During the one- or two-year period, the borrower seeks out additional long-term financing to pay off the bridge loan. Commercial banks have also become major first mortgage lenders for residential real estate but tend not to keep the mortgage loans in their portfolio through maturity. Most of the loans are sold into the secondary market or securitized in bonds following the closing of the loan. Commercial banks have also been active in second-mortgage home equity loans in which homeowners borrow money against the appreciated value of their homes. Commercial banks are chartered either by the federal government or by the state in which the bank is located. Depositors' accounts with commercial banks are insured by the Federal Deposit Insurance Corporation.

bridge loan

Short-term loan with a maturity of one to two years that provides the borrower necessary financing to purchase real property. A bridge loan usually is refinanced by a long-term loan.

Life Insurance Companies

Life insurance companies derive their funds from the premiums paid by their policyholders and investment income that remains after operating expenses and policy claims are paid or provided for. Although life insurance companies engage in a wide variety of lending activity, mortgage loans constitute a large percentage of their investment portfolio.

Most life insurance companies invest money in large long-term loans used to finance the acquisition or construction of commercial and industrial properties. Life insurance companies also invest in residential mortgage loans by purchasing large blocks of government-backed (FHA- and VA-guaranteed) loans from Fannie Mae or other agencies that warehouse such loans for resale on the **secondary mortgage market.**

Many life insurance companies have also ventured into acquisitions in the projects they finance. Life insurance companies are active in joint ventures or partnership arrangements with the real estate developer. In this way, the life insurance company may

secondary mortgage market

Group of investors who purchase mortgage loans from primary mortgage lenders.

make a loan to a developer in which the life insurance company is also a partner or joint venturer on the project. The life insurance company receives interest on the loan and earns a portion of any appreciation in value of the developed property through its partnership relationship.

Credit Unions

Credit unions are nonprofit financial institutions, typically associated with a large corporation or organization, which permit employees of the corporation or members of the organization to deposit savings with the credit union. The credit union not only pays interest on these deposits, but also permits members of the credit union to borrow money from the credit union for personal use. Originally, credit unions made only short-term consumer and home improvement loans, but credit unions now are active in making long-term first- and second-mortgage loans on residential property.

Pension Funds

Pension or retirement plans for large corporations and unions accumulate and invest large sums of money for the retirement of plan participants. Like life insurance companies, pension funds retain some of their money to satisfy retirement benefits and to cover operating expenses and then invest the rest. Pension fund administrators are required by law to make only prudent and safe investments. Mortgage loans on both residential and commercial properties are considered prudent investments, and pension funds have been active in these areas.

Mortgage Banking Companies

Mortgage banking companies originate mortgage loans for insurance companies, commercial banks, pension funds, savings banks, and other investors throughout the country. Mortgage banking companies may originate these loans as a correspondent or agent on behalf of a permanent investor, using the permanent investor's money to fund the loan. Some mortgage banking companies have sufficient funds of their own to make real estate loans that are later sold to investors, with the mortgage company receiving a fee for servicing (collecting the money for) the loans. Mortgage banking companies are involved in all types of real estate loan activities and usually are organized as public or private corporations.

Issuers of Mortgage-Backed Bonds

The latter part of the 1990s witnessed a new type of lender in both the residential and commercial mortgage markets: issuers of mortgage-backed bonds. These lenders originate or buy pools of residential or commercial mortgages. They then package these mortgages as pools into a bond, which pays interest, and sells the bonds in the public securities market. Payment of the bond is secured by the payments on the residential or commercial mortgages in the pool securing the bond. Generally, the interest payable on a mortgage-backed bond is higher than interest payable on a U.S. Treasury security and is attractive to institutional investors such as life insurance companies and pension plans.

This type of lender is known as a **conduit lender** because it does not own or hold the mortgages for the full term of repayment. Instead, the lender transfers the mortgages to the mortgage pool and ultimately sells the risk of repayment to investors who buy the bonds. Conduit lenders have become substantial players in both residential and commercial markets and presently rank equally with life insurance companies and pension funds as the

conduit lender

An issuer of bonds secured by residential or commercial mortgages. The payments on the residential or commercial mortgage loans pay the interest and principal on the bonds.

main source of money for commercial mortgage transactions. The money received from the sale of mortgage-backed bonds is used either to fund the loans in the pool securing the bonds or to repay the conduit lender for the amount of the mortgage loans. The conduit lender generates income through fee income from making the loans and income from the sale of the bonds. In some cases, the mortgage-backed bond will sell for more than the principal amount of the underlying loans used to secure the bond.

TYPES OF LOANS

conventional loan

Mortgage loan in which the risk of repayment of the debt rests solely on the ability of the borrower to pay and the value of the security provided by the mortgage.

A mortgage loan may be identified as either a **conventional loan** or an **insured** or **guaranteed loan.** With a conventional loan, the risk of payment of the debt depends solely on the borrower's ability to pay and the value of the security provided by the mortgage. The risk of repayment of an insured or guaranteed loan is additionally secured through insurance issued by a private mortgage insurance company or guarantees provided by the government through such agencies as the FHA or VA.

insured or **guaranteed loan**

Mortgage loan in which the repayment of the loan is insured or guaranteed by either a government agency or a private insurance company.

Conventional Loans

A lender who makes conventional loans will require the preparation of an appraisal of the value of the real property given as security for the loan. The lender will also review credit reports, financial statements, and other information concerning the prospective buyer's ability to repay the loan.

loan-to-value ratio

Ratio of the amount of a mortgage loan to the value of the secured real property. For example, when the amount of the loan is $80,000 and the market value of the real property pledged as security for the loan is $100,000, the loan-to-value ratio is 80 percent.

The ratio of the debt to the value of the secured real property is known as the **loan-to-value ratio.** A lender who makes conventional loans generally will require a lower loan-to-value ratio than it would otherwise require for an insured or guaranteed loan. Theoretically, the lender has less risk of repayment with a lower loan-to-value ratio. For example, a $60,000 loan secured by a home with an appraised value of $100,000 is a lower risk than a $90,000 loan secured by the same home.

Insured or Guaranteed Loans

private mortgage insurance

Insurance issued by a private company that insures a lender against loss it may suffer in the event the debtor defaults on payment of the loan.

In an insured or guaranteed loan, a third party, government agency, or **private mortgage insurance** company guarantees the lender a repayment of a portion of the loan. Government and private guaranties usually guarantee repayment from 60 to 90 percent of the loan, depending on the government program under which the guaranty is issued or the terms of the private mortgage insurance contract. A number of federal and state agencies offer guaranteed loans under certain terms and conditions; a discussion of three large federal programs follows.

FHA-Insured Loans

Congress designed the FHA-insured mortgage loan in 1934. The FHA was created out of the National Housing Act of 1934 to ensure that quality housing would be made available to all U.S. citizens. The FHA operates under the Department of Housing and Urban Development (HUD). Despite popular belief, a person who wants to obtain a FHA loan does not borrow directly from the FHA, but instead obtains financing from an approved lender who agrees to make the loan, subject to a FHA commitment to insure the lender against losses caused by the loan default. A FHA loan is not made by the agency but is insured or guaranteed by it. The FHA insures loans made up to 97 percent of the loan-to-value ratio of the secured property. The FHA has maximum dollar amounts for loans to be insured, which change from time to time, and sets standards for construction quality and neighborhood and credit requirements for borrowers.

VA-Guaranteed Loans

The Serviceman's Readjustment Act of 1944 authorized the VA to guarantee loans for the purpose of purchasing or constructing homes for eligible veterans. Similarly to the FHA, the VA does not lend money but guarantees loans made by private lending institutions approved by the agency. A VA loan is not made by the agency but is guaranteed by it. Although the VA sets no limit on the amount of the loan a veteran can obtain, the VA does set a limit on the amount of the loan it will guarantee. This limit is 60 percent of the loan amount.

A veteran who is seeking a VA loan must apply for a Certificate of Eligibility. The Certificate of Eligibility does not mean that the veteran will receive a loan, but the certificate does set forth and guarantee the maximum amount of the loan to which the veteran is entitled.

The VA also issues a Certificate of Reasonable Value for the property being purchased, stating its current market value based on a VA-approved appraisal. The certificate establishes the maximum amount of the VA loan allowed for the property. If the purchase price is greater than the amount set forth in the Certificate of Reasonable Value, the veteran must pay the difference in cash. The VA guarantees 60 percent of the amount of the loan up to a loan-to-value ratio of 100 percent, provided the loan amount does not exceed the amount on the Certificate of Reasonable Value.

Small Business Administration—Guaranteed Loans

The U.S. Small Business Administration (SBA) was formed to assist small businesses. One part of this assistance is a guaranty program that enables small business owners to obtain necessary capital to start or continue a small business. In some instances, the SBA lends the money directly to a small business, but in most cases, it does not lend the money but guarantees loans made by a private lending institution approved by the agency. A SBA guaranty usually is between 70 and 85 percent of the loan amount. The SBA sets maximum dollar amounts for loans to be insured and establishes strict criteria for a small business. SBA-guaranteed loans have become a major source of capital for small businesses.

Subprime Lending

Subprime lending is one of the more rapidly growing areas of the residential mortgage market. Subprime lending is the business practice of making mortgage loans to people who do not have a good credit history or stable income. Subprime borrowers generally pay higher interest rates and fees for their mortgage than other borrowers. Subprime borrowers tend to be minority and low-income, less well educated than most borrowers, and more interested in being accepted for a mortgage loan than in obtaining the best interest rate for the loan. Some subprime lenders have been predators on the poor and uninformed in connection with these loans. Due to predatory lending practices of some subprime lenders, both the federal government and many states now regulate these types of loans. A discussion of the Home Ownership Equity Protection Act, which regulates subprime loans at the federal level, and state attempts to regulate predatory lending is found in Chapter 15. More information concerning subprime lending can be found on the Internet using a keyword search on a search engine such as *http://www.google.com*.

Subprime lending can be viewed as both a benefit and an evil. Edward M. Gramlich, a Governor of the Federal Reserve Board, succinctly framed the dilemma in his remarks to the Financial Services Roundtable Annual Housing Policy Meeting in Chicago, Illinois. "The increased availability of subprime mortgage credit has created new opportunities for home ownership and has allowed previously credit-constrained homeowners to borrow against the equity in their homes to meet a variety of needs. At the same time, increased subprime lending has been associated with higher levels of delinquency, foreclosure, and,

subprime lending

The business practice of making mortgage loans to people who do not have a good credit history or stable income.

in some cases, abusive lending practices. On a social level, one questions whether the gains supported by these new market developments outweigh the losses."[1]

Private Mortgage Insurance

A lender may also look to private sources for security that a debtor will pay his or her loan. These private sources or insurance companies will, for the payment of a fee, guarantee the mortgage lender that payment on a loan will be made. If the payments are not made, the mortgage insurance company buys the loan from the lender and enforces the debt against the debtor. With a privately insured lending program, home purchasers can obtain conventional mortgage loans for up to 95 percent of the appraised value at prevailing interest rates and reasonable mortgage insurance premium costs.

SECONDARY MARKET

primary market

Lenders who make mortgage loans directly to borrowers.

There is both a primary and a secondary market for mortgage loans. The **primary market** consists of (a) lenders who, as an investment, supply funds to borrowers and (b) lenders who close or originate loans for the purposes of selling the loans to investors. Paralegals usually are involved with closings in the primary market. Once a mortgage loan is closed in the primary market, the loan can be bought and sold in the secondary market.

interest

Charge by a lender to a borrower for the use of money.

primary mortgage lender

Lender who makes mortgage loans directly to a borrower.

Because a mortgage loan bears **interest,** it is viewed as an investment similar to a bond or a Treasury bill. A number of investors, such as life insurance companies and pension plans, are willing to purchase mortgage loans to receive the interest. Likewise, a number of **primary mortgage lenders** are willing to sell their inventory of mortgage loans. For example, a primary mortgage lender, such as a savings bank, may want to sell numerous loans to raise money for the purpose of making new loans. Secondary mortgage activities are a good source of new funds in the primary mortgage market and are therefore beneficial when money is in short supply.

servicing the loan

Collection of payments from the borrower of a mortgage loan.

When a mortgage loan has been sold on a secondary market, the original lender may continue to collect the payments from the borrower. This arrangement is called **servicing the loan.** The servicing lender passes the payments to the investor who has purchased the loan and charges the investor a fee for servicing the loan.

Fannie Mae and Freddie Mac

A number of large warehousing agencies are active participants in the secondary mortgage market. A warehouse agency purchases a number of mortgage loans and assembles them in one or more packages for resale to investors. Two major warehousing agencies are popularly called **Fannie Mae** and **Freddie Mac;** these names are shorthand for Federal National Mortgage Association and Federal Home Loan Mortgage Corporation, respectively.

Fannie Mae

Federal National Mortgage Association, a quasi-government agency organized for the purpose of investing in FHA and VA loans.

Freddie Mac

Federal Home Loan Mortgage Corporation, a quasi-public corporation that purchases and invests in mortgages.

Fannie Mae and Freddie Mac are publicly owned corporations organized to provide a secondary market for single-family and multifamily residential loans. They raise money to purchase loans by selling government-guaranteed bonds at market interest rates. These bonds are secured by blocks or pools of mortgages acquired through the Fannie Mae or Freddie Mac programs.

Mortgage banking firms, banks, and other lenders are actively involved in selling loans to Fannie Mae or Freddie Mac while retaining the servicing (collection of payment) functions. Fannie Mae and Freddie Mac help millions of Americans purchase or refinance homes and obtain affordable rental housing.

PERMANENT AND CONSTRUCTION LOANS

A **permanent loan** is a long-term loan that finances the acquisition of real property or refinances a **construction loan** on improvements. The payments on a permanent loan are **amortized,** which means that the payment will pay both principal and interest on the loan. The loan will be paid in full at its maturity. A permanent lender's main concerns when underwriting a permanent loan are the market value of the real property given as security for the loan and the financial stability of the borrower. In addition, on commercial permanent loans, the lender considers the amount and reliability of income being produced from the real property and will not make the loan unless the income is sufficient to pay the expenses of management and maintenance of the real property as well as the payments on the loan. The payment of principal and interest on a loan is called **debt service.**

A construction loan is made for the purpose of constructing improvements on real property. Construction loans are short term, with an average maturity of one year or less. The monthly payments of a construction loan are interest only, with a total payment of all principal and interest due at maturity. The source of repaying the construction loan at maturity is the proceeds from a permanent loan. The borrower refinances a construction loan by obtaining a permanent loan. Many construction lenders will not make a construction loan unless the borrower has already obtained a commitment for a permanent loan. Because construction loans are for the purpose of building improvements, construction loans usually are disbursed in installments as the improvements are completed. Most construction lenders only disburse 90 percent of the cost of improvements during construction, retaining 10 percent to protect against cost overruns. The retainage is disbursed when construction is completed. The interest charged on construction loans is tied to the lender's source of funds: usual short-term rates, such as the prime lending rate, or the one-year Treasury bill rate. Because construction loans are riskier than permanent loans, some construction lenders add a premium to the interest rates.

The underwriting concerns for a construction lender involve the construction lender's estimate of the cost of construction. Many construction lenders have staff engineers and contractors who can estimate the cost of building, or they hire professional architects or engineers to perform this service. Construction lenders inspect the real property each time money is requested to make sure the improvements have in fact been completed.

Interest

The sum of money charged for the use of money is called *interest.* Typically, interest is expressed in terms of a certain percentage of the principal that must be paid each year the debt is outstanding. For example, a lender may make a loan of $80,000 at 10 percent interest. The interest on the loan on an annual basis is 10 percent of the principal, or $8,000. The amount of interest due on any one of the installment payment days is calculated by computing the total yearly interest, based on the unpaid balance, dividing that figure by the number of payments made each year. For example, if the outstanding loan balance is $80,000 with interest at the rate of 10 percent per annum and the amount of monthly payments is $750, the interest and principal due on the next installment would be computed as follows: $80,000 times 10 percent equals $8,000 annual interest; $8,000 annual interest divided by 12 equals $666.67 monthly interest; $750 minus $666.67 equals $83.33 monthly principal. Interest may be due either at the end of each payment period

permanent loan

Long-term loan that finances the acquisition of real property or refinances a construction loan on improvements.

construction loan

Mortgage loan made for the purpose of providing money to construct improvements on real property.

amortization

Reduction of a debt by periodic payments covering interest and part of the principal.

debt service

Payment of principal and interest on a loan.

(payment in arrears) or at the beginning of each payment period (payment in advance). Most mortgage loans are paid in arrears.

Interest on a mortgage loan may be either fixed or variable. In a fixed-rate loan, the interest rate is fixed at the beginning of the loan and remains at the same rate throughout the term of the loan. In a variable-rate loan, the interest rate will fluctuate during the term of the loan based upon an index, typically a Treasury bond index. That is, the interest rate will fluctuate based upon a certain spread over 5-year Treasury bonds. For example, a borrower may borrow money at a spread of 200 basis points or 2% over 5-year Treasury bonds. If 10-year Treasury bonds were yielding 5.05% at the time the loan was made, the interest rate on the borrower's loan would be 7.05%. Variable rate loans usually provide for annual adjustments in interest rate. For example, if, one year after the loan is closed, 5-year Treasury bonds are yielding 5.40% interest, the interest on the loan would adjust and increase to 7.40%. Variable-rate loans typically have caps, which provide that the interest rate cannot increase or decrease more than a certain percentage during the term of the loan.

The interest rate and term of repayment on a mortgage loan can directly affect the monthly mortgage payment. Example 9–1 shows how interest rates can affect the monthly mortgage payment on a $200,000 mortgage loan payable over 360 months (30 years). You can see that the monthly mortgage payment on a $200,000 mortgage loan at 8% is over $300 higher than the same payment would be at 5½%. The total interest payable over the term of the 8% loan is $328,310.80 as compared to $208,808.80 for the 5½% loan. When you combine the $200,000 principal repayment with the total interest paid, at 8% a borrower would borrow $200,000 and pay back $528,310.80 over the loan's 30-year term.

Example 9–1

Monthly payment on $200,000 mortgage loans at different interest rates payable over 360 months

Annual Interest Rate	5.5%	6%	6.5%	7%	8%
Monthly Mortgage Payment	$1,135.58	$1,199.10	$1,264.14	$1,330.60	$1,467.53
Total Interest Paid Over Term of Loan	$208,808.80	$231,676.00	$255,090.40	$279,016.00	$328,310.80

Example 9–2 illustrates how the length of the term of repayment of a loan affects the monthly mortgage payment. The monthly mortgage payment of a $200,000 loan at 7% interest rate payable over 180 months (15 years) is $1,797.66, as compared to the monthly mortgage payment of $1,330.60 at the same interest rate payable over 360 months (30 years). If the loan term is extended to 40 years, the monthly payment would be $1,242.86. Although the monthly mortgage payment reduces as the term of repayment is extended, the total interest payable over the loan increases. The interest payable over 15 years on the loan shown in Example 9–2 is $123,578.80, compared to the total interest payable over 30 years of $279,016, or $396,572.80 payable over 40 years. The interest payable on the same amount of borrowed money is three times greater if payable over 40 years than over 15 years. Even though a longer-term loan results in smaller monthly mortgage payments, the total cost of the loan is substantially increased as the term is extended.

Example 9–2

Monthly payment on $200,000 mortgage loans at 7% per annum interest rate, payable over different time periods

Term of Loan	180 months (15 years)	240 months (20 years)	300 months (25 years)	360 months (30 years)	480 months (40 years)
Monthly Payment	$1,797.66	$1,550.60	$1,413.56	$1,330.60	$1,242.86
Total Interest Paid Over Term of Loan	$123,578.80	$172,144.00	$224,068.00	$279,016.00	$396,572.80

Payment Plans

Most mortgage loans are amortized loans. That is, regular payments are applied first to the interest owed and then to the balance of the principal amount, over a term between 20 and 30 years. At the end of loan term, the full amount of principal and all interest due will be paid in full.

Most amortized mortgage loans are paid in monthly installments. Some are paid quarterly or semiannually. Some examples of payment plans are as follows:

1. The most commonly used amortization plan is the **fully amortized loan,** which requires the borrower to pay a constant amount, usually monthly. The amount of each payment is first credited to the interest due, and then the remainder is applied to reduce the principal of the loan. Because each payment is the same, the portion applied toward payment of principal will increase, and the portion accredited toward interest will decrease as the unpaid balance of the loan is reduced. An example of an amortization calculator and schedule are shown at the end of this chapter as Exhibit 9–1 and Exhibit 9–2. Many residential loans are now being paid bimonthly, which results in a substantial reduction in the amount of interest paid over the term of the loan.

    Most residential mortgage loans are fully amortized over 360 months or 30 years; however, in some parts of the country where real property values have substantially increased, such as in California, there are some residential loans that are amortized and paid over a 40-year term.

2. A **straight-line amortized loan** is one in which the borrower pays a different amount for each installment, with each payment consisting of a fixed amount credited toward principal and an additional amount for the interest due on the balance of the principal outstanding since the last payment. The payments become smaller as the loan matures because the amount credited to interest decreases as the principal amount of the loan decreases.

3. A *straight* or **term loan** is one in which the borrower may choose a payment plan that calls for periodic payments of interest only, with the principal being paid in full in one installment at the end of the loan term. Construction loans and interim bridge acquisition loans use this method of payment.

4. A **graduated payment mortgage** is one that permits the borrower to pay lower monthly payments for the first few years of the loan and larger payments for the remainder of the term. These loans typically are used to permit young, less affluent buyers to buy property or to permit buyers in times of high interest rates to purchase real estate on terms they can afford.

fully amortized loan

Loan in which the partial payments of principal and accrued interest, if paid for the stated period of time, will result in the entire loan being paid at maturity.

straight-line amortized loan

Mortgage loan in which the borrower will pay a different amount for each installment, with each payment consisting of a fixed amount credited toward principal and an additional amount for the interest due on the balance of the principal unpaid since the last payment.

term loan

Loan in which the borrower makes periodic payments of interest, with the principal being paid in one installment at the end of the loan term.

graduated payment mortgage

Mortgage loan that permits the borrower to pay lower monthly payments for the first few years and larger payments for the remainder of the term.

balloon payment

Final payment of all unpaid principal and accrued and unpaid interest on the loan, which is greater than the periodic payments on the loan.

partially amortized loan

Loan on which the required payments of principal and interest, if paid for the stated period of time, will not pay the loan in full. Final payment will be the balance due on the loan and will be a larger payment than the previous payments.

negative amortization

Loan on which the payments are not sufficient to pay the interest costs of the loan. The unpaid interest is added to the principal of the loan, resulting in an increase in the principal amount of the loan during the term of repayment.

5. A borrower may make payments on a mortgage loan that will not fully amortize the amount of the loan by the time the final payment is due. The final payment then is a larger amount than the other payments. This payment is called a **balloon,** and this type of loan is called a **partially amortized loan.** For example, a loan is made for $80,000 at 11.5 percent interest computed on a 30-year amortization schedule, but with the final balloon payment due at the end of the twentieth year. In this case, each monthly payment would be $792.24 (the amount taken from a 30-year amortization schedule), with a final balloon payment of $56,340 (the amount of principal still owing after 20 years). The borrower at the time the balloon payment is due must either come up with the cash to pay the balloon payment or refinance the loan.

6. A borrower may make payment on a mortgage loan that will not even fully pay the interest that is due each month on the outstanding principal balance of the loan. This payment plan is known as a **negative amortization loan.** Because the interest is not being paid each month, the unpaid portion of the interest will be added to the principal. The principal balance of a negative amortized loan increases instead of decreases as the loan is repaid. This can result at maturity in the borrower having to pay a balloon payment that may be more than the original principal amount borrowed from the lender. A negative amortized loan is used only on a loan that provides for a variable interest rate, that is, an interest rate that will fluctuate with some index, such as the prime lending rate or the rate on Treasury securities. A negative amortization loan usually is used when interest rates are increasing to such a rate that the average borrower cannot afford additional payments to pay the interest in full. The negative amortization loan gives the borrower the benefit of reduced payments during the period when high interest payments are being made. The borrower's hope in repaying the loan is that the value of the real property serving as security for the loan will increase faster than the amount of the debt not being paid; therefore, the loan can be refinanced with a bigger loan at maturity. Because of the dangers inherent in negative amortization loans, they seldom are used.

7. Recently, there has been a movement toward *interest-only loans* for residential single-family mortgages. Under an interest-only program, a borrower may take out a 30-year mortgage and choose to pay interest only for a shorter period of time, such as 5, 10, or 15 years. For the interest-only period, the monthly payments would readjust and include an amortization of principal over the remaining years of the loan. An interest-only loan means that during the interest-only period, 100 percent of the payment is tax deductible and the monthly payment is lower than on an amortized loan. A disadvantage, however, is that during the interest-only period the borrower is not reducing the debt. At the end of the interest-only period, either the borrower can refinance the loan, or the payments will substantially increase to provide for amortization. Interest-only loans still account for a very small portion of overall single-family mortgage loans.

THE HOUSING RECESSION

Since 2007, the United States has experienced a serious real estate recession resulting in plummeting market values for homes and commercial properties, an increasing number of loan defaults and foreclosures, and rising unemployment due to the contraction of the homebuilding and construction industry. The recession is also having a serious impact on the financial solvency of banks and other financial institutions that have held and invested in mortgage loans. The causes for this recession are complex and even disputed among economists and other financial experts. Most economists, however, agree that at least three factors were instrumental in causing the recession: (1) an unprecedented increase in homeownership through the use of low interest rates, (2) creation of mortgage-backed bonds that securitized the mortgage payment risk, and (3) the growth of subprime lending.

Between 1994 and 2004, the United States experienced a housing boom in which the homeownership rate increased from 64% in 1994 (about where it had been since 1980) to an all-time high of 69.2% in 2004. As homeownership increased, so did housing prices. Between 1997 and 2006, the price of the typical U.S. house increased by 124%. Although personal income growth for consumers was flat during this period of time, interest rates were low, and credit was easy to obtain. This gave homebuyers the ability to pay more for a home and to carry more mortgage debt, creating conditions that led to the creation of both a housing and credit bubble.

During this same time, the number of mortgage-backed securities (MBS) grew rapidly. Mortgage originators increased the number of mortgage loans, packaged them into bonds, and sold them to investors such as pension plans, banks, insurance companies, and foreign investors. Most of the originators held little or no portion of the securities and, therefore, were able to close loans and sell the risk of repayment to other third-party investors. Since mortgage-backed securities offered a higher return than other so-called safe investments, such as Treasury bills or corporate bonds, a large supply of money was available to provide homebuyers with funds to purchase homes.

The increased demand for mortgage-backed securities also led to new types of mortgage loans: the subprime mortgage and the ALT-A mortgage. Subprime lending, previously discussed in this chapter, consisted of loans made to borrowers with low credit scores. Borrowers of ALT-A loans had better credit scores than subprime borrowers but still did not meet Fannie Mae or Freddie Mac purchase guidelines. As loan demand grew, lenders became increasingly careless, granting loans without proper knowledge of the borrower's financial situation. They also started offering enticing loan incentives, such as low initial payments and payment grace periods. These incentives encouraged borrowers to obtain large mortgages in the belief that they could quickly refinance them on more favorable terms due to the rising value of the home.

The first economic problems appeared in such manufacturing hubs in the Midwest as Detroit and Cleveland. As the manufacturing economy started to decline in 2007, defaults in these cities and others started to increase. In addition, housing prices started to stagnate and decline in late 2006 and early 2007, as even cheaply financed home prices reached the peak level of affordability for most buyers. The surplus of unsold homes built by over-optimistic homebuilders also added to the decline in home prices. The resulting collapse of home prices created a situation in which many homeowners had mortgages with unpaid debt higher than the value of their homes, resulting in a zero or negative equity, sometimes known as being "under water on your mortgage." In addition, interest rates, which had been historically very low, were beginning to increase due to inflation in the system caused by higher energy prices. Borrowers with adjustable rate mortgages could no longer make the higher payments when the loans were readjusted to higher rates. Due to the decline in the price of their homes, the "underwater borrowers" could not escape the high payments by refinancing. This vicious cycle of decreasing home prices and increasing interest rates created even more defaults, which drove home prices down further. Defaults also impacted the value of MBS securities held by banks and other investors and seriously affected their ability to continue lending, thus creating a credit crunch. Homebuilders began to stop building homes, and a large segment of the employment growth that had happened over the last 10 years began to stall and decline. Between 2007 and 2009, unemployment rose from about a 5.5% level to a 9.5% level. This loss of jobs and steady income has also led more homeowners to default on their

ETHICS: Overbilling

A paralegal is employed with a law firm that represents a number of lending institutions. The state in which the law firm is located requires that an out-of-state lender be licensed by the state to make loans within the state. The set of rules that control this licensing is complex. The paralegal was involved in a research project researching and outlining the requirements for licensing within the state by an out-of-state lender. The research project consumed more than 40 hours of the paralegal's time, and the paralegal was able to bill one of the firm's clients $100 per hour for each hour spent. The firm now has another out-of-state client that is requesting the same information. The paralegal will spend about two hours reviewing and updating the research information from the last client's existing file. Had the paralegal not performed the research for the previous client, it would take the paralegal 40 hours to perform the services required by the new client. Should the paralegal bill the one or two hours of time necessary to review the existing information to the new client, or should the paralegal bill the full 40 hours?

It is unethical for an attorney or a paralegal to overbill a client for services rendered to the client. If the client has agreed to pay for legal services based on time spent on the matter, it is unethical for the attorney or paralegal to add phantom or additional hours that were not spent on the client's matter. It would be ethical for the law firm and the paralegal in this case to bill the new client only for the additional time spent in revising and preparing the client's requested report or application for a license. It would be unethical to bill the new client for the 40 hours of research performed for a previous client.

mortgages. These defaults have in turn led to an increased number of foreclosures, leaving huge volumes of foreclosed homes held by lenders. These properties compete with homes that are for sale but not in default, thus contributing to a greater decline in prices.

By 2009, the residential recession began to carry over into the commercial real estate market. Lack of employment, reduced consumer spending, and lack of credit has hurt retailers, shopping center developers, hotels, and other segments of the commercial real estate industry. At the time of the publication of this sixth edition, the conditions are still serious, and there is no clear return to normalcy in the near future.

The federal government has launched several programs to try to stabilize the housing situation by making it easier for homeowners to modify or restructure their home loans. Many states have also imposed temporary moratoriums (60–120 days) on the foreclosure of residential loans in order to avoid default.

In order to increase demand for homes and therefore support the market value of existing homes, the federal government has given first-time homebuyers a tax credit. The amount of the credit is the lesser of 10 percent of the home purchase price or $8,000 for married couples filing a joint tax return and $4,000 for individuals. The tax credit is temporary and expires on April 30, 2010. If the market for homes does not improve, the federal government can be expected to provide new credits or use other tax-based incentives to increase demand for homes.

SUMMARY

A paralegal may assist an attorney who represents one of the lending institutions mentioned in this chapter. The loans made by the lender may be construction or permanent loans and have different amortization schedules. The paralegal's chief duty is to make sure all requirements for the loan have been met and that all loan documents are properly prepared.

HELPFUL WEBSITES

Mortgage Banking Association

The Mortgage Bankers Association (MBA) is the trade association for most mortgage lenders, both residential and commercial. The MBA Web site contains information for professionals in the business and some consumer information. The Web site is an excellent source for current events that affect the mortgage lending industry. The Web site can be found at *http://www.mba.org.*

Fannie Mae

The Web site for Fannie Mae contains information about Fannie Mae and consumer information for homeowners and homebuyers. The Web site can be found at *http://www.fanniemae.com.*

Freddie Mac

The Web site for Freddie Mac contains consumer information about mortgages and buying and owning a home. The Web site also contains calculators and tools to compare costs between renting and owning, affordability of a home, and types of mortgages, and to estimate payments and costs. The Web site can be found at *http://www.freddiemac.com.*

KEY TERMS

amortization	fully amortized loan	primary market
balloon payment	graduated payment mortgage	primary mortgage lender
bridge loan	insured or guaranteed loan	private mortgage insurance
conduit lender	interest	secondary mortgage market
construction loan	loan-to-value ratio	servicing the loan
conventional loan	mortgage loan	straight-line amortized loan
debt service	negative amortization	subprime lending
Fannie Mae	partially amortized loan	term loan
Freddie Mac	permanent loan	

REVIEW QUESTIONS

1. What is the difference between a conventional loan and an insured mortgage loan?
2. What is the loan-to-value ratio?
3. What role does the VA play in real estate financing?
4. What service does a private mortgage insurance company provide?
5. Who are the major investors in the secondary mortgage market?
6. What is a construction loan, and how is the construction loan repaid?
7. What does it mean to pay a mortgage loan in arrears?
8. What is the difference between a fully amortized loan and a straight-line amortized loan?
9. What is a balloon payment?
10. What is a negative amortization loan?

CASE PROBLEMS

1. Assume a mortgage loan has an outstanding principal balance of $75,000 and the interest rate is 10.25 percent. Calculate what portion of a $710 monthly payment will be allocated to interest.

2. Assume a mortgage loan with a principal balance of $110,000 and an interest rate of 9.75 percent. The loan is to be repaid over 20 years, and the monthly payment is to be $875. What type of amortization plan is this?

3. Assume a mortgage loan with an outstanding principal balance of $70,000 and an interest rate of 11 percent. The loan is to be repaid over 20 years. The monthly mortgage payment is $291.67 plus accrued interest. What type of amortization payment plan is this?

PRACTICAL ASSIGNMENTS

1. Does your state have any special regulations governing subprime lenders? Search your state's statutes for such regulations. Prepare a short memorandum outlining the regulations and attach the state statutes you found as an addendum.

2. Visit a local residential mortgage lender in your state and obtain information from them regarding all the types of mortgage payment plans they offer to customers. Summarize the features of each plan and discuss the advantages and disadvantages in a short memorandum.

ADDENDUM

Exhibit 9–1 Amortization Calculator

Exhibit 9–2 Amortization Schedule of Direct Reduction Loan

ENDNOTE

[1] Source: *http://www.federalreserve.gov/boarddocs/speeches/2004/2004/20040521/default.htm.*

Student StudyWare™ CD-ROM

Interactive Student CD in the book includes additional quizzing, case studies, and key terms flashcards.

Online Companion™

For additional resources, please go to *www.paralegal.delmar.cengage.com*

Annual interest rate (xx.xxx) ---------------------------------------6.5000000   % (key in decimal)
Use a 365/360 day basis? (Y,N)-- N
Term of loan (in months)---360
Pmt frequency (01=Mo 06=Semi-Annual) -------------------------------- 1
Principal amt (whole dollars)---100000

Interest compounding frequency -- M
Payment amount --632.07
Total of payments-- 227,545.20
Total interest paid-- 127,545.20
Effective interest rate---6.5000004   %

Delmar/Cengage Learning

EXHIBIT 9–1

Amortization Calculator

EXHIBIT 9-2
Amortization Schedule of Direct Reduction Loan

ING Investment Management, Inc.
Schedule of Direct Reduction Loan

Name
Loan Amount 100,000.00
Payment Begins Mar 01 2003
Interest Rate 6.50000%
Maturity Date Feb 01 2033
Payment Amount $632.07
Interest Basis 360/30

PMT Due Date #	Interest	Principal	Principal Balance	Total Interest	Total Principal	Per Diem *** Notes ***	#Days
001 MAR 01 03	541.67	90.40	99,909.60	541.67	90.40	.0000	30
002 APR 01 03	541.18	90.89	99,818.71	1,082.85	181.29	.0000	30
003 MAY 01 03	540.68	91.39	99,727.32	1,623.53	272.68	.0000	30
004 JUN 01 03	540.19	91.88	99,635.44	2,163.72	364.56	.0000	30
005 JUL 01 03	539.69	92.38	99,543.06	2,703.41	456.94	.0000	30
006 AUG 01 03	539.19	92.88	99,450.18	3,242.60	549.82	.0000	30
007 SEP 01 03	538.69	93.38	99,356.80	3,781.29	643.20	.0000	30
008 OCT 01 03	538.18	93.89	99,262.91	4,319.47	737.09	.0000	30
009 NOV 01 03	537.67	94.40	99,168.51	4,857.14	831.49	.0000	30
010 DEC 01 03	537.16	94.91	99,073.60	5,394.30	926.40	.0000	30
*** 2003				5,394.30	926.40	* Calendar Yr. Amounts *	
011 JAN 01 04	536.65	95.42	98,978.18	5,930.95	1,021.82	.0000	30
012 FEB 01 04	536.13	95.94	98,882.24	6,467.08	1,117.76	.0000	30
013 MAR 01 04	535.61	96.46	98,785.78	7,002.69	1,214.22	.0000	30
014 APR 01 04	535.09	96.98	98,688.80	7,537.78	1,311.20	.0000	30
015 MAY 01 04	534.56	97.51	98,591.29	8,072.34	1,408.71	.0000	30
016 JUN 01 04	534.04	98.03	98,493.26	8,606.38	1,506.74	.0000	30
017 JUL 01 04	533.51	98.56	98,394.70	9,139.89	1,605.30	.0000	30
018 AUG 01 04	532.97	99.10	98,295.60	9,672.86	1,704.40	.0000	30
019 SEP 01 04	532.43	99.64	98,195.96	10,205.29	1,804.04	.0000	30
020 OCT 01 04	531.89	100.18	98,095.78	10,737.18	1,904.22	.0000	30
021 NOV 01 04	531.35	100.72	97,995.06	11,268.53	2,004.94	.0000	30
022 DEC 01 04	530.81	101.26	97,893.80	11,799.34	2,106.20	.0000	30
*** 2004				6,405.04	1,179.80	* Calendar Yr. Amounts *	
023 JAN 01 05	530.26	101.81	97,791.99	12,329.60	2,208.01	.0000	30
024 FEB 01 05	529.71	102.36	97,689.63	12,859.31	2,310.37	.0000	30
025 MAR 01 05	529.15	102.92	97,586.71	13,388.46	2,413.29	.0000	30

(continued)

EXHIBIT 9–2

Amortization Schedule of Direct Reduction Loan (continued)

Name Loan Amount Payment Begins PMT Due Date #	100,000.00 Mar 01 2003 Interest	Interest Rate Maturity Date Principal	6.50000% Feb 01 2033 Principal Balance	Payment Amount Interest Basis 360/30 Total Interest	$632.07 Total Principal	*** Notes *** Per Diem	#Days
026 APR 01 05	528.59	103.48	97,483.23	13,917.05	2,516.77	.0000	30
027 MAY 01 05	528.03	104.04	97,379.19	14,445.08	2,620.81	.0000	30
028 JUN 01 05	527.47	104.60	97,274.59	14,972.55	2,725.41	.0000	30
029 JUL 01 05	526.90	105.17	97,169.42	15,499.45	2,830.58	.0000	30
030 AUG 01 05	526.33	105.74	97,063.68	16,025.78	2,936.32	.0000	30
031 SEP 01 05	525.76	106.31	96,957.37	16,551.54	3,042.63	.0000	30
032 OCT 01 05	525.19	106.88	96,850.49	17,076.73	3,149.51	.0000	30
033 NOV 01 05	524.61	107.46	96,743.03	17,601.34	3,256.97	.0000	30
034 DEC 01 05	524.02	108.05	96,634.98	18,125.36	3,365.02	.0000	30
*** 2005				6,326.092	1,258.82	* Calendar Yr. Amounts *	
035 JAN 01 06	523.44	108.63	96,526.35	18,648.80	3,473.65	.0000	30
036 FEB 01 06	522.85	109.22	96,417.13	19,171.65	3,582.87	.0000	30
037 MAR 01 06	522.26	109.81	96,307.32	19,693.91	3,692.68	.0000	30
038 APR 01 06	521.66	110.41	96,196.91	20,215.57	3,803.09	.0000	30
039 MAY 01 06	521.07	111.00	96,085.91	20,736.64	3,914.09	.0000	30
040 JUN 01 06	520.47	111.60	95,974.31	21,257.11	4,025.69	.0000	30
041 JUL 01 06	519.86	112.21	95,862.10	21,776.97	4,137.90	.0000	30
042 AUG 01 06	519.25	112.82	95,749.28	22,296.22	4,250.72	.0000	30
043 SEP 01 06	518.64	113.43	95,635.85	22,814.86	4,364.15	.0000	30
044 OCT 01 06	518.03	114.04	95,521.81	23,332.89	4,478.19	.0000	30
045 NOV 01 06	517.41	114.66	95,407.15	23,850.30	4,592.85	.0000	30
046 DEC 01 06	516.79	115.28	95,291.87	24,367.09	4,708.13	.0000	30
*** 2006				6,241.73	1,343.11	* Calendar Yr. Amounts *	
047 JAN 01 07	516.16	115.91	95,175.96	24,883.25	4,824.04	.0000	30
048 FEB 01 07	515.54	116.53	95,059.43	25,398.79	4,940.57	.0000	30
049 MAR 01 07	514.91	117.16	94,942.27	25,913.70	5,057.73	.0000	30
050 APR 01 07	514.27	117.80	94,824.47	26,427.97	5,175.53	.0000	30
051 MAY 01 07	513.63	118.44	94,706.03	26,941.60	5,293.97	.0000	30
052 JUN 01 07	512.99	119.08	94,586.95	27,454.59	5,413.05	.0000	30

(continued)

EXHIBIT 9–2
Amortization Schedule of Direct Reduction Loan (continued)

Name Loan Amount Payment Begins PMT Due Date #	100,000.00 Mar 01 2003 Interest	Interest Rate Maturity Date Principal	6.50000% Feb 01 2033 Principal Balance	Payment Amount Interest Basis 360/30 Total Interest	$632.07 Total Principal	*** Notes *** Per Diem	#Days
053 JUL 01 07	512.35	119.72	94,467.23	27,966.94	5,532.77	.0000	30
054 AUG 01 07	511.70	120.37	94,346.86	28,478.64	5,653.14	.0000	30
055 SEP 01 07	511.05	121.02	94,225.84	28,989.69	5,774.16	.0000	30
056 OCT 01 07	510.39	121.68	94,104.16	29,500.08	5,895.84	.0000	30
057 NOV 01 07	509.73	122.34	93,981.82	30,009.81	6,018.18	.0000	30
058 DEC 01 07	509.07	123.00	93,858.82	30,518.88	6,141.18	.0000	30
*** 2007				6,151.79	1,433.05	* Calendar Yr. Amounts *	
059 JAN 01 08	508.40	123.67	93,735.15	31,027.28	6,264.85	.0000	30
060 FEB 01 08	507.73	124.34	93,610.81	31,535.01	6,389.19	.0000	30
061 MAR 01 08	507.06	125.01	93,485.80	32,042.07	6,514.20	.0000	30
062 APR 01 08	506.38	125.69	93,360.11	32,548.45	6,639.89	.0000	30
063 MAY 01 08	505.70	126.37	93,233.74	33,054.15	6,766.26	.0000	30
064 JUN 01 08	505.02	127.05	93,106.69	33,559.17	6,893.31	.0000	30
065 JUL 01 08	504.33	127.74	92,978.95	34,063.50	7,021.05	.0000	30
066 AUG 01 08	503.64	128.43	92,850.52	34,567.14	7,149.48	.0000	30
067 SEP 01 08	502.94	129.13	92,721.39	35,070.08	7,278.61	.0000	30
068 OCT 01 08	502.24	129.83	92,591.56	35,572.32	7,408.44	.0000	30
069 NOV 01 08	501.54	130.53	92,461.03	36,073.86	7,538.97	.0000	30
070 DEC 01 08	500.83	131.24	92,329.79	36,574.69	7,670.21	.0000	30
*** 2008				6,055.81	1,529.03	* Calendar Yr. Amounts *	
071 JAN 01 09	500.12	131.95	92,197.84	37,074.81	7,802.16	.0000	30
072 FEB 01 09	499.40	132.67	92,065.17	37,574.21	7,934.83	.0000	30
073 MAR 01 09	498.69	133.38	91,931.79	38,072.90	8,068.21	.0000	30
074 APR 01 09	497.96	134.11	91,797.68	38,570.86	8,202.32	.0000	30
075 MAY 01 09	497.24	134.83	91,662.85	39,068.10	8,337.15	.0000	30
076 JUN 01 09	496.51	135.56	91,527.29	39,564.61	8,472.71	.0000	30
077 JUL 01 09	495.77	136.30	91,390.99	40,060.38	8,609.01	.0000	30
078 AUG 01 09	495.03	137.04	91,253.95	40,555.41	8,746.05	.0000	30
079 SEP 01 09	494.29	137.78	91,116.17	41,049.70	8,883.83	.0000	30
080 OCT 01 09	493.55	138.52	90,977.65	41,543.25	9,022.35	.0000	30
081 NOV 01 09	492.80	139.27	90,838.38	42,036.05	9,161.62	.0000	30
082 DEC 01 09	492.04	140.03	90,698.35	42,528.09	9,301.65	.0000	30

(continued)

EXHIBIT 9–2

Amortization Schedule of Direct Reduction Loan (continued)

Name				Payment Amount		*** Notes ***		
Loan Amount 100,000.00		Interest Rate Mar 01 2003	6.50000% Feb 01 2033	Interest Basis 360/30	$632.07			
Payment Begins		Maturity Date						
PMT Due Date								
#	Interest	Principal	Principal Balance	Total Interest	Total Principal	Per Diem	* Calendar Yr. Amounts *	#Days
*** 2009				5,953.40	1,631.44		* Calendar Yr. Amounts *	
083 JAN 01 10	491.28	140.79	90,557.56	43,019.37	9,442.44	.0000		30
084 FEB 01 10	490.52	141.55	90,416.01	43,509.89	9,583.99	.0000		30
085 MAR 01 10	489.75	142.32	90,273.69	43,999.64	9,726.31	.0000		30
086 APR 01 10	488.98	143.09	90,130.60	44,488.62	9,869.40	.0000		30
087 MAY 01 10	488.21	143.86	89,986.74	44,976.83	10,013.26	.0000		30
088 JUN 01 10	487.43	144.64	89,842.10	45,464.26	10,157.90	.0000		30
089 JUL 01 10	486.64	145.43	89,696.67	45,950.90	10,303.33	.0000		30
090 AUG 01 10	485.86	146.21	89,550.46	46,436.76	10,449.54	.0000		30
091 SEP 01 10	485.07	147.00	89,403.46	46,921.83	10,596.54	.0000		30
092 OCT 01 10	484.27	147.80	89,255.66	47,406.10	10,744.34	.0000		30
093 NOV 01 10	483.47	148.60	89,107.06	47,889.57	10,892.94	.0000		30
094 DEC 01 10	482.66	149.41	88,957.65	48,372.23	11,042.35	.0000		30
*** 2010				5,844.14	1,740.70		* Calendar Yr. Amounts *	
095 JAN 01 11	481.85	150.22	88,807.43	48,854.08	11,192.57	.0000		30
096 FEB 01 11	481.04	151.03	88,656.40	49,335.12	11,343.60	.0000		30
097 MAR 01 11	480.22	151.85	88,504.55	49,815.34	11,495.45	.0000		30
098 APR 01 11	479.40	152.67	88,351.88	50,294.74	11,648.12	.0000		30
099 MAY 01 11	478.57	153.50	88,198.38	50,773.31	11,801.62	.0000		30
100 JUN 01 11	477.74	154.33	88,044.05	51,251.05	11,955.95	.0000		30
101 JUL 01 11	476.91	155.16	87,888.89	51,727.96	12,111.11	.0000		30
102 AUG 01 11	476.06	156.01	87,732.88	52,204.02	12,267.12	.0000		30
103 SEP 01 11	475.22	156.85	87,576.03	52,679.24	12,423.97	.0000		30
104 OCT 01 11	474.37	157.70	87,418.33	53,153.61	12,581.67	.0000		30
105 NOV 01 11	473.52	158.55	87,259.78	53,627.13	12,740.22	.0000		30
106 DEC 01 11	472.66	159.41	87,100.37	54,099.79	12,899.63	.0000		30
*** 2011				5,727.56	1,857.28		* Calendar Yr. Amounts *	
107 JAN 01 12	471.79	160.28	86,940.09	54,571.58	13,059.91	.0000		30
108 FEB 01 12	470.93	161.14	86,778.95	55,042.51	13,221.05	.0000		30
109 MAR 01 12	470.05	162.02	86,616.93	55,512.56	13,383.07	.0000		30
110 APR 01 12	469.18	162.89	86,454.04	55,981.74	13,545.96	.0000		30

(continued)

EXHIBIT 9–2

Amortization Schedule of Direct Reduction Loan *(continued)*

Name		Interest Rate	Payment Amount		*** Notes ***	
Loan Amount 100,000.00		Maturity Date Feb 01 2033	Interest Basis 360/30			$632.07
Payment Begins Mar 01 2003						
PMT Due Date		6.500000%				
#	Interest	Principal	Principal Balance	Total Interest	Total Principal	Per Diem	#Days
---	---	---	---	---	---	---	---
111 MAY 01 12	468.29	163.78	86,290.26	56,450.03	13,709.74	.0000	30
112 JUN 01 12	467.41	164.66	86,125.60	56,917.44	13,874.40	.0000	30
113 JUL 01 12	466.51	165.56	85,960.04	57,383.95	14,039.96	.0000	30
114 AUG 01 12	465.62	166.45	85,793.59	57,849.57	14,206.41	.0000	30
115 SEP 01 12	464.72	167.35	85,626.24	58,314.29	14,373.76	.0000	30
116 OCT 01 12	463.81	168.26	85,457.98	58,778.10	14,542.02	.0000	30
117 NOV 01 12	462.90	169.17	85,288.81	59,241.00	14,711.19	.0000	30
118 DEC 01 12	461.98	170.09	85,118.72	59,702.98	14,881.28	.0000	30
*** 2012				5,603.19	1,981.65	* Calendar Yr. Amounts *	
119 JAN 01 13	461.06	171.01	84,947.71	60,164.04	15,052.29	.0000	30
120 FEB 01 13	460.13	171.94	84,775.77	60,624.17	15,224.23	.0000	30
121 MAR 01 13	459.20	172.87	84,602.90	61,083.37	15,397.10	.0000	30
122 APR 01 13	458.27	173.80	84,429.10	61,541.64	15,570.90	.0000	30
123 MAY 01 13	457.32	174.75	84,254.35	61,998.96	15,745.65	.0000	30
124 JUN 01 13	456.38	175.69	84,078.66	62,455.34	15,921.34	.0000	30
125 JUL 01 13	455.43	176.64	83,902.02	62,910.77	16,097.98	.0000	30
126 AUG 01 13	454.47	177.60	83,724.42	63,365.24	16,275.58	.0000	30
127 SEP 01 13	453.51	178.56	83,545.86	63,818.75	16,454.14	.0000	30
128 OCT 01 13	452.54	179.53	83,366.33	64,271.29	16,633.67	.0000	30
129 NOV 01 13	451.57	180.50	83,185.83	64,722.86	16,814.17	.0000	30
130 DEC 01 13	450.59	181.48	83,004.35	65,173.45	16,995.65	.0000	30
*** 2013				5,470.47	2,114.37	* Calendar Yr. Amounts *	
131 JAN 01 14	449.61	182.46	82,821.89	65,623.06	17,178.11	.0000	30
132 FEB 01 14	448.62	183.45	82,638.44	66,071.68	17,361.56	.0000	30
133 MAR 01 14	447.62	184.45	82,453.99	66,519.30	17,546.01	.0000	30
134 APR 01 14	446.63	185.44	82,268.55	66,965.93	17,731.45	.0000	30
135 MAY 01 14	445.62	186.45	82,082.10	67,411.55	17,917.90	.0000	30
136 JUN 01 14	444.61	187.46	81,894.64	67,856.16	18,105.36	.0000	30
137 JUL 01 14	443.60	188.47	81,706.17	68,299.76	18,293.83	.0000	30
138 AUG 01 14	442.58	189.49	81,516.68	68,742.34	18,483.32	.0000	30
139 SEP 01 14	441.55	190.52	81,326.16	69,183.89	18,673.84	.0000	30
140 OCT 01 14	440.52	191.55	81,134.61	69,624.41	18,865.39	.0000	30

(continued)

EXHIBIT 9–2

Amortization Schedule of Direct Reduction Loan *(continued)*

Name Loan Amount Payment Begins PMT Due Date #	100,000.00 Mar 01 2003 Interest	Interest Rate Maturity Date Principal	6.50000% Feb 01 2033 Principal Balance	Payment Amount Interest Basis 360/30 Total Interest	$632.07 Total Principal	*** Notes *** Per Diem	#Days
141 NOV 01 14	439.48	192.59	80,942.02	70,063.89	19,057.98	.0000	30
142 DEC 01 14	438.44	193.63	80,748.39	70,502.33	19,251.61	.0000	30
*** 2014				5,328.88	2,255.96	* Calendar Yr. Amounts *	
143 JAN 01 15	437.39	194.68	80,553.71	70,939.72	19,446.29	.0000	30
144 FEB 01 15	436.33	195.74	80,357.97	71,376.05	19,642.03	.0000	30
145 MAR 01 15	435.27	196.80	80,161.17	71,811.32	19,838.83	.0000	30
146 APR 01 15	434.21	197.86	79,963.31	72,245.53	20,036.69	.0000	30
147 MAY 01 15	433.13	198.94	79,764.37	72,678.66	20,235.63	.0000	30
148 JUN 01 15	432.06	200.01	79,564.36	73,110.72	20,435.64	.0000	30
149 JUL 01 15	430.97	201.10	79,363.26	73,541.69	20,636.74	.0000	30
150 AUG 01 15	429.88	202.19	79,161.07	73,971.57	20,838.93	.0000	30
151 SEP 01 15	428.79	203.28	78,957.79	74,400.36	21,042.21	.0000	30
152 OCT 01 15	427.69	204.38	78,753.41	74,828.05	21,246.59	.0000	30
153 NOV 01 15	426.58	205.49	78,547.92	75,254.63	21,452.08	.0000	30
154 DEC 01 15	425.47	206.60	78,341.32	75,680.10	21,658.68	.0000	30
*** 2015				5,177.77	2,407.07	* Calendar Yr. Amounts *	
155 JAN 01 16	424.35	207.72	78,133.60	76,104.45	21,866.40	.0000	30
156 FEB 01 16	423.22	208.85	77,924.75	76,527.67	22,075.25	.0000	30
157 MAR 01 16	422.09	209.98	77,714.77	76,949.76	22,285.23	.0000	30
158 APR 01 16	420.96	211.11	77,503.66	77,370.72	22,496.34	.0000	30
159 MAY 01 16	419.81	212.26	77,291.40	77,790.53	22,708.60	.0000	30
160 JUN 01 16	418.66	213.41	77,077.99	78,209.19	22,922.01	.0000	30
161 JUL 01 16	417.51	214.56	76,863.43	78,626.70	23,136.57	.0000	30
162 AUG 01 16	416.34	215.73	76,647.70	79,043.04	23,352.30	.0000	30
163 SEP 01 16	415.18	216.89	76,430.81	79,458.22	23,569.19	.0000	30
164 OCT 01 16	414.00	218.07	76,212.74	79,872.22	23,787.26	.0000	30
165 NOV 01 16	412.82	219.25	75,993.49	80,285.04	24,006.51	.0000	30
166 DEC 01 16	411.63	220.44	75,773.05	80,696.67	24,226.95	.0000	30
*** 2016				5,016.57	2,568.27	* Calendar Yr. Amounts *	
167 JAN 01 17	410.44	221.63	75,551.42	81,107.11	24,448.58	.0000	30

(continued)

EXHIBIT 9–2

Amortization Schedule of Direct Reduction Loan *(continued)*

Name								
Loan Amount 100,000.00			Interest Rate 6.5000000%		Payment Amount $632.07			
Payment Begins Mar 01 2003			Maturity Date Feb 01 2033		Interest Basis 360/30			
PMT Due Date							*** Notes ***	
#		Interest	Principal	Principal Balance	Total Interest	Total Principal	Per Diem	#Days
168 FEB 01 17		409.24	222.83	75,328.59	81,516.35	24,671.41	.0000	30
169 MAR 01 17		408.03	224.04	75,104.55	81,924.38	24,895.45	.0000	30
170 APR 01 17		406.82	225.25	74,879.30	82,331.20	25,120.70	.0000	30
171 MAY 01 17		405.60	226.47	74,652.83	82,736.80	25,347.17	.0000	30
172 JUN 01 17		404.37	227.70	74,425.13	83,141.17	25,574.87	.0000	30
173 JUL 01 17		403.14	228.93	74,196.20	83,544.31	25,803.80	.0000	30
174 AUG 01 17		401.90	230.17	73,966.03	83,946.21	26,033.97	.0000	30
175 SEP 01 17		400.65	231.42	73,734.61	84,346.86	26,265.39	.0000	30
176 OCT 01 17		399.40	232.67	73,501.94	84,746.26	26,498.06	.0000	30
177 NOV 01 17		398.14	233.93	73,268.01	85,144.40	26,731.99	.0000	30
178 DEC 01 17		396.87	235.20	73,032.81	85,541.27	26,967.19	.0000	30
*** 2017					4,844.60	2,740.24	* Calendar Yr. Amounts *	
179 JAN 01 18		395.59	236.48	72,796.33	85,936.86	27,203.67	.0000	30
180 FEB 01 18		394.31	237.76	72,558.57	86,331.17	27,441.43	.0000	30
181 MAR 01 18		393.03	239.04	72,319.53	86,724.20	27,680.47	.0000	30
182 APR 01 18		391.73	240.34	72,079.19	87,115.93	27,920.81	.0000	30
183 MAY 01 18		390.43	241.64	71,837.55	87,506.36	28,162.45	.0000	30
184 JUN 01 18		389.12	242.95	71,594.60	87,895.48	28,405.40	.0000	30
185 JUL 01 18		387.80	244.27	71,350.33	88,283.28	28,649.67	.0000	30
186 AUG 01 18		386.48	245.59	71,104.74	88,669.76	28,895.26	.0000	30
187 SEP 01 18		385.15	246.92	70,857.82	89,054.91	29,142.18	.0000	30
188 OCT 01 18		383.81	248.26	70,609.56	89,438.72	29,390.44	.0000	30
189 NOV 01 18		382.47	249.60	70,359.96	89,821.19	29,640.04	.0000	30
190 DEC 01 18		381.12	250.95	70,109.01	90,202.31	29,890.99	.0000	30
*** 2018					4,661.04	2,923.60	* Calendar Yr. Amounts *	
191 JAN 01 19		379.76	252.31	69,856.70	90,582.07	30,143.30	.0000	30
192 FEB 01 19		378.39	253.68	69,603.02	90,960.46	30,396.98	.0000	30
193 MAR 01 19		377.02	255.05	69,347.97	91,337.48	30,652.03	.0000	30
194 APR 01 19		375.63	256.44	69,091.53	91,713.11	30,908.47	.0000	30
195 MAY 01 19		374.25	257.82	68,833.71	92,087.36	31,166.29	.0000	30
196 JUN 01 19		372.85	259.22	68,574.49	92,460.21	31,425.51	.0000	30
197 JUL 01 19		371.45	260.62	68,313.87	92,831.66	31,686.13	.0000	30

(continued)

EXHIBIT 9–2

Amortization Schedule of Direct Reduction Loan (continued)

# / PMT Due Date	Interest	Principal	Principal Balance	Total Interest	Total Principal	Per Diem	#Days
Name						*** Notes ***	
Loan Amount	100,000.00	Interest Rate	6.50000%	Payment Amount	$632.07		
Payment Begins	Mar 01 2003	Maturity Date	Feb 01 2033	Interest Basis 360/30	Total		
	Interest	Principal	Balance	Total Interest	Principal	Per Diem	#Days
198 AUG 01 19	370.03	262.04	68,051.83	93,201.69	31,948.17	.0000	30
199 SEP 01 19	368.61	263.46	67,788.37	93,570.30	32,211.63	.0000	30
200 OCT 01 19	367.19	264.88	67,523.49	93,937.49	32,476.51	.0000	30
201 NOV 01 19	365.75	266.32	67,257.17	94,303.24	32,742.83	.0000	30
202 DEC 01 19	364.31	267.76	66,989.41	94,667.55	33,010.59	.0000	30
*** 2019				4,465.24	3,119.60	* Calendar Yr. Amounts *	30
203 JAN 01 20	362.86	269.21	66,720.20	95,030.41	33,279.80	.0000	30
204 FEB 01 20	361.40	270.67	66,449.53	95,391.81	33,550.47	.0000	30
205 MAR 01 20	359.93	272.14	66,177.39	95,751.74	33,822.61	.0000	30
206 APR 01 20	358.46	273.61	65,903.78	96,110.20	34,096.22	.0000	30
207 MAY 01 20	356.98	275.09	65,628.69	96,467.18	34,371.31	.0000	30
208 JUN 01 20	355.49	276.58	65,352.11	96,822.67	34,647.89	.0000	30
209 JUL 01 20	353.99	278.08	65,074.03	97,176.66	34,925.97	.0000	30
210 AUG 01 20	352.48	279.59	64,794.44	97,529.14	35,205.56	.0000	30
211 SEP 01 20	350.97	281.10	64,513.34	97,880.11	35,486.66	.0000	30
212 OCT 01 20	349.45	282.62	64,230.72	98,229.56	35,769.28	.0000	30
213 NOV 01 20	347.92	284.15	63,946.57	98,577.48	36,053.43	.0000	30
214 DEC 01 20	346.38	285.69	63,660.88	98,923.86	36,339.12	.0000	30
*** 2020				4,256.31	3,328.53	* Calendar Yr. Amounts *	30
215 JAN 01 21	344.83	287.24	63,373.64	99,268.69	36,626.36	.0000	30
216 FEB 01 21	343.27	288.80	63,084.84	99,611.96	36,915.16	.0000	30
217 MAR 01 21	341.71	290.36	62,794.48	99,953.67	37,205.52	.0000	30
218 APR 01 21	340.14	291.93	62,502.55	100,293.81	37,497.45	.0000	30
219 MAY 01 21	338.56	293.51	62,209.04	100,632.37	37,790.96	.0000	30
220 JUN 01 21	336.97	295.10	61,913.94	100,969.34	38,086.06	.0000	30
221 JUL 01 21	335.37	296.70	61,617.24	101,304.71	38,382.76	.0000	30
222 AUG 01 21	333.76	298.31	61,318.93	101,638.47	38,681.07	.0000	30
223 SEP 01 21	332.14	299.93	61,019.00	101,970.61	38,981.00	.0000	30
224 OCT 01 21	330.52	301.55	60,717.45	102,301.13	39,282.55	.0000	30
225 NOV 01 21	328.89	303.18	60,414.27	102,630.02	39,585.73	.0000	30

(continued)

EXHIBIT 9–2

Amortization Schedule of Direct Reduction Loan (continued)

PMT Due Date #	Loan Amount 100,000.00 Mar 01 2003 Interest	Interest Rate Maturity Date Principal	6.50000% Feb 01 2033 Principal Balance	Payment Amount $632.07 Interest Basis 360/30 Total Interest	Total Principal	*** Notes *** Per Diem	#Days
226 DEC 01 21	327.24	304.83	60,109.44	102,957.26	39,890.56	.0000	30
*** 2021				4,033.40	3,551.44	* Calendar Yr. Amounts *	
227 JAN 01 22	325.59	306.48	59,802.96	103,282.85	40,197.04	.0000	30
228 FEB 01 22	323.93	308.14	59,494.82	103,606.78	40,505.18	.0000	30
229 MAR 01 22	322.26	309.81	59,185.01	103,929.04	40,814.99	.0000	30
230 APR 01 22	320.59	311.48	58,873.53	104,249.63	41,126.47	.0000	30
231 MAY 01 22	318.90	313.17	58,560.36	104,568.53	41,439.64	.0000	30
232 JUN 01 22	317.20	314.87	58,245.49	104,855.73	41,754.51	.0000	30
233 JUL 01 22	315.50	316.57	57,928.92	105,201.23	42,071.08	.0000	30
234 AUG 01 22	313.78	318.29	57,610.63	105,515.01	42,389.37	.0000	30
235 SEP 01 22	312.06	320.01	57,290.62	105,827.07	42,709.38	.0000	30
236 OCT 01 22	310.32	321.75	56,968.87	106,137.39	43,031.13	.0000	30
237 NOV 01 22	308.58	323.49	56,645.38	106,445.97	43,354.62	.0000	30
238 DEC 01 22	306.83	325.24	56,320.14	106,752.80	43,679.86	.0000	30
*** 2022				3,795.54	3,789.30	* Calendar Yr. Amounts *	
239 JAN 01 23	305.07	327.00	55,993.14	107,057.87	44,006.86	.0000	30
240 FEB 01 23	303.30	328.77	55,664.37	107,361.17	44,335.63	.0000	30
241 MAR 01 23	301.52	330.55	55,333.82	107,662.69	44,666.18	.0000	30
242 APR 01 23	299.72	332.35	55,001.47	107,962.41	44,998.53	.0000	30
243 MAY 01 23	297.92	334.15	54,667.32	108,260.33	45,332.68	.0000	30
244 JUN 01 23	296.11	335.96	54,331.36	108,556.44	45,668.64	.0000	30
245 JUL 01 23	294.29	337.78	53,993.58	108,850.73	46,006.42	.0000	30
246 AUG 01 23	292.47	339.60	53,653.98	109,143.20	46,346.02	.0000	30
247 SEP 01 23	290.63	341.44	53,312.54	109,433.83	46,687.46	.0000	30
248 OCT 01 23	288.78	343.29	52,969.25	109,722.61	47,030.75	.0000	30
249 NOV 01 23	286.92	345.15	52,624.10	110,009.53	47,375.90	.0000	30
250 DEC 01 23	285.05	347.02	52,277.08	110,294.58	47,722.92	.0000	30
*** 2023				3,541.78	4,043.06	* Calendar Yr. Amounts *	
251 JAN 01 24	283.17	348.90	51,928.18	110,577.75	48,071.82	.0000	30
252 FEB 01 24	281.28	350.79	51,577.39	110,859.03	48,422.61	.0000	30
253 MAR 01 24	279.38	352.69	51,224.70	111,138.41	48,775.30	.0000	30
254 APR 01 24	277.47	354.60	50,870.10	111,415.88	49,129.90	.0000	30

(continued)

EXHIBIT 9–2

Amortization Schedule of Direct Reduction Loan (continued)

Name	Loan Amount 100,000.00	Interest Rate Maturity Date	6.50000% Feb 01 2033	Payment Amount Interest Basis 360/30	$632.07	*** Notes ***	
Payment Begins Mar 01 2003							
PMT Due Date #	Interest	Principal	Principal Balance	Total Interest	Total Principal	Per Diem	#Days
255 MAY 01 24	275.55	356.52	50,513.58	111,691.43	49,486.42	.0000	30
256 JUN 01 24	273.62	358.45	50,155.13	111,965.05	49,844.87	.0000	30
257 JUL 01 24	271.67	360.40	49,794.73	112,236.72	50,205.27	.0000	30
258 AUG 01 24	269.72	362.35	49,432.38	112,506.44	50,567.62	.0000	30
259 SEP 01 24	267.76	364.31	49,068.07	112,774.20	50,931.93	.0000	30
260 OCT 01 24	265.79	366.28	48,701.79	113,039.99	51,298.21	.0000	30
261 NOV 01 24	263.80	368.27	48,333.52	113,303.79	51,666.48	.0000	30
262 DEC 01 24	261.81	370.26	47,963.26	113,565.60	52,036.74	.0000	30
*** 2024				3,271.02	4,313.82	* Calendar Yr. Amounts *	
263 JAN 01 25	259.80	372.27	47,590.99	113,825.40	52,409.01	.0000	30
264 FEB 01 25	257.78	374.29	47,216.70	114,083.18	52,783.30	.0000	30
265 MAR 01 25	255.76	376.31	46,840.39	114,338.94	53,159.61	.0000	30
266 APR 01 25	253.72	378.35	46,462.04	114,592.66	53,537.96	.0000	30
267 MAY 01 25	251.67	380.40	46,081.64	114,844.33	53,918.36	.0000	30
268 JUN 01 25	249.61	382.46	45,699.18	115,093.94	54,300.82	.0000	30
269 JUL 01 25	247.54	384.53	45,314.65	115,341.48	54,685.35	.0000	30
270 AUG 01 25	245.45	386.62	44,928.03	115,586.93	55,071.97	.0000	30
271 SEP 01 25	243.36	388.71	44,539.32	115,830.29	55,460.68	.0000	30
272 OCT 01 25	241.25	390.82	44,148.50	116,071.54	55,851.50	.0000	30
273 NOV 01 25	239.14	392.93	43,755.57	116,310.68	56,244.43	.0000	30
274 DEC 01 25	237.01	395.06	43,360.51	116,547.69	56,639.49	.0000	30
*** 2025				2,982.09	4,602.75	* Calendar Yr. Amounts *	
275 JAN 01 26	234.87	397.20	42,963.31	116,782.56	57,036.69	.0000	30
276 FEB 01 26	232.72	399.35	42,563.96	117,015.28	57,436.04	.0000	30
277 MAR 01 26	230.55	401.52	42,162.44	117,245.83	57,837.56	.0000	30
278 APR 01 26	228.38	403.69	41,758.75	117,474.21	58,241.25	.0000	30
279 MAY 01 26	226.19	405.88	41,352.87	117,700.40	58,647.13	.0000	30
280 JUN 01 26	223.99	408.08	40,944.79	117,924.39	59,055.21	.0000	30
281 JUL 01 26	221.78	410.29	40,534.50	118,146.17	59,465.50	.0000	30
282 AUG 01 26	219.56	412.51	40,121.99	118,365.73	59,878.01	.0000	30

(continued)

EXHIBIT 9-2

Amortization Schedule of Direct Reduction Loan (continued)

Name Loan Amount Payment Begins PMT Due Date #	100,000.00 Mar 01 2003 Interest	Interest Rate Maturity Date Principal	6.50000% Feb 01 2033 Principal Balance	Payment Amount Interest Basis 360/30 Total Interest	$632.07 Total Principal	*** Notes *** Per Diem	#Days
283 SEP 01 26	217.33	414.74	39,707.25	118,583.06	60,292.75	.0000	30
284 OCT 01 26	215.08	416.99	39,290.26	118,798.14	60,709.74	.0000	30
285 NOV 01 26	212.82	419.25	38,871.01	119,010.96	61,128.99	.0000	30
286 DEC 01 26	210.55	421.52	38,449.49	119,221.51	61,550.51	.0000	30
*** 2026				2,673.82	4,911.02	* Calendar Yr. Amounts *	
287 JAN 01 27	208.27	423.80	38,025.69	119,429.78	61,974.31	.0000	30
288 FEB 01 27	205.97	426.10	37,599.59	119,635.75	62,400.41	.0000	30
289 MAR 01 27	203.66	428.41	37,171.18	119,839.41	62,828.82	.0000	30
290 APR 01 27	201.34	430.73	36,740.45	120,040.75	63,259.55	.0000	30
291 MAY 01 27	199.01	433.06	36,307.39	120,239.76	63,692.61	.0000	30
292 JUN 01 27	196.67	435.40	35,871.99	120,436.43	64,128.01	.0000	30
293 JUL 01 27	194.31	437.76	35,434.23	120,630.74	64,565.77	.0000	30
294 AUG 01 27	191.94	440.13	34,994.10	120,822.68	65,005.90	.0000	30
295 SEP 01 27	189.55	442.52	34,551.58	121,012.23	65,448.42	.0000	30
296 OCT 01 27	187.15	444.92	34,106.66	121,199.38	65,893.34	.0000	30
297 NOV 01 27	184.74	447.33	33,659.33	121,384.12	66,340.67	.0000	30
298 DEC 01 27	182.32	449.75	33,209.58	121,566.44	66,790.42	.0000	30
*** 2027				2,344.93	5,239.91	* Calendar Yr. Amounts *	
299 JAN 01 28	179.89	452.18	32,757.40	121,746.33	67,242.60	.0000	30
300 FEB 01 28	177.44	454.63	32,302.77	121,923.77	67,697.23	.0000	30
301 MAR 01 28	174.97	457.10	31,845.67	122,098.74	68,154.33	.0000	30
302 APR 01 28	172.50	459.57	31,386.10	122,271.24	68,613.90	.0000	30
303 MAY 01 28	170.01	462.06	30,924.04	122,441.25	69,075.96	.0000	30
304 JUN 01 28	167.51	464.56	30,459.48	122,608.76	69,540.52	.0000	30
305 JUL 01 28	164.99	467.08	29,992.40	122,773.75	70,007.60	.0000	30
306 AUG 01 28	162.46	469.61	29,522.79	122,936.21	70,477.21	.0000	30
307 SEP 01 28	159.92	472.15	29,050.64	123,096.13	70,949.36	.0000	30
308 OCT 01 28	157.36	474.71	28,575.93	123,253.49	71,424.07	.0000	30
309 NOV 01 28	154.79	477.28	28,098.65	123,408.28	71,901.35	.0000	30
310 DEC 01 28	152.20	479.87	27,618.78	123,560.48	72,381.22	.0000	30
*** 2028				1,994.04	5,590.80	* Calendar Yr. Amounts *	
311 JAN 01 29	149.60	482.47	27,136.31	123,710.08	72,863.69	.0000	30

(continued)

EXHIBIT 9–2

Amortization Schedule of Direct Reduction Loan *(continued)*

Name Loan Amount Payment Begins PMT Due Date #	100,000.00 Mar 01 2003 Interest	Interest Rate Maturity Date Principal	6.50000% Feb 01 2033 Principal Balance	Payment Amount Interest Basis 360/30 Total Interest	$632.07 Total Principal	*** Notes *** Per Diem	#Days
312 FEB 01 29	146.99	485.08	26,651.23	123,857.07	73,348.77	.0000	30
313 MAR 01 29	144.36	487.71	26,163.52	124,001.43	73,836.48	.0000	30
314 APR 01 29	141.72	490.35	25,673.17	124,143.15	74,326.83	.0000	30
315 MAY 01 29	139.06	493.01	25,180.16	124,282.21	74,819.84	.0000	30
316 JUN 01 29	136.39	495.68	24,684.48	124,418.60	75,315.52	.0000	30
317 JUL 01 29	133.71	498.36	24,186.12	124,552.31	75,813.88	.0000	30
318 AUG 01 29	131.01	501.06	23,685.06	124,683.32	76,314.94	.0000	30
319 SEP 01 29	128.29	503.78	23,181.28	124,811.61	76,818.72	.0000	30
320 OCT 01 29	125.57	506.50	22,674.78	124,937.18	77,325.22	.0000	30
321 NOV 01 29	122.82	509.25	22,165.53	125,060.00	77,834.47	.0000	30
322 DEC 01 29	120.06	512.01	21,653.52	125,180.06	78,346.48	.0000	30
*** 2029				1,619.58	5,965.26	* Calendar Yr. Amounts *	
323 JAN 01 30	117.29	514.78	21,138.74	125,297.35	78,861.26	.0000	30
324 FEB 01 30	114.50	517.57	20,621.17	125,411.85	79,378.83	.0000	30
325 MAR 01 30	111.70	520.37	20,100.80	125,523.55	79,899.20	.0000	30
326 APR 01 30	108.88	523.19	19,577.61	125,632.43	80,422.39	.0000	30
327 MAY 01 30	106.05	526.02	19,051.59	125,738.48	80,948.41	.0000	30
328 JUN 01 30	103.20	528.87	18,522.72	125,841.68	81,477.28	.0000	30
329 JUL 01 30	100.33	531.74	17,990.98	125,942.01	82,009.02	.0000	30
330 AUG 01 30	97.45	534.62	17,456.36	126,039.46	82,543.64	.0000	30
331 SEP 01 30	94.56	537.51	16,918.85	126,134.02	83,081.15	.0000	30
332 OCT 01 30	91.64	540.43	16,378.42	126,225.66	83,621.58	.0000	30
333 NOV 01 30	88.72	543.35	15,835.07	126,314.38	84,164.93	.0000	30
334 DEC 01 30	85.77	546.30	15,288.77	126,400.15	84,711.23	.0000	30
*** 2030				1,220.09	6,364.75	* Calendar Yr. Amounts *	
335 JAN 01 31	82.81	549.26	14,739.51	126,482.96	85,260.49	.0000	30
336 FEB 01 31	79.84	552.23	14,187.28	126,562.80	85,812.72	.0000	30
337 MAR 01 31	76.85	555.22	13,632.06	126,639.65	86,367.94	.0000	30
338 APR 01 31	73.84	558.23	13,073.83	126,713.49	86,926.17	.0000	30

(continued)

EXHIBIT 9–2

Amortization Schedule of Direct Reduction Loan (continued)

Name					*** Notes ***	
Loan Amount 100,000.00	Interest Rate 6.50000%		Payment Amount $632.07			
Payment Begins Mar 01 2003	Maturity Date Feb 01 2033		Interest Basis 360/30			
PMT Due Date						
#	Interest	Principal	Principal Balance	Total Interest	Total Principal	Per Diem	#Days
339 MAY 01 31	70.82	561.25	12,512.58	126,784.31	87,487.42	.0000	30
340 JUN 01 31	67.78	564.29	11,948.29	126,852.09	88,051.71	.0000	30
341 JUL 01 31	64.72	567.35	11,380.94	126,916.81	88,619.06	.0000	30
342 AUG 01 31	61.65	570.42	10,810.52	126,978.46	89,189.48	.0000	30
343 SEP 01 31	58.56	573.51	10,237.01	127,037.02	89,762.99	.0000	30
344 OCT 01 31	55.45	576.62	9,660.39	127,092.47	90,339.61	.0000	30
345 NOV 01 31	52.33	579.74	9,080.65	127,144.80	90,919.35	.0000	30
346 DEC 01 31	49.19	582.88	8,497.77	127,193.99	91,502.23	.0000	30
*** 2031				793.84	6,791.00	* Calendar Yr. Amounts *	
347 JAN 01 32	46.03	586.04	7,911.73	127,240.02	92,088.27	.0000	30
348 FEB 01 32	42.86	589.21	7,322.52	127,282.88	92,677.48	.0000	30
349 MAR 01 32	39.66	592.41	6,730.11	127,322.54	93,269.89	.0000	30
350 APR 01 32	36.45	595.62	6,134.49	127,358.99	93,865.51	.0000	30
351 MAY 01 32	33.23	598.84	5,535.65	127,392.22	94,464.35	.0000	30
352 JUN 01 32	29.98	602.09	4,933.56	127,422.20	95,066.44	.0000	30
353 JUL 01 32	26.72	605.35	4,328.21	127,448.92	95,671.79	.0000	30
354 AUG 01 32	23.44	608.63	3,719.58	127,472.36	96,280.42	.0000	30
355 SEP 01 32	20.15	611.92	3,107.66	127,492.51	96,892.34	.0000	30
356 OCT 01 32	16.83	615.24	2,492.42	127,509.34	97,507.58	.0000	30
357 NOV 01 32	13.50	618.57	1,873.85	127,522.84	98,126.15	.0000	30
358 DEC 01 32	10.15	621.92	1,251.93	127,532.99	98,748.07	.0000	30
*** 2332				339.00	7,245.84	* Calendar Yr. Amounts *	
359 JAN 01 33	6.78	625.29	626.64	127,539.77	99,373.36	.0000	30
360 FEB 01 33	3.39	626.64	.00	127,543.16	100,000.00	.0000	30
*** 2033				10.17	1,251.93	* Calendar Yr. Amounts *	
***							
*** Grand Totals				127,543.16	100,000.00		

chapter | 10

Legal Aspects of Real Estate Finance

Objectives

After reading this chapter, you should be able to:

- Prepare a promissory note
- Prepare a guaranty
- Understand the basic provisions contained in a promissory note
- Understand the basic provisions contained in a guaranty
- List the legal requirements for a mortgage, deed of trust, or security deed
- Understand the risks inherent in a second mortgage
- Identify the various legal remedies available to both the borrower and the lender in the event of a default on a mortgage loan

Outline

Real estate mortgage loans involve large sums of money and numerous risks for both the borrower and the lender. The borrower may be unable to pay the debt and may lose the real property pledged as security for the debt. The lender may not be repaid as promised and may resort to the real property security or other measures to collect on the debt. Over the years, several legal documents have been created to evidence and secure mortgage loan transactions. Paralegals are actively involved in the preparation of these documents and need to be familiar with the different legal documents required to make a loan secured by real property. The main legal documents are a promissory note and a security instrument, which, depending on the location of the real property, may be a mortgage, deed of trust, or security deed. A promissory note is the written promise made by a property owner to repay the money borrowed from a lender or creditor; the security instrument (mortgage, deed of trust, or security deed) is the instrument conveying real property as security for the repayment of the money.

PROMISSORY NOTE

promissory note

Legal document that contains a promise by one party to pay money to another party.

maker

Party to a promissory note who promises to pay money.

payee

Party to a promissory note to whom a promise to pay money has been made.

negotiable note

Written note signed by the maker and containing an unconditional promise to pay a certain sum of money on demand or at a definite time. A negotiable note may be transferred to a holder in due course.

holder

Person who is the owner of a promissory note.

A **promissory note** is a promise by one party to pay money to another party. The parties on a promissory note are referred to as *payor* or **maker** (the party who promises to pay) and **payee** (the party to whom the promise is made). A note may be negotiable or nonnegotiable. The term **negotiable** means that the note is capable of being transferred from the original payee to another person, referred to as a **holder.** A negotiable note can be transferred to a holder in due course. A holder in due course has a privileged status in the ability to collect payment on a note. A holder in due course of a promissory note usually defeats any defenses to payment that the maker of the note may have. For example, Ajax Realty Company sells a home to Mary Stewart. Ajax agrees, as part of the purchase price, to take a note from Mary Stewart in the amount of $100,000 payable over the next 10 years. Ajax Realty Company also warrants to Mary Stewart that the roof of the house will not leak for 10 years. After the sale of the home, the note from Mary Stewart to Ajax Realty Company is transferred to First Bank and Trust, a holder in due course. A year after the closing, the roof begins to leak, causing damage to Mary Stewart's personal possessions. Mary Stewart stops payment on the note. First Bank and Trust sues Mary Stewart for $100,000. Mary Stewart countersues, arguing that the roof is leaking and has damaged her possessions in the amount of $20,000. She argues that she should be entitled to pay only $80,000 on the note. If First Bank and Trust were not a holder in due course, Mary Stewart would be able to set off the $20,000 leaking-roof damages against the payment of the note. Because First Bank and Trust is a holder in due course, Mary Stewart is not able to set off the leaking-roof damages against the payment of the note. First Bank and Trust, as a holder in due course, can collect the full $100,000 from Mary Stewart.

A holder in due course defeats most defenses that a maker on a note would have to the payment of the note. Exceptions to this rule are (a) incapacity of the maker, (b) illegality of the purpose of the note, (c) duress of the maker in signing the note, (d) discharge of the maker in bankruptcy, (e) forgery of the maker's signature, (f) fraud in factum, and (g) material alteration of the note. *Fraud in factum* is a situation in which a party signing the note did not have enough knowledge or reasonable opportunity to determine that a note was being signed. Except for these seven defenses, a holder in due course is entitled to collect payment on a note from a maker.

It is in the best interest of investors and purchasers of promissory notes to be a holder in due course. For a holder in due course situation to exist, the note being held must be a negotiable note, and the holder must have possession of the original note with all the necessary endorsements to establish title in the holder. The holder also must have purchased the note for value and in good faith without notice of any defenses or without notice that the note was overdue or dishonored.

Investors who purchase notes, such as Fannie Mae, Freddie Mac, and other investors in the secondary mortgage market, have a strong interest in being a holder in due course. This strong interest in being a holder in due course means that most notes that are prepared to secure a loan are negotiable. Lawyers and paralegals, therefore, make every effort in the drafting of a note to make the note negotiable.

A negotiable note, by definition, is written, signed by the maker, and contains an unconditional promise to pay a certain sum of money on demand or at a definite time. If any part of this definition is missing, the note is not negotiable. For example, you have a written note in which the maker agrees to pay $100,000 on the completion of a contract. Because it is unknown when and if the contract will be completed, the promise to pay is conditional, and the note is not negotiable.

Negotiability should not be confused with enforceability. As discussed previously, a negotiable note can be transferred to a holder in due course. A nonnegotiable note may be enforceable; that is, a holder of a nonnegotiable note may be able to collect the money from the maker. A nonnegotiable note may be transferred, but it cannot be transferred to a holder in due course. Collection of a nonnegotiable note is subject to whatever defenses the maker may have toward the collection of the note.

Endorsement

Notes often are transferred by the payees. It is not uncommon in a real estate transaction for the original lender—for example, a savings bank—to sell the note to another investor, such as Fannie Mae. A note is transferred and sold by **endorsement**. An endorsement is simply a direction, usually printed on the back of the note or attached to the note, ordering that the money be paid to the order of the new owner of the note. Sample endorsements are shown in Example 10–1.

endorsement

Method of transferring ownership of a promissory note.

Example 10–1

Unqualified Endorsement
FOR VALUE RECEIVED, pay to the order of:

_____

By: _____ (SEAL)

Qualified Endorsement No. 1
FOR VALUE RECEIVED, without recourse, pay to the order of:

_____

By: _____ (SEAL)

Qualified Endorsement No. 2
FOR VALUE RECEIVED, without recourse and warranty, pay to the order of:

_____

By: _____ (SEAL)

An endorser who transfers a note by endorsement incurs certain contractual and warranty liabilities to the new owner of the note. The contractual liability is that the endorser will pay the note according to its terms in the event the maker does not. Contractual liability of an endorser to pay a note is secondary. The holder of the note must first present the note to the maker for payment, and the maker must dishonor (refuse or fail to pay) the note. Once the note has been presented to the maker and the maker has refused or failed to pay, a notice of dishonor must be sent to the endorser within three business days from the date of dishonor. If all these steps are performed by the holder of the note, an endorser is then responsible to pay the note. These three steps—presentment, dishonor, and notice of dishonor—can be waived by an endorser, and this waiver can be contained in the note that is endorsed. The purchaser of a note usually wants the waiver because the waiver will make it easier to collect the note from an endorser. An example of language contained in a note that waives presentment, dishonor, and notice of dishonor is shown in Example 10–2.

Example 10–2

Waiver. Demand, presentment, notice, protest, and notice of dishonor are hereby waived by Borrower and by each and every co-maker, endorser, guarantor, surety, and other person or entity primarily or secondarily liable on this note.

In addition to a contractual obligation to pay the note, an endorser has warranty liabilities to the new owner of the note. An endorser who sells the note by endorsement warrants the following: (a) the endorser has good title to the note; (b) all signatures are genuine and authorized; (c) the note has not been materially altered; (d) there are no defenses to payment of the note; and (e) the endorser has no knowledge of any bankruptcy proceedings against the maker.

An endorser of a note may not want the obligation to pay the note. For example, a savings bank closes a number of residential loans for the purpose of selling the loans to a life insurance company investor. The understanding between the savings bank and the life insurance company is that the life insurance company will rely solely on the credit risks of the individual homeowners for repayment of the notes. There is no intent on the part of the life insurance company to look to the savings bank for payment of the homeowners' notes.

An endorser can escape the contractual liability by giving a qualified endorsement. One type of qualified endorsement is the "without recourse" endorsement, shown as Qualified Endorsement No. 1 in Example 10–1. The "without recourse" endorsement negates contractual liability but still imposes warranty liability on the endorser, with the exception that in connection with the warranty of no defenses, the endorser who makes a "without recourse" endorsement warrants only that he or she has no knowledge of any defenses to the payment of the note.

An endorsement "without recourse and warranty" negates all contractual and warranty liabilities. This endorsement is shown as Qualified Endorsement No. 2 in Example 10–1. This type of endorsement is similar to a quitclaim deed in that it transfers whatever title the endorser has to the note but makes no warranties.

Few investors will purchase notes that contain a "without recourse and warranty" endorsement, and this endorsement seldom is used.

Payment

A maker's promise on a negotiable note is unconditional, and the maker is not released by the sale of the security securing the note. For example, a homeowner signs a note promising to pay $100,000 secured by her home. The homeowner later sells the home. The sale of the home does not release the homeowner from the promise to pay the $100,000 on the note.

In some situations, there is more than one maker on a note, such as in the case of a husband and wife signing a note for the purpose of purchasing a home. In such an event, each maker of the note, referred to as a co-maker, is fully responsible for the payment of the note.

The note can be collected from each of the co-makers in full. This is known as joint and several liability. For example, Stanley White and Martha White purchase a home. As part of the purchase, they borrow $100,000 from First Bank and Trust and sign a note promising to pay the $100,000. The bank can collect the $100,000 in full from either Stanley White or Martha White.

The holder of a note is the only person entitled to payment, and a maker, when paying a note, should be careful to pay only the holder. Another risk arises when the maker leaves the note with the holder after it has been paid. What, other than honesty and integrity, is to prevent the holder from selling the note to a holder in due course after it has been paid? The holder in due course, if unaware that the note has been paid, is entitled by law to collect again from the maker. Therefore, to avoid multiple payments of the same note, it is not uncommon for makers of notes to demand that the original note be returned marked "paid" or "satisfied" at the time of payment.

Prepayment

A note cannot be prepaid before the date established in the note for payment. If the maker of the note wants the privilege to prepay, this privilege must be provided for in the note. It is not unusual for a lender to condition prepayment on the payment of an additional premium or penalty. Some lenders, such as life insurance companies that desire to have their loans outstanding without prepayment for a fixed period of time, may establish a prepayment privilege that is closed for a certain period of time and then is available with a penalty. The prepayment clause is typically used on commercial loans held by life insurance companies and other commercial mortgage loan investors. The prepayment clause basically provides that the lender will receive a sum of money sufficient to invest in an alternate investment, such as a Treasury bill, which will provide the same yield to maturity as the mortgage loan would have yielded without prepayment. An example of such a prepayment clause is shown in Example 10–3.

Example 10–3

Prepayment Privilege. This note may not be prepaid in whole or in part except as herein specifically provided. No prepayment of the principal of this note shall be permitted or allowed prior to the end of the third (3rd) Loan Year, as hereinafter defined. After the end of the third (3rd) Loan Year, this note may be prepaid in whole, but not in part, upon any principal and interest payment date as provided herein, provided that (a) no later than sixty (60) days prior to the date of such prepayment, Borrower delivers written notice to Payee that Borrower intends to prepay the note in full on the date specified in the notice; and (b) Borrower pays to Payee at the time of such prepayment a percentage of the prepaid principal amount of the indebtedness as a prepayment premium. The amount of the prepayment premium shall be the product obtained by multiplying the prepaid principal amount of the indebtedness by the product of the following: (i) the amount obtained by subtracting the annualized yield on a United States Treasury Bill, Note, or Bond with a maturity date that occurs closest to the maturity date of this note, as such annualized yield is reported by *The Wall Street Journal*, on the business day preceding the date of prepayment, from 6.50% multiplied by (ii) the number of years and any fraction thereof remaining between the date of prepayment and the maturity date of this note.

Notwithstanding the foregoing, however, in the event of acceleration of this note at any time, including the period of time prior to the end of the third (3rd) Loan Year, and subsequent involuntary or voluntary prepayment, the prepayment premium as calculated above shall be payable, however, in no event shall it exceed an amount equal to the excess, if any, of (i) interest calculated at the highest applicable rate permitted by applicable law, as construed by courts having jurisdiction thereof, on the principal balance of the indebtedness evidenced by this note from time to time outstanding from the date hereof to the date of such acceleration; over (ii) interest theretofore paid and accrued on this note. Any prepaid amounts specified in any notice shall become due and payable at the time provided in such notice. Under no circumstances shall the prepayment premium ever be less than zero. The amount of prepayment shall never be less than the full amount of the then outstanding principal indebtedness and accrued interest thereon.

A Loan Year for the purposes of this note shall mean each successive twelve (12)-month period, beginning with the date of the first installment payment of principal and interest hereunder, provided, however, that the first (1st) Loan Year shall include the period from the date of this note to the date of such first installment payment of principal and interest.

Borrower further agrees to pay in addition to the above-described prepayment premium, a reinvestment fee of one-half of one percent (½%) of the outstanding prepaid principal indebtedness evidenced by this note to Payee. Borrower agrees that the reinvestment fee together with the prepayment premium shall be due and payable regardless of whether prepayment is made involuntarily or voluntarily.

The case of *Acord v. Jones*, 211 Ga. App. 682, 440 S.E.2d 679 (Ga. 1994), is a good indication of the need for lenders such as life insurance companies to use a prepayment clause in the note.

Usury

usury

Interest rates that are determined to be in excess of the maximum permitted by law.

Most states have statutes that establish a ceiling or maximum rate of interest to be charged on a loan. These statutes are called **usury** statutes. The penalty for usury varies from state to state. It usually is the loss of all interest on the loan, but it can be as extreme as the forfeiture of the entire loan amount. Lenders, therefore, are careful to establish an interest rate that does not violate the usury laws. Most notes contain what is known as a "usury savings clause." This is an attempt by the lender to credit any excess interest to either a reduction of principal or a refund to the borrower. An example of a usury savings clause appears in Example 10–4.

Example 10–4

This note and all provisions hereof and of all documents securing this note conform in all respects to the laws of the State of Georgia so that no payment of interest or other sum construed to be interest or charges in the nature of interest shall exceed the highest lawful contract rate permissible under the laws of the State of Georgia as applicable to this transaction. Therefore, this note and all agreements between Borrower and Payee are limited so that in no contingency or event whatsoever, whether acceleration of maturity of the indebtedness or otherwise, shall the amount paid or agree to be paid to the Payee for the use, forbearance, or detention of the money advanced by or to be advanced hereunder exceed the highest lawful rate permissible under the laws of the State of Georgia as applicable to this transaction. In determining whether or not the rate of interest exceeds the highest lawful rate, the Borrower and Payee intend that all sums paid hereunder that are deemed interest for the purposes of determining usury be prorated, allocated, or spread in equal parts over the longest period of time permitted under the applicable laws of the State of Georgia. If, under any circumstances whatsoever, fulfillment of any provision hereof, or of any other instrument evidencing or securing this Indebtedness, at the time performance of such provision shall be due, shall involve the payment of interest in excess of that authorized by law, the obligation to be fulfilled shall be reduced to the limit so authorized by law, and if under any circumstances Payee shall ever receive as interest an amount that would exceed the highest lawful rate, the amount that would be excessive shall be either applied to the reduction of the unpaid principal balance of the Indebtedness, without payment of any prepayment fee (and not to the payment of interest), or refunded to the Borrower, and Payee shall not be subject to any penalty provided for the contracting for, charging, or receiving interest in excess of the maximum lawful rate regardless of when or the circumstances under which said refund or application was made.

Execution

A note is signed by the maker, but the signature is not required to be witnessed or notarized. A note usually is not recorded, but in some states, such as Louisiana, a copy of the note is attached as an exhibit to the deed of trust and is recorded.

Practice Tips for the Paralegal

A note is an important legal document, and the original of the note is the best evidence of the note at the time of collection. Special care should be taken in preparing a note to make sure it correctly reflects the terms of the loan and the repayment of the money. Corrections on notes should be avoided. If an error on a note is corrected by whiting it out or using some other typing correction technique, the correction should be initialed by the maker. For notes that are more than one page long, the maker should initial each page of the note.

Three note forms are included at the end of this chapter: Exhibit 10–1, Fannie Mae/Freddie Mac Residential Fixed-Rate Note; Exhibit 10–2, Fannie Mae/Freddie Mac Residential Adjustable-Rate Note; and Exhibit 10–3, Commercial Loan Note. The following is a checklist to assist in the preparation of a note.

CASE

Acord v. Jones
211 Ga. App. 682, 440 S.E.2d 679 (Ga. 1994)

JOHNSON, Judge.

Acord appeals from the trial court's grant of Jones' motion for judgment on the pleadings.

Acord gave Jones two promissory notes which were secured by real property. The interest-bearing notes, which were payable in monthly installments and matured in five and ten years, were silent on the issue of prepayment. Acord attempted to pay them off prior to maturity by tendering the outstanding principal plus accrued interest. Jones refused the tender, maintaining that the notes did not allow prepayment and that, even if they did, the amount tendered did not cover the full indebtedness since it did not include unaccrued interest. Acord filed suit to force cancellation of the notes and security deeds since he had tendered what he considered to be the full amount due. Acord filed a motion for summary judgment and/or for judgment on the pleadings. Jones apparently filed a cross-motion for judgment on the pleadings. The trial court denied Acord's motion and granted judgment on the pleadings to Jones. Acord appeals. We reverse the trial court's decision.

In his sole enumeration of error, Acord contends that the trial court erred in holding that the terms of the contract did not allow prepayment. He argues that because the

notes contain the phrase "[i]f not sooner paid,"[1] there is the implication that the notes may be paid prior to maturity. Neither party has cited, and our research has failed to uncover, any cases in which Georgia courts have been called upon to decide whether that language has the effect of allowing prepayment, and if so, whether the lender would be entitled to recover unearned interest.

"In construing contracts . . . the language used must be afforded its literal meaning and plain ordinary words given their usual significance." (Citations and punctuation omitted.) *Twin Oaks Assoc. v. DeKalb Venture,* 190 Ga. App. 854, 855(1) (380 S.E.2d 469) (1989). In its plain ordinary sense, the phrase "if not sooner paid" clearly contemplates the possibility of early repayment. Further, the phrase would have to be construed against Jones as the drafter. *Roswell Properties v. Salle,* 208 Ga. App. 202, 206(3) (430 S.E.2d 404) (1993). Thus, we hold that Acord was entitled to prepay the indebtedness.

However, the issue of whether unaccrued interest can be required as part of the prepayment remains. In the absence of a contractual provision addressing the issue, we must apply existing law. See *State Farm Mutual Automobile Insurance Co. v. Hodges,* 111 Ga. App. 317, 321 (141 S.E.2d 586) (1965); *Jenkins v. Morgan,* 100 Ga. App. 561 (112 S.E.2d 23) (1959). The trial

(continued)

court and Jones rely upon *Cook v. Securities Investment Co.,* 184 Ga. 544 (192 S.E. 179) (1937), for the proposition that the payee of an installment note cannot be compelled to accept prepayment of the principal with interest to date only. *Id.* at 548. A careful reading of that case, however, reveals that it is not dispositive of the issues in the instant case. We note that what Jones refers to as the holding in *Cook* is merely dicta. There is nothing in the opinion in *Cook* which indicates that that case involved language comparable to the "if not sooner paid" phrase in the contracts which are the subject of the instant case. *Cook* involved the rights of a judgment creditor where legal title to the property of the debtor had been conveyed to a third party to secure a debt to the third party; accordingly, that case was decided pursuant to § 39-201 of the Code (now OCGA § 9-113-60), a section which is inapplicable here. *Id.* at 546-548.

Since *Cook* was decided fifty-six years ago, we have held that a contract which provides for the payment of purchase money notes "on or before maturity" does allow the maker to pay principal plus accrued interest at any time prior to maturity and relieves the maker of having to pay unearned interest. *Kuttner v. May Realty Co.,* 220 Ga. 163, 164 (137 S.E.2d 637) (1964). In addition, the legislature has enacted several statutes, such as the Motor Vehicle Sales Finance Act (OCGA § 10-1-30 et seq.), the Retail Installment and Home Solicitation Sales Act (OCGA § 10-1-1 et seq.), and the Industrial Loan Act (OCGA § 7-3-1), all of which, among other things, relieve consumers of the obligation to pay unearned interest when debts are paid off prior to maturity. While not applicable here, these statutes do show consistent recognition of a public policy in favor of allowing prepayment of loans without penalty. To require payment of unearned interest in this case would effectively impose a prepayment penalty where none has been contemplated by the terms of the contracts. The law does not favor penalties. See generally *Southern Guaranty Corp. v. Doyle,* 256 Ga. 790, 792 (353 S.E.2d 510) (1987); *Wasser v. C & S Nat. Bank,* 170 Ga. App. 872, 873 (318 S.E.2d 518) (1984). We hold that, in the absence of an express contractual provision to the contrary, a maker may prepay principal plus accrued interest, without being required to tender unaccrued interest or pay any other penalty. Because Acord was entitled to prepay the debts and since he made a valid tender, Jones was required to accept the payment as satisfaction of the debts and cancel the security deeds.

Judgment reversed. McMurray, P.J., and Blackburn J., concur

---

[1]The notes set forth the amount borrowed, interest rates, dates and amounts of installments and provide for payment of "a like amount on the same day of each succeeding month thereafter to be applied first to any interest due, then to principle [sic] until the total of said indebtedness shall be paid in full. *If not sooner paid* the total balance due hereunder shall be paid at the expiration of ten years from date."

✓ CHECKLIST

Preparation of a Note

☐ I. Parties
　　☐ A. Maker (borrower)
　　☐ B. Payee or holder (lender)

☐ II. Amount of Note

☐ III. Interest Rate to Be Charged on Note
　　☐ A. Fixed rate
　　☐ B. Adjustable rate
　　　　1. Identification of index to be used for adjustment (e.g., prime lending rate, three-year Treasury security)
　　　　2. Intervals of adjustment (e.g., daily, monthly, annually)
　　　　3. Indication of any minimum or maximum interest rates

☐ IV. Payments
  ☐ A. Time and place of payments
  ☐ B. Amount of payments

☐ V. Maker's Right to Prepay
  ☐ A. May prepay in whole or in part at any time
  ☐ B. May prepay in whole at any time after reasonable notice
  ☐ C. No prepayment allowed
  ☐ D. No prepayment allowed for a certain period of time
  ☐ E. Prepayment allowed but on payment of prepayment fee
  ☐ F. No prepayment allowed for a certain period of time and after that period
    of time prepayment allowed only on payment of prepayment fee

☐ VI. Maker's Failure to Pay as Required
  ☐ A. Late charge for overdue payment
    1. Time for late charge to commence (e.g., 10 days, 15 days after
     due date)
  ☐ B. Amount of late charge (e.g., 4 percent of late payment)
  ☐ C. Default for failure to pay
    1. Grace period
    2. Notice of default and period of time to cure default
    3. Acceleration of loan on default
     a. Optional acceleration
    4. Payment of holder's cost and expenses for collection of note
     a. Attorney's fees
     b. Court costs and other reasonable expenses
     c. Default interest rate is higher during periods of default than normal
      note rate.

☐ VII. Identify Security Given for Note
  ☐ A. Mortgage or deed of trust
  ☐ B. Assignment of leases and rents
  ☐ C. Security agreement
  ☐ D. Other documents

☐ VIII. Usury Savings Clause

☐ IX. Choice of Applicable Law

☐ X. Waiver of Homestead Exemption or Other Debtor's Rights

☐ XI. Joint and Several Liability

☐ XII. Waiver of Notice of Default, Presentment of Notice of Dishonor

☐ XIII. Signatures
  ☐ A. Only maker signs note
    1. Corporate maker
     a. Identify name of corporation
     b. Identify the officers of the corporation signing the note by name
      and by title
     c. Affix corporate seal
  ☐ B. Partnership maker
    1. Identify partnership by name
    2. Identify all partners signing the note by name
  ☐ C. Names of all people signing the note should be typed underneath the
    signature line
  ☐ D. Notes are not witnessed or notarized

GUARANTY

guaranty

Legal document that obligates the maker of the document to pay the debt of another person.

guarantor

Person who signs a guaranty promising to pay the debt of another person.

A mortgage lender may require a person other than the debtor to guarantee the payment of the debtor's note. For example, when making a loan to a corporate debtor, a mortgage lender may require the shareholders of the corporation to guarantee the loan. This **guaranty** gives the mortgage lender the right to sue the shareholders for payment of the note and, if necessary, the right to recover the debt from the personal assets of the shareholders.

A guaranty of a note must be written. The written guaranty form is closely interpreted by the courts, and the guarantor's liability is not extended by implication or interpretation. A guaranty may be a "payment guaranty" or a "collection guaranty." The **guarantor** who signs a payment guaranty unconditionally guarantees to pay the note when due without resort to any other party, including the maker of the note. The holder of a note may go directly to a payment guarantor for payment once the note becomes due and payable.

The guarantor who signs a collection guaranty promises to pay the note only after the holder of the note has sued the original maker of the note, has reduced the claim to a judgment, and has attempted to collect against the assets of the maker. A guarantor who signs a collection guaranty is required to pay the note only in the event the maker of the note is insolvent or otherwise lacks assets sufficient to pay the note.

Under the terms of both the payment guaranty and a collection guaranty, a change in the terms of the note being guaranteed without the guarantor's consent releases the guarantor. Therefore, any time that the note is modified or amended in any way, it is necessary that all guarantors consent to the modification and amendment.

A form of a payment guaranty is shown in Exhibit 10–4 at the end of this chapter.

MORTGAGES, DEEDS OF TRUST, AND SECURITY DEEDS

The companion legal document to a promissory note secured by real estate is the security instrument. Depending on the state in which the real property is located, the security interest may be a mortgage, deed of trust, or security deed. Regardless of the form of security instrument being used, its main purpose is to convey real property as security for the repayment of the debt evidenced by the note.

The three basic types of security instruments are (1) **mortgage**, (2) **deed of trust**, and (3) **deed to secure debt**. Mortgage, deed of trust, and deed to secure debt forms are included at the end of this chapter as Exhibit 10–5, Florida Mortgage; Exhibit 10–6, North Carolina Deed of Trust; and Exhibit 10–7, Georgia Commercial Deed to Secure Debt.

mortgage

Legal document that creates an encumbrance on real property to secure a debt.

deed of trust

Legal document that conveys title to real property to a trustee who holds the title as security for a debt to a lender.

deed to secure debt

Legal document that conveys title to real property to a lender to secure a debt.

Mortgage

A mortgage is a pledge of land as security for a debt. The ancient term for this pledge combined the words for *dead* ("mort") and *pledge* ("gage"). A mortgage was a dead pledge. This was based upon the thought that it was doubtful whether the mortgagor would pay on the day the debt was due and if the mortgagor did not pay, then the land he had pledged would be taken away from him forever and would therefore be dead to him. If the mortgagor did pay the money, then the pledge would be dead to the mortgagee.

Early mortgages required the mortgagor to give possession of the pledged land to the mortgagee during the payment of the debt. Once the debt had been paid, possession of the land was returned to the debtor. As the law evolved, it became practice that more debts were paid than were unpaid, and therefore, a theory evolved that the mortgage was no more than a security for a debt and that the mortgagee's rights to the land must be so limited as to insure that he obtained only a security interest in the mortgage. This idea that a mortgage was but a security device was accompanied by the practice of allowing the mortgagor to remain in possession of the land until he defaulted on the payment of the debt. This right to remain in possession while the debt was repaid was called the *mortgagor's equity of redemption,* which was recognized as a property right in ancient English law. The mortgagor's equity of redemption could be terminated by the mortgagee in the event the debt was not paid when due. This body of mortgage law, which became very common at the end of the sixteenth century in England, is similar to the modern mortgage law that currently exists in the United States. Mortgages are still used in a number of states.

Deed of Trust

Several states use a deed of trust form for real estate loans. A deed of trust is a document wherein the owner of the real property conveys title to the real property to a third party, known as a trustee. The trustee then holds the title in trust for the benefit of the lender. If the debt being secured by the deed of trust is not paid, the trustee has the power to sell the title to the real property and to use the proceeds from the sale to pay the debt owed to the lender.

Deed to Secure Debt

A deed to secure debt is a security instrument wherein the owner of the real property conveys legal title directly to the lender as security for the repayment of the debt. The lender is given the power to sell the real property in the event the debt is not paid.

Regardless of which security instrument is used, the owner stays in possession of the real property and can use and enjoy the real property so long as the debt is being paid.

For simplicity of reference, all three security instruments are referred to as a mortgage throughout this chapter. Please keep in mind that, depending on the state in which the real property is located, the security instrument may be a mortgage, deed of trust, or deed to secure debt.

Requirements of a Mortgage

A mortgage must meet all the requirements of a deed, together with a description of the debt being secured. These requirements are (a) names of the parties, (b) words of conveyance or grant, (c) valid description of the property conveyed, (d) proper execution and attestation, and (e) effective delivery to the lender.

The mortgage may grant to the lender the power to sell the property in the event of a default under the mortgage, as well as numerous other provisions designed to protect the lender in every conceivable situation.

Parties to a Mortgage

A mortgage is entered into by two parties: the **mortgagor** and the **mortgagee.** The mortgagor is the owner of the property (the debtor), or borrower, and the mortgagee is the lender, or creditor. A mortgage is given by the owner to the lender. In the case of a deed of trust, the instrument may be entered into by three parties, with the addition of the trustee.

Because it is a fundamental rule that only the owner of real property can pledge the real property as security for a loan, it is important that the title to the real property be examined to determine the correct owner and that the owner be made the mortgagor. If the mortgagor is a corporation, proper corporate authority must be presented not only to authorize the loan and the pledge of real property as security, but also to authorize the corporate officers to sign the mortgage. A mortgage signed by a partnership requires that all partners sign

mortgagor

Person who signs a mortgage pledging real property to secure a debt.

mortgagee

Person who receives a mortgage, that is, a lender.

the mortgage or that a partner authorized by all the partners sign the mortgage. Mortgages given by co-owners of property require the signatures of all owners.

Secured Debt

A valid debt must exist to have a valid mortgage. A mortgage must describe in words and figures the debt secured. The date of the final maturity of the debt also is identified.

A mortgage may be given to secure any and all debt between the mortgagor and the mortgagee, including past debt, present debt, and even future debt incurred after the mortgage is in place. These mortgages are called **open-end** or **dragnet** because of the unlimited amount of debt that can be secured.

For example, on March 15, a borrower enters into a mortgage loan transaction with a lender wherein the borrower borrows $100,000 to buy a parcel of land. The mortgage given to the lender contains an open-end or dragnet provision that makes the mortgage secure any and all debts between the borrower and the lender. At the time the loan is entered on March 15, the borrower only owes $100,000 to the lender, and therefore, the mortgage only secures $100,000. On August 10 of the same year, the borrower goes to the lender and obtains another loan for an unrelated purpose in the amount of $25,000. The borrower signs a note to evidence the debt, but there is no discussion regarding the mortgage or any amendments to the mortgage. Despite the fact that the note does not refer to the mortgage and there are no amendments to the mortgage, the dragnet or open-end effect of the mortgage causes the mortgage to secure the additional $25,000, for a total of $125,000. Furthermore, any future loans the borrower receives from the lender will be secured by the mortgage.

An open-end or dragnet mortgage can create a problem for the borrower because a default under any of the separate loans secured by the mortgage can give the lender the right to foreclose and have the real property sold. In addition, at the time the mortgage is to be paid and satisfied, the lender can require that all the debt between the borrower and the lender be paid in full before the mortgage is released.

A lender may make separate loans to a borrower secured by separate parcels of property. The lender may feel insecure regarding each loan and require that the property for each loan secure the debt of all the loans. This method of collectively securing all loans by all the mortgages is known as cross-collateralization. Each mortgage, in order to have an effective cross-collateralization, must have an open-end or dragnet clause, which is shown in Example 10–5.

open-end or **dragnet**

Mortgage provision that provides that the mortgage will secure any and all debt between the mortgagor and the mortgagee, including past debt, present debt, and even future debt incurred after the mortgage is signed.

Example 10–5

This mortgage is made and intended to secure all indebtedness now or hereafter owing by Mortgagor to Mortgagee, however or whenever created, incurred, arising or evidenced, whether direct or indirect, joint or several, absolute or contingent, or due or to become due, and any and all renewal or renewals, extension or extensions, modification or modifications or any substitution or substitutions for said indebtedness, either in whole or in part.

Secured Property

Any land or interest in land that can be conveyed by ordinary deed may be conveyed by a mortgage. Real property in a mortgage is described with the same degree of accuracy as in a deed. The description usually is prepared from a land survey. Real property can be added to the mortgage by amendment or modification. The priority of the mortgage with respect to the added real property is determined as of the date of the addition and *not* as of the date of the original mortgage.

For example, a mortgage is given on Tract A on March 15. The priority of the mortgage as to Tract A is determined as of March 15. This means that the mortgage is subject to any outstanding property interests, such as other mortgages or easements, that occur before March 15, but it is superior and senior to any property interests created after March 15. On October 10, Tract B is added by amendment to the mortgage. Even though the mortgage is originally dated March 15, it only has priority, as to Tract B, from October 10. Any easements, mortgages, or other property interests that are created or exist against the Tract B project before October 10 have priority over the mortgage.

Assignment of Mortgage

Mortgages are freely assignable and often are assigned. A person who buys a mortgage may exercise any and all powers contained in the mortgage. A transfer of mortgage conveys the real property and the secured debt, even though both may not be mentioned in the transfer. A transfer of the note usually includes a transfer of the mortgage, and a transfer of the mortgage includes a transfer of the note.

Most mortgages are assigned either by the inclusion of transfer or assignment language on the mortgage or by a separate assignment that is executed by the assigning lender and recorded. An example of an assignment is shown in Example 10–6.

Example 10–6

TRANSFER AND ASSIGNMENT

    FOR VALUE RECEIVED, the undersigned hereby transfers, assigns and conveys unto ___

_____

all of its right, title, interest, powers and options in, to and under the within and foregoing Mortgage as well as the Premises described therein and the Indebtedness (without recourse) secured thereby.

    IN WITNESS WHEREOF the undersigned has caused this transfer and assignment to be executed by its officer and its seal affixed hereto this ___ day of ___, 20___.

Signed, sealed and

delivered in the

presence of:

_____   By: _____

Unofficial Witness   Title: _____

    Attest:_____

_____   Title: _____

Notary Public

        _____(Seal)

Helping Families Save Their Homes Act of 2009, Public Law 111-22 that passed into law May 20, 2009 requires a creditor that purchases or takes by assignment a mortgage loan that is secured by the principal dwelling of the consumer, to provide the consumer within thirty days after the date on which the loan was sold or assigned, a written disclosure notifying the consumer of: (i) the identity, address, and telephone number of the new creditor; (ii) the date of transfer; (iii) how to reach an agent or party having authority to act on behalf of the new creditor; (iv) the location of the place where transfer of ownership of the debt is recorded; and (v) any other relevant information regarding the new creditor.

Transfer of Property Encumbered by a Mortgage

The fact that real property is mortgaged does not in itself prohibit the owner from selling the real property. However, close attention should be paid to the actual mortgage document.

due on sale clause

Clause found in a mortgage that prohibits the sale of the real property described in the mortgage without the lender's consent. A sale in violation of this provision is a default of the mortgage.

A provision known as a **due on sale clause** commonly is found in mortgages. This provision prohibits the sale of real property without the mortgagee's consent. A sale in violation of this provision is a default of the mortgage and could result in a foreclosure of the real property.

Example 10–7 shows a mortgage due on sale provision.

Example 10–7

If all or any part of the property or any interest in it is sold or transferred without mortgagee's prior written consent, mortgagee may, at its option, require immediate payment in full of all sums secured by this mortgage.

When the borrower is not a natural person, but instead is a corporation or a partnership, a lender may have a broadened definition of what constitutes a sale. An example of this type of mortgage due on sale provision is shown in Example 10–8.

Example 10–8

Unless the written consent of mortgagee is first obtained, mortgagee shall have the right, at its option, to declare all sums secured hereby immediately due and payable if (a) mortgagor (by deed or contract of sale or otherwise) sells, conveys, transfers, or further encumbers the mortgaged property or any part thereof; or (b) mortgagor suffers its title or interest therein to be divested, whether voluntarily or involuntarily; or (c) mortgagor changes or permits to be changed the character or use of the mortgaged property; or (d) if mortgagor is a partnership and any of the general partner's interests are transferred or assigned, whether voluntarily or involuntarily to an entity that the general partner of the mortgagor is not also a general partner therein; or (e) if mortgagor is a corporation with fewer than 100 stockholders at the date of execution of this mortgage and more than 10% of the capital stock thereof is sold, transferred, or assigned during a twelve (12)-month period. If any of the events enumerated in (a) through (e) above, inclusive, occurs, and if mortgagee consents to the same or fails to exercise its right to declare all sums secured hereby to be due and payable, such consent or failure shall not be deemed or construed as a waiver, and the consent of mortgagee shall be required on all successive occurrences.

"Subject to" versus "Assumption"

Real property may be sold "subject to" or with an "assumption" of an existing mortgage. A purchaser who buys the real property "subject to" a mortgage does not have personal liability for payment of the debt. The new owner will make the loan payments to protect the real property from foreclosure, but the owner cannot be personally sued to recover on the debt. A lender in a "subject to" sale can foreclose and sell the real property in the event the debt is not paid, and the lender can sue the original mortgagor for payment of the debt because a sale of the real property does not release the original mortgagor.

A purchaser who buys real property and "assumes" the mortgage becomes personally liable for the debt. If the loan is in default, the lender can (a) foreclose on the real property, (b) sue the new owner of the real property who has assumed the debt, and (c) sue the original mortgagor. The express words used in the transfer from the original mortgagor to the new owner are determinative of whether the real property has been sold "subject to" or "assumption of" the mortgage. If the words "assume and agree to pay" appear in the deed or any other document that has been signed in connection with the deed, then there is an assumption, and the new owner becomes personally liable.

The original mortgagor who sells the real property is not released from the obligation to pay the debt and will not be released unless a separate, written release from the mortgagee lender is obtained. This assumption of the loan by the new owner and release of the old owner may constitute a novation. A novation is a substitution of parties to a contract to such an extent that the law declares that a new contract has been entered into. A novation can result in a loss of priority of a mortgage lien. The mortgage lien will be deemed to take priority from the date of the novation, not from its original date. To avoid this problem, a lender usually obtains an endorsement to its title insurance policy insuring that the assumption of the loan and the release of the original borrower will not in any manner affect the priority of the mortgage lien.

If the original mortgagor pays the mortgage in a "subject to" transaction, the mortgagor can recover only against the real property. The original mortgagor is substituted or subrogated in place of the lender and has the right to foreclose on the real property to recover on the debt. If the original mortgagor pays the lender in a "loan assumption" transaction, the original mortgagor can recover the payments by foreclosing against the real property, suing the current owner personally for recovery on the debt, or both, until payment is received in full.

Selling real property subject to a prior mortgage or with an assumption of a prior mortgage is a matter of negotiation between the purchaser and the seller. Purchasing real property subject to a mortgage is to the advantage of the purchaser, and purchasing property with a loan assumption is to the advantage of the seller. A lender benefits if the mortgage is assumed because an additional person is obligated on the debt. If the mortgage contains a due on sale provision and the lender's consent to the sale is necessary, it is not unusual for the lender to require that the purchaser assume the mortgage. The chart shown as Example 10–9 illustrates the different remedies a lender has when property is sold "subject to" or with an "assumption" of a mortgage.

[handwritten marginalia:] purchasing real property is subject to a mortgage is to the advantage of the purchaser, and purchasing property with loan assumption is to the advantage of the seller.

Example 10–9

Sale Subject to Existing Mortgage
- The old borrower (seller) remains liable on the debt secured by the existing mortgage.
- The new owner (purchaser) makes payments on, but is not liable for, the debt secured by the existing mortgage.
- The lender may, if mortgage payments are not paid, foreclose on the property or sue the original borrower (seller) for the unpaid debt. The lender cannot sue the new owner (purchaser) for the debt.

Sale with Assumption of Existing Mortgage
- The old borrower (seller) is not released from liability on the debt secured by the existing mortgage unless an express release of liability is obtained from the mortgage lender.
- The new owner (purchaser) makes payments on the debt secured by the existing mortgage and is liable for the debt secured by the mortgage.
- The lender may, if mortgage payments are not paid, foreclose on the property and sue the new owner (purchaser) and/or the old borrower (seller) for the unpaid debt.

Cancellation or Satisfaction of Mortgage

A mortgage is automatically released by full payment of the debt. Full payment of the debt, however, does not release the mortgage of record, and the mortgagee has a duty to file a cancellation or satisfaction of mortgage in the deed records where the mortgage has been recorded. In many states, failure to satisfy or cancel the mortgage of record can result in imposition of a fine on the mortgage lender. Example 10–10 shows mortgage cancellation or satisfaction.

Example 10–10

Satisfaction

The indebtedness which this instrument was given to secure having been paid in full or other arrangements for payment of the indebtedness having been made to the satisfaction of mortgagee, this instrument is hereby cancelled and the clerk of the Superior court of _____ County _____ is hereby authorized and directed to mark it satisfied of record.

This _____ day of _____, 20_____

By: _____

Title: _____

Second Mortgage Loans

estoppel certificate

A written statement generally signed by the holder of a first mortgage and given to the holder of a second mortgage, swearing as to certain facts concerning the first mortgage loan. The estoppel certificate may also obligate the first mortgage holder to notify the second mortgage holder in the event of a default under the first mortgage loan.

A borrower, unless prohibited by the express terms of the mortgage, can mortgage the real property more than once. In fact, a person can mortgage the real property as many times as a lender is willing to take the real property as security for a loan. Today, it is not unusual for home and commercial properties to have more than one mortgage.

A lender who makes a second mortgage loan assumes some risk. The main risk is that the first mortgage (first in time on the real property and superior to the second mortgage) will not be paid. If the first mortgage is not paid, goes into default, and is foreclosed, the second mortgage will be terminated at the foreclosure sale. It is, therefore, not unusual for second mortgage lenders to receive **estoppel certificates** from the first mortgage lender concerning the nature of the outstanding debt. The estoppel certificate provides that the first mortgage lender will not foreclose the loan without first giving a notice of default to the second mortgage lender and providing the second mortgage lender with time to cure the default. A form of estoppel certificate is shown in Example 10–11.

Example 10–11

STATE OF _____

COUNTY OF _____

ESTOPPEL CERTIFICATE

The undersigned hereby certifies as of the date of execution hereof as follows:

(a) That the undersigned (the "Lender") is the holder of a certain Promissory Note dated _____ from _____, in the original principal amount of $_____ (the "Note").

(b) The Note is secured by a Mortgage from _____ to Lender dated _____ and recorded in Deed Book _____, Page _____, _____ County, _____ located in _____ County, _____ (the "Property") more particularly described on Exhibit "A" attached hereto and made a part hereof;

(c) True and correct copies of the Note and Mortgage are attached hereto as Exhibits "B" and "C";

(d) That the Note and Mortgage are in full force and effect and there have been no events of default in connection therewith;

(e) That all payments of interest and principal under the Note and Mortgage are current; that as of this date, the outstanding principal balance due on the Note is $_____, that the last payment received on the Note was on the _____ day of _____, 20____; and that the next payment is due on _____.

(f) Lender understands that _____ is pledging as security the Property to _____ to secure loans in the collective amount of $_____ (the "Security Conveyance"). The Security Conveyance is hereby consented to and approved and shall not constitute an event of default in connection with the Note or the Mortgage;

(g) That there is no failure of compliance, breach, default, or event of default that has occurred in the Note or the Mortgage as of this date;

(h) Lender agrees to provide to _____, notice of any default under the Note or the Mortgage and to permit _____ thirty (30) days to cure any default under the Note or Mortgage, prior to Lender's acceleration of the Note. _____ at its option, shall have the right to purchase the Note and Mortgage in the event the default cannot be cured.

The undersigned acknowledges that _____ is relying on this certificate.

WITNESS my hand and seal this _____ day of _____, 20_____

_____ (Seal)

Signed, sealed, and delivered
in the presence of:

_____

_____ (Seal)

Witness

_____

Notary Public
Sworn to before me this _____
day of _____, 20_____.
My Commission Expires:

_____

A second mortgage lender also wants to provide in the mortgage that a default under any prior mortgage shall constitute an event of default under the second mortgage. The second mortgage lender wants the right to cure any defaults under a prior mortgage and add the cost of curing the defaults to the debt secured by the second mortgage. The lender of a second mortgage takes the assignment of any excess proceeds that may be generated from the foreclosure and sale of a prior mortgage. An example of a mortgage provision providing these safeguards is shown in Example 10–12.

Example 10–12

This Mortgage is subject to a prior mortgage held by _____ (hereinafter called the "Prior Mortgage"). Mortgagor covenants and agrees that it will at all times fully perform and comply with all agreements, covenants, terms, and conditions imposed on the Mortgagor under the Prior Mortgage, and if Mortgagor fails to do so, Mortgagee may (but shall not be obligated to) declare such failure to be an event of default hereunder and or may take any action Mortgagee deems necessary or desirable to prevent or to cure any default by Mortgagor in the performance and compliance with any of Mortgagor's covenants or obligations under the Prior Mortgage. Any sums of money advanced by Mortgagee to cure Mortgagor's defaults under the Prior Mortgage shall be added to the Indebtedness secured hereby. Mortgagor shall immediately on receiving any knowledge or notice of any default under the Prior Mortgage give written notice to Mortgagee. Mortgagor assigns any proceeds that may belong to Mortgagor resulting from the foreclosure sale of the property by the holder of the Prior Mortgage.

The federal government has also passed laws to assist lenders and homeowners who are in need of a loan modification to avoid foreclosure. The Federal Homeowner Affordability and Stability Plan ("Plan"), under the direction of the Treasury Department, provides access through its refinancing program to low cost financing for certain homeowners who are current on their mortgage payments, but who are unable to refinance their mortgage due to falling home prices. In order to participate in the refinancing program, the mortgage loan must be a first lien on a primary residence and the homeowner must be current in his or her payments. Also, the new mortgage loan, including refinancing costs, cannot exceed 105% of the current market value of the home. In addition, the homeowner must have sufficient income to make the new loan payments.

The Plan also contains a program to provide mortgage loan modifications to homeowners who are in default or at risk of imminent default. In order to participate in the modification program, the homeowner must have a mortgage debt-to-income ratio greater than 31%, and the mortgage balance of the loan must exceed the current market value of the home. The homeowner will not be eligible for modification if the total expected cost of the modification to the lender, taking into account government subsidized payments, is expected to be higher than the direct cost of putting the homeowner through foreclosure.

The objective of the modification program is for a mortgage loan to be modified to a sustainable payment level. A lender is required to reduce the mortgage interest rate until a borrower's monthly mortgage payment falls to at least 38% of the borrower's monthly income. Further reductions of the borrower's interest rate can be shared equally by the lender and the Treasury Department to bring the percentage down from 38% to 31%. The new interest rate must be kept in affect for five (5) years, after which it can be gradually stepped up to the conforming loan interest rate at the time of the modification.

Federal and state government programs to address the rising problems of foreclosures are continuously being passed or being modified. A paralegal working on a residential loan foreclosure will need to carefully research both federal law and his or her own state's law concerning requirements placed upon lenders in the foreclosure process of residential homes.

DEBTOR'S REMEDIES AND DEFENSES TO FORECLOSURE

A debtor may have a number of defenses to a lender's foreclosure action. A debtor may be able to show that the loan was not in default, or that the default had been waived by the lender, or that the default had been cured by timely action of the debtor. A debtor may also defend on the basis that the foreclosure sale is not being conducted in a manner required by law.

If a debtor believes that the foreclosure is not justified, the debtor's main remedies are to seek an injunction of the sale or if the sale has been completed to sue the lender for wrongful foreclosure or conversion. A debtor may also file for bankruptcy, which will temporarily stop the foreclosure sale.

Injunction

If a debtor believes a foreclosure is not justified, the debtor has a right to seek an injunction to stop the sale. Grounds for injunctive relief are, for example, invalidity of debt, absence of default, payment of debt, and improperly conducted sale.

The debtor also may void a sale that has already been held on the same grounds as would support a claim for injunctive relief. In some states, a foreclosure sale can be voided if the property brought an inadequate price at the sale.

🏛 ETHICS: Confidentiality of Client Information

The firm that employs you represents a high-profile real estate developer. The attorney you work for has just informed you that the developer has serious financial problems and has asked you to assist in the attempted restructure of a number of bank loans. That evening your spouse asks you if anything interesting happened at the office. Do you tell your spouse about the developer's financial problems, or do you discuss the upcoming firm's spring picnic?

The practice of law often involves the resolution of a client's most intimate personal problems. The client expects his or her attorney to be a trusted confidant. Without this trust, the client would be reluctant or unwilling to disclose to the attorney all the facts necessary for the attorney to evaluate the client's problem and give legal advice. Ethical considerations, therefore, require an attorney and a paralegal to keep all client information and correspondence confidential. When working on a real estate transaction, the paralegal should not discuss any aspects of the transaction with anyone except other members of the paralegal's law firm.

Sometimes a paralegal will be requested by another party in a real estate transaction to disclose confidential information received from a client. For example, a real estate developer client has had a parcel of property under contract for sale for a number of months. The contract has not closed, and the developer considers the contract to be null and void. The developer has applied for a loan on the property. An attorney or paralegal representing the bank mentions to you that he has heard that the property is under contract for sale and that there may be a lawsuit concerning the contract. They ask you to confirm or deny this rumor. In a situation such as this, it is important to remember that only the client can give permission for the release or disclosure of confidential information. When a request for disclosure is made, the paralegal should not make any disclosures until the matter has been discussed with the supervising attorney. It should be the responsibility of the supervising attorney to contact the client and respond to the request for confidential information.

The keeping of a client's confidence requires not only that the paralegal not discuss confidential matters with third parties, but also that the paralegal keep copies of all confidential letters and other documents out of the sight or view of third parties. It is not wise to bring files home from the office and leave them on tables and countertops in view of neighbors, friends, and visitors.

Suit for Conversion or Wrongful Foreclosure

Foreclosing on real property without the legal right to do so is the tort of **conversion** or wrongful foreclosure. A debtor can sue for conversion and recover not only actual damages, but also punitive damages from the foreclosing lender. Generally, the damages for wrongful foreclosure is the value of the debtor's equity in the foreclosed property. For example, if the home that is being foreclosed has a market value of $400,000 and the unpaid balance of the debt secured by the mortgage is $300,000, then the damages for wrongful foreclosure would be $100,000, the value of the debtor's equity.

conversion

Act of taking a person's property without a legal right to do so.

Bankruptcy

Bankruptcy is the debtor's main defense to a foreclosure because the filing of a bankruptcy petition has the effect of an automatic injunction stopping the foreclosure sale.

Bankruptcy law is federal law designed to protect debtors and to give debtors a fresh start. Bankruptcy petitions can be filed voluntarily or involuntarily. Once the bankruptcy petition is filed, the act of filing the petition operates as an automatic injunction, commonly called an "automatic stay," of all litigation against the debtor and efforts to collect claims or enforce liens against the debtor's property, including foreclosure sales. This automatic stay remains in force throughout the bankruptcy proceeding and is not terminated until the case is either closed or dismissed or the debtor's discharge is granted or denied. A creditor, such as a mortgage lender, who wants to seek relief from the automatic stay can bring an action in the bankruptcy court requesting that the court remove the injunction so that the mortgage lender can foreclose against the real property. The grounds for lifting the automatic stay in a bankruptcy proceeding are as follows:

- The mortgage holder is not being "adequately protected" within the bankruptcy proceeding. Loosely defined, this term means that the mortgage security is declining in value in the bankruptcy proceeding. Adequate protection can be achieved by requiring the debtor to maintain the property or make payments on the mortgage loan, keep the property insured, and so on.

- The debtor has no equity interest in the real property (the value of the property is equal to or less than the amount of the debt). For example, an apartment building securing a mortgage loan has a market value of $850,000, but the outstanding balance on the mortgage loan, including accrued and unpaid interest, is $950,000. Since the debt secured by the property exceeds the value of the property, a debtor would not receive any money in the event the property was sold at its fair market value. The debtor in this situation is deemed to have no equity interest in the property.

- The real property is not necessary to an effective reorganization or liquidation of the debtor's estate. For example, the bankrupt debtor is an apartment owner who has four apartment buildings. Three of the apartment buildings are fully rented and generate income that exceeds the expenses incurred in connection with the operation of the apartment building. The fourth building is largely vacant, and the income produced from the rent does not even pay insurance premiums, taxes, and other expenses in connection with the property. This building, because it is a financial drain on the debtor, would not be a property deemed necessary to the effective reorganization of the debtor's estate.

The burden of proof is on the debtor to prove that the stay should remain in full force and effect. The issue of whether the debtor's real property is equal to or less than the value of the debt is an evidentiary burden of the creditor.

SUMMARY

The basic loan documents used to secure a real estate loan are a note and a security instrument, generally referred to as a mortgage. The note is the promise to pay money and is the main document that evidences and enforces the payment of the debt. All notes are written and generally set forth the amount of the debt, the interest rate payable on the debt, and the payment terms for the debt. On some loan transactions, the payment of the note may be secured by a separate loan document known as a guaranty. A guaranty is the promise to pay the debt of another person. For example, an individual majority shareholder of a corporation may promise to pay the debt of a loan made to the corporation. The corporation would sign the note in connection with the debt, and the individual majority shareholder would sign a guaranty promising to pay the note in the event the corporation did not pay.

The companion document to a note on a real estate transaction is the security instrument that conveys or grants an interest in real property to secure the payment of the note.

Depending on where in the country the loan originated, this security instrument may be a mortgage, deed of trust, or deed to secure debt. Although each instrument varies slightly in form and in operation, all perform the same function of conveying an interest in real property and securing the repayment of the note. Failure to pay the note could result in the property being sold or foreclosed by the lender for purposes of paying the note. Although the legal concepts behind a note and mortgage are simple, the actual forms in many instances are complex and vary in format from state to state. Paralegals are actively involved in the preparation of mortgage loan documents and assist attorneys in the mortgage loan closing process.

It is important that the paralegal be familiar with the different forms used in the state in which he or she practices and that the paralegal be aware of the many provisions that can be included in these forms. A more thorough discussion of loan documents and mortgage provisions follows in Chapter 11.

HELPFUL WEBSITES

State Foreclosure Laws
Summaries of each state's foreclosure laws can be found on a number of Web sites such as *http://www.foreclosures.com*, *http://www.realtytrac.com/foreclosure-laws/foreclosure-laws-comparison.asp*, and *http://www.foreclosureuniversity.com*.

KEY TERMS

conversion
deed of trust
deed to secure debt
due on sale clause
endorsement
estoppel certificate
foreclosure
guarantor

guaranty
holder
interpleader
maker
mortgage
mortgagee
mortgagor
negotiable note

open-end or dragnet
payee
power of sale
promissory note
receiver
redemption
usury

REVIEW QUESTIONS

1. Why is the negotiability of a promissory note important?

2. Explain the endorsement process, with its accompanying contractual and warranty liabilities.

3. What is an open-end or dragnet mortgage?

4. What is the importance of being a holder in due course?

5. What is the difference between purchasing real property subject to a mortgage and assuming a mortgage?

6. What risks are inherent in second mortgage loans?

7. What is the difference between a promissory note and a guaranty?

8. What is the difference between a judicial and a nonjudicial power of sale foreclosure?

9. Why is bankruptcy a good debtor's defense to a foreclosure?

10. What remedies other than foreclosure are available to a real estate lender in the event of a default?

CASE PROBLEMS

1. Margo Maker executed and delivered a negotiable promissory note for $10,000 to Acme Bank and Trust. The note, while in Acme's possession, was altered from $10,000 to $100,000. Acme sold the altered note to Wherever Life Insurance Company for $95,000. The endorsement from Acme to Wherever is without recourse. Wherever Life Insurance Company then sells the note to Harrison Holder for $95,000. Wherever's endorsement to Harrison Holder is without recourse and warranty. At maturity, Harrison Holder presents the note to Margo Maker for payment. Can Harrison Holder recover $100,000 from Margo Maker? Does Harrison Holder have a right to recover against Acme Bank and Trust? Does Harrison Holder have a right to recover against Wherever Life Insurance Company?

2. You are a paralegal assisting in the representation of a maker of a negotiable promissory note. The maker wants to pay the note in full and has asked you to obtain the original note marked "paid and satisfied" from the holder of the note. On contact with the holder of the note, you learn that the holder cannot find the original note, claiming that it has been lost. Would you advise the maker of the note to pay the holder anyway?

3. You are assisting in the representation of a lending institution as the holder of a promissory note from the Good Earth Land Company. The note is personally guaranteed by the principal shareholder of Good Earth Land Company, Gooden Earth. The note is being modified to extend the final term for repayment for an additional five (5) years. Is there documentation that you should receive from Gooden Earth in regard to this extension of the note?

4. Ruth Thomas owns a home that has been pledged to First Bank and Trust to secure a mortgage debt of $60,000. Ruth Thomas sells her home to John Kendall, who purchases the home and assumes the mortgage held by First Bank and Trust. John Kendall subsequently sells the home to Mark Murphy, who purchases the home subject to the First Bank and Trust loan. The First Bank and Trust loan goes into default. Can First Bank and Trust Company foreclose on the home? Can First Bank and Trust Company sue Mark Murphy for the debt? Can First Bank and Trust Company sue John Kendall for the debt? Can First Bank and Trust Company sue Ruth Thomas for the debt? In the event Ruth Thomas pays the bank in full, what remedies does she have against John Kendall or Mark Murphy or against the real property?

5. You are assisting a mortgage lender who specializes in making second mortgage loans to homeowners. You have been requested to prepare an estoppel certificate to be signed by the first mortgagee on the home. What types of things would you include in the estoppel certificate to be signed by the first mortgagee?

6. You are a paralegal working for a law firm that represents a lender who specializes in making second mortgage loans. You have been asked to prepare some special stipulations to be contained in the lender's mortgages to protect them against possible problems caused by the first mortgage holders on the secured properties. What types of provisions would you be including in the second mortgage documents?

7. You are a paralegal working for a law firm that represents a large shopping center developer. The developer has come to the firm with a problem with one of its major lenders. It appears that the lender is foreclosing on one of the shopping centers. The developer insists that the loan is not in default and that the foreclosure is being made because of some bad feelings between the developer and the lender. What types of actions can the developer take to stop the foreclosure sale?

8. You are working for a law firm that represents a lender who specializes in second mortgage loans. It has come to your attention that the holder of a first mortgage on one of the properties securing this lender's loans has commenced foreclosure proceedings. Should the second mortgage lender be concerned? If so, what steps could the second mortgage lender take to protect its interest in the property?

9. You are a paralegal in a law firm that handles foreclosures for mortgage lenders. You are attending a power of sale foreclosure. The bidder at the sale bids and buys the property for $100,000 more than the debt owed to the foreclosing lender. You are standing there with the $100,000 in hand and are approached by an individual. The individual tells you that he has a second mortgage on the property in the amount of $50,000 and that he is entitled to that amount of the excess proceeds. Should you give this person the money? What should you do with the excess money?

PRACTICAL ASSIGNMENTS

1. You are a paralegal working for a law firm that represents the American Eagle Mortgage Company. American Eagle Mortgage Company is making a real estate mortgage loan to Constance Morton and Samuel Morton. The amount of the loan is $75,500 payable at an annual interest rate of 8 percent per annum over a period of 30 years. The monthly payment of $553.95 is due and payable on the first day of each month. The note is to be signed on February 23, 20____, with the first payment being due and payable on April 1, 20____. American Eagle Mortgage Company charges a late fee equivalent to 5 percent of the overdue payment if the payment is more than 10 days late. American Eagle Mortgage Company's address is 1050 Cumberland Circle, Anytown, United States 27333.

The purpose of the loan is to enable the Mortons to purchase a home located at 1000 Riverview, Anytown, United States 27333. The legal description for the home is as follows:

All that tract or parcel of land lying and being in Land Lot 6 of the 8th District of Madison County, Your State, and being more particularly described as Lot 3, Block A, Riverview Subdivision, as shown on plat of subdivision recorded at Plat Book 23, Page 19, Madison County, Your State Records.

Prepare a note and deed to secure debt for this loan transaction. You may either use Exhibits 10–1 and 10–7 found at the end of this chapter as forms or the appropriate note and security instruments used in your state as the forms.

2. Research your state's method of foreclosure of a mortgage. Is it a judicial proceeding or a nonjudicial proceeding? Prepare a brief memorandum discussing the procedures for the foreclosure of a mortgage. Attach as an addendum any statutory or case authority you were able to find through your research.

3. Research the usury statutes of your state. Write a brief report indicating the maximum rate of interest that can be charged under these statutes for a mortgage loan. Attach copies of the statutes used to form the conclusions set forth in the report.

4. Research your state's law to determine if it recognizes post-foreclosure redemption rights for mortgagors. If so, what is the redemption price that must be paid? What is the period of time for redemption following a foreclosure sale? Can a right of redemption be waived prior to the foreclosure sale? Can it be waived after the foreclosure sale?

5. Research your state's law to see if there have been any recent statutes passed that limit the rights of lenders to foreclose residential mortgages. Copy the provisions of these laws and discuss in class.

ADDENDUM

Exhibit 10–1 Fannie Mae/Freddie Mac Residential Fixed-Rate Note

Exhibit 10–2 Fannie Mae/Freddie Mac Residential Adjustable-Rate Note

Exhibit 10–3 Commercial Loan Note

Exhibit 10–4 Payment Guaranty

Exhibit 10–5 Florida Mortgage

Exhibit 10–6 North Carolina Deed of Trust

Exhibit 10–7 Georgia Commercial Deed to Secure Debt

Student StudyWare™ CD-ROM

Interactive Student CD in the book includes additional quizzing, case studies, and key terms flashcards.

Online Companion™

For additional resources, please go to *www.paralegal.delmar.cengage.com*

EXHIBIT 10–1

Fannie Mae/Freddie Mac Residential Fixed-Rate Note

_____, _____   _____, _____
              [Date]   [City]   [State]

_____
                   [Property Address]

1. BORROWER'S PROMISE TO PAY

In return for a loan that I have received, I promise to pay U.S. $_____ (this amount is called "Principal"), plus interest, to the order of the Lender. The Lender is _____
_____. I will make all payments under this Note in the form of cash, check or money order.

I understand that the Lender may transfer this Note. The Lender or anyone who takes this Note by transfer and who is entitled to receive payments under this Note is called the "Note Holder."

2. INTEREST

Interest will be charged on unpaid principal until the full amount of Principal has been paid. I will pay interest at a yearly rate of _____%.

The interest rate required by this Section 2 is the rate I will pay both before and after any default described in Section 6(B) of this Note.

3. PAYMENTS

(A) Time and Place of Payments

I will pay principal and interest by making a payment every month.

I will make my monthly payment on the _____ day of each month beginning on _____, _____. I will make these payments every month until I have paid all of the principal and interest and any other charges described below that I may owe under this Note. Each monthly payment will be applied as of its scheduled due date and will be applied to interest before Principal. If, on _____, 20____, I still owe amounts under this Note, I will pay those amounts in full on that date, which is called the "Maturity Date."

I will make my monthly payments at _____
_____ or at a different place if required by the Note Holder.

(B) Amount of Monthly Payments

My monthly payment will be in the amount of U.S. $_____.

4. BORROWER'S RIGHT TO PREPAY

I have the right to make payments of Principal at any time before they are due. A payment of Principal only is known as a "Prepayment." When I make a Prepayment, I will tell the Note Holder in writing that I am doing so. I may not designate a payment as a Prepayment if I have not made all the monthly payments due under the Note.

I may make a full Prepayment or partial Prepayments without paying a Prepayment charge. The Note Holder will use my Prepayments to reduce the amount of Principal that I owe under this Note. However, the Note Holder may apply my Prepayment to the accrued and unpaid interest on the Prepayment amount, before applying my Prepayment to reduce the Principal amount of the Note. If I make a partial Prepayment, there will be no changes in the due date or in the amount of my monthly payment unless the Note Holder agrees in writing to those changes.

5. LOAN CHARGES

If a law, which applies to this loan and which sets maximum loan charges, is finally interpreted so that the interest or other loan charges collected or to be collected in connection with this loan exceed the permitted limits, then: (a) any such loan charge shall be reduced by the amount necessary to reduce the charge to the permitted limit; and (b) any sums already collected from me which exceeded permitted limits will be refunded to me. The Note Holder may choose to make this refund by reducing the Principal I owe under this Note or by making a direct payment to me. If a refund reduces Principal, the reduction will be treated as a partial Prepayment.

Delmar/Cengage Learning

(continued)

EXHIBIT 10–1

Fannie Mae/Freddie Mac Residential Fixed-Rate Note (continued)

---

6. BORROWER'S FAILURE TO PAY AS REQUIRED

(A) Late Charge for Overdue Payments

If the Note Holder has not received the full amount of any monthly payment by the end of _____ calendar days after the date it is due, I will pay a late charge to the Note Holder. The amount of the charge will be _____% of my overdue payment of principal and interest. I will pay this late charge promptly but only once on each late payment.

(B) Default

If I do not pay the full amount of each monthly payment on the date it is due, I will be in default.

(C) Notice of Default

If I am in default, the Note Holder may send me a written notice telling me that if I do not pay the overdue amount by a certain date, the Note Holder may require me to pay immediately the full amount of Principal which has not been paid and all the interest that I owe on that amount. That date must be at least 30 days after the date on which the notice is mailed to me or delivered by other means.

(D) No Waiver By Note Holder

Even if, at a time when I am in default, the Note Holder does not require me to pay immediately in full as described above, the Note Holder will still have the right to do so if I am in default at a later time.

(E) Payment of Note Holder's Costs and Expenses

If the Note Holder has required me to pay immediately in full as described above, the Note Holder will have the right to be paid back by me for all of its costs and expenses in enforcing this Note to the extent not prohibited by applicable law. Those expenses include, for example, reasonable attorneys' fees.

7. GIVING OF NOTICES

Unless applicable law requires a different method, any notice that must be given to me under this Note will be given by delivering it or by mailing it by first class mail to me at the Property Address above or at a different address if I give the Note Holder a notice of my different address.

Any notice that must be given to the Note Holder under this Note will be given by delivering it or by mailing it by first class mail to the Note Holder at the address stated in Section 3(A) above or at a different address if I am given a notice of that different address.

8. OBLIGATIONS OF PERSONS UNDER THIS NOTE

If more than one person signs this Note, each person is fully and personally obligated to keep all of the promises made in this Note, including the promise to pay the full amount owed. Any person who is a guarantor, surety or endorser of this Note is also obligated to do these things. Any person who takes over these obligations, including the obligations of a guarantor, surety or endorser of this Note, is also obligated to keep all of the promises made in this Note. The Note Holder may enforce its rights under this Note against each person individually or against all of us together. This means that any one of us may be required to pay all of the amounts owed under this Note.

9. WAIVERS

I and any other person who has obligations under this Note waive the rights of Presentment and Notice of Dishonor. "Presentment" means the right to require the Note Holder to demand payment of amounts due. "Notice of Dishonor" means the right to require the Note Holder to give notice to other persons that amounts due have not been paid.

10. UNIFORM SECURED NOTE

This Note is a uniform instrument with limited variations in some jurisdictions. In addition to the protections given to the Note Holder under this Note, a Mortgage, Deed of Trust, or Security Deed (the "Security Instrument"), dated the same date as this Note, protects the Note Holder from possible losses which might result if I do not keep the promises which I make in this Note. That Security Instrument describes how and under what conditions I may be required to make immediate payment in full of all amounts I owe under this Note. Some of those conditions are described as follows:

> If all or any part of the Property or any Interest in the Property is sold or transferred (or if Borrower is not a natural person and a beneficial interest in Borrower is sold or transferred) without Lender's prior written consent, Lender may require immediate payment in full of all sums secured by this Security Instrument. However, this option shall not be exercised by Lender if such exercise is prohibited by Applicable Law.

MULTISTATE FIXED RATE NOTE—Single Family—Fannie Mae/Freddie Mac UNIFORM INSTRUMENT   **Form 3200   1/01** *(page 2 of 3 pages)*

(continued)

EXHIBIT 10–1

Fannie Mae/Freddie Mac Residential Fixed-Rate Note (*continued*)

If Lender exercises this option, Lender shall give Borrower notice of acceleration. The notice shall provide a period of not less than 30 days from the date the notice is given in accordance with Section 15 within which Borrower must pay all sums secured by this Security Instrument. If Borrower fails to pay these sums prior to the expiration of this period, Lender may invoke any remedies permitted by this Security Instrument without further notice or demand on Borrower.

WITNESS THE HAND(S) AND SEAL(S) OF THE UNDERSIGNED

_____ (Seal)
                                                    - Borrower

_____ (Seal)
                                                    - Borrower

_____ (Seal)
                                                    - Borrower

[Sign Original Only]

MULTISTATE FIXED RATE NOTE—Single Family—**Fannie Mae/Freddie Mac UNIFORM INSTRUMENT**   **Form 3200** **1/01** *(page 3 of 3 pages)*

EXHIBIT 10–2

Fannie Mae/Freddie Mac Residential Adjustable-Rate Note

ADJUSTABLE RATE NOTE
(1 Year Treasury Index -- Rate Caps)

THIS NOTE CONTAINS PROVISIONS ALLOWING FOR CHANGES IN MY
INTEREST RATE AND MY MONTHLY PAYMENT. THIS NOTE LIMITS THE
AMOUNT MY INTEREST RATE CAN CHANGE AT ANY ONE TIME AND THE
MAXIMUM RATE I MUST PAY.

_____, _____   _____, _____
      [Date]   [City]   [State]

_____
[Property Address]

1. BORROWER'S PROMISE TO PAY

In return for a loan that I have received, I promise to pay U.S. $_____ (this amount is called "Principal"), plus interest, to the order of the Lender. The Lender is _____ _____. I will make all payments under this Note in the form of cash, check or money order.

I understand that the Lender may transfer this Note. The Lender or anyone who takes this Note by transfer and who is entitled to receive payments under this Note is called the "Note Holder."

2. INTEREST

Interest will be charged on unpaid principal until the full amount of Principal has been paid. I will pay interest at a yearly rate of _____%. The interest rate I will pay will change in accordance with Section 4 of this Note.

The interest rate required by this Section 2 and Section 4 of this Note is the rate I will pay both before and after any default described in Section 7(B) of this Note.

3. PAYMENTS

(A) Time and Place of Payments

I will pay principal and interest by making a payment every month.

I will make my monthly payment on the first day of each month beginning on _____, _____. I will make these payments every month until I have paid all of the principal and interest and any other charges described below that I may owe under this Note. Each monthly payment will be applied as of its scheduled due date and will be applied to interest before Principal. If, on _____, 20____, I still owe amounts under this Note, I will pay those amounts in full on that date, which is called the "Maturity Date."

I will make my monthly payments at _____
_____ or at a different place if required by the Note Holder.

(B) Amount of My Initial Monthly Payments

Each of my initial monthly payments will be in the amount of U.S. $_____. This amount may change.

(C) Monthly Payment Changes

Changes in my monthly payment will reflect changes in the unpaid principal of my loan and in the interest rate that I must pay. The Note Holder will determine my new interest rate and the changed amount of my monthly payment in accordance with Section 4 of this Note.

4. INTEREST RATE AND MONTHLY PAYMENT CHANGES

(A) Change Dates

The interest rate I will pay may change on the first day of _____, _____, and on that day every 12th month thereafter. Each date on which my interest rate could change is called a "Change Date."

(B) The Index

Beginning with the first Change Date, my interest rate will be based on an Index. The "Index" is the weekly average yield on United States Treasury securities adjusted to a constant maturity of one year, as made available by the Federal Reserve Board. The most recent Index figure available as of the date 45 days before each Change Date is called the "Current Index."

If the Index is no longer available, the Note Holder will choose a new index which is based upon comparable information. The Note Holder will give me notice of this choice.

MULTISTATE ADJUSTABLE RATE NOTE--ARM 5-1--Single Family--Fannie Mae/Freddie Mac UNIFORM INSTRUMENT   Form 3501 1/01 *(page 1 of 4 pages)*

Delmar/Cengage Learning

(continued)

EXHIBIT 10–2

Fannie Mae/Freddie Mac Residential Adjustable-Rate Note (*continued*)

(C) Calculation of Changes

Before each Change Date, the Note Holder will calculate my new interest rate by adding _____ _____ percentage points (_____%) to the Current Index. The Note Holder will then round the result of this addition to the nearest one-eighth of one percentage point (0.125%). Subject to the limits stated in Section 4(D) below, this rounded amount will be my new interest rate until the next Change Date.

The Note Holder will then determine the amount of the monthly payment that would be sufficient to repay the unpaid principal that I am expected to owe at the Change Date in full on the Maturity Date at my new interest rate in substantially equal payments. The result of this calculation will be the new amount of my monthly payment.

(D) Limits on Interest Rate Changes

The interest rate I am required to pay at the first Change Date will not be greater than _____% or less than _____%. Thereafter, my interest rate will never be increased or decreased on any single Change Date by more than one percentage point (1.0%) from the rate of interest I have been paying for the preceding 12 months. My interest rate will never be greater than _____%.

(E) Effective Date of Changes

My new interest rate will become effective on each Change Date. I will pay the amount of my new monthly payment beginning on the first monthly payment date after the Change Date until the amount of my monthly payment changes again.

(F) Notice of Changes

The Note Holder will deliver or mail to me a notice of any changes in my interest rate and the amount of my monthly payment before the effective date of any change. The notice will include information required by law to be given to me and also the title and telephone number of a person who will answer any question I may have regarding the notice.

5. BORROWER'S RIGHT TO PREPAY

I have the right to make payments of Principal at any time before they are due. A payment of Principal only is known as a "Prepayment." When I make a Prepayment, I will tell the Note Holder in writing that I am doing so. I may not designate a payment as a Prepayment if I have not made all the monthly payments due under the Note.

I may make a full Prepayment or partial Prepayments without paying a Prepayment charge. The Note Holder will use my Prepayments to reduce the amount of Principal that I owe under this Note. However, the Note Holder may apply my Prepayment to the accrued and unpaid interest on the Prepayment amount, before applying my Prepayment to reduce the Principal amount of the Note. If I make a partial Prepayment, there will be no changes in the due dates of my monthly payment unless the Note Holder agrees in writing to those changes. My partial Prepayment may reduce the amount of my monthly payments after the first Change Date following my partial Prepayment. However, any reduction due to my partial Prepayment may be offset by an interest rate increase.

6. LOAN CHARGES

If a law, which applies to this loan and which sets maximum loan charges, is finally interpreted so that the interest or other loan charges collected or to be collected in connection with this loan exceed the permitted limits, then: (a) any such loan charge shall be reduced by the amount necessary to reduce the charge to the permitted limit; and (b) any sums already collected from me which exceeded permitted limits will be refunded to me. The Note Holder may choose to make this refund by reducing the Principal I owe under this Note or by making a direct payment to me. If a refund reduces Principal, the reduction will be treated as a partial Prepayment.

7. BORROWER'S FAILURE TO PAY AS REQUIRED

(A) Late Charges for Overdue Payments

If the Note Holder has not received the full amount of any monthly payment by the end of _____ calendar days after the date it is due, I will pay a late charge to the Note Holder. The amount of the charge will be _____% of my overdue payment of principal and interest. I will pay this late charge promptly but only once on each late payment.

(B) Default

If I do not pay the full amount of each monthly payment on the date it is due, I will be in default.

(C) Notice of Default

If I am in default, the Note Holder may send me a written notice telling me that if I do not pay the overdue amount by a certain date, the Note Holder may require me to pay immediately the full amount of Principal which has not been paid and all the interest that I owe on that amount. That date must be at least 30 days after the date on which the notice is mailed to me or delivered by other means.

(D) No Waiver By Note Holder

Even if, at a time when I am in default, the Note Holder does not require me to pay immediately in full as described above, the Note Holder will still have the right to do so if I am in default at a later time.

(E) Payment of Note Holder's Costs and Expenses

If the Note Holder has required me to pay immediately in full as described above, the Note Holder will have the right

MULTISTATE ADJUSTABLE RATE NOTE--ARM 5-1--Single Family--Fannie Mae/Freddie Mac UNIFORM INSTRUMENT   **Form 3501 1/01** (*page 2 of 4 pages*)

(continued)

EXHIBIT 10–2

Fannie Mae/Freddie Mac Residential Adjustable-Rate Note (*continued*)

to be paid back by me for all of its costs and expenses in enforcing this Note to the extent not prohibited by applicable law. Those expenses include, for example, reasonable attorneys' fees.

8. GIVING OF NOTICES

Unless applicable law requires a different method, any notice that must be given to me under this Note will be given by delivering it or by mailing it by first class mail to me at the Property Address above or at a different address if I give the Note Holder a notice of my different address.

Any notice that must be given to the Note Holder under this Note will be given by delivering it or by mailing it by first class mail to the Note Holder at the address stated in Section 3(A) above or at a different address if I am given a notice of that different address.

9. OBLIGATIONS OF PERSONS UNDER THIS NOTE

If more than one person signs this Note, each person is fully and personally obligated to keep all of the promises made in this Note, including the promise to pay the full amount owed. Any person who is a guarantor, surety or endorser of this Note is also obligated to do these things. Any person who takes over these obligations, including the obligations of a guarantor, surety or endorser of this Note, is also obligated to keep all of the promises made in this Note. The Note Holder may enforce its rights under this Note against each person individually or against all of us together. This means that any one of us may be required to pay all of the amounts owed under this Note.

10. WAIVERS

I and any other person who has obligations under this Note waive the rights of Presentment and Notice of Dishonor. "Presentment" means the right to require the Note Holder to demand payment of amounts due. "Notice of Dishonor" means the right to require the Note Holder to give notice to other persons that amounts due have not been paid.

11. UNIFORM SECURED NOTE

This Note is a uniform instrument with limited variations in some jurisdictions. In addition to the protections given to the Note Holder under this Note, a Mortgage, Deed of Trust, or Security Deed (the "Security Instrument"), dated the same date as this Note, protects the Note Holder from possible losses which might result if I do not keep the promises which I make in this Note. That Security Instrument describes how and under what conditions I may be required to make immediate payment in full of all amounts I owe under this Note. Some of those conditions are described as follows:

If all or any part of the Property or any Interest in the Property is sold or transferred (or if Borrower is not a natural person and a beneficial interest in Borrower is sold or transferred) without Lender's prior written consent, Lender may require immediate payment in full of all sums secured by this Security Instrument. However, this option shall not be exercised by Lender if such exercise is prohibited by Applicable Law. Lender also shall not exercise this option if: (a) Borrower causes to be submitted to Lender information required by Lender to evaluate the intended transferee as if a new loan were being made to the transferee; and (b) Lender reasonably determines that Lender's security will not be impaired by the loan assumption and that the risk of a breach of any covenant or agreement in this Security Instrument is acceptable to Lender.

To the extent permitted by Applicable Law, Lender may charge a reasonable fee as a condition to Lender's consent to the loan assumption. Lender may also require the transferee to sign an assumption agreement that is acceptable to Lender and that obligates the transferee to keep all the promises and agreements made in the Note and in this Security Instrument. Borrower will continue to be obligated under the Note and this Security Instrument unless Lender releases Borrower in writing.

MULTISTATE ADJUSTABLE RATE NOTE--ARM 5-1--Single Family--Fannie Mae/Freddie Mac UNIFORM INSTRUMENT   Form 3501 1/01 (*page 3 of 4 pages*)

(continued)

EXHIBIT 10–2

Fannie Mae/Freddie Mac Residential Adjustable-Rate Note (*continued*)

If Lender exercises the option to require immediate payment in full, Lender shall give Borrower notice of acceleration. The notice shall provide a period of not less than 30 days from the date the notice is given in accordance with Section 15 within which Borrower must pay all sums secured by this Security Instrument. If Borrower fails to pay these sums prior to the expiration of this period, Lender may invoke any remedies permitted by this Security Instrument without further notice or demand on Borrower.

WITNESS THE HAND(S) AND SEAL(S) OF THE UNDERSIGNED.

_____ (Seal)
                                             -Borrower

_____ (Seal)
                                             -Borrower

_____ (Seal)
                                             -Borrower

[Sign Original Only]

MULTISTATE ADJUSTABLE RATE NOTE--ARM 5-1--Single Family--Fannie Mae/Freddie Mac UNIFORM INSTRUMENT   **Form 3501 1/01** *(page 4 of 4 pages)*

EXHIBIT 10–3

Commercial Loan Note

$1,600,000.00

(City), (State)
September 14, 20____

REAL ESTATE NOTE

FOR VALUE RECEIVED, the undersigned HARRIS OFFICE PARK LIMITED PARTNERSHIP, an Ohio limited partnership, hereinafter referred to as "Borrower," promises to pay to the order of WHEREVER INSURANCE COMPANY, an Ohio corporation, hereinafter referred to as "Payee," at the main office of Payee located at _____ _____, or at such other place as Payee shall designate in writing, in lawful money of the United States of America which shall at the time of payment be legal tender for payment of all debts, public and private, the principal sum of ONE MILLION SIX HUNDRED THOUSAND AND NO/100 DOLLARS ($1,600,000.00), together with interest thereon at the rate of ten and one-half percent (10.50%) per annum in two hundred seventy-six (276) consecutive monthly installments, installments 1 to 275 both inclusive, being for the sum of FIFTEEN THOUSAND THREE HUNDRED EIGHTY NINE AND 88/100 DOLLARS ($15,389.88) each, and installment number 276 being for the balance of the principal and interest then owing.

Interest only on the outstanding principal balance of the indebtedness shall be due and payable on October 1, 20____ and the first of said monthly amortized installments of principal and interest shall be due and payable on November 1, 20____, and continue to be due and payable on the first day of each month thereafter, with the final installment of all unpaid principal and unpaid and accrued interest, unless sooner paid, being due and payable on the 1st day of October, 20 ____. Each such amortized installment of principal and interest, when paid, shall be applied first to the payment of interest accrued on the unpaid principal balance and the residue thereof shall be applied toward the payment of principal.

Notwithstanding anything contained in this note to the contrary, Payee shall have the right, at its sole option and discretion, to declare the entire outstanding principal balance of this note and all accrued and unpaid interest thereon to be due and payable in full at the end of the seventh (7th), twelfth (12th), seventeenth (17th), or twenty-second (22nd) Loan Years (hereinafter defined) and each date is hereinafter referred to as a "Call Date". Payee shall give notice of the exercise of such option to Borrower at least six (6) months in advance. In the event Payee shall elect to so declare this note due, then this note shall be and become due and payable in full on the due date of the eighty-fourth (84th), one hundred forty-fourth (144th), two hundred fourth (204th), or two hundred sixty-fourth (264th) installment of principal and interest due hereunder, depending upon whether or not Payee elects to declare this note due, and upon which Call Date Payee exercises the option to declare this Note due. No prepayment premium as hereinafter described shall be due and payable if this Note is prepaid because of Payee's exercise of its rights to declare the Note due pursuant to this paragraph.

Late Charge. Borrower shall pay a late charge of four percent (4%) of any payment of principal and interest which is not paid within fifteen (15) days of the due date thereof. The collection of any such late charge by Payee shall not be deemed a waiver by Payee of any of its rights hereunder or under any document or instrument given to secure this note. During the entire term of this note, Borrower shall pay all costs of collection, including reasonable attorney's fees not to exceed fifteen percent (15%) of the principal and interest due, if collected by or through an attorney-at-law.

Prepayment Privilege. This note may not be prepaid in whole or in part except as herein specifically provided. No prepayment of the principal of this note shall be permitted or allowed prior to the end of the third (3rd) Loan Year, as hereinafter defined. After the end of the third (3rd) Loan Year, this note may be prepaid in whole, but not in part, upon any principal and interest payment date as provided herein, provided that (a) no later than sixty (60) days prior to the date of such prepayment, Borrower delivers written notice to Payee, that Borrower intends to prepay the note in full on the date specified in the notice; and (b) Borrower pays to Payee at

Delmar/Cengage Learning

(continued)

EXHIBIT 10–3

Commercial Loan Note
(*continued*)

the time of such prepayment, a percentage of the prepaid principal amount of the indebtedness as a prepayment premium. The amount of the prepayment premium shall be the product obtained by multiplying the prepaid principal amount of the indebtedness by the product of the following: (i) the amount obtained by subtracting the annualized yield on a United States Treasury Bill, Note or Bond with a maturity date which occurs closest to the next applicable Call Date of this note, as such annualized yield is reported by *The Wall Street Journal*, on the business day preceding the date of prepayment, from 10.50% multiplied by: (ii) the number of years and any fraction thereof remaining between the date of prepayment and the next applicable Call Date of this note.

Notwithstanding the foregoing, however, in the event of acceleration of this note at any time, including the period of time prior to the end of the third (3rd) Loan Year, and subsequent involuntary or voluntary prepayment, the prepayment premium as calculated above shall be payable, however, in no event shall it exceed an amount equal to the excess, if any, of (i) interest calculated at the highest applicable rate permitted by applicable law, as construed by courts having jurisdiction thereof, on the principal balance of the indebtedness evidenced by this note from time to time outstanding from the date hereof to the date of such acceleration; over (ii) interest theretofore paid and accrued on this note. Any prepaid amounts specified in any notice shall become due and payable at the time provided in such notice. Under no circumstances shall the prepayment premium ever be less than zero. The amount of prepayment shall never be less than the full amount of the then outstanding principal indebtedness and accrued interest thereon.

A Loan Year for the purposes of this note shall mean each successive twelve (12) month period, beginning with the date of the first installment payment of principal and interest hereunder, provided, however, that the first (1st) Loan Year shall include the period from the date of this note to the date of such first installment payment of principal and interest.

Borrower further agrees to pay in addition to the above-described prepayment premium, a reinvestment fee of one-half of one (1/2%) percent of the outstanding prepaid principal indebtedness evidenced by this note to Payee. Borrower agrees that the reinvestment fee together with the prepayment premium shall be due and payable regardless of whether the prepayment is made involuntarily or voluntarily.

Collateral. This note is secured by, among other instruments, (i) a Deed of Trust of even date herewith executed by Borrower in favor of Payee (the "Security Deed"), conveying and covering certain real property lying and being in Land Lot 50 of the 17th District, of Simkin County, Ohio, as the same is more particularly described in the Security Deed (the "Premises"), (ii) Security Agreement of even date herewith executed by Borrower in favor of Payee (the "Security Agreement"), conveying a security interest in certain personal property as more particularly described in the Security Agreement, (iii) Assignment of Leases and Rents of even date herewith executed by Borrower in favor of Payee (the "Rent Assignment") covering the Premises.

Default. If Borrower fails to pay when due any amount payable under this note or if Borrower shall be in default under the Security Deed, Security Agreement or Rent Assignment, then Borrower shall be in default under this note. In the event Borrower shall be in default under this note, at the option of Payee and without further demand or further notice of any kind, the entire unpaid principal balance of this note together with accrued interest thereon, may be declared and thereupon immediately shall become due and payable, and the principal portion of such sum shall bear interest at the rate of two percent (2%) per annum in excess of the highest rate of interest then being charged under this note from the date of default until paid, and Payee, at the option of Payee and without demand or notice of any kind, may exercise any and all rights and remedies provided for or allowed by the Security Deed, Security Agreement, Rent Assignment or provided for or allowed by law or inequity. Any acceleration of payment of the indebtedness evidenced by this note pursuant to the terms hereof or pursuant to the terms of the Security Deed shall be considered prepayment of such indebtedness

(*continued*)

authorizing Payee, upon any such acceleration, and in addition to the balance of principal and interest accrued thereon and all other amounts due under this note and the Security Deed, to the extent permitted by applicable law, to recover any amount equal to the prepayment premium provided for hereinabove as if such indebtedness has been prepaid otherwise.

Time. Time is of the essence of this note.

Waiver. Demand, presentment, notice, protest, and notice of dishonor are hereby waived by Borrower and by each and every co-maker, endorser, guarantor, surety, and other person or entity primarily or secondarily liable on this note. Borrower and each and every co-maker, endorser, guarantor, surety, and other person or entity primarily or secondarily liable on this note: (i) severally waives, each for himself and family, any and all homestead and exemption rights by which any of them or the family of any of them may have under or by virtue of the Constitution or laws of the United States of America or of any state as against this note or any and all renewals, extensions, or modifications of, or substitutions for, this note; (ii) hereby transfers, conveys, and assigns to Payee a sufficient amount of such homestead or exemption as may be allowed, including such homestead or exemption as may be set apart in bankruptcy, to pay the indebtedness evidenced by this note in full, with all costs of collection; (iii) does hereby direct any trustee in bankruptcy having possession of such homestead or exemption to deliver to Payee a sufficient amount of property or money set apart as exempt to pay the indebtedness evidenced by this note, and any and all renewals, extensions, and modifications of, and substitutions for, this note; and (iv) does hereby appoint Payee attorney in-fact to claim any and all homestead exemptions allowed by law.

Third Party Liability. With the consent of Payee, this note may be extended or renewed, in whole or in part, without notice to or consent of any co-maker, endorser, guarantor, surety or other person or entity primarily or secondarily liable on this note and without affecting or lessening the liability of any such person or entity, and each such person or entity hereby waives any right to notice of or consent to such extensions and renewals. Failure of Payee to exercise any rights under this note shall not affect the liability of any co-maker, endorser, guarantor, surety or other person or entity primarily or secondarily liable on this note.

Forbearance. Payee shall not be deemed to waive any of Payee's rights or remedies under this note unless such waiver be express, in writing and signed by or on behalf of Payee. No delay, omission, or forbearance by Payee in exercising any of Payee's rights or remedies shall operate as a waiver of such rights or remedies. A waiver in writing on one occasion shall not be construed as a waiver of any right or remedy on any future occasion.

Governing Law and Severability. This note shall be governed by, construed under, and interpreted and enforced in accordance with the laws of the State of Ohio. Wherever possible, each provision of this note shall be interpreted in such manner as to be effective and valid under applicable law, but if any provision of this note shall be prohibited by or invalid under the applicable law, such provision shall be ineffective only to the extent of such prohibition or invalidity, without invalidating the remainder of such provision or the remaining provisions of this note.

This note and all provisions hereof and of all documents securing this note conform in all respects to the laws of the State of Ohio so that no payment of interest or other sum construed to be interest or charges in the nature of interest shall exceed the highest lawful contract rate permissible under the laws of the State of Ohio as applicable to this transaction. Therefore, this note and all agreements between Borrower and Payee are limited so that in no contingency or event whatsoever, whether acceleration of maturity of the indebtedness or otherwise, shall the amount paid or agree to be paid to the Payee of the use, forbearance, or detention of the money advanced by or to be advanced hereunder exceed the highest lawful rate permissible under the laws of the State of Ohio as applicable to this transaction. In determining whether or not the rate of interest exceeds the highest lawful rate, the Borrower and Payee intend that all sums paid hereunder which are deemed interest for the purposes of determining usury be prorated, allocated, or spread in equal parts over the longest period of time permitted under the applicable laws of the State of Ohio. If, under any circumstances whatsoever, fulfillment of

EXHIBIT 10–3

Commercial Loan Note
(*continued*)

(*continued*)

EXHIBIT 10–3

Commercial Loan Note

(*continued*)

any provision hereof, or of any other instrument evidencing or securing this Indebtedness, at the time performance of such provisions shall be due, shall involve the payment of interest in excess of that authorized by law, the obligation to be fulfilled shall be reduced to the limit so authorized by law, and if under any circumstances Payee shall ever receive as interest an amount which would exceed the highest lawful rate, the amount which would be excessive shall be either applied to the reduction of the unpaid principal balance of the Indebtedness, without payment of any prepayment fee, (and not to the payment of interest) or refunded to the Borrower, and Payee shall not be subject to any penalty provided for the contracting for, charging, or receiving interest in excess of the maximum lawful rate regardless of when or the circumstances under which said refund or application was made.

Notices. All notices, requests, demands, and other communications of this note shall be in writing and shall be deemed to have been duly given if given in accordance with the provisions of the Security Deed.

Terms. The word "Borrower" as used herein shall include the legal representatives, successors, and assigns of Borrower as if so specified at length throughout this note, all of which shall be liable for all indebtedness and liabilities of Borrower. The word "Borrower" as used herein shall also include all makers of this note, and each of them, who shall be jointly and severally liable under this note, should more than one maker execute this note; and shall include all endorsers, guarantors, sureties, and other persons or entities primarily or secondarily liable on this note, and each of them; and shall include the masculine and feminine genders, regardless of the sex of Borrower or any of them; and shall include partnerships, corporations, and other legal entities, should such an entity be or become primarily or secondarily liable on this note. The word "Payee" as used herein shall include the transferees, legal representatives, successors, and assigns of Payee, as if so specified at length throughout this note, and all rights of Payee under this note shall inure to the successors and assigns of Payee.

IN WITNESS WHEREOF, Borrower by its duly authorized general partner has executed this note under seal and has delivered this note to Payee, this _____ day of September, 20_____.

BORROWER:

HARRIS OFFICE PARK LIMITED
PARTNERSHIP, an Ohio limited
partnership

General Partner:

_____(SEAL)
Veronica F. Harris

EXHIBIT 10–4

Payment Guaranty

Guaranty

_____ 20____

(City) _____, (State) _____

FOR VALUE RECEIVED, the sufficiency of which is hereby acknowledged, and in consideration of any loan or other financial accommodation heretofore or hereafter at any time made or granted to _____ (hereinafter called the "Debtor") by _____ (hereinafter, together with its successors and assigns, called the "Bank"), the undersigned hereby unconditionally guarantee(s) the full and prompt payment when due, whether by declaration or otherwise, and at all times hereafter, of all obligations of the Debtor to the Bank, however and whenever incurred or evidenced, whether direct of indirect, absolute or contingent, or due or to become due (collectively called "Liabilities"), and the undersigned further agree(s) to pay the following (herein called "Expenses"): (a) all expenses paid or incurred by the Bank in endeavoring to collect the Liabilities or any part thereof from the Debtor, including attorney's fees of 15% of the total amount sought to be collected if the Bank endeavors to collect from the Debtor by law or through an attorney at law; and (b) all expenses paid or incurred by the Bank in collecting this guaranty, including attorney's fees of 15% of the total amount sought to be collected if this guaranty is collected by law or through an attorney at law. The right of recovery against the undersigned is, however, limited to _____ Dollars ($_____) of the principal amount of the Liabilities plus the interest on such amount and plus the Expenses as applicable thereto and as applicable to this guaranty.

Undersigned hereby represents that loans or other financial accommodations by the Bank to the Debtor will be to the direct interest and advantage of the undersigned.

Undersigned hereby transfers and conveys to the Bank any and all balances, credits, deposits, accounts, items and monies of the undersigned now or hereafter with the Bank, and the Bank is hereby given a lien upon security title to and a security interest in all property of the undersigned of every kind and description now or hereafter in the possession or control of the Bank for any reason, including all dividends and distributions on or other rights in connection therewith.

In the event of the death, incompetency, dissolution or insolvency (as defined by the Uniform Commercial Code as in effect at the time in Georgia) of the Debtor, or if a petition in bankruptcy be filed by or against the Debtor, of if a receiver be appointed for any part of the property or assets of the Debtor, or if any judgment be entered against the Debtor, or if the Bank shall feel insecure with respect to Liabilities and if any such event should occur at a time when any of the Liabilities may not then be due and payable, the undersigned agrees to pay to the Bank upon demand the full amount which would be payable hereunder by the undersigned if all Liabilities were then due and payable.

Bank may, without demand or notice of any kind, at any time when any amount shall be due and payable hereunder by any of the undersigned, appropriate and apply toward the payment of such amount, and in such order of application as the Bank may from time to time elect, any property, balances, credits, deposits, accounts, items or monies of such undersigned in the possession or control of the Bank for any purpose.

This guaranty shall be continuing, absolute and unconditional and shall remain in full force and effect as to the undersigned, subject to discontinuance of this guaranty as to any of the undersigned (including, without limitation, any undersigned who shall become deceased, incompetent or dissolved) only as follows: Any of the undersigned, and any person duly authorized and acting on behalf of any of the undersigned, may given written notice to the Bank of discontinuance of this guaranty as to the undersigned by whom or on whose behalf such notice is given, but no such notice shall be effective in any respect until it is actually received by the Bank and

Delmar/Cengage Learning

(continued)

EXHIBIT 10–4

Payment Guaranty

(*continued*)

no such notice shall affect or impair the obligations hereunder of the undersigned by whom or on whose behalf such notice is given with respect to any Liabilities existing at the date of receipt of such notice by the Bank, any interest thereon or any expenses paid or incurred by the Bank in endeavoring to collect such Liabilities, or any part thereof, and in enforcing this guaranty against such undersigned. Any such notice of discontinuance by or on behalf of any of the undersigned shall not affect or impair the obligations hereunder of any other of the undersigned.

The Bank may, from time to time, without notice to the undersigned (or any of them), (a) retain or obtain a security interest in any property to secure any of the Liabilities or any obligation hereunder, (b) retain or obtain the primary or secondary liability of any party or parties, in addition to the undersigned, with respect to any of the Liabilities, (c) extend or renew for any period (whether or not longer than the original period), alter or exchange any of the Liabilities, (d) release or compromise any liability of any of the undersigned hereunder or any liability of any other party or parties primarily or secondarily liable on any of the Liabilities, (e) release its security interest, if any, in all or any property securing any of the Liabilities or any obligation hereunder and permit any substitution or exchange for any such property, and (f) resort to the undersigned (or any of them) for payment of any of the Liabilities, whether or not the Bank shall have resorted to any property securing any of the Liabilities or any obligation hereunder or shall have proceeded against any other of the undersigned or any other party primarily or secondarily liable on any of the Liabilities.

Any amount received by the Bank from whatever source and applied by it toward the payment of the Liabilities shall be applied in such order of application as the Bank may from time to time elect.

The undersigned hereby expressly waive(s): (a) Notice of the acceptance of this guaranty, (b) notice of the existence or creation of all or any of the Liabilities, (c) presentment, demand, notice of dishonor, protest, and all other notices whatsoever, and (d) all diligence in collection or protection of or realization upon the Liabilities or any thereof, any obligation hereunder, or any security for any of the foregoing.

The creation or existence from time to time of Liabilities in excess of the amount to which the right of recovery under this guaranty is limited is hereby authorized, without notice to the undersigned (or any of them), and shall in no way affect or impair this guaranty.

The Bank may, without notice of any kind, sell, assign or transfer all or any of the Liabilities, and in such event each and every immediate and successive assignee, transferee, or holder of all or any of the Liabilities, shall have the right to enforce this guaranty, by suit or otherwise, for the benefit of such assignee, transferee or holder, as fully as if such assignee, transferee or holder were herein by name specifically given such rights, powers and benefits, but the Bank shall have an unimpaired right, prior and superior to that of any such assignee, transferee or holder, to enforce this guaranty for the benefit of the Bank, as to so much of the Liabilities as it has not sold, assigned or transferred.

No delay or failure on the part of the Bank in the exercise of any right or remedy shall operate as a waiver thereof, and no single or partial exercise by the Bank of any right or remedy shall preclude other or further exercise thereof or the exercise of any other right or remedy. No action of the Bank permitted hereunder shall in any way impair or affect this guaranty. For the purpose of this guaranty, Liabilities shall include all obligations of the Debtor to the Bank, notwithstanding any right or power of the Debtor or anyone else to assert any claim or defense, as to the invalidity or unenforceability of any such obligation, and no such claim or defense shall impair or affect the obligations of the undersigned hereunder.

This guaranty is cumulative of and shall not effect, modify or limit any other guaranty executed by the undersigned with respect to any Liabilities.

This guaranty shall be binding upon the undersigned, and upon the heirs, legal representatives, successors and assigns of the undersigned. If more than one party shall execute this guaranty, the term "undersigned" shall mean all parties executing this guaranty, and all such parties shall be jointly and severally obligated hereunder.

(*continued*)

This guaranty has been made and delivered in the State of Georgia, and shall be governed by the laws of that State. Wherever possible each provision of this guaranty shall be interpreted in such manner as to be effective and valid under applicable law, but if any provision of this guaranty shall be prohibited by or invalid under such law, such provision shall be ineffective to the extent of such prohibition or invalidity, without invalidating the remainder of such provision or the remaining provisions of this guaranty.

IN WITNESS WHEREOF the undersigned have hereunto set their hands and affix their seals the day and year above written.

_____ (SEAL)

_____ (SEAL)

_____ (SEAL)

EXHIBIT 10–4

Payment Guaranty

(*continued*)

EXHIBIT 10–5

Florida Mortgage

THIS INDENTURE, made this _____ day of _____ in the year of our Lord two thousand and _____, by and between _____ _____ _____ of the _____, County of _____, and State of Florida, hereinafter called the Mortgagor; and _____; hereinafter called the Mortgagee:

Whereas the said Mortgagor is justly indebted to the said Mortgagee in the principal sum of _____ _____ Dollars, as evidenced by a certain promissory note of even date herewith, executed by _____ _____ and payable to the order of the Mortgagee, with interest and upon terms as provided therein.

Said note provides that all installments of principal and interest are payable in lawful money of the United States of America, which shall be legal tender for public and private debts at the time of payment, at the office of _____, or at such other place as the holder thereof may from time to time designate in writing. Said note also provides that the final installment of principal and interest shall be due and payable on the _____ day of _____, 20_____.

Said note provides that each maker and endorser, jointly and severally, shall pay all costs of collection, including a reasonable attorney's fee, on failure to pay any principal and interest when due thereon, and that all principal due thereunder shall bear interest at the maximum permissible rate per annum from due date until paid.

Said note further provides that if any installment of principal and/or interest shall not be paid when due, then the entire principal sum and accrued interest shall become due and payable at once, at the option of the holder thereof.

NOW THIS INDENTURE WITNESSETH, that the said Mortgagor, to secure said indebtedness and interest thereon, and also for and in consideration of the sum of One Dollar paid by Mortgagee, at or before the ensealing and delivery of these presents, the receipt whereof is hereby acknowledged, has granted, bargained, sold and conveyed and by these presents does grant, bargain, sell and convey unto the Mortgagee all that certain lot, parcel or piece of land lying and being in the County of _____ and State of Florida, more particularly described as _____ _____.

ALSO TOGETHER WITH all buildings and improvements thereon situate or which may hereafter be erected or placed thereon and all and singular the tenements, hereditaments, appurtenances and easements thereunto belonging or in anywise appertaining, and the rents, issues and profits thereof, and together with all heating, ventilating and air conditioning equipment, all plumbing apparatus, fixtures, hot water heaters, water and sprinkler systems and pumps, all lighting fixtures and all screens, awnings, venetian blinds, built-in equipment, and built-in furniture (whether or not affixed to land or building) now or hereafter located in or on said premises, including all renewals, replacements and additions thereto.

TO HAVE AND TO HOLD the above granted and described premises unto the said Mortgagee; its successors or assigns, forever.

And the said Mortgagor hereby covenants with the Mortgagee that the said Mortgagor is indefeasibly seized of said land in fee simple; that the said Mortgagor has full power and lawful right to convey the same in fee simple as aforesaid; that it shall be lawful for the Mortgagee at all times peaceably and quietly to enter upon, hold, occupy and enjoy said land and every part thereof; that the land is free from all encumbrances, except as aforesaid; that said Mortgagor will make such further assurances to prove the fee simple title to said land in said Mortgagee as may be reasonably required, and that said Mortgagor does hereby fully warrant the title to said land and every part thereof and will defend the same against the lawful claims of all persons whomsoever.

Delmar/Cengage Learning

(continued)

PROVIDED ALWAYS, and these presents are on this express condition, that if said Mortgagor shall well and truly pay said indebtedness unto the said Mortgagee, and any renewals or extensions thereof, and the interest thereon, together with all costs, charges and expenses, including a reasonable attorney's fee, which the said Mortgagee may incur or be put to in collecting the same by foreclosure, or otherwise, and shall perform and comply with all other terms, conditions and covenants contained in said promissory note and this mortgage, then these presents and the estate hereby granted shall cease, determine and be null and void.

And the said Mortgagor hereby jointly and severally covenants and agrees to and with the said Mortgagee as follows:

1. To pay all and singular the principal and interest and the various and sundry sums of money payable by virtue of said promissory note and this mortgage, each and every, promptly on the days respectively the same severally become due.

2. To pay all and singular the taxes, assessments, levies, liabilities, obligations and encumbrances of every nature and kind now on said described property, and/or that hereafter may be imposed, suffered, placed, levied or assessed thereupon and/or that hereafter may be levied or assessed upon this mortgage and/or the indebtedness secured hereby, each and every, before they become delinquent, and in so far as any thereof is of record the same shall be promptly satisfied and discharged of record and the original official document (such as, for instance, the tax receipt or the satisfaction paper officially endorsed or certified) shall be placed in the hands of said Mortgagee within ten days after next payment.

3. To keep the buildings now or hereafter situate on said land and all personal property used in the operation thereof continuously insured against loss by fire and such other hazards as may from time to time be requested by Mortgagee, in companies and in amounts in each company as may be approved by and acceptable to Mortgagee; and all insurance policies shall contain the usual standard mortgagee clause making the loss under said policies payable, without contribution, to said Mortgagee as its interest may appear, and each and every such policy shall be promptly delivered to and held by said Mortgagee; and, not less than ten (10) days in advance of the expiration of each policy, to deliver to said Mortgagee a renewal thereof, together with a receipt for the premium of such renewal. Any insurance proceeds, or any part thereof, may be applied by Mortgagee, at its option, either to the indebtedness hereby secured or to the restoration or repair of the property damaged.

4. To keep said land and the buildings and improvements now or hereafter situate thereon in good order and repair, and to permit, commit or suffer no waste, impairment or deterioration of said property or any part thereof.

5. To comply, as far as they affect the mortgaged property, with all statutes, laws, ordinances, decrees and orders of the United States, the State of Florida and of any political subdivision thereof.

6. In case Mortgagor shall fail to promptly discharge any obligation or covenant as provided herein, the Mortgagee shall have the option, but no obligation, to perform on behalf of the Mortgagor any act to be performed by Mortgagor in discharging such obligation or covenant, and any amount which Mortgagee may expend in performing such act, or in connection therewith, with interest thereon at the rate of ten (10) percent per annum and together with all expenses, including reasonable attorney's fees, incurred by Mortgagee shall be immediately payable by Mortgagor and shall be secured by this mortgage; and Mortgagee shall be subrogated to any rights, equities and liens so discharged.

7. That if the principal or interest on the note herein described or any part of the indebtedness secured by this mortgage or interest thereon, be not paid within ten (10) days after they are due, or if default be made in the full and prompt performance of any covenant or agreement herein contained, or if any proceeding be instituted to abate any nuisance on the mortgaged property, or if any proceeding be instituted which might result to the detriment of the use and enjoyment of the said property or upon the rendering by any court of last resort of a decision that an undertaking by the Mortgagor as herein provided to pay any tax, assessment,

(continued)

EXHIBIT 10–5

Florida Mortgage
(*continued*)

levy, liability, obligation or encumbrance is legally inoperative or cannot be enforced, or in the event of the passage of any law changing in any way or respect the laws now in force for the taxation of mortgages or debts secured thereby for any purpose, or the manner of collection of any such tax, so as to affect this mortgage or the debt secured hereby; or if the Mortgagor shall make an assignment for the benefit of creditors, or if a receiver be appointed for the Mortgagor or any part of the mortgaged property, or if Mortgagor files a petition in bankruptcy, or is adjudicated a bankrupt or files any petition or institutes any proceedings under the National Bankruptcy Act, then on the happening of any one or more of these events, this conveyance shall become absolute and the whole indebtedness secured hereby shall immediately become due and payable, at the option of the Mortgagee, and this mortgage may thereupon be foreclosed for the whole of said money, interest and costs; or Mortgagee may foreclose only as to the sum past due, without injury to this mortgage or the displacement or impairment of the remainder of the lien thereof, and at such foreclosure sale the property shall be sold subject to all remaining items of indebtedness; and Mortgagee may again foreclose, in the same manner, as often as there may be any sum past due.

8. Except during such period or periods as the Mortgagee may from time to time designate in writing, the Mortgagor will pay to the Mortgagee on the first day of each month throughout the existence of this mortgage a sum equal to the Mortgagee's estimate of the taxes and assessments next due on the mortgaged property and premiums next payable on or for policies of fire and other hazard insurance thereon, less any sums already paid the Mortgagee with respect thereto, divided by the number of months to elapse before one month prior to the date when such taxes, assessments and premiums become due and payable, such sums to be held by the Mortgagee, without interest, to pay such items. If at any time the estimated sum is insufficient to pay an item when due, the Mortgagor shall forthwith upon demand pay the deficiency to the Mortgagee. The arrangement provided for in this paragraph is solely for the added protection of the Mortgagee and entails no responsibility on the Mortgagee's part beyond the allowing of due credit, without interest, for sums actually received by it. Upon the occurrence of a default under this mortgage, the Mortgagee may apply all or any part of the accumulated funds then held, upon any obligation secured hereby. Upon assignment of this mortgage, any funds on hand shall be turned over to the assignee and any responsibility of the assignor with respect thereto shall terminate. Each transfer of the mortgaged property shall automatically transfer to the grantee all right of the grantor with respect to any funds accumulated hereunder.

9. That in case of default or the happening of any event which would enable the Mortgagee to declare the whole indebtedness secured hereby immediately due and payable, the Mortgagee shall be entitled to the appointment of a receiver of all the rents, issues and profits, regardless of the value of the mortgaged property and the solvency or insolvency of the Mortgagor and other persons liable to pay said indebtedness.

10. That the Mortgagee may collect a "late charge" not to exceed four cents (4¢) for each dollar of each payment due hereunder made more than fifteen (15) days in arrears to cover the extra expense involved in handling delinquent payments.

11. That the words "Mortgagor" and "Mortgagee" when used herein shall be taken to include singular and plural number and masculine, feminine or neuter gender, as may fit the case, and shall also include the heirs, administrators, executors, successors and assigns of the parties hereto. Each and all of the terms and provisions hereof shall extend to and be a part of any renewal or extension of this mortgage.

12. That this mortgage and the note secured hereby constitute a Florida contract and shall be construed according to the laws of that state.

IN WITNESS WHEREOF, the said Mortgagor has hereunto set his hand and seal the day and year first above written.

EXHIBIT 10–6

North Carolina Deed of Trust

SATISFACTION: The debt secured by the within Deed of Trust together with the note(s) secured thereby has been satisfied in full.

This the .... day of ...., 20 ....

Signed: ....

Mail after recording to:

This instrument prepared by:

Recording: Time, Book and Page

NORTH CAROLINA DEED OF TRUST

THIS DEED of TRUST made this   day of   , 20   , by and between:

GRANTOR	TRUSTEE	BENEFICIARY
		SOUTHERN NATIONAL BANK OF NORTH CAROLINA, a national banking association

Enter in appropriate block for each party: name, address, and, if appropriate, character of entity, e.g. corporation or partnership.

The designation Grantor, Trustee, and Beneficiary as used herein shall include said parties, their heirs, successors, and assigns, and shall include singular, plural, masculine, feminine or neuter as required by context.

WITNESSETH: The Grantor is indebted to the Beneficiary in the sum of _____

_____ DOLLARS ($ ....)

(the "Debt") for money loaned, as evidenced by promissory Note(s) of even date herewith, the terms of which are incorporated herein by reference.

NOW, THEREFORE, as security for the Debt, together with interest thereon, and as security for all renewals, extensions, deferments, amortizations and re-amortizations thereof, in whole or in part, together with interest thereon whether at the same or different rates, and for a valuable consideration, receipt of which is hereby acknowledged, the Grantor has bargained, sold, granted and conveyed and does by these presents bargain, sell, grant and convey to the Trustee, his heirs, or

successors, and assigns, the real property situated in the City of _____, _____ Township, _____

County, State of North Carolina, particularly described as follows:

DESCRIPTION SET FORTH HEREINBELOW AND ON SCHEDULE "A", IF ANY, ATTACHED HERETO AND MADE A PART HEREOF

(continued)

EXHIBIT 10–6

North Carolina Deed of Trust

(*continued*)

TO HAVE AND TO HOLD said real property, including all buildings, improvements and fixtures now or hereafter located thereon, with all the rights, privileges and appurtenances thereunto belonging, to the Trustee, his heirs, or successors, and assigns forever, upon the trusts, terms and conditions, and for the uses hereinafter set forth.

If the Grantor shall pay the Debt secured hereby in accordance with the terms of the note(s) evidencing the same, and all renewals, extensions, deferments, amortizations and reamortizations thereof, in whole or in part, together with interest thereon, and shall comply with all the covenants, terms and conditions of the deed of trust, then this conveyance shall be null and void and may be cancelled of record at the request of the Grantor. If, however, there shall be any default in any of the covenants, terms, or conditions of the Note(s) secured hereby, or any failure or neglect to comply with the covenants, terms, or conditions contained in this deed of trust, then and in any of such events, if the default is not made good within (15) days, the Note(s) shall, at the option of the Beneficiary, at once become due and payable without notice, and it shall be lawful for and the duty of the Trustee, upon request of the Beneficiary, to sell the land herein conveyed at public auction for cash, after having first given such notice of hearing as to commencement of foreclosure proceedings and obtaining such findings or leave of court as may be then required by law and giving such notice and advertising the time and place of such sale in such manner as may be then provided by law, and upon such sale and any resales and upon compliance with the then law relating to foreclosure proceedings to convey title to the purchaser in fee simple.

The proceeds of the Sale shall, after the Trustee retains his commission, be applied to the costs of sale, the amount due on the Note(s) hereby secured and otherwise as required by the then existing law relating to foreclosures. The Trustee's commission shall be five per cent of the gross proceeds of the sale or the minimum sum of $ ...., whichever is greater, for a completed foreclosure. In the event foreclosure is commenced, but not completed, the Grantor shall pay all expenses incurred by Trustee and a partial commission computed on five per cent of the outstanding indebtedness or the above stated minimum sum, whichever is greater, in accordance with the following schedule, to wit: one-fourth thereof before the Trustee issues a notice of hearing on the right to foreclose; one-half thereof after issuance of said notice; three-fourths thereof after such hearing; and the greater of the full commission or minimum after the initial sale.

And the said Grantor does hereby covenant and agree with the Trustee and with the Beneficiary as follows:

1. INSURANCE. Grantor shall keep all improvements on said land, now or hereafter erected constantly insured for the benefit of the Beneficiary against loss by fire, windstorm and such other casualties and contingencies, in such manner and in such companies and for such amounts as may be satisfactory to or required by the Beneficiary. Grantor shall purchase such insurance, pay all premiums therefor, and shall deliver to Beneficiary such policies along with evidence of premium payment as long as the Note(s) secured hereby remains unpaid. If Grantor fails to purchase such insurance, pay the premiums therefor or deliver said policies with mortgagee clause satisfactory to Beneficiary attached thereto, along with evidence of payment of premiums thereon, then Beneficiary, at his option, may purchase such insurance. Such amounts paid by Beneficiary shall be added to the Note(s) secured by this Deed of Trust, and shall be due and payable upon demand by Grantor to Beneficiary.

2. TAXES, ASSESSMENTS, CHARGES. Grantor shall pay all taxes, assessments and charges as may be lawfully levied against said premises within thirty (30) days after the same shall become due. In the event that Grantor fails to so pay all taxes, assessments and charges as herein required, then Beneficiary, at his option, may pay the same and the amounts so paid shall be added to the Note(s), secured by this Deed of Trust, and shall be due and payable upon demand by Grantor to Beneficiary.

3. PARTIAL RELEASE. Grantor shall not be entitled to the partial release of any of the above described property unless a specific provision providing therefor is included in this Deed of Trust. In the event a partial release provision is included in this Deed of Trust, Grantor must strictly comply with the terms thereof. Notwithstanding anything herein contained, Grantor shall not be entitled to any release of property unless Grantor is not in default and is in full compliance with all of the terms and provisions of this Deed of Trust, and any other instrument that may be securing said Note(s).

4. WASTE. The Grantor convenants that he will keep the premises herein conveyed in as good order, repair and condition as they are now, reasonable wear and tear excepted, and that he will not commit or permit any waste.

5. WARRANTIES. Grantor covenants with Trustee and Beneficiary that he is seized of the premises in fee simple, has the right to convey the same in fee simple, that title is marketable and free and clear of all encumbrances, and that he will warrant and defend the title against the lawful claims of all persons whomsoever, except for the exceptions hereinafter stated. Title to the property hereinabove described is subject to the following exceptions:

6. CONVEYANCE; ACCELERATION: If Grantor sells, conveys, transfers, assigns or disposes of the hereinabove-described real property or any part thereof or interest therein, by any means or method, whether voluntary or involuntary, without the written consent of Beneficiary, then at the option of Beneficiary and without notice to Grantor, all sums of money secured hereby, both principal and interest, shall immediately become due and payable and in default, notwithstanding anything herein or in the Note(s) secured hereby to the contrary.

7. SUBSTITUTION OF TRUSTEE. Grantor and Trustee covenant and agree to and with Beneficiary that in case the said Trustee, or any successor trustee, shall die, become incapable of acting, renounce his trust, or for other similar or dissimilar reason become unacceptable to the holder of the Note(s), then the holder of the Note(s) may appoint, in writing, a trustee to take the place of the Trustee; and upon the probate and registration of the same, the trustee thus appointed shall succeed to all the rights, powers, and duties of the Trustee.

8. CIVIL ACTION. In the event that the Trustee is named as a party to any civil action as Trustee in this Deed of Trust, the Trustee shall be entitled to employ an attorney at law, including himself if he is a licensed attorney, to represent him in said action and the reasonable attorney's fees of the Trustee in such action shall be paid by Beneficiary and charged to the Note(s) and secured by this Deed of Trust.

9. PRIOR LIENS. Default under the terms of any instrument secured by a lien to which this deed of trust is subordinate shall consitute default hereunder.

IN WITNESS WHEREOF, the Grantor has hereunto set his hand and seal, or if corporate, has caused this instrument to be signed in its corporate name by its duly authorized officers and its seal to be hereunto affixed by authority of its Board of Directors, the day and year first above written.

(Corporate Name)

.... (SEAL)

By: ....

.... President .... (SEAL)

ATTEST: .... (SEAL)

....

.... Secretary (Corporate Seal) .... (SEAL)

USE BLACK INK ONLY

SEAL-STAMP

STATE OF NORTH CAROLINA, COUNTY OF ....

I, ..., a notary public of said county do hereby certify that ....

.... Grantor, personally appeared before me this day and acknowledged the execution of the foregoing instrument. Witness my hand and official stamp or seal, this .... day of ...., 20.........

My commission expires: .... Notary Public

Use Black Ink

SEAL-STAMP

STATE OF NORTH CAROLINA, COUNTY OF ....

I, ..., a Notary Public of the County and State aforesaid, certify that ...., personally came before me this day and acknowledged that .... he is .... Secretary of .... a North Carolina corporation, and that by authority duly given and as the act of the corporation, the foregoing instrument was signed in its name by its .... President, sealed with its corporate seal and attested by ....

.... as its .... Secretary.

Witness my hand and official stamp or seal, this .... day of ....20......... .

My commission expires: .... Notary Public

Use Black Ink

The foregoing Certificate (s) of ....

is/are certified to be correct. This instrument and this certificate are duly registered at the date and time and in the Book and Page shown on the first page hereof.

.... REGISTER OF DEEDS FOR .... COUNTY

By .... Deputy/Assistant - Register of Deeds

EXHIBIT 10–7

Georgia Commercial
Deed to Secure Debt

STATE OF GEORGIA

COUNTY OF_____

SECURITY DEED AND AGREEMENT

THIS INDENTURE is made this _____ day of _____, by
and between _____,
party of the first part, hereinafter referred to as "Grantor"; and _____
_____ party of the second part, hereinafter referred to as "Grantee";

WITNESSETH:

FOR AND IN CONSIDERATION of the financial accommodations to Grantor by Grantee resulting in the
obligation which is hereinafter more particularly described, and in order to secure that obligation, Grantor hereby
grants, bargains, conveys, transfers, assigns and sells unto Grantee the following described land:

TOGETHER WITH ANY AND ALL of the following: (i) all buildings, structures and other improvements now or hereafter
located thereon or on any part or parcel thereof and all fixtures affixed or attached, actually or constructively, thereto; (ii) all
and singular the tenements, hereditaments, easements and appurtenances belonging thereunto or in any wise appertaining
thereto and the reversion and reversions, remainder or remainders thereof; (iii) all rents, issues, income, revenues and profits
accruing therefrom, whether now or hereafter due; (iv) all accounts and contract rights now or hereafter arising in connection
with any part or parcel thereof or any buildings, structures or improvements now or hereafter located thereon, including without
limitation all accounts and contract rights in and to all leases or undertakings to lease now or hereafter affecting the land or any
buildings, structures, or improvements thereon; (v) all minerals, flowers, crops, trees, timber, shrubbery and other emblements
now or hereafter located thereon or thereunder or on or under any part or parcel thereof; (vi) all estates, rights, title and interest
therein, or in any part or parcel thereof; (vii) all equipment, machinery, apparatus, fittings, fixtures whether actually or constructively attached thereto and including all trade, domestic and ornamental fixtures, furniture, furnishings and all personal
property of every kind or description whatsoever now or hereafter located thereon, or in or on the buildings, structures and
other improvements thereon, and used in connection with the operation and maintenance thereof, and all additions thereto
and replacements thereof; and (viii) all building materials, supplies, goods and equipment delivered thereto and placed thereon
for the purpose of being affixed to or installed or incorporated or otherwise used in the buildings, structures or other improvements now or hereafter located thereon or any part or parcel thereof. All of the foregoing are hereinafter sometimes referred
to collectively as the "Premises."

TO HAVE AND TO HOLD the Premises to the only proper use, benefit and behoof of Grantee, forever, in fee simple.

GRANTOR WARRANTS that Grantor has good title to the Premises, that Grantor is lawfully seized and possessed of
the Premises, that Grantor has the right to convey the Premises, that the Premises are unencumbered except as may be
herein expressly provided and that Grantor shall forever warrant and defend the title to the Premises unto Grantee against
the claims of all persons whomsoever.

THIS INSTRUMENT IS A DEED passing legal title pursuant to the laws of the State of Georgia governing deeds to
secure debt and a security agreement granting a security interest pursuant to the Uniform Commercial Code of the State
of Georgia, and it is not a mortgage. This deed and security agreement is made and intended to secure: (i) an obligation of
Grantor to Grantee evidenced as follows:

(ii) any and all renewal or renewals, extension or extensions, modification or modifications thereof, and substitution or substitutions therefor, either in whole or in part; and (iii) all indebtedness now or hereafter owing by Grantor to Grantee,
however or whenever created, incurred, arising or evidenced, whether direct or indirect, joint or several, absolute or contingent,
or due or to become due, and any and all renewal or renewals, extension or extensions, modification or modifications of and
substitution or substitutions for, said indebtedness, either in whole or in part. The obligations which this deed and security
agreement is given to secure are hereinafter sometimes referred to collectively as the "Indebtedness." This deed and security
agreement is hereinafter sometimes referred to as this "Security Deed."

GRANTOR COVENANTS AND AGREES: (1) *Junior Encumbrances:* Grantor shall not create or permit to exist any
liens or encumbrances on the Premises which are junior and inferior in terms of priority to this Security Deed. (2) *Payments
by Grantor:* Grantor shall pay, when due and payable: (i) the Indebtedness in accordance with the terms and conditions of
the instruments evidencing the same; (ii) all taxes, all assessments, general or special, and all other charges levied on or
assessed or placed or made against the Premises, this Security Deed, the Indebtedness or any interest of Grantee in the Premises,
this Security Deed or the Indebtedness; (iii) premiums on policies of fire and casualty insurance covering the Premises, as
required by this Security Deed; (iv) premiums on all life insurance policies now or hereafter pledged as collateral for the
Indebtedness or any part thereof; (v) premiums for all liability, rental, mortgage and flood insurance policies required by this
Security Deed or now or hereafter required by Grantee in connection with the Premises or the Indebtedness or any part of
either; and (vi) all ground rents, lease rentals and other payments respecting the Premises payable by Grantor. Grantor shall
promptly deliver to Grantee, upon request by Grantee, receipts showing payment in full of all the foregoing items; provided, however, that Grantee shall not require a receipt showing payment in full of the Indebtedness. In the event any
state, federal, municipal or other governmental law, order, rule or regulation becomes effective subsequent to the date hereof
and in any manner changes or modifies the laws in force on the date hereof governing the taxation of the Indebtedness or the
manner of collecting the taxes thereon so as to adversely affect Grantee by requiring that a payment or payments be made
or other action be taken to protect Grantee's interest under this Security Deed or the Indebtedness, Grantor shall promptly
pay any amounts required on or before the date the same are due or take any other action required on or before the date any such
action must be taken. (3) *Grantee's Acts on Behalf of Grantor:* In the event Grantor shall either fail or refuse to pay or cause to be
paid, as the same shall become due and payable, any item (including all items specified at Paragraph (2) immediately above) which
Grantor is required to pay hereunder or which Grantor may pay to cure an event of default hereunder, or in the event Grantor shall
either fail or refuse to do or perform any act which Grantor is obligated to do or perform hereunder or which Grantor may do or
perform to cure an event of default hereunder, then Grantee, at Grantee's option, may make such payment or do or perform such
act on behalf of Grantor. All such payments made by Grantee and all costs and expenses incurred by Grantee in doing or performing all such acts shall be and shall also become part of the Indebtedness secured hereby and shall bear interest at the highest rate per
annum then being charged with respect to any part of the Indebtedness secured hereby from the date paid or incurred by Grantee,
and such interest thereon shall also be part of the Indebtedness secured hereby. (4) *Further Assurances:* Grantor shall, at any time
and from time to time upon request by Grantee, make, execute and deliver, or cause to be made, executed and delivered, any and
all other and further instruments, documents, certificates, agreements, letters, representations and other writings which may be
necessary or desirable, in the opinion of Grantee, in order to effectuate, complete, correct, perfect or continue and preserve the
obligations of Grantor under the Indebtedness and the lien and security interest of Grantee hereunder. Grantor shall upon request
by Grantee certify in writing to Grantee, or to any proposed assignee of this Security Deed, the amount of principal and interest
then owing on the Indebtedness and whether or not any set-offs or defenses exist against all or any part of the Indebtedness.

(continued)

EXHIBIT 10–7

Georgia Commercial Deed to Secure Debt *(continued)*

(5) *Rents and Leases:* Grantor hereby transfers, assigns and conveys unto Grantee all of Grantor's right, title and interest in and to all leases or undertakings to lease now or hereafter existing or made, and all other agreements for use or occupancy, with respect to the Premises or any part thereof, and grants to Grantee a security interest in all rents, issues, income, revenues, profits, accounts and contract rights due or to become due thereunder or otherwise deriving from the use and occupancy of the Premises. Grantor shall faithfully perform the covenants of Grantor as lessor under all present and future leases of all or any portion of the Premises and shall not do, neglect to do, or permit to be done, anything which may cause the termination of such leases, or any of them, or which may diminish or impair their value or the rents provided for therein or the interest of Grantor or Grantee therein or thereunder. Grantor, without first obtaining the written consent of Grantee, shall not further assign the rents, issues, income, revenues, profits, accounts or contract rights from the Premises or any part thereof, shall not consent to the cancellation or surrender of any lease of the Premises or any part thereof now existing or hereafter to be made, shall not modify any such lease so as to shorten the unexpired term thereof or so as to decrease the amount of the rent payable thereunder and shall not collect rents from the Premises or any part thereof for more than one month in advance. Grantor shall procure and deliver to Grantee upon request estoppel letters or certificates from each lessee, tenant, occupant in possession and other user of the Premises or any part thereof, as required by and in form and substance satisfactory to Grantee, and shall deliver to Grantee a recordable assignment of all of Grantor's interest in all leases now or hereafter existing or made with respect to the Premises or any part thereof, which assignment shall be in form and substance satisfactory to Grantee, together with proof of due service of a copy of such assignment on each lessee, tenant, occupant in possession or other user of the Premises or any part thereof. (6) *Maintenance and Repair:* Grantor shall maintain the Premises in good condition and repair, shall not commit or suffer any waste to the Premises, and shall comply with, or cause to be complied with, all statutes, ordinances, rules, regulations and directives of any governmental authority relating to the Premises or any part thereof or the use or occupancy of the Premises or any part thereof. No part of the Premises, including but not limited to any buildings, structures, parking lots, driveways or other improvements now or hereafter constructed on the land which is part of the Premises, shall be removed, demolished or materially altered without the prior written consent of Grantee. If at any time during the continuance of the Indebtedness any addition, alteration, change, repair, reconstruction or other work on the Premises of any nature, structural or otherwise, becomes necessary or desirable because of damage to or destruction of the Premises or any part thereof, the entire expense thereof, regardless of when the same shall be incurred or become due, shall be the sole obligation and responsibility of Grantor, and Grantor shall pay the entire expense thereof promptly when due. (7) *Hazard and Liability Insurance:* Grantor shall keep the Premises insured against loss or damage by fire and such other casualties and risks as the Grantee may require from time to time, with such companies, in such amounts and under such forms of policies as Grantee may approve. Such policies shall insure Grantee's interest in the Premises, name Grantee as an insured party thereunder, provide that losses thereunder shall be payable to Grantee pursuant to such forms of loss payable clauses as Grantee may approve and provide that no cancellation or reduction in coverage shall be effective unless the insuror first gives Grantee thirty (30) days prior written notice. Irrespective of the insurance required and approved by Grantee, Grantor shall assign and deliver to Grantee, as additional collateral for the payment of the Indebtedness, all policies of insurance which insure against loss or damage to the Premises, and Grantor hereby grants to Grantee a security interest in the proceeds from any and all such policies. Grantor shall also procure and maintain public liability insurance coverage with such companies, in such amounts and under such forms of policies as Grantee may approve, naming Grantee as an additional insured thereunder and providing that no cancellation or reduction in coverage thereunder shall be effective unless the insuror first gives Grantee thirty (30) days prior written notice. Forthwith upon the issuance of all such policies, Grantor shall deliver the same to Grantee together with evidence satisfactory to Grantee that the premiums therefor have been paid. Within fifteen (15) days prior to the expiration date of each such policy, Grantor shall deliver to Grantee a renewal policy together with evidence satisfactory to Grantee that the premium therefor has been paid. In the event of a foreclosure and sale by Grantee of the Premises, the purchaser of the Premises shall succeed to all rights of Grantor in and to such policies, including the right to the refund of unearned premiums and to dividends thereunder, and Grantee may, at Grantee's election, assign and deliver the policies to such purchaser without any warranty or representation, express or implied, and without recourse. In the event of damage to or destruction of the Premises or any part thereof, Grantee may adjust, settle or compromise claims under such policies, and the proceeds therefrom shall be paid to Grantee. Grantee, at Grantee's option and in Grantee's sole discretion, may either (i) apply the proceeds or any part thereof to the Indebtedness or (ii) require Grantor to repair, replace or reconstruct the Premises or any part thereof and disburse the proceeds to Grantor to be applied against the costs and expenses thereof as incurred or paid by Grantor. (8) *Flood Insurance:* Grantor represents and has certified to Grantee that no part of the Premises lies within a "special flood hazard area" as defined and specified by the United States Department of Housing and Urban Development pursuant to the Flood Disaster Protection Act of 1973. In the event Grantee determines that the rules or regulations of the Federal Reserve Board, the Comptroller of the Currency or any other governing agency licensing or regulating the operations of Grantee require that flood insurance coverage be obtained for the Premises or any part thereof in order for Grantee to comply with such rules or regulations or with the Flood Disaster Protection Act of 1973 as then in effect, then Grantor, upon receiving written notice from Grantee of such determination: (i) shall promptly purchase and pay the premiums for such flood insurance policies as Grantee deems required by such agency or agencies so that Grantee shall be deemed in compliance with the rules and regulations of such agency or agencies and with the Flood Disaster Protection Act of 1973 as then in effect; and (ii) shall deliver such policies to Grantee together with evidence satisfactory to Grantee that the premiums therefor have been paid. Such policies of flood insurance shall be in a form satisfactory to Grantee, shall name Grantee as an insured thereunder, shall provide that losses thereunder be payable to Grantee pursuant to such forms of loss payable clause as Grantee may approve, shall be for an amount at least equal to the Indebtedness or the maximum limit of coverage made available with respect to the Premises under the National Flood Insurance Act of 1968, as amended, whichever is less, and shall be noncancellable as to Grantee except upon thirty (30) days prior written notice given by the insuror to Grantee. Within ten (10) days prior to the expiration date of each such flood insurance policy, Grantor shall deliver to Grantee a renewal policy or endorsement together with evidence satisfactory to Grantee that the premium therefor has been paid. (9) *Condemnation:* To the extent of the Indebtedness, Grantor grants to Grantee a security interest in any and all payments, awards, judgments or settlements, including interest thereon, to which Grantor may be or may become entitled or which Grantee may receive by reason of injury or damage to, or loss of, the Premises or any part thereof as a result of the exercise of the right of eminent domain. Notwithstanding any injury or damage to, or loss of, the Premises or any part thereof as a result of the exercise of the right of eminent domain, Grantor shall continue to pay the Indebtedness. All sums paid or payable to Grantor by reason of any injury or damage to, or loss of, the Premises or any part thereof as a result of the exercise of the right of eminent domain shall be delivered to Grantee and Grantee, at Grantee's option and at Grantee's sole discretion, may either (i) apply the sum or any part thereof to the Indebtedness or (ii) require Grantor to repair, replace or reconstruct the Premises or any part thereof and disburse such sums to Grantor to be applied against the costs and expenses thereof as incurred or paid by Grantor. (10) *Inspection:* Grantor shall permit any person designated by Grantee to visit and inspect the Premises, to examine the books of account and other records of Grantor with respect to the Premises, and to discuss the affairs, finances and accounts of Grantor with and to be advised as to the same by Grantor or a knowledgeable and duly authorized representative of Grantor, all at such reasonable times and intervals as Grantee may desire. (11) *Restriction on Transfer:* Unless Grantee gives its written consent thereto and such consent is recorded in the public deed records of the Clerk of the Superior Court of the county in which this Security Deed is recorded, Grantor shall not grant, bargain, convey, transfer, assign, exchange or sell all or any portion of Grantor's interest in the Premises prior to the satisfaction and release by Grantee of this Security Deed.

EVENTS OF DEFAULT hereunder shall be the occurrence of any one or more of the following: (1) *Payment of Indebtedness:* Failure of Grantor to pay the Indebtedness or any part thereof when and as the same shall become due and payable, whether at the due date thereof or at a date fixed for prepayment or at a date fixed by reason of acceleration of the due date thereof or otherwise; (2) *Other Payments and Terms:* Failure of Grantor to make any payment (other than on the Indebtedness) required hereunder or to observe, perform, or comply with any of the covenants, terms or conditions set forth herein, or in any other instrument, document, agreement, letter or other writing heretofore, concurrently herewith or in the future executed by Grantor in favor of Grantee in connection with any transaction which resulted in the Indebtedness or any part thereof; (3) *False Statements:* If any certificate, representation, warranty, statement or other writing made herein or heretofore, now or hereafter furnished to Grantee by or on behalf of Grantor in connection with any transaction which resulted in the Indebtedness or any part thereof be false, untrue, incomplete or misleading in any respect as of the date made; (4) *Waste:* If the Premises or any part thereof should be subject to actual or threatened waste, or any part thereof be removed, demolished, or materially damaged or altered as a result of which the value of the Premises shall be diminished; (5) *Seizure or Levy:* If the Premises or any part thereof be seized or levied upon under legal process or a receiver be appointed for the Premises or any part thereof or for Grantor; (6) *Liens:* If any Federal tax lien or any claim of lien for labor, material or architectural or engineering services furnished or alleged to have been furnished in the improvement of or with respect to the Premises is filed of record against Grantor or the Premises and is not removed from record by payment or bond within thirty (30) days from the date of such filing; (7) *Priority Claim:* If any person shall assert any claim of priority over this Security Deed in any legal or equitable proceeding, and such claim shall not have been dismissed with prejudice within sixty (60) days after the filing thereof; (8) *Insolvency or Bankruptcy:* If Grantor shall become insolvent or make an assignment for benefit of creditors; or if Grantor should file a petition for bankruptcy or an arrangement pursuant to the Federal Bankruptcy Act or any similar statute, or if Grantor be adjudicated a bankrupt or an insolvent; or if any proceeding is instituted against or on behalf of Grantor alleging that Grantor is insolvent or unable to pay Grantor's debts as they mature; or if a petition for the bankruptcy or arrangement of Grantor, pursuant to the Federal Bankruptcy Act or any similar statute is filed; (9) *Receiver:* If there should be appointed a receiver, liquidator or trustee for Grantor or for any property of Grantor; (10) *Judgments:* If any judgment is rendered against Grantor which is not paid in full and satisfied or is not appealed from within the time allowed for appeals and paid in full and satisfied when it becomes final; (11) *Liquidation or Dissolution:* Should Grantor, if a corporation, be liquidated or dissolved or its articles of incorporation expire or be revoked, or, if a partnership or business association, be dissolved or partitioned, or, if a trust, be terminated or expire.

- 2 -

(continued)

EXHIBIT 10–7

Georgia Commercial
Deed to Secure Debt

(continued)

GRANTEE'S REMEDIES AND POWER OF SALE upon the occurrence of an event of default shall be that, at Grantee's option and election without notice to Grantor, Grantee may declare all or any portion of the Indebtedness to be immediately due and payable, whereupon the same shall be and shall become due and payable forthwith without presentment, demand, protest or notice of any kind, all of which are expressly waived by Grantor, and Grantee, at Grantee's option and election, may do any one or more of the following: (1) *Entry and Possession:* Grantee may enter upon the Premises or any part thereof and take possession thereof, excluding therefrom Grantor and all agents, employees and representatives of Grantor; employ a manager of the Premises or any part thereof; hold, store, use, operate, manage, control, maintain and lease the Premises or any part thereof; conduct business thereon; make all necessary and appropriate repairs, renewals, and replacements; keep the Premises insured; or carry out or enter into agreements of any kind with respect to the Premises. (2) *Collection of Rents:* Grantee may collect and receive all rents, issues, income, revenues, profits, accounts and contract rights from the Premises and apply the same to the Indebtedness, after deducting therefrom all costs, charges, and expenses of taking, holding, managing, and operating the Premises, including the fees and expenses of Grantee's attorneys, and agents. (3) *Payments:* Grantee may pay any sum or sums deemed necessary or appropriate by Grantee to protect the Premises or any part thereof or Grantee's interest therein. (4) *Other Remedies:* Grantee may exercise all rights and remedies contained in any other instrument, document, agreement or other writing, heretofore, concurrently herewith or in the future executed by Grantor in favor of Grantee in connection with the transactions resulting in the Indebtedness or any part thereof. (5) *Appointment of Receiver:* Grantee may make application to any court and be entitled to the appointment of a receiver to take charge of the Premises or any part thereof without alleging or proving, or having any consideration given to, the insolvency of Grantor, the value of the Premises as security for the Indebtedness or any other matter usually incident to the appointment of a receiver. (6) *U.C.C. Remedies:* With respect to the personal property in which a security interest is herein granted, Grantee may exercise any or all of the rights accruing to a secured party under this Security Deed, the Uniform Commercial Code (§§109A-9-101 *et. seq.* of the Ga. Code Annotated) and any other applicable law. Grantor shall, if Grantee requests, assemble all such personal property and make it available to Grantee at a place or places to be designated by Grantee, which shall be reasonably convenient to Grantor and Grantee. Any notice required to be given by Grantee of a public or private sale, lease or other disposition of the personal property or any other intended action by Grantee may be personally delivered to Grantor or may be deposited in the United States mail with postage prepaid duly addressed to Grantor at the address of Grantor last known to Grantee at least five (5) business days prior to such proposed action, and shall constitute reasonable and fair notice to Grantor of any such action. (7) *Power of Sale:* Grantee may sell the Premises, or any part thereof or any interest therein separately, at Grantee's discretion, with or without taking possession thereof, at public sale before the courthouse door of the county in which the Premises, or a part thereof, is located, to the highest bidder for cash, after first giving notice of the time, place and terms of such sale by advertisement published once a week for four weeks (without regard for the number of days) in a newspaper in which advertisements of sheriff's sales are published in such county. The advertisement so published shall be notice to Grantor, and Grantor hereby waives all other notices. Grantee may bid and purchase at any such sale, and Grantee may execute and deliver to the purchaser or purchasers at any such sale a sufficient conveyance of the Premises, or the part thereof or interest therein sold. Grantee's conveyance may contain recitals as to the occurrence of any event of default under this Security Deed, which recitals shall be presumptive evidence that all preliminary acts prerequisite to such sale and conveyance were in all things duly complied with. The recitals made by Grantee shall be binding and conclusive upon Grantor, and the sale and conveyance made by Grantee shall divest Grantor of all right, title, interest and equity that Grantor may have had in, to and under the Premises, or the part thereof or interest therein sold, and shall vest the same in the purchaser or purchasers at such sale. Grantee may hold one or more sales hereunder until the Indebtedness has been satisfied in full. Grantor hereby constitutes and appoints Grantee as Grantor's agent and attorney-in-fact to make such sale, to execute and deliver such conveyance and to make such recitals, and Grantor hereby ratifies and confirms all of the acts and doings of Grantee as Grantor's agent and attorney-in-fact hereunder. Grantee's agency and power as attorney-in-fact hereunder are coupled with an interest, cannot be revoked by insolvency, incompetency, death or otherwise, and shall not be exhausted until the Indebtedness has been satisfied in full. The proceeds of each sale by Grantee hereunder shall be applied first to the costs and expenses of the sale and of all proceedings in connection therewith, including attorney's fees if applicable, then to the payment of the Indebtedness, and the remainder, if any, shall be paid to Grantor. If the proceeds of any sale are not sufficient to pay the Indebtedness in full, Grantee shall determine, at Grantee's option and in Grantee's discretion, the portions of the Indebtedness to which the proceeds (after deducting therefrom the costs and expenses of the sale and all proceedings in connection therewith) shall be applied and in what order the proceeds shall be so applied. Grantor covenants and agrees that, in the event of any sale pursuant to the agency and power herein granted, Grantor shall be and become a tenant holding over and shall deliver possession of the Premises, or the part thereof or interest therein sold, to the purchaser or purchasers at the sale or be summarily dispossessed in accordance with the provisions of law applicable to tenants holding over.

All rights and remedies set forth above are cumulative and in addition to any right or remedy provided for by statute, or now or hereafter existing at law or in equity, including without limitation the right of Grantee to collect or enforce the Indebtedness with or without taking any action with respect to the Premises. Grantee may, at Grantee's election and at Grantee's discretion, exercise each and every such right and remedy concurrently or separately.

ADDITIONAL PROVISIONS of this Security Deed, constituting additional covenants and agreements by Grantor, are as follows: (1) *Applicable Law:* This Security Deed shall be governed by and construed, interpreted and enforced in accordance with the laws of the State of Georgia. (2) *Forbearance:* Grantee shall not be deemed to waive any of Grantee's rights or remedies hereunder unless such waiver be in writing and signed by or on behalf of Grantee. No delay, omission or forbearance by Grantee in exercising any of Grantee's rights or remedies shall operate as a waiver of such rights or remedies, and a waiver in writing on one occasion shall not be construed as a consent to or a waiver of any right or any remedy on any future occasion. (3) *Time:* Time is and shall be of the essence of this Security Deed and the covenants and agreements by Grantor. (4) *Captions:* Any captions or heading preceding the text of separate sections, paragraphs and sub-paragraphs hereof are solely for reference purposes and shall not affect the meaning, construction, interpretation or effect of the text. (5) *Notices:* All notices, requests, demands and other communications hereunder shall be in writing and shall be deemed to have been duly given to Grantor if personally delivered or if mailed in the United States mail, by certified mail with a return receipt requested and with postage prepaid, to Grantor's last address known to Grantee. (6) *Severability:* In the event that any of the terms, provisions or covenants of this Security Deed are held to be partially or wholly invalid or unenforceable for any reason whatsoever, such holding shall not affect, alter, modify or impair in any manner whatsoever any of the other terms, provisions or covenants hereof nor held to be partially or wholly invalid or unenforceable. (7) *Definitions:* The word "Grantor" as used herein shall include the plural should more than one Grantor execute this document; the masculine and feminine gender, regardless of the sex of Grantor or any of them; individuals, partnerships, joint ventures, corporations and other legal entities should such an entity execute this document; and the heirs, legal representatives, successors and assigns of Grantor. If more than one party shall execute this Security Deed, the word "Grantor" shall mean all parties signing, and each of them, and each and every agreement and obligation of Grantor shall be and mean the joint and several undertaking of each of them. The word "Grantee" as used herein shall include the transferees, successors, legal representatives and assigns of Grantee, and all rights of Grantee hereunder shall inure to the benefit of its transferees, successors, legal representatives and assigns. (8) *Other Provisions:* The terms and conditions set forth in Exhibit "B", if any, attached hereto are incorporated herein and made a part hereof by reference.

GRANTOR EXPRESSLY WAIVES the following: (1) *Notice and Hearing:* Any right Grantor may have under the Constitution of the State of Georgia or the Constitution of the United States of America to notice or to a judicial hearing prior to the exercise of any right or remedy provided to Grantee by this Security Deed, and Grantor waives Grantor's rights, if any, to set aside or invalidate any sale under power duly consummated in accordance with the provisions of this Security Deed on the ground (if such be the case) that the sale was consummated without prior notice or judicial hearing or both; and (2) all homestead exemption rights, if any, which Grantor or Grantor's family may have pursuant to the Constitution and laws of the United States, the State of Georgia or any other State of the United States, in and to the Premises as against the collection of the Indebtedness, or any part thereof. All waivers by Grantor in this paragraph have been made voluntarily, intelligently and knowingly by Grantor, after Grantor has been afforded an opportunity to be informed by counsel of Grantor's choice as to possible alternative rights. Grantor's execution of this Security Deed shall be conclusive evidence of the making of such waivers and that such waivers have been voluntarily, intelligently and knowingly made.

IN WITNESS WHEREOF, this Security Deed has been executed and sealed by Grantor the day and year first above written.

Signed, sealed and delivered
in the presence of:

_____ (SEAL)

_____
Unofficial Witness

_____ (SEAL)

_____
Notary Public

_____ (SEAL)

Commercial Loan Department

Security Deed Form No. _____

_____ (SEAL)

First Priority Lien Position

(Second Priority By Attaching Exhibit "B")

chapter | 11

Mortgage Forms and Provisions

Objectives

After reading this chapter, you should be able to:

- Understand the provisions contained in residential and commercial mortgages
- Understand the provisions contained in a construction loan agreement
- Understand the provisions contained in an assignment of leases and rents

Outline

A lthough the primary purpose of a mortgage is to convey real property to a lender to secure repayment of a debt, most mortgage documents address a wide range of issues of importance to the borrower and lender. For example, the lender wants assurance that property taxes will be paid on a current basis and that all buildings and improvements are insured with adequate insurance coverages during the term of the loan. A borrower may want the right to receive a notice of any default under the loan and an opportunity to cure the default before the mortgage is foreclosed. These and other matters are routinely covered in mortgage loan documents.

Mortgage loan documents are signed by a borrower each time a loan is secured by real property. These mortgage loan documents often are prepared by the paralegal as part of the real estate closing process, which is discussed further in Chapters 14 through 16. It is, therefore, important for a paralegal to be familiar with the contents of the various mortgage loan documents used in residential and commercial real estate loan transactions.

RESIDENTIAL MORTGAGE PROVISIONS

The instrument set forth in Exhibit 11–1 is a Fannie Mae/Freddie Mac uniform instrument. It is used to secure most residential loans throughout the nation. A brief explanation of the provisions contained in this mortgage follow.

Part A lists the date of the mortgage.

Part B identifies the "Borrower," who will be the property owner. The borrower's identification should be shown exactly as it appears in the borrower's deed in the chain of title.

Part C identifies the "Lender," which is the lending institution making the loan. The institution's name should be identified as it officially appears on the lender's corporate records.

Part D "Note" describes the debt being secured by the mortgage. The debt typically is described as a debt evidenced by a note the same date of the mortgage that provides a final maturity date. The statute of limitations enforcing a mortgage typically is 20 years from the date of the final maturity of the note. If the final maturity of a note is not revealed in the mortgage, it is 20 years from the date of the mortgage. Because many residential mortgage loans have a maturity greater than 20 years, it is important to show the final maturity date of the note in the mortgage.

Parts E through P contain a list of terms and their definitions that are used in the mortgage.

TRANSFER OF RIGHTS IN THE PROPERTY

This paragraph is the conveyance or transfer of the real property in the mortgage to secure the repayment of the note. This section contains a complete description of the real property. It should match the survey description for the real property as well as the description contained in the borrower's deed. This section also contains a street address for the property.

The conveyance provides that in addition to the real property conveyed as security, all easements, rights, appurtenances, rents, royalties, and mineral and gas rights of borrower are conveyed. The intent is for the lender to receive everything the borrower owns in connection with the real property.

This section also contains a warranty paragraph wherein the borrower sets out the same warranties that are usually found in a general warranty deed.

UNIFORM COVENANTS

The next section of the mortgage is the uniform covenants. These covenants include the following:

1. *Payment of Principal, Interest, Escrow Items, Prepayment Charges, and Late Charges.* This section is a reaffirmation of the promise to pay the debt when it is due, including all other items such as prepayment charges and late charges. This promise is also contained in the note being secured by the mortgage; however, most lenders have the promise repeated in the mortgage.

2. *Application of Payments or Proceeds.* This covenant provides that when the lender receives funds from the borrower it shall apply those funds in the following order of priority: first, to interest due under the note; next, to principal due under the note; and then to amounts due under Section 3 of the mortgage, which are escrow items for taxes and insurance premiums. Any remaining amounts shall be applied first to pay late

EXHIBIT 11–1

Fannie Mae/Freddie Mac Uniform Mortgage

After Recording Return To:

_____

_____

_____

_____

_____ [Space Above This Line For Recording Data] _____

MORTGAGE

DEFINITIONS

Words used in multiple sections of this document are defined below and other words are defined in Sections 3, 11, 13, 18, 20 and 21. Certain rules regarding the usage of words used in this document are also provided in Section 16.

(A) **"Security Instrument"** means this document, which is dated _____, _____, together with all Riders to this document.

(B) **"Borrower"** is _____. Borrower is the mortgagor under this Security Instrument.

(C) **"Lender"** is _____. Lender is a _____ organized and existing under the laws of _____. Lender's address is _____ _____. Lender is the mortgagee under this Security Instrument.

(D) **"Note"** means the promissory note signed by Borrower and dated _____, _____. The Note states that Borrower owes Lender _____ Dollars (U.S. $_____) plus interest. Borrower has promised to pay this debt in regular Periodic Payments and to pay the debt in full not later than _____.

(E) **"Property"** means the property that is described below under the heading "Transfer of Rights in the Property."

(F) **"Loan"** means the debt evidenced by the Note, plus interest, any prepayment charges and late charges due under the Note, and all sums due under this Security Instrument, plus interest.

(G) **"Riders"** means all Riders to this Security Instrument that are executed by Borrower. The following Riders are to be executed by Borrower [check box as applicable]:

☐ Adjustable Rate Rider	☐ Condominium Rider	☐ Second Home Rider
☐ Balloon Rider	☐ Planned Unit Development Rider	☐ Other(s) [specify] _____
☐ 1-4 Family Rider	☐ Biweekly Payment Rider	

IOWA--Single Family--**Fannie Mae/Freddie Mac UNIFORM INSTRUMENT**   **Form 3016   1/01** *(page 1 of 16 pages)*

Delmar/Cengage Learning

(continued)

EXHIBIT 11–1

Fannie Mae/Freddie Mac Uniform Mortgage (*continued*)

(H) "Applicable Law" means all controlling applicable federal, state and local statutes, regulations, ordinances and administrative rules and orders (that have the effect of law) as well as all applicable final, non-appealable judicial opinions.

(I) "Community Association Dues, Fees, and Assessments" means all dues, fees, assessments and other charges that are imposed on Borrower or the Property by a condominium association, homeowners association or similar organization.

(J) "Electronic Funds Transfer" means any transfer of funds, other than a transaction originated by check, draft, or similar paper instrument, which is initiated through an electronic terminal, telephonic instrument, computer, or magnetic tape so as to order, instruct, or authorize a financial institution to debit or credit an account. Such term includes, but is not limited to, point-of-sale transfers, automated teller machine transactions, transfers initiated by telephone, wire transfers, and automated clearinghouse transfers.

(K) "Escrow Items" means those items that are described in Section 3.

(L) "Miscellaneous Proceeds" means any compensation, settlement, award of damages, or proceeds paid by any third party (other than insurance proceeds paid under the coverages described in Section 5) for: (i) damage to, or destruction of, the Property; (ii) condemnation or other taking of all or any part of the Property; (iii) conveyance in lieu of condemnation; or (iv) misrepresentations of, or omissions as to, the value and/or condition of the Property.

(M) "Mortgage Insurance" means insurance protecting Lender against the nonpayment of, or default on, the Loan.

(N) "Periodic Payment" means the regularly scheduled amount due for (i) principal and interest under the Note, plus (ii) any amounts under Section 3 of this Security Instrument.

(O) "RESPA" means the Real Estate Settlement Procedures Act (12 U.S.C. §2601 et seq.) and its implementing regulation, Regulation X (24 C.F.R. Part 3500), as they might be amended from time to time, or any additional or successor legislation or regulation that governs the same subject matter. As used in this Security Instrument, "RESPA" refers to all requirements and restrictions that are imposed in regard to a "federally related mortgage loan" even if the Loan does not qualify as a "federally related mortgage loan" under RESPA.

(P) "Successor in Interest of Borrower" means any party that has taken title to the Property, whether or not that party has assumed Borrower's obligations under the Note and/or this Security Instrument.

TRANSFER OF RIGHTS IN THE PROPERTY

This Security Instrument secures to Lender: (i) the repayment of the Loan, and all renewals, extensions and modifications of the Note; and (ii) the performance of Borrower's covenants and agreements under this Security Instrument and the Note. For this purpose, Borrower irrevocably

IOWA--Single Family--Fannie Mae/Freddie Mac UNIFORM INSTRUMENT   Form 3016   1/01 *(page 2 of 16 pages)*

(continued)

EXHIBIT 11–1

Fannie Mae/Freddie Mac Uniform Mortgage (*continued*)

mortgages, grants and conveys to Lender, with power of sale, the following described property located in the _____ of _____:
              [Type of Recording Jurisdiction]   [Name of Recording Jurisdiction]

which currently has the address of _____
                                                   [Street]
_____, Iowa _____ ("Property Address"):
        [City]   [Zip Code]

TOGETHER WITH all the improvements now or hereafter erected on the property, and all easements, appurtenances, and fixtures now or hereafter a part of the property. All replacements and additions shall also be covered by this Security Instrument. All of the foregoing is referred to in this Security Instrument as the "Property."

BORROWER COVENANTS that Borrower is lawfully seised of the estate hereby conveyed and has the right to grant and convey the Property and that the Property is unencumbered, except for encumbrances of record. Borrower warrants and will defend generally the title to the Property against all claims and demands, subject to any encumbrances of record.

THIS SECURITY INSTRUMENT combines uniform covenants for national use and non-uniform covenants with limited variations by jurisdiction to constitute a uniform security instrument covering real property.

UNIFORM COVENANTS. Borrower and Lender covenant and agree as follows:
    1. Payment of Principal, Interest, Escrow Items, Prepayment Charges, and Late Charges. Borrower shall pay when due the principal of, and interest on, the debt evidenced by the Note and any prepayment charges and late charges due under the Note. Borrower shall also pay funds for Escrow Items pursuant to Section 3. Payments due under the Note and this Security Instrument shall be made in U.S. currency. However, if any check or other instrument received by Lender as payment under the Note or this Security Instrument is returned to Lender unpaid, Lender may require that any or all subsequent payments due under the Note and this Security Instrument be made in one or more of the following forms, as selected by Lender: (a) cash; (b) money order; (c) certified check, bank check, treasurer's check or cashier's check, provided any such check is drawn upon an institution whose deposits are insured by a federal agency, instrumentality, or entity; or (d) Electronic Funds Transfer.

IOWA--Single Family--Fannie Mae/Freddie Mac UNIFORM INSTRUMENT   Form 3016   1/01 *(page 3 of 16 pages)*

(continued)

EXHIBIT 11–1

Fannie Mae/Freddie Mac Uniform Mortgage (*continued*)

Payments are deemed received by Lender when received at the location designated in the Note or at such other location as may be designated by Lender in accordance with the notice provisions in Section 15. Lender may return any payment or partial payment if the payment or partial payments are insufficient to bring the Loan current. Lender may accept any payment or partial payment insufficient to bring the Loan current, without waiver of any rights hereunder or prejudice to its rights to refuse such payment or partial payments in the future, but Lender is not obligated to apply such payments at the time such payments are accepted. If each Periodic Payment is applied as of its scheduled due date, then Lender need not pay interest on unapplied funds. Lender may hold such unapplied funds until Borrower makes payment to bring the Loan current. If Borrower does not do so within a reasonable period of time, Lender shall either apply such funds or return them to Borrower. If not applied earlier, such funds will be applied to the outstanding principal balance under the Note immediately prior to foreclosure. No offset or claim which Borrower might have now or in the future against Lender shall relieve Borrower from making payments due under the Note and this Security Instrument or performing the covenants and agreements secured by this Security Instrument.

2. Application of Payments or Proceeds. Except as otherwise described in this Section 2, all payments accepted and applied by Lender shall be applied in the following order of priority: (a) interest due under the Note; (b) principal due under the Note; (c) amounts due under Section 3. Such payments shall be applied to each Periodic Payment in the order in which it became due. Any remaining amounts shall be applied first to late charges, second to any other amounts due under this Security Instrument, and then to reduce the principal balance of the Note.

If Lender receives a payment from Borrower for a delinquent Periodic Payment which includes a sufficient amount to pay any late charge due, the payment may be applied to the delinquent payment and the late charge. If more than one Periodic Payment is outstanding, Lender may apply any payment received from Borrower to the repayment of the Periodic Payments if, and to the extent that, each payment can be paid in full. To the extent that any excess exists after the payment is applied to the full payment of one or more Periodic Payments, such excess may be applied to any late charges due. Voluntary prepayments shall be applied first to any prepayment charges and then as described in the Note.

Any application of payments, insurance proceeds, or Miscellaneous Proceeds to principal due under the Note shall not extend or postpone the due date, or change the amount, of the Periodic Payments.

⁎ **3. Funds for Escrow Items.** Borrower shall pay to Lender on the day Periodic Payments are due under the Note, until the Note is paid in full, a sum (the "Funds") to provide for payment of amounts due for: (a) taxes and assessments and other items which can attain priority over this Security Instrument as a lien or encumbrance on the Property; (b) leasehold payments or ground rents on the Property, if any; (c) premiums for any and all insurance required by Lender under Section 5; and (d) Mortgage Insurance premiums, if any, or any sums payable by Borrower to Lender in lieu of the payment of Mortgage Insurance premiums in accordance with the provisions of Section 10. These items are called "Escrow Items." At origination or at any time during the term of the Loan, Lender may require that Community Association Dues, Fees, and Assessments, if any, be escrowed by Borrower, and such dues, fees and assessments shall be an Escrow Item. Borrower shall promptly furnish to Lender all notices of amounts to be paid under this Section. Borrower shall pay Lender the Funds for Escrow Items unless Lender waives Borrower's obligation to pay the

Escrow payment

IOWA--Single Family--Fannie Mae/Freddie Mac UNIFORM INSTRUMENT　　　　Form 3016　1/01　*(page 4 of 16 pages)*

(continued)

EXHIBIT 11–1

Fannie Mae/Freddie Mac Uniform Mortgage (*continued*)

Funds for any or all Escrow Items. Lender may waive Borrower's obligation to pay to Lender Funds for any or all Escrow Items at any time. Any such waiver may only be in writing. In the event of such waiver, Borrower shall pay directly, when and where payable, the amounts due for any Escrow Items for which payment of Funds has been waived by Lender and, if Lender requires, shall furnish to Lender receipts evidencing such payment within such time period as Lender may require. Borrower's obligation to make such payments and to provide receipts shall for all purposes be deemed to be a covenant and agreement contained in this Security Instrument, as the phrase "covenant and agreement" is used in Section 9. If Borrower is obligated to pay Escrow Items directly, pursuant to a waiver, and Borrower fails to pay the amount due for an Escrow Item, Lender may exercise its rights under Section 9 and pay such amount and Borrower shall then be obligated under Section 9 to repay to Lender any such amount. Lender may revoke the waiver as to any or all Escrow Items at any time by a notice given in accordance with Section 15 and, upon such revocation, Borrower shall pay to Lender all Funds, and in such amounts, that are then required under this Section 3.

Lender may, at any time, collect and hold Funds in an amount (a) sufficient to permit Lender to apply the Funds at the time specified under RESPA, and (b) not to exceed the maximum amount a lender can require under RESPA. Lender shall estimate the amount of Funds due on the basis of current data and reasonable estimates of expenditures of future Escrow Items or otherwise in accordance with Applicable Law.

The Funds shall be held in an institution whose deposits are insured by a federal agency, instrumentality, or entity (including Lender, if Lender is an institution whose deposits are so insured) or in any Federal Home Loan Bank. Lender shall apply the Funds to pay the Escrow Items no later than the time specified under RESPA. Lender shall not charge Borrower for holding and applying the Funds, annually analyzing the escrow account, or verifying the Escrow Items, unless Lender pays Borrower interest on the Funds and Applicable Law permits Lender to make such a charge. Unless an agreement is made in writing or Applicable Law requires interest to be paid on the Funds, Lender shall not be required to pay Borrower any interest or earnings on the Funds. Borrower and Lender can agree in writing, however, that interest shall be paid on the Funds. Lender shall give to Borrower, without charge, an annual accounting of the Funds as required by RESPA.

If there is a surplus of Funds held in escrow, as defined under RESPA, Lender shall account to Borrower for the excess funds in accordance with RESPA. If there is a shortage of Funds held in escrow, as defined under RESPA, Lender shall notify Borrower as required by RESPA, and Borrower shall pay to Lender the amount necessary to make up the shortage in accordance with RESPA, but in no more than 12 monthly payments. If there is a deficiency of Funds held in escrow, as defined under RESPA, Lender shall notify Borrower as required by RESPA, and Borrower shall pay to Lender the amount necessary to make up the deficiency in accordance with RESPA, but in no more than 12 monthly payments.

Upon payment in full of all sums secured by this Security Instrument, Lender shall promptly refund to Borrower any Funds held by Lender.

4. Charges; Liens. Borrower shall pay all taxes, assessments, charges, fines, and impositions attributable to the Property which can attain priority over this Security Instrument, leasehold payments or ground rents on the Property, if any, and Community Association Dues, Fees, and Assessments, if any. To the extent that these items are Escrow Items, Borrower shall pay them in the manner provided in Section 3.

IOWA--Single Family--Fannie Mae/Freddie Mac UNIFORM INSTRUMENT   Form 3016   1/01 *(page 5 of 16 pages)*

(continued)

EXHIBIT 11-1

Fannie Mae/Freddie Mac Uniform Mortgage (*continued*)

Borrower shall promptly discharge any lien which has priority over this Security Instrument unless Borrower: (a) agrees in writing to the payment of the obligation secured by the lien in a manner acceptable to Lender, but only so long as Borrower is performing such agreement; (b) contests the lien in good faith by, or defends against enforcement of the lien in, legal proceedings which in Lender's opinion operate to prevent the enforcement of the lien while those proceedings are pending, but only until such proceedings are concluded; or (c) secures from the holder of the lien an agreement satisfactory to Lender subordinating the lien to this Security Instrument. If Lender determines that any part of the Property is subject to a lien which can attain priority over this Security Instrument, Lender may give Borrower a notice identifying the lien. Within 10 days of the date on which that notice is given, Borrower shall satisfy the lien or take one or more of the actions set forth above in this Section 4.

Lender may require Borrower to pay a one-time charge for a real estate tax verification and/or reporting service used by Lender in connection with this Loan.

5. Property Insurance. Borrower shall keep the improvements now existing or hereafter erected on the Property insured against loss by fire, hazards included within the term "extended coverage," and any other hazards including, but not limited to, earthquakes and floods, for which Lender requires insurance. This insurance shall be maintained in the amounts (including deductible levels) and for the periods that Lender requires. What Lender requires pursuant to the preceding sentences can change during the term of the Loan. The insurance carrier providing the insurance shall be chosen by Borrower subject to Lender's right to disapprove Borrower's choice, which right shall not be exercised unreasonably. Lender may require Borrower to pay, in connection with this Loan, either: (a) a one-time charge for flood zone determination, certification and tracking services; or (b) a one-time charge for flood zone determination and certification services and subsequent charges each time remappings or similar changes occur which reasonably might affect such determination or certification. Borrower shall also be responsible for the payment of any fees imposed by the Federal Emergency Management Agency in connection with the review of any flood zone determination resulting from an objection by Borrower.

If Borrower fails to maintain any of the coverages described above, Lender may obtain insurance coverage, at Lender's option and Borrower's expense. Lender is under no obligation to purchase any particular type or amount of coverage. Therefore, such coverage shall cover Lender, but might or might not protect Borrower, Borrower's equity in the Property, or the contents of the Property, against any risk, hazard or liability and might provide greater or lesser coverage than was previously in effect. Borrower acknowledges that the cost of the insurance coverage so obtained might significantly exceed the cost of insurance that Borrower could have obtained. Any amounts disbursed by Lender under this Section 5 shall become additional debt of Borrower secured by this Security Instrument. These amounts shall bear interest at the Note rate from the date of disbursement and shall be payable, with such interest, upon notice from Lender to Borrower requesting payment.

All insurance policies required by Lender and renewals of such policies shall be subject to Lender's right to disapprove such policies, shall include a standard mortgage clause, and shall name Lender as mortgagee and/or as an additional loss payee. Lender shall have the right to hold the policies and renewal certificates. If Lender requires, Borrower shall promptly give to Lender all receipts of paid premiums and renewal notices. If Borrower obtains any form of insurance coverage, not otherwise required by Lender, for damage to, or destruction of, the Property, such policy shall

IOWA--Single Family--**Fannie Mae/Freddie Mac UNIFORM INSTRUMENT**   Form 3016   1/01 *(page 6 of 16 pages)*

(continued)

EXHIBIT 11–1

Fannie Mae/Freddie Mac Uniform Mortgage (*continued*)

include a standard mortgage clause and shall name Lender as mortgagee and/or as an additional loss payee.

In the event of loss, Borrower shall give prompt notice to the insurance carrier and Lender. Lender may make proof of loss if not made promptly by Borrower. Unless Lender and Borrower otherwise agree in writing, any insurance proceeds, whether or not the underlying insurance was required by Lender, shall be applied to restoration or repair of the Property, if the restoration or repair is economically feasible and Lender's security is not lessened. During such repair and restoration period, Lender shall have the right to hold such insurance proceeds until Lender has had an opportunity to inspect such Property to ensure the work has been completed to Lender's satisfaction, provided that such inspection shall be undertaken promptly. Lender may disburse proceeds for the repairs and restoration in a single payment or in a series of progress payments as the work is completed. Unless an agreement is made in writing or Applicable Law requires interest to be paid on such insurance proceeds, Lender shall not be required to pay Borrower any interest or earnings on such proceeds. Fees for public adjusters, or other third parties, retained by Borrower shall not be paid out of the insurance proceeds and shall be the sole obligation of Borrower. If the restoration or repair is not economically feasible or Lender's security would be lessened, the insurance proceeds shall be applied to the sums secured by this Security Instrument, whether or not then due, with the excess, if any, paid to Borrower. Such insurance proceeds shall be applied in the order provided for in Section 2.

If Borrower abandons the Property, Lender may file, negotiate and settle any available insurance claim and related matters. If Borrower does not respond within 30 days to a notice from Lender that the insurance carrier has offered to settle a claim, then Lender may negotiate and settle the claim. The 30-day period will begin when the notice is given. In either event, or if Lender acquires the Property under Section 22 or otherwise, Borrower hereby assigns to Lender (a) Borrower's rights to any insurance proceeds in an amount not to exceed the amounts unpaid under the Note or this Security Instrument, and (b) any other of Borrower's rights (other than the right to any refund of unearned premiums paid by Borrower) under all insurance policies covering the Property, insofar as such rights are applicable to the coverage of the Property. Lender may use the insurance proceeds either to repair or restore the Property or to pay amounts unpaid under the Note or this Security Instrument, whether or not then due.

6. Occupancy. Borrower shall occupy, establish, and use the Property as Borrower's principal residence within 60 days after the execution of this Security Instrument and shall continue to occupy the Property as Borrower's principal residence for at least one year after the date of occupancy, unless Lender otherwise agrees in writing, which consent shall not be unreasonably withheld, or unless extenuating circumstances exist which are beyond Borrower's control.

7. Preservation, Maintenance and Protection of the Property; Inspections. Borrower shall not destroy, damage or impair the Property, allow the Property to deteriorate or commit waste on the Property. Whether or not Borrower is residing in the Property, Borrower shall maintain the Property in order to prevent the Property from deteriorating or decreasing in value due to its condition. Unless it is determined pursuant to Section 5 that repair or restoration is not economically feasible, Borrower shall promptly repair the Property if damaged to avoid further deterioration or damage. If insurance or condemnation proceeds are paid in connection with damage to, or the taking of, the Property, Borrower shall be responsible for repairing or restoring the Property only if Lender has released proceeds for such purposes. Lender may disburse proceeds for

IOWA--Single Family--Fannie Mae/Freddie Mac UNIFORM INSTRUMENT   Form 3016   1/01 (*page 7 of 16 pages*)

(*continued*)

EXHIBIT 11–1

Fannie Mae/Freddie Mac Uniform Mortgage (*continued*)

the repairs and restoration in a single payment or in a series of progress payments as the work is completed. If the insurance or condemnation proceeds are not sufficient to repair or restore the Property, Borrower is not relieved of Borrower's obligation for the completion of such repair or restoration.

Lender or its agent may make reasonable entries upon and inspections of the Property. If it has reasonable cause, Lender may inspect the interior of the improvements on the Property. Lender shall give Borrower notice at the time of or prior to such an interior inspection specifying such reasonable cause.

8. Borrower's Loan Application. Borrower shall be in default if, during the Loan application process, Borrower or any persons or entities acting at the direction of Borrower or with Borrower's knowledge or consent gave materially false, misleading, or inaccurate information or statements to Lender (or failed to provide Lender with material information) in connection with the Loan. Material representations include, but are not limited to, representations concerning Borrower's occupancy of the Property as Borrower's principal residence.

9. Protection of Lender's Interest in the Property and Rights Under this Security Instrument. If (a) Borrower fails to perform the covenants and agreements contained in this Security Instrument, (b) there is a legal proceeding that might significantly affect Lender's interest in the Property and/or rights under this Security Instrument (such as a proceeding in bankruptcy, probate, for condemnation or forfeiture, for enforcement of a lien which may attain priority over this Security Instrument or to enforce laws or regulations), or (c) Borrower has abandoned the Property, then Lender may do and pay for whatever is reasonable or appropriate to protect Lender's interest in the Property and rights under this Security Instrument, including protecting and/or assessing the value of the Property, and securing and/or repairing the Property. Lender's actions can include, but are not limited to: (a) paying any sums secured by a lien which has priority over this Security Instrument; (b) appearing in court; and (c) paying reasonable attorneys' fees to protect its interest in the Property and/or rights under this Security Instrument, including its secured position in a bankruptcy proceeding. Securing the Property includes, but is not limited to, entering the Property to make repairs, change locks, replace or board up doors and windows, drain water from pipes, eliminate building or other code violations or dangerous conditions, and have utilities turned on or off. Although Lender may take action under this Section 9, Lender does not have to do so and is not under any duty or obligation to do so. It is agreed that Lender incurs no liability for not taking any or all actions authorized under this Section 9.

Any amounts disbursed by Lender under this Section 9 shall become additional debt of Borrower secured by this Security Instrument. These amounts shall bear interest at the Note rate from the date of disbursement and shall be payable, with such interest, upon notice from Lender to Borrower requesting payment.

If this Security Instrument is on a leasehold, Borrower shall comply with all the provisions of the lease. If Borrower acquires fee title to the Property, the leasehold and the fee title shall not merge unless Lender agrees to the merger in writing.

10. Mortgage Insurance. If Lender required Mortgage Insurance as a condition of making the Loan, Borrower shall pay the premiums required to maintain the Mortgage Insurance in effect. If, for any reason, the Mortgage Insurance coverage required by Lender ceases to be available from the mortgage insurer that previously provided such insurance and Borrower was required to make separately designated payments toward the premiums for Mortgage Insurance, Borrower shall pay

IOWA--Single Family--**Fannie Mae/Freddie Mac UNIFORM INSTRUMENT**   Form 3016   1/01 (*page 8 of 16 pages*)

(continued)

EXHIBIT 11–1

Fannie Mae/Freddie Mac Uniform Mortgage (*continued*)

the premiums required to obtain coverage substantially equivalent to the Mortgage Insurance previously in effect, at a cost substantially equivalent to the cost to Borrower of the Mortgage Insurance previously in effect, from an alternate mortgage insurer selected by Lender. If substantially equivalent Mortgage Insurance coverage is not available, Borrower shall continue to pay to Lender the amount of the separately designated payments that were due when the insurance coverage ceased to be in effect. Lender will accept, use and retain these payments as a non-refundable loss reserve in lieu of Mortgage Insurance. Such loss reserve shall be non-refundable, notwithstanding the fact that the Loan is ultimately paid in full, and Lender shall not be required to pay Borrower any interest or earnings on such loss reserve. Lender can no longer require loss reserve payments if Mortgage Insurance coverage (in the amount and for the period that Lender requires) provided by an insurer selected by Lender again becomes available, is obtained, and Lender requires separately designated payments toward the premiums for Mortgage Insurance. If Lender required Mortgage Insurance as a condition of making the Loan and Borrower was required to make separately designated payments toward the premiums for Mortgage Insurance, Borrower shall pay the premiums required to maintain Mortgage Insurance in effect, or to provide a non-refundable loss reserve, until Lender's requirement for Mortgage Insurance ends in accordance with any written agreement between Borrower and Lender providing for such termination or until termination is required by Applicable Law. Nothing in this Section 10 affects Borrower's obligation to pay interest at the rate provided in the Note.

Mortgage Insurance reimburses Lender (or any entity that purchases the Note) for certain losses it may incur if Borrower does not repay the Loan as agreed. Borrower is not a party to the Mortgage Insurance.

Mortgage insurers evaluate their total risk on all such insurance in force from time to time, and may enter into agreements with other parties that share or modify their risk, or reduce losses. These agreements are on terms and conditions that are satisfactory to the mortgage insurer and the other party (or parties) to these agreements. These agreements may require the mortgage insurer to make payments using any source of funds that the mortgage insurer may have available (which may include funds obtained from Mortgage Insurance premiums).

As a result of these agreements, Lender, any purchaser of the Note, another insurer, any reinsurer, any other entity, or any affiliate of any of the foregoing, may receive (directly or indirectly) amounts that derive from (or might be characterized as) a portion of Borrower's payments for Mortgage Insurance, in exchange for sharing or modifying the mortgage insurer's risk, or reducing losses. If such agreement provides that an affiliate of Lender takes a share of the insurer's risk in exchange for a share of the premiums paid to the insurer, the arrangement is often termed "captive reinsurance." Further:

(a) **Any such agreements will not affect the amounts that Borrower has agreed to pay for Mortgage Insurance, or any other terms of the Loan. Such agreements will not increase the amount Borrower will owe for Mortgage Insurance, and they will not entitle Borrower to any refund.**

(b) **Any such agreements will not affect the rights Borrower has – if any – with respect to the Mortgage Insurance under the Homeowners Protection Act of 1998 or any other law. These rights may include the right to receive certain disclosures, to request and obtain cancellation of the Mortgage Insurance, to have the Mortgage Insurance terminated**

(*continued*)

EXHIBIT 11–1

Fannie Mae/Freddie Mac Uniform Mortgage (*continued*)

automatically, and/or to receive a refund of any Mortgage Insurance premiums that were unearned at the time of such cancellation or termination.

    11. Assignment of Miscellaneous Proceeds; Forfeiture. All Miscellaneous Proceeds are hereby assigned to and shall be paid to Lender.

    If the Property is damaged, such Miscellaneous Proceeds shall be applied to restoration or repair of the Property, if the restoration or repair is economically feasible and Lender's security is not lessened. During such repair and restoration period, Lender shall have the right to hold such Miscellaneous Proceeds until Lender has had an opportunity to inspect such Property to ensure the work has been completed to Lender's satisfaction, provided that such inspection shall be undertaken promptly. Lender may pay for the repairs and restoration in a single disbursement or in a series of progress payments as the work is completed. Unless an agreement is made in writing or Applicable Law requires interest to be paid on such Miscellaneous Proceeds, Lender shall not be required to pay Borrower any interest or earnings on such Miscellaneous Proceeds. If the restoration or repair is not economically feasible or Lender's security would be lessened, the Miscellaneous Proceeds shall be applied to the sums secured by this Security Instrument, whether or not then due, with the excess, if any, paid to Borrower. Such Miscellaneous Proceeds shall be applied in the order provided for in Section 2.

    In the event of a total taking, destruction, or loss in value of the Property, the Miscellaneous Proceeds shall be applied to the sums secured by this Security Instrument, whether or not then due, with the excess, if any, paid to Borrower.

    In the event of a partial taking, destruction, or loss in value of the Property in which the fair market value of the Property immediately before the partial taking, destruction, or loss in value is equal to or greater than the amount of the sums secured by this Security Instrument immediately before the partial taking, destruction, or loss in value, unless Borrower and Lender otherwise agree in writing, the sums secured by this Security Instrument shall be reduced by the amount of the Miscellaneous Proceeds multiplied by the following fraction: (a) the total amount of the sums secured immediately before the partial taking, destruction, or loss in value divided by (b) the fair market value of the Property immediately before the partial taking, destruction, or loss in value. Any balance shall be paid to Borrower.

    In the event of a partial taking, destruction, or loss in value of the Property in which the fair market value of the Property immediately before the partial taking, destruction, or loss in value is less than the amount of the sums secured immediately before the partial taking, destruction, or loss in value, unless Borrower and Lender otherwise agree in writing, the Miscellaneous Proceeds shall be applied to the sums secured by this Security Instrument whether or not the sums are then due.

    If the Property is abandoned by Borrower, or if, after notice by Lender to Borrower that the Opposing Party (as defined in the next sentence) offers to make an award to settle a claim for damages, Borrower fails to respond to Lender within 30 days after the date the notice is given, Lender is authorized to collect and apply the Miscellaneous Proceeds either to restoration or repair of the Property or to the sums secured by this Security Instrument, whether or not then due. "Opposing Party" means the third party that owes Borrower Miscellaneous Proceeds or the party against whom Borrower has a right of action in regard to Miscellaneous Proceeds.

IOWA--Single Family--Fannie Mae/Freddie Mac UNIFORM INSTRUMENT   **Form 3016**   1/01 *(page 10 of 16 pages)*

(continued)

EXHIBIT 11–1

Fannie Mae/Freddie Mac Uniform Mortgage (*continued*)

Borrower shall be in default if any action or proceeding, whether civil or criminal, is begun that, in Lender's judgment, could result in forfeiture of the Property or other material impairment of Lender's interest in the Property or rights under this Security Instrument. Borrower can cure such a default and, if acceleration has occurred, reinstate as provided in Section 19, by causing the action or proceeding to be dismissed with a ruling that, in Lender's judgment, precludes forfeiture of the Property or other material impairment of Lender's interest in the Property or rights under this Security Instrument. The proceeds of any award or claim for damages that are attributable to the impairment of Lender's interest in the Property are hereby assigned and shall be paid to Lender.

All Miscellaneous Proceeds that are not applied to restoration or repair of the Property shall be applied in the order provided for in Section 2.

12. Borrower Not Released; Forbearance By Lender Not a Waiver. Extension of the time for payment or modification of amortization of the sums secured by this Security Instrument granted by Lender to Borrower or any Successor in Interest of Borrower shall not operate to release the liability of Borrower or any Successors in Interest of Borrower. Lender shall not be required to commence proceedings against any Successor in Interest of Borrower or to refuse to extend time for payment or otherwise modify amortization of the sums secured by this Security Instrument by reason of any demand made by the original Borrower or any Successors in Interest of Borrower. Any forbearance by Lender in exercising any right or remedy including, without limitation, Lender's acceptance of payments from third persons, entities or Successors in Interest of Borrower or in amounts less than the amount then due, shall not be a waiver of or preclude the exercise of any right or remedy.

13. Joint and Several Liability; Co-signers; Successors and Assigns Bound. Borrower covenants and agrees that Borrower's obligations and liability shall be joint and several. However, any Borrower who co-signs this Security Instrument but does not execute the Note (a "co-signer"): (a) is co-signing this Security Instrument only to mortgage, grant and convey the co-signer's interest in the Property under the terms of this Security Instrument; (b) is not personally obligated to pay the sums secured by this Security Instrument; and (c) agrees that Lender and any other Borrower can agree to extend, modify, forbear or make any accommodations with regard to the terms of this Security Instrument or the Note without the co-signer's consent.

Subject to the provisions of Section 18, any Successor in Interest of Borrower who assumes Borrower's obligations under this Security Instrument in writing, and is approved by Lender, shall obtain all of Borrower's rights and benefits under this Security Instrument. Borrower shall not be released from Borrower's obligations and liability under this Security Instrument unless Lender agrees to such release in writing. The covenants and agreements of this Security Instrument shall bind (except as provided in Section 20) and benefit the successors and assigns of Lender.

14. Loan Charges. Lender may charge Borrower fees for services performed in connection with Borrower's default, for the purpose of protecting Lender's interest in the Property and rights under this Security Instrument, including, but not limited to, attorneys' fees, property inspection and valuation fees. In regard to any other fees, the absence of express authority in this Security Instrument to charge a specific fee to Borrower shall not be construed as a prohibition on the charging of such fee. Lender may not charge fees that are expressly prohibited by this Security Instrument or by Applicable Law.

If the Loan is subject to a law which sets maximum loan charges, and that law is finally interpreted so that the interest or other loan charges collected or to be collected in connection with

IOWA--Single Family--Fannie Mae/Freddie Mac UNIFORM INSTRUMENT   Form 3016   1/01 (*page 11 of 16 pages*)

(continued)

EXHIBIT 11–1

Fannie Mae/Freddie Mac Uniform Mortgage (*continued*)

the Loan exceed the permitted limits, then: (a) any such loan charge shall be reduced by the amount necessary to reduce the charge to the permitted limit; and (b) any sums already collected from Borrower which exceeded permitted limits will be refunded to Borrower. Lender may choose to make this refund by reducing the principal owed under the Note or by making a direct payment to Borrower. If a refund reduces principal, the reduction will be treated as a partial prepayment without any prepayment charge (whether or not a prepayment charge is provided for under the Note). Borrower's acceptance of any such refund made by direct payment to Borrower will constitute a waiver of any right of action Borrower might have arising out of such overcharge.

15. Notices. All notices given by Borrower or Lender in connection with this Security Instrument must be in writing. Any notice to Borrower in connection with this Security Instrument shall be deemed to have been given to Borrower when mailed by first class mail or when actually delivered to Borrower's notice address if sent by other means. Notice to any one Borrower shall constitute notice to all Borrowers unless Applicable Law expressly requires otherwise. The notice address shall be the Property Address unless Borrower has designated a substitute notice address by notice to Lender. Borrower shall promptly notify Lender of Borrower's change of address. If Lender specifies a procedure for reporting Borrower's change of address, then Borrower shall only report a change of address through that specified procedure. There may be only one designated notice address under this Security Instrument at any one time. Any notice to Lender shall be given by delivering it or by mailing it by first class mail to Lender's address stated herein unless Lender has designated another address by notice to Borrower. Any notice in connection with this Security Instrument shall not be deemed to have been given to Lender until actually received by Lender. If any notice required by this Security Instrument is also required under Applicable Law, the Applicable Law requirement will satisfy the corresponding requirement under this Security Instrument.

16. Governing Law; Severability; Rules of Construction. This Security Instrument shall be governed by federal law and the law of the jurisdiction in which the Property is located. All rights and obligations contained in this Security Instrument are subject to any requirements and limitations of Applicable Law. Applicable Law might explicitly or implicitly allow the parties to agree by contract or it might be silent, but such silence shall not be construed as a prohibition against agreement by contract. In the event that any provision or clause of this Security Instrument or the Note conflicts with Applicable Law, such conflict shall not affect other provisions of this Security Instrument or the Note which can be given effect without the conflicting provision.

As used in this Security Instrument: (a) words of the masculine gender shall mean and include corresponding neuter words or words of the feminine gender; (b) words in the singular shall mean and include the plural and vice versa; and (c) the word "may" gives sole discretion without any obligation to take any action.

17. Borrower's Copy. Borrower shall be given one copy of the Note and of this Security Instrument.

18. Transfer of the Property or a Beneficial Interest in Borrower. As used in this Section 18, "Interest in the Property" means any legal or beneficial interest in the Property, including, but not limited to, those beneficial interests transferred in a bond for deed, contract for deed, installment sales contract or escrow agreement, the intent of which is the transfer of title by Borrower at a future date to a purchaser.

IOWA--Single Family--Fannie Mae/Freddie Mac UNIFORM INSTRUMENT   **Form 3016   1/01** *(page 12 of 16 pages)*

(continued)

EXHIBIT 11–1

Fannie Mae/Freddie Mac Uniform Mortgage (*continued*)

If all or any part of the Property or any Interest in the Property is sold or transferred (or if Borrower is not a natural person and a beneficial interest in Borrower is sold or transferred) without Lender's prior written consent, Lender may require immediate payment in full of all sums secured by this Security Instrument. However, this option shall not be exercised by Lender if such exercise is prohibited by Applicable Law.

If Lender exercises this option, Lender shall give Borrower notice of acceleration. The notice shall provide a period of not less than 30 days from the date the notice is given in accordance with Section 15 within which Borrower must pay all sums secured by this Security Instrument. If Borrower fails to pay these sums prior to the expiration of this period, Lender may invoke any remedies permitted by this Security Instrument without further notice or demand on Borrower.

19. Borrower's Right to Reinstate After Acceleration. If Borrower meets certain conditions, Borrower shall have the right to have enforcement of this Security Instrument discontinued at any time prior to the earliest of: (a) five days before sale of the Property pursuant to any power of sale contained in this Security Instrument; (b) such other period as Applicable Law might specify for the termination of Borrower's right to reinstate; or (c) entry of a judgment enforcing this Security Instrument. Those conditions are that Borrower: (a) pays Lender all sums which then would be due under this Security Instrument and the Note as if no acceleration had occurred; (b) cures any default of any other covenants or agreements; (c) pays all expenses incurred in enforcing this Security Instrument, including, but not limited to, reasonable attorneys' fees, property inspection and valuation fees, and other fees incurred for the purpose of protecting Lender's interest in the Property and rights under this Security Instrument; and (d) takes such action as Lender may reasonably require to assure that Lender's interest in the Property and rights under this Security Instrument, and Borrower's obligation to pay the sums secured by this Security Instrument, shall continue unchanged. Lender may require that Borrower pay such reinstatement sums and expenses in one or more of the following forms, as selected by Lender: (a) cash; (b) money order; (c) certified check, bank check, treasurer's check or cashier's check, provided any such check is drawn upon an institution whose deposits are insured by a federal agency, instrumentality or entity; or (d) Electronic Funds Transfer. Upon reinstatement by Borrower, this Security Instrument and obligations secured hereby shall remain fully effective as if no acceleration had occurred. However, this right to reinstate shall not apply in the case of acceleration under Section 18.

20. Sale of Note; Change of Loan Servicer; Notice of Grievance. The Note or a partial interest in the Note (together with this Security Instrument) can be sold one or more times without prior notice to Borrower. A sale might result in a change in the entity (known as the "Loan Servicer") that collects Periodic Payments due under the Note and this Security Instrument and performs other mortgage loan servicing obligations under the Note, this Security Instrument, and Applicable Law. There also might be one or more changes of the Loan Servicer unrelated to a sale of the Note. If there is a change of the Loan Servicer, Borrower will be given written notice of the change which will state the name and address of the new Loan Servicer, the address to which payments should be made and any other information RESPA requires in connection with a notice of transfer of servicing. If the Note is sold and thereafter the Loan is serviced by a Loan Servicer other than the purchaser of the Note, the mortgage loan servicing obligations to Borrower will remain with the Loan Servicer or be transferred to a successor Loan Servicer and are not assumed by the Note purchaser unless otherwise provided by the Note purchaser.

IOWA--Single Family--Fannie Mae/Freddie Mac UNIFORM INSTRUMENT   **Form 3016**   1/01   (*page 13 of 16 pages*)

EXHIBIT 11-1

Fannie Mae/Freddie Mac Uniform Mortgage (*continued*)

Neither Borrower nor Lender may commence, join, or be joined to any judicial action (as either an individual litigant or the member of a class) that arises from the other party's actions pursuant to this Security Instrument or that alleges that the other party has breached any provision of, or any duty owed by reason of, this Security Instrument, until such Borrower or Lender has notified the other party (with such notice given in compliance with the requirements of Section 15) of such alleged breach and afforded the other party hereto a reasonable period after the giving of such notice to take corrective action. If Applicable Law provides a time period which must elapse before certain action can be taken, that time period will be deemed to be reasonable for purposes of this paragraph. The notice of acceleration and opportunity to cure given to Borrower pursuant to Section 22 and the notice of acceleration given to Borrower pursuant to Section 18 shall be deemed to satisfy the notice and opportunity to take corrective action provisions of this Section 20.

21. Hazardous Substances. As used in this Section 21: (a) "Hazardous Substances" are those substances defined as toxic or hazardous substances, pollutants, or wastes by Environmental Law and the following substances: gasoline, kerosene, other flammable or toxic petroleum products, toxic pesticides and herbicides, volatile solvents, materials containing asbestos or formaldehyde, and radioactive materials; (b) "Environmental Law" means federal laws and laws of the jurisdiction where the Property is located that relate to health, safety or environmental protection; (c) "Environmental Cleanup" includes any response action, remedial action, or removal action, as defined in Environmental Law; and (d) an "Environmental Condition" means a condition that can cause, contribute to, or otherwise trigger an Environmental Cleanup.

Borrower shall not cause or permit the presence, use, disposal, storage, or release of any Hazardous Substances, or threaten to release any Hazardous Substances, on or in the Property. Borrower shall not do, nor allow anyone else to do, anything affecting the Property (a) that is in violation of any Environmental Law, (b) which creates an Environmental Condition, or (c) which, due to the presence, use, or release of a Hazardous Substance, creates a condition that adversely affects the value of the Property. The preceding two sentences shall not apply to the presence, use, or storage on the Property of small quantities of Hazardous Substances that are generally recognized to be appropriate to normal residential uses and to maintenance of the Property (including, but not limited to, hazardous substances in consumer products).

Borrower shall promptly give Lender written notice of (a) any investigation, claim, demand, lawsuit or other action by any governmental or regulatory agency or private party involving the Property and any Hazardous Substance or Environmental Law of which Borrower has actual knowledge, (b) any Environmental Condition, including but not limited to, any spilling, leaking, discharge, release or threat of release of any Hazardous Substance, and (c) any condition caused by the presence, use or release of a Hazardous Substance which adversely affects the value of the Property. If Borrower learns, or is notified by any governmental or regulatory authority, or any private party, that any removal or other remediation of any Hazardous Substance affecting the Property is necessary, Borrower shall promptly take all necessary remedial actions in accordance with Environmental Law. Nothing herein shall create any obligation on Lender for an Environmental Cleanup.

IOWA--Single Family--**Fannie Mae/Freddie Mac UNIFORM INSTRUMENT**   **Form 3016** 1/01 *(page 14 of 16 pages)*

(continued)

EXHIBIT 11–1

Fannie Mae/Freddie Mac Uniform Mortgage (continued)

NON-UNIFORM COVENANTS. Borrower and Lender further covenant and agree as follows:

22. Acceleration; Remedies. Lender shall give notice to Borrower prior to acceleration following Borrower's breach of any covenant or agreement in this Security Instrument (but not prior to acceleration under Section 18 unless Applicable Law provides otherwise). The notice shall specify: (a) the default; (b) the action required to cure the default; (c) a date, not less than 30 days from the date the notice is given to Borrower, by which the default must be cured; and (d) that failure to cure the default on or before the date specified in the notice may result in acceleration of the sums secured by this Security Instrument, foreclosure by judicial proceeding and sale of the Property. The notice shall further inform Borrower of the right to reinstate after acceleration and the right to assert in the foreclosure proceeding the non-existence of a default or any other defense of Borrower to acceleration and foreclosure. If the default is not cured on or before the date specified in the notice, Lender at its option may require immediate payment in full of all sums secured by this Security Instrument without further demand and may foreclose this Security Instrument by judicial proceeding. Lender shall be entitled to collect all expenses incurred in pursuing the remedies provided in this Section 22, including, but not limited to, reasonable attorneys' fees and costs of title evidence.

23. Release. Upon payment of all sums secured by this Security Instrument, Lender shall release this Security Instrument. Lender may charge Borrower a fee for releasing this Security Instrument, but only if the fee is paid to a third party for services rendered and the charging of the fee is permitted under Applicable Law.

24. Waivers. Borrower relinquishes all right of dower and waives all right of homestead and distributive share in and to the Property. Borrower waives any right of exemption as to the Property.

25. HOMESTEAD EXEMPTION WAIVER. I UNDERSTAND THAT HOMESTEAD PROPERTY IS IN MANY CASES PROTECTED FROM THE CLAIMS OF CREDITORS AND EXEMPT FROM JUDICIAL SALE; AND THAT BY SIGNING THIS MORTGAGE, I VOLUNTARILY GIVE UP MY RIGHT TO THIS PROTECTION FOR THIS MORTGAGED PROPERTY WITH RESPECT TO CLAIMS BASED UPON THIS MORTGAGE.

_____   _____ [Date]

_____   _____ [Date]

26. Redemption Period. If the Property is less than 10 acres in size and Lender waives in any foreclosure proceeding any right to a deficiency judgment against Borrower, the period of redemption from judicial sale shall be reduced to 6 months. If the court finds that the Property has been abandoned by Borrower and Lender waives any right to a deficiency judgment against Borrower, the period of redemption from judicial sale shall be reduced to 60 days. The provisions of this Section 26 shall be construed to conform to the provisions of Sections 628.26 and 628.27 of the Code of Iowa.

IOWA--Single Family--Fannie Mae/Freddie Mac UNIFORM INSTRUMENT   Form 3016 1/01 (page 15 of 16 pages)

(continued)

EXHIBIT 11–1

Fannie Mae/Freddie Mac Uniform Mortgage (*continued*)

IMPORTANT: READ BEFORE SIGNING. THE TERMS OF THIS AGREEMENT SHOULD BE READ CAREFULLY BECAUSE ONLY THOSE TERMS IN WRITING ARE ENFORCEABLE. NO OTHER TERMS OR ORAL PROMISES NOT CONTAINED IN THIS WRITTEN CONTRACT MAY BE LEGALLY ENFORCED. YOU MAY CHANGE THE TERMS OF THIS AGREEMENT ONLY BY ANOTHER WRITTEN AGREEMENT.

BY SIGNING BELOW, Borrower accepts and agrees to the terms and covenants contained in this Security Instrument and in any Rider executed by Borrower and recorded with it.

Witnesses:

_____   _____(Seal)
                                                                              - Borrower

_____   _____(Seal)
                                                                              - Borrower

_____   [Space Below This Line for Acknowledgment] _____

IOWA--Single Family--Fannie Mae/Freddie Mac UNIFORM INSTRUMENT   Form 3016   1/01 *(page 16 of 16 pages)* charges; second, to any other amounts due under the mortgage; and then to reduce the principal balance of the note.

3. *Funds for Escrow Items.* This is an escrow provision typically found in most mortgages. A lender is concerned that taxes be paid on the real property, that the real property be insured against fire and other casualties, and, if mortgage insurance is required, that the premiums be kept current. Out of concern for these items, a lender requires the borrower to pay monthly, together with the monthly payments on the note, one-twelfth of the annual taxes, annual insurance premiums, and mortgage insurance premiums. It is escrowed by the lender and used to pay the taxes, insurance premiums, and mortgage insurance premiums when they become due. Typically, the funds are held by a lender in an interest-bearing account and commingled with other funds of the lender. Some states require the lender to pay interest to the borrower on the funds held in escrow.

4. *Charges; Liens.* This covenant requires the borrower to keep the real property lien-free and to pay any and all other charges and assessments that might be assessed against the real property.

5. *Property Insurance.* This covenant requires the borrower to purchase insurance, naming the lender as mortgagee, under a standard loss payable mortgage clause. Because most of the value of the property securing the loan will be in the improvements, which can be destroyed by fire or other casualty, a lender usually provides a detailed description of the insurance requirements in the mortgage. A lender has a right to approve the insurance policy and is entitled to notice before the expiration of the insurance policy. The insurance proceeds usually are jointly payable to the lender and the borrower and may be used either to restore the improvements or to repay the debt.

6. *Occupancy.* This covenant requires the borrower to occupy and use the property as the borrower's principal residence within 60 days after the execution of the mortgage and to agree to continue to use it as a principal residence for at least one year after the date of occupancy.

7. *Preservation, Maintenance, and Protection of the Property; Inspections.* This covenant basically provides that the borrower agrees to maintain the real property and improvements in good repair and not to commit any waste. It also grants to the lender the right to make reasonable entrance upon and to inspect the property. Inspections of residential property are rare unless the real property has been abandoned. In commercial loans, it is not unusual for the lender to make an annual inspection of the property.

8. *Borrower's Loan Application.* This covenant provides that it will be an event of default under the loan if the borrower, in its loan application, gives any materially false or inaccurate information or statements to the lender.

9. *Protection of Lender's Interest in the Property and Rights under This Security Instrument.* This covenant provides that if the borrower fails to perform any of the promises or covenants under the mortgage (e.g., pay taxes and insurance, keep the property in good repair), the lender may pay these charges and take whatever action is necessary to protect the property and its improvements. The cost of doing so is assessed against the borrower and secured by the mortgage.

10. *Mortgage Insurance.* This covenant provides that if payment of the loan is insured by a private mortgage insurance carrier, the borrower will pay the premiums before they become due and delinquent. In the event the mortgage insurance becomes unavailable, the borrower agrees to pay a sum equal to one-twelfth of the yearly mortgage insurance premium each month to the lender to be held as a loss reserve in lieu of mortgage insurance.

11. *Assignment of Miscellaneous Proceeds; Forfeiture.* This covenant covers the application of miscellaneous proceeds, which are defined under Section (L) of the mortgage to mean "any compensation, settlement, award of damages, or proceeds paid by any third party (other than insurance proceeds paid under [an insurance policy] for damage to, or destruction of, the property . . . or condemnation or other taking of all or any part of the Property [or any] . . . conveyance in lieu of condemnation." This provision states that the money will be paid jointly to the lender and borrower and can be used either to restore the real property or to repay the debt. Note that paragraph 11 of the Fannie Mae/Freddie Mac mortgage contains an allocation of monies between the borrower and the lender in the event of a partial taking.

12. *Borrower Not Released; Forbearance by Lender Not a Waiver.* This covenant provides that if a lender extends time for payment, this does not release the borrower from its obligation to make payments. The lender will not waive any rights under the mortgage by delaying time or not exercising rights.

13. *Joint and Several Liability; Cosigners; Successors and Assigns; Borrower.* This paragraph basically states that all the covenants and provisions of the mortgage will bind the successors and assigns of the lender and the borrower and that all borrowers signing the note and mortgage are jointly and severally liable for the debt. Joint and several liability means that each borrower is 100% responsible for the debt. This paragraph also provides that any one who cosigns a security instrument but does not execute the note is not personally obligated for the debt but can lose his or her real property through a foreclosure in the event the debt is not paid.

14. *Loan Charges.* This covenant is a usury savings clause. It provides that if the interest or other charges on the loan should exceed the maximum interest permitted under law, the rate will be reduced to the permitted limit and all sums already collected will be refunded to the borrower or used to repay the debt.

15. *Notices.* This covenant explains how notices are to be given under the mortgage.

16. *Governing Law; Severability; Rules of Construction.* This is a miscellaneous paragraph that covers a number of items. It contains a choice of law paragraph that explains which law will govern. It provides that if any of the provisions should be unenforceable, these provisions will be deleted from the mortgage, leaving the remainder of the mortgage enforceable. It also contains certain rules of construction for the use of words in the mortgage.

17. *Borrower's Copy.* This covenant provides that the borrower is entitled to receive a copy of the note and the mortgage.

18. *Transfer of the Property or a Beneficial Interest in Borrower.* This is a "due on sale" clause. It provides that the real property will not be sold without the lender's consent. If the property is sold without the lender's consent, the lender has the right to require immediate payment in full of all sums secured by the mortgage.

19. *Borrower's Right to Reinstate after Acceleration.* This covenant provides that even though the borrower may be in default and the loan may be accelerated and due and payable in its entirety, if the borrower pays the amount of the delinquent payments plus all expenses, the loan will be reinstated.

20. *Sale of Note; Change of Loan Servicer; Notice of Grievance.* This covenant provides that the note or any partial interest in the note may be sold without prior notice to the borrower. It provides that the borrower will receive notice of such transfer pursuant to the terms of the mortgage and any new name or place where monthly payments are to be sent. The paragraph also provides that neither borrower or lender will commence an

action or be joined in any judicial action alleging that the other party has breached any provision of the mortgage until notice of such alleged breach is given to the defaulting party and the defaulting party is given a reasonable time to take corrective action after being given such notice.

21. *Hazardous Substances.* This covenant provides that the borrower will not cause or permit the presence, use, disposal, storage, or release of hazardous substances on the property. The borrower also agrees to promptly notify the lender of any investigation, claim, demand, lawsuit, or other action taken by any governmental or regulatory agent or private party involving the property and any hazardous substances in connection therewith.

NONUNIFORM COVENANTS

Following the uniform covenants are nonuniform covenants. Nonuniform covenants address matters that vary slightly from state to state. The nonuniform covenants are custom drafted for the state in which the mortgage is to be used. Exhibit 11–1 is an example of one designed for use in Iowa.

22. *Acceleration; Remedies.* This covenant explains what remedies the lender has in the event of a default. The basic remedy is to foreclose and sell the property. The proceeds received from the sale are used by the lender to pay the debt.

23. *Release.* This covenant provides that upon payment in full of the debt, the lender will release the mortgage.

24 and 25. *Waivers* and *Homestead Exemption Waiver.* These paragraphs provide that the borrower relinquishes all right of dower and waives all right of homestead and distributive share in and to the property.

26. *Redemption Period.* The mortgage form is used in Iowa, and Iowa provides for a limited right of redemption. After the foreclosure sale, the borrower has six months in which to buy the property back from the person who purchased it at the sale at a price equal to the amount bid plus a premium.

At the end of the mortgage, there is a place for the signature of the borrower. Each borrower should sign, and the name should be typed beneath the line on each signature. Mortgages use the same formality as deeds and require witnesses or notarization or in some states, both. Mortgages are recorded in the public records of the county in which the real property is located.

COMMERCIAL MORTGAGE PROVISIONS

In addition to the standard provisions found in residential mortgages, mortgages on commercial properties contain a number of other provisions that reflect a lender's concerns regarding a commercial loan transaction. Examples of some of these provisions follow.

Assignment of Rents and Leases

Most commercial mortgages contain an assignment of all rental income and leases in connection with the real property. An example of such a provision is shown in Example 11–1.

Example 11–1

Mortgagor hereby transfers, assigns, and conveys unto Mortgagee all of Mortgagor's right, title, and interest in and to all leases, now or hereafter existing or made, and all other agreements for use or occupancy, with respect to the premises or any part thereof and grants to Mortgagee a security interest in all rents, issues, income, revenue, profits, accounts, and contract rights due or to become due thereunder or otherwise deriving from the use and occupancy of the premises. Mortgagor shall faithfully perform the covenants of Mortgagor or lessor under all present or future leases on all or any portion of the premises and shall not do, neglect to do, or permit to be done anything that may cause the termination of such leases, or any of them, or that may diminish or impair the value of the rents provided for therein or the interest of the Mortgagor or Mortgagee therein or thereunder. Mortgagor, without first obtaining the written consent of Mortgagee, shall not further assign the rents, issues, income, revenue, profits, accounts, or contract rights from the premises or any part thereof, shall not consent to the cancellation or surrender of any lease of the premises or any part thereof now existing or hereafter made, shall not modify any such leases so as to shorten the unexpired term thereof or so as to increase the amount of the rent payable thereunder, shall not collect rents from the premises or any part thereof for more than one month in advance. Mortgagor shall procure and deliver to Mortgagee upon request estoppel letters or certificates from each lessee, tenant, occupant in possession, or other user of the premises or any part thereof as required by and in a form or substance satisfactory to Mortgagee and shall deliver to Mortgagee a recordable assignment of all the Mortgagor's interest in all leases now or hereafter existing or made with respect to the premises or any part thereof, which assignment shall be in a form and substance acceptable to Mortgagee, together with proof of due service of a copy of such assignment on each lessee, tenant, occupant in possession, or other user of the premises or any part thereof.

Security Agreement   *commercial loans*

As security for the loan, a mortgage grants to the lender all real property, including fixtures. Personal property is not covered by a mortgage but by a **security agreement.** A security agreement must be written, identify the debtor, describe the property being covered by the security agreement, and be signed by the debtor. Many lenders incorporate a security agreement within the mortgage to cover any personal property used in connection with the commercial real property. An example of such a provision is shown in Example 11–2.

security agreement

Legal document that pledges personal property as security for a debt.

Example 11–2

Security Agreement. This Security Deed shall constitute a security agreement as defined in the Uniform Commercial Code ("Code") and shall create a security interest within the meaning of the Code in favor of Grantee on the Secured Personal Property and Rents, Leases, and Profits ("Collateral") comprising the Secured Premises. The remedies for any violation of the covenants, terms, and conditions of the agreement herein contained shall be (a) as prescribed herein, or (b) by general law, or (c) as to such part of the security that is also reflected in any financing statement by the specific statutory consequences now or hereafter enacted and specified in the Uniform Commercial Code, all at Grantee's sole election. Grantor and Grantee agree that the filing of such a financing statement and the records normally having to do with personal property shall never be construed as in any way derogating from or impairing this declaration and hereby stated intention of the parties hereto that everything used in connection with the production of income from the Secured Property and/or adapted for use therein is, and at all times and for all purposes and in all proceedings, both legal and equitable, shall be regarded as part of the real estate irrespective of whether (a) any such item is physically attached to the improvements, (b) serial numbers are used for the better identification of certain equipment items capable of being thus identified in a recital contained herein or in any list filed with the Grantee, or (c) any such item is referred to or reflected in any such financing statement so filed at any time.

The name of the record owner of said real estate is the Grantor. Information concerning the security interest created by this instrument may be obtained from the Grantee, as secured party as required by the Code.

Rights under Uniform Commercial Code. In addition to the rights available to a grantee of real property if an Event of Default shall occur, Grantee shall also have all the rights, remedies, and recourse available to a secured party under the Uniform Commercial Code, including the right to proceed under the provisions of the Uniform Commercial Code governing default as to any Secured Personal Property that may be included in the Secured Property or that may be deemed non-realty in a foreclosure of this Security Deed or to proceed as to such Personal Property in accordance with the procedures and remedies available pursuant to a foreclosure of real estate.

Books, Records, and Financial Statements

A source of repayment for most commercial loans is the income generated from the commercial real property pledged as security for the loan. A lender requires current information concerning the financial condition of the commercial real property as well as the financial condition of the mortgagor. Typical mortgage provisions that require a mortgagor to provide annual financial information concerning the real property and mortgagor are shown in Example 11–3.

Example 11–3

Mortgagor covenants and agrees to keep proper records and accounts with full, true, current, and correct entries of all its transactions with respect to the operation of the mortgaged property, in accordance with generally accepted accounting principles consistently applied with such other accounting method as Mortgagee may approve. Mortgagee shall have the right to inspect Mortgagor's books and records at any reasonable time after reasonable prior notice to Mortgagor.

Mortgagor covenants and agrees to furnish to mortgagee quarter-annual operating statements showing all income and all expenditures relative to the mortgaged property. The term "income" shall mean all income, from whatever source, arising out of the operation of the mortgaged property and described in this mortgage given to secure the indebtedness, including without limitation, all rental income, vending machine rentals, and proceeds of the sale, lease, or other disposition of any personal property or fixtures located on or used in connection with the operation of the mortgaged property. These statements shall be due within thirty (30) days after the expiration of each calendar quarter and shall be prepared in accordance with generally accepted accounting principles and certified by a certified public accountant approved by Mortgagee. Mortgagee may with its prior written consent permit Mortgagor to verify the financial statements in lieu of a certified public accountant. If Mortgagor is a corporation or a partnership with a general partner who is a corporation, such verification by Mortgagor shall be by the principal officer of such corporation.

Hazardous Waste

Under federal law and the law of many states, a real property owner can be responsible for the removal of hazardous waste from the real property. In the event a mortgage loan goes into default, a lender can become an owner of the real property through foreclosure and may be responsible for the removal of hazardous waste. Many lenders seek an indemnity from the borrower concerning hazardous waste liability. An example of a commercial mortgage provision with a hazardous waste indemnity is set forth in Example 11–4.

Example 11-4

(a) *Hazardous Waste.* Mortgagor will not, nor will Mortgagor permit or suffer any of its partners, officers, employees, agents, tenants, or any other licensee or invitee or trespasser to cause or to permit any hazardous waste, toxic substances, or related "hazardous materials" (as defined below) to be brought upon, kept, or used or disposed of on, under, in, or about the property.

(b) If Mortgagor breaches the representations, covenants, or obligations stated in this article, and because of such breach the presence of hazardous materials on, under, in, about, or near the property results in a contamination of the property or other properties by hazardous materials, then, in addition to other remedies available to Mortgagee, Mortgagor shall indemnify, defend, and hold Mortgagee and its officers, employees, agents, affiliates, and successors in interest harmless from any and all claims, judgments, damages, penalties, fines, costs, liabilities, and expenses, including actual attorney's fees and the cost of any cleanup, and any losses that arise at any time as a result of such contamination, or allegation thereof by governmental agency, or the determination by any court or governmental agency, or by Mortgagee or its successor in interest, that the uses of the property must be limited or that the hazardous material should be removed and the damage to the property and its environs restored.

(c) The indemnification of Mortgagee and its officers, employees, agents, and successors in interest by Mortgagor contained in this article include, without limitation, costs incurred in connection with any investigation of site conditions, or any cleanup, remedial removal or restoration required by any federal, state, or local governmental agency or political subdivision, or by any insurance company, or by Mortgagee or its successor in interest in the exercise of its reasonable discretion, because of hazardous material present in the improvements, soil, ground, water, air, or otherwise in, on, under, about, or near the property.

(d) Without limiting the foregoing, if the presence of any hazardous material in, on, under, about, or near the property is caused or permitted by Mortgagor, its tenants, or either their successors in interest, officers, employees, agents, licensees or invitees, or by trespassers, and results in any contamination of the property or other properties, Mortgagor shall take all actions at its sole cost and expense that are necessary to return the property to the condition existing prior to the introduction of any such hazardous materials to the property; provided that Mortgagee's approval of such action shall be first obtained, which approval shall not be unreasonably withheld so long as such actions would not have an adverse long-term or short-term effect on the property.

(e) The foregoing cleanup and indemnification obligation shall survive the reconveyance or foreclosure of this mortgage.

(f) Mortgagor also agrees (i) to provide Mortgagee with copies of any communications between Mortgagor, or its tenants, or their officers, employees, agents, predecessors, or successors in interest, licensees, or invitees and any third parties, including, but not limited to, governmental authorities relative to any hazardous material on, under, in, about, or near or affecting the property, and (ii) that Mortgagee is hereby granted the right (but not the obligation) to participate in any proceeding with any governmental agency or court relative to any hazardous materials on, in, under, about, near, or affecting the property.

(g) As used herein the term hazardous materials means any hazardous, toxic, infectious substance, material, gas, or waste that is or becomes regulated by any governmental authority, or the United States government, or any of their agencies, or that has been identified as a toxic, cancer-causing, or otherwise hazardous substance. The term hazardous materials including without limitation, any material or substance that is (a) petroleum, (b) polychlorinated biphenyls (PCB), (c) asbestos, (d) designated a hazardous substance pursuant to Section 307 of the Federal Water Pollution Control Act (3 U.S.C. § 1317), as currently existing or hereafter amended or designated as a hazardous substance pursuant to Section 311 of the Clean Water Act, 33 U.S.C. § 1251 et seq. (33 U.S.C. § 1321), (e) defined as a hazardous waste pursuant to Section 1004 of the Federal Resource Conservation Recovery Act, 42 U.S.C. § 6901 et seq. (42 U.S.C. § 6903), as currently existing or hereafter amended, or (f) defined as a hazardous substance pursuant to Section 101 of the Comprehensive Environmental Response Compensation and Liability Act, 42 U.S.C. § 9601 et seq. (42 U.S.C. § 9601), as currently existing or hereafter amended.

In addition to presenting a potential liability to the lender, hazardous waste has a dramatic effect on the value of the real property. The presence of hazardous waste can cause the security for a loan to decline in value and the loan to become undercollateralized.

Nonrecourse or Exculpation Provisions

Many commercial mortgage loans are negotiated with the understanding that the lender will look only to the security of the mortgaged real property as recovery for the repayment of the loan. This means that in the event there is a default under the mortgage loan, the lender will only foreclose on the real property to recover on its debt and will not personally sue the borrower for payment of the debt or for any deficiency that might result from the sale of the mortgaged property. This type of mortgage loan is called a nonrecourse or **exculpated loan.** A lender who agrees to an exculpated or nonrecourse loan usually makes exceptions to this limitation of liability against the borrower in cases when the borrower has committed fraud, has intentionally injured the real property, or is responsible for hazardous waste cleanup. An example of a nonrecourse or exculpated mortgage provision is set out in Example 11–5.

exculpated loan

A real estate loan in which the borrower is not personally responsible for the repayment of the loan. If the loan is not repaid, the borrower will lose the real property pledged as security for the loan. The borrower will not be personally sued for payment of the loan.

Example 11–5

Mortgagee agrees by accepting this mortgage that it will look solely to the mortgaged property and the rents therefrom for the payment of the indebtedness, and all other amounts required to be paid out of the terms of this mortgage and the note and any other document executed in connection herewith and Mortgagee further agrees not to seek payment of the indebtedness from the Mortgagor. Mortgagee further agrees in connection with any action or foreclosure to enforce any provision of this mortgage or any other document executed in connection herewith, Mortgagee will not seek any deficiency judgment against Mortgagor; provided, however, (a) nothing in this paragraph shall be, or be deemed to be, a release or impairment of said indebtedness or the lien created hereby upon the mortgage property, or prohibit Mortgagee from suing upon the note and foreclosing this mortgage in case of any default or defaults hereunder, or from enforcing any of its rights, except as set out above. Notwithstanding the above, the Mortgagee shall not be precluded from seeking a judgment against Mortgagor to recover: (i) any rents received by or on behalf of Mortgagor from the obligors under the leases of the mortgaged property that have been collected either in violation of the loan documents executed in connection herewith or after the occurrence of any event of default of the loan documents executed in connection herewith; or (ii) any security deposits received by or on behalf of Mortgagor from the obligors under the leases of the mortgaged property; or (iii) any amounts representing intentional damage to or conversion of any part of the mortgaged property by Mortgagor or persons acting on Mortgagor's behalf; or (iv) all condemnation awards or insurance proceeds that are not utilized in accordance with the terms and conditions of this mortgage; or (v) any and all costs, expenses, damages, or liabilities incurred by Mortgagee, including, but not limited to, all reasonable attorney's fees, directly or indirectly arising out of or attributable to the use, generation, storage, release, threatened release, discharge, disposal of, presence on, under, about the mortgaged property of any materials, wastes, or substances defined or classified as hazardous or toxic pursuant to federal, state, or local laws, regulations, including, without limitation, asbestos, lead, PCBs, and herbicides.

Cross-Collateralization and Cross-Default

Many commercial lenders make multiple mortgage loans on multiple parcels of property owned by a single borrower. These loans are sometimes called portfolio loans. The commercial lenders who make these portfolio loans often want the loans to be cross-collateralized and cross-defaulted. This cross-collateralization feature provides in the loan documentation that each parcel of property is security for each and every loan. For example, a lender makes a loan to a borrower in the amount of $3,000,000 secured by Parcel A, a loan to the same borrower in the amount of $5,000,000 secured by Parcel B, and a third loan to the same borrower in the amount of $5,000,000 secured by Parcel C. The cross-collateralization feature of the loan means that each parcel (for example Parcel A) will be security for the entire aggregate amount of the three loans, that is, $13,000,000. The lender would be entitled to receive from a foreclosure sale of each parcel all of the foreclosure proceeds, until the $13,000,000 debt has been paid in full. Cross-collateralization can be accomplished by referring to each loan in each of the mortgage instruments. Using the preceding example, the mortgage on Parcel A would refer to the debt being secured by the mortgage to be a note for $3,000,000 (Parcel A Note), a note for $5,000,000 (Parcel B Note), and a note for $5,000,000 (Parcel C Note). The mortgages on Parcels B and C would likewise refer to the three notes. Cross-collateralization can also be done by a separate cross-collateralization agreement, which states that all the mortgages secure all of the borrower's debts.

A cross-default provision is different from cross-collateralization. Cross-default means that a default under any one loan may be a default under another loan. In the preceding example, if Loans A, B, and C are cross-defaulted, then a default under Loan A would also constitute a default under Loans B and C. A default under Loan A would give the lender the opportunity to foreclose all loans: A, B, and C. This default feature protects the lender from a borrower "giving back" a weak property. The borrower may believe that there is little or no equity in a particular property securing a loan and may be willing to default on the loan instead of spending money to improve the property. With a cross-default provision, however, the borrower cannot stop payments on a loan without the risk of foreclosure on all loans that are cross-defaulted. It is not uncommon in commercial lending situations for portfolio loans to be both cross-collateralized and cross-defaulted.

Attorneys and paralegals who prepare mortgage loan documents often find helpful a checklist outlining the basic terms and provisions of the mortgage. The following checklist incorporates previously discussed issues that should be considered in the preparation of a real property mortgage.

✔ CHECKLIST

Preparation of a Mortgage

☐ I. Parties
  - ☐ A. Mortgagor or grantor—record title owner of the property described in the mortgage
  - ☐ B. Mortgagee or grantee—creditor and holder of the note being secured by the mortgage

☐ II. Description of Property to be Conveyed
  - ☐ A. Accurate description of real property and associated personal property
  - ☐ B. Include easements appurtenant to the secured property
    - 1. Cross-access easements
    - 2. Off-site utility easements

☐ III. Indebtedness
  - ☐ A. Amount of indebtedness
  - ☐ B. Final maturity date for payment of indebtedness
  - ☐ C. Open-ended or future advance provisions

(continued)

☐ IV. Security Agreement
    ☐ A. To be included if personal property is part of the security

☐ V. Assignment of Leases and Rents
    ☐ A. To be included if property is a commercial investment or income-producing property

☐ VI. Miscellaneous Mortgage Covenants
    ☐ A. Payment of indebtedness
    ☐ B. Escrow for taxes and insurance
    ☐ C. Application of payments
    ☐ D. Hazard insurance
    ☐ E. Preservation and maintenance of property
    ☐ F. Lender's right to inspect
    ☐ G. Condemnation
    ☐ H. Lender's right to cure defaults
    ☐ I. Due on sale
    ☐ J. Prohibition on secondary financing
    ☐ K. Financial reporting
    ☐ L. Events of default
    ☐ M. Remedies on default
    ☐ N. Provision for giving notices
    ☐ O. Choice of law
    ☐ P. Forbearance not a waiver
    ☐ Q. Waiver of homestead and other debtor's rights
    ☐ R. Indemnity against hazardous waste
    ☐ S. Any other indemnities or provisions relative to the transaction
    ☐ T. Cross-default with other loan documents such as assignment of leases or construction loan agreements

☐ VII. Signature
    ☐ A. Mortgagor or grantor is only party to sign mortgage
        1. Corporate mortgagor or grantor
            a. Correctly identify name of corporation
            b. Correctly identify by name and title all officers signing on behalf of corporation
            c. Affix official corporate seal
        2. Partnership mortgagor or grantor
            a. Identify the partnership by name
            b. Identify by name all partners signing the mortgage
        3. Limited Liability Company mortgagor or grantor
            a. Identify the limited liability company by name
            b. Identify the names of the managing members signing the mortgage
    ☐ B. Mortgagor or grantor's signature is witnessed and notarized with sufficient formality to permit the mortgage to be recorded
    ☐ C. Mortgage is recorded to protect mortgagee's priority against future purchasers or mortgagees.

MISCELLANEOUS COMMERCIAL LOAN DOCUMENTS

In addition to a mortgage, a lender on a commercial loan may require other loan documents in connection with the transaction. These loan documents usually consist of a Uniform Commercial Code (UCC) financing statement and an assignment of rents and leases. If the loan is a construction loan, a construction loan agreement and assignments of the construction contract and architectural contract are required.

Security Agreement and Financing Statement

A commercial real estate finance transaction may include personal property as security for the loan. Because a mortgage only creates a security interest in the real property and fixtures, a security interest in personal property must be created and perfected by additional documentation. The method for securing a loan with personal property, including fixtures, is provided by Article 9 of the Uniform Commercial Code (UCC), a standardized law that has been passed in all states. Under this article, such a loan is secured by having the debtor sign a security agreement and by filing a UCC-1 **financing statement.** A security agreement is a written agreement conveying a security interest in personal property for purposes of securing a debt. Most mortgage forms include additional language that makes the mortgage a security agreement. An example of that language is contained in Example 11–2.

The UCC mandates a national UCC financing statement form. A copy of the national UCC-1 financing statement form is shown as Exhibit 11–2. The debtor's signature is not required on the national financing statement form. A secured party may file the financing statement as long as it is authorized by the debtor to do so. This authorization may be in the security agreement or, in the case of fixtures, the mortgage entered into between the debtor and the secured party. The financing statement may be filed either electronically or by paper filing. The filing officer who maintains the records for financing statements can dictate which medium of filing it requires.

A financing statement perfecting a security interest in fixtures must be filed in the county where the real property is located. The proper place for filing a financing statement perfecting security interests in collateral other than a fixture is the debtor's location. For corporations, registered limited partnerships, or limited liability companies, the debtor's location is the state in which it was incorporated or registered. For other organizations, the debtor's location is its principal place of business, if it has only one place of business, or its chief executive office, if it has more than one place of business. Individual debtors are considered located in the state of their principal residence. A general filing in the state of the debtor's location will be with the secretary of state, but a state may designate another filing office for the statements.

The information required on a UCC-1 financing statement includes a debtor's name and address, secured party (creditor's) name and address, description of the personal property, and description of the real property on which the personal property is located. The property must be described with specificity so that it can be identified. The debtor must be correctly identified on the financing statement. If the debtor is a registered organization, such as a corporation, a limited liability company, or a limited partnership, the debtor's name must be shown on the financing statement exactly the same way it is shown in its registration with the secretary of state.

The importance of correctly identifying the name of the debtor in a financing statement cannot be overemphasized. The failure to correctly identify the name of the debtor, even a slight variation from the correct name, may result in a financing statement being held invalid and the secured party's security interest not capable of being perfected. Lack of perfection results in the secured party not being protected against future secured creditors of the debtor. In the event of the debtor's bankruptcy, the secured party would be an unsecured creditor, a status that would greatly diminish the secured party's financial return. The correct name of a debtor can be difficult when the debtor is as an individual. The debtor must be stated in the financing statement by his or her legally known name, not a nickname. A bankruptcy court declared a secured party's financing statement invalid when the correct name of the debtor was Terrance Joseph Kinderknecht, but the secured party's financing statement identified the debtor as Terry J. Kinderknecht. The bankruptcy court held

financing statement
Form that is recorded to give notice that there is a security interest in personal property owned by a debtor.

EXHIBIT 11–2

UCC Financing Statement

UCC FINANCING STATEMENT

FOLLOW INSTRUCTIONS (front and back) CAREFULLY

A. NAME & PHONE OF CONTACT AT FILER [optional]

B. SEND ACKNOWLEDGMENT TO: (Name and Address)

THE ABOVE SPACE IS FOR FILING OFFICE USE ONLY

1. DEBTOR'S EXACT FULL LEGAL NAME - insert only one debtor name (1a or 1b) - do not abbreviate or combine names

1a. ORGANIZATION'S NAME				
OR 1b. INDIVIDUAL'S LAST NAME	FIRST NAME	MIDDLE NAME		SUFFIX
1c. MAILING ADDRESS	CITY	STATE	POSTAL CODE	COUNTRY
1d. TAX ID #: SSN OR EIN	ADD'L INFO RE ORGANIZATION DEBTOR	1e. TYPE OF ORGANIZATION	1f. JURISDICTION OF ORGANIZATION	1g. ORGANIZATIONAL ID #, if any ☐ NONE

2. ADDITIONAL DEBTOR'S EXACT FULL LEGAL NAME - insert only one debtor name (2a or 2b) - do not abbreviate or combine names

2a. ORGANIZATION'S NAME				
OR 2b. INDIVIDUAL'S LAST NAME	FIRST NAME	MIDDLE NAME		SUFFIX
2c. MAILING ADDRESS	CITY	STATE	POSTAL CODE	COUNTRY
2d. TAX ID #: SSN OR EIN	ADD'L INFO RE ORGANIZATION DEBTOR	2e. TYPE OF ORGANIZATION	2f. JURISDICTION OF ORGANIZATION	2g. ORGANIZATIONAL ID #, if any ☐ NONE

3. SECURED PARTY'S NAME (or NAME of TOTAL ASSIGNEE of ASSIGNOR S/P) - insert only one secured party name (3a or 3b)

3a. ORGANIZATION'S NAME				
OR 3b. INDIVIDUAL'S LAST NAME	FIRST NAME	MIDDLE NAME		SUFFIX
3c. MAILING ADDRESS	CITY	STATE	POSTAL CODE	COUNTRY

4. This FINANCING STATEMENT covers the following collateral:

5. ALTERNATIVE DESIGNATION [if applicable]	LESSEE/LESSOR	CONSIGNEE/CONSIGNOR	BAILEE/BAILOR	SELLER/BUYER	AG. LIEN	NON-UCC FILING

6. This FINANCING STATEMENT is to be filed [for record] (or recorded) in the REAL ESTATE RECORDS. Attach Addendum [if applicable]	7. Check to REQUEST SEARCH REPORT(S) on Debtor(s) [ADDITIONAL FEE] [optional]	All Debtors	Debtor 1	Debtor 2

8. OPTIONAL FILER REFERENCE DATA

FILING OFFICE COPY — NATIONAL UCC FINANCING STATEMENT (FORM UCC1) (REV. 07/29/98)

Delmar/Cengage Learning

that the financing statement did not sufficiently provide the name of the debtor and was "seriously misleading" and as a matter of law did not perfect the secured party's security interest.

Many states, such as Texas and Tennessee, have passed recent laws establishing criteria for determining a sufficient identity of the debtor in a financing statement. The laws generally provide that, in the case of an individual debtor, the name that appears on the debtor's driver's license will be sufficient to identify the debtor in the financing statement.

Assignment of Rents

In commercial loan transactions, it is common that, in addition to the assignment of leases and rents that may be contained in the mortgage, a separate assignment of rents and leases is executed and delivered by the borrower to the lender. A form of an assignment of rents and leases is included at the end of this chapter as Exhibit 11–3. A rent assignment essentially provides that all leases and rental income from the real property are assigned to the lender. In the event there is a default under the loan, the lender can take possession of the real property and collect the rent directly from the tenants. The assignment of rents and leases also requires the borrower not to collect in advance more than one or two months rent from a tenant and prohibits the borrower from modifying, amending, or changing the leases in any way without the lender's prior written consent. The assignment of leases and rents is cross-defaulted with the mortgage and note; default under any of the documents shall constitute an event of default under all the documents.

An assignment of rents and leases is executed by the property owner and is witnessed, notarized, and recorded along with the mortgage. It contains an exhibit that is a description of the property as well as a list of all leases being assigned. A description of the leases usually includes all current leases shown on the exhibit as well as all future leases.

Construction Loan Agreement

A construction loan poses several risks for a lender. Money is advanced for the purpose of constructing improvements; therefore, the value of the security does not exist until the improvements are completed. A lender must be careful in a construction loan to make sure the money is in fact used for the improvements and that the improvements are built according to plans and specifications previously approved by the lender. In addition, the lender must make sure that all the subcontractors, materials suppliers, and other people who may have potential mechanic's lien claims against the property are being paid during the progress of the construction. Because of these problems, many lenders who make construction loans require the borrowers to execute construction loan agreements. A form of construction loan agreement is included at the end of this chapter as Exhibit 11–4.

Generally, a construction loan agreement will contain a number of representations and warranties made by the borrower to the lender. These representations and warranties may contain recitals that (a) the borrower has good title to the real property; (b) the borrower has all necessary licenses and permits in connection with the proposed construction; (c) all construction will be in accordance with all private restrictive covenants as well as all zoning and building code requirements; (d) the borrower's contracts with the contractor, architect, engineer, and subcontractors are all valid and in full force and effect; (e) true and correct copies of these contracts have been provided to the lender; (f) there is no pending litigation affecting the borrower or the real property; (g) all utilities such as water, electric, and gas are available to the real property; (h) all roads necessary for full utilization of the improvements are available and have been dedicated for public use, or all necessary easements for private use have been obtained; and (i) all necessary insurance has been acquired to insure the construction of the improvements as well as liability for any accidents or other harm that may occur during the construction.

There may also be a requirement that in the event the loan proceeds prove to be insufficient to finish construction of the improvements, the lender may stop advancing money until the borrower has deposited the necessary funds with the lender to complete the construction.

A construction loan agreement will also set forth the requirements for the disbursement of loan proceeds during construction. The lender requires that all requests for proceeds be made on a form approved by the lender. The request explains in full detail how the funds will be spent. The lender retains an inspecting architect to inspect the work as it is completed. The lender may require that a title examination to the real property be updated to check for lien claims. Endorsements to the title insurance are issued, insuring that each advance of the loan proceeds is free and clear of liens. The lender may require that a survey locating the foundation of the improvements be provided. This is important to determine if the improvements are located on the real property and comply with all necessary setback and building line restrictions. It also is not unusual for a lender to advance only a portion of the proceeds, for example, 90 percent of the actual cost of construction. The 10 percent holdback or **retainage** is held by the lender until the construction is completed. This retainage provides the lender with some security in the event there are cost overruns or unpaid bills.

The final advance under a construction loan agreement requires the same conditions as an interim advance and a few additional ones. Most lenders will not make the final advance under a construction loan agreement unless an architect's certificate of substantial completion has been issued. The lender also may require that a **certificate of occupancy** be issued by the appropriate governmental authority having jurisdiction over the improvements. This certificate of occupancy is evidence that the improvements do comply with all zoning and building codes and all health and fire regulations. A final advance usually is conditioned on an inspection made by the permanent lender and the receipt of a final survey showing all completed improvements to be located on the real property. A lender may require full and complete lien waivers from all people who have provided material or labor to the real property.

A construction loan agreement will describe those events that constitute default and identify the remedies in case of defaults. Construction loan agreements typically are cross-defaulted with the note and mortgage, so that a default under any of the documents constitutes a default under all documents. General events of default are as follows:

- A violation by the borrower of any covenant or promise in the construction loan agreement
- The filing of any mechanic's liens for labor or materials or any liens for unpaid taxes
- Any litigation against the borrower or against the real property in connection with the construction
- Abandonment stoppage of construction
- The use of improper materials or not constructing the improvements in accordance with the plans or specifications

A construction loan agreement will provide remedies for the lender in the event of default. The lender has the right to accelerate the indebtedness and to foreclose on the real property. In addition, the lender has the right to take possession of the real property and

---

retainage

Portion of the loan proceeds held by a construction lender until the construction is completed. The term also refers to an owner holding back money from a contractor until construction is completed.

certificate of occupancy

Permit issued by an appropriate governmental authority granting occupancy to newly constructed improvements. The certificate usually is evidence that the improvements comply with all zoning, building codes, and health and fire regulations.

complete construction. The lender has the right to advance retained loan proceeds toward completion of the construction. The lender also has the right to sue the borrower for any deficiencies required to complete the construction of the improvements.

A construction loan agreement will have general conditions. These general conditions usually include a statement to the effect that the construction loan agreement is personal between the borrower and the lender and does not provide any third parties, such as contractors, subcontractors, laborers, or materials suppliers, with any benefits. This is necessary to prevent contractors or subcontractors from suing to obtain payment directly from the lender. A construction loan agreement provides that the lender is not an agent or representative of the borrower and that the lender is not in any way responsible for the construction or for the payment of the cost of the construction. Other typical provisions found in the general conditions include no assignment by borrower, notices, amendments, governing law, and time is of the essence. Construction loan agreements are executed by both the borrower and the lender and are witnessed and notarized. Although construction loan agreements are in recordable form, they are seldom recorded in the public records where the real property is located.

A lender making a construction loan may take an assignment of all construction contracts and architect and engineering contracts in connection with the real property. In the event there is a default or interruption in the construction, this assignment gives the lender the right to take over these contracts and complete the performance.

The assignment of architect, construction, and engineer contracts also must be consented to by the architect, contractor, and engineer.

ROLE OF THE PARALEGAL

Many law firms and other mortgage lenders utilize paralegals in the preparation of mortgage loan documents. A thorough discussion of the role of the paralegal in the closing process, including the preparation of sale and loan documents, is discussed in Chapter 14.

Similar to other legal documents, the preparation of mortgage loan documents requires accuracy and attention to detail. It is important that the correct names for the mortgagor and the mortgage lender and a full and complete description of the real property be provided. The paralegal should check and review all the information against the mortgage loan commitment, title report, and other information to ensure that it is correct.

Most law firms and other mortgage lenders maintain their mortgage forms electronically and create transactional documents using word processing technology. Care must be taken that all the terms of the mortgage loan are incorporated into the documents and that the correct precedent has been accessed. Even the completion of preprinted forms can now be done by computer programs that, after the information is input into the system, can complete and repeat the information on each mortgage form as needed.

A paralegal may also be involved in the foreclosure of a mortgage loan. It is possible that in a larger firm with specialized departments of lawyers, a litigation paralegal would be used in the foreclosure process rather than a real estate paralegal. In smaller firms where both the attorneys and the paralegals are generalists, a real estate paralegal may be utilized to assist in a foreclosure. Foreclosure procedures are governed by state law, and a paralegal should become fully familiar with the foreclosure procedures of his or her state.

🏛 ETHICS: Misrepresentation

A paralegal is employed by a law firm that represents lending institutions. One of the paralegal's duties is to send copies of the note, mortgages, and other loan documents to the borrower for review before closing. The paralegal receives a telephone call from a borrower who has received such a loan package. The borrower states that the documents are quite lengthy and asks if the documents contain a "due on sale" provision that would restrict the borrower's ability to sell the property in the future. The paralegal is not totally familiar with the particular lending institution's documents and indicates to the borrower that she does not believe the documents contain a "due on sale" provision. After the telephone conversation with the borrower, the paralegal discovers by reviewing the mortgage that it does contain a "due on sale" provision. Should the paralegal call the borrower back and tell the borrower that she was mistaken and that the documents do contain a "due on sale" provision or remain silent, assuming that the borrower will discover the "due on sale" provision after he or she has fully read the documents, so that no harm will be done in any event?

A paralegal should never engage in professional misconduct, including dishonesty and willful misrepresentation. Although the statement to the borrower that the mortgage loan documents do not contain a "due on sale" provision was made in good faith at the time, the later discovery of the error needs to be corrected. Remaining silent after having given out false information concerning the content of a legal document constitutes dishonest and even willful misrepresentation. The ethical thing to do is for the paralegal to call the borrower, explain that she was mistaken concerning the "due on sale" provision, and indicate to the borrower that there is such a provision and where it can be found in the loan documents.

SUMMARY

Mortgage loan documents attempt to address every conceivable issue and problem that could arise during the term of the mortgage loan. Numerous issues such as obligations to pay taxes on the mortgaged property, providing insurance on the improvements, the abilities of the owner to sell the property, and rights and remedies for default are set forth in a mortgage. Commercial lenders may, in addition to the mortgage, require from the borrower additional loan documents such as a security agreement, an assignment of rents and leases, and the filing of a UCC financing statement. If the mortgage loan is a construction loan, the lender may also require the borrower to sign a construction loan agreement that documents and governs the disbursement of loan proceeds during the construction process.

The terms of the mortgage loan documents are negotiated between the borrower and the lender. Familiarity with the provisions and their effect on either the borrower or the lender is essential for a paralegal to effectively prepare or review mortgage loan documents and to participate in the loan closing process. Although most mortgage loan documents are prepared to protect the interests of the lender, the lender's safety in a mortgage loan does not end with the mortgage documents. A mortgage loan is only as secure as the borrower's title in the real property described in the mortgage. The chapters that follow discuss various methods a lender or a purchaser of property uses to protect itself from a defective land title. Through the use of both title examinations and title insurance, a lender attempts to protect itself from potential defects in the borrower's title to the collateral property.

HELPFUL WEBSITES

Uniform Commercial Code

A copy of the text of Article 9 of the Uniform Commercial Code that governs security interests and financing statements can be found on the Cornell University Law School Web site at *http://www.law.cornell.edu.* Go to *ucc/ucc.table.html*

Florida Mortgage Forms

Free copies of Florida mortgage forms can be found at *http://www.mortgageinvestments.com.*

KEY TERMS

certificate of occupancy
exculpated loan

financing statement
retainage

security agreement

REVIEW QUESTIONS

1. How can a lender protect itself against a borrower's failure to pay real estate taxes and to keep the secured buildings and improvements insured?

2. What is a security agreement?

3. What is the importance of filing a UCC financing statement?

4. Why do lenders who make construction loans require a borrower to sign a construction loan agreement?

5. What is a nonrecourse loan, and who benefits from it?

6. What is the importance of an assignment of leases and rents to a lender?

7. What representations and warranties are required of a borrower in a construction loan agreement?

8. What is retainage in a construction loan, and why is it important?

9. What remedies does a lender have for a default under a construction loan agreement?

CASE PROBLEMS

1. You are assisting an attorney in the closing of a loan to be secured by an apartment project. Each apartment contains a refrigerator, electric range, oven, and dishwasher. You have been asked to prepare a security agreement and to file a UCC financing statement to perfect the lender's security interest in those items. The apartment project is located in Calhoun County, but the borrower resides in Dobbins County. Where would you file the UCC financing statement?

2. The street in front of Sarah Baker's house is being widened from two lanes to four lanes. The widening will require the county to take approximately 10 feet of Sarah's front yard. The county has promised to pay Sarah $20,000 for the yard being taken. Sarah's home is secured by a loan to First Bank and Trust. You have been requested by the attorney who represents Sarah to review the First Bank and Trust mortgage papers to see if the lender has any claim to the proceeds. What would you look for in the mortgage loan documents, and what would you expect to find?

3. You have been asked to prepare a construction loan agreement for a lender client of the firm. The lender wants the maximum protection against problems as they disburse the loan proceeds. In drafting the construction loan agreement, what requirements would you add for the disbursement of the loan proceeds during construction?

4. You have been asked to prepare a mortgage to secure a real estate loan transaction. You have been asked to use the FNMA/FHLMC Uniform Mortgage. What information do you need to prepare the mortgage?

5. You have a mortgage on your home to First Bank and Trust. The mortgage is a FNMA/FHLMC Uniform Mortgage. You currently have the home under a contract for sale. You want to be able to sell the home and have the purchaser assume the mortgage to First Bank and Trust. Two days before the closing of the sale, you notify First Bank and Trust that you are selling the property and that the purchaser will assume the loan. First Bank and Trust responds that it will not consent to the sale unless you provide financial information concerning the purchaser and pay First Bank and Trust a fee of $1,000. First Bank and Trust also informs you that if you refuse to cooperate and sell the home without its consent, it will call the loan in default and foreclose. Can First Bank and Trust legally do this?

PRACTICAL ASSIGNMENTS

1. Research the Uniform Commercial Code Article 9 rules for your state. Has your state adopted the revised rules? Does your state have any special requirements for filing financing statements that perfect security interests in fixtures, growing crops, or timber? Does your state permit electronic filing of UCC financing statements? Prepare answers to these questions in written report form and attach the appropriate statutes or case authority for your answers.

2. Research the common form of mortgage used in your state. Is it a mortgage, deed of trust, or deed to secure debt? Obtain a copy of the form. Review it carefully and observe its differences and similarities with those forms set out in the book.

3. Research the Uniform Commercial Code of your state to determine if it has passed laws establishing criteria for the proper identification of the name of the debtor in a UCC financing statement.

ADDENDUM

Exhibit 11–3 Assignment of Leases and Rents
Exhibit 11–4 Construction and/or Development
 Loan Agreement

Student StudyWare™ CD-ROM

Interactive Student CD in the book includes additional quizzing, case studies, and key terms flashcards.

Online Companion™

For additional resources, please go to *www.paralegal.delmar.cengage.com*

EXHIBIT 11–3

Assignment of Leases and Rents

STATE OF_____
COUNTY OF _____

 THIS ASSIGNMENT is made and entered into this _____ day of September, 20___, by _____, a _____ (hereinafter referred to as "Assignor"), and it is delivered to _____, a _____ corporation (hereinafter called "Assignee").

WITNESSETH:

 WHEREAS, Assignor is justly indebted to Assignee, and said indebtedness is on the date hereof evidenced by Assignor's Real Estate Note of even date herewith, in the principal amount of _____ NO/100 DOLLARS ($_____), hereinafter called the "Note";

 WHEREAS, the indebtedness evidenced by the Note and other indebtedness of Assignor to Assignee is secured by that certain Deed to Secure Debt and Security Agreement of even date herewith, from Assignor to Assignee, conveying the real property described on Exhibit "A," attached hereto and incorporated herein by reference, hereinafter called the "Property," which Deed to Secure Debt and Security Agreement is incorporated herein by reference and is hereinafter called the "Security Deed";

 WHEREAS, Assignee has required that Assignor assign to Assignee certain of Assignor's rights, title and interest with respect to the Property; and

 WHEREAS, Assignor has agreed to so assign such interests to Assignee and desires to make and deliver this assignment for that purpose.

Delmar/Cengage Learning

(continued)

EXHIBIT 11–3

Assignment of Leases
and Rents (*continued*)

NOW, THEREFORE, in consideration of the foregoing premises, of the indebtedness of Assignor to Assignee and of other good and valuable consideration, all of which Assignor acknowledges constitutes sufficient consideration and value received by Assignor at the time of or before Assignor's execution hereof, Assignor hereby assigns and agrees as follows:

1. *Assignment.* Subject to the terms and conditions hereinafter set forth, Assignor does hereby sell, transfer and assign unto Assignee the Leases and the Rents, as such terms are defined in the Security Deed, and does hereby ratify, affirm, confirm and reaffirm the sale, transfer and conveyance of the Leases and the Rents under and pursuant to the Security Deed. As used herein, the term "Leases" includes, but is not limited to, the lease agreements set forth on Exhibit "B" attached hereto and incorporated herein by reference and all future lease agreements involving the Property.

2. *Purpose of Assignment.* This assignment is made and intended to secure the Indebtedness, as such term is defined in the Security Deed.

3. *Power of Attorney.* Assignor does hereby authorize and empower Assignee, and does hereby irrevocably and duly constitute Assignee, as Assignor's attorney-in-fact, to receive any and all of the Rents, to collect any and all of the Rents by such means and taking such actions as Assignee shall deem necessary, and to act in all other ways with respect to the Rents and the Leases for Assignor and in Assignor's place and stead. Assignee shall have the right, as Assignor's attorney-in-fact, but not the obligation, to take any action hereby authorized in Assignor's name and to exercise any and all of Assignor's rights and remedies, whether available at law or in equity or otherwise, with respect to any of the Rents or the Leases. The foregoing appointment of Assignee as Assignor's attorney-in-fact is coupled with an interest, cannot be revoked by bankruptcy, insolvency, death, dissolution or otherwise and shall not terminate until the Indebtedness has been paid and satisfied in full.

4. *Rents Payable to Assignee.* Assignor hereby directs, instructs and demands each and every person, partnership, corporation, association and other entity or organization now or hereafter owing any of the Rents to Assignor to pay any and all amounts so owed promptly and directly to Assignee upon demand therefor by Assignee. Assignor hereby represents and warrants that all payments so made shall have the same effect in satisfaction of obligations owed to Assignor as if made directly to Assignor, and Assignor shall not question or otherwise contest any tenant for any such payment authorized hereby. By accepting Assignor's delivery of this assignment, however, Assignee agrees that the Rents shall be payable to and collected by Assignor until such time as Assignee may demand payment thereof directly to Assignee and that Assignee shall not demand such payment until after a default occurs under this assignment; provided, however, that Assignee's agreement and Assignor's privilege to continue collecting the Rents shall automatically terminate if Assignor collects any installment of rent or any other payment (by cash, note or otherwise) which is part of the Rents more than one (1) month in advance of the date such rent or other payment is due.

5. *Notification of Obligations.* Promptly upon request by Assignee: (i) Assignor shall deliver to Assignee a copy of any of the Leases which are written; (ii) Assignor shall notify the other party or parties to any of the Leases, whether written or oral, and whether now or hereafter made or executed, of the content and existence of this assignment and of the agreements and obligations of Assignor with respect to payment of the Rents as set forth in paragraphs 3 and 4 hereof; and (iii) Assignor shall obtain and deliver to Assignee a written consent from, and agreement by, any and all such parties, and any and all parties owing any Rents to Assignor, to pay any and all Rents so owed directly to Assignee, and not to Assignor, as provided for by this assignment. Any and all notices, consents and agreements required hereunder shall be in such form and substance as Assignee may prepare.

6. *Default.* If: (i) Assignor should fail to perform its duties and obligations under, or should violate or breach or fail to observe, satisfy or comply with any of the terms, covenants, conditions, agreements, requirements, restrictions or provisions set forth in, this assignment or (ii) any representation or warranty made herein should be false, untrue, incomplete or misleading

EXHIBIT 11–3

Assignment of Leases
and Rents (*continued*)

in any material respect when made; or (iii) Assignor shall otherwise be in default under the Note or the Security Deed then, in any of such events, Assignor shall be in default under this assignment.

7. *Rights on Default.* If Assignor shall be in default under this assignment, Assignee may, at its option and election and without notice to Assignor, do any one or more of the following: (i) exercise any or all of Assignee's rights and remedies under this assignment, the Note or the Security Deed, or any other instrument evidencing or securing all or any part of the Indebtedness; (ii) take possession of the Leases; (iii) take such measures or actions as Assignee deems appropriate or necessary to enforce the payment of all Rents; (iv) contest, litigate and compromise any claim for rebate, setoff, loss, demand, abatement or reduction in connection with the Leases or the Rents; or (v) lease or rent any of the Property and employ and pay a rental agent or a broker a commission to facilitate such leasing or renting, such commission to be added to the Indebtedness. Assignor shall pay all of the costs and expenses incurred by Assignee in exercising or enforcing assignee's rights hereunder. Assignee may use and apply the Rents collected by Assignee under this assignment toward the following purposes, in such order as Assignee shall determine: (i) real property ad valorem taxes, sanitary taxes and charges, and personal property ad valorem taxes, with respect to the Property; (ii) premiums for insurance policies required under the Security Deed; (iii) the costs and expenses of repairing and maintaining the Property in such a manner as Assignee may reasonably determine consistent with prior usage and practice; (iv) the costs and expenses to perform completely Assignor's duties, obligations, responsibilities and liabilities under any of the Leases, and in connection with or with respect to any of the Rents; (v) any and all other costs and expenses incurred by Assignee in connection with the Property, including without limitation any and all costs and expenses incurred by reason of assignee's exercise of its rights under this assignment or the Security Deed or both; (vi) interest and default interest accrued on the Indebtedness; and (vii) the outstanding principal balance of the Indebtedness. All of Assignee's rights and remedies in the event of a default hereunder are cumulative of and in addition to, and not restrictive of or in lieu of, the rights and remedies of Assignee under the Note and the Security Deed, or as may be provided or allowed by law or in equity or otherwise, and Assignee may elect one or more or all of the rights and remedies available under this assignment or otherwise.

8. *Assignor's Covenants.* Assignor covenants that: (i) Assignor will fully and faithfully perform all of the duties and obligations of the lessor, landlord or owner of the Property under the Leases, and observe, satisfy and comply with all of the terms, covenants, conditions, agreements, requirements, restrictions and provisions of the Leases, and do all acts otherwise necessary to maintain and preserve the Rents and prevent any diminishment or impairment of the value of the Leases or the Rents or the interest of Assignor or Assignee therein or thereunder, it being expressly understood and agreed that Assignee neither undertakes nor assumes any of Assignor's liabilities, responsibilities, duties or obligations in connection with the Leases or the Rents; (ii) Assignor will enforce the full and faithful performance of all of the duties and obligations of each of the tenants and lessees under the Leases, and the observance, satisfaction and compliance with all of the terms, covenants, conditions, agreements, requirements, restrictions and provisions of the Leases required to be observed, satisfied or complied with by the tenants and lessees thereunder; (iii) Assignor will appear in and prosecute and defend, as shall be necessary, any action or proceeding arising under, out of, with respect to or in connection with any of the Leases, and, upon request by Assignee, do so in the name of and on behalf of Assignee, and pay all costs and expenses, including attorney's fees, incurred by Assignee in connection therewith; (iv) Assignor will not further assign the Leases or the Rents, shall not terminate, alter, modify or amend in any respect, or accept the surrender of, any of the Leases without the prior written consent of Assignee; (v) Assignor shall be the lessor or landlord under all of the Leases; *provided, however,* that Assignor may appoint a leasing agent to act on its behalf upon prior written notice to Assignee of the identity and mailing address of such leasing agent; (vi) Assignor, shall not permit, consent to or acquiesce in any subleasing, assignment, renewal

(continued)

or extension, in whole or in part, of or under any of the Leases without the prior written consent of Assignee; (vii) Assignor will not relocate or consent to or acquiesce in the relocation of any lessee, tenant or other user or occupant of all or any part of the Property without the prior written consent of Assignee; (viii) Assignor will not collect Rents for more than one (1) month in advance and will not accept any security deposit, damage deposit or similar funds under or in connection with any of the Leases for an amount in excess of one (1) month's rent without the prior written consent of Assignee; (ix) Assignor will keep the Leases and the Rents free from any and all liens, encumbrances and security interests whatsoever, other than the security interest created by this assignment and the Security Deed; and (x) Assignor will promptly pay and discharge all taxes assessed against the Leases or the Rents and all liens which may attach to the Leases or the Rents. The foregoing covenants are cumulative of and in addition to those now or hereafter imposed by law.

9. *Liability of Assignee.* Assignee shall not be liable to Assignor for a failure to collect any part or all of the Rents, and Assignee may be required to account for only such sums as Assignee actually collects.

10. *Forbearance.* Assignee shall not be deemed to waive any of Assignee's rights or remedies under this assignment unless such waiver is express, in writing and signed by or on behalf of Assignee. No delay, omission or forbearance by Assignee in exercising any of Assignee's rights or remedies under this assignment shall operate as a waiver of such rights or remedies. A waiver in writing on one occasion shall not be construed as a waiver of any right or remedy on any future occasion. Neither the existence of this Assignment nor the exercise by Assignee of Assignee's right to collect any of the Rents shall be construed as a waiver by Assignee of any of Assignee's rights to enforce payment of the Indebtedness in strict accordance with the terms and provisions of the Note and the Security Deed.

11. *Term of Assignment.* The term of this assignment shall be until the Indebtedness has been paid in full and the Security Deed has been cancelled and satisfied of record. The cancellation and satisfaction of record of the Security Deed shall automatically constitute a satisfaction, cancellation and release by Assignee of Assignor's obligations and Assignee's rights under this assignment.

12. *Applicable Law.* This assignment shall be governed by, construed under and interpreted and enforced in accordance with the laws of the State of _____.

13. *Time.* Time is and shall be of the essence of this assignment and of each covenant and agreement by Assignor.

14. *Captions.* All captions or headings preceding the text of separate sections, paragraphs and subparagraphs of this assignment are solely for reference purposes and shall not affect the meaning, construction, interpretation or effect of the text.

15. *Not Additional Security.* This assignment shall not be deemed or construed to be merely additional security or collateral for the Indebtedness but rather primary and unconditional security. Assignee may exercise all rights granted hereunder without regard to the existence, value or adequacy of any other collateral or security for the Indebtedness held by Assignee. All collateral and security for the Indebtedness is primary and unconditional collateral and security. Assignor hereby authorizes, directs and instructs any trustee or receiver in bankruptcy having possession of the Leases or the Rents or any of them to deliver the same to Assignee in the event of a default by Assignor and the exercise by Assignee of its rights hereunder.

16. *Notices.* All notices, requests, demands and other communications under this assignment shall be in writing and shall be deemed to have been duly given if given in accordance with the provisions of the Security Deed.

17. *Definitions.* The word "Assignor" as used herein shall include the legal representatives, successors, and assigns of Assignor as if so specified at length throughout this assignment, and all covenants, agreements, duties, obligations, liabilities and responsibilities of Assignor shall be binding upon and enforceable against the legal representatives, successors and assigns

EXHIBIT 11–3

Assignment of Leases and Rents (*continued*)

(continued)

EXHIBIT 11–3

Assignment of Leases
and Rents (*continued*)

of Assignor. The word "Assignee" as used herein shall include the transferees, successors, legal representatives and assigns of Assignee as if so specified at length through this assignment, and all rights of Assignee under this assignment shall inure to the benefit of the transferees, successors, legal representatives and assigns of Assignee. The words "Assignor" and "Assignee" shall include the neuter, masculine and feminine genders, and the singular and the plural.

IN WITNESS WHEREOF, Assignor, by its duly authorized representatives, has executed this assignment under seal and Assignor has delivered this assignment to Assignee, all the day and year first written above.

Signed, sealed and delivered this _____   ASSIGNOR:
day of _____, 20_____, in the
presence of:

_____
Unofficial Witness

_____
Notary Public
My Commission Expires:

_____
[Notarial Seal]

AGREEMENT made by and between the undersigned (hereinafter "Borrower") and _____ Bank, _____ (address).

WITNESSETH:

WHEREAS, Borrower is the owner of certain real property described in a Deed to Secure Debt of even date (the "Deed") given this day in favor of Lender to secure a Construction Loan Note of even date in the original principal amount of $_____ (the "Note"); and

WHEREAS, Borrower intends to fully develop and/or construct improvements upon said real property in accordance with certain "plans and specifications" heretofore delivered by Borrower to the Lender; and

WHEREAS, Borrower has obtained a commitment from the Lender to make Borrower loans and advances, evidenced by the Note, for such development and/or construction on terms and conditions therein contained, which commitment is incorporated herein by reference;

NOW, THEREFORE, in consideration of the premises and the making of the loan to Borrower, the Borrower herein agrees as follows:

1. (a) Unless waived by the Lender, no materials shall have been placed upon the real estate prior to the date hereof, and development and/or construction shall not commence sooner than 24 hours, plus any intervening Saturday, Sunday, or holiday, after date hereof.

(b) Unless otherwise approved in writing by the Lender, development and/or construction shall commence not later than expiration of the applicable commencement period specified below.

2. (a) All development and/or construction shall be fully completed in strict accordance with the plans and specifications heretofore delivered by Borrower to the Lender.

(b) All development and/or construction shall be fully completed within the applicable completion dates set forth below.

3. Lender will from time to time make advances to Borrower pursuant to inspection or certification of progress of construction or development in place, up to the total principal amount of the Note set forth below, provided that:

(a) At the time of the first advance, Borrower shall have complied fully with the provisions of paragraphs 1(a) and 1(b) above.

(b) Borrower has delivered, in form and content satisfactory to the Lender, a Promissory Note duly executed by Borrower.

(c) Borrower has delivered to Lender a Deed to Secure Debt, in form and content satisfactory to the Lender.

(d) Borrower has conveyed to the Lender by Security Agreement, in form and content satisfactory to the Lender (including the execution of a U.C.C. financing statement), a security interest in all personal property of Borrower used in connection with or intended as part of the development and/or construction contemplated herein.

(e) No lien or other interest shall have been permitted to attach to the real estate or other property superior to the legal title of the Lender under the Deed to Secure Debt or Security Agreement.

(f) No event of default, as herein defined, shall have occurred.

(g) Borrower has performed each obligation herein contained or made in the commitment or any other instrument given pursuant hereto or thereto.

(h) All construction up to the date of the advance has been in strict accordance with the plans and specifications heretofore delivered to the Lender, and satisfactory evidence thereof has been furnished to the Lender, and all change orders which have been agreed to between Borrower and Contractor have been approved in writing by the Lender.

EXHIBIT 11–4

Construction and/or Development Loan Agreement

Delmar/Cengage Learning

(continued)

EXHIBIT 11–4

Construction and/or
Development Loan Agreement
(*continued*)

(i) At the time of each advance, the Lender is fully satisfied with the timeliness, progress, and quality of development and/or construction, and, in the sole opinion of the Lender, the estimated cost of development and/or construction in accordance with the plans and specifications does not exceed the balance of the loan to be advanced.

4. Borrower herein represents as follows:

(a) All prior funds advanced shall have been spent only in the development and/or construction of the project or agreed-to soft costs, and satisfactory evidence thereof shall be furnished to the Lender as may be requested from time to time.

(b) The real estate and other property is free and clear of all liens and encumbrances except for the security instruments of the Lender and except for the lien for real estate taxes not yet due and payable.

(c) All evidence, statements, and other writings delivered to the Lender by Borrower in connection with this loan are true and correct and omit no material fact, the omission of which would make such statements and other writings misleading.

(d) All bills for labor, materials, and fixtures used, or on hand to be used, in development and/or construction of the project have been paid in accordance with the terms hereof, and no one is asserting a lien against the real estate or other property with respect thereto.

(e) All terms of the commitment have been complied with in full, insofar as the same are required to be complied with at the time of each advance.

(f) That he will furnish the Lender, upon Lender's request, with satisfactory evidence (certificates or affidavits of architects, contractors, subcontractors, or attorneys) showing:

(1) the value of the development and/or construction then existing;

(2) that all outstanding claims for labor, materials, and fixtures have been paid in accordance with the terms thereof;

(3) that no liens (other than the inchoate lien for real estate taxes not yet due) are outstanding or unpaid superior to the security title of the Lender;

(4) that Borrower has complied with all of the terms hereof, the commitment, the Note, the Deed to Secure Debt, and the other loan documents; and

(5) that all construction has been performed in strict accordance with the plans and specifications.

5. (a) If required by the Lender's commitment, Borrower will immediately deposit all funds advanced by the Lender into a separate account maintained at _____ Bank; and if not required by Lender then in a commercial banking institution or a savings and loan association, the deposits of which are insured by the Federal Deposit Insurance Corporation, to be known as the "Development and/or Construction Account," to be withdrawn and used solely for the payment of bills for labor, materials, and fixtures used in connection with the development and/or construction contemplated hereby, and to furnish the Lender with satisfactory evidence of the establishment of the account specified above and with verified copies of all deposit and withdrawal transactions applicable thereto.

(b) Borrower shall advise Lender of all requests for change orders all of which must be approved in advance by Lender. Borrower shall furnish Lender with copies of all change orders immediately upon their origination.

6. (a) Lender shall have no obligation to make any advance if:

(1) any claim of lien is filed against the real estate or other property;

(2) Borrower breaches or fails to perform, observe, or meet any covenant or condition made herein or made in any instrument or document executed by Borrower pursuant hereto;

(3) any warranty or representation of Borrower made, or agreed to be made, or contained in any instrument or document executed by Borrower pursuant hereto, shall be false or materially misleading;

(4) a levy is made under service of process on, or a receiver is appointed for, the real estate or any other property of Borrower (including Borrower's personal property unconnected with this transaction);

(continued)

(5) any proceedings for relief under Federal or State bankruptcy laws or other laws designed for debtor relief are brought by or against Borrower;

(6) Borrower commits any act of bankruptcy;

(7) Borrower is alleged to be insolvent or unable to pay his debts as they become due in any legal proceeding;

(8) Borrower commits, or omits to do, any act, or any event occurs, as a result of which any obligations of Borrower may be declared immediately due and payable to the holder thereof; or

(9) Borrower fails to pay any other debt on the contractually required due date.

(b) Each of the events recited in provision 6(a) above shall be regarded as, and shall be known as (for purposes of this agreement and all other instruments or documents executed by Borrower pursuant hereto), "events of default," and upon the occurrence of any of them, the Lender may, at its discretion, declare immediately due and payable all evidences of debt given by Borrower to the Lender.

7. (a) Lender may, at its option, collect interest on the sum of advances outstanding from time to time by deducting from the Borrower's loan-in-process account the interest that may become due under the Note.

(b) Interest during the construction and/or development period shall be calculated as and from the day funds are advanced and is due and payable monthly in accordance with the Note terms.

(c) No building shall be occupied by anyone before completion of construction and a final inspection by the Lender without the prior written consent of the Lender, and no building shall be occupied by anyone after completion of construction and a final inspection by the Lender without the prior written consent of the Lender.

(d) No oral or written lease or rental agreement shall be offered or executed by Borrower concerning the real estate or other property without the prior written consent of the Lender.

(e) Progress inspections shall be made by the Lender or by a duly qualified and licensed architect or engineer selected by the Lender in its sole discretion. All inspections, reviews, and certifications shall be performed solely for the benefit of the Lender, and all costs and expenses incurred in connection therewith shall be promptly paid by Borrower.

(f) If at any time during development and/or construction of the project, it is determined by the Lender, in its sole discretion, that the balance of the funds remaining unadvanced from the loan are insufficient to pay for completion of the project in accordance with the plans and specifications, then no further advances shall be required to be made by the Lender until Borrower shall have deposited with the Lender sums sufficient to fully complete the project in accordance with the plans and specifications.

(g) Borrower, upon request by Lender, shall pay various subcontractors and materialmen only ninety percent (90%) of the total contract amount due them for work completed or material furnished at the time of Borrower's request for an advance; the balance of funds due such subcontractors and materialmen shall be retained by the Lender until satisfactory completion of the project.

(h) In the event a mechanic's lien or materialman's lien is filed, or legal proceedings instituted, which lien or proceedings are not satisfied or removed, as the case may be, by Borrower within ten (10) days of written notice thereof from the Lender, Lender may apply the balance remaining in Borrower's loan-in-process account to the payment thereof.

(i) Lender and its agents, at all times during development and/or construction, shall have the full right of entry and free access to the real estate and all improvements erected thereon and the right to inspect all work done, labor performed, and material delivered to and furnished in and about the project and the right to inspect and make copies of all books, ledgers, statements, writings, invoices, and other documents and records of the Borrower pertaining thereto.

EXHIBIT 11–4

Construction and/or Development Loan Agreement (*continued*)

(continued)

EXHIBIT 11–4

Construction and/or
Development Loan Agreement
(*continued*)

(j) Borrower will not store or permit others to store any building materials, equipment, supplies, or fixtures of any kind whatsoever on the real estate described in the Deed which are not intended to be used in, for, or in connection with the project.

(k) Borrower will not enter into any agreement with any other person, firm, or entity concerning or pertaining to the real estate which involves easements, cross-easements, rights-of-way, dedications of facilities, streets, or which in any way diminishes the size or limits the use or other rights in the real estate, without the prior written consent of the Lender.

8. (a) Development and/or construction shall be performed strictly in accordance with all applicable ordinances and statutes (both Federal and State) and in accordance with the requirements of all regulatory authorities having jurisdiction over the project.

(b) Upon Lender's request, Borrower will provide the Lender, at Borrower's expense, with appropriate evidence of compliance with all statutory and regulatory requirements of the appropriate governmental authorities, including, by way of illustration, but not limited to, preliminary reports, certifications, surveys, filings, drawings, plans, specifications, final reports, tests, data, announcements, publications, instruments, or agreements filed with, approved by or proposed to be used in compliance with local health regulations, zoning ordinances, or licensing or permit regulations required by local building authorities, the Federal Interstate Land Sales Act, the Georgia Land Sales Act, the Georgia Condominium Act, or Department of Housing and Urban Development regulations. If requested by the Lender, all statutory or regulatory permits, certificates, licenses, etc., shall be obtained by the Borrower in such form that they are fully transferable to the Lender.

(c) (1) All development and/or construction will be performed in accordance with the standards of good workmanship and will be of "first class quality," and all work will be performed on, and the improvements erected upon, only that real estate described in the Deed; and

(2) Development and/or construction will not encroach upon or overhang any easement or right-of-way or upon the land of others; all improvements erected will be within applicable building restriction lines, however established, and will not violate applicable use or other restrictions contained in prior conveyances, recorded plats, ordinances, or regulations.

(d) Borrower will furnish the Lender from time to time, upon Lender's request, with a current survey, signed, sealed, dated, and certified to the Borrower, and also to the Lender as mortgagee, by a registered land surveyor, showing that all development and/or construction is entirely upon the real estate described in the Deed, is in accordance with the plans and specifications, and that no violation of the provisions of (c) (2) above have occurred; Borrower will, in any event, provide the Lender with a proper survey showing the location of each building foundation upon the lot prior to the first advance of funds after the closing, and upon request by Lender, with a final survey, upon completion of all improvements, showing the location of all streets, sidewalks, walkways, driveways, patios, and other permanent improvements, prior to a request for a final advance.

(e) Borrower will maintain at all times during the term of this Agreement and until construction is fully completed and the Deed in favor of Lender has been satisfied Builder's Risk and such other insurance, including fire, theft, vandalism and extended coverage, as required by Lender. Such insurance shall be in an amount and with a company acceptable to Lender with Lender being named as loss payee. Borrower shall provide to Lender evidence of such insurance prior to the first advance of funds being made to Borrower after the closing.

(f) Borrower represents that it has worker's compensation insurance in place as required by law and that it will maintain such insurance at all times during construction, and further that all of its subcontractors also have such insurance as required by law in place while they are working on the project.

(g) Borrower will provide to Lender on or before the first advance of funds after closing a building permit from the proper governmental authority authorizing Borrower to begin construction and/or development of the project.

(*continued*)

9. Lender shall be entitled to collect from Borrower a fee for each inspection of $_____ per inspection.

10. Lender has had no control over, will have no control over, has not supervised, and will not supervise the construction of improvements on the property. Lender has not, does not, and will not make any representations, warranties, guarantees, or promises concerning the construction, workmanship, materials, or design employed in, to be used in, or constituting the improvements on the property. Lender's relationship to the construction and/or improvements on the property is solely that of a mortgage lender, and all periodic inspections and any appraisals made by the Lender are for the sole purpose of protecting Lender's security interest in the real estate and determining that progress has been made for the disbursement of construction loan funds as work has been completed.

11. In the event that the Lender advances funds for the payment of taxes, insurance, or other expenses related to the protection of the Lender's interest in the property, the Lender may charge a reasonable fee for such service. In the event that a check written by the Borrower is returned for insufficient funds, the Lender may impose a reasonable charge for collecting the amount due from Borrower.

12. (a) If at any time prior to completion of the project, Borrower abandons the project, or if work ceases thereon for a period of more than ten (10) days without the prior written approval of the Lender, the Lender may, without notice to Borrower, declare all sums theretofore advanced immediately due and payable.

(b) In the event of default and at the request of the Lender, Borrower shall transfer and assign, or cause to be transferred and assigned, all permits, registrations, vendor's warranties or guarantees used or obtained in connection with the project, in favor of the Lender or its nominee.

13. Provided Borrower is not in default hereunder, Lender shall release certain portions of the real estate, provided it is in accordance with the release provisions set forth in Lender's commitment letter.

Commencement of work must occur by _____ and be completed by _____.

The maximum amount to be advanced under the Lender's Note is $_____.

IN WITNESS WHEREOF, the undersigned has hereunto set its hand(s) and seal(s).

Date: _____

_____

Borrower

_____

Borrower

LENDER: _____

By: _____

GUARANTEE

The undersigned, being the Contractor for the Borrower named herein, for and in consideration of One Dollar ($1.00) and as an inducement to the Lender named herein to make the loan, hereby guarantees completion of all improvements in full accordance with the plans

EXHIBIT 11–4

Construction and/or Development Loan Agreement (*continued*)

EXHIBIT 11–4

Construction and/or
Development Loan Agreement
(*continued*)

and specifications heretofore submitted to Lender, and hereby guarantees performance by Borrower in accordance with the terms and conditions of the foregoing agreement. The undersigned further guarantees that all bills, invoices, and other charges incurred by the undersigned for labor and material used and to be used in the construction of improvements on the property will be paid in full.

Date: _____

_____
Contractor

DISBURSEMENT AUTHORIZATION

Borrower hereby directs Lender to make all advances under the foregoing agreement directly to the Contractor named below. Borrower further hereby authorizes _____, as the agent of the Contractor named below, to apply for and receive all advances under the foregoing agreement for the purpose of paying all bills for labor and materials employed in the construction and/or development which is the subject of the foregoing agreement.

Date: _____
Borrower

_____
Contractor   Borrower

AUTHORIZATION FOR DIRECT DEPOSIT TO CHECKING ACCOUNT
Construction Loan Department

The undersigned Borrower hereby authorizes the Construction Loan Department of _____ _____ Bank to make direct deposits/advances from Borrower's construction loan funds to Borrower's _____ Bank Checking Account.

Borrower understands and agrees to the following terms and conditions:

   (1) No deposits or advances will be made if the loan account is delinquent on or before the date of the requested deposit.
   (2) No deposits or advances will be made unless all conditions precedent as set forth in the Construction and/or Development Loan Agreement have been satisfied.
   (3) _____ Bank shall not be responsible for any insufficient funds, charges or dishonored items in connection with the above checking account, and Borrower hereby releases Lender from any and all liabilities for such charges. Borrower agrees to assume all liability and responsibility for maintenance of said checking account and for compliance with _____ Bank's stated requirements before any deposits are made.
   (4) This authorization will remain in effect for the term of the loan until rescinded by Borrower in writing.
   (5) (a) All Available Funds
   All available funds will be transferred automatically to the account named below following each requested construction inspection, and in an amount calculated in accordance with the draw schedule adopted by the Construction Loan Department of _____ Bank, based on the progress of construction. _____ Bank will make deposits

(*continued*)

or advances only if all of the above requirements are met and Borrower is in full compliance with all terms of the Construction and/or Development Loan Agreement, Deed to Secure Debt, and Promissory Note in favor of Lender;

<u>or</u>

(b) <u>Amount Requested Only</u>

Funds will be transferred to the account named below, following each requested construction inspection, in an amount requested by the Borrower. The amount transferred, however, shall not be greater than the maximum amount available as calculated in accordance with _____ Bank's draw schedule based on progress of construction in place at each inspection. In no event will funds be transferred until an inspection is made by _____ Bank's Construction Inspector. _____ Bank will make deposits or advances only upon request of the undersigned Borrower, and only if all of the above requirements are met, and Borrower is in full compliance with all terms of the Construction and/or Development Loan Agreement, Deed to Secure Debt, and Promissory Note in favor of Lender.

CHECKING ACCOUNT INFORMATION

Title: _____

Number: _____

Borrower's Name: _____

Loan Number:_____Date:_____

_____
Borrower   Borrower

EXHIBIT 11–4

Construction and/or Development Loan Agreement (*continued*)

chapter | 12

Title Examinations

Objectives

After reading this chapter, you should be able to:

- Recognize the importance of title examinations
- Explain the three types of recording statutes
- Understand the process and procedures involved in conducting a title examination
- Review a title examination report
- Identify potential title problems and know how to solve them

Outline

One of the main responsibilities of a real estate attorney or paralegal is to make certain that a client has good title of ownership to real property. A real estate attorney representing a purchaser will insist that the seller produce satisfactory evidence of good title before the purchase. A real estate attorney representing a lender will insist that the borrower produce satisfactory evidence of good title before the loan is made. Typically, this evidence of good title of ownership is provided by a title examination of the public real property records and the issuance of title insurance.

The role of the paralegal in title examinations varies from state to state and even among law firms within a given state. In some law firms, a paralegal conducts the title examination. A real estate closing paralegal usually does not conduct the examination but is responsible for ordering the title examination, reviewing it, and converting it into a title insurance commitment, as discussed in Chapter 13. Regardless of whether the paralegal is performing, ordering, or reviewing the title examination, an understanding of the process and procedures involved is essential for the paralegal to carry out his or her responsibilities.

BONA FIDE PURCHASER FOR VALUE RULE

Why examine the public records of real property to obtain proof of ownership of property? Why record real estate documents? Warranty deeds, contracts, leases, mortgages, and easements are all enforceable without recording. Real estate attorneys and paralegals, however, spend substantial time preparing these documents and having them executed with the formality required to place the documents on public record. Why? The answer is the common law **bona fide purchaser for value** rule. This rule states that anyone who purchases property in good faith for valuable consideration and without notice of any claim to or interest in the property by any other party is a bona fide purchaser for value and takes the property free and clear of any claims to or interest in the property by other parties.

For example, Sam Owner has pledged his farm to secure a debt owed to Aunt Owner. Sam Owner has executed and delivered to Aunt Owner a mortgage on the farm, but the mortgage was not recorded. Sam Owner sells the farm to Catherine Purchaser. At the time of the sale, Catherine Purchaser is unaware of the unrecorded mortgage to Aunt Owner. Catherine Purchaser is a bona fide purchaser for value and purchases the farm free and clear of Aunt Owner's mortgage. Aunt Owner's mortgage is unenforceable against the farm after the sale to Catherine Purchaser.

A bona fide purchaser must pay something of value for the property, although the consideration paid need not be equal to the market value of the property. The person taking title to property by inheritance or as a recipient of a gift has not given valuable consideration and therefore is not protected as a bona fide purchaser. This means that a person who has inherited real property takes the real property subject to all valid claims against the real property, regardless of whether the person had notice of the claims or whether the claims were recorded.

The bona fide purchaser status provides special protection not only to the bona fide purchaser, but also to anyone purchasing from the bona fide purchaser. The protection is extended to the subsequent purchaser whether or not the subsequent purchaser has notice of any prior adverse claim or interest to the property. The rationale for the extended protection is to permit the bona fide purchaser to sell the property for full value.

A bona fide purchaser for value receives ownership to real property subject to any and all claims of which the bona fide purchaser has actual or constructive notice at the time the property is acquired. **Actual notice** occurs when the purchaser has direct knowledge or information about title matters. Actual notice includes any facts that the

bona fide purchaser for value

Person who purchases real property in good faith for valuable consideration without notice of any claim to or interest in the real property by any other party.

actual notice

Title matters about which a purchaser has direct knowledge or information.

purchaser can see with his or her own eyes, any facts that the purchaser learns about the property, and any information the circumstances of which should put the purchaser on duty to conduct an investigation that would lead to the finding of certain facts in regard to the property.

Constructive notice is a presumption of law that charges a purchaser with the responsibility of learning about all title matters that would result from an inspection of the property or an examination of the public real property records. Possession of land is notice to the world of the possessor's rights therein. For possession to constitute notice, it must be open, notorious, and exclusive. For example, a purchaser of a supposedly vacant lot of real property visits the lot and finds an inhabited mobile home on the lot. The purchaser is placed on notice to inquire about the mobile home inhabitant's rights to the property. If the mobile home inhabitants have a 50-year unrecorded lease of the property, the prospective purchaser would purchase the property subject to the 50-year lease, and the inhabitants of the mobile home would be permitted to remain on the property until the lease terminated. A purchaser of real property has a duty to inquire as to a party in possession's rights to the property. If no inquiries are made, the purchaser takes the property subject to any rights the possessor may have. A prudent purchaser will satisfy the constructive notice requirements of inspection by either inspecting the property or obtaining a full survey of the property by a registered land surveyor, or both.

The second form of constructive notice is in regard to matters that an inspection of the public real property records would reveal. All states maintain public real property records for the purpose of recording real estate documents and establishing ownership to real property. A prudent purchaser will satisfy the constructive notice requirements by examining the public records in which the documents are recorded.

Constructive notice is imparted to the purchaser only to the extent that recorded instruments are in the chain of title. A **chain of title** is the sequence of subsequent owners to a particular parcel of property, beginning with the original owner and moving through all successive grantors and grantees to the current owner. The chain of title concept limits the number of records imparting constructive notice and the number of records that must be examined. Courts in the states of Massachusetts and New York have pronounced views on the definition of chain of title. The laws in other states follow either the Massachusetts or the New York definition. Under the Massachusetts definition of chain of title, a purchaser need only examine conveyances from the point at which each owner received the property and until that owner conveyed the property to another owner. All other transactions are considered to be outside the chain of title and are held not to provide constructive notice to a purchaser. Under the New York definition of chain of title, the purchaser must examine all instruments made by successive owners and not merely the instruments made during the ownership.

Constructive notice also is imparted to unrecorded instruments that are referred to in a recorded instrument. For example, a recorded deed may make reference to an unrecorded mortgage. The purchaser must exercise reasonable diligence and prudence to ascertain the contents of the unrecorded mortgage because he or she may be responsible to pay the debt secured by the mortgage.

In summary, if a person obtains an interest in property by way of being a purchaser, a lender of a security deed or mortgage, the holder of an easement, and so on, then the only way this property interest can be protected against subsequent purchasers is to record the deed, easement, mortgage, or instrument in the proper records. The act of recording the instrument in its proper place will place future purchasers on constructive notice. These future purchasers will purchase the property subject to the rights of the holder of the recorded instrument.

---

constructive notice

A presumption of law that charges a person with notice of all title matters that can be discovered from an inspection of the real property or an examination of public real property records.

chain of title

Historical sequence of all owners to a particular tract of real property beginning with the original owner and including all successive owners who have derived their title from the original owner.

Recording an instrument is essential to impart constructive notice. The time and location for such recording normally are expressed in what is known as a state's *recording statute*. It is not always clear when an instrument is deemed recorded so as to impart constructive notice. Some courts have held that merely depositing the instrument in the office of the recorder is sufficient to impart constructive notice. Other courts have held that to impart constructive notice, the instrument must actually be transcribed in a permanent record book.

There also is a split of authority as to notice when an error has occurred in transcribing the instrument into the permanent record book. Some courts have imposed a duty on the person recording the instrument to make sure that it is correctly recorded, and such person shall bear full risk of the failure of the registrar of deeds to correctly record the instrument. An examination of the title records after the instrument has been recorded is necessary to discharge the duty. The examination is for the purpose of confirming that the recorded document has been correctly recorded and is in the chain of title. Under this view, the registrar of deeds is deemed to be the agent of the recording party. According to this view, an incorrectly recorded instrument does not impart constructive notice.

Other courts have held that when an instrument is filed, constructive notice is given, regardless of whether the instrument was correctly indexed or recorded, provided that the party recording the instrument has complied with the state's recording statute and that the mistake was made by the clerk's or registrar's office.

RECORDING STATUTES

The common law bona fide purchaser for value rule has been modified in many states by **recording statutes.** Recording statutes (a) give the community notice of the changes in ownership of the property; (b) protect subsequent purchasers and encumbrancers of property from the same common grantor by giving them notice of information contained in the recorded documents; and (c) determine priority among conflicting claims to real property.

> **recording statutes**
> State statutes that regulate the recordation of real property documents.

There are three types of recording statutes: race, notice, and race-notice. The first type is used by the smallest number of states. Under the race statute, priority between successive grantees of the same land from a common grantor is determined by who wins the race to the recording office. No notice is imparted to a subsequent purchaser or encumbrancers until the instrument is recorded in the prescribed manner. The first to record an instrument has priority of title, irrespective of whether he or she was a prior or subsequent purchaser. Moreover, a purchaser with actual knowledge of a prior but unrecorded instrument from a common grantor of the same property will have priority if such subsequent purchaser is the first to record his or her instrument. For example, Alice Owner conveys her home to Aaron Purchaser by deed dated March 1. Aaron Purchaser does not record the deed until March 4. Alice Owner on March 2 conveys the same home to Bob Purchaser. Bob receives the deed to the home on March 2 with full knowledge that a deed had been given by Alice Owner on the previous day to Aaron Purchaser. Bob Purchaser records the deed to the home on March 3. Under a race recording statute, Bob Purchaser would be the owner to the property because Bob Purchaser recorded the deed to the property before the recording of the deed by Aaron Purchaser.

The notice type of recording statute relies on the notice given by the recording of the instrument or on the notice obtained through means other than recording. Under the notice statute, the grantee of a deed is not required to record the deed to obtain the priority in title over some subsequent purchaser of the same property. The notice statute provides that an unrecorded instrument is valid to a subsequent purchaser if the purchaser paid value with notice of the unrecorded instrument and is invalid if the subsequent purchaser paid value without notice of the unrecorded instrument. Therefore, actual knowledge by a subsequent purchaser of the existence of a prior unrecorded document serves as notice in the same manner as the proper recording of the document. For example, Aaron Owner conveys his property to Robert Purchaser by deed dated January 1. Robert Purchaser neglects to record the deed promptly. On February 1, Aaron conveys the same property to Cindy Buyer, who has full knowledge of the deed to Robert. Cindy's deed is recorded on February 2. Thereafter, Robert on March 1 records the deed from Aaron dated January 1. Robert has priority of title even though Robert has the later recorded deed. This is so because Cindy had actual knowledge of the conveyance from Aaron to Robert at the time Cindy received Aaron's deed from Aaron.

The race-notice recording statute is the most common type. It combines the theory and recording requirements of both the race recording statute and the notice recording statute. Specifically, the race-notice statute combines the notice principle that knowledge of a prior unrecorded instrument serves as notice in the same manner as the proper recording of the instrument with the recording principle that the first party to record an instrument has priority of title, regardless of whether that person was a prior or subsequent purchaser. Thus, under a race-notice statute, a subsequent purchaser has priority over the holder of a prior but unrecorded instrument if such subsequent purchaser makes the purchase without notice of the prior unrecorded instrument and records the instrument before the recording of the prior instrument. This type of recording statute operates as a pure notice statute until a subsequent purchaser takes title from the common grantor as a bona fide purchaser without notice of the prior recorded instrument. On that occurrence, the race-notice statute operates as a pure race statute in determining priority solely on the basis of which party records first.

The following is an example of the effect of the various recording statutes on the same factual course of events. Alice Owner conveys her home to Ajax Purchaser on March 1. Ajax Purchaser does not record the deed until March 3. On March 2, Alice Owner conveys the same home to Beth Purchaser, who purchases the home on March 2 with no knowledge of the March 1 deed from Alice Owner to Ajax Purchaser. Beth Purchaser does not record her deed until March 4. Under a race-notice statute, Ajax would have priority of title and would be the owner of the home because Ajax purchased the home without notice of any other claims and was the first to record the deed to the home. Under a notice statute, Beth would have priority of title and would be the owner of the home because Beth was a purchaser without notice of the prior unrecorded deed to Ajax, and the subsequent recording by Ajax does not divest the title and ownership existing in Beth. Under a race statute, Ajax would have priority and be the owner of the home because Ajax was the first to record a deed.

City of Richland Hills v. Bertelsen discusses both the concept of bona fide purchaser for value and the policy issues behind recording statutes.

⚖ CASE

City of Richland Hills v. Bertelsen
724 S.W. 2d 428 (Texas 1987)

OPINION

BURDOCK, Justice.

Appellant, the City of Richland Hills, appeals the trial court's denial of its motion for summary judgment and entry of partial summary judgment for appellee. The summary judgment motions arose from appellee, Keith Bertelsen's action for a declaratory judgment seeking to invalidate the city's claim to property owned by him.

We affirm as modified.

Appellee purchased the real property described below from Frank C. Campbell, for $30,000 cash:

Lots A–L inclusive, Block 53, and Lots A–K inclusive, Block 44, Long Addition to the City of Richland Hills, Tarrant County, Texas, according to the revised Plat recorded in Volume 388–68, Page 29, Deed Records of Tarrant County, Texas.

Subsequently, appellee requested that the recorded plat of the land be vacated by the city's Planning and Zoning Commission. Later the city informed appellee it claimed a public park and easement on Lots K and L in Block 53, and Lot K in Block 44 of the property, pursuant to an antecedent unrecorded plat given the city by appellee's grantor.

Appellant, the city, filed a motion for summary judgment, claiming as a matter of law there was a dedicated public park and drainage easement on the property. Appellee filed a motion for partial summary judgment and severance, solely contending that appellant had no valid claim to a public park on the property. The trial court granted appellee's motion for partial summary judgment and severance, removing the cloud placed on the property by appellant's claim to a public park.

In three of its points of error, appellant alleges the trial court erred in finding appellee was a bona fide purchaser of the property for value, and in failing to find Campbell, appellee's grantor, had dedicated the lots as a public park.

[1] Before considering any rights appellee may have in the land in dispute, we must first determine whether or not he was a bona fide purchaser. A person qualifies as a bona fide purchaser for value if he purchases property in good faith for valuable consideration without notice. *Neal v. Holt,* 69 S.W.2d 603, 609 (Tex. Civ. App.—Texarkana 1934, writ ref'd). Since appellant does not allege appellee failed to pay valuable consideration or exhibited bad faith, we must only decide if appellee had notice of the city's claim.

It is elementary doctrine that, independent of valuable consideration and good faith, notice will destroy the character of a bona fide purchaser and defeat the protection otherwise given to him. *Id.* at 609.

Texas law has long favored the purpose of recording acts, which make land title information available to interested persons. *Leonard v. Benford Lumber Co.,* 110 Tex. 83, 216 S.W. 382, 383 (1919); *Hancock v. Tram Lumber Co.,* 65 Tex. 225, 232 (1885). In *Anderson v. Barnwell,* 52 S.W.2d 96, 101 (Tex. Civ. App.—Texarkana 1932), *affirmed,* 126 Tex. 182, 86 S.W.2d 41 (1935), the court stated:

> The intention of the recording acts is to compel every person receiving conveyances of real property to place such an instrument of record, not only that he may thereby protect his own rights, but also those of all others who may afterwards seek to acquire an interest in the same property.

Anderson, 52 S.W.2d at 101.

To be effectively recorded, an instrument relating to real property must be recorded in the public records in the county in which a part of the property is located. TEX. PROP. CODE ANN. sec. 11.001(a) (Vernon 1984). In addition, any conveyance of real property or an interest in real property is void as to a subsequent purchaser for valuable consideration without notice, unless the instrument has been acknowledged and filed for record as required by law. *See* TEX. PROP. CODE ANN. sec. 13.001(a) (Vernon 1984).

[2–4] Constructive notice is described as that notice one is charged with which is given by instruments of record, irrespective of any actual knowledge. 5 Lange, *Texas Land Titles,* sec. 811 (1961). Actual notice, on the other hand, exists when a person actually knows the facts charged to him, or should have known them if he had inquired about them, after learning of facts which put him on inquiry. *West v. Jennings,* 119 S.W.2d 685, 686 (Tex. Civ. App.—San Antonio 1938, no writ); 5 Lange, at sec. 811. We find appellee purchased the property in good faith and for valuable consideration and without constructive notice of appellant's claim.

An examination of the pleadings here shows the only plat on file with the county clerk was a properly acknowledged plat, signed by appellee's grantor. The subsequent unsigned plat which the city relies on was incapable of being recorded, and would only be discovered if appellee had reason to search the city records. Appellee had a right to rely on the records properly recorded in the office of the Tarrant County Clerk. See *Lesley v. City of Rule,* 255 S.W.2d 312, 314 (Tex. Civ. App.—Eastland 1953, writ ref'd n.r.e.).

If the plat held by the city had been recorded, it would have been in appellee's chain of title and sufficiently put appellee on inquiry to inspect the city records. However, since nothing had been filed in the county records which constructively notified appellee of the existence of a dedicated park, we find he had no duty to search the city records. Without actual notice of the existence of a dedicated park, appellee takes the land free of the burden of a dedication to the city. *Pokorny v. Yudin,* 188 S.W.2d 185, 193 (Tex. Civ. App.—El Paso 1945, no writ).

In its third point of error, the city alleges the trial court erred in granting appellee's motion for summary judgment because appellant raised numerous fact issues. Most of appellant's complaints under this third point have already been discussed and overruled in our treatment of the first two points of error.

However, appellant raises one critical issue with its allegation that a fact issue existed regarding appellee's actual notice of the property's status as a city park. Ordinarily, actual notice is a fact question for the jury. *Goodwin v. Abilene State Bank,* 294 S.W. 883, 889 (Tex. Civ. App.— Eastland 1927, writ ref'd).

In support of its third point of error, the city relies in part on certain requests for admissions and their answers. A review of the record reveals that the city's requests for admissions and Bertelsen's answers are not included in the record on appeal pursuant to TEX. R. APP. P. 51, 52. Therefore, they are not before the court.

Even if the requests and answers were properly before the court, appellant's third point of error could not be sustained. In response to appellant's requests for admissions, appellee denied he had either actual or constructive knowledge of the city's claim of a park at the time he purchased the property from Campbell. The pleadings and affidavits filed by appellant do not indicate appellee knew or should have known the property was a park.

AFFIRMED.

PRACTICE TIPS FOR ORDERING A TITLE EXAMINATION

title examination

Examination of the real property records to determine the ownership to a particular tract of real property.

The primary purposes of a **title examination,** as discussed previously, are to ensure that a seller has the ability to convey good title to the purchaser at the time of the closing or that a borrower has good title to the property being pledged as security for a loan. The purchaser's or lender's attorney or paralegal usually orders or conducts the title examination. It is best to have the examination performed as early as possible to allow time for dealing with unexpected complications. In addition, a title "check down" or update usually is done immediately before the closing of the sale or loan. This update ensures that no adverse interest had been recorded against the property between the date of the preliminary title examination and the closing of the transaction for which the examination was made.

Information Needed to Do an Examination

A title examiner should have as much accurate information as possible to perform the examination. The minimum information required is (a) a legal description of the property to be examined, (b) the name of the current owner, and (c) copies of all deeds and surveys, or any prior title examinations or title insurance policies that affect the property. If the examination is being prepared in connection with a sale, the sales contract will have a description of the property to be purchased. The seller of the property should be the current owner. If the examination is being prepared in connection with a mortgage loan, the loan application usually contains a description of the property, and the loan applicant, it is hoped, is the current owner of the property. The property owner should be contacted to see if he or she has information, such as prior title examinations, surveys, or deeds, concerning the property. It is a good idea to use a title order form on which pertinent information may be written. An example of title order form is shown in Exhibit 12–1.

EXAMINING TITLE TO REAL PROPERTY

Place to Search

Title examinations usually are conducted in the courthouse of the county in which the property is located. If the property is located in more than one county, it may be necessary to conduct the examination in each county to have a full title examination. The public official who is responsible for keeping real property records varies from state to state, but he or she usually is the clerk of the court or a registrar of deeds. The real property records typically are kept in a record room located within the county courthouse.

Period of Examination

A title examination searches the owner's chain of title by starting at the present time and working backward to some predetermined point. The examination establishes a source of title for each owner in the chain. Title examinations are classified as either full or limited searches. The length of time for a full search differs from state to state but usually requires that an owner's chain of title be established for 50 or 60 years. Most potential defects in title, both recorded and unrecorded, will have no effect on the current ownership of the property after 50 or 60 years.

A limited search title examination is for a period less than that required for a full search. Limited searches often are performed for loan assumptions and second mortgage closings. The theory supporting a limited search in these situations is an assumption that a full search

Delmar/Cengage Learning

EXHIBIT 12–1

Abstract Order

```
Our File Number: _____ Date Ordered: _____ Need By: _____
Ordered by: _____ Date of Closing: _____
Present Owner/Seller: _____
Name of Purchaser: _____
RE Broker: _____
Brief Legal: _____
           _____
Street Address: _____
Length of Search: _____ .
MISCELLANEOUS INFORMATION KNOWN:
Plat Information: _____
Back Title Policy: ( ) Yes  ( ) No            Back Title Notes: ( ) Yes  ( ) No
With Who: _____          _____
          _____          _____
          _____          _____

PLEASE PROVIDE US WITH ANY BANKRUPTCY INFORMATION: ( ) yes  ( ) no
Other Information:
_____
_____
_____
_____
_____
_____
_____

In Addition, please provide the following:
( ) Copies of applicable Restrictive Covenants of record
( ) Copies of applicable easements of record
( ) Copies of any liens, executions, fi fa, etc. of record
( ) City, State and County Mileage Rates (latest figures available)
( ) _____
( ) _____
( ) _____
```

was performed for the first security mortgage holder and that all defects and objections were cured at that time. A title examination beginning from the recording date of the first mortgage should be sufficient to protect the interest of the parties. A limited search may be possible when the property is covered by a title insurance policy for which the full search was performed or when the examiner can obtain a copy of a previous full title examination. Most title insurance companies issue title insurance based on a limited search from the date of an earlier title insurance policy. The client must be informed of the extent of the title examination in the title examiner's title opinion letter. The client also should be made aware that a limited search does not qualify as a full legal search and does not protect against title matters created before the starting date of the limited search.

What to Search

A title examination involves searching through a grantee index of the owner's chain of title backward in time to some predetermined point to establish a source of title for each owner in the chain. Then, for each grantor in the chain of title, the examiner searches the grantor's index from the date the grantor acquired title to the next grantor in the chain. Finally, the examiner searches other indices to determine whether there are any other recorded claims against the property, such as judgment liens, mechanic's liens, and tax liens.

Grantee and Grantor Indices

Most real property record rooms are indexed by the names of the grantees and the grantors of real property and the interest recorded therein. Each entry referenced in the grantee or grantor index usually provides the following information:

- Name of grantor
- Name of grantee
- Date of instrument
- Date of recording of instrument
- Nature of the instrument (e.g., deed, mortgage, easement)
- Brief description of the property covered
- Place where the instrument can be found so that it can be examined and read (record book and page reference)

grantee index

Alphabetical index of the public real property records that lists the last names of all people who are grantees of real property interest during a given year within the county.

Grantee Index The **grantee index** is an alphabetical index by last name of all people who are grantees of any property interest during a given year within the county. The index is maintained on a year-by-year basis from the beginning of time that the county maintained records. The grantee's property interest consists of purchasers, holders of mortgages and security deeds, easement holders, tenants, holders of liens, and so on.

The grantee index enables an examiner to build a chain of title from the present to the past. The first link in the chain of title is the conveyance to the current owner of the property. To find this first link, the examiner begins in the current year's grantee index and looks for the name of the current owner of the property. The examiner continues to search in each year's grantee index until the examiner finds the name of the current owner. Once this name is located, it is matched to the property in question. The examiner then looks to see who gave the property to the current owner (i.e., who was the grantor of the deed to the current owner); this person then becomes the next link in the chain of the title. The examiner searches the grantee index until this person's name is found. This process continues for 50 or 60 years in the grantee index, at which time the examiner should have a list of successive owners of the property, the dates they acquired ownership, and the dates they transferred ownership away for the 50- or 60-year history. Once this is done, the examiner uses the grantor index.

grantor index

Alphabetical index of the public real property records that lists the last names of all people who are grantors of real property interest during a given year within the county.

Grantor Index A **grantor index** is an annual alphabetical index by last name of all people who are grantors of a real property interest within the county. Grantors of property are sellers, borrowers, mortgagors, grantors of easements, and so on. The examiner begins with the grantor index from the past and follows it to the present. The examiner starts with the last grantee that was found in the grantee index and then examines the grantor index until this person's name is found and there is a transfer of the property from them. For example, if the examiner, at the conclusion of the grantee index search, finds that in 1960 (50-year search beginning in 2010) Mary T. Sneed was the owner of the property, the examiner begins the grantor index searching for the name of Mary T. Sneed. He or she will begin in the 1960 index. The examiner continues the search in 1960, 1961, 1962, and so on until Mary T. Sneed's name is located as the grantor of a deed transferring ownership of the property.

At this juncture, the examiner searches for the name of the grantee of the deed from Mary T. Sneed, and this person becomes the next grantor to be located. The examiner stays with this person until they have conveyed away the property by deed. By reviewing the grantor index, the examiner can discover any easements, mortgages, or other title exceptions to the property.

Plat Index

Most counties maintain a **plat** or **tract index** and copies of all plats that have been recorded within the county. The index to the plats usually is based on one of the following criteria: (a) land lot and district (location designation), (b) name of owner designation, or (c) subdivision designation. For example, title is being examined to property in the Pine Tree Subdivision, which was developed by the Acme Realty Company and was located in Land Lot 100 of the 17th District of Salem County, Virginia. An index to a plat reference (a book and a page where a plat is recorded) for the subdivision can be found in one of three ways. First, there may be an entry under Land Lot 100 of the 17th District for Pine Tree. Second, there may be in the owner index a listing for Acme Realty Company and a list of all plats filed by Acme Realty Company, with a book and a page where the plats are located. Third, there may be a listing in the subdivision index for Pine Tree Subdivision. Once the plat has been found, it should be carefully examined. The plat contains a legal description of the property, and it should match the description being used for the examination. Any discrepancies in the description should be noted. Plats often have restrictive covenants printed on them that are binding on an owner of the property. Plats also show building setback lines, easements, and other matters. Most courthouses have photocopy equipment to enable the examiner to make a copy of the plat. It is advisable to request that a copy be made for the paralegal and the client.

> **plat** or **tract index**
>
> Index of all plats that have been recorded within the county within a given year.

Reviewing the Various Instruments in the Chain of Title

A title examiner carefully examines each instrument's property description to make certain that it is the same as the property that is being examined. Title examiners should note any errors or discrepancies in the legal description. The legal description may change over the course of time because a current parcel of property may have been included within larger tracts in the past history of the property. For example, a title examiner is examining record title to a residential subdivision lot. The lot is described by a plat book and page reference. The residential subdivision lot in its past history was part of a farm that was described by a metes and bounds legal description.

The examiner maps out each property conveyance, including the property conveyed and the property excluded from the conveyance, to determine that the property in question is being transferred each time and that the current legal description is a true description of the property vested in the current record owner. Subtle differences in property description that go undetected early can seriously impair the validity of the title examination.

When reviewing deeds, easements, or mortgages, an examiner usually does the following:

- Notes the identity of the parties to the instrument, the date the instrument was signed, and the date it was filed
- Examines the signature and witnessing requirements
- Makes a notation of what estate was being conveyed (e.g., fee simple, life estate)
- Pays particular attention to any covenants or other requirements that may be set out in the instruments

Most title examiners make copies of all instruments in the chain of title that currently affect the property and attach the copies as exhibits to the title examination report.

Other Things to Examine

In addition to searching the grantee and grantor indices and reviewing various documents contained therein, an examiner must look for other potential title problems. These items may change slightly from state to state but usually include the following.

Judgments

A money debt resulting from a lawsuit is called a *judgment*. A judgment may have been entered against an owner in the chain of title. Once a judgment has been recorded in the public records, it becomes a lien on all property of the judgment debtor. A docket or index for judgments can be found in the real property record room. The docket lists in alphabetical order the names of all people within the county within a given year against whom a judgment has been recorded. The index also refers to a book and page of a judgment book in which a copy of the judgment can be found. The index does not indicate the amount of the judgment or whether the judgment has been paid and satisfied. An examination of a copy of the judgment in the judgment book reveals the amount and whether the judgment has been satisfied. Most clerks print the word "Paid" or "Satisfied" on a judgment when it has been paid. Judgments in most states have only a five- to seven-year lifetime, but they can be renewed for an additional seven years. Because judgments attach at the time of recordation to all property then owned by the judgment debtor or to any property thereafter acquired by the judgment debtor, it is necessary for the examiner to examine the judgment index for the names of all people who have owned the property during the lifetime of a judgment (seven years). For example, Bryan Thompson, Martha Farris, and the Winston Company, Inc. have by the grantee-grantor search been found to be owners at one time or another of the property during the past seven years. All these names should be searched in the judgment index.

Federal and State Tax Liens

The federal and state governments have the right to file a lien against the property of any delinquent taxpayer. A federal tax lien, once filed, becomes a lien on all property owned by the taxpayer at the time of filing as well as all future property acquired by the taxpayer until the lien has been paid in full. Most record rooms maintain a separate index for federal tax liens and a separate book in which the federal tax liens can be examined. The same considerations and procedures for examining judgments apply to federal tax liens, except that a federal tax lien has a 10-year lifetime unless renewed. A state tax lien has its own statute of limitations for enforcement.

Delinquent Taxes

All property is taxed by county or city governments and may be separately assessed for sanitary, sewer, or other services. These tax liabilities and other assessments are liens on the property. Liens for assessments may be found in a tax assessor's or tax collector's office, which may be separate and apart from the real property record room. In many localities, there are specialized tax services that examine tax and assessment records for a reasonable price. Most title examiners and law firms use these services where they are available to determine the tax obligations of a particular piece of property.

Uniform Commercial Code

Many real estate transactions involve both real and personal property. When personal property is involved, it is necessary for the examiner to search the Uniform Commercial Code (UCC) financing statement index to determine if any of the personal property has been pledged as security for a loan. This index is an alphabetical listing of the last name of all debtors who have pledged personal property as security for a loan. In states that also have central filing of UCC financing statements with the secretary of state's office, a state search must be conducted as well as a local search.

Lis Pendens

A lawsuit affecting title to real estate that has not been resolved and is still pending is not a cloud on the title to the property unless a **lis pendens** is filed in the real property records. *Lis pendens* is a combination of two Latin words: "lis," which means an action, suit, or controversy, and "pendens," which means something that is continuing or pending. A lis pendens notice is a notice of a pending lawsuit. A lis pendens charges third parties with notice that an action is pending against certain property and that if they purchase the property or acquire a loan on the property, they will be bound by the subsequent judgment in the lawsuit. Both real and personal property are subject to a lis pendens. A lis pendens is inapplicable in a suit for a personal or money judgment. Lis pendens is applicable only in an action that directly affects title to property. For example, a lis pendens would be applicable to any suit that challenges the current ownership of the property. In addition, a lis pendens would be applicable in a suit for breach of contract against a current owner if the suit is asking for specific performance of the contract. An action for divorce does not ordinarily invoke a lis pendens, except when specific property is sought for either an alimony purpose or a property settlement.

A lis pendens usually is a simple document that gives notice that a lawsuit has been filed as well as information concerning the lawsuit, such as the court in which the lawsuit was filed, the parties involved, a civil action file number, and a brief description of the nature of the lawsuit. If a lis pendens is filed, the property in the lis pendens is subject to the outcome of the lawsuit, and a lis pendens is considered to be a cloud on the title. Most counties maintain separate record for the lis pendens. The record index is maintained alphabetically in the name of the property owner.

lis pendens

Notice recorded in the real property records that informs that a lawsuit affecting title to real property described in the notice has been filed and is pending.

Civil Suits

Technically, a pending civil suit, regardless of its nature, does not have any effect on title to real property unless a lis pendens notice has been recorded. Many title examiners, however, examine the civil dockets for informational purposes. For example, if a client is in the process of purchasing property from a seller and the examiner finds on the civil docket a number of lawsuits against the seller for breach of contract, the client should be advised to be cautious.

Probate Court Records

Property may pass through probate and estate proceedings because of the death of one of the owners. It may be necessary for the examiner to examine the probate court records to make sure that the will is properly probated and that the property has been distributed to the devisees under the will or the heirs at law, in the case of intestate estate. In addition, if property has been sold by the executor of an estate, the title examiner searches the probate or estate records to ascertain if the proper authority for the sale had been obtained by the executor.

Mechanic's Liens

A mechanic's lien or lien given to a contractor, laborer, or material supplier who has contributed to the construction of improvements on real property may be found in the grantor index or in a separate index.

Preliminary Title Report

Once a title examination is completed, the examiner reports in writing the conclusion of the examination. If title insurance is being obtained, the examiner certifies title to the title insurance company, and an insurance commitment or binder is issued before the closing.

At a minimum, the title report should reveal the following: (a) the name of the current record title holder; (b) legal description of captioned property; (c) existing unpaid loans or mortgages; (d) other lien holders; (e) status of taxes; (f) listing of all easements, covenants, and other restrictions; (g) any objections to marketability; (h) other matters that affect title; and (i) requirements for vesting marketable title in the purchaser.

The title examination should be reviewed as soon as it is received. Defects that may take time to cure should be addressed promptly to avoid a delay in closing.

Title Examination Example

An example of a title examination is shown in Example 12–1.

Example 12–1

Property
ALL THAT TRACT or parcel of land lying and being in Land Lot 50 of the 3rd District, Fulton County, Georgia, Lot 3, Block A, Pines Subdivision, per plat recorded at Plat Book 10, Page 64, Fulton County, Georgia Records.

Situation
Your firm represents a purchaser of the above-referenced property who has a contract with John Samson. You have been asked to examine title to the property to determine the title of John Samson. You have in your possession a title policy insuring title to the property under the name of the ABC Company, dated with an effective date of November 4, 1990. You have been asked to do a limited title examination from November 4, 1990, through the current date. The 1990 title policy revealed no exceptions to title.

The following is an example of the title notes taken from this limited title examination:

Grantee Index:
(FIRST ENTRY): 3-1-2007, Samson, John-Sarah T. Davis-3-1-2007-WD-Lot 3, Block A, Pines Subdivision-DB 604, Page 91.
(SECOND ENTRY): 6-9-2001-Davis, Sarah T.-George Farris-6-9-2001-WD-Lot 3, Block A, Pines Subdivision-DB 496, Page 831.
(THIRD ENTRY): 2-7-94-Farris, George-ABC Co.-2-7-94-WD-Lot 3, Block A, Pines Subdivision-DB 291, Page 204.
(FOURTH ENTRY): 11-4-90-ABC Co.-Fred Smith-11-4-90-WD-20 Acres-Pines Subdivision-DB 283, Page 61.

Grantor Index:
(FIRST ENTRY): 11-4-90-Smith, Fred-ABC Co.-11-4-90-WD-20 Acres-Pines Subdivision-DB 283, Page 61.
(SECOND ENTRY): 11-4-90-ABC Co.-First Bank-11-4-90-DSD-20 Acres-Pines Subdivision-DB 283, Page 63.
(THIRD ENTRY): 7-9-92-ABC Co.-Georgia Power-7-9-92-EASE-Pines Subdivision-DB 289, Page 150.
(FOURTH ENTRY): 2-7-94-ABC Co.-George Farris-2-7-94-WD-Lot 3, Block A, Pines Subdivision-Db 291, Page 204.
(FIFTH ENTRY): 2-7-94-Farris, George-S.L. of Tucker-2-7-94-DSD-Lot 3, Block A, Pines Subdivision-DB 291, Page 205.
(SIXTH ENTRY): 6-9-2001-Farris, George-Sarah T. Davis-6-9-2001-WD-Lot 3, Block A, Pines Subdivision-DB 496, Page 831.
(SEVENTH ENTRY): 3-1-2007-Davis, Sarah T.-John Samson-3-1-2007-WD-Lot 3, Block A, Pines Subdivision-DB 604, Page 91.
(EIGHTH ENTRY): 5-10-2008-Samson, John-Acme Finance-5-10-2008-DSD-Lot 5, Block A, Pines Subdivision-DB 608, Page 200.

Explanation of Title Notes

To prepare the title notes in Example 12–1, the title examination would have proceeded as follows:

1. The examiner goes to the Fulton County Courthouse with a description of the property and the current owner's name, John Samson.

2. The examiner first examines the subdivision plat of Pines Subdivision. It is not necessary to use a plat index to locate the plat because a plat book and page number for the plat are part of the legal description. If the plat book or page number for the plat were not provided, it could have been obtained by looking in the subdivision name index under the Pines Subdivision.

3. The plat shows the dimensions of Lot 3. The examiner notes any restrictive covenants, easements, or setback lines that affect Lot 3. The examiner makes a copy of the plat and attaches it to the title report.

4. The examiner is now ready to start searching in the grantee index. The examiner looks in the current year's index under the *S*s for Samson. Because *John Samson* may be a common name in the county, the examiner may find many entries for John Samson, but the examiner is only interested in the entry for John Samson that affects Lot 3, Block A, Pines Subdivision. According to the title notes, the examiner does not find any entries in the current year or any year until 2007. In the 2007 book, the examiner finds an entry dated March 1, 2007, to John Samson from Sarah T. Davis, a warranty deed affecting the property and recorded at Deed Book 604, Page 91. The examiner at this stage stops indexing and goes to Deed Book 604, Page 91, and looks at the deed to make sure that it is in fact the same parcel of property being examined. Once assured that it is the same parcel of property, the examiner returns to the grantee index for further indexing.

5. The next person the examiner looks for in the grantee index is Sarah T. Davis. The examiner look in the 2007 book for Davis because she may have acquired the property the day before she sold it to Samson. The examiner does not find Davis in the 2007 book and looks in the 2006, 2005, 2004, 2003, 2002, and 2001 books. In the 2001 book, the examiner finds an entry to Sarah T. Davis from George Farris, a warranty deed for the same property. Once this deed has been discovered, George Farris becomes the next person to look for in the grantee index. The examiner stays in the same period, 2001, and searches the *F*s for George Farris. The examiner then looks in the indices for 2000, 1999, 1998, 1997, 1996, 1995, and 1994. In the 1994 grantee index, the examiner finds an entry to George Farris from the ABC Co. for this property. ABC Co. then becomes the next grantee, and the examiner searches the indices for ABC Co. all the way back to 1990, where the examiner finds an entry to ABC Co. from Fred Smith.

6. Because the search is limited, this is the end of the grantee indexing. The grantee search gives the following information: ABC Co. owned the property from 11-4-90 to 2-7-94; George Farris owned the property from 2-7-94 to 6-9-2001; Sarah T. Davis owned the property from 6-9-2001 to 3-1-2007; and John Samson bought the property on 3-1-2007 from Sarah T. Davis. The examiner does not know if John Samson is still the owner of the property. This information cannot be determined except for a needle-in-the-haystack type of search from the grantee index. This information is more readily available in the grantor index.

7. The examiner starts searching in the grantor index from the past to the present. The examiner starts in the grantor index for 1990 with the name Fred Smith and finds an entry from Fred Smith to ABC Co. on 11-4-90. The next grantor, then, is ABC Co.,

and the examiner stays with the name in the 1990 book. The examiner finds an entry on the same day to the First Bank. It is a DSD, which is an abbreviation for *deed to secure debt*. The examiner stays with ABC Co. They have not transferred property but have only pledged the property as security for a loan to First Bank. The examiner runs the 1990, 1991, and 1992 books for ABC Co. In the 1992 grantor index, the examiner finds an entry from ABC Co. to Georgia Power, something called an EASE, which is an abbreviation for *easement*. (Many counties abbreviate all the identification of the instruments, and it may take a few days to learn all the abbreviations.) This entry to Georgia Power still does not divest ABC Co. of title of the property, and ABC Co. remains grantor. The examiner searches the 1992, 1993, and 1994 books and finds in the 1994 index for ABC Co. an entry of a warranty deed to George Farris. This entry does divest ABC Co. of title, and George Farris then becomes the next grantor. The examiner then switches in the 1994 index to look under the *F*s and finds an entry from George Farris to the S&L of Tucker. It is another deed to secure debt, which means that George Farris has pledged the property as security for a loan. The examiner stays with George Farris and looks in the 1994, 1995, 1996, 1997, 1998, 1999, 2000, and 2001 grantor index books for George Farris. In the 2001 grantor index, the examiner finds an entry from George Farris to Sarah T. Davis. It is a warranty deed entry, and Sarah T. Davis now becomes the next grantor. The examiner searches Davis in the 2001, 2002, 2003, 2004, 2005, 2006, and 2007 books. In the 2007 book, there is an entry from Davis to John Samson, a warranty deed. John Samson becomes the next grantor. The examiner searches for John Samson in the 2007, 2008, 2009, and 2010 books. In the 2008 book, there is an entry from John Samson to Acme Finance, another deed to secure debt. The property has been pledged another time as security for a loan. The examiner continues to search John Samson forward to the most current date of the examination. Every attempt should be made to examine up to the date of the examination. However, some record rooms may be behind in indexing, and the search can only go as far as the record day. Most clerks post each day the "record date" of the system.

8. Once both the grantee and the grantor search are finished, the examiner can determine from the title notes the following: (a) John Samson owns the property and (b) the property is subject to (i) a deed to secure debt from ABC Co. to First Bank; (ii) an easement from ABC Co. to Georgia Power; (iii) a deed to secure debt from George Farris to S&L of Tucker; and (iv) a deed to secure debt from John Samson to Acme Finance.

9. It is now necessary for the examiner to review each and every document, including every deed in the chain of title. These documents are found by going to the deed book and pages that were discovered during the indexing. Satisfactions of deeds to secure debts or mortgages often are stamped in the book and are difficult to find through the indexing process.

10. Once all the deeds, security deeds, easements, and so on have been examined, the examiner does the other searches regarding judgments, tax liens, lis pendens, and so on.

TITLE DEFECTS AND PROBLEMS

A real estate paralegal should be familiar with common title defects and basic procedures for curing them. Space does not permit more than a short summary of title objections that can arise from a title examination. The exact procedure to be followed in resolving these objections varies from state to state. The course of corrective action also depends on the nature and severity of the defect and the purpose for which the property is being purchased.

A sale or loan closing cannot be completed until title defects and objections have been removed.

Record Title Holder

The owner of the real property as shown in the deed records is known as the **record title holder.** In most cases, the seller named in the sales contract or the borrower who is applying for the loan is the holder of the record title. If the title examination reveals that someone else is the record title holder, there is a problem. Sometimes the problem is simple, as when a husband signs the sales contract but record title is in the wife's name. The closing paralegal can easily verify with the real estate agent if the wife is the real seller. At other times, the problem is not so simple, as when an heir signs the sales contract but the record title holder is the deceased. In this case, an estate probate proceeding may be necessary.

Another situation arises when the seller is not the record title holder but has been in possession of the captioned property for more than the statutory adverse possession period. The closing should not take place until a judicial proceeding, a suit to quiet title, is brought to establish the seller as the record title holder. Another solution is to obtain quitclaim deeds from all parties with a possible interest in the property.

> **record title holder**
>
> Owner of real property as shown on the deed records from a title examination of the property.

Breaks in the Chain of Title

A chain of title is composed of consecutive links of the grantors and grantees of the captioned property: A to b, b to c, c to d, with d holding current record title. Occasionally, there is a missing link: a to b, d to e. The record title does not reveal how b was divested of title or how d acquired title. A break in the chain of title can be caused by any number of factors, such as an unrecorded deed (see diagram), a name change, an unadministered estate, or a foreign divorce decree. Unless the missing link can be reconstructed by verifiable sources outside the record, the defect is a serious cloud on the title.

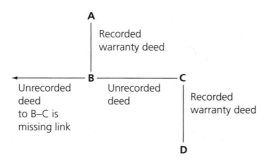

The link must be established before it can be determined what is necessary to protect the record. Often all that can be done is to advise the parties of the problem and require them to establish the missing link. If the current owner and the predecessors in title have satisfied the statutory requirements for adverse possession, a **quiet title action** brought by d against b and his heirs would resolve the problem, assuming that b or his heirs do not have a valid defense.

Under a contract to purchase, the purchaser cannot force the current owner to prosecute a suit to quiet title. Legally, the purchaser can only reject title until the defect is corrected or seek damages in a suit for breach of contract.

> **quiet title action**
>
> Judicial proceeding to establish the ownership of real property.

Errors in Prior Recorded Deeds

Errors in a prior recorded deed in the chain of title, such as an erroneous legal description, misspelled name, or improper execution, must be cured before title is acceptable. When possible, such errors may be cured by a corrective deed from the grantor to the grantee of the defective deed. A corrective deed has the same format as the original deed, with the error corrected and a clause inserted:

> This deed is given to correct [describe error] contained in a prior deed between the parties dated ____, 20____, recorded ____, 20 ____, in the Clerk's Office, Circuit Court of ___ County, Virginia, at deed book ____, page ____.

No consideration is required for a corrective deed.

The corrective deed must be recorded. A corrective deed may not be used to change a greater estate to a lesser estate (i.e., fee simple to life estate), nor can it be used to change the identity of a grantor altogether, although it may correct misspellings. It is the responsibility of the current owner to locate the parties and obtain the corrective deed.

An error in a prior recorded mortgage or deed of trust is of no consequence so long as the mortgage or deed of trust is paid and released before closing.

Name Variances

A name variance, as distinguished from a simple misspelling, is a variation between the name by which a record title holder acquired title to the property and a name by which the holder conveyed the title. If variances in the name of a previous record title holder exist, the current owner should be asked to provide an affidavit from the prior owner that the person whose name appears in the two documents are one and the same person. If the variances are in the name of the current owner, a clause in the deed explaining the variance is sufficient. For example:

> Grantor named herein is one and the same person as John D. Adams, the grantee named in a prior deed dated ____ day, 20____, and recorded ____ day, 20____, in the Clerk's Office, Circuit Court of ____ County, Colorado, in deed book ____, page ____.

Corporations limited liability companies and partnerships can present a similar problem. In the case of the corporation or limited liability company, a certified copy of an amendment changing the name should be obtained from the clerk of the State Corporation Commission. In the case of a general partnership, affidavits from each partner may be required to verify a name change, merger, or death of a partner. When one general partner has power of attorney to act on behalf of the others, a single affidavit may be sufficient. Similarly, in the case of a limited partnership, a single affidavit from the general partner normally is sufficient.

Improper and Missing Power of Attorney

When a deed in the owner's chain of title was signed for the owner by an attorney-in-fact, a properly executed power of attorney should have been recorded with the deed. If it was not, the effect is the same as if the deed itself was not signed. The defect may be cured by having the current owner obtain and record a correction deed or quitclaim deed signed by the prior owner.

Sales Contracts, Options, and Leases

If the title examination reveals that the property is subject to a contract or an option to sell or lease, the owner should provide proof by affidavit or other means that the contract or option has expired. If the contract or option has not expired, the seller should be required to obtain a quitclaim deed from the purchaser or optionee named in the contract. The quit-claim deed should be recorded if the contract or option was recorded.

If the property is subject to a lease or if a lease is discovered during the title examination, all parties should be advised to make inquiry as to possession. Depending on the purchaser's purpose in acquiring the property, the lease may or may not constitute a defect. A lender also should be advised of the outstanding possessory rights of any person other than a purchaser or borrower.

Because leases often are unrecorded or not in writing, the purchaser or lender should always be advised to physically inspect the property well in advance of closing. A discovery that the premises are occupied by someone other than or in addition to the current owner indicates a possible possessory interest in a third party.

Unsatisfied or Unreleased Mortgages

If an existing mortgage or deed of trust is to be assumed by the purchaser, it will be necessary to obtain an assumption package from the lender. If the debt is to be satisfied at closing, it is necessary to obtain a payoff amount from the lender and make certain that the debt is in fact satisfied from the sale proceeds. Sometimes a mortgage or deed of trust in the owner's chain of title will have been satisfied but never released of record. In this situation, the owner should obtain a release from the lender or an affidavit of repayment.

Mortgages and deeds of trust commonly are satisfied by one of two forms of release: (a) a marginal release entered in the margin of the deed book in which the mortgage or deed of trust is recorded or (b) a certificate of satisfaction from the lender to the record title holder recorded in the office in which the mortgage or deed of trust is recorded. Mortgages also may be partially released when more than one parcel of property is secured by a single mortgage or deed of trust. When dealing with a series of parcel releases, it is important to make sure that they constitute a complete release of record of the property in question.

Notice of Lis Pendens

A notice of lis pendens is a recorded notice that there is a pending suit or lien of attachment that may affect the title to the property. Such a notice must be released of record before the property can be sold or pledged as security for a loan. This usually requires that the suit itself for which the lis pendens serves as notice be settled or dismissed with prejudice.

Easements

An easement may be created in property by grant, prescription, implication, or necessity. A full discussion of easements is set forth in Chapter 5. Many title examiners routinely object to all recorded easements as defects in the title. As a practical matter, only those easements that in some way restrict the use of the property by the owner are of any consequence. It is important to note that all easements that may restrict the owner's use may not be recorded. Easements that are not recorded include prescriptive easements, easements of necessity, and implied easements.

Nonrestrictive easements, such as those routinely granted to utility companies to allow a reasonable ingress and egress for the purpose of maintaining utility service, usually do not require further action. When a utility easement has been granted a general description (blanket easement), it is wise to ascertain the manner in which the easement has been exercised in the past to make sure that the exercise will not interfere with the owner's use. It is possible to obtain from many utility companies a containment agreement in which the utility company agrees that its easement rights are limited to the actual location of its lines and an area reasonably surrounding such location to provide for maintenance access to the lines. Easements that do restrict the owner's use in a serious manner or that would prevent certain additions or improvements from being made on the property are serious title defects that do need to be resolved before the closing of the sale or loan.

Restrictive Covenants and Conditions

All unexpired restrictive covenants and conditions should be reported to the parties. These normally are of little significance unless restrictions interfere with the owner's use of the property or unless the covenant contains a reversion or forfeiture clause. A reversion or forfeiture clause provides that on violation of the condition, title reverts to the grantor or is otherwise forfeited by the violation. If such a clause is found, the seller should provide proof by affidavit or other means that there has been no violation. Minor violations of covenants or conditions not subject to reversion or forfeiture may be released or waived by the owners of the property benefited by the restrictions. For example, if the house on the property is shown as violating a private building line, it is possible to obtain a waiver from all other owners in the subdivision that such building line violation is acceptable.

Recorded restrictions may be found in the individual deeds of conveyance, or they may be noted on the recorded subdivision plat, or both. Subdivision restrictions or regulations may not be recorded on every deed; however, restrictions may attach by implication to each parcel conveyed from a common developer if there is evidence of a general plan or scheme of development. This general plan or scheme operates as constructive notice of the possible existence of restrictions on use.

Restrictive covenants and conditions often are limited in duration by their terms. Subdivision regulations also may be limited in duration but may be renewed by the action or lack of action of a majority of the affected landowners. When restrictions are not limited in duration, changing conditions over the years may make them unreasonable and therefore unenforceable. It also is possible to have restrictions on use waived by the owners of the benefited property before any violation, thereby removing an objection that might otherwise be a serious title defect.

 ## Mechanic's and Materialmen's Liens

Recorded mechanic's and materialmen's liens must be treated as adverse claims against the property. A full discussion of mechanic's and materialmen's liens is set forth in Chapter 4. The owner of the property should be required to pay the liens and satisfy them of record or discharge them by filing a proper bond before or at the sale or loan of the property. If the liens are to be satisfied at the closing of a sale, contact must be made with the holders of the lien to obtain the amount of the lien and to arrange for payment. If the owner objects to paying the lien, the owner should be required to post a bond that, in most states, will release the property from the lien.

Unperfected liens also are of concern to the purchaser because the purchaser will take property subject to all mechanic's and materialmen's liens for work or material furnished within the past 60 to 100 days, regardless of whether a claim of lien has been filed. For this reason, a seller should be required to provide an affidavit that no improvements have been made or materials supplied within the necessary statutory period before the date of the sale or loan on the property.

UCC Financing Statements

If an examination of the UCC index reveals a financing statement describing personal property or fixtures that are considered part of the realty being transferred or pledged as security for the loan, the owner should be required to terminate the security interest.

Judgment Liens

Final judgments for money damages ...stitute liens against all real property that the defendant owns or subsequently acqui... title examiner will report such judgments as objections when there is a possibility... the current owner is the named defendant.

When the judgment is k... be or is admitted to be against the current owner, the owner must be required to... the lien before or at closing. The judgment lien holder should be contacted to o... amount of balance due, and care should be taken to make sure the judgment is in... ed from the sale or loan proceeds.

If it is not certai... dgment is against the owner and the owner denies that he is the defendant nam... gment, an affidavit to this effect may be sufficient to protect the title to the p... ample of the language used in the affidavit is as follows.

Affiant d... oath that he is not one and the same person as John D. Adams named... the judgment dated ____, 20____, recorded ____, 20____ in the Cler... Court of ____ County, Indiana, in judgment docket ____, page ____ or of Acme Loan Company, Plaintiff.

...ent prior owners of the captioned property may remain as valid liens e prop... spite the fact that the property has been subsequently conveyed. If nts are... ainst the prior owners that do affect the property, the current seller ired to s... se judgments of record.

...ax Liens

Unpaid cou... property taxes should be paid before or at closing, except for the current year... at are not yet due and payable. It is necessary to obtain payoff figures from the a... tax officials and to supervise that the taxes are in fact paid from the sale or lo... s.

Fe... the... s and state income tax liens of many states, when recorded, are liens agai... property owned or subsequently acquired by the delinquent taxpayer. Ta... handled in the same manner as judgments, except that payoff figures ... Internal Revenue Service or the state's Revenue Commission. The ...al evenue ice will provide a certificate of release or discharge when the lien has ...en satisfied or n... certain circumstances, provide a partial release as to the parcel of proper being sol... ledged for a loan. In situations when the owner of the property has a name milar to that... delinquent taxpayer and it can be verified that the owner is not the same person as the ...uent taxpayer, the Internal Revenue Service will issue certificates of nonattachment th... ease the owner's property from the effect of the tax lien.

Title through Esta...

The title examination... veal that the property has been conveyed by the heirs or representatives of a deceased... title holder. In this situation, the fee title may now be unified in a single record title... or it may be fragmented into separate shares owned by the grantees of the various... or representatives. To be certain that the current owners in fact hold title in fee simp... the property in question, it may be necessary to account for all possible fragments o... est. In most cases, a list of heirs recorded in the county clerk's office or a probate off... ws the title examiner to follow and document these conveyances. If, for some re... list of heirs has been filed, it may be necessary to obtain an affidavit of descent fr... erson with personal knowledge of the decedent and his or her family. An example... affidavit of descent is shown in Example 12–2.

Example 12–2

Affidavit of Descent

STATE OF _____

COUNTY OF _____

Re: PRO___

Deed Boo___

Page _____

_____

The undersig_____,

sworn, deposes and says on oath that (s)he was personally acq____ County Records

deceased, over a period of _____ years; that Deponent is (\ent, being duly

(as a _____); that said decedent died (in)testate, a resident of t____

County of _____, State of _____, on the _____,

20_____, and all debts of the estate have been fully paid; that said __said decedent

_____ time(s) as follows:

Name of each   Age and address, if living married

husband or wife   Date of death, if decease

_____   _____

_____   _____

  Deponent further says on oath that the following are the children eve__

by said decedent:

Name of each child   Age and address, if living

            Date of death, if deceased

_____   _____

_____   _____

_____   _____

_____   _____

_____   _____

_____   _____

  Deponent further says on oath that the following are all the children of \ve c__

who died before the decedent:

Name of each child   Names of deceased Age ar\dr\ss if

        parents   living; of \e\h,

               if dec\d

_____ _____ _____

_____ _____ _____

_____ _____ _____

_____ _____ _____

_____ _____ _____

  Deponent says on oath that the living persons above named\stitute all the \eirs

at law of said decedent, and that all of said heirs are of age a\und mind, ex\ept:

_____

  Deponent's attention has been directed to the fact that the w\ffidavit will be reli\d

upon by prospective purchasers or lenders dealing with the heirs \named.

Sworn to and subscribed before me this

_____ day of _____, 20_____.

_____

Notary Public   Deponent

             Address: _____

ROLE OF A PARALEGAL AND PRACTICE TIPS

A paralegal may be utilized to perform a title examination, order a title examination, and/or review the results of a title examination. The results of an American Bar Association utilization survey indicated that paralegals were not utilized to any great extent in the performance of a title examination. The underutilization of paralegals in this area may be the result of some states' unauthorized practice of law statutes that require title examinations to be performed by licensed attorneys. Several states, however, do not have such requirements, and it would appear that a title examination could be performed by a paralegal. Although the principles involved in a title examination are somewhat simple, the examination process itself is difficult and would be best learned through an apprenticeship of the paralegal with an experienced title examiner. Through this apprenticeship, the paralegal can, under the watchful eye of the examiner, learn the intricacies of title examination and the customs and usages of the various courthouse systems of how title records are organized and searches can be competently conducted. Attention to detail and organization are important requirements of any title examiner. Title examinations are considered from a legal malpractice viewpoint to be a high-risk area, as any items missed or misinterpreted in a title examination could be quite costly to the client.

The same American Bar Association utilization survey indicated that paralegals were used to a great extent by attorneys to order title examinations and to review the results of such examinations. Practice tips on how to order title examinations can be found elsewhere in this chapter. A review of a title examination will involve studying the actual copies of all the items reported in the title examination as exceptions to title. These items generally will include liens, mortgages, restrictive covenants, and easements. A paralegal will need to review each document carefully, including legal descriptions set forth in the document, to determine how these title exceptions affect the marketability and use of the property by the client. Easements will need to be carefully reviewed to determine the location of the easement and the use of which the owner of the easement has in regard to the property. Restrictive covenants need to be carefully reviewed to see what uses are permitted and restricted in regard to the property. In addition, the paralegal should review carefully the enforcement remedies for restrictive covenants. Generally, these enforcement remedies are injunctions or damages for breach of the covenants. Any restrictive covenant that provides for reversion of title in the event of a violation must be brought to the attention of the attorney and the client as a serious title matter. A paralegal, when reviewing a title examination, should also pay attention to those matters described as title defects and problems, discussed previously in this chapter. Although practice varies from law firm to law firm, most paralegals who are charged with the duty of reviewing a title examination will prepare a brief memorandum or summary of the title examination problems for presentation to the attorney and client.

The paralegal should also review carefully the checklist at the end of this chapter for ordering or performing a title examination.

RECORD ROOMS AND ELECTRONIC RECORDS

Local governments are using electronic data technology in designing deed or title records. Title registry offices located in many metropolitan and even rural areas throughout the country have converted to electronic storage of all or a large portion of their title record systems. This electronic storage makes it more convenient for title examiners. Instead of searching through large books, which are updated on an annual basis, the title examiner today may simply run the grantor/grantee indices on a computer screen and also view the documents online. The documents can be printed for a nominal fee. By using an electronic database to store real property records, the record room need not expand in size with the increased activity within the county. It is possible to store a large volume of electronic records within a small physical area inside the courthouse or other government building.

Local counties in many states have also developed Web pages where, for a reasonable subscription fee, a title examiner can access the real estate index for that county or, in some situations, for each county of the state. Using the Internet, a title examiner can run a grantor or grantee index from his or her office and do a limited or, in some cases, a full search on the Internet. Private companies such as Ram Quest™ Software, Inc. have also developed title examination databases that can be accessed for a fee. Private providers generally form partnerships with the county governments to obtain the information and provide the means to do title examinations on the Internet. Private providers generally offer a caveat that their records are not official and do not warrant the accuracy of the information provided on the database.

Many states have also enacted the Uniform Real Property Electronic Recording Act (the Act). The Act allows for the recording of electronic documents involving real property such as deeds, mortgages, easements, and so forth. Electronic documents prepared and filed in accordance with the Act satisfy any requirements as a condition of recording that a document be an original on paper or in writing. Any electronic document prepared and filed in accordance with the Act may be signed by an electronic signature and notarized by an electronic notary signature.

This conversion from paper to electronic technology concerns many lawyers and other groups who rely on the accuracy of the county land records. They are concerned about computer glitches, viruses, and other problems that may destroy the electronic database or alter it. They are also concerned about public access to the record room. As record rooms become more electronic, the only way to access data may be through computer terminals. Counties may incur additional costs to upgrade and maintain these terminals. Having to use terminals may also inhibit people who are not computer literate from using the record room. Although many recognize that using the new technology to preserve land records should be embraced, they also believe that paper records should be maintained. Several states have now passed laws requiring county governments that have committed to the use of electronic land title databases to also maintain a paper archive.

🏛 ETHICS: Document Falsification

A paralegal works with a law firm in the real estate department. One of his duties is to receive title notes from the firm's title examiner and transcribe the notes into a title examination report that is then sent to the client. The paralegal is overloaded with work and receives an extensive set of title notes from a title examiner. The supervisory attorney requests that a written title examination report be sent to the client by the end of the day. While the paralegal is reviewing the title notes, he notices there are about eight utility easements affecting the property. A quick review of these easements leads him to believe that they do not materially affect the property. The paralegal decides that to transcribe the notes into a written report to be sent to the client by the end of the day, he will delete four of the easements from the title examination report. Is this decision a correct one?

A paralegal should never be involved in falsifying a document for any reason. Failure to list all the utility easements in the title examination report makes the report misrepresent record title to the property. It could be considered falsifying a title examination report. Even though the paralegal believes the omitted easements do not materially affect the property, it is improper to omit the easements from the title examination report. An overload of work or time pressures to complete an assignment are not justifiable excuses for preparing a legal document that is false or incomplete.

CHECKLIST

Ordering or Performing a Title Examination

- [ ] I. Purpose of Examination
    - [ ] A. Purchase and sale of property
    - [ ] B. Mortgage loan transaction
    - [ ] C. Acquisition of easement
    - [ ] D. Lease transaction

- [ ] II. Items Required for Examination
    - [ ] A. Current owner's name
        - 1. The seller in the contract for sale
        - 2. The borrower in the application for a loan
        - 3. The landlord of a lease
    - [ ] B. Legal description of property to be examined
    - [ ] C. Plats or survey of property to be examined
    - [ ] D. Prior title insurance policies on property to be examined
    - [ ] E. Prior title examinations or abstracts on property to be examined

- [ ] III. Period of Examination
    - [ ] A. Full examination (50–60 years)
    - [ ] B. Limited examination
        - 1. From date of prior title policy
        - 2. Date of prior mortgage
        - 3. From date of prior title examination

- [ ] IV. Indices to be Checked
    - [ ] A. Plat index
    - [ ] B. Grantee index
    - [ ] C. Grantor index

- [ ] V. Other Records to Be Searched
    - [ ] A. Judgment index and records
    - [ ] B. Federal and State tax lien index and records
    - [ ] C. Lis pendens
    - [ ] D. UCC financing index
    - [ ] E. Tax records
    - [ ] F. Special assessments (sanitary and water)
    - [ ] G. Probate records
    - [ ] H. Civil docket

- [ ] VI. Preliminary Title Examination
    - [ ] A. Certification to title company if title insurance is involved
    - [ ] B. Copies of all title exceptions

- [ ] VII. Title Defects or Problems
    - [ ] A. Breaks in chain of title
    - [ ] B. Errors from prior recorded deeds
    - [ ] C. Name variances
    - [ ] D. Improper or missing power of attorney
    - [ ] E. Sale contracts, options, and leases
    - [ ] F. Unsatisfied or unreleased mortgages or deeds of trust
    - [ ] G. Notices of lis pendens
    - [ ] H. Easements
    - [ ] I. Restrictive covenants and conditions
    - [ ] J. Mechanic's or materialmen's liens
    - [ ] K. Tax liens
    - [ ] L. Unpaid real estate taxes or assessments
    - [ ] M. UCC financing statements
    - [ ] N. Title through estates
    - [ ] O. Judgment liens

SUMMARY

This chapter explains the importance of a bona fide purchaser for value rule and its mandate that deeds, mortgages, easements, or other documents conveying an interest in real property be recorded. This chapter also discusses how the bona fide purchaser for value rule may be changed by state recording statutes. Procedures for examining real property in the public deed records are set forth, including a number of title problems that can be discovered from this examination. The importance of the grantor/grantee indices and other indices, such as for judgment, federal tax liens, and unpaid taxes, which must be reviewed during the title examination is discussed. Although title examinations are mandatory in almost any type of real estate transaction that involves a transfer of ownership or pledge of real property as security for a loan, the efforts of the legal profession to protect and ensure quality of title do not end with the title examination. Most transactions involve the issuance of title insurance, which is discussed in Chapter 13.

HELPFUL WEBSITES

State Title Standards

Many state bar associations establish guidelines, sometimes known as title standards, to assist attorneys and others in the examination of titles. Although the standards are not considered law, they do establish a standard of practice for examining title and provide answers and solutions to problems that may arise during the title examining process.

A copy of the latest title standards for the state of Georgia can be found on the Web site of the Real Property Law Section of the State Bar of Georgia at *http://www .garealpropertylaw.com.*

Other State Bar Title Standards:
Florida Title Standards

See the Web site for the Real Property Probate and Trust Law Section of the Florida Bar at *http://www.rpptl.org.*
Michigan Title Standards

http://www.michbar.org
State Bar of Texas Title Standards

www.oilgas.org

KEY TERMS

actual notice	grantee index	quiet title action
bona fide purchaser for value	grantor index	recording statutes
chain of title	lis pendens	record title holder
constructive notice	plat or tract index	title examination

REVIEW QUESTIONS

1. Why is it important to have a title examination performed?
2. What is the difference between actual and constructive notice?
3. What are the three types of recording statutes, and how do they differ?
4. Identify at least five potential title problems, and explain how to solve them.
5. Explain the bona fide purchaser for value rule.
6. What is the difference between a grantor and a grantee index?
7. What information is required to perform a title examination?
8. What information usually is given in an index entry for a grantor or grantee index?
9. What is a lis pendens? Explain its use.
10. What should a title examiner look for when reviewing the recorded documents in a chain of title?

CASE PROBLEMS

1. John has been using a road over his neighbor Sam's property for the past 20 years. In the state where John and Sam live, the use by John of the road for 20 years gives John a prescriptive easement. There are no written documents evidencing the easement. The road is plainly visible from an inspection of the property. Sam sells his property to Alice. Does Alice have a right to stop John from using the road?

2. Mary owns a small apartment complex. At the time Mary purchased the apartment complex from Sam, she gave Sam a mortgage securing a debt for $100,000. The mortgage was mentioned in the deed from Sam to Mary for the apartment complex, but the mortgage was not recorded. Mary sells the apartment complex to John. Mary does not tell John about the unrecorded mortgage to Sam. After the sale of the apartment complex from Mary to John, is the mortgage held by Sam enforceable against the apartment complex?

3. Would it be easier to find a recorded mortgage from Alice Owner to Sam Seller by looking under Alice Owner's name in the grantor index or by looking under Sam Seller's name in the grantee index?

4. You are assisting an attorney in the closing of a real estate sale transaction. You have in your possession a copy of the contract for the purchase and sale of the property. The contract contains the names of both the purchaser and the seller and a complete legal description of the property being bought and sold, and it has attached as an exhibit a survey of the property. You have been asked to order a title examination on behalf of your client. What information do you need to give to the title examiner?

5. The purchaser and seller have entered into a contract for the sale of real property. Before closing, the seller has refused to honor the contract and decides to sell the property to a third party. The purchaser files suit against the seller for breach of contract. What else should the purchaser do to protect the purchaser's rights against the seller and in the property?

6. You are assisting an attorney in the closing of a real estate transaction. The seller of the property under the contract is known as David F. Farris. The title examination reveals that the title is currently owned by a D. Frank Farris. What measures should you take to ensure that David F. Farris and D. Frank Farris are one and the same person?

PRACTICAL ASSIGNMENTS

1. Research your state's bona fide purchaser for value rule. Is it similar or different from that discussed in this chapter? Prepare a brief memorandum complete with the supporting statutes or cases to support your view.

2. Research your state's method for conducting a title examination. In connection with this research, visit a record room and see how it is organized. Discuss the similarities between how your state conducts title examinations and organizes the record rooms and those discussed in this chapter. Discuss the differences.

3. There is a split of authority as to what notice is given when an error has occurred in transcribing an instrument into the permanent record book. Some states rule that a register of deeds is deemed to be an agent of the recording party and that an incorrectly recorded instrument does not impart constructive notice. Other states have held that when an instrument is filed, constructive notice is given regardless of whether the instrument was correctly indexed or recorded. Research your state's law to determine which view it has concerning incorrectly recorded instruments. Prepare a short memorandum regarding your findings.

ACKNOWLEDGMENTS

Portions of this chapter have been excerpted from Recording Statutes: Their Operation and Effect by Robert S. Maxwell and David B. Summers, *Washburn Law Journal,* Vol. 17, 1978, pages 615–637. Used by permission of the publisher.

Wade W. Berryhill, "Title Examination in Virginia," *University of Richmond Law Review* Vol. 17, no. 2 (1983): 229–255. Reprinted with the permission of the University of Richmond Law Review Association, 17 Univ. Rich. L. Re. 229 (1983).

Student StudyWare™ CD-ROM

Interactive Student CD in the book includes additional quizzing, case studies, and key terms flashcards.

Online Companion™

For additional resources, please go to *www.paralegal.delmar.cengage.com*

chapter | 13

Title Insurance

Objectives

After reading this chapter, you should be able to:

- Recognize the importance of title insurance
- Understand the coverage provided by the American Land Title Association owner's and mortgagee's title insurance policies
- Prepare a title insurance commitment
- Review a title insurance commitment and title insurance policy
- Identify title problems that are not insured by a title insurance policy
- Learn how to delete standard title insurance exceptions

Outline

One of the main responsibilities of a real estate attorney or paralegal is to make certain that the client has good title to real property. This title assurance comes about by the use of three safeguards: (1) general warranty deed of conveyance to the property, (2) title examination before conveyance, and (3) title insurance.

General warranty deeds and title examinations are discussed in Chapters 8 and 12, respectively. Both of these methods for title assurance are highly recommended, and it would be imprudent to proceed without them. However, these methods do have certain limitations.

For example, liability on a warranty deed is difficult to enforce and collect. The grantor of the deed may have died or disappeared or be insolvent. Even if the grantor is present and solvent, in most states, liability under a warranty deed is limited to the original purchase price of the property and does not extend to the value of improvements that were erected on the property or the appreciated value of the property. In many states, attorney's fees and other costs of enforcing a warranty deed are unrecoverable.

A title examination is only as good as the skill and solvency of the examiner. The title examiner may not have the financial ability to pay for errors or mistakes in the examination. Although most title examiners carry malpractice insurance, the limits of this insurance may not be sufficient. In addition, some "remote risks" are not covered by a competent title examination and thus not recoverable from the examiner in a malpractice action. Some of these remote risks are as follows:

- Impersonation of the real owner
- Forged signatures on deeds or releases
- Documents executed under a false power of attorney or a power of attorney that has expired
- Deeds delivered after the death of the grantor or without the consent of the grantor
- Undisclosed or missing heirs
- Wills that have not been probated
- Deeds, mortgages, or easements executed by minors or incompetents
- Mistakes made in the indexing of legal documents (documents are lost in records room)
- Falsification of public records
- Confusion arising from similarity of names
- Titles passing by improperly conducted foreclosure sales

Because of these limitations, American ingenuity devised a product to fill the gap. The product is **title insurance,** and its main function is to eliminate all risks and prevent any loss caused by defects in title to the property.

Title insurance is a contract to indemnify the insured against loss through defects in the insured title or against liens or encumbrances that may affect the insured title at the time the policy is issued.

The main economic justifications of title insurance are to cover the remote risks of title examinations and to add financial substance to the title examination and to the deed warranties. Most title companies have deep pockets of money reserves that are annually audited by state authorities. It is rare that a valid claim is not paid by a title company because the title company lacks the money to pay for the claim.

Title insurance, unlike other forms of insurance, such as life, health, and fire insurance, does not assume risk. The main role for title insurance is risk elimination. A title insurance company will not issue a policy of title insurance unless it has performed an extensive title search and believes that there are no problems to the title. Some practitioners joke that if a title insurance company is willing to issue title insurance, then you probably do not need it because the title is risk-free. Title insurance, therefore, is issued only after a title examination has been conducted. The payment for title insurance is a one-time premium and can range from $1 to $3 per each $1,000 of coverage.

There are many title insurance companies across the country; most of them belong to the American Land Title Association (ALTA), a private trade association of title insurance companies. ALTA has prepared over the years a number of standard form title insurance policies that they request and, in some cases, require the member companies to use. These forms are referred to as ALTA Owner's Policy Form No. B and ALTA Mortgagee-Loan Form No. B. The standard forms enable lawyers to transact a real estate practice on a national basis with a title company that belongs to ALTA. Because most title insurance is issued on ALTA forms, the remainder of this chapter is a discussion of the basic provisions of the ALTA forms.

In June 2006, ALTA adopted a new owner's policy form and loan policy form as well as several new title endorsements to use with the new forms. The ALTA June 2006 forms represent the first major change to its title insurance forms since 1992. The June 2006 ALTA forms can be accessed on the American Land Title Association Web page at *http://www .alta.org.* The 2006 policy forms cover both paper and electronic real estate documents and transactions. Use of the 2006 ALTA forms is not mandatory, and attorneys and insureds will have the opportunity to choose between the 1992 forms and the 2006 forms. This chapter will discuss, for the most part, the basic provisions of the 1992 forms but will also highlight where the 2006 forms differ from the 1992 forms. Copies of the 2006 owner's policy and loan policy are found at the end of this chapter as Exhibits 13–23 and 13–24.

title insurance

Contract to indemnify the insured against loss through defects in the title to real property.

OWNER'S POLICY

The most commonly used **owner's policy** title insurance form is the ALTA Owner's Policy Form B. A copy of this form of policy is included at the end of this chapter as Exhibit 13–1. The ALTA owner's form contains many standard printed provisions concerning, for example, notice of loss and claim provisions and two basic parts known as Schedule A and Schedule B. Schedule A is an identification schedule that sets forth the date of the policy (which usually is the date the deed or other instrument that is insured is filed for record), the amount of insurance covered by the policy, the identity of the insured, the estate or interest covered (whether it is a fee simple, life estate, and so on), the identity of the parties in whom title is vested as shown by the deed records, and a full description of the property insured.

owner's policy

Policy of title insurance that insures an owner's title to real property.

affidavit

Sworn statement of fact.

Schedule B of the policy contains a list of exceptions to coverage. Any item shown on Schedule B is not insured against in the insurance policy. Schedule B typically contains some standard exceptions, such as matters of survey, implied easements, building line restrictions, and rights of persons in possession. These standard exceptions can be deleted by the use of proper **affidavits** and a survey. The title company, when issuing its Schedule B, lists all title exceptions found in the title examination of the property. Because Schedule B items are not insured against, it is important that in reviewing title insurance policies, copies of all the documents that represent Schedule B exceptions are obtained and carefully reviewed.

A chart outlining an owner's title insurance coverages and exclusions is shown in Example 13–1.

Example 13–1

Owner's title insurance	Exclusions from policy insures coverage:	Exceptions to coverage:
• Title to the property is vested in the insured	• Zoning and other government regulations	• Rights of parties in possession
• The property is free of defects, liens, encumbrances, except for the exceptions on Schedule B	• Eminent domain and police power	• Matters of survey
• The property has access to a public road	• Matters created, suffered, assumed, or agreed to by the insured	• Unrecorded easements
• Title to the property is marketable	• Unrecorded title defects not known to the title insurance company	• Mechanics' liens
	• Matters resulting in no loss to the insured	• Taxes and special assessments
	• Title defects that are first created after the effective date of the policy	• Any matters revealed by the title examination that appear on Schedule B to the policy
	• Title matters that would not have resulted in loss if insured had been bona fide purchaser for value	

Insuring Provisions of an ALTA Owner's Policy

marketable title

Title to real property that is free from doubt and enables the owner to hold the real property in peace; free from the hazard of litigation or adverse claims.

There are four basic insuring provisions of an ALTA owner's policy, and it is against loss or damage incurred as a result of these four covered risks that the policy insures. The covered risks are (1) insurance that title to the estate or interest described in Schedule A is vested in the insured; (2) insurance against any defect, lien, or encumbrance on such title; (3) insurance that the property has access to a public road; and (4) insurance that the title is a **marketable title.** The ALTA Form A policy used in some states does not insure marketability.

Vesting of Title

The vesting of title provision insures that the insured owns the real property described in the policy. The insurance of the insured's ownership of the described real property is the most important coverage of an owner's title insurance policy. The other coverages enhance and add to this primary insurance.

Defects, Liens, or Encumbrances on Title

An owner's title insurance policy insures against loss or damage caused by reason of any defect in or lien or encumbrance on the title to the insured property that is not expressly excepted from coverage by Schedule B of the policy. This insurance protects an owner against title defects, liens, or encumbrances that have attached to the title of the real property as of the date of the issuance of the policy. The coverage extends to three different kinds of title flaws—defects, liens, and encumbrances. A title defect is defined by case law as the want or absence of something necessary for completeness or perfection of title or a lapse or absence of something essential to the completeness of title. For example, assume a grantor of a deed had the deed signed by an attorney-in-fact who signed the deed after the power of attorney had expired. The signature of the deed by the unauthorized attorney-in-fact renders the title defective.

A *lien* is generally defined by legal treatises to be a claim or charge on a property given as security for the payment of a debt or the fulfillment of an obligation. The term *encumbrance* is generally defined to include liens but extends to every right or interest in property existing in third parties that diminishes the value of the real property but is consistent with the passing of title, such as restrictive covenants or easements.

Access to and from the Property

An owner's policy insures against loss incurred by the insured by the lack of the right of access to and from the insured property. This coverage protects the insured against any loss resulting from the insured's lack of a legal and enforceable right to get to and from the insured property. This coverage does not insure that a particular way of access is available or that the legal access that is available permits an adequate use of the property. This coverage protects against record title defects in the right of access but not against the physical difficulties that may be associated with getting to and from the property.

This concept that title insurance insures only against title defects and not the defects of the physical condition of the land is illustrated in *Title & Trust Company of Florida v. Barrows*.

If any particular form of access is required by the insured for the full enjoyment of the property, the insured would be well advised to have that access specifically insured by the title insurance policy. This can be accomplished by having additional easement parcels included in the legal description on Schedule A or by endorsing the policy to expressly insure access to the property by way of a described route.

Marketability of Title

An owner's title insurance policy insures marketability of the title to the insured property. A marketable title is title free from doubt. It enables the owner to hold the land in peace, free from the hazards of litigation or adverse claims. This insurance provides protection against the inability to market the title—a legal concept—but not the inability to sell the property. The insured may have marketable legal title but still be unable to sell the property due to economic reasons or specific conditions on the property. Title defects that merely diminish the value of the property do not render the title unmarketable within the meaning of this title insurance coverage.

 **CASE**

Title & Trust Company of Florida v. Barrows
381 So. 2d 1088

McCORD, Acting Chief Judge.

This appeal is from a final judgment awarding money damages to appellees for breach of title insurance policy. We reverse.

Through a realtor, appellees purchased, for $12,500, a lot surrounded on three sides by land owned by others, all of which is a part of a beach subdivision. The fourth side of appellee's lot borders on a platted street called Viejo Street, the right-of-way for which has been dedicated to and accepted by St. Johns County. The right-of-way line opposite appellees' lot abuts a Corps of Engineers' right-of-way in which there is a stone breakwater. The intra-coastal waterway flows on the other side of the breakwater.

The realtor who sold the lot to appellees represented to them that the county would build a road in the right-of-way along Viejo Street when appellees began plans for building on their lot. There have been no street improvements in the dedicated right-of-way, and St. Johns County has no present plans for making any improvements. The "road" is merely a continuation of a sandy beach.

A year after purchasing the land appellees procured a survey which disclosed that the elevation of their lot is approximately one to three feet above the mean high water mark. They later discovered that their lot, along with the Viejo Street right-of-way abutting it, is covered by high tide water during the spring and fall of each year.

At the time appellees purchased their lot, they obtained title insurance coverage from appellant. The title policy covered:

> "Any defect in or lien or encumbrance on the title to the estate or title covered hereby . . . or a lack of a right of access to and from the land;

Appellees' complaint of lack of right of access was founded on the impassable condition of the platted street. After trial without a jury, the trial court entered final judgment finding that appellees did not have access to their property and, therefore, were entitled to recover $12,500 from appellant—the face amount of the policy.

[1–3] Appellant and Florida Land Title Association, appearing as amicus curiae, argue that appellant cannot be held liable on grounds of "lack of right of access to and from the land" since there is no defect shown by the public record as to their right of access; that the public record shows a dedicated and accepted public right-of-way abutting the lot. They contend that title insurance does not insure against defects in the physical condition of the land or against infirmities in legal right of access not shown by the public record. See *Pierson v. Bill*, 138 Fla. 104, 189 So. 679 (1939). They argue that defects in the physical condition of the land such as are involved here are not covered by title insurance. We agree. Title insurance only insures against title defects.

The Supreme Court of North Carolina in *Marriott Financial Services, Inc. v. Capitol Funds, Inc.*, 288 N.C. 122, 217 S.E.2d 551 (1975), construed "right of access" to mean the right to go to and from the public right-of-way without unreasonable restrictions. Compare *Hocking v. Title Insurance & Trust Company*, 37 Cal.2d 644, 234 P.2d 625 (1951), where, in ruling that the plaintiff failed to state a cause of action in a suit brought under her title policy, the court said:

> "She appears to possess fee simple title to the property for whatever it may be worth; if she has been damaged by false representations in respect to the condition and value of the land her remedy would seem to be against others than the insurers of the title she acquired."

In *Mafetone et al. v. Forest Manor Homes, Inc., et al.*, 34 A.D.2d 566, 310 N.Y.S.2d 17 (N.Y. 1970), the plaintiff brought an action against a title insurance company for damages allegedly flowing from a change in the grade of a street. There the court said:

> "The title company is not responsible to plaintiffs for the damages incurred by reason of the change in elevating the abutting street to its legal grade, since the provisions of the standard title insurance policy here in question are concerned with matters affecting *title* to property and do not concern themselves with physical conditions of the abutting property *absent* a specific request by the person ordering a title report and policy . . . ." (Emphasis supplied.)

In *McDaniel v. Lawyers' Title Guaranty Fund,* 327 So.2d 852 (Fla. 2 D.C.A.1976), our sister court of the Second District said:

> "The man on the street buys a title insurance policy to insure against defects in the record title. The title insurance company is in the business of guaranteeing the insured's title to the extent it is affected by the public records."

In the case here before us, there is no dispute that the public record shows a legal right of access to appellant's property via the platted Viejo Street. The title insurance policy only insured against record title defects and not against physical infirmities of the platted street. REVERSED.

New Insured Risks under the 2006 Policy

The 2006 owner and lender policies have included new covered or insured risks for the insured. The policy language relating to new covered risks is set forth and explained as follows:

1. *The lien of real estate taxes or assessments imposed on the Title by a governmental authority due or payable, but unpaid.* This insurance protects the insured against unpaid taxes that are due or payable prior to the effective date of the policy but not for taxes that become due and payable after the effective date of the policy.

2. *Any encroachment, encumbrance, violation, variation, or adverse circumstance affecting the title that would be disclosed by an accurate and complete land survey of the land. The term "encroachment" includes encroachments of existing improvements located on the Land (the property being insured), onto adjoining land, and encroachments onto the Land of existing improvements located on adjoining land.* This new covered risk contains general survey insurance for the insured; however, in the event a survey is not obtained, the title insurance company will provide an exception under Schedule B that will take away the new insurance coverage. In order to obtain survey coverage, it is still necessary to obtain a survey and provide the title insurance company with the survey. The title company will then delete the Schedule B survey exception and will insure only as to matters shown on the provided survey.

3. *The violation or enforcement of any law, ordinance, permit, or governmental regulation (including those related to building and zoning) restricting, regulating, prohibiting, or relating to:*

   a. *the occupancy, use, or enjoyment of the Land;*

   b. *the character, dimensions, or location of any improvement erected on the Land;*

   c. *the subdivision of land; or*

   d. *environmental protection,*

   if a notice, describing any part of the Land, is recorded in the public records setting forth the violation or intention to enforce, but only to the extent of the violation or enforcement referred to in that notice. This new covered risk protects the insured against laws, ordinances, permits, or government regulations in effect on the effective date of the policy provided that a notice of such laws, ordinances, permits, or government regulations has been recorded in the public records. The new covered risk does not insure against laws, ordinances, permits, or government regulations enacted after the date of the policy, nor any such laws, ordinances, permits, or government regulations that cannot be found in a search of the public records.

4. *An enforcement action based on the exercise of a government police power if a notice of the enforcement action, describing any part of the Land, is recorded in the public records, but only to the extent of the enforcement referred to in that notice.* For example, this new coverage would protect an insured against a forfeiture action instituted by the government under a racketeering or organized crime act if a notice of forfeiture had been recorded in the public records.

5. *The exercise of the rights of eminent domain if a notice of the exercise, describing any part of the Land, is recorded in the public records.*

6. *Any taking by a governmental body that has occurred and is binding on the rights of a purchaser for value without knowledge.*

7. *The invalidity, unenforceability, lack of priority, or avoidance of the lien of the Insured Mortgage upon the Title*

a. *resulting from the avoidance in whole or in part, or from a court order providing an alternative remedy, or any transfer of all or any part of the title to or any interest in the Land occurring prior to the transaction creating the lien of the Insured Mortgage because that prior transfer constituted a fraudulent or preferential transfer under federal bankruptcy, state insolvency, or similar creditors' rights laws; or*

b. *because the Insured Mortgage constitutes a preferential transfer under federal bankruptcy, state insolvency, or similar creditors' rights laws by reason of the failure of its recording in the Public Records*

(i) *to be timely, or*

(ii) *to impart notice of its existence to a purchaser for value or to a judgment or lien creditor.*

This new covered risk protects the insured against prior fraudulent conveyances or preferential transfers in the chain of title but does not protect the insured if the current transaction is fraudulent or preferential.

8. *Any defect in, or lien or encumbrance on, the title or other matter included in all of the covered risks that has been created or attached or have been filed or recorded in the Public Records subsequent to the date of the Policy and prior to the recording of the insured deed or mortgage in the public records.* This new insured risk is "gap coverage," which protects against matters that arise in the gap between the closing of the sale or loan and the recordation of the deed or mortgage. For example, an insured lender closes and funds a mortgage loan on July 3, but the mortgage is not recorded until July 8. On July 5, an easement unknown to the insured lender is recorded that affects the insured property. The 2006 insurance policy form will insure that the lender's mortgage, which was closed on July 3 but not recorded until July 8, will have priority over the easement recorded on July 5. The policy will protect the insured lender against any loss of damage the easement may cause to the insured.

Exclusions from Coverage

The ALTA owner's policy contains several exclusions from coverage. These exclusions are not negotiable and generally cannot be deleted from the policy. The exclusions are (a) zoning and other governmental police power rights; (b) rights of eminent domain; (c) matters created, suffered, assumed, or agreed to by the insured; (d) title defects not known to the insurance company and not shown by public records, but known to the insured, either at the date of the policy or when the insured acquired the estate or interest, and not disclosed in writing to the insurance company before the date he became an insured; (e) matters resulting in no loss or damage to the insured; (f) title defects that are first attached or created after the effective date of the policy; and (g) matters resulting in a loss or damage that would not have been sustained if the insured had paid value for the estate or interest insured. The ALTA forms also exclude environmental protection matters.

Zoning and Other Governmental Regulations

This exclusion is primarily designed to indicate that matters of zoning are not insured against by the title policy. Beyond that, the exclusion also relates to building and other use restrictions as well as restrictions concerning the right of occupancy and any government regulations concerning further subdivision of the property. This exclusion reflects the fact that all ownership of property ultimately is subject to control and regulation by the government. It is important that zoning information be independently obtained and reviewed to see if it unreasonably interferes with the proposed use of the real property. It is possible in some states to obtain a zoning **endorsement** from the title insurance company that insures against loss if the zoning classification is other than stated in the endorsement. Another endorsement that is available in some situations protects an insured against loss if the land as currently improved violates zoning or other governmental regulations. A title insurance company will not insure against future changes of government regulations.

Eminent Domain and Police Power

This exclusion recognizes that ownership for private property is subject not only to government control, but also to a government taking of the property by eminent domain or regulation under police power. If a notice of the exercise of such rights appears in the public records as of the effective date of the policy, as, for example, would be the case in a condemnation action, then the title insurance must disclose that fact to the insured or insure against any loss for failure to disclose.

Matters Created, Suffered, Assumed, or Agreed to by the Insured

This policy language excludes from coverage defects, liens, encumbrances, adverse claims, or other matters created, suffered, assumed, or agreed to by the insured claimant. This clause has the effect of limiting the title company's liability when the insured has expressly or implicitly assumed or agreed to various defects, liens, or encumbrances in the course of dealing with the property or when the defect, lien, or encumbrance resulted from the insured's misconduct or inequitable dealings. For example, Pat Purchaser is purchasing real property from Sam Seller. As part of the transaction, Pat Purchaser is to give a mortgage to Sam Seller to secure part of the purchase price that will be paid to Sam Seller over a period of time. The mortgage would be an encumbrance on the property purchased by Pat Purchaser, but it is an encumbrance created by Pat Purchaser and therefore not insured by Pat Purchaser's title insurance policy.

On the other hand, the clause will not operate to limit the insurance company's liability for title defects, liens, or encumbrances resulting from the insured's negligence. The theory is that the title problem must result from the insured's knowing or intentional affirmative act or the insured's intentional failure to prevent the attachment of the adverse item. The courts usually apply this exclusion to protect the insurance company from liability for a loss resulting from the insured's wrongful conduct.

Title Defects Not Known to the Insurance Company

This exclusion, known as the "secret defect" exclusion, covers title matters that are not recorded but that the insured claimant knew about and failed to tell the title insurance company at the time of the transaction. The insured claimant must give written disclosure of all "off record" matters that affect the insured property. This exclusion does not apply to record matters even if the insured knows of their existence. The insured claimant must know about the adverse matter for the exclusion to apply. Knowledge usually means actual knowledge, not constructive knowledge, or notice that may be imputed to an insured by reason of any public records.

If a matter fits into the requirements of this exclusion, the only prudent way for the insured to obtain title insurance protection over the item is to make written disclosure of the item to the title insurance company and cause the title company to provide affirmative insurance against the item.

Matters Resulting in No Loss or Damage to the Insured Claimant

This provision fits into the concept that title insurance is a contract of indemnity. Simply put, if there is no loss, there is nothing on which the indemnification aspects of the insurance obligation can operate.

Title Defects That Are First Attached or Created after the Effective Date of the Policy

Title insurance provides the insured with protection for so long as the insured owns an interest in the insured property. Title insurance coverage is generally paid for by a single premium at the time the title policy is issued. The date of issuance of the title insurance policy is important because the title insurance policy covers only those risks that exist in the title at the time the insured's interest is created. The exclusion for defects, liens, encumbrances, adverse claims, or other matters attaching or created subsequent to the date of the policy makes it clear that the title insurance policy is not prospective in operation and provides no protection for agreements, liens, or problems arising after the policy is issued. The insurance covers only the losses attributable to matters in existence on the date of the policy. Title insurance policies contain an effective date, which usually is the date of the recording of the deed or, in the event of a loan policy, the date of the recording of the mortgage.

Matters Resulting in a Loss or Damage That Would Not Have Been Sustained If the Insured Had Paid Value for the Estate or Interest Insured

This exclusion is an example of how title insurance provisions reflect the protection afforded by the various state recording laws. If the recording laws of a state do not protect a party who takes real property for no consideration against a prior interest in the same property, the title policy will not protect the insured as well. For example, if you are representing someone who is receiving property as a gift, it is necessary to obtain an endorsement to the title policy to delete this exclusion.

New Exclusions from Coverage under the 2006 ALTA Loan Policy

The mechanic's lien exclusion has been deleted. If the title insurance company wishes to except mechanic's lien coverage from its policy, it must now take an exception to the risk in Schedule B of the policy.

Schedule A

Schedule A is an identification schedule that localizes or customizes the title insurance to the transaction. A form of Schedule A is shown in Exhibit 13–2.

Policy Date

The date of the policy is important because of the nature of title insurance. Unlike other insurance that covers the future occurrence of risk, title insurance, with some limited exceptions, insures against risks that have already occurred but that have not manifested themselves. The date of the policy is the cutoff for coverage. The policy date is the date the transaction documents, such as the deed or mortgage, are recorded.

The 2006 policy form provides that the "date of policy" is defined to be the date designated as the date of policy on Schedule A of the title policy.

The 2006 policy forms provide for "gap" risk coverage. It is no longer necessary under the 2006 policy forms that the date of policy be the date of recordation of the deed or the mortgage. Since the recording gap is covered, the insured will be protected against any

OFFICE FILE NUMBER	POLICY NUMBER	DATE OF POLICY	AMOUNT OF INSURANCE
1	2	3	4 $

1. Name of Insured:

2. The estate or interest in the land which is covered by this Policy is:

   Fee Simple

3. Title to the estate or interest in the land is vested in the Insured.

4. The land herein described is encumbered by the following mortgage or trust deed, and assignments:

   and the mortgages or trust deeds, if any, shown in Schedule B hereof.

5. The land referred to in this Policy is described as follows:

EXHIBIT 13–2

Schedule A of Owner's Policy

ALTA forms have been used by permission of the American Land Title Association.

intervening matters between the date of the policy and the date the insured instruments (deed or mortgage) are actually recorded.

Amount of Insurance

The dollar amount of insurance coverage is the maximum loss the title insurer will bear in the event of an occurrence of a covered risk. It also is the prime factor in determining the amount of policy premium. The insured must balance the need to obtain adequate insurance coverage against the cost of the coverage. The amount of title insurance usually is the purchase price of the insured property for an owner's policy and the amount of the loan secured by the insured property for a loan policy.

Occasionally, however, to save premiums, the insured may deliberately underinsure. The title insurance company is aware that the property is being underinsured and that the insured has self-insured a portion of the risk. This situation brings a co-insurance clause into account. Through this clause, the insurer limits its liability to that proportion of the loss, damage, or defense cost that the policy amount bears to the market value of the insured property at the time of the loss. For example, a purchaser buys a $100,000 parcel of property but only insures for $60,000. Under the co-insurance rules, if there is a loss in the amount of $30,000 under the title policy, the title insurance company will only pay 60 percent of the loss ($60,000 versus $100,000), or $18,000.

On the other hand, an insured may want more coverage than would be indicated by the amount of the transaction. An owner may anticipate an increase in the property value caused by natural market forces or because the property will be improved. A lender may want more insurance than the original amount of a loan in situations when negative amortization will occur.

Most title insurance companies are willing to sell additional coverage on the demonstration of a reasonable basis for the requested coverage.

Even after a policy is issued, the insured may approach the insurance company to increase the policy amount. This can be done by an endorsement that either changes or does not change the effective date of the policy.

Some insureds do not want to leave the availability of this coverage to chance. Although they seek adequate insurance at the outset (i.e., insurance in the amount of the purchase price of the property), they want to save the payment of the premium for more insurance until the additional value is added to the property. Although the insurer may be willing to agree to give this insurance, the insurer wants the insured's agreement to purchase the insurance. This is accomplished through an endorsement that contains the insured's agreement to purchase more insurance and the title company's undertaking to increase the policy amount and change the effective date of the policy, subject, however, to exception of matters created, recorded, attaching, or coming to the insured's attention subsequent to the original policy's effective date.

An owner may seek additional coverage to protect against the effects of inflation. This is done through inflation protection increases in the policy amount over time. This inflation protection can easily be built into Schedule A of a policy of insurance insuring residential property so that the insured amount will automatically increase by 10 percent on each of the first five policy anniversary dates.

Inflation protection also can be obtained on commercial policies. This coverage is given by endorsement that raises the policy amount by some index rate, such as the consumer price index. In both residential and commercial policies, the inflated policy amount will not exceed 150 percent of the original amount of insurance.

The Insured

The insured should be correctly identified. It should be noticed that, by definition, the insured extends not only to the named insured, but also to those who succeed to the interest of the insured by operation of law, as distinguished from purchase, including but not limited to heirs, distributees, devises, survivors, personal representatives, next of kin, or a corporate and fiduciary successor.

The 2006 owner policy form expands the definition of "insured owner" to include an insured that has converted to another kind of legal entity, such as a limited partnership that converts to a limited liability company, as well as to the grantee of an insured where the deed is delivered without payment of actual valuable consideration conveying the title.

1. If the stock, shares, memberships, or other equity interests of the grantee are wholly owned by the named insured;
2. the grantee wholly owns the named insured;
3. the grantee is wholly owned by an affiliate entity of the named insured, providing the affiliate entity and the named insured are both wholly owned by the same person or entity; or
4. if the grantee is a trustee or beneficiary of a trust created by a written instrument established by the original insured for estate planning purposes.

This new definition of the insured would mean that insurance coverage will not be lost if an insured transfers the property to a trust in which the insured is the beneficiary of the trust for estate planning purposes or if the insured transfers the property to a special purpose entity, such as a limited liability company, for the purpose of obtaining a loan. Transfers to a trust for estate planning purposes and to a special purpose entity for the purposes of obtaining a loan are very common transactions in today's marketplace. This is an effort by the title insurance industry to accommodate its customers.

A successor insured is subject to the same rights or defenses that the title company had against a named insured.

Because title insurance policies are issued for a one-time premium, it is of economic necessity to the title insurance company that the insurance undertaking be definitionally limited to not extend to those who take by purchase. In other words, an owner's title insurance policy is not transferable to someone who purchases the property from the owner. If the purchaser desires insurance, the purchaser will need to purchase a new policy.

A loan policy of insurance, however, extends the insurance by defining the named insured as the owner of the indebtedness secured by the insured mortgage, each successor in ownership of the indebtedness, and any governmental agency or instrumentality that insures or guarantees the indebtedness. The title insurance industry is aware that mortgage loans often are transferred from one lender to another and to accommodate this industry practice with a minimum of cost has provided that the holder of the insured mortgage will be the named insured under the loan policy.

Insured Property

The policy definition of real property encompasses the real property expressly described in Schedule A and the improvements affixed to the real property. Title to personal property is not included in the coverage of a title insurance policy.

It is of primary importance that the legal description contained in Schedule A be the same real property that the insured is purchasing or using to secure a loan.

The insured property often is made up of several parcels or tracts of land. It is important that the policy description set forth a full description of the parcels that are insured. If these parcels are being consolidated into one parcel, the insured should request that the title insurance company issue an endorsement insuring that the tracts or parcels are contiguous to one another and that no gaps exist between the parcels. In addition, if the insured property involves a fee parcel and an easement for access to the fee parcel, the insured should request the contiguity endorsement. This endorsement insures that the land described in both parcels is contiguous and the areas can be served with no intervening adverse interest.

The 2006 policy forms contain a new definition of the word "title." It is defined to mean the estate or interest described in Exhibit A.

Schedule B

Schedule B of an owner's policy contains exceptions to the insurance coverage. These exceptions are divided into two categories: (1) standard exceptions and (2) exceptions found in the title examination of the insured property. An example of a Schedule B to an owner's policy is shown in Exhibit 13–3.

The standard exceptions to an owner's policy are (a) rights or claims of parties in possession not shown by public records; (b) encroachments, overlaps, boundary line disputes, and any other matters that would be disclosed by an accurate survey and inspection of the premises; (c) easements or claims of easement not shown by the public records; (d) any lien, or right to a lien, for services, labor, or material heretofore or hereafter furnished, imposed by law, and not shown by the public records; and (e) taxes or special assessments not shown as existing liens by the public records.

Rights of Parties in Possession

A title policy does not insure against loss or damage incurred by reason of the rights or claims of parties of possession not shown by the public records. Through this exception, the insurance company is relieved of liability when the defect is caused by a claim of a party

EXHIBIT 13–3

Schedule B of Owner's Policy

ALTA forms have been used by permission of the American Land Title Association.

SCHEDULE B

Policy Number: _____
_____Owners_____

EXCEPTIONS FROM COVERAGE

This policy does not insure against loss or damage (and the Company will not pay costs, attorneys' fees or expenses) which arise by reason of:

General Exceptions:

(1)   Rights or claims of parties in possession not shown by the public records.

(2)   Encroachments, overlaps, boundary line disputes, or other matters which would be disclosed by an accurate survey and inspection of the premises.

(3)   Easements, or claims of easements, not shown by the public records.

(4)   Any lien, or right to a lien, for services, labor, or material heretofore or hereafter furnished, imposed by law and not shown by the public records.

(5)   Taxes or special assessments which are not shown as existing liens by the public records.

Special Exceptions: The mortgage, if any, referred to in Item 4 of Schedule A.

Countersigned

_____
Authorized Signatory

in possession. For example, a small retail shopping center is leased to a number of tenants. The tenants' leases are not recorded. The tenants are in possession of the property and are parties in possession. A purchaser purchases the shopping center for $2,000,000. The purchaser receives a title insurance policy that contains an exception for the rights of parties in possession. It is later discovered that one of the tenants has an option to purchase the shopping center for $1,600,000. The title insurance company does not insure the purchaser against any loss that it might suffer if the tenant should exercise its option to purchase the property.

This exception is based upon the premise that constructive notice of rights in real property can be found by both a search of public records of the property and by an inspection or examination of the property. An insurance company issues its policy based upon only a review of the public records. Neither the title insurance company nor its agents will actually inspect or view the insured property. The insured, however, generally will inspect the property prior to purchase and take adequate steps to protect against such rights. Therefore, under this exception, a title insurance company does not insure against anyone who claims title to the property by way of adverse possession, any person who is a tenant with an unrecorded lease, or any person who exercises unrecorded easement rights over the property.

This exception can be deleted from a title policy by obtaining a title affidavit from the owner of the property. In this affidavit, the owner swears under oath that no other parties are in possession of the property except for the owner. A form of title affidavit is included at the end of this chapter as Exhibit 13–4.

Survey Exception

A title insurance policy does not insure against loss caused by encroachments, overlaps, boundary line disputes, and other matters which would be disclosed by an accurate survey or inspection of the premises. This exception further supports the view that the title insurance company has no liability for matters which are primarily shown by an inspection or visit of the insured property itself.

A simple example of the application of this exception can be found in a situation where the insured purchased property and began to erect an industrial building. The building was placed on the site so as to afford adequate clearance for trucks using the building's loading docks. The owner of the adjoining property erected a fence along the property line at a point some three feet inside the place that the insured believed the line to be, thus blocking the effective use of the loading docks. A lawsuit resulted. It developed that the adjoining owner's survey was right about the location of the property line and the insured's survey was incorrect. A court held in this situation that the survey exception protected the title insurance company from liability over this boundary line dispute.

A general survey exception can be removed by preparing a survey in compliance with title insurance standards and by providing the title insurance company with the survey. On the receipt of a survey prepared according to title standards, a title insurance company usually will remove the standard survey exception but will add special exceptions for matters that appear on the survey.

Unrecorded Easement Exception

Another general exception states that the policy does not insure against loss incurred by the insured by reason of easements or claims of easements not shown by the public records. These easements include implied or prescriptive easements, as discussed in Chapter 5. This exception primarily applies to unrecorded easements or right-of-ways that can only be discovered by a physical inspection of the land.

For example, John is a neighbor of Sam. John has been using a road on Sam's property for access to and from John's property for more than 20 years. In the state where John and Sam live, John has a prescriptive easement to use the road on Sam's property. John's prescriptive easement would be an easement or claim of easement not shown by the public records.

A paralegal should pay close attention to such features as footpaths, driveways, water and power lines, and other like matters that appear on the survey of the insured property because all these features could be evidence of implied or prescriptive easement rights.

The standard unrecorded easement exception can be removed from the policy by providing the title company with a survey showing no easements prepared according to title standards and an affidavit from the owner swearing that no implied or prescriptive easements affect the insured property.

Mechanic's Lien Exception

An owner's policy does not insure against loss by reason of a lien or right to a lien for services, labor, or materials heretofore or hereafter furnished imposed by law and not shown by the public records. Once again, the title insurance policy reflects the insurance of record matters but not nonrecord matters. If a claim of lien has been filed in the public records, it will, as a general rule, be excepted as a special exception under Schedule B or covered by the policy's protection. If it is not reflected of record as of the date of policy, it is, by operation of this general exception, excluded from liability, regardless if the lien relates to work or materials furnished before or after the effective date of the policy.

The mechanic's lien exception may be removed from the title insurance policy. The title insurance company may require, as a condition precedent to the deletion, lien waivers from all contractors, materialmen, and laborers supplying labor or materials to the property, an affidavit that all bills have been paid, or an affidavit that no work has been performed within the period of time required for the filing of a lien.

Taxes and Special Assessments

This general exception states that the policy does not insure against loss or damage incurred by reason of "taxes or special assessments which are not shown as existing liens by the public records." This exception focuses on the public records on the day the policy is issued and covers real estate tax and special assessment laws within the jurisdiction where the real property is located. A title insurance company's liability will preclude liability for special assessments for real estate tax liens that become liens after the effective date of the policy.

Schedule B Special Exceptions

In addition to the standard exceptions, Schedule B contains all defects, encumbrances, liens, covenants, restrictions, or other matters that affect the insured property that were revealed by the title examination to the property. An example of an owner's title insurance policy with completed Schedule A and Schedule B is shown at the end of this chapter as Exhibit 13–5.

MORTGAGE OR LOAN POLICIES

mortgage or loan policy

Policy of title insurance that insures the interest of a mortgagee or lender to the title of real property.

A title insurance **mortgage or loan policy** also can be obtained to insure the interest of the mortgagee or lender who has a mortgage loan secured by real property. A form of ALTA loan policy is included at the end of this chapter as Exhibit 13–6. The ALTA loan policy contains a Schedule A; Schedule B, Part 1; and Schedule B, Part 2.

Schedule A of a loan policy contains much of the same information as Schedule A of an owner's policy: (a) the effective date of the policy; (b) the amount of coverage; (c) the named insured; (d) the fee simple owner of the property; (e) a description of the mortgage or loan deed being insured; and (f) a description of the real property conveyed in the mortgage or loan deed. An example of a Schedule A to a loan title insurance policy is shown in Exhibit 13–7.

Schedule B, Part 1, of a loan policy contains both standard exceptions and special exceptions resulting from a title examination of the insured property. The standard exceptions are the same as the exceptions in an owner's policy and can be deleted from a loan policy in the same manner, that is, by the use of surveys and title affidavits. The special exceptions are the title matters reported in the title examination.

The Schedule B, Part 2, items are exceptions to the title with a priority junior and inferior to the insured loan. An example of a Schedule B, Part 2, exception would be tenants of a commercial property with leases that are expressly subordinate to any mortgage or loan deed on the property.

SCHEDULE A

OFFICE FILE NUMBER	POLICY NUMBER	DATE OF POLICY	AMOUNT OF INSURANCE
1	2	3	4 $

1. Name of Insured:

2. The estate or interest in the land which is encumbered by the insured mortgage is:

    Fee Simple

3. Title to the estate or interest in the land is vested in:

4. The insured mortgage and assignments thereof, if any, are described as follows:

5. The land referred to in this Policy is described as follows:

EXHIBIT 13–7

Schedule A of Loan Policy

Delmar/Cengage Learning

Insurance Provisions

The first four insurance provisions of a loan policy are the same as those of an owner's policy, to wit: (1) title is vested in the borrower or maker of the mortgage or loan deed; (2) the property is free and clear of title defects, liens, and encumbrances, except those shown in Schedule B; (3) the property has access to a public road; and (4) borrower's title to the property is marketable. In addition to these four items, the following insurance provisions are provided in the loan policy: (a) the mortgage is valid and enforceable, and the lender shall have the right to foreclosure in the event the debt is not paid; (b) the priority of the mortgage; (c) the mortgage is insured against any claims that may be asserted by mechanic's or materialmen's liens; and (d) the policy insures the validity and enforceability of any assignment of the mortgage or loan deed.

Validity or Enforceability of the Lien

The ALTA loan policy insures against loss resulting from the invalidity or unenforceability of the lien of the insured mortgage on said estate or interest. This is the most basic form of protection to a lender, insuring that the lien in the mortgage or deed of trust is a valid and enforceable lien on the property described therein.

There are two exceptions that the title insurance company does not insure. Title insurance does not insure against the invalidity or unenforceability of the mortgage lien that arises out of the transaction evidenced by the insured mortgage and is based on (a) a claim of usury or (b) any consumer credit protection or truth-in-lending claim.

Priority

The next area of lender's coverage is the natural complement to insurance of the validity and enforceability of the lien: insurance against priority of any lien or encumbrance over the lien of the insured mortgage. Thus, through these two insurance clauses, the lender obtains coverage for the validity, enforceability, and priority of the insured mortgage. This insurance provision is important because most lenders are concerned that the lien be of a required priority to satisfy regulatory and contractual requirements and that on foreclosure the full value of the secured property is made available to the lender.

Mechanic's Liens

Although mechanic's liens usually appear as a special exception to coverage in an owner's policy, they are expressly insured against in a loan policy.

Validity or Enforceability of an Assignment

The last insurance clause is written in the context of an increasingly active secondary mortgage market. It insures against loss caused by the invalidity or unenforceability of any assignment shown in Schedule A of the insured mortgage and the failure of said assignment to vest title to the insured mortgage in the named assignee free and clear of all liens. This insurance clause is written to anticipate the assignment of the mortgage into the secondary mortgage market simultaneous with the mortgage origination. If the mortgage and assignment documents are recorded, Schedule A of the policy, when issued, will show the record identification of the insured mortgage and the insured assignment. If the assignment is not recorded at the time of the issuance of the loan policy, it will not be described in Schedule A and will not be insured under the insuring clause. Insurance of the assignment must then be obtained by way of endorsement.

A loan policy has the same exclusions to coverage as an owner's policy, with the addition of an exclusion against any unenforceability of the insured mortgage because of the lender's not being qualified to do business within the state in which the property is located.

Miscellaneous Provisions

A loan policy is transferable, and the owner of the mortgage or loan deed being insured will be the insured under the policy. A loan policy usually is for the amount of the loan and decreases as the loan is repaid. This rule can create problems in transactions in which the insured mortgage secures a revolving line of credit loan, such as a home equity loan, or a business line of credit loan, which contemplates that monies secured by the mortgage will be borrowed and repaid, reborrowed and repaid, and so on. A revolving line of credit mortgage requires an endorsement to the title insurance policy providing that the amount of insurance will always be the outstanding balance of the loan, despite the fact that monies have been borrowed and repaid numerous times under the loan.

Endorsements

A title insurance policy may be amended or supplemented by an endorsement to the policy. An endorsement is an amendment or supplement increasing or taking away from the coverage of the insurance policy. Endorsements may be used on both owner's and loan policies, although most endorsements are issued in connection with the loan policy to satisfy certain requirements of lenders. The common endorsements required by lenders on loan title insurance policies are (a) zoning, (b) comprehensive, (c) survey, (d) access, (e) contiguity, (f) usury, (g) utility facility, (h) subdivision, (i) tax parcel, and (j) future advance.

Zoning Endorsement

A title insurance policy, due to its exclusions from coverage, does not insure for matters such as zoning or government regulation. An owner or lender, however, may be interested in knowing if the property is properly zoned and if the use made of the property complies with the zoning requirements. This insurance coverage can be provided by an endorsement that generally insures that the use being made of the property complies with the applicable zoning ordinance, that the property has adequate parking, and that the property does not violate any setback requirements or other zoning requirements. A form of zoning endorsement is shown at the end of this chapter as Exhibit 13–8.

Comprehensive Endorsement

A comprehensive endorsement insures that the property does not violate any restrictive covenants that may be placed on the property and that there are no encroachments of the buildings either onto easements or onto adjoining properties. A form of comprehensive endorsement is shown at the end of this chapter as Exhibit 13–9.

Survey Endorsement

A survey endorsement insures that the property insured in a policy is the same as that shown on a survey and that the location of improvements, easements, and all other matters shown on the survey are correct. A form of survey endorsement is shown at the end of this chapter as Exhibit 13–10.

Access Endorsement

Although all title policies insure access to a public street, many times it is important that a certain form of access to a certain street be insured. This is done through the use of an access endorsement that insures that the property has access to an identified public street. A form of access endorsement is shown at the end of this chapter as Exhibit 13–11.

Contiguity Endorsement

Often a policy of insurance will insure more than one parcel of land. It is important in many instances that these parcels of land be contiguous to each other, that is, that there are no strips, gores, or open spaces between the two parcels. This insurance of contiguity is done by a contiguity endorsement, shown at the end of this chapter as Exhibit 13–12.

Usury Endorsement

Usury is the charging of interest that exceeds the maximum rate of interest permitted by law. The penalty for usury may be the inability to enforce a mortgage securing a loan. Although usury is not a matter of title, many title policies will insure that the loan secured by the mortgage is not usurious. This is done by a usury endorsement, shown at the end of this chapter as Exhibit 13–13.

Utility Facility Endorsement

The connection of property to public utilities such as gas, electric, water, and sewer is important. This connection can be insured by a title insurance policy through a utility facility endorsement. A copy of a utility facility endorsement is shown at the end of this chapter as Exhibit 13–14.

Subdivision Endorsement

Often the property being insured has been created through a subdivision of this property from a much larger parcel of property. Subdivisions are often regulated by law, and an improper subdivision could affect the marketability or use of an insured property. An owner or lender can obtain title insurance that the property has been lawfully subdivided and complies with all subdivision laws and regulations. This is done by a subdivision endorsement, shown at the end of this chapter as Exhibit 13–15.

Tax Parcel Endorsement

It is important to an owner or lender to know that the parcel of property insured by a title insurance policy is a single tax parcel and is not taxed with other parcels not owned by the owner or pledged to the lender as security for the insured mortgage. This insurance coverage can be provided by an endorsement that generally protects the insured against loss or damage sustained by reason of the land being taxed as part of a larger parcel of land or failing to constitute a separate tax parcel for real estate tax purposes. A form of tax parcel endorsement is shown at the end of this chapter as Exhibit 13–16.

Future Advance Endorsement

A lender may have a mortgage which secures a loan providing for advances to be made subsequent to the date of the issuance of the loan title insurance policy. This may be a line of credit loan that permits the borrower to repay the money and then reborrow the money up to a stated amount. A home equity loan is an example of a line of credit loan. A lender in this situation will want assurance from the title insurance company that all advances made under the loan secured by the mortgage have priority over all liens and encumbrances other than those originally set forth on Schedule B of the loan policy. A form of future advance endorsement is shown as the end of this chapter as Exhibit 13–17.

Construction Title Insurance

pending disbursement clause

Clause found in a construction loan title insurance policy that provides that the insurance coverage under the policy will be in the amount of the loan as it is disbursed to the borrower up to and not to exceed the face amount of the policy.

If the loan being insured under a loan policy is a loan to finance the construction of improvements, the title insurance policy will contain a **pending disbursement clause** (Example 13–2). This clause provides that the insurance coverage being provided under the policy will be in the amount of the loan as it is disbursed to the borrower up to and not to exceed the face amount of the policy. The clause also provides that as funds are disbursed to the borrower, the loan deed will be insured free and clear of mechanic's liens and claims, provided no claims and liens are filed of record and the lender has no knowledge of any claims or liens that have been asserted against the property. Many pending disbursement clauses require an endorsement to the policy as the construction advances are made to the borrower. Each endorsement requires a title update from the effective date of the policy and the date of the endorsement to ensure that no lien claims have been filed.

Example 13–2

Pending disbursement of the full proceeds of the loan secured by the mortgage insured, this policy insures only to the extent of the amount actually disbursed without knowledge of any intervening lien or interest but increases as each disbursement is made, up to the face amount of the policy. At the time of each disbursement of the proceeds of the loan, the title must be continued down to such time for possible liens, including mechanic's liens, and other objections, intervening between the date hereof and the date of such disbursement.

CLAIMS PROCEDURES UNDER TITLE INSURANCE POLICIES

Both an owner's and a lender's policy protect the insured against title defects that are not excluded or excepted from the coverage of the policy and that are created or attached before the effective date of the policy. The company settles these title defects or pays in the form of reimbursement to the insured sums of money lost as a result of the title defect up to the amount of the total insurance provided under the policy. A title company also has the obligation to defend, at its own expense, title defects that are insured against. The insured has an obligation to immediately notify the title company once the title defects are discovered and to provide the title company with full information concerning the title defects.

COMMITMENTS FOR TITLE INSURANCE

An owner's title insurance policy cannot be issued until the owner in fact owns the property. That is, the title insurance is a postclosing item that comes after the transaction and sale have been completed. The same is true with a loan policy: A lender cannot be insured until it in fact becomes a lender, which means that the insurance follows the funding and closing of a loan. Because title insurance is essentially a postclosing item, it is necessary that before the closing, the attorney or paralegal representing the proposed insured obtain a pro forma copy of the insurance. This is accomplished by means of the title company issuing a **title insurance commitment** or title binder, a contract to issue insurance once the transaction is closed. An example of a title commitment appears at the end of the chapter as Exhibit 13–18. The commitment is, for the most part, an example of how the actual policy will appear once the transaction is closed. The commitment shows all title exceptions and exclusions that will appear in the policy and contains information concerning the insurance provisions of the policy. The main purpose of the commitment is to assure the proposed purchaser or lender that if it complies with the terms of the commitment, closes the transaction, and pays the necessary insurance premium, the proposed insured will have a title insurance policy subject only to the exceptions that appear in the commitment unless defects, liens, encumbrances, or other matters intervene between the date of the commitment and the date of the policy. It is important that the date of the title commitment be as close as possible to the date of the actual closing of the transaction. In many cases, the title commitment or binder is marked by the title insurance agent at the closing to bring the effective date to the exact minute the deed or mortgage is recorded; to delete Schedule B, Section 1, exceptions; and to make other corrections to the policy as required by the proposed insured. The title agent generally marks the title commitment by handwriting on the face of it the changes requested by the insured. In some states, it is customary to use a pro forma title insurance policy, which is a copy of how the exact title policy will appear at the time of issue. The pro forma will be used instead of a marked binder or commitment.

A commitment for title insurance consists of three basic parts: Schedule A, Schedule B-1, and Schedule B-2. Schedule A shows the effective date of the title commitment (which, in most cases, is the date of the title examination of the property), sets forth the amount of coverage and the type of policy (either a loan or an owner's policy) that will be issued, reflects the current record owner of the property and the type of interest he owns (e.g., fee simple, life estate), and fully describes the property to be covered by the policy.

Schedule B, Section 1, of the commitment sets forth the requirements that must be met before the transaction closes for the title insurance to be issued.

Schedule B, Section 2, is a list of exceptions that will appear in Schedule B of the policy and that will not be insured against.

title insurance commitment

Commitment or contract by a title insurance company to issue a title insurance policy.

Practice Tips for the Preparation and Review of a Title Insurance Commitment

Depending on local custom, a real estate paralegal either reviews title commitments for clients or prepares title commitments from title examinations of the property. In some states, law firms are title agents and issue title insurance commitments and policies.

A title insurance commitment cannot be issued until a title examination has been completed. A common practice is for the examining attorney or paralegal to certify the examination to the title insurance company and to include copies of all title exceptions that were found. A paralegal with this information can then prepare a title commitment.

Preparation of Schedule A proceeds as follows:

Step 1. The effective date of the title commitment is the date of the examination by the examining attorney or paralegal. The examining attorney or paralegal gives this information as part of the examination.

Step 2. The type of policy—either an owner's policy or a loan policy—is dictated by the client. The name of the insured is the name of the purchaser or the name of the lending institution. The amount of the insurance coverage is either the purchase price of the property, which can be obtained from the contract, or the amount of the loan, which can be found in the loan commitment. When issuing commitments without full information, it is permissible to identify the proposed insured as "to be determined" and to show the amounts to be the "purchase price" or the "amount of loan." Once this information is obtained, the commitment can be endorsed or amended to provide the exact information.

Step 3. The name and the estate or interest of the current owner are set out in the commitment. This information is obtained from the title examination. In most instances, the current owner is the seller of the property under the contract or the borrower under a loan transaction.

Step 4. A description of the property, provided by the title examination, is included.

Step 5. Schedule B, Section 1, is an important part of the commitment because it identifies conditions or requirements that must be met for the title insurance to be issued. A paralegal, when reviewing the commitment, should make certain that all these conditions are satisfied before or at closing. A paralegal preparing a title commitment should become familiar with the Schedule B, Section 1, conditions. Standard Schedule B, Section 1, conditions (which often are printed on the commitment form) are as follows:

- *Execution, delivery, and recordation of the instruments necessary to vest title in the named insured.* In the case of the owner's policy, this would be a warranty deed from the current owner of the property to the proposed insured. In the case of a loan policy, this would be the execution of a mortgage or trust deed from the owner of the property to the proposed insured lender. In some transactions, the closings are simultaneous sales and loan closings, in which case both a warranty deed from the current owner of the property to the proposed new owner of the property and a mortgage or loan deed from the new owner of the property to the lender are required.

- *Payment of consideration of the transfer.* Transfers of title or loans are not valid unless consideration has been paid. The title company requires proof of payment of consideration.

- *Payment of all taxes and assessments.*

- *Title affidavit.* Many title companies require this affidavit, which permits them to remove mechanic's or materialmen's liens.

Additional requirements can be obtained from the title examination. For example, if a commitment is being issued to insure a particular lender a first-priority mortgage on the property and the title examination reveals a judgment tax lien and a prior mortgage on the property, it will be necessary to provide in Schedule B, Section 1, of the commitment that the prior tax lien and prior mortgage will be satisfied and cancelled of record before the insurance is issued. The satisfaction and cancellation of these items may take place at closing, and many times, funds are paid out of the closing proceeds to satisfy these items.

Step 6. Schedule B, Section 2, of the commitment includes all the title exceptions that will appear in Schedule B to the policy and that will not be insured against. These are the exceptions that will survive closing. It is a good idea to have copies of these exceptions, so that when the commitment is forwarded to the client, copies of the exceptions can be forwarded as well. The paralegal who reviews a title commitment should pay particular attention to all Schedule B, Section 2, title exceptions. These exceptions should be carefully reviewed to see how they will affect the client, since title insurance coverage will not be provided for these exceptions.

An example of a title commitment that has been prepared from a title examination (Exhibit 13–19) appears at the end of this chapter (Exhibit 13–20). The title commitment is being prepared for the Second Federal Savings and Loan Association. The Second Federal Savings and Loan Association is making a $250,000 first-priority mortgage loan to Tall Oaks, Inc., a Maryland corporation.

PRACTICE TIPS FOR THE PREPARATION AND REVIEW OF A TITLE INSURANCE POLICY

A paralegal employed by a law firm or title insurance company may be responsible for the preparation or review of the final title insurance policy.

A title insurance policy cannot be prepared or issued until the transaction for which the insurance is to be issued has been completed. This will mean that all the documents that have been recorded have been returned from the courthouse and can be examined by the paralegal in connection with the preparation of the policy. In addition, a final title examination is generally conducted to verify that the documents have been recorded and properly indexed and that there have been no matters recorded immediately prior to the consummation of the transaction. Once the paralegal has this final examination and copies or originals of the recorded documents, the paralegal can then prepare the title insurance policy.

The preparation of Schedule A to the policy should proceed as follows:

Step 1. The effective date of the title insurance policy is the date the insured instrument, a deed to the owner for an owner's policy or the mortgage for a loan policy, is recorded. This recordation date should be stamped on the copy or original of the recorded deed or mortgage. Generally, the exact time of recordation—including the day, hour, and minute—will be used as the effective date for the title insurance policy. For example, if a deed on an owner's policy was recorded on September 25, 2010, at 3:16 p.m., the effective date of the owner's policy would be September 25, 2010, at 3:16 p.m.

Step 2. The amount of the insurance policy will be the amount shown from the title commitment, or if the commitment was not issued, it would be the purchase price in the event of an owner's policy and the loan amount in the event of a loan policy.

Step 3. The title number for the title insurance would be the policy number issued by the title insurance company. All policies are consecutively issued. Each policy has its own number.

Step 4. The name of the insured will be taken from the recorded documents. In the event of an owner's policy, the name of the insured would be the grantee of the insured deed, and it would appear exactly as it appears in the deed. The name of the insured for a loan policy would be the lender shown on the recorded mortgage, and it would appear exactly as it is shown in the mortgage.

Step 5. The estate or interest that is covered in the policy will generally be fee simple, but if some other estate such as an estate for years is being insured, then that estate would appear in that information blank.

Step 6. The legal description of the property being insured should be the exact description as shown in the recorded deed or recorded mortgage being insured.

Step 7. On loan policies, the insured mortgage is identified in the title insurance policy. The insured mortgage would be identified exactly as it is recorded, identifying both the name of the grantor and the name of the grantee, which would be the insured lender; the date of the mortgage; the amount of the mortgage; and the book and page number or other reference number for the recordation of the mortgage. An example of how an insured mortgage could be shown on a title insurance policy is as follows: "That certain mortgage from Ajax Realty Company to ABC Life Insurance Company dated March 1, 2008, securing a loan in the amount of $1,000,000 and being recorded on March 1, 2008, at Deed Book 716, Page 643, Knox County, Indiana Records."

Step 8. The preparation of Schedule B is an important part of the title insurance policy because it identifies all title exceptions not being insured against. These title exceptions will be taken from the title commitment and the final title examination. The paralegal must carefully verify that all general exceptions are set forth in the title policy on Schedule B unless proper documents have been given to the title company to delete the general exceptions. These documents generally would be affidavits and an approved survey. The general exception for matters of survey will be deleted upon the presentation of an approved survey; however, matters that appear on the survey will be shown as Schedule B matters. That is, if the survey reveals encroachments or other matters, these will be set forth in detail on Schedule B. Other Schedule B matters include the special exceptions shown in the title examination but not satisfied or deleted at the time of the closing.

A paralegal, when reviewing a title insurance policy on behalf of a client, should have available at the time of the review a copy of the marked title commitment or pro forma policy and a copy of all recorded documents. The paralegal would then review a title policy to verify that it is correct in regard to the identification of the insured, the effective date of the policy, the amount of insurance and the proper identification of the insured deed or mortgage, and the legal description of the property being insured. The paralegal would also match carefully the Schedule B exceptions in the final title policy against the Schedule B exceptions that appeared in the final pro forma policy or marked title insurance binder. The exceptions in the policy should be identical to those agreed to by the title company in the final marked binder or pro forma policy.

If the policy contains endorsements to the coverage, the paralegal needs to verify that all required and approved endorsements have been added to the final title insurance policy. The client should receive from the title insurance company the original final title insurance policy.

See the Checklist at the end of this chapter for a summary of the steps one must follow in preparing a title insurance policy.

🏛 ETHICS: Personal Conflict of Interest

The responsibilities of a paralegal working for a title insurance agency are to review title examinations and prepare title insurance commitments and title insurance policies. While working on a title insurance policy for a real estate sale transaction, the paralegal discovers that a judgment lien is outstanding against the owner/seller of the property. Pursuant to the laws of the state in which the transaction is taking place, the judgment, unless it is levied on or paid, will expire in six months. The seller of the property has requested that the title insurance company insure over the judgment rather than pay the judgment. The title insurance company has agreed to the request but has asked that an amount of money equal to the amount of the judgment plus interest and other costs be deposited with the title insurance company until such time as the judgment expires. The paralegal is personal friends with someone who works for the company that is the judgment creditor. After the transaction has closed, the paralegal calls the friend at the creditor company and informs her that a sum of money is being held by the title insurance company to pay the judgment. Was this an ethical thing for the paralegal to do?

Professional ethics mandate that an attorney or a paralegal shall avoid conflicts of interest that may arise from family relationships or personal or business interests. The paralegal in this particular transaction is working for a title agency whose customer was the owner/seller of the property. This customer/client had requested the title insurance company to not pay the judgment but instead to insure over it and to escrow money in the event the judgment holder should come forth and demand payment. The paralegal's conflict of interest through his or her friendship with an employee of the judgment creditor and the telephone call informing the judgment creditor of the escrowed money is a conflict of interest and a breach of ethics. The paralegal had a duty of loyalty and responsibility to the customer, which is a greater duty than the friendship with the employee of the judgment creditor.

✓ CHECKLIST

Preparation of a Title Insurance Policy

- [ ] I. Purpose of Policy
    - [ ] A. Owner's policy
    - [ ] B. Loan policy

- [ ] II. Conditions Precedent to Issuance of Title Insurance
    - [ ] A. Title examination
    - [ ] B. Title examiner's certification to title company
    - [ ] C. Title commitment
    - [ ] D. Survey
    - [ ] E. Title affidavits

- [ ] III. Owner's Policy Schedule A Information
    - [ ] A. Effective date of title policy
    - [ ] B. Name of insured
    - [ ] C. Amount of insurance
    - [ ] D. Description of property

- [ ] IV. Loan Policy Schedule A Information
    - [ ] A. Effective date of policy—date mortgage was recorded
    - [ ] B. Name of insured
    - [ ] C. Name of record title owner to property—borrower
    - [ ] D. Amount of insurance—loan amount
    - [ ] E. Description of insured property

(continued)

☐ V. Procedures for Deletion of Standard Schedule B Exceptions
 ☐ A. Survey of property according to title insurance company standards
 ☐ B. Title affidavit

☐ VI. Schedule B, Section 2, Exceptions
 ☐ A. Receive copies of all exceptions
 ☐ B. Review exceptions to see if acceptable
 ☐ C. Delete as many exceptions as possible

☐ VII. Special Endorsements
 ☐ A. Zoning
 ☐ B. Contiguous parcels
 ☐ C. Pending disbursement
 ☐ D. Revolving line of credit endorsement
 ☐ E. Condominium endorsement
 ☐ F. Planned unit development endorsement
 ☐ G. Adjustable rate endorsement

SUMMARY

Title insurance is used for protecting a purchaser or lender from economic loss resulting from defects in the title to real property. An owner's policy of title insurance will insure the owner that they have marketable title to the property; that the property is free and clear of liens, encumbrances, or other defects unless shown in the policy as exceptions; and that the property has access to a public road or street. A lender's policy of title insurance will insure that the borrower has all the protections of an owner's policy, as well as insuring the priority of the lender's mortgage on the property. All title insurance has exclusions and exceptions to title. The exclusions generally consist of things that cannot be determined from a title examination or inspection of the property. These exclusions include, but are not limited to, zoning and governmental regulation of property, the ability of the government to take the property by power of eminent domain, unrecorded matters, and matters that the insured either created or agreed to. Exceptions to title insurance policies are those matters shown on a title examination of the property. The exceptions will include almost any recorded document that affects title to the property. These exceptions will generally consist of unpaid taxes, easements, restrictive covenants, and other matters recorded against the property being insured.

A lender or owner can enhance their coverage by obtaining endorsements or amendments to the standard title insurance policy form. These endorsements may insure such things as compliance with zoning, proper subdivision of the property, and access to a particular public street.

Title insurance is a postclosing matter in the sense that an owner cannot be insured until he or she has purchased the property and received title to the property. A prospective owner or lender, however, can be protected against title defects by obtaining a title insurance commitment prior to the purchase of the property. This commitment is a contract by a private title insurance company to issue title insurance and will show to the prospective insured an example of the insurance coverage that will be available once the transaction is completed. Through the use of commitments, purchasers and lenders will close transactions, being assured that acceptable title insurance will be available once the transaction is completed.

Although title insurance is useful in protecting a purchaser or lender, it does not give complete protection to either. It is important in any real estate transaction to completely understand what title matters are not covered by the title insurance. It is equally important to understand what coverages are available from the title insurance company and how standard exceptions can be removed from the title policy. Complete familiarity with title insurance is important for a paralegal who assists in the real estate closing process.

HELPFUL WEBSITES

Title Insurance

Information concerning title insurance issues can be found on the Internet. A helpful Web site is the American Land Title Association at *http://www.alta.org*. Title insurance companies also have Web sites that include news items and accompanying information. They can usually be accessed at (name of the title company).com. For example, information about Chicago Title Insurance Company can be found at *http://www.ctic.com*, Fidelity National Title Insurance Company at *http://www.fntic.com*, and First American Title Insurance Company at *http://www.firstam.com*.

KEY TERMS

affidavit

endorsement

marketable title

mortgage or loan policy

owner's policy

pending disbursement clause

title insurance

title insurance commitment

REVIEW QUESTIONS

1. Identify and discuss the three safeguards that assure a good title.
2. What risks are covered by an ALTA owner's policy?
3. How does an ALTA loan policy differ from an ALTA owner's policy?
4. How are exclusions from coverage on a title insurance policy different from exceptions to title?
5. Why is a review of Schedule B to a title policy so important?
6. What is a title commitment, and why is it important in a real estate transaction?
7. What is the effective date of a title insurance policy, and why is it important?
8. What are the requirements of a title insurance company to pay or defend a claim made under a title insurance policy?
9. What are the standard exceptions to an ALTA title insurance policy?
10. What risks are insured by an ALTA loan policy?

CASE PROBLEMS

1. Kim Buyer is purchasing a home. The purchase price for the home is $125,000. Kim is obtaining a loan from Acme Loan Company for $105,000. What is the amount of title insurance that Kim can purchase? What is the amount of title insurance that Acme Loan Company can purchase?

2. T. Sawyer has purchased a home. T. Sawyer obtained an owner's title insurance policy that insured the home to be free and clear of any liens and encumbrances. T. Sawyer, after purchasing the home, sells the home to B. Thatcher. B. Thatcher does not buy title insurance. Later it is discovered that there is a mortgage on the property held by H. Finn that dates before the effective date of T. Sawyer's title insurance policy. Does B. Thatcher have any claim against the title insurance purchased by T. Sawyer? Would the result be different if B. Thatcher had inherited the property from T. Sawyer on T. Sawyer's death?

3. You are reviewing a title commitment that contains a standard exception for parties in possession. Your client does not want the standard exception to be included in the title insurance policy. What steps can you take to have the title insurance company delete the "parties in possession" exception?

4. You are assisting in a real estate sale transaction. The title examination to the property reveals that there is a mortgage on the property from Sam Owner to Acme Loan Company in the amount of $100,000 and a mortgage

on the property from Sam Owner to First Bank and Trust in the amount of $200,000. The contract for the sale of the property indicates that the purchaser is going to assume the $100,000 mortgage from Sam Owner to Acme Loan Company. You have been asked to prepare a title commitment in connection with the transaction. Would the mortgage from Sam Owner to Acme Loan Company appear on Schedule B-1 or Schedule B-2 of the title commitment? Would the mortgage from Sam Owner to First Bank and Trust appear on Schedule B-1 or Schedule B-2 of the title commitment?

5. You are involved in a real estate sale transaction. The sale took place on December 26, but the deed was not recorded until January 5. When you receive the owner's title insurance policy, you note that the effective date of the policy is December 26. Is this the correct effective date?

6. You are assisting in a real estate transaction. After the transaction has closed, you are reviewing the owner's title insurance policy. You note that the legal description to the property as described in the policy contains a number of typographical errors. Should you be concerned?

PRACTICAL ASSIGNMENTS

Big Bank, N.A., is making a first-priority loan to Jason and Marie Phillips in the amount of $160,000. The loan is to provide Jason and Marie Phillips with money to purchase a home from Arnold Development, Inc., for $200,000. A copy of the title examination that has been completed on the property to be insured is included as Exhibit 13–21 at the end of this chapter. Review the title examination carefully, and prepare a title commitment from the information contained in the examination for both an owner's policy insuring Jason Phillips and Marie Phillips and a loan policy insuring Big Bank, N.A. Blank Schedule A; Schedule B, Section 1; and Schedule B, Section 2 title commitment forms are included as Exhibit 13–22 at the end of this chapter. These forms may be used to complete this practical assignment.

ADDENDUM

Exhibit 13–1 Owner's Policy—ALTA
Exhibit 13–4 Owner's Affidavit
Exhibit 13–5 Completed Owner's Policy of Title Insurance
Exhibit 13–6 Loan Policy
Exhibit 13–8 Zoning Endorsement
Exhibit 13–9 Comprehensive Endorsement
Exhibit 13–10 Survey Endorsement
Exhibit 13–11 Access Endorsement
Exhibit 13–12 Contiguity Endorsement
Exhibit 13–13 Usury Endorsement
Exhibit 13–14 Utility Facility Endorsement
Exhibit 13–15 Subdivision Endorsement

Exhibit 13–16 Tax Parcel Endorsement
Exhibit 13–17 Future Advance Endorsement
Exhibit 13–18 Title Commitment
Exhibit 13–19 Title Opinion
Exhibit 13–20 Sample Title Commitment
Exhibit 13–21 Title Examination Form for Practical Assignment
Exhibit 13–22 Title Commitment Forms for Practical Assignment
Exhibit 13–23 2006 ALTA Owner's Policy
Exhibit 13–24 2006 ALTA Loan Policy

ACKNOWLEDGMENT

ALTA forms have been used by permission of the American Land Title Association.

Student StudyWare™ CD-ROM
Interactive Student CD in the book includes additional quizzing, case studies, and key terms flashcards.

Online Companion™
For additional resources, please go to
www.paralegal.delmar.cengage.com

EXHIBIT 13–1

Owner's Policy—ALTA

ALTA forms have been used by permission of the American Land Title Association.

American Land Title Association	**Owner's Policy** **Revised 10/17/92**

POLICY OF TITLE INSURANCE

Issued by

BLANK TITLE INSURANCE COMPANY

     SUBJECT TO THE EXCLUSIONS FROM COVERAGE, THE EXCEPTIONS FROM COVERAGE CONTAINED IN SCHEDULE B AND THE CONDITIONS AND STIPULATIONS, BLANK TITLE INSURANCE COMPANY, a Blank corporation, herein called the Company, insures, as of Date of Policy shown in Schedule A, against loss or damage, not exceeding the Amount of Insurance stated in Schedule A, sustained or incurred by the insured by reason of:

1.   Title to the estate or interest described in Schedule A being vested other than as stated therein;

2.   Any defect in or lien or encumbrance on the title;

3.   Unmarketability of the title;

4.   Lack of a right of access to and from the land.

     The Company will also pay the costs, attorneys' fees and expenses incurred in defense of the title, as insured, but only to the extent provided in the Conditions and Stipulations.
[Witness clause optional]

BLANK TITLE INSURANCE COMPANY

BY:_____
PRESIDENT

BY:_____
         SECRETARY

1

(continued)

EXHIBIT 13–1

Owner's Policy—ALTA (*continued*)

American Land Title Association   **Owner's Policy**
Revised 10/17/92

EXCLUSIONS FROM COVERAGE

The following matters are expressly excluded from the coverage of this policy and the Company will not pay loss or damage, costs, attorneys' fees or expenses which arise by reason of:

1.   (a)   Any law, ordinance or governmental regulation (including but not limited to building and zoning laws, ordinances, or regulations) restricting, regulating, prohibiting or relating to (i) the occupancy, use, or enjoyment of the land; (ii) the character, dimensions or location of any improvement now or hereafter erected on the land; (iii) a separation in ownership or a change in the dimensions or area of the land or any parcel of which the land is or was a part; or (iv) environmental protection, or the effect of any violation of these laws, ordinances or governmental regulations, except to the extent that a notice of the enforcement thereof or a notice of a defect, lien or encumbrance resulting from a violation or alleged violation affecting the land has been recorded in the public records at Date of Policy.

     (b)   Any governmental police power not excluded by (a) above, except to the extent that a notice of the exercise thereof or a notice of a defect, lien or encumbrance resulting from a violation or alleged violation affecting the land has been recorded in the public records at Date of Policy.

2.   Rights of eminent domain unless notice of the exercise thereof has been recorded in the public records at Date of Policy, but not excluding from coverage any taking which has occurred prior to Date of Policy which would be binding on the rights of a purchaser for value without knowledge.

3.   Defects, liens, encumbrances, adverse claims or other matters:

     (a)   created, suffered, assumed or agreed to by the insured claimant;

     (b)   not known to the Company, not recorded in the public records at Date of Policy, but known to the insured claimant and not disclosed in writing to the Company by the insured claimant prior to the date the insured claimant became an insured under this policy;

     (c)   resulting in no loss or damage to the insured claimant;

     (d)   attaching or created subsequent to Date of Policy; or

     (e)   resulting in loss or damage which would not have been sustained if the insured claimant had paid value for the estate or interest insured by this policy.

4.   Any claim, which arises out of the transaction vesting in the Insured the estate or interest insured by this policy, by reason of the operation of federal bankruptcy, state insolvency, or similar creditors' rights laws, that is based on:

     (a)   the transaction creating the estate or interest insured by this policy being deemed a fraudulent conveyance or fraudulent transfer; or

     (b)   the transaction creating the estate or interest insured by this policy being deemed a preferential transfer except where the preferential transfer results from the failure:

          (i)   to timely record the instrument of transfer; or

2

(continued)

EXHIBIT 13–1

Owner's Policy—ALTA (*continued*)

American Land Title Association	Owner's Policy Revised 10/17/92

(ii)   of such recordation to impart notice to a purchaser for value or a judgment or lien creditor.

3

EXHIBIT 13–1

Owner's Policy—ALTA (*continued*)

American Land Title Association	**Owner's Policy**
	Revised 10/17/92

SCHEDULE A

[File No.   ]   Policy No.

Amount of Insurance $

[Premium $]

a.m.

Date of Policy_____[at   p.m.]

1.   Name of Insured:

2.   The estate or interest in the land which is covered by this policy is:

3.   Title to the estate or interest in the land is vested in:

[4.   The land referred to in this policy is described as follows:]

If Paragraph 4 is omitted, a Schedule C, captioned the same as Paragraph 4, must be used.

4

EXHIBIT 13–1

Owner's Policy—ALTA (*continued*)

American Land Title Association	Owner's Policy Revised 10/17/92

SCHEDULE B

[File No.   ]   Policy No.

EXCEPTIONS FROM COVERAGE

This policy does not insure against loss or damage (and the Company will not pay costs, attorneys' fees or expenses) which arise by reason of:

1.

   [POLICY MAY INCLUDE REGIONAL EXCEPTIONS IF SO

2.   DESIRED BY ISSUING COMPANY]

   [VARIABLE EXCEPTIONS SUCH AS TAXES, EASEMENTS, CC & Rs, ETC.]

3.

4.

5

(continued)

EXHIBIT 13–1

Owner's Policy—ALTA (*continued*)

American Land Title Association   **Owner's Policy**
                                                       Revised 10/17/92

CONDITIONS AND STIPULATIONS

1.   DEFINITION OF TERMS.

   The following terms when used in this policy mean:

   (a)   "insured": the insured named in Schedule A, and, subject to any rights or defenses the Company would have had against the named insured, those who succeed to the interest of the named insured by operation of law as distinguished from purchase including, but not limited to, heirs, distributees, devisees, survivors, personal representatives, next of kin, or corporate or fiduciary successors.

   (b)   "insured claimant": an insured claiming loss or damage.

   (c)   "knowledge" or "known": actual knowledge, not constructive knowledge or notice which may be imputed to an insured by reason of the public records as defined in this policy or any other records which impart constructive notice of matters affecting the land.

   (d)   "land": the land described or referred to in Schedule [A][C], and improvements affixed thereto which by law constitute real property. The term "land" does not include any property beyond the lines of the area described or referred to in Schedule [A][C], nor any right, title, interest, estate or easement in abutting streets, roads, avenues, alleys, lanes, ways or waterways, but nothing herein shall modify or limit the extent to which a right of access to and from the land is insured by this policy.

   (e)   "mortgage": mortgage, deed of trust, trust deed, or other security instrument.

   (f)   "public records": records established under state statutes at Date of Policy for the purpose of imparting constructive notice of matters relating to real property to purchasers for value and without knowledge. With respect to Section 1(a)(iv) of the Exclusions From Coverage, "public records" shall also include environmental protection liens filed in the records of the clerk of the United States district court for the district in which the land is located.

   (g)   "unmarketability of the title": an alleged or apparent matter affecting the title to the land, not excluded or excepted from coverage, which would entitle a purchaser of the estate or interest described in Schedule A to be released from the obligation to purchase by virtue of a contractual condition requiring the delivery of marketable title.

2.   CONTINUATION OF INSURANCE AFTER CONVEYANCE OF TITLE.

   The coverage of this policy shall continue in force as of Date of Policy in favor of an insured only so long as the insured retains an estate or interest in the land, or holds an indebtedness secured by a purchase money mortgage given by a purchaser from the insured, or only so long as the insured shall have liability by reason of covenants of warranty made by the insured in any transfer or conveyance of the estate or interest. This policy shall not continue in force in favor of any purchaser from the insured of either (i) an estate or interest in the land, or (ii) an indebtedness secured by a purchase money mortgage given to the insured.

3.   NOTICE OF CLAIM TO BE GIVEN BY INSURED CLAIMANT.

   The insured shall notify the Company promptly in writing (i) in case of any litigation as set forth in

6

(continued)

EXHIBIT 13–1

Owner's Policy—ALTA (*continued*)

American Land Title Association	Owner's Policy
	Revised 10/17/92

Section 4(a) below, (ii) in case knowledge shall come to an insured hereunder of any claim of title or interest which is adverse to the title to the estate or interest, as insured, and which might cause loss or damage for which the Company may be liable by virtue of this policy, or (iii) if title to the estate or interest, as insured, is rejected as unmarketable. If prompt notice shall not be given to the Company, then as to the insured all liability of the Company shall terminate with regard to the matter or matters for which prompt notice is required; provided, however, that failure to notify the Company shall in no case prejudice the rights of any insured under this policy unless the Company shall be prejudiced by the failure and then only to the extent of the prejudice.

4. <u>DEFENSE AND PROSECUTION OF ACTIONS; DUTY OF INSURED CLAIMANT TO COOPERATE.</u>

(a)   Upon written request by the insured and subject to the options contained in Section 6 of these Conditions and Stipulations, the Company, at its own cost and without unreasonable delay, shall provide for the defense of an insured in litigation in which any third party asserts a claim adverse to the title or interest as insured, but only as to those stated causes of action alleging a defect, lien or encumbrance or other matter insured against by this policy. The Company shall have the right to select counsel of its choice (subject to the right of the insured to object for reasonable cause) to represent the insured as to those stated causes of action and shall not be liable for and will not pay the fees of any other counsel. The Company will not pay any fees, costs or expenses incurred by the insured in the defense of those causes of action which allege matters not insured against by this policy.

(b)   The Company shall have the right, at its own cost, to institute and prosecute any action or proceeding or to do any other act which in its opinion may be necessary or desirable to establish the title to the estate or interest, as insured, or to prevent or reduce loss or damage to the insured. The Company may take any appropriate action under the terms of this policy, whether or not it shall be liable hereunder, and shall not thereby concede liability or waive any provision of this policy. If the Company shall exercise its rights under this paragraph, it shall do so diligently.

(c)   Whenever the Company shall have brought an action or interposed a defense as required or permitted by the provisions of this policy, the Company may pursue any litigation to final determination by a court of competent jurisdiction and expressly reserves the right, in its sole discretion, to appeal from any adverse judgment or order.

(d)   In all cases where this policy permits or requires the Company to prosecute or provide for the defense of any action or proceeding, the insured shall secure to the Company the right to so prosecute or provide defense in the action or proceeding, and all appeals therein, and permit the Company to use, at its option, the name of the insured for this purpose. Whenever requested by the Company, the insured, at the Company's expense, shall give the Company all reasonable aid (i) in any action or proceeding, securing evidence, obtaining witnesses, prosecuting or defending the action or proceeding, or effecting settlement, and (ii) in any other lawful act which in the opinion of the Company may be necessary or desirable to establish the title to the estate or interest as insured. If the Company is prejudiced by the failure of the insured to furnish the required cooperation, the Company's obligations to the insured under the policy shall terminate, including any liability or obligation to defend, prosecute, or continue any litigation, with regard to the matter or matters requiring such cooperation.

5. <u>PROOF OF LOSS OR DAMAGE.</u>

In addition to and after the notices required under Section 3 of these Conditions and Stipulations have been provided the Company, a proof of loss or damage signed and sworn to by the insured claimant shall be furnished to the Company within 90 days after the insured claimant shall ascertain the facts giving rise to the loss or damage. The proof of loss or damage shall describe the defect in, or lien or

7

(continued)

EXHIBIT 13–1

Owner's Policy—ALTA (*continued*)

American Land Title Association	Owner's Policy Revised 10/17/92

encumbrance on the title, or other matter insured against by this policy which constitutes the basis of loss or damage and shall state, to the extent possible, the basis of calculating the amount of the loss or damage. If the Company is prejudiced by the failure of the insured claimant to provide the required proof of loss or damage, the Company's obligations to the insured under the policy shall terminate, including any liability or obligation to defend, prosecute, or continue any litigation, with regard to the matter or matters requiring such proof of loss or damage.

In addition, the insured claimant may reasonably be required to submit to examination under oath by any authorized representative of the Company and shall produce for examination, inspection and copying, at such reasonable times and places as may be designated by any authorized representative of the Company, all records, books, ledgers, checks, correspondence and memoranda, whether bearing a date before or after Date of Policy, which reasonably pertain to the loss or damage. Further, if requested by any authorized representative of the Company, the insured claimant shall grant its permission, in writing, for any authorized representative of the Company to examine, inspect and copy all records, books, ledgers, checks, correspondence and memoranda in the custody or control of a third party, which reasonably pertain to the loss or damage. All information designated as confidential by the insured claimant provided to the Company pursuant to this Section shall not be disclosed to others unless, in the reasonable judgment of the Company, it is necessary in the administration of the claim. Failure of the insured claimant to submit for examination under oath, produce other reasonably requested information or grant permission to secure reasonably necessary information from third parties as required in this paragraph shall terminate any liability of the Company under this policy as to that claim.

6.   <u>OPTIONS TO PAY OR OTHERWISE SETTLE CLAIMS; TERMINATION OF LIABILITY</u>.

In case of a claim under this policy, the Company shall have the following additional options:

(a)   <u>To Pay or Tender Payment of the Amount of Insurance</u>.

(i)   To pay or tender payment of the amount of insurance under this policy together with any costs, attorneys' fees and expenses incurred by the insured claimant, which were authorized by the Company, up to the time of payment or tender of payment and which the Company is obligated to pay.

(ii)   Upon the exercise by the Company of this option, all liability and obligations to the insured under this policy, other than to make the payment required, shall terminate, including any liability or obligation to defend, prosecute, or continue any litigation, and the policy shall be surrendered to the company for cancellation.

(b)   <u>To Pay or Otherwise Settle With Parties Other than the Insured or With the Insured Claimant</u>.

(i)   to pay or otherwise settle with other parties for or in the name of an insured claimant any claim insured against under this policy, together with any costs, attorneys' fees and expenses incurred by the insured claimant which were authorized by the Company up to the time of payment and which the Company is obligated to pay; or

(ii)   to pay or otherwise settle with the insured claimant the loss or damage provided for under this policy, together with any costs, attorneys' fees and expenses incurred by the insured claimant which were authorized by the Company up to the time of payment and which the Company is obligated to pay.

8

EXHIBIT 13–1

Owner's Policy—ALTA (*continued*)

American Land Title Association   **Owner's Policy**
                                                       Revised 10/17/92

Upon the exercise by the Company of either of the options provided for in paragraphs (b)(i) or (ii), the Company's obligations to the insured under this policy for the claimed loss or damage, other than the payments required to be made, shall terminate, including any liability or obligation to defend, prosecute or continue any litigation.

7.   <u>DETERMINATION, EXTENT OF LIABILITY AND COINSURANCE.</u>

This policy is a contract of indemnity against actual monetary loss or damage sustained or incurred by the insured claimant who has suffered loss or damage by reason of matters insured against by this policy and only to the extent herein described.

(a)   The liability of the Company under this policy shall not exceed the least of:

(i)   the Amount of Insurance stated in Schedule A; or,

(ii)   the difference between the value of the insured estate or interest as insured and the value of the insured estate or interest subject to the defect, lien or encumbrance insured against by this policy.

(b)   In the event the Amount of Insurance stated in Schedule A at the Date of Policy is less than 80 percent of the value of the insured estate or interest or the full consideration paid for the land, whichever is less, or if subsequent to the Date of Policy an improvement is erected on the land which increases the value of the insured estate or interest by at least 20 percent over the Amount of Insurance stated in Schedule A, then this Policy is subject to the following:

(i)   where no subsequent improvement has been made, as to any partial loss, the Company shall only pay the loss pro rata in the proportion that the amount of insurance at Date of Policy bears to the total value of the insured estate or interest at Date of Policy; or

(ii)   where a subsequent improvement has been made, as to any partial loss, the Company shall only pay the loss pro rata in the proportion that 120 percent of the Amount of Insurance stated in Schedule A bears to the sum of the Amount of Insurance stated in Schedule A and the amount expended for the improvement.

The provisions of this paragraph shall not apply to costs, attorneys' fees and expenses for which the Company is liable under this policy, and shall only apply to that portion of any loss which exceeds, in the aggregate, 10 percent of the Amount of Insurance stated in Schedule A.

(c)   The Company will pay only those costs, attorneys' fees and expenses incurred in accordance with Section 4 of these Conditions and Stipulations.

8.   <u>APPORTIONMENT.</u>

If the land described in Schedule [A][C] consists of two or more parcels which are not used as a single site, and a loss is established affecting one or more of the parcels but not all, the loss shall be computed and settled on a pro rata basis as if the amount of insurance under this policy was divided pro rata as to the value on Date of Policy of each separate parcel to the whole, exclusive of any improvements made subsequent to Date of Policy, unless a liability or value has otherwise been agreed upon as to each parcel by the Company and the insured at the time of the issuance of this policy and shown by an express statement or by an endorsement attached to this policy.

9

(*continued*)

EXHIBIT 13–1

Owner's Policy—ALTA (*continued*)

American Land Title Association	**Owner's Policy** **Revised 10/17/92**

9.   LIMITATION OF LIABILITY.

(a)   If the Company establishes the title, or removes the alleged defect, lien or encumbrance, or cures the lack of a right of access to or from the land, or cures the claim of unmarketability of title, all as insured, in a reasonably diligent manner by any method, including litigation and the completion of any appeals therefrom, it shall have fully performed its obligations with respect to that matter and shall not be liable for any loss or damage caused thereby.

(b)   In the event of any litigation, including litigation by the Company or with the Company's consent, the Company shall have no liability for loss or damage until there has been a final determination by a court of competent jurisdiction, and disposition of all appeals therefrom, adverse to the title as insured.

(c)   The Company shall not be liable for loss or damage to any insured for liability voluntarily assumed by the insured in settling any claim or suit without the prior written consent of the Company.

10.   REDUCTION OF INSURANCE; REDUCTION OR TERMINATION OF LIABILITY.

All payments under this policy, except payments made for costs, attorneys' fees and expenses, shall reduce the amount of the insurance pro tanto.

11.   LIABILITY NONCUMULATIVE.

It is expressly understood that the amount of insurance under this policy shall be reduced by any amount the Company may pay under any policy insuring a mortgage to which exception is taken in Schedule B or to which the insured has agreed, assumed, or taken subject, or which is hereafter executed by an insured and which is a charge or lien on the estate or interest described or referred to in Schedule A, and the amount so paid shall be deemed a payment under this policy to the insured owner.

12.   PAYMENT OF LOSS.

(a)   No payment shall be made without producing this policy for endorsement of the payment unless the policy has been lost or destroyed, in which case proof of loss or destruction shall be furnished to the satisfaction of the Company.

(b)   When liability and the extent of loss or damage has been definitely fixed in accordance with these Conditions and Stipulations, the loss or damage shall be payable within 30 days thereafter.

13.   SUBROGATION UPON PAYMENT OR SETTLEMENT.

(a)   The Company's Right of Subrogation.

Whenever the Company shall have settled and paid a claim under this policy, all right of subrogation shall vest in the Company unaffected by any act of the insured claimant.

The Company shall be subrogated to and be entitled to all rights and remedies which the insured claimant would have had against any person or property in respect to the claim had this policy not been issued. If requested by the Company, the insured claimant shall transfer to the Company all rights and remedies against any person or property necessary in order to perfect this right of subrogation. The

10

EXHIBIT 13–1

Owner's Policy—ALTA *(continued)*

| American Land Title Association | Owner's Policy
Revised 10/17/92 |

insured claimant shall permit the Company to sue, compromise or settle in the name of the insured claimant and to use the name of the insured claimant in any transaction or litigation involving these rights or remedies.

If a payment on account of a claim does not fully cover the loss of the insured claimant, the Company shall be subrogated to these rights and remedies in the proportion which the Company's payment bears to the whole amount of the loss.

If loss should result from any act of the insured claimant, as stated above, that act shall not void this policy, but the Company, in that event, shall be required to pay only that part of any losses insured against by this policy which shall exceed the amount, if any, lost to the Company by reason of the impairment by the insured claimant of the Company's right of subrogation.

(b)   The Company's Rights Against Non_insured Obligors.

The Company's right of subrogation against non-insured obligors shall exist and shall include, without limitation, the rights of the insured to indemnities, guaranties, other policies of insurance or bonds, notwithstanding any terms or conditions contained in those instruments which provide for subrogation rights by reason of this policy.

14.   ARBITRATION

Unless prohibited by applicable law, either the Company or the insured may demand arbitration pursuant to the Title Insurance Arbitration Rules of the American Arbitration Association. Arbitrable matters may include, but are not limited to, any controversy or claim between the Company and the insured arising out of or relating to this policy, any service of the Company in connection with its issuance or the breach of a policy provision or other obligation. All arbitrable matters when the Amount of Insurance is $1,000,000 or less shall be arbitrated at the option of either the Company or the insured. All arbitrable matters when the Amount of Insurance is in excess of $1,000,000 shall be arbitrated only when agreed to by both the Company and the insured. Arbitration pursuant to this policy and under the Rules in effect on the date the demand for arbitration is made or, at the option of the insured, the Rules in effect at Date of Policy shall be binding upon the parties. The award may include attorneys' fees only if the laws of the state in which the land is located permit a court to award attorneys' fees to a prevailing party. Judgment upon the award rendered by the Arbitrator(s) may be entered in any court having jurisdiction thereof.

The law of the situs of the land shall apply to an arbitration under the Title Insurance Arbitration Rules.

A copy of the Rules may be obtained from the Company upon request.

15.   LIABILITY LIMITED TO THIS POLICY; POLICY ENTIRE CONTRACT.

(a)   This policy together with all endorsements, if any, attached hereto by the Company is the entire policy and contract between the insured and the Company. In interpreting any provision of this policy, this policy shall be construed as a whole.

(b)   Any claim of loss or damage, whether or not based on negligence, and which arises out of the status of the title to the estate or interest covered hereby or by any action asserting such claim, shall be restricted to this policy.

11

(continued)

EXHIBIT 13–1

Owner's Policy—ALTA (*continued*)

American Land Title Association	Owner's Policy Revised 10/17/92

(c)   No amendment of or endorsement to this policy can be made except by a writing endorsed hereon or attached hereto signed by either the President, a Vice President, the Secretary, an Assistant Secretary, or validating officer or authorized signatory of the Company.

16.   <u>SEVERABILITY</u>.

In the event any provision of the policy is held invalid or unenforceable under applicable law, the policy shall be deemed not to include that provision and all other provisions shall remain in full force and effect.

17.   <u>NOTICES, WHERE SENT</u>.

All notices required to be given the Company and any statement in writing required to be furnished the Company shall include the number of this policy and shall be addressed to the Company at (fill in).

NOTE: Bracketed [ ] material optional

12

STATE OF GEORGIA   )
)   ss:
COUNTY OF FULTON   )

The undersigned, being duly sworn, states:

That the undersigned is the President of MARKAM INDUSTRIES, INC., a Georgia corporation (the "Company"), and is duly authorized to execute this affidavit in his capacity on behalf of the Company as well as in his individual capacity;

That the principal place of business, principal office and chief executive office of the Company is located in Gwinnett County, Georgia and has been located in said County at all times since the formation of the Company;

That the Company is the fee simple title owner of the real property described on Exhibit "A" attached hereto and incorporated herein by reference (the "Property").

That the lines and corners of the Property are clearly marked and there are no disputes concerning the location of said lines and corners;

That no improvements or repairs have been made or contracted for by the Company on the Property during the three (3) months immediately preceding the date of this affidavit, for which there are outstanding bills for labor or services performed or rendered, or for material supplied or furnished, or incurred in connection with improvements or repairs on the Property, or for the services of architects, surveyors or engineers in connection with improvements or repairs on the Property;

That, except for the matters set forth on Exhibit "B" attached hereto and incorporated herein by reference, the Property is free and clear of all claims, liens and encumbrances, and there is no outstanding indebtedness for or liens against any equipment or fixtures attached to, installed on, incorporated in or located on, or otherwise used in connection with the operation or maintenance of, the Property or the improvements thereon;

That there are no persons or other parties in possession of the Property who have a right or claim to possession extending beyond the date hereof;

That there are no suits, proceedings, judgments, bankruptcies, liens, or executions against the Company which affect title to the Property, the improvements thereon or the fixtures attached thereto;

That the undersigned is making this affidavit with the knowledge that it will be relied upon by lenders, attorneys, and title insurance companies interested in the title to the Property.

Sworn to and subscribed before me this
_____ day of _____, 20_____.

_____   _____
Notary Public   JIM BAXTER

My Commission Expires:

_____

[Notarial Seal]

EXHIBIT 13–4
Owner's Affidavit

Delmar/Cengage Learning

EXHIBIT 13–5

Completed Owner's Policy of Title Insurance

ALTA forms have been used by permission of the American Land Title Association.

SCHEDULE A

OFFICE FILE NUMBER	POLICY NUMBER	DATE OF POLICY	AMOUNT OF INSURANCE
24290.0029	11 0287 107 00070187	4/18/2010	$ 240,000.00

1.   Name of Insured:

DANIEL H. FARRIS AND MARY S. FARRIS

2.   The estate or interest in the land which is covered by this Policy is:

Fee Simple.

3.   Title to the estate or interest in the land is vested in the Insured.

DANIEL H. FARRIS AND MARY S. FARRIS by virtue of a Warranty Deed from James W. Freeman, dated April 15, 2010, filed for record April 18, 2010, and recorded in Deed Book 4318, Page 98, in the Office of the Clerk of the Superior Court of Dade County, Georgia.

4.   The land herein described is encumbered by the following mortgage or trust deed, and assignments:

Security Deed from Daniel H. Farris and Mary S. Farris to American Life Insurance Company dated April 15, 2010, recorded in Deed Book 4318, Page 101, Dade County, Georgia Records, securing an indebtedness in the original principal amount of $240,000.00.

and the mortgages or trust deeds, if any, shown in Schedule B hereof.

5.   The land referred to in this Policy is described as follows:

All that tract or parcel of land lying and being in Land Lots 5 and 6 of the 18th District of Dade County, Georgia, being Lot 24, Block A, Superior Estates, according to plat recorded in Plat Book 12 at Page 47, in the Office of the Clerk of Court of Dade County, Georgia.

This Policy valid only if Schedule B is attached.

SCHEDULE A
Owner's Form
Reorder Form No. 3529 (Rev. 1/89)

(continued)

EXHIBIT 13–5

Completed Owner's Policy of Title Insurance (*continued*)

SCHEDULE B

Policy Number 11 0287 107 00070187

EXCEPTIONS FROM COVERAGE

This policy does not insure against loss or damage by reason of the following exceptions:

General Exceptions:

(1)   Rights or claims of parties in possession not shown by the public records.

(2)   Easements or claims of easements not shown by the public records.

(3)   Taxes or special assessments which are not shown as existing liens by the public records.

Special Exceptions: The mortgage, if any referred to in Item 4 of Schedule A.

1.   All taxes subsequent to the year 2010.

2.   Building setback line of 50 feet as shown on the plat recorded in Plat Book 7, Page 20, Dade County, Georgia records.

3.   Easement from Salem Land Company to Dade Electric Co., Inc., dated August 2, 1999, and recorded at Deed Book 3997, Page 841, Dade County, Georgia Records, and subsequent years, not yet due and payable, as well as future reassessments of prior years' taxes.

Countersigned

_____

    Authorized Signatory

Schedule B of this Policy consists of _____ page(s).

EXHIBIT 13–6

Loan Policy

ALTA forms have been used by permission of the American Land Title Association.

American Land Title Association	_ **Loan Policy** **Revised 10/17/92**

POLICY OF TITLE INSURANCE

Issued by

BLANK TITLE INSURANCE COMPANY

SUBJECT TO THE EXCLUSIONS FROM COVERAGE, THE EXCEPTIONS FROM COVERAGE CONTAINED IN SCHEDULE B AND THE CONDITIONS AND STIPULATIONS, BLANK TITLE INSURANCE COMPANY, a Blank corporation, herein called the Company, insures, as of Date of Policy shown in Schedule A, against loss or damage, not exceeding the Amount of Insurance stated in Schedule A, sustained or incurred by the insured by reason of:

1. Title to the estate or interest described in Schedule A being vested other than as stated therein;

2. Any defect in or lien or encumbrance on the title;

3. Unmarketability of the title;

4. Lack of a right of access to and from the land;

5. The invalidity or unenforceability of the lien of the insured mortgage upon the title;

6. The priority of any lien or encumbrance over the lien of the insured mortgage;

7. Lack of priority of the lien of the insured mortgage over any statutory lien for services, labor or material:

    (a) arising from an improvement or work related to the land which is contracted for or commenced prior to Date of Policy; or

    (b) arising from an improvement or work related to the land which is contracted for or commenced subsequent to Date of Policy and which is financed in whole or in part by proceeds of the indebtedness secured by the insured mortgage which at Date of Policy the insured has advanced or is obligated to advance;

8. The invalidity or unenforceability of any assignment of the insured mortgage, provided the assignment is shown in Schedule A, or the failure of the assignment shown in Schedule A to vest title to the insured mortgage in the named insured assignee free and clear of all liens.

The Company will also pay the costs, attorneys' fees and expenses incurred in defense of the title or the lien of the insured mortgage, as insured, but only to the extent provided in the Conditions and Stipulations.

[Witness clause optional]

BLANK TITLE INSURANCE COMPANY

BY:_____
PRESIDENT

BY:_____
SECRETARY

Page 1 of 12

(continued)

EXHIBIT 13–6

Loan Policy (*continued*)

American Land Title Association	Loan Policy Revised 10/17/92

EXCLUSIONS FROM COVERAGE

The following matters are expressly excluded from the coverage of this policy and the Company will not pay loss or damage, costs, attorneys' fees or expenses which arise by reason of:

1. (a) Any law, ordinance or governmental regulation (including but not limited to building and zoning laws, ordinances, or regulations) restricting, regulating, prohibiting or relating to (i) the occupancy, use, or enjoyment of the land; (ii) the character, dimensions or location of any improvement now or hereafter erected on the land; (iii) a separation in ownership or a change in the dimensions or area of the land or any parcel of which the land is or was a part; or (iv) environmental protection, or the effect of any violation of these laws, ordinances or governmental regulations, except to the extent that a notice of the enforcement thereof or a notice of a defect, lien or encumbrance resulting from a violation or alleged violation affecting the land has been recorded in the public records at Date of Policy.

    (b) Any governmental police power not excluded by (a) above, except to the extent that a notice of the exercise thereof or a notice of a defect, lien or encumbrance resulting from a violation or alleged violation affecting the land has been recorded in the public records at Date of Policy.

2. Rights of eminent domain unless notice of the exercise thereof has been recorded in the public records at Date of Policy, but not excluding from coverage any taking which has occurred prior to Date of Policy which would be binding on the rights of a purchaser for value without knowledge.

3. Defects, liens, encumbrances, adverse claims or other matters:

    (a) created, suffered, assumed or agreed to by the insured claimant;

    (b) not known to the Company, not recorded in the public records at Date of Policy, but known to the insured claimant and not disclosed in writing to the Company by the insured claimant prior to the date the insured claimant became an insured under this policy;

    (c) resulting in no loss or damage to the insured claimant;

    (d) attaching or created subsequent to Date of Policy (except to the extent that this policy insures the priority of the lien of the insured mortgage over any statutory lien for services, labor or material); or

    (e) resulting in loss or damage which would not have been sustained if the insured claimant had paid value for the insured mortgage.

4. Unenforceability of the lien of the insured mortgage because of the inability or failure of the insured at Date of Policy, or the inability or failure of any subsequent owner of the indebtedness, to comply with applicable doing business laws of the state in which the land is situated.

5. Invalidity or unenforceability of the lien of the insured mortgage, or claim thereof, which arises out of the transaction evidenced by the insured mortgage and is based upon usury or any consumer credit protection or truth in lending law.

6. Any statutory lien for services, labor or materials (or the claim of priority of any statutory lien for services, labor or materials over the lien of the insured mortgage) arising from an improvement or work related to the land which is contracted for and commenced subsequent to Date of Policy and is not financed in whole or in part by proceeds of the indebtedness secured by the insured mortgage which at Date of Policy the insured has advanced or is obligated to advance.

Page 2 of 12

(*continued*)

EXHIBIT 13–6

Loan Policy (*continued*)

American Land Title Association	**Loan Policy**
	Revised 10/17/92

---

7.   Any claim, which arises out of the transaction creating the interest of the mortgagee insured by this policy, by reason of the operation of federal bankruptcy, state insolvency, or similar creditors' rights laws, that is based on:

    (a)   the transaction creating the interest of the insured mortgagee being deemed a fraudulent conveyance or fraudulent transfer; or

    (b)   the subordination of the interest of the insured mortgagee as a result of the application of the doctrine of equitable subordination; or

    (c)   the transaction creating the interest of the insured mortgagee being deemed a preferential transfer except where the preferential transfer results from the failure:

        (i)   to timely record the instrument of transfer; or

        (ii)   of such recordation to impart notice to a purchaser for value or a judgment or lien creditor.

Page 3 of 12

(continued)

EXHIBIT 13–6

Loan Policy (*continued*)

American Land Title Association	Loan Policy Revised 10/17/92

SCHEDULE A

[File No.   ]   Policy No.
                     Amount of Insurance $
                     [Premium $]
                                    a.m.
Date of Policy_____   [at   p.m.]

1.   Name of Insured:

2.   The estate or interest in the land which is encumbered by the insured mortgage is:

3.   Title to the estate or interest in the land is vested in:

4.   The insured mortgage and assignments thereof, if any, are described as follows:

[5.   The land referred to in this policy is described as follows:]

If Paragraph 5 is omitted, a Schedule C, captioned the same as Paragraph 5, must be used.

Page 4 of 12

(*continued*)

EXHIBIT 13–6

Loan Policy (*continued*)

American Land Title Association	**Loan Policy**
	Revised 10/17/92

SCHEDULE B

[File No.   ]   Policy No.

EXCEPTIONS FROM COVERAGE

This policy does not insure against loss or damage (and the Company will not pay costs, attorneys' fees or expenses) which arise by reason of:

PART I

1.

[POLICY MAY INCLUDE REGIONAL EXCEPTIONS IF SO

2.   DESIRED BY ISSUING COMPANY]

[VARIABLE EXCEPTIONS SUCH AS TAXES, EASEMENTS, CC & Rs, ETC.]

3.

4.

Note: If there are matters which affect the title to the estate or interest in the land described in Schedule [A][C], but which are subordinate to the lien of the insured mortgage, Part II of Schedule B must be added, or Part I of Schedule B must contain the following statement:

"Matters which affect the title to the estate or interest, but which are subordinate to the lien of the insured mortgage"

PART II

In addition to the matters set forth in Part I of this Schedule, the title to the estate or interest in the land described or referred to in Schedule [A][C] is subject to the following matters, if any be shown, but the Company insures that these matters are subordinate to the lien or charge of the insured mortgage upon the estate or interest:

Page 5 of 12

(continued)

EXHIBIT 13–6

Loan Policy (*continued*)

American Land Title Association	**Loan Policy** **Revised 10/17/92**

CONDITIONS AND STIPULATIONS

1. DEFINITION OF TERMS.

    The following terms when used in this policy mean:

    (a) "insured": the insured named in Schedule A. The term "insured" also includes

    (i) the owner of the indebtedness secured by the insured mortgage and each successor in ownership of the indebtedness except a successor who is an obligor under the provisions of Section 12(c) of these Conditions and Stipulations (reserving, however, all rights and defenses as to any successor that the Company would have had against any predecessor insured, unless the successor acquired the indebtedness as a purchaser for value without knowledge of the asserted defect, lien, encumbrance, adverse claim or other matter insured against by this policy as affecting title to the estate or interest in the land);

    (ii) any governmental agency or governmental instrumentality which is an insurer or guarantor under an insurance contract or guaranty insuring or guaranteeing the indebtedness secured by the insured mortgage, or any part thereof, whether named as an insured herein or not;

    (iii) the parties designated in Section 2(a) of these Conditions and Stipulations.

    (b) "insured claimant": an insured claiming loss or damage.

    (c) "knowledge" or "known": actual knowledge, not constructive knowledge or notice which may be imputed to an insured by reason of the public records as defined in this policy or any other records which impart constructive notice of matters affecting the land.

    (d) "land": the land described or referred to in Schedule [A][C], and improvements affixed thereto which by law constitute real property. The term "land" does not include any property beyond the lines of the area described or referred to in Schedule [A][C], nor any right, title, interest, estate or easement in abutting streets, roads, avenues, alleys, lanes, ways or waterways, but nothing herein shall modify or limit the extent to which a right of access to and from the land is insured by this policy.

    (e) "mortgage": mortgage, deed of trust, trust deed, or other security instrument.

    (f) "public records": records established under state statutes at Date of Policy for the purpose of imparting constructive notice of matters relating to real property to purchasers for value and without knowledge. With respect to Section 1(a)(iv) of the Exclusions From Coverage, "public records" shall also include environmental protection liens filed in the records of the clerk of the United States district court for the district in which the land is located.

    (g) "unmarketability of the title": an alleged or apparent matter affecting the title to the land, not excluded or excepted from coverage, which would entitle a purchaser of the estate or interest described in Schedule A or the insured mortgage to be released from the obligation to purchase by virtue of a contractual condition requiring the delivery of marketable title.

2. CONTINUATION OF INSURANCE.

    (a) After Acquisition of Title. The coverage of this policy shall continue in force as of Date of Policy in favor of (i) an insured who acquires all or any part of the estate or interest in the land by foreclosure, trustee's sale, conveyance in lieu of foreclosure, or other legal manner which discharges the lien of the insured mortgage; (ii) a transferee of the estate or interest so acquired from an insured corporation, provided the transferee is the parent or wholly-owned subsidiary of the insured corporation, and their corporate successors by operation of law and not by purchase, subject to any rights or defenses the Company may have against any predecessor insureds; and (iii) any governmental agency or governmental instrumentality which acquires all or any part of the estate or interest pursuant to a contract of insurance or guaranty insuring or guaranteeing the

    Page 6 of 12

(continued)

EXHIBIT 13–6

Loan Policy (*continued*)

American Land Title Association | Loan Policy
Revised 10/17/92

---

indebtedness secured by the insured mortgage.

(b)   <u>After Conveyance of Title</u>. The coverage of this policy shall continue in force as of Date of Policy in favor of an insured only so long as the insured retains an estate or interest in the land, or holds an indebtedness secured by a purchase money mortgage given by a purchaser from the insured, or only so long as the insured shall have liability by reason of covenants of warranty made by the insured in any transfer or conveyance of the estate or interest. This policy shall not continue in force in favor of any purchaser from the insured of either (i) an estate or interest in the land, or (ii) an indebtedness secured by a purchase money mortgage given to the insured.

(c)   <u>Amount of Insurance</u>. The amount of insurance after the acquisition or after the conveyance shall in neither event exceed the least of:

(i)   the Amount of Insurance stated in Schedule A;

(ii)   the amount of the principal of the indebtedness secured by the insured mortgage as of Date of Policy, interest thereon, expenses of foreclosure, amounts advanced pursuant to the insured mortgage to assure compliance with laws or to protect the lien of the insured mortgage prior to the time of acquisition of the estate or interest in the land and secured thereby and reasonable amounts expended to prevent deterioration of improvements, but reduced by the amount of all payments made; or

(iii)   the amount paid by any governmental agency or governmental instrumentality, if the agency or instrumentality is the insured claimant, in the acquisition of the estate or interest in satisfaction of its insurance contract or guaranty.

3.   <u>NOTICE OF CLAIM TO BE GIVEN BY INSURED CLAIMANT.</u>

The insured shall notify the Company promptly in writing (i) in case of any litigation as set forth in Section 4(a) below, (ii) in case knowledge shall come to an insured hereunder of any claim of title or interest which is adverse to the title to the estate or interest or the lien of the insured mortgage, as insured, and which might cause loss or damage for which the Company may be liable by virtue of this policy, or (iii) if title to the estate or interest or the lien of the insured mortgage, as insured, is rejected as unmarketable. If prompt notice shall not be given to the Company, then as to the insured all liability of the Company shall terminate with regard to the matter or matters for which prompt notice is required; provided, however, that failure to notify the Company shall in no case prejudice the rights of any insured under this policy unless the Company shall be prejudiced by the failure and then only to the extent of the prejudice.

4.   <u>DEFENSE AND PROSECUTION OF ACTIONS; DUTY OF INSURED CLAIMANT TO COOPERATE.</u>

(a)   Upon written request by the insured and subject to the options contained in Section 6 of these Conditions and Stipulations, the Company, at its own cost and without unreasonable delay, shall provide for the defense of an insured in litigation in which any third party asserts a claim adverse to the title or interest as insured, but only as to those stated causes of action alleging a defect, lien or encumbrance or other matter insured against by this policy. The Company shall have the right to select counsel of its choice (subject to the right of the insured to object for reasonable cause) to represent the insured as to those stated causes of action and shall not be liable for and will not pay the fees of any other counsel. The Company will not pay any fees, costs or expenses incurred by the insured in the defense of those causes of action which allege matters not insured against by this policy.

(b)   The Company shall have the right, at its own cost, to institute and prosecute any action or proceeding or to do any other act which in its opinion may be necessary or desirable to establish the title to the estate or interest or the lien of the insured mortgage, as insured, or to prevent or reduce loss or damage to the insured. The Company may take any appropriate action under the terms of this policy, whether or not it shall be liable hereunder, and shall not thereby concede liability or waive any provision of this policy. If the Company shall exercise its rights under this paragraph, it shall do so diligently.

Page 7 of 12

EXHIBIT 13–6

Loan Policy (*continued*)

American Land Title Association   **Loan Policy**
                                                    Revised 10/17/92

(c)   Whenever the Company shall have brought an action or interposed a defense as required or permitted by the provisions of this policy, the Company may pursue any litigation to final determination by a court of competent jurisdiction and expressly reserves the right, in its sole discretion, to appeal from any adverse judgment or order.

(d)   In all cases where this policy permits or requires the Company to prosecute or provide for the defense of any action or proceeding, the insured shall secure to the Company the right to so prosecute or provide defense in the action or proceeding, and all appeals therein, and permit the Company to use, at its option, the name of the insured for this purpose. Whenever requested by the Company, the insured, at the Company's expense, shall give the Company all reasonable aid (i) in any action or proceeding, securing evidence, obtaining witnesses, prosecuting or defending the action or proceeding, or effecting settlement, and (ii) in any other lawful act which in the opinion of the Company may be necessary or desirable to establish the title to the estate or interest or the lien of the insured mortgage, as insured. If the Company is prejudiced by the failure of the insured to furnish the required cooperation, the Company's obligations to the insured under the policy shall terminate, including any liability or obligation to defend, prosecute, or continue any litigation, with regard to the matter or matters requiring such cooperation.

5.   PROOF OF LOSS OR DAMAGE.

In addition to and after the notices required under Section 3 of these Conditions and Stipulations have been provided the Company, a proof of loss or damage signed and sworn to by the insured claimant shall be furnished to the Company within 90 days after the insured claimant shall ascertain the facts giving rise to the loss or damage. The proof of loss or damage shall describe the defect in, or lien or encumbrance on the title, or other matter insured against by this policy which constitutes the basis of loss or damage and shall state, to the extent possible, the basis of calculating the amount of the loss or damage. If the Company is prejudiced by the failure of the insured claimant to provide the required proof of loss or damage, the Company's obligations to the insured under the policy shall terminate, including any liability or obligation to defend, prosecute, or continue any litigation, with regard to the matter or matters requiring such proof of loss or damage.

In addition, the insured claimant may reasonably be required to submit to examination under oath by any authorized representative of the Company and shall produce for examination, inspection and copying, at such reasonable times and places as may be designated by any authorized representative of the Company, all records, books, ledgers, checks, correspondence and memoranda, whether bearing a date before or after Date of Policy, which reasonably pertain to the loss or damage. Further, if requested by any authorized representative of the Company, the insured claimant shall grant its permission, in writing, for any authorized representative of the Company to examine, inspect and copy all records, books, ledgers, checks, correspondence and memoranda in the custody or control of a third party, which reasonably pertain to the loss or damage. All information designated as confidential by the insured claimant provided to the Company pursuant to this Section shall not be disclosed to others unless, in the reasonable judgment of the Company, it is necessary in the administration of the claim. Failure of the insured claimant to submit for examination under oath, produce other reasonably requested information or grant permission to secure reasonably necessary information from third parties as required in this paragraph, unless prohibited by law or governmental regulation, shall terminate any liability of the Company under this policy as to that claim.

6.   OPTIONS TO PAY OR OTHERWISE SETTLE CLAIMS; TERMINATION OF LIABILITY.

In case of a claim under this policy, the Company shall have the following additional options:

(a)   To Pay or Tender Payment of the Amount of Insurance or to Purchase the Indebtedness.

(i)   to pay or tender payment of the amount of insurance under this policy together with any costs, attorneys' fees and expenses incurred by the insured claimant, which were authorized by the Company, up to the time of payment or tender of payment and which the Company is obligated to pay; or

(continued)

EXHIBIT 13–6

Loan Policy (*continued*)

American Land Title Association	Loan Policy Revised 10/17/92

(ii)   to purchase the indebtedness secured by the insured mortgage for the amount owing thereon together with any costs, attorneys' fees and expenses incurred by the insured claimant which were authorized by the Company up to the time of purchase and which the Company is obligated to pay.

If the Company offers to purchase the indebtedness as herein provided, the owner of the indebtedness shall transfer, assign, and convey the indebtedness and the insured mortgage, together with any collateral security, to the Company upon payment therefore.

Upon the exercise by the Company of either of the options provided for in paragraphs a(i) or (ii), all liability and obligations to the insured under this policy, other than to make the payment required in those paragraphs, shall terminate, including any liability or obligation to defend, prosecute, or continue any litigation, and the policy shall be surrendered to the Company for cancellation.

(b)   <u>To Pay or Otherwise Settle With Parties Other than the Insured or With the Insured Claimant</u>.

(i)   to pay or otherwise settle with other parties for or in the name of an insured claimant any claim insured against under this policy, together with any costs, attorneys' fees and expenses incurred by the insured claimant which were authorized by the Company up to the time of payment and which the Company is obligated to pay; or

(ii)   to pay or otherwise settle with the insured claimant the loss or damage provided for under this policy, together with any costs, attorneys' fees and expenses incurred by the insured claimant which were authorized by the Company up to the time of payment and which the Company is obligated to pay.

Upon the exercise by the Company of either of the options provided for in paragraphs b(i) or (ii), the Company's obligations to the insured under this policy for the claimed loss or damage, other than the payments required to be made, shall terminate, including any liability or obligation to defend, prosecute or continue any litigation.

7.   <u>DETERMINATION AND EXTENT OF LIABILITY</u>.

This policy is a contract of indemnity against actual monetary loss or damage sustained or incurred by the insured claimant who has suffered loss or damage by reason of matters insured against by this policy and only to the extent herein described.

(a)   The liability of the Company under this policy shall not exceed the least of:

(i)   the Amount of Insurance stated in Schedule A, or, if applicable, the amount of insurance as defined in Section 2 (c) of these Conditions and Stipulations;

(ii)   the amount of the unpaid principal indebtedness secured by the insured mortgage as limited or provided under Section 8 of these Conditions and Stipulations or as reduced under Section 9 of these Conditions and Stipulations, at the time the loss or damage insured against by this policy occurs, together with interest thereon; or

(iii)   the difference between the value of the insured estate or interest as insured and the value of the insured estate or interest subject to the defect, lien or encumbrance insured against by this policy.

(b)   In the event the insured has acquired the estate or interest in the manner described in Section 2(a) of these Conditions and Stipulations or has conveyed the title, then the liability of the Company shall continue as set forth in Section 7(a) of these Conditions and Stipulations.

(c)   The Company will pay only those costs, attorneys' fees and expenses incurred in accordance with Section 4 of these Conditions and Stipulations.

Page 9 of 12

(continued)

EXHIBIT 13–6

Loan Policy (*continued*)

American Land Title Association	**Loan Policy** **Revised 10/17/92**

---

8. <u>LIMITATION OF LIABILITY</u>.

    (a)   If the Company establishes the title, or removes the alleged defect, lien or encumbrance, or cures the lack of a right of access to or from the land, or cures the claim of unmarketability of title, or otherwise establishes the lien of the insured mortgage, all as insured, in a reasonably diligent manner by any method, including litigation and the completion of any appeals therefrom, it shall have fully performed its obligations with respect to that matter and shall not be liable for any loss or damage caused thereby.

    (b)   In the event of any litigation, including litigation by the Company or with the Company's consent, the Company shall have no liability for loss or damage until there has been a final determination by a court of competent jurisdiction, and disposition of all appeals therefrom, adverse to the title or to the lien of the insured mortgage, as insured.

    (c)   The Company shall not be liable for loss or damage to any insured for liability voluntarily assumed by the insured in settling any claim or suit without the prior written consent of the Company.

    (d)   The Company shall not be liable for: (i) any indebtedness created subsequent to Date of Policy except for advances made to protect the lien of the insured mortgage and secured thereby and reasonable amounts expended to prevent deterioration of improvements; or (ii) construction loan advances made subsequent to Date of Policy, except construction loan advances made subsequent to Date of Policy for the purpose of financing in whole or in part the construction of an improvement to the land which at Date of Policy were secured by the insured mortgage and which the insured was and continued to be obligated to advance at and after Date of Policy.

9. <u>REDUCTION OF INSURANCE; REDUCTION OR TERMINATION OF LIABILITY</u>.

    (a)   All payments under this policy, except payments made for costs, attorneys' fees and expenses, shall reduce the amount of the insurance pro tanto. However, any payments made prior to the acquisition of title to the estate or interest as provided in Section 2(a) of these Conditions and Stipulations shall not reduce pro tanto the amount of the insurance afforded under this policy except to the extent that the payments reduce the amount of the indebtedness secured by the insured mortgage.

    (b)   Payment in part by any person of the principal of the indebtedness, or any other obligation secured by the insured mortgage, or any voluntary partial satisfaction or release of the insured mortgage, to the extent of the payment, satisfaction or release, shall reduce the amount of insurance pro tanto. The amount of insurance may thereafter be increased by accruing interest and advances made to protect the lien of the insured mortgage and secured thereby, with interest thereon, provided in no event shall the amount of insurance be greater than the Amount of Insurance stated in Schedule A.

    (c)   Payment in full by any person or the voluntary satisfaction or release of the insured mortgage shall terminate all liability of the Company except as provided in Section 2(a) of these Conditions and Stipulations.

10. <u>LIABILITY NONCUMULATIVE</u>.

    If the insured acquires title to the estate or interest in satisfaction of the indebtedness secured by the insured mortgage, or any part thereof, it is expressly understood that the amount of insurance under this policy shall be reduced by any amount the Company may pay under any policy insuring a mortgage to which exception is taken in Schedule B or to which the insured has agreed, assumed, or taken subject, or which is hereafter executed by an insured and which is a charge or lien on the estate or interest described or referred to in Schedule A, and the amount so paid shall be deemed a payment under this policy.

(continued)

EXHIBIT 13–6

Loan Policy (*continued*)

American Land Title Association **Loan Policy**
 Revised 10/17/92

---

11.   PAYMENT OF LOSS.

(a)   No payment shall be made without producing this policy for endorsement of the payment unless the policy has been lost or destroyed, in which case proof of loss or destruction shall be furnished to the satisfaction of the Company.

(b)   When liability and the extent of loss or damage has been definitely fixed in accordance with these Conditions and Stipulations, the loss or damage shall be payable within 30 days thereafter.

12.   SUBROGATION UPON PAYMENT OR SETTLEMENT.

(a)   The Company's Right of Subrogation.

Whenever the Company shall have settled and paid a claim under this policy, all right of subrogation shall vest in the Company unaffected by any act of the insured claimant.

The Company shall be subrogated to and be entitled to all rights and remedies which the insured claimant would have had against any person or property in respect to the claim had this policy not been issued. If requested by the Company, the insured claimant shall transfer to the Company all rights and remedies against any person or property necessary in order to perfect this right of subrogation. The insured claimant shall permit the Company to sue, compromise or settle in the name of the insured claimant and to use the name of the insured claimant in any transaction or litigation involving these rights or remedies.

If a payment on account of a claim does not fully cover the loss of the insured claimant, the Company shall be subrogated to all rights and remedies of the insured claimant after the insured claimant shall have recovered its principal, interest, and costs of collection.

(b)   The Insured's Rights and Limitations.

Notwithstanding the foregoing, the owner of the indebtedness secured by the insured mortgage, provided the priority of the lien of the insured mortgage or its enforceability is not affected, may release or substitute the personal liability of any debtor or guarantor, or extend or otherwise modify the terms of payment, or release a portion of the estate or interest from the lien of the insured mortgage, or release any collateral security for the indebtedness.

When the permitted acts of the insured claimant occur and the insured has knowledge of any claim of title or interest adverse to the title to the estate or interest or the priority or enforceability of the lien of the insured mortgage, as insured, the Company shall be required to pay only that part of any losses insured against by this policy which shall exceed the amount, if any, lost to the Company by reason of the impairment by the insured claimant of the Company's right of subrogation.

(c)   The Company's Rights Against Non-insured Obligors.

The Company's right of subrogation against non-insured obligors shall exist and shall include, without limitation, the rights of the insured to indemnities, guaranties, other policies of insurance or bonds, notwithstanding any terms or conditions contained in those instruments which provide for subrogation rights by reason of this policy.

The Company's right of subrogation shall not be avoided by acquisition of the insured mortgage by an obligor (except an obligor described in Section 1(a)(ii) of these Conditions and Stipulations) who acquires the insured mortgage as a result of an indemnity, guarantee, other policy of insurance, or bond and the obligor will not be an insured under this policy, notwithstanding Section 1(a)(i) of these Conditions and Stipulations.

EXHIBIT 13–6

Loan Policy (*continued*)

American Land Title Association	Loan Policy
	Revised 10/17/92

---

13. ARBITRATION.

Unless prohibited by applicable law, either the Company or the insured may demand arbitration pursuant to the Title Insurance Arbitration Rules of the American Arbitration Association. Arbitrable matters may include, but are not limited to, any controversy or claim between the Company and the insured arising out of or relating to this policy, any service of the Company in connection with its issuance or the breach of a policy provision or other obligation. All arbitrable matters when the Amount of Insurance is $1,000,000 or less shall be arbitrated at the option of either the Company or the insured. All arbitrable matters when the Amount of Insurance is in excess of $1,000,000 shall be arbitrated only when agreed to by both the Company and the insured. Arbitration pursuant to this policy and under the Rules in effect on the date the demand for arbitration is made or, at the option of the insured, the Rules in effect at Date of Policy shall be binding upon the parties. The award may include attorneys' fees only if the laws of the state in which the land is located permit a court to award attorneys' fees to a prevailing party. Judgment upon the award rendered by the Arbitrator(s) may be entered in any court having jurisdiction thereof.

The law of the situs of the land shall apply to an arbitration under the Title Insurance Arbitration Rules.

A copy of the Rules may be obtained from the Company upon request.

14. LIABILITY LIMITED TO THIS POLICY; POLICY ENTIRE CONTRACT.

(a)   This policy together with all endorsements, if any, attached hereto by the Company is the entire policy and contract between the insured and the Company. In interpreting any provision of this policy, this policy shall be construed as a whole.

(b)   Any claim of loss or damage, whether or not based on negligence, and which arises out of the status of the lien of the insured mortgage or of the title to the estate or interest covered hereby or by any action asserting such claim, shall be restricted to this policy.

(c)   No amendment of or endorsement to this policy can be made except by a writing endorsed hereon or attached hereto signed by either the President, a Vice President, the Secretary, an Assistant Secretary, or validating officer or authorized signatory of the Company.

15. SEVERABILITY.

In the event any provision of this policy is held invalid or unenforceable under applicable law, the policy shall be deemed not to include that provision and all other provisions shall remain in full force and effect.

16. NOTICES, WHERE SENT.

All notices required to be given the Company and any statement in writing required to be furnished the Company shall include the number of this policy and shall be addressed to the Company at (fill in).

NOTE: Bracketed [ ] material optional

Page 12 of 12

EXHIBIT 13–8

Zoning Endorsement

ALTA forms have been used by permission of the American Land Title Association.

American Land Title Association   **Endorsement 3 (Zoning)**
                                                        Revised 10/17/98

ENDORSEMENT

Attached to Policy No.

Issued by

BLANK TITLE INSURANCE COMPANY

The Company insures the insured against loss or damage sustained in the event that, at Date of Policy:

1. According to applicable zoning ordinances and amendments thereto, the land is not classified Zone _____.

2. The following use or uses are not allowed under that classification:

There shall be no liability under this endorsement based on:

(a)   Lack of compliance with any conditions, restrictions, or requirements contained in the zoning ordinances and amendments thereto mentioned above, including but not limited to the failure to secure necessary consents or authorizations as a prerequisite to the use or uses.

(b)   The invalidity of the ordinances and amendments thereto mentioned above until after a final decree of a court of competent jurisdiction adjudicating the invalidity, the effect of which is to prohibit the use or uses.

(c)   The refusal of any person to purchase, lease or lend money on the estate or interest covered by this policy.

This endorsement is issued as part of the policy. Except as it expressly states, it does not (i) modify any of the terms and provisions of the policy, (ii) modify any prior endorsements, (iii) extend the Date of Policy, or (iv) increase the Amount of Insurance. To the extent a provision of the policy or a previous endorsement is inconsistent with an express provision of this endorsement, this endorsement controls. Otherwise, this endorsement is subject to all of the terms and provisions of the policy and of any prior endorsements.

[Witness clause optional]

                                BLANK TITLE INSURANCE COMPANY

                                BY:

Page 1 of 1

ENDORSEMENT

ATTACHED TO POLICY NO.

ISSUED BY

The Company insures the owner of the indebtedness secured by the insured mortgage against loss of damage sustained by reason of:

1.   Any incorrectness in the assurance that, at Date of Policy:

   (a) There are no covenants, conditions or restrictions under which the lien of the mortgage referred to in Schedule A can be divested, subordinated or extinguished, or its validity, priority or enforceability impaired.

   (b) Unless expressly excepted in Schedule B:

      (1) There are no present violations on the land of any enforceable covenants, conditions or restrictions, nor do any existing improvements on the land violate any building setback lines shown on a plat of subdivision recorded or filed in the public records.

      (2) Any instrument referred to in Schedule B as containing covenants, conditions or restrictions on the land does not, in addition, (i) establish an easement on the land; (ii) provide a lien for liquidated damages; (iii) provide for a private charge or assessment; (iv) provide for an option to purchase, a right of first refusal of the prior approval of a future purchaser or occupant.

      (3) There is no encroachment of existing improvements located on the land onto adjoining land, nor any encroachment onto the land of existing improvements located on adjoining land.

      (4) There is no encroachment of existing improvements located on the land onto that portion of the land subject to any easement excepted in Schedule B.

      (5) There are no notices of violation of covenants, conditions and restrictions relating to environmental protection recorded or filed in the public records.

2.   Any future violation on the land of any existing covenants, conditions or restrictions occurring prior to the acquisition of title to the estate or interest in the land by the Insured, provided the violation results in:

   (a) Invalidity, loss of priority, or unenforceability of the lien of the insured mortgage; or

   (b) loss of title to the estate or interest in the land if the Insured shall acquire title in satisfaction of the indebtedness secured by the insured mortgage.

3.   Damage to existing improvements, including lawns, shrubbery or trees:

   which are located on or encroached upon that portion of the land subject to an easement excepted in Schedule B, which damage results from the exercise of the right to maintain the easement for the purpose for which it was granted or reserved.

4.   Any final court order or judgment requiring the removal from any land adjoining the land of any encroachment excepted in Schedule B.

5.   Any final court order or judgment denying the right to maintain any existing improvements on the land because of any violation of covenants, conditions or restrictions or building setback lines shown on a plat of subdivision recorded or filed in the public records.

EXHIBIT 13–9

Comprehensive Endorsement

ALTA forms have been used by permission of the American Land Title Association.

(continued)

EXHIBIT 13–9

Comprehensive Endorsement
(*continued*)

Whenever in this endorsement the words "covenants, conditions or restrictions" appear, they shall not be deemed to refer to or include the terms, covenants, conditions or limitations contained in any instrument creating a lease.

As used in paragraphs 1(b)(1) and 5, the words "covenants, conditions or restrictions" shall not be deemed to refer to or include any covenants, conditions or restrictions relating to environmental protection.

This endorsement is made a part of the policy and is subject to all of the terms and provisions thereof and any prior endorsements thereto. Except to the extent expressly stated, it neither modifies any of the terms and provisions of the policy and any prior endorsements, nor does it extend the effective date of the policy and any prior endorsements, nor does it include the face amount thereof.

Dated:

_____

Authorized Signatory

CLTA Endorsement - Form 100.2 (Rev. 3/27/92)
ALTA Endorsement - Form 9

EXHIBIT 13–10

Survey Endorsement

ALTA forms have been used by permission of the American Land Title Association.

American Land Title Association   **Endorsement 25-06 (Same as Survey)**
                                                       Adopted 10-16-08

ENDORSEMENT

Attached to Policy No. _____

Issued by

BLANK TITLE INSURANCE COMPANY

The Company insures against loss or damage sustained by the Insured by reason of the failure of the Land as described in Schedule A to be the same as that identified on the survey made by _____ dated _____, and designated Job No. _____.

This endorsement is issued as part of the policy. Except as it expressly states, it does not (i) modify any of the terms and provisions of the policy, (ii) modify any prior endorsements, (iii) extend the Date of Policy, or (iv) increase the Amount of Insurance. To the extent a provision of the policy or a previous endorsement is inconsistent with an express provision of this endorsement, this endorsement controls. Otherwise, this endorsement is subject to all of the terms and provisions of the policy and of any prior endorsements.

[Witness clause optional]

BLANK TITLE INSURANCE COMPANY

By: _____
      Authorized Signatory

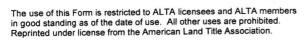

EXHIBIT 13–11

Access Endorsement

ALTA forms have been used by permission of the American Land Title Association.

American Land Title Association   **Endorsement 17-06 (Access and Entry)**
Adopted 6-17-06

ENDORSEMENT

Attached to Policy No. _____

Issued by

BLANK TITLE INSURANCE COMPANY

The Company insures against loss or damage sustained by the Insured if, at Date of Policy (i) the Land does not abut and have both actual vehicular and pedestrian access to and from [insert name of street, road, or highway] (the "Street"), (ii) the Street is not physically open and publicly maintained, or (iii) the Insured has no right to use existing curb cuts or entries along that portion of the Street abutting the Land.

This endorsement is issued as part of the policy. Except as it expressly states, it does not (i) modify any of the terms and provisions of the policy, (ii) modify any prior endorsements, (iii) extend the Date of Policy, or (iv) increase the Amount of Insurance. To the extent a provision of the policy or a previous endorsement is inconsistent with an express provision of this endorsement, this endorsement controls. Otherwise, this endorsement is subject to all of the terms and provisions of the policy and of any prior endorsements.

[Witness clause optional]

BLANK TITLE INSURANCE COMPANY

By: _____
       Authorized Signatory

AMERICAN
LAND TITLE
ASSOCIATION

EXHIBIT 13–12

Contiguity Endorsement

ALTA forms have been used by permission of the American Land Title Association.

American Land Title Association   **Endorsement Form 19.1-06 (Contiguity-Single Parcel)**
                                                                    Adopted 6-17-06

[For use when the Insured desires contiguity coverage between the Land and some other parcel of land]

ENDORSEMENT

Attached to Policy No. _____

Issued by

BLANK TITLE INSURANCE COMPANY

The Company insures against loss or damage sustained by the Insured by reason of:

1. the failure of the Land to be contiguous to **[describe the land that is contiguous to the Land by its legal description or by reference to a recorded instrument – e.g. ". . . that certain parcel of real property legally described in the deed recorded as Instrument No. _____, records of _____ County, State of _____]** along the _____ boundary line[s]; or

2. the presence of any gaps, strips, or gores separating the contiguous boundary lines described above.

This endorsement is issued as part of the policy. Except as it expressly states, it does not (i) modify any of the terms and provisions of the policy, (ii) modify any prior endorsements, (iii) extend the Date of Policy, or (iv) increase the Amount of Insurance. To the extent a provision of the policy or a previous endorsement is inconsistent with an express provision of this endorsement, this endorsement controls. Otherwise, this endorsement is subject to all of the terms and provisions of the policy and of any prior endorsements.

[Witness clause optional]

BLANK TITLE INSURANCE COMPANY

By: _____

     Authorized Signatory

EXHIBIT 13–13

Usury Endorsement

ALTA forms have been used by permission of the American Land Title Association.

American Land Title Association   **Endorsement 27-06 (Usury)**
                                                        Adopted 10-16-08

ENDORSEMENT

Attached to Policy No. _____

Issued by

BLANK TITLE INSURANCE COMPANY

The Company insures against loss or damage sustained by the Insured by reason of the invalidity or unenforceability of the lien of the Insured Mortgage as security for the Indebtedness because the loan secured by the Insured Mortgage violates the usury law of the state where the Land is located.

This endorsement is issued as part of the policy. Except as it expressly states, it does not (i) modify any of the terms and provisions of the policy, (ii) modify any prior endorsements, (iii) extend the Date of Policy, or (iv) increase the Amount of Insurance. To the extent a provision of the policy or a previous endorsement is inconsistent with an express provision of this endorsement, this endorsement controls. Otherwise, this endorsement is subject to all of the terms and provisions of the policy and of any prior endorsements.

[Witness clause optional]

BLANK TITLE INSURANCE COMPANY

By: _____
      Authorized Signatory

AMERICAN
LAND TITLE
ASSOCIATION

EXHIBIT 13–14

Utility Facility Endorsement

ALTA forms have been used by permission of the American Land Title Association.

American Land Title Association   **Endorsement 17.2-06 (Utility Access)**
                                                                                     Adopted 10-16-08

ENDORSEMENT

Attached to Policy No. _____

Issued by

BLANK TITLE INSURANCE COMPANY

The Company insures against loss or damage sustained by the Insured by reason of the lack of a right of access to the following utilities or services: **[CHECK ALL THAT APPLY]**

☐ Water service   ☐ Natural gas service   ☐ Telephone service

☐ Electrical power service   ☐ Sanitary sewer   ☐ Storm water drainage

☐ _____]   ☐ _____]   ☐ _____]

either over, under or upon rights-of-way or easements for the benefit of the Land because of:

(1) a gap or gore between the boundaries of the Land and the rights-of-way or easements;

(2) a gap between the boundaries of the rights-of-way or easements ; or

(3) a termination by a grantor, or its successor, of the rights-of-way or easements.

This endorsement is issued as part of the policy. Except as it expressly states, it does not (i) modify any of the terms and provisions of the policy, (ii) modify any prior endorsements, (iii) extend the Date of Policy, or (iv) increase the Amount of Insurance. To the extent a provision of the policy or a previous endorsement is inconsistent with an express provision of this endorsement, this endorsement controls. Otherwise, this endorsement is subject to all of the terms and provisions of the policy and of any prior endorsements.

[Witness clause optional]

BLANK TITLE INSURANCE COMPANY

By: _____
        Authorized Signatory

AMERICAN LAND TITLE ASSOCIATION

EXHIBIT 13–15

Subdivision Endorsement

ALTA forms have been used by permission of the American Land Title Association.

American Land Title Association **Endorsement 26-06 (Subdivision)**
Adopted 10-16-08

ENDORSEMENT

Attached to Policy No. _____

Issued by

BLANK TITLE INSURANCE COMPANY

The Company insures against loss or damage sustained by the Insured by reason of the failure of the Land to constitute a lawfully created parcel according to the subdivision statutes and local subdivision ordinances applicable to the Land.

This endorsement is issued as part of the policy. Except as it expressly states, it does not (i) modify any of the terms and provisions of the policy, (ii) modify any prior endorsements, (iii) extend the Date of Policy, or (iv) increase the Amount of Insurance. To the extent a provision of the policy or a previous endorsement is inconsistent with an express provision of this endorsement, this endorsement controls. Otherwise, this endorsement is subject to all of the terms and provisions of the policy and of any prior endorsements.

[Witness clause optional]

BLANK TITLE INSURANCE COMPANY

By: _____

Authorized Signatory

EXHIBIT 13–16

Tax Parcel Endorsement

ALTA forms have been used by permission of the American Land Title Association.

American Land Title Association   **Endorsement 18-06 (Single Tax Parcel)**
                                                                Adopted 6-17-06

ENDORSEMENT

Attached to Policy No. _____

Issued by

BLANK TITLE INSURANCE COMPANY

The Company insures against loss or damage sustained by the Insured by reason of the Land being taxed as part of a larger parcel of land or failing to constitute a separate tax parcel for real estate taxes.

This endorsement is issued as part of the policy. Except as it expressly states, it does not (i) modify any of the terms and provisions of the policy, (ii) modify any prior endorsements, (iii) extend the Date of Policy, or (iv) increase the Amount of Insurance. To the extent a provision of the policy or a previous endorsement is inconsistent with an express provision of this endorsement, this endorsement controls. Otherwise, this endorsement is subject to all of the terms and provisions of the policy and of any prior endorsements.

[Witness clause optional]

BLANK TITLE INSURANCE COMPANY

By: _____

     Authorized Signatory

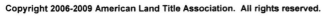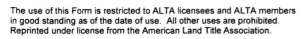

AMERICAN
LAND TITLE
ASSOCIATION

EXHIBIT 13–17

Future Advance Endorsement

ALTA forms have been used by permission of the American Land Title Association.

American Land Title Association

Endorsement 14-06 (Future Advance —Priority)
Adopted 6-17-06

ENDORSEMENT

Attached to Policy No. _____

Issued by

BLANK TITLE INSURANCE COMPANY

1. The insurance for Advances added by Sections 2 & 3 of this endorsement is subject to the exclusions in Section 4 of this endorsement and the Exclusions from Coverage in the Policy, except Exclusion 3(d), the provisions of the Conditions, and the exceptions contained in Schedule B.

   a. "Agreement," as used in this endorsement, shall mean the note or loan agreement secured by the Insured Mortgage or the Insured Mortgage.

   b. "Advances," as used in this endorsement, shall mean only those advances of principal indebtedness made after the Date of Policy as provided in the Agreement, including expenses of foreclosure, amounts advanced pursuant to the Insured Mortgage to pay taxes and insurance, assure compliance with laws, or to protect the lien of the Insured Mortgage before the time of acquisition of the Title, and reasonable amounts expended to prevent deterioration of improvements, together with interest on those advances.

2. The Company insures against loss or damage sustained by the Insured by reason of:

   a. The invalidity or unenforceability of the lien of the Insured Mortgage as security for each Advance.

   b. The lack of priority of the lien of the Insured Mortgage as security for each Advance over any lien or encumbrance on the Title.

   c. The invalidity or unenforceability or loss of priority of the lien of the Insured Mortgage as security for the Indebtedness and Advances resulting from (i) re-Advances and repayments of Indebtedness, (ii) lack of outstanding Indebtedness before an Advance, or (iii) the failure of the Insured Mortgage to comply with the requirements of state law of the state in which the Land is located to secure Advances.

3. The Company also insures against loss or damage sustained by the Insured by reason of:

   a. The invalidity or unenforceability of the lien of the Insured Mortgage resulting from any provisions of the Agreement that provide for (i) interest on interest, (ii) changes in the rate of interest, or (iii) the addition of unpaid interest to the Indebtedness.

   b. Loss of priority of the lien of the Insured Mortgage as security for the Indebtedness, interest on interest, or interest as changed in accordance with the provisions of the Insured Mortgage, which loss of priority is caused by (i) changes in the rate of interest, (ii) interest on interest, or (iii) increases in the Indebtedness resulting from the addition of unpaid interest.

   "Changes in the rate of interest," as used in this endorsement, shall mean only those changes in the rate of interest calculated pursuant to a formula provided in the Insured Mortgage at Date of Policy.

4. This endorsement does not insure against loss or damage (and the Company will not pay costs, attorneys' fees, or expenses) resulting from:

   a. Advances made after a Petition for Relief under the Bankruptcy Code (11 U.S.C.) has been filed by or on behalf of the mortgagor.

   b. The loss of priority of the lien of the Insured Mortgage, as security for Advances, to the lien of real estate taxes or assessments on the Title imposed by governmental authority arising after Date of Policy.

   c. The loss of priority of the lien of the Insured Mortgage as security for any Advance, to a federal tax lien, which Advance is made after the earlier of (i) actual knowledge of the Insured that a

---

AMERICAN
LAND TITLE
ASSOCIATION

EXHIBIT 13–18

Title Commitment

ALTA forms have been used by permission of the American Land Title Association.

AMERICAN LAND TITLE ASSOCIATION COMMITMENT

COMMITMENT FOR TITLE INSURANCE

, herein called the Company, for a valuable consideration, hereby commits to issue its policy or policies of title insurance, as identified in Schedule A, in favor of the proposed Insured named in Schedule A, as owner or mortgagee of the estate or interest covered hereby in the land described or referred to in Schedule A, upon payment of the premiums and charges therefor; all subject to the provisions of Schedules A and B and to the Conditions and Stipulations hereof.

This Commitment shall be effective only when the identity of the proposed Insured and the amount of the policy or policies committed for have been inserted in Schedule A hereof by the Company, either at the time of the issuance of this Commitment or by subsequent endorsement.

This Commitment is preliminary to the issuance of such policy or policies of title insurance and all liability and obligations hereunder shall cease and terminate six months after the effective date hereof or when the policy or policies committed for shall issue, whichever first occurs, provided that the failure to issue such policy or policies is not the fault of the Company.

IN WITNESS WHEREOF, (caused this Commitment to be signed and sealed as of the effective date of Commitment shown in Schedule A, the Commitment to become valid when countersigned by an authorized signatory.

By:

Issued by:

                                                                        President.
ATTEST:

                                                                        Secretary.

_____
Authorized Signatory

(continued)

EXHIBIT 13–18

Title Commitment (*continued*)

COMMITMENT

SCHEDULE A

¹ OFFICE FILE NUMBER		
² COMMITMENT NUMBER	³ EFFECTIVE DATE	⁴ LOAN AMOUNT
		OWNERS AMOUNT

1. Policy or Policies to be issued:
   ALTA LOAN POLICY.
   Proposed Insured:

   ALTA OWNER'S POLICY, Form
   Proposed Insured:

2. The estate or interest in the land described or referred to in this Commitment and covered herein is a fee simple, and title thereto is at the effective date hereof vested in:

3. The Land is described as follows:

Note: This Commitment consists of insert pages labeled in Schedule A, Schedule B-Section 1, and Schedule B-Section 2. This Commitment is of no force and effect unless all schedules are included, along with any Rider pages incorporated by reference in the insert pages.

(continued)

EXHIBIT 13–18

Title Commitment (*continued*)

COMMITMENT

SCHEDULE B — Section 1

Commitment Number

Requirements

The following are the requirements to be complied with:

1. Instrument(s) creating the estate or interest to be insured must be approved, executed and filed for record, to wit:

2. Payment of the full consideration to, or for the account of, the grantors or mortgagors.

3. Payment of all taxes, charges, assessments, levied and assessed against subject premises, which are due and payable.

4. Satisfactory evidence should be had that improvements and/or repairs or alterations thereto are completed; that contractor, subcontractors, labor and materialmen are all paid.

(continued)

EXHIBIT 13–18

Title Commitment (*continued*)

COMMITMENT

SCHEDULE B—Section 2

Commitment Number

Exceptions

Schedule B of the policy or policies to be issued will contain exceptions to the following matters unless the same are disposed of to the satisfaction of the Company.

1. Defects, liens, encumbrances, adverse claims or other matters, if any, created, first appearing in the public records or attaching subsequent to the effective date hereof but prior to the date the proposed Insured acquires for value of record the estate or interest or mortgage thereon covered by this Commitment.

2. Any owner's policy issued pursuant hereto will contain under Schedule B the standard exceptions set forth on the inside cover. Any loan policy will also contain under Schedule B thereof, the standard exceptions set forth on the inside cover of this commitment relating to the owner's policy.

3. Standard Exceptions 2 and 3 may be removed from the policy when a satisfactory survey and inspection of the premises is made.

4. Taxes and assessments for the year   and subsequent years.

Note: On loan policies, junior and subordinate matters, if any, will not be reflected in Schedule B.

(*continued*)

EXHIBIT 13–18

Title Commitment (*continued*)

STANDARD EXCEPTIONS FOR OWNER'S POLICY

The owner's policy will be subject to the mortgage, if any, noted under item one of Section 1 of Schedule B hereof and to the following exceptions: (1) rights or claims of parties in possession not shown by the public records; (2) encroachments, overlaps, boundary line disputes, and any matters which would be disclosed by an accurate survey and inspection of the premises; (3) easements, or claims of easements, not shown by the public records; (4) any lien, or right to a lien, for services, labor, or material heretofore or hereafter furnished, imposed by law and not shown by the public records; (5) taxes or special assessments which are not shown as existing liens by the public records.

CONDITIONS AND STIPULATIONS

1. The term "mortgage," when used herein, shall include deed of trust, trust deed, or other security instrument.

2. If the proposed Insured has or acquires actual knowledge of any defect, lien, encumbrance, adverse claim or other matter affecting the estate or interest or mortgage thereon covered by this Commitment other than those shown in Schedule B hereof, and shall fail to disclose such knowledge to the Company in writing, the Company shall be relieved from liability for any loss or damage resulting from any act of reliance hereon to the extent the Company is prejudiced by failure to so disclose such knowledge. If the proposed Insured shall disclose such knowledge to the Company, or if the Company otherwise acquires actual knowledge of any such defect, lien, encumbrance, adverse claim or other matter, the Company at its option may amend Schedule B of this Commitment accordingly, but such amendment shall not relieve the Company from liability previously incurred pursuant to paragraph 3 of these Conditions and Stipulations.

3. Liability of the Company under this Commitment shall be only to the named proposed Insured and such parties included under the definition of Insured in the form of policy or policies committed for and only for actual loss incurred in reliance hereon in undertaking in good faith (a) to comply with the requirements hereof, or (b) to eliminate exceptions shown in Schedule B, or (c) to acquire or create the estate or interest or mortgage thereon covered by this Commitment. In no event shall such liability exceed the amount stated in Schedule A for the policy or policies committed for and such liability is subject to the insuring provisions, the Exclusions from Coverage and the Conditions and Stipulations of the form of policy or policies committed for in favor of the proposed Insured which are hereby incorporated by reference and are made a part of this Commitment except as expressly modified herein.

4. Any action or actions or rights of action that the proposed Insured may have or may bring against the Company arising out of the status of the title to the estate or interest or the status of the mortgage thereon covered by this Commitment must be based on and are subject to the provisions of this Commitment.

EXHIBIT 13–19

Title Opinion

TO: __LAW FIRM_____   RE: ___TALL OAKS, INC._____
_____   _____825 Collins Hill Road_____
_____   _____Gwinnett County, Maryland_____
_____   _____
_____   _____

    A search of the record of title to the real estate described in Exhibit "A" as of an effective date of __December 19, 2010__ reveals title to be vested in __TALL OAKS, INC., a Maryland corporation__
_____, subject to the exceptions and objections set out on page two herein.

    All questions with reference to the following are expressly excepted from this opinion:

(a) All matters of record subsequent to the date of this opinion;

(b) Matters affecting the title which are not of record, or which, if of record, are not indexed in a proper manner;

(c) Such state of facts as would be disclosed by a competent civil engineer's accurate survey of the property; (A timely survey is preferred so as to determine the existence of encroachments, overhangs, overlaps, that the improvements are within the boundaries of subject property, and that the lines and corners of the property are clearly and properly marked.)

(d) Encroachments, except such as in this Attorney's opinion do not materially affect the value of the property;

(e) Title to that portion of the property within the bounds of any public road;

(f) Riparian rights of abutting owners on any stream running through property;

(g) Adverse claims of tenants in possession;

(h) All zoning laws, ordinances or regulations, municipal or county, and all governmental regulations of the use and occupancy of the property described including the regulations or condemnation of the land or any building or structure thereon;

(i) Taxes due the appropriate county and city authority;

(j) Unrecorded claims of lien for labor or material furnished for the improvement of said property;

(k) Street improvement liens which have not been properly placed of record;

(l) Unpaid and/or past due water bills and sanitation assessments;

(m) Any fee or cost associated with water or sewer systems to the property.

(n) All matters prior to the date of the basis of this opinion.

    The following indices were reviewed for a seven year period (ten years for Federal Tax Liens): General Execution Docket; Lis Pendens Docket; Suit Docket; Federal Tax Lien Docket; Uniform Commercial Code Docket; and OTHER: _____.

    The Following names were run on the above-named indices:

__Tall Oaks, Inc., a Maryland corporation_____
_____
_____
_____

This is a ___60___ year search.

EXHIBIT "A"

    ALL THAT TRACT or parcel of land lying and being in Land Lot 11 of the 7th District of Gwinnett County, Maryland, containing 5.00 acres, same being more particularly described as follows:

    BEGINNING at an iron pin found on the easterly Right-of-Way Line of Collins Road (Eighty (80´) foot Right-of-Way), which iron pin found is located northwesterly a distance of 62.54 feet along said Right-of-Way Line from a Right-of-Way monument which marks the intersection of the easterly Right-of-Way Line of said Collins Road with the northerly Right-of-Way Line of Maryland Highway No. 316 (Three hundred forty (340´) foot Right-of-Way); thence traveling along the easterly Right-of-Way Line of said Collins Road north 34 degrees 31 minutes 28 seconds west a distance of 709.55 feet to an iron pin found on said Right-of-Way Line; thence leaving said Right-of-Way Line and traveling north 55 degrees 40 minutes 26 seconds east a

(continued)

EXHIBIT 13–19

Title Opinion (*continued*)

distance of 320.59 feet to an iron pin set; thence traveling south 30 degrees 00 minutes 08 seconds east a distance of 789.15 feet to an iron pin found; thence traveling south 72 degrees 19 minutes 34 seconds west a distance of 269.96 feet to an iron pin found on the easterly Right-of-Way Line of said Collins Road, which iron pin found is the TRUE POINT OF BEGINNING.

Note: RTV means Tall Oaks, Inc.

EXCEPTIONS and OBJECTIONS

1. Mortgage from Tall Oaks, Inc. to J. H. Patton, dated 12-16-06 recorded 12-16-06 at Deed Book 4985, page 22 in the orig. princ. amt. of $490,000.00.
2. Right of Way Easement-RTV to Jackson Electric Membership Corporation, dated 8-13-98, recorded 9-10-98 at Deed Book 4886, page 17.
3. Septic Sewer Easement-RTV to the Academy, Inc. dated 3-15-96, recorded 3-17-96 at Deed Book 4801, page 301.
4. Easement for Right-of-Way from J. H. Patton to Universal Power Company, dated 2-20-88, recorded 3-6-88 at Deed Book 291, page 591.
5. Right-of-Way Deed from J. H. Patton to Gwinnett County Dept. of Transportation, dated 5-2-78, recorded 5-5-78 at Deed Book 1465, page 220.

This the 27th day of December, 2010.

Sincerely,
TITLE EXAMINER

This is a search coming out of an Owner's Policy of Title Insurance from _____ Title Insurance Company, Policy # _____, dated _____.

This is a limited search coming forward from the latest priority Purchase Money Security Deed, being at Deed Book _____, page _____.

EXHIBIT 13–20

Sample Title Commitment

Title Commitment Progress Form
Schedule A

Number 100

Effective Date
December 19, 2010

1. Policy or Policies to be issued:
     OWNER'S: $
     Proposed Insured:
   LOAN: $250,000.00
   Proposed Insured:
     Second Federal Savings and Loan Association

2. The estate or interest in the land described or referred to in this Commitment and covered herein is a fee simple, and title thereto is at the effective date hereof vested in:
   Tall Oaks, Inc.

3. The land referred to in the Commitment is described in Schedule C.

Schedule B—Section 1

The following are the requirements to be complied with:

1. Instrument(s) creating the estate or interest to be insured must be approved, executed and filed for record, to wit:
   (a) Corporate Resolution from Tall Oaks, Inc. authorizing the loan.
   (b) Mortgage from Tall Oaks, Inc. to Second Federal Savings and Loan Association.

2. Payment of the full consideration to, or for the account of, the grantors or mortgagors.

3. Payment of all taxes, charges, assessments, levied and assessed against subject premises, which are due and payable.

4. Satisfactory evidence should be had that improvements and/or repairs or alterations thereto are completed; that contractor, subcontractors, labor and materialmen are all paid.

5. Payment and satisfaction of record of mortgage from Tall Oaks, Inc. to J. H. Patton, dated 12-16-06 recorded at Deed Book 4985, page 22, Gwinnett County, Maryland Records.

Schedule B—Section 2

Schedule B of the policy or policies to be issued will contain exceptions to the following matters unless the same are disposed of to the satisfaction of the Company.

1. Defects, liens, encumbrances, adverse claims or other matters, if any, created, first appearing in the public records or attaching subsequent to the effective date hereof but prior to the date the proposed Insured acquires for value of record the estate or interest or mortgage thereon covered by this Commitment.

2. Any owner's policy issued pursuant hereto will contain under Schedule B the standard exceptions set forth at the inside cover hereof. Any loan policy will contain under Schedule B standard Exceptions 1, 2 and 3 unless a satisfactory survey and inspection of the premises is made.

3. Right-of-Way Easement—Tall Oaks, Inc. to Jackson Electric Membership Corporation, dated 8-13-98, recorded 9-10-98 at Deed Book 4886, page 17.

4. Septic Sewer Easement—Tall Oaks, Inc., to Academy, Inc. dated 3-15-96, recorded 3-17-96 at Deed Book 4801, page 301.

5. Easement for Right-of-Way from J. H. Patton to Universal Power Company, dated 2-20-78, recorded 3-6-78 at Deed Book 291, page 591.

6. Right-of-Way Deed from J. H. Patton to Gwinnett County Dept. of Transportation, dated 5-2-88, recorded 5-5-88 at Deed Book 1465, page 220.

Delmar/Cengage Learning

(continued)

Schedule C

The land referred to in this Commitment is described as follows:

ALL THAT TRACT or parcel of land lying and being in Land Lot 11 of the 7th District of Gwinnett County, Maryland, containing 5.00 acres, same being more particularly described as follows:

BEGINNING at an iron pin found on the easterly Right-of-Way Line of Collins Road (Eighty (80´) foot Right-of-Way), which iron pin found is located northwesterly a distance of 62.54 feet along said Right-of-Way Line from a Right-of-Way monument which marks the intersection of the easterly Right-of-Way Line of said Collins Road with the northerly Right-of-Way Line of Maryland Highway No. 316 (Three hundred forty (340´) foot Right-of-Way); thence traveling along the easterly Right-of-Way Line of said Collins Road north 34 degrees 31 minutes 28 seconds west a distance of 709.55 feet to an iron pin found on said Right-of-Way Line; thence leaving said Right-of-Way Line and traveling north 55 degrees 40 minutes 26 seconds east a distance of 320.59 feet to an iron pin set; thence traveling south 30 degrees 00 minutes 08 seconds east a distance of 789.15 feet to an iron pin found; thence traveling south 72 degrees 19 minutes 34 seconds west a distance of 269.96 feet to an iron pin found on the easterly Right-of-Way Line of said Collins Road, which iron pin found is the TRUE POINT OF BEGINNING.

EXHIBIT 13–20

Sample Title Commitment (*continued*)

Certificate of Title

TO:

RE: Arnold Development Inc.
Gwinnett County
File No. 4094

Gentlemen:

This to certify that we have examined the record of title to the real estate described in Exhibit A attached to this Certificate and incorporated herein by this reference and made a part hereof, and we find the fee simple title to said property to be vested in Arnold Development, Inc. by virtue of a Warranty Deed from Trust Company Bank of Gwinnett County successor in title to Gwinnett Commercial Bank, dated March 23, 2008, filed March 28, 2008, 3:00 P.M., recorded in Deed Book 2749, page 313, Gwinnett County Records subject to those objections and exceptions set out in Exhibit B attached to this Certificate and incorporated herein by this reference and made a part hereof.

All questions with reference to the following are expressly excepted from this Certificate, and this opinion is limited to the names of married women as they appear in the chain of title and as furnished to examining counsel:

(a) All matters of record subsequent to the date of this Certificate.

(b) Matters affecting the title which are not of record, or which, if they are of record, are not indexed in such a manner that a reasonably prudent search would have revealed them to the examiner.

(c) Such state of facts as would be disclosed from a competent civil engineers accurate survey of said property. (It is always advisable that survey be made in order to determine, if there are encroachments, overhangs, overlaps, that the improvements are within the boundaries of caption, and the lines and corners of caption are clearly marked.)

EXHIBIT 13–21

Title Examination Form for Practical Assignment

Delmar/Cengage Learning

(*continued*)

EXHIBIT 13–21

Title Examination Form for
Practical Assignment
(*continued*)

(d) Encroachments, except such as in our opinion do not materially affect the value of the property.

(e) Title to that portion of the premises within the bounds of any public road.

(f) The riparian rights of abutting owners on any stream running through the premises.

(g) Adverse claims of tenants in possession.

(h) All zoning laws, ordinances or regulations, municipal or county, and all Governmental regulations of the use and occupancy of premises described, including the regulations or condemnation of the land or any building or structure thereon.

(i) Taxes not due and payable at the date of this Certificate, and taxes coming due and payable for all future times.

(j) Unrecorded claims of liens for labor or material furnished for the improvements of said property.

(k) Street improvement liens which have not been properly placed of record.

(l) Past due water bills, which, while not technically liens, will deter the municipal authority form transferring water meters until the bills have been paid.

(m) Pay-as-you-enter water or sewer lines, which, while not technically liens, will be payable upon connection with such lines.

The effective date of this Certificate of Title is October 12, 2010, at 5:00 o'clock P.M.

EXHIBIT "A"

All that tract or parcel of land lying and being in Land Lot 81 of the 5th District of Gwinnett County, Michigan, being Lot 45, Block B, Summerville Subdivision, Unit IV, according to a plat of survey recorded at Plat Book 25, page 11, Gwinnett County Records, which plat is incorporated herein by reference thereto.

EXHIBIT "B"

1. 2010 State and County taxes are paid in the amount of $1046.50 on 65.78 acres.

2. Recorded plat at Plat Book 25, page 11, reveals the following:
   a) 35 foot building setback line;
   b) Protective covenants;
   c) 5 foot drainage easement;
   d) 20 foot drainage easement along rear property line;
   e) Fence along rear property line;
   f) 10 foot side line.

3. Mortgage from Arnold Development, Inc. to Trust Company Bank of Gwinnett County, dated March 23, 2008, filed March 28, 2008, 3:00 P.M., recorded in Deed Book 2749, page 338, Gwinnett County Records, in the amount of $152,000.00.

EXHIBIT 13–22

Title Commitment Forms for Practical Assignment

ALTA forms have been used by permission of the American Land Title Association.

COMMITMENT

SCHEDULE A

1 OFFICE FILE NUMBER		
2 COMMITMENT NUMBER	3 EFFECTIVE DATE	4 LOAN AMOUNT
		OWNERS AMOUNT

1. Policy or Policies to be issued:
   ALTA LOAN POLICY.
   Proposed Insured:

   ALTA OWNER'S POLICY, Form
   Proposed Insured:

2. The estate or interest in the land described or referred to in this Commitment and covered herein is a fee simple, and title thereto is at the effective date hereof vested in:

3. The Land is described as follows:

Note: This Commitment consists of insert pages labeled in Schedule A, Schedule B-Section 1, and Schedule B-Section 2. This Commitment is of no force and effect unless all schedules are included, along with any Rider pages incorporated by reference in the insert pages.

(continued)

EXHIBIT 13–22

Title Commitment Forms for Practical Assignment (*continued*)

COMMITMENT

SCHEDULE B — Section 1

Commitment Number

Requirements

The following are the requirements to be complied with:

1. Instrument(s) creating the estate or interest to be insured must be approved, executed and filed for record, to wit:

2. Payment of the full consideration to, or for the account of, the grantors or mortgagors.

3. Payment of all taxes, charges, assessments, levied and assessed against subject premises, which are due and payable.

4. Satisfactory evidence should be had that improvements and/or repairs or alterations thereto are completed; that contractor, subcontractors, labor and materialmen are all paid.

(*continued*)

EXHIBIT 13–22

Title Commitment Forms for Practical Assignment (*continued*)

COMMITMENT

SCHEDULE B—Section 2

Commitment Number

Exceptions

Schedule B of the policy or policies to be issued will contain exceptions to the following matters unless the same are disposed of to the satisfaction of the Company.

1. Defects, liens, encumbrances, adverse claims or other matters, if any, created, first appearing in the public records or attaching subsequent to the effective date hereof but prior to the date the proposed Insured acquires for value of record the estate or interest or mortgage thereon covered by this Commitment.

2. Any owner's policy issued pursuant hereto will contain under Schedule B the standard exceptions set forth on the inside cover. Any loan policy will also contain under Schedule B thereof, the standard exceptions set forth on the inside cover of this commitment relating to the owner's policy.

3. Standard Exceptions 2 and 3 may be removed from the policy when a satisfactory survey and inspection of the premises is made.

4. Taxes and assessments for the year   and subsequent years.

Note: On loan policies, junior and subordinate matters, if any, will not be reflected in Schedule B.

EXHIBIT 13–23

2006 ALTA Owner's Policy

ALTA forms have been used by permission of the American Land Title Association.

American Land Title Association	Owner's Policy Adopted 6-17-06

OWNER'S POLICY OF TITLE INSURANCE
Issued by
BLANK TITLE INSURANCE COMPANY

Any notice of claim and any other notice or statement in writing required to be given to the Company under this Policy must be given to the Company at the address shown in Section 18 of the Conditions.

COVERED RISKS

SUBJECT TO THE EXCLUSIONS FROM COVERAGE, THE EXCEPTIONS FROM COVERAGE CONTAINED IN SCHEDULE B, AND THE CONDITIONS, BLANK TITLE INSURANCE COMPANY, a Blank corporation (the "Company") insures, as of Date of Policy and, to the extent stated in Covered Risks 9 and 10, after Date of Policy, against loss or damage, not exceeding the Amount of Insurance, sustained or incurred by the Insured by reason of:

1. Title being vested other than as stated in Schedule A.

2. Any defect in or lien or encumbrance on the Title. This Covered Risk includes but is not limited to insurance against loss from

    (a) A defect in the Title caused by

        (i) forgery, fraud, undue influence, duress, incompetency, incapacity, or impersonation;

        (ii) failure of any person or Entity to have authorized a transfer or conveyance;

        (iii) a document affecting Title not properly created, executed, witnessed, sealed, acknowledged, notarized, or delivered;

        (iv) failure to perform those acts necessary to create a document by electronic means authorized by law;

        (v) a document executed under a falsified, expired, or otherwise invalid power of attorney;

        (vi) a document not properly filed, recorded, or indexed in the Public Records including failure to perform those acts by electronic means authorized by law; or

        (vii) a defective judicial or administrative proceeding.

    (b) The lien of real estate taxes or assessments imposed on the Title by a governmental authority due or payable, but unpaid.

    (c) Any encroachment, encumbrance, violation, variation, or adverse circumstance affecting the Title that would be disclosed by an accurate and complete land survey of the Land. The term "encroachment" includes encroachments of existing improvements located on the Land onto adjoining land, and encroachments onto the Land of existing improvements located on adjoining land.

3. Unmarketable Title.

4. No right of access to and from the Land.

5. The violation or enforcement of any law, ordinance, permit, or governmental regulation (including those relating to building and zoning) restricting, regulating, prohibiting, or relating to

---

(continued)

EXHIBIT 13–23

2006 ALTA Owner's Policy (*continued*)

American Land Title Association

Owner's Policy
Adopted 6-17-06

(a) the occupancy, use, or enjoyment of the Land;

(b) the character, dimensions, or location of any improvement erected on the Land;

(c) the subdivision of land; or

(d) environmental protection if a notice, describing any part of the Land, is recorded in the Public Records setting forth the violation or intention to enforce, but only to the extent of the violation or enforcement referred to in that notice.

6. An enforcement action based on the exercise of a governmental police power not covered by Covered Risk 5 if a notice of the enforcement action, describing any part of the Land, is recorded in the Public Records, but only to the extent of the enforcement referred to in that notice.

7. The exercise of the rights of eminent domain if a notice of the exercise, describing any part of the Land, is recorded in the Public Records.

8. Any taking by a governmental body that has occurred and is binding on the rights of a purchaser for value without Knowledge.

9. Title being vested other than as stated in Schedule A or being defective

(a) as a result of the avoidance in whole or in part, or from a court order providing an alternative remedy, of a transfer of all or any part of the title to or any interest in the Land occurring prior to the transaction vesting Title as shown in Schedule A because that prior transfer constituted a fraudulent or preferential transfer under federal bankruptcy, state insolvency, or similar creditors' rights laws; or

(b) because the instrument of transfer vesting Title as shown in Schedule A constitutes a preferential transfer under federal bankruptcy, state insolvency, or similar creditors' rights laws by reason of the failure of its recording in the Public Records
  (i) to be timely, or
  (ii) to impart notice of its existence to a purchaser for value or to a judgment or lien creditor.

10. Any defect in or lien or encumbrance on the Title or other matter included in Covered Risks 1 through 9 that has been created or attached or has been filed or recorded in the Public Records subsequent to Date of Policy and prior to the recording of the deed or other instrument of transfer in the Public Records that vests Title as shown in Schedule A.

The Company will also pay the costs, attorneys' fees, and expenses incurred in defense of any matter insured against by this Policy, but only to the extent provided in the Conditions.

[Witness clause optional]

BLANK TITLE INSURANCE COMPANY

BY: **PRESIDENT**

BY: **SECRETARY**

(*continued*)

EXHIBIT 13–23

2006 ALTA Owner's Policy (*continued*)

American Land Title Association

Owner's Policy
Adopted 6-17-06

EXCLUSIONS FROM COVERAGE

The following matters are expressly excluded from the coverage of this policy, and the Company will not pay loss or damage, costs, attorneys' fees, or expenses that arise by reason of:

1. (a) Any law, ordinance, permit, or governmental regulation (including those relating to building and zoning) restricting, regulating, prohibiting, or relating to

    (i) the occupancy, use, or enjoyment of the Land;

    (ii) the character, dimensions, or location of any improvement erected on the Land;

    (iii) the subdivision of land; or

    (iv) environmental protection;

    or the effect of any violation of these laws, ordinances, or governmental regulations. This Exclusion 1(a) does not modify or limit the coverage provided under Covered Risk 5.

   (b) Any governmental police power. This Exclusion 1(b) does not modify or limit the coverage provided under Covered Risk 6.

2. Rights of eminent domain. This Exclusion does not modify or limit the coverage provided under Covered Risk 7 or 8.

3. Defects, liens, encumbrances, adverse claims, or other matters

    (a) created, suffered, assumed, or agreed to by the Insured Claimant;

    (b) not Known to the Company, not recorded in the Public Records at Date of Policy, but Known to the Insured Claimant and not disclosed in writing to the Company by the Insured Claimant prior to the date the Insured Claimant became an Insured under this policy;

    (c) resulting in no loss or damage to the Insured Claimant;

    (d) attaching or created subsequent to Date of Policy (however, this does not modify or limit the coverage provided under Covered Risk 9 and 10); or

    (e) resulting in loss or damage that would not have been sustained if the Insured Claimant had paid value for the Title.

4. Any claim, by reason of the operation of federal bankruptcy, state insolvency, or similar creditors' rights laws, that the transaction vesting the Title as shown in Schedule A, is

    (a) a fraudulent conveyance or fraudulent transfer; or

    (b) a preferential transfer for any reason not stated in Covered Risk 9 of this policy.

5. Any lien on the Title for real estate taxes or assessments imposed by governmental authority and created or attaching between Date of Policy and the date of recording of the deed or other instrument of transfer in the Public Records that vests Title as shown in Schedule A.

AMERICAN
LAND TITLE
ASSOCIATION

(continued)

EXHIBIT 13–23

2006 ALTA Owner's Policy (*continued*)

American Land Title Association

Owner's Policy
Adopted 6-17-06

SCHEDULE A

Name and Address of Title Insurance Company:

[File No.:   ]   Policy No.:
Address Reference:
Amount of Insurance: $ [Premium: $]
Date of Policy: [at a.m./p.m.]

1. Name of Insured:

2. The estate or interest in the Land that is insured by this policy is:

3. Title is vested in:

4. The Land referred to in this policy is described as follows:

(continued)

EXHIBIT 13–23

2006 ALTA Owner's Policy (*continued*)

American Land Title Association

**Owner's Policy
Adopted 6-17-06**

SCHEDULE B

[File No.   ]   Policy No.

EXCEPTIONS FROM COVERAGE

This policy does not insure against loss or damage, and the Company will not pay costs, attorneys' fees, or expenses that arise by reason of:

1.   [Policy may include regional exceptions if so desired by the issuing Company.]
2.   [Variable exceptions such as taxes, easements, CC&R's, etc., shown here]

(continued)

EXHIBIT 13–23

2006 ALTA Owner's Policy (*continued*)

American Land Title Association	**Owner's Policy** **Adopted 6-17-06**

CONDITIONS

1. DEFINITION OF TERMS

The following terms when used in this policy mean:

(a) "Amount of Insurance": The amount stated in Schedule A, as may be increased or decreased by endorsement to this policy, increased by Section 8(b), or decreased by Sections 10 and 11 of these Conditions.

(b) "Date of Policy": The date designated as "Date of Policy" in Schedule A.

(c) "Entity": A corporation, partnership, trust, limited liability company, or other similar legal entity.

(d) "Insured": The Insured named in Schedule A.

    (i) the term "Insured" also includes

        (A) successors to the Title of the Insured by operation of law as distinguished from purchase, including heirs, devisees, survivors, personal representatives, or next of kin;

        (B) successors to an Insured by dissolution, merger, consolidation, distribution, or reorganization;

        (C) successors to an Insured by its conversion to another kind of Entity;

        (D) a grantee of an Insured under a deed delivered without payment of actual valuable consideration conveying the Title

            (1) if the stock, shares, memberships, or other equity interests of the grantee are wholly-owned by the named Insured,

            (2) if the grantee wholly owns the named Insured,

            (3) if the grantee is wholly-owned by an affiliated Entity of the named Insured, provided the affiliated Entity and the named Insured are both wholly-owned by the same person or Entity, or

            (4) if the grantee is a trustee or beneficiary of a trust created by a written instrument established by the Insured named in Schedule A for estate planning purposes.

    (ii) with regard to (A), (B), (C), and (D) reserving, however, all rights and defenses as to any successor that the Company would have had against any predecessor Insured.

(e) "Insured Claimant": An Insured claiming loss or damage.

(f) "Knowledge" or "Known": Actual knowledge, not constructive knowledge or notice that may be imputed to an Insured by reason of the Public Records or any other records that impart constructive notice of matters affecting the Title.

(g) "Land": The land described in Schedule A, and affixed improvements that by law constitute real property. The term "Land" does not include any property beyond the lines of the area described in Schedule A, nor any right, title, interest, estate, or easement in abutting streets, roads, avenues, alleys, lanes, ways, or waterways, but this does not modify or limit the extent that a right of access to and from the Land is insured by this policy.

(h) "Mortgage": Mortgage, deed of trust, trust deed, or other security instrument, including one evidenced by electronic means authorized by law.

(i) "Public Records": Records established under state statutes at Date of Policy for the purpose of imparting constructive notice of matters relating to real property to purchasers for value and without Knowledge. With respect to Covered Risk 5(d), "Public Records" shall also include

---

(continued)

EXHIBIT 13–23

2006 ALTA Owner's Policy (continued)

American Land Title Association

Owner's Policy
Adopted 6-17-06

---

environmental protection liens filed in the records of the clerk of the United States District Court for the district where the Land is located.

(j) "Title": The estate or interest described in Schedule A.

(k) "Unmarketable Title": Title affected by an alleged or apparent matter that would permit a prospective purchaser or lessee of the Title or lender on the Title to be released from the obligation to purchase, lease, or lend if there is a contractual condition requiring the delivery of marketable title.

2. CONTINUATION OF INSURANCE

The coverage of this policy shall continue in force as of Date of Policy in favor of an Insured, but only so long as the Insured retains an estate or interest in the Land, or holds an obligation secured by a purchase money Mortgage given by a purchaser from the Insured, or only so long as the Insured shall have liability by reason of warranties in any transfer or conveyance of the Title. This policy shall not continue in force in favor of any purchaser from the Insured of either (i) an estate or interest in the Land, or (ii) an obligation secured by a purchase money Mortgage given to the Insured.

3. NOTICE OF CLAIM TO BE GIVEN BY INSURED CLAIMANT

The Insured shall notify the Company promptly in writing (i) in case of any litigation as set forth in Section 5(a) of these Conditions, (ii) in case Knowledge shall come to an Insured hereunder of any claim of title or interest that is adverse to the Title, as insured, and that might cause loss or damage for which the Company may be liable by virtue of this policy, or (iii) if the Title, as insured, is rejected as Unmarketable Title. If the Company is prejudiced by the failure of the Insured Claimant to provide prompt notice, the Company's liability to the Insured Claimant under the policy shall be reduced to the extent of the prejudice.

4. PROOF OF LOSS

In the event the Company is unable to determine the amount of loss or damage, the Company may, at its option, require as a condition of payment that the Insured Claimant furnish a signed proof of loss. The proof of loss must describe the defect, lien, encumbrance, or other matter insured against by this policy that constitutes the basis of loss or damage and shall state, to the extent possible, the basis of calculating the amount of the loss or damage.

5. DEFENSE AND PROSECUTION OF ACTIONS

(a) Upon written request by the Insured, and subject to the options contained in Section 7 of these Conditions, the Company, at its own cost and without unreasonable delay, shall provide for the defense of an Insured in litigation in which any third party asserts a claim covered by this policy adverse to the Insured. This obligation is limited to only those stated causes of action alleging matters insured against by this policy. The Company shall have the right to select counsel of its choice (subject to the right of the Insured to object for reasonable cause) to represent the Insured as to those stated causes of action. It shall not be liable for and will not pay the fees of any other counsel. The Company will not pay any fees, costs, or expenses incurred by the Insured in the defense of those causes of action that allege matters not insured against by this policy.

(b) The Company shall have the right, in addition to the options contained in Section 7 of these Conditions, at its own cost, to institute and prosecute any action or proceeding or to do any other act that in its opinion may be necessary or desirable to establish the Title, as insured, or to

---

AMERICAN
LAND TITLE
ASSOCIATION

(continued)

EXHIBIT 13–23

2006 ALTA Owner's Policy (*continued*)

American Land Title Association   **Owner's Policy**
                                                       Adopted 6-17-06

---

prevent or reduce loss or damage to the Insured. The Company may take any appropriate action under the terms of this policy, whether or not it shall be liable to the Insured. The exercise of these rights shall not be an admission of liability or waiver of any provision of this policy. If the Company exercises its rights under this subsection, it must do so diligently.

(c) Whenever the Company brings an action or asserts a defense as required or permitted by this policy, the Company may pursue the litigation to a final determination by a court of competent jurisdiction, and it expressly reserves the right, in its sole discretion, to appeal any adverse judgment or order.

6. DUTY OF INSURED CLAIMANT TO COOPERATE

(a) In all cases where this policy permits or requires the Company to prosecute or provide for the defense of any action or proceeding and any appeals, the Insured shall secure to the Company the right to so prosecute or provide defense in the action or proceeding, including the right to use, at its option, the name of the Insured for this purpose. Whenever requested by the Company, the Insured, at the Company's expense, shall give the Company all reasonable aid (i) in securing evidence, obtaining witnesses, prosecuting or defending the action or proceeding, or effecting settlement, and (ii) in any other lawful act that in the opinion of the Company may be necessary or desirable to establish the Title or any other matter as insured. If the Company is prejudiced by the failure of the Insured to furnish the required cooperation, the Company's obligations to the Insured under the policy shall terminate, including any liability or obligation to defend, prosecute, or continue any litigation, with regard to the matter or matters requiring such cooperation.

(b) The Company may reasonably require the Insured Claimant to submit to examination under oath by any authorized representative of the Company and to produce for examination, inspection, and copying, at such reasonable times and places as may be designated by the authorized representative of the Company, all records, in whatever medium maintained, including books, ledgers, checks, memoranda, correspondence, reports, e-mails, disks, tapes, and videos whether bearing a date before or after Date of Policy, that reasonably pertain to the loss or damage. Further, if requested by any authorized representative of the Company, the Insured Claimant shall grant its permission, in writing, for any authorized representative of the Company to examine, inspect, and copy all of these records in the custody or control of a third party that reasonably pertain to the loss or damage. All information designated as confidential by the Insured Claimant provided to the Company pursuant to this Section shall not be disclosed to others unless, in the reasonable judgment of the Company, it is necessary in the administration of the claim. Failure of the Insured Claimant to submit for examination under oath, produce any reasonably requested information, or grant permission to secure reasonably necessary information from third parties as required in this subsection, unless prohibited by law or governmental regulation, shall terminate any liability of the Company under this policy as to that claim.

7. OPTIONS TO PAY OR OTHERWISE SETTLE CLAIMS; TERMINATION OF LIABILITY

In case of a claim under this policy, the Company shall have the following additional options:

(a) To Pay or Tender Payment of the Amount of Insurance.

To pay or tender payment of the Amount of Insurance under this policy together with any costs, attorneys' fees, and expenses incurred by the Insured Claimant that were authorized by the Company up to the time of payment or tender of payment and that the Company is obligated to pay.

Upon the exercise by the Company of this option, all liability and obligations of the Company to the Insured under this policy, other than to make the payment required in this subsection, shall terminate, including any liability or obligation to defend, prosecute, or continue any litigation.

AMERICAN
LAND TITLE
ASSOCIATION

(*continued*)

EXHIBIT 13–23

2006 ALTA Owner's Policy (*continued*)

American Land Title Association

Owner's Policy
Adopted 6-17-06

    (b) To Pay or Otherwise Settle With Parties Other Than the Insured or With the Insured Claimant.

        (i) to pay or otherwise settle with other parties for or in the name of an Insured Claimant any claim insured against under this policy. In addition, the Company will pay any costs, attorneys' fees, and expenses incurred by the Insured Claimant that were authorized by the Company up to the time of payment and that the Company is obligated to pay; or

        (ii) to pay or otherwise settle with the Insured Claimant the loss or damage provided for under this policy, together with any costs, attorneys' fees, and expenses incurred by the Insured Claimant that were authorized by the Company up to the time of payment and that the Company is obligated to pay.

    Upon the exercise by the Company of either of the options provided for in subsections (b)(i) or (ii), the Company's obligations to the Insured under this policy for the claimed loss or damage, other than the payments required to be made, shall terminate, including any liability or obligation to defend, prosecute, or continue any litigation.

8. DETERMINATION AND EXTENT OF LIABILITY

    This policy is a contract of indemnity against actual monetary loss or damage sustained or incurred by the Insured Claimant who has suffered loss or damage by reason of matters insured against by this policy.

    (a) The extent of liability of the Company for loss or damage under this policy shall not exceed the lesser of

        (i) the Amount of Insurance; or

        (ii) the difference between the value of the Title as insured and the value of the Title subject to the risk insured against by this policy.

    (b) If the Company pursues its rights under Section 5 of these Conditions and is unsuccessful in establishing the Title, as insured,

        (i) the Amount of Insurance shall be increased by 10%, and

        (ii) the Insured Claimant shall have the right to have the loss or damage determined either as of the date the claim was made by the Insured Claimant or as of the date it is settled and paid.

    (c) In addition to the extent of liability under (a) and (b), the Company will also pay those costs, attorneys' fees, and expenses incurred in accordance with Sections 5 and 7 of these Conditions.

9. LIMITATION OF LIABILITY

    (a) If the Company establishes the Title, or removes the alleged defect, lien, or encumbrance, or cures the lack of a right of access to or from the Land, or cures the claim of Unmarketable Title, all as insured, in a reasonably diligent manner by any method, including litigation and the completion of any appeals, it shall have fully performed its obligations with respect to that matter and shall not be liable for any loss or damage caused to the Insured.

    (b) In the event of any litigation, including litigation by the Company or with the Company's consent, the Company shall have no liability for loss or damage until there has been a final determination by a court of competent jurisdiction, and disposition of all appeals, adverse to the Title, as insured.

    (c) The Company shall not be liable for loss or damage to the Insured for liability voluntarily assumed by the Insured in settling any claim or suit without the prior written consent of the Company.

AMERICAN
LAND TITLE
ASSOCIATION

(*continued*)

EXHIBIT 13–23

2006 ALTA Owner's Policy (*continued*)

American Land Title Association

Owner's Policy
Adopted 6-17-06

---

10. REDUCTION OF INSURANCE; REDUCTION OR TERMINATION OF LIABILITY

All payments under this policy, except payments made for costs, attorneys' fees, and expenses, shall reduce the Amount of Insurance by the amount of the payment.

11. LIABILITY NONCUMULATIVE

The Amount of Insurance shall be reduced by any amount the Company pays under any policy insuring a Mortgage to which exception is taken in Schedule B or to which the Insured has agreed, assumed, or taken subject, or which is executed by an Insured after Date of Policy and which is a charge or lien on the Title, and the amount so paid shall be deemed a payment to the Insured under this policy.

12. PAYMENT OF LOSS

When liability and the extent of loss or damage have been definitely fixed in accordance with these Conditions, the payment shall be made within 30 days.

13. RIGHTS OF RECOVERY UPON PAYMENT OR SETTLEMENT

(a) Whenever the Company shall have settled and paid a claim under this policy, it shall be subrogated and entitled to the rights of the Insured Claimant in the Title and all other rights and remedies in respect to the claim that the Insured Claimant has against any person or property, to the extent of the amount of any loss, costs, attorneys' fees, and expenses paid by the Company. If requested by the Company, the Insured Claimant shall execute documents to evidence the transfer to the Company of these rights and remedies. The Insured Claimant shall permit the Company to sue, compromise, or settle in the name of the Insured Claimant and to use the name of the Insured Claimant in any transaction or litigation involving these rights and remedies.

If a payment on account of a claim does not fully cover the loss of the Insured Claimant, the Company shall defer the exercise of its right to recover until after the Insured Claimant shall have recovered its loss.

(b) The Company's right of subrogation includes the rights of the Insured to indemnities, guaranties, other policies of insurance, or bonds, notwithstanding any terms or conditions contained in those instruments that address subrogation rights.

14. ARBITRATION

Either the Company or the Insured may demand that the claim or controversy shall be submitted to arbitration pursuant to the Title Insurance Arbitration Rules of the American Land Title Association ("Rules"). Except as provided in the Rules, there shall be no joinder or consolidation with claims or controversies of other persons. Arbitrable matters may include, but are not limited to, any controversy or claim between the Company and the Insured arising out of or relating to this policy, any service in connection with its issuance or the breach of a policy provision, or to any other controversy or claim arising out of the transaction giving rise to this policy. All arbitrable matters when the Amount of Insurance is $2,000,000 or less shall be arbitrated at the option of either the Company or the Insured. All arbitrable matters when the Amount of Insurance is in excess of $2,000,000 shall be arbitrated only when agreed to by both the Company and the Insured. Arbitration pursuant to this policy and under the Rules shall be binding upon the parties. Judgment upon the award rendered by the Arbitrator(s) may be entered in any court of competent jurisdiction.

AMERICAN
LAND TITLE
ASSOCIATION

(*continued*)

EXHIBIT 13–23

2006 ALTA Owner's Policy (*continued*)

American Land Title Association	Owner's Policy Adopted 6-17-06

---

15. LIABILITY LIMITED TO THIS POLICY; POLICY ENTIRE CONTRACT

(a) This policy together with all endorsements, if any, attached to it by the Company is the entire policy and contract between the Insured and the Company. In interpreting any provision of this policy, this policy shall be construed as a whole.

(b) Any claim of loss or damage that arises out of the status of the Title or by any action asserting such claim shall be restricted to this policy.

(c) Any amendment of or endorsement to this policy must be in writing and authenticated by an authorized person, or expressly incorporated by Schedule A of this policy.

(d) Each endorsement to this policy issued at any time is made a part of this policy and is subject to all of its terms and provisions. Except as the endorsement expressly states, it does not (i) modify any of the terms and provisions of the policy, (ii) modify any prior endorsement, (iii) extend the Date of Policy, or (iv) increase the Amount of Insurance.

16. SEVERABILITY

In the event any provision of this policy, in whole or in part, is held invalid or unenforceable under applicable law, the policy shall be deemed not to include that provision or such part held to be invalid, but all other provisions shall remain in full force and effect.

17. CHOICE OF LAW; FORUM

(a) Choice of Law: The Insured acknowledges the Company has underwritten the risks covered by this policy and determined the premium charged therefor in reliance upon the law affecting interests in real property and applicable to the interpretation, rights, remedies, or enforcement of policies of title insurance of the jurisdiction where the Land is located.

Therefore, the court or an arbitrator shall apply the law of the jurisdiction where the Land is located to determine the validity of claims against the Title that are adverse to the Insured and to interpret and enforce the terms of this policy. In neither case shall the court or arbitrator apply its conflicts of law principles to determine the applicable law.

(b) Choice of Forum: Any litigation or other proceeding brought by the Insured against the Company must be filed only in a state or federal court within the United States of America or its territories having appropriate jurisdiction.

18. NOTICES, WHERE SENT

Any notice of claim and any other notice or statement in writing required to be given to the Company under this policy must be given to the Company at [fill in].

NOTE: Bracketed [ ] material optional

EXHIBIT 13–24

2006 ALTA Loan Policy

ALTA forms have been used by permission of the American Land Title Association.

American Land Title Association	Loan Policy Adopted 6-17-06

LOAN POLICY OF TITLE INSURANCE
Issued By
BLANK TITLE INSURANCE COMPANY

Any notice of claim and any other notice or statement in writing required to be given to the Company under this Policy must be given to the Company at the address shown in Section 17 of the Conditions.

COVERED RISKS

SUBJECT TO THE EXCLUSIONS FROM COVERAGE, THE EXCEPTIONS FROM COVERAGE CONTAINED IN SCHEDULE B, AND THE CONDITIONS, BLANK TITLE INSURANCE COMPANY, a Blank corporation (the "Company") insures as of Date of Policy and, to the extent stated in Covered Risks 11, 13, and 14, after Date of Policy, against loss or damage, not exceeding the Amount of Insurance, sustained or incurred by the Insured by reason of:

1. Title being vested other than as stated in Schedule A.

2. Any defect in or lien or encumbrance on the Title. This Covered Risk includes but is not limited to insurance against loss from

    (a) A defect in the Title caused by

    (i) forgery, fraud, undue influence, duress, incompetency, incapacity, or impersonation;

    (ii) failure of any person or Entity to have authorized a transfer or conveyance;

    (iii) a document affecting Title not properly created, executed, witnessed, sealed, acknowledged, notarized, or delivered;

    (iv) failure to perform those acts necessary to create a document by electronic means authorized by law;

    (v) a document executed under a falsified, expired, or otherwise invalid power of attorney;

    (vi) a document not properly filed, recorded, or indexed in the Public Records including failure to perform those acts by electronic means authorized by law; or

    (vii) a defective judicial or administrative proceeding.

    (b) The lien of real estate taxes or assessments imposed on the Title by a governmental authority due or payable, but unpaid.

    (c) Any encroachment, encumbrance, violation, variation, or adverse circumstance affecting the Title that would be disclosed by an accurate and complete land survey of the Land. The term "encroachment" includes encroachments of existing improvements located on the Land onto adjoining land, and encroachments onto the Land of existing improvements located on adjoining land.

3. Unmarketable Title.

4. No right of access to and from the Land.

5. The violation or enforcement of any law, ordinance, permit, or governmental regulation (including those relating to building and zoning) restricting, regulating, prohibiting, or relating to

    (a) the occupancy, use, or enjoyment of the Land;

    (b) the character, dimensions, or location of any improvement erected on the Land;

AMERICAN
LAND TITLE
ASSOCIATION

(continued)

EXHIBIT 13–24

2006 ALTA Loan Policy (continued)

American Land Title Association

Loan Policy
Adopted 6-17-06

(c) the subdivision of land; or

(d) environmental protection

if a notice, describing any part of the Land, is recorded in the Public Records setting forth the violation or intention to enforce, but only to the extent of the violation or enforcement referred to in that notice.

6. An enforcement action based on the exercise of a governmental police power not covered by Covered Risk 5 if a notice of the enforcement action, describing any part of the Land, is recorded in the Public Records, but only to the extent of the enforcement referred to in that notice.

7. The exercise of the rights of eminent domain if a notice of the exercise, describing any part of the Land, is recorded in the Public Records.

8. Any taking by a governmental body that has occurred and is binding on the rights of a purchaser for value without Knowledge.

9. The invalidity or unenforceability of the lien of the Insured Mortgage upon the Title. This Covered Risk includes but is not limited to insurance against loss from any of the following impairing the lien of the Insured Mortgage

    (a) forgery, fraud, undue influence, duress, incompetency, incapacity, or impersonation;

    (b) failure of any person or Entity to have authorized a transfer or conveyance;

    (c) the Insured Mortgage not being properly created, executed, witnessed, sealed, acknowledged, notarized, or delivered;

    (d) failure to perform those acts necessary to create a document by electronic means authorized by law;

    (e) a document executed under a falsified, expired, or otherwise invalid power of attorney;

    (f) a document not properly filed, recorded, or indexed in the Public Records including failure to perform those acts by electronic means authorized by law; or

    (g) a defective judicial or administrative proceeding.

10. The lack of priority of the lien of the Insured Mortgage upon the Title over any other lien or encumbrance.

11. The lack of priority of the lien of the Insured Mortgage upon the Title

    (a) as security for each and every advance of proceeds of the loan secured by the Insured Mortgage over any statutory lien for services, labor, or material arising from construction of an improvement or work related to the Land when the improvement or work is either

        (i) contracted for or commenced on or before Date of Policy; or

        (ii) contracted for, commenced, or continued after Date of Policy if the construction is financed, in whole or in part, by proceeds of the loan secured by the Insured Mortgage that the Insured has advanced or is obligated on Date of Policy to advance; and

    (b) over the lien of any assessments for street improvements under construction or completed at Date of Policy.

12. The invalidity or unenforceability of any assignment of the Insured Mortgage, provided the assignment is shown in Schedule A, or the failure of the assignment shown in Schedule A to vest title to the Insured Mortgage in the named Insured assignee free and clear of all liens.

13. The invalidity, unenforceability, lack of priority, or avoidance of the lien of the Insured Mortgage upon the Title

---

AMERICAN
LAND TITLE
ASSOCIATION

(continued)

EXHIBIT 13–24

2006 ALTA Loan Policy (*continued*)

American Land Title Association	Loan Policy Adopted 6-17-06

    (a) resulting from the avoidance in whole or in part, or from a court order providing an alternative remedy, of any transfer of all or any part of the title to or any interest in the Land occurring prior to the transaction creating the lien of the Insured Mortgage because that prior transfer constituted a fraudulent or preferential transfer under federal bankruptcy, state insolvency, or similar creditors' rights laws; or

    (b) because the Insured Mortgage constitutes a preferential transfer under federal bankruptcy, state insolvency, or similar creditors' rights laws by reason of the failure of its recording in the Public Records

        (i)   to be timely, or

        (ii) to impart notice of its existence to a purchaser for value or to a judgment or lien creditor.

14. Any defect in or lien or encumbrance on the Title or other matter included in Covered Risks 1 through 13 that has been created or attached or has been filed or recorded in the Public Records subsequent to Date of Policy and prior to the recording of the Insured Mortgage in the Public Records.

The Company will also pay the costs, attorneys' fees, and expenses incurred in defense of any matter insured against by this Policy, but only to the extent provided in the Conditions.

[Witness clause optional]

BLANK TITLE INSURANCE COMPANY

BY: **PRESIDENT**

BY: **SECRETARY**

(*continued*)

EXHIBIT 13–24

2006 ALTA Loan Policy (*continued*)

American Land Title Association

Loan Policy
Adopted 6-17-06

EXCLUSIONS FROM COVERAGE

The following matters are expressly excluded from the coverage of this policy, and the Company will not pay loss or damage, costs, attorneys' fees, or expenses that arise by reason of:

1. (a) Any law, ordinance, permit, or governmental regulation (including those relating to building and zoning) restricting, regulating, prohibiting, or relating to

    (i) the occupancy, use, or enjoyment of the Land;

    (ii) the character, dimensions, or location of any improvement erected on the Land;

    (iii) the subdivision of land; or

    (iv) environmental protection;

    or the effect of any violation of these laws, ordinances, or governmental regulations. This Exclusion 1(a) does not modify or limit the coverage provided under Covered Risk 5.

    (b) Any governmental police power. This Exclusion 1(b) does not modify or limit the coverage provided under Covered Risk 6.

2. Rights of eminent domain. This Exclusion does not modify or limit the coverage provided under Covered Risk 7 or 8.

3. Defects, liens, encumbrances, adverse claims, or other matters

    (a) created, suffered, assumed, or agreed to by the Insured Claimant;

    (b) not Known to the Company, not recorded in the Public Records at Date of Policy, but Known to the Insured Claimant and not disclosed in writing to the Company by the Insured Claimant prior to the date the Insured Claimant became an Insured under this policy;

    (c) resulting in no loss or damage to the Insured Claimant;

    (d) attaching or created subsequent to Date of Policy (however, this does not modify or limit the coverage provided under Covered Risk 11, 13, or 14); or

    (e) resulting in loss or damage that would not have been sustained if the Insured Claimant had paid value for the Insured Mortgage.

4. Unenforceability of the lien of the Insured Mortgage because of the inability or failure of an Insured to comply with applicable doing-business laws of the state where the Land is situated.

5. Invalidity or unenforceability in whole or in part of the lien of the Insured Mortgage that arises out of the transaction evidenced by the Insured Mortgage and is based upon usury or any consumer credit protection or truth-in-lending law.

6. Any claim, by reason of the operation of federal bankruptcy, state insolvency, or similar creditors' rights laws, that the transaction creating the lien of the Insured Mortgage, is

    (a) a fraudulent conveyance or fraudulent transfer, or

    (b) a preferential transfer for any reason not stated in Covered Risk 13(b) of this policy.

7. Any lien on the Title for real estate taxes or assessments imposed by governmental authority and created or attaching between Date of Policy and the date of recording of the Insured Mortgage in the Public Records. This Exclusion does not modify or limit the coverage provided under Covered Risk 11(b).

AMERICAN
LAND TITLE
ASSOCIATION

(*continued*)

EXHIBIT 13–24

2006 ALTA Loan Policy (*continued*)

American Land Title Association　　　　　　　　　　　　　　**Loan Policy**
　　　　　　　　　　　　　　　　　　　　　　　　　　　　　　Adopted 6-17-06

SCHEDULE A

Name and Address of Title Insurance Company:

[File No.:　　]　　Policy No.:
Loan No.:
Address Reference:
Amount of Insurance: $　　[Premium: $　　　]
Date of Policy:　　　　[at a.m./p.m.]

1. Name of Insured:

2. The estate or interest in the Land that is encumbered by the Insured Mortgage is:

3. Title is vested in:

4. The Insured Mortgage and its assignments, if any, are described as follows:

5. The Land referred to in this policy is described as follows:

[6. This policy incorporates by reference those ALTA endorsements selected below:

4-06	(Condominium)
4.1-06	
5-06	(Planned Unit Development)
5.1-06	
6-06	(Variable Rate)
6.2-06	(Variable Rate--Negative Amortization)
8.1-06	(Environmental Protection Lien) Paragraph b refers to the following state statute(s):
9-06	(Restrictions, Encroachments, Minerals)
13.1-06	(Leasehold Loan)
14-06	(Future Advance-Priority)
14.1-06	(Future Advance-Knowledge)
14.3-06	(Future Advance-Reverse Mortgage)
22-06	(Location) The type of improvement is a _____, and the street address is as shown above.]

AMERICAN
LAND TITLE
ASSOCIATION

(continued)

EXHIBIT 13–24

2006 ALTA Loan Policy (*continued*)

American Land Title Association

Loan Policy
Adopted 6-17-06

SCHEDULE B

[File No.   ]   Policy No.

EXCEPTIONS FROM COVERAGE

[Except as provided in Schedule B - Part II,] t[or T]his policy does not insure against loss or damage, and the Company will not pay costs, attorneys' fees, or expenses that arise by reason of:

[PART I

PART II

In addition to the matters set forth in Part I of this Schedule, the Title is subject to the following matters, and the Company insures against loss or damage sustained in the event that they are not subordinate to the lien of the Insured Mortgage:]

AMERICAN
LAND TITLE
ASSOCIATION

(continued)

EXHIBIT 13–24

2006 ALTA Loan Policy (*continued*)

American Land Title Association   **Loan Policy**
                                                   Adopted 6-17-06

CONDITIONS

1. DEFINITION OF TERMS

The following terms when used in this policy mean:

(a) "Amount of Insurance": The amount stated in Schedule A, as may be increased or decreased by endorsement to this policy, increased by Section 8(b) or decreased by Section 10 of these Conditions.

(b) "Date of Policy": The date designated as "Date of Policy" in Schedule A.

(c) "Entity": A corporation, partnership, trust, limited liability company, or other similar legal entity.

(d) "Indebtedness": The obligation secured by the Insured Mortgage including one evidenced by electronic means authorized by law, and if that obligation is the payment of a debt, the Indebtedness is the sum of

(i) the amount of the principal disbursed as of Date of Policy;

(ii) the amount of the principal disbursed subsequent to Date of Policy;

(iii) the construction loan advances made subsequent to Date of Policy for the purpose of financing in whole or in part the construction of an improvement to the Land or related to the Land that the Insured was and continued to be obligated to advance at Date of Policy and at the date of the advance;

(iv) interest on the loan;

(v) the prepayment premiums, exit fees, and other similar fees or penalties allowed by law;

(vi) the expenses of foreclosure and any other costs of enforcement;

(vii) the amounts advanced to assure compliance with laws or to protect the lien or the priority of the lien of the Insured Mortgage before the acquisition of the estate or interest in the Title;

(viii) the amounts to pay taxes and insurance; and

(ix) the reasonable amounts expended to prevent deterioration of improvements;

but the Indebtedness is reduced by the total of all payments and by any amount forgiven by an Insured.

(e) "Insured": The Insured named in Schedule A.

(i) The term "Insured" also includes

(A) the owner of the Indebtedness and each successor in ownership of the Indebtedness, whether the owner or successor owns the Indebtedness for its own account or as a trustee or other fiduciary, except a successor who is an obligor under the provisions of Section 12(c) of these Conditions;

(B) the person or Entity who has "control" of the "transferable record," if the Indebtedness is evidenced by a "transferable record," as these terms are defined by applicable electronic transactions law;

(C) successors to an Insured by dissolution, merger, consolidation, distribution, or reorganization;

(D) successors to an Insured by its conversion to another kind of Entity;

(E) a grantee of an Insured under a deed delivered without payment of actual valuable consideration conveying the Title

---

AMERICAN
LAND TITLE
ASSOCIATION

(*continued*)

EXHIBIT 13–24

2006 ALTA Loan Policy (*continued*)

American Land Title Association	Loan Policy
	Adopted 6-17-06

---

(1) if the stock, shares, memberships, or other equity interests of the grantee are wholly-owned by the named Insured,

(2) if the grantee wholly owns the named Insured, or

(3) if the grantee is wholly-owned by an affiliated Entity of the named Insured, provided the affiliated Entity and the named Insured are both wholly-owned by the same person or Entity;

(F) any government agency or instrumentality that is an insurer or guarantor under an insurance contract or guaranty insuring or guaranteeing the Indebtedness secured by the Insured Mortgage, or any part of it, whether named as an Insured or not;

(ii) With regard to (A), (B), (C), (D) , and (E) reserving, however, all rights and defenses as to any successor that the Company would have had against any predecessor Insured, unless the successor acquired the Indebtedness as a purchaser for value without Knowledge of the asserted defect, lien, encumbrance, or other matter insured against by this policy.

(f) "Insured Claimant": An Insured claiming loss or damage.

(g) "Insured Mortgage": The Mortgage described in paragraph 4 of Schedule A.

(h) "Knowledge" or "Known": Actual knowledge, not constructive knowledge or notice that may be imputed to an Insured by reason of the Public Records or any other records that impart constructive notice of matters affecting the Title.

(i) "Land": The land described in Schedule A, and affixed improvements that by law constitute real property. The term "Land" does not include any property beyond the lines of the area described in Schedule A, nor any right, title, interest, estate, or easement in abutting streets, roads, avenues, alleys, lanes, ways, or waterways, but this does not modify or limit the extent that a right of access to and from the Land is insured by this policy.

(j) "Mortgage": Mortgage, deed of trust, trust deed, or other security instrument, including one evidenced by electronic means authorized by law.

(k) "Public Records": Records established under state statutes at Date of Policy for the purpose of imparting constructive notice of matters relating to real property to purchasers for value and without Knowledge. With respect to Covered Risk 5(d), "Public Records" shall also include environmental protection liens filed in the records of the clerk of the United States District Court for the district where the Land is located.

(l) "Title": The estate or interest described in Schedule A.

(m) "Unmarketable Title": Title affected by an alleged or apparent matter that would permit a prospective purchaser or lessee of the Title or lender on the Title or a prospective purchaser of the Insured Mortgage to be released from the obligation to purchase, lease, or lend if there is a contractual condition requiring the delivery of marketable title.

2. CONTINUATION OF INSURANCE

The coverage of this policy shall continue in force as of Date of Policy in favor of an Insured after acquisition of the Title by an Insured or after conveyance by an Insured, but only so long as the Insured retains an estate or interest in the Land, or holds an obligation secured by a purchase money Mortgage given by a purchaser from the Insured, or only so long as the Insured shall have liability by reason of warranties in any transfer or conveyance of the Title. This policy shall not continue in force in favor of any purchaser from the Insured of either (i)

(continued)

EXHIBIT 13–24

2006 ALTA Loan Policy (*continued*)

American Land Title Association	Loan Policy
	Adopted 6-17-06

---

an estate or interest in the Land, or (ii) an obligation secured by a purchase money Mortgage given to the Insured.

3. NOTICE OF CLAIM TO BE GIVEN BY INSURED CLAIMANT

The Insured shall notify the Company promptly in writing (i) in case of any litigation as set forth in Section 5(a) of these Conditions, (ii) in case Knowledge shall come to an Insured of any claim of title or interest that is adverse to the Title or the lien of the Insured Mortgage, as insured, and that might cause loss or damage for which the Company may be liable by virtue of this policy, or (iii) if the Title or the lien of the Insured Mortgage, as insured, is rejected as Unmarketable Title. If the Company is prejudiced by the failure of the Insured Claimant to provide prompt notice, the Company's liability to the Insured Claimant under the policy shall be reduced to the extent of the prejudice.

4. PROOF OF LOSS

In the event the Company is unable to determine the amount of loss or damage, the Company may, at its option, require as a condition of payment that the Insured Claimant furnish a signed proof of loss. The proof of loss must describe the defect, lien, encumbrance, or other matter insured against by this policy that constitutes the basis of loss or damage and shall state, to the extent possible, the basis of calculating the amount of the loss or damage.

5. DEFENSE AND PROSECUTION OF ACTIONS

(a) Upon written request by the Insured, and subject to the options contained in Section 7 of these Conditions, the Company, at its own cost and without unreasonable delay, shall provide for the defense of an Insured in litigation in which any third party asserts a claim covered by this policy adverse to the Insured. This obligation is limited to only those stated causes of action alleging matters insured against by this policy. The Company shall have the right to select counsel of its choice (subject to the right of the Insured to object for reasonable cause) to represent the Insured as to those stated causes of action. It shall not be liable for and will not pay the fees of any other counsel. The Company will not pay any fees, costs, or expenses incurred by the Insured in the defense of those causes of action that allege matters not insured against by this policy.

(b) The Company shall have the right, in addition to the options contained in Section 7 of these Conditions, at its own cost, to institute and prosecute any action or proceeding or to do any other act that in its opinion may be necessary or desirable to establish the Title or the lien of the Insured Mortgage, as insured, or to prevent or reduce loss or damage to the Insured. The Company may take any appropriate action under the terms of this policy, whether or not it shall be liable to the Insured. The exercise of these rights shall not be an admission of liability or waiver of any provision of this policy. If the Company exercises its rights under this subsection, it must do so diligently.

(c) Whenever the Company brings an action or asserts a defense as required or permitted by this policy, the Company may pursue the litigation to a final determination by a court of competent jurisdiction, and it expressly reserves the right, in its sole discretion, to appeal any adverse judgment or order.

6. DUTY OF INSURED CLAIMANT TO COOPERATE

(a) In all cases where this policy permits or requires the Company to prosecute or provide for the defense of any action or proceeding and any appeals, the Insured shall secure to the

---

AMERICAN
LAND TITLE
ASSOCIATION

(continued)

EXHIBIT 13–24

2006 ALTA Loan Policy (*continued*)

American Land Title Association

Loan Policy
Adopted 6-17-06

Company the right to so prosecute or provide defense in the action or proceeding, including the right to use, at its option, the name of the Insured for this purpose.

Whenever requested by the Company, the Insured, at the Company's expense, shall give the Company all reasonable aid (i) in securing evidence, obtaining witnesses, prosecuting or defending the action or proceeding, or effecting settlement, and (ii) in any other lawful act that in the opinion of the Company may be necessary or desirable to establish the Title, the lien of the Insured Mortgage, or any other matter as insured. If the Company is prejudiced by the failure of the Insured to furnish the required cooperation, the Company's obligations to the Insured under the policy shall terminate, including any liability or obligation to defend, prosecute, or continue any litigation, with regard to the matter or matters requiring such cooperation.

(b) The Company may reasonably require the Insured Claimant to submit to examination under oath by any authorized representative of the Company and to produce for examination, inspection, and copying, at such reasonable times and places as may be designated by the authorized representative of the Company, all records, in whatever medium maintained, including books, ledgers, checks, memoranda, correspondence, reports, e-mails, disks, tapes, and videos whether bearing a date before or after Date of Policy, that reasonably pertain to the loss or damage. Further, if requested by any authorized representative of the Company, the Insured Claimant shall grant its permission, in writing, for any authorized representative of the Company to examine, inspect, and copy all of these records in the custody or control of a third party that reasonably pertain to the loss or damage. All information designated as confidential by the Insured Claimant provided to the Company pursuant to this Section shall not be disclosed to others unless, in the reasonable judgment of the Company, it is necessary in the administration of the claim. Failure of the Insured Claimant to submit for examination under oath, produce any reasonably requested information, or grant permission to secure reasonably necessary information from third parties as required in this subsection, unless prohibited by law or governmental regulation, shall terminate any liability of the Company under this policy as to that claim.

7. OPTIONS TO PAY OR OTHERWISE SETTLE CLAIMS; TERMINATION OF LIABILITY

In case of a claim under this policy, the Company shall have the following additional options:

(a) To Pay or Tender Payment of the Amount of Insurance or to Purchase the Indebtedness.

(i) To pay or tender payment of the Amount of Insurance under this policy together with any costs, attorneys' fees, and expenses incurred by the Insured Claimant that were authorized by the Company up to the time of payment or tender of payment and that the Company is obligated to pay; or

(ii) To purchase the Indebtedness for the amount of the Indebtedness on the date of purchase, together with any costs, attorneys' fees, and expenses incurred by the Insured Claimant that were authorized by the Company up to the time of purchase and that the Company is obligated to pay.

When the Company purchases the Indebtedness, the Insured shall transfer, assign, and convey to the Company the Indebtedness and the Insured Mortgage, together with any collateral security.

Upon the exercise by the Company of either of the options provided for in subsections (a)(i) or (ii), all liability and obligations of the Company to the Insured under this policy, other than to make the

---

(continued)

EXHIBIT 13–24

2006 ALTA Loan Policy (*continued*)

American Land Title Association   **Loan Policy**
                                                                Adopted 6-17-06

---

payment required in those subsections, shall terminate, including any liability or obligation to defend, prosecute, or continue any litigation.

(b) To Pay or Otherwise Settle With Parties Other Than the Insured or With the Insured Claimant.

(i) to pay or otherwise settle with other parties for or in the name of an Insured Claimant any claim insured against under this policy. In addition, the Company will pay any costs, attorneys' fees, and expenses incurred by the Insured Claimant that were authorized by the Company up to the time of payment and that the Company is obligated to pay; or

(ii) to pay or otherwise settle with the Insured Claimant the loss or damage provided for under this policy, together with any costs, attorneys' fees, and expenses incurred by the Insured Claimant that were authorized by the Company up to the time of payment and that the Company is obligated to pay.

Upon the exercise by the Company of either of the options provided for in subsections (b)(i) or (ii), the Company's obligations to the Insured under this policy for the claimed loss or damage, other than the payments required to be made, shall terminate, including any liability or obligation to defend, prosecute, or continue any litigation.

8. DETERMINATION AND EXTENT OF LIABILITY

This policy is a contract of indemnity against actual monetary loss or damage sustained or incurred by the Insured Claimant who has suffered loss or damage by reason of matters insured against by this policy.

(a) The extent of liability of the Company for loss or damage under this policy shall not exceed the least of

(i) the Amount of Insurance,

(ii) the Indebtedness,

(iii) the difference between the value of the Title as insured and the value of the Title subject to the risk insured against by this policy, or

(iv) if a government agency or instrumentality is the Insured Claimant, the amount it paid in the acquisition of the Title or the Insured Mortgage in satisfaction of its insurance contract or guaranty.

(b) If the Company pursues its rights under Section 5 of these Conditions and is unsuccessful in establishing the Title or the lien of the Insured Mortgage, as insured,

(i) the Amount of Insurance shall be increased by 10%, and

(ii) the Insured Claimant shall have the right to have the loss or damage determined either as of the date the claim was made by the Insured Claimant or as of the date it is settled and paid.

(c) In the event the Insured has acquired the Title in the manner described in Section 2 of these Conditions or has conveyed the Title, then the extent of liability of the Company shall continue as set forth in Section 8(a) of these Conditions.

(d) In addition to the extent of liability under (a), (b), and (c), the Company will also pay those costs, attorneys' fees, and expenses incurred in accordance with Sections 5 and 7 of these Conditions.

(*continued*)

EXHIBIT 13–24

2006 ALTA Loan Policy (*continued*)

American Land Title Association   **Loan Policy**
                                                                    Adopted 6-17-06

---

9. LIMITATION OF LIABILITY

(a) If the Company establishes the Title, or removes the alleged defect, lien, or encumbrance, or cures the lack of a right of access to or from the Land, or cures the claim of Unmarketable Title, or establishes the lien of the Insured Mortgage, all as insured, in a reasonably diligent manner by any method, including litigation and the completion of any appeals, it shall have fully performed its obligations with respect to that matter and shall not be liable for any loss or damage caused to the Insured.

(b) In the event of any litigation, including litigation by the Company or with the Company's consent, the Company shall have no liability for loss or damage until there has been a final determination by a court of competent jurisdiction, and disposition of all appeals, adverse to the Title or to the lien of the Insured Mortgage, as insured.

(c) The Company shall not be liable for loss or damage to the Insured for liability voluntarily assumed by the Insured in settling any claim or suit without the prior written consent of the Company.

10. REDUCTION OF INSURANCE; REDUCTION OR TERMINATION OF LIABILITY

(a) All payments under this policy, except payments made for costs, attorneys' fees, and expenses, shall reduce the Amount of Insurance by the amount of the payment. However, any payments made prior to the acquisition of Title as provided in Section 2 of these Conditions shall not reduce the Amount of Insurance afforded under this policy except to the extent that the payments reduce the Indebtedness.

(b) The voluntary satisfaction or release of the Insured Mortgage shall terminate all liability of the Company except as provided in Section 2 of these Conditions.

11. PAYMENT OF LOSS

When liability and the extent of loss or damage have been definitely fixed in accordance with these Conditions, the payment shall be made within 30 days.

12. RIGHTS OF RECOVERY UPON PAYMENT OR SETTLEMENT

(a) The Company's Right to Recover

Whenever the Company shall have settled and paid a claim under this policy, it shall be subrogated and entitled to the rights of the Insured Claimant in the Title or Insured Mortgage and all other rights and remedies in respect to the claim that the Insured Claimant has against any person or property, to the extent of the amount of any loss, costs, attorneys' fees, and expenses paid by the Company. If requested by the Company, the Insured Claimant shall execute documents to evidence the transfer to the Company of these rights and remedies. The Insured Claimant shall permit the Company to sue, compromise, or settle in the name of the Insured Claimant and to use the name of the Insured Claimant in any transaction or litigation involving these rights and remedies.

If a payment on account of a claim does not fully cover the loss of the Insured Claimant, the Company shall defer the exercise of its right to recover until after the Insured Claimant shall have recovered its loss.

(b) The Insured's Rights and Limitations

(i) The owner of the Indebtedness may release or substitute the personal liability of any debtor or guarantor, extend or otherwise modify the terms of payment, release a portion of the Title

---

(continued)

EXHIBIT 13–24

2006 ALTA Loan Policy (*continued*)

American Land Title Association	Loan Policy Adopted 6-17-06

---

from the lien of the Insured Mortgage, or release any collateral security for the Indebtedness, if it does not affect the enforceability or priority of the lien of the Insured Mortgage.

(ii) If the Insured exercises a right provided in (b)(i), but has Knowledge of any claim adverse to the Title or the lien of the Insured Mortgage insured against by this policy, the Company shall be required to pay only that part of any losses insured against by this policy that shall exceed the amount, if any, lost to the Company by reason of the impairment by the Insured Claimant of the Company's right of subrogation.

(c) The Company's Rights Against Noninsured Obligors

The Company's right of subrogation includes the Insured's rights against non-insured obligors including the rights of the Insured to indemnities, guaranties, other policies of insurance, or bonds, notwithstanding any terms or conditions contained in those instruments that address subrogation rights.

The Company's right of subrogation shall not be avoided by acquisition of the Insured Mortgage by an obligor (except an obligor described in Section 1(e)(i)(F) of these Conditions) who acquires the Insured Mortgage as a result of an indemnity, guarantee, other policy of insurance, or bond, and the obligor will not be an Insured under this policy.

13. ARBITRATION

Either the Company or the Insured may demand that the claim or controversy shall be submitted to arbitration pursuant to the Title Insurance Arbitration Rules of the American Land Title Association ("Rules"). Except as provided in the Rules, there shall be no joinder or consolidation with claims or controversies of other persons. Arbitrable matters may include, but are not limited to, any controversy or claim between the Company and the Insured arising out of or relating to this policy, any service in connection with its issuance or the breach of a policy provision, or to any other controversy or claim arising out of the transaction giving rise to this policy. All arbitrable matters when the Amount of Insurance is $2,000,000 or less shall be arbitrated at the option of either the Company or the Insured. All arbitrable matters when the Amount of Insurance is in excess of $2,000,000 shall be arbitrated only when agreed to by both the Company and the Insured. Arbitration pursuant to this policy and under the Rules shall be binding upon the parties. Judgment upon the award rendered by the Arbitrator(s) may be entered in any court of competent jurisdiction.

14. LIABILITY LIMITED TO THIS POLICY; POLICY ENTIRE CONTRACT

(a) This policy together with all endorsements, if any, attached to it by the Company is the entire policy and contract between the Insured and the Company. In interpreting any provision of this policy, this policy shall be construed as a whole.

(b) Any claim of loss or damage that arises out of the status of the Title or lien of the Insured Mortgage or by any action asserting such claim shall be restricted to this policy.

(c) Any amendment of or endorsement to this policy must be in writing and authenticated by an authorized person, or expressly incorporated by Schedule A of this policy.

(d) Each endorsement to this policy issued at any time is made a part of this policy and is subject to all of its terms and provisions. Except as the endorsement expressly states, it does not (i) modify any of the terms and provisions of the policy, (ii) modify any prior endorsement, (iii) extend the Date of Policy, or (iv) increase the Amount of Insurance.

AMERICAN
LAND TITLE
ASSOCIATION

(continued)

EXHIBIT 13–24

2006 ALTA Loan Policy (*continued*)

American Land Title Association	Loan Policy Adopted 6-17-06

---

15. SEVERABILITY

In the event any provision of this policy, in whole or in part, is held invalid or unenforceable under applicable law, the policy shall be deemed not to include that provision or such part held to be invalid, but all other provisions shall remain in full force and effect.

16. CHOICE OF LAW; FORUM

(a) Choice of Law: The Insured acknowledges the Company has underwritten the risks covered by this policy and determined the premium charged therefor in reliance upon the law affecting interests in real property and applicable to the interpretation, rights, remedies, or enforcement of policies of title insurance of the jurisdiction where the Land is located.

Therefore, the court or an arbitrator shall apply the law of the jurisdiction where the Land is located to determine the validity of claims against the Title or the lien of the Insured Mortgage that are adverse to the Insured and to interpret and enforce the terms of this policy. In neither case shall the court or arbitrator apply its conflicts of law principles to determine the applicable law.

(b) Choice of Forum: Any litigation or other proceeding brought by the Insured against the Company must be filed only in a state or federal court within the United States of America or its territories having appropriate jurisdiction.

17. NOTICES, WHERE SENT

Any notice of claim and any other notice or statement in writing required to be given to the Company under this policy must be given to the Company at [fill in].

NOTE: Bracketed [ ] material optional

AMERICAN
LAND TITLE
ASSOCIATION

chapter | 14

Real Estate Closings

Objectives

After reading this chapter, you should be able to:
- Review a real estate contract and prepare a closing checklist for both the purchaser and the seller
- Review a mortgage loan commitment and prepare a closing checklist for the borrower
- Understand the legal procedures required for the closing of a sale of real property
- Understand the legal procedures required for the closing of a mortgage loan

Outline

Y ou enter a large room. Windows dominate one side of the room, offering the occupants a beautiful view of a downtown skyline. Framed English hunting prints adorn the other three walls. The focal point of the room is a large Queen Anne conference table ringed with a dozen chairs. Two couples are seated across from each other at one end of the table. One couple appears nervous. They look at each other and smile. Although the other couple appears sophisticated and blasé to the events that are taking place, they, too, look uneasy. A middle-aged well-dressed person seated in the corner of the conference room is talking on a cell phone. The caller has an appointment book and appears to be transacting business, oblivious to the other occupants of the room. At the other end of the conference table, there is a large stack of manila folders and papers, a yellow legal pad, and some kind of metal seal or stamp.

As you enter the room, everyone except the caller in the corner, who is still in phone oblivion, immediately looks in your direction. You have just entered that phenomenon known as the Real Estate Closing Zone.

The consummation of a real estate transaction is called a **closing.** Closings may be simple, as in the purchase and sale of a home, or complicated, as in the closing of a purchase and sale of a major resort hotel. The consummation of a loan secured by a mortgage is also called a closing, or **loan closing.** Many transactions involve a simultaneous sale and loan closing.

Real estate closing customs vary from one part of the country to another. In many states, real estate closings are conducted by clients and lawyers in a "face-to-face" conference room setting. The buyer, seller, mortgage lender, attorneys, brokers, and all other parties involved in the transaction attend an in-person closing, usually held in a conference room at a law office or title insurance company office. All the documents are signed by the various parties at this meeting, and the transaction is "closed" in the presence of all the parties.

The custom in other parts of the country is a closing in **escrow.** With a closing in escrow, the buyer, seller, and other parties tender the closing documents to an impartial third party known as an *escrow agent.* An escrow agent is usually a title insurance company but in some states may be a licensed escrow agent. The escrow agent has the legal obligation to safeguard the interests of everyone who is involved in the closing, including buyer, seller, and mortgage lender. The parties to the transaction generally enter into an *escrow agreement* with the escrow agent, which sets forth the escrow agent's duties in connection with the closing. Each party signs the necessary documents needed for the closing in advance and submits these documents to the escrow agent with detailed instructions for their delivery to other parties involved in the closing. For example, a seller may deliver to the escrow agent a signed deed for the property and other affidavits in connection with the sale. The seller's escrow instructions will direct the escrow agent not to deliver the deed and other documents to the buyer or to record the deed unless the seller has received certain documentation and the sale proceeds from the sale of the property. Often a party will give the escrow agent wire instructions for the wire transfer of the sale proceeds to the appropriate account.

An escrow agent's duty in connection with a closing will depend to a large degree upon the instructions given to the escrow agent by the various parties and by custom and usage in the area where the escrow agent operates. The escrow agent is responsible to the third party in the event the escrow agent fails to follow explicit escrow instructions. It is important when drafting escrow instructions that the attorney or party giving the instructions make sure that the instructions are clear and unambiguous so that the escrow agent knows exactly his or her authority to act. A closing in escrow provides a convenient environment in which to close the purchase and sale of real estate and to close any loans involved with such sale. An example of a mortgage lender's escrow instructions is set forth at the end of this chapter as Exhibit 14–9. Regardless of where the closing takes place or whether either an attorney

closing

Consummation of a real estate purchase and sale transaction.

loan closing

Consummation of a loan secured by real property.

escrow

Agreement that requires the deposit of a document or money into the possession of a third party to be held by that party until certain conditions are fulfilled.

or an escrow agent is in charge of the closing, most closings follow the procedures set forth in this chapter. All closings involve a certain amount of due diligence in regard to the inspection of title and other matters concerning the property in the preparation and execution of sale and loan documents.

In many parts of the country, a real estate paralegal is actively involved in helping the attorney or escrow agent in a real estate closing. Although ethical considerations in many states may prohibit a paralegal from actually conducting the closing, all states permit the paralegal to aid in all phases and aspects of the closing. Therefore, most of the discussion in this chapter concerning file creation, information gathering, preparation of legal documents, recording and disbursing, and so forth will be handled by the paralegal. This chapter is designed to provide good practical advice to the paralegal in each of these areas in connection with the real estate closing.

THE PARTIES

As previously mentioned, the parties to a real estate closing will vary depending upon the type of transaction being closed. A sale of a home may only involve the seller, buyer, a mortgage lender, real estate broker, attorney and paralegal.

The closing of a sale and finance of a chain of hotels may involve a seller, buyer, a mortgage lender, real estate broker, representative of a management company, title insurance representative, representative of the hotel franchisor, escrow agent, and each party's attorneys.

In addition, many people are involved in the closing but do not attend, such as real estate appraisers, surveyors, title examiners, insurance agents, and so on. A chart identifying many of the parties involved in a real estate closing is shown in Exhibit 14–1.

THE ENVIRONMENT

Residential real estate transactions do not close in a perfect, stress-free environment. Months have passed since the contract has been signed; frustrations and delays have been encountered at every turn. Credit reports have been lost; appraisals have been difficult to schedule or have turned out to be insufficient and have had to be rescheduled. The sellers desperately need the proceeds check because they have purchased another home and cannot afford two mortgage payments. The purchasers' dream house that looked so pretty two months ago has been slightly tarnished over the passage of time. The rooms appear smaller. There are cracks in the plaster. Everyone is concerned about the rubber raft tied to the third step of the basement. The real estate brokers have spent their commission and desperately need the check to pay creditors. The loan officer is being paid a base salary plus a percentage of all loans closed and is behind on her quota.

Residential loan closings are not a high-fee item for law firms and can only be profitable from a high volume. The real estate attorney often juggles more loan closings than the Karuchi Brothers juggle knives. Everything is done at hyperspeed. It is not unusual for people to arrive in the reception area before the loan package arrives from the lender. The U.S. Postal Service is passed over for more efficient means of delivery, such as courier and fax. Everything resembles the trading floor of a commodities exchange. In this environment, the professional real estate paralegal must maintain order and composure and produce a quality, error-free package. This requires training, discipline, organization, and a good sense of humor.

Closing a commercial transaction is similar to and yet very different from closing a residential transaction. Commercial transactions are easier because the people involved are

EXHIBIT 14–1

Real Estate Closing Participants

Appraiser	Professionally trained person who estimates the value of real property
Attorney	Professionally trained person who provides legal representation to other parties of the closing, that is, seller, buyer, lender, and so forth
Broker/Agent Real Estate	Person who has assisted seller and/or buyer in the purchase and sale of real property
Buyer	The purchaser of the real property
Environmental Engineer	Professionally trained person who performs an inspection of the real property to determine if it contains a hazardous substance; usually involved on most commercial real property transactions
Insurance Agent	Person who arranges for the improvements of the property to be insured against damage caused by fire, flood, and other natural causes
Escrow Agent	Company or person who acts as an agent for buyer, seller, and lender and accepts delivery of documents pursuant to written instructions
Paralegal	Professionally trained person who assists an attorney in the transaction
Management Company	Company or person who manages the property for the owner. This may mean collecting rent, payment of expenses, and maintenance of property; usually found only in commercial rental property transactions
Mortgage Lender	Company that finances the purchase of the property or provides financing for the owner of the property
Property Inspector	Professionally trained person who on behalf of the buyer or the lender, inspects the physical condition of the improvement on the property. A termite inspector is a property inspector
Record Clerk	Government officer who will record all deeds and mortgages in the connection with the closing
Seller	The owner of the property who is selling in connection with the closing
Surveyor	Professionally trained person who prepares a land survey of the real property; usually represents the buyer or lender of the property
Title Examiner	Professionally trained person who prepares a title examination on the real property; usually represents the buyer or lender
Title Insurance Agent or Company	Company that issues title insurance on the real property. The title insurance will insure the buyer or lender, or both

Delmar/Cengage Learning

not strangers to the transaction. They know what they want and what to expect, and they are not under the pressures of having a moving van full of household belongings circling the block waiting for the closing to be completed.

Although commercial closings involve more sophisticated parties, they also involve larger sums of money and larger risks. The legal techniques used for commercial closings are more sophisticated, and translating these techniques into documents that properly set forth in plain, concise language what everyone has agreed to and understands can be difficult. Until you have it right, patient communication is necessary.

Unlike residential transactions, in which most of the documentation is preprinted forms, commercial loan transactions use more negotiated and tailored documentation. Lenders usually start with the basic form, but the form will be negotiated over the course of the loan closing transaction or will be tailored to each particular transaction. Unlike most residential closings, in which purchaser and seller are not represented by counsel and do no more than quickly review the documentation, all parties to commercial transactions usually are represented by competent counsel, and the documents are reviewed many times, negotiated, debated, and changed before or at closing.

Commercial closings offer the luxury of higher fees for a law firm, and therefore, more time can be spent on a single file. This does not mean that commercial loan closings are easier than residential, but it does mean that the paralegal's attention does not have to be divided among 10 or 15 files at the same time, and he or she can concentrate on perhaps two or three deals.

One advantage in closing commercial loans is the opportunity to work with skilled counsel and other skilled paralegals. It is easier to close a transaction if all the participants have a high level of knowledge with regard to real estate law.

Both residential and commercial closings have advantages and disadvantages, and most paralegals specialize in one or the other.

In some states, residential and even commercial closings may be handled by title insurance companies. Unless a paralegal is employed by the title insurance company, he or she may not be directly involved in the closing but only involved in the review of closing documents on behalf of a client. This chapter is based on the assumption that the paralegal is employed by a law firm, corporate legal department, or title insurance company and is directly involved in the preparation for and closing of a real estate transaction.

ANATOMY OF A REAL ESTATE CLOSING

The difference between success and failure in a real estate closing is determined by the amount of preparation that was done before the closing. A real estate closing can be broken down into six areas: (1) file creation; (2) information gathering; (3) document preparation; (4) the closing; (5) disbursement, recording, and transmittal of the closing package; and (6) final closeout. A paralegal may be actively involved in all six areas of the closing.

File Creation

The first step in a real estate closing is the organization of the file. Most law firms that specialize in real estate have as clients lending institutions, such as savings banks, commercial banks, and life insurance companies, that make loans secured by residential and commercial properties. The case is referred to the firm for closing by way of a transmittal package from one of the loan officers at the lending institution or, if there is a rush to close, by telephone call or e-mail. An initial closing package typically includes a copy of the sales contract and a copy of the lender's loan commitment. It is common practice in some areas of the country for the lender to send an entire package of loan documents to the law firm.

Once the case is referred and the package is received, the law firm opens a file for purposes of billing in the name of the client and cross-references the other parties involved, such as the seller, purchaser, and any brokers. The firm monitors and reviews all the names involved in the closing to check for conflicts of interest. If a firm already has as a client one of the other parties, the potential exists for ethical problems or conflicts of interest. If a conflict of interest exists, the firm either declines representation of all parties in connection with the closing or obtains written consent from all parties after full disclosure of the conflict.

Assuming that no conflicts of interest exist, the file is logged onto the firm's computer system for billing, and an internal file is opened. This file may consist of nothing more than a manila folder with a label indicating the names of the parties and a file number for purposes of billing and reference.

It is advisable for a paralegal to maintain his or her own filing system separate and apart from the firm's own internal file system. The separate file provides a convenient source of information to verify what the paralegal has done in respect to a particular transaction.

Information Gathering

Most law firms use paralegals to gather information required to prepare the sale and loan documents and to close the transaction.

A starting point for gathering information is the closing package received by the firm, which usually contains a real estate sales contract and a lender's commitment letter. These two basic documents provide most of the clues for the type of information needed to close the transaction. It is advisable to review the contract and loan commitment promptly on receipt of the file and to prepare a checklist of the items required for the sale and the loan closing. File folders should be prepared for each item shown on the checklist. As the items are received or prepared, they can be placed in their own folders and easily reviewed or recalled when needed.

Reviewing the Real Estate Contract

The real estate contract sets forth the obligations of the purchaser and seller in regard to the sale transaction. It is the main document for a paralegal to review to prepare a sale closing checklist. The contract sets forth the names of the parties (seller, purchaser, broker), the legal description of the property, the purchase price of the property, the amount of the earnest money, the date for closing, and what documents the respective seller and purchaser must furnish to each other at the closing.

The names of the seller, purchaser, and broker should be contained in the real estate contract, along with their addresses, telephone numbers, and e-mail addresses. If telephone numbers and e-mail addresses are not included in the contract, they should be obtained because there will be numerous contacts with each party before closing. It is necessary to verify the correct spelling of each of the names because the seller's and purchaser's names will appear in most of the closing documents.

It is important when reviewing a real estate contract to determine the anticipated date of closing. Most contracts provide a closing date; however, the parties may want to close earlier, or the closing date may have been extended by an amendment. Early verification of the closing date is essential to prioritize activity. For example, if the closing is two weeks away, then the closing does not become a high-priority item, and the information can be gathered in a regular, orderly manner. On the other hand, if the closing is scheduled for the day after tomorrow, then the gathering of the information becomes a high-priority item and must be done in the quickest manner available. The closing date also needs to be verified with the lender's expiration date on its loan commitment. Because of the fluctuation of interest rates, loan commitments have short durations. Although the closing on the contract may not be for a couple of weeks, the loan commitment may be effective only for a week. Therefore, to close under the current terms of the loan, the sale needs to close early. Another problem encountered in residential and commercial transactions is the availability and convenience of the parties. The parties often have a conflict with the date of closing set forth in the contract, and therefore, a different closing date must be scheduled. Although it is not rational, parties to a real estate contract may place other, personal events ahead of the closing. It is not unusual for real estate closings to be scheduled around vacation plans or work schedules. It is recommended that paralegals obtain large calendars or appointment books to schedule all the closing activities for a given month.

[handwritten: scheduling]

The contract should contain a legal description of the property. The legal description is important, since it will be used on all the sale and loan closing documents as well as to order title examinations and surveys.

The real estate contract will probably describe in some detail the documents required by the seller and purchaser at the time of closing. These requirements need to be carefully reviewed, understood, and added to any checklist being prepared. It is not unusual for preprinted broker's contracts, often used on residential transactions, to be sketchy in regard to the documents required at closing. These contracts may refer only to the deed of the seller to the purchaser. On any real estate sale transaction, the seller is required to furnish, at minimum, the following documentation: (a) owner's or title affidavit; (b) corporate resolution, if the seller is a corporation; (c) warranty deed; (d) bill of sale for any personal property included in the transaction; (e) an assignment of all appliance or other manufacturer's warranties in connection with the property, such as roof warranty and furnace warranty; (f) foreign person affidavit; and (g) Form 1099–B. The Internal Revenue Service requires that on all real estate transactions that involve a foreign person, a percentage of the sales proceeds be withheld from the closing and remitted to the Internal Revenue Service. It is the purchaser's responsibility to withhold the funds and to remit them to the government. The purchaser can be relieved of this responsibility by obtaining an affidavit from the seller that the seller is not a foreign person. The purchaser is entitled to rely on the sworn affidavit. A copy of the foreign person affidavit is included in Chapter 16.

[handwritten: required documents — seller]

The Internal Revenue Service also requires that the closing agent, usually the law firm, report all sales of one- to four-family residences to the Internal Revenue Service. This report usually is done by preparing Form 1099–B with all the necessary sale information and having it signed by the seller. A copy of Form 1099–B is included in Chapter 16.

In addition to the preceding minimum requirements, a seller also may be required to provide such things as (a) termite clearance letters, (b) keys, (c) warranties, (d) assignment of leases and security deposits, (e) assignments of service contracts, and (f) estoppel letters from prior lenders and tenants.

[handwritten: Other required docs from seller]

A purchaser under a contract is required to provide money and proof of insurance at closing. The purchaser's checklist may be extended if the contract provides for seller financing, since the purchaser will provide a note and mortgage to the seller at the time of closing.

[handwritten: purchaser checklist]

The closing checklist in Exhibit 14–2 is prepared from the sample contract that follows the checklist.

EXHIBIT 14–2

Real Estate Sales Contract

This Contract is entered into this _____ day of January, 20_____ by and between ACME, INC., as ("Purchaser"), I.M. SELLER ("Seller") and BROKER & ASSOCIATES, as ("Broker").

FOR VALUABLE CONSIDERATION RECEIVED, the receipt and sufficiency of which are hereby acknowledged, the parties hereby agree as follows:

1. Purchaser agrees to buy and Seller agrees to sell subject to the terms and conditions of this Contract as set forth herein ALL THAT TRACT OF PARCEL OF LAND with such improvements as are located thereon lying and being in Land Lot 1135, 2nd District, 2nd Section of _____ County, _____ and being more particularly described on Exhibit "A" attached hereto and made a part hereof (hereinafter referred to as the "Property").

2. **Purchase Price.** The purchase price for the Property shall be SIX HUNDRED FIFTY THOUSAND AND NO/100 DOLLARS ($650,000.00), which shall be paid as follows: Purchaser shall pay to the Seller the sum of $650,000.00 in cash at closing.

3. **Earnest Money.** Purchaser has paid to Broker & Associates, a licensed broker acting on behalf of the Seller, FIVE THOUSAND AND NO/100 DOLLARS ($5,000.00) in the form of a check, the receipt whereof is hereby acknowledged by Broker & Associates as earnest money ("Earnest Money"), which Earnest Money shall be applied as part payment of the purchase price of said Property at the time the sale is consummated or paid to Seller or returned to Purchaser as otherwise provided herein.

4. **Warranties of Title.** Seller warrants that Seller presently has title to said Property and at the time the sale is consummated, agrees to convey good and marketable title to said Property to Purchaser by a general warranty deed subject only to such title exceptions as Purchaser shall agree to.

5. **Title.** Purchaser shall move promptly and in good faith after acceptance of this Contract by Seller to examine the title to said Property and to furnish Seller with a written statement of objections affecting the marketability of said title.

Seller shall have a reasonable time after receipt of said such objections to satisfy all valid objections specified by Purchaser and if Seller fails to satisfy such valid objections within a reasonable time, then Purchaser at Purchaser's option may cancel this Contract by giving Seller written notice of such cancellation and this Contract shall become null and void and Purchaser shall be entitled to a return of the Earnest Money. Marketability of title as used herein shall mean the quality of title which a title insurance company licensed to do business in the State of _____ and a member of the American Land Title Association would insure at its regular rate without exception.

6. **Hazardous Waste Indemnity.** Purchaser's obligation to purchase the Property pursuant to this Contract is contingent upon there being no petroleum hydrocarbons or contaminants contained in the soil, surface or subterranean water which are in violation of local, state, or federal statutes and regulations and that there be no other existence of any hazardous substances or waste located upon the Property. For purposes of this Agreement, the term "hazardous substances or wastes" shall mean petroleum, including crude oil or any fraction thereof, flammable explosives, radioactive materials, asbestos, any material containing polychlorinated biphenyls, and any of the substances defined as "hazardous substances" or "toxic substances" in the Comprehensive Environmental Response, Compensation and Liability Act of 1980, as amended, 42 U.S.C. Section 9601 *et seq.*, Hazardous Materials Transportation Act, 49 U.S.C. Section 1802 *et seq.*, the Resource Conservation and Recovery Act, 42 U.S.C. Section 6901 *et seq.*, and in the Toxic Substance Control Act of 1976, as amended, 15 U.S.C. Section 2601 *et seq.*, or any other federal, state, local or other governmental legislation, statute, law, code, rule, regulation or ordinance identified by its terms as pertaining to the disposal, storage, generation or presence of hazardous substances or waste (the "Environmental Laws"). Purchaser shall at Seller's expense have the Property inspected for purposes of discovering if hazardous substances or wastes exist. If upon inspection, hazardous wastes or substances do exist, Purchaser shall have the option of terminating his contract and receiving a refund of his

Delmar/Cengage Learning

(continued)

EXHIBIT 14–2

Real Estate Sales Contract
(*continued*)

$5,000.00 earnest money down payment. In the alternative, Seller shall have the right at its own expense to remove all hazardous substance or waste from the Property and to conclude the sale with Purchaser.

Seller warrants, represents and agrees that (a) neither Seller nor any person has violated any of the applicable Environmental Laws as defined in the paragraph above relating to or affecting the Property; (b) the Property is presently in compliance with all Environmental Laws, and there are no facts or circumstances presently existing upon or under the Property or relating to the representations and warranties, which violate any of the applicable Environmental Laws, and there is not now pending nor threatened any action, suit, investigation or proceeding against Seller or the Property (or against any other party related to the Property); (c) Seller has obtained all licenses, permits or other governmental regulatory approvals necessary to comply with Environmental Laws and Seller is in full compliance with the terms and provisions of all such licenses, permits or other governmental regulatory approvals; and (d) Seller has received no notice that any municipality or any governmental or quasi-governmental authorities are investigating or has determined that there are any violations of zoning, health, building, fire, pollution, environmental, or other statutes, ordinances, regulations affecting the Property.

7. **Inspection.** Purchaser, its agents and representatives, at Purchaser's expense and at reasonable times during normal business hours, shall have the right to enter upon the Property for purpose of inspection, examining, testing, surveying the Property. Purchaser assumes all responsibility for acts of itself, its agents, representatives, in exercising its rights under this paragraph and agrees to hold Seller harmless for any damages resulting therefrom.

8. **Condition of Improvements.** Seller warrants until the sale is consummated, that the Improvements located on the Property will be in the same condition as they are on the date this Contract is signed by the Seller, natural wear and tear excepted. Should the Improvements located on the Property be destroyed or substantially damaged before the Contract is consummated, then at the election of the Purchaser, (a) the Contract may be cancelled and Earnest Money refunded to Purchaser or (b) Purchaser may consummate the Contract and receive all insurance proceeds paid or due on the claim of loss.

This election is to be exercised within ten (10) days after the Purchaser has been notified in writing by Seller of the amount of the insurance proceeds, if any, Seller shall receive on the claim of loss; if Purchaser has not been notified within forty-five (45) days, subsequent to the occurrence of such damage or destruction, Purchaser may at its option cancel this Contract and receive a refund of its Earnest Money.

9. **Possession.** Seller shall deliver title and possession of the Property to Purchaser at closing free and clear of the claims of any and all tenants and all leases existing on the Property shall be cancelled and terminated by Seller at Seller's expense prior to closing.

10. **Closing.** Closing shall be held at the offices of attorney of Purchaser, _____ _____, 1400 Peachtree Place Tower, 999 Peachtree Street, N.E., _____, _____, or at such location as is agreeable to Purchaser and Seller, on a day selected by Purchaser not later than sixty (60) days from the date Seller can deliver title and possession of the Property free and clear of any and all leases or other rights of tenants in regard to the Property and a date not later than _____, 20____. Purchaser shall give Seller notice of the closing date at least five days prior thereto; provided, if Purchaser gives Seller no such notice of the closing date, then the closing date shall be _____, 20_____.

11. **Execution of Documents.** Seller shall execute and deliver to Purchaser a general warranty deed in recordable form conveying the Property to Purchaser as provided herein and shall execute and deliver to Purchaser all necessary affidavits in order for Purchaser to obtain a title insurance policy without exception and an affidavit indicating Seller's nonforeign status within the meaning of Section 1445(f)(3) of the Internal Revenue Code of 1986 and any and all other documents which may be required by Purchaser to carry out the terms of this Contract.

(continued)

EXHIBIT **14–2**

Real Estate Sales Contract
(*continued*)

12. **Closing Costs.** In connection with the closing, Seller shall pay the real estate Transfer Tax and all costs for the satisfaction, cure and removal of all title exceptions undertaken by the Seller as herein required. All other closing costs incurred by Purchaser in connection with the sale shall be paid by Purchaser. Each party shall pay its own attorney's fees.

13. **Prorations.** At the closing all ad valorem property taxes, water and sewer charges and assessments of any kind on the Property for the year of the closing shall be prorated between Purchaser and Seller as of 12:01 a.m. on the closing date. Such proration shall be based upon the latest ad valorem property tax, water, sewer charge and assessment bills available. If, upon receipt of the actual ad valorem property tax, water, sewer and assessment bills for the Property, such proration is incorrect, then either Purchaser or Seller shall be entitled, upon demand, to receive such amounts from the other as may be necessary to correct such malapportionment. This obligation to correct such malapportionment shall survive the closing and not be merged into any documents delivered pursuant to the closing.

14. **Brokerage Commissions.** Upon consummation of the closing of the sale contemplated herein, a sales commission shall be paid by the Seller to Broker & Associates, Inc., Broker, which commission has been negotiated between Broker and Seller. Purchaser shall have no obligation whatsoever to Broker & Associates, Inc. for any real estate commission. Seller further agrees to indemnify and hold harmless the Purchaser from and by any and all claims or demands with respect to any brokerage fees or agent's commissions or other compensation asserted against any person, firm, or corporation in connection with this Contract or sale or the transactions contemplated hereby arising from actions or alleged commitments of the Seller. This provision shall survive closing and the conveyance of the Property by Seller to Purchaser.

15. **Purchaser Default.** In the event the transaction contemplated hereby is not closed because of Purchaser's default, the Earnest Money shall be paid to Seller as full liquidated damages for such failure to close, the parties acknowledging the difficulty of ascertaining Seller's damages in such circumstances, whereupon neither party hereto shall have any further rights, claims, or liabilities under this Agreement except for the provisions which were made to survive the termination or cancellation of this Agreement. Said liquidated damages shall be Seller's sole and exclusive remedy and Seller shall expressly not have the right to seek specific performance or other damages.

16. **Sellers Default.** If Seller shall be unable to deliver title in accordance with this Agreement, Seller's liability shall be limited to the return of the Earnest Money paid hereunder. In the event Seller fails to perform other covenants of this Agreement or if Seller otherwise defaults hereunder, the Purchaser shall have the right, in addition to all rights and remedies herein provided, to pursue any right or remedy it may have against Seller at law or in equity for such breach and/or default, including without limitation, the right of specific performance of all provisions of this Agreement. Purchaser's monetary damages in the event of such breach and/or default shall be limited to $25,000.00. The parties hereby acknowledge the difficulty of ascertaining Purchaser's monetary damages in such event.

17. **Assignability.** Purchaser shall have the right to assign this Agreement to any corporation or partnership of which Purchaser is a shareholder or partner without notice to and without consent of Seller, and the transaction contemplated by this Agreement shall be consummated in the name of such assignee. Purchaser shall not have the right to assign the Contract to any other party except as mentioned above without the prior written consent of Seller.

18. **Notification.** Any notice or demand under which the terms of this Agreement or under any statute must or may be given or made by the parties hereto shall be made in writing and shall be deemed to have been delivered when hand delivered; as of the date sent by an overnight courier; or as of the date of postmark affixed by the U.S. Postal Service, by mail of same by certified mail, return receipt requested, addressed to the respective parties at the following addresses:

(*continued*)

EXHIBIT 14–2

Real Estate Sales Contract
(*continued*)

TO PURCHASER:

TO SELLER:

TO BROKER:

19. **Time is of the Essence**. Time is of the essence of this Agreement and of each of its provisions.

This instrument shall be regarded as an offer by the Purchaser or Seller who shall first sign this Contract to the other party and is open for acceptance by the other party until _____: _____.m. on the _____ day of _____, 20_____.

The above proposition is hereby accepted this _____ day of _____, 20_____.

IN WITNESS WHEREOF, the undersigned parties hereinto set their hand and seal to this Contract.

PURCHASER:

_____(SEAL)

SELLER:

_____(SEAL)

_____(SEAL)

BROKER

By:_____

CHECKLIST

Closing Documents

1. Title examination
2. Title commitment/policy
3. Survey
4. Hazard insurance
5. Foreign person affidavit
6. Form 1099–B
7. Title affidavit

8. Hazardous waste affidavit
9. Warranty deed
10. Bill of sale
11. Assignment of warranties
12. Broker indemnity
13. Settlement statement

CONTACT WITH SELLER, PURCHASER, AND BROKER BY THE PARALEGAL

One of the first things the paralegal needs to do is verify the correctness of the names that appear in the contract. The seller should be requested to provide any title information or surveys that the seller may have regarding the real property. If the seller is a corporation, copies of the articles of incorporation, bylaws, and a certificate of good standing with the secretary of state's office should be requested. A corporation should provide a corporate resolution with the names and titles of the people who will be signing on behalf of the corporation. The corporate seller should bring the corporate seal to the closing. All of these items are required to ensure that the corporation has the authority to sell the real property.

If the seller is a partnership, a request should be made for copies of the partnership agreement and the names of all the partners who intend to be present at the closing to sign the closing documents. In the situation of a partnership, all partners must sign the documents unless the partnership agreement authorizes an individual partner or group of partners to sign. If fewer than all the partners intend to sign the closing documents, a partnership resolution should be obtained from all the partners giving their consent and authorizing the signature partners to consummate and close the transaction.

If the seller is a limited liability company, a request should be made for copies of the articles of organization and the operating agreement. In addition, the name of the managing member or members who intend to be present at the closing to sign the closing documents should be obtained. Most limited liability companies execute sale documents by authorizing a managing member or group of members of the limited liability company to sign. A limited liability company resolution should be obtained authorizing the signature of the members to consummate and close the transaction.

The seller should be questioned about loan numbers of any outstanding loans on the subject property. These computer loan numbers are necessary to obtain payoff information. In addition, discuss with the seller the approximate date of closing and any special instructions you might need in regard to the closing.

The purchaser should be contacted to verify the names that are to appear on the warranty deed and the name of their insurance agent and to inquire about any special instructions. The purchaser should receive an explanation of the steps in a closing and assurance that closing money figures will be available at least on the day before the closing to give the purchaser adequate time to obtain the necessary funds.

After the purchaser and seller are contacted, the real estate agents should be contacted to notify them of the approximate date of closing and to verify the amount of the real estate commissions due the agents.

Ordering the Title Examination

It is unusual for a closing paralegal to examine the title to the property. Most title examinations are prepared by other members of the firm or by specialized firms that have a retainer relationship with the closing law firm. Title examinations may be handled by title insurance companies in some states. A title examination should be ordered quickly by the paralegal, even though the closing may be several weeks away. The earlier the examination is received, the more time there will be to correct defects that may be revealed by the examination. The title examiner needs, at a minimum, the following information to conduct the examination: (a) the name of the current owner, which usually is the seller under the sale contract; (b) the legal description of the real property; and (c) any title information or surveys available.

The title examiner should be informed of the name of the title company issuing the title insurance so that the title examiner's certification can be prepared and sent to the title company. The title examiner should be instructed to make copies of all exceptions to title. These copies should be provided to both the paralegal and the title insurance company. The title examiner should establish a firm date for completion of the examination. This date should be recorded on a calendar or appointment book. It is a good idea for the paralegal to call or e-mail the title examiner the day before the scheduled date of completion. This inquiry should be made not for the purpose of trying to obtain the title examination a day early but to confirm that the title examination will be available on the date scheduled for completion. The title examiner's response to this preemptive telephone call may be that the title examination has already been completed and can be picked up on the day of the call, which means that the examination is delivered one day early, or the preemptive telephone call may remind the title examiner of the date set for completion and will act as a further reminder to provide the title examination on time.

Ideally, a title examination order is given in writing by using a title examination form. A copy of such a form is shown in Exhibit 14–3. Because of the fast-track nature of most residential closings, title examinations typically are ordered by e-mail. If a telephone request is made, it is a good idea to complete the written title examination form before making the call. This requires collecting the necessary information for the title examination and increases the efficiency of the telephone call or e-mail. Ordering a title examination without completing the form could result in the examiner's receiving incomplete information. This will cause the title examination to be incomplete or necessitate a second call or e-mail to the examiner.

Ordering the Survey

Most law firms have a relationship with a surveying and engineering firm that can prepare surveys to satisfy title and email addresses insurance company and lender client requirements. The names, telephone numbers of these surveyors will be provided to the paralegal. Most surveys are ordered by telephone or e-mail, and a surveyor will need, at a minimum, the following information: (a) the legal description of the property to be surveyed, (b) information regarding previous surveys, (c) the correct names of the purchasers as they appear on the survey, (d) the correct name of the lending institution as it appears on the survey, and (e) any special lender requirements for a survey.

The surveyor will prepare an as-built survey locating the improvements and all easements, setback lines, and so forth on the survey. The surveyor will indicate if the property is located in a flood hazard zone. In some states, the surveyor may prepare a title insurance company inspection report form. If so, the surveyor will need to know which title insurance company is issuing the insurance so that the company's form can be used. At least six prints of the survey should be received, and the surveyor should be reminded to enclose a bill with the survey so that it can be paid at closing.

A firm date for the completion of the survey should be obtained from the surveyor. If possible, a survey should be received at least five business days before closing. The date for completion should be recorded on a calendar or appointment book and a preemptive inquiry made the day before the due date.

Ordering Hazard and Fire Insurance

Insurance against fire and other casualties is a requirement on all real estate closings that involve improved property. Often the insurance will be obtained by the purchaser or by one of the real estate agents in connection with the sale. An insurance company must receive the

EXHIBIT 14–3

Title Examination Form

Abstract Order

Our File Number: _____ Date Ordered: _____ Need By: _____

Ordered by: _____ Date of Closing: _____

Present Owner/Seller: _____

Name of Purchaser: _____

RE Broker: _____

Brief Legal: _____

_____

Street Address: _____

Length of Search: _____

MISCELLANEOUS INFORMATION KNOWN:

Plat Information: _____

Back Title Policy: ( ) Yes ( ) No   Back Title Notes: ( ) Yes ( ) No

With Who: _____   _____

_____   _____

_____   _____

PLEASE PROVIDE US WITH ANY BANKRUPTCY INFORMATION: ( ) yes   ( ) no

Other Information:

_____

_____

_____

_____

_____

_____

_____

_____

In addition, please provide the following:

( ) Copies of applicable Restrictive Covenants of record

( ) Copies of applicable easements of record

( ) Copies of any liens, executions, judgments, etc. of record

( ) City, State and County Millage Rates (latest figures available)

( ) _____

( ) _____

( ) _____

following information: (a) the name of the purchaser; (b) the correct address of the property; (c) the amount of the loan because most lenders require that, at a minimum, the insurance be for the amount of the loan; and (d) the name and address of the lender because the lender will appear as a mortgagee on the insurance policy. This mortgagee endorsement to the insurer policy contains both the name of the mortgagee and its address. If flood insurance is necessary, the agent should be given the finished flood elevation, which can be obtained from the surveyor. The insurance company should be given a date for delivery of the insurance.

Most lenders require the insurance premium to be paid one year in advance from date of closing and the proof of such payment to be provided at closing. The insurance agent will provide a paid receipt for the insurance.

Most residential lenders require that the original policy be available at the time of closing. On commercial transactions, commercial insurance policies are more difficult to obtain, and many lenders are willing to close on a binder or certificate of insurance. The policy will be provided after closing.

In the event the purchaser or real estate agent undertakes the task of obtaining the fire and casualty insurance, it is a good idea to receive from them the name of the agent and to verify with the agent all the necessary information that must appear in the policy. This direct communication with the insurance agent often reduces the number of mistakes in the final policy. Although most mistakes, such as misspelled names and incorrect property addresses, are not serious and usually will not hold up a closing, they do require corrective work after the closing.

Obtaining the Termite Clearance Letter or Bond

In many areas of the United States, termites present special problems for real estate closings. It is not unusual in residential and even in commercial transactions that a termite clearance letter be required within the terms of the contract. These clearance letters or bonds are prepared by licensed pest control companies. The certificate reports that the pest control company has inspected the property in question and has either found no termites, powder-post beetles, or other wood-boring insects or found such insects and treated the property. In addition, termite clearance letters report either that no damage was observed from past infestation of termites, powder-post beetles, or other wood-boring insects or that past damage has been repaired.

Because of the serious nature of termite infestation, it is advisable that termite clearance letters be obtained before the date of closing. By obtaining the termite letter early, any termite infestation problem identified can be corrected by the closing date. Experience shows that a number of closings have been adjourned because termite letters that were delivered at the closing stated that the property had been damaged by infestation of termites. Receiving such a letter at the closing gives the closing attorney little time to react, and the termite inspector who issued the report often is not available to answer questions during the closing. The result is that the closing must be adjourned until more information can be received. Such adjournment wastes time, creates a major inconvenience, and potentially increases the interest rates and charges that the purchaser must pay if the loan commitment expires.

Reviewing the Title Examination

Once the title examination has been received, it should be carefully reviewed by the paralegal for objections to title. All prior loans or debts on the property need to be paid at closing. It will be necessary to obtain from each lender or creditor a payment or satisfaction letter.

Satisfaction of Loans and Liens

Paralegals are generally used to obtain sufficient information to pay prior loans or liens on the property. Most lenders assign a computer number to each loan, and this number is needed to obtain a satisfaction amount for the loan. Some lenders will not give out information concerning any loan over the telephone or even by e-mail or letter without the customer's consent and permission. It is a good idea to anticipate such problems and request the seller to contact his or her lender to obtain loan information or at least approve the paralegal's obtaining such loan information. When requesting a payoff amount, it is necessary to give the lender a closing date and request a per diem interest charge if the sale does not close on the scheduled date. Ideally, loan payoffs should be verified by written communication with the lender; however, because of the fast-track nature of residential loans, many loan payoffs are handled by telephone.

A sample loan payment request is shown in Exhibit 14–4. This form should be used even with a telephone request. It is advisable when receiving a telephone satisfaction amount that the name and telephone number of the person giving the information be obtained. A letter or e-mail can then be sent from the firm to the lender verifying the telephone conversation and requesting to be notified immediately if the information contained in the letter or e-mail is incorrect. A similar letter or e-mail indicating that the check is being sent as payment in full pursuant to a telephone conversation of a certain date should be sent to the lender after closing. If a payoff letter was received, a copy of that letter should be enclosed with the letter accompanying the check.

The amount of unpaid taxes can be obtained by calling the tax collector's office. Most delinquent taxes accrue penalties and interest; thus, a satisfaction amount as of the date of closing with a per diem charge is required.

The satisfaction of judgment liens or mechanic's liens requires a telephone call or email to the attorney representing the judgment creditor or lienor. The attorney's name and address usually appear somewhere on the recorded judgment or lien. It is advisable in obtaining satisfaction of liens and judgments that written information be provided. This is handled by making telephone or e-mail contact and requiring the attorney representing the judgment creditor or lienor to provide a letter setting forth the amount needed for satisfaction. Arrangements also need to be made with judgment creditors and lienors to obtain a written satisfaction of the judgment or lien. This may require the attorney for the creditor or lien holder to attend the closing and tender the written satisfaction of lien or judgment in return for the payment check.

Satisfaction information for federal and state tax liens can be obtained through the Internal Revenue Service for federal tax liens and the state department of revenue for state tax liens. When speaking with the government authorities, full information concerning the lien, such as the date of the lien, the name of the taxpayer, and the place where the lien was filed and recorded, should be given. In addition, the closing date and a per diem interest charge should be provided.

A PARALEGAL'S REVIEW OF THE MORTGAGE LOAN COMMITMENT

loan commitment

Contract between a borrower and a lender to make and accept a mortgage loan secured by real property. The loan commitment sets forth the terms, requirements, and conditions for the mortgage loan.

The mortgage **loan commitment** provides a paralegal with clues about what information and documents are required to close the transaction. A mortgage loan commitment is addressed to the borrower. It indicates the mortgage lender's approval of the borrower's loan application and the lender's commitment to loan the amount requested, provided

EXHIBIT 14-4
Loan Payment Request Form

```
File #_____          Purchaser: _____
                                Phone:      (H)_____    (w)_____
••••••••••••••••••••••••••••••••••••••••••••••••••••••••••••••••••••••••••

( )R.E. AGENTS:   Seller: (    %)                    Phone:
   (     %)       Buyer: (    %)                     Phone:
------------------------------------------------------------------------
( )ABSTRACT:      Date Ordered:        From:
                                                     ()collect at closing
                  Date Received:       Cost:$        ()included in fee
------------------------------------------------------------------------
( )SURVEY:        Date Ordered:        From:
                                                     ()collect at closing
                  Date Received:       Cost:$        ()poc
------------------------------------------------------------------------
( )TERMITE        Date Ordered:        From:
   LETTER                                            ()collect at closing
                  Date Received:       Cost:$        ()poc
                  ( )to be mailed      ( )to be delivered at closing
------------------------------------------------------------------------
( )HAZARD INS:    Date Ordered:        Date Received:
                  From:                               Phone:
                  Address:                            Agent:

                  Amt. of Coverage: $                 Eff. Date:
                                                      ()collect at closing
      ()new     * Yearly Premium:   $                 ()poc
      ()exist.                                        ()collect at closing
      ()trans.   * Additional Prem:  $                ()poc
------------------------------------------------------------------------
( ) FLOOD INS:    Date Ordered:        Date Received:
                  From:                               Phone:
                  Address:                            Agent:

                  Amt. of Coverage: $                 Eff. Date:
                                                      ()collect at closing
      ()new     * Yearly Premium:   $                 ()poc
      ()exist.                                        ()collect at closing
      ()tran.    * Additional Prem:  $                ()poc
------------------------------------------------------------------------
( ) PAYOFFS:      Date Ordered:        Date Received:  Ordered by:

      ()1st:      To:                                  Deed Book:
                  Address:                             Phone:
                                                       Loan No.:
                                                       Attention:
                * Payoff is: $          as of:         Per Diem:$

      ()2nd:      To:                                  Deed Book:
                  Address:                             Phone:
                                                       Loan No.:
                                                       Attention:
                * Payoff is: $          as of:         Per Diem:$

      ()3rd:      To:                                  Deed Book:
                  Address:                             Phone:
                                                       Loan No.:
                                                       Attention:
                * Payoff is: $          as of:         Per Diem:$
------------------------------------------------------------------------
( ) OTHER CHARGES:                                    Paid by:

                  () Attorneys Fees    $        Buyer    Seller
   (P/A/C/LT)     () Title Insurance   $        Buyer    Seller
                  () Toll Charges      $        Buyer    Seller
   ()Loan         () Assignments       $        Buyer    Seller
   ()Owners       () Power of Attorney $        Buyer    Seller
   ()S.1.         () Photo Copies      $        Buyer    Seller
   ()Const.       () Federal Express   $        Buyer    Seller
                  ()                   $        Buyer    Seller
                  ()                   $        Buyer    Seller
```

the borrower agrees to comply with all the conditions listed in the commitment. It is the responsibility of the paralegal to make certain that all the lender's requirements set forth in the loan commitment have been satisfied before or at the time of closing. The commitment is a binding legal agreement and will govern all future disputes between the borrower and the lender and the drafting of the formal loan documents.

The following is a discussion of the conditions and terms that can be found in a mortgage loan commitment. Some of these items can be found in any loan commitment, and others apply only to commercial loan transactions.

Parties

The parties to a loan commitment are the prospective borrower and the lender.

Loan Amount

The amount of the loan should be clearly indicated in every loan commitment. This amount is used throughout in the preparation of all the necessary loan documents, such as notes, mortgages, and assignment of rents and leases.

Interest Rate

The commitment should clearly specify the annual interest rate for the loan. The interest rate will be either a fixed rate or a floating rate that adjusts pursuant to some index.

Term of Loan

The commitment should specify the exact number of years over which the loan must be repaid. The term should commence on the loan closing date or such other date as the loan funds are disbursed to the borrower.

Repayment Terms

The commitment should specify how the loan is to be repaid. It is customary to provide for monthly payments, but payments on any other basis may be agreed on.

Prepayment Terms

The loan commitment should indicate whether the loan can be prepaid before maturity. Most residential loans are prepayable in full or in part, provided the prepayments are made on a date otherwise scheduled for a regular payment of principal and interest. For example, if payments are made on the first day of each month, a prepayment must be made on the first day of each month as well.

Most institutional commercial lenders do not allow a voluntary prepayment of the loan in whole or in part during the first few years of the loan term. Thereafter, it is customary to provide for prepayment subject to the payment of a premium.

Loan can be repaid before

Security

A mortgage loan commitment indicates what security is required by the lender for the loan. As a general rule, the lender requires a valid and enforceable first lien on the real property being offered by the borrower, which, in most situations, is the real property being purchased with the proceeds of the loan. The lender typically requires that it receive fee simple title to the real property. Occasionally, a commercial lender may make a loan based on an estate for years or leasehold interest. The commitment letter indicates what quality of title the lender is requiring as security for the loan.

Appraisal

Most loan commitments require that before closing, the lender be provided with a formal written appraisal of the value of the proposed real property security. This appraisal of value ensures that the lender is not lending more money than the real property security is worth or more money than a percentage of the total fair market value of such real property security versus loan amount.

Insurance

A mortgage loan commitment requires that at or before closing, the borrower deliver to the lender insurance policies indicating that the real property security is covered by the following types of coverages: (a) fire, with extended and additional extended insurance; (b) vandalism and malicious mischief; (c) sprinkler; (d) war (if available); (e) rent or business interruption; (f) public liability; (g) plate glass liability; (h) boiler liability; and (i) flood. The insurance company and the dollar limits of such coverage also are subject to the approval of the lender. With respect to the amount of fire coverage, the general rule is that the policy must be for at least the original amount of the loan or the full amount of the replacement value of the improvements on the real property as determined at regular intervals, whichever is less.

All policies must have a proper mortgagee clause or endorsement attached thereto insuring the lender as the first mortgagee. A lender also may require a carrier to provide that it will not cancel the policy for any reason without prior written notice to the lender. Thirty days is the time period often required for such notice.

With respect to the payment of insurance proceeds, most lenders require a standard **mortgagee loss payable clause** to a policy whereby the insured and carrier agree that any and all proceeds payable under the policy are to be paid by the carrier directly to the lender or to a mutually agreed on third party. Thereafter, the loan documents allow the lender to use such proceeds either as an offset of the borrower's outstanding indebtedness or for restoration of the real property security.

mortgagee loss payable clause

Endorsement to a policy of fire and hazard insurance whereby the owner of the insured property and the insurance company agree that any and all proceeds payable under the policy are to be paid directly to the lender who has a mortgage on the insured property.

Escrow for Taxes and Insurance

A commitment may require that at closing, the borrower establishes with the lender an escrow account to assure the lender that all real estate taxes, special assessments, and insurance premiums relating to the security will be paid when due. The borrower is required to make monthly deposits to such account in the amount of one-twelfth of the annual taxes, assessments, and hazard insurance premiums as estimated by the lender. Thereafter, all tax, assessment, and insurance premium payments are made by the lender, and a failure to make the requisite monthly deposits may be deemed a loan default by the borrower. No interest is paid on such deposits, and they are not held in trust but may be commingled with the general assets of the lender.

Title Insurance

Most loan commitments require that the borrower obtain a mortgagee (loan) title insurance policy insuring that the proposed mortgage or deed of trust creates a valid first lien on the title to the real property security.

Survey

Most mortgage loan commitments require that an as-built survey of the real property be prepared. An as-built survey shows not only the perimeter lines of the subject property and all improvements located thereon, but also the location and path of any and all easements of record or those evident from an inspection of the property.

Compliance with Law

Most loan commitments require that the lender be provided with proof that all improvements on the real property (and their uses) comply fully with any and all applicable zoning and building laws, ordinances, and regulations and all other applicable federal, state, and municipal laws, rules, and regulations.

Financial Documents

Most loan commitments require that all financial information submitted by the borrower to the lender in connection with the mortgage loan application be recertified by the borrower at the time of closing. This typically is done by an affidavit of no adverse change wherein the borrower swears that all financial information previously submitted to the lender is true and correct and that there has been no adverse material change in its financial condition since the application.

Documents

The commitment specifies what loan documents are needed to close the loan. These documents include a note, a mortgage or deed of trust, and, in the case of a commercial loan, an assignment of leases and rents, a security agreement, and a Uniform Commercial Code (UCC) financing statement. Construction mortgage loan commitments also may require a construction loan agreement and assignments of the construction contract and the architects' and engineers' contracts.

Defaults and Late Charges

A loan commitment provides that the loan documents include default provisions. Most default provisions are subject to reasonable notice and grace periods to cure before the various remedies available to the lender can be invoked. With respect to monetary defaults, such as failure to pay the debt or pay taxes or pay insurance premiums, a five- or ten-day right to cure is common. In the case of nonmonetary defaults, the borrower may be given 20 to 30 days to cure such default.

A loan commitment may specify a late fee for note payments not made on time. This fee reimburses the lender the cost of processing late payments. In addition to a late fee, the loan commitment may require that a default rate of interest be applied to the unamortized portion of the loan at the date of default. Default rates are substantially higher than the interest rate applicable to the loan when the borrower is not in default.

Commitment Fee

Most loan commitments require the borrower to deliver to the lender before closing a specified sum of money as consideration for the issuance of the commitment. This fee may be called a commitment fee deposit, standby fee, earnest money, or a similar name.

Loan Expenses

The commitment provides that all expenses, fees, and costs incurred with respect to the loan, including but not limited to lender's attorney fees, title insurance fees, survey costs, recording and filing fees, mortgage taxes or other taxes on the note and mortgage, cost of appraisals, and personal inspections, be paid by the borrower.

Closing and Commitment Expiration Date

A loan commitment indicates the date on which the loan closing is to be held and the lender is to disburse the loan proceeds. The closing is conditioned on the borrower's having complied with all conditions of the commitment to the satisfaction of the lender and its counsel.

In addition to the loan closing date, a commitment may set forth a commitment expiration date, which may or may not coincide with the closing date.

Disbursement of Loan Proceeds

A loan commitment specifies how the proceeds of the loan are to be disbursed on closing to the borrower, whether by cash, lender's check, check on federal funds, bank wire, or wire of federal funds. The lender may place good funds in the closing attorney's escrow account, and the closing attorney will disburse all checks from that account.

Acceptance of a Loan Commitment

A loan commitment is not effective or binding until it has been accepted by the borrower.

Assignability

A loan commitment is personal to the borrower and cannot be assigned without the lender's consent.

A review of the loan commitment provides the paralegal with a checklist of items needed to close and fund the loan. A checklist of closing requirements compiled from an example of a loan commitment for a residential loan (Exhibit 14–5) follows.

The following is a checklist of closing requirements compiled from Exhibit 14–6.

✓ CHECKLIST

Loan Commitment for a Residential Loan

1. Title commitment/insurance
2. Survey
3. Hazard insurance
4. Truth-in-lending statement
5. Borrower's affidavit
6. Note
7. Mortgage
8. Settlement statement

EXHIBIT 14–5

Loan Commitment for
Residential Loan

American Eagle Mortgage Company
March 7, 20 __

Ms. Helen Davis
849 Mentelle Drive, N.E.
Atlanta, Georgia 30308

Re: Mortgage Loan Commitment—$100,000.00 at 6.5% for thirty (30) years

Dear Ms. Davis:

American Eagle Mortgage Company (the "Company") is pleased to inform you that it has acted upon your application and has approved a loan to you, subject to all terms and conditions of this letter. The loan will be in the principal sum of $100,000.00 at an annual rate of 6.5%, to be repaid as follows:

In equal consecutive monthly installments of $632.07 per month for thirty (30) years. Each installment, when paid, shall be applied first to the payment of accrued interest and then to the unpaid principal balance.

The holder may collect a "late charge" not to exceed an amount equal to four percent (4%) of any installment which is not paid within fifteen (15) days of the due date thereof, to cover the extra expenses involved in handling delinquent payments.

The loan proceeds shall be used for the acquisition of improved real estate (the "Property") located at 5167 Tilly Mill Road, Atlanta, Georgia.

The loan shall be secured by a first priority lien on the Property and on all improvements now or hereafter existing thereon. The Company's agreement to make the loan to you is subject to satisfaction of the following conditions, all at your sole cost and expense and in a manner acceptable to the Company.

1. The Company shall procure a standard form ALTA mortgagee's policy of title insurance insuring the loan as a first priority lien against the Property, showing there is to be no other encumbrances against the Property which render it unmarketable.

2. You shall provide the Company prior to closing with a recent plat of survey of the Property, together with a surveyor's certificate in form satisfactory to the Company's title insuror, depicting and certifying all improvements on the Property to be completely within the boundary lines of the Property and to be in compliance with all applicable building or setback line restrictions.

3. You shall provide the Company prior to closing with fire, lightning and extended coverage insurance issued by a company or companies and upon terms acceptable to the Company in at least the sum of $100,000.00. Premiums for such insurance shall be paid by you for not less than one year in advance. All policies shall be issued with a mortgagee clause in favor of and acceptable to the Company and shall be non-cancellable without at least ten (10) days prior written notice to the Company.

4. The Company shall select an attorney to close the loan and to prepare all documents deemed necessary or appropriate by the Company to evidence the loan and to establish the Company's first priority lien against the Property and the Policy. All such loan documents will be in form and substance satisfactory to the Company's closing attorney.

5. All actual fees or expenses (including, without limitation, such closing attorney's fees, title insurance premiums, cost of title examination, abstract of title fee, document preparation fee, cost of survey, appraisal fee, recording fees and intangibles or other taxes) incurred in connection with reviewing your loan application, or with closing, servicing, collecting or cancelling the loan, shall be paid by you.

(continued)

EXHIBIT 14–5

Loan Commitment for
Residential Loan (*continued*)

6. The loan may be assumed by a transferee of the Property, provided the Company gives prior written consent thereto; but any transfer of title to all or any part of the Property whatsoever, or any further encumbrance or other lien imposed against the Property without the Company's prior written consent, will authorize the Company to declare the loan immediately due and payable. Any such assumption, transfer or encumbrance to which the Company shall consent shall be upon such terms and conditions as the Company shall determine and approve.

7. You shall pay a non-refundable commitment fee of $1000.00 to the Company upon your acceptance of this commitment letter.

8. You shall provide the Company with photographs of all buildings or other structural improvements on the Property prior to closing.

9. You shall pay an appraisal fee to the Company in the amount of $450.00.

10. The loan is to be escrowed for taxes and insurance premiums.

Very truly yours,
AMERICAN EAGLE MORTGAGE COMPANY

By: _____
    J. Perry Drake
    Treasurer

✓ CHECKLIST

Loan Commitment for a Commercial Loan

1. Title examination and title commitment
2. Survey and surveyor's inspection report
3. Fire insurance
4. Borrower's attorney's opinion
5. Copy of personal property list
6. Copies of all leases
7. Tenant estoppel letters for all leases
8. Subordination and nondisturbance attornment agreement for all leases
9. Certificate of occupancy for all leases
10. Certified articles of incorporation and bylaws—Acme, Inc.
11. Certificate of good standing—Acme, Inc.
12. Corporate resolution—Acme, Inc.
13. Environmental audit
14. Photograph of improvements
15. Federal tax ID number
16. Zoning letter
17. Utility letters
18. Letter from regional office of Environmental Protection Agency
19. Borrower's affidavit
20. Promissory note
21. Deed to secure debt
22. Assignment of rents and leases
23. Security agreement
24. UCC financing statement
25. Rental achievement escrow
26. Loan closing statement

EXHIBIT 14–6

Commercial Loan Commitment Letter

RE: First Mortgage Loan—$1,150,000
Acme, Inc., Mortgagor
10¾% 25 year amortization
Call options in year 10, 15, 20

Dear

We are pleased to advise that our Investment Review Committee has approved the above captioned first mortgage loan. The loan will be in the amount of $1,150,000 at an interest rate of 10¾% per annum, and is to be amortized over a period of twenty-five (25) years by equal monthly installments of $11,068.75, including interest. Lender reserves the right to declare the entire amount of outstanding principal and all unpaid accrued interest thereon to be immediately due and payable on any one of the following dates: ten (10), fifteen (15), or twenty (20) years from the first installment of principal and interest. Such right shall be exercised by lender by giving written notice to borrower at least six (6) months prior to date on which said payment of all principal and interest shall be due and payable.

An interest bearing escrow account is to be established in the amount of $300,000 with an escrow agent acceptable to lender, with all interest accruing in the name of the borrower. Said escrow will be held until such time that 23,089 square feet is leased at an average of $12.50 per square foot, net of free rent or other rental concessions, producing a gross income of at least $288,613 annually. Said leases are to be for a minimum term of one year and shall be acceptable to lender. If the above requirements have not been met prior to January 31, 20__ the $300,000 shall be applied to reduce the principal balance of the loan without penalty and in inverse order to the normal monthly payments owing.

This commitment is issued subject to the following conditions:

1. The loan is to be secured by a valid first lien on the fee simple title to the following described property, together with the improvements thereon, located in the city limits of _____
_____. Said property is a rectangle that contains approximately 2.11 acres with 248 feet of frontage on Carpenter Drive. The physical address is 275 Carpenter Drive.

We are to be provided with a complete and accurate legal description subject to our approval prior to closing of this loan.

2. All loan documents, agreements or other instruments used in connection with this transaction shall first have the approval of our Legal Department and must be prepared by an attorney designated by our Legal Department.

3. All legal fees and other expenses in connection with the closing of this loan are to be paid by the mortgagor. It is further understood that the mortgagor will pay any expenses incident to this transaction should for any reason the loan not be closed after said expenses have been incurred.

4. Fire and extended coverage insurance policies are to be furnished in an amount at least equal to the amount of the loan and not less than the full insurable value of the improvements, issued by a company or companies satisfactory to us. If the policy carries a co-insurance clause or other clause limiting the amount of coverage under certain conditions the insurance must be in such an amount as to give full coverage under all conditions. All insurable buildings and personal property or easily removable real estate items or fixtures included in the security instrument must be covered by such insurance.

5. The loan documents shall contain the following items or provisions:

a. No prepayment of the principal of this note shall be allowed prior to the fifth anniversary of the date hereof. After the fifth anniversary of the date hereof, the principal of this note may be prepaid in whole but not in part, on any interest payment date herein, provided that: (1) not later than sixty (60) days prior to such prepayment, Applicant delivers written notice to Holder, and that Applicant intends to prepay the note in full on the date specified in such notice; and (2) Applicant pays to Holder at the time of such prepayment, a percentage of the prepaid

(continued)

EXHIBIT 14–6

Commercial Loan Commitment
Letter (*continued*)

principal amount as a prepayment premium. Such percentage shall be the product obtained by multiplying the prepaid principal amount by the product of the following:

(i) the amount obtained by subtracting the annualized yield on a United States Treasury Bill, Note or Bond with maturity date which occurs closest to the next applicable call date of this Note, as such annualized yield is reported by *The Wall Street Journal* on the business day preceding the date of prepayment from 10¾% multiplied by:

(ii) the number of years and fraction thereof remaining between the date of prepayment and the next applicable call date of this note.

Notwithstanding the foregoing, however, in the event of acceleration of the Note at any time and subsequent involuntary or voluntary prepayment, the Prepayment Premium shall be payable, however in no event shall it exceed an amount equal to the excess, if any, of (i) interest calculated at the highest applicable rate permitted by applicable law, as construed by courts having jurisdiction thereof, on the principal balance of the Note from time to time outstanding from the date hereof to the date of such acceleration, over (ii) interest theretofore paid and accrued on the Note. Any prepaid amounts specified in such notice shall become due and payable at the time provided in such notice. A "Loan Year" for the purposes of this Note shall mean each successive twelve (12) month period beginning with the date of the first installment payment of interest hereunder provided however, that the first Loan Year shall include the period from the date of this Note to the date of such first installment payment of interest. Under no circumstances shall the prepayment premium ever be less than zero. The amount of prepayment shall never be less than the full amount of the then outstanding principal and interest.

In addition to the above described prepayment penalty, a reinvestment fee of ½ of 1% of the outstanding loan balance will be due in the event of prepayment prior to the maturity of this loan.

b. An assignment of rents in a form satisfactory to our Legal Department.

c. The holder may collect a "late charge" not to exceed an amount equal to four percent (4%) of any installment which is not paid within fifteen (15) days of the due date thereof, to cover the extra expense involved in handling delinquent payments, provided that collection of said late charge shall not be deemed a waiver by the holder of any of its other rights under this note.

d. The Lender is to be furnished with a certified, itemized statement of annual income and expenses on the property covered by this loan within 90 days following the end of each fiscal or calendar year.

e. The usual covenant requiring monthly escrow deposits for annual payment of ad valorem taxes and hazard insurance premiums.

f. It shall be a default under the mortgage if, without the Lender's prior written consent, the real property security for this loan or any part thereof is sold, transferred, conveyed or encumbered in any way. Notwithstanding the above, Lender hereby agrees to allow a one-time transfer of ownership and assumption of this loan by a qualified borrower acceptable to Lender. As consideration for this transfer and assumption, the Lender will receive a non-refundable 1% fee based on the then outstanding balance, payable at the time of transfer.

g. Installments shall be due and payable on the first day of each month.

h. The Promissory Note taken in this transaction will include a provision which reads "Subject to the terms of the next succeeding paragraph and notwithstanding anything to the contrary otherwise contained in this Note, it is agreed that the promise of Maker to pay the principal indebtedness and the interest on this Note shall be for the sole purpose of establishing the existence of an indebtedness; Holder's source of satisfaction of said indebtedness and of Maker's other obligations hereunder and under the Loan Documents is limited solely to (a) the property described in the Mortgage, (b) Holder's receipt of the rents, issues and profits from the property described in the Mortgage and (c) any separate agreements guaranteeing the payment of the amounts due hereunder and under the Loan Documents and Makers' performance hereunder and under the Loan Documents; Holder shall not seek to procure

(continued)

EXHIBIT 14–6

Commercial Loan Commitment
Letter (*continued*)

payment out of any other assets of Maker, or to procure any judgment against Maker for any amount which is or may be payable under this Note, the Mortgage or any of the other Loan Documents or for any deficiency remaining after foreclosure of the Mortgage; provided, however, that nothing herein contained shall be deemed to be a release or impairment of said indebtedness or the security therefor intended by the Mortgage, or be deemed to preclude Holder from foreclosing the Mortgage or from enforcing any of Holder's rights thereunder, or in any way or manner affecting Holder's rights and privileges under any of the Loan Documents or any separate agreements guaranteeing Maker's payment and performance hereunder and under the Loan Documents.

Notwithstanding the foregoing limitation of liability provision, it is expressly understood and agreed that Maker shall be personally liable for the payment to the Holder of:

(a) all security deposits of tenants, any rents that are collected more than one (1) month in advance, and all income, rents, issues, profits and revenues derived from the property described in the Mortgage which are not promptly applied to payment of the indebtedness evidenced by the Note and/or to the costs of normal maintenance and operation of such property;

(b) any loss due to fraud or misrepresentations to Holder by Maker (or by any of its general partners, by any of the general partners of any of its general partners or by any of its or their agents, if applicable);

(c) the misapplication of (i) proceeds paid under any insurance policies by reason of damage, loss or destruction to any portion of the property described in the Mortgage to the full extent of such misapplied proceeds, or (ii) proceeds of awards resulting from the condemnation or other taking in lieu of condemnation of any portion of such property, to the full extent of such misapplied proceeds or awards;

(d) any loss due to waste of the property described in the Mortgage or any portion thereof, and all costs, including reasonable attorneys' fees, incurred by Holder to protect such property and any other security for the indebtedness evidenced by this Note or to enforce such Note, the Mortgage and any of the other Loan Documents; and

(e) any taxes, assessments and insurance premiums for which Maker is liable under this Note, the Mortgage or any of the other Loan Documents and which are paid by Holder; and

(f) arising under the hazardous substance indemnification and hold harmless agreement and the borrower's hazardous substances covenant's warranties and representations provisions contained in the attached as Exhibits "A & B."

6. Prior to closing, the Borrower must furnish to the Lender, at the Borrower's sole cost and expense, the original of an environmental audit and certification addressed to Lender and Lender's successors and assigns, with form acceptable to Lender, and prepared by a licensed engineer and geotechnical consultant ("Engineer") or either including field reconnaissance, site history records survey, tenant use history record survey, and an examination of the Compensation and Liability Systems Record in the State in which the property is located, to establish that a thorough investigation of those records and an inspection of the property site and improvements reveal no evidence of any pollutant or other toxic or hazardous substance, as defined under the Comprehensive Environmental Response, Compensation, and Liability Act ("CERCLA"), 42 U.S.C. 9601 *et seq.*, as amended, or any other federal, state or local law ("Hazardous Substance"). In the event the Engineer determines in his or her professional judgment that an examination of the sub-surface soils is necessary, then the parties contemplate that Borrower will require that the Engineer provide the Borrower with an estimate of the additional charges which will be incurred in such examination. In the event that Borrower provides Lender with written notice, received by Lender within five (5) days of the Borrower's receipt of the estimate, that Borrower has determined that the additional charges are not acceptable, then Borrower may simultaneously provide Lender with Borrower's written election to cancel this Commitment Letter in which event the commitment fee will be refunded to Borrower and neither Borrower nor Lender will thereafter have any liability to the other under this Commitment Letter. In the event that Borrower either: (i) fails to provide Lender with receipt of written notice within

EXHIBIT 14–6

Commercial Loan Commitment Letter (*continued*)

the said five (5) days of receiving said estimate, or, (ii) determines that the additional charges are acceptable, then the Borrower will be deemed to have elected to close without regard to such additional charges and said audit and certificate must be provided to Lender by Borrower and must include a subsurface soils examination or any other examination deemed necessary and the cost thereof will be paid by Borrower. In any event, the charges for the environmental audit and certification will be paid in full by Borrower.

With respect to any Hazardous Substance found on the property, the environmental audit must indicate the nature of the substance, the statutory control over the removal process, the time and costs of removal, and the assessment of risk.

The loan documents will contain the Borrower's covenants, representations, warranties and indemnities, in the identical form of the wording attached hereto as Exhibit "A & B."

The Borrower must, at the Borrower's sole cost and expense, obtain and provide to Lender at or before closing the original of a letter addressed to Lender from the Regional Office of the Environmental Protection Agency establishing whether the property or property in the vicinity of the property has been the location of a hazardous waste site.

In the event that the environmental audit or the letter from the Environmental Protection Agency reveals that the property has or has had any Hazardous Substance located on or in the property or the improvements located on the property, or any other condition which Lender determines to be objectionable, then Lender, may at its option elect not to close this loan. If Lender, after reviewing any item required of Borrower under this provision, determines not to close this loan, then this Commitment Letter will be canceled and the commitment fee will be refunded to Borrower and neither Borrower nor Lender will thereafter have any liability to the other under this Commitment Letter.

7. The financing statement covering the fixtures and equipment will be properly executed and recorded, and the properly executed security agreement delivered to us.

8. We are to be furnished with an engineer's survey, certified to by a registered surveyor, dated within 90 days prior to closing, showing no encroachments other than those approved by us and showing the improvements to be within lot and building lines.

9. We are to be furnished with a mortgagee title insurance policy issued by a company approved by us, or an endorsement to a previously issued title policy, which will insure that the Lender has a first lien without exceptions, other than those specifically approved by us.

10. Any outstanding unpaid taxes and assessments are to be paid prior to our disbursement of the loan proceeds.

11. We will require loss of rent insurance in an amount not less than nine (9) months gross rental.

12. In order to comply with IRS Regulation TD 8047, we are to be furnished with the social security number, in the case of an individual mortgagor, or the tax identification number for all other mortgagors. We must be provided with this number prior to the closing of this loan.

13. We are to be furnished a current written opinion of counsel for the Borrower, satisfactory to Lender, to the effect that the subject loan is not usurious or otherwise illegal under applicable law and that all loan documents are valid and binding upon Borrower and are enforceable in accordance with their terms.

14. We have tentatively scheduled this loan for closing sometime during the month of January, 20___, and this commitment shall expire January 31, 20___.

15. Provided this commitment is acceptable, you are to forward your check, within ten (10) business days from the date hereof, in the amount of $34,500. This amount plus $11,500 previously received from you will be held by us in a non-interest bearing account as a commitment fee. If and when this loan is closed under the terms and conditions of this commitment letter, $43,500 of the above $46,000 commitment fee will be refunded. However, if this loan is not closed, it is agreed and understood that upon expiration or cancellation of this commitment this fee will be retained by Lender as consideration for this commitment. If Borrower should elect to do so, Lender will accept $23,000 of the above fee in the form of a Letter of Credit. The

(continued)

EXHIBIT 14–6

Commercial Loan Commitment Letter (*continued*)

Letter of Credit must be drawn on an institution and be in a form acceptable to Lender with an expiration date no earlier than March 31, 20___.

16. Lender reserves the right to cancel this commitment and terminate its obligations hereunder at any time upon the happening of any of the following events:

    a. Borrower's failure to comply with any of the applicable conditions of this commitment within the time specified.

    b. Non-payment of any of the fees or expenses to be paid by the Borrower in connection with this commitment.

    c. Any infirmity in Borrower's title to the real estate, filed by or against Borrower any petition in bankruptcy or insolvency or for the reorganization of Borrower or appointment of a receiver or trustee or the making of an assignment for the benefit of creditors.

17. This agreement is made for the sole protection of the Borrower and the Lender, its successors and assigns and no other person or persons shall have any right of action thereon, and this commitment is not assignable or transferable by Borrower.

    Lender reserves the absolute right to partially or totally assign this commitment to a third party lending institution for the purpose of facilitating a participation loan. By acceptance of this commitment letter, Borrower acknowledges and agrees that this loan may be a loan in which an additional lender may act as a participating lender at the time of funding.

    We appreciate your offering us the opportunity to make this loan and trust that it will be handled to your entire satisfaction.

Sincerely,

SPECIAL PROVISIONS IN A CONSTRUCTION LOAN COMMITMENT

A commitment for a construction loan may contain special provisions in addition to the regular provisions found in other loan commitments.

A lender in a construction loan wants the right to (a) review and approve all preliminary and final plans or specifications; (b) be consulted on and approve any and all changes in such plans of specification; (c) establish minimum standards for construction; (d) establish a time schedule for the various stages of construction from commencement to completion; (e) receive periodic progress reports; (f) undertake periodic inspections of the construction; (g) be supplied with a certificate of the architect as to the satisfactory completion of the work in accordance with the plans and specification; (h) be supplied with a certificate of borrower as to the total construction costs required for the project; (i) be supplied with a certificate of borrower stating that all utility lines (electricity, gas, water, and sanitary sewers) are completed, connected, and adequate; and (j) be supplied with pictures of the project as construction progresses.

These additional construction requirements may necessitate submission of the following items to the lender before closing: (a) a copy of the construction contract; (b) a copy of all major subcontracts; (c) a copy of the building permit; (d) utility letters; (e) final plans and specifications; (f) the architect's contract; (g) the engineer's contract; (h) a cost breakdown of all construction components; and (i) the retention of a construction supervisor or inspector.

In addition, construction loans require other forms of documentation. For example, a construction loan agreement and an assignment of all major contracts are required. Copies of these forms are included in Chapter 11. The title insurance policy contains a pending disbursement clause and may require periodic title change checkdowns and endorsements to insure the loan in full as construction progresses. The fire and casualty insurance is in the form of builder's risk insurance. Builder's risk insurance insures the risk of a building during the stages of construction. Liability insurance and workers' compensation insurance are required on construction projects.

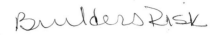

Most construction loans are paid from a refinancing of the construction loan with a permanent loan. Therefore, a construction loan commitment provides that the permanent commitment must be in existence before the funding of the construction loan. A construction lender may require an assignment of the permanent commitment along with the permanent lender's consent to the assignment. This permits the construction lender, in the event there is a default during construction, to take over the project, finish it, and deliver the permanent loan, thereby receiving the proceeds from the permanent loan.

Hazardous Waste

Most loan commitments provide that the borrower will indemnify the lender against damage or liability caused by hazardous waste located in or on the property. These indemnities are carried over and included in the loan documents.

Leasehold Loans

If the loan commitment contemplates taking as security a leasehold interest, it will contain several additional provisions. The commitment requires an assignment of the borrower's interest as tenant under the lease as well as an assignment of borrower's interest in any underlying subleases, licenses, or other agreements. The loan commitment requires the borrower to supply the lender at closing with a certificate from the landlord of the ground lease stating (a) the ground lease is in full force and effect; (b) it has not been modified, supplemented, or amended except as set forth in such certificate; (c) the rent payments are current and have not been paid in advance except as required by such lease; (d) the tenant is not in default under any of the terms or provisions of such lease; or (e) if tenant is in default, the nature of such default is explained.

The loan commitment requires that the unexpired term of the lease being offered for security be of sufficient duration to cover the term of the loan.

With respect to a ground lease taken as security, the lender requires its counsel to review such lease. In some instances, the lender requests that the ground lessor subordinate its interest to the mortgage loan by signing the mortgage documents. This permits the lender, in the event of default, to foreclose on the leasehold as well as the fee and to obtain fee simple title at foreclosure.

A leasehold loan commitment may require the borrower, as a condition of closing, to give to the lender a document providing that the ground lessor will give written notice of any default by tenant or borrower under the lease to lender and allow lender adequate time to cure any such default. A lender may require that in the event the ground lease terminates, the landlord will enter into a new lease with the lender for the unexpired term of the ground lease on the same terms and conditions as the ground lease.

THE CLOSING AND AFTERMATH

By the time the closing day arrives, it is hoped that most of the requirements and all the loan and sale documents have been prepared by the paralegal. All the parties (seller, purchaser, and brokers) have been notified of the date, time, and place of the closing. The purchaser knows the exact amount of money to bring to the closing and has been instructed to bring good funds in the form of a certified or cashier's check or by wire transfer into the firm's escrow account.

Most closing proceeds are disbursed through the law firm's or title insurance company's escrow account. The purchaser, therefore, should be instructed to bring funds in the form of a cashier's check made payable to the law firm or title insurance company or arrange for wire transfer to the account.

Closings usually take place in a conference room of the law firm handling the closing or at the office of the title insurance company. After the introduction of the parties to one another, the closing usually commences with the closing attorney explaining the sale documents to the seller and the purchaser. Ideally, the seller and purchaser have received copies of all documents and have already reviewed and approved them. In many residential transactions, this ideal is not met, and the parties may be seeing the documents for the first time at the closing table. Additional copies of each document should be prepared so that each party will have its own copy to review while the documents are being explained. The item of prime interest is the closing statement, in which all the closing disbursements and costs have been outlined. The seller is interested in making certain that all payoffs and satisfaction of prior liens are correct according to his or her records and that brokerage commissions and other expenses he or she are required to pay are in the correct amounts. The agents are interested in determining that commission amounts are true and correct. It is not unusual for adjustments to be made at the time of closing. Unpaid charges, such as cleanup bills or other expenses that need to be reimbursed between the parties, may not be brought to the closing attorney's attention until the date of closing. Sums of money allocated to pay for termite protection, hazard insurance, and surveys may have already been paid and need to be deleted from the closing statement. Most seasoned closing attorneys review the closing statement first; if changes are to be made, they are taken care of while the closing is progressing. This results in a new and corrected closing statement at the end of the closing, which can then be signed.

The usual sequence of events for most closings is to handle the sale aspects first, with the seller signing all the transfer documents. Then the loan transaction takes place, with the purchaser signing all the loan documents.

It may be desirable and prudent on some commercial transactions for the loan closing to take place before the sale. Many commercial borrowers do not want the seller to know what terms were arranged for financing the property. If this is desired by the parties, then two closings will be scheduled: first the loan closing and then the sale closing.

The closing is finished after all the documents have been signed, witnessed, and notarized; good funds have been verified from the purchaser and the lender; and all checks have been cut and disbursements made to those parties present at closing. At many residential transactions, the seller delivers keys to the purchaser, and the dates for vacating and occupying the property are clearly understood between the parties. Purchaser and seller should receive copies of all closing documents signed by the seller and purchaser in connection with the closing. Most brokers require that only a copy of the closing statement be given to them.

Representatives of the lenders for residential closings seldom attend the closing. Representatives of the lender for a commercial closing may be present at the closing. This is important because last-minute details in the loan often are negotiated at the closing table. Documents that are changed at closing should be either retyped or altered at the table. All alterations should be initialed by all parties affected by the alterations.

Disbursing, Recording, and Transmitting Final Documents

After the purchaser, seller, and agent have gone home, the closing paralegal still has much to do before the job is done. Checks have already been disbursed to the seller and real estate agents at closing. The next checks to disburse immediately after closing are the checks to pay off all prior mortgages, liens, or encumbrances against the real property. Before disbursing any monies, the paralegal should be satisfied that the check received from the purchaser will be honored by the bank on which it is drawn and satisfied that the check provided by the lender will be honored when it is presented. Because most firms disburse all monies through their escrow accounts and all checks paid from closing will be firm checks, it is required that lenders, purchasers, or anyone supplying funds for the closing provide either cashier's or certified checks drawn on a federal reserve bank. If funds are to be wired into the firm's escrow account, they should be sent by federal wire. It is important when issuing checks that a ledger card be used to balance the funds received against the funds paid out.

The custom in some states is to record all the documents before disbursements are made. If the paralegal is closing in a state that has this custom, he or she would then record the documents before making any disbursements to the parties in connection with the transaction.

Otherwise, all closing documents that are to be recorded should be recorded immediately after closing. This usually includes the deed of conveyance from seller to purchaser and the mortgage from purchaser or borrower to the lender. It also may include assignments for rents and leases, UCC financing statements, satisfaction of liens, or other matters that may be recorded in connection with a particular transaction. Most firms use couriers to deliver the recorded documents to the clerk's office. In some parts of the country, rush recording is available for an additional fee. With rush recording, the clerk's office can index, record, and copy the documents and return the originals the same day.

All monies to pay off liens or satisfactions should be sent with a transmittal letter. The transmittal letter should include a statement that the money being sent constitutes payment in full of the debt and that the check is being cashed based on that assumption. It is a good idea to request that all satisfactions and releases of mortgages or liens be returned to the paralegal. The paralegal should provide a self-addressed, stamped envelope for the return. It also is advisable to call the person to whom satisfaction money has been sent to make sure that he or she has received it and that the sum is sufficient to pay off the debt.

Most lenders require that a loan document package consisting of all the original documents except those documents that have been sent to record be delivered to them the day after the closing. The transmittal package to the lender is important because it reveals the quality of the firm's work. There should be no errors, and all the lender's instructions should be followed to the letter. Making errors or not following instructions could lead to the law firm's being removed from the lender's approved list and could seriously affect the firm's economic viability.

Final Closeout by the Paralegal

After all deeds, mortgages, and other loan documents have been recorded and returned from the clerk's office and all cancellations and other satisfactions have been returned and recorded, it is time to close out the file. Original recorded documents need to be sent to the parties entitled to receive them. The purchaser is entitled to receive the warranty deed, and the lender is entitled to receive the recorded mortgage, assignment of rents, UCC financing statements, and so on.

Another aspect of the closeout is the issuance of the final title insurance policies. A final title examination is necessary to verify that the deed and loan documents have in fact been recorded and do properly appear in the index of the record room. A final title examination also searches for the recorded satisfactions on all prior liens and security deeds.

Most lenders will not accept title policies unless the general standard exceptions for parties in possession, matters of survey, unrecorded easements, and mechanic's liens are deleted. In addition, if any restrictive covenants are set forth in Schedule B, most lenders require the inclusion of an affirmative provision in the policy stating that said restrictive covenants have not been violated to date and that any future violation will not result in the forfeiture or reversion of title.

The title policy should follow the commitment exactly. The effective date of the owner's policy is the date of the recording of the deed, and the effective date of the loan policy is the date of the recording of the mortgage.

✓ CHECKLIST

Real Estate Closing Tasks

☐ I. File Creation
  ☐ A. Open file
    1. Client name
    2. Client number
    3. Billing information
    4. Cross reference and conflict check

☐ II. Information Gathering
  ☐ A. Review real estate contract
    1. Name of seller
    2. Name of purchaser
    3. Name of broker
    4. Description of real property
    5. Date of closing
    6. Requirements of seller
    7. Requirements of purchaser
  ☐ B. Prepare closing checklist from review of real estate contract
  ☐ C. Review loan commitment
    1. Name of lender
    2. Name of borrower
    3. Amount of loan
    4. Commitment expiration date
    5. Loan closing requirements
  ☐ D. Prepare a loan closing checklist
  ☐ E. Order title examination and title policy
    1. Description of real property
    2. Date when examination is required
    3. Name of title company
    4. Name of insured
    5. Insured amount
  ☐ F. Order survey
    1. Legal description of property
    2. Information regarding previous survey
    3. Name of purchaser and other names to appear on survey
    4. Name of lending institution to appear on survey

(continued)

      5. Flood hazard certification

      6. Other special requirements for survey

      7. Date of completion for survey

☐   G. Order hazard and fire insurance

      1. Name of insured

      2. Proper address of property

      3. Amount of insurance

      4. Proof insurance premium has been paid one year in advance

      5. Name of lender for mortgagee clause

      6. Date for delivery of insurance policy

☐ **III. Preclosing Procedures**

  ☐ A. Review title examination and title policy

  ☐ B. Obtain copies of all title exceptions

  ☐ C. Request satisfaction amounts from any mortgages, liens, or encumbrances to be paid at closing

  ☐ D. Review survey

      1. Do improvements encroach over property line?

      2. Is survey in compliance with purchaser and lender requirements?

  ☐ E. Verify that all sale obligations have been met by both purchaser and seller

  ☐ F. Verify that all mortgage loan commitment requirements have been satisfied

☐ **IV. Document Preparation**

  ☐ A. Preparation of all purchase and sale documents

  ☐ B. Preparation of all loan documents

☐ **V. Closing**

  ☐ A. Inform all parties (purchaser, seller, broker, lender representatives) of the date, time, and place of closing

  ☐ B. Inform purchaser of proper amount of proceeds needed for closing and instruct purchaser to bring good funds

  ☐ C. Verify that lender has deposited loan proceeds with firm

  ☐ D. Reserve conference room

  ☐ E. Prepare closing packet of documents for purchaser and seller

☐ **VI. Disbursing, Recording, and Transmittal of Final Documents**

  ☐ A. Transmit deed, mortgage, and other documents to be recorded to courthouse for recording

  ☐ B. Transmit money necessary to pay prior liens, mortgages, and encumbrances to proper parties

  ☐ C. Prepare final package for purchaser and seller

  ☐ D. Prepare final loan package for lender

☐ **VII. Final Closeout**

  ☐ A. Obtain all deeds, mortgages, and other documents recorded from courthouse

  ☐ B. Obtain all satisfactions and cancellations for prior mortgages, liens, and encumbrances

  ☐ C. Order final title examination and verify proper recording and indexing of deed, mortgage, and other recorded documents

  ☐ D. Obtain and review title insurance policy

  ☐ E. Transmit recorded deed and title insurance policy to purchaser

  ☐ F. Transmit recorded mortgage and other loan documents and title insurance policy to lender

  ☐ G. Final review of file to verify that all closing procedures have been completed

  ☐ H. Close file and send to storage

After the title policies have been prepared and sent to the lender with the recorded mortgage and to the purchaser with the recorded warranty deed, the file should be rechecked to make sure that everything has been taken care of and that all checks have been disbursed, ledger cards balanced, all documents recorded and delivered to the proper parties, and all liens and other debts satisfied and cancelled. The entire transaction is now completed, and the file can be sent to storage.

It is not unusual for four to six weeks to elapse between the closing and the final completion of the file.

A real estate closing is a complicated procedure, and it is essential that the paralegal be organized and pay attention to detail. The best method to achieve organization and attention to detail is to prepare a checklist for all the items required in a real estate closing. As previously discussed, each real estate closing is unique and has its own checklist. The checklists that appear earlier in the chapter are examples of the types of things one would expect to find in a real estate closing. The following checklist is a general outline of all the aspects of a real estate closing.

USE OF E-MAIL

In many law firms and other businesses, electronic mail or e-mail has replaced most other forms of communication, such as letters, telephone calls, and telephone facsimiles. The ease and rapidity of e-mail has made its use the favorite of all communication methods required for a closing. Even legal documents, which may be changed electronically, may be e-mailed between parties as attachments to other e-mail communications.

When using e-mail, a paralegal should remember that it is a written form of communication and is the same as a letter. Even though you may hit the delete button and erase the e-mail from your computer screen, the e-mail generally is not destroyed and may later be retrieved. In the event there is litigation involving a closing, e-mails are discoverable as evidence in the litigation. With these general rules in mind, a paralegal should consider the following thoughts in regard to any e-mail communication.

The first issue to be considered is whether an e-mail is the appropriate way to deliver the message. If the matter is urgent and requires a quick response, a telephone call or even a personal visit (especially if the other person is a member of your firm) may be more practical than an e-mail. If the subject matter of the e-mail is sensitive or very complex, a telephone call or a personal visit may also be appropriate. A paralegal should always think: "Is there anything in the e-mail that you would not want anyone else involved in the transaction to see?" If there is, then the e-mail is probably an inappropriate way to deliver the message.

A paralegal needs to be careful about what is said in an e-mail. Since all e-mails may later be discoverable in any future litigation, you may be asked to explain what was written in the e-mail. It is recommended that before you draft an e-mail, you make sure that the content is accurate, complete, and presented in an organized manner. You should also be aware of the tone of voice in the message, especially in communicating with other participants in a closing. E-mails should be respectful, avoiding sarcasm and humor. It is a good idea not to send an e-mail if you are angry. Wait until you have calmed down before you send it. E-mails should be written using the same formality and grammar that you would use in a business letter. Always avoid any derogatory or inflammatory remarks involving any of the participants in the closing. When sending an e-mail, you should also avoid sending multipage string e-mails. If the e-mail you are forwarding contains a string of previous e-mails, you may want to take the time to send it as a single e-mail without the trail.

Another issue a paralegal should consider is selecting the audience for the e-mail. The paralegal should limit distribution of e-mails to only those people who need to know.

When issuing an e-mail with potentially sensitive or confidential information for the first time to a party, make sure the e-mail address has been verified by a telephone call or other means. You also need to use the same discretion when responding to an e-mail. If you wish to respond to only one person on the e-mail, then respond to that person and avoid hitting the "respond to all" button.

A paralegal should always be aware of the attorney-client privilege when using an e-mail. When sending an e-mail to a client, a notation should be made on the e-mail that it is "Privileged and Confidential" and is an attorney-client communication.

Finally, as previously mentioned, the e-mail can be discovered if there is litigation. E-mail discovery can be very expensive. When using e-mail, use it only for communication that is necessary for the transaction, thereby reducing your total number of e-mails and saving any future discovery costs for the client.

TECHNOLOGY FOR DOCUMENT PRODUCTION

The representation of a seller, purchaser, or lender in connection with a real estate closing involves the preparation of numerous legal documents. Computerized automated document preparation systems have been in existence for several years. These systems become more sophisticated each year as technology advances in the area. The automated document preparation systems generally in use today are either older fill-in-the-blank, search-for-the-code document systems or intelligent document assembly systems. The older technology uses generic forms that have blanks for variable information such as the names of the parties, loan amounts, and legal descriptions. It is necessary for the user of this system to type in the variable information and then to identify on each form where this information is to be inserted by the computer. The computer then prints the forms with the variable information included. Residential closings using standard FNMA forms and an automated database generally involve this type of fill-in-the-blank software. This traditional automated system requires considerable manual input for it to work.

Document assembly software enables lawyers and paralegals to develop their own set of standard forms. The software then permits these forms to be assembled and disassembled, rearranged, and used in any number of ways to create customized documents. A document assembly program allows the paralegal to create his or her own documents through the use of clause libraries. Once these clause libraries are established, the user can then select from the various clauses within the library to create custom forms. Most of the document assembly programs ask the user questions in order to assemble the necessary documents. A paralegal using a document assembly program would answer the questions and input variables to produce a highly complicated and sophisticated document for the lawyer's final review.

Document assembly software requires manual input and work to create the custom forms. Once these forms are created, however, the software permits the manipulation of this information and allows the lawyer or paralegal to create sophisticated real estate documents efficiently.

Some of the closing software systems enable a paralegal to prepare a HUD-1 settlement statement, title insurance documents, and other transaction documents. Some programs will perform trust account balancing and will even enable a paralegal to do check writing and any 1099 tax reporting that is required. Many of the programs permit electronic transfer of data to and from a lender or client. Some closing programs are flexible enough so that you can tailor a program for closing practices in any particular jurisdiction. For example, local recording fees and transfer tax formulas may be input into the system, and the program will then automatically compute the amounts for each transaction.

In addition to software technology, most law firms also make use of the technological advances in computer hardware. One useful hardware tool is the scanner or imaging system. A scanner is a piece of hardware that can scan (read) a written document and convert it into an electronic file. The file then can be revised and printed from one's own computer system. Scanners generally do not make perfect copies, so the computer copy needs to be carefully read against the original for mistakes or imperfections.

By using technology, attorneys are able to generate more documents efficiently and at a lower cost. This lower cost is often passed on to the client in the form of lower fees for the services performed, although some of the lower cost is retained by the firm to enhance its profits in maintaining a real estate closing practice.

It is critical that any paralegal working in real estate have computer skills. Being able to type and being familiar with various computer software systems is as important as having real estate knowledge and other skills. Although many corporations and firms may have training programs for paralegals that are not computer literate, many do not, and therefore, the paralegal is encouraged to obtain these computer skills at college or through other training sources.

A new trend in closing technology is an online resource that creates software that helps coordinate all of the resources for conducting real estate closings. This software and closing Web sites are offered by a number of vendors such as Settlement Room (*http://www .settlementroom.com*) and Bridgespan (*http://www.bridgespan.com*). These Web sites enable parties to communicate with one another during a closing about such things as common checklists that can be updated by way of computer, deadline date tracking, online document posting, and online message posting. These Web sites permit the parties to communicate through the Internet. These sites can be very helpful when numerous parties are involved in the closing or when parties are located in several different geographic areas.

ETHICS: Conflicts of Interest

You are a paralegal with a firm that represents a bank. The bank makes a number of consumer home loans. You have received a new loan and have just contacted the purchasers for the purpose of going over the closing checklist. During your conversation, you realize that the purchasers think you represent them in the transaction. Should you keep quiet, or quickly inform the purchasers that you represent the bank and advise the purchasers to obtain their own legal representation?

Attorneys cannot accept employment in those situations in which the attorney's own interest might impair his or her independent professional judgment. This means that an attorney cannot represent a client in which the attorney has a financial interest or represent two clients in the same transaction. The residential real estate attorney faces these conflicts of interest daily. In many transactions that involve residential real estate, the attorney represents the lender but is the only attorney involved in the transaction. The seller and purchaser often look to this attorney for advice and even believe that the attorney is representing their interests in the transaction. It is necessary for the attorney and the paralegal to be aware of this potential conflict of interest. Law firms and bar associations have different ways of resolving the conflict. Some law firms resolve the conflict by informing the parties early in the transaction as to the firm's representation. For example, a firm that represents the lender would notify, at the beginning of the transaction, both the seller and the purchaser that the attorney is representing the lender's interest. The attorney would invite both the seller and the purchaser to seek their own counsel in connection with the transaction. This early disclosure can help to resolve the conflicts of interest problem.

SUMMARY

The real estate closing is the main fee-generating transaction for most real estate attorneys. A real estate closing is a real-life event that requires the practical use of all the real estate attorney's or paralegal's knowledge about title examinations, surveys, deeds, mortgages, and general real estate law. Although the accumulated knowledge of all real estate law is required to accomplish a successful closing, the closing process has its own identity with its own set of rules and procedures. The activities involved in a real estate closing can generally be divided into six areas: (1) file creation; (2) information gathering; (3) document preparation; (4) the closing; (5) disbursement, recording, and transmittal of the closing package; and (6) final closeout. The paralegal is generally actively involved in all six areas.

Information gathering or due diligence involves obtaining the necessary investigation and information to successfully close the transaction. A paralegal will be actively involved in this area in ordering and reviewing title examinations, title insurance commitments, surveys, fire and casualty insurance, termite letters, and other documents required by the sale contract or loan commitment. A checklist of the due diligence items needed to close the transaction can generally be obtained by a careful reading of the real estate contract or loan commitment involved in connection with the transaction to be closed. Once all of the due diligence or information gathering has been completed, loan and sale documents will be prepared by the paralegal. The paralegal will use this information to prepare the required sale and loan documents. A checklist of the necessary documents will also be obtained by a careful review of the real estate contract and loan commitment. Once the transaction has been closed, the paralegal will also be involved in disbursing the necessary sale and loan proceeds and recording the sale and transfer documents. A thorough knowledge of local customs concerning recording fees and expenses will be required by the paralegal to competently perform these tasks. A paralegal is also generally responsible for receiving all the necessary closing documents from the recorder's office and other places and transmitting these to the purchaser, seller, and lender involved in the transaction.

Examples of many of the legal forms used in a residential real estate closing follow in Chapter 16.

HELPFUL WEBSITES

The following are Web sites to look at for commercial real estate law:

Commercial Real Estate Law
www.real-estate-law.com

Commercial Real Estate Law Newsletter
www.reprofile.com

KEY TERMS

closing
escrow

loan closing
loan commitment

mortgagee loss payable clause

REVIEW QUESTIONS

1. Explain some of the general differences between residential and commercial real estate closings.

2. What helpful information with respect to a real estate closing can a paralegal obtain from reviewing the real estate contract?

3. What helpful information with respect to a real estate loan closing can a paralegal obtain from reviewing the loan commitment?

4. What is the minimum documentation that a seller must furnish at a real estate closing?

5. What minimum documentation does the purchaser need to provide at the real estate closing?

6. What information does the surveyor need to prepare a survey?

7. What is the importance of hazard and fire insurance, and what is a mortgagee loss payable clause?

8. Why is it important for a paralegal to prepare a checklist of documents and procedures to be followed in a real estate closing?

9. What special requirements are found in a construction loan commitment?

10. What is a prepayment fee or premium, and how is it different from a late charge?

PRACTICAL ASSIGNMENTS

1. You are a paralegal representing a firm responsible for the closing of a real property sale transaction. You have been provided with a copy of a contract for closing between Daniel B. Farris as purchaser and Acme Inc. as seller, said contract being shown as Exhibit 14–7 at the end of this chapter. Review the contract carefully, and prepare a closing checklist of all documents or other items that will be required from both purchaser and seller to close the sale.

2. You are a paralegal involved in the closing of a mortgage loan. You have been provided with a copy of the mortgage loan commitment shown as Exhibit 14–8 at the end of this chapter. Review the commitment carefully, and prepare a closing checklist of all documents and other items that will be required to close the mortgage loan.

3. Arrange to attend a real estate closing. Observe carefully the formalities and procedures that take place. Prepare a short memorandum discussing your observations.

ADDENDUM

Exhibit 14–7 Sample Contract for Closing Checklist
Exhibit 14–8 Mortgage Loan Commitment

Exhibit 14–9 Escrow Instruction Letter

ACKNOWLEDGMENTS

Portions of this chapter have been excerpted from *The Residential Real Estate Closing* by Daniel J. Falligant, *Real Estate Practices and Procedures Program Materials*, Pages 5a.1–5a.11; Institute of Continuing Legal Education of Georgia, 1985, Athens, Georgia. Used by permission of the Publisher.

Portions of this chapter have been excerpted from A Practical Guide to Mortgage Loan Commitments by George J. Walsh, III, *Real Estate Law Journal*, Vol. 8, Number 3, 1980, pages 195–229. Used by permission of Publisher.

Student StudyWare™ CD-ROM

Interactive Student CD in the book includes additional quizzing, case studies, and key terms flashcards.

Online Companion™

For additional resources, please go to *www.paralegal.delmar.cengage.com*

EXHIBIT 14–7

Sample Contract for Closing Checklist

Real Estate Sales Contract

This Contract is entered into this _____ day of January, 20_____ by and between DANIEL B. FARRIS, as ("Purchaser"), ACME, INC., a Delaware corporation (collectively "Seller") and BROKER & ASSOCIATES, as ("Broker").

FOR VALUABLE CONSIDERATION RECEIVED, the receipt and sufficiency of which are hereby acknowledged, the parties hereby agree as follows:

1. Purchaser agrees to buy and Seller agrees to sell subject to the terms and conditions of this contract as set forth herein ALL THAT TRACT OF PARCEL OF LAND with such improvements as are located thereon lying and being in Land Lot 1135, 2nd District, 2nd Section of _____ County, _____ and being more particularly described on Exhibit "A" attached hereto and made a part hereof (hereinafter referred to as the "Property").

2. **Purchase Price.** The purchase price for the Property shall be SIX HUNDRED FIFTY THOUSAND AND NO/100 DOLLARS ($650,000.00) which shall be paid as follows: (a) Purchaser shall pay to the Seller the sum of $150,000.00 in cash at closing; and (b) the balance of $500,000.00 shall be paid over a period of thirty (30) years with interest at the rate of ten percent (10%) per annum represented by a purchase money note and deed to secure debt encumbering the Property as security for payment thereof. The purchase money note shall bear interest at the rate of ten percent (10%) per annum and principal and interest shall be payable semi-annually over a period of thirty (30) years. The semi-annual payments shall begin six (6) months after closing, with each payment being applied first to interest on the unpaid principal and the balance to the principal. The note shall be an exculpated, nonrecourse note to Purchaser. The note shall contain a notice of default and fifteen (15) day right to cure default for monetary default and a notice of default and thirty (30) day right to cure for nonmonetary defaults. The note is to contain provisions that it can be prepaid at any time in whole or in part without penalty or premium. The note shall be in a form substantially similar to that note attached hereto as Exhibit "B".

The note shall be secured by a first lien purchase money deed to secure debt encumbering the Property in a form substantially similar to the form attached hereto as Exhibit "C". The purchase money deed to secure debt shall also contain provisions as follows: (a) if all or any part of the Property or any interest in it is sold or transferred without prior written consent of Grantee, Grantee may at its option, require immediate payment in full of all sums secured by the purchase money deed to secure debt. Notwithstanding the above, the purchase money deed to secure debt shall provide that the Property may be transferred by Purchaser ("Grantor") to a corporation or partnership of which Purchaser is a shareholder or partner and there shall be no prohibition or restrictions on Purchaser's right to place junior deeds to secure debt on the Property to secure other debts. The Purchaser shall have the right to alter or improve the improvements located on the Property, including grading of the site on the Property without Seller's prior written consent, so long as such alteration, improvements or grading shall not in any way cause a decline in value to the Property as security for the note.

3. **Earnest Money.** Purchaser has paid to Broker & Associates, a licensed broker acting on behalf of the Seller, FIVE THOUSAND AND NO/100 DOLLARS ($5,000.00) in the form of a check, the receipt whereof is hereby acknowledged by Broker & Associates as earnest money ("Earnest Money"), which Earnest Money shall be applied as part payment of the purchase price of said Property at the time the sale is consummated or paid to Seller or returned to Purchaser as otherwise provided herein.

4. **Warranties of Title.** Seller warrants that Seller presently has title to said Property and at the time the sale is consummated, agrees to convey good and marketable title to said Property to Purchaser by a general warranty deed subject only to such title exceptions as Purchaser shall agree to.

5. **Title.** Purchaser shall move promptly and in good faith after acceptance of this Contract by Seller to examine the title to said Property and to furnish Seller with a written statement of objections affecting the marketablility of said title.

Delmar/Cengage Learning

(continued)

EXHIBIT 14–7

Sample Contract for Closing Checklist (*continued*)

Seller shall have a reasonable time after receipt of said such objections to satisfy all valid objections specified by Purchaser and if Seller fails to satisfy such valid objections within a reasonable time, then Purchaser at Purchaser's option may cancel this Contract by giving Seller written notice of such cancellation and this Contract shall become null and void and Purchaser shall be entitled to a return of the Earnest Money. Marketability of title as used herein shall mean the quality of title which a title insurance company licensed to do business in the State of _____ and a member of the American Land Title Association would insure at its regular rate without exception.

6. **Hazardous Waste Indemnity.** Purchaser's obligation to purchase the Property pursuant to this Contract is contingent upon there being no petroleum hydrocarbons or contaminants contained in the soil, surface or subterranean water which are in violation of local, state, or federal statutes and regulations and that there be no other existence of any hazardous substances or waste located upon the Property. For purposes of this Agreement, the term "hazardous substances or wastes" shall mean petroleum, including crude oil or any fraction thereof, flammable explosives, radioactive materials, asbestos, any material containing polychlorinated biphenyls, and any of the substances defined as "hazardous substances" or "toxic substances" in the Comprehensive Environmental Response, Compensation and Liability Act of 1980, as amended, 42 U.S.C. Section 9601 *et seq.*, Hazardous Materials Transportation Act, 49 U.S.C. Section 1802 *et seq.*, the Resource Conservation and Recovery Act, 42 U.S.C. Section 6901 *et seq.*, and in the Toxic Substance Control Act of 1976, as amended, 15 U.S.C. Section 2601 *et seq.*, or any other federal, state, local or other governmental legislation, statute, law, code, rule, regulation or ordinance identified by its terms as pertaining to the disposal, storage, generation or presence of hazardous substances or waste (the "Environmental Laws"). Purchaser shall at Seller's expense have the Property inspected for purposes of discovering if hazardous substances or wastes exist. If upon inspection, hazardous wastes or substances do exist, Purchaser shall have the option of terminating his contract and receiving a refund of his $5,000.00 earnest money down payment. In the alternative, Seller shall have the right at its own expense to remove all hazardous substance or waste from the Property and to conclude the sale with Purchaser.

Seller warrants, represents and agrees that (a) neither Seller nor any person has violated any of the applicable Environmental Laws as defined in the paragraph above relating to or affecting the Property; (b) the Property is presently in compliance with all Environmental Laws, and there are no facts or circumstances presently existing upon or under the Property or relating to the representations and warranties, which violate any of the applicable Environmental Laws, and there is not now pending nor threatened any action, suit, investigation or proceeding against Seller or the Property (or against any other party related to the Property); (c) Seller has obtained all licenses, permits or other governmental regulatory approvals necessary to comply with Environmental Laws and Seller is in full compliance with the terms and provisions of all such licenses, permits or other governmental regulatory approvals; and (d) Seller has received no notice that any municipality or any governmental or quasi-governmental authorities are investigating or has determined that there are any violations of zoning, health, building, fire, pollution, environmental, or other statutes, ordinances, regulations affecting the Property.

7. **Inspection.** Purchaser, its agents and representatives, at Purchaser's expense and at reasonable times during normal business hours, shall have the right to enter upon the Property for purpose of inspection, examining, testing, surveying the Property. Purchaser assumes all responsibility for acts of itself, its agents, representatives, in exercising its rights under this paragraph and agrees to hold Seller harmless for any damages resulting therefrom.

8. **Condition of Improvements.** Seller warrants until the sale is consummated, that the Improvements located on the Property will be in the same condition as they are on the date this Contract is signed by the Seller, natural wear and tear excepted. Should the Improvements located on the Property be destroyed or substantially damaged before the Contract is consummated, then at the election of the Purchaser, (a) the Contract may be cancelled and Earnest

EXHIBIT 14–7

Sample Contract for Closing
Checklist (*continued*)

Money refunded to Purchaser or (b) Purchaser may consummate the Contract and receive all insurance proceeds paid or due on the claim of loss.

This election is to be exercised within ten (10) days after the Purchaser has been notified in writing by Seller of the amount of the insurance proceeds, if any, Seller shall receive on the claim of loss; if Purchaser has not been notified within forty-five (45) days, subsequent to the occurence of such damage or destruction, Purchaser may at its option cancel this Contract and receive a refund of its Earnest Money.

9. **Possession.** Seller shall deliver title and possession of the Property to Purchaser at closing free and clear of the claims of any and all tenants and all leases existing on the Property shall be cancelled and terminated by Seller at Seller's expense prior to closing.

10. **Closing.** Closing shall be held at the offices of attorney of Purchaser, _____ _____, or at such location as is agreeable to Purchaser and Seller, on a day selected by Purchaser not later than sixty (60) days from the date Seller can deliver title and possession of the Property free and clear of any and all leases or other rights of tenants in regard to the Property and a date not later than _____, 20___. Purchaser shall give Seller notice of the closing date at least five days prior thereto; provided, if Purchaser gives Seller no such notice of the closing date, then the closing date shall be _____, 20___.

11. **Execution of Documents.** Seller shall execute and deliver to Purchaser a general warranty deed in recordable form conveying the Property to Purchaser as provided herein and shall execute and deliver to Purchaser all necessary affidavits in order for Purchaser to obtain a title insurance policy without exception and an affidavit indicating Seller's nonforeign status within the meaning of Section 1445(f)(3) of the Internal Revenue Code of 1986 and any and all other documents which may be required by Purchaser to carry out the terms of this Contract.

12. **Closing Costs.** In connection with the closing, Seller shall pay the _____ real estate Transfer Tax and all costs for the satisfaction, cure and removal of all title exceptions undertaken by the Seller as herein required. Seller shall pay the Intangibles Tax on the purchase money note and deed to secure debt. All other closing costs incurred by Purchaser in connection with the sale shall be paid by Purchaser. Each party shall pay its own attorney's fees.

13. **Prorations.** At the closing all ad valorem property taxes, water and sewer charges and assessments of any kind on the Property for the year of the closing shall be prorated between Purchaser and Seller as of 12:01 a.m. on the closing date. Such proration shall be based upon the latest ad valorem property tax, water, sewer charge and assessment bills if available. If, upon receipt of the actual ad valorem property tax, water, sewer and assessment bills for the Property, such proration is incorrect, then either Purchaser or Seller shall be entitled, upon demand, to receive such amounts from the other as may be necessary to correct such malapportionment. This obligation to correct such malapportionment shall survive the closing and not be merged into any documents delivered pursuant to the closing.

14. **Brokerage Commissions.** Upon consummation of the closing of the sale contemplated herein, a sales commission shall be paid by the Seller to Broker & Associates, Inc., Broker, which commission has been negotiated between Broker and Seller. Purchaser shall have no obligation whatsoever to Broker & Associates, Inc. for any real estate commission. Seller further agrees to indemnify and hold harmless the Purchaser from and by any and all claims or demands with respect to any brokerage fees or agent's commissions or other compensation asserted against any person, firm, or corporation in connection with this Contract or sale or the transactions contemplated hereby arising from actions or alleged commitments of the Seller. This provision shall survive closing and the conveyance of the Property by Seller to Purchaser.

15. **Purchaser Default.** In the event the transaction contemplated hereby is not closed because of Purchaser's default, the Earnest Money shall be paid to Seller as full liquidated damages for such failure to close, the parties acknowledging the difficulty of ascertaining Seller's damages in such circumstances, whereupon neither party hereto shall have any further rights,

(continued)

EXHIBIT 14–7

Sample Contract for Closing
Checklist (*continued*)

claims, or liabilities under this Agreement except for the provisions which were made to survive the termination or cancellation of this Agreement. Said liquidated damages shall be Seller's sole and exclusive remedy and Seller shall expressly not have the right to seek specific performance or other damages.

16. **Sellers Default.** If Seller shall be unable to deliver title in accordance with this Agreement, Seller's liability shall be limited to the return of the Earnest Money paid hereunder. In the event Seller fails to perform other covenants of this Agreement or if Seller otherwise defaults hereunder, the Purchaser shall have the right to, in addition to all rights and remedies herein provided, to pursue any right or remedy it may have against Seller at law or in equity for such breach and/or default, including without limitation, the right of specific performance of all provisions of this Agreement. Purchaser's monetary damages in the event of such breach and/or default shall be limited to $25,000.00. The parties hereby acknowledge the difficulty of ascertaining Purchaser's monetary damages in such event.

17. **Assignability.** Purchaser shall have the right to assign this Agreement to any corporation or partnership of which Purchaser if a shareholder or partner without notice to and without consent of Seller, and the transaction contemplated by this Agreement shall be consummated in the name of such assignee. Purchaser shall not have the right to assign the Contract to any other party except as mentioned above without the prior written consent of Seller.

18. **Notification.** Any notice or demand under which the terms of this Agreement or under any statute must or may be given or made by the parties hereto shall be made in writing and shall be deemed to have been delivered when hand delivered; as of the date sent by an overnight courier; or as of the date of postmark affixed by the U.S. Postal Service, by mail of same by certified mail; return receipt requested, addressed to the respective parties at the following addresses:

TO PURCHASER:

TO SELLER:

TO BROKER:

19. **Time is of the Essence.** Time is of the essence of this Agreement and of each of its provisions.

This instrument shall be regarded as an offer by the Purchaser or Seller who shall first sign this Contract to the other party and is open for acceptance by the other party until _____ : _____ __.m. on the _____ day of _____, 20___.

The above proposition is hereby accepted this _____ day of _____, 20___.

IN WITNESS WHEREOF, the undersigned parties hereinto set their hand and seal to this Contract.

PURCHASER:

_____(SEAL)

SELLER:

_____(SEAL)

_____(SEAL)

BROKER

By:_____

EXHIBIT 14–8

Mortgage Loan Commitment

RE: First Mortgage Loan—$1,600,000
Mortgagor—Acme, Inc.
Property—
Rate—10.5%
Term—23 years, callable by lender
7th, 12th, 17th, and 22nd loan years

Dear

We are pleased to advise that our Investment Review Committee has approved the above captioned first mortgage loan. The loan will be in the amount of $1,600,000 at an interest rate of 10.5% per annum, and is to be amortized over a period of 23 years by equal monthly installments of $15,389.88, including interest. Lender receives the right to declare the entire amount of outstanding principal and all unpaid accrued interest thereon to be immediately due and payable on any one of the following dates: seven (7), twelve (12), seventeen (17), and twenty-two (22) years from the first installment of principal and interest. Such right shall be exercised by Lender by giving written notice to Borrower at least six (6) months prior to date on which said payment of all principal and interest shall be due and payable.

This commitment is issued subject to the following conditions:

1. The loan is to be secured by a valid first lien on the fee simple title to the following described property, together with the improvements thereon, located in the city limits of _____ _____. The property is located at _____. The site is irregular in shape with approximately 200 feet of frontage on _____, a 25 foot wide easement from the property to _____ roughly 580 feet of depth, and with a total land area of 3.11 acres. The site contains five (5) office buildings containing a total of approximately 54,500 gross square feet or 47,400 net square feet.

We are to be provided with a complete and accurate legal description subject to our approval prior to closing of this loan.

2. All loan documents, agreements or other instruments used in connection with this transaction shall first have the approval of our Legal Department and must be prepared by an attorney designated by our Legal Department.

3. All legal fees and other expenses in connection with the closing of this loan are to be paid by the mortgagor. It is further understood that the mortgagor will pay any expenses incident to this transaction should for any reason the loan not be closed after said expenses have been incurred.

4. Fire and extended coverage insurance policies are to be furnished in an amount at least equal to the amount of the loan and not less than the full insurable value of the improvements, issued by a company or companies satisfactory to us. Such policies are to be obtained and held by you. If the policy carries a co-insurance clause or other clause limiting the amount of coverage under certain conditions the insurance must be in such amount as to give full coverage under all conditions. All insurable buildings and personal property or easily removable real estate items or fixtures included in the security instrument must be covered by such insurance.

5. The loan documents shall contain the following items or provisions:

a. No prepayment of the principal of this note shall be allowed prior to the third (3rd) anniversary of the date hereof. After the third (3rd) anniversary of the date hereof, the principal of this note may be prepaid in whole but not in part, on any interest payment date herein, provided that: (1) not later than sixty (60) days prior to such prepayment, Applicant delivers written notice to Holder, and that Applicant intends to prepay the note in full on the date specified in such notice; and (2) Applicant pays to holder at the time of such prepayment, a percentage of the prepaid principal amount as a prepayment premium. Such percentage shall be the product obtained by multiplying the prepaid principal amount by the product of the following:

(i) the amount obtained by subtracting the annualized yield on a United States Treasury Bill, Note or Bond with maturity date which occurs closest to the next call option date of

Delmar/Cengage Learning

(continued)

Exhibit 14–8

Mortgage Loan Commitment
(*continued*)

this Note, as such annualized yield is reported by *The Wall Street Journal* on the business day preceding the date of prepayment, from 10.5% multiplied by:

(ii) the number of years and fraction thereof remaining between the date of prepayment and the next call option date of this note.

Notwithstanding the foregoing, however, in the event of acceleration of the Note at any time and subsequent involuntary or voluntary prepayment, the Prepayment Premium shall be payable, however in no event shall it exceed an amount equal to the excess, if any, of (i) interest calculated at the highest applicable rate permitted by applicable law, as construed by courts having jurisdiction thereof, on the principal balance of the Note from time to time outstanding from the date hereof to the date of such acceleration, over (ii) interest theretofore paid and accrued on the Note. Any prepaid amounts specified in such notice shall become due and payable at the time provided in such notice. A "Loan Year" for the purposes of this Note shall mean each successive twelve (12) month period beginning with the date of the first installment payment of interest hereunder provided, however, that the first Loan Year shall include the period from the date of this Note to the date of such first installment payment of interest. Under no circumstances shall the prepayment premium ever be less than zero. The amount of prepayment shall never be less that the full amount of the then outstanding principal and interest.

In addition to the above-described prepayment penalty, a reinvestment fee of ½ of 1% of the outstanding loan balance will be due in the event of prepayment prior to the maturity of this loan.

b. An assignment of rents in a form satisfactory to our Legal Department.

c. The holder may collect a "late charge" not to exceed an amount equal to four percent (4%) of any installment which is not paid within fifteen (15) days of the due date thereof, to cover the extra expense involved in handling delinquent payments, provided that collection of said late charge shall not be deemed a waiver by the holder of any of its other rights under this note.

d. The Lender is to be furnished with a certified, itemized statement of annual income and expenses on the property covered by this loan within 90 days following the end of each fiscal or calender year.

e. The usual covenant requiring monthly escrow deposits for annual payment of ad valorem taxes and hazard insurance premiums.

f. It shall be a default under the mortgage if, without the Lender's prior written consent, the real property security for this loan or any part thereof is sold, transferred, conveyed or encumbered in any way. Notwithstanding the above, Lender, hereby agrees to allow the transfer of ownership and assumption of this loan by a qualified borrower of equal or greater financial strength, credit standing and management expertise. As consideration for this transfer and assumption, the Lender will receive a non-refundable one percent (1%) fee based on the then outstanding balance, payable at the time of transfer.

g. Installments shall be due and payable on the first day of each month.

h. The Promissory Note taken in this transaction will include a provision which reads "Subject to the terms of the next succeeding paragraph and notwithstanding anything to the contrary otherwise contained in this Note, it is agreed that the promise of Maker to pay the principal indebtedness and the interest on this Note shall be for the sole purpose of establishing the existence of an indebtedness; Holder's source of satisfaction of said indebtedness and of Grantors' other obligations hereunder and under the Loan Documents is limited solely to (a) the property described in the Mortgage, (b) Holder's receipt of the rents, issues and profits from the property described in the Mortgage and (c) any separate agreements guaranteeing the payment of the amounts due hereunder and under the Loan Documents and Makers' performance hereunder and under the Loan Documents; Holder shall not seek to procure payment out of any other assets of Maker, or to procure any judgment against Maker for any amount which is or may be payable under this Note, the Mortgage or any of the other

Loan Documents or for any deficiency remaining after foreclosure of the Mortgage; provided, however, that nothing herein contained shall be deemed to be a release or impairment of said indebtedness or the security therefor intended by the Mortgage, or be deemed to preclude Holder from foreclosing the Mortgage or from enforcing any of Holder's rights thereunder, or in any way or manner affecting Holder's rights and privileges under any of the Loan Documents or any separate agreements guaranteeing Maker's payment and performance hereunder and under the Loan Documents.

Notwithstanding the foregoing limitation of liability provision, it is expressly understood and agreed that Maker shall be personally liable for the payment to the Holder of:

(a) all security deposits of tenants, any rents that are collected more than one (1) month in advance, and all income, rents, issues, profits and revenues derived from the property described in the Mortgage which are not promptly applied to payment of the indebtedness evidenced by the Note and/or to the costs of normal maintenance and operation of such property;

(b) any loss due to fraud or misrepresentations to Holder by Maker (or by any of its general partners, by any of the general partners of any of its general partners or by any of its or their agents, if applicable);

(c) the misapplication of (i) proceeds paid under any insurance policies by reason of damage, loss or destruction to any portion of the property described in the Mortgage to the full extent of such misapplied proceeds, or (ii) proceeds of awards resulting from the condemnation or other taking in lieu of condemnation of any portion of such property, to the full extent of such misapplied proceeds or awards;

(d) any loss due to waste of the property described in the Mortgage or any portion thereof, and all costs, including reasonable attorneys' fees, incurred by Holder to protect such property and any other security for the indebtedness evidenced by this Note or to enforce such Note, the Mortgage and any of the other Loan Documents; and

(e) any taxes, assessments and insurance premiums for which Maker is liable under this Note, the Mortgage or any of the other Loan Documents and which are paid by Holder; and

(f) arising under the hazardous substance indemnification and hold harmless agreement and the borrower's hazardous substances covenant's warranties and representations provisions contained in the Loan Documents.

6. Prior to closing, the Borrower must furnish to the Lender, at the Borrower's sole cost and expense, the original of an environmental audit and certification addressed to Lender and Lender's successors and assigns, with form acceptable to Lender, and prepared by a licensed engineer and geotechnical consultant (Engineer) or either including field reconnaissance, site history records survey, tenant use history record survey, and an examination of the Compensation and Liability Systems Record in the State in which the Property is located, to establish that a thorough investigation of those records and an inspection of the Property site and improvements reveal no evidence of any pollutant or other toxic or hazardous substance, as defined under the Comprehensive Environmental Response, Compensation, and Liability Act ("CERCLA"), 42 U.S.C. 9601 *et seq.*, as amended, or any other federal, state or local law ("Hazardous Substance"). In the event the Engineer determines in his or her professional judgment that an examination of the subsurface soils is necessary, then the parties contemplate that Borrower will require that the Engineer provide the Borrower with an estimate of the additional charges which will be incurred in such examination. In the event that Borrower provides Lender with written notice, received by Lender within five (5) days of the Borrower's receipt of the estimate, that Borrower has determined that the additional charges are not acceptable, then Borrower may simultaneously provide Lender with Borrower's written election to cancel this Commitment Letter in which event the commitment fee will be refunded to Borrower and neither Borrower nor Lender will thereafter have any liability to the other under this Commitment Letter. In the event that Borrower either: (i) fails to provide Lender

EXHIBIT 14–8

Mortgage Loan Commitment (*continued*)

(continued)

EXHIBIT 14–8

Mortgage Loan Commitment
(*continued*)

with receipt of written notice within the said five (5) days of receiving said estimate, or, (ii) determines that the additional charges are acceptable, then the Borrower will be deemed to have elected to close without regard to such additional charges and said audit and certificate must be provided to Lender by Borrower and must include a subsurface soils examination or any other examination deemed necessary, and the cost thereof will be paid by Borrower. In any event, the charges for the environmental audit and certification will be paid in full by Borrower.

With respect to any Hazardous Substance found on the Property, the environmental audit must indicate the nature of the substance, the statutory control over the removal process, the time and costs of removal, and the assessment of risk.

The loan documents will contain the Borrower's covenants, representations, warranties and indemnities, in the identical form of the wording attached hereto as Exhibit "A's".

The Borrower must, at the Borrower's sole cost and expense, obtain and provide to Lender at or before closing the original of a letter addressed to Lender from the Regional Office of the Environmental Protection Agency establishing whether the Property or property in the vicinity of the Property has been the location of a hazardous waste site.

In the event that the environmental audit or the letter from the Environmental Protection Agency reveals that the Property has or has had any Hazardous Substance located on or in the Property or the improvements located on the Property, or any other condition which Lender determines to be objectionable, then Lender, may at its option elect not to close this loan. If Lender, after reviewing any item required of Borrower under this provision, determines not to close this loan, then this Commitment Letter will be canceled and the commitment fee will be refunded to Borrower and neither Borrower nor Lender will thereafter have any liability to the other under this Commitment Letter.

7. We are to be furnished with an engineer's survey, certified to by a registered surveyor, dated within 90 days prior to closing, showing no encroachments other than those approved by us and showing the improvements to be within lot and building lines.

8. We are to be furnished with a mortgagee title insurance policy issued by a company approved by us, or an endorsement to a previously issued title policy, which will insure that the Lender has a first lien without exceptions, other than those specifically approved by us.

9. Any outstanding unpaid taxes and assessments are to be paid prior to our disbursement of the loan proceeds.

10. The financing statement covering the fixtures and equipment will be properly executed and recorded, and the properly executed security agreement delivered to us.

11. We will require that all the lessees be advised in writing of the existence of the assignment of said leases. We specifically agree, however, not to exercise any such assignments until such time as a default exists in the terms of the mortgage.

12. We will require an Estoppel and Subordination Letter from each tenant. The form of these letters must be approved by our Legal Department.

13. We will require loss of rent insurance in an amount not less than nine (9) months gross rental.

14. In order to comply with IRS Regulation TD 8047, we are to be furnished with the social security number, in the case of an individual mortgagor, or the tax identification number for all other mortgagors. We must be provided with this number prior to the closing of this loan.

15. We are to be furnished a current written opinion of counsel for the Borrower, satisfactory to Lender, to the effect that the subject loan is not usurious or otherwise illegal under applicable law and that all loan documents are valid and binding upon Borrower and are enforceable in accordance with their terms.

16. The property site is to be inspected and approved by a duly authorized agent of Lender.

17. Lender requires that the site and improvements be inspected by an engineer or other qualified party to determine if there is deferred maintenance on the property and to determine the cost to cure the identified deferred maintenance. The inspecting party(s) must be approved

(*continued*)

EXHIBIT 14–8
Mortgage Loan Commitment
(*continued*)

by the lender. The Borrower is responsible for the cost of this inspection and is to pay the bills directly.

18. If the inspection report identified in item 17 above identifies deferred maintenance, then lender will require an escrow account be established for the amount identified. The borrower will have six (6) months to complete all identified items and if all work is not done at that point then lender will apply the escrowed funds to the loan balance without penalty and in reverse order to payments owing. If all identified work is completed within six (6) months, then the borrower may obtain all the escrowed funds at the point of completing the work. Borrower must provide the lender with sufficient information to prove that bills in conjunction with this work are paid and that no liens have been filed against the property, prior to receiving the escrowed funds.

19. We have tentatively scheduled this loan for closing sometime during the month of August, 20__, and this commitment shall expire August 31, 20___.

20. Lender will retain and has earned a loan processing fee of $4,000 or ¼% of the loan amount. Lender acknowledges receipt of $4,250 for the loan processing fee. Lender will apply the balance ($250) to the below referenced refundable commitment fee.

21. Provided this commitment is acceptable, you are to forward your check, within ten (10) business days from the date hereof, in the amount of $46,750. This amount plus $17,250 previously received from you will be held by us in a non-interest bearing account as a commitment fee. If and when this loan is closed under the terms and conditions of this commitment letter, the above $64,000 commitment fee will be refunded. However, if this loan is not closed, it is agreed and understood that upon expiration or cancellation of this commitment this fee will be retained by Lender as consideration for this commitment. If Borrower should elect to do so, Lender will accept $32,000 of the above fee in the form of a Letter of Credit. The unconditional irrevocable Letter of Credit must be drawn on an institution and be in a form acceptable to Lender, with an expiration date no earlier than October 31, 20__.

22. Lender reserves the right to cancel this commitment and terminate its obligations hereunder at any time upon the happening of any of the following events:

   a. Borrower's failure to comply with any of the applicable conditions of this commitment within the time specified.

   b. Non-payment of any of the fees or expenses to be paid by the Borrower in connection with this commitment.

   c. Any infirmity in Borrower's title to the real estate, filed by or against Borrower any petition in bankruptcy or insolvency or for the reorganization of Borrower or appointment of a receiver or trustee or the making of an assignment for the benefit of creditors.

   This agreement is made for the sole protection of the Borrower and the Lender, its successors and assigns and no other person or persons shall have any right of action thereon, and this commitment is not assignable or transferable by Borrower. Lender reserves the absolute right to partially or totally assign this commitment to a third party lending institution for the purpose of facilitating a participation loan. By acceptance of this commitment letter, Borrower acknowledges and agrees that this loan may be a loan in which an additional lender may act as a participating lender at the time of funding.

   We appreciate your offering us the opportunity to make this loan and trust that it will be handled to your entire satisfaction.

   Sincerely,

EXHIBIT 14–9

Escrow Instruction Letter

DEED, BLACKACRE & FEE
Attorneys at Law
604 Main Street
Silverville, California

_____, 20___

_____
Senior Escrow Officer
National Commercial Services
Escrow Title Insurance Company
1000 Mt. Diablo Blvd., Suite 500
Walnut Creek, California 94596

ESCROW INSTRUCTION LETTER

RE: $2,000,000 Secured Loan
   Borrower: Farris Investments LLC
   Lender: American Eagle Mortgage Company
   Premises: 604 Mason Mill Road, Dublin, California
   Your Escrow
   Account No.:   _____

Dear _____:

   We represent American Eagle Mortgage Company ("Lender"), which is making the loan described herein.

A. Closing Documents. In connection with the making of a loan in the amount of $2,000,000 to Farris Investments LLC ("Borrower"), by Lender under the above-referenced escrow, the execution copy of each of the following documents is enclosed (except as otherwise indicated below) for the purpose of closing the above-referenced escrow:
   1. Promissory Note ("Note") in the amount of $2,000,000;
   2. Deed of Trust, Security Agreement, Financing Statement, and Fixture Filing ("Deed of Trust");
   3. Assignment of Rents and Leases ("Assignment of Rents");
   4. UCC Financing Statement (Fixture Filing);
   5. UCC Financing Statement (Secretary of State);
   6. Environmental Indemnification Agreement;
   7. Limited Guaranty;
   8. Form of Borrower's Counsel Opinion (executed original, dated as of the date of the closing, to be provided by Borrower's counsel); and
   9. Certificate of Borrower.
      Funds in the loan amount of $2,000,000 from Lender will be transmitted by wire transfer, in accordance with your instructions as shown on Schedule 1 attached hereto.
B. Conditions of Closing. You may close the above-referenced escrow upon fulfillment of Lender's requirements and satisfaction of the conditions set forth below:

Delmar/Cengage Learning

(continued)

1. You have printed all of the listed documents and confirmed that each is complete, legible, and in the form transmitted. Adobe Acrobat version 5.0 or higher must be used to print the documents.

Please note that in the Note and the Deed of Trust slip pages will be provided to complete those instruments once the closing date is confirmed.

2. You hold the documents referred to in Division A above, duly executed by the Borrower and/or other appropriate party, and acknowledged and notarized where required, and you hold the funds referred to in Division A above, plus any funds from Borrower necessary to comply with these instructions. Note that the Note and the Deed of Trust are to be signed inside the document (page 6 of the Note and page 32 of the Deed of Trust) as well as at the end. You may be receiving directly from counsel for the Borrower counterpart signature pages to the Loan Documents. You are directed to substitute those items for the counterpart pages enclosed herewith. Only the signature pages are to be substituted, however, and the Loan Documents transmitted herewith as printed by you are not to be otherwise altered.

3. You have sent to us by e-mail (preferred) or by facsimile transmission: this letter, fully executed, the fully executed Note, and the fully executed closing statement (signed by Borrower and by you).

4. Escrow Title Insurance Company (the "Title Company") is irrevocably committed to issue its ALTA Loan Policy, dated as of the date and time of recording, in the form approved by me (the "Title Policy").

5. You have confirmed that the legal description in the Title Policy is identical to the legal description set forth in Exhibit A to the Deed of Trust. You have also confirmed that Exhibit A is attached not only to the Deed of Trust, but to all other documents which refer to Exhibit A.

6. You have obtained Borrower's acceptance of these instructions and instructions from Borrower confirming that the loan proceeds are to be wired by Lender in accordance with the above.

7. You have confirmed to us via e-mail or fax that all of the foregoing conditions have been satisfied (other than your receipt of the funds from Lender).

C. **Closing Procedures.** In closing this escrow, please strictly adhere to the procedures set forth herein. All requirements with respect to closing shall be considered as having taken place simultaneously, and no delivery or payment shall be considered as having been made until all deliveries, payments and closing transactions have been accomplished. *Please date all of the documents, including the legal opinion, as of the date of funding.*

1. Record the Deed of Trust, the Assignment of Rents, and the UCC Financing Statement (Fixture Filing), with the appropriate filing office of Alameda County, California in such a manner as will enable you to issue the Title Policy. Please be certain that the instruments to be recorded have been properly dated.

2. File by mail the UCC Financing Statement (Secretary of State) with the Office of the Secretary of State of California, Uniform Commercial Code Division, and enclose an acknowledgment copy to be file-stamped and returned to the undersigned.

3. Obtain, within sixty (60) days after closing for delivery to the undersigned a UCC Search Report, with copies of any filings shown on the report, from the Office of the Secretary of State of California, Uniform Commercial Code Division, to show all filings including the new filing referred to in item 2 above. Please provide the undersigned with a copy of this search report request, when made.

4. Disburse the funds received pursuant to Division A above as follows:

(a) Disburse to the designated parties in the amount shown on the settlement statement prepared by you and approved by Lender prior to disbursement.

(b) Disburse the balance, if any, as directed in writing by Borrower, and all as to be set forth in a settlement sheet to be approved by the Lender prior to closing.

EXHIBIT 14–9

Escrow Instruction Letter
(*continued*)

(continued)

EXHIBIT 14–9

Escrow Instruction Letter
(*continued*)

5. Send to the undersigned by overnight courier for delivery to this office on the first business day after the funding of the loan:

    (a) The original Note;

    (b) The original Limited Guaranty;

    (c) The original and two copies of all other original documents referred to in Division A above which do not have to be filed or recorded;

    (d) Two copies of all documents referred to in Division A but not returned to us pursuant to (a) or (b) above, file-stamped and certified by you as being true copies submitted for filing or recording, specifying the date submitted and to what office, together with, if possible, filing or recording information as to reference numbers;

    (e) The fully signed original of this letter;

    (f) An executed copy of the borrowing resolutions;

    (g) A copy of your disbursement (settlement) statement indicating the amount and payee of all funds disbursed by you at the direction of the Borrower.

7. Deliver to Borrower's counsel, William A. Law, 8515 Creek Plaza, Dublin, CA 94541, a copy of the loan documents.

8. As soon as possible after those original documents in Division A above (including any SNDAs) which have to be filed or recorded have been filed or recorded, such filed or recorded documents, and the original Title Policy, should be delivered to the undersigned. Please advise us as to the anticipated length of time between closing and our receipt of the filed or recorded documents and the Title Policy.

D. General Instructions.

1. All costs and expenses for payment of prior encumbrances, the Title Policy, endorsements, escrow fees, photocopying, recording fees, mortgage taxes, title company services, and all other fees, charges and taxes with respect to the closing of this transaction shall be paid by Borrower, and Lender and the undersigned law firm shall have no responsibility or liability for any such costs or expenses. Copies of documents desired by any of the parties should be arranged for at the time of closing. Neither the Lender nor this law firm will be supplying copies.

2. We understand that in connection with this escrow you may be receiving instructions from the attorney for the Borrower. You may comply with those instructions so long as said instructions do not conflict with any provisions of these instructions.

3. This escrow instructions agreement may be executed in counterparts, each of which shall be deemed to be a duplicate original.

Very truly yours,

DEED, BLACKACRE & FEE

The undersigned hereby consents to the foregoing instructions on behalf of Borrower. Borrower instructs Lender to wire the funds in accordance with Division A of this letter and authorizes the disbursement of funds as set forth above. Borrower agrees to pay interest at the rate set forth in the Note on the loan proceeds wired by Lender to escrow from the date funds are first wired, regardless of whether the funds are available for disbursement or reinvestment on the date of such wire.

(continued)

FARRIS INVESTMENTS LLC, a
California limited liability company

By:_____
       Mary Farris
       Title: Managing Member

The undersigned acknowledges receipt of the written escrow instructions and agrees to proceed in accordance therewith.

Escrow Title Insurance Company

By:_____
Name:_____
Title:_____

EXHIBIT 14–9

Escrow Instruction Letter
(*continued*)

chapter | 15

Government Regulation of Real Estate Closings

Objectives

After reading this chapter, you should be able to:

- Understand the purposes of the Real Estate Settlement Procedures Act, the Truth-in-Lending Act, the Home Ownership Equity Protection Act, and the Adjustable Rate Mortgage Disclosure Requirements
- Identify real estate loans that require a right of rescission
- Prepare right of rescission notice forms
- Prepare adjustable rate disclosure forms

Outline

Real property closings have become increasingly controlled by federal regulation. Most federal regulations focus on lenders, and many have a direct impact on the real property closing. Regulatory bodies such as the Federal Reserve Bank, the Federal Home Loan Bank Board, the Office of the Controller of the Currency, the Federal Deposit Insurance Corporation, the Federal Savings and Loan Insurance Corporation, and Housing and Urban Development (HUD) have promulgated and enforced such regulations as the Truth-in-Lending Act, Real Estate Settlement Procedures Act, Regulation B Equal Credit Opportunity Act, National Flood Insurance Act, Fair Credit Reporting Act, Fair Debt Collection Practices Act, Fair Housing Act, Community Reinvestment Act, Home Mortgage Disclosure Act, Home Ownership Equity Protection Act, and Right to Financial Privacy Act. All these regulations affect how real estate closings take place.

The area has become so inundated with regulations that real estate attorneys and real estate paralegals must work hard to keep abreast of the changes. This discussion does not provide an in-depth review of all the regulations. Rather, it is a cursory overview of the main regulations that must be complied with when lenders make residential real estate loans.

REAL ESTATE SETTLEMENT PROCEDURES ACT

The **Real Estate Settlement Procedures Act (RESPA),** passed in 1974, was designed to reform the real estate closing or settlement process to ensure that consumers receive more information about the settlement and to protect consumers from unnecessarily high settlement costs. RESPA requires advance disclosure of **settlement costs,** eliminates kickbacks and referral fees, and mandates the maximum amount that may be required to be placed in escrow accounts for payment of recurring charges or assessments that affect the lender's real property security.

Real Estate Settlement Procedures Act (RESPA)

A federal law designed to reform the real estate settlement process and to ensure that consumers receive more information about real estate settlement costs.

settlement costs

All costs involved in the settlement or closing of a real estate transaction. Such items include but are not limited to attorney's fees, surveyor's fees, title insurance premiums, recording fees, and appraisal fees.

Transactions Subject to RESPA

A real estate transaction that involves a federally related mortgage loan secured by a first lien on residential real property (defined as real property improved with a one- to four-family dwelling) is subject to RESPA. The term "federally related mortgage loan" is broadly defined. It includes loans that are:

(a) made by a lender regulated by a federal agency or whose deposits are insured by a federal agency (such as a federal bank with deposits insured by the Federal Deposit Insurance Corporation or a federal savings and loan association with deposits insured by the Federal Savings and Loan Insurance Corporation);

(b) made, insured, guaranteed, supplemented, or assisted by a federal agency. Loans that would fall within this category are loans guaranteed by the Veterans Administration or by the Federal Housing Administration;

(c) intended to be sold to Fannie Mae or Freddie Mac; or

(d) made by a creditor who makes or invests more than $1 million per year in residential real estate loans.

Exemptions from RESPA

The following are federally regulated mortgage loans that are exempted from RESPA's coverage:

- A loan to finance the purchase or transfer of 25 or more acres
- A home improvement loan, refinance loan, or other loan that does not involve a legal transfer of title

- A vacant lot loan in which no proceeds are used for construction of a one- to four-family structure
- Assumption transactions, except the conversion of a construction loan to a permanent loan to finance the purchase of a home by a first user
- Construction loans, except when the construction loan is used or converted to a permanent loan to finance the purchase by a first user

Required Disclosures and Prohibitions of RESPA

RESPA provides for the following disclosures and prohibitions.

Special Information Booklet

A special information booklet written by HUD is to be distributed by lenders to each loan applicant within three business days after the application for credit. The booklet explains to consumers the costs related to real estate settlements.

Good Faith Estimates

Lenders are required to give the loan applicant an estimate of the amounts and types of costs the applicant can expect to incur to consummate the loan and close the purchase. The estimated costs must bear a reasonable relation to the actual charges. In addition, the applicant must be informed that additional costs may be charged. The estimate must be given to the applicant within three business days after the application for credit.

Uniform Settlement Statement

HUD–1

Uniform settlement statement required by the Real Estate Settlement Procedures Act for all real estate transactions that involve a federally related mortgage loan.

RESPA requires the use of a uniform settlement statement (**HUD–1**) for all transactions that involve a federally related mortgage loan (see Exhibit 15–1 at the end of this chapter). All charges imposed on borrowers and sellers must be conspicuously and clearly itemized. HUD has prescribed regulations that contain line-by-line instructions for the correct completion of the forms.

One-Day Advance Inspection

On request of the borrower, the settlement agent (attorney) shall permit the borrower to inspect those settlement cost items known to the settlement agent during the business day immediately preceding the closing date. The settlement agent must provide the settlement form in as complete a condition as possible.

Escrow Limitation

RESPA permits a lender to establish an advance deposit escrow account to ensure the payment of recurring charges or assessments that affect the lender's security. Typical escrow items include various taxes, insurance, and assessments. The lender may escrow an amount sufficient for the lender to pay the charges as they become due, plus a cushion of one-sixth (two months) of the estimated annual total charges. The lender is permitted to collect one-twelfth of the estimated annual total charges for escrow items with each monthly mortgage installment. For example, a mortgage loan closes on April 15, and the current year's tax bills are due on October 1. The first payment under which the lender will receive one-twelfth of the tax amount will be made on June 1. At closing, the lender then can collect 10 months of the current year's tax bill. How is this calculated? By indicating that 12 months end on

October 1, the lender will receive one-twelfth on June 1, one-twelfth on July 1, one-twelfth on August 1, and one-twelfth September 1, or four-twelfths in total. The lender needs twelve-twelfths on October 1, so the lender will be eight months short. Because RESPA permits a lender to accumulate two additional months, the lender can collect 10 months tax escrow at closing (see Example 15–1).

Example 15–1

Loan Closes: April 15
Taxes Due: October 1
First Payment Due on Loan: June 1
Tax Bill: $1,200
$1,200 amount of tax bill divided by 12 = $100/mo. escrow
$100 paid June 1, July 1, August 1, September 1 ($400 total)
$1,200 due October 1 minus $400 = $800 needed
$800 + $200 (two months additional escrow permitted under RESPA) $1,000 collected
   at closing

Title Insurance

A seller, as a condition of sale, shall not require title insurance from any particular company. A violation of this regulation results in a seller's being liable for three times the title insurance charge paid by the purchaser.

Kickbacks

RESPA provides that no person shall give and no person shall accept any fee, **kickback,** or thing of value pursuant to any agreement or understanding, oral or otherwise, that involves the referral of business incident to or part of a real estate settlement involving a federally related loan. For example, (a) a lender cannot pay a real estate broker or another originating party a kickback to obtain business; (b) a real estate broker cannot pay a lender a kickback to obtain a loan for the client; (c) a title company cannot pay an attorney, abstractor, real estate broker, or lender a kickback to obtain business; (d) an attorney cannot pay a kickback to a lender, real estate broker, title company, abstractor, or others to obtain business; and (e) an insurance agent, surveyor, or termite inspector cannot pay a kickback to any party to obtain business.

kickback

Payment of money or something of value to a person for the purpose of obtaining business from that person.

Unearned Fees

RESPA provides that no person shall give and no person shall accept any portion, split, or percentage of any charge made or received for the rendering of a real estate settlement service in connection with a transaction that involves a federally related mortgage loan other than for services actually performed. A split payment for services actually performed is permitted by RESPA.

Penalties

The civil and criminal penalties for violation of RESPA are severe. The violator may be fined $10,000 and sentenced to one year imprisonment. In addition, violators are liable for civil penalties in an amount equal to three times the amount of the fees wrongfully charged plus court costs and reasonable attorneys' fees.

New RESPA Rules

In November 2008, the Department of Housing and Urban Development (HUD) announced new rules updating the requirements of the Real Estate Settlement Procedures Act (RESPA). The new rules require a standardized "good faith estimate" (GFE) for borrowers, explaining rates, fees, and any prepayment penalties and other matters that the borrower is likely to incur to obtain the loan. A lender must issue a GFE no later than three business days after the lender receives an application for a loan. If circumstances change that would require new fees or costs or would make the GFE inaccurate, a lender is required to issue a revised GFE within three business days of receiving information sufficient to establish a changed circumstance. The new rules also create a new HUD–1 form that must be provided to borrowers before they sign loan documents. The new forms must be used by January 1, 2010. Information and copies of the new good faith estimate and HUD–1 form can be found at *http://www.hud .gov/offices/hsg/sfh/res/respa_hm.cfm.*

A paralegal's main exposure to RESPA is in the preparation of the uniform settlement statement at the time of closing. Instructions for completing the uniform settlement statement appear in Chapter 16.

TRUTH-IN-LENDING ACT

The **Truth-in-Lending Act** was passed by the U.S. Congress on July 1, 1969. It was aimed at economically stabilizing and strengthening the competition among financial institutions by providing a means for the informed use of credit. Another purpose of the Act was to protect consumers against inaccurate and unfair billing practices and to facilitate the informed use of credit by requiring the disclosure of credit terms in such a manner that consumers could readily compare the various terms available from different lenders.

The Truth-in-Lending Act continues to undergo periodic amendments.

Disclosures for Closed-End Real Property Transactions

Who Must Make Disclosures?

The regulation requires that a creditor must make the disclosures. For purposes of closed-end credit (the lender makes a one-time advance), the regulations define "creditor" as a person to whom an obligation is payable and who regularly extends consumer credit that is subject to a **finance charge** or is payable by written agreement in more than four installments. For purposes of transactions secured by a home, a person "regularly extends consumer credit" only if credit has been extended more than four times in the preceding or current calendar year. **Consumer credit** is credit offered or extended primarily for personal, family, or household purposes.

Who Must Receive the Disclosure?

The disclosure must be made to the consumer or borrower. The regulations define **consumer** as a natural person to whom consumer credit is offered.

When Must Disclosures Be Made?

In residential mortgage transactions subject to RESPA, the creditor must make a good faith estimate of the disclosure no later than three business days after receiving the consumer's written application for credit. For real estate transactions not subject to RESPA, the disclosures must be made before the consummation of the transaction. The creditor should redisclose before consummation if early disclosures become inaccurate. **Consummation**

Truth-in-Lending Act

Federal law designed to provide consumers with information for an informed use of credit. The Truth-in-Lending Act requires creditors to disclose to consumers the true costs of a consumer loan.

finance charge

Term used in the Truth-in-Lending Act to mean any charge or fee payable directly or indirectly by the consumer to obtain a consumer loan.

consumer credit

Term used in the Truth-in-Lending Act to mean a loan offered or extended primarily for personal, family, or household purposes.

consumer

Term used in the Truth-in-Lending Act to mean a natural person to whom a loan for personal, family, or household purposes is offered.

consummation

Term used in the Truth-in-Lending Act to mean the time a consumer becomes contractually obligated under state law to make payments under a loan.

is narrowly defined by the regulations to mean the time when a consumer becomes contractually obligated under state law to make payments under a credit transaction. In most real estate loan transactions, this would be at the time the promissory note is signed by the consumer or borrower.

What Format Must Be Used for Disclosure?

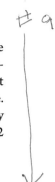

The disclosures must be made clearly and conspicuously in writing and in a form that the consumer may keep. The disclosures must be segregated from all nondisclosure information. To comply with this requirement, the disclosure should be made on a separate sheet of paper or must be circumscribed from other information with a bold print dividing line. The Federal Reserve Board has provided a series of standard disclosure forms to be used by lenders to comply with the regulations. A copy of a disclosure form is shown in Exhibit 15–2 at the end of this chapter.

What Must Be Disclosed?

Disclosure must be based on the terms of the legal obligation between the borrower and the lender. The note and mortgage establish the legal obligation. Disclosures that are not relevant to the transaction may be omitted.

The law allows the following items to be disclosed at the option of the lender: the date of the transaction, the consumer's name and address, the consumer's account number, and an acknowledgment of receipt of the disclosure.

The following disclosures *must* be made.

Creditor. The creditor must be identified by name. The creditor's address and telephone number must be included.

Amount Financed. The amount financed is the amount of credit provided to the customer. The amount financed usually is the loan amount less the prepaid finance charges. Prepaid finance charges are discussed later in this chapter.

Finance Charge. Finance charge is the cost of credit as a dollar amount. Subject to certain exceptions, the finance charge includes any charge or fee payable directly or indirectly by the consumer and imposed directly or indirectly by the creditor as an incident to or condition of an extension of credit. The finance charge must be disclosed more conspicuously than other disclosure items. The finance charge on most residential real estate loans is the total of all monthly payments made under the loan together with any loan discount or loan origination fees charged by the lender to make the loan.

Annual Percentage Rate

The annual percentage rate is the cost of credit as a yearly rate. A calculation of the annual percentage rate is a technical computation. Most law firms use calculators that have special programs designed to compute the annual percentage rate. The tolerance for inaccurate disclosure is one-eighth of one percentage point above or below the correct annual percentage rate.

Prepaid Finance Charge

The following items are prepaid finance charges that must be subtracted from the loan amount to arrive at the *amount financed* and added to the total payments made under the loan to arrive at the *finance charge:* (a) interest on the loan, (b) loan discount points, (c) service or carrying charges, (d) loan fees, (e) appraiser's fees or credit reporting costs, and (f) the cost of guaranty of insurance to protect the creditor against consumer defaults, such as credit life insurance or private mortgage insurance.

Variable Rate Disclosure

When the annual percentage rate may increase after consummation of the transaction, such as would happen under an interest rate that varies according to some index such as three-year treasury bills, the creditor must disclose the circumstances under which the rate may increase, any limitation on the increase, the effect of an increase, and an example of the payment terms that would result from an increase. No variable rate disclosure needs to be made if the payment schedule is known and fixed before consummation.

Payment Schedule

The creditor must disclose the number, amount, and timing of the payment schedule to repay the obligation. The payment schedule should include not only the repayment of principal, but also all elements of any finance charges imposed.

Total of Payments

The total of payments is the total amount the consumer will have paid if all scheduled payments are made.

Demand Feature

If the obligation has a demand feature—that is, it becomes due before its normal amortization—such demand feature must be disclosed.

Prepayment Provisions

The creditor is required to disclose whether or not a penalty will be assessed against a consumer if the obligation is prepaid in full before its normal maturity. In addition, the creditor must state whether the consumer will be entitled to a refund of part of a precomputed finance charge in the event of early prepayment.

Late Payment Charges

The creditor must disclose any charges that may be imposed for individual late payments before the maturity of the loan.

Security Interest

The creditor must describe any security interest taken as part of the transaction. If the security interest is in property being purchased with the proceeds of the transaction, disclosure need only provide a general identification. If the security interest is taken in property in a nonpurchase money transaction, the property in which the security interest is taken must be identified by item or type.

Insurance Charges

If the contractual relationship between the creditor and the borrower requires property insurance coverage, that fact must be disclosed. In addition, a written disclosure is required of credit-related insurance, such as credit life or credit disability insurance, to exempt the cost of such insurance from the calculation of the finance charge.

Exempt Transactions from Truth-in-Lending

Truth-in-lending applies only to consumer transactions. If the loan or extension of credit is made to an entity other than a natural person, such as a corporation, a partnership, or a joint venture, truth-in-lending does not apply. If the purpose of the loan is for business, commercial, or agricultural purposes, truth-in-lending does not apply. The primary purpose of a transaction must be ascertained by reviewing the transaction as a whole.

Right of Rescission

In addition to the disclosure of credit terms, truth-in-lending provides the consumer home-owner with a right of **rescission.** The right of rescission gives the consumer, whose principal dwelling may be encumbered to secure a real estate loan, a three-business-day cooling-off period to think over the transaction and to cancel it for any reason without penalty.

Loans created or retained to finance the acquisition or initial construction of a dwelling are exempt from the rescission rights.

A loan transaction in which a state agency is a creditor and advances under a preexisting open-end credit plan (such as a home equity loan) are exempt from the rescission rights, if the security interest has already been retained and the advances are in accordance with a previously established credit limit for the plan.

rescission

Act of repealing or voiding something or some action.

Who Has the Right to Rescind?

Any natural person with an ownership interest in a dwelling who uses it as a principal residence has the right to rescind if that ownership is or may be encumbered in connection with the real estate loan transaction. Any person who has the right to rescind may rescind a transaction on behalf of others with the right with or without the consent of the other parties. For example, a husband and wife own a home; either the husband or the wife may rescind the transaction without the other's permission.

Notice of the Right to Rescind

The creditor must give two copies of the notice of the right to rescind to each consumer who is entitled to rescind the transaction. The notice must be on a separate document that identifies the transaction. The transaction may be identified by simply giving its date. The notice also must disclose the following information: (a) the retention or acquisition of a security interest in the consumer's principal dwelling, (b) the consumer's right to rescind, (c) how the right of rescission may be exercised, (d) the effects of rescission, and (e) the date at midnight when the three-business-day rescission period expires.

The Federal Reserve Board provides sample notices of the right to rescind for use in transactions (see Exhibit 15–3 at the end of this chapter). It also is a good practice to obtain an affidavit from the consumers indicating that they have not rescinded at the expiration of the three-day period (see Exhibit 15–4 at the end of this chapter).

How a Consumer Rescinds

A consumer may rescind a transaction by notifying the creditor in writing during the rescission period. A consumer has until midnight of the third business day following the receipt of a notice of right to rescind in which to rescind the transaction. For example, if a loan is closed on a Tuesday and the notice of right of rescission is given on the same day, the consumer has until midnight of Friday in which to rescind the loan. The rescission is effective on mailing of the notice, not on receipt.

Effect of Rescission

If the rescission is effective, the security interest giving rise to the right of rescission becomes void as of the time of rescission. The creditor has 20 days to terminate the security interest and return any money or property that has been given to any person in connection with the transaction.

Waiver of the Right to Rescind

The consumer may waive the right to rescind to permit performance during the rescission period. The consumer must inform the creditor in writing that the extension of credit is needed to meet a bona fide personal financial emergency period. This waiver, which cannot be on a preprinted form, must describe the emergency and must be signed and dated by all consumers who have a right to rescind.

The Federal Reserve Board has asserted that it believes that the waiver of the right to rescind should not be a routine matter. Creditors are not insulated from liability for failing to provide a rescission right because they rely on a borrower's waiver. Creditors must make a reasonable investigation to make sure that the waiver is bona fide.

Disbursement of Money before Expiration of Rescission Period

A creditor's obligation does not end with the providing of the notice of the right to rescind. A creditor must be reasonably satisfied that any consumer with the right to rescind has not rescinded before any money or property is delivered or any services are performed under the transaction. A creditor will not disburse the loan proceeds until the rescission period has expired and the statement of nonrescission (see Exhibit 15–4) has been received.

The Mortgage Disclosure Improvement Act

The Mortgage Disclosure Improvement Act (the Act), which became law on July 30, 2008, has amended Regulation Z requirements for truth-in-lending disclosures for mortgage loans. The Act has expanded initial truth-in-lending disclosure requirements to all dwelling-secured loans that are subject to RESPA. The initial truth-in-lending disclosure must be provided within three (3) business days of application for the loan and at least seven (7) business days before closing of the loan. If an initial truth-in-lending disclosure is out of tolerance, a final truth-in-lending disclosure must be received by the consumer at least three (3) business days before loan closing. If the final truth-in-lending disclosure is mailed, the consumer is deemed to have received it three (3) business days after mailing. In the event of a bona fide personal emergency, the consumer may waive the waiting period applicable to the initial and final disclosure. The waiver can only take place if the consumer has already received the disclosure at the time of the waiver. The initial and final truth-in-lending disclosure must include the following notice: "You are not required to complete this agreement merely because you have received these disclosures or signed a loan application." A new truth-in-lending form is being created. The changes are effective October 1, 2009, including the use of the new truth-in-lending form.

HOME OWNERSHIP EQUITY PROTECTION ACT

The Truth-in-Lending Simplification Reform Act was amended in 1994 to include new provisions known as the Home Ownership Equity Protection Act (HOEPA). HOEPA primarily targets for protection consumers who enter into "subprime loans." These are nonpurchase mortgage loans with high interest rates or up-front fees. These high-cost mortgages are typically aimed at homeowners with limited incomes who have developed equity in their homes as a result of paying down their first mortgages, or receiving an inheritance, or by a rise in real estate values.

Loans Regulated by HOEPA

These include loans secured by a consumer's principal dwelling where the annual percentage rate on the loan at consummation is more than 10 percentage points above the yield on Treasury securities that have comparable periods of maturity to the loan maturity. In addition, loans in which the total points or fees payable by the consumer at or before the loan is closed that exceed the greater of 8% of the total loan amount or $465.00 are regulated by HOEPA.

HOEPA Disclosure and Prohibition

HOEPA requires that certain disclosures be made by the lender, including a statement that the lender will have a mortgage on the consumer's home and a warning that the consumer could lose the home and any money they put into it if they do not meet their obligations under the loan. The disclosures must also include the annual percentage rate and the amount of the regular monthly payment. If the loan is a variable interest rate loan, the following must be disclosed: (a) the potential increase in the interest rate and monthly payment and (b) the amount of a single maximum monthly payment based on the maximum interest rate increase.

In addition, HOEPA prohibits certain terms and mortgage transactions that it regulates. HOEPA prohibits a balloon payment for a loan with a term of less than five years. It also prohibits negative amortized loans, that is, loans with a schedule of regular periodic payments that causes the principal balance to increase. HOPEA does not allow default-rate interest (an interest rate that would increase after a default on the loan). In addition, HOEPA prohibits any penalty or excessive charge to be assessed against a borrower who pays the loan in full ahead of schedule.

HOEPA and Higher-Priced Mortgage Loans

The Federal Reserve Board adopted on July 14, 2008 new rules which bring under the jurisdiction of the Home Ownership and Equity Protection Act (HOEPA) a new category of residential loans identified as "higher-priced mortgage loans." Higher-priced mortgage loans which are now subject to HOEPA are consumer credit transactions secured by a consumer's principal dwelling that for first priority mortgage liens, have an interest rate 1.5% points above the "Prime Offer Rate" and for second mortgage liens, have an interest rate 2.5% points over the "Prime Offer Rate." "Prime Offer Rate" is an average prime offer rate established by Freddie Mac, and such rates will be published at least weekly. Higher-priced mortgage loans include home purchase, home improvement loans, and refinances. The new rules prohibit certain acts in connection with higher-priced mortgage loans. These prohibited acts include: (1) extending credit without determining that the borrower has the ability to repay; (2) relying on income and/or assets and failing to verify them using reasonably reliable third-party documentation; (3) there can be no prepayment penalty if the loan payment can change in the initial four years from closing. If the loan payment cannot be changed in the initial four years, the prepayment penalty cannot last beyond the first two years from loan closing or be applicable to refinancing by the creditor or its affiliate.

The new rules require impounding for property taxes and homeowner's insurance for all first lien higher-priced mortgage loans during the first 12 months of the loan. Creditors may offer the borrower the opportunity to cancel the escrow payments after one year. There is a limited exemption for condominiums and cooperatives when the association or board pays the insurance under a master policy.

The Act is effective for all loan applications on or after October 1, 2009 and for all loans consummated on or after January 1, 2010.

ADJUSTABLE INTEREST RATE DISCLOSURES

The past several years have ushered in an unprecedented era of interest rate volatility. It is not unusual for interest rates to go up or down more than one percentage point in a given year. This interest rate volatility has caused many lenders and even many consumer borrowers to desire to have their interest rates on loans tied to some interest rate index. These loans are generally referred to as adjustable rate mortgage (ARM) loans. The rate of interest under an ARM adjusts based on an index such as the Treasury bill rate or prime lending rate. As this index increases or decreases due to the volatility of interest rates in the market, the interest rate on the loan will increase or decrease. During periods of increasing interest rates, the borrower will experience an increase in the mortgage payment, and during periods of decreasing interest rates, the borrower will experience a decrease in the mortgage payment. The federal government, believing that a borrower should be made aware of the risks and rewards inherent in an adjustable interest rate loan, has enacted laws that require mortgage lenders to disclose the terms of an adjustable interest rate loan.

Types of Loans Covered by ARM Disclosure Requirements

The disclosure requirements apply to ARMs that are secured by the consumer's principal one- to four-family residence and that have a term of more than one year. The loan must be extended primarily for personal, family, or household purposes.

When Must ARM Disclosures Be Made?

ARM disclosures are required at the time an application form is provided to a consumer or before the consumer pays a nonrefundable fee for the loan, whichever is earlier.

Content of the Disclosure

A consumer or borrower entering into an ARM loan is entitled to a copy of the *Consumer Handbook on Adjustable Rate Mortgages,* which is issued by the Federal Reserve Board. The borrower also is entitled to receive the following information: (a) the fact that the interest rate, payment, or term of the loan may change; (b) the index or formula used in making adjustments and a source of information about the index or formula; (c) an explanation of how the interest rate and payment will be determined, including an explanation of how the index is adjusted; (d) a statement that the consumer should ask about the current margin value or current interest rate; (e) if applicable, the fact that the interest rate will be discounted and a statement that the consumer should ask about the amount of the interest rate discount; (f) the frequency of interest rate and payment changes; (g) any rules relating to changes in the index, interest rate, payment amount, and outstanding loan balance, including, for example, an explanation of interest rate or payment limitations, any negative amortization, or interest rate carryover permitted; (h) a historical example based on a $10,000 loan amount that illustrates how payments and the loan balances would have been affected by interest rate changes implemented according to the terms of the loan program, based on the most recent 15 years of index values, including all significant loan program terms that would have been affected by the index movement during the period; (i) an explanation of how the consumer may calculate the payments for the loan amount based on the most recent payments shown on the historical example; (j) the maximum interest rate and payment for a $10,000 loan originated at the most recent interest rate shown on the historical sample and assuming the maximum periodic increases in rates and payments under the program, including the initial interest rate and payment for that loan; (k) the fact that the loan program contains a demand feature, if it does; and (l) the type of information that will be provided and notices of adjustments and the timing of such notices.

Subsequent Disclosures

The lender periodically must send to the consumer an adjustment notice. An adjustment notice must be sent at least once each year during which an interest rate adjustment is made without an accompanying payment change. If any payment change accompanies the interest rate adjustment, the lender must send an adjustment notice at least 25 calendar days but not more than 120 calendar days before a payment at the new level is due. An adjustment notice must contain the following information: (a) the current and prior interest rates; (b) the index values on which the current and prior interest rates are based; (c) the extent to which the creditor has forgone any increase in the interest rate; (d) the contractual effects of the adjustment, including the payment due after the adjustment is made and the statement of the loan balance; and (e) if the payment is different from that referred to in subsection (d), the monthly amount required to fully amortize the loan at the new interest over the remainder of the loan term.

Index Requirements

The ARM disclosure law also regulates the type of index that can be used for the adjustment in the interest rate. The requirements provide that the loan documents must specify an index to which the changes in the interest rate will be linked. The index must be readily available to and verifiable by the consumer and must be beyond the control of the lender. For example, a bank could not use its own prime lending rate as an index. A bank would have to use another bank's prime lending rate or the rate on Treasury bills.

Interest Rate Cap

The Competitive Equality Banking Act of 1987 requires that any ARM loan secured by a lien on a one- to four-family dwelling originated by a national bank must include a lifetime cap on the interest rate.

The maximum interest rate to be charged must be included in the initial ARM disclosure and in the loan documents. The interest cap must be stated in a manner that allows the consumer to easily ascertain what the rate ceiling will be over the term of the loan. For example:

The maximum rate will not exceed ____%.

The interest rate will never be higher than ____ percentage points above the initial rate of ____ percent.

PREDATORY LENDING LAWS

Subprime lending, as discussed in Chapter 9, is the business practice of making mortgage loans to people who do not have a good credit history or stable income. Subprime borrowers generally pay higher interest rates and fees for their mortgages than other borrowers. Loans from subprime lenders have enabled many people with poor or nonexistent credit history to obtain loans to buy a house. Some subprime lenders, however, have been guilty of preying on minorities, the poor, the less educated, and the elderly. Several states, in order to protect their citizens from predatory lending mortgage practices, have enacted predatory lending laws to prohibit the use of certain abusive mortgage loan practices. These predatory lending laws may vary in content from state to state, but there are certain general concepts that can be found throughout most of the laws.

The predatory lending laws generally regulate high-interest-rate or high-fee mortgages. The definition of a high-interest-rate or high-fee mortgage is defined in the laws. Predatory lending laws generally:

- Cap the amount of prepayment fees that can be charged for an early payment of the high-cost loan.
- Prohibit the loan documents from allowing an increase in the interest rate after default.

✓ CHECKLIST

Disclosure Forms

The disclosures listed in the following checklist are to be given to a borrower at the time the borrower obtains a consumer loan secured by the borrower's residence.

☐   I. Real Estate Settlement Procedures Act
  A. Special Information Booklet. This booklet is given by the lender to the consumer or borrower within three business days after the consumer's application for the loan.
  B. Good Faith Estimate. This estimate must be provided by the lender to the consumer or borrower within three days after the borrower's application for the loan.
  C. Uniform Settlement Statement (HUD–1). This uniform settlement statement must be used at the closing of all residential loan transactions that involve a federally related mortgage loan. The HUD–1 must be made available to the borrower for inspection at least one day before closing.

☐   II. Truth-In-Lending Act
  A. Truth-In-Lending Disclosure Statement. A truth-in-lending disclosure statement must be given to the borrower at least three (3) business days before the time the borrower signs the promissory note.
  B. Right of Rescission Notice. The right of rescission notice must be given to a consumer/borrower before the time the borrower signs a note. The right of rescission notice is given only on loans secured by the borrower's residence that are not being made for the purpose of purchasing or constructing the residence. The borrower has three business days from receiving the right of rescission to rescind.
  C. Affidavit of No Rescission. This form should be obtained from a consumer/borrower who has received a notice of rescission after the three-business-day period has expired. This form should be received before the disbursement of any loan proceeds to the borrower.

☐   III. ARM Disclosure Requirements
  A. Consumer Handbook on Adjustable Rate Mortgages. This booklet should be given by the lender to the borrower at the time the borrower applies for an ARM loan.
  B. ARM Loan Program Disclosure Form. This form should be given to a borrower on an ARM loan before the time the borrower signs the note. When interest rates on an ARM change, the lender is required to give an adjustment notice.

- Prevent the lender from charging the borrower any fees or other charges to modify, renew, extend or amend a high-cost loan or to defer any payment due under the terms of the high-cost loan.

- Predatory lending laws may contain a number of other prohibitions, depending upon the concerns of the particular state legislature.

Most predatory lending laws prohibit the practice of *flipping*. Flipping occurs when a creditor makes a high-cost home loan to a borrower who refinances an existing home loan that has been consummated within the prior five years and the new high-cost loan does not provide reasonable tangible net benefits to the borrower, taking into account factors including the terms of both the new and refinanced loan, the cost of the new loan, and the borrower's circumstances. In other words, flipping is when a lender talks a borrower into refinancing a lower-cost loan with a higher-cost loan.

Most predatory lending laws subject violators to damages that may equal two times the interest paid under the loan or, in some cases, forfeiture of all interest under the loan. Many of the laws also pay for the borrower's attorneys' fees incurred in enforcing their rights under the laws. Because the state predatory lending laws are not uniform, it is very difficult for many lenders to operate a national mortgage business and comply with all the various state laws. There have been recent requests for a single federal statute regulating predatory lending that would preempt the state laws and provide one set of nationwide rules.

MORTGAGE FRAUD

The favorable interest rate environment that has existed during the last several years has helped many people achieve home ownership and has resulted in a significant increase in the purchase and sale of single-family homes. This torrid pace in residential sales, loan closings, and refinancings of existing loans has also resulted in an increase in mortgage fraud. Mortgage fraud can take many shapes and scenarios. Mortgage fraud includes, among other schemes, the use of false appraisals, phony borrower, stolen identities, forged deeds, and forged credit reports.

Some mortgage fraud involves a network of appraisers, mortgage brokers, real estate agents, people known as "straw buyers," and even lawyers in a scheme to artificially inflate the prices of homes. The straw buyers buy and sell the homes among themselves—a practice known as "house flipping"—because the houses change hands multiple times within a period of months, escalating in value at each sale as they pass in rapid succession from one straw buyer to another. The success of this crime requires appraisers who will make fake appraisals that inflate property values; mortgage brokers and loan officers willing to take false applications for loans; and lawyers willing to close the flipped sales. The result is that on each sale the straw buyer obtains a maximum loan against the property that far exceeds the value of the property.

The fake borrowers then take the loan money and flee the community, leaving the home empty. Mortgage fraud not only costs the mortgage and title insurance industry millions of dollars, but it also damages many neighborhoods that end up with several vacant homes that become magnets for vandalism and other criminal acts. Mortgage fraud also causes an appreciation in the value of properties, which may cause government authorities to increase the taxes for the honest homeowners based on the fraudulent inflated sales prices.

Many states are addressing mortgage fraud by enacting mortgage fraud statutes making certain acts committed in the sale or closing of a mortgage loan a criminal offense. These statutes often authorize district attorneys to investigate and prosecute cases of mortgage fraud. Typically, a fraud statute will provide that any person commits the offense of mortgage fraud when such person, with the intent to defraud, knowingly makes any deliberate misstatement, misrepresentation, or omission during the mortgage loan process with the intention for it to be relied on by a mortgage lender, borrower, or any other party to the mortgage lending process. Mortgage fraud is generally a felony and can result in imprisonment or a fine.

ETHICS: Communication with Parties Represented by an Attorney

A paralegal works for a law firm assisting attorneys in the closing of residential loans. The paralegal is responsible for preparing the documents and obtaining necessary information to close the loans. This work involves contact between the paralegal and the borrowers. Many borrowers are not represented by attorneys and frequently call the paralegal to ask for information and nonlegal advice. On one transaction, the paralegal is aware that the borrowers are represented by an attorney. The attorney has requested that all documents be forwarded to her for review before closing and has had other telephone and written communication with the paralegal. The paralegal, in the process of closing the loan, has a number of questions that need answers from the borrowers. The paralegal, rather than requesting this information from the attorney representing the borrowers, calls the borrowers directly to obtain the information. Did the paralegal act ethically in this respect?

Professional ethics require that attorneys and paralegals shall not communicate or cause another to communicate with a party the attorney or paralegal knows to be represented by a lawyer in a pending matter without the prior consent of the lawyer representing such party. This ethical restriction is necessary to protect the confidential relationship between a client and an attorney and to protect a party from having opposing counsel attempt to obtain information, exert undue influence, or take some advantage of the party. The paralegal in this situation is fully aware that the parties are represented by an attorney and did act unethically in contacting the parties directly to obtain information. The paralegal should have spoken with the attorney first to see if direct contact with the client was permissible or request the information through the attorney.

SUMMARY

A paralegal involved in the closing of a residential real estate loan transaction must be aware of the various federal laws that regulate the transaction. Most law firms have the necessary forms to comply with the federal laws, and a paralegal need only make certain that the forms are properly completed and the necessary disclosures are made to the consumer or borrower at the appropriate times.

HELPFUL WEBSITES

RESPA
The latest news and other interesting information about RESPA can be found on the Web site at *http://www.respanews.com.*

Truth-in-Lending and Reg. Z
Information about the Truth-in-Lending Act and Reg. Z can be found on the government Web site at *http://www.fdic .gov/regulations/laws/rules/6500-1400.html.*

Home Ownership Equity Protection Act (HOEPA)
Information about HOEPA can be found at *http://www .mbaa.org/. HomeOwnershipEquityProtectionActHOEPA.htm*

KEY TERMS

consumer
consumer credit
consummation
finance charge

HUD–1
kickback
Real Estate Settlement Procedures
   Act (RESPA)

rescission
settlement costs
Truth-in-Lending Act

REVIEW QUESTIONS

1. What is the purpose of RESPA?

2. What transactions are subject to RESPA? Which transactions are exempt?

3. Why are kickbacks prohibited under RESPA?

4. What is the purpose of the Truth-in-Lending Act?

5. What real estate transactions are subject to the Truth-in-Lending Act?

6. Which transactions are exempt from the Truth-in-Lending Act?

7. What disclosures does the Truth-in-Lending Act require before the closing of a residential real estate loan transaction?

8. What is the purpose of the right of rescission under the Truth-in-Lending Act?

9. What disclosures must be made under the adjustable interest rate disclosure requirements?

10. What residential loans are exempt from the right of rescission under the Truth-in-Lending Act?

CASE PROBLEMS

1. You are assisting an attorney in the closing of a loan made by a federally insured savings and loan association to facilitate the purchase of a home. The loan is closing on October 15. The first payment under the loan will be due December 1. The real estate taxes on the home for the current year were due and payable on September 1, and they have been paid in the amount of $1,800. If the lender requests that you escrow taxes under its loan, how much money do you need to collect for the escrow at the closing on October 15?

2. The firm you work with closes a number of real estate loans with a Federal Deposit Insurance Company–insured bank. The firm does not do its own title examination work but instead retains an independent title examiner to do the title examinations. The firm at closing charges a title examination fee, of which 75 percent goes to the title examiner and 25 percent is retained by the firm to compensate the firm for reviewing the title examination and typing the title examination from the title examiner's notes. Is this practice legal under RESPA?

3. How many copies of the right to rescind must be given in a loan transaction secured by a vacation home owned by a husband and wife?

4. You are assisting in a real estate closing that closes on July 2. The closing is subject to the truth-in-lending right of rescission. On what day does the right of rescission expire?

5. Check your state laws to see if your state has passed a mortgage fraud act. Copy the statute and write a short report summarizing the content of your state's mortgage fraud act. The report should cover such things as what actions constitute mortgage fraud and what the penalties for mortgage fraud are.

ADDENDUM

Exhibit 15–1 HUD–1 Settlement Statement
Exhibit 15–2 Truth-in-Lending Disclosure Statement

Exhibit 15–3 Rescission Model Form (General)
Exhibit 15–4 Nonrescind Statement

ACKNOWLEDGMENT

Portions of this chapter have been excerpted from *Lending in a Changing Environment*, by Robert R. Stubbs, *Real Estate Practices and Procedures Program Materials*, Pages 4.1-4.44; Institute of Continuing Legal Education in Georgia, 1985, Athens, Georgia. Used by permission of the Publisher.

Student StudyWare™ CD-ROM

Interactive Student CD in the book includes additional quizzing, case studies, and key terms flashcards.

Online Companion™

For additional resources, please go to *www.paralegal.delmar.cengage.com*

EXHIBIT 15–1

HUD–1 Settlement Statement

OMB Approval No. 2502-0265

U.S. DEPARTMENT OF HOUSING AND URBAN DEVELOPMENT

A. Settlement Statement (HUD-1)

B. Type of Loan

1. ☐ FHA	2. ☐ RHS	3. ☐ Conv. Unins.	6. File Number:	7. Loan Number:	8. Mortgage Insurance Case Number:
4. ☐ VA	5. ☐ Conv. Ins.				

C. Note: This form is furnished to give you a statement of actual settlement costs. Amounts paid to and by the settlement agent are shown. Items marked "(p.o.c.)" were paid outside the closing; they are shown here for informational purposes and are not included in the totals.

D. Name & Address of Borrower:	E. Name & Address of Seller:	F. Name & Address of Lender:
G. Property Location:	H. Settlement Agent:	I. Settlement Date:
	Place of Settlement:	

J. Summary of Borrower's Transaction		K. Summary of Seller's Transaction	
100. Gross Amount Due from Borrower		**400. Gross Amount Due to Seller**	
101. Contract sales price		401. Contract sales price	
102. Personal property		402. Personal property	
103. Settlement charges to borrower (line 1400)		403.	
104.		404.	
105.		405.	
Adjustment for items paid by seller in advance		**Adjustments for items paid by seller in advance**	
106. City/town taxes to		406. City/town taxes to	
107. County taxes to		407. County taxes to	
108. Assessments to		408. Assessments to	
109.		409.	
110.		410.	
111.		411.	
112.		412.	
120. Gross Amount Due from Borrower		**420. Gross Amount Due to Seller**	
200. Amounts Paid by or in Behalf of Borrower		**500. Reductions In Amount Due to Seller**	
201. Deposit or earnest money		501. Excess deposit (see instructions)	
202. Principal amount of new loan(s)		502. Settlement charges to seller (line 1400)	
203. Existing loan(s) taken subject to		503. Existing loan(s) taken subject to	
204.		504. Payoff of first mortgage loan	
205.		505. Payoff of second mortgage loan	
206.		506.	
207.		507.	
208.		508.	
209.		509.	
Adjustments for items unpaid by seller		**Adjustments for items unpaid by seller**	
210. City/town taxes to		510. City/town taxes to	
211. County taxes to		511. County taxes to	
212. Assessments to		512. Assessments to	
213.		513.	
214.		514.	
215.		515.	
216.		516.	
217.		517.	
218.		518.	
219.		519.	
220. Total Paid by/for Seller		**520. Total Reduction Amount Due Seller**	
300. Cash at Settlement from/to Borrower		**600. Cash at Settlement to/from Seller**	
301. Gross amount due from borrower (line 120)		601. Gross amount due to seller (line 420)	
302. Less amounts paid by/for borrower (line 220)	( )	602. Less reductions in amount due seller (line 520)	( )
303. Cash ☐ From ☐ To Borrower		**603. Cash** ☐ To ☐ From Seller	

The Public Reporting Burden for this collection of information is estimated at 35 minutes per response for collecting, reviewing, and reporting the data. This agency may not collect this information, and you are not required to complete this form, unless it displays a currently valid OMB control number. No confidentiality is assured; this disclosure is mandatory. This is designed to provide the parties to a RESPA covered transaction with information during the settlement process.

Previous editions are obsolete   Page 1 of 3   HUD-1

Delmar/Cengage Learning

(continued)

L. Settlement Charges

		Paid From Borrower's Funds at Settlement	Paid From Seller's Funds at Settlement
700. Total Real Estate Broker Fees			
Division of commission (line 700) as follows:			
701. $ to			
702. $ to			
703. Commission paid at settlement			
704.			
800. Items Payable in Connection with Loan			
801. Our origination charge $	(from GFE #1)		
802. Your credit or charge (points) for the specific interest rate chosen $	(from GFE #2)		
803. Your adjusted origination charges	(from GFE A)		
804. Appraisal fee to	(from GFE #3)		
805. Credit report to	(from GFE #3)		
806. Tax service to	(from GFE #3)		
807. Flood certification	(from GFE #3)		
808.			
900. Items Required by Lender to Be Paid in Advance			
901. Daily interest charges from to @ $ /day	(from GFE #10)		
902. Mortgage insurance premium for months to	(from GFE #3)		
903. Homeowner's insurance for years to	(from GFE #11)		
904.			
1000. Reserves Deposited with Lender			
1001. Initial deposit for your escrow account	(from GFE #9)		
1002. Homeowner's insurance months @ $ per month $			
1003. Mortgage insurance months @ $ per month $			
1004. Property taxes months @ $ per month $			
1005. months @ $ per month $			
1006. months @ $ per month $			
1007. Aggregate Adjustment –$			
1100. Title Charges			
1101. Title services and lender's title insurance	(from GFE #4)		
1102. Settlement or closing fee $			
1103. Owner's title insurance	(from GFE #5)		
1104. Lender's title insurance $			
1105. Lender's title policy limit $			
1106. Owner's title policy limit $			
1107. Agent's portion of the total title insurance premium $			
1108. Underwriter's portion of the total title insurance premium $			
1200. Government Recording and Transfer Charges			
1201. Government recording charges	(from GFE #7)		
1202. Deed $ Mortgage $ Releases $			
1203. Transfer taxes	(from GFE #8)		
1204. City/County tax/stamps Deed $ Mortgage $			
1205. State tax/stamps Deed $ Mortgage $			
1206.			
1300. Additional Settlement Charges			
1301. Required services that you can shop for	(from GFE #6)		
1302. $			
1303. $			
1304.			
1305.			
1400. Total Settlement Charges (enter on lines 103, Section J and 502, Section K)			

EXHIBIT 15–1

HUD–1 Settlement Statement (*continued*)

(*continued*)

EXHIBIT 15–1

HUD–1 Settlement Statement
(*continued*)

Comparison of Good Faith Estimate (GFE) and HUD-1 Charges		Good Faith Estimate	HUD-1
Charges That Cannot Increase	**HUD-1 Line Number**		
Our origination charge	# 801		
Your credit or charge (points) for the specific interest rate chosen	# 802		
Your adjusted origination charges	# 803		
Transfer taxes	#1203		

Charges That in Total Cannot Increase More Than 10%		Good Faith Estimate	HUD-1
Government recording charges	# 1201		
	#		
	#		
	#		
	#		
	#		
	#		
	#		
Total			
Increase between GFE and HUD-1 Charges		$ or	%

Charges That Can Change		Good Faith Estimate	HUD-1
Initial deposit for your escrow account	#1001		
Daily interest charges	# 901 $ /day		
Homeowner's insurance	# 903		
	#		
	#		
	#		

Loan Terms

Your initial loan amount is	$ _____
Your loan term is	_____ years
Your initial interest rate is	_____ %
Your initial monthly amount owed for principal, interest, and any mortgage insurance is	$ _____ includes ☐ Principal ☐ Interest ☐ Mortgage Insurance
Can your interest rate rise?	☐ No. ☐ Yes, it can rise to a maximum of ___%. The first change will be on _____ and can change again every _____ after _____. Every change date, your interest rate can increase or decrease by ___%. Over the life of the loan, your interest rate is guaranteed to never be **lower** than ___% or **higher** than ___%.
Even if you make payments on time, can your loan balance rise?	☐ No. ☐ Yes, it can rise to a maximum of $ _____.
Even if you make payments on time, can your monthly amount owed for principal, interest, and mortgage insurance rise?	☐ No. ☐ Yes, the first increase can be on _____ and the monthly amount owed can rise to $ _____. The maximum it can ever rise to is $ _____.
Does your loan have a prepayment penalty?	☐ No. ☐ Yes, your maximum prepayment penalty is $ _____.
Does your loan have a balloon payment?	☐ No. ☐ Yes, you have a balloon payment of $ _____ due in _____ years on _____.
Total monthly amount owed including escrow account payments	☐ You do not have a monthly escrow payment for items, such as property taxes and homeowner's insurance. You must pay these items directly yourself. ☐ You have an additional monthly escrow payment of $ _____ that results in a total initial monthly amount owed of $ _____. This includes principal, interest, any mortgage insurance and any items checked below: ☐ Property taxes ☐ Homeowner's insurance ☐ Flood insurance ☐ _____ ☐ _____ ☐ _____

Note: If you have any questions about the Settlement Charges and Loan Terms listed on this form, please contact your lender.

Form 82-17

EXHIBIT 15–2

Truth-in-Lending Disclosure Statement

CREDITOR:

FEDERAL TRUTH IN LENDING ACT DISCLOSURE STATEMENT
ADJUSTABLE RATE MORTGAGE

Borrowers name(s) _____

Mailing address of subject property _____

ANNUAL PERCENTAGE RATE	FINANCE CHARGE	Amount Financed	Total of Payments
The cost of your credit as a yearly rate.	The dollar amount the credit will cost you.	The amount of credit provided to you or on your behalf.	The amount you will have paid after you have made all payments as scheduled.
_____ %	$ _____	$ _____	$ _____

Your payment schedule will be:

Number of Payments	Amount of Payments	When Payments Are Due
*		

* Assuming maximum rate change

Insurance: Hazard insurance and flood insurance (if the property lies within a flood plain) is required. You may obtain this insurance from anyone you want that is acceptable to Creditor.

Security: You are giving a security interest in the property being purchased.

Late Charge: If a payment is received more than 15 days after it is due, you will be charged ____ % of the payment.

Prepayment: If you payoff early, you

☐ may ☐ will not have to pay a penalty.

☐ may ☐ will not be entitled to a refund of part of the Finance Charge.

Assumption: Someone buying your home

☐ may, subject to conditions be allowed to assume the remainder of the mortgage on the original terms.

☐ cannot assume the remainder of the mortgage on the original terms.

See your contract documents for any additional information about nonpayment, default, any required repayment in full before the scheduled date, and prepayment refunds and penalties.

_____
"e" means an estimate

Type of Disclosure and Certificate or Acknowledgement (check applicable box)

☐ **Original Disclosure.** The undersigned representative of the Creditor certifies that the Real Estate Settlement Procedures Act (RESPA) Information Booklet, "The RESPA Good Faith Estimate of Settlement Costs," and the above Federal Truth in Lending Act Disclosure Statement appropriately completed so as to reflect the mortgage loan for which Borrower(s) have applied to Creditor were on the date indicated below deposited in the U.S. Mail, first class postage prepaid addressed to the Borrower(s) at the following mailing address:

_____

Date: _____   _____
                         Signature of Creditor's Representative

☐ **Corrective Redisclosure.** Borrower(s) have applied to Creditor for a mortgage loan the proceeds of which will be used to purchase a dwelling. Shortly after receiving Borrower(s) application the Creditor provided to Borrower(s) a Federal Truth in Lending Act Disclosure Statement (the "Original Disclosure Statement") which contained important information about the mortgage loan for which Borrower(s) have applied. Some of the disclosures contained in the Original Disclosure Statement do not accurately reflect certain details of the actual mortgage loan that Borrower(s) are receiving from Creditor. This is due to the fact that certain disclosures contained in the Original Disclosure Statement were based on estimates or due to the fact that certain details of the requested mortgage loan have changed since the date the Original Disclosure Statement was prepared. The purpose of this Corrective Redisclosure Statement is to provide Borrower(s) with disclosures that accurately reflect the actual mortgage loan that Borrower(s) are receiving from creditor. The undersigned hereby acknowledge receipt of a copy of this Federal Truth in Lending Disclosure Statement this date.

_____   _____
Signature of Borrower   Date

_____   _____   _____
Witness   Signature of Co-Borrower   Date

EXHIBIT 15–3

Rescission Model Form
(General)

NOTICE OF RIGHT TO CANCEL

Your Right to Cancel

You are entering into a transaction that will result in a [mortgage/lien/security interest] [on/in] your home. You have a legal right under federal law to cancel this transaction without cost, within three business days from whichever of the following events occurs last:

(1)   the date of the transaction, which is _____; or

(2)   the date you received your Truth-in-Lending disclosures; or

(3)   the date you received this notice of your right to cancel.

If you cancel the transaction, the [mortgage/lien/security interest] is also cancelled. Within 20 calendar days after we receive your notice, we must take the steps necessary to reflect the fact that the [mortgage/lien/security interest] [on/in] your home has been cancelled, and we must return to you any money or property you have given to us or to anyone else in connection with this transaction.

You may keep any money or property we have given you until we have done the things mentioned above, but you must then offer to return the money or property. If it is impractical or unfair for you to return the property, you must offer its reasonable value. You may offer to return the property at your home or at the location of the property. Money must be returned to the address below. If we do not take possession of the money or property within 20 calendar days of your offer, you may keep it without further obligation.

How to Cancel

If you decide to cancel this transaction, you may do so by notifying us in writing at:

   (creditor's name and business address)

You may use any written statement that is signed and dated by you and states your intention to cancel, and/or you may use this notice by dating and signing below. Keep one copy of this notice because it contains important information about your rights. If you cancel by mail or telegram, you must send the notice no later than midnight of (date) (or midnight of the third business day following the latest of the three events listed above). If you send or deliver your written notice to cancel some other way, it must be delivered to the above address no later than that time.

I WISH TO CANCEL

_____   _____

Consumer's Signature   Date

EXHIBIT 15–4

Nonrescind Statement

With the intention that _____

_____ rely

on this statement, the undersigned does hereby certify that (s)he (they) has(ve) not rescinded, attempted to rescind or otherwise attempted to notify _____

_____ _____ of any intention to rescind the

loan transaction involving a security interest in his(er) (their) residence known as:

_____

_____

_____   _____

                                      Date

_____   _____

                                      Date

chapter | 16

Real Estate Closing Forms and Examples

Objectives

After reading this chapter, you should be able to:

- Understand and prepare various kinds of affidavits
- Understand and prepare various real estate closing documents such as deeds, bills of sale, assignment of warranties, assignment of leases, and assignment of contracts
- Understand the importance and particular use of such real estate documents as corporate resolutions, agreements regarding survival of loan commitments, indemnities of fees, attorney's opinions, and compliance agreements
- Prepare a HUD–1 Uniform Settlement Statement
- Understand the documentation involved in the closing of a residential sale and loan transaction

Outline

At a real estate closing, ownership of real property is transferred from seller to purchaser. At a loan closing, a loan is consummated between the lender and the borrower. The purchaser at a closing expects to receive good title to the real property that he or she has agreed to buy and to obtain whatever warranties and assurances the seller has made in the real estate sale contract. The seller at a closing expects to be paid the contract price for the real property and not obligate himself or herself to perform any duty not required under the contract. In the case of a loan closing, the borrower expects to receive the loan proceeds from the lender, and the lender expects to receive good security for its loan as well as the satisfaction of all the borrower's promises and covenants contained in the loan commitment.

A real estate attorney uses a number of legal documents at the closing to accomplish and satisfy all the expectations of the parties involved. A real estate paralegal prepares many of the legal documents required. These legal documents are numerous and vary in form from state to state. The paralegal should become familiar with the various legal forms used in the locality in which he or she works. This information can be obtained from the law firm that employs the paralegal.

Some of the basic forms that are used in residential and commercial real estate closing transactions are discussed in this chapter. Many forms, such as deeds, notes, and mortgages, have already been discussed. References are made to the chapters in which these forms can be found.

All forms referred to in the sections on affidavits, sale and transfer documents, and miscellaneous closing documents appear at the end of the latter section.

AFFIDAVITS

affidavit

Sworn statement of fact.

An **affidavit** is a written statement of fact that is sworn to by the person making the statement (affiant) under oath as a true statement of facts. The person who administers the oath to the affiant is a notary public. The notary's signature usually appears on the affidavit as well as the notary seal. Giving a false affidavit is perjury. Perjury can result in both civil and criminal penalties.

Affidavits are used for many purposes in a real estate closing transaction. Some of the more common affidavits used by the real estate attorney or paralegal are discussed in this section.

Title Affidavit

Most purchasers of real property require the seller to execute a title affidavit at the time of the sale. In addition, most lenders require the borrower to execute a title affidavit at the time the lender acquires a mortgage on the borrower's real property. The title affidavit is helpful in removing standard exceptions from title insurance policies. A title affidavit is a statement of facts swearing to the following: (a) the affiant owns the real property described in the affidavit; (b) the boundary lines of the real property are certain and not in dispute; (c) the affiant has a right to possession of the real property; (d) there are no liens, encumbrances, easements, or leases affecting the real property unless they are identified in the affidavit; (e) there are no judgments, bankruptcies, or other restrictions against the affiant owner of the real property; and (f) the affidavit is being made by the affiant with knowledge that it will be relied on by purchasers, lenders, and title insurance companies involved with the real property.

Exhibit 16–1 shows a title affidavit. Other title affidavits can be found in Chapter 13.

Hazardous Waste Affidavit

The presence of hazardous waste materials on real property can create serious problems for the property owner. Federal and state laws impose on the owner of real property liability for all damage caused by hazardous waste as well as the cost of the hazardous waste cleanup.

EXHIBIT 16–1

Affidavit of Title

STATE OF _____
COUNTY OF _____

The undersigned, _____, being
duly sworn, states:

That the undersigned is the fee simple title owner of the real property described on Exhibit "A" attached hereto and incorporated herein by reference (the "Property");

That the lines and corners of the Property are clearly marked and there are no disputes concerning the location of said lines and corners;

That no improvements or repairs have been made or contracted for on the Property during the three (3) months immediately preceding the date of this affidavit, for which there are outstanding bills for labor or services performed or rendered, or for materials supplied or furnished, or incurred in connection with improvements or repairs on the Property, or for the services of architects, surveyors or engineers in connection with improvements or repairs on the Property;

That, except for the matters set forth on Exhibit "B" attached hereto and incorporated herein by reference, the Property is free and clear of all claims, liens and encumbrances, and there is no outstanding indebtedness for or liens against any equipment or fixtures attached to, installed on, incorporated in or located on, or otherwise used in connection with the operation or maintenance of, the Property or the improvements thereon;

That there are no persons or other parties in possession of the Property who have a right or claim to possession extending beyond the date hereof, except for tenants under terms of written leases disclosed on Exhibit "C" attached hereto and incorporated herein by reference;

That there are no suits, proceedings, judgments, bankruptcies, liens, or executions against the undersigned which affect title to the Property, the improvements thereon or the fixtures attached thereto;

That the undersigned is making this affidavit with the knowledge that it will be relied upon by lenders, attorneys, and title insurance companies interested in the title to the Property.

Sworn to and subscribed before
me this _____ day of _____,
20___.

_____   _____ (SEAL)
Notary Public
My Commission Expires:

_____

[NOTARY SEAL]

Delmar/Cengage Learning

Liability is imposed on any owner of real property, regardless of whether that owner was responsible for the creation of the hazardous waste material. A full discussion of hazardous materials is found in Chapter 4. Most purchasers and lenders will not purchase or make a loan on real property without having a hazardous waste inspection done by a professional inspection firm. In addition to the independent inspection for hazardous waste, most purchasers and lenders require the seller or borrower to sign a hazardous waste affidavit at the time of the sale or loan closing (see Exhibit 16–2).

Affidavit of No Change

It is not uncommon in loan transactions for several weeks to pass between the time the loan application is made and the time the loan is closed. Many lenders require the borrower, at the time of the loan closing, to sign an affidavit swearing that the borrower's financial

EXHIBIT 16–2

Hazardous Waste Affidavit

STATE OF _____)
) ss:
COUNTY OF _____)

The undersigned is the fee simple title owner of the real property described in Exhibit "A" attached hereto and incorporated herein by reference (the "Property").

That no pollutants or other toxic or hazardous substances, as defined under the Comprehensive Environmental Response, Compensation, and Liability Act ("CERCLA"), 42 U.S.C. § 9601 *et seq.*, or any other federal or state law, including any solid, liquid, gaseous, or thermal irritant or contaminant, such as smoke, vapor, soot, fumes, acids, alkalis, chemicals or waste (including materials to be recycled, reconditioned or reclaimed) (collectively "Substances") have been or shall be discharged, disbursed, released, stored, treated, generated, disposed of, or allowed to escape (collectively referred to as the "incident") on or from Property.

That no asbestos or asbestos-containing materials have been installed, used, incorporated into, or disposed of on the Property.

That no polychlorinated biphenyls ("PCBs") are located on or in the Property, in the form of electrical transformers, fluorescent light fixtures with ballasts, cooling oils, or any other device or form.

That no underground storage tanks are located on the Property or were located on the Property and subsequently removed or filled.

That no investigation, administrative order, consent order and agreement, litigation, or settlement (collectively referred to as the "action") with respect to substances is proposed, threatened, anticipated or in existence with respect to the Property.

That the Property and undersigned's operations at the Property are in compliance with all applicable federal, state and local statutes, laws and regulations. No notice has been served on undersigned, from any entity, governmental body, or individual claiming any violation of any law, regulation, ordinance or code, or requiring compliance with any law, regulation, ordinance or code, or demanding payment or contribution for environmental damage or injury to natural resources.

That the undersigned are making this affidavit with the knowledge that it will be relied upon by lenders, interested in the title to the Property.

_____ (SEAL)

Sworn to and subscribed before
me this _____ day of _____,
20___.

Notary Public
My Commission Expires:

_____
Notarial Seal

Delmar/Cengage Learning

condition has not materially changed from the date the loan application was made (see Exhibit 16–3).

Same Name Affidavit

An owner of property may be referred to in the chain of title or in a transaction in a number of ways. For example, a person named William Charles Smith may be referred to as W. C. Smith in some of the closing documents or the documents within the chain of title. It is important to make certain that W. C. Smith and William Charles Smith are one and the same person. Often an affidavit to that effect is used (see Exhibit 16–4).

EXHIBIT 16–3

Affidavit of No Material Change

STATE OF _____)
) ss:
COUNTY OF _____)

    The undersigned, being duly sworn, state:

    That the undersigned have received from SECOND FEDERAL SAVINGS AND LOAN ASSOCIATION a loan Commitment letter dated August 25, 20___, amended by letter dated December 13, 20__ ("Commitment Letter"), to finance the construction of a 62,128 square foot shopping center located in Gulfport, Mississippi;

    That no adverse change has taken place in the undersigneds' business or financial condition or in connection with the property serving as collateral for the loan;

    That the undersigned are making this affidavit with the knowledge that it will be relied upon by SECOND FEDERAL SAVINGS AND LOAN ASSOCIATION in making the loan set forth in the commitment letter.

                                              _____ (SEAL)
                                              _____ (SEAL)

Sworn to and subscribed before me this
_____ day of _____, 20__.

_____
Notary Public
My Commission Expires:

_____
Notarial Seal

Delmar/Cengage Learning

EXHIBIT 16–4

Same Name Affidavit

STATE OF _____
COUNTY OF _____

    Before me came in person William Charles Smith who, being duly sworn, on oath says:

    Deponent states that William Charles Smith (s)he is one and the same person as W.C. Smith and is the same person as named in Warranty Deed dated November 14, 1998 and recorded at Deed Book 156, page 242, _____ County, State of _____.

                                   _____
                                     William Charles Smith

Sworn to and subscribed before me this
_____ day of _____, 20__.

_____
Notary Public

Delmar/Cengage Learning

Similar Name Affidavit

It is not unusual for a common name such as William Smith to appear on the judgment index during a title examination. The judgments may be against a person with the name of William Smith other than the borrower or seller of the real property involved in the real estate transaction. To clear up the matter, most title companies will accept an affidavit signed by the real property owner indicating that the real property owner is not the same person mentioned in the judgments (see Exhibit 16–5). On receipt of this affidavit, the title company will insure the real property free and clear of the judgments.

EXHIBIT 16–5

Similar Name Affidavit

STATE OF _____

COUNTY OF _____

    Before me, the undersigned attesting officer, came in person _____, who, after having been first duly sworn, deposes and on oath says that deponent is not the _____ referred to in the following:

    That there are no judgments or executions of any kind or nature outstanding against deponent; and

    That this affidavit is made for the purpose of inducing _____ to make a loan secured by a loan deed on or to purchase property known as:

_____

_____

                              _____

Sworn to and subscribed before me this
_____ day of _____, 20___.

_____
Notary Public

Delmar/Cengage Learning

Foreign Person Affidavit

The Internal Revenue Service requires that a purchaser of real property from a foreign person withhold 10 percent of the purchase price and pay it to the Internal Revenue Service. If the purchaser fails to withhold the 10 percent, the purchaser will be responsible for any tax assessed against the foreign person on account of the sale. The purchaser is not excused from this obligation unless the purchaser obtains an affidavit from the seller to the effect that the seller is not a foreign person (see Exhibit 16–6). The foreign person affidavit has become standard on all real estate transactions.

SALE AND TRANSFER DOCUMENTS

The sale and transfer of real property requires the use of a number of legal documents. The type of real property being transferred often dictates what documents are required. For example, the sale of a home requires less documentation than the sale of a resort hotel. On most real estate transactions, the sale and transfer at least requires the use of a deed, bill of sale, and assignment of warranties, and, on commercial contracts, an assignment of leases and assignment of contracts.

Deed

A deed is a legal document that transfers ownership of real property from one person to another. A full discussion of deeds, together with several examples of different types of deeds, can be found in Chapter 8.

Bill of Sale

A deed only transfers ownership to real property. If the real estate transaction involves both real and personal property, which is the case in most residential and commercial transactions, then a separate legal document must be used to transfer ownership of the

Delmar/Cengage Learning

EXHIBIT 16–6

Foreign Person Affidavit

STATE OF _____

COUNTY OF _____

    The undersigned, being duly sworn, deposes, certifies and states on oath as follows:

    That the undersigned is not a "foreign person" as such term is defined in the United States Internal Revenue Code of 1986, as amended (the "Code") and regulations promulgated there under, and is not otherwise a "foreign person" as defined in Section 1445 of the Code;

    That the undersigned's United States taxpayer identification number is; _____

_____ :

    That the undersigned is making this Affidavit pursuant to the provisions of Section 1445 of the Code in connection with the sale of the real property described on Exhibit "A" attached hereto and incorporated herein by reference, from the undersigned to   , which sale constitutes the disposition of the undersigned of a United States real property interest, for the purpose of establishing that   is not required to withhold tax pursuant to Section 1445 of the Code in connection with such sale;

    That the undersigned acknowledges that this Affidavit may be disclosed to the Internal Revenue Service by   , that this Affidavit is made under penalty of perjury, that any false statement made herein could be punished by fine, imprisonment, or both.

    Under penalty of perjury, I declare that I have examined the foregoing Affidavit and hereby certify that it is true, correct and complete.

Sworn to and subscribed before
me this _____ day of _____,
20__.

_____   _____

Notary Public

---

personal property. The legal document that transfers ownership to personal property is a **bill of sale.** A bill of sale, similar to a deed, can either contain warranties of title or be a quitclaim bill of sale without warranties. A general warranty bill of sale usually contains warranties that (a) the seller lawfully owns and is possessed of the personal property being sold; (b) the seller has a right to sell, transfer, and convey the personal property to the purchaser; (c) the personal property is free and clear of any and all encumbrances or security interests; and (d) the seller will warrant and forever defend the title of the personal property against the claims of any and all people whomsoever. The bill of sale usually is signed with the same formality as a deed, witnessed, and notarized. A bill of sale usually is not recorded. An example of a general warranty bill of sale appears as Exhibit 16–7.

bill of sale

Legal document that transfers ownership to personal property.

Assignment of Warranties

A number of warranties may exist in connection with the improvements located on real property. For example, a home may have a 20-year roof warranty and a 10-year furnace warranty. On commercial properties, there may be warranties that involve the air-conditioning system, the furnace, the asphalt sealant on the parking lot, and so on. Most purchasers of the real property require that the right to enforce these warranties be assigned to them as part of the sale. This is done by an assignment of warranties signed by the seller. The assignment of warranties usually is prepared with the same formality as a deed, and the seller's signature is witnessed and notarized. The assignment of warranties usually is not recorded. An example of an assignment of warranties appears as Exhibit 16–8.

EXHIBIT 16–7

General Warranty Bill of Sale

STATE OF
COUNTY OF

FOR AND IN CONSIDERATION of the sum of Ten and NO/100 Dollars ($10.00) and other good and valuable consideration in hand paid to _____ (hereinafter referred to as "Seller") by _____ (hereinafter referred to as "Purchaser"), Seller hereby sells and conveys to Purchaser, her successors and assigns, any and all existing fixtures, equipment, furniture, appliances and other personal property owned by Seller and used in connection with and being situated on or within certain improved real estate of Seller located in _____ County, _____, and more particularly described on Exhibit "A" attached hereto and by this reference incorporated herein and made a part hereof.

Seller hereby covenants with and represents and warrants to Purchaser as follows:

1. That Seller is lawfully seized and possessed of said personal property.
2. That Seller has the right to sell, transfer and convey the same;
3. That same is free and clear of any and all encumbrances; and
4. That Seller warrants and will forever defend the title to same against all claims whatsoever.

IN WITNESS WHEREOF, Seller has hereunto caused its hand and seal to be applied this _____ day of _____, 20__.

Signed, sealed and delivered this

_____ day of _____, 20__, in the

presence of:

(Seal)

_____

_____
Witness

_____
Notary Public
My Commission Expires:

_____

Delmar/Cengage Learning

Assignment of Leases

The sale of a commercial real property with tenants involves the transfer of the tenant leases from the seller to the purchaser. Most purchasers require that all leases be assigned to them together with all security deposits that must be returned to the tenant on the expiration of the leases. The purchaser also requires that the seller indemnify the purchaser against any claims that the tenants may have against the seller or the purchaser as a result of defaults under the leases that have happened before the date of the sale. Most sellers require that the purchaser indemnify the seller against all claims that may be made by the tenants against the seller because of defaults under the leases that occur after the date of the sale. An assignment of leases usually is signed by both purchaser and seller, and their signatures are witnessed and notarized. The assignment of leases is not recorded unless the leases have been recorded. Exhibit 16–9 is an example of an assignment of leases.

Assignment of Contracts

The sale of commercial property may involve the assignment of certain service contracts that are an integral part of the real property. For example, an apartment project may have a contract with a landscape service to take care of the grounds or a contract with a pool

For good and valuable consideration, the undersigned, hereby transfers and assigns unto

_____

_____ all right, title and interest of the undersigned, in and to any and all equipment, construction, and appliances warranties of any nature whatsoever pertaining to all or part of the real property described in Exhibit "A" attached hereto and incorporated herein by reference and in or pertaining to all or any of the improvements located on such real property.

This Assignment is made without warranty by the undersigned and without recourse, it being the intention of the undersigned and the purpose of this document only to transfer and assign unto _____ whatever right, title and interest that the undersigned may have in such warranties, if any, nothing more.

IN WITNESS WHEREOF, the undersigned, have hereunto set their hands and seals this _____ day of _____, 20__.

Signed, sealed and delivered this _____   _____ (SEAL)

day of _____, 20___.

In the presence of: _____ (SEAL)

_____

Witness

_____

Notary Public
My Commission Expires:

_____

Notarial Seal

EXHIBIT 16–8

Assignment of Warranties

Delmar/Cengage Learning

STATE OF _____)

) ss:

COUNTY OF _____)

THIS INDENTURE, made and entered into this _____ day of _____, 20__, by and between _____

_____ (hereinafter referred

to as "Assignor") and _____

_____, its suc-

cessors and assigns (hereinafter referred to as "Assignee").

WITNESSETH:

WHEREAS, Assignor has on even date herewith conveyed to Assignee certain improved real property located in _____ County, _____ (hereinafter referred to as the "Property"), more particularly described on Exhibit "A" attached hereto and made a part hereof, and in connection therewith Assignor desires to transfer and assign to Assignee the tenant leases and security deposits in existence with regard to the improvements located on the Property;

NOW, THEREFORE, for and in consideration of the sum of TEN AND NO/100 ($10.00) DOLLARS and other good and valuable consideration, the receipt and sufficiency of which are hereby acknowledged, Assignor and Assignee covenant and agree as follows:

1. Assignment of Leases.

Assignor hereby transfers and assigns to Assignee all of Assignor's right, title and interest as landlord or lessor in and to each of the leases described on Exhibit "B" attached hereto and made a part hereof (hereinafter referred to as the "Leases") affecting all or any part of the Property.

EXHIBIT 16–9

Assignment of Leases and Security Deposits

Delmar/Cengage Learning

(continued)

EXHIBIT 16–9

Assignment of Leases and
Security Deposits

(continued)

2. Indemnification of Assignee.

Assignor indemnifies, defends and holds Assignee, its successors and assigns, harmless from and against any claim against or liability of Assignee, its successors and assigns, arising out of the covenants and duties of the lessor/landlord under the Leases to be performed before the date hereof by Assignor.

3. Assignment of Security Deposit.

Assignor hereby transfers and conveys to Assignee all of Assignor's right, title and interest in and to all security deposits collected by Assignor under the Leases, said security deposits being more particularly described on Exhibit "B" attached hereto and made a part hereof.

4. Indemnification of Assignor.

Assignee indemnifies, defends, and holds Assignor harmless from any and all claims against or liabilities of Assignor arising out of the covenants and duties of Assignor to return the security deposits and fees assigned herein and assumes the obligation of landlord or lessor and agrees to perform under the Leases pursuant to the conditions contained in the Leases.

5. Successors and Assigns.

This Assignment shall be binding upon and inure to the benefit of the Assignor and Assignee and their respective successors and assigns.

6. Governing Law.

This Assignment shall be governed and construed in accordance with the laws of the State of _____.

    IN WITNESS WHEREOF, the undersigned parties have hereunto set their hands and seals, as of the day and year first above written.

ASSIGNOR:

Signed, sealed and delivered in the presence of:

_____ (SEAL)

_____
Witness

_____
Notary Public
My Commission Expires:

_____
Notarial Seal

ASSIGNEE:

Signed, sealed and delivered in the presence of:

_____ (SEAL)

_____
Witness

_____
Notary Public
My Commission Expires:

_____
Notarial Seal

service to take care of the recreational area. The sale of a hotel may have any number of contracts that involve, for example, ice machine, pool maintenance, landscaping, and janitorial services that are to be either terminated at the time of closing or transferred from seller to purchaser. It is not unusual for contracts to be terminated at the time of closing so that the purchaser may enter into its own contractual relations to provide these services. If the contracts are not to be terminated, they are assigned by the seller to the purchaser. The assignment usually contains an indemnity from the seller to the purchaser indemnifying the purchaser against any claims or losses the purchaser may suffer because of defaults under the contracts before the date of the sale. The purchaser likewise indemnifies the seller for any claims or losses incurred by the seller because of defaults under the contracts after the date of the sale. An assignment of contracts is signed by both the seller and the purchaser, and their signatures are witnessed and notarized. The assignment of contracts is not recorded. Exhibit 16–10 is an example of an assignment of contracts.

STATE OF _____)
) ss:
COUNTY OF _____)

    THIS INDENTURE, made and entered this _____ day of _____, 20___, by and between _____
_____ (hereinafter referred to as "Assignor") and _____
_____, its successors and assigns (hereinafter referred to as "Assignee").

WITNESSETH:

    WHEREAS, Assignor has on even date herewith conveyed to Assignee certain improved real property located in _____ County, _____ (hereinafter referred to as the "Property"), more particularly described on Exhibit "A" attached hereto and made a part hereof, and in connection therewith Assignor desires to transfer and assign to Assignee the service contracts in existence with regard to the improvements located on the Property;

    NOW, THEREFORE, for and in consideration of the sum of TEN AND NO/100 ($10.00) DOLLARS and other good and valuable consideration, the receipt and sufficiency of which are hereby acknowledged, Assignor and Assignee covenant and agree as follows:

1. Assignment of Contracts.

Assignor hereby transfers and assigns to Assignee all of Assignor's right, title and interest in and to each of the service contracts described on Exhibit "B" attached hereto and made a part hereof (hereinafter referred to as the "Contracts") affecting all or any part of the Property.

2. Indemnification of Assignee.

Assignor indemnifies, defends and holds Assignee, its successors and assigns, harmless from and against any claims against or liability of Assignee, its successors and assigns, arising out of the covenants and duties of the Assignor under the Contracts to be performed before the date hereof by Assignor.

3. Indemnification of Assignor.

Assignee indemnifies, defends, and holds Assignor harmless from any and all claims against or liabilities of Assignor arising out of the covenants and duties of Assignor and assumes the obligations and agrees to perform under the Contracts pursuant to the conditions contained in the Contracts.

4. Successors and Assigns.

This Assignment shall be binding upon and inure to the benefit of the Assignor and Assignee and their respective successors and assigns.

EXHIBIT 16–10
Assignment of Contracts

Delmar/Cengage Learning

(continued)

EXHIBIT 16–10

Assignment of Contracts
(continued)

5. Governing Law.

This Assignment shall be governed and construed in accordance with the laws of the State of
_____.

    IN WITNESS WHEREOF, the undersigned parties have hereunto set their hands and seals, as of the day and year first above written.

ASSIGNOR:

Signed, sealed and delivered in the presence of:

_____ (SEAL)

_____
Witness

_____
Notary Public
My Commission Expires:

_____

Notarial Seal

ASSIGNEE:

Signed, sealed and delivered in the presence of:

_____ (SEAL)

_____
Witness

_____
Notary Public
My Commission Expires:

_____

Notarial Seal

Loan Documents

A real estate transaction that involves a loan secured by the real estate requires a number of loan documents. The basic loan documents are a note and a mortgage. On commercial properties, the note and mortgage may be supplemented by an assignment of leases and rents, a security agreement, and a Uniform Commercial Code financing statement. If the loan is a construction loan, a construction loan agreement and an assignment of construction and architect's contracts are required. A full explanation of loan documents and several examples of loan document forms are included in Chapter 11.

MISCELLANEOUS REAL ESTATE CLOSING DOCUMENTS

Corporate Resolution

The sale of real property that involves either a corporate seller or a corporate purchaser requires the corporate entity to provide a corporate resolution. The corporate resolution authorizes the sale or purchase of the real property and empowers certain officers of the company to sign the purchase and sale documents on behalf of the corporation.

Examples of corporate resolutions are shown as Exhibits 16–11, 16–12, and 16–13.

A real estate loan transaction that involves a corporate borrower also requires a corporate resolution. The resolution should authorize the corporation to borrow the money and empower officers to sign the loan documents.

I, Zack A. Collins, Secretary of Acme International, Inc. (the "Company"), do hereby certify as follows:

1. Attached hereto as Exhibit "A" is a true and correct copy of resolutions which were duly adopted at a special meeting of the Board of Directors on July 31, 20___, at which a quorum was present and acting throughout and which have not been amended, modified or rescinded in any respect and are in full force and effect on the date hereof.

2. The below named persons have been fully elected and have been qualified and at all times have been and this day are officers of the Company holding the respective offices below set opposite their names and signatures set opposite their names are their genuine signatures.

| Mary R. Farris | President | _____ |
| Zack A. Collins | Secretary | _____ |

Witness my hand and seal of the Company, this _____ day of _____, 20___.

_____
Zack A. Collins, Secretary
[CORPORATE SEAL]

EXHIBIT "A"

RESOLVED, that Acme International, Inc. (hereafter called the "Company") sell the real property described on Exhibit "B" attached hereto and made a part of hereof to Richard Money pursuant to the real estate contract dated May 10, 20__, a copy of which is attached as Exhibit "C" and made a part hereof;

FURTHER RESOLVED, that the President of the Company, Mary R. Farris, is hereby authorized and directed to execute and deliver on behalf of the Company any and all documentation required in connection with the sale of the property.

EXHIBIT 16–11

Certificate

Delmar/Cengage Learning

I, Zack A. Collins, Secretary of Acme International, Inc. (the "Company"), do hereby certify as follows:

1. Attached hereto as Exhibit "A" is a true and correct copy of resolutions which were duly adopted at a special meeting of the Board of Directors on July 31, 20__, at which a quorum was present and acting throughout and which have not been amended, modified or rescinded in any respect and are in full force and effect on the date hereof.

2. The below named persons have been duly elected and have been qualified and at all times have been and this day are officers of the Company holding the respective offices below set opposite their names and signatures set opposite their names are their genuine signatures.

| Mary R. Farris | President | _____ |
| Zack A. Collins | Secretary | _____ |

Witness my hand and seal of the Company, this _____ day of _____, 20__.

_____
Zack A. Collins, Secretary
[CORPORATE SEAL]

EXHIBIT "A"

RESOLVED, that Acme International, Inc. (hereafter called the "Company") purchase the real property described on Exhibit "B" attached hereto and made a part of from Richard Money pursuant to the real estate contract dated May 10, 20__, a copy of which is attached as Exhibit "C" and made a part hereof;

FURTHER RESOLVED, that the President of the Company, Mary R. Farris, is hereby authorized and directed to execute and deliver on behalf of the Company any and all documentation required in connection with the purchase of the property.

EXHIBIT 16–12

Certificate

Delmar/Cengage Learning

EXHIBIT 16–13

Certificate

I, Zack A. Collins, Secretary of Acme International, Inc. (the "Company"), do hereby certify as follows:

1. Attached hereto as Exhibit "A" is a true and correct copy of resolutions which were duly adopted at a special meeting of the Board of Directors on July 31, 20__, at which a quorum was present and acting throughout and which have not been amended, modified or rescinded in any respect and are in full force and effect on the date hereof.

2. The below named persons have been fully elected and have been qualified and at all times have been and this day are officers of the Company holding the respective offices below set opposite their names and signatures set opposite their names are their genuine signatures.

Mary R. Farris	President	_____
Zack A. Collins	Secretary	_____

Witness my hand and seal of the Company, this _____ day of _____, 20__.

_____
Zack A. Collins, Secretary
[CORPORATE SEAL]

EXHIBIT "A"

RESOLVED, that Acme International, Inc. (hereafter called the "Company") borrow money from Second National Bank as outlined by Commitment Letter dated July 31, 20__, a copy of which is attached as Exhibit "B" and made a part hereof;

FURTHER RESOLVED, that the President of the Company, Mary R. Farris, is hereby authorized and directed to execute and deliver on behalf of the Company any and all documentation required in connection with the loan.

Delmar/Cengage Learning

EXHIBIT 16–14

Agreement Regarding Loan Commitment

FOR VALUABLE CONSIDERATION, the receipt and sufficiency of which are hereby acknowledged, the undersigned hereby agrees that certain Commitment Letter from Second Federal Savings and Loan Association, dated August 25, 20__, amended by letter dated December 13, 20__, a copy of which is attached hereto as Exhibit "A" and made a part hereof, the terms of which have not been satisfied at closing of the loan, shall survive the closing of the loan and shall remain in full force and effect until such time as the loan committed for therein has been paid in full.

IN WITNESS WHEREOF, the undersigned have hereunto set their hands and seals this _____ day of December, 20__.

ACME ASSOCIATES, INC., a Delaware corporation
By: _____
Janice Acme, President

Attest: _____
Aaron Acme, Secretary

[CORPORATE SEAL]

Delmar/Cengage Learning

Agreement Regarding Survival of Loan Commitment

A commitment for a loan, in addition to containing many terms and requirements for the loan, often imposes financial reporting obligations and other conditions on a borrower to be performed after the loan closes. It is not unusual for a lender to have a simple agreement prepared that provides that the conditions and terms for the loan commitment that have not been satisfied at closing will survive closing and remain in full force and effect until the loan has been paid in full. An agreement for this purpose is shown in Exhibit 16–14.

FOR VALUE RECEIVED, the undersigned Seller and Purchaser of the real property described on Exhibit "A" attached hereto and made a part hereof (the "Property"), hereby indemnify and agree to hold each other harmless and their successors, assigns, agents, employees, and attorneys, against any and all claims for brokerage fees or commissions claimed by, through or under either of the undersigned and arising from the purchase and sale of the Property.

IN WITNESS WHEREOF, the undersigned have hereunto set their hands and seals this _____ day of _____, 20__.

SELLER:

BY: _____ (SEAL)

PURCHASER:

BY: _____ (SEAL)

EXHIBIT 16–15

Indemnity Agreement—Purchaser-Seller

Delmar/Cengage Learning

FOR VALUE RECEIVED, the undersigned hereby indemnifies and agrees to hold harmless SECOND FEDERAL SAVINGS AND LOAN ASSOCIATION, its successors, assigns, agents, employees, and attorneys, against any and all claims for brokerage fees or commissions claimed by, through or under the undersigned and arising from the issuance of Second Federal Savings and Loan Association's Commitment Letter, dated August 25, 20__, as amended by letter dated December 13, 20__, to the undersigned or in connection with the loan committed for therein.

IN WITNESS WHEREOF, the undersigned has by its duly authorized officers, hereunto set his hand and seal this day of December, 20__.

ACME ASSOCIATES, INC., a Delaware corporation

By: _____
Janice Acme, President

Attest: _____
Aaron Acme, Secretary

[CORPORATE SEAL]

EXHIBIT 16–16

Indemnity Agreement—Borrower-Lender

Delmar/Cengage Learning

Indemnity of Fees

It is not unusual on a real estate sale or loan transaction that brokers and agents representing the seller, purchaser, and borrower are involved. These agents also are entitled to fees usually paid by the person who has hired them—the seller, purchaser, or borrower. The parties to a real estate transaction who have not retained these agents may require indemnities from the other parties concerning the payment of fees to these agents. These indemnities usually take the form of a seller and purchaser each indemnifying the other against brokers' commissions that involve brokers retained by them. Indemnities involved in a loan transaction usually are from the borrower, who indemnifies the lender against any brokers' fees or loan fees for which the borrower is responsible. Examples of a purchaser-seller indemnity and a borrower-lender indemnity appear in Exhibits 16–15 and 16–16, respectively.

Attorney's Opinion

A lender may require on a commercial loan that the borrower's attorney render an opinion involving certain aspects of the loan transaction. A form of opinion is shown as Exhibit 16–17. This borrower's attorney's opinion usually involves an opinion by

EXHIBIT 16–17

Attorney's Opinion

To Be Transcribed on Letterhead
for Counsel of Borrower

Date

American Eagle Mortgage Company
Independent Boulevard
U.S.A.

Gentlemen:

We have acted as counsel for Acme, Inc., a Delaware corporation, the "Borrower," in connection with the Loan hereinafter described. The Loan (the "Loan") is secured by a first deed to secure debt in the stated principal sum of One Million and No/100 Dollars ($1,000,000.00). The Loan has been made by American Eagle Mortgage Company ("Lender") as a loan pursuant to Lender's commitment dated October 18, 20___, as modified by letter dated November 18, 20___. The Loan is evidenced and secured by the following instruments (herein generally called the "Loan Documents"), each dated as of _____
_____, 20___, and each being executed by Borrower.

A. The Loan is evidenced by the Promissory Note (the "Note") made by Borrower in the stated principal amount of _____ / 100 Dollars ($ _____) bearing interest at the rate set out therein, due in regular installments with a final payment due on _____ _____, payable to the order of Lender.

B. The Loan is secured by a Deed to Secure Debt and Security Agreement (with Assignment of Rents) (the "Security Deed") made by Borrower to Lender, as grantee, encumbering certain improved real property, furniture, furnishings, and equipment (all herein generally called the "Premises") owned by Borrower in _____ County, _____.

C. The Loan is also secured by an Assignment of Lessor's Interest in Rents and Leases (the "Assignment") made by Borrower, as assignor, to Lender as assignee, assigning all of the rents, issues, profits, and avails of the Premises, and all of the leases now or hereafter in effect with respect to the Premises.

D. The Loan is also secured by a certain Security Agreement and Financing Statement ("Security Agreement") as evidenced by a certain Financing Statement ("Financing Statement") made by Borrower, as debtor, to Lender, as secured party, creating and perfecting a security interest in personal property, fixtures, and equipment comprising part of the Premises.

In connection with the foregoing, we have examined and reviewed the documents referred to in paragraphs A through D above and such other matters as we determined appropriate and necessary for the formulation and rendition of the opinions hereinafter expressed with the knowledge that Lender is making the loan in reliance on said opinion.

Based on the foregoing, we are of the opinion that:

1. Acme, Inc. is a validly formed corporation under the laws of the State of Delaware and is duly authorized to transact business in the State of _____. Acme, Inc. is in good standing under the laws of Delaware and _____.

2. Each of the Loan Documents constitutes the legal, valid and binding obligation and agreement of the Borrower, properly and validly executed and enforceable in accordance with its terms (except as such enforcement may be affected by bankruptcy, insolvency, or other like laws affecting generally the rights of creditors).

(continued)

3. The Loan is governed by the laws of the State of _____, and under such laws the Loan, including the interest rate reserved or charged in the Note, and all fees and charges paid or to be paid by or on behalf of Borrower or received or to be received by Lender are wholly lawful and not usurious or violative of any law or regulation of the State of _____ governing the payment or receipt of interest.

4. The Security Deed, Assignment, and Financing Statement when duly recorded and/ or filed in such places as are required under the laws of the State of _____ will constitute good and valid liens against the Premises and property covered by said Security Deed, Assignment, Security Agreement and Financing Statement.

5. No further approval, consent, order, or authorization of or designation, resignation, declaration, or filing with any governmental authority is required in connection with the valid execution and delivery of the Note, Security Deed, Assignment, Security Agreement, and Financing Statements, the carrying out of the liens created by the Security Deed, Assignment, Security Agreement and Financing Statements, except the future filing by the secured party thereunder of Continuation Statements with respect to the Financing Statements at the times and in the manner specified in the Uniform Commercial Code of the State of _____.

6. We have examined all of the provisions of the Loan Documents and Lender's commitment with Borrower, and we have no knowledge of any event of default which exists under any of them, and we have no knowledge of any facts that exist which but for notice and/or passage of time would constitute an event of default under any of them, and we have been advised by Borrower that Borrower intends to borrow the full amount of the loan.

7. The execution and delivery of the Loan Documents, the fulfillment of the respective terms and conditions thereof, and the communication of the respective transactions therein contemplated do not conflict with, or constitute a breach of or default under any agreement, indenture or other instrument to which Borrower is a party and is duly authorized by the requisite partnership or corporate authority governing Borrower.

8. The real property and improvements thereon comprised within the Premises are properly zoned for the uses and purposes to which they are presently devoted; and the use and occupancy of the Premises for the business presently conducted thereon are wholly lawful and not violative of any zoning, use building, or environmental protection laws, ordinances, and regulations applicable thereto.

9. All licenses, permits, and authorizations necessary for the use and occupancy of the Premises by Borrower for its business as presently conducted thereon are in full force and effect.

10. All water, gas, electric, storm and sanitary sewer and other utilities necessary for the Premises and the improvements constructed thereon are available to the Premises, and the utility companies or municipalities providing such service have agreed to make available such services to the Premises and the improvements constructed thereon; and there are no pending, or to the best of our knowledge, threatened proceedings before any governmental agency or moratoria which would interfere with or enjoin the furnishing of any utility service to the Premises and such improvements.

11. To the best of our knowledge, there are not threatened or pending actions against the Borrower at law, equity, or bankruptcy.

Very truly yours,

EXHIBIT 16–17

Attorney's Opinion
(*continued*)

borrower's counsel that (a) if the borrower is a corporation, it is created and existing in the laws of a certain state; (b) the borrower has the authority to enter into the loan transaction; (c) the loan transaction does not violate or conflict with any provision of the borrower's certificate of incorporation, bylaws, or any other documents to which the borrower is a party or to which it is subject; (d) all loan documents have been validly authorized, executed, and delivered by the borrower and, assuming the due authorization, execution, and delivery thereof by all other parties, constitute binding, enforceable obligations of the borrower; (e) all loan documents are valid and enforceable according to their terms; (f) the interest charged on the loan is not usurious; (g) the property is properly zoned for the use intended; and (h) the attorney knows of no title problems or regulatory matters that would impair the lender's security.

Compliance Agreements

A large number of documents are executed in connection with any residential or commercial sale and loan closing. Even the most careful paralegal and attorney can make mistakes in the preparation of the documents. Most lenders require the borrower to sign a compliance agreement. This agreement essentially states that if there are typographical errors or other mistakes made in preparing the documents, the borrower agrees to execute corrective documents. An example of a compliance agreement is shown as Exhibit 16–18.

EXHIBIT 16–18

Compliance Agreement

STATE OF _____
COUNTY OF _____

BORROWER(S):
LENDER:
PROPERTY:

    The undersigned borrower(s), in consideration of the lender disbursing funds today for the closing of property located at _____ agrees, if requested by lender or someone acting on behalf of said lender, to fully cooperate and adjust for clerical errors, any and all loan closing documentation deemed necessary or desirable in the reasonable discretion of lender to enable lender to sell, convey, seek guaranty or market said loan to any entity, including but not limited to an investor, Federal National Mortgage Association (FNMA), Government National Mortgage Association (GNMA), Federal Home Loan Mortgage Corporation, Department of Housing and Urban Development, Veterans Administration, or any Municipal Bonding Authority.

    The undersigned borrower(s) do hereby so agree and covenant in order to ensure that the loan documentation executed this date will conform and be acceptable in the marketplace in the instance of transfer, sale or conveyance by lender of its interest in and to said loan documentation.

    Dated effective this _____ day of _____, 20__.

_____
Borrower

_____
Borrower

_____
Notary Public
My commission expires:

EXHIBIT 16–19

Information for Real Estate 1099-B Report Filing as required by the Internal Revenue Service

---

Section 6045 of the Internal Revenue Code, as amended by the Tax Reform Act of 1986, requires the reporting of certain information on every real estate transaction. From the information you provide below, a Form 1099–B will be produced, and a copy of it will be furnished to the I.R.S. and to you no later than January 31 of the next year. If you fail to furnish adequate information (in particular, a taxpayer ID number), then you will be subject to all I.R.S. Regulations, including the possible withholding of twenty percent (20%) of the current sales price.

FILE NUMBER: _____   FILE NAME: _____

SELLER'S NAME:

_____

_____

SELLER'S MAILING ADDRESS:

_____

_____

SOCIAL SECURITY NO.: _____

OR

FEDERAL TAX ID NO.: _____

CLOSING DATE: _____

PROPERTY ADDRESS: _____

_____

SALES PRICE: _____

WAS THIS YOUR PRINCIPAL RESIDENCE?:   Yes _____   No _____

I (We) certify that the above information is correct and understand that it will appear on a Form 1099 that will be sent to me and to the Internal Revenue Service.

DATE _____   _____
                                                                                     SELLER'S SIGNATURE

     _____
                                                                                     SELLER'S SIGNATURE

1099-B Report Form

The Internal Revenue Service requires that settlement agents report sales of real estate transactions to the Internal Revenue Service. The settlement agent, in most situations, is the real estate attorney. The failure to provide the informational form subjects the settlement agent to penalties. A 1099-B reporting form is shown as Exhibit 16–19.

Settlement or Closing Statement   — *Escrow agent*

Know the differences Corporate Buyer and Individual Buyer.

A settlement or closing statement sets forth the financial terms of a sale or loan closing. The statement indicates all the money involved and to whom the funds have been disbursed. The settlement and closing statement forms vary, depending on the type of transaction involved. Law firms and even individual lawyers have their own favorite forms they like to use. The Real Estate Settlement Procedures Act of 1974 requires that on all federally related loans, which means residential consumer loans secured by one- to four-family residences, the HUD–1 form be used. Instructions on how to prepare the HUD–1 form follow. These instructions are keyed to the section and line numbers of the HUD–1 form shown as Exhibit 16–20.

Section A—Heading   The heading of the closing statement that appears at the top of page 1 should be completed as follows.

EXHIBIT 16–20

Settlement Statement

OMB Approval No. 2502-0265

A. **Settlement Statement (HUD-1)**

U.S. DEPARTMENT OF HOUSING AND URBAN DEVELOPMENT

B. Type of Loan

| 1. ☐ FHA   2. ☐ RHS   3. ☐ Conv. Unins. | 6. File Number: | 7. Loan Number: | 8. Mortgage Insurance Case Number: |
| 4. ☐ VA   5. ☐ Conv. Ins. | | | |

C. Note: This form is furnished to give you a statement of actual settlement costs. Amounts paid to and by the settlement agent are shown. Items marked "(p.o.c.)" were paid outside the closing; they are shown here for informational purposes and are not included in the totals.

D. Name & Address of Borrower:	E. Name & Address of Seller:	F. Name & Address of Lender:

G. Property Location:	H. Settlement Agent:	I. Settlement Date:
	Place of Settlement:	

J. Summary of Borrower's Transaction		**K. Summary of Seller's Transaction**	
100. Gross Amount Due from Borrower		**400. Gross Amount Due to Seller**	
101. Contract sales price		401. Contract sales price	
102. Personal property		402. Personal property	
103. Settlement charges to borrower (line 1400)		403.	
104.		404.	
105.		405.	
Adjustment for items paid by seller in advance		**Adjustments for items paid by seller in advance**	
106. City/town taxes to		406. City/town taxes to	
107. County taxes to		407. County taxes to	
108. Assessments to		408. Assessments to	
109.		409.	
110.		410.	
111.		411.	
112.		412.	
120. Gross Amount Due from Borrower		**420. Gross Amount Due to Seller**	
200. Amounts Paid by or in Behalf of Borrower		**500. Reductions In Amount Due to Seller**	
201. Deposit or earnest money		501. Excess deposit (see instructions)	
202. Principal amount of new loan(s)		502. Settlement charges to seller (line 1400)	
203. Existing loan(s) taken subject to		503. Existing loan(s) taken subject to	
204.		504. Payoff of first mortgage loan	
205.		505. Payoff of second mortgage loan	
206.		506.	
207.		507.	
208.		508.	
209.		509.	
Adjustments for items unpaid by seller		**Adjustments for items unpaid by seller**	
210. City/town taxes to		510. City/town taxes to	
211. County taxes to		511. County taxes to	
212. Assessments to		512. Assessments to	
213.		513.	
214.		514.	
215.		515.	
216.		516.	
217.		517.	
218.		518.	
219.		519.	
220. Total Paid by/for Seller		**520. Total Reduction Amount Due Seller**	
300. Cash at Settlement from/to Borrower		**600. Cash at Settlement to/from Seller**	
301. Gross amount due from borrower (line 120)		601. Gross amount due to seller (line 420)	
302. Less amounts paid by/for borrower (line 220)	( )	602. Less reductions in amount due seller (line 520)	( )
303. Cash ☐ From ☐ To Borrower		**603. Cash** ☐ To ☐ From Seller	

The Public Reporting Burden for this collection of information is estimated at 35 minutes per response for collecting, reviewing, and reporting the data. This agency may not collect this information, and you are not required to complete this form, unless it displays a currently valid OMB control number. No confidentiality is assured; this disclosure is mandatory. This is designed to provide the parties to a RESPA covered transaction with information during the settlement process.

Delmar/Cengage Learning

(continued)

EXHIBIT 16–20
Settlement Statement
(*continued*)

L. Settlement Charges

700. Total Real Estate Broker Fees		Paid From Borrower's Funds at Settlement	Paid From Seller's Funds at Settlement
Division of commission (line 700) as follows:			
701. $ to			
702. $ to			
703. Commission paid at settlement			
704.			

800. Items Payable in Connection with Loan			
801. Our origination charge $	(from GFE #1)		
802. Your credit or charge (points) for the specific interest rate chosen $	(from GFE #2)		
803. Your adjusted origination charges	(from GFE A)		
804. Appraisal fee to	(from GFE #3)		
805. Credit report to	(from GFE #3)		
806. Tax service to	(from GFE #3)		
807. Flood certification	(from GFE #3)		
808.			

900. Items Required by Lender to Be Paid in Advance			
901. Daily interest charges from to @ $ /day	(from GFE #10)		
902. Mortgage insurance premium for months to	(from GFE #3)		
903. Homeowner's insurance for years to	(from GFE #11)		
904.			

1000. Reserves Deposited with Lender				
1001. Initial deposit for your escrow account		(from GFE #9)		
1002. Homeowner's insurance months @ $ per month $				
1003. Mortgage insurance months @ $ per month $				
1004. Property taxes months @ $ per month $				
1005. months @ $ per month $				
1006. months @ $ per month $				
1007. Aggregate Adjustment –$				

1100. Title Charges			
1101. Title services and lender's title insurance	(from GFE #4)		
1102. Settlement or closing fee $			
1103. Owner's title insurance	(from GFE #5)		
1104. Lender's title insurance $			
1105. Lender's title policy limit $			
1106. Owner's title policy limit $			
1107. Agent's portion of the total title insurance premium $			
1108. Underwriter's portion of the total title insurance premium $			

1200. Government Recording and Transfer Charges			
1201. Government recording charges	(from GFE #7)		
1202. Deed $ Mortgage $ Releases $			
1203. Transfer taxes	(from GFE #8)		
1204. City/County tax/stamps Deed $ Mortgage $			
1205. State tax/stamps Deed $ Mortgage $			
1206.			

1300. Additional Settlement Charges			
1301. Required services that you can shop for	(from GFE #6)		
1302. $			
1303. $			
1304.			
1305.			

1400. Total Settlement Charges (enter on lines 103, Section J and 502, Section K)			

(continued)

EXHIBIT 16–20

Settlement Statement

(*continued*)

Comparison of Good Faith Estimate (GFE) and HUD-1 Charges		Good Faith Estimate	HUD-1
Charges That Cannot Increase	**HUD-1 Line Number**		
Our origination charge	# 801		
Your credit or charge (points) for the specific interest rate chosen	# 802		
Your adjusted origination charges	# 803		
Transfer taxes	#1203		

Charges That in Total Cannot Increase More Than 10%		Good Faith Estimate	HUD-1
Government recording charges	# 1201		
	#		
	#		
	#		
	#		
	#		
	#		
	#		
Total			
Increase between GFE and HUD-1 Charges		$ or %	

Charges That Can Change		Good Faith Estimate	HUD-1
Initial deposit for your escrow account	#1001		
Daily interest charges	# 901 $ /day		
Homeowner's insurance	# 903		
	#		
	#		
	#		

Loan Terms

Your initial loan amount is	$
Your loan term is	▓▓▓ years
Your initial interest rate is	▓▓▓ %
Your initial monthly amount owed for principal, interest, and and any mortgage insurance is	$ ▓▓▓▓▓ includes ☐ Principal ☐ Interest ☐ Mortgage Insurance
Can your interest rate rise?	☐ No. ☐ Yes, it can rise to a maximum of ▓▓%. The first change will be on ▓▓▓▓▓ and can change again every ▓▓▓▓▓ after ▓▓▓▓▓ . Every change date, your interest rate can increase or decrease by ▓▓%. Over the life of the loan, your interest rate is guaranteed to never be **lower** than ▓▓ % or **higher** than ▓▓ %.
Even if you make payments on time, can your loan balance rise?	☐ No. ☐ Yes, it can rise to a maximum of $ ▓▓▓▓▓ .
Even if you make payments on time, can your monthly amount owed for principal, interest, and mortgage insurance rise?	☐ No. ☐ Yes, the first increase can be on ▓▓▓▓▓ and the monthly amount owed can rise to $ ▓▓▓▓▓ . The maximum it can ever rise to is $ ▓▓▓▓▓ .
Does your loan have a prepayment penalty?	☐ No. ☐ Yes, your maximum prepayment penalty is $ ▓▓▓▓▓ .
Does your loan have a balloon payment?	☐ No. ☐ Yes, you have a balloon payment of $ ▓▓▓▓▓ due in ▓▓ years on ▓▓▓▓▓ .
Total monthly amount owed including escrow account payments	☐ You do not have a monthly escrow payment for items, such as property taxes and homeowner's insurance. You must pay these items directly yourself. ☐ You have an additional monthly escrow payment of $ ▓▓▓▓▓ that results in a total initial monthly amount owed of $ ▓▓▓▓▓ . This includes principal, interest, any mortgage insurance and any items checked below: ☐ Property taxes ☐ Homeowner's insurance ☐ Flood insurance ☐ ▓▓▓▓▓ ☐ ▓▓▓▓▓ ☐ ▓▓▓▓▓

Note: If you have any questions about the Settlement Charges and Loan Terms listed on this form, please contact your lender.

Previous editions are obsolete	Page 3 of 3	HUD-1

Section A U.S. Department of Housing and Urban Development Settlement Statement.

Section B Type of loan, file number, loan number, and mortgage insurance case number. The choices for type of loan are a Federal Housing Administration (FHA) insured loan, a Veterans Administration (VA) insured loan, a Rural Housing Service (RHS) insured loan, a conventional uninsured loan, and a conventional insured loan. In a conventional insured loan, there is no government participation, but the payments of the loan are insured by a private mortgage insurance company. In a conventional uninsured loan, there is no government participation, and the payments of the loan are not insured. The file number is the law firm's internal file number for the loan transaction. The loan number is the lender's loan number for the transaction. Most lenders give a loan number to a particular loan when they issue a commitment. The mortgage insurance case number is the file number for mortgage insurance, if mortgage insurance exists. Mortgage insurance referred to in paragraph B is the private mortgage insurance that insures the payments of the mortgage.

Section C Explanatory note printed on all HUD–1 statements. This note explains that the form is being furnished to give the borrower a statement of actual settlement costs. The amounts paid to and by the settlement agent are shown. The items marked p.o.c. (paid outside of closing) were paid outside the closing. They are shown here for informational purposes and are not included in the total.

Section D Name and address of the borrower, who also is the purchaser of the property in a sale transaction. If the purchaser is buying the home to live in, the home address may be used as the address of the borrower.

Section E Name and address of the seller. The forwarding address for the seller should be used.

Section F Name and address of the lender.

Section G Description of the property. A street address is acceptable.

Section H Identification of the settlement agent and the place of settlement. This is the law firm and the law firm's address.

Section I Settlement date, which is the date of the closing.

Section J Summary of the borrower's (purchaser's) transaction. It is broken into three separate columns, known as the 100 column, 200 column, and 300 column. The *100 column* is a summary of the gross amount of money due from the borrower (purchaser) in connection with the transaction. The *200 column* is a summary of all moneys previously paid either by the borrower (purchaser) or by other parties in connection with the transaction or credits that the borrower (purchaser) is entitled to as part of the transaction. *Column 300* is a summary of columns 100 and 200 and determines whether the borrower (purchaser) gets cash from the closing or brings cash to the closing.

Instructions for the various line numbers within each column follow.

Line 101 Contract sales price. This amount is determined from the contract.

Line 102 Any money in addition to the contract sales price that is to be paid by the borrower for any personal property to be used in connection with the real property. If personal property is not being purchased or the personal property is included within the contract sales price, line 102 remains blank.

Line 103 Total of all settlement charges to the borrower. The amount that appears on line 103 is the amount that appears on line 1400. Instructions for arriving at the amount for line 1400 follow.

Lines 104 and 105   Used for additional items owed by the borrower that are not on any good faith estimate provided by the lender and items paid by the seller prior to settlement and being reimbursed to the seller from the borrower at settlement.

Lines 106, 107, and 108   Used to calculate the purchaser's portion of the real estate taxes, assessments, and sanitary taxes for the current year, if the taxes have been paid in advance by the seller. These amounts are calculated by obtaining copies of the tax report and calling the sanitary tax office. The real property taxes are prorated by a formula that allocates to the seller the seller's portion of the tax year and to the purchaser the purchaser's portion of the tax year. The amount of the real estate taxes or sanitary taxes is divided by 365, the number of days in a year, to obtain a daily tax rate. The daily tax rate is then multiplied by the number of days in the tax year the purchaser or seller owned the property. These amounts are then entered on lines 106, 107, and 108. Lines 106, 107, and 108 are used only if the seller has already paid the taxes at the time of closing or if the taxes are due and payable at the time of closing and will be paid from the seller's funds at that time. For example, if the sale closes on October 15 of a given year and county taxes in the amount of $1,400 have already been paid by the seller, the purchaser's portion of the county tax bill is $291.84. This amount is entered on line 107 and is arrived at by the following computation: $1,400 ÷ 365 = $3.84 per day; October 16–December 31 = 76 days; $3.84 × 76 = $291.84.

Note that tax prorations are based on the tax year and not the calendar year. For many taxing authorities, the tax year is the calendar year, with the first day of the tax year being January 1 and the last day of the tax year being December 31. In the event the tax year is different, it will be necessary to know what the tax year is to arrive at the proration. For example, assume a tax year of March 1 to February 28. The closing takes place on October 15, and the seller has paid the taxes for the year. The purchaser's share of the taxes would be the number of days from October 16 (sale day usually being a seller's day) through February 28, or 135 days. The 135 days would then be multiplied by the daily tax rate to arrive at the purchaser's share of the tax bill.

Lines 109, 110, 111, and 112   Used to itemize any adjustments other than taxes or assessments that were paid to the seller in advance.

Line 120   Total of lines 101 through 112.

Line 201   Amount of any earnest money or deposit that has already been paid by the purchaser. The real estate contract should indicate this amount.

Line 202   Principal amount of any new loans that the purchaser is obtaining to buy the property. The loan commitment should indicate this amount.

Line 203   Used only if the purchaser is buying the property and assuming an existing loan. An estoppel letter from the existing lender gives the amount needed for line 203.

Lines 204, 205, 206, 207, 208, and 209   Used to itemize any amount unique to the transaction paid by or in behalf of the borrower.

Lines 210, 211, and 212   Tax prorations. These are used if the taxes have not been paid in advance by the seller and are due and payable. The proration is the reverse of the proration used to obtain the numbers for lines 106, 107, and 108. For example, the closing takes place on April 15, and the county taxes are $1,400. The purchaser is entitled to a credit for the seller's portion of the year, January 1 through April 15, or 105 days. The purchaser's credit is $403.20. The computation to arrive at $403.20 is as follows: $1,400 ÷ 365 = $3.84; $3.84 × 105 = $403.20.

Lines 213, 214, 215, 216, 217, 218, and 219   Used to itemize items other than taxes and assessments unpaid by the seller.

Line 220   Total of lines 201 through 219.

Line 301   Repeat of line 120.

Line 302   Repeat of line 220. Line 301 usually is greater than line 302, and the difference is entered on line 303 as cash required from the borrower at closing. If, for some reason, line 302 is greater than line 303, this indicates that the borrower will receive cash at closing.

Section K   Summary of the seller's transaction. It consists of three columns, column 400, column 500, and column 600. *Column 400* is the gross amount of money due to the seller pursuant to the real estate contract. *Column 500* lists reductions in the amount of money due to the seller at closing. *Column 600* is a summary of columns 400 and 500 and indicates the amount of money the seller will take from the closing or, in some rare cases, the amount of money the seller will need to close. Instructions for the individual lines are as follows.

Line 401   Contract sales price. This amount is taken from the sales contract.

Line 402   Amount of money paid for any personal property in addition to the contract sales price.

Lines 403, 404, and 405   Repeat of any amounts that appear on lines 104 and 105.

Lines 406, 407, 408, 409, 410, 411, and 412   Repeat of any amounts that appear on lines 106, 107, 108, 109, 110, 111, and 112.

Line 420   Total of lines 401 through 412.

Line 501   Amount of earnest money paid by the purchaser. Same amount as line 201.

Line 502   All settlement charges due from the seller, which is the total that appears on line 1400. Instructions for obtaining this amount follow.

Line 503   Amount of any loans that are being assumed by the purchaser at the time of closing. This line would be used only if the property is being sold subject to an existing loan that is not being paid at the time of closing. This amount is the same as that shown on line 203 and is obtained in the same method.

Line 504   Payoff of any existing first mortgage loan on the property. This amount is obtained from a satisfaction letter from the mortgage lender.

Line 505   Payoff of any second mortgage loan on the property. This amount is obtained by a satisfaction letter from the mortgage lender.

Lines 506 through 509   Payment of any other liens or matters that must be paid out of the seller's proceeds at the time of closing.

Lines 510, 511, 512, 513, 514, 515, 516, 517, 518, and 519   Repeat of the tax proration amounts that appear on lines 210, 211, 212, 213, 214, 215, 216, 217, 218, and 219.

Line 520   Total of lines 501 through 519.

Line 601   Amount taken from line 420.

Line 602   Amount taken from line 520. Line 601 normally is greater than line 602, and the difference is shown on line 603 as cash to seller. If line 602 is greater than line 601, then line 603 indicates the amount of money needed by the seller to close.

Section L Breakdown of all settlement charges or closing costs in connection with the sale and loan transaction. The section is divided into two columns, a borrower's column and a seller's column. The responsibility to pay for settlement costs usually is negotiated between the buyer and the seller in the real estate contract. It is not uncommon for a seller to agree to pay the real estate commissions and the loan and closing costs of a purchaser.

700 Series Amount of the real estate commission. This amount is taken from the real estate contract.

Lines 701 and 702 Division of the real estate commission and the identity of the brokers receiving the money. A listing broker often obtains from the seller the permission to place the property on the market, and a selling broker, a broker who found the purchaser, sells the property. These brokers may split the commission. The real estate contract should provide this information.

Line 703 Total amount of commissions paid at closing. This is usually a seller-paid item.

800 Series Items payable in connection with the loan. These items can be obtained from the loan commitment letter or instruction letter from the lender. They consist of loan origination fees, loan discount, appraisal fees, credit reports, and any other fees or other charges that might be assessed by the lender. These items usually are paid by the borrower, but the contract should be checked to make sure that the seller has not agreed to pay them.

Line 801 This line includes all charges received by a loan originator. The amount on line 801 also includes all amounts received for any service, including administrative and processing services, performed by or on behalf of the lender or any mortgage broker. All origination fees or points to obtain a loan must be shown on line 801. The designation should follow "Our Origination Charge" either by adding the language (Includes Origination Point (% or $____) on line 801 or by placing an asterisk (*) and adding the language at the bottom of the page.

Example: 801 Our Origination Charge (Includes Origination Point 1% or $1000.00 $2500.00).

Line 802 If the borrower is to obtain a "no cost" loan, the amount of the charges shown in line 801 which are to be provided to the borrower at "no cost" must be totaled and shown as a credit on line 802.

Line 803 Subtract any credit shown on line 802 from line 801, and this balance is shown on line 803.

Lines 804 through 808 Fees paid to a third party such as appraiser, tax service, credit reports, and so forth are listed on lines 804–808.

900 Series List of items required by the lender to be paid in advance at the time of closing.

Line 901 Interest adjustment. The interest on most mortgage loans is paid in arrears. For example, a mortgage payment due on May 1 would pay interest for the month of April. Most lenders require that the payments start on the first day of the second month after the closing. For example, if a closing is on April 15, the first mortgage payment would not be until June 1. The June 1 payment would pay interest from May 1 through May 31 but would not pay the April interest. Therefore, it is necessary at the time of closing to collect interest for the month of closing, April 15 through April 30. A lender may give the per diem interest charge, and it is only necessary to multiply this per diem interest charge by the number of days left in the month, in this case 16. If the lender does not give a per diem interest charge, it can be calculated by multiplying the loan amount by the interest rate and dividing by 365 or 360. Some lenders calculate interest based on a 360-day year. The amount from said computation equals the per diem interest, which then can be multiplied by the number of days to be collected. For example, a loan in the amount of $80,000 at 10 percent interest closes on April 15. The amount of money needed to be collected from the borrower at closing for interest for the remaining part of April, April 15 through April 30 (16 days), is $355.52 and is calculated as follows: $80,000 × .10 = $8,000; $8,000 ÷ 360 = $22.22; $22.22 × 16 = $355.52.

Line 902   Used only when a private mortgage insurance company is insuring the payments on the loan. The amount to be entered on this line is given in the lender's instruction letter.

Line 903   Name of the insurance company issuing the fire insurance and the amount of the annual premium. If the borrower has already paid for the first year's insurance premium, then the notation p.o.c. is inserted. If the borrower has not paid for the insurance premium, then the amount of the insurance premium must be shown on this line.

Lines 904   Other items required to be paid by the lender in advance, such as flood insurance premiums that are due. This would be used only if the property is in a flood hazard zone.

1000 Series   Summary of all the insurance and tax reserves required by the lender at closing.

Line 1001   Total of all escrow items contained in the 1000 series of the HUD-1.

Line 1002   Amount of money necessary to establish an insurance escrow. This amount is arrived at by taking the annual premium for fire insurance and dividing it by 12 to get a monthly amount. Then the number of monthly amounts needed before the next due date on the insurance premium is calculated. The number of payments to be received monthly is subtracted from the number needed and that yields the amount to be collected and entered on line 1001. For example, a closing takes place on April 15, and insurance is paid for one year. The first payment under the loan is not due until June 1; therefore, one-twelfth of the hazard insurance premium will not be received by the lender until June 1. The lender then will receive one-twelfth on the first day of each month thereafter. The lender will receive eleven payments before the next year's April 15 premium due date. It would be necessary to collect at least one payment to have enough money on April 15 of the next year to pay the insurance premium. Lenders usually collect an escrow for insurance premiums for two months.

Line 1003   Computes the private mortgage insurance and is determined by multiplying the loan amount by the factor from a private mortgage insurance factor table. This number is given in the lender's instruction letter.

Line 1004   Escrows necessary to pay real estate taxes and assessments. The amounts to be entered on these lines are determined by first looking at the tax report to determine the annual taxes. It also is necessary to know when the tax bill becomes due. Then the tax bill is divided by 12 to arrive at a monthly tax amount. Then the number of payments of these monthly tax amounts that will be received before the due date of the tax bill is determined, and that amount is subtracted from the number of payments needed to pay the tax bill. For example, a loan closes on April 15, and the taxes are due October 1. The lender's first payment is due under the loan on June 1 and on the first day of each month thereafter. The lender receives in the due course of servicing the loan one-twelfth of the taxes of June 1, July 1, August 1, and September 1 before the October 1 due date. The lender will need eight monthly payments collected at closing to have an adequate amount of money in escrow to pay the taxes.

Lines 1005 and 1006 Used for any reserves other than insurance and taxes required to be escrowed by lender.

1100 Series

Line 1101 All title service fees are to be shown on line 1101. These fees include fees for title examination and evaluation, preparation of title commitment and title policies, clearance of title matters, document preparation, notary, and so forth.

Line 1102 Any closing or fee for settlement escrow is shown on line 1102. If a law firm handles the settlement, its legal fees are shown on line 1102.

Line 1103 The title premium for the owner's title insurance policy is shown on line 1103.

Line 1104 The title premium for the lender's title insurance policy is shown on line 1104.

Line 1105 The amount of the lender's title insurance policy is shown on line 1105.

Line 1106 The amount of the owner's title insurance policy is shown on line 1106.

Line 1107 If a title insurance agent receives a portion of the title insurance premium, that amount is to be shown on line 1107.

Line 1108 The amount of the title insurance premium that belongs to the title insurance company that issues the policy is shown on line 1108.

1200 Series Summary of all government recording and transfer charges. These charges vary from state to state, and it is necessary to know the local charges in the place where the documents are to be recorded.

1300 Series

Line 1301 The total of all charges for third-party settlement services that the lender required but for which the borrower was permitted to select the service provider. The charges on line 1301 are shown on the borrower's column.

Line 1400 Summary of all total settlement charges and the amounts from line 1400 are entered on behalf of the purchaser on line 103, Section J, and on behalf of the seller on line 502, Section K.

Page 3 of the HUD-1 Form that must be used after January 1, 2010 contains information comparing the good faith estimates charges with the HUD-1, setting forth charges that in total cannot increase more than 10% and charges that can increase more than 10%. Page 3 also provides for a summary of the terms of the loan for which the HUD-1 has been issued. The lender is required to provide to the preparer of the HUD-1 the good faith estimate given to the borrower and other information necessary to complete page 3.

RESIDENTIAL CLOSING EXAMPLE

This closing example involves a sale of a residence by a corporate seller, Markam Industries, Inc., to an individual, Helen Davis. Exhibits 16–21 through 16–34 appear at the end of this chapter. Helen Davis is obtaining a loan from the American Eagle Mortgage Company for a portion of the purchase price. A review of the sales contract between Markam Industries, Inc. and Helen Davis (see Exhibit 16–21) and the loan commitment

✓ CHECKLIST

Residential Closing Example

1. Title examination
2. Title commitment and policy
3. Survey
4. Corporate resolution
5. Foreign person affidavit
6. 1099-B form
7. Owner's affidavit
8. Transfer tax certificate
9. Warranty deed
10. Bill of sale
11. Termite letter
12. Truth-in-Lending disclosure statement
13. Borrower's affidavit
14. Promissory note
15. Deed to secure debt
16. Hazard and fire insurance
17. Settlement statement

(see Exhibit 16–22) from American Eagle Mortgage Company to Helen Davis produces the checklist above.

After preparing the checklist, a paralegal would approach the checklist in the following manner.

Title Examination

The title examination should be ordered the same day the file is opened. The title examiner needs a legal description of the property and the current owner's name. In addition, the title examiner should be informed of the title company that will issue the insurance so that the examination can be certified in favor of the title company. The title examiner should be given a date for the completion of the examination. This date should be at least three to five business days before the closing date. The examiner should be instructed to provide copies of all title exceptions and a copy of any plat involving the property. The seller's name and a description of the property can be taken from the real estate sales contract. The seller in this case is Markam Industries, Inc., and the property is Lot 12, Bassett Hall Subdivision, pursuant to the plat recorded at Plat Book 68, Page 79, lying and being in Land Lot 359 of the 18th District of Fulton County, Georgia. A copy of the title examination report is shown as Exhibit 16–23.

Title Commitment

The title insurance company issuing the title commitment needs to be informed that a title examination is being prepared and will be delivered to it. The title company also needs to know the types of policies to be issued, the owners or lenders, the names of the insureds, and the amount of the insurance. The title company should be provided with the date for the issuance of the title commitment. In this case, assuming that both an owner's and a lender's policy will be issued, the title company should be instructed to issue a commitment for an $80,000 loan policy to American Eagle Mortgage Company and an owner's commitment for $100,000 to Helen Davis.

Survey

The survey should be ordered as soon as possible. The surveyor needs the legal description and the names of the parties to whom the survey should be certified. The survey typically is certified in the names of the purchaser and the lending institution. In this example, these would be Helen Davis and American Eagle Mortgage Company. The surveyor also should indicate on the survey if the property is in a flood zone. The surveyor should provide the title company with a surveyor's inspection report form so that the title company can delete its standard survey exception. The date for completion of the survey, which should be three to five business days before the closing, should be given to the surveyor. The surveyor also should be instructed to provide the paralegal with a minimum of six prints of the survey.

Corporate Resolution

Markam Industries, Inc. is a corporation, and a corporate seller of property requires a resolution of the board of directors authorizing the sale of the property and the signatures on the various documents. A form of corporate resolution is shown as Exhibit 16–24.

Foreign Person Affidavit

The Internal Revenue Service requires that the purchaser withhold 10 percent of the sale proceeds if the seller is a foreign corporation. An affidavit is used to indicate that the seller is not a foreign person or foreign corporation so that withholding is not required. The foreign person affidavit is shown as Exhibit 16–25.

Owner's Affidavit

The owner's affidavit is a title affidavit wherein the owner of the property, Markam Industries, Inc., swears that they own the property and that the property is free and clear of all liens and encumbrances except those shown on the exhibit attached. The liens and encumbrances that appear on the exhibit are those that appear from the title examination. The owner's affidavit is shown as Exhibit 16–26.

Transfer Tax Certificate

The transfer tax certificate is required by Georgia law (see Exhibit 16–27). Georgia requires a transfer tax to be assessed on deeds. The tax is 10 cents for each $100 of consideration for the property being transferred. The certificate is filed in duplicate with the deed. Several other states have recording fees and requirements, and it is not unusual for some type of certificate to be provided to the clerk indicating the amount of tax due on the recordation of the deed.

Warranty Deed

The property is transferred by warranty deed, and in this case, the deed is from Markam Industries, Inc. to Helen Davis. The only title exceptions that will appear on the warranty deed are those title exceptions that survive closing: taxes for the current year and the two easements from the title examination. The warranty deed is shown as Exhibit 16–28.

Bill of Sale

The warranty deed transfers only title to real property. The personal property included in the sale is transferred by bill of sale (see Exhibit 16–29).

Termite Letter

In many states, termites are a problem. This sales contract requires a termite letter indicating that the property is free and clear of termites or that a termite bond be provided at closing.

Truth-in-Lending Disclosure Statement

Federal law requires on a residential loan that the borrower, Helen Davis, be informed of all the costs of the loan before the closing of the loan. The truth-in-lending disclosure statement is shown as Exhibit 16–30.

Borrower's Affidavit

This title affidavit is similar to the owner's affidavit signed by Markam Industries, Inc. (see Exhibit 16–31). This affidavit is signed by Helen Davis.

Promissory Note

This note is the promise to pay money from Helen Davis to American Eagle Mortgage Company. The note should be prepared from the information found in the lender's commitment letter. Typically, payments will begin on the first day of the second month after closing. Only one original note is signed at closing. The promissory note is shown as Exhibit 16–32.

Deed to Secure Debt

This deed is the security document conveying to American Eagle Mortgage Company the real property as security for the note (see Exhibit 16–33). The grantor of the security deed is Helen Davis, and the grantee is American Eagle Mortgage Company. All the necessary information to complete the form can be obtained from the contract for sale and the lender's commitment letter.

Hazard Insurance

The lender requires that the real property be insured and that the lender, American Eagle Mortgage Company, appear as a mortgagee on the policy. The original insurance policy together with an endorsement showing American Eagle Mortgage Company as a mortgagee and a statement that the premium has been paid one year in advance must be made available at closing.

Settlement Statement

The settlement statement form is the HUD–1 required by the Real Estate Settlement Procedures Act. It is an outline and disclosure of all costs involved in the closing of the sale of the loan.

The form of HUD–1 used for the Helen Davis–Markam Industries, Inc. transaction is shown as Exhibit 16–34. The following explanation is a line-item-by-line-item explanation of how the numbers that appear on the settlement statement were arrived at. The discussion begins with a computation of the settlement costs in Schedule L, which appears on the second page of the settlement statement.

Line 700 is used to compute the seller's broker commissions. These commissions are found in the contract of sale between the seller and buyer. The contract provides that the commission will be 7 percent of the sales price of $100,000, or $7,000. The commission is to be split in half between Ajax Realty Company and Northside Realty Co., Inc. Northside has received the $1,000 earnest money at closing and will retain the $1,000 as a credit against the commission owed to it. Therefore, total commissions paid at closing will be $7,000, less the $1,000 earnest money retained by Northside, or $6,000. The $6,000 is placed under the seller's column.

Line 800 items are payable in connection with the loan. These items are found in the lender's commitment letter. On this particular transaction, only the items shown on lines 801 and 803 are payable in connection with the loan, and they are payable by the borrower.

Line 900 items are required by the lender to be paid in advance at closing. This loan is closing on April 25, but the first payment is not due until June 1. The June 1 payment will pay interest in arrears from May 1 through May 31. It will, therefore, be necessary to collect, at closing, interest for the remainder of April. Interest will be collected from the date of closing through the end of April, or from April 25 to April 30 (six days). A lender may in a commitment letter give a per diem interest charge. This loan amount has not been shown, and the method for calculating the charges is as follows:

Loan Amount: $100,000 $\times$ interest rate 8% = $8,000.

Divide the $8,000 by 365 (360 in some cases) to get $21.92.

Multiply $21.92 by the number of days (6) = $131.52.

The amount of $131.52 should be entered on line 901 under the borrower's column.

Line 1000 items are reserves deposited with the lender for taxes and insurance. To calculate the insurance reserve, take the total insurance bill for the year (see Example 16–1) and divide it by 12 ($480.00 divided by 12 equals $40.00 per month). Because the premium has been paid for one year in advance of the date of closing, the next premium on the insurance is not due until April 25 of the next year. The lender requires that one-twelfth of the insurance premium be paid each month, with the monthly payments beginning on June 1. Calculate the number of these payments from June 1 until April 25 of next year, and 11 payments will be made. The lender will need to collect at least one month's insurance to have enough to pay the bill. The lender can, under federal law, collect two months insurance and usually does.

Lines 1003 and 1004 are the tax escrows. Tax bills can be obtained from the title report (Exhibit 16–23). Divide this tax bill by 12 to show a monthly amount. You will need to know when the tax bills are due to set up the escrow reserves. Tax bills in the example are due October 1, and the lender is going to receive one-twelfth of the taxes with each monthly payment—June, July, August, and September, or four payments. Therefore, it will be necessary to escrow at least eight payments to have enough money when the bills are due. The computation for this is as follows: city taxes $1,560.00 divided by 12 = $130.00 per month $\times$ 8 = $1,040.00; county taxes $1,850.00 divided by 12 = $154.17 per month $\times$ 8 = $1,233.36.

Line 1100 items are title charges and attorneys' fees. These are invoiced by the providers of the title charges. For this example, the charges are given on the expense sheet (Example 16–1).

Line 1200 items are recording and transfer charges. Recording fees vary from state to state. For this example, the recording fees are given on the expense sheet (Example 16–1).

Settlement charges are always allocated between borrower and seller and totaled. The contract indicates which charges are assessed to the seller and which to the buyer.

Section J contains a summary of the borrower's transaction. Line 101 is the contract sales price, which can be found in the contract or, in this case, $100,000.

Paragraph 103 contains the settlement charges allocated to the borrower from line 1400—$5,638.88.

Paragraph 120 is a total of lines 101 and 103, or $105,638.88.

The *200 columns* are amounts paid by the borrower or on behalf of the borrower. These amounts reduce the borrower's cash requirements at closing.

Line 201 is any earnest money that has been paid. A review of the contract reveals an earnest money check of $1,000. This amount is entered on line 201.

Line 202 is the principal amount of any new loan, which in this case is the loan of $80,000 from American Eagle Mortgage Company. This amount is entered on line 202.

Lines 210 and 211 are prorations of city and county taxes between seller and buyer. The seller is responsible for the current year's taxes for the number of days the seller has owned the property. The computation is made by taking the tax bill for the entire year from the title examination and dividing the bill by 365. The amount received from that computation is then multiplied by the number of days the seller has owned the property to arrive at the appropriate credit amount for the borrower.

Annual tax bill for county real estate taxes is $1,560 divided by 365 = $4.27 per day, multiplied by the number of days that the seller owned the property during the tax year, which is the number of days from January 1 through the closing April 25, for a total of 115 days = $491.05.

The calculation for the county tax bill of $1,850 divided by 365 = $5.07 per day. Multiply the $5.07 per day by the number of days, again using 115 days = $583.05.

Since the taxes have not been paid in the current year, the purchaser will receive a credit for these amounts in columns 210 and 211.

All 200 items are totaled and placed on line 220.

Line 300 is the summation of the borrower's transaction and discloses the amount of money needed from the borrower at closing. In this example, the borrower needs $23,564.78. The borrower should be made aware of this as early as possible and should be informed to bring a cashier's check made payable to the law firm.

Section K is a summary of the seller's transaction. Line 401 is the amount of the sales contract, or $100,000.

Section 500 is reductions from the amount of the sales price due to the seller.

Line 501 is the earnest money deposit of the purchaser.

Line 502 is the total of settlement charges due to the seller from line 1400, or $6,103.00.

Line 504 is a payoff of the existing first loan of $82,460 on the property. This amount is shown on the expense sheet (Example 16–1).

Example 16–1

FEES

Attorneys' Fees	$650.00
Title Insurance	$400.00
Survey	$350.00
Hazard Insurance Premium	$480.00 per year
Recording Fees	$2.00 per page
	$1.00 per instrument
Transfer Tax—paid by seller	.10 per $100.00 of purchase price
Intangibles Tax—paid by purchaser	$1.50 per $500.00 of loan amount
1st Mortgage Payoff	$82,460.00

Jim Baxter is President of Markam Industries, Inc.
Floyd Knox is Secretary of Markam Industries, Inc.

Lines 510 and 511 are the same prorations under lines 210 and 211.

All of the *500 items* are totaled, and the sum is entered on line 520.

The *600 column* is the settlement of the seller's transaction and reveals that the seller will leave the closing with $9,362.90.

After a settlement statement is prepared, it is necessary to do a cash reconciliation to make sure that cash in equals cash out. An example of the cash reconciliation for this transaction is shown in Example 16–2.

Example 16–2

Cash In:

$ 80,000.00—American Eagle Mortgage Company
$ 23,564.78—Helen Davis
$103,564.78

Cash Out:

$ 82,460.00 —Payment of first loan
$ 9,362.90 —Payment to seller
$ 6,000.00 —Real estate commission
$ 1,000.00 —Commitment fee to American Eagle Mortgage Company
$ 500.00 —Appraisal fee to American Eagle Mortgage Company
$ 131.52 —Prepaid interest to American Eagle Mortgage Company
$ 80.00 —Insurance reserves to American Eagle Mortgage Company
$ 1,040.00 —Reserves for city property taxes to American Eagle Mortgage Company
$ 1,233.36 —Reserves for county property taxes to American Eagle Mortgage Company
$ 650.00 —Attorney's fees (law firm)
$ 400.00 —Title premium (title company)
$ 17.00 —Recording fees
$ 240.00 —Intangible tax
$ 100.00 —Transfer tax
$ 350.00 —Survey
$103,564.78

Closing procedures and document preparation, like other aspects of business life, have been computerized. Software applications exist to assist the paralegal in preparing a HUD–1 settlement sheet, printing loan documents on residential transactions, and even printing checks for disbursement to the seller, purchaser, and lender. Most law firms that do a reasonable volume of residential work own such software applications. Many of the software applications claim that an entire residential loan package can be completed within 30 minutes, which is far less than the usual three or four hours required without a software package. Software applications also assure accuracy not only in making the computations necessary for the closing statement, but also in the repetitive use of data in the various closing documents. Once the correct data is entered into the software, it is accurately and correctly redistributed on the various closing documents.

🏛 ETHICS: Case Problem

Ann is a real estate paralegal in a large law firm. Her primary responsibility is to assist two attorneys who represent a bank in the closing of real estate loans. She has developed a good working relationship with the bank's loan officers. In fact, the loan officers send most of their new loans directly to Ann. On receipt from the bank, Ann prepares file opening memorandums for the supervising attorneys' signatures.

It is late Wednesday afternoon, and Ann receives a new loan file from the bank as well as a telephone call from the loan officer. The loan officer indicates that the loan has to close no later than Friday and that it is a high-priority matter. A conflicts check on the loan reveals that the borrower had several years ago been represented by one of the lawyers in the firm. It appears that there has been no activity with this client for the past three years. Ann calls the attorney to check out the situation but finds that the attorney is on vacation and will not be back until Monday. The attorney's secretary does not know anything about the client. Ann decides that the expedient thing to do is to go ahead and open the file and proceed for a closing.

Thursday morning Ann calls the borrower to go over the closing requirements. Once Ann identifies herself and the firm for which she works, the borrower is relieved to know that she works for the firm that represents him. The borrower is cooperative in providing information for the closing. After receiving all the necessary information, Ann prepares the closing documents and schedules the closing for 3:00 P.M. on Friday. Ann attempts a number of times to meet with her supervising attorney so that she can review the loan documents but is not successful.

On Friday, Ann receives a call from the borrower, who indicates that he has a surprise business appointment out of town and must leave in an hour. He would like Ann to come to his office and have him sign the papers. Ann immediately goes to the office. When she arrives, she finds that the borrower has left to pick up airline tickets and will not be back for about 45 minutes. The borrower's secretary asks that the documents be left with her, and she would make sure that the borrower signed them before he left town. She would then courier them back over to Ann. Ann agrees and goes back to the office.

Later that afternoon, the documents arrive in Ann's office, and none of them has been notarized. Ann calls the secretary to discuss this fact, and the secretary indicates that she saw the borrower sign the documents. She asks Ann to notarize the documents since everything is okay. Ann, to close the transaction on time, notarizes the documents.

Later, as Ann is putting the package together for transmittal back to the bank client, her supervising attorney stops by. The attorney would like to review the file before the 3:00 P.M. closing. Ann tells her that the closing has already taken place. Ann tells her about the developer's unexpected trip out of town and the trip to his office and the closing at the office. Ann neglects to tell the attorney the part about leaving the documents for signature and her notarization of the documents.

What legal ethics or codes of professional responsibility have been violated in this example?

SUMMARY

Many law firms ask the paralegal to prepare the documents used in a real estate closing transaction. The paralegal should be familiar not only with what types of forms must be used, but also with the content of these forms. When preparing the forms, the paralegal must be careful not to make mistakes that will change the transaction or require corrective work. It is important that legal documents be carefully reviewed and proofread to minimize mistakes.

HELPFUL WEBSITES

Some good general information real estate related links can be found at:

ABA Real Property, Probate and Trust Law, *www.abanet .org/rppt/home.html*

Law Journal Extra Real Estate Law, *www.legaline.com/ real.htm*

DIRT, an Internet real estate discussion group led by Professor Patrick A. Randolph, Jr., *http://dirt.umkc.edu*

KEY TERMS

affidavit

bill of sale

REVIEW QUESTIONS

1. What statement of facts usually is included in a title affidavit?

2. What is the purpose of a hazardous waste affidavit? Why is it important to a purchaser of real property?

3. Why is a foreign person affidavit important to a purchaser?

4. What is the purpose of an assignment of warranties? An assignment of leases? An assignment of contracts?

5. When is a corporate resolution required in a closing transaction, and why is it important?

6. A lender may require the borrower's attorney to render an opinion as to certain aspects of the loan transaction. What are some of the items that may be covered in an attorney's opinion?

CASE PROBLEMS

1. You are a paralegal involved in a real estate sale transaction. The seller of the property is Susan T. Clarke. The title examination of the property reveals that there are five judgments against Susan Clarke, S. T. Clarke, and Sue Clarke. You call the seller, Susan T. Clarke, and tell her about the judgments. She informs you on the phone that she is not the Susan Clarke mentioned in the judgments. What do you do to protect the purchaser in the closing?

2. You are a paralegal representing a purchaser of a home. You have been asked to prepare the sale closing papers. What documents does the Internal Revenue Service require you to prepare in connection with the sale? What information do you need from the various parties to prepare this documentation?

3. You are a paralegal involved in a real estate sale transaction. The seller is a corporation. You have asked the president of the corporation to bring a corporate resolution authorizing the sale and the execution on behalf of the corporation of the various real estate closing documents. The president of the corporation delivers to you

a corporate resolution signed only by the president that authorizes only the president to sign all the documents. Is there any additional documentation that you should request from the president to evidence his or her authority to sign the loan closing documents?

4. You are assisting in a real estate sale transaction. The title examination reports that there is an outstanding loan to Second Bank and Trust on the property. The loan is to be satisfied at closing. You believe that the closing will take place on July 10. You obtain from Second Bank and Trust a satisfaction payoff letter indicating how much money is needed to pay the loan as of July 10. The loan closing is delayed and does not take place until July 15. Is there any additional information that you may need from Second Bank and Trust for the July 15 closing?

5. You are preparing a title affidavit for a real estate closing. Exhibit A to the affidavit is a legal description of the real property, and Exhibit B is a list of title exceptions to the real property. Where would you get the information to complete Exhibits A and B?

PRACTICAL ASSIGNMENTS

1. You are a paralegal involved in a real estate sale transaction. The sale is to close on September 10. The title examination reports that county real estate taxes have been paid by the seller for the current year in the amount of $1,640. The tax year for the county begins February 1 and ends January 31. You have been asked to calculate the tax proration between purchaser and seller. What is the amount of the tax proration, and on which lines of the HUD–1 would the amount appear?

2. You are a paralegal working on a real estate sale transaction. The title examination reports that real estate taxes for the current year are unpaid in the amount of $1,350 and that they are due November 15 of the year. Your closing is taking place on May 10. The closing also involves a loan in which the lender wants taxes escrowed. The lender's first payment under the note will be July 1. Calculate the tax proration between seller and purchaser. Calculate the amount of taxes to be escrowed for the lender. Are the amounts the same? If not, should they be?

3. You are a paralegal involved in a real estate sale transaction. The contract provides that the real estate commission is to be 6 percent of the contract price for the real property. The contract price for the real property is $116,000. The contract also indicates that two brokers are involved, Ajax Realty Company and Beta Realty Company. The commission is to be split 50/50 between these two companies. In addition, Ajax Realty Company has $2,500 earnest money from the purchaser. What information do you need from the parties to prepare lines 700, 701, and 702 of the HUD Uniform Settlement Statement?

4. You are assisting in a real estate closing transaction. The loan is $80,000 at an interest rate of 6 percent per annum. The loan is closing on March 14, and the lender wants the first payment on the loan to begin on May 1. The lender also requires the borrower to pay in advance all interest accruing during March. How much interest would you collect from the borrower at closing?

5. You are assisting in the closing of the sale of a home. The contract price for the home is $86,500. The seller owes a real estate broker a commission of 6 percent of the sales price and other closing costs of $600. In addition, there is an outstanding loan on the property that is to be paid at closing in the amount of $28,400. In addition, real property taxes for the current year in the amount of $2,150 are unpaid. The tax year is the calendar year, and the closing is taking place on August 15. In preparing the Uniform Settlement Statement, how much net money would the seller take home from the closing?

6. You are assisting in the purchase of a home. The contract purchase price is $115,000. The settlement costs allocated to the purchaser are $3,230. Taxes for the current year in the amount of $1,650 have been paid by the seller. The calendar tax year is the calendar year, and the closing takes place on September 25. The purchaser has paid an earnest money deposit of $5,000 for the property and has obtained a loan to purchase the property for $90,000. You are preparing the Uniform Settlement Statement. How much money, if any, does the purchaser need to bring to closing to consummate the sale?

ADDENDUM

Exhibit 16–21 Sales Contract
Exhibit 16–22 Loan Commitment
Exhibit 16–23 Title Examination
Exhibit 16–24 Corporate Resolution
Exhibit 16–25 Foreign Person Affidavit
Exhibit 16–26 Owner's Affidavit
Exhibit 16–27 Transfer Tax Certificate

Exhibit 16–28 Warranty Deed
Exhibit 16–29 General Warranty Bill of Sale
Exhibit 16–30 Truth-in-Lending Disclosure Statement
Exhibit 16–31 Owner's Affidavit
Exhibit 16–32 Promissory Note
Exhibit 16–33 Security Deed
Exhibit 16–34 HUD–1 Settlement Statement

Student StudyWare™ CD-ROM

Interactive Student CD in the book includes additional quizzing, case studies, and key terms flashcards.

Online Companion™

For additional resources, please go to *www.paralegal.delmar.cengage.com*

EXHIBIT 16–21

Sales Contract

ATLANTA REAL ESTATE BOARD
Commercial Sales Contract
September, 1972

January 15, _____ , 20____

As a result of the efforts of __Northside Realty Co., Inc._____ ,

a licensed Broker, the undersigned Purchaser agrees to buy, and the undersigned Seller agrees to sell, all that tract or parcel of land, with such improvements as are located thereon, described as follows: all that tract or parcel of land lying and being in Land Lot 359 of the 18th District of Fulton County, Georgia, being Lot 12 of Bassett Hall Subdivision, as per plat recorded in Plat Book 68, Page 79, Fulton County, Georgia, being improved property with a house located thereon known as 5167 Tilly Mill Road, Atlanta, Georgia 30302.

together with all electrical, mechanical, plumbing, air-conditioning, and any other systems or fixtures as are attached thereto and all plants, trees, and shrubbery now on the premises.

The purchase price of said property shall be:

__One Hundred Thousand and No/100_____ DOLLARS, $ _100,000.00_____ ,

to be paid as follows:
All cash at closing

Purchaser has paid to the undersigned, __One Thousand Dollars --------------------------------__ , as Broker,

$ _1,000.00_____ ( ) cash (X) check, receipt whereof is hereby acknowledged by Broker, as earnest money, which earnest

money is to be promptly deposited in Broker's escrow account and is to be applied as part payment of purchase price of said property at the time sale is consummated.

Seller warrants that he presently has title to said property, and at the time the sale is consummated, he agrees to convey good and marketable title to said property to Purchaser by general warranty deed subject only to (1) zoning ordinances affecting said property, (2) general utility easements of record serving said property, (3) subdivision restrictions of record, and (4) leases, other easements, other restrictions and encumbrances specified in this contract. In the event leases are specified in this contract, the Purchaser agrees to assume the Seller's responsibilities thereunder to the tenant and to the Broker who negotiated such leases.

The Purchaser shall move promptly and in good faith after acceptance of this contract to examine title and to furnish Seller with a written statement of objections affecting the marketability of said title. Seller shall have reasonable time after receipt of such objections to satisfy all valid objections and if Seller fails to satisfy such valid objections within a reasonable time, then at the option of the Purchaser, evidenced by written notice to Seller, this contract shall be null and void. Marketable title as used herein shall mean title which a title insurance company licensed to do business in the State of Georgia will insure at its regular rates, subject only to standard exceptions unless otherwise specified herein.

Seller and Purchaser agree that such papers as may be necessary to carry out the terms of this contract shall be executed and delivered by such parties at time the sale is consummated.

Purchaser, its agents, or representatives, at Purchaser's expense and at reasonable times during normal business hours, shall have the right to enter upon the property for the purpose of inspecting, examining (including soil boring), testing, and surveying the property. Purchaser assumes all responsibility for the acts of itself, its agents, or representatives in exercising its rights under this paragraph and agrees to hold Seller harmless for any damages resulting therefrom.

Seller warrants that when the sale is consummated the improvements on the property will be in the same condition as they are on the date this contract is signed by the Seller, natural wear and tear excepted. However, should the premises be destroyed or substantially damaged before the contract is consummated, then at the election of the Purchaser: (a) the contract may be cancelled, or (b) Purchaser may consummate the contract and receive such insurance as is paid on the claim of loss. This election is to be exercised within ten (10) days after the Purchaser has been notified in writing by Seller of the amount of the insurance proceeds, if any, Seller will receive on the claim of loss; if Purchaser has not been notified within forty-five (45) days subsequent to the occurrence of such damage or destruction, Purchaser may, at its option, cancel the contract.

In negotiating this contract, Broker has rendered a valuable service for which reason Broker is made a party to enable Broker to enforce his commission rights hereunder against the parties hereto on the following basis: Seller agrees to pay Broker the full commission when the sale is consummated and in the event the sale is not consummated because of Seller's inability, failure or refusal to perform any of the Seller's covenants herein, then the Seller shall pay the full commission to Broker, and Broker, at the option of Purchaser, evidenced by written notice to Seller, this contract shall be null and void. Purchaser agrees that if Purchaser fails or refuses to perform any of Purchaser's covenants herein, Purchaser shall forthwith pay Broker the full commission; provided that Broker may first apply one-half of the earnest money toward payment of, but not to exceed, the full commission and may pay the balance thereof to Seller as liquidated damages of Seller, if Seller claims balance as Seller's liquidated damages in full settlement of any claim for damages, whereupon Broker shall be released from any and all liability for return of earnest money to Purchaser. If this transaction involves exchange of real estate, the full commission shall be paid in respect to the property conveyed by each party to the other and notice of the dual agency is hereby given and accepted by Seller and Purchaser. The commission on an exchange shall be calculated on the amount on the basis of which each property is taken in such exchange, according to the contract between the parties, and if no value is placed on any property exchange, then according to the reasonable value thereof. In the event of an exchange, each party shall be regarded as Seller as to the property conveyed by each party.

Commission to be paid in connection with this transaction has been negotiated between Seller and Broker and shall be _____

__7% of the purchase price._____ .

Time is of essence of this contract.

This contract shall inure to the benefit of, and be binding upon, the parties hereto, their heirs, successors, administrators, executors and assigns.

The interest of the Purchaser in this contract shall not be transferred or assigned without the written consent of Seller.

This contract constitutes the sole and entire agreement between the parties hereto and no modification of this contract shall be binding unless attached hereto and signed by all parties to this agreement. No representation, promise, or inducement not included in this contract shall be binding upon any party hereto.

The following stipulations shall, if conflicting with printed matter, control:

(continued)

EXHIBIT 16–21

Sales Contract

(*continued*)

SPECIAL STIPULATIONS

1. Real Estate taxes on said property shall be prorated as of the date of closing.
2. Seller shall pay State of Georgia property transfer tax.
3. Sale shall be closed on or before ___April 25, 20___.
4. Possession of premises shall be granted by Seller to Purchaser no later than ___April 25, 20___.
5. Seller warrants that all appliances remaining with the dwelling and the heating and air conditioning systems will be in normal operating condition at time of closing. Purchaser shall have the privileges and responsibility of making inspections of said equipment and systems prior to closing of sale.
6. Seller shall provide at time of closing of the transaction a clearance letter from a licensed pest control operator, certified in wood destroying organisms, certifying the property is free from termites and other wood destroying organisms and from structural damage caused thereby and carrying a guarantee that the property will be treated for a period of one year from the date of issuance of said letter.

* continued

This instrument shall be regarded as an offer by the Purchaser or Seller who first signs to the other and is open for acceptance by the other until _____O'clock ___ M., on the ____ day of_____,20___ ; by which time written acceptance of such offer must have been actually received by Broker, who shall promptly notify other party, in writing of such acceptance.

The above proposition is hereby accepted this _____ day of _____ , 20 ____.

_____
(Purchaser)   Helen Davis

_____
(Purchaser)

_____
(Seller)   Markam Industries, Inc.

_____
(Seller)

By: Northside Realty Co., Inc.
        (Broker)

* continued

7. All kitchen appliances are included in the sales price.
8. This contract is in cooperation with Ajax Realty Co. and the commission is to be divided 50/50.
9. This contract is subject to the Purchaser obtaining a loan in the principal amount of not less than $80,000.00, shall bear interest at a rate not to exceed 11% per annum and a term of not less than 25 years.

OR IN LIEU OF SAID LETTER

Seller shall provide a Termite Contract that is in full force with a licensed pest control company that may be transferred to the Purchaser, providing said contract covers both ADDITIONAL TREATMENT and REPAIR OF DAMAGE.

FORM 203

IVAN ALLEN CO., ATLANTA

To

From

Commercial Sales Contract

ATLANTA REAL ESTATE BOARD
September, 1972

EXHIBIT 16–22

Loan Commitment

AMERICAN EAGLE MORTGAGE COMPANY

March 7, 20__

Ms. Helen Davis
849 Mentelle Drive, N.E.
Atlanta, Georgia 30308

Re: Mortgage Loan Commitment—$80,000 at 8% for thirty (30) years

Dear Ms. Davis:

American Eagle Mortgage Company (the "Company") is pleased to inform you that it has acted upon your application and has approved a loan to you, subject to all terms and conditions of this letter. The loan will be in the principal sum of $80,000 at an annual rate of 8%, to be repaid as follows:

In equal consecutive monthly installments of $588.00 per month for thirty (30) years. Each installment, when paid, shall be applied first to the payment of accrued interest and then to the unpaid principal balance.

The holder may collect a "late charge" not to exceed an amount equal to four percent (4%) of any installment which is not paid within fifteen (15) days of the due date thereof, to cover the extra expenses involved in handling delinquent payments.

The loan proceeds shall be used for the acquisition of improved real estate (the "Property") located at 5167 Tilly Mill Road, Atlanta, Georgia.

The loan shall be secured by a first priority lien on the Property and on all improvements now or hereafter existing thereon. The Company's agreement to make the loan to you is subject to satisfaction of the following conditions, all at your sole cost and expense and in a manner acceptable to the Company.

1. The Company shall procure a standard form ALTA mortgagee's policy of title insurance insuring the loan as a first priority lien against the Property, showing there is to be no other encumbrances against the Property which render it unmarketable.
2. You shall provide the Company prior to closing with a recent plat of survey of the Property, together with a surveyor's certificate in form satisfactory to the Company's title insuror, depicting and certifying all improvements on the Property to be completely within the boundary lines of the Property and to be in compliance with all applicable building or setback line restrictions.
3. You shall provide the Company prior to closing with fire, lightning and extended coverage insurance issued by a company or companies and upon terms acceptable to the Company in at least the sum of $80,000. Premiums for such insurance shall be paid by you for not less than one year in advance. All policies shall be issued with a mortgagee clause in favor of and acceptable to the Company and shall be non-cancellable without at least ten (10) days prior written notice to the Company.
4. The Company shall select an attorney to close the loan and to prepare all documents deemed necessary or appropriate by the Company to evidence the loan and to establish the Company's first priority lien against the Property and the Policy. All such loan documents will be in form and substance satisfactory to the Company's closing attorney.
5. All actual fees or expenses (including, without limitation, such closing attorney's fees, title insurance premiums, cost of title examination, abstract of title fee, document preparation fee, cost of survey, appraisal fee, recording fees and intangibles or other taxes) incurred in connection with reviewing your loan application, or with closing, servicing, collecting or cancelling the loan, shall be paid by you.
6. The loan may be assumed by a transferee of the Property, provided the Company gives prior written consent thereto; but any transfer of title to all or any part of the Property whatsoever, or any further encumbrance or other lien imposed against the Property without

Delmar/Cengage Learning

(continued)

EXHIBIT 16–22

Loan Commitment

(*continued*)

the Company's prior written consent, will authorize the Company to declare the loan immediately due and payable. Any such assumption, transfer or encumbrance to which the Company shall consent shall be upon such terms and conditions as the Company shall determine and approve.

7. You shall pay a non-refundable loan origination fee of $1,000.00 to the Company upon your acceptance of this commitment letter.
8. You shall provide the Company with photographs of all buildings or other structural improvements on the Property prior to closing.
9. You shall pay an appraisal fee to the Company in the amount of $500.00.
10. The loan is to be escrowed for taxes and insurance premiums.

Very truly yours,

AMERICAN EAGLE MORTGAGE COMPANY

By: _____

J. Perry Drake

Treasurer

EXHIBIT 16–23

Title Examination

RE: 5167 Tilly Mill Road, Atlanta, Georgia

A search of the above referenced property as of April 20, 20__ at 5:00 P.M., reveals title to be vested in Markam Industries, Inc., subject to the following objections:

1. Easement between Sam Turner and Georgia Power Company dated August 6, 1959 recorded at Deed Book 2898, page 25, Fulton County Records.

2. Easement between Markam Industries, Inc. and Georgia Power Company dated February 11, 1998 and recorded in Deed Book 5106, page 810 aforesaid records.

3. Deed to Secure Debt from Markam Industries, Inc. to The Southern National Bank dated March 3, 20__ recorded in Deed Book 5508, page 83, aforesaid recording securing the original principal amount of $85,000.

4. County taxes have been paid through 20__ but are unpaid for 20__, in the amount of $1,850.00—due on October 1, 20__.

5. City of Atlanta taxes paid through 20__; 20__ due in the amount of $1,560.00 and due on October 1, 20__.

EXHIBIT 16–24

Corporate Resolution

CERTIFICATE

I, FLOYD KNOX, Secretary of MARKAM INDUSTRIES, INC., a Georgia Corporation (the "Company") do hereby certify as follows:

1. Attached hereto as Exhibit "A" is a true and correct copy of resolutions which were duly adopted at a special meeting of the Board of Directors on _____, 20__, at which a quorum was present and acting throughout and which have not been amended, modified or rescinded in any respect and are in full force and effect from the date hereof.

2. The below-named persons have been duly elected and are qualified and at all times have been and this day are officers of the Company, holding the respective offices below set opposite their names, and signatures set opposite their names are their genuine signatures.

JIM BAXTER

President   _____

FLOYD KNOX

Secretary   _____

(*continued*)

EXHIBIT 16–24

Corporate Resolution

(*continued*)

WITNESS my hand and seal of the Company this _____ day of _____, 20__.

_____ (SEAL)
FLOYD KNOX
Secretary
[CORPORATE SEAL]

EXHIBIT "A"

RESOLVED, that MARKAM INDUSTRIES, INC., a Georgia Corporation (hereinafter called the "Company"), sell that certain real property more particularly described on Exhibit "B" attached hereto and made a part hereof to HELEN DAVIS pursuant to Contract for Sale dated January 15, 20__;

FURTHER RESOLVED, that the President of the Company, JIM BAXTER, is hereby authorized and directed to execute and deliver on behalf of Company any and all documentation required to sell the property to HELEN DAVIS, including but not limited to, any and all warranty deeds, affidavits, bills of sale and closing statements.

EXHIBIT "B"

All that tract or parcel of land lying and being in Land Lot 359 of the 18th District of Fulton County, Georgia, being Lot 12 of Bassett Hall Subdivision as per plat recorded of Plat Book 68, page 79, Fulton County, Georgia Records.

EXHIBIT 16–25

Foreign Person Affidavit

Does not Benefit Seller

STATE OF _____)
) ss:
COUNTY OF _____)

The undersigned is the President of MARKAM INDUSTRIES, INC., a Georgia corporation (the "Transferor"), and is duly authorized to execute this Certificate and Affidavit in his representative capacity on behalf of the Transferor, as well as in his individual capacity;

That the principal place of business, principal office and chief executive office of the Transferor is located at 210 Corporate Square, Atlanta, Fulton County, Georgia 30303;

That the Transferor is a corporation duly organized and validly existing under the laws of the State of Georgia;

That the Transferor is not a "foreign corporation," as such term is defined in the United States Internal Revenue Code of 1986, as amended (the "Code") and Regulations promulgated thereunder, and is not otherwise a "foreign person," as defined in § 1445 of the Code;

That the Transferor's United States taxpayer identifying number is 58–1004212;

That the undersigned is making this Certificate and Affidavit pursuant to the provisions of § 1445 of the Code in connection with the sale of the real property described on Exhibit "A", attached hereto and incorporated herein by reference, by the Transferor to HELEN DAVIS (the "Transferee"), which sale constitutes the disposition by the Transferor of a United States real property interest, for the purpose of establishing that the Transferee is not required to withhold tax pursuant to § 1445 of the Code in connection with such disposition; and

That the undersigned acknowledges that this Certificate and Affidavit may be disclosed to the Internal Revenue Service by the Transferee, that this Certificate and Affidavit is made under penalty of perjury, and that any false statements made herein could be punished by fine, imprisonment, or both.

Under penalty of perjury, I declare that I have examined the foregoing Certificate and Affidavit and hereby certify that it is true, correct and complete.

_____ (SEAL)
JIM BAXTER

Delmar/Cengage Learning

(continued)

Certified, sworn to and subscribed before me
this _____ day of _____, 20__.

_____
Notary Public
My Commission Expires:

_____
[Notarial Seal]

EXHIBIT "A"

All that tract or parcel of land lying and being in Land Lot 359 of the 18th District of Fulton County, Georgia, being Lot 12 of Bassett Hall Subdivision as per plat recorded of Plat Book 68, page 79, Fulton County, Georgia Records.

EXHIBIT 16–25
Foreign Person Affidavit
(*continued*)

STATE OF _____)
) ss:
COUNTY OF _____)

The undersigned, being duly sworn, states:

That the undersigned is the President of MARKAM INDUSTRIES, INC., a Georgia corporation (the "Company"), and is duly authorized to execute this affidavit in his capacity on behalf of the Company as well as in his individual capacity;

That the principal place of business, principal office and chief executive office of the Company is located in Fulton County, Georgia, and has been located in said County at all times since the formation of the Company;

That the Company is the fee simple title owner of the real property described on Exhibit "A" attached hereto and incorporated herein by reference (the "Property").

That the lines and corners of the Property are clearly marked and there are no disputes concerning the location of said lines and corners;

That no improvements or repairs have been made or contracted for by the Company on the Property during the three (3) months immediately preceding the date of this affidavit, for which there are outstanding bills for labor or services performed or rendered, or for materials supplied or furnished, or incurred in connection with improvements or repairs on the Property, or for the services of architects, surveyors or engineers in connection with improvements or repairs on the Property;

That, except for the matters set forth on Exhibit "B" attached hereto and incorporated herein by reference, the Property is free and clear of all claims, liens and encumbrances, and there is no outstanding indebtedness for or liens against any equipment or fixtures attached to, installed on, incorporated in or located on, or otherwise used in connection with the operation or maintenance of, the Property or the improvements thereon;

That there are no persons or other parties in possession of the Property who have a right or claim to possession extending beyond the date hereof;

That there are no suits, proceedings, judgments, bankruptcies, liens, or executions against the Company which affect title to the Property, the improvements thereon or the fixtures attached thereto;

That the undersigned is making this affidavit with the knowledge that it will be relied upon by lenders, attorneys, and title insurance companies interested in the title to the Property.

Sworn to and subscribed before me
this _____ day of _____, 20__.

_____   _____
Notary Public   JIM BAXTER

EXHIBIT 16–26
Owner's Affidavit

Delmar/Cengage Learning

(*continued*)

EXHIBIT 16–26

Owner's Affidavit

(*continued*)

My Commission Expires:

_____

[Notarial Seal]

EXHIBIT "A"

All that tract or parcel of land lying and being in Land Lot 359 of the 18th District of Fulton County, Georgia, being Lot 12 of Bassett Hall Subdivision as per plat recorded of Plat Book 68, page 79, Fulton County, Georgia Records.

EXHIBIT "B"

1. All taxes for the current year.
2. Easement between Sam Turner and Georgia Power Company dated August 6, 1959, recorded at Deed Book 2898, page 25, Fulton County, Georgia Records.
3. Easement between Markam Industries, Inc., and Georgia Power Company dated February 11, 1998 and recorded at Deed Book 5106, page 810, aforesaid records.
4. Deed to Secure Debt from Markam Industries, Inc., to The Southern National Bank dated March 3, 20___, recorded at Deed Book 5508, page 83, aforesaid records securing the original principal amount of $85,000.00.

EXHIBIT 16–27

Transfer Tax Certificate

PT-61 (Rev. 10/92) (PLEASE TYPE OR PRINT)

SECTION A - SELLER'S INFORMATION	SECTION E - TAX COMPUTATION	
1. NAME Markam Industries, Inc.	1. Actual value of consideration received by seller (Fill out below only when actual value is not known)	$100,000.00
2. MAILING ADDRESS (STREET & NUMBER) 210 Corporate Square	1a. Estimated fair market value of Real and Personal property conveyed	
3. CITY, STATE, ZIP CODE Atlanta, Georgia 30324 / **4. DATE OF SALE**	2. Fair market value of Personal property only conveyed	
	3. Amount of Liens and Encumbrances not removed by transfer	
SECTION B - BUYER'S INFORMATION	4. Net Taxable Value (1 or 1a minus 2 minus 3)	$100,000.00
1. NAME Helen Davis	5. TAX DUE at 10¢ per $100 or fraction thereof (Minimum $1.00)	100.00

2. MAILING ADDRESS FOR TAX NOTICES, BILLS, ETC. (STREET & NUMBER)
5167 Tilly Mill Road

3. CITY, STATE, ZIP CODE
Atlanta, Georgia 30302   **4. INTENDED USE** [ ] [ ] [ ] [ ] R A C I

SECTION F - CERTIFICATIONS

SELLER: I hereby certify that all the items of information entered on this transfer form PT-61 are true and correct to the best of my knowledge and belief.

Signature _____
(Seller or Authorized Agent)   (Date)

SECTION C - PROPERTY INFORMATION

1. LOCATION (STREET, ROUTE, HWY., ETC.)
5167 Tilly Mill Road   **2. COUNTY** Fulton

3. CITY (IF APPLICABLE)
Atlanta   **4. MAP & PARCEL NUMBER**

5. ACRES	6. DISTRICT 18	7. LAND LOT 359	8. SUB LOT & BLOCK

BUYER: I hereby certify that all information on this form is true and correct to the best of my knowledge and belief. I acknowledge that if the above property is taxable and is subdivided or improved during the year of this transfer, that I must return if for taxation the following year, but if there are no changes and I do not elect to file a return, I will be deemed to have returned the property at the same valuation as was finally determined for the year of this transfer. I further acknowledge that this form does not relieve me of the responsibility of filing a return for personal property or of applying for homestead or other exemptions.

Signature _____
(Buyer or Authorized Agent)   (Date)

SECTION D - RECORDING INFORMATION

1. DATE	2. DEED BOOK	PAGE	3. PLAT BOOK	PAGE

CLERK OF COURT: I hereby certify that the recording information in Section D is correct and that the tax due in Section E5 is computed correctly based upon the information supplied in Section E by the seller or authorized agent.

Signature _____
(Clerk or Deputy of Superior Court)   (Date)

REVENUE COPY

Delmar/Cengage Learning

EXHIBIT 16–28
Warranty Deed

STATE OF GEORGIA

COUNTY OF FULTON

WARRANTY DEED

THIS INDENTURE made this   25th day of   April   20___   by and between
MARKAM INDUSTRIES, INC., a Georgia corporation
party or parties of the first part, hereinafter referred to as "Grantor", and

HELEN DAVIS
party or parties of the second part hereinafter referred to as "Grantee", the words "Grantor" and "Grantee" to
include the neuter, masculine and feminine genders, the singular and the plural;

WITNESSETH :

FOR AND IN CONSIDERATION of the sum of Ten Dollars in hand paid and other good and valuable
consideration delivered to Grantor by Grantee at and before the execution, sealing and delivery hereof, the receipt and
sufficiency of which is hereby acknowledged, Grantor, has and hereby does grant bargain, sell and convey unto
Grantee and the heirs, legal representatives, successors and assigns of Grantee

All that tract or parcel of land lying and being in Land Lot 359 of the 18th
District of Fulton County, Georgia, being Lot 12 of Bassett Hall Subdivision,
as per plat recorded at Plat Book 68, Page 79, Fulton County, Georgia Records.

SUBJECT TO:

Ad valorem taxes for the year 20___ and subsequent years.

Easement between Sam Turner and Georgia Power Company dated August 6, 1959,
recorded at Deed Book 2898, Page 25, Fulton County, Georgia Records.

Easement between Markam Industries, Inc. and Georgia Power Company dated
February 11, 1998 and recorded at Deed Book 5106, Page 810, aforesaid records.

TO HAVE AND TO HOLD said tract or parcel of land, together with any and all of the rights, members and appurtenances thereof to the same being, belonging or in anywise appertaining to the only proper use, benefit and behoof of the
Grantee and the heirs, legal representatives, successors and assigns of Grantee, forever, in fee simple.

GRANTOR SHALL WARRANT and forever defend the right and title to said tract or parcel of land unto the Grantee
and the heirs, legal representatives, successors and assigns of Grantee, against the claims of all persons   whomsoever.

IN WITNESS WHEREOF, the Grantor has signed and sealed this deed, the day and year first above written.

Signed, Sealed and Delivered in the presence of: MARKAM INDUSTRIES, INC.

_____   By: _____ (SEAL)
(Unofficial Witness)   Jim Baxter, President
                                               Attest: _____ (SEAL)
_____   Floyd Knox, Secretary
(Notary Public)
                                                    [CORPORATE SEAL]

Delmar/Cengage Learning

EXHIBIT 16–29

General Warranty Bill of Sale

STATE OF _____)
) ss:

COUNTY OF _____)

     In consideration of the sum of Ten and No/100 ($10.00) Dollars, and other good and valuable consideration in hand paid to MARKAM INDUSTRIES, INC., a Georgia corporation (hereinafter referred to as "Seller") by HELEN DAVIS (hereinafter referred to as "Purchaser"), Seller hereby sells and conveys to Purchaser, its successors and assigns, all personal property, appliances and fixtures located on or used in connection with the property described on Exhibit "A" attached hereto and made a part hereof.

     Seller hereby covenants with and represents and warrants to Purchaser as follows:

1. That Seller is lawfully seized and possessed of said personal property;
2. That Seller has a right to sell, transfer and convey the same;
3. That the same is free and clear of any and all encumbrances or security interests;
4. That Seller warrants and forever will defend the title to same against any and all claims whatsoever.

     IN WITNESS WHEREOF, Seller, by its duly authorized officers, has hereunto set its hand and seal this the _____ day of _____, 20___.

                                MARKAM INDUSTRIES, INC.,
                              a Georgia corporation
                              By: _____ (SEAL)
                                  JIM BAXTER
                                President
                              Attest: _____ (SEAL)
                                  FLOYD KNOX
                                  Secretary

Signed, sealed and delivered in the presence
of this _____ day of _____, 20___.

_____
Unofficial Witness

_____
Notary Pubic
My Commission Expires:

_____
[Notarial Seal]

EXHIBIT "A"

     All that tract or parcel of land lying and being in Land Lot 359 of the 18th District of Fulton County, Georgia, being Lot 12 of Bassett Hall Subdivision as per plat recorded of Plat Book 68, page 79, Fulton County, Georgia Records.

EXHIBIT 16–30

Truth-in-Lending Disclosure Statement

TRUTH-IN-LENDING MORTGAGE DISCLOSURE STATEMENT

Lender: AMERICAN EAGLE MORTGAGE COMPANY   **Borrower's Name and Address:** Helen Davis
5167 Tilly Mill Road
Atlanta, Georgia 30302

APPLICATION #   DATE OF DISCLOSURE

(In this disclosure statement, the words "I," "me," "my," and "mine" refer to each consumer listed above. The words "you," "your," and "lender" refer to American Eagle Mortgage Company

ANNUAL PERCENTAGE RATE The cost of my credit as a yearly rate,	FINANCE CHARGE The dollar amount the credit will cost me,	Amount Financed The amount of credit provided to me or on my behalf.	Total of Payments The amount I will have paid after I have made all payments as scheduled, based on the current annual interest rate
8.25 %	$ 132,680.00	$ 79,000.00	$ 211,680.00

My payment schedule will be:

Number of Payments	Amount of Payments	When Payments Are Due
360	$588.00	First day of each month commencing on June 1, 20__

☐ **Construction Loan:** Interest on the amount of credit advanced during the construction period will be paid for _____ based on the outstanding balance. After the construction period I will pay payments as shown above.

☐ **Variable Rate:**

Security: I am giving you a mortgage on real estate located at
5167 Tilly Mill Road, Atlanta, Georgia 30302

Late Charge: If payment is ____15____ days late, I will be charged ____4____% of the interest and principal payment.
Assumption:
☐ Someone buying my home may be allowed to assume the remainder of the mortgage on the original terms, subject to conditions.
☐ Someone buying my house cannot assume the remainder of the mortgage on the original terms.

Prepayment: If I pay off early, I _____ have to pay a penalty, and I will not be entitled to a rebate of part of the finance charge.
☐ If this space is checked, all above numerical disclosures except for the late charge are estimates.
See contract documents for any additional information about nonpayment default, any required repayment in full before the scheduled date, and prepayment refunds and penalties.
e means an estimate

Recording Fees: $ _____.

Insurance: I may obtain all required property insurance (including any required flood insurance) from anyone I want that is acceptable to the lender.

Itemization of Amount Financed: ($ _____) (c minus d):

(a) $ _____ Amount given to me directly
(b) $ _____ Amount applied to indebtedness of mine with the lender
(c) $ _____ Principal amount of loan (total of a + b)
(d) $ _____ Prepaid finance charge (itemized below)

$ _____ for "points" paid by me
$ _____ for _____ days prepaid interest
$ _____ for _____

Delmar/Cengage Learning

(continued)

EXHIBIT 16–30

Truth-in-Lending Disclosure Statement (*continued*)

Insurance: Credit life insurance and credit disability insurance are not required to obtain credit, and will not be provided unless I sign and agree to pay the additional cost. No such insurance will be in force until I have completed an application, the insurance company has issued the policy, the effective date of that policy has arrived and the required premium has been paid.

TYPE	PREMIUM	SIGNATURE
Credit Life		I want to apply for Credit Life Insurance
Credit Disability		I want to apply for Disability Insurance
Credit Life & Credit Disability		I want to apply for Credit Life and Disability Insurance

These disclosures are summaries of important provisions of the mortgage loan documents. This form is not a contract itself. The note and the mortgage deed contain the basic contract terms. I understand that the above disclosures do not describe all aspects of the mortgage transaction.

Everyone signing below acknowledges receiving a filled-in copy of this disclosure statement.

_____ _____   _____ _____
DATE   SIGNATURE   DATE   SIGNATURE
                          LENDER'S COPY   HELEN DAVIS

EXHIBIT 16–31

Owner's Affidavit

STATE OF _____)
) ss:
COUNTY OF _____)

The undersigned, being duly sworn, states:

That the undersigned is the fee simple title owner of the real property described on Exhibit "A" attached hereto and incorporated herein by reference (the "Property").

That the lines and corners of the Property are clearly marked and there are no disputes concerning the location of said lines and corners;

That no improvements or repairs have been made or contracted for by the undersigned on the Property during the three (3) months immediately preceding the date of this affidavit, for which there are outstanding bills for labor or services performed or rendered, or for materials supplied or furnished, or incurred in connection with improvements or repairs on the Property, or for the services of architects, surveyors or engineers in connection with improvements or repairs on the Property;

That, except for the matters set forth on Exhibit "B" attached hereto and incorporated herein by reference, the Property is free and clear of all claims, liens and encumbrances, and there is no outstanding indebtedness for or liens against any equipment or fixtures attached to, installed on, incorporated in or located on, or otherwise used in connection with the operation or maintenance of, the Property or the improvements thereon;

That there are no persons or other parties in possession of the Property who have a right or claim to possession extending beyond the date hereof;

That there are no suits, proceedings, judgments, bankruptcies, liens, or executions against the undersigned which affect title to the Property, the improvements thereon or the fixtures attached thereto;

Delmar/Cengage Learning

(*continued*)

EXHIBIT 16–31

Owner's Affidavit
(*continued*)

That the undersigned is making this affidavit with the knowledge that it will be relied upon by lenders, attorneys, and title insurance companies interested in the title to the Property.

Sworn to and subscribed before me this
day of _____, 20____.

_____   _____
Notary Public   HELEN DAVIS
My Commission Expires:

_____
[Notarial Seal]

EXHIBIT "A"

All that tract or parcel of land lying and being in Land Lot 359 of the 18th District of Fulton County, Georgia, being Lot 12 of Bassett Hall Subdivision as per plat recorded of Plat Book 68, page 79, Fulton County, Georgia Records.

EXHIBIT "B"

1. All taxes for the current year.
2. Easement between Sam Turner and Georgia Power Company dated August 6, 1959, recorded at Deed Book 2898, page 25, Fulton County, Georgia Records.
3. Easement between Markam Industries, Inc. and Georgia Power Company dated February 11, 1998 and recorded at Deed Book 5106, page 810, aforesaid records.

EXHIBIT 16-32

Promissory Note

NOTE

_____, 20____   Atlanta_____, Georgia
April 25   20
     [Date]   [City]   [State]

5167 Tilly Mill Road, Atlanta, Georgia 30302
_____
                                   [Property Address]

1. BORROWER'S PROMISE TO PAY

In return for a loan that I have received, I promise to pay U.S. $ __80,000.00__ (this amount is called "Principal"), plus interest, to the order of the Lender. The Lender is __AMERICAN EAGLE MORTGAGE COMPANY__ _____. I will make all payments under this Note in the form of cash, check or money order.

I understand that the Lender may transfer this Note. The Lender or anyone who takes this Note by transfer and who is entitled to receive payments under this Note is called the "Note Holder."

2. INTEREST

Interest will be charged on unpaid principal until the full amount of Principal has been paid. I will pay interest at a yearly rate of __eight (8)__ %.

The interest rate required by this Section 2 is the rate I will pay both before and after any default described in Section 6(B) of this Note.

3. PAYMENTS

(A) **Time and Place of Payments**

I will pay principal and interest by making a payment every month.

I will make my monthly payment on the __1st__ day of each month beginning on __June 1__, 20__. I will make these payments every month until I have paid all of the principal and interest and any other charges described below that I may owe under this Note. Each monthly payment will be applied as of its scheduled due date and will be applied to interest before Principal. If, on __May 1__, 20____, I still owe amounts under this Note, I will pay those amounts in full on that date, which is called the "Maturity Date."

I will make my monthly payments at __ADDRESS OF AMERICAN EAGLE MORTGAGE COMPANY__ _____ or at a different place if required by the Note Holder.

(B) **Amount of Monthly Payments**

My monthly payment will be in the amount of U.S. $ __588.00__ .

4. BORROWER'S RIGHT TO PREPAY

I have the right to make payments of Principal at any time before they are due. A payment of Principal only is known as a "Prepayment." When I make a Prepayment, I will tell the Note Holder in writing that I am doing so. I may not designate a payment as a Prepayment if I have not made all the monthly payments due under the Note.

I may make a full Prepayment or partial Prepayments without paying a Prepayment charge. The Note Holder will use my Prepayments to reduce the amount of Principal that I owe under this Note. However, the Note Holder may apply my Prepayment to the accrued and unpaid interest on the Prepayment amount, before applying my Prepayment to reduce the Principal amount of the Note. If I make a partial Prepayment, there will be no changes in the due date or in the amount of my monthly payment unless the Note Holder agrees in writing to those changes.

5. LOAN CHARGES

If a law, which applies to this loan and which sets maximum loan charges, is finally interpreted so that the interest or other loan charges collected or to be collected in connection with this loan exceed the permitted limits, then: (a) any such loan charge shall be reduced by the amount necessary to reduce the charge to the permitted limit; and (b) any sums already collected from me which exceeded permitted limits will be refunded to me. The Note Holder may choose to make this refund by reducing the Principal I owe under this Note or by making a direct payment to me. If a refund reduces Principal, the reduction will be treated as a partial Prepayment.

MULTISTATE FIXED RATE NOTE—Single Family—Fannie Mae/Freddie Mac UNIFORM INSTRUMENT   **Form 3200**   1/01 *(page 1 of 3 pages)*

(continued)

EXHIBIT 16–32

Promissory Note (*continued*)

6. **BORROWER'S FAILURE TO PAY AS REQUIRED**

   (A) **Late Charge for Overdue Payments**

   If the Note Holder has not received the full amount of any monthly payment by the end of __15__ calendar days after the date it is due, I will pay a late charge to the Note Holder. The amount of the charge will be __4__% of my overdue payment of principal and interest. I will pay this late charge promptly but only once on each late payment.

   (B) **Default**

   If I do not pay the full amount of each monthly payment on the date it is due, I will be in default.

   (C) **Notice of Default**

   If I am in default, the Note Holder may send me a written notice telling me that if I do not pay the overdue amount by a certain date, the Note Holder may require me to pay immediately the full amount of Principal which has not been paid and all the interest that I owe on that amount. That date must be at least 30 days after the date on which the notice is mailed to me or delivered by other means.

   (D) **No Waiver By Note Holder**

   Even if, at a time when I am in default, the Note Holder does not require me to pay immediately in full as described above, the Note Holder will still have the right to do so if I am in default at a later time.

   (E) **Payment of Note Holder's Costs and Expenses**

   If the Note Holder has required me to pay immediately in full as described above, the Note Holder will have the right to be paid back by me for all of its costs and expenses in enforcing this Note to the extent not prohibited by applicable law. Those expenses include, for example, reasonable attorneys' fees.

7. **GIVING OF NOTICES**

   Unless applicable law requires a different method, any notice that must be given to me under this Note will be given by delivering it or by mailing it by first class mail to me at the Property Address above or at a different address if I give the Note Holder a notice of my different address.

   Any notice that must be given to the Note Holder under this Note will be given by delivering it or by mailing it by first class mail to the Note Holder at the address stated in Section 3(A) above or at a different address if I am given a notice of that different address.

8. **OBLIGATIONS OF PERSONS UNDER THIS NOTE**

   If more than one person signs this Note, each person is fully and personally obligated to keep all of the promises made in this Note, including the promise to pay the full amount owed. Any person who is a guarantor, surety or endorser of this Note is also obligated to do these things. Any person who takes over these obligations, including the obligations of a guarantor, surety or endorser of this Note, is also obligated to keep all of the promises made in this Note. The Note Holder may enforce its rights under this Note against each person individually or against all of us together. This means that any one of us may be required to pay all of the amounts owed under this Note.

9. **WAIVERS**

   I and any other person who has obligations under this Note waive the rights of Presentment and Notice of Dishonor. "Presentment" means the right to require the Note Holder to demand payment of amounts due. "Notice of Dishonor" means the right to require the Note Holder to give notice to other persons that amounts due have not been paid.

10. **UNIFORM SECURED NOTE**

   This Note is a uniform instrument with limited variations in some jurisdictions. In addition to the protections given to the Note Holder under this Note, a Mortgage, Deed of Trust, or Security Deed (the "Security Instrument"), dated the same date as this Note, protects the Note Holder from possible losses which might result if I do not keep the promises which I make in this Note. That Security Instrument describes how and under what conditions I may be required to make immediate payment in full of all amounts I owe under this Note. Some of those conditions are described as follows:

   > If all or any part of the Property or any Interest in the Property is sold or transferred (or if Borrower is not a natural person and a beneficial interest in Borrower is sold or transferred) without Lender's prior written consent, Lender may require immediate payment in full of all sums secured by this Security Instrument. However, this option shall not be exercised by Lender if such exercise is prohibited by Applicable Law.

MULTISTATE FIXED RATE NOTE—Single Family—Fannie Mae/Freddie Mac UNIFORM INSTRUMENT   Form 3200   1/01 (*page 2 of 3 pages*)

(continued)

EXHIBIT 16–32

Promissory Note (*continued*)

> If Lender exercises this option, Lender shall give Borrower notice of acceleration. The notice shall provide a period of not less than 30 days from the date the notice is given in accordance with Section 15 within which Borrower must pay all sums secured by this Security Instrument. If Borrower fails to pay these sums prior to the expiration of this period, Lender may invoke any remedies permitted by this Security Instrument without further notice or demand on Borrower.

WITNESS THE HAND(S) AND SEAL(S) OF THE UNDERSIGNED

_____ (Seal)
HELEN DAVIS   - Borrower

_____ (Seal)
                                               - Borrower

_____ (Seal)
                                               - Borrower

[Sign Original Only]

EXHIBIT 16–33

Security Deed

After Recording Return To:

_____

_____

_____

_____

_____ **[Space Above This Line For Recording Data]** _____

SECURITY DEED

DEFINITIONS

Words used in multiple sections of this document are defined below and other words are defined in Sections 3, 11, 13, 18, 20 and 21. Certain rules regarding the usage of words used in this document are also provided in Section 16.

(A) **"Security Instrument"** means this document, which is dated April 25, _____, 20__, together with all Riders to this document.

(B) **"Borrower"** is HELEN DAVIS _____. Borrower is the grantor under this Security Instrument.

(C) **"Lender"** is AMERICAN EAGLE MORTGAGE COMPANY _____. Lender is a _____ organized and existing under the laws of _____ _____. Lender's address is 10 Piedmont Center, Atlanta, _____ Georgia 30017 _____. Lender is the grantee under this Security Instrument.

(D) **"Note"** means the promissory note signed by Borrower and dated April 25, 20__, _____. The Note states that Borrower owes Lender Eighty Thousand and No/100 _____ Dollars (U.S. $ 80,000.00) plus interest. Borrower has promised to pay this debt in regular Periodic Payments and to pay the debt in full not later than May 1, 20__ .

(E) **"Property"** means the property that is described below under the heading "Transfer of Rights in the Property."

(F) **"Loan"** means the debt evidenced by the Note, plus interest, any prepayment charges and late charges due under the Note, and all sums due under this Security Instrument, plus interest.

(G) **"Riders"** means all Riders to this Security Instrument that are executed by Borrower. The following Riders are to be executed by Borrower [check box as applicable]:

☐ Adjustable Rate Rider   ☐ Condominium Rider   ☐ Second Home Rider
☐ Balloon Rider   ☐ Planned Unit Development Rider   ☐ Other(s) [specify] _____
☐ 1-4 Family Rider   ☐ Biweekly Payment Rider

GEORGIA--Single Family--**Fannie Mae/Freddie Mac UNIFORM INSTRUMENT**   **Form 3011** 1/01 *(page 1 of 16 pages)*

(continued)

EXHIBIT 16–33

Security Deed (*continued*)

(H) "Applicable Law" means all controlling applicable federal, state and local statutes, regulations, ordinances and administrative rules and orders (that have the effect of law) as well as all applicable final, non-appealable judicial opinions.

(I) "Community Association Dues, Fees, and Assessments" means all dues, fees, assessments and other charges that are imposed on Borrower or the Property by a condominium association, homeowners association or similar organization.

(J) "Electronic Funds Transfer" means any transfer of funds, other than a transaction originated by check, draft, or similar paper instrument, which is initiated through an electronic terminal, telephonic instrument, computer, or magnetic tape so as to order, instruct, or authorize a financial institution to debit or credit an account. Such term includes, but is not limited to, point-of-sale transfers, automated teller machine transactions, transfers initiated by telephone, wire transfers, and automated clearinghouse transfers.

(K) "Escrow Items" means those items that are described in Section 3.

(L) "Miscellaneous Proceeds" means any compensation, settlement, award of damages, or proceeds paid by any third party (other than insurance proceeds paid under the coverages described in Section 5) for: (i) damage to, or destruction of, the Property; (ii) condemnation or other taking of all or any part of the Property; (iii) conveyance in lieu of condemnation; or (iv) misrepresentations of, or omissions as to, the value and/or condition of the Property.

(M) "Mortgage Insurance" means insurance protecting Lender against the nonpayment of, or default on, the Loan.

(N) "Periodic Payment" means the regularly scheduled amount due for (i) principal and interest under the Note, plus (ii) any amounts under Section 3 of this Security Instrument.

(O) "RESPA" means the Real Estate Settlement Procedures Act (12 U.S.C. §2601 et seq.) and its implementing regulation, Regulation X (24 C.F.R. Part 3500), as they might be amended from time to time, or any additional or successor legislation or regulation that governs the same subject matter. As used in this Security Instrument, "RESPA" refers to all requirements and restrictions that are imposed in regard to a "federally related mortgage loan" even if the Loan does not qualify as a "federally related mortgage loan" under RESPA.

(P) "Successor in Interest of Borrower" means any party that has taken title to the Property, whether or not that party has assumed Borrower's obligations under the Note and/or this Security Instrument.

TRANSFER OF RIGHTS IN THE PROPERTY

This Security Instrument secures to Lender: (i) the repayment of the Loan, and all renewals, extensions and modifications of the Note; and (ii) the performance of Borrower's covenants and agreements under this Security Instrument and the Note. For this purpose, Borrower does hereby grant and convey to Lender and Lender's successors and assigns, with power of sale, the following

GEORGIA--Single Family--Fannie Mae/Freddie Mac UNIFORM INSTRUMENT   **Form 3011   1/01** *(page 2 of 16 pages)*

(continued)

EXHIBIT 16–33

Security Deed (*continued*)

described property located in the _____ of
[Type of Recording Jurisdiction]

_____ :
[Name of Recording Jurisdiction]

All that tract or parcel of land lying and being in Land Lot 359 of the 18th District of Fulton County, Georgia, being Lot 12 of Bassett Hall Subdivision, as per plat recorded in Plat Book 68, Page 79, Fulton County, Georgia Records, being improved property with a house located thereon known as 5167 Tilly Mill Road, Atlanta, Georgia 30302.

which currently has the address of ___5167 Tilly Mill Road,_____
[Street]

___Atlanta_____, Georgia ___30302_____ ("Property Address"):
[City]   [Zip Code]

TO HAVE AND TO HOLD this property unto Lender and Lender's successors and assigns, forever, together with all the improvements now or hereafter erected on the property, and all easements, appurtenances, and fixtures now or hereafter a part of the property. All replacements and additions shall also be covered by this Security Instrument. All of the foregoing is referred to in this Security Instrument as the "Property."

BORROWER COVENANTS that Borrower is lawfully seised of the estate hereby conveyed and has the right to grant and convey the Property and that the Property is unencumbered, except for encumbrances of record. Borrower warrants and will defend generally the title to the Property against all claims and demands, subject to any encumbrances of record.

THIS SECURITY INSTRUMENT combines uniform covenants for national use and non-uniform covenants with limited variations by jurisdiction to constitute a uniform security instrument covering real property.

UNIFORM COVENANTS. Borrower and Lender covenant and agree as follows:
1. Payment of Principal, Interest, Escrow Items, Prepayment Charges, and Late Charges. Borrower shall pay when due the principal of, and interest on, the debt evidenced by the Note and any prepayment charges and late charges due under the Note. Borrower shall also pay funds for Escrow Items pursuant to Section 3. Payments due under the Note and this Security Instrument shall be made in U.S. currency. However, if any check or other instrument received by Lender as payment under the Note or this Security Instrument is returned to Lender unpaid, Lender may require that any or all subsequent payments due under the Note and this Security Instrument be made in one or more of the following forms, as selected by Lender: (a) cash; (b) money order;

GEORGIA--Single Family--Fannie Mae/Freddie Mac UNIFORM INSTRUMENT   Form 3011   1/01 (*page 3 of 16 pages*)

(continued)

EXHIBIT 16–33

Security Deed (*continued*)

(c) certified check, bank check, treasurer's check or cashier's check, provided any such check is drawn upon an institution whose deposits are insured by a federal agency, instrumentality, or entity; or (d) Electronic Funds Transfer.

Payments are deemed received by Lender when received at the location designated in the Note or at such other location as may be designated by Lender in accordance with the notice provisions in Section 15. Lender may return any payment or partial payment if the payment or partial payments are insufficient to bring the Loan current. Lender may accept any payment or partial payment insufficient to bring the Loan current, without waiver of any rights hereunder or prejudice to its rights to refuse such payment or partial payments in the future, but Lender is not obligated to apply such payments at the time such payments are accepted. If each Periodic Payment is applied as of its scheduled due date, then Lender need not pay interest on unapplied funds. Lender may hold such unapplied funds until Borrower makes payment to bring the Loan current. If Borrower does not do so within a reasonable period of time, Lender shall either apply such funds or return them to Borrower. If not applied earlier, such funds will be applied to the outstanding principal balance under the Note immediately prior to foreclosure. No offset or claim which Borrower might have now or in the future against Lender shall relieve Borrower from making payments due under the Note and this Security Instrument or performing the covenants and agreements secured by this Security Instrument.

2. Application of Payments or Proceeds. Except as otherwise described in this Section 2, all payments accepted and applied by Lender shall be applied in the following order of priority: (a) interest due under the Note; (b) principal due under the Note; (c) amounts due under Section 3. Such payments shall be applied to each Periodic Payment in the order in which it became due. Any remaining amounts shall be applied first to late charges, second to any other amounts due under this Security Instrument, and then to reduce the principal balance of the Note.

If Lender receives a payment from Borrower for a delinquent Periodic Payment which includes a sufficient amount to pay any late charge due, the payment may be applied to the delinquent payment and the late charge. If more than one Periodic Payment is outstanding, Lender may apply any payment received from Borrower to the repayment of the Periodic Payments if, and to the extent that, each payment can be paid in full. To the extent that any excess exists after the payment is applied to the full payment of one or more Periodic Payments, such excess may be applied to any late charges due. Voluntary prepayments shall be applied first to any prepayment charges and then as described in the Note.

Any application of payments, insurance proceeds, or Miscellaneous Proceeds to principal due under the Note shall not extend or postpone the due date, or change the amount, of the Periodic Payments.

3. Funds for Escrow Items. Borrower shall pay to Lender on the day Periodic Payments are due under the Note, until the Note is paid in full, a sum (the "Funds") to provide for payment of amounts due for: (a) taxes and assessments and other items which can attain priority over this Security Instrument as a lien or encumbrance on the Property; (b) leasehold payments or ground rents on the Property, if any; (c) premiums for any and all insurance required by Lender under Section 5; and (d) Mortgage Insurance premiums, if any, or any sums payable by Borrower to Lender in lieu of the payment of Mortgage Insurance premiums in accordance with the provisions of Section 10. These items are called "Escrow Items." At origination or at any time during the term of the Loan, Lender may require that Community Association Dues, Fees, and Assessments, if any,

GEORGIA--Single Family--**Fannie Mae/Freddie Mac UNIFORM INSTRUMENT** Form 3011 1/01 *(page 4 of 16 pages)*

EXHIBIT 16-33

Security Deed (*continued*)

be escrowed by Borrower, and such dues, fees and assessments shall be an Escrow Item. Borrower shall promptly furnish to Lender all notices of amounts to be paid under this Section. Borrower shall pay Lender the Funds for Escrow Items unless Lender waives Borrower's obligation to pay the Funds for any or all Escrow Items. Lender may waive Borrower's obligation to pay to Lender Funds for any or all Escrow Items at any time. Any such waiver may only be in writing. In the event of such waiver, Borrower shall pay directly, when and where payable, the amounts due for any Escrow Items for which payment of Funds has been waived by Lender and, if Lender requires, shall furnish to Lender receipts evidencing such payment within such time period as Lender may require. Borrower's obligation to make such payments and to provide receipts shall for all purposes be deemed to be a covenant and agreement contained in this Security Instrument, as the phrase "covenant and agreement" is used in Section 9. If Borrower is obligated to pay Escrow Items directly, pursuant to a waiver, and Borrower fails to pay the amount due for an Escrow Item, Lender may exercise its rights under Section 9 and pay such amount and Borrower shall then be obligated under Section 9 to repay to Lender any such amount. Lender may revoke the waiver as to any or all Escrow Items at any time by a notice given in accordance with Section 15 and, upon such revocation, Borrower shall pay to Lender all Funds, and in such amounts, that are then required under this Section 3.

Lender may, at any time, collect and hold Funds in an amount (a) sufficient to permit Lender to apply the Funds at the time specified under RESPA, and (b) not to exceed the maximum amount a lender can require under RESPA. Lender shall estimate the amount of Funds due on the basis of current data and reasonable estimates of expenditures of future Escrow Items or otherwise in accordance with Applicable Law.

The Funds shall be held in an institution whose deposits are insured by a federal agency, instrumentality, or entity (including Lender, if Lender is an institution whose deposits are so insured) or in any Federal Home Loan Bank. Lender shall apply the Funds to pay the Escrow Items no later than the time specified under RESPA. Lender shall not charge Borrower for holding and applying the Funds, annually analyzing the escrow account, or verifying the Escrow Items, unless Lender pays Borrower interest on the Funds and Applicable Law permits Lender to make such a charge. Unless an agreement is made in writing or Applicable Law requires interest to be paid on the Funds, Lender shall not be required to pay Borrower any interest or earnings on the Funds. Borrower and Lender can agree in writing, however, that interest shall be paid on the Funds. Lender shall give to Borrower, without charge, an annual accounting of the Funds as required by RESPA.

If there is a surplus of Funds held in escrow, as defined under RESPA, Lender shall account to Borrower for the excess funds in accordance with RESPA. If there is a shortage of Funds held in escrow, as defined under RESPA, Lender shall notify Borrower as required by RESPA, and Borrower shall pay to Lender the amount necessary to make up the shortage in accordance with RESPA, but in no more than 12 monthly payments. If there is a deficiency of Funds held in escrow, as defined under RESPA, Lender shall notify Borrower as required by RESPA, and Borrower shall pay to Lender the amount necessary to make up the deficiency in accordance with RESPA, but in no more than 12 monthly payments.

Upon payment in full of all sums secured by this Security Instrument, Lender shall promptly refund to Borrower any Funds held by Lender.

GEORGIA--Single Family--**Fannie Mae/Freddie Mac UNIFORM INSTRUMENT**   Form 3011   1/01 *(page 5 of 16 pages)*

(continued)

EXHIBIT 16–33

Security Deed (*continued*)

4. Charges; Liens. Borrower shall pay all taxes, assessments, charges, fines, and impositions attributable to the Property which can attain priority over this Security Instrument, leasehold payments or ground rents on the Property, if any, and Community Association Dues, Fees, and Assessments, if any. To the extent that these items are Escrow Items, Borrower shall pay them in the manner provided in Section 3.

Borrower shall promptly discharge any lien which has priority over this Security Instrument unless Borrower: (a) agrees in writing to the payment of the obligation secured by the lien in a manner acceptable to Lender, but only so long as Borrower is performing such agreement; (b) contests the lien in good faith by, or defends against enforcement of the lien in, legal proceedings which in Lender's opinion operate to prevent the enforcement of the lien while those proceedings are pending, but only until such proceedings are concluded; or (c) secures from the holder of the lien an agreement satisfactory to Lender subordinating the lien to this Security Instrument. If Lender determines that any part of the Property is subject to a lien which can attain priority over this Security Instrument, Lender may give Borrower a notice identifying the lien. Within 10 days of the date on which that notice is given, Borrower shall satisfy the lien or take one or more of the actions set forth above in this Section 4.

Lender may require Borrower to pay a one-time charge for a real estate tax verification and/or reporting service used by Lender in connection with this Loan.

5. Property Insurance. Borrower shall keep the improvements now existing or hereafter erected on the Property insured against loss by fire, hazards included within the term "extended coverage," and any other hazards including, but not limited to, earthquakes and floods, for which Lender requires insurance. This insurance shall be maintained in the amounts (including deductible levels) and for the periods that Lender requires. What Lender requires pursuant to the preceding sentences can change during the term of the Loan. The insurance carrier providing the insurance shall be chosen by Borrower subject to Lender's right to disapprove Borrower's choice, which right shall not be exercised unreasonably. Lender may require Borrower to pay, in connection with this Loan, either: (a) a one-time charge for flood zone determination, certification and tracking services; or (b) a one-time charge for flood zone determination and certification services and subsequent charges each time remappings or similar changes occur which reasonably might affect such determination or certification. Borrower shall also be responsible for the payment of any fees imposed by the Federal Emergency Management Agency in connection with the review of any flood zone determination resulting from an objection by Borrower.

If Borrower fails to maintain any of the coverages described above, Lender may obtain insurance coverage, at Lender's option and Borrower's expense. Lender is under no obligation to purchase any particular type or amount of coverage. Therefore, such coverage shall cover Lender, but might or might not protect Borrower, Borrower's equity in the Property, or the contents of the Property, against any risk, hazard or liability and might provide greater or lesser coverage than was previously in effect. Borrower acknowledges that the cost of the insurance coverage so obtained might significantly exceed the cost of insurance that Borrower could have obtained. Any amounts disbursed by Lender under this Section 5 shall become additional debt of Borrower secured by this Security Instrument. These amounts shall bear interest at the Note rate from the date of disbursement and shall be payable, with such interest, upon notice from Lender to Borrower requesting payment.

GEORGIA--Single Family--Fannie Mae/Freddie Mac UNIFORM INSTRUMENT   Form 3011   1/01 *(page 6 of 16 pages)*

(continued)

EXHIBIT 16–33

Security Deed (*continued*)

All insurance policies required by Lender and renewals of such policies shall be subject to Lender's right to disapprove such policies, shall include a standard mortgage clause, and shall name Lender as mortgagee and/or as an additional loss payee. Lender shall have the right to hold the policies and renewal certificates. If Lender requires, Borrower shall promptly give to Lender all receipts of paid premiums and renewal notices. If Borrower obtains any form of insurance coverage, not otherwise required by Lender, for damage to, or destruction of, the Property, such policy shall include a standard mortgage clause and shall name Lender as mortgagee and/or as an additional loss payee.

In the event of loss, Borrower shall give prompt notice to the insurance carrier and Lender. Lender may make proof of loss if not made promptly by Borrower. Unless Lender and Borrower otherwise agree in writing, any insurance proceeds, whether or not the underlying insurance was required by Lender, shall be applied to restoration or repair of the Property, if the restoration or repair is economically feasible and Lender's security is not lessened. During such repair and restoration period, Lender shall have the right to hold such insurance proceeds until Lender has had an opportunity to inspect such Property to ensure the work has been completed to Lender's satisfaction, provided that such inspection shall be undertaken promptly. Lender may disburse proceeds for the repairs and restoration in a single payment or in a series of progress payments as the work is completed. Unless an agreement is made in writing or Applicable Law requires interest to be paid on such insurance proceeds, Lender shall not be required to pay Borrower any interest or earnings on such proceeds. Fees for public adjusters, or other third parties, retained by Borrower shall not be paid out of the insurance proceeds and shall be the sole obligation of Borrower. If the restoration or repair is not economically feasible or Lender's security would be lessened, the insurance proceeds shall be applied to the sums secured by this Security Instrument, whether or not then due, with the excess, if any, paid to Borrower. Such insurance proceeds shall be applied in the order provided for in Section 2.

If Borrower abandons the Property, Lender may file, negotiate and settle any available insurance claim and related matters. If Borrower does not respond within 30 days to a notice from Lender that the insurance carrier has offered to settle a claim, then Lender may negotiate and settle the claim. The 30-day period will begin when the notice is given. In either event, or if Lender acquires the Property under Section 22 or otherwise, Borrower hereby assigns to Lender (a) Borrower's rights to any insurance proceeds in an amount not to exceed the amounts unpaid under the Note or this Security Instrument, and (b) any other of Borrower's rights (other than the right to any refund of unearned premiums paid by Borrower) under all insurance policies covering the Property, insofar as such rights are applicable to the coverage of the Property. Lender may use the insurance proceeds either to repair or restore the Property or to pay amounts unpaid under the Note or this Security Instrument, whether or not then due.

6. Occupancy. Borrower shall occupy, establish, and use the Property as Borrower's principal residence within 60 days after the execution of this Security Instrument and shall continue to occupy the Property as Borrower's principal residence for at least one year after the date of occupancy, unless Lender otherwise agrees in writing, which consent shall not be unreasonably withheld, or unless extenuating circumstances exist which are beyond Borrower's control.

7. Preservation, Maintenance and Protection of the Property; Inspections. Borrower shall not destroy, damage or impair the Property, allow the Property to deteriorate or commit waste

GEORGIA--Single Family--**Fannie Mae/Freddie Mac UNIFORM INSTRUMENT**   Form 3011   1/01 *(page 7 of 16 pages)*

(continued)

EXHIBIT 16–33

Security Deed (*continued*)

on the Property. Whether or not Borrower is residing in the Property, Borrower shall maintain the Property in order to prevent the Property from deteriorating or decreasing in value due to its condition. Unless it is determined pursuant to Section 5 that repair or restoration is not economically feasible, Borrower shall promptly repair the Property if damaged to avoid further deterioration or damage. If insurance or condemnation proceeds are paid in connection with damage to, or the taking of, the Property, Borrower shall be responsible for repairing or restoring the Property only if Lender has released proceeds for such purposes. Lender may disburse proceeds for the repairs and restoration in a single payment or in a series of progress payments as the work is completed. If the insurance or condemnation proceeds are not sufficient to repair or restore the Property, Borrower is not relieved of Borrower's obligation for the completion of such repair or restoration.

Lender or its agent may make reasonable entries upon and inspections of the Property. If it has reasonable cause, Lender may inspect the interior of the improvements on the Property. Lender shall give Borrower notice at the time of or prior to such an interior inspection specifying such reasonable cause.

8. Borrower's Loan Application. Borrower shall be in default if, during the Loan application process, Borrower or any persons or entities acting at the direction of Borrower or with Borrower's knowledge or consent gave materially false, misleading, or inaccurate information or statements to Lender (or failed to provide Lender with material information) in connection with the Loan. Material representations include, but are not limited to, representations concerning Borrower's occupancy of the Property as Borrower's principal residence.

9. Protection of Lender's Interest in the Property and Rights Under this Security Instrument. If (a) Borrower fails to perform the covenants and agreements contained in this Security Instrument, (b) there is a legal proceeding that might significantly affect Lender's interest in the Property and/or rights under this Security Instrument (such as a proceeding in bankruptcy, probate, for condemnation or forfeiture, for enforcement of a lien which may attain priority over this Security Instrument or to enforce laws or regulations), or (c) Borrower has abandoned the Property, then Lender may do and pay for whatever is reasonable or appropriate to protect Lender's interest in the Property and rights under this Security Instrument, including protecting and/or assessing the value of the Property, and securing and/or repairing the Property (as set forth below). Lender's actions can include, but are not limited to: (a) paying any sums secured by a lien which has priority over this Security Instrument; (b) appearing in court; and (c) paying reasonable attorneys' fees to protect its interest in the Property and/or rights under this Security Instrument, including its secured position in a bankruptcy proceeding. Securing the Property includes, but is not limited to, making repairs, replacing doors and windows, draining water from pipes, and eliminating building or other code violations or dangerous conditions. Although Lender may take action under this Section 9, Lender does not have to do so and is not under any duty or obligation to do so. It is agreed that Lender incurs no liability for not taking any or all actions authorized under this Section 9.

Any amounts disbursed by Lender under this Section 9 shall become additional debt of Borrower secured by this Security Instrument. These amounts shall bear interest at the Note rate from the date of disbursement and shall be payable, with such interest, upon notice from Lender to Borrower requesting payment.

GEORGIA--Single Family--Fannie Mae/Freddie Mac UNIFORM INSTRUMENT   **Form 3011**   **1/01** *(page 8 of 16 pages)*

(continued)

EXHIBIT 16–33

Security Deed (*continued*)

If this Security Instrument is on a leasehold, Borrower shall comply with all the provisions of the lease. If Borrower acquires fee title to the Property, the leasehold and the fee title shall not merge unless Lender agrees to the merger in writing.

10. Mortgage Insurance. If Lender required Mortgage Insurance as a condition of making the Loan, Borrower shall pay the premiums required to maintain the Mortgage Insurance in effect. If, for any reason, the Mortgage Insurance coverage required by Lender ceases to be available from the mortgage insurer that previously provided such insurance and Borrower was required to make separately designated payments toward the premiums for Mortgage Insurance, Borrower shall pay the premiums required to obtain coverage substantially equivalent to the Mortgage Insurance previously in effect, at a cost substantially equivalent to the cost to Borrower of the Mortgage Insurance previously in effect, from an alternate mortgage insurer selected by Lender. If substantially equivalent Mortgage Insurance coverage is not available, Borrower shall continue to pay to Lender the amount of the separately designated payments that were due when the insurance coverage ceased to be in effect. Lender will accept, use and retain these payments as a non-refundable loss reserve in lieu of Mortgage Insurance. Such loss reserve shall be non-refundable, notwithstanding the fact that the Loan is ultimately paid in full, and Lender shall not be required to pay Borrower any interest or earnings on such loss reserve. Lender can no longer require loss reserve payments if Mortgage Insurance coverage (in the amount and for the period that Lender requires) provided by an insurer selected by Lender again becomes available, is obtained, and Lender requires separately designated payments toward the premiums for Mortgage Insurance. If Lender required Mortgage Insurance as a condition of making the Loan and Borrower was required to make separately designated payments toward the premiums for Mortgage Insurance, Borrower shall pay the premiums required to maintain Mortgage Insurance in effect, or to provide a non-refundable loss reserve, until Lender's requirement for Mortgage Insurance ends in accordance with any written agreement between Borrower and Lender providing for such termination or until termination is required by Applicable Law. Nothing in this Section 10 affects Borrower's obligation to pay interest at the rate provided in the Note.

Mortgage Insurance reimburses Lender (or any entity that purchases the Note) for certain losses it may incur if Borrower does not repay the Loan as agreed. Borrower is not a party to the Mortgage Insurance.

Mortgage insurers evaluate their total risk on all such insurance in force from time to time, and may enter into agreements with other parties that share or modify their risk, or reduce losses. These agreements are on terms and conditions that are satisfactory to the mortgage insurer and the other party (or parties) to these agreements. These agreements may require the mortgage insurer to make payments using any source of funds that the mortgage insurer may have available (which may include funds obtained from Mortgage Insurance premiums).

As a result of these agreements, Lender, any purchaser of the Note, another insurer, any reinsurer, any other entity, or any affiliate of any of the foregoing, may receive (directly or indirectly) amounts that derive from (or might be characterized as) a portion of Borrower's payments for Mortgage Insurance, in exchange for sharing or modifying the mortgage insurer's risk, or reducing losses. If such agreement provides that an affiliate of Lender takes a share of the insurer's risk in exchange for a share of the premiums paid to the insurer, the arrangement is often termed "captive reinsurance." Further:

GEORGIA--Single Family--**Fannie Mae/Freddie Mac UNIFORM INSTRUMENT**   **Form 3011**   1/01 (*page 9 of 16 pages*)

(*continued*)

EXHIBIT 16–33

Security Deed (*continued*)

(a) Any such agreements will not affect the amounts that Borrower has agreed to pay for Mortgage Insurance, or any other terms of the Loan. Such agreements will not increase the amount Borrower will owe for Mortgage Insurance, and they will not entitle Borrower to any refund.

(b) Any such agreements will not affect the rights Borrower has – if any – with respect to the Mortgage Insurance under the Homeowners Protection Act of 1998 or any other law. These rights may include the right to receive certain disclosures, to request and obtain cancellation of the Mortgage Insurance, to have the Mortgage Insurance terminated automatically, and/or to receive a refund of any Mortgage Insurance premiums that were unearned at the time of such cancellation or termination.

11. **Assignment of Miscellaneous Proceeds; Forfeiture.** All Miscellaneous Proceeds are hereby assigned to and shall be paid to Lender.

If the Property is damaged, such Miscellaneous Proceeds shall be applied to restoration or repair of the Property, if the restoration or repair is economically feasible and Lender's security is not lessened. During such repair and restoration period, Lender shall have the right to hold such Miscellaneous Proceeds until Lender has had an opportunity to inspect such Property to ensure the work has been completed to Lender's satisfaction, provided that such inspection shall be undertaken promptly. Lender may pay for the repairs and restoration in a single disbursement or in a series of progress payments as the work is completed. Unless an agreement is made in writing or Applicable Law requires interest to be paid on such Miscellaneous Proceeds, Lender shall not be required to pay Borrower any interest or earnings on such Miscellaneous Proceeds. If the restoration or repair is not economically feasible or Lender's security would be lessened, the Miscellaneous Proceeds shall be applied to the sums secured by this Security Instrument, whether or not then due, with the excess, if any, paid to Borrower. Such Miscellaneous Proceeds shall be applied in the order provided for in Section 2.

In the event of a total taking, destruction, or loss in value of the Property, the Miscellaneous Proceeds shall be applied to the sums secured by this Security Instrument, whether or not then due, with the excess, if any, paid to Borrower.

In the event of a partial taking, destruction, or loss in value of the Property in which the fair market value of the Property immediately before the partial taking, destruction, or loss in value is equal to or greater than the amount of the sums secured by this Security Instrument immediately before the partial taking, destruction, or loss in value, unless Borrower and Lender otherwise agree in writing, the sums secured by this Security Instrument shall be reduced by the amount of the Miscellaneous Proceeds multiplied by the following fraction: (a) the total amount of the sums secured immediately before the partial taking, destruction, or loss in value divided by (b) the fair market value of the Property immediately before the partial taking, destruction, or loss in value. Any balance shall be paid to Borrower.

In the event of a partial taking, destruction, or loss in value of the Property in which the fair market value of the Property immediately before the partial taking, destruction, or loss in value is less than the amount of the sums secured immediately before the partial taking, destruction, or loss in value, unless Borrower and Lender otherwise agree in writing, the Miscellaneous Proceeds shall be applied to the sums secured by this Security Instrument whether or not the sums are then due.

If the Property is abandoned by Borrower, or if, after notice by Lender to Borrower that the Opposing Party (as defined in the next sentence) offers to make an award to settle a claim for

GEORGIA--Single Family--Fannie Mae/Freddie Mac UNIFORM INSTRUMENT   Form 3011   1/01 *(page 10 of 16 pages)*

(continued)

EXHIBIT 16–33

Security Deed (*continued*)

damages, Borrower fails to respond to Lender within 30 days after the date the notice is given, Lender is authorized to collect and apply the Miscellaneous Proceeds either to restoration or repair of the Property or to the sums secured by this Security Instrument, whether or not then due. "Opposing Party" means the third party that owes Borrower Miscellaneous Proceeds or the party against whom Borrower has a right of action in regard to Miscellaneous Proceeds.

Borrower shall be in default if any action or proceeding, whether civil or criminal, is begun that, in Lender's judgment, could result in forfeiture of the Property or other material impairment of Lender's interest in the Property or rights under this Security Instrument. Borrower can cure such a default and, if acceleration has occurred, reinstate as provided in Section 19, by causing the action or proceeding to be dismissed with a ruling that, in Lender's judgment, precludes forfeiture of the Property or other material impairment of Lender's interest in the Property or rights under this Security Instrument. The proceeds of any award or claim for damages that are attributable to the impairment of Lender's interest in the Property are hereby assigned and shall be paid to Lender.

All Miscellaneous Proceeds that are not applied to restoration or repair of the Property shall be applied in the order provided for in Section 2.

12. Borrower Not Released; Forbearance By Lender Not a Waiver. Extension of the time for payment or modification of amortization of the sums secured by this Security Instrument granted by Lender to Borrower or any Successor in Interest of Borrower shall not operate to release the liability of Borrower or any Successors in Interest of Borrower. Lender shall not be required to commence proceedings against any Successor in Interest of Borrower or to refuse to extend time for payment or otherwise modify amortization of the sums secured by this Security Instrument by reason of any demand made by the original Borrower or any Successors in Interest of Borrower. Any forbearance by Lender in exercising any right or remedy including, without limitation, Lender's acceptance of payments from third persons, entities or Successors in Interest of Borrower or in amounts less than the amount then due, shall not be a waiver of or preclude the exercise of any right or remedy.

13. Joint and Several Liability; Co-signers; Successors and Assigns Bound. Borrower covenants and agrees that Borrower's obligations and liability shall be joint and several. However, any Borrower who co-signs this Security Instrument but does not execute the Note (a "co-signer"): (a) is co-signing this Security Instrument only to mortgage, grant and convey the co-signer's interest in the Property under the terms of this Security Instrument; (b) is not personally obligated to pay the sums secured by this Security Instrument; and (c) agrees that Lender and any other Borrower can agree to extend, modify, forbear or make any accommodations with regard to the terms of this Security Instrument or the Note without the co-signer's consent.

Subject to the provisions of Section 18, any Successor in Interest of Borrower who assumes Borrower's obligations under this Security Instrument in writing, and is approved by Lender, shall obtain all of Borrower's rights and benefits under this Security Instrument. Borrower shall not be released from Borrower's obligations and liability under this Security Instrument unless Lender agrees to such release in writing. The covenants and agreements of this Security Instrument shall bind (except as provided in Section 20) and benefit the successors and assigns of Lender.

14. Loan Charges. Lender may charge Borrower fees for services performed in connection with Borrower's default, for the purpose of protecting Lender's interest in the Property and rights under this Security Instrument, including, but not limited to, attorneys' fees, property inspection and valuation fees. In regard to any other fees, the absence of express authority in this Security

GEORGIA--Single Family--Fannie Mae/Freddie Mac UNIFORM INSTRUMENT   Form 3011   1/01 (*page 11 of 16 pages*)

(continued)

EXHIBIT 16–33

Security Deed (*continued*)

Instrument to charge a specific fee to Borrower shall not be construed as a prohibition on the charging of such fee. Lender may not charge fees that are expressly prohibited by this Security Instrument or by Applicable Law.

If the Loan is subject to a law which sets maximum loan charges, and that law is finally interpreted so that the interest or other loan charges collected or to be collected in connection with the Loan exceed the permitted limits, then: (a) any such loan charge shall be reduced by the amount necessary to reduce the charge to the permitted limit; and (b) any sums already collected from Borrower which exceeded permitted limits will be refunded to Borrower. Lender may choose to make this refund by reducing the principal owed under the Note or by making a direct payment to Borrower. If a refund reduces principal, the reduction will be treated as a partial prepayment without any prepayment charge (whether or not a prepayment charge is provided for under the Note). Borrower's acceptance of any such refund made by direct payment to Borrower will constitute a waiver of any right of action Borrower might have arising out of such overcharge.

15. Notices. All notices given by Borrower or Lender in connection with this Security Instrument must be in writing. Any notice to Borrower in connection with this Security Instrument shall be deemed to have been given to Borrower when mailed by first class mail or when actually delivered to Borrower's notice address if sent by other means. Notice to any one Borrower shall constitute notice to all Borrowers unless Applicable Law expressly requires otherwise. The notice address shall be the Property Address unless Borrower has designated a substitute notice address by notice to Lender. Borrower shall promptly notify Lender of Borrower's change of address. If Lender specifies a procedure for reporting Borrower's change of address, then Borrower shall only report a change of address through that specified procedure. There may be only one designated notice address under this Security Instrument at any one time. Any notice to Lender shall be given by delivering it or by mailing it by first class mail to Lender's address stated herein unless Lender has designated another address by notice to Borrower. Any notice in connection with this Security Instrument shall not be deemed to have been given to Lender until actually received by Lender. If any notice required by this Security Instrument is also required under Applicable Law, the Applicable Law requirement will satisfy the corresponding requirement under this Security Instrument.

16. Governing Law; Severability; Rules of Construction. This Security Instrument shall be governed by federal law and the law of the jurisdiction in which the Property is located. All rights and obligations contained in this Security Instrument are subject to any requirements and limitations of Applicable Law. Applicable Law might explicitly or implicitly allow the parties to agree by contract or it might be silent, but such silence shall not be construed as a prohibition against agreement by contract. In the event that any provision or clause of this Security Instrument or the Note conflicts with Applicable Law, such conflict shall not affect other provisions of this Security Instrument or the Note which can be given effect without the conflicting provision.

As used in this Security Instrument: (a) words of the masculine gender shall mean and include corresponding neuter words or words of the feminine gender; (b) words in the singular shall mean and include the plural and vice versa; and (c) the word "may" gives sole discretion without any obligation to take any action.

17. Borrower's Copy. Borrower shall be given one copy of the Note and of this Security Instrument.

GEORGIA--Single Family--Fannie Mae/Freddie Mac UNIFORM INSTRUMENT   Form 3011   1/01 *(page 12 of 16 pages)*

EXHIBIT 16–33

Security Deed (*continued*)

18. **Transfer of the Property or a Beneficial Interest in Borrower.** As used in this Section 18, "Interest in the Property" means any legal or beneficial interest in the Property, including, but not limited to, those beneficial interests transferred in a bond for deed, contract for deed, installment sales contract or escrow agreement, the intent of which is the transfer of title by Borrower at a future date to a purchaser.

If all or any part of the Property or any Interest in the Property is sold or transferred (or if Borrower is not a natural person and a beneficial interest in Borrower is sold or transferred) without Lender's prior written consent, Lender may require immediate payment in full of all sums secured by this Security Instrument. However, this option shall not be exercised by Lender if such exercise is prohibited by Applicable Law.

If Lender exercises this option, Lender shall give Borrower notice of acceleration. The notice shall provide a period of not less than 30 days from the date the notice is given in accordance with Section 15 within which Borrower must pay all sums secured by this Security Instrument. If Borrower fails to pay these sums prior to the expiration of this period, Lender may invoke any remedies permitted by this Security Instrument without further notice or demand on Borrower.

19. **Borrower's Right to Reinstate After Acceleration.** If Borrower meets certain conditions, Borrower shall have the right to have enforcement of this Security Instrument discontinued at any time prior to the earliest of: (a) five days before sale of the Property pursuant to any power of sale contained in this Security Instrument; (b) such other period as Applicable Law might specify for the termination of Borrower's right to reinstate; or (c) entry of a judgment enforcing this Security Instrument. Those conditions are that Borrower: (a) pays Lender all sums which then would be due under this Security Instrument and the Note as if no acceleration had occurred; (b) cures any default of any other covenants or agreements; (c) pays all expenses incurred in enforcing this Security Instrument, including, but not limited to, reasonable attorneys' fees, property inspection and valuation fees, and other fees incurred for the purpose of protecting Lender's interest in the Property and rights under this Security Instrument; and (d) takes such action as Lender may reasonably require to assure that Lender's interest in the Property and rights under this Security Instrument, and Borrower's obligation to pay the sums secured by this Security Instrument, shall continue unchanged. Lender may require that Borrower pay such reinstatement sums and expenses in one or more of the following forms, as selected by Lender: (a) cash; (b) money order; (c) certified check, bank check, treasurer's check or cashier's check, provided any such check is drawn upon an institution whose deposits are insured by a federal agency, instrumentality or entity; or (d) Electronic Funds Transfer. Upon reinstatement by Borrower, this Security Instrument and obligations secured hereby shall remain fully effective as if no acceleration had occurred. However, this right to reinstate shall not apply in the case of acceleration under Section 18.

20. **Sale of Note; Change of Loan Servicer; Notice of Grievance.** The Note or a partial interest in the Note (together with this Security Instrument) can be sold one or more times without prior notice to Borrower. A sale might result in a change in the entity (known as the "Loan Servicer") that collects Periodic Payments due under the Note and this Security Instrument and performs other mortgage loan servicing obligations under the Note, this Security Instrument, and Applicable Law. There also might be one or more changes of the Loan Servicer unrelated to a sale of the Note. If there is a change of the Loan Servicer, Borrower will be given written notice of the change which will state the name and address of the new Loan Servicer, the address to which payments should be made and any other information RESPA requires in connection with a notice

GEORGIA--Single Family--Fannie Mae/Freddie Mac **UNIFORM INSTRUMENT**   Form 3011   1/01 *(page 13 of 16 pages)*

(continued)

EXHIBIT 16–33

Security Deed (*continued*)

of transfer of servicing. If the Note is sold and thereafter the Loan is serviced by a Loan Servicer other than the purchaser of the Note, the mortgage loan servicing obligations to Borrower will remain with the Loan Servicer or be transferred to a successor Loan Servicer and are not assumed by the Note purchaser unless otherwise provided by the Note purchaser.

Neither Borrower nor Lender may commence, join, or be joined to any judicial action (as either an individual litigant or the member of a class) that arises from the other party's actions pursuant to this Security Instrument or that alleges that the other party has breached any provision of, or any duty owed by reason of, this Security Instrument, until such Borrower or Lender has notified the other party (with such notice given in compliance with the requirements of Section 15) of such alleged breach and afforded the other party hereto a reasonable period after the giving of such notice to take corrective action. If Applicable Law provides a time period which must elapse before certain action can be taken, that time period will be deemed to be reasonable for purposes of this paragraph. The notice of acceleration and opportunity to cure given to Borrower pursuant to Section 22 and the notice of acceleration given to Borrower pursuant to Section 18 shall be deemed to satisfy the notice and opportunity to take corrective action provisions of this Section 20.

21. Hazardous Substances. As used in this Section 21: (a) "Hazardous Substances" are those substances defined as toxic or hazardous substances, pollutants, or wastes by Environmental Law and the following substances: gasoline, kerosene, other flammable or toxic petroleum products, toxic pesticides and herbicides, volatile solvents, materials containing asbestos or formaldehyde, and radioactive materials; (b) "Environmental Law" means federal laws and laws of the jurisdiction where the Property is located that relate to health, safety or environmental protection; (c) "Environmental Cleanup" includes any response action, remedial action, or removal action, as defined in Environmental Law; and (d) an "Environmental Condition" means a condition that can cause, contribute to, or otherwise trigger an Environmental Cleanup.

Borrower shall not cause or permit the presence, use, disposal, storage, or release of any Hazardous Substances, or threaten to release any Hazardous Substances, on or in the Property. Borrower shall not do, nor allow anyone else to do, anything affecting the Property (a) that is in violation of any Environmental Law, (b) which creates an Environmental Condition, or (c) which, due to the presence, use, or release of a Hazardous Substance, creates a condition that adversely affects the value of the Property. The preceding two sentences shall not apply to the presence, use, or storage on the Property of small quantities of Hazardous Substances that are generally recognized to be appropriate to normal residential uses and to maintenance of the Property (including, but not limited to, hazardous substances in consumer products).

Borrower shall promptly give Lender written notice of (a) any investigation, claim, demand, lawsuit or other action by any governmental or regulatory agency or private party involving the Property and any Hazardous Substance or Environmental Law of which Borrower has actual knowledge, (b) any Environmental Condition, including but not limited to, any spilling, leaking, discharge, release or threat of release of any Hazardous Substance, and (c) any condition caused by the presence, use or release of a Hazardous Substance which adversely affects the value of the Property. If Borrower learns, or is notified by any governmental or regulatory authority, or any private party, that any removal or other remediation of any Hazardous Substance affecting the Property is necessary, Borrower shall promptly take all necessary remedial actions in accordance with Environmental Law. Nothing herein shall create any obligation on Lender for an Environmental Cleanup.

GEORGIA--Single Family--Fannie Mae/Freddie Mac UNIFORM INSTRUMENT   Form 3011   1/01 *(page 14 of 16 pages)*

EXHIBIT 16–33

Security Deed (*continued*)

NON-UNIFORM COVENANTS. Borrower and Lender further covenant and agree as follows:

22. Acceleration; Remedies. Lender shall give notice to Borrower prior to acceleration following Borrower's breach of any covenant or agreement in this Security Instrument (but not prior to acceleration under Section 18 unless Applicable Law provides otherwise). The notice shall specify: (a) the default; (b) the action required to cure the default; (c) a date, not less than 30 days from the date the notice is given to Borrower, by which the default must be cured; and (d) that failure to cure the default on or before the date specified in the notice may result in acceleration of the sums secured by this Security Instrument and sale of the Property. The notice shall further inform Borrower of the right to reinstate after acceleration and the right to bring a court action to assert the non-existence of a default or any other defense of Borrower to acceleration and sale. If the default is not cured on or before the date specified in the notice, Lender at its option may require immediate payment in full of all sums secured by this Security Instrument without further demand and may invoke the power of sale granted by Borrower and any other remedies permitted by Applicable Law. Borrower appoints Lender the agent and attorney-in-fact for Borrower to exercise the power of sale. Lender shall be entitled to collect all expenses incurred in pursuing the remedies provided in this Section 22, including, but not limited to, reasonable attorneys' fees and costs of title evidence.

If Lender invokes the power of sale, Lender shall give a copy of a notice of sale by public advertisement for the time and in the manner prescribed by Applicable Law. Lender, without further demand on Borrower, shall sell the Property at public auction to the highest bidder at the time and place and under the terms designated in the notice of sale in one or more parcels and in any order Lender determines. Lender or its designee may purchase the Property at any sale.

Lender shall convey to the purchaser indefeasible title to the Property, and Borrower hereby appoints Lender Borrower's agent and attorney-in-fact to make such conveyance. The recitals in the Lender's deed shall be prima facie evidence of the truth of the statements made therein. Borrower covenants and agrees that Lender shall apply the proceeds of the sale in the following order: (a) to all expenses of the sale, including, but not limited to, reasonable attorneys' fees; (b) to all sums secured by this Security Instrument; and (c) any excess to the person or persons legally entitled to it. The power and agency granted are coupled with an interest, are irrevocable by death or otherwise and are cumulative to the remedies for collection of debt as provided by Applicable Law.

If the Property is sold pursuant to this Section 22, Borrower, or any person holding possession of the Property through Borrower, shall immediately surrender possession of the Property to the purchaser at the sale. If possession is not surrendered, Borrower or such person shall be a tenant holding over and may be dispossessed in accordance with Applicable Law.

23. Release. Upon payment of all sums secured by this Security Instrument, Lender shall cancel this Security Instrument. Borrower shall pay any recordation costs. Lender may charge Borrower a fee for releasing this Security Instrument, but only if the fee is paid to a third party for services rendered and the charging of the fee is permitted under Applicable Law.

24. Waiver of Homestead. Borrower waives all rights of homestead exemption in the Property.

GEORGIA--Single Family--Fannie Mae/Freddie Mac UNIFORM INSTRUMENT   Form 3011   1/01 (*page 15 of 16 pages*)

(*continued*)

EXHIBIT 16–33

Security Deed (*continued*)

25. Assumption Not a Novation. Lender's acceptance of an assumption of the obligations of this Security Instrument and the Note, and any release of Borrower in connection therewith, shall not constitute a novation.

26. Security Deed. This conveyance is to be construed under the existing laws of the State of Georgia as a deed passing title, and not as a mortgage, and is intended to secure the payment of all sums secured hereby.

BORROWER ACCEPTS AND AGREES to the terms and covenants contained in this Security Instrument and in any Rider executed by Borrower and recorded with it.

IN WITNESS WHEREOF, Borrower has signed and sealed this Security Instrument.

Signed, sealed and delivered in the presence of:

_____   _____(Seal)
Unofficial Witness   HELEN DAVIS   - Borrower

_____   _____(Seal)
                                                                                                                  - Borrower

Notary Public, _____ County

_____ **[Space Below This Line For Acknowledgment]** _____

EXHIBIT 16–34

HUD–1 Settlement Statement

A. SETTLEMENT STATEMENT

U.S. Department of Housing and Urban Development

OMB No. 2502-0265

B. Type of Loan

1. ___ FHA	2. ___ FmHA	3. X Conv. Unins.	6. File Number	7. Loan Number	8. Mortgage Insurance Case No.#
4. ___ VA	5. ___ Conv. Ins.				

C. NOTE: This form is furnished to give you a statement of actual settlement costs. Amounts paid to and by the settlement agent are shown. Items marked (P.O.C.) were paid outside the closing; they are shown here for information purposes and are not included in the totals.

D. Name and Address of Borrower	E. Name and Address of Seller	F. Name and Address of Lender
HELEN DAVIS 5167 Tilly Mill Road Atlanta, Georgia 30302	MARKAM INDUSTRIES, INC. 210 Corporate Square Atlanta, Georgia 30303	AMERICAN EAGLE MORTGAGE COMPANY 10 Piedmont Center Atlanta, Georgia 30317

G. Property Location	H. Settlement Agent	
5167 Tilly Mill Road Atlanta, Georgia 30302	Place of Settlement	I. Settlement Date 4/25/20__ RD:

J. SUMMARY OF BORROWER'S TRANSACTION:		K. SUMMARY OF SELLER'S TRANSACTION:	
100. Gross Amount Due From Borrower		**400. Gross Amount Due To Seller**	
101. Contract sales price	100,000.00	401. Contract sales price	100,000.00
102. Personal property		402. Personal property	
103. Settlement charges to borrower (line 1400)	5,638.88	403.	
104.		404.	
105.		405.	
Adjustments for items paid by seller in advance		**Adjustments for items paid by seller in advance**	
106. City/town taxes to		406. City/town taxes to	
107. County taxes to		407. County taxes to	
108. Assessments to		408. Assessments to	
109.		409.	
110.		410.	
111.		411.	
112.		412.	
120. GROSS AMOUNT DUE FROM BORROWER	105,638.88	420. GROSS AMOUNT DUE TO SELLER	100,000.00
200. Amounts Paid By or In Behalf of Borrower		**500. Reductions In Amount Due To Seller**	
201. Deposit or earnest money	1,000.00	501. Excess Deposit (see instructions) (EM)*	1,000.00
202. Principal amount of new loan(s)	80,000.00	502. Settlement charges to seller (line 1400)	6,103.00
203. Existing loan(s) taken subject to		503. Existing loan(s) taken subject to	
204.		504. Payoff of first mortgage loan	82,460.00
205.		505. Payoff of second mortgage loan	
206.		506. *Earnest Money	
207.		507.	
208.		508.	
209.		509.	
Adjustments for items unpaid by seller		**Adjustments for items unpaid by seller**	
210. City/town taxes 1/1 to 4/25 (115)	491.05	510. City/town taxes 1/1 to 4/25 (115)	491.05
211. County taxes 1/1 to 4/25 (115)	583.05	511. County taxes 1/1 to 4/25 (115)	583.05
212. Assessments to		512. Assessments to	
213.		513.	
214.		514.	
215.		515.	
216.		516.	
217.		517.	
218.		518.	
219.		519.	
220. TOTAL PAID BY/FOR BORROWER	82,074.10	520. TOTAL REDUCTION AMOUNT DUE SELLER	90,637.10
300. Cash At Settlement From or To Borrower		**600. Cash At Settlement To or From Seller**	
301. Gross amount due from borrower (line 120)	105,638.88	601. Gross amount due to seller (line 420)	100,000.00
302. Less amounts paid by/for borrower (line 220)	82,074.10	602. Less reduction amount due seller (line 520)	90,637.10
303. CASH FROM BORROWER	23,564.78	603. CASH TO SELLER	9,362.90

(continued)

EXHIBIT 16–34

HUD–1 Settlement Statement (*continued*)

| U.S. DEPARTMENT OF HOUSING AND URBAN DEVELOPMENT | SETTLEMENT STATEMENT | | PAGE 2 |

L. SETTLEMENT CHARGES: FILE NO.#:	PAID FROM BORROWER'S FUNDS AT SETTLEMENT	PAID FROM SELLER'S FUNDS AT SETTLEMENT
700. TOTAL SALES/BROKER'S COMMISSION based on price $100,000.00 @7% = 7,000.00		
Division of commission (line 700) as follows:		
701. $ 3,500.00 to Ajax Realty Co.		
702. $ 3,500.00 to Northside Realty Co., Inc.		
703. Commission paid at Settlement $1,000.00 Earnest Money retained by Northside		6,000.00
704. Realty Co.		
800. ITEMS PAYABLE IN CONNECTION WITH LOAN		
801. Loan Origination Fee 1 % American Eagle Mortgage Company	1,000.00	
802. Loan Discount %		
803. Appraisal Fee to American Eagle Mortgage Company	500.00	
804. Credit Report to		
805. Lender's Inspection Fee to		
806. Mtg. Ins. Application Fee to		
807. Assumption Fee to		
808.		
809.		
810.		
811.		
812.		
813.		
814.		
815.		
900. ITEMS REQUIRED BY LENDER TO BE PAID IN ADVANCE		
901. Interest from 4/25 to 5/1 @ $ 21.92 /day	131.52	
902. Mortgage Insurance Premium for to		
903. Hazard Insurance Premium for yrs to		
904.		
905.		
1000. RESERVES DEPOSITED WITH LENDER FOR		
1001. Hazard Insurance 2 mo.@$40.00 /mo.	80.00	
1002. Mortgage Insurance mo.@$ /mo.		
1003. City Property Taxes 8 mo.@$130.00 /mo.	1,040.00	
1004. County Property Taxes 8 mo.@$154.17 /mo.	1,233.36	
1005. Annual Assessments mo.@$ /mo.		
1006. mo.@$ /mo.		
1007. mo.@$ /mo.		
1008. mo.@$ /mo.		
1100. TITLE CHARGES		
1101. Settlement or closing fee to		
1102. Abstract or title search to		
1103. Title examination to		
1104. Title insurance binder to		
1105. Document Preparation to		
1106. Notary Fees to		
1107. Attorney's fees to Law Firm	650.00	
(includes above items No: 1101, 1102, 1103, 1104, 1105 and 1106)		
1108. Title Insurance to Title Company	400.00	
(includes above items No:)		
1109. Lender's coverage $ 80,000.00 ----		
1110. Owner's coverage $ 100,000.00 ----		
1111.		
1112.		
1113.		
1200. GOVERNMENT RECORDING AND TRANSFER CHARGES		
1201. Recording Fees: Deed $ 3.00 ; Mortgage $ 11.00 ; Releases $ 3.00	14.00	3.00
1202. City/county tax/stamps: Deed $; Mortgage $		
1203. State Tax/stamps: Deed $ 100.00 ; Mortgage $ 240.00	240.00	100.00
1204.		
1205.		
1300. ADDITIONAL SETTLEMENT CHARGES		
1301. Survey to Survey Company	350.00	
1302. Pest Inspection to		
1303.		
1304.		
1305.		
1306.		
1307.		
1308.		
1400. TOTAL SETTLEMENT CHARGES (enter on lines 103 and 502, Sections J and K)	5,638.88	6,103.00

chapter | 17

Condominiums and Cooperatives

Objectives

After reading this chapter, you should be able to:

- Understand the condominium form of property ownership
- Understand the cooperative form of property ownership
- Understand the time-sharing form of property ownership
- Understand the difference between the condominium and the cooperative form of ownership
- Understand the requirements for condominium declarations and condominium plats
- Understand the content of the legal documents required to create a condominium

Outline

A merica's first 200 years of growth and settlement as a nation depended, to a large extent, on an abundance of cheap land. Early landowners were able to obtain individual tracts of land on which to construct homes and other improvements. Early development of the country was horizontal, across the surface of the land. Early cities consisted of rows of individually owned homes and businesses. Multifamily housing in the early cities was rental housing with a building being owned by a single landowner and the various apartments or living spaces being leased to tenants. During the late nineteenth century, land—especially that in urban areas—became more expensive, and landowners, including residential landowners, began to build vertically on the surface of the land. These early "high-rise" apartments were also under single ownership with the living spaces leased to tenants. As the wealth of the tenants grew and these high-rise apartments became more desirable, new concepts of ownership began to develop—the condominium and the cooperative. Condominium and cooperative ownership have become popular, and condominiums and cooperatives exist in most states. Some are in high-rise or multistory buildings, and some are in low-rise or cluster-detached housing. The condominium and cooperative concept extends beyond residential use. Condominium office buildings are commonplace in many areas.

It is essential, to assist in the representation of a client who is buying, selling, or making a loan on a condominium or cooperative, that a paralegal understand the basic rules and concepts of condominium and cooperative property ownership.

CONDOMINIUM

The word *condominium* is a combination of two Latin words: *con,* meaning "one or more persons," and *dominium,* meaning "control over an object or property." Similar to its name, the **condominium** concept of property ownership is a combination of individual and joint ownership. A condominium owner individually owns his or her unit, which usually is located in a multiunit building. In addition, together with the other individual condominium owners, he or she has joint ownership and control over the common property, sometimes referred to as the **common areas** or common elements of the condominium. The common areas usually consist of exterior walls of buildings, stairwells, elevators, walks, yards, roofs, entryways, and so on. In many residential condominiums, the common areas may include recreational areas, swimming pools, and, in some cases, even a golf course. The common areas are used by all the condominium owners and are jointly owned and maintained by the condominium owners.

The laws that govern and define condominium ownership are both statutory and contractual. All states have passed laws commonly referred to as condominium acts that set forth a comprehensive legal framework for the creation and governance of condominium ownership. In addition to the state regulation, condominium developers prepare a comprehensive set of contractual covenants, known as a **condominium declaration,** that will govern the ownership and control the governance of the condominium. The declaration is recorded, and each condominium owner is bound by its terms.

BIRTH OF A CONDOMINIUM

A developer can create a condominium either by purchasing an apartment building and converting it into a condominium or by developing and constructing a new condominium. In either situation, the developer is required by state law to prepare for each condominium a condominium declaration that sets forth the rules and regulations of the condominium and a **condominium plat** that shows the location of all individual units as well as the common areas and to create a condominium homeowners' association that will govern the condominium property on final completion and sale of the units by the developer. The declaration, plat, and homeowners' association must be in place before the project can be considered a condominium and before individual units can be sold.

The declaration, sometimes called a master deed or master lease, is the most important legal document in the creation of a condominium. It is prepared and signed by the condominium developer and recorded in the county where the condominium is located. The declaration describes and defines the boundaries of the units and the common areas or elements, creates or provides for the creation of the condominium government, and imposes restrictive covenants on the owners that regulate the use of the units and common areas. Most states' condominium acts require that the declaration contain certain express provisions for the condominium to be properly created. A unit owner may find it difficult to resell or obtain financing on a unit when the declaration is defective and does not comply with state law. An example of state condominium act requirements for the contents of a declaration is shown in Exhibit 17–1 at the end of this chapter.

---

condominium

Form of property ownership in which the owner owns an individual unit in a multiunit building and is a tenant in common with other owners of units in the building in certain common areas.

common areas

That portion of the condominium property that is owned in common by all the owners of units in the condominium.

condominium declaration

Legal document required by state condominium acts to create a condominium.

condominium plat

Plat of survey of condominium property required by state condominium acts. The plat must show in sufficient detail the location and dimensions of the real property, as well as all condominium units located on the real property.

In general, a condominium declaration contains the following information:

1. Name of the condominium, which in many states is required to contain the word *condominium* or to be followed by the words *a condominium*

2. Legal description of the entire property being submitted to the condominium form of ownership

3. Description or delineation of the boundaries of the individual condominium units, including horizontal, upper, lower, vertical, and lateral boundaries

4. Description or delineation of all common areas, including a designation of limited common areas

A **limited common area** is a common area that, by the declaration, is limited in use to one or more of the condominium owners. For example, an enclosed backyard or patio in a low-rise condominium project may be a limited common area assigned for use only to the property owner whose unit adjoins the patio or enclosed yard. Although the use of the limited common area is assigned only to a particular unit owner, the limited common areas are owned in common by all the owners in the condominium project.

limited common area

Common area of a condominium that is limited in use to one or more condominium unit owners.

5. Creation of a governing body for the condominium or the requirement that one be created

The governing body usually is a nonprofit corporation in which each owner is entitled to one vote. These corporations often are referred to as condominium associations.

6. Limitations or restrictions on the power of the condominium association
7. Allocation of a share of liability for common area expenses to each condominium unit
8. Statement of all restrictive covenants in the general use of the units and common areas
9. Description of how the condominium can be expanded

It is not unusual for some developers to do phase condominiums. In a phase condominium, the developer may develop only a portion of the condominium to test the market. If the condominium sells, the developer will then add new units over a period of time. The declaration must spell out in detail how this phase of additional units will be accomplished.

10. Statement of how the condominium form of ownership can be terminated

An example of a condominium declaration appears as Exhibit 17–2 at the end of this chapter. A condominium developer, in addition to preparing and recording a declaration, must prepare and record a plat of the condominium improvements. The plat must show in sufficient detail the location and dimensions of the submitted property; the location and dimensions of all structural improvements located on any portion of the submitted property; the intended location and dimensions of all contemplated structural improvements committed to be provided by the declaration; and the location and dimensions of all easements appurtenant to the submitted property or otherwise submitted to the condominium form of ownership. An example of a state condominium act's requirements for a condominium plat appears as Exhibit 17–3 at the end of this chapter.

Articles and Bylaws of a Condominium Association

The internal operations of a condominium are governed by a homeowners' association or **condominium association.** The association takes the legal form of a nonprofit corporation, with each owner of a unit being entitled to a vote in the affairs of the association.

condominium association

Governing body of a condominium, the members of which are owners of condominium units. The condominium association usually is in the form of a nonprofit corporation.

A condominium association, like any other corporation, is governed by two legal documents: articles of incorporation and bylaws. The articles of incorporation form the basic corporate constitution or charter and are filed with the secretary of state's office in the state where the association is located. The articles of incorporation contain the following information:

- Name of the association
- Purpose of the association
- Duration of the corporation's existence
- Initial directors of the corporation
- Registered agent and registered office of the corporation
  The registered agent is the person on whom service of process can be served for the corporation, and the registered office is the address for the registered agent.
- Criteria for becoming an owner or member of the association and the name of the incorporator
  The incorporator usually is the developer or an attorney for the developer.

An example of articles of incorporation for a condominium association is shown as Exhibit 17–4 at the end of this chapter. The bylaws of a condominium association are the rules and regulations by which the association is governed. Bylaws contain more detail about the association than do the articles of incorporation. The bylaws provide for the following:

- Selection of the board of directors
- How meetings are to be held and conducted
- How officers are to be appointed or elected
- How votes are to be counted in the governance of the corporation; particularly, whether resolutions must be passed by a simple majority or a three-fourths or two-thirds majority
- Regulation of the common elements
- Rights and responsibilities of unit owners
- Assessment and collection of monthly charges
- Other relevant matters

Bylaws usually are not required to be recorded or filed with a state agency. They must, however, be provided to a purchaser of a unit before the time of purchase. An example of condominium bylaws is set forth as Exhibit 17–5 at the end of this chapter.

A developer usually retains control of the condominium association until such time as either all the units or a percentage of units have been sold to purchasers. Most condominium associations that provide for this limited period of developer control have two levels of membership in the association: the owner's level of membership, with one vote for each unit owned, and the developer's voting rights, which usually consist of all the voting rights as long as the developer is a member. The developer usually turns over control to the unit owners on the sale of a set number of units, typically not less than 75 percent.

The costs and expenses of operating a condominium are borne by the condominium owners. Expenses include taxes on the individual units, taxes on the common elements, maintenance and repair of the common elements, and insurance.

Taxes on the individual units are paid by the individual unit owners. The units can be returned to the tax authorities for taxes the same as a single-family home or other property. Tax on the common elements, however, is an expense of the association and a joint obligation of all the owners. The repair and maintenance of the common area are also joint responsibilities and expenses of the owners. In addition, most condominium declarations and even some condominium acts require that the insurance on both the units and the common area be under one master policy and that such insurance be the expense of the condominium association and, indirectly, the joint expense of all the owners.

The joint responsibility for paying common area expenses such as taxes, maintenance, and insurance is handled by the use of an **assessment** against each owner's unit to cover that unit owner's share of the common area expenses.

assessment

Sum of money owed by a condominium owner for monthly upkeep of the common areas of the condominium.

The amount of the assessment is determined by the condominium association. The determination is made based on an operating budget for the year's expenses in regard to the common areas and allocation of this operating budget to the number of units in the association. If a condominium is composed of different sized units, the owner of a larger unit may be allocated a greater portion of the common area expense assessment than the owner of a smaller unit. The method for imposing assessments is determined both by state law and by condominium declaration.

If a common area assessment is not voluntarily paid by a unit owner, the association may have a lien against the unit for unpaid assessments. A lien is a debt payable in money that may attach to property owned by the debtor. The holder of the lien may enforce collection and payment of the debt by selling the attached property of the debtor. A condominium association lien, like any other lien, can be enforced by having the delinquent condominium owner's condominium unit sold for the purpose of paying the lien. The association, in addition to imposing the lien, can sue an owner directly for nonpayment of delinquent assessments. It has been held in many states that an owner's obligation to pay is unconditional. This means that the owner is obligated to pay the assessment even if the association is not providing all the services required by the association. The policy behind this rule is explained in *Forest Villas Condominium Assoc. v. Camerio,* which follows.

Unpaid assessments are also imposed on a purchaser of a unit if the assessments are unpaid at the time of purchase. It is prudent, when representing a condominium purchaser, to inquire of the association if assessments are unpaid on the unit being purchased. These unpaid assessments often are not in the form of a lien that is recorded, and therefore, the only method of determining if unpaid assessments exist is to inquire of the association.

Condominium owners also have a joint and several liability for damage or harm caused to person or property in connection with the common areas. This liability is often covered by liability insurance that insures both the individual unit owners and the association. In some states, an owner's liability for injury or harm that takes place on the common areas may be limited to the owner's pro rata share of the common area. For example, if an owner has a 2 percent share of the common areas and there is liability caused by negligence, such as a slip and fall at the swimming pool, then this owner's liability for the harm would be limited to 2 percent.

Insurance covering casualty of the condominium improvements is usually in the form of a master policy that insures all unit owners and the condominium association. The insurance covers both the individual units and the common areas. State law and condominium declarations usually require that insurance money be used for restoration of the condominium improvements unless a specified number of homeowners—usually not less than 75 percent—agree not to restore. In the event restoration does not take place, the insurance proceeds would be paid to the owners according to their interest in the condominium. In the event insurance proceeds are insufficient to totally repair or restore the premises, it would be the joint obligation of the owners to contribute money necessary to complete the construction. This contribution could be imposed in the form of an assessment lien, the same as assessments for common area expenses and maintenance.

CASE

Forest Villas Condominium Association, Inc. v. Camerio et al.
205 Ga. App. 617, 422 S.E.2d 884 (Ga. App. 1992)

BEASLEY, Judge.

The central issue is the construction of OCGA § 44-3- 80(d), part of the Georgia Condominium Act.

Forest Villas Condominium Association, Inc., sued Camerio and Elliot, owners of 23 of the 94 units in the Association, to recover an arrearage of condominium fees. In addition to the accrued $28,060, the Association sought interest on the arrearage and the remaining assessments for the year.

Defendants denied the allegations of the complaint, alleged a number of affirmative defenses, and filed a counterclaim which asserted that the Association failed to honor its obligations to perform maintenance and make repairs on the units owned by defendants; the Association had discriminated against defendants and their units because they were rental units as opposed to owner-occupied; and the Association had mismanaged the funds paid to it by defendants. Defendants also alleged that due to the Association's failure to make certain repairs they had been forced to pay for those repairs themselves. They sought an accounting of the monies handled by the Association; a reimbursement by the Association for all expenses they incurred due to the association's breach of duty; a declaration that certain unspecified actions of the Association in contravention of Georgia law and the condominium declaration, bylaws, and rules be declared null and void; attorney fees; and the enjoining of the Association from expending its funds to install certain water meters.

The Association moved for summary judgment, contending that it was entitled to recover the fees because OCGA § 44-3-80(d) did not permit a unit owner any exemption from liability for assessments. It also urged that defendants' counterclaim sounded in equity and thus was beyond the authority of the state court. The Association also filed a motion in limine to preclude defendants from introducing any evidence relating to their counterclaim for the same reason.

The trial court denied the Association's motion for summary judgment altogether, concluding that there were genuine issues of material fact and that "the word 'exempt' found in OCGA § 44-3-80(d) does not mean that the Defendants in this case could never have any justification for withholding the assessments charged to them." The court denied the motion in limine, holding that the counterclaim defenses could be presented before it.

1. The first question is whether the court correctly construed OCGA § 44-3-80(d), contrary to the Association's contention that it misinterpreted plain and unambiguous language.

[1] The statutory subsection provides: "No unit owner other than the association shall be exempted from any liability for any assessment under this Code section or under any condominium instrument for any reason whatsoever, including, without limitation, abandonment, nonuse, or waiver of the use or enjoyment of his unit or any part of the common elements."

[2] The language is plain and susceptible of only one interpretation insofar as it relates to the defenses. See *Lunda Constr. Co. v. Clayton County,* 201 Ga. App. 106, 107, 410 S.E.2d 446 (1991). There is no legal justification for a condominium owner to fail to pay valid condominium assessments. This reflects a clear choice by the legislature that the owner's obligation to pay assessments be absolute and a condominium unit owner involved in a dispute with the condominium Association about its services and operations may not exert leverage in that controversy by withholding payment but must seek other remedy. The obligation to pay the assessment is independent of the Association's obligations to provide services. This is necessary because the communal business of the condominium Association for the benefit in common of all condominium owners continues unabated during the pendency of any such individual dispute. The public policy expressed in the statute assures that fulfillment of obligations and the functioning of a condominium Association as a whole not be jeopardized or compromised by individual disputes, which may or may not be meritorious. See *Rivers Edge Condo. Assn. v. Rere,* 390 Pa. Super. 196, 568 A.2d 261 (1990). See also *Newport West Condo. Assn. v. Veniar,* 134 Mich. App. 1, 350 N.W.2d 818 (1984).

The state court misinterpreted OCGA § 44-3-80(d) insofar as the defenses or "exemptions" urged by defendants are concerned. They do not assert, nor is there any evidence, that the condominium instruments were anything other than lawful, see OCGA § 44-3-76, or that the subject assessments were made other than in compliance with the condominium instruments and law. See OCGA §§ 44-3-71(5) and 44-3-76. Whether such would be a defense permitted under OCGA § 44-3-80(d) in a suit for unpaid fees is not before us. Cf. *San Antonio etc. Homeowners Assn. v. Miller,* 761 S.W.2d 460 (Tex. App. 1988). Plaintiff Association was entitled to summary judgment on defendants' liability for unpaid assessments.

Subcondominium

Many states now permit the creation of a subcondominium within a condominium project. A subcondominium is where the owner of a condominium unit divides the unit into separate subcondominium units. A subcondominium property can only be created if the master condominium declaration so provides. The owner of the condominium unit being subdivided shall be considered the declarant of the subcondominium. The subcondominium will have its own subcondominium declaration and will be governed by its own subcondominium owners association.

Typically, you will find subcondominiums in large mixed-use condominium projects. For example, you may have a high-rise building turned into a condominium. The condominium may only have three units, a unit 1 for the first floor that is to be used only for retail, a unit 2 for the next few floors that is to be used only for offices, and a unit 3 for the remainder of the building that is to be used only for residences. Each of these units may be converted into a subcondominium and then sold to retail stores, office owners, and residential purchasers. When the project is completed, you will have a master condominium of three units and a subcondominium comprised of several retail units, another subcondominium comprised of office units, and a third subcondominium comprised of residences.

Practice Tips for the Paralegal

A paralegal may assist an attorney in the formation of a condominium. This person may be responsible for drafting and preparing the condominium declaration and the articles of incorporation and bylaws of the condominium association. The preparation of condominium formation documents requires careful attention to detail in regard to the name of the condominium, number of units, and other factual issues concerning the formation of the condominium. Because condominium declarations are recorded and condominium articles of incorporation are generally filed with the secretary of state's office in the state where the association is located, any mistakes made in these documents will require rerecordation and/or refiling.

A paralegal may also be involved in assisting an attorney in representing a purchaser, seller, or lender of a condominium unit. The paralegal, to adequately assist in the representation of this client, must be knowledgeable of the condominium laws in the state where the condominium is located. In addition, the paralegal should obtain copies of all the condominium documentation, such as the declaration, plat, articles of incorporation, and bylaws of the condominium association, and review them carefully.

The checklist that follows addresses issues and questions that need to be asked and answered when representing a condominium unit purchaser or lender.

✔ CHECKLIST

Condominium Fundamentals

☐ 1. Does the developer or builder have a good reputation? The reputation of the condominium developer or builder is related to the success of the developer's projects. A good reputation means that the builder builds good-quality condominium units that usually are trouble-free. The quality of construction in a condominium unit can greatly affect the cost of maintaining the unit and the resale value of the unit.

☐ 2. Does the condominium documentation comply with state law? A condominium declaration that is defective or does not comply with state law can affect the marketability and cloud the title of the condominium unit. Purchasers may not want to purchase property that is not technically in compliance with the state condominium laws, and lenders may decline to make loans on such property. It is

(continued)

possible in some states to obtain an endorsement from a title insurance company ensuring that the condominium has been properly formed and is in compliance with the state condominium act.

3. Carefully review the assessments while a developer is still in control of the condominium project. Not uncommonly, the developer, while in control, may subsidize the condominium budget and keep assessments artificially low during this period of ownership. It is important to obtain copies of the actual budget, if available, from the developer to determine what the assessments will be once the developer has sold the units and left the project.

4. Who controls the board of directors? During the development, it is not unusual for the developer to have control over the board of directors. The developer usually retains control until such time as a minimum number of units have been sold, usually not less than 75 percent of the units. Although it is not unusual for a developer to control the association during the period of development, the property owner needs to know when control will be turned over to the owners and to be aware that for a period of time, he or she may have little say in the internal affairs of the association.

5. Review the restrictions on use of the unit and common areas. A condominium contains restrictive covenants that affect the use of units and the common areas by the owners. These restrictive covenants are enforceable so long as they do not violate some public policy, such as racial discrimination. A potential condominium purchaser must be made aware that these covenants are enforceable and that there probably is someone in the condominium project who enforces them. If a condominium purchaser has trouble with any of the restrictive covenants, he or she needs to rethink the purchase.

6. Is there any control on the resale of the property? A few condominium declarations contain rights of first refusal restrictions on an owner's ability to resell his or her unit. The right of first refusal usually requires that the owner offer the unit first to the condominium association before it can be resold. The association seldom exercises these rights of first refusal, but this practice can affect an owner's ability to sell the unit or present problems at a closing in the event a notice of the sale was not sent to the association.

COOPERATIVE

cooperative

Form of ownership of real property in which a corporation owns a multiunit building and leases living space in the building to the shareholders of the corporation.

The **cooperative** form of ownership, despite its popularity in Europe and other parts of the world, has had limited success in the United States. Cooperatives usually are found in urban areas along the East Coast. In the late 1960s and early 1970s, they were used to provide publicly assisted housing. A limited number of these properties can still be found throughout the United States.

Cooperative ownership is quite different from condominium ownership. In a cooperative, a corporation owns the land, the building, and all common areas. A person who wants to become an owner purchases from the cooperative corporation shares of stock in the corporation. These shares of stock entitle the person to enter into a long-term lease for his or her cooperative unit with the corporation. A cooperative owner is, in essence, both a tenant under a long-term lease with the corporation and an owner, because the person owns shares in the landlord cooperative corporation. The owner participates with other owners, who are also members of the corporation, in the governance of the corporation. The shares of stock and lease are transferable and, therefore, offer a cooperative owner, like a condominium owner, an opportunity to build value in his or her investment. Ownership in a cooperative usually is considered ownership of personal property rather than of real property.

Differences between Condominiums and Cooperatives # 5

The main difference between a cooperative and a condominium is financing. With a condominium, each owner obtains his or her own financing and pledges the unit as security for the loan. In cooperative financing, there is a blanket mortgage on all the cooperative property, including the living units and common areas. The cooperative purchaser agrees to pay his or her share of the blanket mortgage payments, which is based on the percentage of ownership of the total cooperative. At the time of purchase, a cooperative owner may also be required to make a substantial down payment, which typically is greater than a condominium down payment. A condominium owner usually can purchase a unit with a down payment of only 10 to 20 percent of the purchase price, whereas it is not unusual for a cooperative owner to have to pay as much as one-third of the purchase price as a down payment. Financing for the down payment is available to a cooperative purchaser. The lender will either take an assignment of the cooperative owner's lease or an assignment of the owner's stock in the cooperative corporation as security for the loan. The master financing of a cooperative versus individual financing of a condominium creates another set of problems for the cooperative owner. A cooperative owner could be making his or her payments each month to the cooperative corporation for his or her share of the common mortgage, but the other cooperative owners could be defaulting on their payment obligations. These collective defaults of other owners could cause the blanket mortgage to go into default and could threaten the foreclosure of the master mortgage on the cooperative owner's home.

Cooperative owners commonly have more restricted rights of resale than do condominium owners. Most condominium owners can resell their units without the consent of the condominium association. Cooperative owners usually cannot sell their cooperative interests unless the board of directors of the cooperative corporation approves the new owners. This approval process is necessary because of the collective mortgage and the requirement that the cooperative owners work more closely together in a cooperative effort so that each cooperative owner can prosper and be protected in his or her ownership of a unit.

The financing difficulties and the restrictions on resale have caused the cooperative form of ownership to be less popular than the condominium form of ownership.

TIME-SHARES

You like to ski, and each year you go to your favorite ski resort for a week. You enjoy the trip very much and think it might be a good idea to own property in the area of the ski resort. You are hesitant to buy a vacation condominium or home because you will only be using it one or two weeks of the year. You are not certain if the unit can be rented the other 50 weeks to cover your costs and expenses of ownership. Would it be nice if you could just buy a condominium or home in the ski area for one or two weeks a year? It is this desire and demand that an industry known as time-sharing was created to satisfy. **Time-share** ownership, also called interval ownership, is a popular marketing device for resort developments in the United States. Under a time-sharing arrangement, a person purchases the right to use a home or condominium at a resort area for a limited period each year.

time-share

Form of ownership of real property in which an owner owns the property for a short period, usually one or two weeks of each year. Time-share ownership typically is used for vacation or recreational property.

🏛 ETHICS: Paralegal Correspondence

You are a closing paralegal employed in a busy real estate department of a law firm. Your work requires a great deal of correspondence, and you share a secretary with your supervising attorney. Your secretary has taken a day's vacation, and you are working with a temporary secretary. You have a number of letters that need to go out, and you notice that the temporary secretary has used firm letterhead for all your correspondence and has typed your name in such a way that it appears you are an attorney for the firm. It is late in the day, and it will take more than an hour to retype the letters. Do you send the letters or have them retyped?

Many states provide that to the extent necessary to perform functions properly delegated to a paralegal and to the extent that these functions do not fall within the definition of the practice of law, the paralegal may correspond on the law firm letterhead in the paralegal's own name. If a paralegal in the employ of a member of the bar is permitted by the member to correspond on the law firm letterhead, the paralegal must clearly identify his or her status by the use of an appropriate designation, such as "paralegal" or "law clerk." Failure to do so might constitute a representation on the part of the law firm that the paralegal is a member of the state bar and authorized to practice law within the state.

Time-share ownership comes in a number of legal forms. A time-share may be a cooperative in which the developer owns a corporation and each owner of the time-share purchases stock in the corporation. The amount of stock owned by the purchaser permits the owner to use units within the development during a certain period of the year. A time-share may be based on a form of interval ownership in which an owner of a time-share actually owns the unit for a certain time each year. A time-share may also be structured in such a way that the purchaser enters into a tenancy in common arrangement with other time-share owners for the entire resort development. This arrangement permits the owner to use a particular residential unit during a portion of the year.

rescission

Right to terminate a contract.

Time-shares have been subject to abuse and fraud by developers and are heavily regulated by state law. The purchaser of a time-share is entitled to full disclosure concerning all operations of the time-share and is given a period of **rescission** after a contract to buy a time-share has been signed. During this period, usually five to seven days, the purchaser can change his or her mind and terminate the agreement.

SUMMARY

The condominium and cooperative forms of property ownership combine individual and joint ownership. A condominium owner individually owns his or her unit and, together with other individual owners, has joint ownership and control over the common property. A cooperative owner has a lease on his or her living unit and owns stock in a cooperative corporation that owns the building in which the unit is located.

Generally, each state has a condominium act that governs and regulates the creation, governance, and regulation of the condominium form of ownership. The condominium must be created in substantial compliance with the state regulatory acts. Most condominiums are created by the preparation and filing of a condominium declaration and a condominium plat. Condominiums are also generally governed by a condominium association, which usually takes the form of a nonprofit corporation. The individual owners of the condominium units are shareholders or members of this condominium association.

Cooperatives are generally governed by a board of directors of the corporation owning the cooperative building. Each individual cooperative owner is a member or shareholder of this corporation and is entitled to vote for the board of directors.

A paralegal who assists in the preparation and formation of a condominium or cooperative or who represents a purchaser, seller, or lender of condominium or cooperative property must be familiar with the rules and regulations involving condominiums and cooperatives.

HELPFUL WEBSITES

Condominiums

How to Buy a Condominium

Good information on how to buy, insure, and inspect a condominium can be found on the eHow Web site at *http://www.ehow.com*.

Cooperatives

The National Association of Housing Cooperatives Web site contains information on buying and managing a cooperative.

Most information is available only to members, but some free information is available at *http://www.coophousing.org*.

A good article on "How Housing Cooperatives Work" can be found on the HowStuff Works Web site at *http://money.howstuffworks.com*.

KEY TERMS

assessment

common areas

condominium

condominium association

condominium declaration

condominium plat

cooperative

limited common area

rescission

time-share

REVIEW QUESTIONS

1. What is the difference between a common area and a limited common area in a condominium? Give an example of each.

2. What information is contained in a condominium declaration?

3. How are common area expenses paid for in a condominium?

4. What is a cooperative?

5. How does a cooperative differ from a condominium?

CASE PROBLEM

You are a paralegal employed by a law firm who is representing a purchaser of a condominium unit. You have been asked to assist an attorney in the closing of the sale. What documentation in regard to the condominium would you request from the seller? What issues do you want answered from the seller or from a review of the condominium documentation?

PRACTICAL ASSIGNMENTS

1. Research your own state's condominium act. How does your state's requirements for a condominium declaration differ from those contained in the condominium declaration statute shown as Exhibit 17–1 at the end of this chapter? How does your state's requirements for a condominium plat differ from those in the statute shown as Exhibit 17–3 at the end of this chapter?

2. Review the condominium declaration shown as Exhibit 17–2 at the end of this chapter in conjunction with your state's condominium act. Does the declaration satisfy all requirements of your state's condominium act? If not, list the areas in which the condominium declaration is deficient or areas that would need to be added to the condominium declaration.

ADDENDUM

Exhibit 17–1 State Condominium Act Requirements for Declaration

Exhibit 17–2 Condominium Declaration

Exhibit 17–3 State Condominium Act Requirements for Condominium Plat

Exhibit 17–4 Articles of Incorporation

Exhibit 17–5 Condominium Association Bylaws

Student StudyWare™ CD-ROM

Interactive Student CD in the book includes additional quizzing, case studies, and key terms flashcards.

Online Companion™

For additional resources, please go to *www.paralegal.delmar.cengage.com*

EXHIBIT 17–1

State Condominium Act Requirements for Declaration

44-3-77. Contents of declaration.

(a) The declaration for every condominium shall contain the following:

(1) The name of the condominium, which name shall include the word "condominium" or be followed by the words "a condominium";

(2) The name of the county or counties in which the condominium is located;

(3) A legal description by metes and bounds of the submitted property, including any horizontal, upper, and lower boundaries as well as the vertical, lateral boundaries;

(4) A description or delineation of the boundaries of the units, including any horizontal, upper, and lower boundaries as well as the vertical, lateral boundaries;

(5) A description or delineation of any limited common elements showing or designating the unit or units to which each is assigned;

(6) A description or delineation of all common elements that may subsequently be assigned as limited common elements together with a statement that they may be so assigned and a description of the method whereby any such assignments shall be made;

(7) The allocation to each unit of an undivided interest in the common elements;

(8) The allocation to each unit of a number of votes in the association;

(9) The allocation to each unit of a share of the liability for common expenses;

(10) Any limitations or restrictions on the powers of the association and the board of directors;

(11) The name and address of the attorney or other person who prepared the declaration;

(12) A statement of any and all restrictions on the general use of the condominium or a statement that there are no such restrictions; and

(13) Such other matters not inconsistent with this article as the declarant deems appropriate.

(b) If the condominium is an expandable condominium, the declaration shall also contain the following:

(1) The explicit reservation of an option or options to expand the condominium;

(2) A time limit or date not exceeding seven years from the recording of the declaration upon which all options to expand the condominium shall expire, together with a statement of any circumstances which will terminate any such option prior to the expiration of the time limit so specified; provided, however, that, if the condominium instruments so provide, the unit owners of units to which two-thirds of the votes in the association appertain, exclusive of any vote or votes appurtenant to any unit or units then owned by the declarant, may consent to the extension of any such option within one year prior to the date upon which the option would otherwise have expired;

(3) A statement of any other limitations on the option or options or a statement that there are no such limitations;

(4) A legal description by metes and bounds of the additional property, including any horizontal, upper, and lower boundaries as well as the vertical, lateral boundaries;

Delmar/Cengage Learning

(continued)

(5) A statement as to whether portions of the additional property may be added to the condominium at different times, together with any limitations fixing the boundaries of those portions by legal descriptions setting forth the metes and bounds thereof or regulating the order in which they may be added to the condominium, or a statement that there are no such limitations;

(6) A statement of any limitations as to the location of any improvements that may be made on any portions of the additional property or a statement that there are no such limitations;

(7) A statement of the maximum number of units that may be created on the additional property. If portions of the additional property may be added to the condominium and the boundaries of those portions are fixed in accordance with paragraph (5) of this subsection, the declaration shall also state the maximum number of units that may be created on each such portion added to the condominium. If portions of the additional property may be added to the condominium and the boundaries of those portions are not fixed in accordance with paragraph (5) of this subsection, then the declaration shall also state the maximum average number of units per acre that may be created on any such portion added to the condominium;

(8) With regard to the additional property, a statement of whether any units may be created therein that may not be restricted exclusively to residential use and, if so, a statement of the maximum extent thereof or a limitation as to the extent of such nonresidential use;

(9) A statement of the extent to which any structures erected on any portion of the additional property added to the condominium will be compatible with structures on the submitted property in terms of quality of construction, the principal materials to be used, and architectural style or a statement that no assurances are made in those regards;

(10) A description of all other improvements that will be made on any portion of the additional property added to the condominium, or a statement of any limitations as to what other improvements may be made thereon, or a statement that no assurances are made in that regard;

(11) A statement that any units created on any portion of the additional property added to the condominium will be substantially identical to the units on the submitted property, or a statement of any limitations as to what types of units may be created thereon, or a statement that no assurances are made in that regard;

(12) A description of the declarant's reserved right, if any, to create limited common elements within any portion of the additional property or to designate common elements therein which may subsequently be assigned as limited common elements, in terms of the types, sizes, and maximum number of such limited common elements within each such portion, or a statement that no limitations are placed on that right; and

(13) A statement of a formula, ratio, or other method whereby, upon the expansion of any expandable condominium, there shall be reallocated among the units the undivided interests in the common elements, the votes in the association, and the liability for common expenses.

Plats or plans may be recorded with the declaration of any amendment thereto and identified therein to supplement or provide information required to be furnished pursuant to this subsection; and provided, further, that paragraph (8) of this subsection need not be complied with if none of the units on the submitted property are restricted exclusively to residential use.

(c) If the condominium contains any convertible space, the declaration shall also contain a statement of a formula, ratio, or other method whereby, upon the conversion of all or any portion of a convertible space, there shall be allocated among the units created therefrom such undivided interest in the common elements, such number of votes in the association, and such liability for common expenses as previously pertained to such convertible space.

(d) If the condominium is a leasehold condominium, with respect to any ground lease, other lease, or other instrument creating the estate for years, the expiration or termination of which may terminate or reduce the condominium, the declaration shall set forth the county or counties

(continued)

EXHIBIT 17–1

State Condominium Act
Requirements for Declaration
(*continued*)

wherein the same are recorded and the deed book and page number where the first page of each such lease or other instrument is recorded. The declaration shall also contain the following:

(1) The date upon which such leasehold or estate for years is due to expire;

(2) A statement of whether any property will be owned by the unit owners in fee simple and, if so, a legal description by metes and bounds of any such property. With respect to any improvements owned by the unit owners in fee simple, the declaration shall contain a statement of any rights the unit owners shall have to remove the improvements after the expiration or termination of the leasehold or estate for years involved or a statement that they shall have no such rights;

(3) A statement of the name and address of the person or persons to whom payments of rent must be made by the unit owners unless such rent is collected from the unit owners as a part of the common expenses; and

(4) A statement of the share of liability for payments under any such lease or other instrument which are chargeable against each unit.

(e) Whenever this Code section requires a legal description by metes and bounds of submitted property or additional property, such requirement shall be deemed to include a requirement of a legally sufficient description of any easements that are submitted to this article or that may be added to the condominium, as the case may be. In the case of any such easement, the declaration shall contain the following:

(1) A description of the permitted use or uses;

(2) If the benefit of the easement does not inure to all units and their lawful occupants, a statement of the relevant restrictions and limitations on utilization; and

(3) If any person other than those entitled to occupy any unit may use the easement, a statement of the rights of others to such use.

Notwithstanding any other provision of this subsection, the foregoing requirements may be satisfied by attaching a true copy of any such easement to the declaration.

(f) Whenever this Code section requires a legal description by metes and bounds of submitted property or additional property, such requirement shall be deemed to include a separate legal description by metes and bounds of all property in which the unit owners collectively shall or may be tenants in common or joint tenants with any other persons. No units shall be situated on any such property, however, and the declaration shall describe the nature of the unit owners' estate therein. No such property shall be shown on the same plat or plats showing other portions of the condominium but shall be shown instead on separate plats unless such property is specifically shown and labeled as being owned subject to such a tenancy.

(g) Wherever this article requires a statement of a method for allocation or reallocation of undivided interests in the common elements, votes in the association, and the liability for common expenses, such method shall be so related to the physical characteristics of the units affected or otherwise so stated as to enable any person to determine the interest, vote, or share in such matters pertaining to any particular unit upon such allocation or reallocation. Certain spaces within the units, including, without limitation, attic, basement, and garage space, may but need not be omitted from such calculation or partially discounted by the use of a ratio so long as the same basis of calculation is employed for all units in the condominium. In the event that the declaration allocates or provides for the allocation to any unit of a different share of undivided interests in common elements than is allocated for liability for common expenses, such difference shall be based upon a good faith estimate of the declarant regarding the approximate relative maintenance or other costs occasioning such disparity, and the basis of such determination shall be stated in the declaration; provided, however, that no unit owner or other person may require any reallocation on account of any disparity between actual costs and the determination reflected in the declaration. Subject to the foregoing sentence of this subsection, nothing contained in this article shall be construed to require that the proportions of undivided interest in the common elements, of votes in the association, or of liability for common expenses assigned and allocated to each unit be equal, it being intended that such proportions may be independent. (Ga. L. 1975, p. 609, § 14; Ga. L. 1982, p. 3, § 44.)

EXHIBIT 17–2
Condominium Declaration

STATE OF _____
COUNTY OF _____

DECLARATION OF CONDOMINIUM
FOR
CLAIREMONT OAKS, A CONDOMINIUM

This Declaration is made by The Farris Corporation (herein called the "Declarant").

WITNESSETH:

WHEREAS, Declarant is the fee simple owner of that certain tract or parcel of land lying and being in Land Lot 55 of the 6th District of Wayne County, _____(State)_____ , as more particularly described in Exhibit "A" attached hereto and incorporated herein by reference, hereinafter called the "Property" subject to the matters set forth on Exhibit "B" attached hereto; and

WHEREAS, certain improvements have been constructed on the Property as shown on the Plat and the Plans which are referenced in Section 5.01(a) and (b) hereof and the matters attached hereto as Exhibit "C"; and

WHEREAS, Declarant has duly incorporated Clairemont Oaks Condominium Association, Inc. as a nonprofit membership corporation under the laws of the State of _____, copies of the Articles of Incorporation, By-Laws and Organizational Meeting being attached hereto as Exhibits "D", "E" and "F"; and

WHEREAS, the Declarant desires to submit the Property to the condominium form of ownership pursuant to the provisions of the ___(State)___ Condominium Act, as the same is in effect on the date hereof (as amended, hereinafter called the "Act"), the terms, conditions and provisions of which are incorporated herein by express reference, and the terms and conditions hereinafter set out.

NOW, THEREFORE, the Declarant does hereby make, declare and publish its intention and desire to submit, and does hereby submit, the Property to the condominium form of ownership pursuant to, subject to and in accordance with the provisions of the Act and the terms and conditions hereinafter set forth.

ARTICLE 1
Name

1.01 The name of the condominium shall be CLAIREMONT OAKS, A CONDOMINIUM (the "Condominium").

ARTICLE 2
Description of Submitted Property

2.01 The Property is located in Wayne County, ___(State)___, in Land Lot 55 of the 6th District, and is more particularly described in Exhibit "A" attached hereto and incorporated herein by reference.

2.02 The Property is subject to the easements and other matters which are set forth on Exhibit "B" attached hereto and by reference made a part hereof.

ARTICLE 3
Definitions

3.01 The terms defined in Official Code of ___(State)___, Section _____ shall have the meanings specified therein and wherever they appear in the condominium instruments unless the context otherwise requires.

Delmar/Cengage Learning

(continued)

EXHIBIT 17–2

Condominium Declaration
(*continued*)

ARTICLE 4

Convertible Space; Expandable Condominium

4.01 Convertible Space. The Condominium does not contain any convertible space.

4.02 Expansion of Condominium. This Condominium shall contain sixty (60) residential units, and is not expandable beyond that amount.

ARTICLE 5

Unit Information and Boundaries

5.01 The buildings and structures situated upon the property are:

(a) located thereon as shown on that certain plat of Clairemont Oaks, A Condominium, dated _____, prepared by _____, which plat has been prepared in accordance with Official Code of _____(State)_____, Section _____ and has been filed contemporaneously herewith in Condominium Plat Book _____, Page _____, Wayne County, ____(State)____ Records a copy of which is attached hereto as Exhibit "C" (hereinafter said condominium plat as recorded is referred to as the "Plat" or the "Condominium Plat");

(b) divided into sixty (60) residential units intended for independent ownership and use and as substantially shown upon those certain Plans for Clairemont Oaks, dated _____, by _____, and filed contemporaneously herewith in the Condominium Floor Plans Cabinet _____, Folder _____, _____ County, ____(State)____ Records (hereinafter said plans are referred to as the "Plans" or the "Condominium Plans").

5.02 Unit Number. Each unit shall have the identifying number allocated to it in accordance with the Plat and the Plans.

5.03 Boundaries. The boundaries of the units are the floors, ceilings and walls delineated in the Plans.

5.04 Appurtenant Surfaces. If any chute, flue, duct, conduit, wire, bearing wall, bearing column or any other apparatus lies partially within and partially outside the designated boundaries of a unit, any portions thereof serving only that unit shall be deemed a part of that unit, and any portions thereof serving more than one unit or any portion of the common elements shall be deemed a part of the common elements.

5.05 Subdivision and Partition of Units; Relocation of Boundaries. The boundaries between adjoining units may be relocated from time to time, but no unit may be subdivided for the purpose of creating two or more units, therefrom and no owner shall have the right of partition of a unit.

ARTICLE 6

Limited Common Elements

6.01 Generally. Any shutter, awning, window box, doorstep, porch, balcony or patio, and any other apparatus designed to serve a single unit, shall be deemed to be a limited common element appertaining to that unit exclusively.

ARTICLE 7

Allocation of Undivided Interest in the Common Elements

7.01 The undivided interest in the common elements allocated to each unit is set forth on Exhibit "G" attached hereto and incorporated herein by reference.

(*continued*)

EXHIBIT 17–2

Condominium Declaration
(*continued*)

ARTICLE 8
Allocation of Votes in the Association

8.01 Generally. The number of votes in the Clairemont Oaks Condominium Association, Inc. for each unit shall be as designated on Exhibit "G" attached hereto.

8.02 Method of Voting. The persons entitled to exercise such votes at meetings of the Association, the method by which such votes may be exercised and the rights and obligations generally of members of the Association with regard to voting shall be in accordance with the By-Laws of the Association.

ARTICLE 9
Allocation of Liabilities, Common Expenses and Utility Fees

9.01 Derivation of Amounts. The share of liability for each unit of the common expenses of the Association is shown on Exhibit "D" attached hereto and incorporated herein by reference.

9.02 Liability for Assessments. The owner of each unit shall, by acceptance of a deed from the Declarant or any direct or remote successor-in-interest to Declarant in any unit, be personally liable for and shall pay to the Association:

(a) any assessment with respect to all expenditures made or incurred by or on behalf of the Association in the operation, management and maintenance of the Property, including but not limited to: fees for management and supervision; printing, mailing, office equipment, all legal and accounting fees as required, secretarial and other expenses related to the conduct of the affairs of the Association and the Board of Directors; insurance; all utility charges in connection with the common elements, including gas, electric, water, sewerage and telephone charges; all expenses in connection with maintenance and repair of all common elements; security; and water, sewer, sanitary, gas and electric services and other similar charges for all units.

(b) any assessment, payable monthly or as otherwise billed, for utility fees chargeable to each unit for the providing of electricity, gas and such other utility service as may from time to time be provided to or for the unit.

(c) pursuant to the By-Laws of the Association, assessments may be made more often than annually, may be made for the purpose of defraying, in whole or in part, utilities, operating expenses, the cost of any construction or reconstruction, or unexpected repair or replacement of capital improvements in respect to the common elements.

The Declarant shall be liable for all common area and other assessments and utility fees on units owned by Declarant. The Declarant shall not be liable for any other assessments or expenses provided in this Article 9 of this Declaration prior to the date of the first unit sale.

9.03 Equitable Assessment for Limited Common Area Expenses. Any common expenses which:

(a) are incurred through or occasioned by the use or enjoyment of any common elements which benefits or is intended to benefit less than all the units, shall not be assessed against all the units pursuant to Section 9.01 hereof, but shall be specifically assessed equitably among those units which are so benefited or intended to be benefited; and

(b) are incurred by the conduct of less than all of those entitled to occupy all of the units or by the licensees or invitees of any such unit or units shall be especially assessed against the condominium unit or units, the conduct of any occupant, licensee or invitee of which occasioned any such common expenses.

9.04 Assessment for Exclusive Benefit of Particular Units. Any common expenses which relate to limited common elements assigned to any unit or units and reserved for the exclusive use of those entitled to the use of such unit or units shall be assessed against such unit or units only.

(*continued*)

9.05 Lien Rights of Association. The Board of Directors shall have the authority to establish general rules applicable to all units providing that the lien for assessments shall include any one or more of the following: (i) a late or delinquency charge (not in excess of $10.00 or ten percent of the amount of each assessment or installment thereof not paid when due, whichever is greater), (ii) interest on each assessment or installment thereof, and any delinquency or late charge appertaining thereto, from the date the same was first due and payable, at a rate not in excess of ten percent per annum, (iii) the costs of collection, including court costs, the expenses of sale, any expenses required for the protection and preservation of the unit, and reasonable attorneys' fees actually incurred, and (iv) the fair rental value of the condominium unit from the time of the institution of suit until the sale of the condominium unit at foreclosure (or until the judgment rendered in such suit is otherwise satisfied).

ARTICLE 10

Association

10.01 Creation. The Declarant has caused the Clairemont Oaks Condominium Association, Inc., to be duly incorporated as a nonprofit membership corporation.

10.02 Powers Generally. The limitations and restrictions on the powers of the Association and on the Board of Directors of the Association are set out in the By-Laws of the Association.

10.03 Enforcement. The Association shall be empowered, in order to enforce compliance with the lawful provisions of the condominium instruments, including any rules or regulations contained in or promulgated in accordance with the By-Laws of the Association, to impose and assess fines and to suspend temporarily the right of use of certain of the common elements.

10.04 Restrictions on Powers. The Association shall have, except to the extent restricted herein, all those powers permitted by the provisions of Official Code of ____(State)____ , Section _____ , and except to the extent that it may not without the written consent of two-thirds of the unit owners (excluding Declarant) sell or transfer the common elements (excluding the grant of easements for public utilities or for any other public purposes consistent with the intended use of the common elements by the unit owners).

ARTICLE 11

Easements, Covenants and Use of the Condominium

11.01 Purposes. The Condominium is formed for residential purposes only and units shall be occupied and used by the owners thereof only as private residences for the owners and the families, tenants, invitees, and guests of such owners and for no other purposes whatsoever. Without derogating from the generality of the foregoing, no business shall be maintained or conducted in or from any unit.

11.02 Common Elements. All occupants of units and their guests shall have a nonexclusive right to use the common elements for the purposes for which they are intended, subject, however, to the following provisions:

(a) No such use shall enter or encroach upon the lawful rights of other persons; and

(b) The right of the Association to restrict the use and govern the operation of the common elements by promulgating reasonable rules and regulations with respect thereto, including, without limitation, the right to charge reasonable monthly fees for the use thereof by unit owners as the Association deems necessary or appropriate.

11.03 Strict Compliance. The owners of the units shall be entitled to all of the rights but shall be subject to all of the obligations provided for in the Act and all owners shall comply strictly with the provisions of the Condominium instruments including any restrictions, rules or regulations contained in or promulgated in accordance with the By-Laws of the Association.

(*continued*)

11.04 Maintenance of Offices. The provisions of Section 10.01 hereof shall not affect the right of the Declarant and its duly authorized agents, representatives and employees to enjoy the easement provided for in Official Code of ___(State)___, Section _____ for the maintenance of sales and leasing offices and/or model units on the submitted property.

11.05 Construction Easement. The Property shall be subject to a nonexclusive easement in favor of Declarant and its officers, employees, agents, independent contractors and invitees for entry upon and passage over the Property for purposes of constructing the units and other improvements described herein.

11.06 Utility Easements. There shall be appurtenant to each unit a nonexclusive easement for use of all pipes, wire cables, conduits, utility lines, flues and ducts serving such unit and situated in any other unit. Each unit shall be subject to an easement in favor of other units for use of all pipes, wire, cables, conduits, utility lines, flues and ducts situated in such unit and serving such other units.

11.07 Encroachments. If any portion of the common elements now encroaches upon any unit, or if any unit now encroaches upon any other unit or upon any portion of the common element, or if any such encroachment shall occur hereafter as a result of (i) settling of a unit or units; (ii) repair, alteration or reconstruction of the common elements made by or with the consent of the Association; (iii) repair or reconstruction of a unit or units following damage by fire or other casualty; or (iv) condemnation or eminent domain proceedings, a valid easement shall exist for such encroachment and for the maintenance of the same so long as the Property remains subject to the Act.

11.08 Right of Access. The Association shall have the irrevocable right, to be exercised by the Board of Directors, to have access to each unit from time to time during reasonable hours as may be necessary for the maintenance, repair or replacement of any of the common elements therein or accessible therefrom, or for making emergency repairs therein necessary to prevent damage to the common elements or to another unit.

11.09 Maintenance of Common Elements. The necessary work of maintenance, repair and replacement of the common elements and the making of any additions or improvements thereto shall be carried out only as provided in the Act, this Declaration and the By-Laws.

11.10 Prohibited Work. No owner shall do any work which would jeopardize the soundness or safety of the Property, reduce the value thereof or impair any easement or hereditament without in every such case unanimous consent of all other owners being first obtained.

ARTICLE 12

Insurance and Casualty Losses

12.01 Insurance Coverage. The Association shall obtain and maintain in full force and effect, at all times, the following insurance coverages:

(a) Insurance covering all of the insurable improvements on the property (with the exception of improvements and betterments made by the respective unit owners or occupants) and all personal property as may be owned by the Association, against loss or damage by fire and other hazards covered by the standard extended coverage endorsement, and such other risk as from time to time shall be customarily covered with respect to buildings similar in construction, location and use as the units, including, but not limited to, vandalism and malicious mischief in an amount equal to the maximum insurable replacement value thereof (exclusive of excavation and foundations), as determined annually by the Association;

(b) Comprehensive public liability insurance covering all of the common elements and insuring against all damage or liability caused by the acts of the Association, its officers, directors, agents and employees, all unit owners and other persons entitled to occupy any unit or

EXHIBIT 17–2

Condominium Declaration
(*continued*)

any other portion of the condominium, with liability limits in amounts authorized from time to time by the Association, but in no event less than the amounts required in the Act;

(c) Such other types and amounts of insurance as may from time to time be deemed necessary, desirable or proper, and be authorized by the Association by action of the Board of Directors or in its By-Laws.

12.02 Payment of Insurance Premiums. Premiums for all insurance carried by the Association shall be common expenses and shall be paid by the Association.

12.03 Policy Standards.

(a) All insurance coverage obtained by the Association shall be written in the name of the Association as trustee for, and for the use and benefit of, each of the unit owners and their mortgagees as their interest may appear, and their respective percentages of undivided interest in and to the common elements. Each such insurance policy shall be issued by an insurer authorized under the laws of the State of _____ to do business in _____(State)_____ and to issue the coverage provided by the policy, and shall provide for the issuance of a certificate of insurance to each unit owner and its mortgagee, if any, which shall specify the proportionate amount of such insurance attributable to the particular unit owner's interest in the property.

(b) The Association shall use its best efforts to cause all of such insurance policies to contain: (i) a waiver of subrogation by the insurer as to any claims against the Association, any officer, director, agent or employee of the Association, the unit owners and their employees, agents, tenants and invitees, and a waiver of any defenses based on co-insurance or on invalidity arising from the acts of the insured; (ii) a waiver by the insurer of its right to repair and reconstruct instead of paying cash; (iii) a provision that the policy cannot be cancelled, invalidated or suspended on account of the conduct of any unit owner or any employee, agent, tenant or invitee of any unit owner, or any officer, director, agent or employee of the Association, without a prior demand in writing and delivered to the Association to cure the defect and the allowance of reasonable time thereafter within which the defect may be cured by the Association, any unit owner or any mortgagee; (iv) a provision that any "other insurance" clause in the policy shall exclude from its scope any policies of the individual unit owners; (v) a provision that the coverage may not be cancelled or substantially modified (including cancellation for nonpayment of premium) without at least thirty days written notice to any and all of the insured thereunder, including mortgagees; and (vi) a provision that the coverage will not be prejudiced by any act or neglect of the owners of the units when said act or neglect is not within the control of the Association, or any failure of the Association to comply with any warranty or condition regarding any portion of the property over which the Association has no control.

12.04 Adjustment of Losses. Exclusive authority to adjust losses under insurance policies obtained by the Association shall be vested in the Association; provided, however, that no mortgagee shall be prohibited from participating in the settlement negotiations, if any, related thereto.

12.05 Individual Insurance by Unit Owners. It shall be the individual responsibility of each unit owner, at its sole cost and expense, to provide, as it sees fit any insurance coverage not required to be maintained by the Association. Any unit owner who obtains an individual insurance policy rejecting any risk as to which insurance is carried by the Association shall file a copy of such individual policy with the Association within thirty days after the purchase thereof.

12.06 Handling of Casualty Insurance Proceeds. All insurance policies purchased by and in the name of the Association shall provide that proceeds covered in casualty loss shall be paid to the Association. The Association shall receive such proceeds as are paid and delivered to it and hold the same in trust for the benefit of the unit owners and their mortgagees as follows:

(a) Proceeds on account of damage to the common elements not involving a unit shall be held to the extent of the undivided interest of each unit owner, for each unit owner, such interest to be equal to the undivided interest of each unit owner in and to the common elements.

(b) Proceeds on account of damage to units (or on account of damage to common elements involving a unit) shall be held for the owners of the damaged units in proportion to the cost of repairing the damage suffered by each unit owner, which cost shall be determined by the Board of Directors.

(c) In the event a mortgagee endorsement has been issued as to any unit under the policy under which such proceeds are paid, the share of that unit owner shall be held in trust for the unit owner and the mortgagee, as their interest may appear. Unless a determination is made not to repair or reconstruct pursuant to Section 12.07(b) hereof, and such proceeds, or such portion thereof as may be required for such purpose, shall be disbursed by the Association as payment of the cost and any expenses of repair or reconstruction, as hereinafter provided. Any proceeds remaining after payment of all cost and expenses of repair or reconstruction shall be common profits.

12.07 Damage and Destruction.

(a) Immediately after any damage or destruction by fire or other casualty to all or any portion of the property covered by insurance written in the name of the Association, the Association shall proceed with the filing and adjustment of all claims and losses arising under such insurance and obtain reliable and detailed estimates of the cost of repair or reconstruction of the damaged or destroyed property. Repair or reconstruction, as used in this paragraph, means repairing or restoring the property to substantially the same condition that existed prior to the fire or other casualty with each unit and the common elements having the same vertical and horizontal boundaries as before the casualty.

(b) Any damage or destruction shall be repaired or reconstructed unless: (i) the condominium is terminated pursuant to, subject to and in accordance with the provisions of the Act and this Declaration; (ii) the damaged or destroyed portion of the property is withdrawn from the condominium pursuant to, subject to and in accordance with the provisions of the Act; or (iii) the unit owners of the damaged or destroyed units, if any, and their mortgagees, together with the unit owners of other units to which two-thirds of the votes in the Association appertain and the mortgagees, exclusive of the votes appertaining to any damaged or destroyed units, agree not to repair or reconstruct such damage or destruction, pursuant to, subject to and in accordance with the provisions of the Act. Any such determination shall be conclusively made, if at all, not more than ninety days after the date of the casualty. Should a determination be made to terminate the condominium, as herein provided, then the insurance proceeds paid to the Association and held by it on account of such casualty shall be common profits, to be held and disbursed pursuant to, subject to and in accordance with Section 12.06 hereof. Should a determination be made to withdraw from the condominium the damaged portion of the property or not to repair or reconstruct the damage or destruction, as herein provided, then the insurance proceeds paid to the Association and held by it on account of such casualty shall be disbursed by the Association in accordance with the manner in which such proceeds are held by the Association, pursuant to Section 12.06 hereof. Any remittances with respect to units as to which mortgagee endorsements have been issued on the policies under which the proceeds were paid shall be payable to the unit owner and its mortgagee jointly, as their interest may appear.

(c) If the damage or destruction for which the insurance proceeds are paid is to be repaid and such proceeds are not sufficient to defray the cost thereof, the Association may levy an additional assessment against all unit owners in sufficient amounts to provide funds to pay such excess cost of repair or reconstruction. Further, additional assessments may be made in a like manner and any time during or following the completion of any repair or reconstruction. The proceeds from insurance and assessments, if any, received by the Association hereunder when the damage or destruction is to be repaired or reconstructed shall be disbursed as provided for in Section 12.06 hereof.

EXHIBIT 17–2

Condominium Declaration (*continued*)

(continued)

EXHIBIT 17–2

Condominium Declaration
(*continued*)

12.08 Non-Liability and Indemnity of Officers and Directors of the Association and Declarant. The officers and directors of the Association and Declarant shall not be personally liable to any unit owner for any mistake of judgment or for any other act or omission of any nature whatsoever in administering the Association, except for acts or omission which constitute gross negligence or willful misconduct. The Association shall indemnify and hold harmless each of the officers and directors of the Association and Declarant and their respective legal representatives, successors and assigns, from any liability, cost or expense arising out of any act or omission in administering the Association which is not deemed to be gross negligence or willful misconduct.

ARTICLE 13
Damage or Destruction

13.01 Obligation to Rebuild. In the event of damage to or destruction of the whole or any part of the building, the Association shall repair, rebuild or restore the building or such part as has been damaged or destroyed.

13.02 Compliance With Condominium Instruments. Such reparation, rebuilding or restoration shall be carried out in accordance with the provisions of the Act and the By-Laws of the Association.

ARTICLE 14
Sale or Leasing of Units

14.01 Notice Provisions. Any owner who sells or who leases his unit shall give notice in writing to the Board of Directors of such sale or of such lease stating the name and address of the purchaser or lessee and such other information as the Board may reasonably require. The Board of Directors shall have authority to make and to enforce reasonable rules and regulations in order to enforce this provision, including the right to impose fines constituting a lien upon the unit sold or leased, pursuant to the Act; provided, however, no rule or regulation may create a right of first refusal in the Association or any other third party, this paragraph solely creating the obligation of an owner to give notice to sell or lease. Notice, as required herein, shall be given, in the case of a lease, not later than fifteen (15) days after commencement of the lease and, in the case of a sale, not later than the closing of the sale.

14.02 Leasing Provision. Units may be rented only in their entirety; no fraction or portion may be rented. There shall be no subleasing of units or assignment of leases. With the exception of a lender in possession of a condominium unit following a default in a first mortgage, a foreclosure proceeding, or any deed or other arrangement in lieu of foreclosure, no unit owner shall be permitted to lease his unit for transient or hotel purposes. All leases and lessees are subject to the provisions of the condominium units and rules and regulations adopted pursuant thereto. Any lease agreement shall be required to provide that the terms of a lease shall be subject in all respects to the provisions of the Declaration and By-Laws and that any failure by the lessee to comply with the terms of such documents shall be a default under the lease. All leases shall be in writing. Other than units owned by the Declarant and with the exception of a lender in possession of a condominium unit following a default in a first mortgage, a foreclosure proceeding, or any deed or other arrangement in lieu of foreclosure, all rentals must be for a term of no less than one year. The unit owner must make available to the tenant copies of the Declaration, By-Laws and Rules and Regulations.

14.03 Any unit owner or person having executed a lease or a contract for the purchase of a condominium unit requesting a recordable statement certifying to the receipt by the Association of the notice herein specified, or the waiver of the Association's rights to receive such notice shall be furnished such a statement. Any such statement shall be binding on the Association and every unit owner. Payment of a fee, not exceeding $25.00, may be required as a prerequisite to the issuance of such a statement.

(*continued*)

ARTICLE 15

Eminent Domain

15.01 If any portion of the Condominium property is taken by eminent domain, the award shall be allocated as provided in Official Code of _____(State)_____ , Section _____ .

ARTICLE 16

Amendment of Condominium Instruments

16.01 By Owners. The Condominium instruments, including this Declaration, shall be amended only by the agreement of both the owners and mortgagees of units to which two-thirds (2/3) of the votes in the Association appertain, as provided in the By-Laws.

ARTICLE 17

Termination of the Condominium

17.01 Clairemont Oaks, a Condominium, shall be terminated only by the agreement of four-fifths (4/5) of the owners of the units and of all mortgagees of such units unless, in the case of the destruction of the entire development by fire or other casualty, following which the owners of the units decide not to rebuild, in which case the provisions of the By-Laws and the Declaration shall apply.

ARTICLE 18

Control by Declarant

18.01 Generally. The Declarant is hereby authorized in accordance with the By-Laws of the Association, incorporated herein by reference, to appoint and remove any member or members of the Board of Directors and any officer or officers of the Association with or without cause until the first of the following two occur:

(a) The third anniversary of the date of recording of this Declaration, or

(b) The date as of which units to which seventy percent (70%) of the undivided interests in the common elements have been conveyed by Declarant to unit owners other than a person or persons constituting Declarant, or

(c) The date as of which the Declarant surrenders the authority to appoint and remove all members of the Board of Directors by express amendment to the Declaration executed and recorded by the Declarant.

ARTICLE 19

Perpetuities

19.01 Should any of the provisions of this Declaration be unlawful, void or voidable for violation of the rule against perpetuities, then such provision shall continue only until twenty-one (21) years after the date that is ninety (90) years from and after the date of this Declaration.

ARTICLE 20

Miscellaneous

20.01 Notices. Notices provided for in the Act, this Declaration or the Articles or By-Laws shall be in writing, and shall be addressed to any unit owner at his/her or their unit at the condominium or at such other address as hereinafter provided. Notices to the Association shall be in writing and addressed to the President of the Association at his or her unit at the condominium, or to such other address as may hereafter be provided for and a written notice of such change of address furnished to all unit owners. Any unit owner may designate a different address for notices to him by giving written notice to the Association. Notices addressed as above shall be deemed delivered three business days after mailing by U. S. registered or certified mail, or when delivered in person. Upon written request to the Association, the holder

EXHIBIT 17–2

Condominium Declaration (*continued*)

(continued)

EXHIBIT 17–2

Condominium Declaration
(*continued*)

of any interest in any unit shall be given a copy of all notices to be given to the owner whose unit is subject to such interest.

20.02 Right to Notice, Attend Meetings and Inspection of Records. The owner of any interest in any unit, including any mortgagee, and any insurer or grantor of such mortgage, in addition to the rights set forth in the Act, shall have the right to inspect the books and records of the Association, including financial records, upon reasonable notice, and the right to attend and speak at any meeting of the Association, provided, however, no person other than a member as such shall have any voting rights. If the owner of any such interest files with the Association a written request, the Association shall have the right to notify such party of any violation by the owner of such unit, provided, however, that in no event shall the Association agree with any such party to furnish such notice unless such party agrees in writing that in no event shall the Association be liable for any claim or damages as a result of any failure to give such notice. Upon written request, any mortgagee shall have the right to receive a financial statement for the immediately preceding fiscal year.

20.03 Headings. The headings, sections and subsections in this Declaration and the Articles and By-Laws are for convenience or reference only and shall not in any way be deemed to limit or construe the intent of the parties or interpret the meaning of any document.

20.04 Number and Gender. As used in this Declaration, the singular shall include the plural, the masculine, feminine and neuter pronouns shall be fully interchangeable, where the context so requires.

20.05 Severability. If any provision of this Declaration or the Articles or By-Laws is held invalid, the validity of the remainder of this Declaration and the Articles and By-Laws shall not be affected thereby, and the remainder thereof shall be construed as if such invalid part was never included herein or therein.

20.06 Rights and Obligations. Each successor in title of the Declarant with respect to any part of the property, by the acceptance of a Deed of Conveyance, accepts the same subject to all restrictions, conditions, covenants, reservations, liens and charges created or reserved by this Declaration. All rights, benefits and privileges hereby imposed shall be deemed and taken to be covenants running with the land, and shall be binding inured to the benefit of any person having any interest or estate in the property, or any portion thereof.

ARTICLE 21

Author

21.01 This Declaration was prepared by _____ , with an office address of_____

_____

IN WITNESS WHEREOF, the Declarant has executed this Declaration under seal on the _____ day of _____ , 20___.

DECLARANT:

Signed, sealed and delivered in the
presence of:

THE FARRIS CORPORATION

_____

_____

Unofficial Witness

_____

By: _____

Notary Public

President

County of Appointment:

Attest: _____

Expiration of Commission:

[Notary Seal]

Secretary

[CORPORATE SEAL]

44-3-83. Recording of plats and plans; contents; completion of structural improvements; certification by registered architect or engineer.

(a) Prior to the first conveyance of a condominium unit, there shall be recorded one or more plats of survey showing the location and dimensions of the submitted property; the location and dimensions of all structural improvements located on any portion of the submitted property; the intended location and dimensions of all contemplated structural improvements committed to be provided by the declaration on any portion of the submitted property; and, to the extent feasible, the location and dimensions of all easements appurtenant to the submitted property or otherwise submitted to this article as part of the common elements. With respect to all such structural improvements, the plats shall indicate which, if any, have not been begun by use of the phrase "Not Yet Begun." No structural improvement which contains or constitutes all or part of any unit or units and which is located on any portion of the submitted property shall be commenced on any portion of the submitted property after the recording of the plats. The declarant shall complete all structural improvements depicted on the plats, subject only to such limitations, if any, as may be expressly stated in the declaration with respect to those labeled "Not Yet Begun" on the plats, provided that, within six months after written notice from the association, the declarant shall be obligated to complete within a reasonable time every structural improvement actually commenced on the submitted property, notwithstanding any provision of the declaration, unless the declarant removes within a reasonable time all portions of any such structural improvement and restores the surface of the land affected thereby to substantially the same condition as that which existed prior to commencement of any such structural improvement; and provided, further, that nothing contained in this sentence shall exempt the declarant from any contractual liability to complete any such structural improvement. If the submitted property consists of noncontiguous parcels, the plats shall indicate the approximate distances between such parcels unless such information is disclosed in the declaration. If, with respect to any portion or portions, but less than all, of the submitted property, the unit owners are to own only a leasehold or estate for years, the plats shall show the location and dimensions of any such portion or portions and shall label each such portion by use of the phrase "Leased Land." To the extent feasible, the plats shall show all easements to which the submitted property or any portion thereof is subject. The plats shall also show all encroachments by or on any operation of the submitted property. In the case of any units which have vertical boundaries lying wholly or partially outside of structures for which plans pursuant to subsection (b) of this Code section are recorded, the plats shall show the location and dimensions of the vertical boundaries to the extent that they are not shown on the plans; and the units or portions thereof thus depicted shall bear their identifying numbers. Each plat shall be certified as to its accuracy and compliance with this subsection by a registered land surveyor. The specification within this subsection of items that shall be shown on the plats shall not be construed to mean that the plats shall not also show all other items customarily shown or required by law to be shown for land title surveys.

(b) There shall be recorded prior to the first conveyance of a condominium unit:

(1) Plans which have been prepared, signed, and sealed by a registered architect or registered engineer of every structure which contains or constitutes all or part of any unit or units located on or within any portion of the submitted property, which plans shall show:

(A) The location and dimensions of the exterior walls and roof of such structures;

(B) The walls, partitions, floors, and ceilings as constitute the horizontal boundaries, if any, and the vertical boundaries of each unit, including convertible space, to the extent that such boundaries lie within or coincide with the boundaries of such structures; and

(C) The identifying numbers of all units or portions thereof depicted on the plans; and

EXHIBIT 17–3

State Condominium Code Requirements for Condominium Plat

Delmar/Cengage Learning

(continued)

(2) A certification by such architect or engineer to the effect that he has visited the site and viewed the property and that, to the best of his knowledge, information, and belief:

(A) The exterior walls and roof of each structure are in place as shown on the plans; and

(B) Such walls, partitions, floors, and ceilings, to the extent shown on said plans, as constitute the horizontal boundaries, if any, and the vertical boundaries of each unit, including convertible space, have been sufficiently constructed so as to establish clearly the physical boundaries of such unit.

In addition, each convertible space depicted in the plans shall be labeled as such by use of the phrase "CONVERTIBLE SPACE." Unless the condominium instruments expressly provide otherwise, it shall be presumed that, in the case of any unit not wholly contained within or constituting one or more of the structures, the horizontal boundaries extend, in the case of each unit, at the same elevation with regard to any part of such unit lying outside of such structures, subject to the following exception: in the case of any unit which does not lie over any other unit other than basement units, it shall be presumed that the lower horizontal boundary, if any, of that unit lies at the level of the ground with regard to any part of that unit lying outside of the structures.

(b.1) There shall be recorded prior to the first conveyance of a condominium unit plans of every structure which contains or constitutes all or part of any unit or units located on or within any portion of the submitted property and a certification by a registered architect or registered engineer to the effect that he has visited the site and viewed the property and that, to the best of his knowledge, information, and belief:

(1) The foundation, structural members, exterior walls, and roof of each such structure are complete and in place as shown on the plans;

(2) The walls, partitions, floors, and ceilings, to the extent shown on the plans, as constituting or coinciding with the vertical and horizontal boundaries of each unit, including convertible space, within each such structure, are sufficiently complete and in place to establish clearly the physical boundaries of such unit and that such physical boundaries are as shown on the plans; and

(3) Each such structure, to the extent of its stage of completion at that time, is constructed substantially in accordance with such plans.

The plans shall show the location and dimensions of the horizontal boundaries, if any, and the vertical boundaries of each unit to the extent that such boundaries lie within or coincide with the boundaries of such structures, and the units, or portions thereof, thus depicted shall bear their identifying numbers. In addition, each convertible space depicted in the plans shall be labeled as such by use of the phrase "CONVERTIBLE SPACE." Unless the condominium instruments expressly provide otherwise, it shall be presumed that, in the case of any unit not wholly contained within or constituting one or more of the structures, the horizontal boundaries extend, in the case of each unit, at the same elevation with regard to any part of such unit lying outside of such structures, subject to the following exception: in the case of any unit which does not lie over any other unit other than basement units, if shall be presumed that the lower horizontal boundary, if any, of that unit lies at the level of the ground with regard to any part of that unit lying outside of the structures. This subsection shall apply to any condominium created prior to July 1, 1980, or to the expansion of any such condominium.

(c) Prior to the first conveyance of a condominium unit located on any portion of any additional property being or having been added to an expandable condominium, there shall be recorded new plats of survey conforming to the requirements of subsection (a) of this Code section and, with regard to any structures on the property being or having been added, plans conforming to the requirements of subsection (b) of this Code section or certifications, conforming to the certification requirements of subsection (b) of this Code section, of plans previously recorded.

(d) When converting all or any portion of any convertible space into one or more units or limited common elements, the declarant shall record, with regard to the structure or portion thereof constituting that convertible space, plans showing the location and dimensions of the horizontal boundaries, if any, and the vertical boundaries of each unit formed out of such

(*continued*)

space. The plans shall be certified by a registered architect or registered engineer in accordance with the certification requirements of subsection (b) of this Code section.

(e) When any portion of the submitted property is withdrawn, there shall be recorded a plat or plats showing the portion of the submitted property withdrawn and the remaining submitted property, which plat or plats shall be certified as provided in subsection (a) of this Code section.

EXHIBIT 17–3

State Condominium Code Requirements for Condominium Plat (*continued*)

ARTICLES OF INCORPORATION

OF

CLAIREMONT OAKS CONDOMINIUM ASSOCIATION, INC.

ARTICLE 1

The name of the corporation shall be:

CLAIREMONT OAKS CONDOMINIUM ASSOCIATION, INC.

ARTICLE 2

The corporation is organized pursuant to the provisions of the ____(State)____ Nonprofit Corporation Code.

ARTICLE 3

The corporation shall have perpetual duration.

ARTICLE 4

The corporation shall have no stock or stockholders; it is not organized and shall not operate for profit or pecuniary gain; and no part of the net earnings of the corporation shall inure to the benefit of any member, director, officer of any private individual except that, pursuant to proper authorization, reasonable compensation may be paid for services rendered to or for the corporation affecting one or more of its purposes. No substantial part of the activities of the corporation shall be for carrying on of propaganda, or otherwise attempting to influence legislation, and the corporation shall not participate in or intervene in (including publishing or distributing statements) any political campaign on behalf of any candidate for public office.

ARTICLE 5

The purposes for which the corporation is organized are: to provide for the administration of a condominium to be known as Clairemont Oaks, A Condominium; to provide for the maintenance, repair, replacement and operation of portions of the condominium; to promote the health, safety and welfare of the owners and occupants of the condominium; to exercise all rights and privileges and perform all duties and obligations of the corporation as set forth in the ____(State)____ Condominium Act and in the Declaration for Clairemont Oaks, A Condominium to be recorded in the Office of the Clerk of the Superior Court of Wayne County, ____(State)____; and to perform such related functions as the board of directors of the corporation shall from time to time determine.

ARTICLE 6

In addition to, but not in limitation of, the general powers conferred by law, the corporation shall have the power to own, acquire, construct, operate and maintain property, buildings, structures and other facilities incident thereto; to supplement municipal or governmental

EXHIBIT 17–4

Articles of Incorporation

(continued)

EXHIBIT 17–4

Articles of Incorporation
(*continued*)

services; to fix and collect assessments to be levied against and with respect to the condominium units and the owners thereof which assessments shall be a lien and permanent charge on said units as well as the personal obligation of said owners; to enforce any and all covenants, restrictions and agreements applicable to the condominium; to buy, hold, lease, sell, rent, manage and otherwise deal in property of every kind and description, whether real or personal; to borrow money, issue promissory notes and other obligations and evidences of indebtedness and to secure the same by mortgage, deed, security deed, pledge or otherwise; and, insofar as permitted by law, to do any other thing that, in the opinion of the board of directors, will promote, directly or indirectly, the health, safety, welfare, common benefit or enjoyment of the unit owners and occupants of said units; enhance, preserve or maintain property values within the condominium; enhance, preserve or maintain the appearance of the condominium and its surroundings; or be necessary, proper, useful or incidental to the carrying out of the functions for which the corporation is organized.

ARTICLE 7

The address of the initial registered office of the corporation shall be c/o _____ at _____ , and the name of its original agent at such address is _____ .

ARTICLE 8

The directors of the corporation shall be elected or appointed at the time and in the manner as provided in the By-Laws of the corporation as the same may from time to time be amended.

ARTICLE 9

The initial board of directors of the corporation shall number _____ (____) and the name and address of each person who is to serve as a member thereof is as follows:

Name	Address
_____	_____
	_____
_____	_____
_____	_____
	_____

ARTICLE 10

The corporation shall have one class of members. Each owner of a condominium unit comprising a portion of Clairemont Oaks, A Condominium, shall automatically be a member of the corporation, which membership shall continue during the period of ownership by such unit owner Pursuant to the provisions of the ____(State)____ Condominium Act, the number of votes in the corporation allocated to each condominium unit is set forth in the Declaration for Clairemont Oaks, A Condominium. Said votes shall be cast under such rules and procedures as may be prescribed in the By-Laws of the corporation, as amended from time to time, or by law.

ARTICLE 11

These Articles of Incorporation may be amended as by law provided pursuant to resolution duly adopted by the board of directors and by at least two-thirds of the votes which

(*continued*)

members present in person or by proxy at a duly called meeting are entitled to cast; provided, however, that no members shall be entitled to vote on amendments to these Articles of Incorporation for the sole purpose of complying with the requirements of any governmental or quasi-governmental entity authorized to fund or guarantee mortgages on individual condominium units, as such requirements may exist from time to time, which amendments may be adopted only at a meeting of the board of directors upon receiving the vote of a majority of the directors then in office.

ARTICLE 12

The corporation may be dissolved as by law provided pursuant to resolution duly adopted by the board of directors and by at least four-fifths of the votes of the members of the corporation.

ARTICLE 13

The name of the incorporator is _____, whose address is _____.

IN WITNESS WHEREOF, the incorporator has executed these Articles of Incorporation.

_____

CONSENT TO APPOINTMENT AS REGISTERED AGENT

To: Secretary of State

    Ex-Officio Corporation

    Commissioner

    State of _____

I, _____, do hereby consent to serve as registered agent for the corporation Clairemont Oaks Condominium Association, Inc.

This _____ day of _____ , 20_____.

_____

Address of Registered Agent:

_____

_____

_____

EXHIBIT 17–4

Articles of Incorporation (*continued*)

EXHIBIT 17–5

Condominium
Association Bylaws

BYLAWS OF

CLAIREMONT OAKS CONDOMINIUM ASSOCIATION, INC.

ARTICLE 1

Name and Location

Section 1. Name. The name of the association is Clairemont Oaks Condominium Association, Inc., a ____(State)____ nonprofit membership corporation, hereinafter referred to as the "Association."

Section 2. Location. The principal office of the Condominium shall be located in Wayne County, __(State)__. Meetings of members and directors may be held at such places within the State of _____, County of Wayne as may be designated from time to time by the Board of Directors.

ARTICLE 2

Definitions

Section 1. General. The terms used in these Bylaws, unless otherwise specified or unless the context otherwise requires, shall have the meanings specified in Official Code of __(State)__, Section _____ and the Declaration for Clairemont Oaks, A Condominium (hereinafter called the "Declaration"). Statutory references shall be construed as meaning the referenced statute or portion thereof as the same may exist from time to time.

ARTICLE 3

Membership and Voting Rights

Section 1. Membership. Each unit owner shall automatically be a member of the Association, which membership shall continue during the period of ownership by such unit owner.

Section 2. Voting Rights. The Association shall have one class of voting membership which shall consist of all unit owners. Such owners shall be entitled to exercise voting rights as provided in the __(State)__ Condominium Act, the Declaration and as prescribed herein. The number of votes allocated to each unit is as set forth in the Declaration. When a unit is owned by other than one or more natural persons, the person entitled to cast the vote for such unit shall be designated by a certificate signed by the record owner of such unit and filed with the Secretary. Each such certificate shall be valid until revoked, superseded by a subsequent certificate or a change occurs in the ownership of such unit. When a unit is owned by more than one natural person, they may, without being required to do so, designate the person entitled to cast the vote for such unit as provided above. In the event they do not designate such a person, the following provisions shall apply:

(a) If only one is present at a meeting, the person present shall be counted for purposes of a quorum and may cast the vote for the unit, just as though he owned it individually, and without establishing the concurrence of the absent person or persons.

(b) If more than one of such owners, whether or not all of them, are present at a meeting and concur, any one of the owners may cast the vote for the owners.

(c) If more than one of such owners, whether or not all of them, are present at a meeting and are unable to concur in their decision upon any subject requiring a vote, they shall lose their right to vote on that subject at that meeting. The votes of the unit owners shall be cast under such rules and procedures as may be prescribed in the Declaration or in these Bylaws, as amended from time to time, or by law.

Section 3. Suspension of Voting Rights. During any period in which a unit owner shall be in default in payment of any assessment, the voting rights of such unit owner may be suspended by the Board of Directors until such assessment has been paid. Such rights of a unit owner may also be suspended, for a period not to exceed 30 days, for violation of any rules and regulations established by the Board of Directors.

Delmar/Cengage Learning

(continued)

ARTICLE 4

Meetings of Unit Owners

Section 1. Annual Meetings. The first annual meeting of the unit owners shall be called by the President upon request of the Declarant and shall be held within 12 months following the incorporation of the Association. Each subsequent regular annual meeting of the owners shall be held on the same day of the same month of each year thereafter unless otherwise provided by the unit owners at any previous meeting. If the day for the annual meeting of the unit owners is a legal holiday, the meeting will be held on the first day following which is not a legal holiday.

Section 2. Special Meetings. Special meetings of the unit owners may be called at any time by the President or by the Board of Directors, or upon written request of the unit owners who are entitled to vote at least _____ (____%) of the votes of the membership.

Section 3. Notice of Meetings. Written notice of each meeting of the unit owners shall be given by, or at the direction of, the Secretary or person authorized to call the meeting at least 21 days in advance of any annual or regularly scheduled meeting, and at least seven days in advance of any other meeting, stating the time, place and purpose of such meeting. Such notice shall be delivered personally or sent by United States mail, postage prepaid, to all unit owners of record at such address or addresses as any of them may have designated, or, of no other address has been so designated, at the address of their respective units. Such notice shall also be sent by United States mail, postage prepaid, to each institutional holder of a first mortgage on a unit having theretofore requested same in writing. Each such holder shall be permitted to designate a representative to attend each such meeting without voice or vote except pursuant to Section 5 of this Article 4.

Section 4. Quorum. The presence at the meeting of unit owners and/or proxies entitled to cast more than one-third of the votes of the membership shall constitute a quorum for any action except as otherwise expressly provided in the ____(State)____ Condominium Act or in the Declaration. If, however, such quorum shall not be present or represented at any meeting, the unit owners and/or proxies entitled to cast a majority of the votes thereat shall have the power to adjourn the meeting from time to time, without notice other than announcement at the meeting, until a quorum as aforesaid shall be present or be represented.

Section 5. Proxies. Subject to the provisions of Article 3, Section 2, hereof, at all meetings of the unit owners, each unit owner may vote in person or by proxy. All proxies shall be in writing and filed with the Secretary. Each proxy shall be revocable, shall automatically cease upon conveyance by a unit owner of his unit and shall be effective only for the meeting specified therein and any adjournment thereof.

Section 6. Order of Business. The order of business at all annual meetings of the owners shall be as follows:

        (a) Roll call.

        (b) Proof of notice of meeting.

        (c) Reading of minutes of preceding meeting.

        (d) Reports of officers.

        (e) Report of Board of Directors.

        (f) Reports of committees.

        (g) Election of Directors.

        (h) Unfinished business.

        (i) New business.

Section 7. Decisions of Unit Owners. Unless otherwise expressly provided in the ____(State)____ Condominium Act, the Declaration or these Bylaws, a majority of the votes cast on any particular issue shall be necessary to adopt decisions at any meeting of the unit

EXHIBIT 17–5

Condominium Association Bylaws (*continued*)

(*continued*)

EXHIBIT 17–5

Condominium
Association Bylaws
(*continued*)

owners. When the _____(State)_____ Condominium Act, the Declaration or these Bylaws require the approval or consent of all or a specified percentage of mortgagees and/or other lien holders, no decision or resolution duly adopted by the unit owners shall be effective or valid until such approval or consent shall be obtained. During such time as the Declarant has the right to control the Association pursuant to the provisions of Official Code of _____(State)_____, Section _____, no decision or resolution duly adopted by the unit owners shall be effective or valid until the Declarant's approval or consent shall have been obtained.

Section 8. Conduct of Meetings. The President shall preside over all meetings of the unit owners and the Secretary shall keep the minutes of the meetings and record in a minute book all resolutions duly adopted as well as a record of all transactions occurring at such meetings. The latest edition of Roberts Rules of Order shall govern the conduct of all meetings of the unit owners when not in conflict with the _____(State)_____ Condominium Act, the Declaration or these Bylaws.

ARTICLE 5
Board of Directors

Section 1. Number and Qualifications. Following expiration of the period of the Declarant's right to control the Association pursuant to the provisions of Official Code of _____(State)_____, Section _____, the Board of Directors of the Association shall be composed of three persons. With the exception of those persons appointed as directors by the Declarant pursuant to the provisions of Official Code of _____(State)_____, Section _____, each such person shall be a member of the Association or the spouse of a member.

Section 2. Election and Term of Office. Upon the termination of the Declarant's right to control the Association pursuant to the provisions of Official Code of _____(State)_____, Section _____, the Declarant shall give at least seven days' written notice to each member of a special meeting of the members, to be held not more than 30 days after the date of such termination, to elect a new board of directors. At such meeting, and at each annual meeting thereafter the unit owners shall elect three directors for a term of one year each. Except in the case of death, resignation or removal, each director elected by the members shall serve until the annual meeting at which his term expires and until his successor has been duly elected and qualified. Persons receiving the largest number of votes at any election of directors shall be elected whether or not such number constitutes a majority of the votes cast. Cumulative voting shall not be permitted.

Section 3. Removals; Vacancies. Following expiration of the period of the Declarant's right to control the Association pursuant to the provisions of Official Code of _____(State)_____, Section _____, any director may be removed from the Board of Directors with or without cause, by a majority vote of the unit owners theretofore entitled to elect such director. In the event of death or resignation of a director, his successor shall be selected by the remaining members of the board. In the event of removal of a director, his successor shall be elected by the unit owners theretofore entitled to elect such director. Any such successor shall serve for the unexpired term of his predecessor.

Section 4. Annual Organization Meeting. The first meeting of the Board of Directors following each annual meeting of the unit owners shall be held within ten days thereafter, at such time and place as shall be fixed by the newly elected directors at such annual meeting, and no notice shall be necessary in order legally to constitute such meeting.

Section 5. Regular Meetings. Regular meetings of the Board of Directors may be held at such time and place as shall be determined from time to time by the Board of Directors. Notice of the time and place of regular meetings shall be given to every director by mail or telephone at least three days prior to the date of such meeting.

Section 6. Special Meetings. Special meetings of the Board of Directors may be called by the President on two days notice to every director given by mail or telephone and stating the time, place and purpose of the meeting. Special meetings shall be called by the President or

(*continued*)

Secretary in like manner and on like notice on the written request of directors entitled to cast at least two votes at such meetings.

Section 7. Waiver of Notice; Action without Meeting. Whenever notice of a meeting of the Board of Directors is required to be given under any provision of these Bylaws, a written waiver thereof, executed by a director before or after the meeting and filed with the Secretary, shall be deemed equivalent to notice to the director executing the same. Attendance at a meeting by the director shall constitute a waiver of notice of such meeting by the director if such director attends the meeting without protesting prior thereto or at the meeting's commencement the lack of notice to him. Neither the business to be transacted at, nor the purpose of, any meeting of the Board of Directors need be specified in any written waiver of notice. Any action required or permitted to be taken at any meeting of the Board of Directors may be taken without a meeting provided that all directors consent to the action in writing and the written consents are filed with the records of the proceedings of the Board of Directors. Such consents shall be treated for all purposes as a vote at a meeting.

Section 8. Voting; Quorum of the Board; Adjournment of Meetings. At all meetings of the Board of Directors, each director shall be entitled to cast one vote. The presence in person of directors representing at least two-thirds of the votes of the Board of Directors shall be a quorum at any Board of Directors meeting and a majority of the votes present and voting shall bind the Board of Directors and the Association as to any matter within the powers and duties of the Board of Directors.

Section 9. Powers and Duties. The Board of Directors shall have the powers and duties necessary for administration of the affairs of the Association and may do all such acts and things except as by law or the Declaration may not be delegated to the Board of Directors by the unit owners. In exercising its powers and duties, the Board of Directors shall take as its standard the maintenance of the general character of the condominium as a residential community of the first class in the quality of its maintenance, use and occupancy. Such powers and duties of the Board of Directors shall be exercised in accordance with and subject to all provisions of the ___(State)___ Condominium Act, the Declaration and these Bylaws and shall include without limitation powers and duties to:

(a) Operate, care for, maintain, repair and replace the common elements and employ personnel necessary or desirable therefor.

(b) Determine common expenses of the Association.

(c) Collect assessments from the unit owners.

(d) Adopt and amend rules and regulations covering the details of the operation and use of the condominium.

(e) Open bank accounts on behalf of the Association and designate the signatories required therefor.

(f) Manage, control, lease as lessor, and otherwise deal with the common elements, including power to make shut-offs of common services and other interruptions of the normal functioning of the buildings to facilitate performance of any maintenance or repair work or the making of additions, alterations or improvements by the Association or the unit owners pursuant to provisions of the Declaration. The Board of Directors shall use reasonable efforts to disrupt the unit owners and occupants as little as possible in exercising such authority to effect shut-offs and other interruptions.

(g) Purchase, lease or otherwise acquire units offered for sale or lease or surrendered by their unit owners to the Association.

(h) Own, sell, lease, encumber, and otherwise deal in, but not vote with respect to, units owned by the Association.

(i) Obtain and maintain insurance for the condominium pursuant to the provisions of the Declaration.

EXHIBIT 17–5

Condominium Association Bylaws

(*continued*)

(*continued*)

(j) (1) Make additions and improvements to and alterations of the common elements, and (2) make repairs to and restoration of the property after damage or destruction by fire or other casualty, or as a result of condemnation.

(k) Enforce by any legal or equitable remedies available all obligations of the unit owners or any of them to the Association. Such enforcement power shall include, without limitation, the power to levy, as assessments, fines against unit owners for default in the performance of said obligations in such amounts as from time to time the Board of Directors may deem proper in the circumstances, but not in excess of $_____ for any one violation, counting each day a violation continues after notice from the Board of Directors as a separate violation. If any owner fails to pay a fine within ten days after notification thereof, the Board of Directors may levy, as assessments, additional fines to enforce payment of the initial fine.

(l) Appoint auditors of the Association.

(m) Employ a manager or managing agent and delegate thereto any duties of the Board of Directors under subparagraphs (a), (c), (e), (i) and (o) of this Section 9.

(n) Conduct litigation and be subject to suit as to any cause of action involving the common elements or arising out of the enforcement of the provisions of the ___(State)___ Condominium Act, the Declaration or these By-Laws.

(o) Make contracts in connection with the exercise of any of the powers and duties of the Board of Directors.

(p) Take all other actions the Board of Directors deems necessary or proper for the sound management of the condominium and fulfillment of the terms and provisions of the ___(State)___ Condominium Act, the Declaration and these Bylaws.

In the case of those powers and duties specified in the foregoing clauses (d), (g), (h), (j), (l), and (m), the Board of Directors need exercise the same only to the extent, if any, it deems necessary or desirable or is required to do so by vote of the unit owners. The Board of Directors shall not be obligated to take any action or perform any duty imposed upon it requiring an expenditure of funds unless in its opinion it shall have funds of the Association sufficient therefor.

ARTICLE 6
Officers

Section 1. Designation. The Principal officers of the Association shall be the President, the Vice President, the Secretary and the Treasurer, all of whom shall be elected by the Board of Directors. One person may hold the office of Secretary and Treasurer simultaneously. The Board of Directors may appoint an assistant treasurer, an assistant secretary, and such other officers as in its judgment may be necessary. The Vice President may also hold the office of assistant secretary and perform the functions thereof in the absence of the Secretary. The President and Vice President shall be members of the Board of Directors. Any other officers may be, but shall not be required to be, members of the Board of Directors.

Section 2. Election of Officers. The officers of the Association shall be elected annually by the Board of Directors at the organization meeting of each new Board of Directors and shall hold office at the pleasure of the Board of Directors. Any vacancy in an office shall be filled by the Board of Directors at a regular meeting of the Board of Directors, or at any special meeting of the Board of Directors called for such purpose.

Section 3. Removal of Officers. Upon the affirmative vote of a majority of the votes of the Board of Directors, any officer may be removed, either with or without cause, and his successor may be elected at any regular meeting of the Board of Directors, or at any special meeting of the Board of Directors called for such purpose.

Section 4. Multiple Offices. The offices of Secretary and Treasurer may be held by the same person. No person shall simultaneously hold more than one of any of the other offices except in the case of special offices created pursuant to Section 1 of this Article 6.

(*continued*)

Section 5. President. The President shall be the chief executive of the Association. He shall preside at all meetings of the unit owners and of the Board of Directors. He shall have all of the general powers and duties which are incident to the office of president of a corporation, including, but not limited to, the power to appoint committees from among the unit owners from time to time as he may, in his sole discretion, deem appropriate to assist in the conduct of the affairs of the Association.

Section 6. Vice President. The Vice President shall take the place of the President and perform his duties whenever the President shall be absent or unable to act. If neither the President nor the Vice President is able to act, the Board of Directors shall appoint some other member of the Board of Directors to act in the place of the President on an interim basis. The Vice President shall also perform such other duties as shall, from time to time, be imposed upon him by the Board of Directors or by the President.

Section 7. Secretary. The Secretary shall keep the minutes of all meetings of the unit owners and of the Board of Directors and shall have charge of such books and papers as the Board of Directors may direct. He shall, in general, perform all the duties incident to the office of secretary of a corporation and such other duties as shall, from time to time, be imposed upon him by the Board of Directors or by the President.

Section 8. Treasurer. The Treasurer shall have the responsibility for Association funds and securities and shall be responsible for keeping full and accurate financial records and books of account showing all receipts and disbursements, and for the preparation of all required financial data; he shall be responsible for the deposit of all monies and other valuable effects in the name of the Association, in such depositories as may from time to time be designated by the Board of Directors, and he shall, in general, perform all the duties incident to the office of treasurer of a corporation and such other duties as shall, from time to time, be imposed upon him by the Board of Directors or by the President.

Section 9. Compensation. Unless otherwise expressly provided by the Board of Directors, no officer shall receive compensation from the Association for acting as such, but shall be entitled to reimbursement from the Association as a common expense for reasonable out-of-pocket disbursements made by him in the performance of his duties. No officer shall be obligated to make any such disbursements.

ARTICLE 7

Officers and Directors: General Provisions

Section 1. Contracts with Interested Parties. No contract or transaction between the Association and one or more of its officers or directors, or between the Association and any other entity in which one or more of the association's officers or directors are officers, directors, partners or trustees, or have a financial interest, shall be void or voidable solely for this reason, or solely because the Association's officer or director is present at or participates in the meeting of the Board of Directors which authorizes the contract or transaction, or solely because his or their votes are counted for such purpose, if (a) the material facts as to his interest and as to the contract or transaction are disclosed or are known to the Board of Directors and the Board of Directors in good faith authorized the contract or transaction by a vote sufficient for such purpose without counting the vote or votes of the interested director or directors; or (b) the material facts as to his interest and as to the contract or transaction are disclosed or are known to the unit owners entitled to vote thereon, and the contract or transaction is specifically approved or ratified in good faith by vote of such unit owners; or (c) the contract or transaction is fair as to the Association as of the time it is authorized, approved or ratified by the Board of Directors or the unit owners. Interested directors may be counted in determining the presence of a quorum at a meeting of the Board of Directors which authorizes the contract or transaction.

EXHIBIT 17–5

Condominium Association Bylaws (*continued*)

(*continued*)

EXHIBIT 17–5

Condominium
Association Bylaws
(*continued*)

Section 2. Indemnification. Pursuant to the provisions of Section 12.08 of the Declaration, the Association shall indemnify its officers and directors to the extent provided in and subject to the limitations of the Declaration.

ARTICLE 8
Books and Records

Section 1. Books and Records. The Association shall keep such books and records as by law provided and shall make same available for inspection by any unit owner, any institutional holder of a first mortgage on a unit, and their respective agents and attorneys, for any proper purpose at any reasonable time. In addition, an annual report of the receipts and expenditures of the Association, based upon an audit made by an independent public accountant, shall be rendered by the Board of Directors to all unit owners, and to each institutional holder of a first mortgage on a unit having theretofore requested same in writing, within three months after the end of each fiscal year.

ARTICLE 9
Amendments

Section 1. Amendments. These Bylaws may be amended only by the owners of the units to which two-thirds (2/3) of the votes in the Association cast their vote in person or by proxy at a meeting duly called for such purpose, written notice of which shall be delivered or sent to all unit owners not less than 21 days in advance of the meeting stating the time, place and purpose of such meeting and the subject matter of the proposed amendment or, in lieu of such vote, these Bylaws may be amended by an instrument duly executed by unit owners having at least two-thirds (2/3) of the entire voting interest of all unit owners. Amendments to these Bylaws for the sole purpose of complying with the requirements of any governmental or quasi-governmental entity authorized to fund or guarantee mortgages on individual condominium units, as such requirements may exist from time to time, may be effected by an instrument duly executed by a majority of the directors of the Association. Each such amendment shall be effective when adopted or at such later date as may be specified therein.

ARTICLE 10
Miscellaneous

Section 1. Conflicts. In the event of any conflict between the Declaration and these Bylaws, the Declaration shall control.

Section 2. Association Seal. The Association shall have a seal in circular form having within its circumference the words: _____.

Section 3. Fiscal Year. The fiscal year of the Association shall begin on the first day of January and end on the 31st day of December of every year, except that the first fiscal year shall begin on the date on which the Association was incorporated under the laws of the State of _____.

chapter | 18

Leases

Objectives

After reading this chapter, you should be able to:

- Review a commercial lease and understand its key provisions
- Define the various ways to compute rent under a lease
- Understand the legal differences between an assignment of lease and a sublease
- Recognize a landlord's remedies for a tenant's default under a lease
- Recognize a tenant's remedies for a landlord's default under a lease

Outline

lease

Legal document that transfers possession of real property from one party to another. The lease also may contain numerous terms and conditions involving the use and possession of the property.

residential lease

A lease for the possession and use of a residence such as an apartment or a house.

commercial lease

A lease for the possession and use of a business or commercial enterprise such as a retail store, warehouse, or office.

Paralegals often are involved in the preparation and review of **leases.** Although in many instances a paralegal is furnished with either a preprinted form or a form prepared by a law firm to review or to use as a guide in the preparation of the new lease, it is important that the paralegal understand the legal theories and concepts of leases as well as be aware of the general provisions found in most leases.

A lease may be a **residential lease** for use in a residential situation for the possession and use of an apartment or house. A lease may also be a **commercial lease** and used in a commercial setting for the possession and use of a business or commercial enterprise such as a retail store, warehouse, or office. Because of the legal expense involved, most paralegals are involved in the preparation and review of commercial leases. For this reason, most of the discussion in this chapter pertains to commercial leases. Many of the issues discussed, however, have equal application to a residential apartment or home lease. Examples of residential and commercial lease forms are included at the end of this chapter.

COMMON LAW AND LEASES

The English common law treated a lease as a combination of property and contract law. Because a lease transfers possession and, in some cases, is an estate for years, it is deemed to be a conveyance of real property. In addition, leases contain numerous terms and conditions that involve the use and possession of the property. In this respect, the lease is a contract and enforceable according to the general terms of contract law.

The common law of leases made a major departure from contract law in holding that lease covenants were independent. This meant that the landlord's promises were independent from the tenant's, and the failure of one party (such as a landlord) to perform its obligations was not an excuse for the other party, the tenant, not to perform. For example, a lease may require the landlord to provide basic utility services to the premises and the tenant to pay rent.

The landlord refuses or fails to provide utility services. Does this excuse the tenant from its obligation to pay rent? The common law theory of independent covenants said no. The tenant must continue to pay rent even though the landlord refuses to perform its obligations. The tenant is left with the remedy of suing the landlord to perform or to compensate the tenant for damages caused by nonperformance. Historically, the common law theory of independent lease covenants has worked to the disadvantage of the tenant. Many states, especially in the area of residential leases, have modified the independent theory of lease covenants. For example, many states impose in residential leases a warranty of habitability on the landlord. This means that the landlord warrants to the tenant that the premises are capable of human habitation. This usually means that the landlord must provide basic utility services, such as water, sewer, and heat. In the event the premises prove not to be habitable, this excuses the tenant from payment of rent. Nevertheless, the common law theory of independent covenants is the law in most states as it pertains to commercial leases.

COMMERCIAL LEASE PROVISIONS

A paralegal who is involved in the preparation and review of a commercial lease must be familiar with the various terms commonly found in commercial leases.

Parties to Lease

landlord or **lessor**

Generally the owner of real property who transfers possession and use of the real property under a lease to a tenant or lessee.

tenant or **lessee**

Person who receives possession and use of property pursuant to a lease.

The parties to a lease are **landlord** or **lessor** and **tenant** or **lessee.** The landlord usually is the fee owner of the property. In making the lease, the landlord is transferring the possession and use of the property to the tenant. The landlord must have title to the property to grant

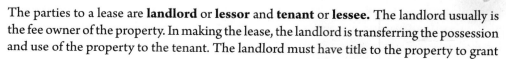

the lease, and the title must be sufficient to cover the lease term. For example, a landlord who had only a life estate in the property could not necessarily grant a lease for 20 years. If the landlord died during the 20 years, the lease would terminate when the landlord's title terminated.

A lease also is subject to all the landlord's title defects. It is prudent in many cases, when representing a tenant, to examine the landlord's title before entering into the lease. A tenant should pay particular attention to any zoning or restrictive covenants that may affect the use of the leased property. Another area of concern for the tenant is any prior mortgages that may exist on the property. A mortgage that is in existence at the time the lease is entered into is senior to the lease. If the loan payments are not made and the mortgage is foreclosed, the lease will terminate. This could place a tenant at a great disadvantage, including tremendous expense, in moving or renegotiating the terms of the lease with the purchaser at the foreclosure sale.

The tenant under the lease is the party to whom possession and use of the property are being transferred. Particular attention is paid to the financial ability of a tenant. It is crucial that the tenant have the ability to perform all the lease covenants. In many cases, it may be necessary that corporate tenants obtain a **lease guaranty** from the principal shareholders of the corporation or a subsidiary corporation obtain a guaranty from the parent corporation to assure financial ability.

Premises

A lease must describe the property that is being rented. The property being rented in a lease often is referred to as the **premises.** Paralegals should pay careful attention when preparing or reviewing a lease to make sure that the premises described are exactly those that are being transferred to the tenant and that the landlord intends to transfer. Important questions in a premises clause are: (a) Where is the premises located? (b) What is the size of the premises? (c) How is the size of the premises to be determined or confirmed? If the lease covers other premises, such as hallways, streets, bathrooms, or parking privileges, all this should be described and covered in the lease. Many times a lease of real property includes the use of certain personal property; if so, the personal property should be described and listed within the lease.

The location of the premises within a building or project should already be the subject of the parties negotiated understanding by the time the paralegal starts to prepare or review the lease. The only real concern should be to review the lease to make sure that the lease accurately documents that understanding. A comparable degree of specificity and precision should be used in leases in describing the premises as is used in conveyancing documents such as a deed. The lease should, at a minimum, provide a method whereby the precise size and location of the premises can be (or will be) determined and verified. Legal descriptions, plats of survey, plans and specifications, street addresses, and suite numbers are all used under different circumstances (and in different combinations) to accomplish this task.

In many situations, the premises will be space that is to be built in a proposed office building or shopping center. When the space is to be built, the tenant should be provided a reasonable means and opportunity to review and confirm the landlord's stated square footage. Many leases contain a provision that the landlord's architect will measure the premises when they are completed, and the determination of the landlord's architect will be binding on both parties. The lease may provide the tenant with a procedure for objecting or contesting the landlord's architect's measurement.

---

lease guaranty

A legal document that obligates the maker of the document to perform the obligations of a tenant under the lease including, but not limited to, the payment of the rent by the tenant to the landlord.

premises

Land and the buildings located on the land. The term often is used to describe real property covered by a lease.

Use

The use the tenant intends to make of the premises should be specified in the lease. The tenant wants a specific use identified in the lease and permission to use the premises for any lawful purpose. A landlord, on the other hand, probably wants to be more restrictive and require that the tenant's use of the premises be only that use set forth in the lease and no other use without prior written consent of landlord.

Term

With respect to the term of a lease, the better practice is to set out the exact commencement and termination dates, rather than merely state a term of years. To the extent renewal options are part of the transaction, this clause also should describe with specificity the term and type of notice required to exercise the renewal option. The length of the term of the lease usually is the subject of the parties' negotiated understanding, and in reviewing a lease, this point should only have to be verified by the paralegal.

Possession and Commencement of the Lease

A lease should provide for a precise beginning and ending date. The lease may provide that possession will begin in the future. Many developers, when constructing new shopping centers or office buildings, prelease the property before the time of completion. A lease that provides for future possession should clearly state that the lease becomes effective when signed, but possession will be delayed until a date in the future. The exact time of possession should be carefully described within the lease. As a practical note, a date of possession can be crucial to a tenant. Most tenants are at some other location and will have to go to the expense of closing that location and moving to the new premises. If, for some reason, possession is delayed, this can cause a disruption of business and considerable expense. A tenant may try to negotiate a provision that requires the landlord to pay an amount of money for each day possession is late.

Rent

rent

Money paid by a tenant to a landlord for the use and possession of property pursuant to a lease.

Rent is the sum of money the tenant pays to the landlord for the use and possession of the premises. It usually is payable in advance and in installments. Rent can be paid at any interval (e.g., annually, semiannually, daily, weekly, monthly). In most commercial and residential properties, the landlord's mortgage on the leased premises has payment due monthly, and because the landlord uses the rent to make the payments, rent is due monthly.

A tenant has a contractual obligation to pay rent. This obligation continues even if the tenant has transferred its interest to the premises or has vacated the premises. The obligation to pay rent, as earlier discussed, usually is independent of the landlord's promises and covenants under the lease. Even though the landlord may be in default under the lease, a tenant must still pay the rent.

Percentage Rent

percentage rent

Rent based on a percentage of sales from a specific location. Percentage rent often is found in retail store leases.

Rent typically is paid in a fixed amount of dollars and is due and payable on a certain day of the month. Rent, however, may be based on a percentage of sales; this type of rental provision commonly is found in retail store leases. A **percentage rent** clause provides that a percentage of the gross sales sold from the premises will be the amount of the rent. Many leases provide for a minimum rent, or base rent, to be paid plus a percentage of sales over a certain amount. These leases are percentage sales leases with a minimum base of sales guaranteed.

For example, if the landlord believes that the tenant will sell $1 million in merchandise from the location in a given year and the landlord wants a 3 percent percentage rent, the landlord will ask that $30,000 of rent (3 percent of $1 million) be payable in 12 equal installments of $2,500 per month. The rent figure is expressed in the lease as a fixed $2,500 per month together with 3 percent of all sales in excess of $1 million.

A percentage rent clause permits a landlord to earn additional rental income based on the amount of a retail tenant's gross sales or net sales from the premises. Such clauses usually are drafted to calculate the tenant's percentage rent obligations on an annual basis. The reason percentage rent has traditionally been due on an annual basis is because each lease year or calendar year (depending on which annual period is used in a given lease) must occur and conclude, and the final gross sales figures must be calculated before the actual percentage rent obligation for the year can be determined. It is not uncommon for leases today to provide for quarterly or even monthly payments of percentage rent. Such payments during the year are stated as payments "made against" the tenant's obligation for percentage rent, which is subject to a final determination. If necessary, a payment adjustment of some amount will be made after the close of the annual period.

Some of the key terms in percentage rent clauses are (a) a percentage rent rate; (b) the percentage rent breakpoint; (c) the amount and definition of gross sales; (d) the amount and nature of permitted exclusions or deductions from gross sales; and (e) the procedure or mechanism for verifying and, if necessary, adjusting payments of percentage rent.

Percentage rent rate and percentage breakpoint are concepts that are interrelated with the base rent obligation. A percentage rent rate is a mutually agreed on amount of the tenant's total annual gross sales that the tenant owes as percentage rent. This amount customarily is stated as a percentage. Different segments of the retail industry appeared to have settled on the "appropriate" percentage rate for their kind of store through negotiations over the years, and no attempt is made here to comment on what rate is appropriate for any given tenant.

The **percentage breakpoint** is the level of gross sales made during the year at which the percentage rent obligation commences. Thereafter, the percentage rent rate applies to all additional gross sales above the breakpoint. The two concepts are interrelated to the base rent because a natural percentage rent breakpoint is an amount determined by dividing the base rent by the percentage rent rate expressed as a number instead of a percentage.

percentage breakpoint

Level of gross sales made during a year at which time a percentage rent obligation will commence.

Required inclusions in gross sales and permitted exclusions or deductions from gross sales are fundamental to the percentage rent clause. The starting point of most lease forms is that the proceeds received from or attributed to everything and anything sold for cash or on credit (including lay-away sales, credit card sales, and sales paid for by checks that ultimately are no good) should be included in gross sales.

Most retailers and landlords agree that some or most of the following items should be excluded or deducted from gross sales: (a) the amount of any sales of fixtures, equipment, and property that is not carried as inventory; (b) the sale price of merchandise sold to tenant's employees at a discount; (c) the amount of any finance, insurance, or service charges on credit sales; (d) charges to customers for making deliveries or repairs to merchandise; (e) the amount of any cash or credit refund made on any sale in which the merchandise sold or some part thereof is thereafter returned by the purchaser and accepted by the tenant; and (f) any sums collected and paid out by the tenant for any sales or excise tax based on gross sales, to the extent such taxes have been included in the gross sales price.

Regardless of whether the tenant is paying percentage rent on a monthly, quarterly, or annual basis, the tenant is obligated to provide a written statement of its gross sales for such a period within a prescribed number of days after the period closes. Timing requirements for reports should be reviewed with the tenant to be sure that they comport with the tenant's current practice of keeping books. Similarly, many percentage rent clauses delineate the specific kinds of books and records of gross sales (including the kinds of cash registers, cash register tapes, and sales slips required) that must be kept and maintained by the tenant and made available to the landlord so that the accuracy of the tenant's report of gross sales can be verified. These details must be reviewed and accepted by the tenant. Finally, many percentage clauses require the tenant to keep its books and records of gross sales at the premises. This may not be workable with a tenant who has multiple locations. Most landlords will, in such circumstances, permit the tenant to keep its records at a central office but will require the tenant to produce them at the premises after an agreed notice (5 or 10 days) requesting such production has been given by the landlord to the tenant.

Many leases also require that annual statements of gross sales either be audited by an independent certified public accountant or be certified as true and correct by the chief financial officer of the tenant, at the landlord's option. Because most tenants would not go to the expense of such an audit for their own purpose, a tenant may negotiate to limit the applicability of this requirement to situations in which the tenant's annual statement of gross sales for a prior annual period has been understated by a certain percentage (e.g., 3 percent or 5 percent), which is mutually agreed to be sufficiently indicative of improper or poor record-keeping practices to trigger the audit obligation.

Most percentage lease provisions permit the landlord to inspect or audit the tenant's books and records of gross sales. If the inspection discloses an understatement of percentage rents by a certain percentage (e.g., 3 percent or 5 percent) or more, the tenant bears the cost of the audit. If either the tenant's preparation of its annual statement of gross sales or the landlord's audit of the tenant's records of gross sales reveals that an overpayment has occurred, most leases provide that the tenant will receive a credit against percentage rent thereafter due.

A lease that contains a percentage rent clause may have a covenant that the tenant will operate and actively conduct the business from the premises. Retail leases often establish the hours the store must be open, such as 10 A.M. through 9 P.M. Monday through Saturday. Percentage sales leases may contain restrictions on assignment and subletting. A percentage sales lease may contain a **radius clause.** A radius clause prohibits a tenant from opening another store within a certain geographical radius of the leased premises. This is a way of protecting a market area for the location and ensuring a particular volume of sales. Example 18–1 shows a percentage rent clause.

radius clause

Clause contained in a lease that prohibits a tenant from operating another retail store or business within a certain geographical radius of the leased premises.

Example 18–1

Percentage Rent

(a) In addition to Minimum Rent, Tenant shall pay to Landlord a sum equal to the amount, if any, by which ____ (___%) percent of Tenant's gross sales for any whole or partial lease year exceeds the Minimum Rent payable for such lease year (hereinafter referred to as "Percentage Rent"). Percentage Rent shall be due and payable on or before the tenth (10th) day of each calendar month during the term hereof and on or before the tenth (10th) day of the first (1st) calendar month following the termination hereof. On or before the tenth (10th) day of each calendar month during the term hereof, Tenant shall furnish Landlord with a written statement certified to be correct by Tenant showing the amount of gross sales in the Premises from the beginning of the lease year to the end of the previous calendar month or portion thereof. If, by the end of any such preceding calendar month, ____ (___%) percent of the gross sales in the Premises shall have exceeded the Minimum Rent payable for such lease year, Tenant shall pay Landlord the Percentage Rent due hereunder on the basis of such sales less the aggregate of Percentage Rent previously paid by Tenant during the lease year.

(b) The term "gross sales" as used herein shall be construed to include the entire sales price, whether for cash or otherwise, of all merchandise sold (including gift and merchandise certificates) and services rendered, and all other receipts whatsoever of all business conducted in or from the Premises whether made by Tenant or any permissible subtenant, concessionaire or licensee. Each sale upon installment or credit shall be treated as a sale for the full price in the month during which such sale was made, and there shall be no deduction from gross sales for uncollected or noncollectable credit accounts. Gross sales shall not include sums collected and paid out for any sales or retail excise tax imposed by any duly constituted governmental authority.

(c) Tenant shall maintain at the Premises and shall cause any permissible subtenants, concessionaires or licensees to keep and maintain accurate books and records which shall disclose separately for each business day of the term all information required to determine gross sales (including but not limited to inventories and receipts of merchandise, telephone and mail order slips, all federal, state and local sales tax returns, records of daily bank deposits of the entire receipts from transactions in, at, or from the Premises, sales slips, daily dated cash register tapes, sales books and bank statements). Such books and records shall be open to inspection and audit at the Premises by Landlord or its duly authorized agents at any time within two years following the close of the lease year in question. If such audit shall disclose a deficiency in rent, Tenant shall promptly pay such deficiency. If such audit shows gross sales to be understated by two (2%) percent or more, Tenant shall pay the cost of such audit in addition to any deficiency and if such audit shows gross sales to be understated by five (5%) percent or more, Landlord shall have the right to terminate this Lease upon five (5) days written notice to Tenant, in addition to any other remedies provided for Tenant's default hereunder. Tenant shall keep and preserve said records for not less than twenty-five (25) months after the close of each lease year.

(d) Tenant shall submit to Landlord on or before the thirtieth (30th) day following the end of the lease year a complete statement signed by Tenant and either certified under oath by a duly authorized officer of Tenant or certified by a Certified Public Accountant, showing accurately and in reasonable detail the amount of gross sales made by Tenant and any permissible sublessees, concessionaires, or licensees, upon and within the Premises during the preceding lease year.

Use Clauses
(a) Use.

(a) Tenant covenants and agrees to use the Premises only for the Permitted Uses and for no other purposes; to operate its business in the Premises under the Tenant's Trade Name (or such other trade name as is adopted by a majority of stores operating under the Trade Name); and to conduct its business at all times in a dignified manner and in conformity with the highest standards of practice obtaining among superior type stores, shops or concerns dealing in the same or similar merchandise and in such manner as to produce the maximum volume of Gross Sales and to help establish and maintain a high reputation for the Shopping Center.

(b) Tenant covenants and agrees to continuously and uninterruptedly use, occupy and operate for retail sales purposes all of the Premises other than such minor portions thereof as are reasonably required for storage and office purposes; to use such storage and office space only in connection with the business conducted by Tenant in the Premises; to furnish and install all trade fixtures and permitted signs; to carry a full and complete stock of seasonable merchandise; to maintain an adequate number of trained personnel for efficient service to customers; to open for business and remain open continuously during the entire Term from at least 10:00 A.M. to 9:30 P.M. Mondays through Saturdays and 12:30 P.M. to 5:30 P.M. Sundays, and to light its display windows and signs during those hours and on those days when the covered mall is kept illuminated by Landlord (but Tenant shall not be obligated to keep the same illuminated beyond 11:00 P.M. on any day). Tenant shall, if not in conflict with any governmental requirements, and provided that (i) at least one Department Store is open on such day and (ii) Landlord shall agree to cause the Shopping Center to remain open for such hours, also open for business for additional hours.

(b) Radius Clause.

Except for existing stores, Tenant shall not, nor shall any officer, director, shareholder, affiliate, franchisee or licensee or the like of Tenant, directly or indirectly operate, manage or have any interest in any other store or other facility for the sale at retail of merchandise or services similar to what is permitted under "Permitted Use" within ____ miles of the Shopping Center. Without limiting Landlord's remedies in the event Tenant should violate this covenant, Landlord may, at its option, include the Gross Sales of such other store in the Gross Sales transacted in the Premises for the purpose of computing Percentage Rent due hereunder. In the event Landlord so elects, all of the provisions of Section ____ hereof (relating to Tenant's records) shall be applicable to all records pertaining to such other store.

Gross versus Net Lease

gross lease

Lease wherein the tenant pays rent only; the operating expenses of the leased premises, such as taxes, utility costs, and insurance, are paid by the landlord.

net lease

Lease in which the tenant is responsible for all expenses of the leased premises, such as utilities, taxes, and insurance.

Lease rent may be gross or net. A **gross lease** is one under which the tenant pays rent only; the ordinary and necessary operating expenses of the premises, such as taxes, utility costs, and insurance, are paid by the landlord.

In a **net lease,** the tenant pays a fixed amount of money to the landlord that is net to the landlord, and the tenant is responsible for all expenses of the property, such as utilities, taxes, and insurance.

Exhibits 18–1 and 18–2 show the duties of landlord and tenant under both a gross lease and a net lease. Some leases may be a hybrid between the pure gross lease and the pure net lease. These leases may obligate the tenant to pay a fixed amount of rent to the landlord and then to pay certain escalations in the expenses of the property. It is not uncommon for

EXHIBIT 18–1

Landlord and Tenant's Duties under a Residential Apartment Lease (Gross Lease)

Tenant's Duties	*Landlord's Duties*
1. Pay rent to landlord.	1. Duty of quiet enjoyment
2. Keep interior of property in good repair.	2. Keep property and common area in good repair.
3. Assign or sublet the lease only with land-lord's consent.	3. Insure property and common area.
4. Surrender premises in original condition less ordinary wear and tear at the end of the lease.	4. Pay taxes.

Delmar/Cengage Learning

EXHIBIT 18–2

Landlord and Tenant's Duties and Obligations under a Commercial Lease (Net Lease)

Tenant's Duties	*Landlord's Duties*
1. Pay rent to landlord.	1. Insure exterior of property.
2. Pay percentage interest of real estate taxes.	2. Maintain roof and exterior walls.
3. Pay percentage interest of insurance premiums.	3. Duty of quiet enjoyment.
4. Maintain the interior and exterior of the property.	
5. Insure tenant's contents.	
6. Assign or sublet the premises only with landlord's consent.	
7. At the termination of the lease surrender the premises in the original condition less ordinary wear and tear.	

Delmar/Cengage Learning

leases of this type to contain tax escalation, insurance escalation, and operating expense escalation provisions. These provisions operate on a theory that the landlord is responsible for the amount of taxes, insurance premiums, and operating expenses during the first year of the lease. All increases in taxes, insurance, and operating expenses that occur during the term of the lease will be paid by the tenant. Sample provisions of tax, insurance, and operating expense escalation clauses are set forth in Example 18–2.

Example 18–2

Tenant shall pay upon demand, as additional rental during the term of this Lease, or any extension or renewal thereof, the amount by which all taxes, insurance premiums insuring the improvements and charges to maintain the common area, exceed the cost of all taxes, insurance premiums and common area charges for the year _____. In the event the Premises are less than the entire property assessed for such taxes, insurance and common area charges for any such year, then the assessment for any such year applicable to the Premises shall be determined by proration on the basis that the rental floor area of the Premises bear to the rental floor area of the entire property assessed. Tenant's pro rata portion of the increased taxes, insurance premiums or common area charges, as provided herein, shall be payable within fifteen (15) days after receipt of notice from Landlord as to the amount due.

Rent Escalation Clauses

During periods of inflation, a lease may require an adjustment in the tenant's rent by tying rent to an inflation-based index, such as the consumer price index (CPI). The tenant's rent increases as the index increases. The use of an inflator index protects the landlord's purchasing power of the rent dollar.

A CPI clause typically is an annual rental adjustment mechanism that uses some versions of the CPI or some other governmental or independently determined inflation-measuring statistic to determine the amount of each annual increase in the base or minimum rent. When reviewing a CPI clause, one should be careful to determine when the clause first "kicks in" if it is a "one-way or two-way escalator" and if potential adjustments are limited, or "capped."

Many (if not most) CPI clauses are drafted to operate on a calendar basis, and the effect of this fact must be considered.

If a tenant's lease term commences in the middle or latter part of a calendar year, then the first adjustment (with a CPI) usually is drafted to be effective "as of January 1," even if not determined until sometime thereafter. This arguably occurs prematurely because the tenant has not received the benefit of a year (or close to a year) of base rental payments at the original amount. A reasonable compromise that accommodates both landlord and tenant is to leave the adjustment mechanism intact as far as how it operates and what measuring period (e.g., calendar year) it uses but to have the first adjustment be postponed until the first anniversary of the commencement date of the lease instead of January 1. Subsequent adjustments can be treated similarly and be effective as of subsequent anniversary dates of the lease.

A CPI clause should adjust the minimum rate downward if the CPI declines over the relative measuring period. Although the historical trends of the past several decades belie the likelihood of this occurring, there is no conceptual reason why adjustment should not operate in both directions.

Tenants may try to limit the amount of any potential increase for any single measuring period. This usually is accomplished with language that establishes a ceiling, or cap, on any single adjustment by fixing it at no more than an agreed percentage (e.g., 4 percent or 5 percent of the prior year's adjusted base rent). Tenants also may try to limit the total "lifetime adjustments" (to some agreed-on percentage) of the original scheduled minimum rent. A sample CPI clause is shown in Example 18–3.

Example 18–3

The annual rental hereunder shall be increased by an amount equal to the product of a (a) $___ X (b) the difference expressed as a percentage between the Consumer Price Index, as herein below defined, published for the month of ___ of the year ___.

"Consumer Price Index," as used herein, shall be the "Consumer Price Index for all urban consumers, U.S., City average, all items (1967) equal 100" issued by the U.S. Bureau of Labor Statistics. If the Consumer Price Index, published by the U.S. Bureau of Labor Statistics is discontinued, then the Consumer Price Index published by the U.S. Department of Commerce shall be used (with proper adjustment), and if the U.S. Department of Commerce Index is discontinued, then Landlord and Tenant shall in good faith agree on a suitable substitute.[1]

Another mechanism used to adjust base rent is a negotiated "set," or "bump," increase. Under this provision, the minimum rent usually is scheduled to increase a predetermined amount effective as of each anniversary date of the commencement date of the lease term.

Maintenance and Alterations of Premises

Most leases prohibit a tenant from conducting any use or making any modification that would in any way (a) violate a certificate of occupancy, (b) make void or voidable any insurance in force with respect to the premises or make it impossible to obtain such insurance, (c) cause structural injury to all or any part of the premises or to any improvements constructed thereon, or (d) constitute a public or private nuisance. Under appropriate circumstances, the landlord may want to consider granting the tenant the right to make nonstructural additions and modifications after receiving prior notice and detail concerning these additions or modifications. Most leases provide that all modifications, additions, or improvements made by the tenant to the premises shall be done in compliance with all applicable building codes and zoning ordinances and that the tenant shall permit no mechanic's liens to be filed against the premises. Example 18–4 shows a maintenance and alteration provision.

Example 18–4

Tenant shall not make or suffer to be made any alterations, additions, or improvements in, on, or to the premises or any part thereof without the prior written consent of Landlord; and any such alterations, additions, or improvements in, on, or to said premises, except to Tenant's movable furniture and equipment, shall immediately become Landlord's property and, at the end of the Term hereof, shall remain on the premises without compensation to Tenant. In the event Landlord consents to the making of any such alterations, additions, or improvements by Tenant, the same shall be made by Tenant, at Tenant's sole cost and expense, in accordance with all applicable laws, ordinances, and regulations and all requirements of Landlord's and Tenant's insurance policies, and in accordance with plans and specifications approved by Landlord, and any contractor or person selected by Tenant to make the same and all subcontracts must first be approved in writing by Landlord, or, at Landlord's option, the alteration, addition or improvement shall be made by Landlord for Tenant's account and Tenant shall reimburse Landlord for the cost thereof upon demand. Upon the expiration or sooner termination of the Term, Tenant shall upon demand by Landlord, at Tenant's sole cost and expense, forthwith and with all due diligence remove any or all alterations, additions, or improvements made by or for the account of Tenant, designated by Landlord to be removed, and Tenant shall forthwith and with due diligence, at its sole cost and expense, repair and restore the premises to their original condition.

Most leases also identify the party obligated for repairs, maintenance, and general management of the premises. Items such as foundations, roofs, utility systems, and other major structural mechanical components usually are maintained by the landlord. All other items, including any items that benefit only the premises, usually are maintained and repaired by the tenant.

Most leases provide that the tenant will not permit any lien to be filed with respect to the premises or the building, and in the event such lien is filed based on work performed for or materials supplied to the tenant, the tenant will cause the lien to be satisfied, bonded, or discharged immediately.

Insurance

Most leases impose on a tenant the requirement to carry appropriate kinds of insurance coverage in stated minimum amounts with a carrier specified in the lease. A commercial tenant's insurance obligation should, at a minimum, encompass fire and extended coverage and comprehensive public liability insurance, including property damage. The tenant may be required to insure not only contents, but also the actual premises as well. This is especially true in a freestanding structure in which the tenant leases the entire premises. Any policies of insurance required to be obtained by the tenant pursuant to the terms of the lease should provide by endorsement that losses are payable to the landlord and tenant as their respective interest appear. In addition, each policy required under the lease should contain an agreement by the insurer that such policy will in no event be canceled without at least 30 days prior written notice to each party. The lease may permit the landlord to pay any insurance premiums not promptly paid by the tenant and to assess that cost to the tenant.

In addition, most lease provisions release and hold harmless both the landlord and the tenant from each other's actions in regard to the cause of any casualty to the premises that is covered by insurance. This release and hold harmless impairs an insurance company's right of **subrogation.** An insurance company has a right when it pays a claim to be subrogated or substituted to the party paid and obtain any rights this party may have against the party causing the accident to recover damages. For example, a tenant negligently starts a fire on the premises that causes substantial damage. The insurance carrier pays the landlord the cost of the damage. The insurance carrier then is subrogated or substituted in place of the landlord to proceed against the tenant and recover for the tenant's negligence in destruction of the premises.

When a lease holds both parties harmless from any action that may damage the premises covered by insurance, this release and hold harmless impairs the insurance company's right of subrogation. When subrogation is impaired, an insurance company does not have to pay a claim under the policy. It is easy to see how this situation can create a serious problem. If subrogation is impaired under the policy, then the insurance company pays no claim for the damage, and if the landlord and tenant have already waived rights against each other, the landlord or tenant has no right to recover for the damage either. The damage, therefore, is unrecoverable, and the expense of it must be borne totally by the landlord or the tenant. This potentially dangerous problem can be resolved by having the insurance company waive its rights of subrogation. This is routinely done, and waivers of subrogation often are already built into the "boilerplate"

subrogation

Right to be substituted to the rights of another person. For example, an insurance carrier who pays a claim to the insured is given the rights of the insured to proceed against any party who caused the damage resulting in the claim.

terms and conditions of a commercial insurance policy. The paralegal, when reviewing a lease that includes hold harmless language, should review all the appropriate insurance policies to make sure that the right of subrogation has been waived by the insurance carrier.

Damage or Destruction to the Premises

Under common law, a lease continued even after the premises had been damaged and destroyed, and the tenant was obligated to continue paying rent. The common law rule has been changed by statute in many states and often is changed within the lease agreement. It is not unusual for a lease to contain a fire damage clause that provides that the lease will terminate or rent will abate if the building or premises are destroyed by fire. Leases do provide, however, that a tenant is obligated for any damage that the tenant causes to the premises by the tenant's negligence or intentional conduct.

It also should be noted that many leases obligate a tenant to return the premises in the same condition as the tenant received it. This affirmative obligation would require the tenant to keep the premises in good repair throughout the term of the lease and to even protect it against casualties caused by fire or other risk.

A lease typically provides that if there is substantial destruction to the premises, either the landlord or the tenant may terminate the lease. The lease also provides that if there is partial or temporary destruction to the premises, the lease will not be terminated, and the premises will be restored. The rent, however, will abate (not be due and payable) during the period of restoration or will abate in proportion to the amount of the premises that cannot be used. For example, a tenant leases 10,000 square feet of space. A fire causes 1,000 square feet of the space to be unusable, but the remaining 9,000 square feet is usable. Under the restoration and abatement provisions in most leases, a tenant would only be responsible for 90 percent of the rent during the restoration of the 1,000 square feet of damaged space.

Obligation of Repair

Under common law, a landlord was not responsible for repair of the premises. The tenant leased the premises "as is," with full obligations to repair. The common law not only made the landlord not responsible for the repair of the premises, but also the landlord was not responsible for any injuries caused by the condition of the premises or the lack of repair. An exception to the common law rule was that a landlord was responsible for hidden defects that were known to exist. A hidden defect is a defect that the landlord knew about but did not disclose to the tenant and is a defect that the tenant would not discover on reasonable investigation or inspection of the property.

This common law rule is still followed in many states. Under certain types of leases, such as residential leases, state statutes have made the landlord responsible for defective premises. Under these statutes, the tenant does have an obligation to make the landlord aware of defects and to give the landlord a reasonable time to repair defects before the landlord will be responsible for any injuries caused by the defects. A landlord also usually is responsible for injuries and accidents that occur in the common premises under the landlord's possession and control, such as hallways, stairs, and parking lots.

Condemnation and Eminent Domain

A lease ordinarily provides for what happens in the event that a specified amount of the leased premises is taken by condemnation, eminent domain, or other governmental right. If this happens, the landlord or the tenant usually has an option to terminate the lease. In the event an election to terminate is not made, the rent is apportioned in accordance with the proportion of the premises remaining tenable.

Default

Most leases contain provisions that indicate what shall constitute an event of default under the lease. At minimum, a tenant will be in default under the lease if the tenant (a) fails to pay any installment of rent or any other sum payable by the tenant under the lease, within a certain number of days after the due date; (b) fails to perform or observe any covenant, term, or condition under the lease, which failure continues for a certain period of days beyond the period of time necessary to cure if diligently pursued; (c) fails to continue its business as a going concern or tenant vacates or abandons the premises; or (d) fails to maintain certain evidence of financial stability.

Landlord's Remedies for Tenant's Default   #5

A landlord's basic remedies for a tenant's default are to (a) sue the tenant for performance, (b) terminate the lease and sue for damages, and (c) dispossess the tenant and sue for damages. A landlord may sue a tenant for performance in the event of a default on the lease. For example, a landlord may sue a tenant for the rent, although this may require a suit brought each month, or the landlord may permit the rent to accumulate for a period of time before bringing suit. A landlord may sue a tenant for a nonmonetary default and ask the tenant to perform, or the landlord may cure the default and sue for reimbursement of the expense. For example, a landlord may sue a tenant to remove an unauthorized sign placed on the premises, or the landlord may remove the sign and sue the tenant for the cost of removal.

A landlord has the right to terminate the lease and evict a tenant for the tenant's default. Once the lease is terminated, rental under the lease ceases, and the landlord may only recover damages. The damage usually is the amount calculated by what the rent for the remainder of the term would have been less a reasonable rent that could be obtained for the remainder of the term by releasing the premises.

Most leases provide that a landlord may evict and remove a tenant from possession of the premises and not terminate the lease. The landlord then may act as the tenant's agent for purposes of reletting or releasing the space. The tenant remains responsible for the rent less any new rent received through reletting.

A lease may provide that the landlord has the right to serve notice of termination on the tenant that will accelerate all rent and other costs and charges reserved to the landlord under the lease.

An accelerated rent remedy is a provision whereby all the future, unearned rent is accelerated and made immediately due and payable at the election of the landlord in the event that an uncured event of default occurs under the lease.

A typical default paragraph may provide that on receipt of a termination notice, the tenant will peacefully quit and surrender the premises.

Landlord's Right to Perform Tenant's Obligations

Most leases give the landlord the right to cure tenant defaults under the lease and to charge the tenant with expenses incurred by the landlord. For example, a tenant may fail to insure the property. The landlord can obtain insurance and charge the tenant with the cost of the premium. Most leases also proved that the cure of a tenant's default by the landlord does not waive the default and allows the landlord despite the cure to exercise all lease remedies for a tenant default.

A lease provision covering the tenant's default and the landlord's remedies appears in Example 18–5.

Example 18–5

The following events shall be deemed to be events of default by Tenant under this Lease:

(1) Tenant shall fail to pay when or before due any sum of money, becoming due to be paid to Landlord hereunder, whether such sum be any installment of the rental herein reserved, any other amount treated as additional rental hereunder, or any other payment or reimbursement to Landlord required herein, whether or not treated as additional rental hereunder, and such failure shall continue for a period of five (5) days from the date such payment was due; or

(2) Tenant shall fail to comply with any term, provision or covenant of this Lease other than failing to pay when or before due any sum of money becoming due to be paid to Landlord hereunder, and shall not cure such failure within twenty (20) days (forthwith, if the default involves a hazardous condition) after written notice thereof to Tenant; or

(3) Tenant shall abandon any substantial portion of the leased premises; or

(4) Tenant shall fail to vacate the leased premises immediately upon termination of this Lease, by lapse of time or otherwise, or upon termination of Tenant's right to possession only; or

(5) If, in spite of the provisions hereof, the interest of Tenant shall be levied upon under execution or be attached by process of law or Tenant shall fail to contest diligently the validity of any lien or claimed lien and give sufficient security to landlord to insure payment thereof or shall fail to satisfy any judgment rendered thereon and have the same released, and such default shall continue for ten (10) days after written notice thereof to Tenant.

(b) Upon the occurrence of any such events of default described in this paragraph or elsewhere in this Lease, Landlord shall have the option to pursue any one or more of the following remedies without any notice or demand whatsoever:

(1) Landlord may, at its election, terminate this Lease or terminate Tenant's right to possession only, without terminating the Lease.

(2) Upon any termination of this Lease, whether by lapse of time or otherwise, or upon any termination of Tenant's right to possession without termination of this Lease, Tenant shall surrender possession and vacate the leased premises immediately, and deliver possession thereof to Landlord, and Tenant hereby grants to Landlord full and free license to enter into and upon the leased premises in such event with or without process of law and to repossess Landlord of the leased premises as of Landlord's former estate and to expel or remove Tenant and any others who may be occupying or within the leased premises and to remove any and all property there from, without being deemed in any manner guilty of trespass, eviction or forcible entry or detainer, and without incurring any liability for any damage resulting therefrom, Tenant hereby waiving any right to claim damage for such re-entry and expulsion and without relinquishing Landlord's right to rent or any other right given to Landlord hereunder or by operation of law.

(3) Upon termination of this Lease, whether by lapse of time or otherwise, Landlord shall be entitled to recover as damages, all rental, including any money treated as additional rental hereunder, and other sums due and payable by Tenant on the date of termination, plus the sum of (i) an amount equal to the then-present value of the rental, including any amounts treated as additional rental hereunder, and other sums provided herein to be paid by Tenant for the residue of the stated term hereof, less the fair rental value of the leased premises for such residue (taking into account the time and expense necessary to obtain a replacement tenant or tenants, including expenses hereinafter described in subparagraph (b)(4) relating to recovery of the leased premises, preparation for reletting and for reletting itself), and (ii) the cost of performing any other covenants which would have otherwise been performed by Tenant.

(4)(i) Upon any termination of Tenant's right to possession only without termination of the Lease, Landlord may, at Landlord's option, enter into the leased premises, remove Tenant's signs and other evidences of tenancy, and take and hold possession thereof as provided in subparagraph (b)(2) above, without such entry and possession terminating the Lease or releasing Tenant, in whole or in part, from any obligation, including Tenant's obligation to pay the rental, including any amounts treated as additional rental, hereunder for the full Term. In any such case, Tenant shall pay forthwith to Landlord if Landlord so elects, a sum equal to the entire amount of the rental, including any amounts treated as additional rental hereunder, for the residue of the stated Term hereof, plus any other sums provided herein to be paid by Tenant for the remainder of the Lease Term;

(ii) Landlord may, but is not required to relet the leased premises, or any part thereof, for such rent and upon such terms as Landlord in its sole discretion shall determine (including the right to relet the leased premises for a greater or lesser term than that remaining under this Lease, the right to relet the leased premises as a part of a larger area, and the right to change the character and use made of the leased premises) and Landlord shall not be required to accept any substitute tenant offered by Tenant or to observe any instructions given by Tenant about such reletting. In any such case, Landlord may make repairs, alterations and additions in or to the leased premises, and redecorate the same to the extent Landlord deems necessary or desirable, and Tenant shall, upon demand, pay the cost thereof, together with Landlord's expenses for reletting including, without limitation, any broker's commission incurred by Landlord. If the consideration collected by Landlord upon any such reletting plus any sums previously collected from Tenant are not sufficient to pay the full amount of all rental, including any amounts treated as additional rental hereunder and other sums reserved in this Lease for the remaining Term hereof, together with the costs of repairs, alterations, additions, redecorating, and Lessor's expenses of reletting and the collection of the rental accruing therefrom (including attorneys' fees and broker's commissions), Tenant shall pay to Landlord the amount of such deficiency upon demand and Tenant agrees that Landlord may file suit to recover any sums falling due under this section from time to time.

(5) Landlord may, at Landlord's option, enter into and upon the leased premises, with or without process of law, if Landlord determines in its sole discretion that Tenant is not acting within a commercially reasonable time to maintain, repair or replace anything for which Tenant is responsible hereunder and correct the same, without being deemed in any manner guilty of trespass, eviction or forcible entry and detainer and without incurring any liability for any damage resulting therefrom and Tenant agrees to reimburse Landlord, on demand, as additional rental, for any expenses which Landlord may incur in thus effecting compliance with Tenant's obligations under this Lease.

(6) Any and all property which may be removed from the leased premises by Landlord pursuant to the authority of the Lease or of law, to which Tenant is or may be entitled, may be handled, removed and stored, as the case may be, by or at the direction of Landlord at the risk, cost and expense of Tenant, and Landlord shall in no event be responsible for the value, preservation or safekeeping thereof. Tenant shall pay to Landlord, upon demand, any and all expenses incurred in such removal and all storage charges against such property so long as the same shall be in Landlord's possession or under Landlord's control. Any such property of Tenant not retaken by Tenant from storage within thirty (30) days after removal from the leased premises shall, at Landlord's option, be deemed conveyed by Tenant to Landlord under this Lease as by a bill of sale without further payment or credit by Landlord to Tenant.

(c) Pursuit of any of the foregoing remedies shall not preclude pursuit of any of the other remedies herein provided or any other remedies provided by law (all such remedies being cumulative), nor shall pursuit of any remedy herein provided constitute a forfeiture or waiver of any rental due to Landlord hereunder or of any damages accruing to Landlord by reason of the violation of any of the terms, provisions and covenants herein contained. No act or thing done by Landlord or its agents during the Term shall be deemed a termination of this Lease or an acceptance of the surrender of the leased premises, and no agreement to terminate this Lease or accept a surrender of said premises shall be valid unless in writing signed by Landlord. No waiver by Landlord of any violation or breach of any of the terms, provisions and covenants herein contained shall be deemed or construed to constitute a waiver of any other violation or breach of any of the terms, provisions and covenants herein contained. Landlord's acceptance of the payment of rental or other payments hereunder after the occurrence of an event of default shall not be construed as a waiver of such default, unless Landlord so notifies Tenant in writing. Forebearance by Landlord in enforcing one or more of the remedies herein provided upon an event of default shall not be deemed or construed to constitute a waiver of such default or of Landlord's right to enforce any such remedies with respect to such default or any subsequent default. If, on account of any breach or default by Tenant in Tenant's obligations under the terms and conditions of this Lease, it shall become necessary or appropriate for Landlord to employ or consult with an attorney concerning or to defend any of Landlord's rights or remedies hereunder, Tenant agrees to pay reasonable attorneys' fees so incurred.

(d) Without limiting the foregoing, to the extent permitted by law, Tenant hereby: (i) appoints and designates the leased premises as a proper place for service of process upon Tenant, and agrees that service of process upon any person apparently employed by Tenant upon the leased premises or leaving process in a conspicuous place within the leased premises shall constitute personal service of such process upon Tenant (provided, however, Landlord does not hereby waive the right to serve Tenant with process by any other lawful means); (ii) expressly waives any right to trial by jury; and (iii) expressly waives the service of any notice under any existing or future law of the State of Georgia applicable to landlords and tenants.

Landlord's Lien

Some leases provide that a landlord has a lien against the personal effects of a tenant stored on the leased premises to secure the performance of the tenant under the lease. This lien often is created as a security interest and is perfected by the filing of the Uniform Commercial Code financing statement. If the tenant defaults, the landlord has the right to repossess the tenant's personal property and sell it to pay the tenant's obligations under the lease.

Grace Periods

Most landlords are willing to accept a 5- to 10-day notice and cure period for monetary defaults such as failure to pay rent, taxes, or other expenses required of the tenant. Many landlords, however, request that such a notice and cure as to monetary defaults be limited to an obligation to provide such a notice an agreed number of times (e.g., two or three times in any 12 consecutive-month period). This provision prevents a repeat offender from taking advantage of the notice requirement by repeatedly paying monetary obligations only after notices of default have been received.

Other defaults under the lease that are nonmonetary often are more difficult to cure because the requirements for cure may not be solely within the control of the tenant. For example, a lease obligates a tenant to operate its business in full compliance of all health, safety, and fire codes. The tenant installs electrical equipment that requires part of the premises to be rewired. The rewiring is not approved by the building inspector. The tenant is in default under the lease and must not only have the wiring replaced, but also schedule another inspection. A longer period of notice and cure (usually 20 or 30 days) is commonplace for nonmonetary defaults.

Tenant's Remedies for Landlord's Default

As previously mentioned, the covenants of a commercial lease are independent, so that a tenant does not have the right to offset or not pay the rent due to a landlord's default under the lease. This leaves the tenant with only the remedy of suing the landlord to perform or for damages caused by nonperformance.

Quiet Enjoyment

Most leases provide that the landlord covenants that the tenant will peacefully and quietly enjoy the premises without hindrance or interference by the landlord for the entire duration of the lease term, subject to each party's performance of the provisions of the lease. A sample of a quiet enjoyment provision is shown in Example 18–6.

Example 18–6

Landlord agrees that if Tenant shall perform all the covenants and agreements herein required to be performed by Tenant, Tenant shall, subject to the terms of this Lease, at times during the continuance of this Lease, have the peaceable and quiet enjoyment and possession of the Demised Premises.

Surrender of the Premises

A tenant is usually required at the end of the lease to surrender the premises in the original condition, less allowances for ordinary wear and tear. The tenant usually has a right to remove trade fixtures at the termination of the lease. This right to remove trade fixtures, however, often is limited to the following provisions: (a) the tenant can remove trade fixtures before the termination of the lease; (b) the trade fixtures cannot be removed if the tenant is in default; and (c) the tenant must repair all damage to the premises caused by the removal of the trade fixtures. Most leases provide that if trade fixtures remain in the premises on termination of the lease, the landlord has the right to remove the trade fixtures and store them. The landlord has no liability for any damage caused to the trade fixtures during the removal and storage, and the landlord can recover from the tenant the cost of such removal and storage. A sample provision regarding surrender of the premises is shown in Example 18–7.

Example 18–7

(a) Tenant shall, at least one hundred eighty (180) days before the last day of the Lease Term, give to Landlord a written notice of intention to surrender the premises on that date, but nothing contained therein or in the failure of Tenant to give such notice shall be construed as an extension of the Term, or as consent of Landlord to any holding over by Tenant.

(b) At the end of the Term, or any renewal thereof, or other sooner termination of this Lease, the Tenant peaceably will deliver to the Landlord possession of the premises, together with all improvements or additions upon or belonging to the same, by whomsoever made, in the same condition as received, or first installed, ordinary wear and tear, damage by fire, earthquake, act of God or the elements alone excepted. Tenant may, upon the termination of this Lease, remove all movable furniture and equipment belonging to Tenant, at Tenant's sole cost, title to which shall be in the name of Tenant until such termination, repairing any damage caused by such removal. Property not so removed shall be deemed abandoned by the Tenant, and title to the same shall thereupon pass to Landlord. Upon request by Landlord, unless otherwise agreed to in writing by Landlord, Tenant shall remove, at Tenant's sole cost, any or all permanent improvements or additions to the premises installed by or at the expense of Tenant and all movable furniture and equipment belonging to Tenant which may be left by Tenant and repair any damage resulting from such removal.

(c) The voluntary or other surrender of this Lease by Tenant, or a mutual cancellation thereof, shall not work a merger, and shall, at the option of the Landlord, terminate all or any existing subleases or subtenancies or may, at the option of Landlord, operate as an assignment to it of any or all such subleases or subtenancies.

Estoppel Certificate

It is not unusual for a lease to provide that the tenant shall, on request, provide to the landlord or to a person at the landlord's direction a sworn statement of facts concerning the lease, commonly referred to as an **estoppel certificate.** An institutional lender that is making a loan to the landlord and taking the premises as security will request estoppel certificates from the tenants.

estoppel certificate

Written statement signed by either a landlord or a tenant swearing to certain facts concerning a lease.

A purchaser of the premises from the landlord will likewise request estoppel certificates from the tenants. An estoppel certificate usually states that (a) the lease is in full force and effect; (b) the lease has not been modified; (c) the lease is not in default; and (d) the tenant has no defense or setoffs against the landlord. An estoppel certificate may attach a copy of the lease as an exhibit. An estoppel certificate is shown as Exhibit 18–5 at the end of this chapter.

Memorandum of Lease

Most leases are not recorded. In some instances, to protect the tenant's interest in the lease or if the lease contains certain additional provisions such as options to purchase the premises by the tenant, a memorandum of lease is recorded. A memorandum of lease includes all operative terms of the lease as well as any purchase options, renewals, and first refusals of additional space. Recording the memorandum in the real estate records will provide notice of the lease to any third parties such as purchasers or lenders who may acquire an interest in the leased property in the future. An example of a short-form memorandum prepared for recordation is shown in Exhibit 18–6 at the end of this chapter.

Example 18–8

SHORT-FORM LEASE. LESSOR and LESSEE hereby agree to enter into a Short-Form Lease setting out (a) the names of the parties hereto, (b) the description of Demised Premises as the same appears in Exhibit A hereof (c) the dates of this Lease Agreement and of its initial and extension or renewal terms and (d) LESSEE's rights upon termination of this Lease Agreement; such Short-Form Lease shall be in writing, duly executed by all the parties hereto on the date hereof or at any time thereafter as prepared and requested by either party hereof, and shall be properly attested and acknowledged for recording in Ohio.

Limitation on the Landlord's Liability

Landlords in commercial leases strive to minimize personal liability. It is not unusual for the lease to provide that the landlord is not responsible for any damage done to the tenant or to the tenant's property or personal effects because of the landlord's failure to perform the landlord's obligations under the lease and that any recovery for any liability of whatever nature under the lease can only be made against the landlord's interest in the premises. This type of provision protects the landlord but does leave the tenant in a precarious situation of not being able to recover for any of the landlord's defaults under the lease.

A limitation of landlord's liability clause may contain an exception for the landlord's intentional misconduct or gross negligence.

ASSIGNMENT, SUBLETTING, OR MORTGAGING OF THE LEASED PREMISES

assignment

With regard to a lease, it is when the tenant transfers all his or her interest under the lease and retains nothing.

sublet

In regard to a lease, it is when the tenant transfers only a portion of his or her interest under the lease, and the tenant retains some interest.

The general rule is that a tenant may assign, sublet, or mortgage his or her interest in the lease. An **assignment**, by definition, is when the tenant transfers all his or her interest under the lease and retains nothing. A **sublet** is when a tenant transfers only a portion of his or her interest under the lease and the tenant retains some interest. For example, if a tenant leased the premises for five years, a sublet may be when he or she transfers possession for only two of those five years. Another example might be a tenant who has leased 10,000 square feet of space and in turn sublets 5,000 square feet of this space to another person.

Restrictions on assignment or subletting of the lease are strictly construed. This means that if the lease prohibits only assignments, then subletting is permissible. If the lease prohibits only subletting, then assignments are permissible. It is not unusual for leases to provide that both assignments and subletting are prohibited or can only take place with the landlord's prior written consent.

An assignment or sublet in violation of a lease restriction could result in the lease being in default. If the landlord accepts rent from an assignee or subtenant after a nonauthorized assignment, the landlord may waive its right to declare the lease in default.

The original tenant, after an assignment or sublet, remains responsible on the lease for rent and other lease obligations unless the lease provides otherwise.

An assignee of a lease has the responsibility for rent as long as the assignee is in possession and is responsible for lease covenants that run with the land. Although the definition and interpretation of lease covenants that run with the land vary from state to state, they usually include any type of use restrictions. An assignee, by express agreement, can be required to assume all obligations under the lease. An express assumption of all lease obligations makes the assignee as responsible as the original tenant. The assumption of lease covenants by an assignee, however, does not release the original tenant. The landlord can sue both the original tenant and the assignee in the event of a default.

A subtenant or sublessee has no responsibility to the original landlord under the lease for either rent or any of the lease covenants. A sublessee is responsible only to the tenant and responsible only pursuant to the terms of the sublease. Great care should be taken when drafting subleases to make sure that the sublease does not conflict with the main lease and that the tenant has full rights to enforce performance of the main lease covenants against the sublessee. This is important because the original tenant is responsible to the landlord for any acts of the subtenant under the sublease. Exhibits 18–3 and 18–4 show the liabilities of the parties under an assignment and sublease. Example 18–9 shows an assignment and subletting provision.

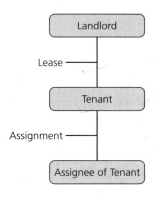

EXHIBIT 18–3

Assignment of Tenant's Interest in Lease

EXHIBIT 18–4

Sublease of Tenant's Interest in Lease

Example 18–9

(a) Tenant shall not sell, assign, encumber or otherwise transfer by operation of law or otherwise this Lease, or any interest herein, nor shall Tenant sublet the premises or any portion thereof, or suffer any other person to occupy or use the premises or any portion thereof, without the prior written consent of Landlord as provided herein, nor shall Tenant permit any lien to be placed on the Tenant's interest by operation of law. Tenant shall, by written notice, advise Landlord of its desire from and after a stated date (which shall not be less than thirty (30) days nor more than ninety (90) days after the date of Tenant's notice) to sublet the premises or any portion thereof for any part of the Term ("Subletting Notice"); and supply Landlord with such information, financial statements, verifications and related materials as Landlord may request or desire to evaluate the written request to sublet or assign. In such event, Landlord shall have the right, to be exercised by giving written notice to Tenant (Landlord's "Termination Notice") within ten days after receipt of Tenant's Subletting Notice, to terminate this Lease as to the portion of the premises described in Tenant's Subletting Notice and this Lease shall thereupon be terminated with respect to the portion of the premises therein described as of the date stated in Tenant's Notice. Tenant's Subletting Notice shall state the name and address of the proposed subtenant, and Tenant shall deliver to Landlord a true and complete copy of the proposed sublease with such Notice. If such Subletting Notice shall indicate that Tenant desires to sublet all of the premises and Landlord shall give its Termination Notice with respect thereto, this Lease shall terminate on the date stated in Tenant's Subletting Notice. If, however, this Lease shall terminate pursuant to the foregoing with respect to less than all the premises, the rental, as defined and reserved hereinabove and as adjusted pursuant to Paragraph 2, shall be adjusted on a pro rata basis according to the number of square feet retained by Tenant, and this Lease as so amended shall continue thereafter in full force and effect. If Landlord, upon receiving Tenant's Subletting Notice with respect to any of the premises, shall not exercise its right to terminate, Landlord will not unreasonably withhold its consent to Tenant's subletting the premises as requested in such Subletting Notice. Tenant shall, at Tenant's own cost and expense, discharge in full any outstanding commission obligation on the part of Landlord with respect to this Lease, and any commissions which may be due and owing as a result of any proposed assignment or subletting, whether or not the Lease is terminated pursuant hereto and rented by Landlord to the proposed subtenant or any other tenant.

(b) Any subletting or assignment hereunder by Tenant shall not result in Tenant being released or discharged from any liability under this Lease. As a condition to Landlord's prior written consent as provided for in this paragraph, the assignee or subtenant shall agree in writing to comply with and be bound by all of the terms, covenants, conditions, provisions and agreements of this Lease, and Tenant shall deliver to Landlord promptly after execution, an executed copy of each sublease or assignment and an agreement of said compliance by each sublessee or assignee.

(c) Landlord's consent to any sale, assignment, encumbrance, subletting, occupation, lien or other transfer shall not release Tenant from any of Tenant's obligations hereunder or be deemed to be a consent to any subsequent occurrence. Any sale, assignment, encumbrance, subletting, occupation, lien or other transfer of this Lease which does not comply with the provisions of this Paragraph shall be void.

A tenant may mortgage the leasehold interests or rights under a lease. The mortgage is subject to the terms of the lease and will terminate if the lease terminates. It is not unusual for lenders who take as security a tenant's obligation under a lease to enter into an agreement with the landlord to provide that the landlord will not terminate the lease unless notice is given to the leasehold mortgagee and the leasehold mortgagee has a right to cure all defaults. It also is important in representing leasehold mortgagees to obtain permission from the landlord to foreclose the mortgage and to accept an assignment of the lease and take over possession of the premises. A landlord often will agree and will recognize anyone who forecloses the leasehold mortgage as the new tenant under the lease. These agreements are called **attornment and nondisturbance agreements.** A form of attornment and non-disturbance agreement can be found at the end of this chapter as Exhibit 18–7.

The landlord also can mortgage its interest in the fee. The landlord's mortgage will be either subordinate or superior to the lease, depending on the time the mortgage was placed on the premises. The mortgage on the premises at the time the lease was entered into will be superior, and the mortgage that was placed on the premises after the lease will be subordinate. These rules can change by contract and lease provision. It is not unusual for leases to provide an automatic subordination that states that the lease will be subordinate to any mortgage on the premises, regardless of when it is placed. Example 18–10 shows a subordination clause.

Example 18–10

Tenant's rights shall be subject to any bona fide mortgage or deed of trust which is now, or may hereafter be, placed upon the Premises by Landlord. Tenant shall, if requested by Landlord, execute a separate agreement reflecting such subordination.

A superior mortgage on the leased premises creates a problem for the tenant if the mortgage is foreclosed because the lease will terminate. A tenant often will try to obtain attornment agreements from the landlord's mortgagee, asking the mortgagee to agree that if it forecloses and the tenant is not in default under the lease, the lender will honor the lease.

Special Sublease Issues

A sublease does not change the relationship between the landlord and the original tenant. The original tenant is still responsible for the performance of all the terms of the prime lease. A default by the tenant on the prime lease that would cause its termination will also terminate the sublease.

A sublease does not create any relationship between the landlord of the prime lease and the sublessee. The landlord of the prime lease cannot require the sublessee to perform either the prime lease or the sublease. Likewise, the sublessee has no right to require the landlord to perform its obligations under the prime lease.

Due to this lack of legal relationship between the landlord and sublessee, the rights of the sublessee are fully dependent upon the performance of the prime lease by the tenant of the prime lease. If the tenant defaults on the prime lease causing it to terminate, the sublease will terminate as well.

Provisions Normally Contained in a Sublease

A sublessor should provide in the sublease that it is not responsible to the sublessee for any failure of the landlord of the prime lease to perform. The sublessor should provide in the sublease that all covenants and provisions of the prime lease are incorporated in the sublease. The sublessor must be certain that any act or failure to act by the sublessee that results in a default of the prime lease is also a default of the sublease. The sublessor may even want the sublessee to indemnify them for damages caused by acts or failure to act of the sublessee that cause a default under the prime lease.

The sublessee should try to obtain from the landlord of the prime lease a consent to the sublease and an agreement to honor the sublease if the prime lease is terminated for any reason. The sublessee may want to have the landlord of the prime lease agree to send notice to the sublessee of any default of the prime lease and agree to accept action by the sublessee to cure the defaults.

Lease Guaranty

It is not unusual for a tenant's obligation under a lease to be guaranteed by some other party. This may happen when the tenant is a corporation with little or no assets or an individual without substantial financial reserve. For example, a landlord may require that the principal shareholders of a corporate tenant guarantee the tenant's performance under the lease. A form of lease guaranty can be found at the end of this chapter as Exhibit 18–8.

A lease guaranty usually is unconditional, and the guarantor agrees to perform all obligations of the tenant under the lease, including but not limited to all monetary obligations of the tenant such as payment of rent, taxes, insurance, utilities, or maintenance charges as well as all other obligations of the tenant, such as maintenance and repair obligations. It is not unusual for a guaranty to be limited in term. The major risks of tenant default normally are in the early years of the lease. It is common for a guaranty of a long-term lease to be applicable only to the first few years of the lease. For example, a subsidiary corporation enters into a 10-year lease with a landlord. The landlord may negotiate with the parent corporation to guarantee the first three years of the subsidiary's obligations under the lease.

Most guarantors agree to pay all costs of collection or enforcement of the guaranty, including attorney's fees and court costs.

Rejection of Leases in Bankruptcy

A debtor's bankruptcy can affect leases on real property. For example, an owner of a shopping center may be seriously in default on its loan to a bank. The shopping center is partially leased but contains a number of vacancies. The owner is desperately trying to sell the shopping center but has no prospective buyers. The bank begins foreclosure proceedings against the shopping center. The owner of the shopping center, to defend against the foreclosure proceedings, files bankruptcy. The bankruptcy stops the bank from foreclosing but raises a number of interesting questions concerning the shopping center leases.

A debtor's bankruptcy confers on the bankruptcy trustee, or the bankrupt debtor in some bankruptcy proceedings, the right to reject unexpired leases.

A bankruptcy trustee in a Chapter 7 bankruptcy or the bankrupt debtor in a Chapter 11 bankruptcy has the power to reject unexpired leases. An unexpired lease is a lease that has a term remaining at the time the bankruptcy petition is filed. The trustee or debtor has one hundred twenty (120) days after the bankruptcy petition has been filed to either reject the leases or assume them. If nothing is done within the 120–day period, the leases are deemed automatically rejected.

If a lease is to be assumed, which means that the lease remains in full force and effect during the bankruptcy proceeding, all current defaults under the lease must be cured, and adequate assurance of future performance must be provided.

If an unexpired lease is rejected and the bankrupt debtor is the tenant, this gives the landlord (nonbankrupt party) the right to have the lease immediately terminated, and the tenant must leave the premises. The landlord has a right to file a claim in the tenant's bankrupt estate for the damages caused by the rejection. Damages usually are limited to one year's rental. If a lease is rejected and the bankrupt debtor is the landlord, the tenant (nonbankrupt party) under the lease is given the option of treating the lease as terminated and may leave, or the tenant may remain in possession for the balance of the lease term. If the tenant decides to remain in possession for the balance of the lease term, the tenant is required to perform all duties under the lease, including those of the bankrupt landlord.

The tenant may, however, set off against any rent that is due the landlord the costs of non-performance caused by the landlord's bankruptcy.

Uniform Residential Landlord and Tenant Act

The common law rules regarding the landlord and tenant relationship have been modified in a number of states for leases of residential property by the passage of either part or all of the Uniform Residential Landlord and Tenant Act (URLTA). URLTA can be considered consumer legislation since it has the effect of tempering or modifying some of the harsher effects of common law regarding the landlord and tenant relationship. URLTA attempts to balance the playing field between landlords and tenants in residential situations by giving the tenants more rights than they would otherwise have under the general common law. Some examples of this moderation of the common law are hereafter discussed.

URLTA requires an obligation of good faith in landlord and tenant dealings. This means that every duty under URLTA and every act that must be performed as a condition precedent to the exercise of relief under URLTA imposes an obligation of good faith in its performance or enforcement. An example of this obligation of good faith is that URLTA prohibits a retaliatory eviction by a landlord because a tenant has made complaints to public authorities about the condition of the premises or has made complaints to the landlord about its obligation to repair the premises.

Under URLTA, rent is generally payable monthly and is due at the beginning of each month. Unless the rental agreement fixes a definite term, the tenancy is a month-to-month tenancy. If the rental agreement provides for a term longer than one year, it is effective for only one year.

A lease may also be enforceable even though it may not be fully signed by both the landlord and the tenant. An acceptance of rent without reservation by a landlord gives the rental agreement the same effect as if it had been signed and delivered by the landlord. Possession of the premises and payment of rent by a tenant without reservation gives the rental agreement the same effect as if it had been signed and delivered by the tenant.

URLTA prohibits certain provisions in a rental agreement. For example, the rental agreement may not provide that the tenant:

1. Agrees to waive or forgo rights or remedies under URLTA
2. Authorizes any person to confess judgment on a claim arising out of the rental agreement
3. Agrees to pay the landlord's attorney's fees
4. Agrees to the exculpation or limitation of any liability of a landlord arising under law or to indemnify the landlord for that liability or the cost connected therewith

URLTA also provides that if a landlord deliberately uses a rental agreement containing provisions known by the landlord to be prohibited, the tenant may recover in addition to his or her actual damages an amount up to three months periodic rent and reasonable attorney's fees.

URLTA provides that a landlord may not command or receive a security deposit in an amount in excess of one months rent. It also provides that upon termination of the lease, the security deposit held by the landlord may be applied to the payment of accrued rent and the amount of damages that a landlord has suffered by reason of the tenant's noncompliance with certain terms of the lease. An itemization of costs must be given by the landlord in a written notice to the tenant together with the amount due within 14 days after termination of the lease.

URLTA provides for a comprehensive division of landlord and tenant responsibilities concerning the use and occupancy of the premises. URLTA imposes a duty on the landlord to keep the premises in good repair, particularly as it materially affects the health and safety of the tenant. A tenant may terminate the lease for the landlord's failure to keep the premises in good repair. A willful or negligent failure on the part of the landlord to provide heat, hot water, or other essential services gives the tenant a right to terminate the lease.

A landlord's remedy to elect to terminate or evict a tenant for failure of the tenant to perform under a lease has also been modified from common law and is regulated under URLTA. Under URLTA, a landlord cannot terminate a lease because of the tenant's default without a written notice to the tenant stating the default and giving the tenant 30 days to cure the default.

A copy of the Uniform Residential Landlord and Tenant Act, including a list of states that have adopted portions of the Act, can be found at the following Web sites:

http://www.lectlaw.com
http://www.law.cornell.edu

Other Web sites can be found by typing in Uniform Residential Landlord and Tenant Act at *http://www.google.com.*

Protection of Residential Tenants from Eviction after a Foreclosure Sale

A lease on property that is mortgaged at the time the lease is entered into is subject to the mortgage. If the mortgage goes into default and the property is sold at a foreclosure sale, the lease will terminate, and the tenant can be promptly evicted from the property.

The recent recession with its increased foreclosures has caused both the federal government and many state governments to pass laws designed to protect resident tenants from being evicted without notice following a foreclosure sale.

The Helping Families Save Their Homes Act of 2009, effective May 20, 2009, provides that in the case of any foreclosure on a federally-related mortgage loan on any dwelling or residential real property, any purchaser at the sale shall assume the property subject to the rights of any bona fide tenant. The purchaser must give the tenant at least 90 days notice before the tenant is required to vacate the premises, even if the tenancy is month-to-month or without a lease. However, if a bona fide lease was entered into prior to the foreclosure, then the tenant is entitled to remain in the premises until the end of the lease term.

The only exception is that the lease may be terminated if the property is sold at the foreclosure sale to a purchaser who will occupy the property as a primary residence, but the tenant must still be given 90 days notice to vacate.

✔ CHECKLIST

Preparation of a Residential Lease

- [ ] I. Parties to Lease
  - [ ] A. Landlord—fee owner of leased premises
  - [ ] B. Tenant—person who intends to take possession and use the leased premises
- [ ] II. Description of Premises
  - [ ] A. Adequate description of leased premises and any associated personal property

(continued)

☐   B. Common areas
    1. Hallways
    2. Elevators
    3. Parking lots

☐ III. Term

☐ IV. Rent
  ☐   A. Fixed amount
  ☐   B. Rent commencement date

☐ V. Utilities
  ☐   A. What utilities tenant pays
  ☐   B. What utilities landlord pays

☐ VI. Maintenance and Repair Obligations
  ☐   A. Identify obligations of landlord and tenant to maintain and repair leased premises
  ☐   B. Identify tenant's rights to alter leased premises

☐ VII. Insurance
  ☐   A. Identify insurance obligations of landlord and tenant

☐ VIII. Damage or Destruction of Leased Premises
  ☐   A. Termination on total destruction
  ☐   B. Renovate on partial destruction
  ☐   C. Termination on partial destruction

☐ IX. Assignment and Subletting
  ☐   A. Free right to assign and sublet
  ☐   B. Restriction—no right to assign and sublet
  ☐   C. No assignment or subletting without permission of landlord

☐ X. Events of Default
  ☐   A. Failure to pay rent
  ☐   B. Failure to comply with lease covenants
  ☐   C. Notice and grace periods
  ☐   D. Landlord's right to cure tenant's default

☐ XI. Landlord's Remedies
  ☐   A. Sue for performance
  ☐   B. Cure default and seek reimbursement
  ☐   C. Terminate lease
  ☐   D. Evict and repossess tenant and relet leased premises as agent for tenant

☐ XII. Tenant's Remedies for Landlord's Default
  ☐   A. Withhold rent
  ☐   B. Sue to enforce
  ☐   C. Sue for money damages
  ☐   D. Cure default and offset costs against rent

☐ XIII. Quiet Enjoyment

☐ XIV. Surrender of Leased Premises
  ☐   A. Tenant must vacate before lease term expires

☐ XV. Holding Over
  ☐   A. Tenant is deemed to be month-to-month tenant
  ☐   B. Tenant to pay same rent as during rent term
  ☐   C. Tenant pays additional rent during holdover period
A form of residential lease can be found at the end of the chapter in Exhibit 18–9.

☑ **CHECKLIST**

Preparation of a Commercial Lease

☐ I. Purpose of Lease
- ☐ A. Retail space
- ☐ B. Office space
- ☐ C. Retail space—shopping center

☐ II. Parties to Lease
- ☐ A. Landlord—fee owner of lease premises
- ☐ B. Tenant—entity that intends to take possession and use the property
- ☐ C. Broker—party to lease to enforce commission rights

☐ III. Description of Property to Be Leased
- ☐ A. Adequate description of leased premises and any associated personal property
- ☐ B. Common area property
  1. Hallways
  2. Elevators
  3. Parking lots
  4. Mall
  5. Restaurants

☐ IV. Term
- ☐ A. Fixed term
- ☐ B. Option renewals
- ☐ C. Term to commence in future
  1. Open for business
  2. Fixed future date
  3. Procedure and remedies for unavailability of space at commencement of term

☐ V. Use
- ☐ A. Specified use
- ☐ B. Any lawful purpose

☐ VI. Rent
- ☐ A. Fixed amount
- ☐ B. Percentage rent
  1. What is included
  2. Definition of gross sales
  3. Exclusions from gross sales
  4. Record-keeping
  5. When is percentage rent payable
  6. Landlord's right to audit and inspect books
  7. Agreement to operate
  8. Radius clause
- ☐ C. Rent escalation (tax, insurance, expenses)
- ☐ D. Gross rent
- ☐ E. Net rent
- ☐ F. Inflators (CPI)
- ☐ G. When is rent due

☐ VII. Maintenance and Alterations
- ☐ A. Identify obligations of landlord and tenant to maintain and repair premises
- ☐ B. Identify tenant's rights to alter premises
- ☐ C. Alterations and maintenance to be lien-free

(continued)

- [ ] VIII. Insurance
  - [ ] A. Allocate responsibilities for insurance between landlord and tenant
  - [ ] B. Waiver of subrogation in insurance policies

- [ ] IX. Damage or Destruction to Premises
  - [ ] A. Termination on total destruction
  - [ ] B. Rent abatement on partial destruction
  - [ ] C. Termination on partial destruction

- [ ] X. Condemnation—Eminent Domain
  - [ ] A. Termination on total taking
  - [ ] B. Abatement of rent on partial taking
  - [ ] C. Termination on partial taking
  - [ ] D. Allocation of condemnation award between landlord and tenant

- [ ] XI. Assignment and Subletting
  - [ ] A. Free right to assign and sublet
  - [ ] B. Restriction—no right to assign and sublet
  - [ ] C. No assignment or subletting without permission of landlord

- [ ] XII. Subordination and Nondisturbance
  - [ ] A. Lease period
  - [ ] B. Lease subordinate to mortgages
  - [ ] C. Lease subordinate to mortgages but with attornment and subordination agreement

- [ ] XIII. Events of Default
  - [ ] A. Failure to pay rent
  - [ ] B. Failure to comply with lease covenants
  - [ ] C. Notice and grace period
  - [ ] D. Landlord's right to cure tenant's default
  - [ ] E. Tenant's payment of all expenses of enforcement of lease
    1. Attorney's fees
    2. Court costs
    3. Reimbursement to landlord for expenses to cure or remedy default

- [ ] XIV. Landlord's Remedies
  - [ ] A. Sue for performance
  - [ ] B. Cure default and seek reimbursement
  - [ ] C. Terminate lease
  - [ ] D. Evict and repossess tenant and relet premises as agent for tenant
  - [ ] E. Accelerate rent
  - [ ] F. Landlord's lien against tenant's personal property to secure payment of rent

- [ ] XV. Tenant's Remedies for Landlord's Default
  - [ ] A. Sue to enforce
  - [ ] B. Sue for money damages
  - [ ] C. Cure default and offset cost against rent
  - [ ] D. Withhold rent

- [ ] XVI. Quiet Enjoyment

- [ ] XVII. Surrender of Premises
  - [ ] A. Tenant must vacate before lease term expires
  - [ ] B. Tenant may remove trade fixtures
    1. If tenant is not in default
    2. Repair damage to premises caused by removal
    3. Remove before termination of lease

(continued)

XVIII. Holding Over
- A. Tenant is deemed to be month-to-month tenant
- B. Tenant to pay same rent as during lease term
- C. Tenant pays additional rent for holdover period

XIX. Estoppel Certificate
- A. Tenant obligated to give estoppel certificate on landlord's demand
  1. To purchasers of leased premises
  2. Mortgage lender

XX. Short-Form Lease
- A. Short-form lease to be prepared
- B. Short-form lease to be recorded
- C. No recordation of total lease

XXI. Limitation on Landlord's Liability
- A. No liability for landlord's failure to perform
- B. Liability limited to recovery against the leased premises
- C. Total landlord's liability
- D. Landlord liability for intentional misconduct or gross negligence

XXII. Other Lease Considerations
A form of small commercial retail space lease can be found at the end of this chapter in Exhibit 18–10.

ETHICS: Legal Needs of the Poor

Attorneys have always considered it a professional obligation to volunteer legal services for the poor. The rules of professional responsibility and conduct that govern attorneys in most states require a public service obligation as part of the ethical requirements of being an attorney. This obligation, often called pro bono participation, taken from the Latin phrase *pro bono publico,* which means "for the public good," should not be limited just to attorneys. A paralegal should consider voluntary pro bono participation as a necessary part of his or her professional life.

One of the major problems of the U.S. justice system is the unmet civil legal needs of the poor. The right to legal counsel in civil cases usually is provided by a number of quasi-governmental or voluntary associations that usually depend on a combination of full-time and part-time paid staff and volunteers to provide the necessary legal services.

Pro bono participation can provide the paralegal with an opportunity to develop and improve skills in an area in which the paralegal specializes. Many poor have landlord-tenant problems, and therefore, a knowledge of lease law can be applied by a paralegal in a pro bono situation. The pro bono experience may also offer the paralegal an opportunity to work in areas of the law in which he or she would not otherwise have the opportunity.

SUMMARY

Leasing is an important aspect of the real estate business. As the chapter points out, there are many issues to be considered in a lease transaction. Although lease negotiations are not adversarial in nature, it is obvious that a landlord and tenant do not have mutual interests in negotiating the lease. It is not always possible to please all the parties in a lease transaction.

Even in the fairest and most reasonable of leases, some provisions favor the landlord, and some favor the tenant. When reviewing or preparing a lease, the paralegal should keep in mind the effect of any lease provision on the client. Knowledge and experience are the essential ingredients to becoming competent in the area of lease transactions.

HELPFUL WEBSITES

Landlord—Tenant Laws
Summaries of landlord-tenant laws for all 50 states can be found at *http://www.rentlaw.com*.

An overview of landlord-tenant law with links to primary and secondary source material can be found on Cornell Law School's Legal Information Web site at *http://topics.law .cornell.edu*.

KEY TERMS

assignment
attornment and nondisturbance
    agreement
commercial lease
estoppel certificate
gross lease
landlord or lessor

lease
lease guaranty
net lease
percentage breakpoint
percentage rent
premises
radius clause

rent
residential lease
sublet
subrogation
tenant or lessee

REVIEW QUESTIONS

1. Explain the theory of independent covenants.
2. What title concerns should a tenant have when entering into a lease with a landlord?
3. Identify the main concerns that a landlord has when entering into a lease with a tenant.
4. What is the value of a CPI escalation rent clause?
5. Identify and briefly discuss the basic remedies of a landlord for a tenant's default under a lease.
6. What is the difference between a gross rent lease and a net rent lease?

7. What is the difference between an assignment and a sublease?
8. Under what circumstances would a tenant want a subordination-attornment agreement?
9. Identify and briefly discuss the basic remedies of a tenant for a landlord's default under a lease.
10. What is a lease guaranty, and when would it be used by a landlord?

CASE PROBLEMS

1. Ajax Stores, as a tenant, is negotiating a lease with Farris Realty Company. Ajax intends for the leased premises to be its main store location and is negotiating a 20-year lease. In addition, Ajax is anticipating that it will spend approximately $250,000 in trade fixtures and other improvements to the leased premises. Ajax conducts a title examination of the leased premises and discovers that Farris Realty Company has encumbered the leased premises with a mortgage to First Bank and Trust to secure a debt of $1.5 million. As a paralegal working for a law firm that represents Ajax, you have been made aware of the mortgage to First Bank and Trust. Should Ajax be concerned about the mortgage to First Bank and Trust? If so, what safeguards can you think of to protect Ajax?

2. As a landlord, is a gross lease or a net lease more favorable to you? Are there any factors to be considered in answering this question?

3. You are a paralegal with a law firm that represents a chain of retail jewelry stores. All the stores lease space in shopping malls. The jewelry store chain is large enough that it creates its own standard form lease for submission to prospective landlords in each of the shopping malls. The jewelry stores know that the landlords are expecting a percentage rent clause to be contained in the standard form lease. You have been asked to assist in the preparation of the standard form lease. What factors should you take into account when drafting the percentage rent clause?

4. You are a paralegal in a law firm representing the owner of a shopping center. The shopping center is being refinanced, and the new lender has requested that the owner obtain estoppel certificates from each of the tenants of the shopping center. You have been asked to prepare the estoppel certificate form. Briefly list the items you intend to include in the form.

5. Toni Tenant entered into a lease with Larry Landlord. The lease contains a provision obligating the tenant to keep the premises insured and to pay a rent of $500 each month. In addition, the lease prohibits assignment of the lease by the tenant. Toni Tenant possesses the premises for a couple of months and then decides to leave town. Toni finds Alice Assignee, who is willing to accept an assignment of the premises from Toni. Toni assigns all her rights, title, and interest in the premises to Alice Assignee, who accepts the assignment and assumes the obligation of Toni Tenant under the lease. The assignment is made without the landlord's consent. The landlord discovers the assignment when the rent check is received next month from Alice Assignee, and the landlord cashes the rent check and raises no objections to the assignment. Alice Assignee continues in this relation for the next couple of months, paying her rent each month to the landlord. Each month the landlord cashes the check. After a few months, Alice Assignee is approached by Samantha Subtenant, who wants to sublease the entire premises, but only for two months. Alice Assignee, thinking about a Mediterranean vacation, agrees and subleases the premises to Samantha for two months. During the two-month period, Samantha fails to pay rent to the landlord. The building burns down. The landlord discovers that the building is not insured. The landlord sues Toni, Alice, and Samantha for unpaid rent and for the value of the premises because of their breach of the promise to insure the premises. Can the landlord recover against Toni? Can the landlord recover against Alice? Can the landlord recover against Samantha? What are the rights, liabilities, and responsibilities among Alice, Toni, and Samantha?

PRACTICAL ASSIGNMENTS

1. Research your state law concerning a landlord's remedies for a tenant's default. Provide both statutory and case authority for the use of these remedies. Compare these remedies with the remedies discussed in this chapter. How are they different, and how are they similar?

2. Does your state provide for an acceleration of rent in the event of a tenant's default? Research the issue thoroughly and provide authority either for accelerated rent or for the denial of accelerated rent.

ADDENDUM

ACKNOWLEDGMENT

Portions of this chapter have been excerpted from *Office and Retail Leases—Representing the Smaller Tenant* by Phillip G. Skinner, *Real Property Law Institute,* Pages 8.1–8.63; Institute of Continuing Legal Education in Georgia, 1988, Athens, Georgia. Used by permission of the Publisher.

Student StudyWare™ CD-ROM

Interactive Student CD in the book includes additional quizzing, case studies, and key terms flashcards.

Online Companion™

For additional resources, please go to *www.paralegal.delmar.cengage.com*

EXHIBIT 18–5

Estoppel Certificate

Date: _____

Re: _____

Gentlemen:

It is our understanding that _____

_____ (hereinafter called "Purchaser") intends to purchase the above-captioned premises, and as a condition precedent, such Purchaser requires that this certification be made by the undersigned (hereinafter called "Tenant").

1. Tenant presently leases approximately _____ square feet of retail space located on the above-referenced Property, pursuant to the terms and provisions of that certain Lease Agreement dated _____, by and between _____, as Landlord and Tenant as Lessee, a copy of said Lease being attached hereto and made a part hereof as Exhibit "A" (the "Lease").

2. Said Lease is in full force and effect and Tenant is primarily liable as Lessee thereunder, and the documents attached hereto as Exhibit "A" constitute a full, complete and accurate copy of said Lease, and said Lease has not been modified, supplemented or amended in any way, and there are no other promises, obligations, understandings, agreements, or commitments between Landlord and Tenant with respect to said Property other than as expressly set forth in said Lease.

3. All contingencies and conditions precedent to the commencement, effectiveness, validity and enforceability of said Lease have been satisfied, and Tenant hereby ratifies said Lease. All duties of an inducement nature and all work required under said Lease to be performed by Landlord have been satisfactorily completed in accordance with the provisions of said Lease, and Tenant claims no offsets, rebates, concessions, abatements, recoupments, or defenses against or with respect to rent, additional rent, or other sums payable under the terms of said Lease, and there are no breaches or defaults under the terms of said Lease, and no event has occurred which, with the passage of time or the giving of notice or both, shall constitute a default by Landlord or Tenant under the terms of said Lease.

4. The base monthly rental presently payable by Tenant under the terms of said Lease is ($_____) Dollars per month, which monthly rental installments have been paid to Landlord through _____ and no other rent has been prepaid to Landlord or any other party, and there has been a security deposit in the amount of ($_____) Dollars paid to and presently held by Landlord with respect to said Lease.

Delmar/Cengage Learning

(continued)

EXHIBIT 18–5

Estoppel Certificate (*continued*)

5. The Lease Term pursuant to said Lease commenced on _____, and shall expire on _____.

6. Tenant has no interest, rights or claims with respect to said Property other than the interest, rights, or claims arising out of or with respect to said Lease.

7. Tenant is a corporation and is in good standing with the State of _____, and has full authority to execute the within document.

8. The undersigned officers of Tenant have full authority to execute and deliver this certificate as agents for and on behalf of Tenant.

9. Tenant is presently in actual, full and complete physical occupancy and possession of said Property, and Tenant has accepted said Property as suitable for all uses and purposes contemplated or intended under said Lease.

10. Upon acquisition of said Property by Purchaser, Tenant shall attorn to Purchaser and recognize Purchaser as Tenant's Lessor and Landlord pursuant to said Lease.

Very truly yours,

By: _____

EXHIBIT 18–6

Short-Form Memorandum

Memorandum of Lease Agreement

THIS MEMORANDUM OF LEASE AGREEMENT ("Memorandum") is entered into as of this 23rd day of March, 20__ by and between HARROLD ROBERTS AND THOMAS CLARK, whose address is 235 East Paces Ferry Road, Stanton, Ohio 60315 (collectively "Lessor"), and ACME CORPORATION, whose address is 6065 Roswell Road, Suite 120, Stanton, Ohio 60305 ("Lessee").

Recitals

By Lease Agreement dated March 23, 20__ ("Lease Agreement"), Lessor has leased to Lessee certain real property located at 5 West Paces Ferry Road, according to the present numbering system in Stanton, Knox County, Ohio, and being more particularly described on Exhibit A attached hereto and incorporated herein by reference, together with all buildings, structures, driveways, parking areas and all other improvements now or hereafter located thereon ("Demised Premises").

TO HAVE AND TO HOLD the Demised Premises for an initial term of approximately ten (10) years and three (3) months commencing on the date of the Lease Agreement and expiring approximately on July 31, 20__, together with the option to extend the initial term for one (1) additional term of five (5) years commencing immediately upon the expiration of the initial term, all on the terms and conditions contained in the Lease Agreement, which terms and conditions are made a part hereof by reference.

Pursuant to the terms of Paragraph 18 of the Lease Agreement, Lessor has the right, after the fifth (5th) anniversary of the Commencement Date of the Initial Term, to terminate the Lease Agreement under certain circumstances. In the event of any such termination, Lessee has an option, under certain circumstances, to lease space in the new development located on the property of which the Demised Premises are a part, under the terms and conditions set forth in that Paragraph of the Lease Agreement.

In addition to the terms referred to above, the Lease Agreement contains numerous other terms, covenants and conditions which affect the Demised Premises, and notice is hereby given that reference should be had to the Lease Agreement directly with respect to the details of such terms, covenants and conditions. Copies of the Lease Agreement are kept at the offices of Lessor and Lessee at the addresses set forth above. This Memorandum does not alter, amend, modify or change the Lease Agreement or the exhibits thereto in any respect. It is executed by the parties solely for the purpose of being recorded in the public records of Knox County, Ohio,

(continued)

and it is the intent of the parties that it shall be so recorded and shall give notice of and confirm the Lease Agreement and exhibits thereto and all of its terms to the same extent as if all of the provisions of the Lease Agreement and exhibits thereto were fully set forth herein. The Lease Agreement and all exhibits thereto are hereby incorporated by reference in this Memorandum and the parties hereby ratify and confirm the Lease Agreement as if said Lease Agreement were being presently re-executed by both parties and being recorded. In the event of any conflict between the provisions of the Memorandum and the Lease Agreement, the provisions of the Lease Agreement shall control.

IN WITNESS WHEREOF, Lessor and Lessee have set their hands and seals herewith and have caused this instrument to be executed in their names and their seals to be affixed hereunto by duly authorized officials thereof, the day and year first above written.

LESSOR:

_____ (SEAL)

HARROLD ROBERTS

_____ (SEAL)

THOMAS CLARK

LESSEE:

ACME CORPORATION, an Ohio Corporation

By: _____
                              its President
[CORPORATE SEAL]

EXHIBIT 18–6
Short-Form Memorandum
(*continued*)

THIS AGREEMENT is made as of _____, 20__, by and among _____, a _____ ("Lessor"), whose address is _____, and _____, a _____ ("Lessee"), whose address is _____, and _____ , a _____ corporation ("Lender"), whose address is _____ _____ .

A. The Property.

The term "Property," as used herein, shall mean the real property situated in the County of _____, State of _____, legally described in Exhibit "A" attached hereto and by this reference made a part hereof, together with all buildings, structures, improvements and fixtures now or hereafter located thereon, and together with all easements and other rights appurtenant thereto.

B. The Lease.

Pursuant to the terms and provisions of a lease dated _____, between Lessor and Lessee (the "Lease"), for a term of _____, the Property has been leased to Lessee.

C. The Loan; Security Documents; Security Deed.

Lessor proposed to borrow certain sums from Lender to be evidenced by a promissory note. Lessor proposes to encumber the Property as security for payment of its obligations to Lender and, for such purpose, shall enter into various instruments and documents (collectively the "Security Documents"), including without limitation a Deed to Secure Debt and Security Agreement (the "Security Deed") from Lessor to Lender and an Assignment of Leases and Rents (the

EXHIBIT 18–7
Subordination, Attornment, and Nondisturbance Agreement

Delmar/Cengage Learning

(*continued*)

"Collateral Assignment"), which Security Deed and Collateral Assignment will be recorded in the real property records of _____ County.

D. Purposes.

In connection with the above-mentioned transactions, Lessor and Lessee have agreed to offer certain assurances and representations to the Lender, and all parties agree to provide for (i) the subordination of the Lease to the Security Documents; (ii) the continuation of the Lease notwithstanding any foreclosure of the Security Deed subject to certain conditions; and (iii) Lessee's attornment to the Lender or to such other parties as may acquire title to the Property as a result of any foreclosure or any conveyance of the Property in lieu of foreclosure.

AGREEMENT

NOW, THEREFORE, in consideration of the mutual terms and provisions hereinafter contained and other good and valuable consideration received by any party from any other, the receipt and sufficiency of which are hereby acknowledged, the parties agree as follows:

1. Notices of Default to Lender.

Notwithstanding anything to the contrary in the Lease, Lessee shall personally deliver or mail to Lender, at Lender's address set forth above, written notice of any default under the Lease by Lessor, and if within the time provided in the Lease for curing thereof by Lessor, Lender performs or causes to be performed all such obligations with respect to which Lessor is in default which can be cured by the payment of money, any right of Lessee to terminate the Lease by reason of such default shall cease and be null and void.

2. Subordination of Lease to Security Documents.

Lessee hereby subordinates its leasehold estate in the Property and all of Lessee's right under the Lease to the Security Documents and to all extensions, renewals, modifications, consolidations and replacements thereof, to the full extent of all obligations secured or to be secured thereby including interest thereon and any future advances thereunder.

3. Non-Disturbance of Lessee.

Lender agrees that, for so long as Lessee shall perform and satisfy all obligations of Lessee under the Lease in accordance with its terms, neither the Lease nor Lessee's rights pursuant thereto shall be disturbed or affected by any foreclosure of the Security Deed or conveyance in lieu of foreclosure.

Lender's obligations under this Section 3 shall be null and void if Lessee shall, at any time, default in the timely performance of the Lessee's obligations under the Lease of this Agreement and not cure such default within the time, if any, allowed in the Lease.

4. Lender as Landlord after Foreclosure.

In the event that the Lender (or any other party) shall acquire title to the Property or shall succeed to Lessor's interest in the Lease, whether through foreclosure of the Security Deed, conveyance in lieu of foreclosure, or otherwise, Lender (or such other party) shall thereupon, and without the necessity of attornment or other act or agreement, be substituted as Lessee's landlord under the Lease, and shall be entitled to the rights and benefits and subject to the obligations thereof; provided that neither Lender nor any other party shall be:

(a) liable for any act or omission of any prior landlord under the Lease (including Lessor); or

(b) subject to any offsets or defenses which Lessee might have against any prior landlord (including Lessor); or

(c) bound by Lessee's payment of any rent or additional rent beyond the then current rent period to any prior landlord under the Lease (including Lessor); or

(continued)

(d) bound by any amendment, modification, extension or supplement of the Lease made without Lender's prior written consent; or

(e) bound by any representations or warranties made by any prior landlord under the Lease (including Lessor) whether such representations are set forth in the lease or in any other writing or were made orally, regardless of the knowledge of Lender or such other party of the existence and substance of any such representations or warranties;

and Lessee hereby agrees to attorn to and recognize such Lender (or such other party) as Lessee's landlord.

5. Payment of Rent upon Default.

Lessee has been advised that the Security Documents give Lender the right to collect rent and other sums payable under the Lease directly from Lessee upon the occurrence of a default thereunder, and that upon the receipt from Lender of notice of any such default, Lessee will thereafter pay all rent and other sums payable under the Lease directly to Lender (or as Lender shall direct) as they become due and payable.

6. Application of Insurance and Condemnation Proceeds.

Lessee has been advised that the insurance and condemnation provisions of the Security Documents give Lender certain rights to require that insurance and condemnation proceeds be applied to payment of the indebtedness secured thereby and not to restoration or re-building; and Lessee hereby waives any terms of such Lease with respect to the application of insurance and condemnation proceeds which are inconsistent with the terms of the Security Documents.

7. Estoppel.

Lessee hereby certifies to Lender as follows:

(a) Lessee is the lessee under the Lease, a true and correct copy of which, together with any amendments thereto, is attached hereto;

(b) Except as set forth in the amendment(s), if any, attached hereto, the Lease has not been amended, modified or supplemented and the Lease is in full force and effect;

(c) All of the improvements contemplated by the Lease have been entirely completed as required therein, the leased premises and the improvements thereon have been accepted by Lessee with Lessee in occupancy thereof and all sums, if any, payable by Lessor to Lessee in connection with the construction of such improvements have been paid in full and all conditions precedent to Lessee's obligations under the Lease have occurred;

(d) The term of the Lease commenced on _____, 20__, and will end, if not sooner terminated according to the terms of the Lease, on _____, 20__;

(e) Rent commenced to accrue under the Lease on _____, and there are presently no offsets or credits against rents thereunder and no payments are due from Lessor to Lessee under the Lease;

(f) Lessee has not prepaid (and will not prepay) any rent which is not yet due and payable under the Lease and no concessions, rebates, allowances or other considerations for free or reduced rent in the future have been granted;

(g) Lessee acknowledges that the Lease and the rentals thereunder have been (or will be) pledged to Lender and that Lessee has no knowledge of any assignment, hypothecation or pledge of the Lease or of any rentals thereunder, other than to Lender;

(h) Lessee has no knowledge of (a) any present defaults of the Lessor under the Lease or (b) any present condition or state of facts which by notice or the passage of time, or both, would constitute a default by Lessor under the Lease; and

(i) The party executing this agreement on behalf of Lessee is fully authorized and empowered to do so.

EXHIBIT 18–7

Subordination, Attornment, and Nondisturbance Agreement (*continued*)

(continued)

8. Binding Effect.

The provisions of this Agreement shall be covenants running with the Property, and shall be binding upon and shall inure to the benefit of the parties hereto and their respective heirs, representatives, successors and assigns.

IN WITNESS WHEREOF, the parties hereto have executed and sealed this Agreement as of the day and year first above written.

LESSOR:
[Individual]

_____ (SEAL)

Signed, sealed and delivered this _____ day of _____, 20___, in the presence of:

_____ (SEAL)

[corporation or partnership]

_____

_____
Witness

By: _____

Title: _____

_____
Notary Public
My Commission Expires:

[CORPORATE SEAL]

_____
[Notarial Seal]

LESSEE:

[Individual]

_____ (SEAL)

_____ (SEAL)

[corporation or partnership]

Signed, sealed and delivered this _____ day of _____, 20___, in the presence of:

_____

_____
Witness

By: _____

Title: _____

[CORPORATE SEAL]

_____
Notary Public
My Commission Expires:

_____
[Notarial Seal]

LENDER:
By: _____
Name: _____
Title: _____

(continued)

Attest: _____

Name: _____

Title: _____

[CORPORATE SEAL]

Signed, sealed and delivered this _____
day of _____, 20___, in the
presence of:

_____

Witness

_____

Notary Public
My Commission Expires:

_____

[Notarial Seal]

(continued)

For and in consideration of the leasing by _____
_____ (referred to as "Landlord"), of certain Premises (hereinafter referred to as the "Premises") to _____
_____
(hereinafter referred to as "Tenant"), pursuant to the terms and provisions of that certain Lease
Agreement dated _____ by and between Landlord and Tenant (hereinafter collectively
referred to as the "Lease"), and in further consideration of the sum of Ten and No/100 Dollars
($10.00) to the undersigned paid by Landlord, the receipt and sufficiency of which are hereby
acknowledged, the undersigned (hereinafter collectively referred to as "Guarantor") hereby
unconditionally guarantees to Landlord the full and prompt payment of any and all rents,
percentage rent, if any, or additional rental (hereinafter collectively referred to as "rent") payable by Tenant under the Lease, and hereby further guarantees the full and timely performance and observance of all of the covenants and terms therein provided to be performed
and observed by Tenant; and Guarantor, to the same extent as Tenant, hereby agrees that if
default or breach shall at any time be made by Tenant in the payment of rent under the Lease,
or if Tenant should default in the performance and observance of any of the covenants and
terms contained in the Lease, Guarantor shall pay the rent and any arrears thereof, to Landlord, and shall faithfully perform and fulfill all such covenants and terms of the Lease, and shall
forthwith pay to Landlord all damages that may arise or are incident to or in consequence of
any default or breach by Tenant under the Lease, and/or by the enforcement of this Guaranty,
including without limitation, all attorneys' fees, court costs, and other expenses and costs incurred by Landlord.

    This Guaranty shall be enforceable by Landlord in a joint action against Guarantor and
Tenant or in a separate and independent action against Guarantor without the necessity of any
suit, action, or proceeding by Landlord of any kind or nature whatsoever against Tenant because of Tenant's default or breach under the Lease, and without the necessity of any other
notice or demand to Guarantor to which Guarantor might otherwise be entitled, all of which

EXHIBIT 18–8

Guaranty of Lease

Delmar/Cengage Learning

(continued)

EXHIBIT 18–8

Guaranty of Lease (*continued*)

notices Guarantor hereby expressly waives; without limiting the generality of the foregoing, Guarantor hereby expressly waives any statutory right pursuant to _____ to require Landlord to take action against Tenant. Guarantor hereby agrees that the validity of this Guaranty and the obligations of Guarantor hereunder shall not be terminated, affected, diminished, or impaired by reason of the assertion or the failure to assert by Landlord against Tenant any of the rights or remedies reserved to Landlord pursuant to the provisions of the Lease or any other remedy or right which Landlord may have at law or in equity or otherwise, the obligations of Guarantor being independent of the obligations of Tenant under the Lease.

Guarantor hereby further covenants and agrees that this instrument constitutes a continuing guaranty, and the liability of Guarantor hereunder shall in no way be affected, modified, or diminished by reason of any assignment, renewal, modification, or extension of the Lease or any modification or waiver of or change in any of the covenants and terms of the Lease by agreement of Landlord and Tenant, or by any unilateral action or either Landlord or Tenant, or by any extension of time that may be granted by Landlord to Tenant or any indulgence of whatever kind granted to Tenant, or any dealings or transactions or matter or thing occurring between Landlord and Tenant, including without limitation, any adjustment, compromise, settlement, accord and satisfaction, or release, or any bankruptcy, insolvency, reorganization, arrangement, assignment for the benefit of creditors, receivership, or trusteeship affecting Tenant. Guarantor does hereby expressly waive any suretyship defense it may have by virtue of any statute, law, ordinance of any state or other governmental authority, and further waives any and every defense of tenant, including, without limitation, any defense arising by reason of any disability of Tenant or by reason of the cessation from any cause whatsoever of the liability of Tenant.

In the event that other agreements similar to this Guaranty are executed from time to time by other entities or persons with respect to the Lease, this Guaranty shall be cumulative of any such other agreements to the effect that the liabilities and obligations of Guarantor hereunder shall be joint and several with those of each other such guarantor, and the liabilities and obligations of Guarantor hereunder shall in no event be affected or diminished by reason of any such other agreement.

All of Landlord's rights and remedies under the Lease or under this Guaranty are intended to be distinct, separate, and cumulative and no such right and remedy therein or herein is intended to be to the exclusion of or a waiver of any other.

Guarantor hereby expressly waives presentment, demand for performance, notice of non-performance, protest, notice of protest, notice of dishonor, and notice of acceptance.

Landlord may, without notice, assign this Guaranty in whole or in part, and/or may assign all of its interests in and to the Lease, and, in such event, each and every successive assignee of the Lease and/or of this Guaranty shall have the right to enforce this Guaranty, by suit or otherwise, for the benefit of such assignee as fully as if such assignee were named herein.

Guarantor warrants and represents that they have the legal right and capacity to execute this Guaranty. This Guaranty shall be governed by and construed in accordance with the laws of the State of _____ .

This Guaranty shall be binding upon Guarantor and the successors, heirs, executors, and administrators of Guarantor, and shall inure to the benefit of Landlord, Landlord's representatives, successors, and assigns. If more than one party shall execute this Guaranty, all such parties shall be jointly and severally obligated hereunder and are herein collectively referred to as "Guarantor."

IN WITNESS WHEREOF, Guarantor have executed, sealed, and delivered this Guaranty, this _____ day of _____, 20__.

_____ (SEAL)

_____ (SEAL)

EXHIBIT 18–9
Apartment Lease

FORM 207
IVAN ALLEN CO., ATLANTA

APARTMENT LEASE CONTRACT

THIS AGREEMENT, made this   day of   , 20   , among

(hereinafter referred to as "Lessor")   (hereinafter referred
to as "Lessee"), and   (hereinafter referred to as "Agent"),

WITNESSETH: That in consideration of the mutual covenants hereinafter set forth, the parties do hereby covenant and agree as follows:

Premises and Term

1.   Lessor does hereby lease to Lessee and Lessee does hereby lease from Lessor Apartment No.   (hereinafter referred to as "Premises") in Lessor's apartment house situated at

in metropolitan Atlanta,   County, Georgia, according to the present system of numbering buildings in metropolitan

Atlanta,   County, Georgia, for a term commencing on the   day of   , 20   , and ending at

midnight on the   day of   , 20

Rental

2.   Lessee shall pay to Lessor, through   at its office in Atlanta, Georgia, promptly on the first day of each month in advance during the term of this Lease, a monthly rental of $ If such rental is not received by the fifth day of each month, Lessee shall pay to Agent a late charge in the amount of 10% of the monthly rental; Lessee shall also pay Agent a charge for any returned checks of Lessee in the amount of $5.00 for each returned check.

Security Deposit

3.   Lessee herewith deposits with Agent the sum of $ (hereinafter referred to as "Security Deposit") as evidence of good faith on the part of Lessee in the fulfillment of all the terms of this Lease, which Security Deposit shall be held by Lessor during the term of this Lease or any renewal thereof and for fifteen days thereafter. Lessor shall have the right to use said Security Deposit to pay, as fully as possible, the expense of any unpaid rentals, of any accumulated late charges or returned check charges, of any unreturned keys, as well as the expense of repairing any damage to Premises, except reasonable wear and tear occurring from normal use of Premises. Lessor's right to recover additional sums from Lessee for damages to Premises shall not be limited by the amount of said Security Deposit. In no event shall Lessee be entitled to apply the Security Deposit to any rental payment due hereunder.

Utilities

4.   Lessor shall furnish Lessee with the utilities checked as follows:☐ cold water;☐ hot and cold water;☐ heat;☐ all utilities for use in Premises. Lessor shall not be responsible for failure to furnish such utilities if the failure to do so is due to any cause beyond Lessor's control. Lessee shall pay all bills for utilities other than those checked hereinabove and used by Lessee in Premises, but all utilities shall be used only for ordinary household purposes. Lessee shall make a written request for any repairs or services to such utilities to Agent or any representative of Lessor at Premises, except in an extreme emergency in which event such notice may initially be given by telephone and later confirmed in writing. Lessor shall not be obligated to furnish any utilities paid for by Lessor to Premises at any time at which Lessee is in default hereunder. Lessor shall not be responsible for stopped-up plumbing, drains or disposals where such stoppage is caused by the introduction of foreign objects not intended for sewer disposal, and Lessee shall pay on demand all charges for repair of such stoppage.

Occupancy

5.   Premises will be occupied only by the following adults and minors:

No persons other than those named above (occasional overnight guests excepted) shall occupy or share Premises with Lessee. In no event shall more persons than the number of persons listed above occupy Premises.

Pets

6.   Pets may be permitted at the discretion of Agent and Lessor; provided that such pets do not constitute a nuisance to other tenants and provided that Lessee deposits with Lessor an additional damage deposit of $. Lessee recognizes that "reasonable wear and damage" as specified in this Lease does not include damage caused by pets and that Lessor's judgment shall be the sole factor in determining such pet damage. Pets must be on leash when outside of Premises and cannot be tied to anything outside of Premises. Lessee shall be limited to one dog or cat weighing not more than twenty-five pounds. Pets must be approved by Agent and Lessor, and such approval is contingent upon Lessee's observance of the foregoing conditions of this Lease and can be withdrawn at any time.

Extension Terms

7.   Unless another Lease is signed by the parties hereto or unless written notice of termination is given by either party at least thirty calendar days before expiration of the term of this Lease, this Lease shall be automatically extended on a year-to-year basis after the expiration of the initial term hereof without the execution of any new Lease or other instrument whatsoever. If Lessor desires to increase the rental payable hereunder for any such upcoming extension term hereof, Lessor shall give Lessee notice of such increased rental at least thirty days prior to the commencement of such extension term and, unless Lessee promptly otherwise notifies Lessor or Agent, then Lessor and Lessee shall enter in a new lease for such extension term at such increased rental. If Lessee does promptly notify Lessor or Agent that Lessee will not accept such increased rental, then the term of this Lease shall not be extended and shall terminate as set forth herein.

Lessor's Failure to Give Possession

8.   Lessor shall not be liable to Lessee for failure to deliver possession of Premises at the commencement of the term of this Lease, but Lessor shall use Lessor's best efforts to give Lessee timely possession of Premises; if failure to do so is caused by any tenant holding over, Lessor will use all customary means to oust the old tenant. Lessee may secure a transfer of and prosecute in Lessee's name any cause of action which Lessor may have against such tenant holding over, and Lessee shall be entitled to retain all amounts recovered in such action.

Use of Premises; Maintenance; Indemnity

9.   Premises shall be used as Lessee's residence only and for no other purposes whatsoever; nor shall Premises be used in violation of any laws, ordinances, restrictions or regulations of any governmental body, nor so as to create a nuisance, nor to vitiate or increase the rate of insurance thereon. Lessee accepts Premises in its present condition and as suited for residential use by Lessee. Lessor shall not be required to make any repairs or improvements to Premises, except that, after receipt of written notice from Lessee of any damage or defect rendering Premises unsafe or untenantable, Lessor shall remedy such defective condition or, if the damaged or defective Premises is unfit for occupancy and if Lessor decides not to repair Premises, then upon written notice from Lessor to Lessee this Lease shall terminate, with rent prorated and any balance due Lessee refunded. Lessee shall be liable for, indemnify and hold Lessor and Agent harmless for any claim of damage or injury to the person or property of Lessee, Lessor's other tenants and any other party whatsoever, if such damage or injury be due to the act or neglect of Lessee, any guest of Lessee or anyone in Lessee's control or employ or brought into Premises by Lessee or if such damage or injury be due to any failure of Lessee to report in writing to Lessor any such defective condition. Lessee shall maintain Premises in good condition and repair and shall do no damage thereto. If Premises are rendered untenantable by fire, storm, earthquake or other casualty whatsoever, this Lease shall terminate as of the date of such destruction or damage and rental shall be accounted for as of that date.

Assignment and Subletting

10. Lessee shall not assign this Lease or sublet Premises or any part thereof or secure a replacement for Lessee hereunder without first obtaining the written approval of Lessor or Agent.

Fixtures and Furniture

11. Lessee may (if not in default hereunder), prior to the termination of this Lease, remove all fixtures, personalty and equipment which Lessee has placed in Premises; provided that Lessee restores Premises to its condition prior to the installation of such fixtures. Lessor shall not be liable for any loss of or damage to any property whatsoever, and Lessee shall at all times cause Lessee's fixtures, personalty and equipment to be insured in amounts satisfactory to Lessee.

Agent's Commission

12. Agent's commission under this Lease shall be paid by Lessor under the terms of a separate agreement between Lessor and Agent. If any rent owing under this Lease is collected by or through an attorney at law, Lessee agrees to pay fifteen per cent of the total amount so collected as attorney's fees. Lessee hereby waives and assigns to Lessor all homestead rights and exemptions which Lessee may have under any law as against any obligation owing under this Lease.

Delmar/Cengage Learning

(continued)

EXHIBIT 18–9

Apartment Lease (*continued*)

Lessee's Conduct; Common Areas; Inspection

13. Lessee, Lessee's family and guests shall not act in a disorderly, boisterous nor unlawful manner and shall not disturb the rights, comforts or convenience of other persons in the building or complex in which Premises is located. The swimming pool, if any, and all other common areas will be used only in compliance with present and future written rules and regulations furnished to Lessee or posted in the common areas, and such pool and common areas are to be used wholly at the risk of the persons making use thereof. Lessor reserves the right to control the method, manner, and time of parking in parking spaces and to control and limit the entry to Premises by agents, messengers, delivery men, solicitors and salesmen. If Lessee or any member of Lessee's family or guest is present in Premises, then Lessor, Lessor's representatives or servicemen may enter Premises at all reasonable times for any reasonable business purpose. If such parties are not present in Premises, then Lessor's representatives or servicemen may enter Premises at all reasonable times (so long as written notice of such entry is left in the apartment after such entry) for the following purposes: repairs, extermination, preventive maintenance, failure to return tools or appliances within prescribed time, emergency, safety or fire inspections and building inspection by fire marshals, mortgage lenders, prospective purchasers or residents or insurance agents.

Lessee's Transfer

14. In the event Lessee is transferred or obtains employment outside of the Metropolitan Atlanta area (such Metropolitan Atlanta area being defined for the purposes of this Lease as any point within sixty miles in any direction from the intersection of Marietta and Peachtree Streets in downtown Atlanta, Fulton County, Georgia), then Lessee shall be released from further obligations under this Lease after Lessee completes the following conditions precedent to such release: (a) Lessee shall provide Agent with written notice of Lessee's intention to seek such release hereunder by virtue of such transfer or new employment at least thirty calendar days prior to termination hereof, and (b) such notice shall be valid only if accompanied by an affidavit from Lessee's employer confirming such transfer or new employment and by Lessee's payment of all rentals and charges whatsoever due under this Lease, including without limitation charges for any damage and repairs to Premises which are the obligation of Lessee under this Lease, and (c) Lessee shall release all Lessee's rights to any Security Deposit made under this Lease as liquidated damages for such cancellation of this Lease. This provision is for the benefit of Lessee, and the foregoing conditions hereof must be strictly complied with by Lessee in order to effectuate such release hereunder.

Premature Cancellation

15. This Lease shall be prematurely cancelled by Lessor as of the first day of any month during the term hereof, if (a) Lessee has given Agent written notice of such desired cancellation at least thirty calendar days prior thereto, and (b) if such notice is accompanied by Lessee's payment of all rental and other charges whatsoever hereunder, including without limitation charges for any damage and repairs to Premises which are the obligation of Lessee under this Lease, due up to such proposed date of cancellation of this Lease and by payment of liquidated damages for such premature cancellation in the amount of one additional month's rental hereunder. In such event any Security Deposit posted by Lessee shall be retained by Lessor as additional liquidated damages hereunder.

Termination and Reletting by Lessor or Agent

16. If Lessee defaults for three calendar days after written notice from Lessor or Agent of default by Lessee in the payment of rental due or otherwise defaults under any term, condition or provision of this Lease; or if Lessee fails to reimburse Lessor for any damages, repairs or plumbing service costs when due under this Lease; or if Lessee shall abandon Premises; or if Lessee or any other occupant or guest in Premises shall violate or fail to comply with any term, condition or provision of this Lease or any of the Apartment Rules and Regulations hereinafter set forth in this Lease, as such rules may be reasonably changed or additional rules imposed and Lessee notified thereof, then Lessor or Agent shall have the option to either terminate this Lease by written notice to Lessee or, without terminating this Lease, to enter upon and take possession of Premises, removing all persons and property therefrom and, as Lessee's agent, to rerent Premises at the best price obtainable by reasonable effort, without advertisement and by private negotiations and for any term Lessor or Agent deems proper; Lessee shall be liable to Lessor for any deficiency between all rental due hereunder and the price obtained by Lessor on such reletting. Such termination shall not release Lessee from liability for any unpaid rentals under this Lease, past or future.

Surrender of Premises

17. Whenever under the terms hereof Lessor is entitled to possession of Premises, Lessee shall at once surrender Premises to Lessor and shall remove all of Lessee's effects therefrom; and Lessor may forthwith re-enter Premises and repossess itself thereof, removing all persons and effects therefrom and using such force as may be necessary, without being guilty of forcible entry or detainer, trespass or other tort. Lessee shall not remain in possession of Premises after the expiration of the final term of this Lease. Any holding of Premises by Lessee after the expiration of this Lease (except pursuant to a new lease, or the expiration hereof as provided in paragraph #7 hereof) shall not constitute a tenant-at-will interest on behalf of Lessee, but Lessee shall be a tenant at sufferance. Unless this Lease is extended pursuant to provision of paragraph #7 , there shall be no renewal or extension of this Lease by operation of law or otherwise.

Service of Notices

18. Lessee hereby appoints as Lessee's agent to receive service of all dispossessory or other legal proceedings and notices thereunder,and all notices required under this Lease, the person occupying Premises at the time such notice is given, and, if no person be occupying the same, then such service or notice may be made by attaching the same on the front entrance to Premises. A copy of all notices under this Lease shall also be sent to Lessee's last known address if different from Premises.

Signs; Carding

19. Lessee shall place no signs, placards, or other advertisements of any character on Premises. Lessor may card Premises "For Rent" at any time within sixty days prior to the expiration of this Lease and during such sixty day period may exhibit Premises to prospective tenants.

Storage and Garage

20. If Lessor makes available to Lessee any storage space or garage outside Premises, anything placed therein by Lessee shall be stored wholly at the risk of Lessee, and Lessor shall have no responsibility in respect thereof. If Lessor makes available to Lessee any space for use as a garage or for parking cars, Lessor shall not be responsible for any damage to or loss of any vehicle stored or parked therein, nor for any part or accessory of such vehicle, nor for any property of any kind stored or left in said garage or vehicle.

Keys

21. All keys issued to Lessee hereunder shall be returned or the replacement cost thereof paid by Lessee when Lessee vacates Premises.

Definitions

22. "Lessor" as used in this Lease shall include Lessor, Lessor's heirs, executors, administrators, legal representatives, assigns and successors in title to Premises; "Lessee" shall include Lessee, Lessee's heirs, executors, administrators, legal representatives and, if this Lease shall be validly assigned or sublet, shall also include Lessee's assignees and sub-lessees. "Agent" shall include Agent, successors and assigns. Lessor, Lessee and Agent include male, female, singular, plural, corporation, partnership or individual, as may fit the particular parties. The captions used herein are merely descriptive of some matters contained therein and do not necessarily describe the contents of each paragraph.

Miscellaneous

23. Except for the commission agreement between Lessor and Agent referred to hereinabove, this Lease contains the entire agreement of the parties and no representation, inducement, promises or agreements, oral or otherwise, between the parties not embodied herein shall be of any force or effect. No failure of Lessor to exercise any power given Lessor hereunder, or to insist upon strict compliance by Lessee of any obligation hereunder, including without limitation any acceptance of partial payments of rental or other amounts due hereunder, and no custom or practice of the parties at variance with the terms hereof, shall constitute a waiver of Lessor's right to demand exact compliance with the terms hereof. Time is of the essence of this agreement. Lessee's rights under this Lease shall be subject to any bona fide mortgage or deed to secure debt which is now or may hereafter be placed upon Premises.

Special Stipulations

In so far as the following special stipulations conflict with any of the foregoing provisions of this Lease, the following shall control:

IN WITNESS WHEREOF, the parties have executed or caused this Lease to be executed by authorized officials in duplicate, the day and year first above written.

Individually and as Agent for Lessor

BY: ______________________________   X ______________________________ (SEAL)
Lessee

RULES AND REGULATIONS OF APARTMENTS

Lessee shall:

1. Not obstruct sidewalks, courts, entry passage, halls, and stairways, nor allow children to loiter or play in them, nor use them for any purpose except ingress and egress, nor leave bicycles or other vehicles therein. Children shall confine their playing to area designated by Lessor.
2. Not cover or obstruct skylights and windows that reflect or admit light to public space.
3. Not use water closets, drains or other plumbing apparatus for any other purposes than those for which they were constructed and not throw sweepings, rubbish, rags, ashes or other substances therein.
4. Be responsible for damage to plumbing, cooling, or heating apparatus, and other equipment from misuse by Lessee.
5. Throw nothing out of the windows or doors, or down the passage, or skylight of the building.
6. Close windows when it rains or snows, and be responsible for any injury to premises or other tenants due to failure so to do.
7. Not alter premises nor change any partition, door, or window, nor add locks thereto, nor paint, paper, bore or screw upon or in the walls, ceiling, floors, woodwork or plaster.
8. Keep whole all glass, locks and trimmings in or upon the door and windows, and immediately replace or repair such thereof as may be broken or out of order under the direction and to the satisfaction of the Lessor.
9. Erect no awnings or shades outside or inside the windows unless approved by Lessor or his agent.
10. Confine his use of porches or balconies in that portion thereof directly in front of his apartment if any and shall keep them clean and shall not use them for storage purposes.
11. Discontinue all phonographs, television, pianos, radios and other musical devices at eleven o'clock P.M. and shall not practice on musical instruments at any time, nor give music lessons, vocal or instrumental, at any time.
12. Preserve perfect order at all times and permit no boisterous conduct.
13. Observe such other and reasonable rules as Lessor in his judgment may from time to time promulgate for the safety, care and cleanliness of the premises, the building, and for the preservation of good order therein.
14. Not hang washing, clothing, bed covers or linen from the windows, or porches, or in any yard space, except that, if any, which Lessor may provide for the specific purpose.
15. Not place flower pots, boxes or other receptacles in hallways or in windows, or porch railings or where they may possibly cause injury to any person, nor place any objects in windows, hallways, or porch railings deemed unsightly by Lessor.
16. No water beds shall be allowed in Premises.
17. No two wheel motor vehicles, nor any tearing down or repairing of any motor vehicles whatsoever, nor any storage or abandonment of inoperative motor vehicles shall be allowed in Premises or on any part of Lessor's real property on which Lessee's Apartment is located.

EXHIBIT 18–10

Small Commercial Retail Space Lease

_____ , 20 ___

THIS LEASE, made this _____ day of _____ , 20 _____ , by and between _____ , first party, (hereinafter called "Landlord"); and _____ , second party, (hereinafter called "Tenant"); and _____ third party, (hereinafter called "Agent");

WITNESSETH:

Premises

1. The Landlord, for and in consideration of the rents, covenants, agreements and stipulations hereinafter mentioned, provided for and contained, to be paid, kept and performed by the Tenant, has leased and rented, and by these presents leases and rents, unto the said Tenant, and said Tenant hereby leases and takes upon the terms and conditions which hereinafter appear, the following described property (hereinafter called "Premises"), to wit:

and being known as _____
No easement for light or air is included in the Premises.

Term

2. The Tenant shall have and hold the Premises for a term of _____ beginning on the _____ day of _____ 20 ____ , and ending on the _____ day of _____ , 20 ____ . at midnight, unless sooner terminated as hereinafter provided.

Rental

3. Tenant agrees to pay to Landlord, by payments to _____ Agent of Landlord, who negotiated this Lease, at the office of Agent in Atlanta, Georgia, an annual rental in the amount of $_____ , which shall be paid promptly on the first day of each month in advance during the term of this Lease, in equal monthly installments of $_____

Agent's Commission

4. Agent has rendered Landlord and Tenant a valuable service by assisting in the creation of the Landlord-Tenant relationship hereunder. For this reason, Agent is made a party to this Lease and is given a special lien on the interest of the Landlord and the interest of the Tenant in the Premisess in order to enable Agent to enforce its commission rights against the Premises as well as against the other parties hereto as herein provided and as otherwise provided by law or equity. The commission to be paid in conjunction with the creation of the aforesaid Landlord-Tenant relationship by this Lease has been negotiated between Landlord and Agent, and Landlord hereby agrees to pay Agent, as compensation for Agent's services in procuring this Lease and creating the aforeseaid Landlord-Tenant relationship, as follows:

If the Tenant becomes a tenant at will or at sufferance pursuant to Paragraph 25 hereof, or if the term of this Lease is extended or if this Lease is renewed or if a new lease is entered into between Landlord and Tenant covering either the Premises, or any part thereof, or covering any other premises as an expansion of, addition to, or substitution for, the Premises, regardless of whether such premises are located adjacent to or in the vicinity of the Premises, Landlord, in consideration of Agent's having assisted in the creation of the Landlord-Tenant relationship, agrees to pay Agent Additional Commissions as set forth below; it being the intention of the parties that Agent shall continue to be compensated so long as the parties hereto, their successors and/or assigns continue the relationship of Landlord and Tenant which initially resulted from the efforts of Agent, whether relative to the Premises or any expansion thereof, or addition thereto or substitution therefor, or relative to any other premises leased by Landlord to Tenant from time to time, whether the rental therefore is paid under this Lease or otherwise:

Landlord, with the consent of Tenant, hereby authorizes Agent to deduct its commission from each rental payment it collects from Tenant; but nothing herein shall relieve Landlord from his obligation to pay to Agent his commission if Tenant fails to pay any rental payment.

Agent agrees that, in the event Landlord sells the Premises, and upon Landlord's furnishing Agent with an agreement signed by Purchaser assuming Landlord's obligations to Agent under this Lease, Agent will release original Landlord from any further obligations to Agent hereunder. Tenant agrees that if this Lease is assigned by him he will secure from assignee an agreement in writing recognizing the assignment of the commissions owed to Agent and agreeing to pay rental to Agent during the continuation of the Landlord-Tenant relationship between or among said assignee, its successors and/or assigns, and Landlord, its successors and/or assigns, whether relative to the Premises or any expansion thereof or substitution therefor, or relative to any other property leased by Landlord to Tenant from time to time, whether rental therefor is paid under this Lease or otherwise. Voluntary cancellation of this Lease shall not nullify Agent's right to collect the commission due for the remaining term of this Lease and the provisions contained hereinabove relative to Additional Commissions shall survive any cancellation or termination of this Lease. In the event that the Premises are condemned, or sold under threat of and in lieu of condemnation, Agent shall, on the date of receipt by Landlord of the condemnation award or sale proceeds, be paid Agent's commission, reduced to its present cash value at the then existing legal rate of interest, which would otherwise be due to the end of the term contracted for under paragraph 2 above.

Purchase of Property by Tenant

5. In the event that Tenant acquires title to the Premises or any part thereof, or any other premises as an expansion of, addition to, or substitution for, the Premises, at any time during the term of this Lease, any renewals thereof, or within six months after the expiration of the term hereof or the extended term hereof, then Landlord shall pay Agent a commission on the sale of the Premises in lieu of any further commissions which otherwise would have been due under this Lease.

Such commission, as negotiated between parties, is to be _____

Utility Bills

6. Tenant shall pay all utility bills, including, but not limited to water, sewer, gas, electricity, fuel, light, and heat bills, for the Premises, and Tenant shall pay all charges for garbage collection services or other sanitary services rendered to the Premises or used by Tenant in connection therewith. If Tenant fails to pay any of said utility bills or charges for garbage collection or other sanitary services, Landlord may pay the same, and such payment shall be added to and become part of the next rental payment due under this Lease.

Use of Premises

7. Premises shall be used for _____
purposes and no other. Premises shall not be used for any illegal purposes, nor in any manner to create any nuisance or trespass, nor in any manner to vitiate the insurance or increase the rate of insurance on premises.

Abandonment of the Premises

8. Tenant agrees not to abandon or vacate the Premises during the period of this Lease and agrees to use the Premises for the purposes herein leased until the expiration hereof.

Repairs by Landlord

9. Landlord agrees to keep in good repair the roof, foundations, and exterior walls of the Premises (exclusive of all glass and exclusive of all exterior doors), and underground utility and sewer pipes outside the exterior walls of the building, except repairs rendered necessary by the negligence of Tenant, its agents, employees or invitees. Landlord gives to Tenant exclusive control of the Premises and shall be under no obligation to inspect said Premises. Tenant shall promptly

Delmar/Cengage Learning

(continued)

EXHIBIT 18–10

Small Commercial Retail Space
Lease (*continued*)

report in writing to Landlord any defective condition known to it which Landlord is required to repair, and failure so to report such conditions shall make Tenant responsible to Landlord for any liability incurred by Landlord by reason of such conditions.

Repairs by Tenant

10. Tenant accepts the Premises in their present condition and as suited for the uses intended by Tenant. Tenant shall, throughout the initial term of this Lease and any extension or renewal thereof, at its expense, maintain in good order and repair the Premises, including the building, heating and air conditioning equipment (including but not limited to replacement of parts, compressors, air handling units and heating units), and other improvements located thereon, except those repairs expressly required to be made by Landlord hereunder. Tenant further agrees to care for the grounds around the building, including the mowing of grass, paving, care of shrubs and general landscaping. Tenant agrees to return the Premises to Landlord at the expiration, or prior to termination, of this Lease in as good condition and repair as when first received, natural wear and tear, damage by storm, fire, lightning, earthquake or other casualty alone excepted.

Tax Escalation

11. Tenant shall pay upon demand, as additional rental during the term of this Lease and any extension or renewal thereof, the amount by which all taxes (including, but not limited to, ad valorem taxes, special assessments and any other governmental charges) on the Premises for each tax year exceed all taxes on the

Premises for the tax year _____. In the event the Premises are less than the entire property assessed for such taxes for any such tax year, then the tax for any such year applicable to the Premises shall be determined by proration on the basis that the rentable floor area of the Premises bears to the rentable floor area of the entire property assessed. If the final year of the lease term fails to coincide with the tax year, then any excess for the tax year during which the term ends shall be reduced by the pro rata part of such tax year beyond the lease term. If such taxes for the year in which the Lease terminates are not ascertainable before payment of the last month's rental, then the amount of such taxes assessed against the property for the previous tax year shall be used as a basis of determining the pro rata share, if any, to be paid by Tenant for that portion of the last lease year. Tenant's pro rata portion of increased taxes, as provided herein, shall be payable within fifteen days after receipt of notice from Landlord or Agent as to the amount due. The Agent's commission shall not apply to any such additional rental resulting from the provisions of this paragraph unless billing and collection thereof is handled by Agent at the request of the Landlord.

Destruction of or Damage to Premises

12. If the Premises are totally destroyed by storm, fire, lightning, earthquake or other casualty, this Lease shall terminate as of the date of such destruction, and rental shall be accounted for as between Landlord and Tenant as of that date. If the Premises are damaged but not wholly destroyed by any such casualties, rental shall abate in such proportion as use of the Premises has been destroyed, and Landlord shall restore Premises to substantially the same condition as before damage as speedily as is practicable, whereupon full rental shall recommence.

Indemnity

13. Tenant agrees to, and hereby does, indemnify and save Landlord harmless against all claims for damages to persons or property by reason of Tenant's use or occupancy of Premises, and all expenses incurred by Landlord because thereof, including attorney's fees and court costs. Supplementing the foregoing and in addition thereto, Tenant shall during all terms of this Lease, and any extension or renewal thereof, and at Tenant's expense maintain in full force and effect comprehensive general liability insurance with limits of $500,000.00 per person and $1,000,000.00 per accident, and property damage limits of $100,000.00, which insurance shall contain a special endorsement recognizing and insuring any liability accruing to Tenant under the first sentence of this Paragraph 13; such insurance policy shall contain a clause expressly waiving any right of the insurer of subrogation against Landlord. Prior to the commencement of the term of this Lease, Tenant shall furnish Landlord with a certificate of such insurance which shall show the waiver of subrogation, and the endorsement required hereby. Such certificate shall provide that Landlord will be given ten (10) days written notice prior to cancellation or expiration of the insurance evidenced thereby.

Governmental Orders

14. Tenant agrees, at his own expense, promptly to comply with all requirements of any legally constituted public authority made necessary by reason of Tenant's occupancy of the Premises. Landlord agrees promptly to comply with any such requirements if not made necessary by reason of Tenant's occupancy. It is mutually agreed, however, between Landlord and Tenant, that if in order to comply with such requirements, the cost to Landlord or Tenant, as the case may be, shall exceed a sum equal to one year's rent, then Landlord or Tenant who is obligated to comply with such requirements may terminate this Lease by giving written notice of termination to the other party, by registered mail, which termination shall become effective sixty (60) days after receipt of such notice, and which notice shall eliminate necessity of compliance with such requirement by party giving such notice unless party receiving such notice of termination shall, before termination becomes effective, pay to party giving notice all cost of compliance in excess of one year's rent, or secure payment of said sum in manner satisfactory to party giving notice.

Condemnation

15. If the whole of the Premises, or such portion thereof as will make the Premises unusable for the purposes herein leased, be condemned by any legally constituted authority for any public use or purpose, then in either of said events the term hereby granted shall cease from the date when possession thereof is taken by public authorities, and rental shall be accounted for as between Landlord and Tenant as of said date. Such termination, however, shall be without prejudice to the rights of either Landlord or Tenant to recover compensation and damage caused by condemnation from the condemnor. It is further understood and agreed that neither the Tenant nor Landlord shall have any rights in any award made to the other by any condemnation authority notwithstanding the termination of the Lease as herein provided. Landlord agrees to pay to Agent, from the award made to Landlord under condemnation, the balance of lease commissions, reduced to their present cash value, as provided in paragraph 4 hereof, and Agent may become a party to the condemnation proceeding for the purpose of enforcing its rights under this paragraph.

Assignment and Subletting

16. Tenant may sublease portions of the Premises to others provided such sublessee's operation is a part of the general operation of Tenant and is under the supervision and control of Tenant, and provided such operation is within the purposes for which the Premises shall be used. Except as provided in the preceding sentence, Tenant shall not, without the prior written consent of Landlord endorsed hereon, assign this Lease or any interest hereunder, or sublet the Premises or any part thereof, or permit the use of the Premises by any party other than Tenant. Consent to any assignment or sublease shall not impair this provision, and all later assignments or subleases shall be made likewise only on the prior written consent of Landlord. Assignee of Tenant, at option of Landlord, shall become directly liable to Landlord for all obligations of Tenant hereunder, but no sublease or assignment by Tenant shall relieve Tenant of any liability hereunder.

Removal of Fixtures

17. Tenant may (if not in default hereunder) prior to the expiration of this Lease, or any extension or renewal thereof, remove all fixtures and equipment which he has placed in the Premises, provided Tenant repairs all damage to the Premises caused by such removal.

Events of Default

18. The happening of any one or more of the following events (hereinafter any one of which may be referred to as an "Event of Default") during the term of this Lease, or any renewal or extension thereof, shall constitute a breach of this Lease on the part of the Tenant: (1) Tenant fails to pay the rental as provided for herein; (2) Tenant abandons or vacates the Premises; (3) Tenant fails to comply with or abide by and perform any other obligation imposed upon Tenant under this Lease; (4) Tenant is adjudicated bankrupt; (5) a permanent receiver is appointed for Tenant's property and such receiver is not removed within sixty (60) days after written notice from Landlord to Tenant to obtain such removal; (6) Tenant, either voluntarily or involuntarily, takes advantage of any debtor relief proceedings under any present or future law, whereby the rent or any part thereof is, or is proposed to be, reduced or payment thereof deferred; (7) Tenant makes an assignment for benefit of creditors; or (8) Tenant's effects are levied upon or attached under process against Tenant, which is not satisfied or dissolved within thirty (30) days after written notice from Landlord to Tenant to obtain satisfaction thereof.

Remedies Upon Default

19. Upon the occurrence of any Event of Default, Landlord may pursue any one or more of the following remedies, separately or concurrently, without any notice (except as specifically provided hereafter) and without prejudice to any other remedy herein provided or provided by law: (a) if the Event of Default involves nonpayment of rental, and Tenant fails to cure such default within ten days after receipt of written notice thereof from Landlord, or if the Event of Default involves a default in performing any of the terms or provisions of this Lease other than the payment of rental, and Tenant fails to cure such default within thirty (30) days after the receipt of written notice of default from Landlord, Landlord may terminate this Lease by giving written notice to Tenant, and upon such termination, shall be entitled to recover from the Tenant damages in an amount equal to all rental which is then due and which would otherwise have become due throughout the remaining term of this Lease, or any renewal or extension thereof (as if this Lease had not been terminated); or (b) if the Event of Default involves any matter other than those set forth in item (a) of this Paragraph 19, the Landlord may terminate this Lease by giving written notice to Tenant, and upon such termination, shall be entitled to recover from the Tenant damages in an amount equal to all rental which is then due and which would otherwise have become due throughout the remaining term of this Lease, or any renewal or extension thereof (as if this Lease had not been terminated); or (c) upon any Event of Default, Landlord may give to Tenant written notice of such default and advise Tenant that unless such default is cured within ten days after receipt of such notice, the entire amount of the rental for the remainder of the term of this Lease, or any renewal or extension thereof, shall immediately become due an payable upon the expiration of the ten day period, and thereafter, unless all the terms and provisions of this Lease are fully complied with by the Tenant within said ten-day period, the entire amount of said rental shall thereupon become immediately due and payable without further notice to Tenant; or (d) upon any Event of Default, Landlord, as Tenant's agent, without terminating this Lease may enter upon and rent the Premises, in whole or in part, at the best price obtainable by reasonable effort, without advertisement and by private negotiations and for any term Landlord deems proper, with Tenant being liable to Landlord for the deficiency, if any, between Tenant's rent hereunder and the price obtained by Landlord on reletting; provided, however, that Landlord shall not be considered to be under any duty by reason of this provision to take any action to mitigate damages by reason of Tenant's default.

Exterior Signs

20. Tenant shall place no signs upon the outside walls or roof of the Premises except with the written consent of the Landlord. Any and all signs placed on the Premises by Tenant shall be maintained in compliance with rules and regulations governing such signs, and the Tenant shall be responsible to Landlord for any damage caused by installation, use, or maintenance of said signs. Tenant, upon the expiration of this Lease, and any extension or renewal thereof, shall remove said signs and agrees upon removal of said signs to repair all damage incident to such removal.

Entry for Carding, etc.

(continued)

reasonable hours to exhibit same to prospective purchasers or tenants and to make repairs required of Landlord under the terms hereof, or to make repairs to Landlord's adjoining property, if any.

Effect of Termination of Lease

22. No termination of this Lease prior to the normal ending thereof, by lapse of time or otherwise, shall affect Landlord's right to collect rent for the period prior to termination thereof.

Mortgagee's Rights

23. Tenant's rights shall be subject to any bona fide mortgage or deed to secure debt which is now, or may hereafter be, placed upon the Premises by Landlord. Tenant shall, if requested by Landlord, execute a separate agreement reflecting such subordination.

No Estate in Land

24. This Lease shall create the relationship of Landlord and Tenant between the parties hereto; no estate shall pass out of Landlord. Tenant has only a usufruct, not subject to levy and sale, and not assignable by Tenant except by Landlord's consent.

Holding Over

25. If Tenant remains in possession of the Premises after expiration of the term hereof, with Landlord's acquiescence and without any express agreement of parties, Tenant shall be a tenant at will at the rental rate which is in effect at end of Lease; and there shall be no renewal of this Lease by operation of law. If Tenant remains in possession of the Premises after expiration of the term hereof without Landlord's acquiescence, then Tenant shall be a tenant at sufferance and, commencing on the date following the date of such expiration, the monthly rental payable under Paragraph 3 hereof shall, for each month or fraction thereof during which Tenant so remains in possession, be twice the monthly rental otherwise payable under Paragraph 3 hereof.

Attorney's Fees and Homestead

26. If any rent or other sum owing under this Lease is collected by or through an attorney at law, Tenant agrees to pay fifteen percent (15%) thereof as attorneys' fees. Tenant waives all homestead rights and exemptions which he may have under any law as against any obligation owing under this Lease. Tenant hereby assigns to Landlord his homestead exemption.

Rights Cumulative

27. All rights, powers and privileges conferred hereunder upon parties hereto shall be cumulative and not restrictive of those given by law.

Service of Notice

28. Tenant hereby appoints as his agent to receive service of all dispossessory or distraint proceedings and notices hereunder, and all notices required under this Lease, the person in charge of the Premises at the time, or occupying the Premises; and if no person is in charge of, or occupying the Premises, then such service or notice may be made by attaching the same on the main entrance to the Premises. A copy of all notices under this Lease shall also be sent to Tenant's last known address, if different from the Premises.

Waiver of Rights

29. No failure of Landlord to exercise any power given Landlord hereunder, or to insist upon strict compliance by Tenant of his obligations hereunder, and no custom or practice of the parties at variance with the terms hereof shall constitute a waiver of Landlord's right to demand exact compliance with the terms hereof.

Disclosure of Ownership

30. The owner of the Premises is _____

whose address is _____

and the person authorized to manage the Premises is _____ , whose address is

Service of process and demands and notices as to the Landlord shall be made on _____ , whose address is

_____

who is authorized to acknowledge the receipt of same.

Limitation on Agent's Services

31. Agent is a party to this Lease solely for the purpose of enforcing his rights under Paragraph 4 of this Lease, and it is understood by all parties hereto that Agent is acting solely in the capacity as agent for Landlord, to whom Tenant must look as regards all covenants, agreements and warranties herein contained, and that Agent shall never be liable to Tenant in regard to any matter which may arise by virtue of this Lease. It is understood and agreed that the commissions payable to Agent under Paragraph 4 of this Lease are compensation solely for Agent's services in assisting in the creation of the Landlord-Tenant relationship hereunder; accordingly, Agent is not obligated hereunder on account of payment of such commissions, to furnish any management services for the Premises.

Time of Essence

32. Time is of the essence of this Lease.

Definitions

33. "Landlord" as used in this Lease shall include first party, his heirs, representatives, assigns and successors in title to the Premises. "Tenant" shall include second party, his heirs and representatives, and if this Lease shall be validly assigned or sublet, shall include also Tenant's assignees or sublessees, as to the Premises covered by such assignment or sublease. "Agent" shall include third party, his successors, assigns, heirs and representatives. "Landlord," "Tenant," and "Agent" include male and female, singular and plural, corporation, partnership or individual, as may fit the particular parties.

Special Stipulations

In so far as the following stipulations conflict with any of the foregoing provisions, the following shall control:

This Lease contains the entire agreement of the parties hereto and no representations, inducements, promises or agreements, oral or otherwise, between the parties, not embodied herein, shall be of any force or effect.

IN WITNESS WHEREOF, the parties herein have hereunto set their hands and seals, in triplicate, the day and year first above written.

Signed, sealed and delivered as
to Landlord, in the presence of:

_____   _____ (SEAL)
                                             (Landlord)

_____ (SEAL)
Notary Public   (Landlord)

Signed, sealed and delivered as
to Tenant, in the presence of:

_____   _____ (SEAL)
                                               (Tenant)

_____ (SEAL)
Notary Public   (Tenant)

Signed, sealed and delivered as
to Agent, in the presence of:

_____   By: _____ (SEAL)

_____

_____
Notary Public

EXHIBIT 18–10

Small Commercial Retail Space
Lease (*continued*)

glossary

actual notice   Title matters about which a purchaser has direct knowledge or information.

ad valorem taxes   Taxes assessed against an owner of real property in an amount based upon the value of the property.

adverse possession   Method of acquiring ownership to real property by possession for a statutory time period.

affidavit   Sworn statement of fact.

agent   A person who has the power and authority to act on behalf of another person. An authorized agent's actions will bind the person on whose behalf the agent is acting.

amortization   Reduction of a debt by periodic payments covering interest and part of the principal.

appropriation   In regard to water law, doctrine stating that water belongs to the person who first makes beneficial use of it.

appurtenant easement   Easement created to benefit a particular parcel of real property. The easement transfers automatically with a transfer of the ownership of the real property benefited by the easement.

as-built survey   Survey that locates all physical improvements on the land in relation to the boundary lines of the land.

assessment   Sum of money owed by a condominium owner for monthly upkeep of the common areas of the condominium.

assignment   With regard to a lease, it is when the tenant transfers all his or her interest under the lease and retains nothing.

attornment and nondisturbance agreement   An agreement, usually entered into between a tenant and a holder of a mortgage on the leased premises, wherein each party agrees to recognize the other in the event of a foreclosure of the mortgage. The mortgage holder also agrees not to terminate the lease or disturb the tenant's possession in the event of a foreclosure of the mortgage.

balloon payment   Final payment of all unpaid principal and accrued and unpaid interest on the loan, which is greater than the periodic payments on the loan.

bank wire transfer   Electronic transfer of money from one bank account to another bank account.

baseline   Imaginary east-west survey line used in the government survey system to establish township lines.

bill of sale   Legal document that transfers ownership to personal property.

blanket easement   Easement that covers real property without a specific location of the easement.

bona fide purchaser for value   Person who purchases real property in good faith for valuable consideration without notice of any claim to or interest in the real property by any other party.

bridge loan   Short-term loan with a maturity of one to two years that provides the borrower necessary financing to purchase real property. A bridge loan usually is refinanced by a long-term loan.

building codes   Public laws that regulate methods and materials to be used in the construction of improvements.

call   Course and distance describing a boundary line of land in a metes and bounds land description.

caption   Portion of the deed that indicates the county and state in which the deed was signed by the grantor.

cashier's check   Check issued by a bank, the payment of which is guaranteed by the full faith and credit of the bank.

caveat emptor   A doctrine which provides that a seller, absent some express warranty, is not liable to a buyer or any conditions regarding the title or improvements to the land existing at the time of transfer.

certificate of occupancy   Permit issued by an appropriate governmental authority granting occupancy to newly constructed improvements. The certificate usually is evidence that the improvements comply with all zoning, building codes, and health and fire regulations.

certified check   Personal check in which the bank certifies that the funds are in the account and that the check will be honored on presentment for payment. Also called a *treasurer's check*.

chain of title   Historical sequence of all owners to a particular tract of real property beginning with the original owner and including all successive owners who have derived their title from the original owner.

chord   Straight line drawn from the beginning point of an arc to the ending point of an arc.

closing   Consummation of a real estate purchase and sale transaction.

closing date   Date set forth in a real estate contract on which the parties agree to perform all the promises of the contract. The date on which ownership of the real property is transferred from seller to purchaser and the purchaser pays the seller the purchase price for the real property.

color of title   A form of adverse possession where the original possession of the property by a prescriber is based upon a written instrument such as a deed or court decree.

commercial lease   A lease for the possession and use of a business or commercial enterprise such as a retail store, warehouse, or office.

common areas   That portion of the condominium property that is owned in common by all the owners of units in the condominium.

community property   Rule of law in states following the civil law of Spain and France, which provides that real property acquired during marriage is owned equally by the husband and wife.

Comprehensive Environmental Response, Compensation and Liability Act (CERCLA)   Also known as Superfund, this federal legislation created a trust fund designed to finance the activities of the Environmental Protection Agency and gave the Environmental Protection Agency the authority to recover cleanup costs for contaminated properties from the responsible parties for the contamination.

condition precedent   Condition in a contract that must be satisfied in accordance with the terms of the contract before one or both of the parties are required to perform their contractual obligations.

condominium association   Governing body of a condominium, the members of which are owners of condominium units. The condominium association usually is in the form of a nonprofit corporation.

condominium declaration   Legal document required by state condominium acts to create a condominium.

condominium plat   Plat of survey of condominium property required by state condominium acts. The plat must show in sufficient detail the location and dimensions of the real property, as well as all condominium units located on the real property.

condominium   Form of property ownership in which the owner owns an individual unit in a multiunit building and is a tenant in common with other owners of units in the building in certain common areas.

conduit lender   An issuer of bonds secured by residential or commercial mortgages. The payments on the residential or commercial mortgage loans pay the interest and principal on the bonds.

consideration   Something of value given to make the promises of a contract enforceable. Consideration also is something of value given by the grantee for a deed.

construction loan   Mortgage loan made for the purpose of providing money to construct improvements on real property.

constructive notice   A presumption of law that charges a person with notice of all title matters that can be discovered from an inspection of the real property or an examination of public real property records.

consumer credit   Term used in the Truth-in-Lending Act to mean a loan offered or extended primarily for personal, family, or household purposes.

consumer   Term used in the Truth-in-Lending Act to mean a natural person to whom a loan for personal, family, or household purposes is offered.

consummation   Term used in the Truth-in-Lending Act to mean the time a consumer becomes contractually obligated under state law to make payments under a loan.

contract   Agreement between two or more persons consisting of a promise or mutual promises that the law will enforce or the performance of which the law recognizes as a duty.

contribution   Right of a co-owner of real property to receive reimbursement from other co-owners for their share of expenses that are common to the real property.

conventional loan   Mortgage loan in which the risk of repayment of the debt rests solely on the ability of the borrower to pay and the value of the security provided by the mortgage.

conversion   Act of taking a person's property without a legal right to do so.

conveyance   The transfer of title or some or all of the ownership rights to real property from one person to another. A conveyance is usually by an instrument such as a deed, lease, mortgage, or other encumbrance.

cooperative   Form of ownership of real property in which a corporation owns a multiunit building and leases living space in the building to the shareholders of the corporation.

corporation   A legal entity wherein the owners do not have personal liability for the debts or actions of the entity.

counteroffer   A response to an offer by the offeree stating terms of acceptance different from the offer. Counteroffer terminates the original offer and becomes an offer of its own to be accepted or rejected.

course   In a metes and bounds legal description, it is the direction of a property boundary line.

covenant or warranty   Promise that a fact is true or that an event will take place.

curtesy   Interest in real property of the wife that the law in some states gives to the surviving husband at the time of the wife's death.

debt service   Payment of principal and interest on a loan.

deed   Written document that transfers ownership of real property from one person to another.

deed of trust   Legal document that conveys title to real property to a trustee who holds the title as security for a debt to a lender.

deed to secure debt   Legal document that conveys title to real property to a lender to secure a debt.

devise   Transfer of real property by means of a last will and testament.

distance   In a metes and bounds legal description, it is the length of a property boundary line, usually measured in feet and hundredths of a foot; example: 82.13 feet.

dominant tenement   Parcel of land benefited by an appurtenant easement.

dower Widow's interest in real property of her husband that provides a means of support after the husband's death.

due on sale clause Clause found in a mortgage that prohibits the sale of the real property described in the mortgage without the lender's consent. A sale in violation of this provision is a default of the mortgage.

earnest money Money paid by the purchaser at the time the real estate contract is signed. The money may be used as a down payment on the purchase price or may be retained by the seller for damages in the event the purchaser defaults on the contract.

easement Right granted to a nonowner of real property to use the real property for a specific purpose. For example, a right given to an electric utility company to locate an electric line on real property is an easement.

easement by necessity Easement for access to a public street that is necessary for the use and enjoyment of the property benefited by the easement.

easement in gross Easement granting the owner of the easement the right to use real property for a particular purpose. The easement does not benefit a parcel of real property owned by the owner of the easement.

elective share Right given to a widow in many states to elect, at her husband's death, to receive either dower or some ownership (fee simple) share of her husband's real property.

electronic signature A person's signature created electronically by a computer.

eminent domain Power of government to take private property for public use.

encumbrance A claim, charge, or liability on property, such as a lien or mortgage that lowers its value.

endorsement Amendment to a title insurance policy that generally modifies existing coverage or adds special coverage to the policy.

endorsement Method of transferring ownership of a promissory note.

escrow Agreement that requires the deposit of a document or money into the possession of a third party to be held by that party until certain conditions are fulfilled.

estate at will Estate of real property the duration of which is for an indefinite period. An estate at will can be terminated at the will of the parties.

estate for years Estate of real property the duration of which is for a definite period.

estoppel certificate A written statement generally signed by the holder of a first mortgage and given to the holder of a second mortgage, swearing as to certain facts concerning the first mortgage loan. The estoppel certificate may also obligate the first mortgage holder to identify the second mortgage holder in the event of a default under the first mortgage loan.

estoppel certificate Written statement signed by either a landlord or a tenant swearing to certain facts concerning a lease.

estoppel letter Sworn statement of fact.

exculpated loan A real estate loan in which the borrower is not personally responsible for the repayment of the loan. If the loan is not repaid, the borrower will lose the real property pledged as security for the loan. The borrower will not be personally sued for payment of the loan.

execution Signature of a party to a legal document. The act of signing a legal document.

express authority Authority that has been clearly given by the principal to the agent.

Fannie Mae Federal National Mortgage Association, a quasi-government agency organized for the purpose of investing in FHA and VA loans.

fee simple determinable Estate of real property with potential infinite duration. The ownership of a fee simple determinable is subject to a condition, the breach of which can result in termination of the estate. A fee simple determinable automatically expires on the nonoccurrence or occurrence of a condition.

fee simple on condition subsequent Estate of real property with potential infinite duration. The ownership of a fee simple on condition subsequent is subject to a condition, the breach of which can result in termination of the estate. A fee simple on condition subsequent continues in existence until an action is brought to recover the property.

fee simple or fee simple absolute Estate of real property with infinite duration and no restrictions on use.

fiduciary Person who holds a special relationship of confidence and trust to a principal and owes to the principal a duty to exercise all of the affairs of the principal in good faith and with loyalty.

finance charge Term used in the Truth-in-Lending Act to mean any charge or fee payable directly or indirectly by the consumer to obtain a consumer loan.

financing statement Form that is recorded to give notice that there is a security interest in personal property owned by a debtor.

fixture Item of personal property that becomes real property because of its attachment to the land or a building.

foreclosure Sale brought by a holder of a mortgage, deed of trust, or security deed of the real property conveyed in the instrument for the purposes of paying the debt secured by the real property.

Freddie Mac Federal Home Loan Mortgage Corporation, a quasi-public corporation that purchases and invests in mortgages.

fully amortized loan Loan in which the partial payments of principal and accrued interest, if paid for the stated period of time, will result in the entire loan being paid at maturity.

general partnership An association of two or more persons to carry on a business for profit as co-owners.

general warranty deed Deed containing full warranty of title.

graduated payment mortgage   Mortgage loan that permits the borrower to pay lower monthly payments for the first few years and larger payments for the remainder of the term.

grant deed   A type of limited warranty deed commonly used in California.

grantee   Person to whom real property has been transferred by deed.

grantee index   Alphabetical index of the public real property records that lists the last names of all people who are grantees of real property interest during a given year within the county.

grantor   Transferor of real property by deed.

grantor index   Alphabetical index of the public real property records that lists the last names of all people who are grantors of real property interest during a given year within the county.

gross lease   Lease wherein the tenant pays rent only; the operating expenses of the leased premises, such as taxes, utility costs, and insurance, are paid by the landlord.

guarantor   Person who signs a guaranty promising to pay the debt of another person.

guaranty   Legal document that obligates the maker of the document to pay the debt of another person.

habendum   Clause found in a deed that indicates what estate in real property is being transferred by the deed.

holder   Person who is the owner of a promissory note.

HUD–1   Uniform settlement statement required by the Real Estate Settlement Procedures Act for all real estate transactions that involve a federally related mortgage loan.

implied authority   Implied authority is implied by law to be those things necessary and proper for the agent to carry out the duties of the agency.

implied easement   Easement created by the conduct of the parties to the easement, not by written agreement.

inheritance   Ability to acquire ownership to real property because of one's kinship to a deceased property owner who dies without a will.

insured or guaranteed loan   Mortgage loan in which the repayment of the loan is insured or guaranteed by either a government agency or a private insurance company.

interest   Charge by a lender to a borrower for the use of money.

interpleader   Judicial proceeding in which money is paid into the court and all parties who claim an interest in the money are allowed to process their claims to the money in the court proceeding.

joint tenancy with right of survivorship   Ownership of real property by two or more persons. Joint tenants with the right of survivorship own equal interest in the real property, and on the death of any owner, the deceased owner's interest in the real property will pass to the surviving owner.

judgment   Money debt resulting from a lawsuit. Judgments are liens on real property owned by the judgment debtor.

kickback   Payment of money or something of value to a person for the purpose of obtaining business from that person.

landlord or lessor   Generally the owner of real property who transfers possession and use of the real property under a lease to a tenant or lessee.

lease guaranty   A legal document that obligates the maker of the document to perform the obligations of a tenant under the lease including, but not limited to, the payment of the rent by the tenant to the landlord.

lease   Legal document that transfers possession of real property from one party to another. The lease also may contain numerous terms and conditions involving the use and possession of the property.

legal description   Description of real property by a government survey, metes and bounds, or lot numbers of a recorded plat, which description is complete enough that a particular parcel of land can be located and identified.

license   A revocable privilege or permission to do an act or series of acts on land possessed by another.

lien   Money debt attached to real property. The holder of the lien can sell the real property to pay the debt.

life estate   Estate of real property the duration of which is measured by the life or lives of one or more persons.

limited common area   Common area of a condominium that is limited in use to one or more condominium unit owners.

limited liability company   An entity which offers the tax advantages of a partnership and the limited liability of a corporation.

limited or special warranty deed   Deed wherein the grantor covenants and warrants only against the lawful claims of people claiming by, through, or under the grantor.

limited partnership   A legal entity made up of two classes of ownership: general partners and limited partners. The general partners have full liability for the debts and obligations of the limited partnership, and the limited partners have liability limited to the extent of their investment in the partnership.

liquidated damages   Amount of money agreed on by the parties to a contract to be the damages in the event of a default of the contract.

lis pendens   Notice recorded in the real property records that informs that a lawsuit affecting title to real property described in the notice has been filed and is pending.

listing agreement   Agreement entered into between an owner and a real estate broker retaining the real estate broker to assist the owner in selling real property.

loan closing   Consummation of a loan secured by real property.

loan commitment   Contract between a borrower and a lender to make and accept a mortgage loan secured by real property. The loan commitment sets forth the terms, requirements, and conditions for the mortgage loan.

loan-to-value ratio   Ratio of the amount of a mortgage loan to the value of the secured real property. For example, when the amount of the loan is $80,000 and the market value of the real property pledged as security for the loan is $100,000, the loan-to-value ratio is 80 percent.

maker   Party to a promissory note who promises to pay money.

marketable title   Title to real property that is free from doubt and enables the owner to hold the real property in peace; free from the hazard of litigation or adverse claims.

mechanic's or materialmen's lien   Lien imposed by law on real property to secure payment for work performed or materials furnished for the construction, repair, or alteration of improvements on the real property.

mortgage   Legal document that creates an encumbrance on real property to secure a debt.

mortgage loan   Loan secured by real property.

mortgage or loan policy   Policy of title insurance that insures the interest of a mortgagee or lender to the title of real property.

mortgagee loss payable clause   Endorsement to a policy of fire and hazard insurance whereby the owner of the insured property and the insurance company agree that any and all proceeds payable under the policy are to be paid directly to the lender who has a mortgage on the insured property.

mortgagee   Person who receives a mortgage, that is, a lender.

mortgagor   Person who signs a mortgage pledging real property to secure a debt.

negative amortization   Loan on which the payments are not sufficient to pay the interest costs of the loan. The unpaid interest is added to the principal of the loan, resulting in an increase in the principal amount of the loan during the term of repayment.

negotiable note   Written note signed by the maker and containing an unconditional promise to pay a certain sum of money on demand or at a definite time. A negotiable note may be transferred to a holder in due course.

net lease   Lease in which the tenant is responsible for all expenses of the leased premises, such as utilities, taxes, and insurance.

offer   A contractual promise to do something.

offeree   A person to whom an offer to contract has been made.

offeror   A person who makes an offer to contract.

open-end or dragnet   Mortgage provision that provides that the mortgage will secure any and all debt between the mortgagor and the mortgagee, including past debt, present debt, and even future debt incurred after the mortgage is signed.

option   A contract by which an owner of property, usually called the optionor, agrees with another person, usually called the optionee, that the optionee shall have the right to buy the owner's real property at a fixed price within a certain time on agreed terms and conditions.

owner's policy   Policy of title insurance that insures an owner's title to real property.

parol evidence rule   Rule of evidence that provides that a written agreement is the best and only evidence of the agreement between the parties and that the parties are not permitted to bring in oral testimony regarding other agreements concerning the transaction.

partially amortized loan   Loan on which the required payments of principal and interest, if paid for the stated period of time, will not pay the loan in full. Final payment will be the balance due on the loan and will be a larger payment than the previous payments.

partition   Method by which co-owners of real property can divide the common property into separate ownerships. Partition may be by voluntary agreement of the co-owners or by court action.

payee   Party to a promissory note to whom a promise to pay money has been made.

pending disbursement clause   Clause found in a construction loan title insurance policy that provides that the insurance coverage under the policy will be in the amount of the loan as it is disbursed to the borrower up to and not to exceed the face amount of the policy.

percentage breakpoint   Level of gross sales made during a year at which time a percentage rent obligation will commence.

percentage rent   Rent based on a percentage of sales from a specific location. Percentage rent often is found in retail store leases.

permanent loan   Long-term loan that finances the acquisition of real property or refinances a construction loan on improvements.

Phase I   An examination of real property to determine if it contains environmental contamination.

Phase II   A more intensive environmental examination of property, usually including the testing of soil and water for evidence of contamination.

plat   Survey of real property that often is recorded.

plat or tract index   Index of all plats that have been recorded within the county within a given year.

possession   Occupation of land evidenced by visible acts such as enclosure, cultivation, the construction of improvements, or the occupancy of existing improvements.

power of attorney   Written document authorizing another person to act as one's agent.

power of sale   The power given to a lender or to a trustee on behalf of the lender to sell the mortgaged property in the event of a default under the mortgage.

preamble   Portion of the deed that sets forth the parties to the deed and the date of the deed.

premises   Land and the buildings located on the land. The term often is used to describe real property covered by a lease.

prenuptial (or antenuptial) agreement   Agreement entered into by a married couple that, among other things, outlines an agreement between the couple regarding the division and ownership of property in the event of separation or divorce.

prescriptive easement   Easement created when a person uses real property for a period of time without the owner's permission.

primary market   Lenders who make mortgage loans directly to borrowers.

primary mortgage lender   Lender who makes mortgage loans directly to a borrower.

principal   A person who appoints an agent to act on his or her behalf.

principal meridians   Imaginary north and south lines used in a government survey system. Meridians intersect the baselines to form a starting point for the measurement of land under that system.

private mortgage insurance   Insurance issued by a private company that insures a lender against loss it may suffer in the event the debtor defaults on payment of the loan.

promissory note   Legal document that contains a promise by one party to pay money to another party.

quiet title action   Judicial proceeding to establish the ownership of real property.

quitclaim deed   Deed that contains no warranties of title. A quitclaim deed transfers only the interest that the grantor has in the land without warranty.

radius clause   Clause contained in a lease that prohibits a tenant from operating another retail store or business within a certain geographical radius of the leased premises.

range lines   Division of a state in a government survey system being a 6-mile-wide row of townships running north and south.

Real Estate Settlement Procedures Act (RESPA)   A federal law designed to reform the real estate settlement process and to ensure that consumers receive more information about real estate settlement costs.

receiver   Third party appointed by a court to take possession of real property in the event of a mortgage default. A receiver acts as a caretaker for the property.

record title holder   Owner of real property as shown on the deed records from a title examination of the property.

recording statutes   State statutes that regulate the recordation of real property documents.

redemption   Right of a property owner to buy back his property after a foreclosure.

rent   Money paid by a tenant to a landlord for the use and possession of property pursuant to a lease.

rescission   Act of repealing or voiding something or some action.

rescission   Remedy for default of a real estate contract wherein the contract is terminated and the defaulting party must reimburse the injured party for expenses incurred in connection with the contract.

residential lease   A lease for the possession and use of a residence such as an apartment or a house.

retainage   Portion of the loan proceeds held by a construction lender until the construction is completed. The term also refers to an owner holding back money from a contractor until construction is completed.

riparian rights   Rights of the owners of lands adjoining streams, rivers, and lakes relating to the water and its use.

secondary mortgage market   Group of investors who purchase mortgage loans from primary mortgage lenders.

section   Division or parcel of land on a government survey comprising 1 square mile, or 640 acres.

security agreement   Legal document that pledges personal property as security for a debt.

servicing the loan   Collection of payments from the borrower of a mortgage loan.

servient tenement   Parcel of land on which an appurtenant easement is located.

settlement costs   All costs involved in the settlement or closing of a real estate transaction. Such items include but are not limited to attorney's fees, surveyor's fees, title insurance premiums, recording fees, and appraisal fees.

specific performance   Remedy for breach of real estate contract that requires a defaulting party to perform the promises made in the contract.

straight-line amortized loan   Mortgage loan in which the borrower will pay a different amount for each installment, with each payment consisting of a fixed amount credited toward principal and an additional amount for the interest due on the balance of the principal unpaid since the last payment.

sublet   In regard to a lease, it is when the tenant transfers only a portion of his or her interest under the lease, and the tenant retains some interest.

subprime lending   The business practice of making mortgage loans to people who do not have a good credit history or stable income.

subrogation   Right to be substituted to the rights of another person. For example, an insurance carrier who pays a claim to the insured is given the rights of the insured to proceed against any party who caused the damage resulting in the claim.

survey   Visual presentation of the physical boundaries of real property. The survey is used to describe real property.

tacking   The addition of possession periods by different adverse possessors.

tenancy by the entirety   Ownership of real property by a husband and wife. The husband and wife are treated as a single owner, and neither the husband nor the wife can transfer the property without the other's consent.

tenancy in common   Co-ownership of real property by two or more persons. Each owner's interest in the property is capable of inheritance.

tenant or lessee   Person who receives possession and use of property pursuant to a lease.

term loan   Loan in which the borrower makes periodic payments of interest, with the principal being paid in one installment at the end of the loan term.

testimonium   Portion of the deed where the grantor signs and the signature is witnessed or notarized.

time is of the essence   Provision contained in a contract that requires strict performance of the contract by the date or dates provided therein.

time-share   Form of ownership of real property in which an owner owns the property for a short period, usually one or two weeks of each year. Time-share ownership typically is used for vacation or recreational property.

title examination   Examination of the real property records to determine the ownership to a particular tract of real property.

title insurance   Contract to indemnify the insured against loss through defects in the title to real property.

title insurance commitment   A commitment or a contract by a title insurance company to issue a title insurance policy.

township lines   Lines in a government rectangular survey system that run east and west at 6-mile intervals parallel with baselines and that form strips of land or tiers called townships.

township   In a government survey, it is a square tract of land 6 miles on each side, containing 36 square miles.

Truth-in-Lending Act   Federal law designed to provide consumers with information for an informed use of credit. The Truth-in-Lending Act requires creditors to disclose to consumers the true costs of a consumer loan.

usury   Interest rates that are determined to be in excess of the maximum permitted by law.

waste   Action or nonaction that causes a loss of value to real property.

will   Legal document by which a person disposes of his property. A will takes effect on the death of the maker of the will.

zoning   Legitimate police power of governments to regulate the use of real property.

index